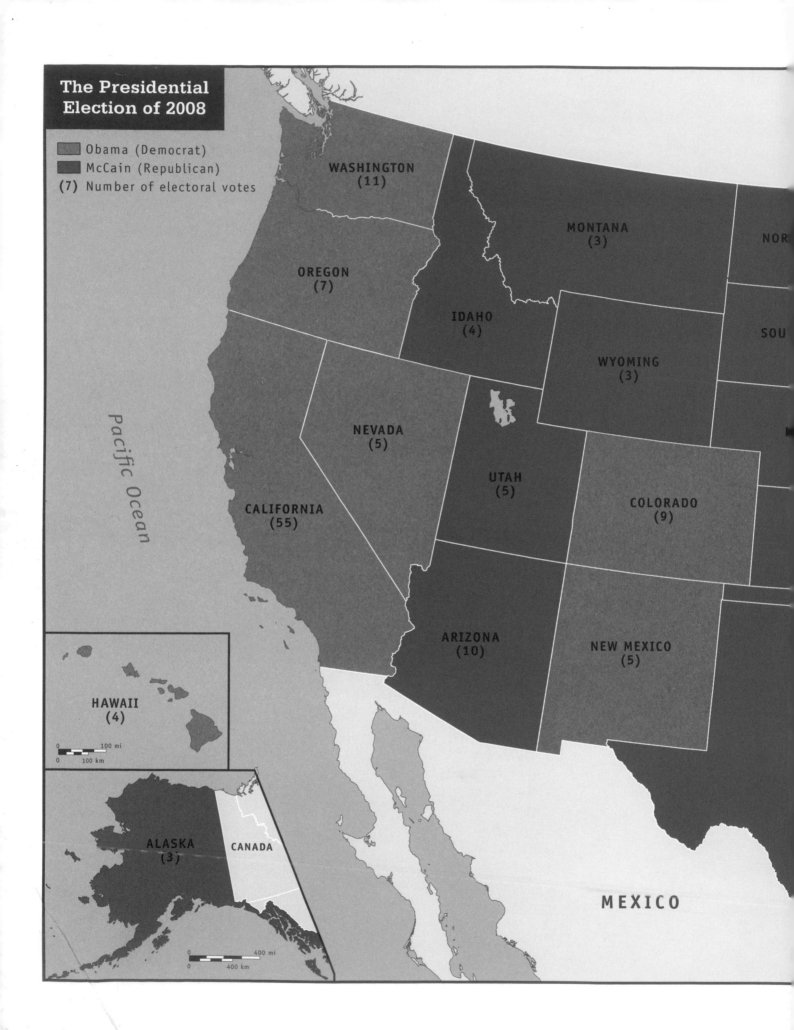

The Presidential Election of 2008

Obama (Democrat)
McCain (Republican)
(7) Number of electoral votes

Pacific Ocean

WASHINGTON
(11)

OREGON
(7)

MONTANA
(3)

NOR

IDAHO
(4)

WYOMING
(3)

SOU

NEVADA
(5)

UTAH
(5)

COLORADO
(9)

CALIFORNIA
(55)

ARIZONA
(10)

NEW MEXICO
(5)

HAWAII
(4)

0   100 mi
0   100 km

ALASKA
(3)

CANADA

0   400 mi
0   400 km

MEXICO

CANADA

MINNESOTA (10)

WISCONSIN (10)

MICHIGAN (17)

MAINE (4)

VT (3)

NH (4)

NEW YORK (31)

MA (12)

CT (7)

RI (4)

IOWA (7)

PENNSYLVANIA (21)

NEW JERSEY (15)

1

ILLINOIS (21)

INDIANA (11)

OHIO (20)

WEST VIRGINIA (5)

DELAWARE (3)

MARYLAND (10)

Washington, D.C. (3)

MISSOURI (11)

VIRGINIA (13)

KENTUCKY (8)

NORTH CAROLINA (15)

S

AHOMA (7)

ARKANSAS (6)

TENNESSEE (11)

SOUTH CAROLINA (8)

ALABAMA (9)

GEORGIA (15)

MISSISSIPPI (6)

LOUISIANA (9)

Atlantic Ocean

FLORIDA (27)

Gulf of Mexico

| 0 | 150 | 300 mi |
| 0 | 150 | 300 km |

BAHAMAS

CORE EDITION

American Politics Today

CORE EDITION

American Politics Today

William T. Bianco
INDIANA UNIVERSITY, BLOOMINGTON

David T. Canon
UNIVERSITY OF WISCONSIN, MADISON

W. W. NORTON AND COMPANY
NEW YORK • LONDON

GREEN EDITION

Planet-friendly publishing
Learn more at www.greenedition.com

Made in the United States
Printed on Recycled Paper

W. W. Norton & Company has been independent since its founding in 1923, when William Warder Norton and Mary D. Herter Norton first published lectures delivered at the People's Institute, the adult education division of New York City's Cooper Union. The Nortons soon expanded their program beyond the Institute, publishing books by celebrated academics from America and abroad. By mid-century, the two major pillars of Norton's publishing program—trade books and college texts—were firmly established. In the 1950s, the Norton family transferred control of the company to its employees, and today—with a staff of four hundred and a comparable number of trade, college, and professional titles published each year—W. W. Norton & Company stands as the largest and oldest publishing house owned wholly by its employees.

Editors: Steve Dunn and Aaron Javsicas
Managing editor, College: Marian Johnson
Project editor: Sarah Mann
Editorial assistant: Carly Fraser
Copyeditors: Sarah Mann and Ellen Lohman
Production manager: Ben Reynolds
Design director: Rubina Yeh
Photo researchers: Trish Marx, Patty Cateura, and Julie Tesser
Composition by TexTech, Inc.
Page layout by Sue Carlson
Manufacturing by Courier—Kendallville, IN

Library of Congress Cataloging-in-Publication Data

Bianco, William T., 1960–

American politics today / William T. Bianco, David T. Canon. — 1st core ed.
p. cm.
Includes bibliographical references and index.

ISBN 978-0-393-93286-7 (pbk.)

1. United States—Politics and government. I. Canon, David T. II. Title.

JK275.B53 2009
320.473—dc22

2008046714

W. W. Norton & Company, Inc., 500 Fifth Avenue, New York, NY 10110
www.wwnorton.com

W. W. Norton & Company, Ltd., Castle House, 75/76 Wells Street, London W1T3QT

1 2 3 4 5 6 7 8 9 0

About the Authors

WILLIAM T. BIANCO is professor of political science at Indiana University, Bloomington, and Co-chair of the Working Group on Sustainable Democracy at the Workshop in Political Theory and Policy Analysis. He is the author of *Trust: Representatives and Constituents, American Politics: Strategy and Choice*, and numerous articles on American politics. He has received three National Science Foundation grants. He has also served as a consultant to congressional candidates and party campaign committees, as well as to the U.S. Department of Energy, the U.S. Department of Health and Human Services, and other state and local government agencies.

DAVID T. CANON is professor of political science at the University of Wisconsin, Madison. His teaching and research interests focus on American political institutions, especially Congress, and racial representation. He is the author of *Actors, Athletes, and Astronauts: Political Amateurs in the U.S. Congress; Race, Redistricting, and Representation: The Unintended Consequences of Black Majority Districts* (winner of the Richard F. Fenno Prize); *The Dysfunctional Congress?* (with Kenneth Mayer); and various articles and book chapters. He is the Congress editor of *Legislative Studies Quarterly*. Professor Canon is the recipient of a University of Wisconsin Chancellor's Distinguished Teaching Award.

For our families,
Regina, Anna, and Catherine,
Sarah, Neal, Katherine, and Sophia,
who encouraged, empathized, and
helped, with patience,
grace, and love.

Contents in Brief

Contents

3. Federalism 62

Part II: Politics

5. Public Opinion 140

6. The Media 182

7. Political Parties 216

8. Elections 256

9. Interest Groups 306

Part III: Institutions

10. Congress 342

11. The Presidency 386

Part IV: Civil Rights

14. Civil Rights   496

Appendix

Boxed Features

Nuts and Bolts

Politics Is Everywhere

Challenging Conventional Wisdom

You Decide

Comparing Ourselves to Others

Preface

This book is based on three simple premises: politics is everywhere, political process matters, and politics is conflictual. It reflects our belief that politics is explainable, that political outcomes can be understood in terms of decisions made by individuals—and that the average college undergraduate can make sense of the political world in these terms. It focuses on contemporary American politics, the events and outcomes that our students have lived through and know something about. The result, we believe, is a book that provides an accessible but rigorous account of the American political system.

The book is also the product of our dissatisfaction with existing texts. Twenty years ago we were assistant professors at the same university, assigned to teach the introductory class in alternate semesters. While our graduate training was quite different, we found that we shared a deep disappointment with available texts. Their wholesale focus on grand normative concepts such as civic responsibility, or their use of analytic themes such as collective action, left students with little idea of how American politics really works, how events in Washington affect their everyday lives, and how to piece together all the facts about American politics into a coherent explanation of why things happen as they do. These texts did not engender excitement, fascination, or even passing interest. What they did was put students to sleep.

This book breaks new ground in both approach and content. Our themes embody our belief that it is possible to make sense of American politics—that we can move beyond simply describing what happens in political life to predicting and explaining behavior and outcomes, and, moreover, that this task can be accomplished in the introductory class. In part we wish to counter the widespread belief among students that politics is too complicated, too chaotic, or too secretive to make sense of. More than that, we want to empower our students, to demonstrate that everyday American politics is relevant to their lives. This emphasis is also a response to the typical complaint about American Government textbooks—that they are full of facts but devoid of useful information, and that after students finish reading, they are no better able to answer "why" questions than they were before they cracked the book.

Throughout the text, we emphasize common sense, showing students that politics inside the Beltway is often strikingly similar to their everyday interactions. For example, what sustains policy compromises made by members of Congress? The fact that the members typically have long careers, that they interact frequently with each other, and that they only deal with colleagues who have kept their word in the past. These strategies are not unique to the political world. Rather, they embody rules of thumb that most people follow (or are at least aware of) in their everyday interactions. In short, we try to help students understand American politics by emphasizing how it is not all that different from the world they know.

This focus on common sense is coupled with many references to the political science literature. We believe that contemporary research has something to say about prediction and explanation of events that students care about—and that these insights can be taught without turning students into formal theorists or statisticians. This emphasis has the secondary benefit of tying the introductory course to the wider political science discipline, including the American politics subfield and work on democracies more generally.

We do not frame the text in terms of any one theory or approach. We present the essential insights of contemporary research, motivated by real-world political phenomena and explained using text or simple diagrams. This approach gives students a set of tools for understanding politics, provides an introduction to the political science literature, and matches up well with students' common-sense intuitions about everyday life. Moreover, by showing that academic scholarship is not a blind alley or irrelevant, this approach helps to bridge the gap between an instructor's teaching and his or her research.

While we do not ignore American history, our stress is on contemporary politics—on the debates, actions, and outcomes that most college students are aware of. The text is, as one of us put it, "ruthlessly contemporary." Focusing on recent events emphasizes the utility of the concepts and insights that we develop in the text. It also goes a long way to establishing the relevance of the intro class.

Finally, our book offers an individual-level perspective on America's government. The essential message is that politics—elections, legislative proceedings, regulatory choices, and everything else we see—is a product of the decisions made by real flesh-and-blood people. This approach grounds our discussion of politics in the real world. Many texts focus on abstractions such as "the eternal debate," "the great questions," or "the pulse of democracy." The problem with these constructs is that they don't explain where the debate, the questions, or even democracy come from. Nor do they help students to understand what's going in Washington and elsewhere, as it's not obvious that the participants care much about these sorts of abstractions—quite the opposite, in fact.

We replace these constructs with a focus on real people and actual choices. The primary goal is to make sense of American politics by understanding why politicians, bureaucrats, judges, and citizens act as they do. That is, we are grounding our description of American politics at the most fundamental level—an individual facing a decision. How, for example, does a voter choose among candidates? Stated that way, it is reasonably easy to talk about where the choice came from, how the individual might evaluate different options, and why one choice might look better than the others. Voters' decisions may be understood by examining the different feasible strategies they employ (issue voting, retrospective evaluations, stereotyping, etc.), and why some voters use one strategy while others use a different one.

By focusing on individuals and choices, we can place students in the shoes of the decision makers, and in doing so, give them insight into why these people act as they do. We can discuss, for example, why a House member might favor enacting wasteful pork-barrel spending, even though a proposal full of such projects will make his constituents economically worse off—and why constituents might reward such behavior, even if they suspect the truth. By taking this approach, we are not trying to let legislators off the hook. Rather, we believe that any real understanding of the political process must begin with a sense of the decisions the participants make and why they make them.

Focusing on individuals also segues naturally into a discussion of consequences, allowing us to move from examining decisions to describing and evaluating outcomes. In this way, we can show students how large-scale outcomes in politics, such as inefficient programs, don't happen by accident or because of malfeasance. Rather, they are the predictable results of choices made by individuals (here, politicians and voters).

The policy chapters—on civil rights in both the Full and Core versions of the text, and on economic policy, social policy, and foreign policy in the Full version— also represent a distinctive feature of this book. The discussion of policy at the end of an intro class often fits awkwardly with the material covered earlier. It is supposed to be a culmination of the semester-long discussion of institutions, politicians, and political behavior, but instead it often becomes an afterthought that gets discarded when time runs out in the last few weeks of the class. Our policy chapters explicitly draw on previous chapters' discussions of the actors that shape policy: the president, Congress, the courts, interest groups, and parties. By doing so, they deliver on the promise of showing how all the pieces of the puzzle fit together.

Finally, this book reflects our experience as practicing scholars and teachers, as well as interactions with over fifteen thousand students in introductory classes at several universities. Rather than thinking of the intro class as a service obligation, we believe it offers a unique opportunity for faculty to develop a broader sense of American politics and American political science, while at the same time giving students the tools they need to behave as knowledgeable citizens or enthusiastic political science majors. We hope that it works for you as well as it does for us.

Features of the Text

THE BOOK'S "THREE KEY IDEAS"—politics is everywhere, political process matters, and politics is conflictual—are fully integrated throughout the text.

 Politics Is Everywhere Debates over what government should do or who should be in charge are not separate from society or from Americans' everyday lives. Politics is a fundamental part of everyone's life, governing what people can and cannot do, their quality of life, and how they think about events, other people, and situations.

 Political Process Matters Governmental actions result from conscious choices made by voters, elected officials, and bureaucrats. The media often cover political issues in the same way they do sporting events, and while this makes for entertaining news, it also leads citizens to overlook the institutions, rules, and procedures that have a decisive influence on American life. Politics really is not just a game.

 Politics Is Conflictual The questions debated in elections, and the policy options considered by people in government, are generally marked by disagreement at all levels. Making policy typically involves important issues on which people disagree, sometimes strongly; so compromise, bargaining, and tough choices about trade-offs are central parts of the process.

CHAPTERS BEGIN WITH ENGAGING ANECDOTES or a case study and an overview of what students are expected to learn, including the "why" and "what" questions that are explained in the chapter. Chapter introductions reinforce the relevance of the three key ideas by showing how they relate to real-world situations.

KEY IDEA SIDEBARS point out where a discussion in the text is relevant to one of the three key ideas. This feature allows students to quickly zero in on the key ideas when studying for an exam or reading the chapter for the first time.

SECTION SUMMARIES appear as numbered lists after each major discussion within the chapters, giving students a chance to review what they have learned at logical interim touchdown points before moving on to the next topic.

BOXED FEATURES further reinforce the three key ideas while introducing other important ways to think about American politics. Specifically, the boxes distill critical concepts (**"Nuts and Bolts"**), offer more real-world applications (**"Politics Is Everywhere"**), provoke students to think critically by presenting alternative perspectives on many issues that are often taken for granted (**"Challenging Conventional Wisdom"**), prompt students to think analytically by making their own political decisions (**"You Decide"**), and introduce students to relevant political and governmental issues in other countries (**"Comparing Ourselves to Others"**).

CRITICAL THINKING is further encouraged with a set of questions at the end of each chapter, and the charts, figures, and tables are accompanied by analytical questions that encourage students to probe the deeper meaning of the data.

Teaching and Learning Supplements

 STUDENT STUDYSPACE
wwnorton.com/studyspace

Students have free and open access to the online StudySpace, which offers review materials (chapter summaries, flash cards, and quizzes) and additional tools for student enrichment such as:

Everydaypoliticsblog.com
This current, engaging blog provides discussions of political news and events from a variety of perspectives and ties directly into the main themes and core concepts of Norton's American government texts.

Critical Thinking Exercises
These exercises help students understand the analytical framework of the text through a variety of online resources and critical thinking activities.

Video Exercises
Streaming video selections that relate to key ideas in the text are paired with questions for thought and analysis.

INSTRUCTOR'S MANUAL

Mike Wagner, University of Nebraska, Lincoln

Offers extensive lecture outlines and additional lecture topics, video ideas to engage a too-quiet classroom, and class activities organized around the three key ideas.

TEST BANK AND COMPUTERIZED TEST BANK

Scott McClurg, Southern Illinois University, Carbondale

Features over 1,500 multiple-choice and essay questions. Available in both print and *ExamView® Assessment Suite* formats.

NORTON AMERICAN POLITICS DVD

This DVD offers more than one hundred brief video clips (thirty seconds to five minutes long) from a range of classic and contemporary sources, including popular culture content, recent election ads from candidates and political action committees, and clips from documentaries and historical footage.

ALSO AVAILABLE:

Lecture PowerPoints
Art PowerPoints
Image gallery of art from the text
Blackboard/WebCT coursepack, web quizzes, and test bank

Acknowledgments

This text is dedicated to our families, who deserve acknowledgement many more times than our page limits will allow. Our wives, Regina and Sarah, graciously accommodated our writing and editing schedules, served as thoughtful sounding boards, and were very patient with how long it took to complete the project. Our five children were vaguely aware of what was going on ("what, you are still working on that book?") and provided us with frequent and appreciated excuses for not working on the book *too* much.

Our colleagues at Indiana University and the University of Wisconsin (and before that, Duke University for both of us), provided many opportunities to talk about American politics and teaching this course.

Bill thanks his colleagues at Indiana University, including Christine Barbour, Ted Carmines, Jeff Isaac, Mike Ensley, Russ Hansen, Lin Ostrom, Gerry Wright, and Regina Smyth for sharp insights and encouragement at crucial moments. He is also grateful to the legion of teaching assistants who have helped him organize and teach the intro class at three universities.

David gives special thanks to Ken Mayer whose daily "reality checks" and consistently thoughtful professional and personal advice are greatly appreciated. John Coleman, Barry Burden, Ken Goldstein, Ben Marquez, Byron Shafer, Charles Franklin, John Witte, Dave Weimer, Kathy Walsh, and all the great people at Wisconsin have provided a wonderful community within which to teach and research American politics. David would also like to thank the students at the University of Debrecen in Hungary where he taught American politics as a Fulbright Scholar in 2003–04. The Hungarian students' unique perspective on democracy, civil liberties, and the role of government required David to think about American politics in a different way.

Both of us are grateful to the political science faculty at Duke University who, in addition to providing us with our first academic jobs, worked to construct a hospitable and invigorating place to research and to teach. In particular, Rom Coles, Ruth Grant, John Aldrich, Tom Spragens, Taylor Cole, and David Barber were model colleagues and scholars. We both learned to teach by watching them, and we are the better teachers and scholars for it.

Special thanks as well to the authors of the book's supplementary materials. Scott McClurg of Southern Illinois University at Carbondale created our test bank; Mike Wagner of the University of Nebraska wrote the instructor's manual; Jacob Samuel Bower-Bir and Nathaniel Birkhead of Indiana University created the content for the Student StudySpace; Jamie Carson of the University of Georgia, Peter Francia of East Carolina University, Lynn Vavreck of UCLA, and Martin Saiz of Cal State, Northridge, produced the Norton American Politics DVD; and Scott Lemieux of Hunter College, Laura McKenna of Ramapo College, David Watkins of Seattle University, and Mike Xenos of Louisiana State University all contribute to Everydaypoliticsblog.com, providing commentary that links our text with American politics as it happens (we also look forward to contributing).

The outstanding people at W. W. Norton made this a much better book than we could have produced on our own. Steve Dunn was responsible for getting the process started and providing good commentary and encouragement from beginning to end. Aaron Javsicas took over editing in midstream, and has been a graceful taskmaster and insightful editor throughout the process. Sarah Mann handled copy-editing with an amazing combination of rigor, sensitivity, and substantive knowledge, and Ellen Lohman came on late in the project to help us meet a fast-approaching manuscript deadline. Carly Fraser made sure everyone had the right versions of everything, and applied her formidable research skills at precisely the right moments. Emily Huang did a great job with fact checking. Dan Jost skillfully helmed the electronic media program, and assembled the crackerjack blog team. Trish Marx, Julie Tesser, Patty Cateura, and Laura Musich put together an excellent photo program, and Megan Jackson cleared reprint permissions for the figures and tables. Ben Reynolds handled production with efficiency and good humor, Rubina Yeh created a beautiful design, and Sue Carlson did a great job with page layout. Thanks also to Peter Lesser, another early advocate at Norton, and to Roby Harrington, the head of Norton's college department. The entire crew at Norton has been incredibly professional and supportive. We feel very fortunate to work with them.

We are also indebted to the many reviewers who have commented on the text. Their suggestions spanned presentation and content, highlighting the places where our arguments were too hard to follow, and where we made errors of fact and interpretation.

REVIEWERS

Dave Adler, Idaho State University
Rick Almeida, Francis Marion University
Jim Bailey, Arkansas State University, Mountain Home
Todd Belt, University of Hawaii, Hilo
Scott Buchanan, Columbus State University
Randy Burnside, Southern Illinois University, Carbondale
Carolyn Cocca, SUNY College at Old Westbury
Tom Dolan, Columbus State University
Dave Dulio, Oakland University
Matt Eshbaugh-Soha, University of North Texas
Kevin Esterling, University of California, Riverside
Peter Francia, East Carolina University
Scott Frisch, California State University, Channel Islands
Sarah Fulton, Texas A&M University
Keith Gaddie, University of Oklahoma
Joe Giammo, University of Arkansas, Little Rock
Kate Greene, University of Southern Mississippi
Steven Greene, North Carolina State University
Phil Habel, Southern Illinois University, Carbondale
Charles Hartwig, Arkansas State University, Jonesboro
Ted Jelen, University of Nevada, Las Vegas
Jennifer Jensen, Binghamton University (SUNY)
Terri Johnson, University of Wisconsin, Green Bay
Luke Keele, Ohio State University
Linda Keith, University of Texas, Dallas
Chris Kelley, Miami University
Jason Kirksey, Oklahoma State University
Jeffrey Kraus, Wagner College
Chris Kukk, Western Connecticut State University
Mel Kulbicki, York College
Joel Lieske, Cleveland State University
Steve Light, University of North Dakota

Baodong (Paul) Liu, University of Utah
Ken Long, Saint Joseph College, Connecticut
Michael Lynch, University of Kansas
Cherie Maestas, Florida State University
Tom Marshall, University of Texas, Arlington
Scott McClurg, Southern Illinois University, Carbondale
Jonathan Morris, East Carolina University
Jason Mycoff, University of Delaware
Sean Nicholson-Crotty, University of Missouri, Columbia
Timothy Nokken, Texas Tech University
Sandra O'Brien, Florida Gulf Coast University
John Orman, Fairfield University
L. Marvin Overby, University of Missouri, Columbia
Catherine Paden, Simmons College
Dan Ponder, Drury University
Paul Posner, George Mason University
David Redlawsk, University of Iowa
Russell Renka, Southeast Missouri State University
Travis Ridout, Washington State University
Andy Rudalevige, Dickinson College
Denise Scheberle, University of Wisconsin, Green Bay
Tom Schmeling, Rhode Island College
Pat Sellers, Davidson College
Dan Smith, Northwest Missouri State University
Dale Story, University of Texas, Arlington
John Vile, Middle Tennessee State University
Mike Wagner, University of Nebraska
Dave Wigg, St. Louis Community College
Maggie Zetts, Purdue University

It is a humbling experience to have so many smart people looking over our shoulders. Their efforts helped us to make this book what it is, and we are profoundly thankful.

William T. Bianco
David T. Canon
October 2008

CORE EDITION

American Politics Today

1

UNDERSTANDING AMERICAN POLITICS

The premise of this book is simple: *American Politics makes sense.* What happens in elections, in Congress, in the White House, and everywhere else in the political process, has a logical and often simple explanation.

This claim may seem unrealistic or even naive. On the surface, American politics is full of bewildering complexities, from the enumerated powers in the Constitution to the unwritten rules that govern how Congress works. Many policy questions, from reforming Social Security to deciding what to do in Iraq, seem hopelessly intractable. Election outcomes look random or even chaotic. Politicians seem more interested in publicizing their disagreements than solving them.

Many people, we believe, have given up on American politics because they don't understand the political process, feel helpless to influence elections or policy making, and believe that politics is irrelevant to their lives. Since you are taking a class on American politics, we hope you have not given up on politics entirely. It is *not* our goal to turn you into a political junkie or a policy expert. It isn't necessary to be completely immersed in politics to make sense of it, but we hope that you will have a basic understanding of the political process after finishing this book.

Another goal of the book is to help you take an active role in the political process. A functioning democracy allows citizens to defer complicated policy decisions to their elected leaders, but it also requires them to monitor what politicians are doing and to hold those leaders accountable at the voting booth. This book will help you accomplish this important duty by providing the analytical skills you will need to make sense of politics, even when it initially appears senseless.

Consider a congressional appropriation in 2005 of $453 million for the construction of two bridges in Alaska. One of them, the infamous "bridge to nowhere," would have connected Ketchikan, Alaska, a town with 8,600 residents, with Gravina Island, population fifty. This bridge would have been nearly as long as the Golden Gate Bridge and taller than the Brooklyn Bridge. Assuming traffic of 1,000 cars a day (which is generous), the cost in tax dollars per trip would be $43.15 for the projected life of the bridge. One commentator called the bridge a "national embarrassment" and said that it "has become an object of national ridicule and a symbol of . . . fiscal irresponsibility."[1] The bridge was funded as part of a $286.5 billion transportation bill, which passed by large margins in the House and Senate and included a record 6,371 earmarks—specific local projects identified in the legislation[2]—totaling $24 billion, so the "bridge to nowhere" was not alone.

FIGURE 1.1   **THE BRIDGE TO NOWHERE**

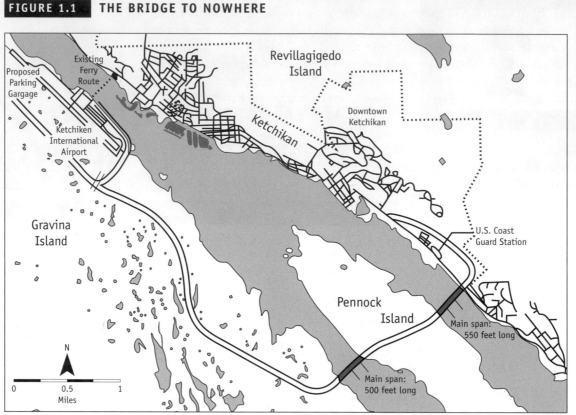

SOURCE: Taxpayers for Common Sense, "The Gravina Access Project: A Bridge to Nowhere," February 9, 2005, available at http://www.taxpayer.net/Transportation/gravinabridge.pdf.

If the story ended here, it could be seen as just another example of members of Congress taking care of their constituents by dishing out generous servings of federal spending. However, the story took on theatrical proportions when, shortly after approving the transportation bill, the Senate was struggling to pay for rebuilding the highways and bridges destroyed by Hurricane Katrina. Senator Tom Coburn, a Republican from Oklahoma, proposed rescinding the $453 million earmarked for the Alaskan bridges and redirecting some of the money to highway repair projects in New Orleans. In response, Senator Ted Stevens of Alaska made an impassioned speech in defense of the spending, and the Senate rejected Coburn's proposal by an 82 to 15 vote.[3] The next development in the saga came a few weeks later when the House–Senate conference committee voted to eliminate the official earmarks for the two bridges, but allotted the same amount of money to the governor of Alaska to spend on any transportation project in the state, including the bridges.[4] President Bush complained about the size of the bill, but ultimately signed it. Nearly two years after the bill was signed into law, despite maintaining that the Gravina–Ketchikan bridge was necessary for local economic development and spending nearly $26 million on the initial phases of construction, Governor Sarah Palin (later the 2008 Republican vice presidential nominee) announced that it would not be built.[5]

How did this happen? How did such a wasteful project get approved, then survive an effort to redirect spending to a seemingly more worthy cause, waste nearly $26 million in taxpayers' money, and then get canceled? The bridge to nowhere seems like a classic example of government waste, and it can certainly seem hard to understand how this project was approved by our elected leaders.

However, some supposed pork-barrel spending, which is the informal term given to wasteful spending of federal money on local projects, is more worthy than it appears. One recent example of pork was the federally funded purchase of a wind-powered ice sled for the sheriff of Ashland County, Wisconsin. The cover of President Bush's 2003 budget request featured a picture of the sled, and Bush vowed that he would not allow spending like that in the future. But as the *Washington Post* explained, "the funding had been secured by Representative David R. Obey (D-Wis.), after an Ashland teenager fell through the ice of Lake Superior and drowned as sheriff's deputies, firefighters, and his father watched helplessly from shore."[6] If they had had the ice sled, they might have been able to rescue the victim. As the old saying goes, "One person's pork is another person's essential spending."

The "bridge to nowhere" may be more difficult to justify than an emergency rescue sled, but the project had its defenders.[7] They pointed out that the bridge would allow much-needed economic development in Ketchikan, which is hemmed in by mountains and has nowhere to expand except to Gravina Island. The bridge also might have increased the traffic flow through Gravina's local airport, bringing jobs to the region. These proponents saw the bridge as an investment in the future and would probably argue that its critics ignored the long-term benefits. Indeed, in the governor's announcement that the bridge project was being canceled, she said, "Much of the public's attitude toward Alaska bridges is based on inaccurate portrayals of the projects here."[8]

The bridge also had friends in high places. At the time the bill was enacted, Alaska Representative Don Young was Chair of the House Transportation Committee, and Alaska Senator Ted Stevens was Chair of the Senate Commerce Committee. Of the $24 billion in earmarks in the transportation bill, nearly $1 billion went to Alaska. Only California and Illinois received more earmarked funds, despite Alaska's ranking as the forty-seventh state in terms of population (whereas California is first and Illinois is fifth).[9]

Finally, the "bridge to nowhere" can also be explained by two features of the legislative process. First, funding for the bridge was a relatively small part of a huge bill that included spending for all federal transportation projects for the next five years. The perception among members of Congress was that America's transportation

▲ The proposed "bridge to nowhere" is often held up as the most egregious example of wasteful government spending. Though the bridge was not built (this is a digitized image), many critics of the project were outraged that Congress considered funding the bridge in light of more pressing needs, such as rebuilding the areas devastated by Hurricane Katrina.

infrastructure was in serious need of repair and that the bill was an important step toward addressing these problems. From this perspective, it would make little sense to sink the bill over a few hundred million dollars.[10] Second, the congressional norm of reciprocity guarantees that some wasteful projects will be funded even though they could not stand on their own merits. This approach of "you scratch my back and I'll scratch yours" means that members can count on each other's support for their pet projects and to help each other get reelected.

This example shows how digging below the surface of political events can help to explain why things happen in American politics. While you still may be relieved that bridge will not be built (and we agree), you now have a sense of why such a project may be approved, without assuming that members of Congress are clueless or single-minded. Our goal is to give you a similar understanding of the entire range of American politics. We are not going to spend much time talking about how American politics should be. Rather, our focus will be on explaining American politics as it is. Here are some other questions we will examine:

- Why do some people participate in the political system while others do not?
- How does the Constitution structure our rights and liberties and the broader political system?
- Why do people vote as they do?
- Why do so many people mistrust politicians and the political system?
- Why do most members of Congress get reelected?
- How do Supreme Court justices decide cases?
- Why do presidents sometimes appear all-powerful, but look powerless other times?
- How much do the media, interest groups, judges, and bureaucrats influence policy decisions and why?

We will answer these questions and many others by applying three key ideas about the nature of politics: politics is everywhere, the political process matters, and politics is conflictual. But before we outline those themes, we need to explore an even more basic question.

Why Do We Have a Government?

TO PROVIDE ORDER

At a basic level, the answer to this question seems obvious: without **government** there would be chaos. As the seventeenth-century British philosopher Thomas Hobbes said, life in the "state of nature" (that is, without government) would be "solitary, poor, nasty, brutish, and short."[11] Without government, there would be no laws—people could do whatever they wanted. Even if people tried to develop informal rules, there would be no way to enforce them without some type of government. This crucial governmental role is noted by the Founders of our government in the preamble to the Constitution: two of the central goals of government are to "provide for the common defense" and to "insure domestic Tranquility." The former refers to military protection (by the Army and Navy at the time of the Founding; it now also includes the Marines, Coast Guard, and Air Force) against foreign invasion and the defense of our common security interests. The latter refers to law enforcement within the nation, which today includes the National Guard,

government The system for implementing decisions made through the political process.

FBI, Department of Homeland Security, state and local police, and courts. So at a minimal level, government is necessary to provide security.

However, there's more to it than that. The Founders also cited the desire to "establish Justice . . . promote the general Welfare, and secure the Blessings of Liberty to ourselves and our Posterity." But do we need government to do these things? It may be obvious that the police power of the state is required to prevent anarchy, but can't people take care of each other and secure their own welfare and prosperity? In a utopian world, maybe, but the Founders had a more realistic view of human nature. As the Founder James Madison said, "But what is government itself, but the greatest of all reflections on human nature? If men were angels, no government would be necessary. If angels were to govern men, neither external nor internal controls on government would be necessary."[12] Furthermore, Madison continued, people have a variety of interests that have "divided mankind into parties, inflamed them with mutual animosity, and rendered them much more disposed to vex and oppress each other than to co-operate for their common good."[13] That is, without government, we would quickly be headed toward Hobbes's nasty and brutish state of nature. Madison's view of human nature might sound pessimistic, but it is also realistic. He assumes that people are self-interested: we want what is best for ourselves and our families, and to satisfy those interests, we tend to form groups with like-minded people. Madison saw these groups, which he called **factions**, as being opposed to the public good, and his greatest fear was of tyranny by a majority faction imposing its will on the rest of the nation. For example, if one group took power and established an official state religion, that faction would be tyrannizing people who practiced a different religion. This type of oppression is precisely why many of the early American colonists fled Europe in the first place.

So government is necessary to avoid the anarchy of the state of nature, and the *right kind* of government is needed to avoid the tyranny of the majority. As discussed in Chapters 2 and 3, America's government was set up to control the effects of factions by dividing government power in three main ways. First, the **separation of powers** divides the government into three branches, the judicial, executive, and legislative, and assigns distinct duties to each branch. Second, the system of **checks and balances** gives each branch some power over the other two. (For example, the president can veto legislation passed by Congress, Congress can impeach the president, and the Supreme Court has the power to interpret laws written by Congress to determine whether they are constitutional.) Third, **federalism** divides power yet again by allotting different responsibilities to local, state, and national government. With power divided in this fashion, Madison reasoned, no single faction could dominate the government.

factions Groups of like-minded people who try to influence the government. American government is set up to avoid domination by any one of these groups.

separation of powers The division of government power across the judicial, executive, and legislative branches.

checks and balances A system in which each branch of government has some power over the others.

federalism The division of power across the local, state, and national levels of government.

▲ *Two important government functions are to "provide for the common defense" and "insure domestic tranquility." The military and local police are two of the most obvious ways in which the government plays those roles.*

public goods Services or actions (such as protecting the environment) that, once provided to one person, become available to everyone. Government is typically needed to provide public goods because they will be under-produced by the free market.

collective action problem A situation in which the members of a group would benefit by working together to produce some outcome, but each individual is better off refusing to cooperate and reaping benefits from those who do the work.

free rider problem The incentive to benefit from others' work without contributing that leads individuals in a collective action situation to refuse to work together.

positive externalities Benefits created by a public good that are shared by the primary consumer of the good and by society more generally.

Another implication of Madison's argument is that the federal government exists to address hard problems that Americans cannot solve on their own, such as taking care of the poor, the sick, or the aged, and dealing with global issues like climate change, terrorist threats, and helping to raise the standard of living in other countries. Government is not inevitable—people can decide that these problems aren't worth solving. But if people *do* want to address these large problems, government action is necessary because **public goods** such as these are not efficiently provided by the free market, either because a **collective action problem** prevents the good from being provided, or because the good will be under-produced by the market.

The eighteenth-century Scottish philosopher David Hume explained the problem of collective action:

> Two neighbours may agree to drain a meadow which they possess in common [so they would be able to use it to grow crops] because 'tis easy for them to know each others mind and each must perceive that the immediate consequence of his failing in his part is the abandoning the whole project. But 'tis very difficult and indeed impossible that a thousand persons shou'd agree in any such action; it being difficult for them to concert so complicated a design and still more difficult for them to execute it while each seeks a pretext to free himself of the trouble and expence and wou'd lay the whole burden on others. Political society easily remedies both these inconveniences.[14]

That is, it is easy for two people to tackle a common problem without the help of government, but a thousand people, to say nothing of the more than 300 million in the United States today, will suffer from a **free rider problem**: it is in everyone's interest to "lay the whole burden on others," and because everyone thinks that way, the meadow cannot be drained. As Hume notes, "political society"—government—can "remedy those inconveniences" by draining the meadow and providing the desired public good. A government representing 300 million people can provide public goods, such as protecting the environment, that could not be provided by all those people acting on their own, so they elect leaders and pay taxes to provide those public goods.

Some types of public goods cannot be provided by the free market and must be provided by the government because once the good is produced, anyone can consume it without paying for it. The classic example provided by economists is a lighthouse. Once it is built, any passing ship benefits from its beacon, and it would be impossible for a private lighthouse owner to charge every ship on the ocean that used its light. Therefore the government must levy a tax on ship owners to provide the lighthouse. Similarly, a private company could not provide national defense because the free rider problem means we cannot rely on each citizen to decide individually to pay for a military; the existence and effectiveness of the military would become unacceptably uncertain. Therefore, the government must defend our country.

The free market may provide other types of public goods, but they will be underproduced because of what economists call **positive externalities**, which means that the benefits from the good are shared by the primary consumer of the good and by society at large. Education is a great example. You benefit personally from your college education in terms of the knowledge and experience you gain, and perhaps the higher salary that you will earn because of your college degree. However, society also benefits from your education. Your employer will benefit from your knowledge and skills, as will people you interact with. If education were solely provided by the free market, those who could afford schooling would go, but the rest would not,

▲ *A lighthouse is a classic example of a public good—a service or product that could not be produced by private markets because once the good is provided, anyone can benefit from it without paying. Supplying public goods is one way that the government provides for the public welfare.*

Forms of Government

The Greek political philosopher Aristotle, writing in the fourth century B.C., developed a classification scheme for governments that is still surprisingly useful today. He distinguished three pure types of government based on the number of rulers versus the number ruled: monarchy (rule by one), aristocracy (rule by the few), and polity (rule by the many, more specifically the property-owning middle class). The only modifications to this typology in the past 2,000 years changed the last category to republicanism (representative democracy with a constitution) and expanded participation beyond the middle class.

Additional distinctions can be made within Aristotle's third type, constitutional republican governments, based on how they allocate power between the executive, legislative, and judicial branches. Presidential systems such as the United States tend to follow a strict separation of power between the three branches, while parliamentary systems such as the United Kingdom elect the chief executive from the legislature, so there is much closer coordination between those two branches.

Aristotle's third type can be further refined by considering the relationships between different levels of the government. In a federal system, power is shared between the local, state, and national levels of government. In a unitary system, all power is held at the national level. A confederation is a less common form of government in which states retain their sovereignty and autonomy but form a loose association at the national level.

leaving a large segment of society with little or no education and therefore unemployable. So, public education, like many important services, benefits all levels of society and must be provided by the government for the general welfare.

Now that we understand *why* we have a government, the next question is, *what* does the government do to accomplish the Founders' goals of "insuring domestic tranquility" and "promoting general welfare"? Many visible components of the government promote these goals, from the police and armed services, to the Internal Revenue Service, the Post Office, the Social Security Administration, the National Aeronatics and Space Administration, the Department of Education, and the Food and Drug Administration. More generally, the government does several things:

- It creates and enforces laws and protects private property through the criminal justice system.
- It establishes a common currency and regulates commerce among the states and trade with other nations.
- It provides public goods that would not be produced or would be under-supplied by the free market, including national defense, an interstate highway system, and national parks.
- It regulates the market to promote the general good, specifically by addressing market failures in areas such as environmental pollution and product safety.
- It protects individual civil liberties, such as the freedom of speech and the free exercise of religion.

SECTION SUMMARY

1. Government is necessary to establish justice, promote the general welfare, and secure liberty.
2. The separation of powers and the system of checks and balances prevent the tyranny of the majority.
3. Government is necessary to overcome collective action problems and provide public goods.

What Is Politics?

We define **politics** as the process that determines what government does. You may consider politics the same thing as government, but we view politics as being much broader; it includes ways of behaving and making decisions that are common in everyday life. Many aspects of our discussion of politics will probably sound familiar because your life involves politics on a regular basis. This may sound a little abstract, but it should become clear in light of the three key ideas of this book.

First, *politics is everywhere.* Decisions about what government should do or who should be in charge are integral to society and they influence the everyday lives of ordinary Americans. Politics helps to determine what people can and cannot do, their quality of life, and how they think about events, people, and situations. Moreover, people's political thought and behavior are driven by the same types of calculations and decision-making rules that shape beliefs and actions in other parts of life. For example, deciding which presidential candidate to vote for is similar to deciding which college to attend. In the first instance you might consider issue positions, character, and leadership ability, while in the latter you will weigh which school fits your academic goals, how much tuition you can afford, and where different schools are located. In both cases you are making a decision that will satisfy the criteria that are important to you.

Second, *political process matters.* Governmental actions don't happen by accident— they result from conscious choices made by elected officials and bureaucrats. Politics, as the process that determines what governments do, is also the process that puts certain individuals into positions of power and makes the rules that structure their choices. The media often covers political campaigns the way they would report on a boxing match or the Super Bowl. This focus on competition and rivalries generates entertaining stories, but it leads people to overlook the institutions, rules, and procedures that often have a decisive influence on politics.

Third, *politics is conflictual.* The questions debated in elections and the options considered by policy makers are generally marked by disagreement at all levels. The federal government does not spend much time resolving issues that everyone agrees should be decided in a particular way. Rather, making government policy involves issues on which people disagree, sometimes strongly, which makes compromise difficult—and this is a normal, healthy part of politics.

KEY IDEA 1: POLITICS IS EVERYWHERE

From coverage of campaigns, legislative proceedings, and presidential pronouncements, to debates over policy, most of us think about some aspect of politics every day. Even though most Americans have a relatively weak interest in politics, most of us absorb politics without really trying, simply by considering information that falls in our laps as we do other things. When you read the paper, watch TV, surf the Web, or listen to the radio, you'll almost surely encounter a political story. Similarly, when you walk down the street, you may see billboards, bumper stickers, posters, or T-shirts advertising a candidate, a political party, an interest group, or an issue position. Someone may ask you to sign a petition. You may walk past a vacant building or a homeless person and wonder whether the government is doing anything about these problems—or whether a winning candidate followed through on her promise to help. You may see an Army recruiting office or glance at a newspaper headline about the war in Iraq, and wonder whether members of Congress and the president were right to pursue this policy. Or you may be going to the post office to mail your tax return, and wonder what you're getting for your money.

Many people have an active interest in putting politics in front of us on a daily basis. Interest groups, political parties, and candidates work to raise public awareness of the political process and to shape what people know and want. The news media offer extensive coverage of politics, both stories about elections and governing and about the consequences of government actions in the ways policies affect ordinary Americans.

The broad reach of politics can also be seen in the concerns that prompt ordinary Americans to look for information. Table 1.1 shows the top ten stories on Google News in mid-January 2008. Of the ten stories, nine have a clear connection to the federal government, from the 2008 presidential race to military operations and actions taken by government agencies. The lone exception concerns a tiger attack at the San Francisco Zoo—and even here, federal regulations determine who can import dangerous animals into the country.

Politics is also a fundamental part of how Americans think about themselves. While most people don't know a lot about politics and governing, virtually everyone can name their party identification, whether they are a Democrat, a Republican, or independent.[15] Most Americans are able to place their own views on a continuum between liberal and conservative.[16] These beliefs shape our views; Americans often look at the world through a partisan or ideological lens. For example, surveys conducted after Hurricane Katrina found Democrats more likely than Republicans to

TABLE 1.1   POLITICS IS EVERYWHERE: TOP STORIES ON GOOGLE NEWS, JANUARY 17, 2008

STORY	FEDERAL GOVERNMENT INVOLVEMENT
Cold Remedies Risky for Kids under Two	Warning issued by the Food and Drug Administration
Landing Temporarily Paralyzes Heathrow	Federal Aviation Administration involved in the subsequent investigation
Gates Ruffles NATO Feathers over Afghan War Readiness	Conflict between U.S. and allies over sending troops to Afghanistan
In South Carolina, the Campaign Mud Arrived before Santa	2008 presidential race
Dozens Report Seeing UFOs over Tiny Texas Town	These UFOs were actually Air Force F-16s
Clinton, Obama Battle for Upper Hand in Nevada	2008 presidential race
Judge Hears Zoo Arguments	—
Navy Chopper Crashes in Texas, Killing Three Crew	Military training mission
Former Congressman Is Indicted over Ties to Islamic Charity	Actions of former legislator
House Panel Criticizes CIA Tape Destruction	Conflict between Congress and the executive branch

SOURCE: Google News search, 1/17/08.

give the federal government poor marks for its efforts to help people whose homes were damaged or lost due to the storm.[17] That is, a typical Democrat seeing the same events as a typical Republican would evaluate the situation differently.

Politics is everywhere in another important way: government actions touch virtually every aspect of your life. As the ironic saying goes, "No man's life, liberty, or property is safe while the Legislature is in session."[18] Some people claim that "the personal is political," meaning that even our most private, personal rights and thoughts are affected by the political process and government actions.[19] The most obvious examples include abortion, gay marriage, and laws governing child custody and other aspects of divorce.

One measure of the government's capacity to influence our lives is its size. As Nuts and Bolts 1.2 shows, the federal government spent about 2.6 trillion dollars in 2006, accounting for 20 percent of the American economy. Over 11 million people receive a paycheck from the federal government, either directly, as a civil servant or member of the military, or because they work for a company funded by a government contract, work for a project funded by a federal grant, or work for the postal service. Federal bureaucrats also issue thousands of pages of new regulations every year. Even in terms of these broad measures, the federal government's reach into the lives of ordinary Americans is extraordinary.

The impact of policy outcomes becomes clear when you think about your typical day. If you attend a public university, you might wake up in a dorm that was partially funded with taxpayers' money, or maybe your apartment was built with federal housing subsidies. Your breakfast was subject to regulation by the Food and Drug Administration. Your clothing was likely manufactured overseas and may have been subject to federal tariffs and other regulations before it was sold. The television you watch and the radio you listen to are regulated by the Federal Trade Commission, the Consumer Products Safety Commission, and the Federal Communications Commission. When you're checking your e-mail or an online weather report, remember that the Internet was developed under contract with an agency in the Department of Defense, and that the National Weather Service provides the satellite imagery used to generate local weather forecasts.

▶ *The idea that "politics is everywhere" is most evident when government policies influence highly personal decisions, such as those about marriage, divorce, and abortion. Gay marriage has been controversial, and many states have passed laws and constitutional amendments defining marriage as being between a man and a woman. In 2004 the city of San Francisco defied California's ban on same sex marriages, issuing marriage licenses to gay and lesbian couples.*

The Size of the Federal Government

Federal Spending	$2.771 trillion (19.6% of GDP)
Federal Taxes	$2.416 trillion (17.1% of GDP)
Federal Workforce	1.8 million civil servants
	1.4 million military personnel
	5.1 million employees of government contractors
	2.9 million people paid through government grants
	800,000 Postal Service employees
Federal Regulations	78,000 new pages in 2006

SOURCES: Congressional Budget Office, "Fiscal Year 2007 Mid-Session Review Budget of the United States," available at http://www.whitehouse.gov/omb/budget/fy2007/pdf/07msr.pdf, and "The Budget and Economic Outlook: Fiscal Years 2008–2018," available at http://www.cbo.gov/ftpdocs/89xx/doc8917/01-23-2008_BudgetOutlook.pdf. Paul Light, "Fact Sheet on the New True Size of Government," Brookings Institution, September 5, 2003, available at http://www.brookings.edu/dybdocroot/gs/cps/light20030905.pdf.

As you walk out the door, consider that government regulations developed by bureaucrats in the Environmental Protection Agency determine how clean the air is—and the costs that companies pay for environmental cleanup and protection. The design of your car was influenced by fuel economy legislation; the price you pay to fill your gas tank is affected by America's foreign policy. And if you drive on a highway, it was likely paid for, at least in part, by a federal highway bill. Suppose you are on your way to class. Most universities and colleges receive money from the federal government in the form of faculty research grants and funding for institutes and laboratories. And many college students receive direct governmental assistance as student loans or grants.

You can ignore what government does, refuse to participate in elections, and have nothing to do with any elected officials, bureaucrats, or judges, but the government's influence over your life is impossible to avoid. Opting out simply ensures that you have no influence over government policy—the decisions that affect your life still get made.

Finally, the idea that politics is everywhere has a deeper meaning: people's political behavior is similar to their behavior in the rest of their lives. You may think that politicians and bureaucrats may as well be a separate species, or that the political world operates according to its own unique set of rules. In fact, the opposite is true. The more you learn about politics, the more you see politics embedded in your everyday life.

As we discuss in Chapter 8, Elections, many voters form judgments about candidates by focusing on a candidate's appearance, including his race, gender, or age. Such stereotyping also shapes people's judgments about individuals who they meet in other areas of life. Inside politics and out, the same mechanisms apply.

Similarly, in Chapter 9, Interest Groups, we will examine one of the biggest problems faced by groups from the Sierra Club to the National Rifle Association: getting organized. Convincing like-minded individuals to contribute time or money to a group's lobbying efforts is no easy task. Each would-be contributor also has the opportunity to be a free rider who refuses to participate yet reaps the benefits of others' participation. Because of these difficulties, some groups of people with common goals remain unorganized, as in David Hume's example of the failure to drain a meadow for farm land when the cooperation of a large number of people is required. College students, many of whom want more student aid and lower interest rates on government-subsidized student loans but fail to organize politically toward those ends, are a good example.

▲ While the price of gasoline is largely beyond government control, policies can have some impact on the price. A foreign policy that creates instability in oil-producing regions can cause gas prices to rise, while domestic policies encouraging more exploration and oil production may stabilize oil and gas prices.

The same kinds of collective action problems occur in everyday life as well. For example, when you live with roommates, keeping common areas neat and clean presents a collective action problem, since everyone has an interest in a clean area, but each person is also inclined to let someone else do the work. The same principles help us to understand campus protests of tuition hikes, alcohol bans, or changes in graduation requirements in terms of which kinds of issues and circumstances foster cooperation. In each case, individual free riders acting in their own self-interest may undermine the outcome that most people prefer.

This similarity between behavior in political situations and in the rest of life is no surprise; everything that happens in politics is the result of individuals' choices. And the connections between politics and everyday life mean you know more about politics than you realize.

KEY IDEA 2: POLITICAL PROCESS MATTERS

The political process is often described as though it were a version of the Super Bowl or the World Series, with a focus on strategies and tactics and ultimately on "winning." In fact, a politics news show on CNN has a daily segment titled "The Play of the Day," which sounds a lot like the rundown of the home runs and best fielding plays of the day on ESPN. This focus overlooks an important point: politics is the process that determines what government does, none of which is inevitable. Public policy—from defending the nation to building "bridges to nowhere"—is up for grabs. And the political process determines these government actions. It really is not just a game.

Elections are an excellent example of the importance of the political process. Elections allow voters to give fellow citizens the power to enact laws, write budgets, and appoint senior bureaucrats and federal judges, so it matters who gets elected. George W. Bush, a Republican, was president from January 2001 to January 2009. Republicans held a majority of the seats in Congress for most of his first six years,[20] but the balance shifted when Democrats gained control of Congress in the 2006 elections.

Many of the policies enacted during the first six years of Bush's presidency would look quite different if Democrats had controlled the House or Senate. For example, the Partial-Birth Abortion Ban Act, enacted in 2003, probably would not exist. While Republican majorities in Congress repeatedly voted to approve the ban in the 1990s, it was always vetoed by President Bill Clinton, a Democrat. Even after the bill was signed into law by President Bush, the Supreme Court might have declared it unconstitutional were it not for two new justices of the Court, John Roberts and Samuel Alito (appointed by President Bush and confirmed by the Republican-controlled Senate), who voted to uphold the ban. Justice Sandra Day O'Connor, whom Justice Alito replaced when he joined the Court, probably would have voted against the ban, changing the outcome of the justices' 5–4 vote.[21]

All of this goes to show that the political process matters: while late-term abortions are relatively rare, supporters of abortion rights see the ban on the procedure as a significant erosion of a woman's right to choose, and opponents view the procedure as a particularly objectionable form of abortion. The ban is the result of a complex political process, and it clearly has consequences for many Americans.

Though election outcomes can be quite far-reaching, politics is more than elections. As you will see, many members of the federal bureaucracy have considerable influence over what government does by virtue of their roles in developing and implementing government policies. The same is true for federal judges, who review government actions to see if they are consistent with the Constitution and other federal

▲ Nancy Pelosi (D-CA) became the new Speaker of the House in January 2007, after Democrats took control of the U.S. House of Representatives for the first time in twelve years. Having Democrats in charge of both the House and Senate made President Bush's last two years in office much more difficult for him.

laws. These individuals' decisions are part of the political process, even though they are not elected to their positions.

Ordinary citizens are also part of politics. They can vote; donate time or money to interest groups, party organizations, or individual candidates; or demand action from these groups or individuals. All of these actions can influence government policy, either by determining who holds the power to change policy directly, or by signaling to policy makers what sorts of choices have public support.

Another important element of politics is the web of rules and procedures that determine who has the power to make choices about government policy. These rules range from the requirement that the president has to have been born in the United States, to the rules that structure debates and voting in the House and the Senate, to the procedures for approving new federal regulations. Seemingly innocuous rules can have an enormous impact on what can happen or what does happen, which means that choices about these rules are actually disguised choices about outcomes. For example, the Constitution's rule that only natural-born citizens may become president means that Governor Arnold Schwarzenegger of California cannot run for the office, since he was born in Austria.

You can debate in the abstract whether this restriction is a good or bad idea. Perhaps those born in the United States are more likely to have its best interests at heart than those born outside the country, or perhaps not. However, abstract debates about rules do not capture their real impact on elections and policies. In the modern era, it's impossible to debate the merits of the presidential citizenship requirement without considering its impact on Schwarzenegger's political prospects, because many people believe that he would be a viable presidential candidate if he were allowed to run.

Another example is the cloture rule for ending debate in the Senate, which means that it takes 60 votes out of 100 to enact a new law, not just a simple majority of 51. During the part of George W. Bush's presidency when Democrats were the minority party in the Senate but the Republican majority fell short of 60 votes, cloture gave the Democrats real power over government policy.

The ability to determine political rules empowers the people who make those choices. To paraphrase a favorite saying of Representative John Dingell, a long-serving Democrat from Michigan, "If you let me decide procedure and I let you decide substance, I'll beat you every time."

KEY IDEA 3: POLITICS IS CONFLICTUAL

Most people do not like conflict, either in their personal lives or in politics. You probably have heard the saying, "Three topics you cannot discuss in polite company are money, religion, and politics." Rather than talking about controversial subjects that may make people uncomfortable, many people simply avoid those topics—and apply their disdain for conflict to politics. "Why is there so much partisan bickering?" our students frequently ask. "Why can't they just get along and compromise?" But conflict cannot be avoided in politics the way it can in polite company. In most instances, politics *requires* conflict to arrive at policies that are in the nation's best interest.

Furthermore, political conflict is rooted in Americans' disagreements on policy questions. These conflicts often involve trade-offs, situations in which compromise is impossible, or scenarios in which giving one group something means that another group gets nothing. It is wrong-headed to claim that there would be no conflict in politics if politicians would just listen to the public. The war in Iraq is a good example. Responses to a 2006 survey of Americans on the future of U.S. involvement

▲ The composition of the Supreme Court can have an important impact on the outcome of closely divided cases. This was certainly true of the Partial-Birth Abortion Ban Act, which the Court upheld after Samuel Alito replaced Justice Sandra Day O'Connor.

▲ California Governor Arnold Schwarzenegger, shown here on the night of his solid reelection victory in 2006, cannot run for president because he is not a natural born U.S. citizen. Such rules may restrict the range of political choices.

in Iraq showed a profound lack of consensus. No matter which policy option you pick, from increasing troop levels significantly to withdrawing troops immediately, a large proportion of Americans prefer a different policy.

Abortion is another example of an issue on which public opinion is fragmented. Abortion rights have been a perennial issue in elections and in Washington since a 1973 Supreme Court decision held that state laws banning abortion were unconstitutional. Surveys about abortion rights show public support spread across a wide range of options, with little agreement about which policy is best. In Chapter 5, Public Opinion, we will look more closely at the political implications of this kind of broad disagreement. In such cases, the problem is not that citizens or politicians like to fight or are inherently unwilling to compromise. Rather, these conflicts reflect sharp, intense differences of opinion among both citizens and elected officials that are rooted in self-interest, ideology, and personal beliefs. You might expect that given enough time, politicians will find ways to compromise, but this is not always true. The problem is the need for trade-offs. In many cases, there may be no policy choice that satisfies even a slight majority of elected officials or citizens.

Such conflict should be no surprise. Situations in which everyone (or almost everyone) agrees about what government should be doing are easy to resolve: either a popular new policy is enacted or an unpopular issue is avoided and the policy debate naturally moves off the political agenda. For example, in the 1980s, a consensus emerged among scientists that chlorofluorocarbons (CFCs), chemicals used in refrigerators, air conditioners, and other machinery, were damaging the atmosphere's ozone layer, which blocks the sun's harmful ultraviolet rays. After minimal debate (all but the most trivial policies have *some* opposition), a combination of international treaties, legislation, and regulations were enacted to strictly limit the use of CFCs and favor the available alternatives in most applications. The result? The ozone layer is strengthening, and CFCs are no longer discussed, either in government or across the nation.[22]

While consensus issues are dealt with quickly and disappear, conflictual issues remain on the agenda as winners try to extend their gains and losers work to roll back policies. Thus, one reason that abortion rights is a perennial issue in campaigns and congressional debates is that there is no national consensus on when abortions should be allowed, no indication that the issue is becoming less important to citizens or elected officials, and no sign of a compromise policy that would attract widespread support.

▶ *Public opinion on abortion is deeply divided. People who believe that "abortion kills" are not going to be swayed by arguments to "keep your laws off my body," and vice versa. Consequently, some issues such as abortion are not very amenable to political compromise.*

An important implication of the inevitable conflicts in American politics is that compromise and bargaining are essential to getting things done. A politician who bargains with opponents is not necessarily abandoning his principles; striking a deal may be the only way to make some of the policy changes he wants. Only in a limited set of circumstances can anyone in government act unilaterally. Enacting a law, for example, requires majority support in the House and the Senate and the president's approval—or two-thirds majorities in both the House and the Senate to override the president's veto. The president's power is also limited. Although he is commander in chief of America's armed forces, members of Congress can control military operations by means of budget restrictions or by invoking the War Powers Act, a 1973 law designed to give Congress greater control over the deployment of troops.

Finally, while conflict is an essential part of American politics, it is important to remember that agreement sometimes exists in the midst of controversy. For example, the survey about abortion cited earlier found strong support for measures such as requiring parental notification when a minor has an abortion, mandating a twenty-four-hour waiting period before an abortion, or requiring doctors who perform the procedure to present their patients with information on alternatives such as adoption. Similarly, public opinion data on the war in Iraq show that relatively few people favored an immediate withdrawal. Instead, most of them were considering when the withdrawal should occur and what should be done in the meantime.

SECTION SUMMARY

1. **Politics is everywhere.** This key idea has two components: politics is a fundamental part of everyone's life—and the ways people think and act politically are driven by the same types of calculations and decision-making rules that govern beliefs and actions in other parts of their lives.
2. **The political process matters.** Politics is the process that determines what governments do. Governmental actions are the result of conscious choices made by elected officials and bureaucrats.
3. **Politics is conflictual.** Making government policy typically involves issues on which people disagree, sometimes strongly, about what should be done. Although this means that compromises are hard to find, conflict is a normal and healthy part of politics.

Sources of Conflict in American Politics

Where does political conflict come from? As mentioned earlier, most people avoid conflict, so you might think politicians would try to minimize it. The reality is that their disagreements are often intractable because of inherent differences between people and their opinions about government and politics.

ECONOMIC INTERESTS, CULTURE, IDENTITY, AND IDEOLOGY

Economic Interests Relative economic equality was a defining characteristic of our nation's early history, at least among white men, since small land-owners, businessmen, craftsmen, and their families comprised a large majority of the nation's population.

Compared to our European counterparts, the United States has been relatively free from class-based politics. Over time, our nation became more stratified by class, to the point that the United States now ranks about fiftieth among the world's 194 countries in terms of income equality, but a commitment to the **free market** and **economic individualism** remain central parts of our national identity.

Despite this basic consensus on economic principles and a history relatively free of class-based politics, there are important differences among American citizens, interest groups, and political parties in terms of their economic interests and favored economic policies. As we discuss in Chapter 7, Political Parties, Democratic politicians and activists tend to favor more **redistributive tax policies** and social spending on programs for the poor. Democrats are also more inclined to regulate industry on issues such as protecting the environment and worker and product safety. Republicans favor lower taxes and less spending on social policies. They are also more supportive than Democrats of the free market and less inclined to interfere with business interests.

Cultural Values In the past several elections, political analysts focused considerable attention on the **culture wars** in the United States between "red-state Americans" who have strong religious beliefs and "blue-state Americans" who tend to be more secular. (The color coding of the states comes from the election-night maps of the United States on network news that show the states carried by Republican candidates in red and those won by Democrats in blue—but see Figure 1.2, "Purple America," for a more nuanced take on this). After George W. Bush was reelected in 2004, leaders of the Christian right claimed that they had delivered the election for Bush and wanted action on their issues, which raised the level of conflict on a broad range of issues.[23]

While the precise makeup and impact of "values voters" is still being debated, there is no doubt that many Americans disagree on cultural and moral issues including the broad category of "family values" (including whether and how to regulate pornography, gambling, and media obscenity and violence), supplementing the teaching of evolution in public schools with the perspectives of intelligent design and creationism, gay marriage, abortion, stem cell research, school prayer, vouchers for parochial schools, and religious displays in public places. These are all

▶ *The importance of cultural values in politics shows in the influence of Americans with strong religious beliefs. Former Senate Majority Leader Bill Frist (R-TN), appeared via teleconference at a Christian rally called Justice Sunday in Louisville, Kentucky, urging churchgoers to support President Bush in his fight with congressional Democrats over judicial nominees.*

◀ Civil and voting rights policies contributed to the realignment of the South in the second half of the twentieth century, as more whites began supporting the Republican Party, and the Democratic Party came to be seen as the champion of minority rights. Here, African American voters head to the polls in South Carolina after a Supreme Court ruling determined they had previously been illegally deprived of the right to vote.

hot-button issues that interest groups and activists on both sides attempt to keep at the top of the policy agenda. Gay marriage and intelligent design have become high-profile, controversial issues more recently than many of the others, but all of them are sure to elicit strong opinions.

Identity Politics Racial, ethnic, and gender differences can also contribute to groups' political interests. Over the last generation, about 90 percent of African Americans have been strong supporters of Democratic candidates. Other racial groups are less cohesive in their voting than blacks, with their support for a particular party falling between in the 55 to 70 percent range. Whites tend to vote Republican; Latinos tend to vote Democratic with the exception of Cuban Americans, who tend to vote Republican; Asian Americans tend to vote Democratic but less consistently than even Latinos. A gender gap in national politics is also evident, with women more likely to vote for Democrats and men for Republicans. Of course, these tendencies are not fixed. In the nineteenth century, African Americans were enthusiastic supporters of Republicans, the "party of Lincoln."[24] Southern whites solidly voted Democratic from the mid-nineteenth century until the 1960s, and now they solidly vote Republican. The gender gap did not consistently appear until 1980—before then men and women tended to have similar voting patterns. Clearly the political implications of racial, ethnic, and gender differences change over time.

One of the enduring debates in American politics concerns whether ethnic and racial differences *should* be tied to political interests. One perspective is rooted in the melting pot image of America, which holds that as different racial and ethnic groups come to this country, they should mostly leave their native languages, customs, and traditions behind. This perspective focuses on the assimilation of various groups into American culture, with the belief that while groups will maintain some native traditions, our common bonds as Americans are more important. Supporters of this view advocate making English the country's official language and oppose bilingual public education.[25]

The alternatives to the melting pot view range from racial separatists, such as the Nation of Islam who see white-dominated society as oppressive and discriminatory, to multiculturalists who argue that there is strength in diversity. The latter perspective advocates mutual tolerance and respect for different traditions and backgrounds.[26] Though debates will continue about the policies best suited to our nation's diverse population, our multiracial makeup is clear, as shown in Table 1.2.

melting pot The idea that as different racial and ethnic groups come to America, they should assimilate into American culture, leaving their native languages, customs, and traditions behind.

ideology A cohesive set of ideas and beliefs used to organize and evaluate the political world.

By 2050, whites will no longer comprise a majority of the U.S. population (this is already true in five states). The extent to which this racial and ethnic diversity continues to be a source of political conflict depends on the broader role of race in our society. As long as there are racial differences in employment, education, health, housing, and crime, and as long as racial discrimination is present in our society, race will continue to matter for politics. The long-running debate over immigration reform is strong evidence that racial and ethnic issues in politics are not going to disappear any time soon.

Many of the same observations apply to gender and politics. The women's movement is usually viewed as beginning in 1848 at the first Women's Rights Convention at Seneca Falls, New York. The fight for women's suffrage and legal rights dominated the movement through the late nineteenth and early twentieth centuries. In the 1960s and 1970s, feminism and the women's liberation movement called attention to a broad range of issues: workplace issues including maternity leave, equal pay, and sexual harassment; reproductive rights and abortion; domestic violence; and sexual violence. While much progress has been made on many of these issues, gender remains an important source of political disagreement and identity politics.

Ideology The final source of differences in interests that we will discuss is **ideology**—a cohesive set of ideas and beliefs that allows you to organize and evaluate the political world. Ideology may seem most obviously related to political

TABLE 1.2 THE RACIAL COMPOSITION OF THE UNITED STATES

These census data show the racial diversity of the United States. Only 75 percent of Americans describe themselves as white. Moreover, the proportion of Hispanics and Latinos in the population is 12.5 percent and rising, although this category contains many distinct subgroups.

RACE	NUMBER	PERCENT
Total U.S. population	281,421,906	100
One race	274,595,678	97.6
Two or more races	6,826,228	2.4
White	211,460,626	75.1
Black or African American	34,658,190	12.3
American Indian and Alaska Native	2,475,956	0.9
Asian	10,242,998	3.6
Native Hawaiian and other Pacific Islander	398,835	0.1
Hispanic or Latino (of any race)	35,305,818	12.5
Mexican	20,640,711	7.3
Puerto Rican	3,406,178	1.2
Cuban	1,241,685	0.4
Other, Hispanic or Latino	10,017,244	3.6
Some other race	15,359,073	5.5

SOURCE: U.S. Census Bureau, Census 2000 Summary File 1.

interests through political parties since Republicans tend to be **conservative** and Democrats tend to be **liberal**. While this is true in a relative sense (most Republicans are more conservative than most Democrats), few Americans consider their own views ideologically extreme. On a seven-point scale, with one being extremely liberal and seven extremely conservative, less than 10 percent of all Americans placed themselves at either one or seven and more than half identified as moderates (a three, four, or five on the scale).[27]

Ideology shapes specific beliefs; conservatives favor lower taxes, a free market, and more limited government, while liberals support stronger government programs and more market regulation. However, the picture gets a little cloudier if you look more closely. **Libertarians**, for example, prefer very limited government serving only for national defense and a few other narrowly defined responsibilities. Because they are at the extreme end of the ideological continuum on this issue, libertarians are extremely conservative on issues such as social welfare policy, environmental policy, and government funding for education, but very liberal on issues involving personal liberty such as free speech, abortion, and the legalization of drugs. For libertarians, the consistent ideological theme is limiting the role of government in our lives.

Also, personal ideologies are not always consistent. Someone could be a fiscal conservative (favoring balanced budgets) and a social liberal (favoring the pro-choice position on abortion and marital rights for gays), or liberal on foreign policy issues (supporting humanitarian aid and opposing the war in Iraq) but conservative on moral issues (pro-life on abortion and opposing stem cell research). Ideology is a significant source of conflict in politics, and it does not always operate in a straightforward manner. In Chapter 5, Public Opinion, we address the question of whether America is becoming more ideological and polarized, deepening conflicts and making compromise more difficult. You may be surprised to find that the American public has fairly centrist views, and there are relatively few systematic differences between residents of blue states and red states on a broad range of policies. For example, political scientist Morris Fiorina finds that red-state and blue-state residents have very similar views on immigration, English as the official

conservative One side of the ideological spectrum defined by support for lower taxes, a free market, and a more limited government; generally associated with Republicans.

liberal One side of the ideological spectrum defined by support for stronger government programs and more market regulation; generally associated with Democrats.

libertarians Those who prefer very limited government and therefore tend to be quite conservative on issues such as welfare policy, environmental policy, and public support for education, but very liberal on issues of personal liberty like free speech, abortion, and the legalization of drugs.

◀ *Debate continues between the advocates of the American cultural "melting pot" and those favoring a multicultural perspective on ethnic heritage. Should our diverse cultures be assimilated into a single, uniquely American identity? Does our diversity make us stronger, or do our differences push us apart?*

language, environmental policy, school vouchers, affirmative action, equal rights for women, and tolerance of others' views. Although politics is conflictual, and differences are somewhat larger on gay rights, abortion, gun control, and the death penalty, even on these issues, views are not as polarized as you might think. (Out of thirteen issues, only two—gay rights and abortion—showed differences of 10 percent or more between red-state and blue-state respondents).[28]

Figure 1.2 illustrates this finding with data from the 2008 presidential election. The map shows the relative strength by state of John McCain and Barack Obama, with the reddest states showing the strongest Republican support and the bluest states showing the Democratic strongholds. As you can see, most of the country is purple, which indicates a geographic intermixing between the parties and their associated ideological beliefs. One of the themes of Barack Obama's 2008 presidential campaign was that we should focus less on blue states and red states and recognize that we are all Americans rather than partisans. This appeal seemed to work, as Obama made significant inroads in states that had been solidly red, such as Indiana, Virginia, and North Carolina.

FIGURE 1.2   **PURPLE AMERICA: THE 2008 PRESIDENTIAL ELECTION**

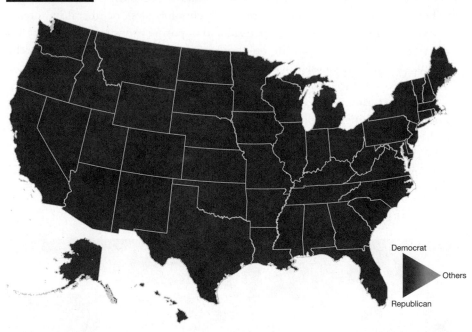

SOURCE: Provided by Robert J. Vanderbei, Princeton University.

SECTION SUMMARY

1. Some disagreements in politics are intractable because of inherent differences between people and their attitudes toward government and politics.
2. American political conflicts are rooted in citizens' different economic interests; cultural values; racial, ethnic, and gender identities; and ideologies.
3. Despite these differences, Americans tend toward moderate views on most issues, producing a "purple America" rather than clear divisions between so-called red states and blue states.

Conclusion

By understanding that politics is everywhere, that it's rooted in process, and it's conflictual, you will see that modern American political life makes more sense than you might think. Along the way, you will learn important "nuts and bolts" of the American political process as well as some political history. In general, though, we focus on real, contemporary questions, debates, and examples to illustrate broader points about our political system. After all, American politics in its current form is the politics that will have the greatest impact on your life.

While there will be many aspects of American politics with which you disagree, and some that will make you angry, our goal is to provide you with the tools you need to understand *why* government operates as it does. We are not arguing that the federal government is perfect, or that failures such as the inadequate response to Hurricane Katrina or funding for the "bridge to nowhere" are inevitable. Rather, we believe that any attempt to explain these outcomes, or to devise ways to prevent similar problems in the future, requires an understanding of why they happened in the first place. After reading this book, you will have a better sense of how American politics works.

CRITICAL THINKING

1. What are some examples from your life that illustrate that "politics is everywhere"? How do government policies affect the things you do every day? Can you think of past decisions or experiences that you may not have seen as political, but illustrate this idea as well?

2. Consider the observation by Representative John Dingell (D-MI) that "If you let me decide procedure and I let you decide substance, I'll beat you every time." Do you think Dingell is right? What are some instances in which process was more important than substance in determining an outcome?

3. What are your views on the role of conflict in politics? What types of issues are most likely to be resolved through political conflict and compromise, and which issues will be more resistant to compromise?

KEY TERMS

checks and balances (p. 7)
collective action problem (p. 8)
conservative (p. 21)
culture wars (p. 18)
economic individualism (p. 18)
factions (p. 7)
federalism (p. 7)
free market (p. 18)
free rider problem (p. 8)
government (p. 6)
ideology (p. 20)
liberal (p. 21)
libertarians (p. 21)
melting pot (p. 19)
politics (p. 10)
positive externalities (p. 8)
public goods (p. 8)
redistributive tax policies (p. 18)
separation of powers (p. 7)

SUGGESTED READING

Dahl, Robert, *On Democracy*. New Haven, CT: Yale University Press, 1998.

Fiorina, Morris P., with Samuel J. Abrams and Jeremy C. Pope. *Culture War? The Myth of a Polarized America*, 2nd ed. New York: Pearson, Longman, 2006.

Gutman, Amy. *Identity in Democracy*, Princeton, NJ: Princeton University Press, 2003.

Schattschneider, E. E. *The Semi-Sovereign People: A Realist's View of Democracy in America*. New York: Holt, Reinhart, and Winston, 1960.

THE CONSTITUTION AND THE FOUNDING

One of our graduate students was famous for carrying around a pocket-sized copy of the Constitution. He would whip it out to settle classroom disputes or consult it during political discussions in the student lounge. Though you may not be quite so intensely dedicated to the document, thorough knowledge of the Constitution is necessary for understanding the American political system. Consider these examples.

As November 7, 2000 unfolded, it soon became evident that this would not be a typical election night. Instead, the close battle between Vice President Al Gore and Texas governor George W. Bush only got tighter as votes started rolling in. Late into the night, many states remained too close for the bleary-eyed broadcasters to call. Florida quickly became the focus, as several networks called the state in for Gore early in the evening, only to put it back up for grabs an hour later. Early Wednesday morning, the networks called Florida for Bush, giving him enough electoral votes to win the presidency. Gore called Bush at about 3 A.M. to concede the election, then as Gore was on his way to make his concession speech, the networks decided once again that the election was too close to call. Gore called Bush again to retract his concession. The nation woke up on Wednesday to find that Gore had a national popular vote lead of several hundred thousand votes, while Bush led in Florida by 1,210 votes. With Florida's twenty-five electoral votes still up for grabs, Gore also led in the electoral college, but neither candidate had the 270 electoral votes needed to win the presidency.

The situation only escalated over the next few days. An electronic recount of the Florida vote showed Bush with a narrow lead of 327 votes. In the mean time, dozens of African American registered voters claimed that they had not been allowed to vote, and later the U.S. Commission on Civil Rights found that thousands of Florida voters had been improperly removed from the voter rolls by an effort to purge felons from the lists. A confusing "butterfly ballot" in Palm Beach County caused several thousand voters to accidentally select the Reform Party candidate, Pat Buchanan, rather than Gore, and thousands of ballots in other counties were discarded uncounted because the "chads" on the punch-card ballots were not entirely detached, making the ballots unreadable by the tabulating machines.

Over the next month, the dispute bounced between the state and federal courts as the Republican legal team tried to stop the recounts and certify Bush's lead while the Democratic lawyers tried to buy more time to recount votes. After two Florida

▲ Election officials in Broward County, Florida, examine ballots during the 2000 presidential election recount. The election outcome remained in doubt until the Supreme Court ended the recount, giving George W. Bush a razor-thin 537-vote win in a state that cast nearly 6 million votes.

State Supreme Court rulings that were favorable to Gore, the U.S. Supreme Court stepped in and stopped the recount, giving the election to Bush. Democrats fumed that the Court had acted in a blatantly partisan fashion while Republicans argued that only the Supreme Court could legitimately decide what was basically a tied election.

Throughout this drama, the American public received a crash course on the constitutional and electoral laws pertaining to presidential elections. Many Americans were only vaguely aware that the popular-vote winner could lose the election, or even that the president is not actually elected on Election Day in November, but more than a month later when the electoral votes are tabulated in Congress. This contentious election also raised many subtle legal questions. What would have happened had the state legislature certified one slate of electors giving George Bush the presidency, based on the original electronic recount, and the state Supreme Court certified another slate giving Al Gore the presidency based on the partial manual recount? Most Constitutional scholars agree that Congress had the authority to pick one slate over the other, but this is not entirely clear. Did the federal government have the right to determine the rules for counting and recounting votes, or was this the domain of the state and local governments? Did the equal protection clause of the 14th Amendment, which grants all citizens equal protection of the laws, mean that the recount could not continue because not all votes were being recounted, as the Supreme Court ultimately held? These difficult questions had many legal experts dusting off their pocket-sized copies of the Constitution.

The second example illustrates the importance of the Constitution in a very different way. Here, the constitutional and legal questions were less complex and the most important interpreter of the Constitution was the American people, rather than the Supreme Court. On January 21, 1998, the *Washington Post* dropped a political bombshell on the nation, revealing that President Bill Clinton had an inappropriate sexual relationship with White House intern Monica Lewinsky, and lied about it under oath in a sexual harassment suit regarding an unrelated incident that occurred when Clinton was governor of Arkansas. Pundits speculated that Clinton would have to resign within the month. However, Clinton maintained his innocence and his approval rating actually increased by nine points to 67 percent after the story broke. When physical evidence linking Clinton to Lewinsky was later leaked to the press, Clinton admitted the relationship and apologized to the nation. Two weeks later, Independent Counsel Kenneth Starr sent his report to Congress arguing that it provided the grounds for impeachment.[1] Republicans were convinced that the public would agree with their disgust at Clinton's conduct and support removing him from office. The report was published on the Internet, complete with the sordid details of the relationship.

Although the public thought Clinton's conduct was immoral, most did not consider it the kind of "high crime or misdemeanor" specified by the Constitution as grounds for

▲ A selection of newspaper headlines report President Clinton's admission that he had sexual relations with Monica Lewinsky and "misled people, including even [his] wife." Despite the scandal, Clinton survived impeachment and an attempt to remove him from office because a majority of the American public approved of the job he was doing as president.

POLITICS IS EVERYWHERE

"You Are Free to Go"

Skeptics may respond to the constitutional questions posed by the 2000 presidential election and President Clinton's impeachment with, "OK, sure. Those events are important and I should understand what happened. But how does the Constitution *really* affect me?" There are many constitutional rights that protect you that you may not be entirely aware of. The 4th Amendment's protection from illegal searches and seizures; various protections in the Bill of Rights for legal due process, such as the right to a fair trial, the right to confront witnesses, and the freedom from self-incrimination; and the 14th Amendment's guarantee that states cannot deny you the equal protection of the laws are just a few of the constitutional protections that affect millions of Americans every day.

However, sometimes it is important to know your constitutional rights, as shown by the Supreme Court's decision in *Ohio v. Robinette*.[a] The case involved a man, Mr. Robinette, who was stopped for speeding

Police officers make millions of traffic stops every year. You might find it useful to know your constitutional rights during a traffic stop.

and given a verbal warning. When returning Mr. Robinette's driver's license, the officer asked him if he had any "illegal drugs, weapons, or contraband" in the car. He said that he didn't and consented to a search of the car, in which the officer then found a small amount of marijuana and a methamphetamine pill. He was found guilty

of "knowing possession of a controlled substance" by a lower court, but his conviction was overturned by the Ohio Court of Appeals' ruling that the search was illegal because the officer did not inform Mr. Robinette that he was legally free to go after receiving verbal warning and having his license returned. The Ohio State Supreme Court agreed with that view, but was overruled by the U.S. Supreme Court which said, "The 4th Amendment does not require that a lawfully seized defendant be advised that he is 'free to go' before his consent to search will be recognized as voluntary." That is, the defendant *was* free to go, but the officer was not obligated to tell him so. If Mr. Robinette had had a better understanding of the Constitution, he never would have been arrested. We are not urging you to study the Constitution in order to get away with illegal activities. (Besides, we are sure you would never find yourself in a comparable position with a police officer.) However, knowing your constitutional rights may unexpectedly come in handy. ■

impeachment and removal from office. Congressional Republicans pressed ahead with the impeachment case despite strong public support for the president; the Democrats even picked up seats in the 1998 midterm election, something the president's party had done only once in the previous 156 years. In a largely party-line vote, the House approved articles of impeachment on December 19, 1998—the same day Clinton's public approval rating peaked at 73 percent! The Senate took the hint and after five weeks of testimony, throughout which two-thirds of the public continued to favor Clinton remaining in office, they voted to acquit.

What do these events show about the Constitution and the political system? At a minimum, citizens need to know the basics about the electoral college and the grounds for impeachment to make sense of what happened. Even citizens whose involvement goes no deeper than watching news of these events unfold still played key roles in both cases. When the Supreme Court decided that the 2000 recount should stop and that George Bush would be president, Americans accepted the decision because of their faith in the Constitution and the Supreme Court. Sure, Democratic partisans were outraged, liberal columnists said that the integrity of the Supreme Court was permanently damaged, and Al Gore was certainly disappointed, but there were no riots, no one stormed the Capitol, and neither Al Gore nor other Democratic leaders contested the Court's decision. The impeachment example illustrates a very different relationship between the people, political officials, and the Constitution. Here, rather than deferring, the people imposed their interpretation of the Constitution on the experts. While most Americans did not have a good grasp of the congressional debates over the meaning of "high crimes and misdemeanors," their gut-level interpretation of the framers' intent—that impeachment should be used for *political* abuses of power rather than personal failings—kept Bill Clinton in office.

Other than illustrating the importance of understanding the Constitution, these examples also highlight a central point of this chapter: there are multiple interpreters of the Constitution. While the Supreme Court often has the final word, the president and members of Congress also must interpret the Constitution on a daily basis. For example, when President George W. Bush decided whether to seek Congress's approval to invade Iraq, he and his advisers had to assess the extent to which the Constitution defines the war powers as shared between the president and Congress. Can the president, as commander in chief, use the military unilaterally, or does Congress's power to declare war mean that they must approve any military invasion? Likewise, when members of Congress write laws, they must decide, for example, whether the Constitution's commerce clause gives them the power to limit the possession of guns within 1,000 feet of a school or to mandate that businesses provide access to handicapped people, or whether the 1st Amendment prevents them from regulating the Internet. Average citizens can also influence constitutional interpretation, as the Clinton impeachment example demonstrates. Indeed, the Constitution begins, "We the people of the United States," deriving its legitimacy directly from the people and conferring important responsibilities on Americans to understand and appreciate the document.

However, recent polls suggest that many Americans are unfamiliar with the Constitution's basic provisions. One reporter observed, "The future of American liberty rests in the hands of young people more familiar with the Three Stooges than the three branches of government." Indeed, a national poll found that 59 percent of thirteen- to seventeen-year-olds could identify Larry, Moe, and Curly, but only 41 percent could name the legislative, executive, and judicial branches. Another survey found that adults' knowledge of the Constitution was depressingly sketchy: 24 percent could not name any First Amendment rights, 52 percent did not know that the Senate has 100 members, and one-sixth thought that the Constitution created a Christian nation.[2]

Despite a lack of detailed knowledge about the Constitution, most Americans support the central values of the document. In a poll by the National Constitution Center, 87 percent said that decisions should be made by the majority, but that minority rights must be protected, and 50 percent said that it is as important to protect the rights of the accused as to put the guilty in jail and an additional 18 percent hold this view "even if this means that some guilty people are let go."[3] However, even these broad statements of support are somewhat fragile when probed more deeply. For example, when asked whether Nazis should be allowed to demonstrate publicly, whether someone accused of child molestation should be given due process rights, or even if movies with sex and swearing should be banned, large majorities of Americans hold distinctly

POLITICS IS CONFLICTUAL

Rather than serving as the final word on matters of the law, the Constitution sets the stage for political conflict. Because there are multiple interpreters of the Constitution, interpretations are bound to vary, which makes conflict between the branches necessary to sort out which view wins.

unconstitutional views. This chapter will give you deeper understanding of this important document by answering the following questions:

- What were the politics behind the drafting of the Constitution?
- How and why did the framers arrive at the specific language of the Constitution?
- How do the Constitution's central ideas shape our government?
- How is the Constitution relevant today?

As the supreme law of the land, the Constitution's influence is everywhere. It establishes the basic rules for our institutions of government, prevents the government from doing certain things to citizens (such as denying them freedom of speech), and guarantees specific individual rights. In other words, the Constitution determines the ground rules for the process that guides politics. The Constitutional Convention demonstrated that politics is conflictual. Those hot summer days in Philadelphia in 1787 involved battles between many competing interests over which topics would be included, which would be ignored, and how future political differences would be resolved. The sweeping influence of the Constitution also shows that politics is everywhere. The document shapes every aspect of national politics, which in turn influences many parts of your life. We will return to these themes throughout this chapter.

Finally, and perhaps surprisingly, the Constitution is highly readable. You do not have to be a lawyer or political philosopher to understand it. It contains only 4,608 words, about the length of a fifteen-page term paper, and while the language is somewhat old-fashioned in places, it uses everyday language rather than the legalese that one would confront in a modern document of this type. If you have never read it, or if it has been a few years since you looked at it, you should flip to the back of the book and read it now.

Conflict at the Constitutional Convention

The Constitution was created through conflict and compromise, and it is important to understand the historical context within which that process took place. Therefore we focus on the interests and ideas that were at stake for the framers and the compromises and decisions that they made. What were the different factions among the framers, and how did their views shape decisions at the Constitutional Convention? How would things be different today if they had made different choices? Understanding the historical context can help clarify *why* specific choices were made. And exploring the consequences of alternative choices is one way of seeing how politics matters.

Key historical events shaped the Constitutional Convention, including the Revolutionary War and problems with the first form of government in the United States, the Articles of Confederation. The events leading up to the Revolutionary War and the war itself led to widespread support for popular control of government through a **republican democracy**, a rejection of **monarchy**, and limitations on government power that would protect against tyranny. While there were a few Tories, supporters of the British monarchy, in the Revolutionary and post-Revolutionary era, most Americans were eager to sever ties with the oppressive British government and establish a new nation that rejected the trappings of royalty.

republican democracy A form of government in which the interests of the people are represented through elected leaders.

monarchy A form of government in which power is held by a single person, or monarch, who comes to power through inheritance rather than election.

FIGURE 2.1 CONSTITUTIONAL TIME LINE

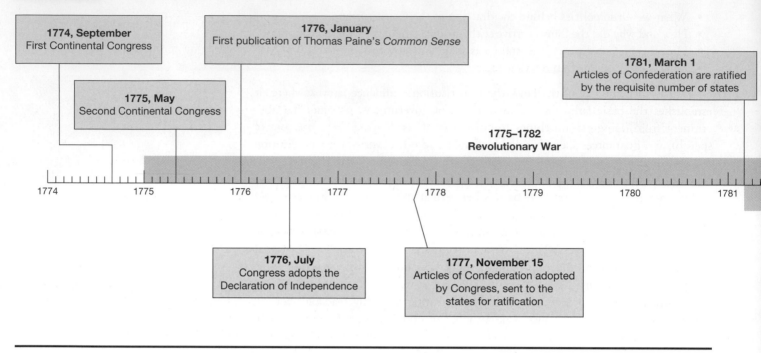

ARTICLES OF CONFEDERATION: THE FIRST ATTEMPT AT GOVERNMENT

The first attempt to structure an American government, the **Articles of Confederation**, swung too far in the direction of **limited government**. The Articles were written in the summer of 1777 during the Second Continental Congress, which also authorized and approved the Declaration of Independence. The Articles were submitted to all thirteen states in 1777 for approval, but they did not formally go into effect until the last state ratified them in 1781. However, in the absence of any alternative, the Articles of Confederation served as the basis for organizing the government during the Revolutionary War.

In their zeal to reject monarchy, the authors of the Articles did not even include a president or any other executive leader. All national power was given to a Congress in which each state had a single vote. Members of Congress were elected by state legislatures rather than directly by the people. There was no judicial branch; all legal matters were left to the states, with the exception of disputes among the states, which would be resolved by special panels of judges appointed on an as-needed basis by Congress. In their eagerness to limit the power of government the authors of the Articles gave each state veto power over any changes to the Articles and required approval from nine of the thirteen states on any legislation. Even more importantly, the states maintained autonomy and did not sacrifice any significant power to the national government. Powers granted to the national government, such as making treaties and coining money, were not exclusive powers; that is, they were not denied to the states. Congress also lacked any real authority over the states. For example, they could suggest the amount of money that each state owed to support the Revolutionary army, but they could not make the states pay. General Washington's troops were in very bad shape, lacking food and clothing to say nothing about the

Articles of Confederation Written in 1776, these were the first attempt at a new American government. It was later decided that the Articles restricted national government too much, and they were replaced by the Constitution.

limited government A system in which the powers of the government are restricted to protect against tyranny.

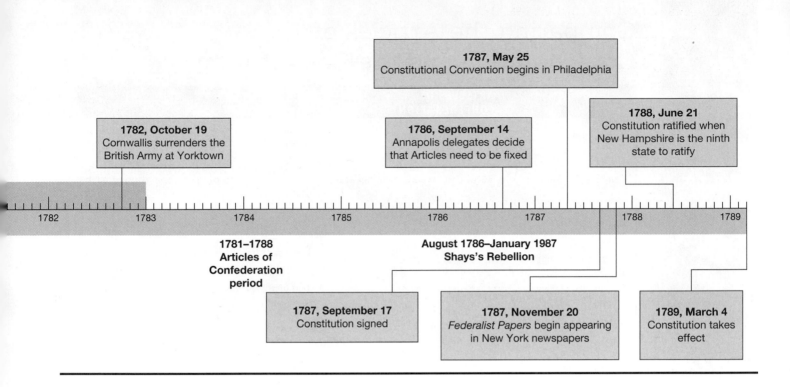

1787, May 25
Constitutional Convention begins in Philadelphia

1782, October 19
Cornwallis surrenders the British Army at Yorktown

1786, September 14
Annapolis delegates decide that Articles need to be fixed

1788, June 21
Constitution ratified when New Hampshire is the ninth state to ratify

1782   1783   1784   1785   1786   1787   1788   1789

1781–1788
Articles of Confederation period

August 1786–January 1987
Shays's Rebellion

1787, September 17
Constitution signed

1787, November 20
Federalist Papers begin appearing in New York newspapers

1789, March 4
Constitution takes effect

arms and munitions they needed to defeat the British. The severe winter of 1780 led to an attempted mutiny in Morristown, New Jersey. At first Congress tried to compel the states to support their own troops, but this appeal failed. Desperate for funds, in 1781 Congress tried to give itself the power to raise taxes, but the measure was vetoed by Rhode Island, which represented less than 2 percent of the nation's population! If France had not come to the aid of the American army with much-needed funds and troops, the weakness of the national government could have led to defeat.[4]

After the Revolutionary War ended, the same weaknesses continued to plague Congress. The new government owed millions of dollars in war debts to foreign governments and domestic creditors, so Congress came up with a plan to repay the debts over twenty-five years, but again had no way to make the states pay their share. Instead, Congress proposed an amendment to the Articles that would allow them to collect import duties—but New York, which had the busiest port in the nation, did not want to share its revenue and vetoed the amendment. Foreign trade also suffered because of the weak national government. If a foreign government negotiated a trade arrangement with the Congress, it could be vetoed or amended by a state government, so that a foreign country wanting to conduct business with the United States might have to negotiate separate agreements with the Congress and each state legislature! Disputes with foreign countries about land boundaries also were complex and contentious because of the Articles. When Spain threatened to close trade routes on the Mississippi River and Great Britain disputed the U.S.–Canadian border, it was not clear whether state governments or Congress could resolve the disputes. Even trade among the states was complicated and inefficient. Each state could make its own currency, exchange rates varied, and many states charged tolls and fees to export goods across state lines. Just imagine how difficult interstate commerce would be today if you had to exchange currency at every state line.

Comparing the Articles of Confederation and the Constitution

ISSUE	ARTICLES OF CONFEDERATION	CONSTITUTION
Legislature	Unicameral Congress	Bicameral Congress divided into the House of Representatives and the Senate
Members of Congress	Between two and seven per state	Two Senators per state; Representatives apportioned according to population of each state
Voting in Congress	One vote per state	One vote per Representative or Senator
Selection of members	Appointed by state legislatures	Representatives elected by popular vote; Senators appointed by state legislatures
Term of legislative office	One year	Two years for Representatives; six years for Senators
Term limit for legislative office	No more than three out of every six years	None
Congressional pay	Paid by states	Paid by the federal government
Executive	None	President
National judiciary	Maritime judiciary established, no general federal courts	Supreme Court; Congress authorized to establish national judiciary
Settle disputes between states	Congress	Supreme Court
New States	Admitted with approval of nine states	Admitted with approval of Congress
Amendments to the document	When approved by all states	When approved by three-fourths of the states
Power to coin money	Federal government and the states	Federal government only
Taxes	Apportioned by Congress, collected by the states	Apportioned and collected by Congress
Ratification	Unanimous consent required	Consent of nine states required

A small group of leaders decided that something must be done. A group from Virginia urged state legislatures to send delegates to a convention on interstate commerce in Annapolis, Maryland, in September 1786. Eight states agreed, but only five ended up sending delegates. Alexander Hamilton and James Madison salvaged something from the convention by getting those delegates to agree to convene again in Philadelphia the following May. They also proposed expanding the scope of the next convention to examine the defects of the current government and "devise such further provisions as shall appear to them necessary to render the Constitution of the Federal Government adequate to the exigencies of the Union."[5]

The issues that motivated the Annapolis Convention gained new urgency as events unfolded over the next several months. In the years after the war economic chaos led to a depression, and many farmers lost their land because they could not pay their debts or state taxes. Frustration mounted, and early in 1787, a former captain in the Revolutionary army, Daniel Shays, led a force of a thousand farmers in an attempt to take over the Massachusetts state government arsenal in Springfield and force the state courts to stop prosecuting debtors and taking their land, but they were repelled by a state militia. Similar protests on a smaller scale happened at the same time in Pennsylvania and Virginia. Some state legislatures gave in to the debtors' demands, causing national leaders to fear that Shays's Rebellion had exposed fundamental discontent with the new government. The very future of the fledgling nation was at risk.

POLITICAL THEORIES OF THE FRAMERS

Although the leaders who gathered in Philadelphia in the summer of 1787 to write the Constitution were chastened by the failure of the Articles of Confederation, they still shared many of the principles that motivated the Revolution.

Republicanism First among these principles was rejection of monarchy in favor of a form of government based on self-rule. Specifically, they supported **republicanism** in which elected leaders would represent the views of the people. Thomas Paine, an influential political writer of the Revolutionary era, wrote a pamphlet entitled *Common Sense* in 1776 that was a widely read[6] and influential indictment of monarchy and endorsement of the principles that fueled the Revolution and underpinned the thinking of the framers. Paine wrote that a monarchy was the "most bare-faced falsity ever imposed on mankind" and that the common interests of the community would be served by elected representatives. The best expression of these core principles is found in the Declaration of Independence:

> We hold these truths to be self-evident, that all men are created equal, that they are endowed by their Creator with certain unalienable Rights, that among these are Life, Liberty, and the pursuit of Happiness. That to secure these rights, Governments are instituted among Men, deriving their just powers from the consent of the governed. That whenever any Form of Government becomes destructive of these ends, it is the Right of the People to alter or to abolish it, and to institute new Government.

Three crucial ideas are packed into this passage: equality, self-rule, and natural rights. Equality was not given much attention in the Constitution (later chapters discuss how the problem of slavery was handled), but the notion that a government gains its legitimacy from the **"consent of the governed"** and that its central purpose is to uphold the "unalienable" or **natural rights** of the people were central to the framers. The "right of the people to alter or abolish" a government that did not protect these rights served both to justify the revolt against the British and to remind the framers of their continuing obligation to make sure that those needs were met. The leaders who met in Philadelphia thought the Articles of Confederation had become "destructive to those ends" and had to be altered.

Paine, Jefferson, Madison, and the other political thinkers of the American Founding broke new ground in laying out the principles of republican democracy, but they also built on the ideas of political philosophers of their era. As mentioned in Chapter 1, the philosopher Thomas Hobbes argued that government was necessary to prevent people from living in an anarchic "state of nature" in which life would be "nasty, brutish, and short." He also believed that leaders gained legitimacy through the consent of the governed. However, Hobbes's central conclusion

republicanism The belief that a form of government in which the interests of the people are represented through elected leaders is the best form of government.

"consent of the governed" The idea that government gains its legitimacy through regular elections in which the people living under that government participate to elect their leaders.

natural rights Also known as "unalienable rights," the Declaration of Independence defines them as "Life, Liberty, and the pursuit of Happiness." The Founders believed that upholding these rights should be the government's central purpose.

▲ *Seventeenth-century political philosopher John Locke had a great influence on the Founders. Many ideas discussed in Locke's writing appear in the Declaration of Independence and the Constitution.*

was undemocratic: he believed that a single king must rule because any other form of government would produce warring factions. Another seventeenth-century philosopher, John Locke, took this same notion of the consent of the governed in determining a government's legitimacy in a more democratic direction. A great influence on the framers, Locke discussed many of the ideas that appeared in the Declaration of Independence and Constitution, including natural rights, property rights, the need for a vigorous executive branch that would be checked by a legislative branch, and self-rule through elections.[7]

HUMAN NATURE AND ITS IMPLICATIONS FOR DEMOCRACY

The framers did not trust popular majorities to control government (so-called populist democracy), and this distrust led to many undemocratic features of the Constitution, but this was not entirely because they doubted the political capacity of the average citizen. Rather, their view of human nature as basically self-interested led to James Madison's assessment that, "In framing a government which is to be administered by men over men, the great difficulty lies in this: you must first enable the government to control the governed; and in the next place oblige it to control itself." This analysis is often considered the clearest articulation of the need for republican government and a system of separated powers. Madison saw the central problem for government as the need to control **factions**, which he defined as, "A number of citizens, whether amounting to a majority or a minority of the whole, who are united and actuated by some common . . . interest, adverse to the rights of other citizens, or to the permanent and aggregate interests of the community." In today's terms this would refer to an interest group that works for self-serving goals rather than the broader interests of the community.

Madison goes on to argue that governments cannot control the causes of factions because such differences of opinion—based on the fallibility of reason; differences in wealth, property, and native abilities; and attachments to different leaders—are part of human nature. The only way to eliminate factions would be to either remove liberty or try to make everyone the same. The first remedy Madison called "worse than the disease" while the second he found "as impracticable as the first would be unwise." The experiences of Communist nations such as China and the former Soviet Union demonstrate the wisdom of Madison's insight. Forced collectivization of agriculture in which farmers worked for the state rather than themselves; abolition of private property, strict limits on citizens' speech, travel, and religion; and the "reeducation" programs that led to the torture and death of millions are strong testimonies to the costs of trying to eliminate factions. Because people are driven by self-interest, which sometimes conflicts with the common good, government must, however, try to control the effects of factions. This was the task facing the framers at the Constitutional Convention.

ECONOMIC INTERESTS

Political ideas were clearly central in shaping the framers' thinking at the Constitutional Convention, but economic interests were equally important. Both the economic status of the framers themselves and the broader economic context of late eighteenth-century America are relevant here. One constitutional scholar addressed the relative importance of economic interests and political ideas for the framers, noting they "did not promote a new form of government to satisfy an abstract political theory. The framers were men of affairs who sought to advance their fortunes and careers as well as the interests of the states." This view was most famously expressed

factions Groups of like-minded people who try to influence the government. American government is set up to avoid domination by any one of these groups.

by Charles Beard nearly 100 years ago in his economic interpretation of the constitution. Beard argued that the framers wanted to revise the Articles of Confederation and strengthen the national government largely to protect their property holdings and investments.[8] Some undemocratic features of the Constitution probably can be explained by the relatively privileged position of the framers. After all, broad political participation and control are more popular among the lower classes who see an equal voice in government as a path to improved economic standing, whereas the privileged class tends to be more concerned with solidifying its own political position. However, Beard's argument has been countered by research showing, among other things, that the opponents of the Constitution also came from the upper class. (If both the supporters and opponents of the document shared the same economic background, it is difficult to claim that the framers' wealth explains the nature of the new system.) Most

▲ The economic context of the American Founding had an important impact on the Constitution. Most Americans worked on small farms or as artisans or business owners, which meant that economic power was broadly distributed. This woodcut shows New York City (in the distance, upper right) around the time the Constitution was written, viewed from upper Manhattan, probably about where Harlem is today.

constitutional scholars now view the Constitution as the product of both ideas and interests. This balanced perspective is summarized by David Robertson who says, "The delegates who made the Constitution were first and foremost politicians, not philosophers or real estate investors."[9]

The broader economic context of the American Founding was more important than the individual interests of the delegates. First, while there were certainly class differences among Americans in the late eighteenth century, they were insignificant compared to class distinctions in Europe. Most importantly, America did not have the history of feudalism that created tremendous levels of inequality in Europe between landowners and propertyless serfs who worked the land. In some European nations a few families owned as much as a third of the land. In contrast, most Americans owned small farms or worked as middle-class artisans and craftsmen. Thus, while political equality did not figure prominently in the Constitution, citizens' relative economic equality influenced the overall context of debates at the Constitutional Convention.

Second, despite Americans' general economic equality, there were significant regional economic differences. The southern part of the country was largely agricultural with large cotton and tobacco plantations that depended on slave labor. The South favored free trade because of its export-based economy (bolstered by westward expansion), and of course slavery. The middle Atlantic and northern states had smaller farms and a broad economic base that included manufacturing, fishing, and trade. These states favored government-managed trade and commercial development. Other economic divisions cut across regional lines, such as debtors versus creditors and states that had large property claims on western states (such as Connecticut, Massachusetts, and Virginia) and those that did not. States with large port cities, such as New York, Massachusetts, and Pennsylvania also were at odds with neighboring states when it came to national control of tariffs. States with ports wanted to maintain control over this important source of revenue.

Despite these regional and sector-based economic differences, a diverse population with various economic interests favored a stronger national government and reform of the Articles of Confederation. Creditors wanted a government that could pay off its debts to them, southern farmers wanted free trade that could only be efficiently promoted by a central government, and manufacturers and traders desperately

POLITICS IS CONFLICTUAL

 Political ideas, human nature, and economic interests all produced conflict at the Constitutional Convention, but one of the deepest sources of conflict was between the Federalist and Antifederalist views about the proper relationship between the national government and the states.

Federalists Those at the Constitutional Convention who favored a strong national government over strong state governments.

Antifederalists Those at the Constitutional Convention who favored strong state governments over a strong national government.

wanted a single national currency and uniform interstate commerce regulations to promote trade across state lines. However there was a deep division between the supporters of empowering the national government to a greater degree and those who still favored relatively strong state governments. These two groups came to be known as the Federalists and the Antifederalists. The stage was set for a productive but contentious convention.

SECTION SUMMARY

1. After the failed Articles of Confederation, the framers knew that they had to create a stronger national government that would be better able to deal with the economic problems of the new nation.

2. While the framers agreed that the new government should be a representative democracy with the consent of the governed, their concerns about the self-interested nature of people and about individual and regional economic interests set the stage for a contentious Constitutional Convention.

The Politics of Compromise at the Constitutional Convention

The central players at the convention were James Madison, Gouverneur Morris, Edmond Randolph, James Wilson, Benjamin Franklin, and George Washington, the unanimous choice to preside over the convention. Several of the important leaders of the Revolution were not present. Patrick "Give me Liberty, or give me Death!" Henry was selected to attend, but he opposed any changes in the Articles, saying he "smelled a rat," and Thomas Jefferson and John Adams were working overseas as U.S. diplomats. Thomas Paine was back in England, and John Hancock and Samuel Adams were not selected to attend. The delegates met in secret to encourage open, uncensored debate, and convention proceedings were not published until more than thirty years later. James Madison's notes provide the best record of the debates and offer insight into the delegates' compromises and decisions.

While there was broad consensus among the convention delegates that the Articles of Confederation needed to be changed, there were many tensions surrounding the nature of the changes that required political compromise:

POLITICAL PROCESS MATTERS

☑ The decision to keep the Constitutional Convention deliberations secret shows how process can shape politics. By keeping the public out, the framers believed that they could minimize outside political pressures and allow more vigorous and honest debates.

- majority rule versus minority rights,
- large states versus small states,
- legislative versus executive power (and how to elect the executive),
- national versus state and local power,
- and slave states versus nonslave states.

This complex set of competing interests meant that the delegates had to focus on pragmatic solutions that *could* be accomplished rather than ideal proposals that represented particular groups' ideals but could not gain majority support. Robert Dahl argues that it was impossible for the Constitution to "reflect a coherent, unified theory of government" because so much compromising and vote-trading was required to find common ground.[10] Instead, the delegates tackled the problems one at a time, holding lengthy debates and multiple votes on most issues.

MAJORITY RULE VERSUS MINORITY RIGHTS

A central problem for any representative democracy is protecting minority rights within a system ruled by the majority. Today we often think of this issue in terms of racial and ethnic minorities, but these groups clearly were not the concern of the framers. Instead, they thought in terms of regional and economic minorities' interests. How could they be sure that small landowners and poorer people would not impose onerous taxes on the wealthier minority? How could they guarantee that the dominant agricultural interests would not impose punitive tariffs on manufacturing while allowing free export of farmed commodities? The answers to these questions can be found in Madison's writings on the problem of factions.

Recall that Madison defined a faction as a group motivated by selfish interests against the common good. If these interests prevailed, it could produce the very kind of tyranny that the Americans fought to escape during the Revolutionary War. Madison was especially concerned about tyranny by majority factions because in a democracy, minority tyranny would be controlled by the republican principle: the majority could simply vote out the minority faction. If, on the other hand, the majority always rules, majority tyranny could be a real problem. Given the understanding of selfish human nature that Madison so clearly outlined, a populist, majoritarian democracy would not necessarily produce the common good. On the other hand, if too many protections were provided to minority and regional interests, the collective interest would not be served because constructive changes could be vetoed too easily, as under the Articles of Confederation.

Madison's solution to this problem provided the justification for our form of government. To control majority tyranny, he argued that factions must be set against one another to counter each other's ambitions and prevent the tyranny of any single majority faction. This was to be accomplished through what Madison called the "double protection" of the separation of powers within the national government in the form of checks and balances, and also by further dividing power across the levels of the state and local governments. Madison also argued that additional protection against majority tyranny came from the "size principle." That is, the new nation would be a large and diverse republic in which majority interests would be less likely to cohere, and therefore less able to dominate. In a small territory, such as a state, "the more frequently will a majority be found of the same party," and "the more easily will they concert and execute their plans of oppression." However, in a large republic this was less likely to happen. Madison says, "Extend the sphere, and you take in a greater variety of parties and interests; you make it less probable that a majority of the whole will have a common motive to invade the rights of other citizens; or if such a common motive exists, it will be more difficult for all who feel it to discover their own strength, and to act in unison with each other."[11] This insight provides the basis for modern **pluralism**, a political theory that makes the same argument about the cross-cutting interests of groups today.

The precise contours of Madison's solution still had to be hammered out at the convention, but the general principle pleased both the Antifederalists and the Federalists because state governments maintained some autonomy, but the national government would become stronger than it had been under the Articles. The issue

POLITICS IS EVERYWHERE

The potential for majority tyranny is inherent in any majority-ruled institution or system. Even deciding among friends which movie to watch or how to spend a Saturday night creates winners who are in the majority and losers who are in the minority.

pluralism The idea that having a variety of parties and interests within a government will strengthen the system, ensuring that no group possesses total control.

here was striking the appropriate balance: none of the framers favored a pure populist majoritarian democracy and few wanted to protect minority rights to the extent that the Articles had.

SMALL STATES VERSUS LARGE STATES

The question of the appropriate balance came to an immediate head in a debate between small states and large states over representation in the national legislature. Under the Articles every state had a single vote, but this did not seem fair to large states that instead were pushing for representation based on population. This proposal was formally made in the Virginia Plan, along with other proposals to strengthen the national government. The small states countered with the **New Jersey Plan**, which proposed maintaining equal representation for every state. Rhode Island, the smallest state in the nation, was so concerned about small-state power that they boycotted the process and did not even send delegates to the convention. Tensions were running high; this issue appeared to have all the elements of a deal breaker, and there seemed to be no way to break the impasse.

Just as it appeared that the convention might grind to a halt before it really got started, Connecticut proposed what came to be known as the **Great Compromise** or the Connecticut Compromise, which suggested that Congress would be comprised of two houses. The Senate would have two senators for every state, and in the House of Representatives each state's number of representatives would be based on its population. Interestingly, Connecticut's population was ranked seventh of the thirteen states. Therefore it was in a perfect position to offer a compromise because it did not have strong vested interests in the plans offered by either the small states or the large states.

Virginia Plan A plan proposed by the larger states during the Constitutional Convention in which representation in the national legislature was based on population. The plan also included a variety of other proposals to strengthen the national government.

New Jersey Plan In response to the Virginia Plan, smaller states at the Constitutional Conventions offered this plan in which each state would receive equal representation in the national legislature, regardless of size.

Great Compromise A compromise between the large and small states, proposed by Connecticut, in which Congress would have two houses: a Senate with two legislators per state and a House of Representatives in which each state's representation would be based on population (also known as the Connecticut Compromise).

POLITICAL PROCESS MATTERS

☑ The two houses of Congress created by the Great Compromise are an example of how process shapes politics. Because each state is represented equally in the Senate, the interests of small states will have stronger influence over legislation in the Senate than in the House.

LEGISLATIVE VERSUS EXECUTIVE POWER

An equally difficult task facing the framers was how to divide power at the national level. Here the central issues revolved around the executive, which in our system is the president. How much power should the president have relative to the legislative branch? (The courts also figured into the discussions, but they were less central.) And how would the president be elected? One of the central problems was that the delegates did not have any positive role models for the executive. Recall that under the Articles of Confederation there was no chief executive, and for the most part, the state governors were very weak. The delegates knew what they did not want: the King of England and his colonial governors were viewed as tramplers of liberty. The only one who actually favored a monarchy was Alexander Hamilton. He said that "the English model was the only good one" and proposed that a single executive and the Senate should "hold their places for life, or at least in good behavior."[12] Hamilton's extreme views on this topic meant that he was largely marginalized at the convention.

Many delegates rejected outright the idea of a single executive because they were not convinced it was possible have an executive who would not be oppressive. When the idea of including an executive was first raised at the convention, Madison's notes reveal the strong reservations:

> Charles Pinckney rose to urge a "vigorous executive." James Wilson followed Pinckney by moving that the executive consist of a single person, Pinckney seconded him. A

sudden silence followed. A considerable pause. A single executive . . . There was menace in the words, some saw monarchy in them. A single executive for the national government conjured up visions from the past—royal governors who could not be restrained, a crown, ermine, a scepter.

Edmund Randolph proposed a three-person executive for this reason, arguing that a single executive would be the "fetus of monarchy." The Virginia Plan envisioned a single executive who would share some legislative power with federal judges in a Council of Revision with the power to veto legislation passed by Congress (however, the veto could be overridden by a simple majority vote in Congress). The delegates finally agreed on the single executive because he would have the most "energy, dispatch, and responsibility for the office," but they constrained the president's power through the system of checks and balances. One significant power they granted to the executive was the veto. While a presidential veto could be overridden by Congress, this could only be done with the support of a super-majority, meaning two-thirds of both chambers. This requirement gave the president a significant role in the legislative process.

In addition to Hamilton, the other New Yorkers, Morris, Livingston, and Jay also favored a strong executive. This was probably because the governor of New York closely resembled the type of executive that the Constitution envisioned. He was elected by the people rather than the legislature, served for three years, and was eligible for reelection. The New York governor also had a legislative veto power and considerable control over appointments to politically controlled jobs. The arguments they made on behalf of the strong executive relied heavily on the philosophy of John Locke. Locke saw the general superiority of a government of laws and by legislatures, but he also saw the need for an executive with more flexible leadership powers, or what he called "prerogative powers." Legislatures are unable, Locke wrote, "to foresee, and so by laws to provide for all accidents and necessities." They also are, by virtue of their size and unwieldiness, too slow to alter and adapt the law in a time of crisis. In these circumstances, the executive can step in to pursue policies in the public's interest. Prerogative power, then, is "the people's permitting their rulers to do several things of their own free choice where the law was silent, and sometimes too, against the direct letter of the law, for the public good, and their acquiescing in it when so done." The check on the use of such power was to be whether the legislature would decide to go along with it.[13]

While there was support for this view, the Antifederalists were concerned that if such powers were viewed as open-ended, they could give rise to the type of oppressive leader the framers were trying to avoid. Madison attempted to reassure the opponents of executive power, arguing that any prerogative powers would have to be clearly enumerated in the Constitution. In fact, the Constitution provides only one extraordinary executive power: the right to grant reprieves and pardons, which means the president can forgive any crimes against the federal government. While Congress was clearly viewed as the premier branch of government by all but the strongest supporters of the executive, the president was given significant powers as well.

The second contentious issue concerning the executive was the method of selecting a president. As one delegate, James Wilson, explained, "This subject has greatly divided the House [the convention], and will also divide the people out of doors. It is in truth the most difficult of all on which we have had to decide."[14] The problem was so severe because it cut across many of the other central tensions facing framers. The way the president was elected incorporated the issues of majority rule and minority rights, state versus national power, and the nature of executive power itself. Would the president be elected by the nation as a whole, by the states,

Small States, Big States, and Crafting a Constitution

The European Union (EU) is tackling some of the same issues the Founders faced concerning how to represent states of dramatically different sizes. The EU expanded from fifteen to twenty-five members in May 2004, added two more members in January 2007, and is trying to ratify a new constitution. The first attempt failed when France and the Netherlands rejected the proposed constitution and seven other nations refused to vote on it (ratification was required by all twenty-seven nations). In December 2007, the EU member nations came up with a new draft, the Treaty of Lisbon, that was submitted to member nations for ratification by 2009, but the proposed voting system (discussed below) would not be implemented until 2014.

VOTING WEIGHTS IN THE COUNCIL OF THE EUROPEAN UNION

	ACCESSION DATE	POPULATION (MILLIONS)	PERCENT OF EU POPULATION	PERCENTAGE OF COUNCIL	VOTES
Germany	1957	82	16.7	8.4	29
France	1957	63	12.8	8.4	29
UK	1973	60	12.3	8.4	29
Italy	1957	59	11.9	8.4	29
Spain	1986	44	8.9	7.8	27
Poland	2004	38	7.7	7.8	27
Romania	2007	22	4.4	4.1	14
Netherlands	1957	16	3.3	3.8	13
Greece	1981	11	2.3	3.5	12
Portugal	1986	11	2.1	3.5	12
Belgium	1957	11	2.1	3.5	12
Czech Republic	2004	10	2.1	3.5	12
Hungary	2004	10	2.0	3.5	12
Sweden	1995	9.0	1.8	2.9	10
Austria	1995	8.3	1.7	2.9	10
Bulgaria	2007	7.7	1.6	2.9	10
Denmark	1973	5.4	1.1	2.0	7
Slovakia	2004	5.4	1.1	2.0	7
Finland	1995	5.3	1.1	2.0	7
Ireland	1973	4.2	0.9	2.0	7
Lithuania	2004	3.4	0.7	2.0	7
Latvia	2004	2.3	0.5	1.2	4
Slovenia	2004	2.0	0.4	1.2	4
Estonia	2004	1.3	0.3	1.2	4
Cyprus	2004	0.77	0.2	1.2	4
Luxembourg	1957	0.46	0.1	1.2	4
Malta	2004	0.40	0.1	0.9	3
EU total		493	100		345

SOURCE: The Council of the European Union, available at http://europa.eu/institutions/inst/council/index_en.htm.

In many ways the EU faces a far more difficult task than the Founders, but the issue of state size is equally vexing. Clearly, tiny states like Luxembourg, with its population of 453,000, cannot receive the same representation on the EU Council of Ministers as the 82.5 million Germans, just as Delaware and Rhode Island could not demand representation on par with New York and Virginia. However, the current allocation of voting rights favors the small and medium-sized EU member states. As the table shows, all nations smaller than Romania receive a disproportionately large share of votes, while large nations—especially Germany—do not receive their fair share.

The current proposal, the Treaty of Lisbon, would change this by allowing most kinds of measures to pass the Council with the support of 55 percent of the nations, as long as they have at least 65 percent of the EU population (although some issues, including taxation and most foreign policy matters, would require a unanimous vote). This rule would prevent the smaller nations from passing legislation not supported by the larger nations. In fact, the "big four"— United Kingdom, Germany, France, and Italy—would have nearly enough votes between them to block any measure proposed under the new 55/65 rule, while Poland, Spain, and the other middle-sized and smaller countries would lose voting power.

Many other complicated issues must also be resolved, including proposals for a common defense policy, enhancing the powers of the European Parliament, and revamping the European Commission. The sheer length of the rejected constitution is a testament to the complexity of the issues: the failed draft was 69,196 words and about 263 pages long (depending on what language you read it in), compared to the 4,608 words of the U.S. Constitution.[a] ■

or by coalitions within Congress? If the state-level governments played a central role, would this mean that the president could not speak for national interests? If the president was elected by Congress, could the executive still provide a check on the legislative branch?

Most Americans do not realize how unique our presidential system is and how close we came to having a parliamentary system, which is the form of government in most other established democracies. In a **parliamentary system**, the executive branch depends on the support of the legislative branch. The Virginia Plan proposed that the president be elected by Congress, just as the British prime minister is elected by parliament, and this was the preferred solution for the first two months of the convention. However, there were lingering concerns that the president would be too beholden to Congress, so the matter was referred back to a committee in late August. On September 4, the committee recommended that the president should be selected by an electoral college, representation in which would be based on the number of representatives and senators in each state's legislature. Each state's legislature would also determine the method for choosing their state's electors.[15] Ten days before the convention adjourned, the delegates approved this recommendation by a vote of 9–2.

Why did the delegates favor this complicated, indirect way of electing the president? One prominent political scientist argues that they had simply run out of alternatives and this was the only widely acceptable solution. He says, "What this strange record suggests to me is a group of baffled and confused men who finally settle on a solution more out of desperation than confidence."[16] As with all good compromises, all sides could claim victory to some extent. Advocates of state power were happy because state legislatures played a central role in presidential elections; those who worried about the direct influence of the people liked the indirect manner of election; and the proponents of strong executive power were satisfied that the president would not simply be an agent of Congress. However, the solution had its flaws and clearly did not work out the way that the framers intended. First, if the electoral college was supposed to provide an independent check on the voters, it never played this role because the framers did not anticipate the quick emergence of political parties. Electors quickly became agents of the parties, as they remain today, rather than independent actors who would use their judgment to pick the most qualified candidate for president. Second, the emergence of parties also created what was arguably the biggest technical error in the Constitution: the provision that had electors cast two votes, electing the candidate with the most votes as president and the second-place finisher as vice president. With the rise of political parties, the electors each cast two votes for the presidential and vice-presidential candidates of their own party, which created a tie in the 1800 presidential election when Thomas Jefferson and Aaron Burr each received seventy-three electoral votes. The problem was easily fixed by the 12th Amendment, which required that electors cast separate ballots for president and vice president.

NATIONAL POWER VERSUS STATE AND LOCAL POWER

Tensions about the balance of power cut across virtually every debate at the convention: presidential versus legislative power, whether the national government could supercede state laws, apportionment in the legislature, slavery, regulation of commerce and taxation, and the amending process. The overall compromise that addressed these tensions was the second of Madison's "double protections," the system of federalism, which divided power between autonomous levels of government that controled different areas of policy.

parliamentary system A system of government in which legislative and executive power are closely joined. The legislature (parliament) selects the chief executive (prime minister) who forms the cabinet from members of the parliament.

Federalism is such an important topic that we devote the entire next chapter to it, but two brief points about it are important here. First, federalism is an example of how nuanced and careful compromises can alter the Constitution's meaning by changing a single word. The 10th Amendment, which was added to the Constitution as part of the Bill of Rights shortly after ratification, was a concession to the Antifederalists who were concerned about the national government gaining too much power in the new political system. The 10th Amendment says, "The powers not delegated to the United States by the Constitution, nor prohibited by it to the States, are reserved to the States respectively, or to the people." This was viewed as setting outer limits on the reach of national power. However, the Antifederalists were not happy with this wording because of the removal of a single word; they wanted the 10th Amendment to read, "The powers not *expressly* delegated to the United States," which would have more explicitly restricted national power. With the word "expressly" removed, the amendment became much more ambiguous and less restrictive of national power. Indeed, the amendment was largely ignored as too broad and vague until the Supreme Court revived it starting in the mid-1990s. (See the discussion in Chapter 3 of the Supreme Court's preference for state-centered federalism.) Second, the **national supremacy clause** of the Constitution (Article VI) says that any national law is the supreme law of the land and takes precedent over any state law that conflicts with it. This is especially important in areas where the national and state governments have overlapping responsibilities for policy.

SLAVE STATES VERSUS NONSLAVE STATES

Slavery was another nearly insurmountable issue for the delegates. Southern states would not agree to any provisions limiting slavery. While the nonslave states opposed the practice, they were not willing to scuttle the entire Constitution by taking a principled stand. Even after these basic divisions had been recognized, many unresolved issues remained between the slave and nonslave states. Could the importation of slaves be restricted in the future? How would northern states deal with runaway slaves? And most importantly, how would the slave population be counted for purposes of slave states' representation in Congress?

The deals that the delegates cut on the issue of slavery illustrate the two most common forms of compromise: splitting the difference and logrolling (trading votes). The first is familiar to anyone who has haggled over the price of a car or bargained for something at a flea market. Let's say the list price on the car is $20,000. You walk into the car dealership armed with the dealer invoice price, which is $18,500. You also know that there is a factory–dealer incentive of $500, which goes directly to the dealer, reducing its costs to $18,000. The highest price you are willing to pay is $18,500, so you start with an offer of $18,000 and the dealer counters with $19,000. You end up meeting halfway, or splitting the difference, and you buy the car for $18,500. Logrolling is when politicians trade votes for one another's pet projects.

The delegates went through similar negotiations over how slaves would be counted for purposes of states' Congressional representation. The states had been through this debate once before, when they addressed the issue of taxation under the Articles of Confederation. At that point, the slave states argued that slaves should not be counted because they did not receive the same benefits as citizens and were not the same burden to the government. Nonslave states countered that slaves should be counted the same way as citizens when

POLITICS IS EVERYWHERE

Compromise, either in the form of splitting the difference or logrolling, is a necessary part of everyday life. Splitting household chores, choosing a movie or restaurant, or settling on the price of a car all involve compromise.

▲ *Slavery created several problems at the Constitutional Convention: would there be limits on the importation of slaves? How would runaway slaves be dealt with by nonslave states? And how would slaves be counted for the purposes of Congressional representation? The pictures show a slave auction in Virginia and slaves picking cotton.*

determining a state's fair share of the tax burden. They ended up agreeing on a figure of three-fifths. That is, slaves would count as three-fifths of a person for purposes of taxation. The arguments on the issue of representation were even more contentious at the constitutional convention. Here the positions were precisely reversed, with slave states arguing that slaves should count like everyone else for the purposes of determining the number of House representatives for each state. When feelings run high on both sides, it may be difficult to reach a compromise, but once again both sides managed to agree on the **Three-fifths Compromise** (it passed by a vote of 6 to 2, with two states divided evenly, so their votes did not count; a motion to count slaves the same as citizens was voted down 8 to 2).

The other two issues, the importation of slaves and dealing with runaway slaves, were handled by logrolling with an element of splitting the difference as well. Logrolling is more likely than splitting the difference when the issue cannot be neatly divided. For example, northern states either would be obligated to return runaway slaves to their southern owners or they would not. There was no way to split the difference. On issues with no clear middle ground, opposing sides will look for other issues on which they can trade votes. The nonslave states wanted more national government control over commerce and trade than under the Articles, a change that slave states opposed. So a logroll, or vote trade, developed as a way to compromise the competing regional interests of slavery and regulation of commerce. Northern states agreed to return runaway slaves, while the southern states agreed to allow Congress to regulate commerce and tax imports with a simple majority vote (rather than the super-majority required under the Articles).

The importation of slaves was also included as part of this logroll, along with some split-the-difference negotiating. Northern states wanted to allow future Congresses to ban the importation of slaves (a likely prospect because the southern states did not control a House or Senate majority). Southern states wanted to allow the importation of slaves to continue indefinitely, arguing that slavery was essential to produce their labor-intensive crops. The committee that examined this issue recommended that the slave trade not be restricted until after 1800, but this was extended to 1808 after further negotiations between the states. The final language resulting from this part of the logroll was inserted in Article I, Section 9.[17]

From a modern perspective it is difficult to understand how the framers could have taken such a purely political approach to the moral issue of slavery. Many of the delegates believed slavery was immoral, yet they were willing to negotiate for

Three-fifths Compromise The states' decision during the Constitutional Convention to count each slave as three-fifths of a person for the purposes of determining the number of House districts per state based on population.

southern states' support of the Constitution. Some southern delegates were apologetic about slavery, even as they argued for protecting their interests. Madison's notes give this example of a delegate from Virginia:

> He urged strenuously that express security ought to be provided for including slaves in the ratio of Representation [this refers to the Three-fifths Compromise]. He lamented that such a species of property existed. But as it did exist the holders of it would require this security.[18]

Many constitutional scholars view the convention's treatment of slavery as its central failure. In fairness to the delegates, it is not clear that they could have done much better if the goal was to create a document that all states would support. However, the delegates' inability to resolve this issue meant that it would simmer below the surface for the next seventy years, finally boiling over into the bloodiest of all American wars, the Civil War.

POLITICS IS CONFLICTUAL

The debates over slavery revealed some of the deepest conflicts at the Constitutional Convention. Compromises suppressed the issue for several decades, but eventually it was settled through the Civil War.

NUTS AND BOLTS

2.2

Major Compromises at the Constitutional Convention

	POSITION OF THE LARGE STATES	POSITION OF THE SMALL STATES	COMPROMISE
Apportionment in Congress	By population	State equality	Great Compromise created the Senate and House
Method of election to Congress	By the people	By the states	Lower house elected by the people; upper house by the state legislatures
Electing the executive (president)	By the states	By Congress	By the electoral college
Who decides federal–state conflicts?	Some federal authority	State courts	State courts to decide*
	POSITION OF THE SLAVE STATES	**POSITION OF THE NONSLAVE STATES**	**COMPROMISE**
Control over commerce	By the States	By Congress	By Congress, but with twenty-year exemption for the importation of slaves
Counting slaves toward apportionment	Counted 1:1 like citizens	Not counted	Three-Fifths Compromise
	POSITION OF THE FEDERALISTS	**POSITION OF THE ANTIFEDERALISTS**	**COMPROMISE**
Protection for individual rights	Secured by state constitutions, national Bill of Rights not needed	National Bill of Rights needed	Bill of Rights passed by the 1st Congress and was ratified by all states as of December 1791

*This was changed by the Judiciary Act of 1789, which provided for appeals from state to federal courts.

Ratification

The convention ended on a relatively harmonious note with Benjamin Franklin moving adoption. Franklin's motion was worded ambiguously to allow those who still had reservations to sign the Constitution anyway. Franklin's motion was in the "following convenient form," "Done in Convention by the unanimous consent of the States present the 17th of September . . . In Witness whereof we have hereunto subscribed our names." His clever wording meant that signers were only bearing witness to the approval by the states and therefore could still, in good faith, oppose substantial parts of the document. Franklin's motion passed with ten ayes, no nays, and one delegation divided. All but three of the delegates signed.

Article VII of the Constitution, which described the process for ratifying the document, was also designed to maximize its chance of success. Only nine states were needed to ratify, rather than the unanimity rule that had applied to changing the Articles of Confederation. Equally important, ratification votes would be taken in state conventions set up specifically for that purpose, bypassing the state legislatures, which would be more likely to resist some of the Constitution's state–federal power-sharing arrangements.

The near-unanimous approval at the convention's end masked very strong opposition that remained. Many delegates simply left the convention when it became clear that things were not going their way. Rhode Island sent no delegates and refused to appoint a ratification convention; more ominously, New York seemed dead set against the Constitution, and Pennsylvania, Virginia, and Massachusetts were split. The ratifying conventions in each state subjected the Constitution to intense scrutiny, as attendees examined every sentence for possible objections. A national debate raged over the next nine months.

The Antifederalists had many concerns about the Constitution, but they were most worried about the role of the president, the transfer of power from the states to the national government, and the lack of specific guarantees of civil liberties. In short, they feared that the national government would become tyrannical. The doubts about the single central executive were expressed by Patrick Henry, a leading Antifederalist. Speaking to the Virginia ratifying convention, Henry was mocking in his indictment, "Your president may easily become a king. There will be no checks, no real balances in this government. What can avail your specious, imaginary balances, your rope dancing, chain rattling, ridiculous ideal checks and contrivances."[19] Even Thomas Jefferson complained that the president seems like a "bad edition of a Polish King," in that he would control the armed forces and also could be reelected indefinitely.[20] State power and the ability to regulate commerce were also central concerns. States such as New York would lose substantial revenue if they could no longer charge states tariffs on goods that came into their port.

▲ *Confederate dead lie on the battlefield at Gettysburg, Pennsylvania, in July 1863. The inability of the framers to resolve the issue of slavery allowed tensions over the issue to grow throughout the early nineteenth century, culminating in the Civil War.*

▲ On September 17, 1787, forty-one of the the fifty-five delegates who attended the Constitutional Convention assembled to sign the document. Junius Brutus Stearns's famous painting captures the scene with George Washington holding the Constitution.

Other states were especially concerned that they would pay a disproportionate share of national taxes.

The Antifederalists' most important objection was the lack of protections for civil liberties in the new political system. Other than ducking the problem of slavery, this was perhaps the biggest failure of the Constitutional Convention and the one most difficult to understand. Most state constitutions protected freedom of speech, freedom of the press, right to a trial by a jury, and other civil liberties. Given the political climate, the delegates should have anticipated that these individual rights would be an important issue. Motions had been offered at the convention to protect various civil liberties, but they were voted down on the grounds that these matters should be left to the states. However, many Antifederalists still wanted assurances that the *national* government would not trample their rights.

The Federalists counterattacked on several fronts. First, supporters of the Constitution gained the upper hand in the debate by claiming the term "federalist." It is a common tactic in debates to co-opt a strong point of the opposing side as a positive for your side. The opponents to the Constitution probably had a stronger claim than its supporters to being federalists, that is, those who favored and emphasized the autonomous power of the state governments. Today, for example, the Federalist Society is a conservative group organized around the principles of states' rights and limited government. By calling themselves "Federalists," the supporters of the Constitution asserted that they were the true protectors of states' interests, which irritated the Antifederalists to no end. The Antifederalists also had the rhetorical disadvantage of having "anti" attached to their name, defining them in terms of their opponents' position rather than their own. But the problem was more than just rhetorical—the Federalists were quick to point out that the Antifederalists did not have their own plan to solve the problems created by the Articles.

Second, the Federalists published a series of eighty-five articles that came to be known as the *Federalist Papers*, written by Alexander Hamilton, James Madison, and John Jay. Since these articles were aimed at the New York delegation, they were originally published in New York newspapers, but they were widely read throughout the nation. The *Federalist Papers* should be viewed as political propaganda because they were one-sided arguments aimed at changing public opinion; the authors downplayed potentially unpopular aspects of the new system, such as the power of the president, while emphasizing points that they knew would appeal to the opposition. Despite their biased arguments, the *Federalist Papers* are the best comprehensive discussion of the political theory underlying the Constitution and the framers' interpretations of many of its key provisions.

Third, the Federalists agreed that the new Congress's first order of business would be to add a **Bill of Rights** to the Constitution to protect individual rights and liberties. This promise was essential for securing the support of New York, Massachusetts, and Virginia. The ninth state, New Hampshire, ratified the Constitution on June 21, 1788, but New York and Virginia were still dragging their heels, and the United States needed their support. By the end of the summer, both Virginia and New York finally voted for ratification, the latter by a narrow 30–27 vote. Two remaining states, Rhode Island and North Carolina, refused to ratify until Congress made good on their promise of a Bill of Rights. The 1st Congress

POLITICAL PROCESS MATTERS

 The process for approving the Constitution, from the language of Franklin's motion to adopt the document to the ratification process, was critical. A different process easily could have led to its defeat.

Federalist Papers A series of eighty-five articles written by Alexander Hamilton, James Madison, and John Jay that sought to sway public opinion toward the Federalists' position.

Bill of Rights The first ten amendments to the Constitution; they protect individual rights and liberties.

submitted the ten amendments to the states and they were ratified by all the states as of December 15, 1791.

SECTION SUMMARY

1. Despite the hard work of the framers at the Constitutional Convention, ratification of the document was far from assured.
2. The Antifederalists worried that the president would be too powerful, that too much power was being transferred from the states to the national government, and that the document lacked specific guarantees of civil liberties.
3. The *Federalist Papers*, written by Alexander Hamilton, James Madison, and John Jay, helped convince the skeptics, and by June 1788 the Constitution was ratified.

The Constitution: A Framework for Government

The Constitution certainly has its flaws, primarily its undemocratic qualities such as the indirect election of senators and the president, the compromises that suppressed the issue of slavery, and the absence of any general statement about citizens' right to vote. However, given the delegates' political context and the various factions that had to be satisfied, the Constitution's accomplishments are substantial. The document's longevity is testimony to the framers' foresight in crafting a flexible framework for government. Perhaps its most important feature is the system of separation of powers and checks and balances that prevent majority tyranny, while maintaining sufficient flexibility for decisive leadership during times of crisis, such as the Civil War, the Great Depression, and World War II. At the national level, the system of checks and balances means that each branch of government has certain exclusive powers, some shared powers, and the ability to check the other two branches (see Nuts and Bolt 2.3).

EXCLUSIVE POWERS

The framers viewed Congress as the "first branch" of government and granted it significant exclusive powers. With the popularly elected House of Representatives and the Senate indirectly elected by state legislatures, Congress was designed to be both the voice of the people and an elite institution with a significant role in domestic and foreign policy. Congress was given the power to raise revenue for the federal government through taxes and borrowing, regulate interstate and foreign commerce, coin money, establish post offices and roads, grant patents and copyrights, declare war, "raise and support armies," make rules for the military, and create and maintain a navy. The most important of these powers is the so-called "power of the purse"— control over taxing and spending—given to Congress in Article I, Section 9, of the Constitution: "No money shall be drawn from the Treasury, but in consequence of appropriations made by law." Or as Madison put it, "the legislative department alone has access to the pockets of the people." Congress's exclusive powers take on

▲ *Two of Congress's exclusive powers are to raise and support armies and the power of the purse. The war in Iraq has produced congressional struggles over whether the power to deny war funding should be used to force the executive branch to agree to a timetable for bringing troops home. Here, a convoy of U.S. armored vehicles heads toward Iraq's border.*

Checks and Balances

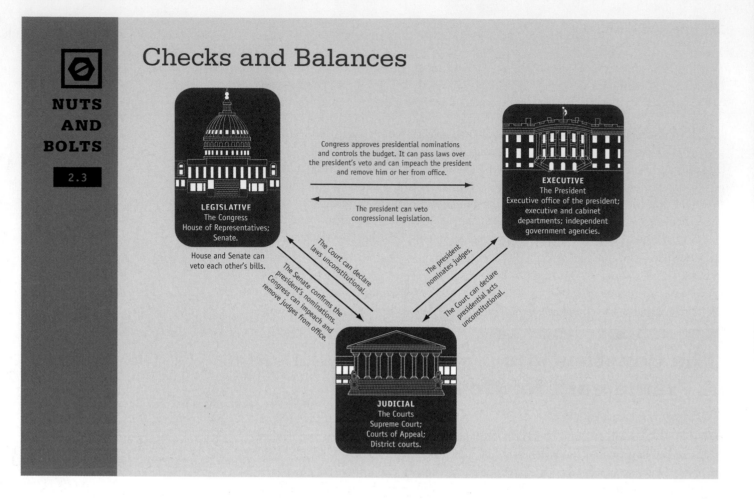

Congress approves presidential nominations and controls the budget. It can pass laws over the president's veto and can impeach the president and remove him or her from office.

The president can veto congressional legislation.

LEGISLATIVE
The Congress
House of Representatives;
Senate.

House and Senate can veto each other's bills.

The Court can declare laws unconstitutional.

The Senate confirms the president's nominations. Congress can impeach and remove judges from office.

EXECUTIVE
The President
Executive office of the president; executive and cabinet departments; independent government agencies.

The president nominates judges.

The Court can declare presidential acts unconstitutional.

JUDICIAL
The Courts
Supreme Court;
Courts of Appeal;
District courts.

---

additional significance through the **elastic clause**, also known as the necessary and proper clause, which gives Congress the power to "make all Laws which shall be necessary and proper for carrying into Execution the foregoing Powers, and all other Powers vested by this Constitution in the Government of the United States, or in any Department or Officer thereof." This broad grant of power meant that Congress could pass laws related to any of its exclusive powers. For example, while the Constitution did not explicitly mention Congress's right to compel people to serve in the military, its power to enact a draft was clearly given by the elastic clause, in conjunction with its power to "raise and support armies."

Congress's exclusive powers are far more numerous and specific than the limited powers granted to the president. The president, as the commander in chief of the armed forces, has power to receive ambassadors and foreign ministers and to issue pardons. The president's most important power is to ensure "that the laws are faithfully executed." As we will see later in the chapter, this executive powers clause has given the president most of his power.

The courts did not receive nearly as much attention in the Constitution as either Congress or the president. The framers devoted only six short paragraphs to the third branch of government. Alexander Hamilton argued in *Federalist* 78 that the Supreme Court would be the "least dangerous branch," because it had "neither the power of the purse nor the sword." The most important positive powers that the framers gave the Supreme Court were lifetime tenure for justices in good behavior and relative independence from the other two branches. The critical negative power of judicial review, the ability to strike down the laws and actions of other branches, will be discussed below.

elastic clause Part of Article I, Section 8, of the Constitution that grants Congress the power to pass any law that is related to one of its expressed powers

SHARED POWERS

Along with dividing the exclusive powers between branches, checks and balances also designate some shared powers, areas where no branch has exclusive control. For example, the president has the power to negotiate treaties and make appointments to the federal courts and other government offices, but these executive actions are to be undertaken with the "advice and consent" of the Senate, which means they were intended to be shared powers. In the twentieth century, these particular powers have become executive-centered, with the Senate providing almost no advice to the president and routinely giving their consent (often disapprovingly called "rubber stamping"). However, the Senate can assert its shared power as shown recently by Senate Democrats who blocked several of President George W. Bush's appointments to the lower federal courts.

The war powers, which include decisions about when and how to use military force, were also intended to be shared, but have become executive-dominated powers. The framers disagreed about who should control the war powers. Some wanted to keep the arrangement set up by the Articles of Confederation in which nine of the thirteen states had to agree before Congress could declare war. Others wanted to follow the British system in which the executive branch controlled war powers. The resulting compromise shows checks and balances at work, with the president serving as the commander in chief of the armed forces, while Congress has the power to declare war and to appropriate the funds to conduct a war. At the Constitutional Convention, the original proposal gave Congress the power to "make war" rather than "declare war." Clearly this would have been a far more significant grant of power, suggesting an ongoing role for Congress in the conduct of a war, but the framers decided that this could potentially cause conflict with the president and too much micromanagement by Congress in times of crisis.

Since very early in our nation's history, the president has taken a lead role in the war powers, relegating Congress to the role of sideline critic or supporter. Presidents have authorized the use of American troops on hundreds of occasions, but Congress has declared war only five times. Of these five, Congress debated the merits of entering only one war, the War of 1812. The other "declarations" of war recognized a state of war that already existed. For example, after Japan bombed Pearl Harbor, Hawaii, in 1941 Congress's subsequent declaration of war formally recognized what everyone already knew. Instead, the president usually takes the lead in the decision to use military force. As the 2003 invasion of Iraq demonstrated, if a president is intent on going to war, Congress must go along or get out of the way.

In a few instances, however, Congress wanted to declare war and the president resisted. For example, in 1895 and 1896 when Grover Cleveland was president, tensions were mounting in the United States over Cuba's struggle for independence from Spain. Congressional leaders tried to convince Cleveland of the merits of entering the war to help Cuba, but he refused. When a congressman reminded him that Congress had the power to declare war, Cleveland countered that he was the commander in chief saying, "I will not mobilize the army. I happen to know that we can buy the Island of Cuba from Spain for $100 million and a war will cost vastly more than that. . . . It would be an outrage to declare war."[21]

Examples such as this are interesting because they are unusual. It would be impossible today for Congress to declare war without a willing commander in chief. However, since

▲ John Roberts (with his back to the camera) is sworn in before the Senate Judiciary Committee at his confirmation hearing to become the Chief Justice of the Supreme Court. The president and the Senate share the appointment power to the federal courts: the president makes the nominations, while the Senate provides its "advice and consent."

the Vietnam War, Congress has tried to redress the imbalance in the war powers in other ways. In 1970, during the Vietnam War, Congress passed a resolution that prevented any funds from supporting ground troops in Laos or Cambodia (nations that bordered Vietnam). In 1973 they attempted to gain more control over the use of U.S. troops in "undeclared wars" by passing the War Powers Act. This attempt largely failed and will be discussed in more detail in Chapter 17, Foreign Policy. Then in the 1980s, Democrats in Congress prevented President Ronald Reagan from using any appropriated funds to support the Contra rebels in their fight against the Sandanista government in Nicaragua.[22] These examples show that while the president continues to dominate the war powers, Congress can assert its joint power when it has the will, just as it can by advising the president in treaty negotiations or withholding approval of the president's nominees for appointed positions.

NEGATIVE OR CHECKING POWERS

The last leg of the system of checks and balances is the negative power that the branches have over each other. Congress has two important negative checks on the other two branches: impeachment and the power of the purse. **Impeachment** was based on the British practice of removing unpopular or corrupt ministers of the king through a vote of no confidence, but the framers made one important change. The president, vice president or other "officers of the United States" (including federal judges) could not be removed for political reasons, but rather only for abuses of power, specifically "Treason, Bribery, or other High Crimes or Misdemeanors." Some framers wanted impeachment to be a political vote of no confidence that could be initiated by a majority of the state legislatures or, in another proposed version, the state governors. Instead, they decided to place this central check with Congress as part of the overall move toward centralizing power at the national level.

The **power of the purse** can be an important check as well. Congress can punish executive agencies by freezing or cutting their funding or holding hearings on, investigations of, or audits of their operations to make sure money is being spent properly. Though the Constitution prevents Congress from lowering the judges' salaries, they can freeze salaries to show displeasure with court decisions. Congress also has the power to alter the jurisdiction of the federal courts, limiting the issues they can consider, an extreme step that it has taken on several occasions. Congress can limit the discretion of judges in other ways, such as setting federal sentencing guidelines that recommend a range of years in prison that should be served for various crimes. Frustrated that some federal judges are ignoring the guidelines and handing out too many sentences more lenient than the recommendations, in 2003 Congress passed a law that requires the Justice Department to keep information on the sentencing record of every federal judge and forward this information to the House and Senate Judiciary Committees. This law drew a strong rebuke from then-Chief Justice William Rehnquist, who saw it as a threat to judicial independence. In his 2003 year-end report, Rehnquist said the law "could appear to be an unwarranted and ill-considered effort to intimidate individual judges in the performance of their judicial duties."[23] Even today the system of checks and balances is not fixed in stone, but evolves according to the changing political climate.

The framers placed important checks on Congressional power as well, and the president's most important check on Congress is the veto. Again there was very little agreement among the framers on this topic. The Antifederalists argued that it is "a political error of the greatest magnitude, to allow the executive power a negative, or in fact any kind of control over the proceedings of the legislature." On the other hand, the Federalists worried that Congress would slowly strip away presidential

impeachment A negative or checking power of Congress over the other branches allowing them to remove the president, vice president, or other "officers of the United States" (including federal judges) for abuses of power.

power of the purse The constitutional power of Congress to raise and spend money. Congress can use this as a negative or checking power over the other branches by freezing or cutting their funding to punish executive agencies.

powers and leave the president too weak. Addressing this fear, Madison argued that the veto would "restrain the legislature from encroaching on the other coordinate departments, or on the rights of the people at large, or from passing laws unwise in their principle or incorrect in their form." In the end, the Federalist view that the president needed some protections against the "depredations" of the legislature won the day. However, the veto has developed into a major policy-making tool for the president, which is probably broader than the check against "depredations" envisioned by the framers.

The president does not have any formal check on the courts other than the power to appoint judges (which does not always work out the way that presidents plan). However, presidents have, at various times, found unconventional ways to try to influence the courts. For example, Franklin D. Roosevelt tried to "pack the Court" by expanding the size of the Supreme Court with justices who would be sympathetic with his New Deal policies. More recently, George W. Bush attempted to expand the reach of executive power in the War on Terror by taking over some functions within the executive branch that previously had been performed by the courts. However, the Supreme Court struck down some of these policies as unconstitutional violations of defendants' due process rights. Critics are concerned that the expansion of executive power in order to fight terrorism has threatened the institutional balance of power by giving the president too much control over functions previously carried out by the courts.

The Constitution did not provide the Supreme Court with any negative checks on the other two branches. Instead, the practice of **judicial review**, the ability of the Supreme Court to strike down a law or an executive-branch action as unconstitutional, was asserted by the Court much later, in the landmark decision of *Marbury v. Madison* in 1803. Some of the framers clearly favored explicitly granting the Supreme Court the power of judicial review, but it proved to be too contentious an issue to handle at the convention. In several states, aggressive courts had struck down state laws, and delegates from those states resisted giving an unelected national court similar power over the entire country. While judicial review is not explicitly mentioned in the Constitution, supporters of the practice point to the supremacy clause, which states that the "Constitution, and the Laws of the United States which shall be made in Pursuance thereof . . . shall be the supreme law of the land." As Chief Justice John Marshall argued in *Marbury v. Madison*, in order to enforce the Constitution as the supreme law of the land, the Court must determine which laws are "in pursuance thereof." Critics of judicial review argue that the Constitution is supreme because it gains its legitimacy from the people, and therefore elected officials—Congress and the president—should be the primary interpreters of the Constitution rather than the courts. This dispute may never fully be resolved, but Marshall's bold assertion of judicial review made the Supreme Court an equal partner in the system of separated powers and checks and balances rather than "the least dangerous branch" that the framers described.

POLITICS IS CONFLICTUAL

The systems of checks and balances sets up inherent conflict in our political system as each branch attempts to limit the power of the others.

SECTION SUMMARY

1. The most important feature of the Constitution is the system of separation of powers and checks and balances. These arrangements prevent majority tyranny while maintaining sufficient flexibility for decisive leadership during times of crisis.

judicial review The Supreme Court's power to strike down a law or executive branch action that it finds unconstitutional.

2. At the national level, the system of checks and balances gives each branch of government certain exclusive powers, some shared powers, and the ability to check the power of the other two branches.

The Question of Relevance: Is the Constitution a "Living Document"?

W. E. Gladstone, a great British prime minister of the late nineteenth century, called the American Constitution "the most wonderful work ever struck off at a given time by the brain and purpose of man."[24] On the other hand, Robert Dahl, a leading democratic theorist of the twentieth century, takes a more pragmatic view in asking, "Why should we feel bound today by a document produced more than two centuries ago by a group of fifty-five mortal men, actually signed by only thirty-nine, a fair number of whom were slaveholders, and adopted in only thirteen states by the votes of fewer than two thousand men, all of whom are long since dead and mainly forgotten?"[25]

Can the Constitution provide the blueprint for modern democratic governance? If so, how has it remained relevant after more than 200 years? The answer to the first question, in our opinion, is clearly yes. While the United States falls short on many measures of an ideal democracy, the Constitution remains relevant in part because it embodies many of the central values of American citizens: liberty and freedom, majority rule and minority rights, equal protection for all citizens under the laws, and a division of power across and within levels of government. The Constitution presents a list of substantive values, largely within the Bill of Rights, aimed at legally protecting certain individual rights that we still consider basic and necessary. The Constitution also sets out the institutional framework within which the government operates.

But these observations beg the question of *why* the Constitution remains relevant today. Why does this framework of government still work? How can the framers' values still be meaningful to us? There are at least four reasons that the Constitution continues to be a "living document": a willingness over the years to simply ignore the parts that become irrelevant, ambiguity in central passages that allows flexible interpretation, the amending process, and the document's own designation of multiple interpreters of the Constitution. These factors have allowed the Constitution to evolve with the changing values and norms of the nation.

POLITICS IS EVERYWHERE

Because the Constitution is a living document, it remains relevant for the daily lives of all Americans.

TURNING A BLIND EYE

Some parts of the Constitution are ignored today because they have no meaning in a modern context. For example, Article I, Section 4 says that "Congress shall assemble at least once in every year, and such meeting shall be on the first Monday in December," but the modern Congress is in session throughout the year (with various recesses). Nobody pays attention to this passage anymore because it simply does not matter. Another example is the 3rd Amendment's prohibition against the quartering of troops in someone's house without their consent. Today the idea that National Guard officers would roll up to your house and ask to sleep on your couch

The U.S. Constitution as a Model for Other Nations

Albert P. Blaustein, a Rutgers law professor who helped draft more than forty constitutions worldwide, called the Constitution "America's most important export." He argues, "Since that seventeenth day of September 1787, a one-document constitution has been deemed an essential characteristic of nationhood. Today, of the 192 independent nations of the world, all but a very few have such a constitution or are committed to having one." Many of those that do not have constitutions, such as the United Kingdom, New Zealand, and Israel, are democratic nations with "sophisticated constitutional jurisprudence but no one specific document that can be called a constitution." Blaustein also argues that the American Constitution influenced the development of federalism in Latin America: Venezuela, Argentina, Mexico, and Brazil are federal states.[a]

While this conventional view is correct in a limited sense—most nations do have constitutions, and our nation led the way—it is profoundly incorrect to view the United States as a model for the democracies around the world. As Graham Wilson points out, "No other advanced industrial democracy has emulated the American system."[b] Nearly every other democracy has some version of parliamentary government, in which the chief executive is a prime minister who is selected by the majority party (or coalition of parties) in the legislature. Very few nations have our system of congressional single-member district elections and none share our unique institution of the electoral college. Instead, most have some version of proportional representation in which a broader range of parties compete for votes. Even the practice of judicial review that allows the courts to strike down actions taken by the legislative and executive branches is almost unique to the United States. (Germany, France, and Italy are among the few nations that have judicial review.)

The Iraqi people's extreme difficulties establishing a democracy illustrate the problems associated with exporting two important features of our political system. The separation of church and state was crucial to the American settlers who were fleeing religious persecution in Europe. But in many democracies around the world, the state embraces a specific religion, including Islam, Catholicism, and the Anglican Church of England. Religious leaders in Iraq have as much power, or more, than elected leaders. Placing control of the armed services in the hands of elected leaders is a foreign concept in many parts of the world where military leaders and elected officials operate with rival power bases. Sectarian militias in Iraq clashing with Iraq's government and U.S. troops are a stark reminder that civilian control of the military is another American export that does not always travel well. ■

Many countries have no separation of church and state. Religious leaders are powerful political players in Iraq's fledgling democracy. This picture show Iraqis holding posters of radical Shiite cleric Muqtada al-Sadr during a service in Kufa, Iraq, on March 28, 2008.

(or worse, kick you out of your bed) is absurd, but this was a real concern when the Constitution was written.

The tendency to ignore (or at least flexibly interpret) relevant passages can come into play in more meaningful ways as well. In the 2000 presidential election, George W. Bush and Dick Cheney nearly ran afoul of the part of the 12th Amendment, which says that electors in the electoral college shall "vote by ballot for President and Vice-President, one of whom, at least, shall not be an inhabitant of the same state with themselves." This would have put the Texas electors in a bind because both Bush and Cheney lived in Dallas, but Cheney changed his official state of residence to Wyoming. The courts dismissed legal challenges to this move, allowing the Texas electors to cast their votes for both Bush and Cheney. Whether this example demonstrates the courts' willingness to be flexible in their interpretation of the Constitution or a biased reading of the facts in Cheney's favor depends on your own interpretation.

AMBIGUITY

The second and far more important characteristic of the Constitution that has kept the document relevant is its ambiguity. Key passages were written in very general and therefore indeterminate language, which has allowed the Constitution to grow and evolve along with changing norms, values, and political contexts. This ambiguity was by design and political necessity, since the framers were well aware that the document would need to survive for generations, but in many instances the specific language that was written down was simply the wording that could be agreed upon.

Three of the most important parts of the Constitution are also among its most ambiguous: the elastic clause (also called the necessary and proper clause), the **executive powers clause**, and the **commerce clause**. As discussed earlier, the elastic clause gives Congress an extremely open-ended power to enact laws that are related to its **enumerated powers**, or those that are explicitly granted. But what does "necessary and proper" mean? Congress for the most part gets to answer that question. The executive powers clause is even more sparse in its language. Article II of the Constitution begins, "The executive Powers shall be vested in a President of the United States of America." While it may not seem like much, this sentence has been used to justify a broad range of presidential actions, such as issuing executive orders or forming executive agreements with other nations. It is a broad delegation of power because it does not define any boundaries for the "executive powers" it grants. This vague wording was necessary because the convention delegates could not agree on a definition of executive power. While this general wording was expedient for the framers, it also had the desirable consequence of making Article II flexible enough to serve the country, both in times that require strong presidential action, such as the Civil War, the Great Depression or World War II, and also in times when the president was not as central, like the "golden age of Congress" in the late nineteenth century.

Perhaps the best illustration of the importance of ambiguity in the Constitution is the commerce clause, which gives Congress "the power to regulate commerce . . . among the several States." Again, the key words are not defined. What is "commerce," and what exactly does "among the states" mean? This ambiguity has allowed for different interpretations reflecting the prevailing norms of the time. In the nineteenth century, when the national government was relatively weak and more power was held at the state level, the Supreme Court interpreted the clause to mean that Congress could not regulate commerce that was entirely within the boundaries of a single state (intrastate commerce, as opposed to interstate commerce between states). Because manufacturing typically occurred within the boundaries of a given state, this ruling lead to a distinction between manufacturing and commerce, which had significant implications. For example, Congress could not regulate working hours, worker safety, or child labor given that these were defined as part of manufacturing rather than commerce. In the New Deal era of the mid-1930s, the Court adopted a more expansive interpretation of the commerce clause that largely

executive powers clause Part of Article II, Section 1, of the Constitution that states, "The executive Power shall be vested in a President of the United States of America." This broad statement has been used to justify many assertions of presidential power.

commerce clause Part of Article I, Section 8, of the Constitution that gives Congress "the power to regulate Commerce . . . among the several States." The Supreme Court's interpretation of this clause has varied, but today it serves as the basis for much of Congress's legislation.

enumerated powers Powers explicitly granted to Congress, the president, or the Supreme Court in the first three articles of the Constitution. Examples include Congress's power to "raise and support armies" and the president's power as commander in chief.

obliterated the distinction between intrastate and interstate commerce. This view was strengthened in the 1960s when the Supreme Court upheld a civil rights law that, among other things, prevented owners of hotels from discriminating against African Americans. As we will discuss more fully in Chapter 3, Federalism, for nearly sixty years this interpretation held, but more recently the Supreme Court has tightened the scope of Congress's powers to regulate commerce. The commerce clause has been unchanged since 1789, but its ambiguous wording has been used to justify or restrict a varying array of legislation.

CHANGING THE CONSTITUTION

The most obvious ways that the Constitution keeps up with the times is by allowing for changes to its language. The idea behind Article V, which lays out the formal process for amending the Constitution, was broadly supported by the framers: the people must control their own political system, which included the ability to change it through a regular, nonviolent process. George Washington called constitutional amendments "explicit and authentic acts" and Thomas Jefferson was adamant that each generation needed to have the power to change the Constitution. Toward the end of his life, he wrote in a letter to James Madison:

> Some men look at constitutions with sanctimonious reverence, and deem them like the ark of the covenant, too sacred to be touched. They ascribe to the men of the preceding age a wisdom more than human, and suppose what they did to be beyond amendment. I knew that age well; I belonged to it and labored with it. . . . It was very like the present . . . Let us not weakly believe that one generation is not as capable as another of taking care of itself.[26]

While there was strong consensus on including in the Constitution a set of provisions for amending it, there was no agreement on exactly how this should be done. The Virginia Plan envisioned a relatively easy process of changing the Constitution "whensoever it shall seem necessary" by means of ratification by the people, while the New Jersey plan proposed a central role for state governments. James Madison suggested the plan that was eventually adopted, which once again accommodated the views of those who wanted a stronger national government and those who favored the states. Article V describes the two steps necessary to change the Constitution, proposal and ratification. Congress may propose an amendment that has the approval of two-thirds of the members in both houses, or an amendment may be proposed by a national convention that has been called by two-thirds of the states' legislatures. In either case, the amendment must be ratified by three-fourths of the states' legislatures or state conventions (see Nuts and Bolts 2.4). A national convention has never been used to propose an amendment and every amendment except for the twenty-first, which repealed Prohibition, has been ratified by state legislatures rather than state conventions.

Article V was a brilliant compromise that struck a balance between opposing views at the convention and made it neither too difficult nor too easy to amend the Constitution. However, the amending process has its flaws. First, one reason that a new constitutional convention has never been called is fear of a "runaway convention." Some scholars argue that nothing in Article V would constrain the convention to consider a single issue, so it is possible that the convention could start from scratch, the way the framers did, even proposing a new method of ratification. Others dispute this view, but we have come close to finding out on several occasions. In the 1960s, thirty-five states, one short of the necessary two-thirds, called for a

Amending the Constitution

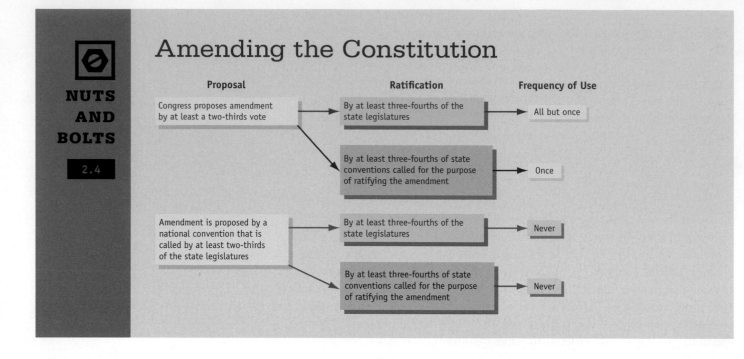

Proposal	Ratification	Frequency of Use
Congress proposes amendment by at least a two-thirds vote	By at least three-fourths of the state legislatures	All but once
	By at least three-fourths of state conventions called for the purpose of ratifying the amendment	Once
Amendment is proposed by a national convention that is called by at least two-thirds of the state legislatures	By at least three-fourths of the state legislatures	Never
	By at least three-fourths of state conventions called for the purpose of ratifying the amendment	Never

convention to propose a constitutional amendment that would overturn a Supreme Court decision concerning legislative redistricting. In the late 1970s, thirty states called for a convention to propose an amendment requiring a balanced federal budget. Article V also does not specify voting procedures for a constitutional convention. Would votes be apportioned equally so that each state would have one vote (as was true at the 1787 convention), or would the voting power be based on population, or perhaps some mixture of the two, as in the electoral college? Article V is also silent on the mechanism for choosing delegates to attend the state conventions. Thus, there is a wide range in the different states' methods of selection. Delegates may be appointed by the governor, elected by the people, or comprised of the current state legislators.

Article V also does not address the question of time limits on amendments; rather, this issue has been left up to Congress. Some amendments have been approved by Congress and sent to the states for ratification without time limits on the ratification process. This led to the odd situation surrounding the 27th Amendment, which required that no legislation granting a congressional pay raise could go into effect until after the following election. This amendment was originally proposed in 1789 as part of the original Bill of Rights. It sat unratified for more than eighty years until Ohio ratified it to protest a congressional pay hike; however, no other states followed Ohio's lead. It sat for another 100 years until 1978, when Wyoming ratified the amendment. Then, in the early 1980s, the amendment gained national attention. From 1983 to 1992, enough states ratified the amendment to add it to the Constitution on May 7, 1992, after a lag of more than 202 years!

Most amendments have been wider-reaching than the 27th Amendment, but they have ranged from fairly narrow, technical corrections of errors in the original document (11th and 12th Amendments), to important topics such as the abolition of slavery, mandating equal protection of the laws for all citizens, providing for the popular election of senators, giving blacks and then women the right to vote, and allowing a national income tax. Potential Constitutional amendments have addressed many other issues, with over 10,000 proposed; of those thirty-three were sent to the states, and twenty-seven have made it through the amending process (with the first ten coming at once in the Bill of Rights). Table 2.1 shows several significant amendments that were sent to the states but not ratified. The You Decide box outlines the debate over when it is appropriate to amend the Constitution.

MULTIPLE INTERPRETERS

The final way that the Constitution maintains its relevance is through changing interpretations of the document by multiple interpreters. As the discussion of the commerce clause pointed out, there have been significant changes over time in the way that the Constitution structures the policy-making process, even though the pertinent text of the Constitution has not changed.[27] This point is best understood by examining the concept of implied powers, that is, powers that are not explicitly stated in the Constitution but can be inferred from an enumerated power. The Supreme Court often defines the boundaries of implied powers, but Congress, the president, and the public can also play key roles.

Three of the earliest examples of implied powers show the president, the Supreme Court, and Congress each interpreting the Constitution and contributing to its evolving meaning. The first example involved the question of how active the president should be in stating national foreign policy principles. In issuing his famous proclamation of neutrality in 1793, George Washington unilaterally set forth a national foreign policy, even though the president's power to do so is not explicitly stated in the Constitution. Alexander Hamilton defended the presidential power to make such a proclamation as implied in both the executive powers clause and the president's explicitly granted powers in the area of foreign policy (receiving ambassadors, negotiating treaties, and serving as commander in chief). Thomas Jefferson, on the other hand, thought it was terrible idea for presidents to have that kind of power, preferring that such general policy statements be left to Congress.

The Supreme Court made its mark on the notion of implied powers in an early landmark case involving the creation of a national bank. In *McCulloch v. Maryland* (1819) the Court ruled that the federal government had the power to create a national bank and denied the state of Maryland the right to tax a branch of that bank. The Court said it was not necessary for the Constitution to expressly grant Congress the power to create the bank; rather, it was implied in Congress's power over financial matters and from the elastic clause of the Constitution.

Congress got into the act with an early debate over the president's implied power to remove appointed officials. The Constitution clearly gives the president the power to make appointments to cabinet positions and other top executive branch offices, but it is silent on how these people can be removed. This was one of the most difficult issues in the first Congress, and members spent more than a month debating the topic. The record of the debate is the most thorough examination of implied powers ever conducted in Congress. The logical implication of the president's appointment power, which requires Senate approval, would be that the advice and consent of the Senate would also be required for removal. This was Alexander Hamilton's view, as he stated in *Federalist* 77, but others disagreed. Madison proposed that in three executive branch departments, War, Treasury, and Foreign Affairs, appointments would require the consent of the Senate, but removal would be up to the president alone. He argued that this would make the president more responsible for the conduct of the departments. The Senate was divided with at least five proposals on removal power having some support, ranging from those who wanted removal power left to the courts, to those who wanted the president to have unilateral removal power. Others wanted a role for the Senate, or supported some combination of several positions. Congress ended up not taking any action on the issue, which left the president's removal power implicit in the Constitution.

Issues concerning implied powers have continued to surface frequently. The president's appointment powers have evolved in the last twenty years as the Senate has played a much more aggressive role in providing its "advice and consent" on presidential nominations to the federal courts. As we will explore more fully in Chapter 14, in the past twenty years the Senate has blocked court appointments at a significantly higher rate than it did in the first half of the twentieth century. The relevant language in the Constitution is the same, yet the Senate's understanding of its role in this important process has changed.

Public opinion and social norms also influence the prevailing interpretation of the Constitution, as evident in the evolving meanings of capital punishment and

Amending the Constitution

In a typical Congress there are between fifty and one hundred proposals to amend the Constitution. Some of the proposed amendments reflect efforts to overturn particularly controversial Supreme Court decisions. Recent examples include amendments to prohibit abortion, guarantee the right to obtain an abortion, make flag desecration a crime, and permit prayer in public school. Some amendments are designed to change the government's basic structure and process, such as proposals to replace the electoral college with a direct popular vote, choose presidential electors at the congressional-district level, repeal the 22nd amendment (which limits presidents to two terms), require a two-thirds

Some people argue that the Constitution should not be used to make policy, but for broader purposes such as expanding political rights or protecting equality. The 18th Amendment, ratified in 1919, prohibited the consumption of alcohol and is often upheld as an example of a failed policy attempt. In this 1933 photo, a beer distributor readies his first shipment following ratification of the 21st Amendment, repealing Prohibition.

congressional vote to raise taxes, impose term limits on Representatives and Senators, or repeal the 16th Amendment (which permitted a federal income tax). And some proposed amendments would guarantee specific benefits or create new classes of constitutionally guaranteed rights like affordable housing, quality health care, a clean environment, or full employment. Perhaps the most specific proposal is the one that would replace the 8th Amendment with, "Excessive bail shall not be required, nor excessive fines imposed, nor cruel and unusual punishments (including incarceration, before or after trial, for minor traffic offenses) inflicted." This proposed amendment was specifically designed to overturn the 2001 Supreme Court decision *Atwater v. Lago Vista*, in which the Court held in a 5–4 vote that the police can arrest and detain individuals for minor violations, such as not wearing a seatbelt, even if the violation itself would not result in a jail sentence. The amendment died in committee.

The only thing that cannot be changed in the Constitution is the equal apportionment of states' votes in the Senate (two senators per state).[a] Anything short of that is fair game, but many constitutional scholars argue that the amending process should not be used to address short-term, narrow policy issues such as term limits, burning the flag, balanced budgets, or the Pledge of Allegiance. The only adopted amendments that fall into this category are Prohibition (which was subsequently repealed with another amendment) and the long-delayed 27th Amendment regarding Congressional pay raises. The other amendments address broader pol-

icy concerns, expand or protect individual rights and liberties, modify electoral laws and institutions, or address basic concerns about the working of government. Constitutional scholar Kathleen Sullivan is critical of efforts to alter the Constitution. Constitutional principles should not, she concludes, be "up for grabs" or politicized, but should be slow to change; amendments should be reserved for setting out the basic structure of government and defining "a few fundamental political ideals."[b] The alternative perspective chides those who "treat the Constitution like an untouchable religious text and the republic's founders as omniscient," and maintains that "meaningful democratic politics requires an aggressive constitutional politics."[c]

One area of debate concerns gay marriage. Many states have amended their constitutions to define marriage to exclude same-sex couples. Advocates of this view are pushing for an amendment to the U.S. Constitution to define marriage the same way at the national level. Would you support such an amendment? Try to separate your view on the specific issue, gay marriage, from your position on the question of amending the Constitution. If you oppose gay marriage, is it possible that the better path of action would be through the state legislatures? What kinds of policies would you favor addressing through Constitutional amendments? Do you agree that amendments should be reserved for a "few fundamental political ideas"—things like the right to vote and the structure of government—or that more frequent amendments are necessary for "meaningful democratic politics"? ■

▲ *The 8th Amendment's ban on "cruel and unusual punishment" is generally viewed as excluding capital punishment, but the execution of juveniles and the mentally retarded has been found unconstitutional. This picture shows the electric chair in the Southern Ohio Correctional Facility in Lucasville, Ohio.*

the freedom of speech. When the Constitution was written, capital punishment was broadly accepted, even for horse thieves. The framers were only concerned that people not be "deprived of life, liberty, or property without the due process of law." Therefore the prohibition in the 8th Amendment against "cruel and unusual punishment" certainly did not mean to the framers that the death penalty was unconstitutional. However, in 1972 the Supreme Court struck down capital punishment as unconstitutional because it was being applied arbitrarily.[28] Subsequently, after procedural changes were made, the Court once again upheld the practice. However, the Court has since decided that capital punishment for a mentally retarded man constituted cruel and unusual punishment—a decision that reflects modern sensibilities but not the thinking of the framers. Similarly, the text of the 1st Amendment protections for freedom of speech has never changed, but the Supreme Court has been willing to uphold significant limitations on free speech, especially in wartime. However, when external threats are less severe, the Court has been more tolerant of controversial speech, which reflects society's relative levels of tolerance in peacetime and during war.

The line between a new interpretation of the Constitution and constitutional change is difficult to define. Clearly not every new direction taken by the Court or new interpretation of the constitutional roles of the president or Congress is comparable to a Constitutional amendment. In one respect, a Constitutional amendment is much more permanent than a new interpretation by the Court. For example, the Supreme Court could not unilaterally decide that eighteen-year-olds, women, and African Americans no longer have the right to vote. Constitutional amendments expanded the right to vote to include these groups, and only further amendments could either expand or restrict the right to vote. However, gradual changes in constitutional interpretation are probably just as important as the amending process in explaining the Constitution's ability to keep pace with the times. Even the large "revolutions" in Constitutional change have occurred by both means: the Civil War led to a **constitutional revolution** that was accomplished through three important amendments, while the New Deal constitutional revolution happened without changing a single word of the document.

SECTION SUMMARY

1. The Constitution embodies many of the central values of American citizens: liberty and freedom, majority rule and minority rights, equal protection of the laws, and a division of power across and within levels of government.

2. The Constitution has remained a "living document" that evolves with the changing values and norms of the nation for four main reasons: willingness to ignore the parts that become irrelevant, ambiguity in central passages that allows flexible interpretation, the amending process, and multiple interpreters of its meaning.

constitutional revolution A significant change in the Constitution that may be accomplished either through amendments (as in after the Civil War) or shifts in the Supreme Court's interpretation of the Constitution (as in the New Deal era).

Conclusion

To return to Dahl's challenge to the relevance of the Constitution, why should we pay attention to this document? One answer can be found in the events that opened this chapter: the 2000 presidential election and Clinton's impeachment. The Constitution proved critical for resolving both of those issues. In the first instance, the

Supreme Court's interpretation of the Constitution determined the resolution of an electoral crisis. In the latter, the people decided that Clinton's lies about his sexual transgressions did not rise to the level of a "high crime or misdemeanor," and he retained the presidency.

A leading constitutional scholar, Walter Murphy, addresses the relevance issue saying, "The ideals that it enshrines, the processes it prescribes, and the actions it legitimizes must either help to change its citizenry or, at a minimum, reflect their current values. If a constitution does not articulate at least in general terms, the ideals that form or will reform its people and express the political character they have, it will soon be replaced or atrophy." The Constitution's ability to change with the times and reflect its citizens' values has allowed it to remain relevant and important today.

CRITICAL THINKING

1. Should the Constitution be a "living document" that evolves with changes in our society, or should interpretation of the Constitution follow more closely the original intentions of the framers?
2. If you were at the Constitutional Convention, which part of the document would you have worked to change? How would you have negotiated a compromise to make that change possible?
3. The Clinton impeachment scandal can be considered an example of how the public's interpretation of the Constitution influenced the way an event played out. What are some other examples of events changed by the public's interpretation of the Constitution?

KEY TERMS

Antifederalists (p. 36)
Articles of Confederation (p. 30)
Bill of Rights (p. 46)
commerce clause (p. 54)
"consent of the governed" (p. 33)
constitutional revolution (p. 60)
elastic clause (p. 48)
enumerated powers (p. 54)
executive powers clause (p. 54)
factions (p. 34)
Federalist Papers (p. 46)
Federalists (p. 36)
Great Compromise (p. 38)
impeachment (p. 50)
implied powers (p. 58)
judicial review (p. 51)

limited government (p. 30)
monarchy (p. 29)
national supremacy clause (p. 42)
natural rights (p. 33)
New Jersey Plan (p. 38)
parliamentary system (p. 41)
pluralism (p. 37)
power of the purse (p. 50)
republican democracy (p. 29)
republicanism (p. 33)
Three-fifths Compromise (p. 43)
Virginia Plan (p. 38)

SUGGESTED READING

Currie, David P. *The Constitution of the United States: A Primer for the People*, 2nd ed. Chicago: University of Chicago Press, 2000.

Dahl, Robert A. *How Democratic Is the American Constitution?* New Haven, CT: Yale University Press, 2001.

Davis, Sue. *Corwin and Peltason's Understanding the Constitution*, 17th ed. Boston: Wadsworth Publishing, 2007.

Hamilton, Alexander, James Madison, and John Jay. *The Federalist Papers*. 1788. Reprint, 2nd ed., edited by Roy P. Fairfield. Baltimore, MD: Johns Hopkins University Press, 1981.

Ketcham, Ralph. *The Anti-Federalist Papers and the Constitutional Convention Debates*. New York: Signet Classics, 2003.

Rossiter, Clinton. *1787: The Grand Convention*. New York: MacMillan, 1966.

Sunstein, Cass R. *Designing Democracy: What Constitutions Do*. New York: Oxford University Press, 2001.

Wood, Gordon S. *The Creation of the American Republic*. New York: W.W. Norton, 1969.

FEDERALISM

In 1981, twenty-nine states and the District of Columbia allowed people over the age of either eighteen or nineteen to drink some types of alcohol. However, under intense lobbying from Mothers Against Drunk Driving and other organizations, Congress passed a law in 1984 that would with-hold 5 percent of federal highway funds in 1986 and 10 percent for every year after that from any state that did not raise the drinking age to twenty-one. Why did Congress take this indirect route? Why didn't they simply pass a law making the national drinking age twenty-one? Establishing the drinking age had been viewed as a state power since the ratification of the 21st Amendment in 1933, which repealed the 18th Amendment, Prohibition. Therefore, the only way that Congress could get states to change their laws was by using its "power of the purse" to coerce them. The legislation put conservative Republicans in a difficult position because they typically would support states' rights over the heavy hand of the national government. However, forty-five of the fifty-five Republicans supported the bill when it passed in the Senate by an 81–16 vote. It also passed in the House, and Republican President Ronald Reagan signed the bill saying, "This problem is bigger than the individual states. It's a grave national problem and it touches all of our lives. With the problem so clear-cut and the proven solution at hand, we have no misgiving about this judicious use of federal power. I'm convinced that it will help persuade the state legislators to act in the national interest."[1]

Several states resisted, taking their case to the courts. However, in 1987 the Supreme Court ruled that while Congress did not have the power to directly implement a national drinking age, it was acceptable for Congress to "encourage" the states to adopt the drinking age of twenty-one.[2] It took twelve years for every state to fall in line (Louisiana was the last, ending its holdout in 1996).

Statistics support President Reagan's view: the law appears to be in the nation's interest. According to the National Highway Traffic Safety Administration (NHTSA), 50 percent of fatalities from car accidents in 1988 were alcohol-related. That number fell to 38 percent ten years later. From 1988 until 1998, the NHTSA showed that drivers who were between sixteen and twenty years old experienced the largest decrease in intoxication rates in fatal crashes (33 percent) for any age group in that period. Before 1986, young adults who lived in states with a drinking age of twenty-one drove to nearby states with lower age limits, leading to what came to be known as "blood borders." As these intoxicated teens drove home, thousands were killed in accidents. Eliminating these blood borders helped reduce alcohol-related fatalities, saving as many as 1,250 lives a year.

In an effort to improve upon these gains, the anti-drunk driving lobby continued its push to make highways safer. Significant discrepancies remained among states' definitions of the blood alcohol content (BAC) at which someone was legally too drunk to drive; legal intoxication thresholds ranged from .05 to .1. The activists lobbied Congress to use the same coercive technique to require every state to adopt a BAC limit of at least .08 or lose highway funds. In 1998 Congress passed the Transportation Equity Act for the 21st Century that required states to adopt the .08 standard, pass a ban on open containers of alcohol in cars, and toughen their punishments for repeat drunk drivers by October 2000—or lose 1.5 percent of their highway funds in the first two years and 3 percent after that. In addition, the federal government made millions of dollars in "incentive grants" available to states that complied. Every state is now in compliance with the .08 BAC standard, but eleven states still do not have open container laws.[3]

Drinking laws illustrate the importance of our federal system. Federalism can be defined as a form of government that divides sovereign power across at least two political units. Sovereign power simply means that each unit of government (in the U.S. context, the national and state governments) has some degree of authority and autonomy, so states can do some things that the national government would not agree with, and in other areas, the national government holds sway over the states.

As discussed in the previous chapter, this division of power across levels of government is central to our system of separated powers. While the concept of dividing power across levels of government is simple, the political battles over *how* that power will be divided have been intense. Indeed, disputes at the heart of both the Constitutional Convention and the Civil War focused on this same principle, and these fights continue today in legislatures and courts.

The results of these battles have tremendous consequences for all citizens. Not only must politicians and judges choose between emphasizing national power or state power, but decentralizing power across levels of government provides a much broader range of *individual-level* choices than a unitary system. For example, a retiree trying to decide where to live could choose between low-tax, low-service states such as Texas or Alaska and high-tax, high-service states such as New York or Wisconsin. Business owners often decide where to locate a new office

▶ The group Mothers Against Drunk Driving has urged Congress to pass tougher drunk driving laws. While Congress cannot pass national legislation concerning drinking, they can pressure states to change their laws by withholding federal highway funding. Such pressure induced all fifty states to make twenty-one the legal drinking age and to set a legal blood alcohol content limit under 0.08 for drivers.

or factory based on the balance between statewide income and education levels and an attractive "business climate," which depends on the corporate tax structure, environmental laws, regulatory policy, and levels of unionization of the workforce. States offer different balances between these factors because our federal system gives states autonomy to choose policies that meet their residents' needs.

Of course, the Constitutional Convention and the Civil War were a long time ago, and you probably do not own a business, so how does federalism affect your life? Answering this question illustrates that politics is everywhere. For example, if you attend a public university or college you are influenced by a broad range of state and national-level policies. Your university may be the product of a "land grant" to the state from the national government, the cost of operating the university is paid partly by state taxpayers, and the state legislature probably sets tuition levels (this varies by state). College admissions decisions are regulated by national laws, including a recent Supreme Court decision that allows an applicant's race to be considered a "plus factor" in the admissions process.[4] Even students at private universities are affected by national policies. You or your parents may have saved for your college education tax-free using a 529 College Savings Plan. You may have a work-study job, Pell Grant, or federally guaranteed student loan, which are all products of national policies. Thus, your college experience has been shaped by state and national policies and is indirectly a product of our federal system.

▲ *Trying to stop violence against women has been an important issue at the national and state levels. Students from Columbia College rallied at the South Carolina statehouse to protest insensitive comments about domestic violence made by State Representative John Altman.*

This chapter also illustrates the key idea that politics is conflictual. Controversial issues that have come up in recent years include whether the national government should be able to prevent states from allowing marijuana use for medical purposes or from allowing assisted suicides. Should Congress be able to prevent state governments from discriminating against their employees based on age or disability? Can Congress compel states to ban guns within or around public schools? Does Congress have the power to provide stronger penalties for violence against women than the states? These questions involve defining the frequently disputed boundaries between what the states and national government are allowed to do. Much of U.S. history has been rooted in this struggle to define American federalism: will it be more state-centered or nation-centered?

The drinking laws, like many other examples in this chapter, also illustrate how much the political process matters. Congress's indirect route to affect changes in state laws through a combination of coercive penalties and incentive grants shows how the process of changing policy in a federal system can be quite slow and cumbersome. Because states control policy in many areas, it is difficult for the national government to get the states to change. If we had a single national government that could decide policy for the entire country, changes could be made much more easily.

This chapter begins by defining federalism and showing how the balance between state and national power has evolved throughout our history, culminating with an examination of the particular tensions that have emerged in the past twenty years: while the national government still dominates the political system, states have been resurgent in many areas. We will also consider how the Supreme Court has shaped recent battles over federalism.

What Is Federalism?

A distinguishing feature of federalism is that each level of government has some degree of autonomy from the other levels; that is, each level can carry out some policies that may not be preferred by the other levels. In the United States, this means that the national and state governments have distinct powers and responsibilities. The national government, for example, is responsible for national defense and foreign policy. State and local governments have primary responsibility for education and law enforcement. In other areas, such as transportation, the different levels of government share responsibilities in what are typically called the **concurrent powers** (see Nuts and Bolts 3.1). The national government has also taken on additional responsibilities through implied powers that are inferred from the powers explicitly granted in the Constitution (this will be discussed in more detail later in the chapter).

Local governments—cities, towns, school districts, and counties—are not autonomous units of government and therefore have a different place within our federal system than the national and state governments. Local governments are creatures of the state government. That is, state governments

POLITICS IS EVERYWHERE

Some advocates of our federalist system of government argue that local government is "closest to the people," and therefore, policies that are implemented at the local level are more desirable or effective than state or national policies. Whether or not you agree with this argument, local policies have a big impact on your life.

NUTS AND BOLTS

3.1

National and State Responsibilities

National Government Powers

- Print money
- Regulate interstate commerce and international trade
- Make treaties and conduct foreign policy
- Declare war
- Provide an army and navy
- Establish post offices
- Make laws necessary and proper to carry out these powers

State Government Powers

- Issue licenses
- Regulate intrastate (within the state) businesses
- Conduct elections
- Establish local governments
- Ratify amendments to the Constitution
- Promote public health and safety
- May exert powers the Constitution does not delegate to the national government or prohibit the states from using

Concurrent Powers

- Collect taxes
- Build roads
- Borrow money
- Establish courts
- Make and enforce laws

- Charter banks and corporations
- Spend money for the general welfare
- Take private property for public purposes, with just compensation

POWERS DENIED TO THE NATIONAL GOVERNMENT AND STATE GOVERNMENTS

Denied to the National Government

- May not violate the Bill of Rights
- May not impose export taxes among states
- May not use money from the Treasury without an appropriation from Congress
- May not change state boundaries

Denied to State Governments

- May not enter into treaties with other countries
- May not print money
- May not tax imports or exports
- May not interfere with contracts
- May not suspend a person's rights without due process

Source: GPO Access: Guide to the U.S. Government, available at http://bensguide.gpo.gov/3-5/government/federalism/html.

create local governments and control the types of activities they can engage in, by specifying in the state charter either what they *can* do or only what they *cannot* do—that is, they are allowed to do anything not specifically prohibited in the charter. This lack of autonomy does not imply that local governments are unimportant. Indeed they play the central role in providing public education, police and fire departments, and land use policies. They raise money through property taxes, user fees, and in some cases local sales taxes. But overall, local governments do not directly share power within our federal system with the state and national governments because of their lack of autonomy.

▲ *In unitary governments, power is centralized at the national level. For example, the British Parliament (the House of Commons is shown here) has complete authority over England, Scotland, Wales, and Northern Ireland.*

FEDERALISM IN COMPARATIVE PERSPECTIVE

This same observation about the place of local governments within our system may be made with respect to state governments by comparing U.S. federalism to forms of government in other countries. Just because a nation is comprised of states does not mean that it is a federal system. The key point again is the autonomy of the political subunit. The United Kingdom, for example, is comprised of England, Scotland, Wales, and Northern Ireland. In 1998, the British Parliament created a new Scottish government and gave it authority in a broad range of areas. However, the Parliament could unilaterally dissolve the Scottish government, therefore the subunit (Scotland) is not autonomous. This type of government in which power is centralized within the national government is called a **unitary government**. Unitary governments are the most common in the modern world (about 80%); other examples include Israel, Italy, France, Japan, and Sweden. While federalism is not as common, many other nations including Australia, Austria, Canada, Germany, and Switzerland, share this form of government with the United States (see Comparing Ourselves to Others).

At the opposite end of the spectrum from a unitary government is a **confederal government**, in which the states have most of the power and often even have veto power over the actions of the central government. This was the first type of government in the United States under the Articles of Confederation. As discussed in Chapter 2, there were many problems associated with having such a weak national government, thus there are few modern examples. The Commonwealth of Independent States (CIS), which was formed on December 21, 1991 after the breakup of the former Soviet Union, has had some success in coordinating the economic activity and security needs of twelve independent states.[5] The Commonwealth has a Council of Heads of State and Council of Heads of Government that produced hundreds of treaties and agreements in its first five years.[6] Over time, however, rifts among the member states have created problems, and today the CIS is viewed as largely ineffective.

While true confederations are rare, intergovernmental organizations have proliferated in the past several decades. More than 1,200 multilateral organizations have been created by member nations seeking to coordinate their policies on, for example, economic activity, security, or environmental protection. The United Nations (UN), International Monetary Fund (IMF), and North Atlantic Treaty Organization (NATO) are some important examples. The European Union is an example of an intergovernmental organization that began as a loose confederation, but it is

POLITICAL PROCESS MATTERS

Whether a country has a confederal, federal, or unitary structure has a big impact on how policies are made and even on whether the nation survives or is dissolved.

unitary government A system in which the national, centralized government holds ultimate authority. It is the most common form of government in the world.

confederal government A form of government in which states hold power over a limited national government.

Unitary versus Federal Systems

Unitary systems are about four times more common than federal systems. Why is this the case? The simplest reason is that federal systems are much more complicated and often involve disagreements over the division of power between the central and regional governments (in the United States, these disputes usually must be resolved in the courts). Second, some economists argue that decentralized federal systems undermine prudent financial management, producing slower economic growth and larger budget deficits than unitary systems. However, there is conflicting evidence on the impact of federalism on growth and budget deficits. One recent study found that if federal systems become more reliant on intergovernmental transfers (that is, grants from the central government to the states) and if states retain the ability to borrow independently, budget deficits tend to be higher. In contrast if the central government in a federal system imposes borrowing restrictions on the states, or if states have a strong degree of autonomy for both taxing and borrowing, balanced budgets are more common. Unitary systems do not have to worry as much about lower levels of governments as a source of na-

Federalism helps democracies deal with ethnic and national differences within their populations. For example, Canada's federal system provides French Canadians with autonomy in Quebec province.

tional debt because the states have less fiscal autonomy.[a]

Another potential drawback of federalism relative to unitary systems is that it promotes regional and ethnic separation. The former communist states of eastern Europe demonstrate this point. Of those nine states, six were unitary and three were federal. The six unitary states have remained intact (in fact, they are now five states because East Germany has reunited

with the Federal Republic of Germany), while the three federal states—Yugoslavia, the USSR, and Czechoslovakia—have fractured into twenty-two independent states! Furthermore, most of the conflict in this region has occurred in these states."[b]

On the other hand, federalist systems are a necessary tool for dealing with ethnic and national differences within countries. There are many multi-ethnic countries in the world, but very few of them are democracies—usually the iron fist of totalitarianism keeps these different factions together. In Iraq, for example, the Sunnis, Shiites, and Kurds were held together as one nation by Saddam Hussein's oppressive rule. When he was removed from power, the nation degenerated into sectarian violence as these groups struggled for power. Federalism made the fledgling democracy possible (the Kurds would never have agreed with the constitution without substantial autonomy), but the country may still split apart. There are several success stories of multinational or multi-ethnic democracies and all are federal: Switzerland, Canada, Belgium, Malaysia, India, and Spain.[c] Federalism allows each group, such as the French Canadians in Quebec, to have autonomy while remaining part of the larger country. ■

becoming more federalist in its decision-making process and structure. Its relative success, compared to the failure of the CIS, can be explained in part by this move toward a more federal structure, while the CIS maintained its confederal structure.

SECTION SUMMARY

1. Federalism divides certain powers and responsibilities between the national and state governments, but some concurrent powers are shared.
2. Under federalism each level of government has some degree of autonomy and independence.
3. This federal system is in contrast to the more common unitary system and the less common confederal system.

Balancing National and State Power in the Constitution

While the Founders wanted a national government that was stronger than it had been under the Articles of Confederation, they also wanted to preserve the autonomy of the states. These goals are reflected in different parts of the Constitution, which provides ample evidence for advocates of both state-centered and nation-centered federalism. The nation-centered position can point to the preamble of the Constitution, which begins, "We the People of the United States," compared to the Articles of Confederation that began, "We the undersigned delegates of the States." The Constitution's phrasing emphasizes the nation as a whole over the separate states.

Other aspects of the Constitution also support the nation-centered perspective. The Founders wanted a strong national government to provide national security and a healthy and efficient economy. As discussed in the previous chapter, Congress was granted the power to raise and support armies, declare war, and "suppress Insurrections and repel Invasion," while the president, as commander in chief of the armed forces, would oversee the conduct of war. Giving Congress the power to regulate interstate commerce centralized an important economic power at the national level, and many restrictions on state power had similar effects. States were *prohibited* from entering into "any Treaty, Alliance, or Confederation" or keeping troops or "ships of war" during peace time. They also could not coin money or impose duties on imports or exports (see Article I, Section 10). These provisions ensured that states would not interfere with the smooth operation of interstate commerce or create problems for national defense. Imagine, for example, that Texas had the power to tax oil produced in other states or that California decided to create its own army. This would create inefficiencies and potential danger for the rest of the country.

The elastic clause of the Constitution, Article I, Section 8, which says that Congress has the power "To make all Laws which shall be necessary and proper for carrying into Execution the foregoing Powers," was a broad grant of power to the national government. The national supremacy clause, Article VI of the Constitution, says that the Constitution and all laws and treaties that are made under the Constitution shall be the "supreme Law of the Land" and "the Judges in every State shall be bound thereby, any Thing in the Constitution or Laws of any State to the Contrary notwithstanding." This is perhaps the clearest statement of the nation-centered focus of the Constitution. If any state law or constitution conflicts with national law or the Constitution, the national perspective wins.

Despite these clear examples of the Founders' nation-centered bias, many parts of the Constitution also address state powers and limits on national power. Article II gives the states the power to choose the electors for the electoral college, and Article V grants the states a central role in the process of amending the Constitution. Three-fourths of the states must ratify any constitutional amendment (either through conventions or the state legislatures, as specified by Congress), but the states can also bypass Congress in proposing amendments if two-thirds of the states call for a convention. This route to amending the Constitution has never been used, but the Founders clearly wanted to provide an additional check on national power. There are also limitations on Congress's authority to regulate interstate commerce. For example, it cannot favor one state over another in regulating commerce and it cannot impose a tax on any good that is shipped from one state to another. Also Congress could not prohibit slavery until 1808, but it was allowed to impose a duty of up to $10 per slave.

Article I of the Constitution enumerates many specific powers for Congress, but the list of state powers is much shorter. This could be interpreted as more evidence for the nation-centered perspective, but at the time of the Founding, the default position was to keep most power at the state level. Therefore, the federal powers that were exceptions to this rule had to be clearly specified while state governments were given authority over all other matters. This view is supported by the 10th Amendment which says, "The powers not delegated to the United States by the Constitution, nor prohibited by it to the states, are reserved to the states respectively, or to the people."

The 11th Amendment, the first one passed after the Bill of Rights, was another important affirmation of state sovereignty. Antifederalists were concerned that the part of Article III that gave the Supreme Court authority over cases involving a "State and Citizens of another State" would undermine state sovereignty by giving the Court too much power over state laws. Federalists, including Hamilton and Madison, assured them this would not happen, but the Supreme Court ruled in *Chisholm v. Georgia* (1793) that citizens of one state could sue the government of another state. The majority opinion ridiculed the "haughty notions of state independence, state sovereignty, and state supremacy." The states struck back by adopting the 11th Amendment, which made such lawsuits unconstitutional. While the Supreme Court lost this skirmish over state power, it continued to serve as the umpire in disputes between the national and state governments.

Lastly, the **full faith and credit clause** of the Constitution is also very important for federalism and has elements that favor both the state- and nation-centered perspectives. Article IV specifies that states must respect each other's laws, granting citizens the "Full Faith and Credit" of their state's laws if they move to another state. For example, a legal marriage in one state must be honored by another state. However, divorce is a bit more complicated. If a divorce is granted in a state in which the couple does not have a legal residence, that divorce does not have to be honored by their home state. Article IV has also fueled the ongoing controversy over same-sex marriages. In 1996, after Hawaii courts gave homosexual marriages most of the same legal rights as heterosexual marriages, many states passed laws saying they would not have to honor those marriages. In response, Congress passed the Defense of Marriage Act in 1996, which said that states would not have to recognize same-sex marriages. Hawaii courts have since overturned the decision to recognize same-sex marriages, but as of this writing, nine states and the District of Columbia recognize civil unions between homosexual partners and two (Massachusetts and Connecticut) allow gay marriages.[7] Nancy Wilson and Paula Schoenwether, who married in Massachusetts then moved to Florida where gay marriage is banned, asked a federal court to overturn the act. However, the court ruled that the full faith and credit clause did not apply, citing the "policy exception."[8]

Under the **privileges and immunities clause** of Article IV, the citizens of each state are also "entitled to all Privileges and Immunities" of citizens in the other states, which means that states must treat visitors from other states the same as their own residents. This part of the Constitution favors a nation-centered perspective because it was intended to promote free travel and economic activity between the states. For example, Michigan could not charge the owner of a lake cabin different property taxes depending on whether she lived in Chicago or in Detroit. States also may not deny new residents welfare benefits or deny police protection to visitors even though they do not pay state taxes. For example, a 1992 law in California limited the cash welfare benefit to new residents to the level of benefits that they had been receiving in the state from which they had just moved. The law was intended to save California's government money and also discourage people from moving to California just

full faith and credit clause Part of Article IV of the Constitution requiring that each state's laws be honored by the other states. For example, a legal marriage in one state must be recognized across state lines.

privileges and immunities clause Part of Article IV of the Constitution requiring that states must treat non-state residents within their borders as they would treat their own residents. This was meant to promote commerce and travel between states.

to get the higher benefit—particularly since California's cash benefit for a mother and one child was $456 a month in 1992, but in the neighboring state of Arizona it was only $275.[9] The Supreme Court ruled that the state law violated the privileges and immunities clause and the right to travel freely between the states.

However, states are allowed to make some distinctions between residents and nonresidents. For example, states do not have to permit nonresidents to vote in state elections, and public colleges and universities may charge out-of-state residents higher tuition than in-state residents. This provision cuts both ways on the question of the balance of power because it allows the states to determine and uphold these laws autonomously, but it also emphasizes that national citizenship is more important than state citizenship.

The Constitution sets the boundaries for the battles over federalism. For example, Kentucky cannot decide to print its own currency, and the United States government cannot take over any public school district in the country. But within those broad boundaries, the balance between national and state power at any given point in history will be a political decision, the product of choices made by elected leaders and the courts. Decisions by the Supreme Court have figured prominently in this evolution.

POLITICAL PROCESS MATTERS

The Constitution sets certain guarantees about treating citizens of various states equally under the law, but each state still gets to make its own laws, which produces great variation across the states.

SECTION SUMMARY

1. The Founders wanted a national government that was stronger than it had been under the Articles of Confederation, but they also wanted to preserve the autonomy of the states.
2. The elastic clause, supremacy clause, and extensive specific powers granted to Congress in Article I demonstrate the nation-centered focus of the Constitution.
3. The 10th Amendment, which grants all undelegated powers to the states; the 11th Amendment, which prohibits citizens from suing the government of a state other than their own; and other specific state powers demonstrate the state-centered focus of the Constitution.

The Evolving Concept of Federalism

FEDERALISM IN THE EARLY YEARS: ESTABLISHING NATIONAL SUPREMACY

As the United States gained its footing, several clashes between the advocates of state-centered and nation-centered federalism quickly evolved into a partisan struggle. The Federalists, the party of George Washington and Alexander Hamilton, controlled the new government for its first twelve years and favored strong national power. Their opponents, the Democratic-Republicans, led by Thomas Jefferson and James Madison, favored state power. The first confrontation came when the Federalists established a national bank in 1791, over the objections of Jefferson. This controversy did not come to a head until Congress chartered the second national bank in 1816. The state of Maryland, which was controlled by the

Democratic-Republicans, tried to tax the National Bank out of existence, but the head cashier of the bank refused to pay the tax and the case eventually ended up at the Supreme Court. The Court had to decide whether Congress had the power to create the bank, and if it did, whether Maryland had the right to tax the bank. In the landmark decision *McCulloch v. Maryland* (1819) the Court ruled in favor of the national government on both counts. In deciding whether Congress could create the bank, the Court held that even though the word "bank" does not appear in the Constitution, Congress's power to create one is implied through its enumerated powers—such as the power to coin money, levy taxes, and borrow money. They also ruled that Maryland did not have the right to tax the bank because of the national supremacy clause of the Constitution, which says the Constitution and national laws take precedent over state laws if there is a conflict. Both the concept of implied powers and the validation of national supremacy were critical for establishing the centrality of the national government.

A few years later, the Supreme Court decided another case that cemented Congress's power to act based on the commerce clause in the Constitution. In *Gibbons v. Ogden* (1824) the Supreme Court said that Congress has broad power to regulate interstate commerce and struck down a New York law that had granted a monopoly to a private company operating steamboats on the Hudson River between New York and New Jersey. By granting this monopoly, the ruling stated, New York was interfering with interstate commerce.

Another important, early clash over federalism concerned the Sedition Act of 1798 passed by a majority-Federalist Congress. The act banned "any false, scandalous writing against the government of the United States." The stated purpose of the law was to prevent the rejection of authority and mass political movements that were sweeping through France from taking hold in the United States. But Jeffersonians argued, rightly, that the law was an attempt to silence dissent and criticism of the government and was a clear violation of the 1st Amendment protection of freedom of speech. Indeed, under this law ten Democratic-Republican newspaper editors were arrested, fined, and jailed. The issue was important in the 1800 presidential election, and when Jefferson was elected he pardoned everyone convicted under the law.

The Sedition Act is important for our purposes because of a political tactic that Jefferson devised to try to overturn the law before he became president. His opponents controlled Congress and the Supreme Court, so there was not much hope of using the normal political channels to change the law. Thus, he and Madison came up with an idea to circumvent the national government by working through the states. They convinced the Kentucky and Virginia legislatures to pass resolutions challenging the national government's power to pass the Sedition Act through an idea they called the **doctrine of interposition**. Under this doctrine, if the national government passes an unconstitutional law, the people of the states can interpose or insert themselves between the law and the national government and declare the law void. This doctrine views the Constitution as a contract between the states. Although the tension over the Sedition Act was defused when Jefferson was elected president in 1800, this approach to federalism had important implications for national power.[10]

The idea of interposition regained significance as the basis for the southern states' push for broader **states' rights** on issues such as tariffs and slavery. John Calhoun, an important South Carolina senator, used the term "nullification" to refer to the same principle, urging South Carolina to ignore a tariff law passed by Congress in 1832. The states' rights perspective was at the center of the dispute between southern and northern states over slavery, which ultimately led to the secession of the states of the Confederacy and subsequently the Civil War. The stakes were enormous in the

doctrine of interposition The idea that if the national government passes an unconstitutional law, the people of the states (through their state legislatures) can declare the law void. This idea provided the basis for southern secession and the Civil War.

states' rights The idea that states are entitled to a certain amount of self-government, free of federal government intervention. This became a central issue in the lead up to the Civil War.

battles over federalism: about 527,000 died in the bloodiest of American wars (including battle deaths and soldiers who died from disease and infection).[11] As Abraham Lincoln so forcefully argued, concepts such as nullification and states' rights, when taken to their logical extremes, were too divisive to be allowed to stand. If states were allowed to ignore national laws, the basis of the United States would fall apart.

DUAL FEDERALISM

The ideas of states' rights and nullification did not produce the Civil War by themselves. They had some help from the Supreme Court's infamous *Dred Scott* decision, but before explaining the significance of that case, we will take a brief look at some key players in the evolution of the Court's approach to federalism. The first two-thirds of the nineteenth century saw an incredible period of stability in the leadership of the Court. Only two chief justices served during this time: John Marshall from 1801 to 1835, and Roger Taney from 1835 to 1864, and they had very different ideas about federalism. Marshall was a Federalist and a thorn in the side of states' rights advocates while Taney was a supporter of states' rights. The series of decisions under Marshall's leadership outlined earlier secured the place of the national government within our federal system, but in the years that followed, Taney was able to limit the reach of the national government through his vision of federalism, which is known as dual federalism.

Under **dual federalism** the national and state governments were viewed as distinct with little overlap in their activities or the services they provided. In this view, the national government's activities are confined to powers strictly enumerated in the Constitution, despite the elastic clause and the implied powers endorsed in *McCulloch v. Maryland*. While Taney developed the idea of dual federalism, one decision toward the end of Marshall's tenure endorsed a notion of "dual citizenship" in which an individual's rights as a U.S. citizen under the Bill of Rights did not apply to that same person under state law. That decision, *Barron v. Baltimore* (1833), held that a man whose wharf in the Baltimore harbor had been ruined by the city's dumping of sand and gravel could not sue the city for violating the 5th Amendment's prohibition of taking property without due process. The Court ruled that the 5th Amendment only applied to the U.S. Congress and not to state and local governments.

The Taney court expanded the power of the states over commerce in ways that would not be accepted today, including giving the mayor of New York City the right to control immigration by requiring shipmasters to post bonds for foreign passengers who would later go on welfare[12] and allowing the city of Philadelphia to require ships to use local captains when entering the harbor.[13] The state-centered views of the Taney Court also produced a tragic decision, *Dred Scott v. Sandford*, (1857). Dred Scott was a slave who had lived for many years with his owner in the free Wisconsin Territory, but was living in Missouri, a slave state, when his master died. Scott petitioned for his freedom under the Missouri Compromise, which said that slavery was illegal in any free state. The majority decision held that slaves were not citizens but private property, and therefore the Missouri Compromise violated the 5th Amendment because it deprived people (slave owners) of property without the due process of law. This unfortunate decision contributed to the Civil War, which started four years later, because it indicated that there could not be a political solution to the problem of slavery.

▲ *In ruling on Dred Scott's petition to become a free man, the Supreme Court said that slaves were property, not U.S. citizens, and that Congress did not have the power to prohibit slavery in any state. This decision, which was rooted in a view of state-centered federalism, hastened the start of the Civil War.*

dual federalism The form of federalism favored by Chief Justice Roger Taney in which national and state governments are seen as distinct entities providing separate services. This model limits the power of the national government.

The Civil War ended the dispute over slavery, but it did not resolve the basic questions about the balance of power between the national and state systems. Right after the Civil War, the Constitution was amended to ensure that the Union's views on states' rights were the law of the land. The Civil War Amendments banned slavery (the 13th), prohibited states from denying citizens due process or equal protection of the laws (14th), and gave newly freed male slaves the right to vote (15th). The 14th Amendment was the most important in terms of federalism because it was the constitutional basis for many of the civil rights laws passed by Congress during Reconstruction.

However, the Supreme Court soon stepped in again to limit the power of the national government. In 1873 the Supreme Court reinforced the notion of dual federalism, ruling that the 14th Amendment did not change the balance of power between the national and state governments, despite its clear language aimed at state action. Endorsing the notion of dual citizenship, the Court ruled that the 14th Amendment right to due process and equal treatment under the law only applied to individuals' rights as citizens of the United States, not to their state citizenship.[14] By extension, freedom of speech, freedom of the press, and the other liberties protected in the Bill of Rights only applied to laws passed by Congress, not to state laws. This distinction between state and national citizenship sounds odd today partly because the 14th Amendment has long been viewed as the basis for making sure that states do not violate basic rights.

Ten years later, the Court overturned the 1875 Civil Rights Act, arguing that the 14th Amendment did not give Congress the power to regulate private conduct, such as whether a white restaurant owner had to serve a black customer, but only applied to the conduct of state governments.[15] This narrow view of the 14th Amendment left the national government powerless to prevent southern states from implementing state and local laws that led to complete segregation of the races in the South—under the Jim Crow laws—and the denial of many basic rights to blacks after the northern troops left the South at the end of Reconstruction.

Early Landmark Supreme Court Decisions on Federalism

CASE	HOLDING AND SIGNIFICANCE
Chisholm v. Georgia (1793)	Citizens of one state could sue another state; led to the 11th Amendment, which prohibited such lawsuits.
McCulloch v. Maryland (1819)	Upheld the national government's right to create a bank and reaffirmed the idea of "national supremacy."
Barron v. Baltimore (1833)	Endorsed a notion of "dual federalism" in which the rights of a U.S. citizen under the Bill of Rights did not apply to that same person under state law.
Dred Scott v. Sandford (1857)	Sided with southern states' view that slaves were property and ruled that the Missouri Compromise violated the 5th Amendment, since making slavery illegal in some states deprived slave owners of property. Contributed to the start of the Civil War.
National Labor Relations Board v. Jones & Laughlin Steel Corporation (1937)	Upheld the National Labor Relations Act of 1935 as consistent with Congress's commerce clause powers, reversing the Court's more narrow interpretation of that clause.

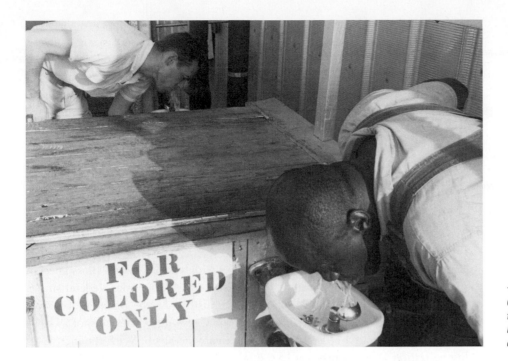

◀ *After the Supreme Court struck down the 1875 Civil Rights Act, southern states were free to impose Jim Crow laws. These state and local laws led to complete racial segregation, even for public drinking fountains.*

The other area in which the Supreme Court limited the reach of the national government concerned Congress's power to regulate the economy through its com-**merce clause powers**. In a series of cases in the late nineteenth and early twentieth centuries the Supreme Court endorsed a view of *laissez faire* capitalism—French for "leave alone"—aimed at protecting business from regulation by the national government. To this end, the Court defined clear boundaries between *inter*state and *intra*state commerce, ruling that Congress could not regulate any economic activity that occurred *within* a state. The Supreme Court allowed some national legislation that was connected to interstate commerce, such as limiting monopolies through the Sherman Antitrust Act (1890). However, when the national government tried to use this act to break up a cartel of four sugar companies that controlled 98 percent of the nation's sugar production, the Court ruled that Congress did not have this power. According to the decision, the commerce clause only dealt with the transportation of goods, not their manufacture, and the sugar in question was made within a single state. Even if the sugar was sold throughout the country, this was seen as "incidental" to its manufacture.[16] On the same grounds the Court also struck down attempts by Congress to regulate child labor.[17] In some instances, the Court's *laissez faire* perspective also led them to strike down state laws, as in one case that ruled unconstitutional a New York law limiting working hours of bakers to no more than sixty hours a week or ten hours a day.[18] Therefore, the limits that the Court placed on Congress during this antiregulation phase did not necessarily tip the balance to the state governments. Rather, big business was the clear winner over both national and state government.

COOPERATIVE FEDERALISM

The Progressive Era policies of the early twentieth century and the New Deal policies of the 1930s ushered in a new era of American federalism in which the national government became much more involved in activities formerly reserved for the states, such as education, transportation, civil rights, agriculture, social welfare, and management–labor relations. At first, the Supreme Court resisted this broader reach of national power, clinging to its nineteenth-century conception of dual federalism.[19] But as commerce became more national, the distinction between interstate and

commerce clause powers The powers of Congress to regulate the economy granted in Article I, Section 8, of the Constitution.

intrastate commerce, and between manufacture and transportation, became increasingly difficult to sustain. Starting in 1937, the Supreme Court largely discarded these distinctions and gave Congress far more latitude in shaping economic and social policy for the nation.[20]

A few years later the Court made it clear that there was virtually no limit on what could be construed as interstate commerce, ruling that a farmer who grew more wheat than he was supposed to under an acreage quota law, but fed all of it to his own livestock, was nonetheless engaged in interstate commerce. The Court ruled that the farmer was undermining Congress's ability to regulate interstate commerce because even if he did not sell his extra wheat, no matter how small the amount, he would have had to buy more wheat to support his livestock had he not exceeded his growing quota.[21]

The type of federalism that emerged in the Progressive Era and blossomed in the late 1930s is called **cooperative federalism**, or "marble cake" federalism, as opposed to the "layer cake" model of dual federalism.[22] As the image of a marble cake suggests, the boundaries of state and national responsibilities are not as well-defined under cooperative federalism as under dual federalism. With the increasing industrialization and urbanization of the late 1930s and the 1940s, more complex problems arose that could not be solved at one level of government. Cooperative federalism adopts a more practical focus on intergovernmental relations and how to efficiently provide services. State and local governments maintained a level of influence as the implementers of national programs, but the national government played an enhanced role as the initiator of key policies.

Cooperative federalism accurately describes this important shift in national–state relations in the first half of the twentieth century, but it does not begin to capture the complexity of modern federalism. The marble cake metaphor falls short in one important way: the lines of authority and patterns of cooperation are not as messy as implied by the gooey flow of chocolate through white cake. Instead the metaphor of **picket fence federalism**, which became popular in the 1960s, is a better description of cooperative federalism in action. As shown in Figure 3.1, each picket of the fence represents a different policy area, and the horizontal boards that hold the pickets together represent the different levels of government. This is certainly a much more orderly image than the marble cake, and it has important implications about how policy is made across levels of government. The most important point is that activity within the cooperative federal system occurs *within* pickets of the fence, that is within policy areas. Policy makers within a given policy area will have more in common with others in that area at different levels of government than with people at the same level of government who work on different issues. For example, someone working in the state education department will have more contact with people working in local school districts and the national Department of Education than with the people who also work at the state level but focus on transportation policy.

Cooperative federalism, then, is most likely to emerge within policy areas rather than across them. This may create problems for the chief executives who are trying to run the show (mayors, governors, and the president) as rivalries develop between policy areas competing for funds. Also, contact within policy areas is not always cooperative. Everyone is familiar with detective shows in which the FBI arrives to investigate a local crime and pulls rank on the town sheriff, creating tension and provoking resentment from the local law enforcement officials who would rather handle their problems without interference from the feds. This is the inefficient

POLITICS IS EVERYWHERE

Congress's power to regulate commerce serves as the basis for justifying a broad range of national legislation.

cooperative federalism A form of federalism in which national and state governments work together to provide services efficiently. This form emerged in the late 1930s, representing a profound shift toward less concrete boundaries of responsibility in national–state relations.

picket fence federalism A more refined and realistic form of cooperative federalism in which policy makers within a particular policy area work together across the levels of government.

FIGURE 3.1 **VERSIONS OF FEDERALISM**

The marble cake and picket fence versions of federalism depict very different images of the relationships among local, state, and national governments. Which version seems more efficient?

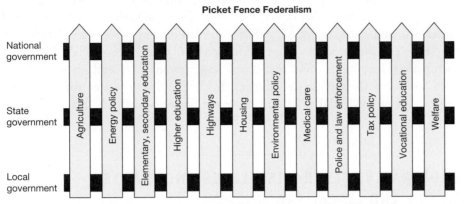

Picket Fence Federalism

National government

State government

Local government

Horizontal boards represent levels of government that connect the different policy areas (pickets).

The Marble Cake of American Federalism

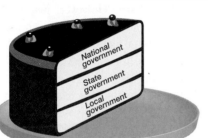

Layer cake: No interactions between the levels of government.

Marble cake: Interactions between the levels of government are common.

side of picket fence federalism in action. But overall, this version of federalism provides great opportunities for coordination and the development of expertise within policy areas.

SECTION SUMMARY

1. From our nation's early history through the early 1930s, the country operated under dual federalism in which the national and state governments were viewed as very distinct. There was little overlap in their activities or the services they provided.

2. The more active role for the national government that started with the New Deal policies of the 1930s ushered in a period of cooperative federalism based on a more practical focus on intergovernmental relations and how to efficiently provide services.

3. Picket fence federalism is a version of cooperative federalism emphasizing that policy makers within a given area will have more in common with others in their area at different levels of government than with people at the same level of government who work on different issues.

Federalism Today

This overview of the evolution of federalism within U.S. political history will help you understand federalism today, which is a complex mix of all of the elements we have experienced in the past. Our system is predominantly characterized by cooperative federalism, but it has retained strong elements of national supremacy, dual federalism, and states' rights. So, rather than categorizing types of federalism into neat time periods, it makes sense to characterize the dominant tendency within each period, keeping in mind that competing versions of federalism have always been just below the surface; see Table 3.1. In the past twenty years, the competing versions are so evident that this period could be considered the "era of balanced federalism."[23]

COOPERATIVE FEDERALISM LIVES ON: GRANTS IN AID AND FISCAL FEDERALISM

The cooperative relationship between the national and state governments is rooted in the system of transfer payments or grants from the national government to lower levels of government, which is called **fiscal federalism**. However, just because money flows from Washington does not ensure cooperation. That is, depending on how the money is transferred, the national government can either help local and state governments achieve their own goals or use its fiscal power to impose its will. This may sound familiar. When your parents let you use the car or lent you $50, did they expect something in return, such as help with the yard work or washing the car—or was it "no strings attached"? Even in the era of dual federalism these kinds of questions arose between different levels of government, but they were far less frequent simply because the national government provided very little aid to the states.

Today, most aid to the states comes in one of two forms. **Categorical grants** are provided for specific purposes—they have strings attached—and therefore will be discussed below in the section on coercive federalism. **Block grants** are financial aid to states to be used within a specific policy area, but within that area the states have a fair amount of discretion on how the money will be spent.

A third type of grant, **general revenue sharing (GRS)**, was tried briefly in the 1970s and 1980s and was preferred by the states because it came with *no* strings attached at all. GRS was started by President Richard Nixon in 1972 as part of his New Federalism program to return more control over programs to the states. At its peak in 1979, the federal government granted $6.8 billion (1.4 percent of federal spending) to the states through this program, which would be more than $25 billion in today's budget. However, the state component of the program was phased out beginning in 1980, and it was terminated in 1986 when Treasury Secretary James Baker reported that the federal government had no more revenue to share (that was a period of large national budget deficits). The political support for GRS was difficult to sustain because it was opposed by conservatives who wanted a smaller national government and by liberals who preferred more targeted spending.[24]

Instead, advocates of cooperative federalism promoted block grants as the best way for the levels of government to work together to solve problems. With block grants the national government identified problem areas, then provided money to the states to help solve them. Between 1966, when the first block grant was created, and 1994, there were twenty-three block grants established.[25] For example,

fiscal federalism A form of federalism in which federal funds are allocated to the lower levels of government though transfer payments or grants.

categorical grants Federal aid to state or local governments that is provided for a specific purpose, such as a mass transit program within the transportation budget or a school lunch program within the education budget.

block grants Federal aid provided to a state government to be spent within a certain policy area, which the state can decide how to spend within that area.

general revenue sharing (GRS) A type of grant used in the 1970s and 1980s in which the federal government provided state governments with funds to be spent at each state's discretion. These grants provided states with more control over programs.

TABLE 3.1	COMPETING VERSIONS OF FEDERALISM	
TYPE OF FEDERALISM	**PERIOD**	**CHARACTERISTICS**
Dual federalism (layer cake)	1789–1937	The national and state governments were viewed as very distinct with little overlap in their activities or the services they provided. Within this period, federalism could have been state-centered or nation-centered, but relations were largely separate.
Cooperative federalism (marble cake)	1937–present	Greater cooperation and collaboration between the levels of government, but with policy changes typically coming from the national government in large bursts (the New Deal and Great Society programs).
Picket fence federalism	1961–present	A version of cooperative federalism emphasizing that policy makers within a given policy area will have more in common with others in their area at different levels of government than with people at the same level of government who work on different issues.
Fiscal federalism	1937–present	The system of transfer payments or grants from the national government to lower-level governments involves varying levels of national control over how the money is spent. Categorical grants give the national government a great deal of control, block grants involve less national control, and revenue sharing was a "no strings attached" grant of funds to the states.
New Federalism	1969–present	An attempt to shift power to the states by consolidating categorical grants into block grants and giving the states authority over programs such as welfare.
Coercive federalism	1970s–present	System of federal preemptions of state and local authority and unfunded mandates on state and local governments to force the states to change their policies to match national goals or policies established by Congress.

Community Development Block Grants were started in 1974 to help state and local governments revitalize their communities; such grants may support ongoing programs or help with large capital expenditures, such as building a waste treatment plant or a highway. Since the 1970s, grants to the states as a proportion of the size of the national economy (gross domestic product, or GDP) has been relatively constant, while the rate of state and local spending has continued to inch up (see Figure 3.2)

New Federalism Richard Nixon's New Federalism seemed to be a brief experiment in state-centered fiscal federalism, but then it was revived during the presidency of Ronald Reagan in the 1980s. Reagan's 1981 inaugural address emphasized that, "All of us need to be reminded that the federal government did not create the states. The states created the federal government." This classic statement of the states' rights position is similar to Antifederalists' position at the Constitutional Convention. Reagan's goal of returning more power to the states was centered around consolidating seventy-seven categorical grants into nine general block grants that gave the local politicians more control over how money was spent. This change was based on the belief that because state and local politicians were closer to the people,

POLITICAL PROCESS MATTERS

✓ The manner in which federal money is distributed to the states largely determines how much discretion states have over how the money will be spent.

Since the early 1950s, federal spending as a percentage of the overall size of the economy has been flat, while the share of state and local spending has more than doubled. What does this say about the debates between nation-centered and state-centered federalism?

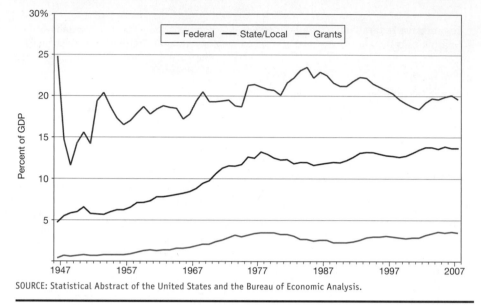

SOURCE: Statistical Abstract of the United States and the Bureau of Economic Analysis.

they would know better how to spend the money (see Politics Is Everywhere). However, this increase in state control came with a 25 percent cut in the amount of federal money granted to the states. Critics of this process dubbed it "shift and shaft," but it did have the effect of giving state and local governments more control. A second part of his proposal that was not adopted because it was seen as too radical was to give responsibility for welfare programs to the states while taking over responsibility for Medicaid, the program that funds health care for the poor, at the national level. As it turns out this would have been a great deal for the states because the costs of Medicaid have risen much faster than welfare costs in recent years.

The next phase of New Federalism came when Republicans won control of the U.S. Congress in 1994. Working with President Clinton, a moderate Democrat, Republicans passed several pieces of significant legislation that shifted power toward the states in what came to be known as the Devolution Revolution, that is, devolving power to the states. In 1996 the Personal Responsibility and Work Opportunity Act reformed welfare by creating a block grant to the states, Temporary Assistance to Needy Families (TANF), to replace the largest nationally administered welfare program. The 1996 Prison Litigation Reform Act ended federal court supervision of state and local prison systems. And the Unfunded Mandate Reform Act of 1995 made it more difficult for Congress to impose unfunded mandates on the states by requiring a separate vote on mandates that imposed costs of more than $50 million and requiring a Congressional Budget Office estimate of exactly how much such mandates would cost the states. While this law could not prevent unfunded mandates, Republicans hoped that bringing more attention to the practice would create political pressure against them.

While the shift from categorical grants to block grants was an important part of New Federalism after Reagan, it has not substantially affected the balance of

unfunded mandates Federal laws that require the states to do certain things but do not provide state governments with funding to implement these policies.

Federalism and Local Politics

A central claim of the state-centered perspective on federalism is that "the best government is closest to the people," and it is certainly true that local government has a big impact on your daily life. While the national government is certainly more important when it comes to national defense, retirement security through Social Security and Medicare, your local government is likely to affect a broader range of your daily activities.

Start with transportation. Your city is responsible for building and maintaining city streets, plowing snow in the winter (if it snows where you live); establishing bike paths, running the system of public transportation (if the city has one); regulating traffic laws, including speed limits, stop signs, and traffic signals; allocating parking permits; and setting and enforcing parking regulations. Your local government is also responsible for creating and maintaining city parks, establishing zoning laws that

regulate residential and economic development, creating and supporting schools, picking up the trash, and supporting the fire and police departments. Some of these responsibilities may be shared, at least financially, with the state and national governments, but all of these important activities are carried out by local governments.

There are also far more opportunities for individuals to influence local policies and regulations than national policy. The tradition of public involvement in local politics goes back to the time of the first town hall meetings in New England (these are still held in many areas), in which the citizens directly decided policies after extended discussion and debate.[a] This obviously would not work the same way for larger towns and cities, but even those local governments routinely solicit public opinion before deciding on a policy. For example, when a developer proposes new apartment building or shopping mall, local public officials meet with neighborhood groups to

discuss concerns such as traffic and safety issues. When school attendance area boundaries have to be changed to reflect shifts in population, school board members consult with the affected residents. Dozens of interest groups promote connections between citizens and their local governments, including Public Interest Groups, League of Women Voters, Urban League, local chapters of environmental groups such as the Sierra Club, and the Local Government Commission. These groups often organize letter-writing or e-mail campaigns on a given issue or help get citizens to public meetings with local officials.

Two examples of the impact of citizen involvement on local policy come from personal experience. Author David Canon's family lives on a relatively busy but narrow street where cars regularly drove much too fast, especially given the number of small children who lived on the block. A group of neighbors got in touch with the neighborhood association, which contacted the local city council member. The council member arranged a series of meetings with the neighbors and city officials, and the city agreed to put in a traffic circle at the intersection to slow down the traffic on the block. This whole process took less than a year.

Another issue was resolved even more quickly. The house is also close to a neighborhood bar that always emptied the recycling bins after closing, around 2:30 A.M. The clanging and shattering bottles woke up the neighborhood every night, especially during the summer when people sleep with their windows open. All it took to resolve the problem was a call to find out about local noise ordinances, a call to the city council member, and a meeting with the bar owner who agreed not to empty the bins until the morning. Local government can change your daily life and sometimes it isn't that hard to influence policies you care strongly about. ■

New Federalism is rooted in the idea that state and local governments are closer to the people than the national government.   For example, it is easier for local residents to protest a decision in their own city rather than Washington, DC.   These demonstrators at Chicago's City Hall are urging the city council to require "big-box" mega-retailers to pay their workers a living wage.

power between the national and state governments. The amount of money going to the states through block grants has been surpassed by categorical grants since 1982, despite shifting welfare spending to the states through the sizable TANF block grant. The reason for this should be clear, and we will look more closely at it in the next section: Congress prefers categorical grants because they have more control over how the money is spent.

NATIONAL SUPREMACY REIGNS?
THE RISE OF COERCIVE FEDERALISM

Despite the overall shift toward cooperative federalism, strong overtones of national government supremacy remain. Three important characteristics of American politics in the past forty years have reinforced the role of the national government: (1) turning to the national government in times of crisis and war, (2) the rights revolution of the 1950s and 1960s, and Great Society programs of the 1960s, and (3) the rise of coercive federalism.

The first point is the most obvious and has always been a characteristic of American politics. Even in the 1800s, during the period of dual federalism and strong state power, the national government's strong actions were needed during the Civil War to hold the nation together. More recently, following the September 11, 2001, terrorist attacks, most Americans expected the national government to improve national security and retaliate for the attack. Even Republicans, who normally opposed increasing the size of government, largely stood behind President Bush's proposal to create a new cabinet-level Department of Homeland Security.

Second, the "rights revolution" created by the Supreme Court and Lyndon Johnson's Great Society programs contributed to more national control over state policies. Landmark Court decisions thrust the national government into policy areas that had typically been reserved to the states. In the school desegregation and bussing cases of the 1950s and 1960s, the Court upheld the national goal of promoting racial equality and fighting discrimination over the earlier norm of local control of school districts.[26] The "one person, one vote" decisions, which required that the populations of legislative districts be equalized when district lines were redrawn, put the federal courts at the center of another policy area that had always been left to the states.[27] The rights revolution also applied to police powers, another area of traditional state control, including protection against self-incrimination and preventing illegally obtained evidence from being used in a criminal trial.[28]

▼ *The Americans with Disabilities Act of 1990 requires that public accommodations and commercial facilities be handicapped accessible, and recent Supreme Court rulings have held that the law applies to state and local government buildings. Disabled activists are shown in the U.S. Capitol lobbying for stronger legislation.*

These Court actions were paralleled by a burst of legislation from Congress and the President. Often dubbed the Great Society legislation, these laws tackled civil rights, education, the environment, medical care for the poor, and housing. Specific Great Society policies will be discussed in detail in Chapter 16, Social Policy. For now, the important point is that they gave the national government much more leverage over policy areas previously controlled by state and local governments. In some cases, the national powers were far-reaching. For example, the 1965 Voting Rights Act sent federal marshals to the South to make sure that African Americans were allowed to vote. Another part of this act required local governments to submit any changes in their electoral practices, including the boundaries of their voting districts, to the Justice Department to make sure they did not have a discriminatory impact.

During this period, the national government also expanded its reach through an explosion in categorical grants, which the states sorely needed even though they came with strings attached. For example, the 1964 Civil Rights Act required non-discrimination as a condition for receiving any kind of federal grants. The Elementary and Secondary Education Act of 1965 gave the federal government more control over public education than ever before by attaching federal grant money to certain conditions. Requiring a state drinking age of twenty-one before granting federal highway funds, as discussed at the beginning of this chapter, is another example.

Categorical grants aimed at a broad national goal are part of the third trend that has reinforced national supremacy in past several decades, **coercive federalism**. As the name implies, this version of federalism refers to the use of federal regulations, mandates, or conditions to force or entice the states to change their policies to match national goals or policies established by Congress. The Clean Air and Water Acts, the Americans with Disabilities Act that promoted handicapped access to public buildings and commercial facilities, and the "Motor Voter Act" that required states to provide voter registration services at drivers' license departments, are all laws that forced states to change their policies. The laws most objectionable to the states were unfunded mandates that required states to do certain things, but forced them to come up with the money on their own.

Along with these mandates, federal preemption is the other most direct method of coercive federalism. Derived directly from the Constitution's national supremacy clause, **federal preemptions** are the imposition of national priorities on the states. One study found that more than half of the four hundred and thirty-nine explicit preemptions of state laws between 1789 and 1991 occurred after 1969 (233 or 53 percent). Many of the preemptions also include unfunded mandates, making the state and local governments pick up the tab for policies that the national government wants them to implement. While the 1995 unfunded mandate reform may have slowed the trend, it certainly has not eliminated mandates. The U.S. Conference on Mayors has identified ten federal mandates that consume 11.3 percent of cities' budgets and the National Association of Counties estimates that twelve mandates account for 12.3 percent of their budgets. Many of the most expensive items are environmental laws aimed at goals that a majority of Americans share. However, state and local governments complain that they should not have to shoulder so much of the burden.[29] These are among the most controversial assertions of national power because they impose such high costs on state and local governments.

The presidency of George W. Bush provides strong evidence of this shift toward national power. Beyond the obvious centralization of power associated with fighting terrorism, President Bush pushed the national government into more areas that had been dominated by the states, including significant mandates and preemptions in education testing, sales tax collection, emergency management, infrastructure, and elections administration. This is particularly noteworthy because it happened when Republicans, who have traditionally supported states' rights, controlled the presidency and Congress (in the House for six of Bush's eight years and in the Senate for four and a half years).[30]

THE STATES FIGHT BACK

Most Americans support the national policies that have been imposed on the states: racial equality, clean air and water, a fair legal process, safer highways, and equal access to the voting booth. At the same time, there has always been strong support for state and local governments. In fact, in most national surveys, Americans

coercive federalism A form of federalism in which the federal government pressures the states to change their policies by using regulations, mandates, and conditions (often involving threats to withdraw federal funding).

federal preemptions Impositions of national priorities on the states through national legislation that is based on the Constitution's supremacy clause.

State versus National Power in the War on Terror

Do state and local governments still matter in a post–September 11 world? The conventional view is that the War on Terror and the war in Iraq have caused Americans to look increasingly to the national government to solve problems rather than to the states. The swift passage of the USA PATRIOT Act, the creation of the Department of Homeland Security, and executive orders concerning enemy combatants, military tribunals, and domestic surveillance certainly seem to support that view. These changes resemble policy responses to the other major crises of the twentieth century—the Great Depression's New Deal policies and the massive mobilization for World War II—which dramatically shifted the balance of power toward Washington.

However, the War on Terror and the war in Iraq appear to differ from these earlier crises. While there was certainly an initial focus on centralizing power in Washington in response to the terrorist attacks, that centralization has not been sustained. Instead, as a 2002 study of all levels of government responses to the terrorist attacks found national, state, and local governments "demonstrated a capacity and energy to marshal resources in a time of urgency."[a] States did not sit back and wait for Washington to take charge, but acted independently to ensure the safety of their citizens, suggesting that a successful homeland security

An antiterrorism training drill in Hillsborough County, Florida.

policy is likely to be rooted in cooperation between levels of government. One study found that "regional organizational structures" that promoted communication across levels of governments "are most effective in promoting intergovernmental cooperation and preparedness."[b]

Public perceptions of the different levels of government appear to be relatively unchanged from pre–September 11 levels. On the basic question of "trust and confidence in government" 68 percent of Americans have a "great deal" or "fair amount" of trust in local government, 67 percent in state government, and about 62 percent in national government. Though polls showed a spike in support for the national government after September 11,

these more recent numbers are quite similar to those before September 11.[c] In general, polls show that, as they did before the attacks, more people think they "get the least for their money" from the federal government (36.4 percent in 2005) than the number who feel this way about state or local government (29.3 percent and 20.9 percent, respectively). The number of respondents with this negative view of the national government dipped a bit following September 11, but has now returned to the 1989 level (which is still a bit lower than in the 1990s). Similarly, people are much more likely to think that the national government "has too much power today" than to hold this belief about state and local government (the numbers are 62 percent for national government compared to 15 percent for state and 7 percent for local government). Soon after the attacks, this question registered a similar temporary increase of support for national power, which has since subsided.[d]

Overall then, despite the threat posed by terrorism most Americans still trust their state and local governments more than the national government, think that the national government is relatively more likely to waste their money, and believe the national government has too much power. Furthermore, rather than focusing exclusively on strengthening power at the national level, homeland security policies have involved efforts across levels of government. ■

typically say that they trust state and local government more than the national government, and they believe their tax dollars are spent more efficiently at the lower levels of government. While it would be impossible to apply the nineteenth-century concept of dual federalism in the twenty-first century, the popular preference for government that is "closer to the people" has always created political support for state-centered federalism, like New Federalism and other devolution policies. The balance may have changed since September 11, with one national poll showing that slightly more people trust the national government "to do a good job" than their state government (68 percent to 65 percent). It remains to be seen whether this high level of support for the national government will persist and some evidence indicates that state and local governments are reasserting their power, even in the War on Terror (see Challenging Conventional Wisdom).

States appear to be reversing their traditional role of resisting change and protecting the status quo. In recent years, states have taken lead on environmental policy, refusing to accept national pollution standards that are too lenient and a lack of national action on issues such as global warming. Many policies to address climate change, including development of renewable energy sources, carbon emissions limits, and carbon "cap and trade" programs, have been advocated at the state level. States have also taken the lead on fighting electronic waste, mercury emissions, and air pollution more generally.[31]

States have one important advantage over the national government when it comes to experimenting with new policies: their numbers. The fact that there are fifty states potentially trying a mix of different policies is another reason that advocates of state-centered federalism see states as the proper repository of government power. In this view, such a mix of policies produces **competitive federalism**—the competition between states to provide the best policies to attract businesses, create jobs, and maintain a healthy social fabric. Supporters point out that competitive federalism is also a check on tyranny because people will "vote with their feet"—that is, move to a different state—if they do not like a given state's policies. One advocate of this view argues that it "disciplines government and forces the states to compete for the citizens' business, talents, and assets" which makes government act more like a free market.[32]

But just as competitive federalism can produce a good mix of policies, it can also create a "race to the bottom" as states compete in a negative way. Cass Sunstein points out that when states compete for businesses and jobs, they may do so by eliminating more environmental or occupational regulations than would be desirable. A desire to keep taxes low may also lead to cuts in benefits to those who can least afford it, such as welfare or Medicaid recipients.[33]

While there are two sides to the argument, there is no doubt that competition between states provides citizens with a broad range of choices about the type of government they prefer. Choices by different state leaders about tax policies, levels of support for public schools and parks, and how much to regulate business all provide a range of options for businesses deciding where to locate or expand, and to citizens considering a move. Because different citizens prefer different policies, this is generally viewed as an overall advantage to American democracy.

POLITICS IS EVERYWHERE

Federalism provides citizens with a broad range of policies to choose from. You can "vote with your feet" by moving to a low-tax, low-service state or a high-tax, high-service state

SECTION SUMMARY

1. Cooperative federalism lives on today through fiscal federalism, the system of transfer payments or grants from the national government to lower levels of government.
2. New Federalism attempted to return more policy control to the states by giving them more control over spending money and implementing programs.
3. Coercive federalism involves the national government's attempts to compel the states to follow national policy priorities through unfunded mandates and other techniques. However, the states have been fighting back in recent years, attempting to assert their own priorities in some policy areas.

competitive federalism A form of federalism in which states compete to attract businesses and jobs through the policies they adopt.

Fighting for States' Rights: The Role of the Modern Supreme Court

Just as the Supreme Court played a central role in defining the boundaries of dual federalism in the nineteenth and early twentieth centuries and in opening the door to a more nation-centered cooperative federalism in the late 1930s, today's Court is once again reshaping federalism. But this time the move is decidedly in the direction of state power. In the *New York Times*, Linda Greenhouse summarized the rising tension in the Court over federalism in these terms: "There are dissenting opinions at the Supreme Court, and then there are declarations of war. These days, federalism means war."[34] This "war" has had clear consequences for the balance of power between the national and state governments. As the next sections show, in a little over a decade (the late 1980s to the late 1990s), the Supreme Court invalidated more national laws on federalist grounds than in the previous two centuries.[35]

THE 10TH AMENDMENT

On paper, it seems that the 10th Amendment would be at the center of any resurgence of state power since it ensures that all powers not delegated to the national government are reserved to the states or to the people. However, in practice, the amendment has had little significance except during the early 1930s and in the past decade. Twenty-five years ago, a leading text on the Constitution said the 10th Amendment "does not alter the distribution of power between the national and state governments. It adds nothing to the Constitution."[36] To understand why, consider the following example. State and local governments have always controlled their own public schools. Thus, public education is a power reserved to the states under the 10th Amendment. However, a state law concerning public education is void if it conflicts with the Constitution—as racial segregation conflicted with the equal protection clause of the 14th Amendment—or with a national law that is based on an enumerated power. For example, a state could not compel an eighteen-year-old to attend school if the student had been drafted to serve in the Army. Under the 10th Amendment, the constitutionally enumerated national power to "raise and support armies" would trump the reserved state power to support public education.

This view was validated as recently as 1985 when the Court ruled that Congress had the power to impose a national minimum wage law on state governments, even if this was an area of traditional state power.[37] How times change! With the appointment of three conservative justices who favored a stronger role for the states (Antonin Scalia in 1986, Anthony Kennedy in 1988, and Clarence Thomas in 1991), the Court started to limit Congress's reach. One technique was to require that Congress provide an unambiguous statement of their intent to overrule state authority. For example, the Court ruled that the Missouri Constitution, which requires state judges to retire by age seventy, did not violate the Age Discrimination in Employment Act because Congress did not make their intentions "unmistakably clear in the language of the statute."[38] In another case showing that the 10th Amendment still had some life, the Court ruled that Congress may not "commandeer" state regulatory processes by ordering states to dispose of low-level radioactive waste (under the Low-Level Radioactive Waste Policy Act).[39] The Court also ruled that Congress cannot require local law enforcement officers to perform background checks on prospective handgun purchasers, thus striking down part of the 1993 Brady Handgun Violence Prevention Act (Brady Bill).[40]

THE 11TH AMENDMENT

Another important source of the federalism revolution is the 11th Amendment, which protects state governments from being sued by other states' residents, as mentioned earlier in the chapter. Few Americans have even the foggiest notion about the 11th Amendment—and for good reason. There was very little litigation based on this amendment for the past century, until this recent shift by the Court. The Amendment says, "The Judicial power of the United States shall not be construed to extend to any suit in law or equity, commenced or prosecuted against one of the United States by Citizens of another State, or by Citizens or Subjects of any Foreign State."

In a flurry of cases beginning with *Seminole Tribe v. Florida* (1996), the Supreme Court used the 11th Amendment to strengthen states' sovereign immunity. In the *Seminole* case, the Court said that Congress could not compel Florida to negotiate with Indian tribes about gaming and casinos, even though the Constitution explicitly gives Congress the power to "regulate commerce with . . . Indian tribes" (Article I, Section 8).[41]

A few years later, three cases decided on the same day expanded state immunity even further. In two companion cases, the Court ruled that companies could not sue the state government for infringing on their patents or engaging in false advertizing in violation of federal law.[42] In the third case, the Court ruled that a group of state employees could not sue the state of Maine for violating the overtime pay provisions of the federal Fair Labor Standards Act.[43] One important difference between this case and previous cases is that it came to the Supreme Court through the *state* courts whereas the other cases involved the *federal* courts. Thus, if a state employee is not paid overtime, in violation of federal law, he or she has no recourse in federal *or* state court. The federal government could still sue the state for violating federal law, but as a practical matter these suits are quite rare. The national government has counted on private lawsuits to bring attention to violations of the law.

The farthest-reaching 11th Amendment case was *Federal Maritime Commission v. South Carolina Ports Authority* (2002). This case involved a boat with casinos on board that was denied access to a marina owned by the state of South Carolina. The boat owner filed a complaint with the Federal Maritime Commission saying that the state had discriminated against him under federal law. South Carolina claimed immunity from the suit under the 11th Amendment. However, there was an important difference between this case and the preceding ones: the complaint was brought in a federal *agency* rather than a federal *court*. This case was more far-reaching than the others because most of the implementation of laws happens in federal agencies, not the courts. However, the Supreme Court ruled that because of the judicial functions of the agency, the 11th Amendment applied. One critic of the decision said, "The decision finds little support in the Constitution's text; it is the sort of interpretive leap that, were it taken by liberal judges, conservatives would denounce it as 'activist.' And its cramped view of federal power could harm vulnerable people who need federal agencies to protect them from abuse by the states."[44]

These decisions concerning the 11th Amendment seem rather abstract and remote. Why would they matter to you? For example, imagine you were a state employee who discovered a violation of the Clean Water Act by a large corporation. It turns out that corporation is a large contributor to the governor, so the governor wants the infraction hushed up. You are fired when you refuse to keep quiet, and you seek help from the U.S. Department of Labor under a federal labor law that

states' sovereign immunity Described in the 11th Amendment, this means that state governments cannot be sued in federal court.

POLITICAL PROCESS MATTERS

☑ If citizens cannot work through the courts to protect their rights from being violated by state governments, they have to rely on the federal government to protect those rights.

would protect you from arbitrary firing without cause (because your state does not have a strong "whistle-blower" law). Based on recent Court decisions, that option is no longer open to you. In fact, you may have no options at all if state law does not cover your situation. Another example would be that a state could fire someone because they are sixty years old and the worker has no redress against the state. More unlikely but still legal, a state university could photocopy a copyrighted textbook, sell it to students and pay the author nothing. Critics of this line of cases joked, "Perhaps financially strained state colleges and universities might consider selling Microsoft Windows to alleviate their condition."[45]

THE 14TH AMENDMENT

One response to these concerns would be, "I feel sorry for those state employees, but the rest of us aren't affected by this stuff." Fair enough. The decisions we have reviewed thus far mostly affect the 5 million Americans who work for state governments. However, many cases involving the 14th Amendment concern state action against any citizen and Congress's power under the Constitution's commerce clause to pass legislation regulating nonstate action as well. These cases affect all Americans.

As we noted earlier, the 14th Amendment was intended to give the national government broad control over the potentially discriminatory laws of southern states after the Civil War. Specifically, Section 1 of the 14th Amendment guarantees that no state shall make or enforce any law depriving any person of "life, liberty, or property, without due process of law," or denying any person the "equal protection of the laws," while Section 5 empowers Congress "to enforce" those guarantees by "appropriate legislation." The Supreme Court narrowly interpreted the 14th Amendment in the late nineteenth century, severely limiting Congress's ability to affect state policy. However, throughout most of the twentieth century, the Court interpreted Section 5 to give Congress broad discretion to pass legislation to remedy bad state laws. For example, discriminatory application of literacy tests prevented millions of African Americans from voting in the South before the Voting Rights Act was passed in 1965. As part of the federalism revolution of the 1990s, the Court started to chip away at Congress's 14th Amendment powers.

In one important case in 1997 the Supreme Court struck down the Religious Freedom Restoration Act as an overly broad attempt to curtail state-sponsored harassment based on religion. This case established a new standard to justify **remedial legislation**—that is, national legislation that fixes discriminatory state law—under Section 5, saying, "There must be a congruence and proportionality between the injury to be prevented or remedied and the means adopted to that end."[46] Two applications of this logic also applied the 11th Amendment. The Court ruled that the Age Discrimination in Employment Act of 1967 could not be applied to state employees because it was not "appropriate legislation."[47] The Supreme Court also struck down the portion of the Americans with Disabilities Act (ADA) that applied to the states. Passed in 1990 with nearly unanimous support to protect the 45 million Americans who have some type of disability, the ADA required employers, including state agencies, to make "reasonable accommodations" for a "qualified individual with a disability." However, the majority opinion said that states could refuse to hire people in wheelchairs, or deaf or blind people, as "States are not required . . . to make special accommodations for the disabled."[48] Three years later, the Court made a narrow exception to this ruling, saying that states did need to provide access for the disabled to courthouses.[49]

In another exception to the federalism revolution the Court also upheld Congress's power to apply the 1993 Family Leave Act to state employees as "appropriate

remedial legislation National laws that address discriminatory state laws. Authority for such legislation comes from Section 5 of the 14th Amendment.

legislation" under Section 5 of the 14th Amendment.[50] The key difference between this case and the age or disability cases is that in passing the Family Leave Act, Congress explicitly recognized the gender inequality of family care. That is, when a family member gets sick, the mother or wife typically bears the burden. Constitutional protections for discrimination based on age or disability are much weaker than discrimination based on gender or race.

THE COMMERCE CLAUSE

The final area of cases leading to more state power concerns the commerce clause of the Constitution. The first Court case to limit Congress's commerce powers since the New Deal of the 1930s, came in 1995. The case involved the Gun-Free School Zones Act of 1990, which Congress passed in response to the increase in school shootings around the nation. The law made it a federal offense to have a gun within 1,000 feet of a school. Congress assumed that it had the power to pass this legislation, given the Court's expansive interpretation of the commerce clause over the previous fifty-five years, even though it concerned a traditional area of state power. While it was a bit of a stretch to claim that carrying a gun in or around a school was related to interstate commerce, Congress might have been able to demonstrate the point by showing that most guns are made in one state and sold in another (thus commercially crossing state lines), that crime affects the economy and commerce, and that the quality of education, which is also crucial to the economy, is harmed if students and teachers are worrying about guns in their schools. However, they did not present this evidence.

Alfonso Lopez, a senior at Edison High School in San Antonio, Texas, was arrested for carrying a concealed .38 caliber handgun with five bullets in it. Lopez moved to dismiss the charges, arguing that the law was unconstitutional because carrying a gun in a school could not be regulated as "interstate commerce." The Court agreed in *United States v. Lopez*,[51] and the ruling was widely viewed as a warning shot over Congress's bow. If Congress wanted to encroach on the states' turf in the future, they would have to demonstrate that the law in question was a legitimate exercise of the commerce clause powers.

Congress learned its lesson. The next time it passed legislation that affected law enforcement at the state level, they were careful to document the impact on interstate commerce. The Violence Against Women Act (VAWA) was passed in 1994 with strong bipartisan support (unanimously in the House and by an overwhelming margin in the Senate) after weeks of testimony and thousands of pages of evidence were entered into the record showing the links between violence against women and commerce. Despite the evidence Congress presented, the Supreme Court ruled that Congress did not have the power under the commerce clause to make a national law regarding gender-based crimes.[52]

Another far-reaching case that limited Congress's power relative to the states upheld an Alabama law requiring applicants for drivers' licenses to take the written examination in English. This means that individuals who believe they have been subjected to a state law that has a discriminatory effect (rather than one inflicting direct, intentional discrimination) based on race, color, or national origin can no longer sue a state under Title VI of the 1964 Civil Rights Act. Instead, the Court concluded that Congress intended these regulations to be directly enforceable only by the Office of Civil Rights—a political body with very limited resources.

POLITICS IS CONFLICTUAL

In the mid-1990s, the Supreme Court began adding new limits to Congress's commerce clause powers. This is likely to lead to more conflict between the Court and Congress over the next few decades as the boundaries of this important power are reshaped.

Recent Important Supreme Court Decisions on Federalism

CASE	HOLDING AND SIGNIFICANCE
Gregory v. Ashcroft (1991)	The Missouri Constitution's requirement that state judges retire by age seventy did not violate the Age Discrimination in Employment Act.
United States v. Lopez (1995)	Carrying a gun in a school did not fall within "interstate commerce," thus Congress could not prohibit the possession of guns on school property.
Seminole Tribe v. Florida (1996)	Used the 11th Amendment to strengthen states' sovereign immunity, ruling that Congress could not compel a state to negotiate with Indian tribes about gaming and casinos.
Printz v. United States (1997)	Struck down part of the Brady Handgun Violence Prevention Act by saying that Congress cannot require local law enforcement officers to perform background checks on prospective handgun purchasers.
City of Boerne v. Flores (1997)	Struck down the Religious Freedom Restoration Act as an overly broad attempt to curtail the state-sponsored harassment of religion, saying that national legislation aimed at remedying states' discrimination must be "congruent and proportional" to the harm.
Alden v. Maine (1999)	State employees could not sue the state of Maine for violating the overtime pay provisions of the federal Fair Labor Standards Act.
United States v. Morrison (2000)	Struck down the Violence Against Women Act, saying that Congress did not have the power under the commerce clause to provide a national remedy for gender-based crimes.
Kimel et al. v. Florida Board of Regents (2000)	The Age Discrimination in Employment Act of 1967 could not be applied to state employees because it was not considered "appropriate legislation" under Section 5 of the 14th Amendment.
Alabama v. Garrett (2001)	Struck down the portion of the Americans With Disabilities Act (ADA) that applied to the states, saying that state governments are not required to make special accommodations for the disabled.
Federal Maritime Commission v. South Carolina Ports Authority (2002)	The 11th Amendment prevents the Federal Maritime Commission pursuing a claim on behalf of a gambling boat owner denied access to a marina owned by the state of South Carolina.
Nevada Department of Human Resources v. Hibbs (2003)	Upheld Congress's power to apply the 1993 Family Leave Act to state employees as "appropriate legislation" under Section 5 of the 14th Amendment.

The significance of this line of federalism cases is enormous. Not only has the Supreme Court set new limits on Congress's ability to address national problems (the "congruence and proportionality" test), but it has also clearly stated that the Court alone will determine which rights warrant protection by Congress. The cases have also been quite controversial on the bench. The introduction to this section mentioned that on the Court, federalism means "war." Nearly all of the cases mentioned here were decided by 5–4 votes, with extremely intense and persistent dissents. In many instances the dissenters took the unusual step of reading their opinions from the bench.

This account of recent federalism cases is consistent with the views of many constitutional experts, who see these rulings as an important shift of power from the national government to the states. However, it is important to recognize that the Court does not consistently rule against Congress; it often rules against the states because of broader Constitutional principles or general public consensus behind a specific issue. The clearest example of the Court ruling against the states for Constitutional reasons was *U.S. Term Limits v. Thornton* that struck down Arkansas's three-term limit for members of Congress.[53] In a narrow reading of the Constitution, the Court ruled by a 5–4 margin that states could not impose any additional limits on the qualifications for being a member of Congress beyond those in the Constitution. Another ruling against a state was *Romer v. Evans*, which struck down a state-wide initiative passed by a small majority of Colorado voters in 1992. The law banned state and local action of any type (executive, judicial, or legislative) that prohibited discrimination against lesbians and gays based on their sexual orientation.[54] The Court held that the initiative violated the equal protection clause of the 14th Amendment. Our final example of a case decided against the states is more difficult to ground in the Constitution. Instead it is an example of the "living Constitution" approach to the law, which will be discussed further in Chapter 13. This approach recognizes public consensus on important issues even when that consensus is not consistent with a narrow reading of the Constitution. The Court ruled that the death penalty for the mentally retarded is "cruel and unusual punishment" and thus prohibited by the 8th Amendment despite the fact that the Constitution clearly recognizes the death penalty as legitimate if due process is followed.[55] The ruling struck down the practice, which previously was allowed by twenty states.

Based on these cases, some would also argue that the shift in power toward the states has been relatively marginal. Furthermore, the national government still has the upper hand in the balance of power and has many tools at its disposal to blunt the impact of a Court decision. First, Congress can pass new laws to clarify their legislative intent and overturn any of the Court cases that involved statutory interpretation. Second they can use their financial power to impose their will on the states, as they did with raising the drinking age. So, for example, Congress could pass a law stating that before a state could receive money from the federal government, it had to agree to abide by the American with Disabilities Act or the Age Discrimination in Employment Act.

▲ The *Lopez* decision struck down the 1990 Gun-Free School Zones Act, ruling that Congress did not have the power to forbid people to carry guns near schools. After the shooting of twelve students and one teacher at Columbine High School in Jefferson County, Colorado on April 20, 1999, there were renewed calls nationwide for strengthening gun control laws.

SECTION SUMMARY

1. The Court has enhanced state sovereignty by resurrecting the 10th Amendment's limitation against Congressional encroachments on states' turf and by revitalizing and expanding the 11th Amendment's grant of state immunity from law suits.

2. The Court has limited Congress's power to use the commerce clause and the 14th Amendment to achieve its goals. This line of cases does not enhance the power of the states, but it prevents the national government from encroaching on traditional areas of state power or imposing a state responsibility to protect new national-level rights.

Assessing Federalism

Up to this point, issues concerning federalism seem to break down along traditional liberal and conservative lines. Liberals generally favor strong national power to fight discrimination against women, minorities, disabled people, gays, and the elderly and push for progressive national policies on issues like protecting the environment and supporting the poor. Conservatives tend to favor limited intrusion from the national government and allowing the states to decide their own mix of social welfare and regulatory policies including how aggressively they will protect various groups from discrimination.

However, assessing federalism is not so simple. In recent years the tables have turned, and in many cases liberals are suddenly arguing for states' rights while conservatives advocate the virtues of uniform national laws. On a broad range of new issues, such as medical uses of marijuana, gay marriage, cloning, and assisted suicide, state governments are passing socially liberal legislation.[56] And the Court's earlier, state-centered rulings give it little precedent for striking down these laws. The Court's conservative majority will either have to continue applying its state-centered federalism and uphold these liberal state laws, or strike them down on ideological grounds, which would undermine the Court's credibility. One potential solution, from a socially conservative perspective, involves passing congressional legislation banning, for example, cloning or gay marriage. This approach would also be difficult for the Court to sustain, however, given their earlier, narrow definition of "economic activity" under the commerce clause. The most interesting of these cases in many ways pertain to the medical use of marijuana and assisted suicide (see You Decide). In these court cases, apparently political ideology and policy views about the drug laws and the right to die were more important for most of the justices than consistency on questions of federalism.[57]

In addition to pointing out the ideological complexities of federalism, any assessment of federalism today must consider the advantages and disadvantages for our political system. The advantages of a strong role for the states can be summarized in four main points: states can be laboratories of democracy, state and local government is closer to the people, states provide more access to the political system, and states provide an important check on national power.

The first point refers to the role that states play as the source of policy diversity and innovation. If many states are trying to solve problems creatively, they can complement the efforts of the national government. Successful policies first adopted at the state level often percolate up to the national level. The most important recent example is welfare reform. Many states had great success in helping people get off of welfare by providing worker training, education assistance, health benefits, and child care. The national government decided that states were doing a better job than it was doing and, through the TANF block grant mentioned earlier, devolved welfare funding and responsibility to the states.

Second, government that is closer to the people encourages participation in the political process. Local politicians will know better what their constituents want than farther-removed national politicians will. If the voters want higher taxes to pay for more public benefits, like public parks and better schools, they can enact these changes at the state and local levels. Also, local government provides a broad range of opportunities for direct involvement in politics, from working on local political campaigns to attending school board or

▼ *Thirteen people died and about 100 more were injured when a bridge in Minneapolis, Minnesota, collapsed on August 1, 2007. Necessary repairs on bridges and highways will cost hundreds of billions of dollars over the next decade, requiring significant financial assistance from the national government.*

Medical Marijuana and Assisted Suicide

The debate over devolving power from the national government to the states has grown increasingly complicated in the past several years. The partisan nature of the debate has shifted, the Courts have played a larger but inconsistent role, and issues of states' rights increasingly cut across normal ideological and partisan divisions. In the 1990s, Republicans continued to favor greater state control, and Democratic president Bill Clinton also supported devolution to the states in several areas including welfare policy. Since the mid-1990s, the Supreme Court has played a central role in the shift of power to the states, but two recent cases involving medical marijuana (*Raich v. Gonzales*, 2005) and assisted suicide (*Gonzales v. Oregon*, 2006) show how the typical debate between national and state power can shift when a moral dimension is introduced.

In both cases, state voters supported liberal policies. In 1996, California voters passed the Compassionate Use Act, by a margin of 56 to 44 percent. This law allowed seriously ill Californians, typically AIDS and cancer patients, to use marijuana as part of their medical treatment with the permission of a doctor. Oregon voters approved the Death with Dignity Act in 1994 by a margin of 51 to 49 percent. This law allows physicians to prescribe a lethal drug dosage to a patient with a terminal illness. A court order delayed implementation of the law until 1997, the same year that the matter was put before the voters again, but they rejected repealing the law by a margin of 60 to 40 percent. Both of these states' laws were challenged in federal court in classic con-

Federal drug enforcement agents raid a medical marijuana club.

frontations between the states' rights and national power perspectives. Surprisingly, the Supreme Court ruled against medical marijuana and in favor of assisted suicide (this over-simplifies the legal arguments, but these were the bottom-line outcomes).

Should Congress be able to tell a state that it cannot allow the use of medical marijuana? Can the attorney general interpret a congressional law as a prohibition of assisted suicide? Unlike most of the cases discussed in this chapter, the states' rights position in these cases represented the liberal perspective, rather than the conservative position typically associated with state-centered federalism. Social liberals tended to support both the medical marijuana law and the assisted suicide law, while social conservatives tended to oppose them both. However, if you examine these cases in terms of the question of federal versus state power, a central ideological divide in this nation since the Constitutional Convention, the traditional liberal and conservative perspectives both look more complex.

That is, a national-power liberal and a social conservative would agree that the national government should regulate medical marijuana and assisted suicide. Likewise, states'-rights conservatives and social liberals would share the view that the states should decide these issues on their own.

Somewhat surprisingly, there was almost no consistency among the eight justices who voted on both cases (William Rehnquist was replaced by John Roberts between the two cases). Only Justice O'Connor supported the states' rights position in both cases while Scalia voted as a moral conservative against both laws—and counter to his previously articulated views on national power and federalism. The other six justices mixed their views voting to uphold one of the laws and to strike down the other. The resulting rulings were inconsistent on the question of federalism as well. In the medical marijuana case, the Court upheld Congress's power to regulate the medical use of marijuana under the Controlled Substances Act. But in the assisted suicide case, the Court said that under that same congressional law, the U.S. attorney general did not have the power to limit the drugs that doctors in Oregon could prescribe for use in an assisted suicide.

As a matter of policy, should doctors be able to prescribe marijuana to alleviate pain? Should they be able to prescribe lethal drugs to terminally ill patients? Do you tend to support a state-centered or nation-centered perspective on federalism? Now revisit your answers to the first two questions. Are your positions more consistent with your views on federalism or with your policy concerns? ■

city council meetings. When citizens are able to directly affect policies, they are more likely to get involved in the political process.

Third, our federalist system provides more potential paths to address problems. The court system allows citizens to pursue complaints under state or federal law. Likewise, cooperative federalism can draw on the strengths of different levels of government to solve problems. A local government may recognize a need and

FIGURE 3.3 TYPES OF TAXES PER CAPITA BY STATE, 2007

Tax rates vary dramatically by state. What are some of the advantages and disadvantages of living in a low-tax state or in a high-tax state? Which type of state would you rather live in?

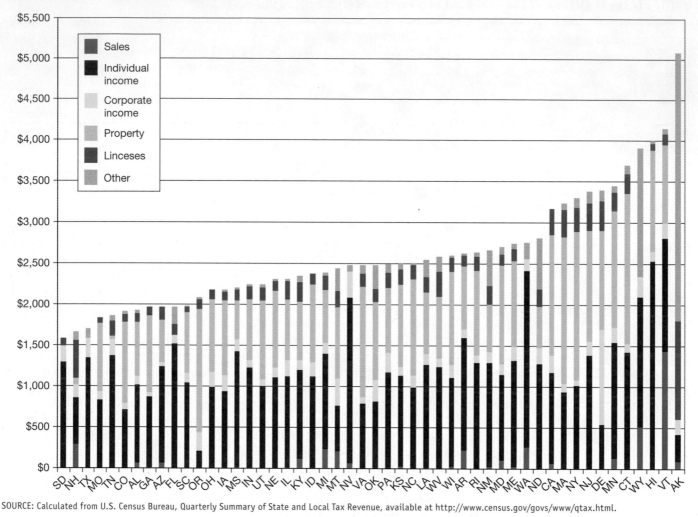

SOURCE: Calculated from U.S. Census Bureau, Quarterly Summary of State and Local Tax Revenue, available at http://www.census.gov/govs/www/qtax.html.

respond to it more quickly than the national government, but if it needs additional resources to address the problem, it may be able to turn to the state or national government for help. Finally, federalism can provide a check on national tyranny. Competitive federalism ensures that Americans will have a broad range of social policies, levels of taxation and regulation, and public services to choose from (Figure 3.3). When people "vote with their feet" by deciding whether to move and where to live, they encourage healthy competition between states that would be impossible under a unitary government.

On the other hand, there are problems with a federalist system that gives too much power to the states: unequal distribution of resources across the states, unequal protection for civil rights, and competitive federalism that produces a "race to the bottom." Also, one puzzle that will be considered in more detail in other chapters is that more people vote in national elections than state and local elections. Turnout at the local level is often ridiculously low. If people support local government so strongly, why aren't they more interested?

One central problem of giving too much responsibility to the states is the huge variation in the distribution of resources. Without federal funding, poor states simply cannot provide an adequate level of benefits because they have the greatest needs (Figure 3.4a) and the lowest incomes (Figure 3.4b), which leads to great disparities in important areas. For example, the wealthiest states spend more than twice as much per capita on education as the poorest states. Citizens of poor states are still citizens of the United States, and one important role for the national government is to ensure that all people have some kind of safety net. The resource problem becomes more acute in dealing with national-level problems that are intractable at the local or state level. For example, pollution spills across state lines and the deteriorating public infrastructure, like the highway system, crosses state boundaries. One study estimated that 45 percent of U.S. bridges are structurally deficient and

---

FIGURE 3.4a **POVERTY RATES BY STATE, 2007**

There are huge differences between the wealthiest states and the poorest states in terms of their income levels and poverty rates. What do these disparities imply about the role of the national government in terms of supporting a "social safety net"? How do recent developments in federalism support or undermine the notion of a social safety net?

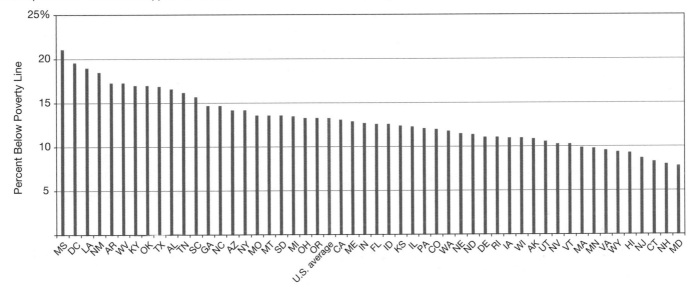

FIGURE 3.4b **PER CAPITA INCOME BY STATE, 2007**

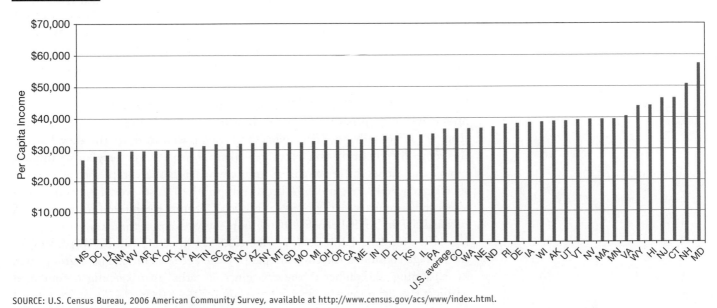

SOURCE: U.S. Census Bureau, 2006 American Community Survey, available at http://www.census.gov/acs/www/index.html.

126,000 are seriously unsafe; two-thirds of the highway system is in need of major repair and 25 percent of mass transit needs to be updated. Solving these problems will cost hundreds of billions of dollars, vastly outstripping the resources of state and local governments.

The second problem, unequal civil rights protection, was evident in the discussion of the various federalism cases before the Supreme Court, which clearly show that states are not uniformly willing to protect the civil liberties and civil rights of their citizens. Without national laws, there will be large differences in the levels of protection against discrimination based on age, disability, and sexual orientation. Finally, as discussed earlier in the chapter, competitive federalism can create a "race to the bottom" as states attempt to lure businesses by keeping taxes and social spending low. This can create an unfair burden on states that take a more generous position toward the poor.

SECTION SUMMARY

1. In recent years traditional positions on federalism have sometimes been reversed, with liberals suddenly arguing for states' rights while conservatives advocate the virtues of uniform national laws, as the cases concerning the medical use of marijuana and assisted suicide demonstrate.

2. The advantages of a strong role for the states are that states are "laboratories of democracy," state and local government is "closer to the people," states provide more access to the political system, and states provide an important check on national power.

3. On the other hand, giving too much power to the states may produce unequal protection for civil rights and competitive federalism that produces a "race to the bottom." Unequal distribution of resources across the states means that states are not equally able to deal with problems.

Conclusion

Alexis de Tocqueville, a French observer of American politics in the early nineteenth century, noted the tendency of democratic governments to centralize. This is especially true during wartime or times of crisis, as in the aftermath of the September 11 attacks, but it is also true during normal political times. Powerful interest groups have an incentive to claim national importance for their causes to increase their likelihood of success. As the political scientist E. E. Schattschneider noted more than a half-century ago, any participant in a conflict who is losing a fight has an incentive to expand the scope of conflict. He uses the example of a street fight in which the person suffering the beating will have an incentive to expand the scope of conflict—that is, bring in his three friends who are down the alley. Placing this more directly in the context of federalism, Michael Greve explains, "Interest groups and parties thrive on redistribution, which is best accomplished at a highly centralized level of government—because it spreads the costs over a larger number of losers and eliminates exit options for them."[58] That is, when interest groups get a national law passed that benefits their group, say for example the dairy price support legislation for dairy farmers, which increases the price of milk by 26 percent for the average consumer, the costs are paid by the entire country. These groups win by expanding the conflict to the entire nation rather than keeping it contained within a specific state.

The drinking age example at the beginning of the chapter also illustrates this point. Mothers Against Drunk Driving would have had a much more difficult task going to all twenty-nine states that allowed drinking at age eighteen or nineteen and convincing each state legislature to change its law. Instead, they were able to convince Congress to pressure the states, and they accomplished their objective more efficiently. This scenario is repeated again and again across a broad range of issues and creates a powerful centralizing force. Within that general pattern of government centralization, however, there have been lengthy periods when the states' rights held sway over the national government.

But this evolving balance of power between the national government and the states obscures a broader reality of federalism: we are citizens of several levels of government simultaneously. Martha Derthick, a leading scholar of American federalism, says that the basic question of federalism involves choices about how many communities we will be.[59] If you asked most people in our nation about their primary geopolitical community they would probably not say, "I am a Montanaian or I am a Arizonian." Most people would likely say, "I am an American." Yet, we have strong attachments to our local communities and state identities. Most Texans would not be caught dead wearing a styrofoam cheesehead, but thousands of football fans in Green Bay, Wisconsin, regularly don the funny-looking things in Lambeau Field to watch their beloved Packers. We are members of multiple communities, which has had an indelible impact on our political system. The beauty of our federal system is that despite its complex and evolving nature, it makes a lot of sense.

▲ One of the strengths of federalism is that it allows regional diversity to flourish. Green Bay Packers fans proudly wear their cheesehead hats at Lambeau Field, showing that what passes for normal behavior in one part of the country would be viewed differently in other areas.

CRITICAL THINKING

1. On which issues is the national government particularly well-suited to serve the people's interests? Which issues are the states better suited to handle? Explain the reasons for your choices.
2. How would our country be different if it were a unitary system? Do you think we would be better or worse off?

KEY TERMS

block grants (p. 78)
categorical grants (p. 78)
coercive federalism (p. 83)
commerce clause powers (p. 75)
competitive federalism (p. 85)
concurrent powers (p. 66)
confederal government (p. 67)
cooperative federalism (p. 76)
doctrine of interposition (p. 72)
dual federalism (p. 73)
federal preemptions (p. 83)
fiscal federalism (p. 78)
full faith and credit clause (p. 70)
general revenue sharing (GRS) (p. 78)
picket fence federalism (p. 76)
privileges and immunities clause (p. 70)
remedial legislation (p. 88)
states' rights (p. 72)
states' sovereign immunity (p. 87)
unfunded mandates (p. 80)
unitary government (p. 67)

SUGGESTED READING

Beer, Samuel. *To Make a Nation: The Rediscovery of American Federalism.* Cambridge, MA: Harvard University Press, 1993.

Conlan, Timothy. *From New Federalism to Devolution: Twenty-Five Years of Intergovernmental Reform.* Washington, DC: Brookings Institution, 1998.

Derthick, Martha. *Keeping the Compound Republic: Essays on American Federalism.* Washington, DC: Brookings Institution, 2001.

Elkins, Stanley and Eric McKitrick. *The Age of Federalism: The Early American Republic, 1788–1800.* New York: Oxford University Press, 1993.

Grodzins, Martin. *The American System: A New View of Government in the United States.* Chicago: Rand McNally, 1966.

Manna, Paul. *School's In: Federalism and the National Education Agenda.* Washington, DC: Georgetown University Press, 2006.

McDonald, Forrest. *States' Rights and the Union: Imperium in Imperia, 1776–1876.* Lawrence, KS: University Press of Kansas, 2000.

Nagel, Robert F. *The Implosion of American Federalism.* New York: Oxford University Press, 2001.

Peterson, Paul E. *The Price of Federalism.* Washington, DC: Brookings Institution, 1995.

Posner, Paul L. *The Politics of Unfunded Mandates: Whither Federalism?* Washington, DC: Georgetown University Press, 1998.

Scheberle, Denise. *Federalism and Environmental Policy: Trust and the Politics of Implementation*, 2nd ed. Washington, DC: Georgetown University Press, 2004.

4

CIVIL LIBERTIES

The claim is often made that "everything changed" after the terrorist attacks of September 11, 2001. While the breadth of the claim can certainly be challenged, Americans became less concerned about freedom in the wake of the attacks and more worried about security. Sixty percent of respondents in a national survey taken shortly after the terrorist attacks said that high school teachers do not have the "right to criticize America's policies toward terrorism" and instead should "defend America's policies in order to promote loyalty to our country." Forty-five percent of respondents said they would be willing to "give up some civil liberties" in order to curb terrorism.[1] Another survey showed that 49 percent of the public thinks that "the 1st Amendment goes too far in the rights that it guarantees," an increase of 10 percent from the previous year.[2]

The government's position toward suspected terrorists also changed dramatically after the attacks. An internal memo by then–White House counsel Alberto Gonzales, who became attorney general during George W. Bush's second term, outlined a "new paradigm" that "places a high premium on . . . the ability to quickly obtain information from captured terrorists and their sponsors in order to avoid further atrocities against American civilians." Vice President Dick Cheney expanded on these sentiments on the television news show *Meet the Press* five days after the attacks, saying that the government needed to "work through, sort of, the dark side." Cheney said,

> A lot of what needs to be done here will have to be done quietly, without any discussion, using sources and methods that are available to our intelligence agencies, if we're going to be successful. That's the world these folks operate in. And so it's going to be vital for us to use any means at our disposal, basically, to achieve our objective.[3]

Former Supreme Court Justice Sandra Day O'Connor had predicted this shift in a speech shortly after the attacks, saying, "we're likely to experience more restrictions on our personal freedom than has ever been the case in our country."[4]

Despite these warnings and the expectation that our government should aggressively pursue suspected terrorists, it still came as a surprise when disturbing stories surfaced about people taken from airports or their homes by government agents. In the process called "extraordinary rendition," suspected terrorists were arrested in the United States and taken to a foreign country that is less protective of civil liberties than the United States, such as Egypt, Syria, Jordan, or Morocco, where foreign agents working with the CIA would try to extract the information needed by the United States. Usually, following their arrest, the suspects disappeared—family members had no idea what happened to them. Survivors of this process have reported a very similar chain of events: they are taken to a foreign country by a Special Removal Unit in a Gulfstream V jet. If interrogations fail to reveal useful information, they may be beaten, kept in tiny underground cells, shocked with cattle prods, and even water boarded (a process in which the suspect is tied to a board on an incline with his head lower than his feet. Water is poured over the suspect's face, immediately producing a gag reflex that makes the person believe he is drowning). Most have been released without charges. One, a Canadian engineer named Maher Arar, was held in a "grave cell" measuring six feet long, seven feet high, and three feet wide, and was tortured for ten months in Syria. Arar sued the U.S. government but a federal judge dismissed the case because it raised sensitive questions of national security and foreign relations.[5] While it is impossible to get precise numbers, as many as 150 people have been subjected to this process.[6] The government has admitted to "rendering" people to other countries, but says it did not participate in or know of the torture.

Early in 2005, a bill called the Torture Outsourcing Prevention Act was introduced in the House of Representatives to prohibit the practice of extraordinary rendition. This bill died in committee, but continued public outrage over rendition and the torture of detainees at Abu Ghraib prison in Iraq and the U.S. base in Guantanamo Bay, Cuba, lead to a high-stakes confrontation between Republican senator John McCain and President Bush. McCain attached an amendment to a military spending bill that banned cruel and inhumane treatment of prisoners in American custody anywhere in the world. The amendment passed by a 90–9 vote in the Senate despite a veto threat from the president. The House later passed a resolution supporting McCain's amendment by a 308–122 vote in one of the strongest rebukes of Bush's foreign policy.[7]

Perhaps because of revelations about the rendition program, domestic spying without a court order, and the compilation of the phone records of millions of Americans, support for **civil liberties**, the political freedoms that protect against

▶ These "enemy combatants" from Afghanistan wait in a holding area before being placed in the detention center at the U.S. naval base in Guantanamo Bay, Cuba. The detention facility has come under increasing criticism from human rights groups and some members of Congress who think the facility should be shut down.

FIGURE 4.1   SUPPORT FOR CIVIL LIBERTIES, 1996–2008

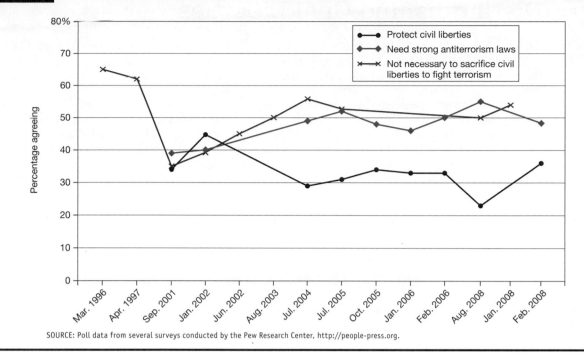

SOURCE: Poll data from several surveys conducted by the Pew Research Center, http://people-press.org.

arbitrary and abusive government actions, is strengthening. Figure 4.1 shows the percentage of respondents saying civil liberties should not be sacrificed to fight terrorism hit a low of 35 percent following the terrorist attacks, but by early 2007 it was back up to 54 percent. About three-fourths of Americans have consistently opposed government monitoring of Americans' phone calls, e-mail, and credit records.[8] On the other hand, more people are concerned that "the government will fail to enact strong, new antiterrorism laws" than laws that "excessively restrict the average person's civil liberties," and this percentage has grown since September 2001.

While Americans tend to support specific civil liberties, such as privacy for phone calls, extraordinary rendition raises a critical point about civil liberties: *there are no absolutes*. Even the strongest critic of state-sponsored torture would have to admit that in some instance it might be justified. For example, if a nuclear device was set to detonate in Manhattan in three hours, few would insist on protecting the civil liberties of someone who knew where the bomb was hidden. Because there are no absolutes, defining our constitutionally protected civil liberties involves balancing interests and drawing lines. The chapter begins with some examples of these tensions.

Most of this chapter describes how the Supreme Court has continually engaged in balancing interests and drawing lines to define and redefine the freedoms and liberties at the core of the American political system. Every time the Supreme Court decides whether a national security concern outweighs a particular freedom of speech, it makes a political decision with broad implications. The evolution of the meaning of civil liberties, as largely defined by the courts, is a great example that the political process matters. Civil liberties also are an excellent illustration of "politics is everywhere." Freedom of speech, religion, and assembly; privacy rights; and the rights of criminal defendants generate great public interest because they are so obviously central to our political system and the daily lives of millions of Americans.

Distinguishing Civil Liberties
from Civil Rights

The terms *civil rights* and *civil liberties* are often used interchangeably, but there are some important differences. Civil liberties refer to the freedoms guaranteed in the Bill of Rights and the "due process" protection of the 14th Amendment, while civil rights protect all persons from discrimination and are rooted in laws and the "equal protection" clause of the 14th Amendment. Another difference is that civil liberties primarily restrict what the government can do to you ("*Congress* shall make no law . . . abridging the freedom of speech") whereas civil rights protect you from discrimination both by the government and by individuals. To oversimplify a bit, civil liberties are about freedom and civil rights are about equality. Given that civil liberties are rooted in the Bill of Rights, it may have been less confusing if they had called it the "Bill of Liberties." (This distinction is discussed further in Chapter 14, Civil Rights.)

Civil Liberties: Balancing
Interests and Drawing Lines

Civil liberties are deeply rooted in our key idea that politics is conflictual and involves trade-offs. When the Supreme Court rules on civil liberties cases, it must balance an individual's freedom with government interests and the public good. In some cases, the Court must not only balance these interests but "draw a line" between permissible and illegal conduct concerning a specific liberty.

BALANCING INTERESTS

Extraordinary rendition and the War on Terror provide particularly contentious examples of balancing civil liberties against competing interests: to what extent should we sacrifice liberties to enhance our security? Other interests that compete with civil liberties include public safety or public health. For example, in the mid-twentieth century some Christian fundamentalist churches regularly handled dangerous snakes in their services, but many states and cities have laws against "the handling of poisonous reptiles in such manner as to endanger the public health, safety, and welfare." These conflicting interests collided in a 1947 case in which members of the Zion Tabernacle Church in Durham, North Carolina, were each fined $50 for handling a poisonous copperhead snake in a church service. They appealed all the way to the North Carolina Supreme Court, arguing that the local ordinance "impinges on the freedom of religious worship." The court rejected this view saying that "public safety is superior to religious practice."[9] Similarly, in some states Amish people are forced to place bright orange "slow-moving vehicle" triangles on their horse-drawn carriages, even if it violates their religious beliefs, because of the paramount concern for public safety.[10] On the other hand, the Amish were not forced to send their children to public schools despite a state law requiring all children to attend school through age sixteen. The Court said this law presented "a very real threat of undermining the Amish community and religious practice as it exists today." However the majority opinion made it clear that this ruling would *not* apply to "faddish new sects or communes."[11]

DRAWING LINES

Along with balancing competing interests, court rulings draw the lines defining the limits of permissible conduct by the government or an individual in the context of a specific civil liberty. For example, despite the 1st Amendment protection of freedom of speech it is obvious that some speech cannot be permitted; the classic example is yelling "fire" in a crowded theater. Therefore, the courts must interpret the law to draw the line between protected speech and impermissible speech. The same can be said of other civil liberties such as the establishment of religion, freedom of the press, freedom from illegal searches, or other due process rights. For example, the 1st Amendment prohibits the government from establishing an official religion, which has been carefully interpreted by the Court over the years to avoid "excessive entanglement" between any religion and the government. On these grounds, prayer in public schools has been banned since the early 1960s (we will examine these important cases later in the chapter). But sometimes it is difficult to draw the line between acceptable and impermissible government involvement concerning religion in schools. One such ruling allowed taxpayer subsidies to fund parochial schools for buying books, but not maps. This odd hair-splitting led the late Senator Daniel Patrick Moynihan to quip, "What about atlases?"[12] Another difficult issue is the 4th Amendment prohibition against "unreasonable searches and seizures" and the role of drug-sniffing dogs. Here the line-drawing involves deciding whether a sniff is a search, and if so, under what circumstances it is reasonable (see You Decide). Search and seizure cases also involve balancing interests: in this case, the individual freedoms of the target of police action and the broader interests in public order and security.

The Origins of Civil Liberties

Courts define the boundaries of civil liberties, but the other branches of government and the public often get involved as well. The skirmishes between President

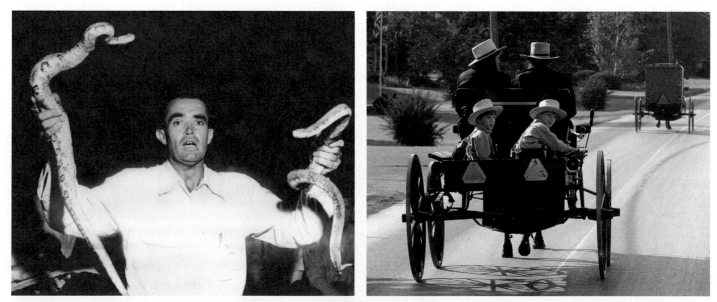

How can conflicts between civil liberties and other legitimate interests, such as public safety and public health, be resolved? Sometimes religious freedom is forced to give way. Courts have upheld bans on the religious practice of snake handling and laws requiring the Amish to display reflective triangles when driving slow-moving buggies on public roads, despite religious objections to doing so.

Drawing Lines and the 4th Amendment

The Supreme Court has ruled that police do not need a search warrant to have drug sniffing dogs search luggage at an airport, or a car that has been stopped for a traffic violation unrelated to drugs. Lower courts have also ruled that sniffs are not considered searches in a hotel hallway, school locker, outside a passenger train's sleeper compartments, or outside an apartment door. However, lower courts have been split on whether drug sniffing dogs may be used outside a home without a warrant, due, in part, to a Supreme Court precedent giving homes stronger 4th Amendment protection than cars, lockers, or other areas. For example, in 2001 the Court ruled that police needed a warrant to use a thermal imaging device outside a home in an attempt to detect marijuana growing under heat lamps inside. A recent case provided an opportunity for the Court to sort out the lower court conflict by determining which precedent from its own decisions was most relevant (the thermal imaging case involv-

Federal agents use a drug-sniffing dog to inspect a car.

ing homes or the dog sniffing cases about airports and cars).

The case involved a Houston man, David Smith, who was arrested when a trained dog smelled methamphetamine in his garage. Based on the dog's positive indication, the police obtained a search warrant and found the meth and other evidence of criminal activity. Smith was sentenced to thirty-seven years in prison, but has appealed the conviction saying that the evidence against

him was illegally obtained. His lawyers argued to the Supreme Court that the thermal imaging case was the relevant precedent and that the charges should be thrown out, saying, "No distinction exists between a thermal imaging device and drug sniffing dog in that they are both sense-enhancing and permit information regarding the interior of a home to be gathered which could not otherwise be obtained without a physical intrusion into a constitutionally protected area." The district attorney, urging the Court to reject the appeal, said that the thermal imaging case was not relevant because the Court's ruling in that case was focused on protecting the original meaning of the 4th Amendment from erosion by new technology. He said that in contrast to thermal imaging devices, "The use of a drug detection dog does not constitute the use of any technology, let alone advanced technology."[a] The Supreme Court declined to hear the case, which means the conviction stands, and offered no explanation why. If you had to decide this case, how would you have ruled? ■

Bush and Congress over torture and domestic spying are recent examples of this broad political debate. The earliest debates during the American Founding also illustrate the basic questions involved in defining civil liberties. Should government be limited by an explicit statement of individual liberties? Would these limitations apply to the state governments or just the national government? How should these freedoms evolve as our society changes?

ORIGINS OF THE BILL OF RIGHTS

As we discussed in Chapter 2, the Founders did not include protection of civil liberties in the Constitution. There were a couple of attempts to do so, including one by George Mason and Elbridge Gerry five days before the Constitutional Convention adjourned. Mason said, "It would give great quiet to the people; and with the aid of the State declarations, a bill might be prepared in a few hours." But their motion to appoint a committee to draft a bill of rights was rejected. Two days later Charles Pinckney and Gerry tried to add a provision to protect the freedom of the press, but that too was rejected.[13]

Mason and Gerry opposed ratification of the Constitution, in part because it did not include a bill of rights, and many Antifederalists echoed this view as the battle for ratification raged in the thirteen states. In a letter to James Madison, Thomas Jefferson predicted that four states would withhold ratification until a bill of rights was added.[14] Some states ratified the Constitution, but urged Congress to draft specific protections for individuals' and states' rights. In some states, the Antifederalists who lost the ratification battle continued making their case to the public and Congress. One of the most famous statements opposing the Constitution came from the Antifederalists on the losing side of Pennsylvania's 46–23 vote for ratification. Their address was printed in local papers, reprinted in various states, and became "a semi-official statement of anti-federalist objections to the new Constitution."[15] One key passage complained about the omission of a bill of rights, which was needed to "fundamentally establish those unalienable and personal rights of men, without the full, free, and secure enjoyment of which there can be no liberty, and over which it is not necessary for a good government to have the control."[16] Their statement went on to outline many of those civil liberties that became the basis for the Bill of Rights.

POLITICAL PROCESS MATTERS

Including the Bill of Rights was an important step in the ratification of the Constitution. Without this guarantee of basic rights and liberties, several states would not have ratified the document.

James Madison and other supporters of the Constitution agreed that the first Congress would take up the issue. State conventions submitted 124 amendments to Congress for their consideration. That list was whittled down to seventeen by the House and then further reduced to twelve by the Senate. That even dozen was approved by the House and sent to the states, which ratified the ten amendments that became the Bill of Rights.[17] Constitutional scholar Akhil Reed Amar notes the significance of the unintended way that things worked out: the ten amendments created a kind of decalogue of ten commandments with an overall impact greater than the sum of its parts.[18]

Despite the profound significance of the Bill of Rights, one important point limited its reach: it applied only to the national government and not the states. For example, the 1st Amendment says that "*Congress* shall make no law" infringing on freedom of religion, speech, and the press, among others. Madison submitted another amendment, which he characterized as "the most valuable of the whole list," requiring states to protect some civil liberties: "The equal rights of conscience, the freedom of speech or of the press, and the right of trial by jury in criminal cases shall not be infringed by any State."[19] Antifederalists feared another power grab by the Federalists in limiting states' rights, so it was voted down in Congress as the amendments were being written. This decision proved consequential because the national government was quite weak for the first half of our nation's history and had much less impact on the daily lives of citizens than did state and local governments. Therefore, protecting civil liberties from the national government's actions protected citizens less than limits on state power would have.

CIVIL LIBERTIES BEFORE THE CIVIL WAR

When the Bill of Rights was ratified, the common understanding was that it applied only to the national government. However, Madison and others soon came to believe that these restrictions should also apply to the states.[20] Ultimately, the Supreme Court had to sort this out. In the last decision of his thirty-three years on the Court, the great Chief Justice John Marshall wrote in *Barron v. Baltimore* that indeed the Bill of Rights only applied to the national government and not to the states (see Chapter 3). In this case, John Barron sued the city of Baltimore when its street paving project diverted streams and sent sand and gravel into the harbor area

The Bill of Rights: A Statement of Our Civil Liberties

1st Amendment	Freedom of religion, speech, press, and assembly; the separation of church and state; and the right to petition the government.
2nd Amendment	Right to bear arms.
3rd Amendment	Protection against the forced quartering of troops in one's home.
4th Amendment	Protection from unreasonable searches and seizures; requirement of "probable cause" for search warrants.
5th Amendment	Protection from forced self-incrimination or double-jeopardy (being tried twice for the same crime); no person can be deprived of life, liberty, or property without due process of law; private property cannot be taken for public use without just compensation; and no person can be tried for a crime without the indictment of a grand jury.
6th Amendment	Right of the accused to a speedy and public trial by an impartial jury, to an attorney, to confront witnesses, to a compulsory process for obtaining witnesses in his or her favor, and to counsel in all felony cases.
7th Amendment	Right to a trial by jury in civil cases involving common law.
8th Amendment	Protection from excessive bail, excessive fines, and cruel and unusual punishment.
9th Amendment	The enumeration of specific rights in the Constitution shall not be construed to deny other rights retained by the people. This has been interpreted to include a general right to privacy and other fundamental rights.
10th Amendment	Powers not delegated by the Constitution to the national government, nor prohibited by it to the states, are reserved to the states or to the people.

he owned, making it impossible for ships to use his once-valuable wharf. Barron claimed that the city owed him the lost value of his property because the 5th Amendment says that private property may not be "taken for public use without just compensation." The Maryland state constitution did not have a similar provision, so Barron sued under the U.S. Constitution. He won in district court but lost on appeal. The Supreme Court agreed with the appeals court, saying that the Bill of Rights "demanded security against the apprehended encroachments of the General Government—not against those of the local governments," and "contain no expression indicating an intention to apply them to the state governments."[21]

As a consequence, the Bill of Rights played a surprisingly trivial role for more than a century. The Supreme Court used it only once before 1866 to invalidate a federal action—in the infamous *Dred Scott* case that contributed to the onset of the Civil War. Further evidence that the Bill of Rights was relatively insignificant in our nation's early history comes from a review of newspapers published in 1841 that could not find a single mention of the fiftieth anniversary of the Bill of Rights.[22]

SELECTIVE INCORPORATION AND THE 14TH AMENDMENT

Civil War Amendments The 13th, 14th, and 15th Amendments to the Constitution, which abolished slavery and granted civil liberties and voting rights to freed slaves after the Civil War.

The significance of the Bill of Rights increased somewhat with the ratification of the 14th Amendment in 1868. It was one of the three **Civil War Amendments** that attempted to guarantee the newly freed slaves equal rights as citizens of the United States. (The other two Civil War Amendments were the 13th, which abolished slavery, and the 15th, which gave male former slaves the right to vote.) Northern politicians were concerned that southerners would deny basic rights to the former slaves, so the sweeping language of the 14th Amendment was adopted. Section 1 says:

> All persons born or naturalized in the United States, and subject to the jurisdiction thereof, are citizens of the United States and of the State wherein they reside. No State shall make or enforce any law which shall abridge the privileges or immunities of citizens of the United States; nor shall any state deprive any person of life, liberty, or property without the due process of law; nor deny to any person within its jurisdiction the equal protection of the laws.

The authors of this amendment and its supporters intended this language to require all states to protect their citizens' civil liberties as guaranteed by the Bill of Rights.[23] The **due process clause**, which forbids any state from denying "life, liberty, or property without the due process of law," was an especially important expansion of civil liberties. The similar clause of the 5th Amendment had previously been interpreted by the Court to only apply to the federal government.

However, in its first opportunity to interpret the 14th Amendment, the Court disagreed. The case involved a group of approximately 1,000 butchers and slaughterhouse owners in Louisiana who were about to be run out of business by a law passed by the corrupt state legislature, which effectively gave a slaughterhouse monopoly to a single firm. The owners of rival slaughterhouses sued the state under the "privileges and immunities" clause of the 14th Amendment, arguing that the state government was denying their basic rights. Despite the clear language of the Amendment saying that "no state shall make or enforce any law" limiting citizens legal "privileges or immunities," the court embraced the "dual citizenship" idea set forth in *Barron v. Baltimore* and stated that the 14th Amendment only protected U.S. citizens against the actions of the national government, not the state governments. The court also rejected the plaintiffs' claim that the state was denying them "the equal protection of the laws" on the grounds that the 14th Amendments was intended to strike down laws that discriminated against blacks.[24] One constitutional scholar observed that all that remained of the 14th Amendment after this decision was a vague, general understanding that it was intended to give citizenship to the newly freed slaves.[25] In other words, all that remained was the first sentence!

Over the next fifty years a minority of justices tried mightily to restore the power of the 14th Amendment and use it to protect civil liberties against state government action. The first step was an 1897 case in which the Court ruled that the 14th Amendment's due process clause forbade a railroad from taking a person's property without just compensation. However, the decision did not specifically mention the 5th Amendment's compensation clause.[26] The next step came about ten years later in a self-incrimination case in which a state judge gave jury instructions that included references to the fact that the accused did not take the stand in his defense. The Supreme Court upheld his conviction, but said, "It is possible that some of the personal rights safeguarded in the first eight amendments against National action may also be safeguarded against state action, because a denial of them would be a denial of the due process of law."[27] Thus, in both the property and self-incrimination cases, the Supreme Court started to use the 14th Amendment to

due process clause Part of the 14th Amendment that forbids states from denying "life, liberty or property" to any person without the due process of law. (A nearly identical clause in the 5th Amendment applies only to the national government.)

POLITICAL PROCESS MATTERS

☑ The due process clause establishes the importance of the courts in protecting basic civil liberties. The state cannot take away a person's life, liberty, or property without going through the proper legal steps.

Selective Incorporation

AMENDMENT	ISSUE	CASE
1st Amendment	Freedom of speech	*Gitlow v. New York* (1925)
	Freedom of the press	*Near v. Minnesota* (1931)
	Freedom of assembly	*DeJonge v. Oregon* (1937)
	Right to petition the government	*Hague v. CIO* (1939)
	Free exercise of religion	*Hamilton v. Regents of the University of California* (1934), *Cantwell v. Connecticut* (1940)
	Separation of church and state	*Everson v. Board of Education of Ewing Township* (1947)
4th Amendment	Protection from unreasonable search and seizure	*Wolf v. Colorado (1949), Mapp v. Ohio* (1961)
5th Amendment	Protection from forced self-incrimination	*Malloy v. Hogan* (1964)
	Protection from double jeopardy	*Benton v. Maryland* (1969)
6th Amendment	Right to a public trial	*In re Oliver 333 U.S. 257* (1948)
	Right to a fair trial and an attorney in death-penalty cases	*Powell v. Alabama* (1932)
	Right to an attorney in all felony cases	*Gideon v. Wainwright* (1963)
	Right to an attorney in cases involving jail time	*Argersinger v. Hamlin* (1972)
	Right to a jury trial in a criminal case	*Duncan v. Louisiana* (1968)
	Right to cross-examine a witness	*Pointer v. Texas* (1965)
	Right to compel witnesses to testify who are vital for the defendant's case	*Washington v. Texas* (1967)
8th Amendment	Protection from cruel and unusual punishment	*Robinson v. California* (1962)[a]
	Protection from excessive bail	*Schilb v. Kuebel* (1971)[b]
9th Amendment	Right to privacy and other non-enumerated, fundamental rights	*United States v. Griswold* (1969)[c]

NOT INCORPORATED

2nd Amendment	Right to bear arms	
3rd Amendment	Prohibition against the quartering of troops in private homes	
5th Amendment	Right to indictment by grand jury	
7th Amendment	Right to a jury trial in a civil case	
8th Amendment	Prohibition against excessive fines	

[a] Some sources list *Louisiana ex rel. Francis v. Resweber* (1947) as the first case that incorporated the 8th Amendment. While the decision mentioned the 5th and 8th Amendments in the context of the due process clause of the 14th Amendment, this argument was not included in the majority opinion which upheld as constitutional the bizarre double-electrocution of Willie Francis (the electric chair malfunctioned on the first attempt, but was successful on the second attempt; see Abraham and Perry, *Freedom and the Court*, pp. 71–2).

[b] Justice Blackmun "assumed" in this case that "the 8th Amendment's proscription of excessive bail [applies] to the states through the 14th Amendment," but later decisions did not seem to share this view. However, Justices Stevens and O'Connor agreed with Blackmun's view in *Browning-Ferris v. Kelco Disposal* (1989). Some sources argue that the excessive bail clause of the 8th Amendment is unincorporated.

[c] Justice Goldberg argued for explicit incorporation of the 9th Amendment in a concurring opinion joined by Justices Warren and Brennan. The opinion of the Court referred more generally to a privacy right rooted in five amendments, including the 9th, but did not explicitly argue for incorporation.

prohibit state governments from violating individual rights, but without specific reference to the Bill of Rights.

This logical progression finally culminated in the 1925 case *Gitlow v. New York*, in which the Court said for the first time that the 14th Amendment incorporated one of the amendments in the Bill of Rights and applied it to the states. The case involved Benjamin Gitlow, a radical Socialist convicted under New York's Criminal Anarchy Act of 1902 for advocating the overthrow of the government. The Court upheld his conviction, arguing that his writings were the "language of direct incitement," but also warned state governments that there were limits on such suppression of speech:

> For present purposes we may and do assume that freedom of speech and of the press—which are protected by the First Amendment from abridgement of Congress—are among the fundamental personal rights and "liberties" protected by the due process clause of the Fourteenth Amendment from impairment by the states.[28]

Slowly over the next fifty years, most civil liberties covered in the Bill of Rights were applied to the states on a case by case basis through the 14th Amendment. However, this process of **selective incorporation** was not smooth and incremental; rather it progressed in surges. The first flurry of activity came in the 1930s when most of the 1st Amendment was incorporated, requiring the states to allow a free press, the right to assemble, free exercise of religion, and the right to petition. The next flurry came in the 1960s with a series of cases on criminal defendants' rights and due process. Why the gap of nearly a quarter century (with only two exceptions)?[29] A case involving the "double jeopardy" clause of the 5th Amendment determined that some rights were so fundamental that they could not be denied by the states, while if others were denied, such as being tried twice for the same crime, it would not undermine our sense of "ordered liberty."[30] The example the Court gave of these fundamental rights was the "freedom of thought and speech." By elevating certain rights later referred to as the Honor Roll of Superior Rights, this ruling meant that civil liberties would be *selectively* incorporated by the 14th Amendment rather than applied as a group to the states. Thus, for the next twenty-five years, the Court largely confined selective incorporation to the 1st Amendment. However, this did not allow the states to ignore the due process of law. By choosing which cases to hear, the Court continued to monitor the states for conduct, that in the words of Justice Felix Frankfurter "shocked the conscience," or in the blunt language of Justice Holmes, "[makes] you vomit."[31]

The second flurry of activity moved away from this idea of fundamental rights and more broadly applied the 14th Amendment to the Bill of Rights. Indeed, the only significant amendment that has not been incorporated is the 2nd Amendment right to bear arms (see Nuts and Bolts 4.3). As a result, the Bill of Rights has evolved from the nineteenth century's relatively inconsequential limitations on national government action to a robust set of protections for freedom and liberty.

selective incorporation The process through which the civil liberties granted in the Bill of Rights were applied to the states on a case-by-case basis through the 14th Amendment.

POLITICS IS EVERYWHERE

The process of selective incorporation gradually applied the Bill of Rights to the states through an increasingly inclusive interpretation of the 14th Amendment, greatly expanding the protection of civil liberties.

SECTION SUMMARY

1. Civil liberties are those freedoms that define what the government cannot do to its citizens.

2. The battle over ratification of the Constitution led to the adoption of the Bill of Rights, which outlines Americans' basic freedoms.

3. Early interpretation of the Constitution protected citizens only against the relatively weak national government, not the states, which limited the significance of the Bill of Rights.
4. Through the process of selective incorporation, the Court's interpretation of the 14th Amendment has gradually broadened to apply most of the civil liberties in the Bill of Rights to state governments as well.

The 1st Amendment: Freedom of Speech, Assembly, and Press

The 1st Amendment's ringing words are the most famous statement of personal freedoms in the Constitution: "Congress shall make no law respecting an establishment of religion, or prohibiting the free exercise thereof; or abridging the freedom of speech or of the press, or the right of the people peaceably to assemble, and to petition the Government for a redress of grievances." You may think that the 1st Amendment's position reflects its importance, but it actually ended up first through an accident of history. Twelve amendments were submitted to the states for ratification, but the first two were not ratified, so the original 3rd Amendment became the first.[32] As we noted earlier, defining the scope of our civil liberties depends on balancing interests and drawing lines. This is especially true of 1st Amendment freedoms, which can be best envisioned on a continuum from most to least protected, based on the Court cases that have tested their limits.

PROTECTED EXPRESSION

Any time you attend a religious service, go to a political rally, write an article for your student paper, or express a political idea, you are being protected by the 1st Amendment. However, the nature of this protection is not set in stone but continually evolving due to political forces and shifting constitutional interpretations. For much of our nation's history, the freedom of speech and press were not strongly protected. Only recently have the courts developed a complex continuum ranging from strongly protected political speech (including symbolic speech such as flag burning) to less protected speech such as obscenity, commercial speech, libel, and fighting words.

Political Speech Freedom of speech got off to a rocky start when in 1798, just a few years after the Bill of Rights was ratified, Congess passed the Alien and Sedition Acts. The especially controversial Sedition Act made it a crime to "write, print, utter or publish . . . any false, scandalous and malicious writing or writings against the government of the United States." Supporters of the four acts claimed they were necessary to strengthen the national government in response to the French Revolution. In reality they were an attempt by the governing Federalist Party to neutralize the opposition Democratic-Republican Party. As many as twenty-five people, mostly newspaper editors, were tried under the law and ten were jailed, including Benjamin Franklin's grandson. The outcry against the laws helped propel Thomas Jefferson to the presidency in 1800. Jefferson pardoned the convicted editors, Congress repealed one of the Acts in 1802, and the others were allowed to expire before the Supreme Court had a chance to rule them unconstitutional.

The next big challenge to freedom of speech came from the states rather than the national government. During the battles over slavery in the first half of the nineteenth century, northern states outlawed positive statements about slavery, while southern states prohibited criticizing slavery. By the end of the nineteenth century, such sedition laws prohibiting behavior considered subversive were quite common at the state level and hundreds of people had been jailed for criticizing the government and its policies (recall that the 1st Amendment did not apply to the states in the nineteenth century).

World War I prompted the harshest crackdowns on free speech since the Sedition Act of 1798. The most important case from this period involved the general secretary of the Socialist Party, Charles Schenk. Schenk strongly opposed U.S. involvement in the war and had printed 15,000 leaflets that he was in the process of mailing to young men who had been drafted to serve in the Army. The leaflet advocated resisting the draft, saying that it was unconstitutional under the 13th Amendment prohibition of "involuntary servitude" and that the war was a "monstrous wrong against humanity, in the interest of Wall Street's chosen few." Schenk was arrested under the Espionage Act of 1917 that prohibited "interfering with military or naval operations," including the draft. He appealed all the way to the Supreme Court, arguing that the 1st Amendment permitted him to protest the war and urge others to resist the draft, but the Court sustained his conviction, noting that free speech is not an absolute right:

> The most stringent protection of free speech would not protect a man in falsely shouting fire in a theatre and causing a panic. . . . The question in every case is whether the words used are used in such circumstances and are of such a nature as to create a clear and present danger that they will bring about the substantive evils that Congress has a right to prevent.[33]

◀ Many American socialists opposed U.S. involvement in World War I. Socialist leader Charles Schenk was prosecuted for encouraging young men to resist the draft, and another socialist, Eugene Debs, was jailed merely for speaking out against the war.

clear and present danger test Established in *Schenk v. United States*, this test allows the government to restrict certain types of speech deemed dangerous.

This clear and present danger test meant that the government could suppress speech they thought was dangerous (in this instance, preventing the government from fighting the war). Critics of this decision argue that Schenk's actions were not dangerous for the country and certainly not equivalent to shouting fire in a theater, which does not allow people a chance to think before panicking.[34] While Schenk's actions would have been legal under the current standard for protecting speech, things would get worse for supporters of the 1st Amendment before they got better. Another socialist leader, Eugene V. Debs, was sentenced to ten years in federal prison for making a speech in 1918 that condemned U.S. involvement in World War I, and two newspaper publishers were jailed for publishing articles critical of the war. Both high-profile convictions were sustained by the Court.[35] Then Congress passed the even more restrictive Sedition Act of 1918, which outlawed any "disloyal, profane, scurrilous, or abusive language about the form of government, the Constitution, soldiers and sailors, flag or uniform of the armed forces" and any words that favored the cause of the German empire or opposed the cause of the United States. In the first test case for the new law, the Court upheld the conviction of six anarchists who supported the cause of the Bolsheviks in Russia and urged the "workers of the world" to strike.

POLITICS IS CONFLICTUAL

Q The tendency to restrict the freedom of speech during wartime stems from the desire to reduce political conflict and strengthen support for the war effort. The government tends to view political speech against an ongoing war as supporting the enemy and thus wants to restrict that speech.

The great Justice Oliver Wendell Holmes, author of the *Schenk* decision and the clear and present danger test, had had enough. He dissented in the anarchists' case, arguing that the "surreptitious publishing of a silly leaflet by an unknown man" posed no danger to the country. In one of the most famous statements of the importance of the freedom of speech, he touted the "free trade in ideas" saying, "The best of truth is the power of the thought to get itself accepted in the competition of the market . . . we should be eternally vigilant against attempts to check the expression of opinion that we loathe and believe to be fraught with death."[36] This notion of the marketplace of ideas in which good ideas triumph over bad is still central to modern defenses of the 1st Amendment. Holmes correctly pointed out that if freedom of speech is to have any meaning, we must protect the right to utter "words that we loathe" that are "fraught with death" as well as those that we agree with and that pose no danger.

Over the next several decades the Court struggled to draw the line between dangerous speech and words that were simply unpopular. For example, during the Red Scare of the late 1940s and early 1950s, Senator Joseph McCarthy and others roused the nation against the Communist threat, presenting the Court with many opportunities to defend unpopular speech. But for the most part they declined. The Communist threat was real but exaggerated, and hundreds of innocent Americans had their careers and lives ruined by false accusations and guilt by association. The legal issue facing the Court was whether the Smith Act, which attempted to restrict the Communist Party by banning the advocacy of force or violence against the United States, violated the 1st Amendment. In 1951 the Court upheld the conviction of eleven members of the Communist Party under the Smith Act.[37]

The strongest protection for free speech, and the one that remains in force today, was put into place in 1969. This case involved a leader of the Ku Klux Klan, Clarence Brandenburg, who made a threatening speech at a cross-burning rally that was subsequently shown on television. Twelve hooded

▲ *Senator Joseph McCarthy stands in front of a map purporting to show Communist activity in the United States. McCarthy was a central figure in the post–World War II Red Scare, during which Americans suspected of supporting Communism were persecuted and imprisoned.*

figures were shown on the film, many with weapons. The speech said that "reven-gence" [sic] might be taken if "our president, our Congress, our Supreme Court continues to suppress the white, Caucasian race." He continued, "We are marching on Congress July the Fourth, four hundred thousand strong." Brandenburg was convicted under the Ohio law banning "sabotage, violence, or unlawful methods of terrorism as a means of accomplishing industrial or political reform," but the Court unanimously reversed his conviction, arguing that threatening speech could not be suppressed just because it sounded dangerous. Specifically, the **direct incitement test** holds that speech is protected "except where such advocacy is directed to incit-ing or producing imminent lawless action and is likely to incite or produce such action."[38] Under this standard, most, if not all, of the sedition convictions during World War I and the Red Scare would have been overturned.

Symbolic Speech The use of signs, symbols, or other unspoken acts or methods to communicate in a political manner—**symbolic speech**—enjoys many of the same protections as regular speech. For example, during the Vietnam War the Court protected the 1st Amendment right of a war protestor to wear an American flag patch sewn on the seat of his pants,[39] and high school students' right to wear an armband to protest the war,[40] or tape a peace symbol on the flag and fly it upside-down outside an apartment window.[41] Lower courts convicted these protestors under state laws that protected the American flag, or in the armband case, under a school policy that explicitly prohibited wearing armbands to protest the Vietnam War. In the flag desecration case involving the peace symbol, the Court clearly stated that protected "speech" need not be verbal, saying that even though the appellant did not use words, "there can be little doubt that appellant communicated through the use of symbols."[42]

A 1989 case provided the strongest protection for symbolic speech yet. The case involved a man, Gregory Johnson, who burned a flag outside the 1984 Re-publican national convention in Texas, chanting along with a group of protestors, "America the red, white, and blue, we spit on you. You stand for plunder, you will go under." The Court refrained from critiquing Johnson's jingle, but its 5–4 decision overturned his conviction under Texas's flag desecration law on the grounds that symbolic political speech is protected by the 1st Amendment.[43] In response to this extremely unpopular decision, Congress passed the Flag Protection Act of 1989, which the Court also struck down as an unconstitutional infringement on political expression.[44] Congress then attempted to pass a constitutional amendment to over-turn the Court decision; the House passed the amendment in 1995, 2000, and 2005 but each time the measure failed by a narrow margin in the Senate.

While flag burning and other forms of symbolic speech have been protected by the Court, there are limits, especially when the symbolic speech conflicts with another substantial governmental interest. For example, Vietnam War protestors who burned their draft cards were not protected by the 1st Amendment because their actions interfered with Congress's constitutional right to "raise and support" armies through the draft. Just because someone is expressing an idea doesn't mean that symbolic action associated with that idea will be protected speech.[45] Another important exception involved Joseph Frederick, a high school student from Juneau, Alaska, who was suspended from school for unfurling a fourteen-foot banner on a public sidewalk that said "Bong Hits 4 Jesus." The incident occurred just outside school grounds, as the Olympic torch relay passed through Juneau on its way to the 2002 Winter Games in Salt Lake City, Utah. Frederick sued the school claim-ing his 1st Amendment rights were violated, but the Supreme Court agreed with the school, saying "It was reasonable for [the principal] to conclude that the banner promoted illegal drug use—and that failing to act would send a powerful message

▲ The American flag is a popular target for protesters: it has been spat upon, shredded, turned into underwear, and burned, as it was during this 2004 demonstration at the Democratic National Convention in Boston. Despite multiple efforts in Congress to ban flag desecration, these activities remain constitutionally protected symbolic speech.

direct incitement test Established in *Bran-denberg v. Ohio*, this test protects threatening speech under the 1st Amendment unless that speech aims to and is likely to cause imminent "lawless action."

symbolic speech Nonverbal expression, such as the use of signs or symbols. It benefits from many of the same constitutional protections of verbal speech.

to the students in her charge." The dissenters lamented the invention of "a special 1st Amendment rule permitting the censorship of any student speech that mentions drugs," based on "a silly, nonsensical banner."[46]

According to the Court, spending money in political campaigns can also be considered symbolic speech since it provides the means for more conventional types of political speech. Here the central question is whether the government can control campaign contributions and spending or whether such laws violate the 1st Amendment rights of candidates or their supporters. You probably have heard the old saying "money talks," which implies that money is speech. Given the importance of advertizing in modern campaigns, limitations on raising and spending money could limit the ability of candidates and groups to reach voters with their message. The Court has walked a tightrope on this one, balancing the public interest in honest and ethical elections and the 1st Amendment rights of candidates and their advocates. The Court has upheld individuals' right to spend their own money in federal elections, but presidential candidates give up that right if they accept federal campaign funds (taxpayers' money) in a presidential election. Also, candidates in federal elections are subject to limits on the types and size of contributions that they can receive, and they must report all contributions and spending to the Federal Election Commission. More recently, the Court upheld a ban on so-called soft money (this term will be discussed in more detail in Chapter 8; at this point it is sufficient to note that it was seen by the Court as the type of contribution with the most potential for corruption because soft money contributions were previously unlimited).[47]

Spending as a form of symbolic speech struck closer to home in a case in 2000 involving student activity fees at the University of Wisconsin. A group of students argued that they should not have to pay student fees to fund groups whose activities they opposed, including a student environmental group, a gay and bisexual student center, a community legal office, an AIDS support network, a campus women's center, and the Wisconsin Student Public Interest Research Group. In a unanimous opinion, the Court ruled that mandatory student fees could continue to support the full range of groups as long as the process for allocating money was "viewpoint neutral." The Court also said that student referendums that could add, cut, or even eliminate money for specific groups violated viewpoint neutrality. The potential for the majority to censor unpopular views was unacceptable to the Court, since "The whole theory of viewpoint neutrality is that minority views are treated with the same respect as are majority views."[48]

POLITICS IS EVERYWHERE

Symbolic political speech is all around you, from political patches, American flags, arm bands, and signs to campaign contributions and student activity fees.

Hate Speech Free speech has been a hot topic on many college campuses since the mid-1980s in the context of hate speech. Do people have a right to say things that are offensive or abusive, especially in terms of race, gender, and sexual orientation? By the mid-1990s more than 350 public colleges and universities said no by regulating some forms of hate speech.[49] One example was a speech code adopted at the University of Michigan that prohibited "Any behavior, verbal or physical, that stigmatizes or victimizes an individual on the basis of race, ethnicity, religion, sex, sexual orientation, creed, national origin, ancestry, age, marital status, handicap, or Vietnam veteran status," and "Creates an intimidating, hostile, or demeaning environment for educational pursuits, employment or participation in University-sponsored extra-curricular activities."[50] The Supreme Court has yet to rule definitively on this issue, but lower courts struck down the University of Michigan's speech code as well as similar rules at the University of Wisconsin, and several other universities. If the Court took up any of these cases, they would be likely to strike down the speech codes because they are not "content neutral" regulations and

hate speech Expression that is offensive or abusive, particularly in terms of race, gender, or sexual orientation. It is currently protected under the 1st Amendment.

they do not meet the direct incitement test of targeting only expressions that would spur imminent violence.

One final significant issue combines the topics of symbolic speech and hate speech. Can a person who burned a cross on a black family's lawn be convicted under a city ordinance that prohibited conduct "arous[ing] anger, alarm, or resentment in others on the basis of race, color, creed, religion, or gender"? Or is the ordinance an unconstitutional limit on 1st Amendment rights? In a unanimous decision the Court said the cross burner could be punished for arson, terrorism, trespassing, or other violations of the law, but he could not be convicted under this St. Paul, Minnesota, ordinance because it was overly broad and vague. The Court said, "Let there be no mistake about our belief that burning a cross in someone's front yard is reprehensible. But St. Paul has sufficient means at its disposal to prevent such behavior without adding the First Amendment to the fire."[51] The city ordinance was unconstitutional because it took selective aim at a disfavored message, or in the legal jargon of the Court, it constituted "viewpoint discrimination." However, the Court has since upheld more carefully worded bans of cross burning. Eleven years after the St. Paul case, the Court ruled that Virginia could prohibit cross burning if there was an intent to intimidate, but that determining intent depends on the context. For example, burning a cross on an African American family's front lawn would be illegal under this law, but burning a cross at a Ku Klux Klan rally to symbolize white supremacist political views would still be protected by the 1st Amendment.[52]

▲ Are laws banning hate speech constitutional? Sometimes yes, but the threshold is relatively high. These Ku Klux Klan members are free to hold rallies, preach racism and xenophobia, and burn crosses, as long as they do not directly incite violence or display an "intent to intimidate."

Freedom of Assembly The right to assemble peaceably has been consistently protected by the Supreme Court. In an important 1937 case that applied this part of the 1st Amendment to the states for the first time, the Court upheld the right to teach Communist doctrine in public meetings, saying that the right to assemble is "one that cannot be denied without violating those fundamental principles which lie at the base of all civil and political institutions."[53] Peaceful civil rights protestors who were arrested for disturbing the peace had their convictions overturned when the Court said the state of South Carolina could not "make criminal the peaceful expression of unpopular views."[54] Perhaps the most famous assembly case involved a neo-Nazi group that wanted to march in Skokie, Illinois, a suburb of Chicago that then had about 70,000 residents of whom nearly 60 percent were Jewish. Many of the residents were Holocaust survivors and strongly opposed the march. The village passed three ordinances that effectively banned the group from marching. In defense of these laws, the village government argued that residents would be so upset by the Nazi marchers that they might become violent, and the local government could not ensure the safety of the marchers. But the lower courts did not accept this argument, ruling that as long as the marchers engaged in protected speech (that is, they didn't incite imminent violence among *their* followers), then the village had to protect the marchers. They ruled that if "the audience is so offended by the ideas being expressed that it becomes disorderly and attempts to silence the speaker, it is the duty of the police to attempt to protect the speaker, not to silence his speech."[55] The Court elaborated on this responsibility to protect expressions of unpopular views by striking down another town's ordinance that allowed them to charge a higher permit fee to groups whose march would likely require more police protection.[56]

While broad protection is provided for peaceable assemblies, governments may regulate the time, manner, and place of expression as long as the regulation is content-neutral, not favoring certain groups or messages over others. For example, anti-abortion protestors were not allowed to picket a doctor's home in Brookfield, Wisconsin. The Court ruled that the ordinance banning all residential picketing was content-neutral and that there was a government interest in preserving the "sanctity of the home, the one retreat to which men and women can repair to escape from the tribulations of their daily pursuits."[57] "Time, manner, and place" restrictions also may be invoked for practical reasons. If the Ku Klux Klan planned to hold a march around the football stadium on the day of a game, the city council could deny them a permit and suggest they choose another day that would be more convenient. The legal standard for these regulations is that they are "reasonable." While vague, this standard allows the courts to balance the right to assemble against other practical considerations.

Freedom of the Press The task of balancing interests is central to many 1st Amendment cases involving the freedom of the press. Which is more important, the 1st Amendment freedom of the press to disclose details about current events or the 6th Amendment right to a fair trial, which may require keeping important information out of the public eye? When do national security concerns prevail over journalists' right to keep citizens informed? The general issue here is **prior restraint**, the government's right to prevent the media from publishing something. When applied to information concerning a ongoing trail, the prohibition to publish is called a **gag order**. Prior restraint has never been clearly defined by the Court, but several landmark cases have set a very high bar for applying it. The first involved a Minnesota law that banned "obscene, lewd and lascivious" publications or "malicious, scandalous and defamatory" content. Under this law, the state shut down a racist, bigoted publication by Jay Near that railed against many groups of people. The Court subsequently struck down the law saying, "The fact that the liberty of the press may be abused by miscreant purveyors of scandal does not make any less necessary the immunity of the press from previous restraint."[58] However, the Court did not specify when prior restraint would be acceptable (it simply said that there would have to be "exceptional circumstances").

The next major opportunity to clarify the issue came in 1971 with the Pentagon Papers case, which involved disclosure of parts of the top-secret report on internal planning for the Vietnam War. The incredibly divided case had nine separate written opinions! By a 6–3 vote the Court decided that the government could not prevent the publication of the Pentagon Papers, but at least five justices supported the view that under some circumstances the government could use prior restraint—though they could not agree on the standard. For some of the justices, a crucial consideration was that the papers revealed that the U.S. government had lied about its involvement in and the progress of the Vietnam War. Justice Hugo Black noted the importance of this point saying, "Only a free and unrestrained press can effectively expose deception in government."[59] This ended up being an amazing prediction of the role of the press in the next several years in uncovering the Watergate scandal that brought down the Nixon presidency.

Prior restraint has taken on new significance in the War on Terror. The media, especially the *New York Times*, skirmished with the Bush administration over publishing stories on various classified programs, including extraordinary rendition of suspected terrorists, domestic surveillance, and the Terrorist Finance Tracking Program, which monitors all large financial transactions in the international banking system. Supporters of the media point to the Pentagon Papers case as precedent for the role of journalists in holding the government accountable. They argue that these

prior restraint A limit on freedom of the press that allows the government to prohibit the media from publishing certain materials.

gag order An aspect of prior restraint that allows the government to prohibit the media from publishing anything related to an ongoing trial.

programs may violate domestic or international law and the public has the right to know about them. Furthermore, these stories are not published without serious consideration of the consequences; the *New York Times* sat on the domestic telephone surveillance story for a year before publishing it. Critics of the media argue that revealing classified programs is irresponsible and may threaten national security. The Justice Department investigated leaks from the National Security Administration believed to be the source of some of the *New York Times* stories and promised to prosecute the leakers and the journalists. Congress responded by trying to pass the Free Flow of Information Act of 2007, which would have given journalists some protection of confidential sources and information. The bill passed the House by a 398–21 vote in October 2007 but was killed in July 2008 when the Senate failed to get enough votes to prevent a filibuster.

Keeping sources confidential has always been an important aspect of the freedom of the press since many sources would not talk to reporters if they thought their names would appear on the front page the next day. But the need to protect sources sometimes conflicts with criminal investigations or trials. For example, Judith Miller a *New York Times* reporter, was jailed for eighty-five days in 2005 for refusing to reveal her sources for several articles to the grand jury investigating the leak of a CIA operative's name by White House officials. She was released when she agreed to provide limited testimony to the grand jury concerning conversations with Dick Cheney's aide, Lewis "Scooter" Libby, without revealing her other sources.

Prior restraint also may be an issue in media coverage of a trial, but gag orders are allowed only when media coverage would make it impossible for the defendant to have a fair trial. In a 1976 case involving a multiple murder in Nebraska, the Court struck down a gag order that prevented the press from describing the facts of the case. The Court said, "the protection against prior restraint should have particular force as applied to reporting of criminal proceedings."[60] Gag orders that prohibit participants in a trial (jury members, witnesses, lawyers, law enforcement officials) from talking to the media operate under more complicated precedents that depend on whether this media contact would undermine a fair trail.[61]

LESS PROTECTED SPEECH AND PUBLICATIONS

Some forms of speech do not warrant the same level of protection as political speech because they do not contribute to public debate or express ideas that have important social value. Four categories of speech may be more easily regulated by the government than political speech: fighting words, libel and slander, commercial speech, and obscenity.

Fighting Words Governments may regulate fighting words, "which by their very utterance inflict injury or tend to incite an immediate breach of the peace." [62] Such laws must be narrowly written; it is not acceptable to ban all foul language, and the prohibited speech must target a single person rather than a group. At first the question of whether certain words provoke a backlash doesn't seem like a very logical test because it depends on the reaction of the targeted person. Inflammatory words directed at Archbishop Emeritus Desmond Tutu would not be fighting words because he would turn the other cheek, whereas the same words yelled at musician Busta Rhymes or actor Sean Penn *would* be fighting words because they would probably deck you. The Court has further clarified the test, based on "what persons of common intelligence would understand to be words likely to cause an average addressee to fight," [63] but the fighting words doctrine has still been difficult to apply and is not widely used by the Court.

▲ *In July of 1971, Daniel Ellsberg testified before Congress that he had leaked the classified Pentagon Papers to reporters, revealing Department of Defense plans and strategies for conducting the Vietnam War. The Supreme Court determined that the government could not prevent publication of the papers, despite their classified status.*

Slander and Libel A more extensive line of cases prohibiting speech concerns slander, spoken false statements that damage someone's reputation, and libel, written statements that do the same thing. As in many areas of 1st Amendment law, it is difficult to draw the line between permissible speech and slander or libel. One text on the subject calls the topic a "veritable public-law snake pit." The current legal standard distinguishes between speech about a public figure, such as a politician or celebrity, and about a regular person. In short, public figures have to have much thicker skin than the average person because it is much more difficult for them to prove libel. To win a libel suit a public figure has to demonstrate that the defamatory statement was made with "actual malice" and "with knowledge that it was false or with reckless disregard of whether it was false or not."[64] One of the most famous libel cases was brought against *Hustler* magazine by Reverend Jerry Falwell, a famous televangelist and political activist. Falwell sued *Hustler* for libel and emotional distress after the magazine published a parody of a liquor advertisement depicting him in a "drunken incestuous rendezvous with his mother in an outhouse" (this quote is from the Supreme Court case).[65] The lower court said that the parody wasn't believable, so *Hustler* couldn't be sued for libel, but they awarded Falwell damages for emotional distress. The Courts unanimously overturned this decision saying that public figures and public officials have to put up with such things and compared the parody to outrageous political cartoons, which have always been protected by the 1st Amendment. While the Court sided with the magazine in this case, other rulings have narrowed the concept of a "public figure" making it easier for a broader range of citizens to prove libel.[66]

Commercial Speech Commercial speech, which mostly refers to advertising, has evolved from having almost no protection under the 1st Amendment to having quite strong protection. One early case involved a business owner who distributed leaflets to advertise rides on his submarine that was docked in New York City. Under city ordinances, leafleting was only permitted if it was devoted to "information or a public protest," but not for a commercial purpose. The plaintiff changed the leaflet to have his advertisement on one side and a statement protesting the city's policies on the other side (clever guy!). He was arrested anyway, and the Court upheld his conviction saying that the city council had the right to regulate the distribution of leaflets.[67] The Court became much more sympathetic to commercial speech starting in the 1970s when it struck down a law against advertising prescription drug prices and one prohibiting placing newspaper racks on city streets to distribute commercial publications such as real estate guides.[68] The key decision came in 1980 and established a test that is still central today. The Court ruled that the government may regulate commercial speech if it concerns an illegal activity, if the advertisement is misleading, or if regulating speech directly advances a substantial government interest and the regulation is not excessive. In practice, this test means that commercial speech can be regulated, but that the government has to have a very good reason to do it. Even public health concerns have not been allowed to override over commercial speech rights. For example, the Court struck down a Massachusetts regulation that limited the content of advertisements aimed at children (the ban on R. J. Reynolds's Joe Camel character is the classic example) in a manner that was more restrictive than federal law.[69]

▲ *Joe Camel peddles his wares on a New York City billboard. Commercial speech, as a general category, is not as strongly protected by the 1st Amendment as political speech, but advertising can only be limited by the government in specific circumstances.*

Obscenity One area in which the press has never experienced complete freedom is in the publication of pornography and material considered obscene. The difficulty, once again, arises in deciding where to draw the line. Nearly everyone would agree that child pornography should not be published,[70] and that pornography should not be available to minors. However, beyond these points there is not much consensus. Some people are offended by nude paintings in art museums, while others enjoy watching hardcore X-rated movies. For example, President Bush's first attorney general, John Ashcroft, disliked giving press conferences under the bare breast of the Spirit of Justice statue that has decorated the Great Hall of the Department of Justice since the building opened in 1936. So the statue (and her male counterpart, Majesty of Law, who already wore a loin cloth) were hidden behind a blue velvet curtain at a cost of $8,650.[71]

Defining obscenity has proven difficult for the courts. In an often-quoted moment of frustration, Justice Potter Stewart wrote that he could not define obscenity, but "I know it when I see it."[72] In its first attempt to provide a framework for limiting obscenity, the Court ruled that a particular publication could be banned if an "average person, applying contemporary community standards" would find that the material appeals to prurient interests and was "utterly without redeeming social importance."[73] This standard proved unworkable because lower courts differed in their interpretation of both "redeeming social importance" and the "community standard" (some assumed a single national community and others applied local standards). The Court took another stab at it in 1973 in *Miller v. California*, the case that gave rise to **Miller test**, which is still applied today. The test has three standards which must all be met in order for material to be banned as obscene. Using the same average person/contemporary community point of reference, material can be banned if it appeals to prurient interests, is "patently offensive," and the work as a whole lacks serious literary, artistic, political, or scientific value. The Court also clarified that *local* community standards were to apply rather than a single national standard, reasoning that what passes for obscenity in Sioux City, Iowa, probably would be considered pretty tame in Las Vegas. Despite providing a more solid foundation for subsequent cases on this topic, there are still some difficulties with the test. As Kathleen Sullivan, the former dean of Stanford University Law School points out, "The first two parts of this test are incoherent: to put it crudely, they require the audience to be turned on and grossed out at the same time."[74]

Congress and the president also get in on the act of controlling obscenity. In general, Congress and the president take a more conservative approach—seeking legislation to limit obscenity, whereas the Court focuses on whether certain speech is protected. Furthermore, the Court tends to rein in Congress and the president when they try to limit obscene speech. In 1967, Congress created a Commission on Obscenity and Pornography that completed its work in 1970 and concluded that there was no link between sexually explicit materials and criminal behavior. President Nixon, who inherited the commission from the previous administration, was upset with the report, saying, "So long as I am in the White House there will be no relaxation of the national effort to control and eliminate smut from our national life . . . I totally reject this report."[75] Sixteen years later President Reagan established the Meese Commission on the same subject. The commission issued strong warnings about the negative effects of pornography on society, but the report was widely criticized for its bias and lack of scientific evidence to back up its claims.

One interesting aspect of the Meese Commission and other attempts to ban obscenity is the odd political coalition of the extreme right and left, between Christian conservatives and feminists, who both hate pornography but for very different reasons. Having failed in the courts to limit pornography as much as they would like, this coalition continued to press its case in Congress. They have tried novel approaches, such as pushing for the Pornography Victims' Compensation Act of 1991. Rather than banning pornography outright, this law would have

Miller test Established in *Miller v. California*, the Supreme Court uses this three-part test to determine whether speech meets the criteria for obscenity. If so, it can be restricted by the government.

allowed victims of sexual crimes to sue publishers, if it could be shown that the criminal was a consumer of the publishers' pornographic material. The bill did not become law.

More recent efforts have focused on the newest pornography medium, the Internet. Congress passed the Communications Decency Act in 1996, which criminalized the use of any computer network to display "indecent" material, unless the provider could provide an effective way of screening out potential users under the age of eighteen. The Court struck down the law in 1997 because it was overly vague, and because it is technically impossible to limit access to Web sites based on age. This ruling gives the Internet the same free speech protection as print,[76] but Congress wasn't going to give up without a fight. In 1998 the Child Online Protection Act (COPA) was signed into law by President Clinton. It prohibited commercial Web sites from distributing material that is "harmful to minors," using the language of the Miller test to specify what this means. The law bounced around in federal courts for six years, twice making it to the Supreme Court, which ultimately struck it down arguing that the government could achieve the same goals using "less restrictive alternatives" to COPA and that the law carried a potential for extraordinary harm and a serious chill upon protected speech."[77]

SECTION SUMMARY

1. Determining the specific meaning of the freedom of speech, assembly, and the press involves balancing interests and drawing lines. Balancing interests is when the Court must choose between competing constitutional rights, such as the right to protest against the Vietnam War by burning your draft card or Congress's right to raise and support armies. Drawing lines refers to the Court defining the range of permissable conduct concerning a specific liberty, such as the freedom of speech.
2. The Court has drawn the lines in various places throughout history and those lines will continue to evolve over the coming decades in important areas such as national security and regulation of the Internet.
3. Political speech, assembly, and press have received stronger protection from the courts than commercial or other nonpolitical activity.

The 1st Amendment: Freedom of Religion

The 1st Amendment has two parts that deal with religion: the **establishment clause**, which says that Congress cannot sponsor or endorse any particular religion, and the **free exercise clause**, which states that Congress cannot interfere in the practice of religion. The establishment clause is primarily concerned with drawing lines. Does a prayer at a public high school football game or a nativity scene on government property constitute state sponsorship of religion? The free exercise clause has more to do with balancing interests; recall the earlier examples of balancing public safety concerns against snake handling in religious services and the use of Amish buggies on highways. The combination of the establishment and free exercise clauses results in a general policy of noninterference and government neutrality

establishment clause Part of the 1st Amendment that states, "Congress shall make no law respecting an establishment of religion," which has been interpreted to mean that Congress cannot sponsor or favor any religion.

free exercise clause Part of the 1st Amendment stating that Congress cannot prohibit or interfere with the practice of religion.

toward religion. As Thomas Jefferson put it in 1802, the 1st Amendment provides a "wall of eternal separation between church and state." Though this language is not part of any law, it continues to be cited frequently in Court cases[78] in which religion and politics intersect. Since both of these areas tend to carry great moral weight and emotional charge, it's no wonder that the vehement debates continue over the appropriateness of the saying "In God We Trust" on our currency, the White House Christmas tree, the movement to "put Christ back into Christmas," and whether public schools should teach evolution and "intelligent design." Since politics is everywhere, the boundaries of religious expression remain difficult to draw.

THE ESTABLISHMENT CLAUSE AND SEPARATION OF CHURCH AND STATE

Determining the boundaries between church and state—the central issue of the establishment clause—is very difficult. As a leading text on civil liberties put it, the words of the establishment clause—"Congress shall make no law respecting an establishment of religion"—are commanding and clear, but their meaning is entirely unclear. What does the clause allow or forbid?[79] We know that the Founders did not want an official state religion nor for the government to favor one religion over another, but beyond that, it's hard to say. Jefferson's "eternal wall of separation" comment has been used in Court decisions that prohibit state aid for religious activities, but lately the Court has been moving toward a more "accommodationist" perspective that sometimes allows religious activity in public institutions.

The prohibition of prayer in public schools has proven to be the most controversial establishment clause issue. It exploded onto the political scene in 1962 when the Court ruled that the following prayer, written by the New York Board of State Regents and read every day in the state's public schools,[80] violated the separation of church and state: "Almighty God, we acknowledge our dependence upon Thee, and we beg Thy blessing upon us, our parents, our teachers, and our country." Banning the prayer caused a huge public outcry protesting the perceived attack on religion.

Over the next forty years Congress repeatedly tried to amend the Constitution to allow school prayer, but these amendments never received the two-thirds vote in both houses necessary to send them to the states for ratification. Meanwhile, the Court continued to take a hard line on school-sponsored prayer. In 1985 the Court struck down the practice of observing a one-minute moment of silence for "meditation or voluntary prayer" in the Alabama public schools.[81] More recently the Court said that benedictions or prayers at public school graduations and a school policy that allowed and elected student representative to lead a prayer at a high school football game also violated the establishment clause.[82] On the other hand, the Court upheld the practice of opening every session of Congress with a prayer and let stand without comment a lower court ruling that allowed a prayer that was planned and led by students (rather than being school policy) at a Texas high school graduation.[83]

The Court has had an even more difficult time coming up with principles to govern aid to religious organizations, either directly, through tax dollars, or indirectly, through the use of public space. One early attempt was known as the **Lemon test**, after one of the parties in a 1971 case involving government support for religious schools. This case said that a practice violated the establishment clause if it (1) did not have a "secular legislative purpose," (2) either advanced or inhibited religion,

Lemon test Established in *Lemon v. Kurtzman*, the Supreme Court uses this test to determine whether a practice violates the 1st Amendment's establishment clause.

▲ The establishment clause of the Constitution requires the separation of church and state. However, the Supreme Court has ruled that religious symbols are permitted on government property as long as they are part of larger, secular displays. Here the Ten Commandments are displayed on one of the forty monuments outside the Texas state capitol in Austin.

or (3) fostered "an excessive government entanglement with religion."[84] The first two parts of the test are pretty straightforward, but the third was open to interpretation by lower courts and therefore led to conflicting rulings.

While the Lemon test still has not been completely abandoned, the Court started to move away from it in a 1984 case involving a creche owned by the city of Pawtucket, Rhode Island and displayed in a park owned by a nonprofit corporation. The Court allowed the Nativity display, saying, "The Constitution does not require complete separation of church and state; it affirmatively mandates accommodation, not merely tolerance, of all religions, and forbids hostility toward any."[85] Later rulings upheld similar religious displays, especially if they conformed to what observers have labeled the "three plastic animals rule"—if the baby Jesus is surrounded by Rudolph the red-nosed reindeer and other secular symbols, the overall display is considered sufficiently nonreligious to pass constitutional muster.[86] This picture became even more muddled in 2005 when the Court said that the Ten Commandments could not be posted in two Kentucky courthouses, but could be displayed on a monument outside the capitol in Austin, Texas. However, there was some consistency between the seemingly contradictory rulings on the Commandments and the "three plastic animals rule." Justice Breyer noted that Austin's monument was one of forty on the capitol grounds, so the display served a "mixed but primarily non-religious purpose," whereas the Kentucky courthouses' displays were clearly religious.[87]

The Court has also applied the accommodationist perspective to funding for religious schools by looking more favorably on providing tax dollars to students' families to subsidize tuition costs rather than funding the parochial schools directly. For example, a 2002 case upheld an Ohio school voucher program that distributed scholarships to needy students so they could attend the Cleveland school of their choice, including private, religious schools. The Court said the program did not violate the establishment clause because it allowed students and their families "to exercise genuine choice among options public and private, secular and religious."[88] Critics of the decision pointed out that 96 percent of the students participating in the scholarship program were enrolled in religiously affiliated schools, which amounted to state-sponsorship of religious education, something that the Court had not previously allowed. There are several cases in which the Court has approved direct public support for specific programs in religious schools or organizations. One case involved tax-dollar support for a sign language interpreter for a deaf student who attended a parochial school. A deeply divided Court ruled that this was acceptable because the benefit given to the school was minimal. The dissenters pointed out that this was the first time that tax dollars had directly paid for an instructional employee at a religious school.[89] The Court also ruled that it was acceptable to use federal funds to buy computers and other educational equipment to be used in public and private schools for "secular, neutral, and nonideological programs."[90]

Another important case involved a clash between the 1st Amendment's free speech and establishment clauses. The University of Virginia denied a student's request for $5,862 from student fees to fund his Christian newspaper, *Wide Awake*, because of its religious content (despite funding 118 other student organizations with a broad range of views), and the student sued the university for violating his freedom of speech. The Court ruled that free speech concerns trumped possible establishment issues, so that refusing to fund the Christian paper while funding so many others amounted to "viewpoint discrimination." The school was not obligated under the establishment clause to deny funding (as the dissenters claimed) because the student activity fund in question was neutral toward religion.[91]

THE FREE EXERCISE CLAUSE

While the freedom of belief is absolute, freedom of religious conduct cannot be unrestricted. That is, you can believe whatever you want without government interference but if you *act* on those beliefs, the government may regulate your behavior. And while the government has restricted religious conduct in dozens of cases, the freedom of religion has been among the most consistently protected civil liberties.

There is one prominent example of when the Court restricted the free exercise of religion, but then quickly corrected its error. The case concerned the children in a Jehovah's Witness family, twelve-year-old Lillian Gobitis and her ten-year-old brother William, who were kicked out of a public school in Minersville, Pennsylvania, for refusing to recite the Pledge of Allegiance.[92] The children cited Exodus 20:3, "you shall have no other Gods before Me," in explaining why they refused to recite the Pledge and salute the flag. The Court surprised the experts by siding with the school—until, three years later, they reversed course and ruled that the school could not force anyone to say the Pledge, especially when it served no important government interest, such as protecting public safety.[93]

There are literally dozens of different topics and hundreds of cases that have come before the Court in the area of the free exercise of religion. Here are a smattering of the important questions:[94] May Amish parents be forced to send their children to schools beyond the eighth grade? (no); may religion serve as the basis for attaining "conscientious objector" status and avoiding the draft? (generally yes, but with many qualifications); is animal sacrifice as part of a religious ceremony protected by the 1st Amendment? (generally yes); may Christian Scientists be committed to a mental institution and compelled to take drugs? (no); may Mormons have multiple wives? (no); may the Amish be compelled to follow traffic laws and put license plates on their buggies? (yes); may people be forced to work on Friday night and Saturday if those are their days of worship? (no); may a city levy licensing fees that target the selling of religious books? (no); may a city ban or tax door-to-door religious canvassing and proselytizing? (no); does the 1st Amendment protect distributing religious leaflets on public streets? (yes), and religious meetings in public parks? (yes, subject to "time, manner, and place" restrictions); may religious dress be regulated? (generally not, but in some contexts, such as the military, yes); are all prison inmates entitled to hold religious services? (apparently yes, but this is still an open question); and are religious organizations subject to child labor laws? (yes). Whew! Keep in mind, this list is by no means exhaustive.

One case addressing a seemingly minor question ended up having broad implications that defined the general basis for government restrictions of religious expression. The 1990 case addressed whether the state may deny unemployment benefits to someone who is fired for taking illegal drugs as part of a religious ceremony. The plaintiffs practiced a Native American religion in which peyote, a hallucinogenic cactus, is consumed during some services. The Court ruled that the state of Oregon had not violated the free exercise clause in denying unemployment benefits to the plaintiffs because they were fired from their jobs in a drug rehabilitation clinic for using peyote. If the case had ended with this simple ruling, it would be just another example of religious conduct that the government had an interest in regulating (in this case, consuming an illegal drug). The broader significance of the ruling came with the Court's announcement of a new interpretation of the free exercise clause: the government does not need a "compelling interest" in regulating a particular behavior to justify a law that limits a religious practice.[95] In other words, after this decision, it would be easier for the government to limit the exercise of religion because the Court would no longer require a "compelling" reason for the restrictions, just a good one.

The case caused an uproar, and Congress responded by passing the Religious Freedom Restoration Act in 1993, reinstating the need to demonstrate a "compelling state interest" before limiting religious freedoms; the act also specified exceptions to the Controlled Substances Act to allow the use of peyote in religious ceremonies. The Court replied in a 1997 decision that Congress could not usurp its power to define the constitutional protections for religion and that the 1993 law did not apply to the states.[96] Congress wouldn't give up and passed another more narrowly written law, the Religious Land Use and Institutionalized Persons Act, in 2000 that only concerned zoning and the religious rights of people in prisons and government-run mental institutions. Under their power to regulate commerce and control spending, Congress told states that if they accepted federal tax dollars they would have to reinstate the "compelling interest" standard when restricting religious practices in these two areas.

The Supreme Court gave partial support to this law in the context of a case involving the religious freedoms of prison inmates in Ohio, without ruling on some of the underlying questions.[97] The Court also upheld the law in allowing a small religion in New Mexico, União do Vegetal, to use a hallucinogenic tea in their services even though the tea is considered a controlled substance by the federal government. The Court unanimously ruled that the government had not demonstrated a compelling interest in barring the sacramental use of the tea,[98] indicating a shift back toward the stricter standard for justifying limits on religious practice. The struggle between Congress and the Court in defining civil liberties illustrates the importance of the political process. When Congress decides to tackle an important civil liberty such as religious freedom, they can influence outcomes in an area that is usually dominated by the courts.

SECTION SUMMARY

1. The freedom of religion in the United States is protected by the establishment clause and the free exercise clause of the 1st Amendment.

2. In interpreting the establishment clause, the Court has moved from a strict separation between church and state to allowing them to intermingle in many areas.

3. Defining the free exercise clause often involves balancing different interests, illustrating our key idea that politics is conflictual and involves trade-offs.

4. Congress has required that the government show a "compelling interest" in regulating a particular behavior before religious practices may be limited.

The 2nd Amendment:
The Right to Bear Arms

Until recently, the right to bear arms was the only civil liberty that the Supreme Court had played a relatively minor role in defining. Between 1791 when the 2nd Amendment was ratified and 2007, the Court issued only four rulings directly pertaining to the 2nd Amendment. The federal courts had always interpreted the 2nd Amendment's somewhat awkward phrasing—"A well regulated militia, being necessary to the security of a free state, the right of the people to keep and bear arms, shall not be infringed"—as a right to bear arms within the context of serving in a militia, rather than an individual right to own a gun. For example, the Court decided in 1939 that the right to own a sawed-off shotgun was not protected by the 2nd Amendment because it was not related to "the preservation or efficiency of a well regulated militia."[99] In thirty-two instances since the 1939 ruling, appeals courts affirmed this focus on a collective right (in the context of a militia) rather than an individual right to bear arms, recognizing an individual right only twice.[100]

This all changed with the landmark ruling in June 2008 that recognized for the first time an individual right to bear arms for self defense and hunting.[101] The decision struck down the District of Columbia's ban on handguns, while noting that state and local governments could enforce ownership restrictions, such as preventing felons or the mentally impaired from buying guns. The Court did not apply the 2nd Amendment to the states but strongly hinted that subsequent decisions would address that issue. The dissenters in the strongly divided 5–4 decision lamented the Court's activism in reopening a legal question considered settled since 1939 and pointed out that defining the new limits on gun control would require a flood of litigation.

While legal conflict over gun ownership intensified recently, battles over guns have always been intense in the broader political realm.[102] Interest groups such as the National Rifle Association have long asserted that the 2nd Amendment guarantees an individual right to bear arms. Critics of this view emphasize the first clause of the amendment and point to the frequent mentions of state militias in congressional debates at the time the Bill of Rights was adopted. They argue that the 2nd Amendment was adopted to reassure Antifederalist advocates of states' rights that state militias, not a national standing army, would provide national security. In this view, the national armed forces and the National Guard have made the 2nd Amendment obsolete.

Before the Court's recent entry into this debate, Congress and state and local lawmakers had largely defined gun ownership and carrying rights, creating a great deal of variation among the states. Wyoming and Montana have virtually no restrictions on gun ownership, including allowing sales to minors and carrying concealed weapons, whereas California and Connecticut have many ownership restrictions. At the national level, Congress tends to respond to crime waves or high-profile assassinations by passing new gun control laws. One of the first was passed in 1934 in response to the upsurge of organized crime during Prohibition. The broadest federal gun control law, the Gun Control Act of 1968, was passed in the wake of the assassinations of Robert Kennedy and Martin Luther King Jr. and remains in effect today. The law set standards for gun dealers, banned the sale of weapons through the mail, restricted the sale of new machine guns, and included many other provisions.

Following the assassination attempt on President Reagan in 1981, the push for stronger gun control laws intensified, led by the Brady Campaign to Prevent Gun Violence. The head of this group was Sarah Brady, whose husband, James Brady, was Reagan's press secretary and was wounded and disabled in the assassination

▶ *The attempted assassination of President Ronald Reagan by John Hinckley outside the Washington Hilton Hotel prompted calls for stronger gun control laws. Nearly thirteen years later, Congress passed the Brady Bill, which mandated a background check and five-day waiting period before purchasing a handgun. The law was revised in 1998 to require a computerized background check that can usually be done in minutes.*

attempt. It took nearly thirteen years for the campaign to bear fruit, but in 1993 Congress passed and President Clinton signed the Brady Bill, which mandated a background check and a five-day waiting period for any handgun purchase. The next year Congress passed a major crime bill that included a provision banning the sale of nineteen kinds of semi-automatic weapons. This law was allowed to expire in 2004. Given the strong public support for gun ownership—there are about 195 million privately owned guns in the United States—and the Supreme Court's endorsement of an individual right to bear arms, stronger gun control at the national level is essentially dead. However, as noted above, extensive litigation will be necessary to define the acceptable boundaries of gun control and which state and local restrictions will be allowed to stand.

Law, Order, and the Rights of Criminal Defendants

Every advanced democracy protects the rights of people who have been accused of a crime. In the United States, the **due process rights** of the 4th, 5th, 6th, and 8th Amendments include the right to a fair trial, right to a consult a lawyer, freedom from self-incrimination, knowing what crime you are accused of, the right to confront the accuser in court, and freedom from unreasonable police searches, all of which are routinely ignored in nondemocratic countries. But even in the United States, many people support these civil liberties more in the abstract than in practice. For example, most people recognize the value of such principles as "innocent until proven guilty" and agree that the state should have the burden of proving guilt "beyond all reasonable doubt" in a criminal case. Similarly, most people endorse the abstract principle of "due process of law" and general ideas such as requiring that police legally obtain any evidence used in court. However, when the Supreme Court started more aggressively protecting the rights of the accused during the Warren Court years of the late 1950s and early 1960s, there was public outrage. An "Impeach Earl Warren" movement started in part because of rulings seen as "soft on criminals"; his critics believed too many suspects were going free on "legal technicalities," such as having to inform a suspect of his right to talk to an attorney

due process rights The idea that laws and legal proceedings must be fair. The Constitution guarantees that the government cannot take away a person's "life, liberty, or property, without due process of law." Other specific due process rights are found in the 4th, 5th, 6th, and 8th amendments, such as protection from self-incrimination and freedom from illegal searches.

before being questioned by the police. Is this a legal technicality or a fundamental civil liberty? What does it mean to value due process, but reject specific examples of adherence to due process procedures?

The difficulty in applying abstract principles of due process to concrete situations is not a failure of the American public. It *is* hard to define precisely what due process is, especially in a way that protects civil liberties without jeopardizing order. The roots of the idea of due process go all the way back to the Magna Carta of 1215, one of the earliest statements of legal rights, which stated, "No free man shall be taken, outlawed, banished, or in any way destroyed, nor will we proceed against or prosecute him, except by the lawfull [sic] judgement of his peers and by the law of the land." The 5th and 14th Amendments specify that life, liberty and property may not be denied "without the due process of law." In general, this language refers to *procedural* restrictions on what government can do and is based on the idea of fairness and justice. The difficulty comes, of course, in defining what is fair or just. The first aspect of due process discussed in the next section is a perfect example: the 4th Amendment protection against "*unreasonable* searches and seizures."

THE 4TH AMENDMENT: UNREASONABLE SEARCHES AND SEIZURES

The 4th Amendment says, "The right of the people to be secure in their persons, houses, papers, and effects, against unreasonable searches and seizures, shall not be violated." Defining "unreasonable" puts us back in the familiar position of drawing lines and balancing interests. Police searches inherently involve a clash between public safety and the private freedom from government intrusions. These issues came to the fore again with the passage of the USA PATRIOT Act of 2001 after the terrorist attacks of September 11. (The act's name is capitalized this way because it is actually an acronym for "Uniting and Strengthening America by Providing Appropriate Tools Required to Intercept and Obstruct Terrorism.") Several of the most controversial parts of the act strengthen police surveillance powers; make it easier to conduct "sneak and peek" searches (which means that the police enter a home with a warrant, look for evidence, and do not tell the suspect of their search until many months later); broaden Internet surveillance; increase the government's access to library, banking, and medical records; and permit roving wiretaps for suspected terrorists (by which a single warrant legalizes surveillance of all possible forms of communication for that individual). Congress extended the Patriot Act in 2006 with some stronger protections for civil liberties. Temporary provisions of the law are now set to expire at the end of 2009.

Given the abusive practices of the British governors in the colonies, the Founders had strong opinions about the "right of the people to be secure in their persons, houses, papers, and effects." Over the years the Court provided strong protections against searches within a person's physical space, typically defined as his or her home. With the introduction of new technology—first telephones and wiretapping, and then more sophisticated listening and searching devices—the Court had to confront a broad array of complicated questions. The Court has attempted to achieve a balance between security and privacy by requiring court approval for search warrants, while carving out limited exceptions to this general rule. Under most circumstances, a law enforcement official seeking a search warrant must provide the court with "personal

▼ *The USA PATRIOT act strengthened the government's ability to conduct surveillance. This cartoon expresses concern that civil liberties have been weakened to pursue the War on Terror.*

The Politics of Domestic Surveillance

The debate over the trade-off between civil liberties and security intensified early in 2006 when a White House-approved domestic surveillance program was revealed. Since the terrorist attacks of September 11, the National Security Agency (NSA) has been monitoring the phone calls of many U.S. citizens who have had contact with suspected terrorists overseas (thus, the Bush administration's preferred label for the program was "terrorist surveillance" rather than "domestic spying"). These calls were intercepted without the approval of the Foreign Intelligence Surveillance Court, which was created by Congress in 1978 specifically for the purpose of approving the interception of calls. A few months later, another more extensive NSA program aimed at creating a database of every phone call made within the borders of the United States was revealed. Phone companies AT&T, Verizon, and BellSouth were reported to have turned over records of millions of customers' phone calls to the government.[a] Not much is known about the details of these programs, but critics in Congress want to know more.

The NSA is at the center of this controversy. Created during the Korean War in 1952 by President Harry Truman, the agency was initially kept so secret that for many years the government even denied its existence. Insiders joked that the NSA stood for "No Such Agency." Today the NSA is responsible for surveillance that is aimed at national security (while the FBI is in charge of spying related to criminal activity, and the CIA overseas foreign intelligence gathering). The Bush administration argued that their activities were legal and that the appropriate members of Congress had been briefed.

Critics warn that phone surveillance may be the tip of the iceberg as the government may be monitoring travel, credit card, and banking records on a more widespread basis than is commonly believed. Government agencies have previously skirted the restrictions in the Privacy Act of 1974 and the 4th Amendment by purchasing this information from businesses, since the Privacy Act only requires disclosure of how the government is using personal information when the government itself collects the data. The Justice Department, which includes the FBI, spent $19 million in 2005 to purchase commercially gathered data on American citizens according to a report by the Government Accountability Office. These data are then used to search for suspicious patterns of behavior in a process known as data mining.[b]

The debate over domestic surveillance has generated intense disagreement. At one extreme, critics of the surveillance program conjure up images of George Orwell's classic novel *1984* in which Big Brother, a reclusive totalitarian ruler, watches the characters' every move. They see the surveillance as a threat to civil liberties and to our system of checks and balances and separation of powers. By refusing to obtain warrants through the FISA court, the surveillance programs place too much power in the hands of the executive branch to determine what is in the nation's interests. On the other side, supporters of the program argue that getting a court order is too burdensome and may take too long, jeopardizing the surveillance necessary to protect the country. Supporters also are extremely critical of the "leakers" who revealed these programs to journalists, saying that they are helping the terrorists by divulging the U.S. government's tactics. Some members of Congress not only support the ongoing surveillance programs, but want to expand them. James Sensenbrenner (R-WI), the ranking minority member of the House Judiciary Committee, introduced legislation that would require Internet service providers to compile information on their customers' Web-surfing habits to help with government investigations. Executives of companies who failed to comply with the law could be imprisoned for up to one year. This bill was not passed.

"Politics is everywhere" may take on ominous overtones in this case if you are concerned about protecting your civil liberties, or it may provide comforting reassurance if you are more concerned about national security. Either way, this issue will remain significant in your daily life for the foreseeable future.

knowledge" of a "probable cause" of specific criminal activity and outline the evidence that is the target of the search. In other words, broad, general "fishing expeditions" for evidence are not allowed. The exceptional cases in which the Court will allow a warrantless search include:

- A search that happens at the time of a legal arrest and "is confined to the immediate vicinity of the arrest."
- Collecting evidence that was not included in the search warrant but is out in the open in plain view.
- Setting up police roadblocks as long as they stop all drivers, not just those who fit a particular profile.

- Searching containers in cars, if the officer has probable cause to suspect criminal activity. For example, police saw a man drive away from a known drug dealer's apartment after putting a brown paper bag in his trunk that resembled a typical marijuana package. This would give the police grounds, without a warrant, to stop the car and order the suspect to open the trunk and the bag.
- Searching the passenger area of a car if the driver has been stopped for a traffic offense, and passengers may also be searched. Automobiles do not have the same 4th Amendment protections as homes.
- Searches conducted using aerial photography are legal.
- Searching an area where the officer thinks there is either a crime in progress or an "armed and dangerous" suspect.
- Searching school lockers, with probable cause.
- Searching for weapons and/or to prevent the destruction of evidence.[103]

▲ *Drug testing is generally allowed in the workplace and has become increasingly common in professional sports. Star pitcher Roger Clemens testified before the House Oversight and Government Reform Committee hearing on drug use in baseball on February 13, 2008.*

A second set of cases are concerned with figuring out what to do if the police illegally obtain evidence. Here the need to balance security and privacy becomes quite concrete. Either you exclude the evidence from a criminal trial to protect privacy rights, or you allow the evidence to support conviction of the suspect.

In 1961 the 4th Amendment was incorporated (applied to the states through the 14th Amendment) in a case that established the **exclusionary rule** for all courts, which had previously applied only at the national level).[104] The rule states that illegally obtained evidence cannot be used in a criminal trial. In the landmark case, police broke into Dollree Mapp's residence without a warrant looking for a suspect thought to be hiding in the house. The officers did not find him, but in searching the house they found some illegal pornography material, and Mapp was convicted of possessing it. Her lawyer tried to defend her on 1st Amendment grounds, claiming she had the right to own the pornography, but instead the Court used the opportunity to apply the 4th Amendment to the states. The Court threw out Mapp's conviction not because of any right to own the material but because the police did not have a search warrant, arguing that applying the 4th Amendment only to the national government and not the states didn't make any sense: why should a state's attorney be able to use illegally obtained evidence while a federal prosecutor could not? They ruled that in order for the exclusionary rule to deter illegal searches and seizures, it must apply to law enforcement at both state and national levels.

As part of the backlash against the Warren Court decisions that strictly upheld suspects' due process rights, subsequent Courts started weakening the exclusionary rule. The public was concerned that too many criminals were being set free because of the limits on obtaining and using evidence, and a majority of justices agreed. In 1974 the Court allowed use of illegally obtained evidence in grand jury testimony.[105] Several years later it relaxed the general rule to allow the use of evidence if the "totality of circumstances" suggests that the police officer's action was justified.[106] The following year the Court established a "good faith exception" to the exclusionary rule allowing evidence to be used as long as the officer believed that he conducted a legal search. In the specific case, the officer had a warrant that turned out to have errors on it, such as the wrong address.[107] Another case established an exception allowing use of evidence that was initially obtained in an illegal search but subsequently acquired with a valid warrant.[108] The bottom line is that the exclusionary rule remains in effect, but in the last several decades it has become easier for prosecutors to use evidence obtained under questionable circumstances.

Another area of 4th Amendment law concerns drug testing. The clause granting people the right "to be secure in their persons" certainly seems to cover drug testing.

exclusionary rule The principle that illegally or unconstitutionally acquired evidence cannot be used in a criminal trial.

On the other hand, the courts have long recognized the right of private companies to test their employees for illegal drugs, and in professional sports, testing for performance-enhancing drugs is increasingly common. Tour de France winner Floyd Landis was stripped of his title in 2006 after testing positive for artificially elevated testosterone levels, and major league baseball is struggling to rein in steroid use by many of its players, including stars such as Roger Clemens and Barry Bonds. What about drug testing by the state? The Court has upheld random drug testing for high school athletes and mandatory drug testing for any junior high or high school students involved in extracurricular activities.[109] In the case of athletes, proponents of the policy were able to make the case that safety concerns should preclude a 260-pound lineman or pitcher with a 90 miles per hour fastball from using drugs. However, the same arguments could not be made for members of the choir, band, debate club, social dance, or the chess club so this decision was a particularly strong endorsement of schools' anti-drug policies.

Federal employees first became subject to drug testing in 1986, when Ronald Reagan issued an executive order requiring all employees to refrain from using illegal drugs, on or off duty, as a condition of federal employment, and directed each agency to implement drug testing for sensitive positions. Two years later, Congress passed the Drug-Free Workplace Act applying the same rule to all executive agencies, the uniformed services, and any service providers under contract with the federal government. Despite these broad prohibitions, drug testing of federal employees is actually limited to about 400,000 people who hold security clearances, carry firearms, or work in public safety or national security. Some employees receive random tests, while others are tested only when they apply for a job, if they are involved in a workplace accident, or show signs of drug use. Many states have adopted similar drug testing policies,[110] and the Court has upheld drug testing of public employees, with one exception. It struck down a Georgia law that would have required all candidates for state office to pass a drug test within thirty days of announcing a run for office because candidates are not public employees.[111] Rather than appealing to the courts, Sen. Ernest Hollings of South Carolina had a different approach to avoid drug testing. When his opponent, Rep. Tommy Hartnett, challenged him to take a drug test, the senator shot back, "I'll take a drug test if you take an I.Q. test."

POLITICAL PROCESS MATTERS

Individuals have general privacy rights, but the government can require drug testing in certain circumstances involving public safety, in schools, and for public employees.

THE 5TH AMENDMENT: SELF-INCRIMINATION

The familiar phrase "I plead the 5th" has been part of our criminal justice system since the Bill of Rights was ratified, ensuring that a suspect cannot be compelled to provide court testimony that would cause her to be prosecuted for a crime. However, what about outside a court of law? If a police officer coerces a confession out of a suspect, does that amount to self-incrimination? Such police interrogations were allowed until a landmark case in 1966. Ernesto Miranda had been convicted in an Arizona court of kidnapping and rape, on the basis of a confession extracted after two hours of questioning in which he was not read his rights. The Court overturned the conviction, saying that a police interrogation "is inherently intimidating" and in these circumstances, "no statement obtained from the defendant can truly be the product of his free choice."[112] To make sure a confession is truly a free choice, the Court came up with the well-known Miranda rights described in Nuts and Bolts 4.4. If police do not read the suspect these rights, nothing the suspect says can be used in court.

Miranda rights The list of civil liberties described in the 5th Amendment that must be read to a suspect before anything the suspect says can be used in a trial.

Just as we saw with the exclusionary rule about illegally obtained evidence, the Court has carved out exceptions to the Miranda rights requirement because the practice was viewed by the public as "coddling criminals" and letting too many people go free on legal technicalities. In one case, police failed to read a suspect his Miranda rights until after frisking him, finding an empty holster, and asking him where his gun was. The suspect led police to a gun. The lower court dismissed the charges because the gun had been used as incriminating evidence in the trial, but the Supreme Court reinstated the conviction saying, "concern for public safety must be paramount to adherence to the literal language of the Miranda rule."[113] A second case created an "inevitable discovery" exception to the Miranda rule. In this case, a murder suspect who had been read his rights and had consulted with his lawyer, who advised him not to answer any questions until the lawyer was present. While taking the suspect to meet with his lawyer, the detectives in the squad car appealed to the suspect's conscience, saying that the "parents of this little girl should be entitled to a Christian burial for the little girl who was snatched away from them on Christmas [E]ve and murdered."[114] After thinking about it, he led them to the body. The Court said that did not violate the Miranda rule because a search party of 200 people was already in the vicinity of the body and would have found it anyway. While the Court has been willing to carve out limited exceptions to the Miranda rule, in 2000 the Court rejected Congress's attempt to overturn *Miranda* by designating all voluntary confessions as legally admissible evidence; the Court ruled that it, and not Congress, had the power to determine Constitutional protections for criminal defendants. They also affirmed their intent to protect the Miranda rule, saying, "*Miranda* has become embedded in routine police practice to the point where the warnings have become part of our national culture."[115]

Another 5th Amendment protection for defendants is preventing people from being tried more than once for a particular crime, a circumstance known as **double jeopardy** because the suspect is "twice put in jeopardy of life or limb" for a single offence. This prohibition was extended to the states in 1969.[116] However, prosecutors can exploit two loopholes in this civil liberty: (1) a suspect may be tried in federal

double jeopardy Being tried twice for the same crime. This is prevented by the 5th Amendment.

POLITICS IS EVERYWHERE

The 5th Amendment Miranda rights are among the most well-known civil liberties because they are read every time someone is taken into police custody.

NUTS AND BOLTS

4.4

The Miranda Warning

This is a typical example of the card that police officers carry with them and read to a suspect after an arrest.

DEFENDANT	LOCATION

SPECIFIC WARNING REGARDING INTERROGATIONS

1. YOU HAVE THE RIGHT TO REMAIN SILENT.

2. ANYTHING YOU SAY CAN AND WILL BE USED AGAINST YOU IN A COURT OF LAW.

3. YOU HAVE THE RIGHT TO TALK TO A LAWYER AND HAVE HIM PRESENT WITH YOU WHILE YOU ARE BEING QUESTIONED.

4. IF YOU CANNOT AFFORD TO HIRE A LAWYER ONE WILL BE APPOINTED TO REPRESENT YOU BEFORE ANY QUESTIONING, IF YOU WISH ONE.

SIGNATURE OF DEFENDANT	DATE
WITNESS	TIME

☐ REFUSED SIGNATURE   SAN FRANCISCO POLICE DEPARTMENT   PR.9.1.4

Property Rights, "Takings," and the 5th Amendment

Anyone who has watched television courtroom dramas is familiar with the phrase "I plead the 5th," which refers to the 5th Amendment's protection against self-incrimination. Another part of the amendment that is not well known is at the heart of a hot legal debate over property rights; the clause says, "nor shall private property be taken for public use, without just compensation." For most of American history, this civil liberty has been noncontroversial. When the government needs private property for a public use such as building a highway or a park, the 5th Amendment states that it may take the property by the practice of eminent domain, but it must pay the property owner the fair market value. This bit of conventional wisdom has never been challenged.

A new, controversial interpretation of the 5th Amendment's "takings" clause has attempted to expand the principle of just compensation to cover not only "physical takings," but also "regulatory takings." For example, if the Endangered Species Act protects an animal whose habitat is on your land, you would not be able to develop that property. Thus, its market value would probably be lower than if the endangered species did not live on your land. Therefore, the argument goes, because of this law the government has "taken" some of the value of your land by legally protecting the species, so it should compensate you for your loss.

One key Court case decided that if a regulation "deprives a property owner of all beneficial use of his property," the owner must receive compensation. This case involved a man who bought two residential lots on the Isle of Palms, a South Carolina barrier island. His plan was to build single-family homes on the lots, but shortly after his purchase the state legislature enacted a law banning "permanent habitable structures" on this part of the barrier islands to prevent further erosion and destruction of the vulnerable land. The owner sued in state court and won a large monetary judgment, and the Supreme Court upheld this ruling.[a] Another case concerned a takings claim based on a regulation that limited

▲ Greenpeace activists chained themselves to bulldozers and set up roadblocks in Alaska's Tongass National Forest to call attention to logging of old-growth forests. Logging is forbidden if it threatens endangered species, raising questions about whether the economic loss this causes should be compensated under the takings clause of the 5th Amendment.

development in a coastal wetlands area in Rhode Island. Here the key legal issue was whether it mattered that the regulation was on the books *before* the plaintiff purchased the land. In a divisive 5–4 ruling, the Court said that a regulatory takings claim could still be made despite the argument that market forces would have already factored in the regulatory loss.[b]

A more controversial interpretation of the 5th Amendment challenges a long-standing practice of deferring to elected leaders' decisions about government takings of privately owned land for public use (of course, with compensation). This new challenge to the conventional wisdom urges the Court to prohibit certain takings, even with compensation, if they do not meet a more narrow definition of public use than the previous standard of "plausible public use." The issue was raised in a case involving a development project in New London, Connecticut, in which a ninety-acre working-class neighborhood would be sold to a private developer with a ninety-nine-year lease, to build a waterfront hotel, office space, and higher-end housing. One home owner sued the city to stop the development, saying that she shouldn't have to sell her home just because the city wants to develop the area, because transferring property from one private owner to another is not "public use." However, the Court ruled in a 5–4 decision that these issues should be decided by the

local government rather than the Court. Justice Stevens noted that "promoting economic development is a traditional and long accepted function of government" so a "plausible public use" is satisfied. Justice O'Connor wrote a strong dissent, saying that the "specter of condemnation hangs over all property. Nothing is to prevent the State from replacing any Motel 6 with a Ritz-Carlton, any home with a shopping mall, or any farm with a factory."[c]

These property rights cases reflect the broader "Constitution in Exile" movement that would like to return Constitutional interpretation to the pre-New Deal era in which Congress's power to regulate commerce through laws and regulations was much more restricted.[d] By expanding the definition of regulatory taking, it would make it much more expensive to pass many laws, because any time a public policy imposed a cost on someone—say an employer who had to pay a higher wage—that person would have to be compensated. Therefore, it would likely become impossible to maintain a broad range of social and environmental legislation, including parts of the Clean Air Act, Clean Water Act, rent control, workplace safety regulations, and even minimum wage laws and Social Security if the argument is taken to its logical extreme. In this area the stakes in debating the conventional wisdom are much higher than in a typical academic dispute. ■

court and state court for the same crime, and (2) if a suspect is found innocent of one set of *criminal* charges brought by the state, he or she may still be found guilty of the same or closely related offenses based on *civil* charges brought by a private individual. Usually these loopholes are exploited only in high-profile cases in which there is public or political pressure to get a conviction. For example in 1992, four Los Angeles police officers were acquitted of beating Rodney King, a driver they had chased for speeding. Before the trial, a bystander's video of the beating had been widely broadcast, and at news of the acquittal massive riots broke out. More than 2,000 people were hurt, about sixty killed, more than a thousand buildings were destroyed, and Los Angeles saw about $1 billion in property damage over three days. Responding to political pressure, President George H. W. Bush urged federal prosecutors to retry the officers not for the *criminal* use of excessive force but for violating Rodney King's *civil* rights (two were found guilty and two were acquitted). A similar pattern of prosecution followed in the trial of football star O. J. Simpson for the murder of his wife and her friend. Simpson was acquitted of first-degree murder, but found guilty on civil charges brought by victims' families.

THE 6TH AMENDMENT: THE RIGHT TO LEGAL COUNSEL AND A JURY TRIAL

One of the key civil liberties when it comes to criminal law is the right to an attorney because the legal system is too complicated for a layperson to navigate. An old expression among lawyers is, "Only a fool has himself for a client." However, until 1963 poor people were required to defend themselves in court if accused of a felony because those who could not pay did not have a right to an attorney (except in cases involving the death penalty).[117] This changed in one of the most celebrated cases in U.S. history, *Gideon v. Wainwright*. Clarence Gideon was accused of breaking into a pool hall and stealing beer, wine, and money from a vending machine. He could not afford an attorney, so he tried to defend himself. He did a pretty good job— calling witnesses, cross-examining the prosecutor's witnesses, and providing a good summary argument. However, he was convicted and sentenced to five years in jail, based largely on the testimony of the person who turned out to be the guilty party. The Court unanimously overturned his conviction saying, "in our adversary system of criminal justice, any person hailed into court who is too poor to hire a lawyer cannot be assured a fair trial unless counsel is provided for him."[118]

Unlike the exclusionary rule and the protection against self-incrimination, the right to an attorney has been strengthened over time, both through legislation and subsequent Court rulings. One year after *Gideon*, Congress passed the Criminal Justice Act that provided better legal representation for criminal defendants in federal court, and within two years twenty-three states had taken similar action. The Court has defined a general right to *effective* counsel and more recently mandated that defense attorneys must conduct any reasonable investigation into possible lines of defense when presenting evidence that could help the defendant.[119]

The 6th Amendment also protects the right to a speedy and public trial by an impartial jury in criminal cases. The Court affirmed the right to a speedy trial in 1967,[120] and in 1974 Congress strengthened the protection of this right when they passed, and then amended in 1979, the Federal Speedy Trial Act. The law requires that a trial begin within seventy days of the defendant's arrest or first appearance in court. This law was further strengthened by a more recent Court decision stating that a defendant may not waive the right to a speedy trial.[121] The most important legal disputes over the other key 6th Amendment issue, defining an "impartial jury," concern the process of jury selection and peremptory challenges, in which lawyers from each side are allowed to eliminate a certain number of people from the jury pool without providing any reason. Specifically, the Court has ruled that race and gender may not be the basis for a peremptory challenge.[122]

THE 8TH AMENDMENT: CRUEL AND UNUSUAL PUNISHMENT

The Founders would be surprised by the intense debates over whether the 8th Amendment prohibition against "cruel and unusual punishment" applies to the death penalty. Clearly, the death penalty was accepted in their time (even stealing a horse was a capital offense!) and the language of the Constitution reflects that. Both the 5th and 14th Amendments says that a person may not be "deprived of life, liberty or property without the due process of laws," which implies that someone *could* be deprived of life as long as the state follows due process. The death penalty remains popular in the United States, with support from about two-thirds of the public, and thirty-six states still allow capital punishment. However, times change, and in the past decade, dozens of countries have abolished the death penalty (see Comparing Ourselves to Others).

The Supreme Court remained silent in the death penalty debate for nearly two centuries. But then in 1972, in one of the longest opinions in its history (243 pages), the Court said that the death penalty was unconstitutional because the process of applying it was far too inconsistent (two justices held that capital punishment was always "cruel and unusual" while three others took this more procedural position). Congress and thirty-five states rushed to make their laws compliant with the Court decision. The typical fix was to say more explicitly which crimes were punishable by death and to make capital sentencing a two-step process: first the determination of guilt or innocence and then a separate sentencing phase if the suspect was found guilty. Four years later, the Court approved these changes and allowed states to bring back the death penalty.[123]

While never challenging the basic constitutionality of the death penalty, the Court has chipped away at its edges for the past two decades. The Court struck down state laws that mandated the death penalty in murder cases and another law requiring a death sentence for rape, prohibited the execution of insane prisoners, and then abolished the death penalty for the mildly retarded (2002), for juveniles under the age of eighteen (2005), and for child rapists (2008).[124] The ruling on juveniles canceled the death sentences of seventy-three people for crimes committed before age eighteen, changing them to sentences of life in prison.

These recent cases have shown that the Court responds to public opinion and political changes (this is sometimes called the "living constitution" perspective, as discussed in Chapter 13). In his opinion in the juvenile death penalty case, Justice Anthony Kennedy noted that thirty states forbid the death penalty for offenders younger than eighteen, which was an increase of five states since the court upheld the juvenile death penalty in 1989. Similarly, the number of states banning the death penalty for the mildly retarded grew from fourteen in 1989 (when the practice was upheld) to twenty-five in 2002 (when it was struck down). One observer noted that the Court shows sensitivity to the " 'evolving standards of decency that mark the progress of a maturing society,' and looks to state legislation and jury verdicts to decide whether a 'national consensus' has developed against a previously accepted practice."[125]

However, in 2008, the Court signalled that there were limits on how far they would go to restrict the death penalty, ruling that execution by lethal injection was not necessarily "cruel and unusual punishment."[126] The Court also rejected a

Are Our Civil Liberties Outside the Mainstream?

The United States prides itself on its strong protection for individual liberties and freedom, and in many instances that pride is well-deserved. Our protections for the freedom of speech, freedom of the press, free exercise of religious beliefs, and criminal defendant rights are among the strongest in the world. So for most civil liberties, we may be outside the mainstream, but that's a good thing.

However, the United States is outside the global mainstream on the side of restricting civil liberties when it comes to the death penalty. As of early in 2005, eighty-five nations have abolished the death penalty for all crimes, eleven countries only have the death penalties for exceptional crimes such as treason during wartime, and twenty-four countries have abolished the death penalty in practice (the law is still on the books, but these countries have had no executions in at least ten years). Japan is the only other developed nation that has maintained the death penalty. In contrast, the death penalty is still used China, Cuba, Liberia, Lybia, North Korea, Saudi Arabia, Sudan, Syria, Uganda, Vietnam, and Yemen. This is not a line-up of countries with which the United States is usually associated; indeed, these are some of the worst human rights violators in the world.

In March 2005, the Supreme Court took note of the United State's international standing in overturning a sixteen-year-old precedent that allowed the execution of minors. The case involved Christopher Simmons, who, at the age of seventeen, murdered a woman by tying her up with electrical wire,

▲ Christopher Simmons was removed from death row when the Supreme Court ruled that executing people who were convicted as juveniles is not permitted under the 8th Amendment.

wrapping her head with duct tape, and throwing her off a bridge into a river. He was tried and sentenced to death as an adult under Missouri law. The Missouri Supreme Court overturned the sentence, and the Court upheld their ruling, saying that the decision "finds confirmation in the stark reality that the United States is the only country in the world that continues to give official sanction to the juvenile death penalty."[a] One Court observer noted that, "For the Supreme Court itself, perhaps the most significant effect of yesterday's decision is to reaffirm the role of international law in constitutional interpretation."[b] The European Union, human right lawyers from Great Britain, and several Nobel Peace Prize winners had filed briefs urging the Court to strike down the juvenile death penalty. The majority opinion recognized this expression of international opinion, saying that it "provide[s] respected and significant confirmation for our own

conclusions."[c] The three dissenters, led by Justice Scalia, strongly objected to the role played by international opinion. They criticized the majority for "proclaim[ing] itself sole arbiter of our Nation's moral standards—and in the course of discharging that awesome responsibility purport[ing] to take guidance from the views of foreign courts and legislatures." Scalia also chastised the majority for selectively paying attention to international opinion, while ignoring it on other issues (such as abortion). "To invoke alien law when it agrees with one's own thinking, and ignore it otherwise, is not reasoned decisionmaking," he thundered, "but sophistry."[d]

Conservatives in Congress were also outraged that a Court decision would give such weight to international law and opinion, and several have introduced legislation that would ban such practices. Scalia rose to defend his institution, essentially telling Congress to back off. "It's none of your business," he told Congress. "No one is more opposed to the use of foreign law than I am, but I'm darned if I think it's up to Congress to direct the Court how to make its decisions." He went on to say that the proposed legislation, "is like telling us not to use certain principles of logic. Let us make our mistakes just as we let you make yours."[e]

Whether the United States Supreme Court should pay attention to international opinion and law is certainly a matter of debate. However, it illustrates the importance of "comparing ourselves to others" and being aware of how our political system may be in step with or outside of the mainstream. ■

significant challenge to the constitutionality of the death penalty in a case concerning racial bias in capital punishment. Extensive research has demonstrated that the death penalty is applied with a bias based on the *race of the victim* rather than the race of the murderer. Someone who kills a white person is much more likely to be sentenced to death than someone who kills a black person. One study by a University of Iowa law professor found that even considering 230 variables that could explain the sentencing outcomes on nonracial grounds (such as whether a police officer was killed, whether rape and kidnapping were part of the murder, etc.), disparities based on the victim's race were huge. In Florida, a black man was thirty-seven times more likely to be sentenced to death for killing a white person than for killing a black person. In Georgia, the disparity was thirty-three to one and in Texas eighty-four to one. Overall, 22 percent of the murder cases involving black defendants and white victims yielded a death sentence, compared to 8 percent of cases involving white defendants and white victims, 1 percent of cases involving black defendants and black victims, and 3 percent of cases involving white defendants and black victims. However, the Court ruled that in order to overturn a death sentence, evidence of racial bias had to be specific to the case at hand rather than a general statistical pattern, so it rejected the argument that the death penalty's racial bias made it unconstitutional.[127] The House of Representatives responded to this decision by passing the Racial Justice Act in 1994 to address racial disparities in capital sentencing, but the provision was taken out of the final version of the bill when the Senate objected.[128]

SECTION SUMMARY

1. The civil liberties described in this section are central to defining the nature of our adversarial legal system.
2. The Constitution protects the accused's right to the due process of law, including freedom from unreasonable police searches, the right to a fair trial, right to a consult a lawyer, freedom from self-incrimination and from being tried twice for the same crime, the right to know what crime you are accused of and to confront the accuser in court, and freedom from cruel and unusual punishment.
3. These civil liberties, like all others, are continually evolving as the courts and Congress respond to different political forces.

Privacy Rights

You may be surprised to learn that there are no explicit **privacy rights** in the Constitution. The right was first developed in a 1965 case that questioned the constitutionality of an 1879 Connecticut law against using birth control. Estelle Griswold, the director of Planned Parenthood in Connecticut, was arrested nine days after opening a clinic that dispensed contraceptives. She was fined $100 and appealed her conviction. Though she lost in state court, she appealed all the way to the Supreme Court, which overturned her conviction. In a very fractured decision (there were six different opinions), the Court agreed the law was outdated—even the dissenters called it an "an uncommonly silly law" that was "obviously unenforceable"—but the justices agreed on little else. Even those who based their opinions on an implied constitutional right to privacy cited various constitutional roots. Justice Douglas wrote the main opinion, but his reasoning was endorsed in its entirety by only one

privacy rights Liberties protected by several amendments in the Bill of Rights that shield certain personal aspects of citizens' lives from governmental interference, such as the 4th Amendment's protection against unreasonable searches and seizures.

other justice. Douglas argued that the "penumbras" (the surrounding fringes or shadows) of the Bill of Rights create "zones of privacy." Specifically, he found privacy implicit in the 1st Amendment right of association, the 3rd's protection against the quartering of troops, the 4th's prohibition against unreasonable searches and seizures, the 5th's protection against self-incrimination, and in the 9th's catch-all statement, "The enumeration of rights in the Constitution shall not be construed to deny or disparage others retained by the people."[129] These all seem like pretty reasonable grounds for implicit privacy rights except the 1st Amendment right of association—since the Founders clearly meant political association, not an association with your spouse in bed.

The Griswold case was significant for establishing the constitutional basis for a right to privacy, but the dissenters in the case were concerned about where this right would lead. Justice Black warned that privacy "is a broad, abstract and ambiguous concept" that can be shrunken or expanded in subsequent decisions. He said that Douglas's argument required

> judges to determine what is or is not constitutional on the basis of their own appraisal of what laws are unwise or unnecessary. The power to make such decisions is of course that of a legislative body. Surely it has to be admitted that no provision of the Constitution specifically gives such blanket power to courts to exercise such a supervisory veto over the wisdom and value of legislative policies and to hold unconstitutional those laws which they believe unwise or dangerous.[130]

Justice Black's prediction came true eight years later in the landmark ruling in *Roe v. Wade*, which struck down laws in forty-six states that limited abortion. Twelve of those states allowed abortions for pregnancies due to rape or incest, to protect the life of the mother, and in cases of severe fetal handicap. The much-criticized trimester analysis in the *Roe* ruling said that states could not limit abortions in the first trimester; in the second trimester, states could regulate abortions in the interests of the health of the mother; and in the third trimester, states could forbid all abortions except those necessary to protect the health or life of the mother. The justices cited a constitutional basis for abortion rights in the general right to privacy outlined in *Griswold*, the concept of "personal liberty" in the 14th Amendment's due process clause; and the "rights reserved to the people" by the 9th Amendment.[131] Subsequent decisions have upheld *Roe* but endorsed various state restrictions on abortion, such as requiring parental consent, a waiting period, or counseling sessions aimed at convincing the woman not to have an abortion.[132] Since *Roe*, most political action concerning abortion has taken place in the courts, but that could all change if the Supreme Court overturns this decision. Such a possibility became more likely when Justice Sandra Day O'Connor retired from the Court in 2006 and was replaced by Justice Samuel Alito. For example, in 2007 Alito voted to uphold a national ban on "partial-birth abortion" while O'Connor had previously voted to strike down a similar law.[133] Opponents of abortion are hoping that *Roe* will be overturned, which would shift the politics of abortion back to state legislatures and make it an even more contested political issue.

Privacy rights have also become central in debates over the right to die, in which two types of political issues have been hotly debated. The first involves the right of a person who is brain dead or in a persistent vegetative state to refuse medical treatment so he may die. Courts have approved living wills in which a person can document his or wishes in

▼ Privacy rights are not clearly articulated in the Constitution, but the federal courts are increasingly asked to rule on questions concerning intensely personal decisions such as abortion and the right to die. Terri Schiavo's case drew national attention in 2005 when her husband and her parents disagreed about whether she should be removed from life support after living in a vegetative state for fifteen years.

advance about end-of-life medical care. The problem comes when a person who can no longer communicate has not left instructions on how much medical intervention they should receive. Thousands of families every month have to make these decisions during the last few weeks of a patient's life, in consultation with their doctors. Most of the time the decisions are extremely difficult but without legal conflict. The high-profile case of Terri Schiavo illustrated how complicated these issues can get. After a heart failure that resulted in severe brain damage, Schiavo remained in a persistent vegetative state for fifteen years. Her husband, Michael, said she would not have wanted to be kept alive in that condition, but Schiavo's parents wanted to do everything possible to keep her alive. After the federal courts refused to intervene, she was taken off life support at her husband's request. Given this precedent, the courts seem unlikely to get involved in matters traditionally resolved between a family and their doctor.

The second right to die issue is more complicated. May states allow assisted suicide for people with terminal illnesses even if that practice conflicts with federal law? The case involved Oregon's Death with Dignity Act, discussed in Chapter 3, which allows a terminally ill patient to get a prescription from their doctor to end their life. The law was approved twice by the state's voters (first by a 51–49 margin in 1994 and then by a 60–40 margin in 1997, when it went into effect). In the law's first seven years, 166 people ended their lives through this procedure.[134] Oregon is the only state with such a law, and it has been highly controversial; Attorney General John Ashcroft attempted to revoke the medical licenses of doctors who prescribed the drugs. According to Ashcroft's interpretation of the federal Controlled Substances Act, use of prescription drugs in doctor-assisted suicide is not a "legitimate medical purpose" of the drugs, and therefore not allowed under the law. However, the Supreme Court upheld the Oregon law in a recent case, ruling that the attorney general should not be given the "extraordinary authority" to "criminalize even the actions of registered physicians, whenever they engage in conduct he deems illegitimate."[135]

POLITICS IS CONFLICTUAL

The Supreme Court's decisions concerning abortion and the right to die have been among its most controversial rulings. The conflict over the Court's abortion rulings has spread throughout partisan and electoral politics.

SECTION SUMMARY

1. There is no explicit privacy right in the Constitution, but the Court has cited implied privacy protections in their rulings allowing access to birth control, abortion rights, and the right to die.
2. If the Supreme Court overruled *Roe v. Wade,* the controversial decision protecting the right to an abortion, political debates over abortion laws would instead play out in the state legislatures.
3. Political and legal debates also rage concerning the right to privacy and the need for government surveillance in the War on Terror.

Conclusion

There probably isn't a day that goes by in which you are not affected in some way by your civil liberties. Speaking in a public place, going to church, being searched at an airport, participating in a political demonstration, writing or reading an article in your school newspaper, being free from illegal police searches in your home, and all of the due process protections that you have if you ever are accused of a crime (we hope *that* part doesn't happen very often!). Because civil liberties are defined as those things that the government *cannot* do to us, defining our civil liberties is a political process. Often this process is confined to the courts, but on many issues, including free speech, freedom of the press, pornography, criminal rights, abortion and gun control, these debates take place in the broader political world where defining civil liberties involves balancing competing ideals and interest and drawing lines by interpreting and applying the law. To return to the example of the introduction, how should we balance national security and personal liberties? Debates over the boundaries of these freedoms—whether newspapers should publish stories about classified programs that may threaten civil liberties; whether government surveillance powers should be strengthened to fight terrorism—will rage for years to come. As with all political questions, there are no easy answers. These continually evolving liberties lie at the core of our political system.

CRITICAL THINKING

1. What is the proper balance between national security and civil liberties? Is it appropriate to restrict civil liberties during a time of war? If so, how much? And if not, why?
2. Do you support complete freedom of speech for the most despicable group you can think of? When should speech be limited, if at all?
3. Has the Supreme Court balanced protection for the free exercise of religion without allowing the state establishment of religion, or have they swung too far in one direction? Which rulings support your conclusion?
4. Do you support due process rights for defendants in criminal cases, even if this means that some potentially guilty people go free? If so, why? If not, are you concerned about convicting innocent people?

KEY TERMS

civil liberties (p. 100)
Civil War Amendments (p. 106)
clear and present danger test (p. 112)
commercial speech (p. 118)
direct incitement test (p. 113)
double jeopardy (p. 131)
due process clause (p. 107)
due process rights (p. 126)
establishment clause (p. 120)
exclusionary rule (p. 129)
fighting words (p. 117)
free exercise clause (p. 120)
gag order (p. 116)
hate speech (p. 114)
Lemon test (p. 121)
libel (p. 118)
Miller test (p. 119)
Miranda rights (p. 130)
prior restraint (p. 116)
privacy rights (p. 136)
selective incorporation (p. 109)
slander (p. 118)
symbolic speech (p. 113)

SUGGESTED READING

Abraham, Henry J. and Barbara A. Perry. *Freedom and the Court: Civil Rights and Liberties in the United States*, 8th ed. Lawrence, KS: University Press of Kansas, 2003.

Amar, Akhil Reed. *The Bill of Rights*. New Haven, CT: Yale University Press, 1998.

Lewis, Anthony. *Gideon's Trumpet*. New York: Random House, 1964.

Moynihan, Daniel Patrick. *Secrecy: The American Experience*. New Haven, CT: Yale University Press, 1998.

Posner, Richard A. *Not a Suicide Pact: The Constitution in a Time of National Emergency*. New York: Oxford University Press, 2006.

Pritchett, C. Herman. *Constitutional Civil Liberties*. Englewood Cliffs, NJ: Prentice Hall, 1984.

Schweber, Howard. *Speech, Conduct, and the First Amendment*. New York: Peter Lang Publishing, 2003.

PUBLIC OPINION

Most Americans have only a minor interest in politics and public policy. And yet, the fundamental assumption of democracy is that citizens have an idea of what they want government to do, and incorporate this information into their voting decisions about many complex issues. How can voters form valid opinions—with some basis in fact—to guide their behavior?

The short answer is that the political knowledge of the average American may surprise you. Consider Figure 5.1 on the next page, which shows data from the Pew Trust's surveys between 2003 and 2008 on the percentage of Americans who believed that the war in Iraq was going "very well" or "well," which has trended downward since the invasion and overthrow of Saddam Hussein's government. However, opinions have shifted in response to events. The percentage of people believing that the war was going well increased after the capture of Saddam Hussein and decreased in months when American casualties were high, as well as after publication of pictures showing American troops abusing prisoners. This percentage increased again after the 2007 "surge" of additional American troops and the resulting decrease in insurgent attacks. As this decrease continued through the summer and fall of 2008, public evaluations of the war gradually became more positive, although they never reached the levels of optimism seen during 2003.

The figure also suggests the political consequences of these opinions. At the time George Bush ran for reelection in 2004, a slim majority of Americans believed that the war was going well. However, by November 2006, that group had shrunk to only about 30 percent, and many Republican representatives and senators who had strongly supported the war lost their races for reelection. One argument about these elections is that many Americans voted for Democratic congressional candidates *because* they opposed the war in Iraq.[1] This conclusion makes sense only if most Americans held opinions about the war that shaped their voting decisions.

While this example may suggest that Americans know something about political events, and their opinions can influence elections, the war in Iraq has been an unusually dominant issue in American politics and media coverage in the last several years, and will likely remain so for years to come. Is public opinion on Iraq the exception or the rule in American politics?

In every election, candidates, political parties, journalists, and political scientists take thousands of polls. For the politicians and their allies, these polls are aimed at

FIGURE 5.1   PUBLIC OPINION ON THE WAR IN IRAQ

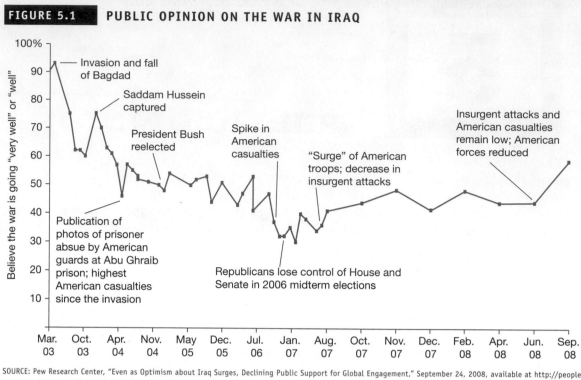

SOURCE: Pew Research Center, "Even as Optimism about Iraq Surges, Declining Public Support for Global Engagement," September 24, 2008, available at http://people-press.org/reports/pdf/453.pdf.

determining who is likely to vote; what sorts of arguments, slogans, and platforms would find favor with these voters; and which candidates are likely to win. News organizations, foundations, political scientists, and others conduct polls addressing these same questions, as well as where these opinions and preferences come from.[2] And yet some scholars have argued that most Americans make up their responses to survey questions, have no firm opinions about government policy, and are easily swayed by candidates, advocacy groups, or the media.[3]

In contrast, this chapter shows that Americans really do hold measurable opinions on a wide range of topics, and these opinions shape their political behavior. We examine the sources of public opinion from everyday events to what politicians say and do, as well as group characteristics such as race, gender, and ethnicity. Finally, we will see how politicians take account of public opinion—how their campaign strategies, as well as their actions in office, are shaped by information about what the public wants or might want in the future. As you will see, process matters: the way individual opinions are formed and the tools used to measure public opinion shape what people demand from government and how politicians respond to those demands.

Studying public opinion reveals a new angle on the idea that politics is everywhere. That is, most Americans are not policy experts, but people do tend to think about politics the same way they think about most things in their lives. Aside from a few broad principles, such as party identification, that are typically formed early in life, opinions take form only when they are needed, such as when people vote on Election Day or answer a survey question.

Finally, opinion data show that Americans disagree about government policy. Examining American public opinion allows us to describe these disagreements in detail and better understand the political conflicts they raise. Perhaps surprisingly, we will also see that while Americans disagree about some important issues, *profound* polarization is relatively rare. On a wide range of policy questions, most Americans hold opinions that are squarely in the middle of the political spectrum.

What Is Public Opinion?

public opinion Citizens' views on politics and government actions.

Public opinion describes what the population thinks about politics and government—what government should be doing, evaluations of what government *is* doing, and judgments about elected officials and others who participate in the political process, as well as the wider set of beliefs that shape these opinions.

Public opinion matters for three reasons. First, citizens' political actions—including voting, contributing to campaigns, writing letters to senators, and other kinds of activism—are driven by their opinions.[4] For example, as we discuss in more detail in Chapter 7, party identification shapes voting decisions. A voter who thinks of herself as a Democrat is more likely to vote for Democratic candidates compared to a voter who identifies as a Republican.[5] Similarly, a voter who believes in small government would likely oppose new programs such as the Medicare Prescription Drug Benefit enacted in 2003. Therefore, if we want to explain either an individual's behavior or broader political outcomes, such as who wins an election or the fate of a legislative proposal, we need good data on public opinion.

The second reason for examining public opinion is to explain the behavior of candidates, political parties, and other political actors. Other chapters in this book, particularly Chapter 8, Elections, and Chapter 10, Congress, show that the link between citizens' opinions and candidates' campaign strategies and actions in office is very strong. Politicians look to public opinion to determine what citizens want them to do, and to determine how happy citizens are with their behavior in office. For example, in Chapter 10 we will see how the opinions of ordinary citizens exert a strong influence on the ways that their representatives in the House and Senate choose to vote. Legislators are reluctant to cast votes that are inconsistent with what their constituents want, especially on issues that constituents consider important. Therefore, to explain a legislator's votes, you need to begin with data on constituents' opinions.

POLITICS IS CONFLICTUAL

Differences in what people want—their opinions, beliefs, and preferences—drive their political behavior.

Third, because public opinion plays a key role in understanding what motivates both citizens and political officials, it can also shed light on the reasons for specific policy outcomes. For example, changes in the policy mood—the public's demand for new policies—are linked to changes in government spending.[6] When people want government to do more, spending increases faster; when people want less from the government, spending goes down (or increases more slowly). Thus, to explain what government does and why, we need to measure and understand public opinion.

Calvin and Hobbes   by Bill Watterson

▲ Politicians read public opinion polls closely to gauge whether their behavior will anger or please constituents. Few politicians always follow survey results—but virtually none would agree with Calvin's father that polls should be ignored entirely.

THE POLITICAL SCIENCE OF PUBLIC OPINION

level of conceptualization The amount of complexity in an individual's beliefs about government and policy, and the extent to which those beliefs are consistent with each other and remain consistent over time.

Though it may sound strange, early studies of public opinion, based on surveys conducted during the 1950s, found little evidence that the public's political opinions existed at all.[7] The surveys revealed high levels of inconsistency; many people expressed liberal responses to some questions and conservative responses to others. Responses also varied across time: many people who said in one survey that they favored an activist government switched to favoring a limited government when asked two years later. Few respondents could say why they liked a particular candidate, or why they were conservative, liberal, or moderate. Americans also had low levels of factual information, such as knowing which party held majorities in the House and Senate. One author estimated that up to 70 percent of survey respondents were either completely making up their responses—in other words, they answered more or less at random—and were unable to say anything meaningful. As he put it, "large portions of the electorate do not have meaningful beliefs, even on issues that have formed the basis for intense political controversy among elites for substantial periods of time."[8] Only a small fraction of the electorate, perhaps 5 percent or less, were categorized as having the highest **level of conceptualization**, which required holding principles and preferences that were consistent with one another and stable over time.

Some modern studies seem to support these claims. One recent study found that people are more likely to know the names of characters on *The Simpsons* than to know which individual liberties are guaranteed by the Bill of Rights.[9] Another found that a majority of Americans could not name any members of the Supreme Court.[10] And in a 2007 survey, nearly 20 percent of college students thought that Martin Luther King's 1963 "I have a dream" speech was aimed at abolishing slavery rather than securing voting rights and ending the "separate but equal" system of public accommodations in southern states.[11] If these early studies and modern examples were the last word, there would be little need to study public opinion since most people would have little to say, many others would make up their responses, and, most importantly, what little public opinion you might discern would have little impact on individual behavior or government actions.

THE NEW THEORY OF PUBLIC OPINION

Three arguments forced changes in the old view of public opinion. Some scholars argued that it was no surprise to find that people have trouble talking about politics.[12] After all, only a few Americans monitor political events or think about politics every day. Another important factor in interpreting survey results is that some survey

▲ Are Americans poorly informed about politics? One survey found that more Americans could identify characters on *The Simpsons* than knew which liberties the Bill of Rights guarantees, and another found most respondents unable to name any Supreme Court justices.

questions are ambiguous and open to interpretation.[13] As a result, people may have trouble answering even seemingly simple questions about politics or public policy.

A second critique focused on the timing of the early public opinion studies of the 1950s. Analysis of surveys taken in the 1960s and afterward found that many opinions remained stable over time.[14] Later surveys also found higher levels of factual knowledge in the American electorate.[15] Both findings suggest that even if the early findings about public opinion were true, at best they described only the American public of the 1950s, not contemporary public opinion.

The third and most important argument was that in order to accurately capture public opinion, scholars needed to expand their picture of what it might look like. Early surveys looked for evidence that citizens had beliefs that were internally consistent, stable, and based on a rationale that allowed them to explain why they held those beliefs. The new work began with the premise that none of these conditions were necessary, and that earlier scholars failed to find evidence of public opinion because they were looking for the wrong thing, rather than because it didn't exist.[16]

Describing Public Opinion Modern theories of public opinion distinguish between two types of opinions. The first are broad expressions such as how a person thinks about politics, what a citizen wants from government, or principles that apply across a range of issues. These kinds of beliefs are typically formed early in life and remain stable over time. Nuts and Bolts 5.1 shows part of a Pew Research Center survey that

NUTS AND BOLTS

5.1

Surveying Political Principles

This is a portion of a Pew Research Center questionnaire that asks about a range of public opinion principles, from the government's role in protecting morality to party identification and liberal–conservative ideology. For each topic, respondents are given a range of possible answers to capture the direction and intensity of their opinions.

Statement 1	Strongly agree	Agree		Agree	Strongly agree	Statement 2
The government should do more to protect morality in society.	☐	☐		☐	☐	I worry the government is getting too involved in the issue of morality.
Homosexuality is a way of life that should be accepted by society.	☐	☐		☐	☐	Homosexuality is a way of life that should be discouraged by society.
The government should do more to help needy Americans, even if it means going deeper into debt.	☐	☐		☐	☐	The government today can't afford to do much more to help the needy.
Religion is a very important part of my life.	☐	☐		☐	☐	Religion is not that important to me.
Elected officials in Washington lose touch with the people pretty quickly.	☐	☐		☐	☐	Elected officials in Washington try hard to stay in touch with voters back home.

In politics today, do you consider yourself a Republican, Democrat, or Independent?

Strong Democrat	Democrat	Independent, lean Democrat	Independent, no leaning	Independent, lean Republican	Republican	Strong Republican
☐	☐	☐	☐	☐	☐	☐

In general, would you describe your political views as very conservative, conservative, moderate, liberal or very liberal?

Very liberal	Liberal	Moderate	Conservative	Very conservative
☐	☐	☐	☐	☐

SOURCE: Pew Research Center, "Beyond Red vs. Blue," available at http://typology.people-press.org/typology.

lists a number of such opinions. Some of these beliefs are obviously political, such as party identification, ideology, and judgments about whether elected officials lose touch with citizens. Others, such as beliefs about homosexuality or religion, may seem irrelevant to politics, but their presence on the Pew questionnaire illustrates an important finding: Americans' political opinions are shaped by a wide range of beliefs and ideas, including many influences that are not inherently political.

One important opinion measured by the Pew survey is **liberal–conservative ideology,** which describes whether a respondent identifies as a liberal, moderate, conservative, or something between these categories. As the responses in Figure 5.2 show, Americans are spread out across the ideological range, with most people identifying as either liberal or conservative, but not strongly so. Liberal–conservative ideology is a good example of a stable opinion: the best way to predict an American's ideology at age forty is to assume it will match his ideology at age twenty, and the same is true for party identification. However, even these typically stable opinions sometimes change in response to events. For example, while party identification is formed during early adulthood and adolescence, and often persists throughout an individual's life, it can change as new issues arise or when candidates' positions contradict a citizen's notion of the differences between parties.[17] In a later section, we will look more closely at how such opinions are formed and why they change.

Many Opinions Are Latent The most important thing to understand about public opinion is that while ideology and party identification are largely consistent over time, they are the exceptions to the rule.[18] The average person does not maintain a set of fully formed opinions on all political topics, such as evaluations of all the state- or city-wide candidates for office or assessments of the entire range of

---

FIGURE 5.2   LIBERAL–CONSERVATIVE IDEOLOGY IN AMERICA

Many commentators describe politics in America as highly conflictual, with most Americans holding either liberal or conservative points of view and very few people in between. Do opinion data confirm or disprove this description?

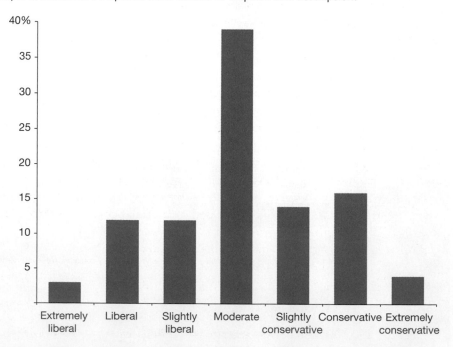

SOURCE: Data from 2006 General Social Survey, available at http://sda.berkeley.edu/archive.htm.

government programs. Instead, most Americans' political judgments are **latent opinions** constructed only when they are needed, such as when answering a survey question or deciding just before Election Day how to vote. For example, when an individual is first asked about his opinions on global warming, he will probably not have a specific response in mind. He simply will not have thought much about the question, and might have, at best, some vague ideas about the subject. His opinions on global warming become more specific and concrete only when he is asked to describe them.

People who follow politics closely have more pre-formed opinions than the average American, whose interest in politics is relatively low. But very few people are so informed that they have ready opinions, judgments, and evaluations across a wide range of political questions. Moreover, even when people do form opinions in advance, they may not remember every factor that influenced them. This way of forming opinions, called **on-line processing,** happens when someone forms an opinion, such as whether she likes or dislikes a particular candidate or policy, and remembers the opinion itself but not the events, experiences, or other data that influenced her assessment.[19] Thus, an individual may identify as a liberal or a conservative, or as a supporter of a particular party, but may be unable to explain specific reasons for these ideological leanings.[20]

When opinions are formed on the spot, they are based on **considerations,** the pieces of relevant information—such as ideology, party identification, religious beliefs, personal circumstances, or other factors—that come to mind when the opinion is requested.[21] The process of forming an opinion usually is not thorough or systematic, since most people don't take into account everything they know about the issue.[22] Rather, they only use considerations that come to mind immediately.[23] Highly informed people who follow politics use this process, as do those with low levels of political interest and knowledge.[24]

To see this process at work, consider how people decide whether they approve of the job the president is doing. Surveys on this topic typically ask respondents whether they approve or disapprove of the president's performance, although their wording varies. Figure 5.3 shows approval ratings for President Bush from the time he assumed office in 2001 through the 2008 presidential election. His approval ratings were highest just after the September 11 attacks, and they reached a second, lower peak in May 2003, just after the invasion of Iraq. As a rule, presidents enjoy higher approval ratings during times of crisis, although the effect is usually short-lived, as in this example. Political scientist John Mueller first identified this pattern and labeled it the "rally 'round the flag" phenomenon.[25]

The two peaks in Bush's approval ratings show the opinion formation process at work. The overall decline in Bush's approval ratings reflects a variety of considerations that shaped public opinion through most of Bush's presidency, including the unpopular war in Iraq and declining economic growth. However, immediately after the September 11 attacks, and again after the start of the Iraq war, many Americans appear to have based their approval judgment on a new consideration—the need for national unity—that led more respondents to express support for the president. Over time, however, the importance of this consideration declined, leading to the pattern seen in the figure.

Many studies of public opinion support the idea that opinions are mostly formed on the spot using a wide range of considerations. Attitudes about immigration are shaped by evaluations of the state of the economy.[26] People judge government spending proposals differently depending on whether a Republican or a Democrat made the proposal, using their own party identification as a consideration.[27] Evaluations of

latent opinion An opinion formed on the spot, when it is needed (as distinct from a deeply held opinion that is stable over time).

on-line processing A way of forming a political opinion in which a person develops a preference regarding a candidate, party, or policy but does not remember the original reasons behind the preference.

considerations The many pieces of information a person uses to form an opinion.

POLITICS IS EVERYWHERE

 A wide range of considerations shape public opinion, including events, thoughts, and ideas that have no clear connection to politics.

FIGURE 5.3

APPROVAL RATINGS FOR PRESIDENT GEORGE W. BUSH, 2001–2008

The dots show presidential approval as measured in a particular poll; the line tracks the average approval rating in all the polls taken at a particular time. Scholars claim that presidential approval is shaped by wars and similar events that lead Americans to "rally 'round the flag." Can you identify these influences in these data on approval of President Bush?

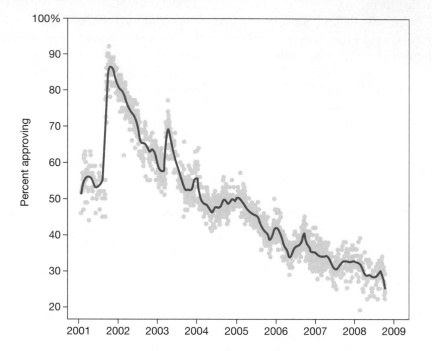

SOURCE: Data aggregated and graphed by Charles H. Franklin, *Political Arithmetik,* October 5, 2008, available at http://politicalarithmetik .blogspot.com.

affirmative action programs vary depending on whether the survey question reminds respondents that they may be hurt by these programs—that is, these preferences are influenced by considerations of personal economic well-being.[28] Voters' party identification and ideology influence their evaluations of candidates.[29] Individuals' willingness to allow protests and other expressions of opinions they disagree with depends on their belief in tolerance.[30] And if people feel obligated to help others in need, they are more likely to support government programs that benefit the poor.[31]

Sometimes competing or contradictory considerations influence the opinion-formation process. In the case of abortion laws, for example, many people believe in protecting human life but also value allowing women to make their own medical decisions.[32] When someone with both of these beliefs is asked for his opinion about abortion laws, his response will depend on which of these considerations comes to mind and seems most relevant as he is answering the question. Opinions about other morally complex issues such as "right to die" legislation, or race-related issues like affirmative action, are also often based on competing considerations.[33]

Events can also become considerations. Following the September 11 attacks, the Pew Research Center began surveying Americans about their fears of another terrorist attack. As Table 5.1 shows, every time a terrorist attack occurred in the next few years, regardless of its location, the percentage of Americans answering that they were "very worried" about a future attack rose significantly. After the July 2005 bombings in London, the "very worried" segment of the U.S. population increased from 17 to 26 percent, showing just shy of a 50 percent increase.

TABLE 5.1   FEARS OF TERRORIST ATTACK: BEFORE AND AFTER SEPTEMBER 11, 2001

In this chapter, we argue that opinions are often sensitive to new information or events. Is this true of worries about a future terrorist attack?

	FOLLOWED VERY CLOSELY	VERY WORRIED[a] BEFORE	AFTER
Terrorist attacks in New York and Washington, DC (9/01)	74%	—	28%
Thwarted British terrorist plot (8/06)	54	17	25[b]
Terrorist bombings in London (7/05)	48	17	26
Terrorist bombings in Madrid (3/04)	34	13	20
Arrest of alleged "dirty bomber" (6/02)	30	20	32
Terrorist bombings in Kenya (12/02)	21	20	31
Failed shoe bombing on Paris flight (1/02)	20	13	20

[a] Percent very worried there will soon be another terrorist attack on the United States. 'Before' figures from closest available survey prior to incident, 'after' and news interest from closest survey following incident.
[b] 'Before' figure from Aug 9: 'After' and news interest from August 10–13.

SOURCE: Pew Research Center, "American Attitudes Hold Steady in Face of Foreign Crises," August 16, 2006, available at http://people-press.org/reports/display.php3?ReportID=285.

Most Americans form opinions—legitimate, meaningful opinions—when they are needed. Though they don't usually seek out new information or take account of everything they know, their opinions reflect at least some of their knowledge of politics, as well as their bedrock ideological beliefs, and ideas about what they want from government.

One of the most appealing features of this description of public opinions about politics is how closely it resembles the way most people think about other aspects of their lives. Do you prefer blue or black jeans? Coke or Pepsi? Jon Stewart or Stephen Colbert? Facebook or MySpace? These decisions are probably easy precisely because you face them every day and, as a result, are likely to have highly accessible opinions about which option you prefer. You don't have to think much to form your opinion. Now think about a different question: What kind of house would you like to own? You probably have not thought much about this one. New or old? Ranch, split, colonial, bungalow, Victorian, or contemporary? Granite counters, slate, Formica, or Corian? Oil, gas, or electric heat—or solar? How do you feel about walkout basements, decks, wall color, floor coverings, and appliances? The list is virtually endless.

If someone asked you to describe your preferred house, you probably could only begin to answer the question. You'd probably base your response on a relatively small set of ideas, using a few mental snapshots of your image of the perfect house. You would probably say something very different if you had time to think, or even if you were asked on a different day. This strategy is exactly how most Americans form their opinions about politics. When someone is asked for an opinion on a political question they know little about, their

▲ Images of intense confrontation between pro-life and pro-choice protesters may conceal the more nuanced, conflicting considerations that underlie many Americans' opinions about abortion. Most Americans believe that the decision to have an abortion should be left up to the woman, but are uncomfortable allowing unrestricted access to the procedure.

response is based on a few general, simple considerations. A question about who should provide health insurance—government or private insurers—may call to mind a fight with an insurance company over a medical claim, recent dealings with government bureaucrats, or how good insurance helped a family member survive cancer. These considerations may not lead to the most thoughtful answer, but they may be all that people use to form their opinions.

This description of how most people think about politics explains many of the anomalies in early studies of public opinion. People have trouble expressing their opinions since they are often devising these opinions on the spot. Although people cannot often provide a rationale for their beliefs, this doesn't mean the beliefs are baseless; rather, such information may not be remembered. And it makes sense that opinions change over time, as people vary the considerations they use.

Thinking about opinions in terms of considerations implies that public opinion cannot simply be measured once and for all. Even if nothing major happens—no big events, new proposals, or other high-profile political activity—opinions may change as people call up different considerations to form them. Such variation does not mean that people are indecisive or that they do not understand what they are being asked. Rather, it reflects how the average person thinks and develops opinions.

SECTION SUMMARY

1. Public opinion describes what Americans think about current government policies, evaluations of elected officials, and demands for policy change, as well as the wider set of beliefs and ideas that shape these evaluations.
2. For most Americans, opinions are latent. They are formed only when they are required to make a decision or to express a preference.
3. The considerations that are used to construct opinions can vary from day to day, depending on events, statements by politicians, personal experiences and other factors. As a result, the opinions a person expresses often depend on when he is asked.

Where Do Opinions Come From?

This section describes the sources of public opinion. Some of these influences come from early life experiences, such as exposure to the beliefs of parents, relatives, or teachers, while others result from later life events. Politicians also play a critical role in the opinion-formation process.

SOCIALIZATION: FAMILIES AND COMMUNITIES

Theories of **political socialization** show that many people's political opinions start with what they learned from their parents. These principles include a liberal–conservative ideology, level of trust in others, class identity, and ethnic identity.[34] There is also a high correlation between both the party identification and the liberal–conservative ideology of parents and those of their children.[35] These principles are not permanent; in fact, people sometimes respond to events by modifying their opinions, even those developed early in life. Even so, for many people, ideas learned

political socialization The process by which an individual's political opinions are shaped by other people and the surrounding culture.

during childhood continue to shape the way they think about politics throughout their lives.[36]

People are also socialized by their communities, the people they interact with while growing up, such as neighbors, teachers, clergy, and others.[37] Support for democracy as a system of government and for American political institutions is higher for individuals who took a civics class in high school.[38] Growing up in a homogenous community, one where many people share the same cultural, ethnic, or political beliefs, increases an adult's sense of civic duty—their belief that voting or other forms of political participation are things that people ought to do.[39] Volunteering in community organizations as a child also shapes political beliefs and participation in later life.[40] Engaging in political activity as a teenager, such as volunteering in a presidential campaign, generates higher levels of political interest as an adult; it also strengthens the belief that people should care about politics and participate in political activities.[41]

POLITICS IS EVERYWHERE

Americans learn about politics, in the form of principles and other considerations, from their parents and their communities.

EVENTS

While socialization often influences individuals' fairly stable core beliefs, public opinion is not fixed. People can revise their opinions in response to what happens to them and in the world around them. All kinds of events, from everyday interactions to traumatic, life-changing disasters, can capture a person's attention and force him to revise his fundamental understanding of politics and the role of government. For example, while an individual's initial partisan affiliation is likely to reflect the leanings of his parents, this starting point will change as a function of subsequent events, such as who runs for office, what platforms they campaign on, and their performance in office.[42]

Some events that shape beliefs are specific, individual experiences. For example, someone who believes that he managed to get a college degree only because of receiving government grants and guaranteed student loans might believe that it is a good thing to have a large, activist government that provides a wide range of benefits to its citizens. Other events shape the beliefs of large numbers of people in similar ways. Political realignments are a good example. A realignment is a nationwide shift in which large numbers of people move from identifying with one

▲ *While events such as wars, economic upheavals, and major policy changes certainly influence public opinion, research shows that most Americans acquire some political opinions early in life from parents, friends, teachers, and others in their community.*

▲ *Americans who came of age during World War II generally report higher levels of support for and trust in the federal government. In many cases, these opinions reflect military service as well as the government's post-war support for veterans, including G.I. Bill housing and tuition benefits.*

political party to identifying with another (see Chapter 7).[43] Beginning in the early 1960s, large numbers of white southerners shifted their party identification from Democratic to Republican. This gradual change in principles was driven by national events, including support of civil rights and voting rights legislation by many Democratic elected officials in Washington.[44]

Many observers have argued that military service during World War II also shaped the opinions of many Americans, giving veterans higher levels of trust in government and greater satisfaction with the performance of the federal government.[45] Others have suggested that the change in opinions was not the result of military service, but of the government's efforts to help veterans after the war through programs such as the G.I. Bill, which funded college education for veterans after they left the military.[46]

Recent events have also shaped beliefs. Scholars have shown that after the September 11 terrorist attacks, many citizens became more willing to restrict civil liberties to reduce the chances of future attacks.[47] Support for restrictions increased soon after September 11 and remained elevated even five years later, suggesting a long-term change in public opinion. Similarly, large numbers of Americans responded to the mismanagement of disaster relief after Hurricane Katrina and depictions of the storm's impact on the poor by becoming more concerned about poverty in America.[48] However, this effect faded in subsequent surveys.

Events hold a similar sway over other opinions, such as presidential approval, which is driven by factors such as changes in the economy. Presidents are more likely to have high approval ratings when economic growth is high, and inflation and unemployment are low, wheras approval ratings fall when growth is negative, and unemployment and inflation are high. Many of these factors shape attachments

▶ *While few Americans are economic policy experts, most people's judgments about economic conditions, based on everyday events and their personal economic circumstances, are remarkably accurate.*

to political parties, both at the level of individual citizens and when partisanship is measured in the aggregate.[49]

Some events have a greater impact on public opinion than others, and some people are more likely than others to change their views. Political scientist John Zaller showed that opinion changes generated by an event or some other piece of new information are more likely when an individual considers the event or information important and when it is unfamiliar, meaning that the individual does not have a set of preexisting principles or other considerations with which to interpret the event. Changes in opinions are also more likely for people who do not have strong feelings about what they believe than for people with strong opinions.[50]

GROUP IDENTITY

Another influence on an individual's opinions are social categories or groups, such as gender, race, or education level. These characteristics might shape opinions in three ways. First, as noted in the discussion of socialization, people learn about politics from the people around them. Therefore, people who live in the same region, or who were born in the same era might have similar beliefs because they experienced the same historical events at similar points in their lives, or learned political viewpoints from each other. In the United States, opinions on many issues are highly correlated with the state or region where a person grew up. For example, until the 1970s relatively few native white southerners identified with the Republican Party.[51] Even today, native white southerners tend to have distinctly different attitudes about many issues, such as support for affirmative action policies, and hold different principles, such as lower support for government involvement in creating racial equality, when compared to people of other races and from different regions of the country.[52]

People also may rely on others who "look like" them as a source of opinions. Political scientists Green, Palmquist, and Schickler, for example, argue that group identities shape partisanship: when someone is trying to decide between being a Republican or a Democrat, she thinks about which demographic groups are associated with each party, and picks the party that has more members from the groups she thinks she is a part of.[53]

A more practical reason for looking at group variations in public opinion is that candidates and political consultants often formulate their campaign strategies in terms of groups. Karl Rove, President George W. Bush's chief political advisor, described Republican and Democratic voters this way:

> First of all, there is a huge gap among people of faith. . . . You saw it in the 2000 exit polling, where people who went to church on a frequent and regular basis voted over-whelmingly for Bush. . . . Another part of the [Republican] coalition is the growing entrepreneurial class, which is increasingly nonwhite. [. . .] I'm not sure exactly why, but if you're married and with kids you are far more likely to be a Republican than to be a Democrat.[54]

Rove identifies groups of Americans, such as regular churchgoers, who he believes are more likely to be Republicans than Democrats. One should keep in mind that Rove is a Republican operative, so his statements may tend to flatter Republicans, but if what he says is true, Republicans should target the groups he identifies because they are likely to be sympathetic to the party's platform.

Table 5.2 reports data on the variation in opinions across different groups of Amer-

TABLE 5.2 THE IMPORTANCE OF GROUPS

Knowing an individual's group characteristics often allows scholars to predict some of that person's opinions. For other opinions, however, these characteristics provide very little information. Can you find an example of both statements in this table?

		"The Bible is the actual Word of God and is to be taken literally, word for word." (Percentage who agree.)	"Men are better suited [than women] for politics." (Percentage who agree.)	"Should government reduce the income differences between the rich and the poor." (Percentage who strongly agree.)
Gender	Male	28%	28%	18%
	Female	38	23	22
Age	18–30	32	24	22
	31–40	34	26	20
	41–55	35	17	22
	Over 55	36	34	17
Education	High school or less	35	25	19
	Bachelor's degree	25	23	11
	Advanced degree	11	23	19
Race	White	30	26	16
	African American	65	21	39
	Other	34	25	27
Family income	Below mean	46	26	28
	Mean	37	26	28
	Above mean	29	24	16
Region	New England	12	22	30
	Middle Atlantic	20	25	23
	Midwest	37	22	22
	South	42	25	26
	Mountain	27	21	12
	Pacific	27	30	15

SOURCE: Data from 2004 General Social Survey, available at http://sda.berkeley.edu/archive.htm.

icans, as measured in the General Social Survey. The table shows group differences on three broad questions: an individual's feelings about the Bible, the role of women in politics, and whether government should redistribute income (tax some people and give the money to others as credits or benefits). These data reveal two important facts about group affiliations and public opinion. First, they show sharp differences between groups on some questions. People tend to respond very differently to the question about the Bible depending on their education level: of the people with a high-school education or less, about a third agree with the statement shown in the table, versus only 10 percent of the people with an advanced degree. Similar disparities arise between racial groups on the income redistribution question.

These data also show a great deal of consensus. There is little variation in different groups' opinions on the role of women in politics. Moreover, no one group holds strong views on all three issues. For example, the table shows that opinions on the

Bible vary with a person's education level, but education level seems unrelated to responses to the women in politics questions, and shows only a weak correlation to opinions about redistribution.

These data show that group characteristics can be important predictors of some of an individual's opinions, but they are not the whole story.[55] The opinions that Americans hold are a product of their socialization and their life experiences as well as their group characteristics. A person's group characteristics may tell us something about their opinions on some issues but reveal little about their thoughts on other issues, and these group memberships are only one factor that influences public opinion.

POLITICIANS AND OTHER POLITICAL ACTORS

Opinions and changes in opinion are also influenced by politicians and other political actors, such as political parties and party leaders, interest groups, and even the leaders of religious, civic, and other large organizations. In part, this link exists because Americans look to these individuals for information because of their presumed expertise. You may not know what to think about the war in Iraq or health care reform, so you might find someone who knows more than you do about the issues and, if that person's opinions seem reasonable, adopt them as your own.[56] Of course, people do not search haphazardly for advice; they only take account of a particular expert's opinions on an issue when they believe they generally agree with the expert, perhaps because they are both conservatives, or Democrats, or the individual has some other basis for thinking their preferences are alike.

Politicians and other political actors also work to shape public opinion. Political scientists Lawrence Jacobs and Robert Shapiro argue that politicians describe proposals using arguments and images designed to tap the public's strong opinions, with the goal of winning support for these proposals.[57] These authors argue that public opposition in 1994 to President Bill Clinton's health care reform proposals did not arise because Americans opposed health care reform or because they disliked what the Clinton plan would do; rather, opposition arose in reaction to the way the proposal was described by legislators who opposed it.

Of course, these attempts are not always successful. In 2005, President Bush and his staff expended much time and effort to promote Social Security reform, giving dozens of public speeches, holding rallies across the nation, briefing legislators, and expressing their willingness to negotiate with Democratic lawmakers on the issue.[58] However, no presidential proposal was formally submitted to Congress, nor did Congress vote on reforms. Why not?

The answer is simple: at no time did a majority of Americans favor reforming Social Security.[59] True, polls showed that many Americans were worried about the future of the program and whether benefits would be available for them when they retired. But none of the options that were debated at the time, such as privatizing the program, reducing future benefits, increasing contributions, or investing Social Security funds in the stock market, attracted more than minority support. In fact, as Bush made more speeches, the proposals attracted less support.

Faced with a public that was suspicious or downright opposed to Social Security reform, members of Congress either publicly announced their opposition to Social Security reform, or informally made it clear that they would support changes only if the president could convince the public that reform was a good idea.[60] In the end, President Bush abandoned his effort—not because he was distracted by other matters or because he had changed his mind about Social Security reform, but because public opposition meant that there was no chance of enacting a reform proposal.

1. An individual's opinions come from a variety of sources, including socialization, historical events and personal experiences, group identities, and the actions and statements of politicians and other national figures.
2. While socialization and early life events play a key role in shaping political opinions, most political opinions continually evolve throughout a person's life.
3. An individual's group characteristics, such as race, gender, age, and religious beliefs, are an important predictor of their political opinions.

Measuring Public Opinion

For the most part, information about public opinion comes from **mass surveys**, in-person or phone interviews with hundreds or even thousands of voters. The aim of a mass survey is to measure the attitudes of a particular **population** or group of people, such as the residents of a particular congressional district, evangelicals, senior citizens, or even the entire adult population in America. For large groups such as these, it would be impossible to survey everyone. So, surveys typically involve **samples** of between a few hundred and several thousand individuals.

Large-scale surveys such as the National Election Study (NES), which is conducted every election year, use various types of questions to measure citizens' opinions and preferences. In presidential election years, participants in the NES are first asked whether they voted for president. If they say they did, they are asked which candidate they voted for: either a major party candidate, Barack Obama or John McCain in 2008; an independent candidate; or some other candidate. The survey does not verify whether someone who says they voted actually did so, or if people really voted for the person they say they did.

Another type of survey question measures people's preferences using an **issue scale**. In a recent National Election Study, for example, respondents were asked to express their opinions about health insurance: should government provide insurance, or should Americans buy insurance on their own? These views were placed at opposite ends of a 7-point scale, and the person being surveyed was asked to choose a position on the scale that reflects her opinion. If she strongly believes in government-provided insurance, she takes position 1; if she believes in private insurance, she takes position 7; and if her position is somewhere in the middle, she picks an intermediate position on the scale.

Surveys are composed of **random samples**, small subsets of the population being studied, in which every member of the population under study has an equal chance of being surveyed. Statistical analysis shows that even small random samples can provide very precise estimates of the opinions held by people in a large population.

Nuts and Bolts 5.2 shows how the **sampling error** or margin of error for a random sample decreases as the size of the sample increases. These errors result from using samples to measure the beliefs of an entire population. Increasing the sample size lowers the sampling error, but the only way to eradicate sampling error is to survey the whole population.

For example, in surveys with 1,000 respondents the sampling error is 2 percent, meaning that 95 percent of the time, the results of a 1,000-person survey will fall within the range of 2 percentage points above or below the actual percentage

mass survey A way to measure public opinion by interviewing a large sample of the population.

population The group of people that a researcher or pollster wants to study, such as evangelicals, senior citizens, or Americans.

sample Within a population, the group of people surveyed in order to gauge the whole population's opinion. Researchers use samples because it would be impossible to interview the entire population.

issue scale A survey response format in which respondents select their answers from a range of positions between two extremes.

random sample A subsection of a population chosen to participate in a survey through a selection process in which every member of the population has an equal chance of being chosen. This kind of sampling improves the accuracy of public opinion data.

sampling error A calculation that describes what percentage of the people surveyed may not accurately represent the population being studied. Increasing the number of respondents lowers the sampling error.

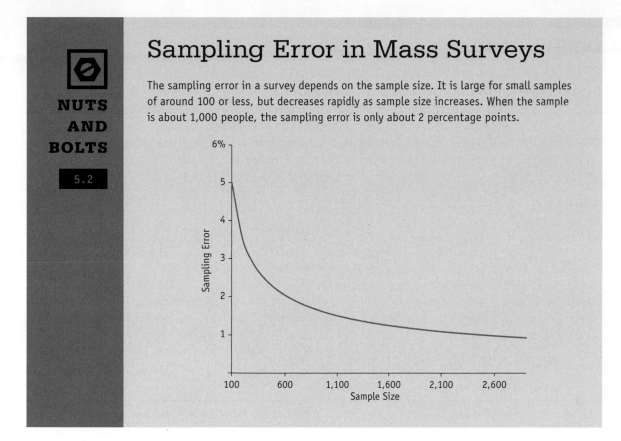

Sampling Error in Mass Surveys

NUTS AND BOLTS

5.2

The sampling error in a survey depends on the sample size. It is large for small samples of around 100 or less, but decreases rapidly as sample size increases. When the sample is about 1,000 people, the sampling error is only about 2 percentage points.

in the population that holds a particular opinion surveyed. If the sample size was increased to 5,000 people, the sampling error would decline to 0.5 percent.

Sampling errors need to be taken into account when interpreting what a poll says about public opinion. For example, suppose a 1,000-person survey about a congressional race finds that 60 percent of the sample favors candidate Smith, while 40 percent support candidate Jones. Since the difference in support for the two candidates (twenty points) exceeds the sampling error (four points), it is reasonable to conclude that Smith has more supporters in the population compared to Jones and should be considered the favorite to win the election. In addition, the fact that the sampling error is four points means that there is a 95 percent chance that the actual level of support for Smith in the population falls between 62 and 58 percent—and that Jones's true level of support is between 38 and 42 percent.

In contrast, suppose the poll found a narrow 51 to 49 percent split slightly favoring Smith over Jones. Since the difference in support is smaller than the sampling error, it would be a mistake to conclude that Smith is the likely winner. Even though Smith is ahead among the sample surveyed in the poll, Jones may have more supporters in the population. Put another way, given the sampling error, the survey results tell us that there is a 95 percent chance that Smith's support in the population is between 49 and 53 percent, and Jones is between 47 and 51 percent. In other words, when a poll shows a difference in support smaller than the sampling error, the only thing that poll tells us is that neither candidate is the clear favorite.

PROBLEMS MEASURING PUBLIC OPINION

Survey results need to be read with caution. The problems begin with the difficulty building a random sample. One standard tactic is to choose households at random from census data and send interviewers out for face-to-face meetings with

Polls and Surveys

Most of the survey questions mentioned in this chapter are overtly political: what Americans want from government, which candidate they support, or the principles and preferences that underlie these opinions. However, mass surveys are used to measure data on an extraordinarily wide range of topics, many of which may appear to have little to do with politics. Consider the list of survey reports prepared by the Gallup Poll organization, shown below. For virtually every topic you can think of, there are polling data describing how Americans think.

Who commissions these polls? Media outlets, from major newspapers to specialized magazines, write stories about polling data, both to inform Americans about public opinion and to support arguments made in their coverage. Corporations use opinion data to gauge demand for their products, and academics track shifts in public opinion to investigate what causes them and how markets and governments respond.

While many survey topics have little connection to the functioning of government, the process by which these opinions are formed is the same as described in the rest of this chapter. Apart from simple questions of fact (have you flown on an airliner in the past year?), most responses to opinion questions are devised on the spot from a small set of considerations. As a result, answers such as self-assessments of body weight will vary across time, as people use different considerations to form their opinions. ■

POLLING FROM A TO Z: SOME GALLUP POLL SURVEY TOPICS

Topic	Question
Airlines	How many air trips, if any, have you taken on a commercial airliner in the past twelve months?
Computers and the Internet	How much time, if any, do you spend using the Internet?
Guns	Do you have a gun in your house, or not?
General Mood of the Country	In general, are you satisfied or dissatisfied with the way things are going in the United States at this time?
Illegal Drugs	Do you think that the use of marijuana should be made legal, or not?
Most Admired Man and Woman	What man [woman] have you heard about or read about, living in any part of the world today, do you admire most?
Personal Weight Situation	How would you describe your personal weight situation right now—very overweight, somewhat overweight, about right, somewhat underweight, or very underweight?
Religion	Did you, yourself, happen to attend church or synagogue in the last seven days?
Sports	What is your favorite college football team?
Tobacco and Smoking	Have you, yourself, smoked any cigarettes in the past week?
Work and Workplace	Are you satisfied or dissatisfied with your relations with your coworkers?

Source: Gallup, "Topics A to Z," available at http://www.galluppoll.com/topics.

random digit dialing A method of random sampling used in telephone surveys, in which the interviewers call respondents by dialing random telephone numbers in order to include those with unlisted numbers.

the selected respondents. Another is to contact people by telephone using **random digit dialing**, which allows surveyors to contact people who have either listed or unlisted phone numbers. While each of these techniques in theory produces a random sample, in practice they may end up including different kinds of people. For example, since laws forbid pollsters from calling cell phone numbers (because many respondents would be charged for the call), polling by phone excludes individuals who do not have a land line in their home. Similarly, face-to-face interviewing loses households in which both adults work during the day because they are less likely to be available to participate.

In order to keep costs down, some organizations have used Internet polling, in which volunteer respondents log on to a Web site to participate in a survey, or **robo-polls**, in which a computer program phones people and interviews them. While these survey techniques are cheaper than face-to-face interviewing or calling respondents, there are serious doubts about the randomness of the samples these techniques produce.[61] (Push polls, in which a campaign uses biased survey questions as a way of driving support away from an opponent, are discussed in Chapter 8.)

Question wording can also bias survey results. Table 5.3 shows Americans' opinions on abortion rights as measured by several recent surveys and reveals that regardless of how the question is asked, about a quarter to a third of Americans take a strong position in favor of access to abortion, and about a fifth to a quarter take a strong anti-abortion position. For the rest of the population, almost a majority,

robo-poll A type of survey in which a computer program, rather than a live questioner, interviews respondents by telephone.

TABLE 5.3   THE IMPACT OF QUESTION WORDING: ATTITUDES ON ABORTION

In many cases, the way people respond to survey questions depends on how the question is asked. How does question wording shape how people respond to surveys concerning abortion rights?

NBC/*Wall Street Journal* (May 2005)

Which of the following best represents your views about abortion . . . The choice on abortion should be left up to the woman and her doctor, abortion should be legal only in cases in which pregnancy results from rape or incest or when the life of the woman is at risk, or abortion should be illegal in all circumstances.

Should be left up to woman and her doctor	Legal only in cases of rape/ incest/risk to woman's life	Illegal in all circumstances	Not sure
55%	29%	14%	2%

CBS News (April 2005)

Which of these comes closest to your view—abortion should be generally available to those who want it, OR abortion should be available but under stricter limits than it is now, OR abortion should not be permitted?

Generally available to those who want it	Available, but under stricter limits than now	Should not be permitted	Don't know
36%	38%	24%	2%

CBS News (July 2005)

What is your personal feeling about abortion? It should be permitted in all cases. It should be permitted, but subject to greater restrictions than it is now. It should be permitted only in cases such as rape, incest, and to save the woman's life, or it should only be permitted to save the woman's life.

Permitted in all cases	Permitted, but greater restrictions than now	Permitted only if rape, incest, or to save woman's life	Only permitted to save the woman's life/Not permitted at all	Don't know
25%	15%	38%	18%	5%

ABC News/*Washington Post* (April 2005)

Do you think abortion should be legal in all cases, legal in most cases, illegal in most cases or illegal in all cases?

Legal in all cases	Legal in most cases	Illegal in most cases	Illegal in all cases	No Opinion
20%	36%	27%	14%	3%

SOURCE: Pew Research Center, "Abortion, the Court, and the Public," October 3, 2005, available at http://people-press.org/commentary/display.php3? AnalysisID=119.

opinions depend on how the question is asked and which considerations are called to mind.[62] In particular, support for abortion rights goes up if a question mentions medical conditions, economic hardship, or consultation with a doctor. Support goes down if abortion rights are described as a purely personal choice.

Another problem with surveys is that people are sometimes reluctant to reveal their opinions. Rather than speaking truthfully, people often give socially acceptable answers, or the ones that they believe the interviewer wants to hear. In the case of voter turnout in elections, up to one-third of the people who say they voted when surveyed actually did not vote at all[63] (the percentage of survey respondents who say they voted for the winning candidate is generally higher than the actual percentage of votes counted for the winner). A significant percentage of the population, probably 10 to 20 percent, are reluctant to express their racial prejudices, or to admit that they would not vote for a female or minority or gay political candidate.

Pollsters use various techniques to address the problem of unreliable respondents. One is to verify answers whenever possible. The American National Election Studies used to check with County Boards of Election to see if respondents who said they voted had actually gone to the polls, although they stopped doing so because of cost. When there is concern that respondents will try to hide their prejudices, pollsters sometimes frame a question in terms of the entire country rather than the respondent's own beliefs. For example, during the 2008 presidential primaries, rather than asking respondents whether they were willing to vote for a Mormon candidate (such as Republican Mitt Romney), pollsters asked the question in a variety of indirect ways, including whether a respondent believed that the country was ready for a Mormon president.

Opinion researchers also have to contend with the opinion formation process discussed earlier. Since many people develop their opinions on the fly, their answers will depend on the considerations that come to mind at the moment they are asked. As a result, the answer a person gives may change a day, a week, or a month later. This problem often arises in polls taken early in a presidential campaign; the results vary from week to week not necessarily because of what the candidates have done, but because opinions are based on very little information, and can shift based on very small changes in what people know.[64]

THE ACCURACY OF PUBLIC OPINION

As noted earlier, early theories of public opinion held that the average American's opinions and beliefs about politics were incomplete at best, and at worst wildly inaccurate. Modern theories have revised these conclusions. It is true that many Americans have significant gaps in factual information, like which party controls the House or the Senate, or the name of the chief justice of the Supreme Court.[65] Americans also routinely overestimate the amount of federal money spent on government programs such as foreign aid, as shown in Table 5.4. Note that the amount of error in opinions about foreign aid is extremely large: on average, people believe that the government spends more than ten times the amount that it actually does. However, rather than reflecting ignorance, these misperceptions often result from survey design or how people interpret survey questions.

In some cases, inaccurate or outlandish survey results are due to the fact that some people don't take surveys seriously. They agree to participate, but are distracted and not really interested in explaining their beliefs to a stranger. So, faced with a long list of questions, they give quick, thoughtless responses, saying anything they can to end the interview as quickly as possible. Misperceptions may also result from

TABLE 5.4	BELIEFS ABOUT FOREIGN AID	
"What percentage of the federal budget is spent on aid to other nations"		20%
"What percentage of the federal budget should be spent on aid to other nations?"		10%
Actual percentage spent		1%

SOURCE: Program on International Policy Attitudes, "Americans on Foreign Aid and World Hunger: A Study of U.S. Public Attitudes," February 2, 2001, available at http://65.109.167.118/pipa/pdf/feb01/ForeignAid_Feb01_rpt.pdf.

forming opinions based on whatever considerations come to mind. This strategy means that in many cases, people exclude important pieces of information from the opinion formation process.

Consider claims about Saddam Hussein's role in the September 11 attacks. In a 2005 survey conducted by Harris Polling, 47 percent of those surveyed believed that Saddam Hussein helped plan and support the attacks, and 26 percent believed that some of the attackers were Iraqi.[66] There is no solid evidence for any of these claims, but there is also no reason to expect that many Americans have even considered the questions, since they are not relevant to their everyday lives. When asked for an opinion as part of a survey, there is no time for respondents to do research or think things through. Thus, it's no surprise that a significant percentage of respondents say that Hussein or other Iraqis were involved in the September 11 attacks: some people who guess an answer say yes, and some say no.

Incomplete or inaccurate responses to survey questions may also result from a respondent's unwillingness to say they don't know about something. There is good evidence that survey participants sometimes make up responses in order to not appear ill-informed.[67] Thus, when asked about Hussein and September 11, a respondent might affirm that a link existed even if they know little or nothing about the situation.

Moreover, leaving aside all of these factors, opinions about Saddam Hussein and September 11 could be influenced by politicians and others. As noted earlier, in the months prior to the invasion of Iraq, President Bush and other administration officials argued many times that there was some sort of ongoing relationship between Iraq and Al Qaeda, although they stopped short of claiming that Hussein directly participated in or had advance knowledge of the attacks. Thus, when survey respondents say that Iraq was involved in the September 11 attacks, it may reflect opinions formed after listening (or half-listening) to these public figures.

A final response to claims about errors in public opinion is that many supposed facts are actually "contested truths," meaning that it is reasonable for individuals to hold a wide range of views.[68] For example, the 2005 Harris survey asked Americans whether they thought that Iraqis were better off at the time the survey was taken than they were under Saddam Hussein, and 76 percent of the people surveyed said yes.[69] There is no right answer to this question. A person could reasonably think that Iraqis are better off because they are no longer governed by a dictator, or worse off because of the hardships and violence that followed Hussein's removal from power.

Such problems do not arise in all areas of public opinion. Studies show that a respondent's ability to express an opinion, as well as the accuracy of her opinions, rises if the questions being asked have something to do with everyday life.[70] Thus, the average American would be more likely to have an accurate sense of the state

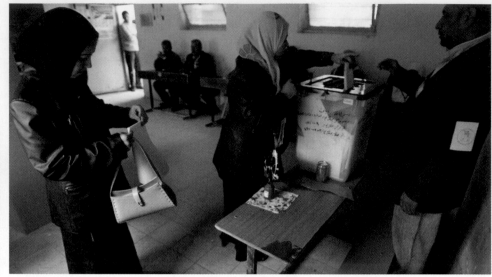

▲ *Often there are no right answers to polling questions. Are Iraqis better off because of the war? Perhaps they are, considering that the country is rid of Saddam Hussein, a ruthless dictator, and has held elections. But how should respondents weigh these advances against insurgent attacks, the collapse of many basic utilities, and the new government's inability to secure Iraq's borders?*

of the economy than the situation in Iraq. Everyday life gives us information about the economy; we learn about Iraq only if we take time to gather information. For example, Figure 5.4 contains two plots of data for the last thirty years; one is the percentage of Americans who said the economy was the most important problem, while the other plots the Misery Index, which is simply the annual rate of inflation plus the annual unemployment rate. Many politicians and other observers use the Misery Index as a broad measure of economic conditions (see Chapter 15). The figure shows that as the Misery Index goes up—meaning that the economy is in worse shape—the percentage of people who say the economy is the most important problem also increases. In other words, people are not giving random answers. They have well-formed opinions and are responding to the conditions around them.

HOW USEFUL ARE SURVEYS?

Mass opinion surveys are a powerful tool for measuring public opinion, but, as discussed earlier, their results must be interpreted carefully. Surveys often ask about complex issues that respondents may not have thought about. Samples may be biased, despite considerable efforts to randomize them. People may also be reluctant to admit some opinions to an interviewer, and many opinions change from day to day. The way people respond to a survey may reflect the wording of the questions, the timing of the survey (including events on the day the survey was carried out), and how familiar people are with the topics of the questions. Even if all of these problems could be solved, surveys that use a sample of the population can only measure public opinion within a margin of error, as we have seen. For all of these reasons, survey data may not give an accurate picture of what a population thinks. These issues also raise a fundamental question: how seriously should you (and political scientists and the media) take poll results? Or, to put it another way, how should survey results be interpreted and used, given all of their pitfalls?

When should you believe a survey result? Results are most likely to be accurate when they are based on a simple, easily understood question about a topic familiar to most Americans, such as their evaluation of the president or their opinion on the state of the economy. You can be even more confident if multiple surveys that ask about the same topic in slightly different ways produce similar findings, since no

FIGURE 5.4 **THE MISERY INDEX AND COMPLAINTS
ABOUT THE ECONOMY**

Most Americans know few details about economic conditions. Does this lack of knowledge
mean that they cannot make reasonably accurate judgments about the state of the economy?

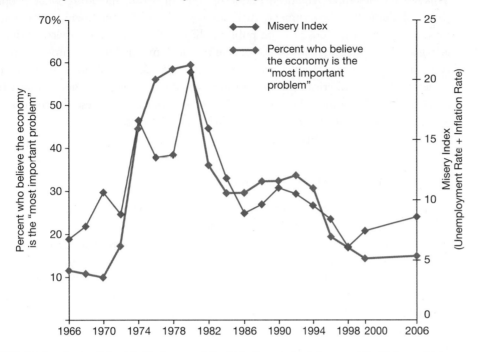

SOURCE: Data from American National Election Survey, available at http://www.electionstudies.org, and the U.S. Bureau of Labor
Statistics, available at http://www.bls.gov.

one survey or survey question provides a complete and accurate picture of public
opinion. If a survey asks about a complex, unfamiliar topic—replacing the income
tax with a national sales tax, for example—then the results may not provide much
insight into public opinion, especially without data from other surveys that ask the
same question in different ways or at different points in time. The same is true if
a survey asks a hypothetical question or tries to get people to express unpopular or
immoral opinions.

SECTION SUMMARY

1. Mass surveys are a powerful tool for measuring public opinion. Even relatively
   small random samples (1,000 people) can, in theory, provide accurate estimates
   of public opinion in the entire nation.
2. People's responses to survey questions are often influenced by the timing of
   the survey, the wording of the questions, people's knowledge about the topic,
   and whether they hold unpopular opinions.
3. While surveys sometimes reveal voters' misinformation and ignorance, particularly about the details of many public policies, they show that in many
   other areas, Americans have good information about the problems facing the
   nation.

ideological polarization The effect on public opinion when many citizens move away from moderate positions and toward either end of the political spectrum, identifying themselves as either liberals or conservatives.

Characteristics of American Public Opinion

This section describes American public opinion in detail, including what people think of the federal government, their ideological beliefs, and many other opinions, along with their positions on public policy questions, such as abortion rights and global warming. These opinions drive public demands for government action, from spending to regulations and other types of public policy. So, if we want to understand what America's national government does and why, we have to start by determining what Americans ask of it. The other priority is to describe the differences of opinion that divide Americans, from specific questions of public policy to general statements of belief.

IDEOLOGICAL POLARIZATION

We begin our discussion by examining liberal–conservative ideology and party identification to see if historical data show evidence of polarization. Are there fewer moderates and more strong liberals and conservatives compared to a generation ago? Figure 5.5 shows data from the General Social Survey on Americans' ideological opinions from the 1970s until the present, aggregated or grouped by decade. The liberal category in the figure combines people who said they were either "extremely liberal" or "liberal." Similarly, the group of conservatives includes respondents calling themselves either "extremely conservative" or "conservative." Finally, moderates said they were either "moderate," "slightly liberal," or "slightly conservative." The plots in Figure 5.5 show no evidence of **ideological polarization**. Over the last several decades, a strong majority of Americans have continued to say they are moderates, with less than 40 percent saying they are liberal or conservative. There is also no evidence that the degree of ideological polarization has increased; the percentage of liberals and of conservatives has remained relatively constant.[71]

Next, Figure 5.6 shows decade-by-decade data about how citizens describe their party identification using General Social Survey data and combining "strong Democrats" with "Democrats," "strong Republicans" with "Republicans," and classifying

---

FIGURE 5.5 **LIBERAL–CONSERVATIVE IDEOLOGY IN AMERICA, 1970–2006**

Many observers claim that American public opinion is increasingly polarized—with more liberals and conservatives, and fewer moderates. Does survey evidence back up these claims?

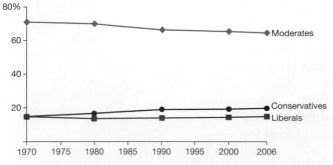

SOURCE: Data from 2006 General Social Survey, available at http://sda.berkeley.edu/archive.htm.

FIGURE 5.6 **PARTY IDENTIFICATION IN AMERICA, 1970–2006**

Party identification is another place to look for evidence of an increasingly polarized America. Do these data show evidence of polarization?

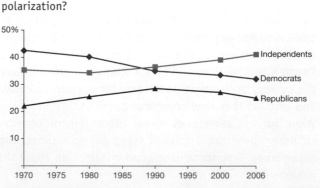

SOURCE: Data from 2006 General Social Survey, available at http://sda.berkeley.edu/archive.htm.

everyone else as an independent. Here again, there is little evidence of polarization. Since 1970, the percentage of Republicans has increased slightly, while the percentage of Democrats has declined significantly. The number of independents, people who have no strong attachment to either party, also increased. As with the plots for ideology, the trend for party identification is towards moderation and no strong attachments to parties.

Looking more closely at opinion polarization, Table 5.5 shows responses to questions that tap a set of important principles, from foreign policy to domestic issues, civil liberties, and morality, all taken from a Pew Trust survey. Principles such as these form the basis for opinions people express in surveys or act on when they vote or engage in other political behavior.

While the responses in Table 5.5 show considerable conflict in American public opinion, it is important to understand that this particular survey was *designed* to divide people into categories based on what they believe and what they want from government. Moreover, on each principle, the survey asked people to choose between two reasonable points of view described in neutral language, and all of the questions tap subjects of impassioned debate during recent political campaigns. Like most surveys, this one did not ask about the many noncontroversial issues in American politics.

POLITICS IS CONFLICTUAL

Because survey questions generally focus on conflictual issues, they tend to overstate the policy or ideological disagreements among the American public.

Until 1998, the General Social Survey (GSS) asked people whether they believed that "women should take care of home not country."[72] In 1974, over a third of respondents agreed, but by 1998, agreement had declined to only about 15 percent, which is why the question isn't asked anymore. There is no reason to gather data on issues about which the vast majority of Americans hold the same opinion. Around the same time, the GSS also stopped asking whether people believed that white people had the right to a segregated neighborhood—not out of moral considerations, but because American public opinion data showed an almost universally antisegregation perspective, whether everyone truly thought that way or not.

Finally, survey responses that reveal public opinion about broad principles do not tell us whether differences in these opinions translate into conflicts over specific policy questions. As we have discussed, public opinion about specific policy questions reflects multiple considerations and principles assembled into a response or evaluation of a policy option. While the data on broad principles show some evidence of polarization in American public opinion, they do not suggest deep, profound disagreements. In some cases, the data even reveal considerable, widespread consensus.

EVALUATIONS OF GOVERNMENT AND OFFICEHOLDERS

Another set of opinions that are important for American politics address how people view their government: how well or poorly they think government is doing, whether they trust the government, and their evaluations of individual politicians, most notably their own representatives in the House and the Senate. These opinions matter for several reasons. A citizen's judgments about the government's overall performance may shape their evaluations of specific policies, especially if the citizen does not know much about the program.[73] Evaluations of specific policies may also be shaped by how much a citizen trusts the government, and as you would expect, more trust brings higher evaluations.[74] Trust in government and overall evaluations might also influence a citizen's willingness to vote for incumbent congressional representatives or a president seeking reelection.[75]

Table 5.6 shows citizen evaluations of government as measured in a Pew Trust survey, revealing that the average American is fairly disenchanted with their

TABLE 5.5 **MEASURING AMERICAN PUBLIC OPINION: EXAMPLES OF PRINCIPLES**

If polarization is not evident in ideological or party identification, perhaps it can be found in responses to specific questions about principles. Do responses to these questions show consistent evidence of polarization? Why might opinion surveys overstate the amount of polarization in the population?

	Strongly Agree	Agree	Neither, don't know	Agree	Strongly Agree	
Government regulation of business is necessary to protect the public interest	32%	17%	10%	11%	30%	Government regulation of business usually does more harm than good
This country should do whatever it takes to protect the environment	63	14	5	12	18	This country has gone too far in its efforts to protect the environment
Racial discrimination is the main reason why many black people can't get ahead these days	18	9	12	16	44	Blacks who can't get ahead in this country are mostly responsible for their own condition
The growing number of newcomers from other countries threatens traditional American values and customs	29	11	10	16	34	The growing number of newcomers from other countries strengthens American society
Homosexuality is a way of life that should be accepted by society	35	14	7	6	38	Homosexuality is a way of life that should be discouraged by society
Books that contain dangerous ideas should be banned from public school libraries	38	6	5	10	41	Public school libraries should be allowed to carry any books they want
The best way to ensure peace is through military strength	25	5	15	9	46	Good diplomacy is the best way to ensure peace
We should all be willing to fight for our country, whether it is right or wrong	39	7	8	8	38	It's acceptable to refuse to fight in war if you believe it is morally wrong
Americans need to be willing to give up more privacy and freedom in order to be safe from terrorism	24	11	5	9	51	Americans shouldn't have to give up privacy and freedom in order to be safe from terrorism

SOURCE: Pew Research Center, "Beyond Red and Blue," May 10, 2005, available at http://people-press.org/reports/display.php3?ReportID=242.

government. A majority believes that elected officials lose touch with the people and don't care what average people think, and that corporations have too much power. A near-majority believes that government is almost always wasteful and inefficient. These evaluations are nothing new; many surveys over the last two generations show similar responses.[76]

TABLE 5.6	MEASURING AMERICAN PUBLIC OPINION: BELIEFS ABOUT GOVERNMENT					

Surveys show that Americans generally like their elected representatives in Congress. Presidents are sometimes extremely popular. Do Americans have positive feelings about government itself?

	Strongly Agree	Agree	Neither, don't know	Agree	Strongly Agree	
Government is almost always wasteful and inefficient.	39%	49%	8%	17%	28%	Government often does a better job than people give it credit for.
Too much power is concentrated in the hands of a few large companies.	46	7	8	14	25	The largest companies do not have too much power.
Elected officials in Washington lose touch with the people pretty quickly.	54	12	8	11	15	Elected officials in Washington try hard to stay in touch with voters back home.
Most elected officials care about what people like me think.	19	13	8	52	11	Most elected officials don't care about what people like me think.

SOURCE: Pew Research Center, "Beyond Red and Blue," May 10, 2005, available at http://people-press.org/reports/display.php3?ReportID=242.

This impression of a disenchanted and disapproving public is amplified by Figure 5.7, which shows levels of trust in government declining steadily since the 1960s. All-time lows were recorded in the mid-1970s during the Watergate scandal and impeachment of then-president Nixon, and in the early 1990s, although trust has increased somewhat in recent years. As noted earlier, many scholars have argued that low levels of trust make it harder for elected officials to enact new policies, especially those that require large expenditures.[77] More profoundly, some scholars argue that low levels of trust raise questions about the future of democracy in America.[78] How can we say that American democracy is a good or popular form of government when so many people are unhappy with the performance of elected officials and bureaucrats?

One important response is that while Americans don't like their government in general, they tend to be far happier with their own representatives in Washington (see Chapter 10). One possibility is that putting a human face on government by asking about specific individuals improves evaluations because it calls to mind different considerations. Asking about "the government" may call to mind a vast room of bureaucrats pushing paperwork from one desk to another, while asking about "your representative" may lead people to think of someone working on their behalf.

In addition, members of Congress work hard to convince their constituents that they are doing everything they can to satisfy their demands. Sometimes, members blame the institution of Congress and the government bureaucracy for shortcomings, setting themselves up as standing between their constituents and an inept, inefficient government. As one scholar put it, "House members run for Congress by running against Congress."[79] In fact, members who deviate from this strategy while running for reelection by trying to convince their constituents that Congress does a good job are more likely to be defeated—not because they do a worse job than their colleagues, but because their statements call to mind unfavorable impressions of government that constituents consider when deciding whether to vote for the representative.[80]

▲ Trust in government reached its lowest recorded levels during the mid-1970s. The decline partly reflected the economic downturn and conflict over the Vietnam War, but opinions were also shaped by the discovery that then-president Richard Nixon lied about his involvement in the Watergate scandal. Here Nixon resigns from office to avoid impeachment.

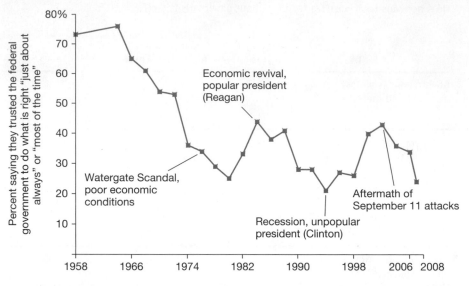

FIGURE 5.7   TRUST IN GOVERNMENT

In America, trust in government varies widely over time. What factors drive these changes?

Percent saying they trusted the federal government to do what is right "just about always" or "most of the time"

- Economic revival, popular president (Reagan)
- Watergate Scandal, poor economic conditions
- Recession, unpopular president (Clinton)
- Aftermath of September 11 attacks

SOURCE: Pew Research Center, "Trends in Political Values and Core Attitudes, 1987–2007," March 27, 2007, available at http://people-press.org/reports/pdf/312.pdf.

POLICY PREFERENCES

In a diverse country of more than 300 million, people care about a wide range of government policies. One useful summary measure of Americans' policy preferences is the **policy mood** mentioned earlier, which captures the public's collective demands for government action on domestic policies.[81] Policy mood measures are constructed from surveys that ask about opinions on a wide range of policy questions.[82] Changes in the policy mood in America have led to changes in defense spending, environmental policy, and race-related policies among others—and have influenced elections.[83] Figure 5.8 shows that when the policy mood leans in a liberal direction, such as in the early 1960s, conditions are ripe for an expansion of the federal government involving more spending and new programs. On the other hand, when the American policy mood leans conservative, such as in the late 1970s and early 1980s, elected officials are likely to enact smaller increases in government spending and fewer new programs. Thus, the Democratic takeover of Congress in the 2006 elections makes sense in light of the increase in support for government action since 2000.

Turning to specific issues, surveys conducted in the past few years show that most Americans are focused on the same set of issues: Iraq, terrorism, economic conditions, energy policy, health care, immigration, global warming, abortion, and gay rights.[84] The remainder of this section presents opinion data on these issues, some of which show significant levels of conflict, with large numbers of people on both sides of the question. In other cases, either most people hold similar opinions, or the level of conflict depends on how the question is asked, meaning that most people's opinions are not very strong.

Iraq The war in Iraq has influenced American politics since American troops invaded the country in March 2003, and public opinion on the conflict has changed

POLITICS IS CONFLICTUAL

Public opinion data on many controversial issues, including the war in Iraq, the War on Terror, and abortion laws, show that the level of conflict revealed by a survey depends on how the questions are worded.

policy mood The level of public support for expanding the government's role in society; whether the public wants government action on a specific issue.

What Do Citizens in Other Countries Think about American Democracy?

Americans may not be happy with their government, but they stand by the idea of democracy. Even though many Americans don't bother to vote and few people pay attention to politics on a daily or even weekly basis, support for our democratic system of government is nearly universal, to the extent that most surveys have stopped asking the question. Most Americans consider the advantages of democracy obvious.

Of course, Americans' enthusiasm for democracy does not imply that people elsewhere will feel the same way. Many of us were born into this democracy and have known no other system of government. For us, support for democracy may be more a matter of habit or socialization than a firm, informed preference. People who have not experienced free and fair elections, or the slow, conflictual process of policy making by elected officials, may have very different views on the merits and disadvantages of a democratic system.

In 2003, the Pew Charitable Trust funded a survey of public opinion in more than forty countries to find out what people elsewhere thought about some of the values generally associated with American democracy. In particular, respondents were asked whether it was "very important" to live in a country that permitted citizens to freely criticize the government, had a trustworthy two-party system, and allowed the media to report without censorship. The table below shows that there is majority support in these regions for all three elements of democracy. Importantly, the differences between predominantly Muslim countries and others in the sample are fairly small. Even among those countries, few of which have strong, stable democracies or a tradition of democratic elections, nearly seven in ten respondents see freedom of speech and honest elections as critical. Of course, put another way, about a third of the population in those nations does not see these factors as very important.

It is also important not to over-read these survey findings. The respondents who favor these particular democratic institutions are not expressing support for America or American-style democracy, and a substantial fraction of the respondents are not strong supporters of democracy in any form. Thus, it would be a mistake for Americans to believe that everyone in other countries wants to copy the American model of democracy, or that other countries would either accept the imposition of democracy or express gratitude for American attempts to change their political system. ■

OPINIONS ABOUT DEMOCRACY IN OTHER NATIONS

Surveys of Americans show strong support for democracy and civil liberties. Is this support something unique to established democracies such as the United States or is it shared by people throughout the world?

VERY IMPORTANT TO LIVE IN A COUNTRY WHERE . . .

	People can openly criticize the government	There are honest, two-party elections	The media can report without censorship
Latin America	71%	66%	67%
Sub-Saharan Africa	71	73	63
Eastern Europe	57	60	60
Muslim countries	67	71	53

SOURCE: Pew Research Center, "World Publics Welcome Global Trade–But Not Immigration," Pew Global Attitudes Project, available at http://pewglobal.org/reports/pdf/258.pdf.

profoundly since the invasion. Given the pessimistic tone of public opinion at the time of the 2006 midterm elections, it makes sense that the war was a central issue in many congressional campaigns, and that Democratic candidates, who generally took antiwar positions, gained support. By the 2008 election, with public opinion on Iraq less negative and many Americans worried about the economy, candidates' positions on the war were not a decisive factor in most races.

Public opinion about Iraq is often considered representative of the high levels of disagreement in America over policy questions.[85] However, Iraq is actually a good example of the way levels of conflict vary with how opinion is measured. Consider the two charts in Figure 5.9 from a late-2006 Pew Trust survey. In the left chart,

FIGURE 5.8   POLICY MOOD

As the labels in the figure indicate, sharp changes in the policy mood often precede changes in the composition of Congress or the party that holds the presidency. Could you have used the recent policy mood data to predict the outcomes of the 2008 presidential and congressional elections?

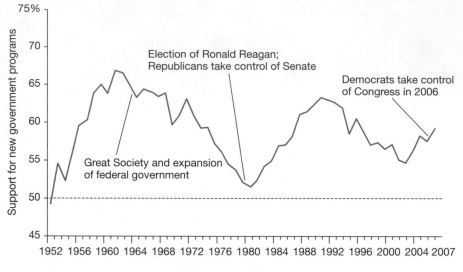

SOURCE: James Stimson, University of North Carolina, Chapel Hill, available at http://www.unc.edu/~jstimson.

people were offered two policy options: bring the troops home or keep them in Iraq. The result was a nearly even 50–44 split, suggesting a profound division in the American public between people who supported the current policy and those who favored withdrawal. However, look at the chart on the right, in which the same people were given more specific options to consider. Very few people supported immediate withdrawal, and very few liked the current policy. Most people fell between these extremes, with many favoring a gradual withdrawal. Moreover, of the people who wanted to keep troops in Iraq, almost half believed that additional forces should be sent to the region.

Terrorism As we discussed earlier, since the September 11 attacks, Americans have become more concerned about the possibility of a terrorist attack. In addition, a majority supports restricting civil liberties as a tactic for fighting terrorism. However, the extent of this support depends on the specific restriction. There is majority support for national identification cards and profiling at airports—but majority opposition to government monitoring of phone calls, e-mails, and credit card transactions.

These data highlight the difficulty of measuring public opinion using nonspecific questions. When people are asked the general question, whether they favor civil liberties restrictions to fight terrorism, a majority says yes. When they are asked about specific restrictions, however, they favor some but not others. Thus, the way people respond to general questions about government policy may have little to do with their opinions on implementing specific policies.

Economic Conditions The data presented earlier showed how Americans' evaluations of the state of the economy related to actual economic conditions. However, it is no exaggeration to say that Americans are always worried about the economy.

POLITICS IS CONFLICTUAL

The fact that Americans agree on the cause of a problem, such as the high price of health care, does not mean that they will agree on how to address the problem.

During late 2006, President Bush approved a "surge" of additional troops to Iraq. At that time, did Americans favor or oppose Bush's policy? Does the answer depend on how the question was asked?

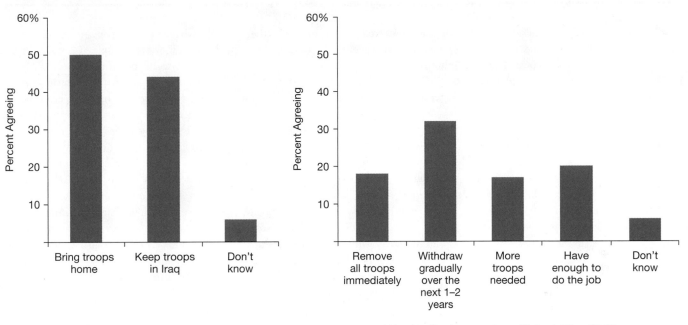

SOURCE: Pew Research Center, "Baker-Hamilton Report Evokes Modest Public Interest," December 12, 2006, available at http://people-press.org/reports/display.php3?ReportID=297.

Even when other pressing issues, such as the war in Iraq or terrorism, surpass the economy as the most important problems to Americans, the economy is typically listed second or third.

Recent history shows evidence of this pattern. Throughout 2006 and 2007, more than one-third of Americans rated the war in Iraq as the most important problem, while the economy ranked a distant second, cited by only 10 percent of respondents.[86] However, conditions began to change in late 2007: the combination of a collapse of housing prices and the disruption of credit markets, along with improving conditions in Iraq, led many Americans to revise their opinions. A February 2008 survey by the Pew Research Center revealed deep doubts about the economy, as shown in Table 5.7. Less than one-fifth of respondents rated economic conditions as "good" or "excellent," whereas a year before, more than one-third of those surveyed had given one of these ratings. Moreover, by early 2008 less than half believed that their personal economic conditions were either "excellent" or "good," and more than one-third said the economy was the country's most important problem, compared to only 27 percent who cited Iraq.

TABLE 5.7 **AMERICANS' EVALUATIONS OF ECONOMIC CONDITIONS, FEBRUARY 2008**

Rating of U.S. Economy	Nov. 2007	Jan. 2008	Feb. 2008
Excellent	3%	3%	1%
Good	20	23	16
Only fair	44	45	36
Poor	32	28	45
Don't know	1	1	2
Rating of Personal Finances			
Excellent/good	50%	49%	45%
Only fair/poor	49	49	53
Don't know	1	2	2

SOURCE: Pew Research Center, "Economic Discontent Deepens as Inflation Concerns Rise," February 14, 2008, http://people-press.org/reports/display.php3?ReportID=395.

Responding to Public Opinion on the Iraq War

lected officials in America work hard to cast votes and propose policies that their constituents will like, which, at first glance, seems easy. All a politician needs to do is take a poll to measure public opinion in her state or district, and comply with the demands expressed in the survey responses.

Actually, carrying out constituents' wishes is far more complex, because public opinion is hard to measure. How does a representative find out what her constituents want? Everything you have learned in this chapter suggests that it's not as easy as taking a poll. Poll results need interpretation and may not provide clear guidance.

Consider public opinion on the war in Iraq. Suppose a member of the House of Representatives serves a district where public opinion on the war mirrors the national data in Figure 5.9. Suppose this representative believes that the most important thing she can do is to behave in accordance with opinion in her district. What sort of guide does the survey data provide? As a policy advisor, how would you interpret these results, and what would you tell the representative to do?

The first problem is that the survey suggests different responses depending on which question you look at. Based on the left-hand chart, the district is sharply divided, with a narrow majority favoring keeping troops in Iraq, so it seems the representative should vote in favor of continuing the current policy. However, look at the right-hand plot, where respondents are given a wider range of options. Now a strong majority wants to change America's Iraq policy, with nearly 40 percent favoring a gradual withdrawal.

The data reveal two problems with reading public opinion for guidance. For one thing, sometimes the American public, either in a district or across the nation, is so divided that survey responses offer little guidance about what to do. Moreover, even when providing more options makes opinion look less divided, the most popular option may be the first choice of relatively few people. No matter which option a representative picks, most of the people in her district will wish she had done something else.

Another issue with interpreting surveys stems from the way opinions are typically formed on the spot and based on relatively little information. As a result, the representative cannot use just one survey as a guide to what her constituents think. Opinions might look very different on a survey taken a day later, even if the situation in Iraq remained unchanged. Small changes in question wording or in how the sample was constructed may also yield very different opinion data. And finally, opinions may be different a month or a year later, as Americans refine their views in light of events and new information.

In sum, even in the case of the Iraq conflict, which has dominated media politial coverage as well as many people's everyday lives, public opinion is hard to measure. Even if a representative wants to act according to her constituents' opinions, those opinions may provide little clear guidance. ■

It is important to understand that not everyone who mentions "the economy" as a problem means the same thing. Consider Table 5.8, which shows the answers that the same Pew survey respondents gave when asked to be more specific about their diagnoses of economic problems. These data show little consensus about particular economic difficulties. One of the most frequently cited problems, prices, was mentioned by only one-fourth of the sample—and even within this category, respondents expressed concern about price increases in several different industries, such as energy and health care. Respondents also cited a variety of other types of problems, including unemployment, taxes, and the cost of the war in Iraq.

These data make sense given what we know about the opinion-formation process. Most Americans base their judgments about the economy on whatever considerations come to mind when they are asked for an opinion—from personal circumstances to long-held values or information from a recent news broadcast. Since these individual considerations vary, so do people's judgments about the economy and their diagnoses of the problems.

These differences in opinion have an important policy implication: policies designed to improve economic conditions may prove widely unpopular if they do not address the considerations that lead individuals to worry. For example, policies that reduce energy prices will find favor with people who see the high price of energy

TABLE 5.8 AMERICANS' DIAGNOSES OF ECONOMIC PROBLEMS, FEBRUARY 2008

Prices	**24%**
Gasoline/oil/energy	11
Healthcare/medical	9
Cost of living/inflation	5
Jobs	**18%**
Unemployment/lack of jobs/low wages	14
Jobs moving overseas/outsourcing	4
Housing	**13%**
Affordable housing/Real estate	9
Mortgage problems/foreclosures	6
Government	**11%**
Budget/deficit/government spending	4
Taxes	3
Government officials	2
Social Security	1
Not enough spending at home	1
Spending on war in Iraq	10
Debt/credit issues/bankruptcy	4
Economy (general)	3
Immigration	3
Other social issues	3
Other	17
None/no problem	1
Don't know	10

Source: Pew Research Center, "Economic Discontent Deepens as Inflation Concerns Rise," February 14, 2008, available at http://people-press.org/reports/display.php3?ReportID=395.

as a drag on the American economy—but these changes will not satisfy people who consider high taxes or the cost of the war in Iraq to be the culprit.

Health Care Health care is another important concern for many Americans, a majority of whom are worried about being unable to afford health insurance or losing their insurance coverage. Over a quarter of Americans have put off treatment because of cost concerns, and almost the same percentage have had trouble paying their medical bills.[87] These opinions raise a puzzling question: if a majority of Americans are unhappy with the current health care system, why has it stayed in place, despite many reform proposals?[88] Figure 5.10 offers an answer. The first two bars show responses when people are asked whether they favor reform in the abstract, and the next four bars show the same group's answers about whether they still favor reform given consequences such as higher costs. The figure shows that universal coverage attracts more support than the current system—until people

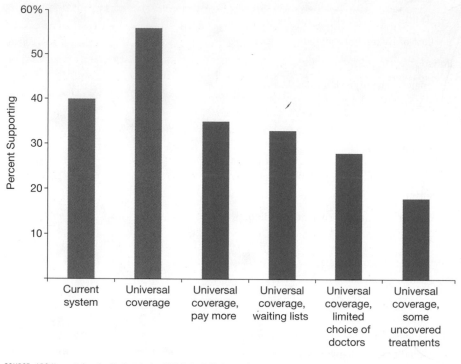

FIGURE 5.10 SUPPORT FOR HEALTH CARE REFORMS

The far left bar shows that only 40 percent of Americans are satisfied with the current health care system. Does this dissatisfaction imply support for universal coverage? Does support depend on how the question is asked?

SOURCE: ABC News, Kaiser Family Foundation/*USA Today* Poll, "As Health Care Costs Take a Toll, Some Changes Win Broad Backing," October 6, 2006, available at http://abcnews.go.com/images/Politics/1021a1HealthCare.pdf.

consider that they could face higher costs, waiting lists for treatment, limited choice of doctors, or lack of coverage for some treatments. With these disadvantages, all of which are possible under universal coverage, the current system, despite its drawbacks, receives more support. These data provide a simple explanation for the lack of health care reform: while many people do not like the current system, they show even less support for realistic transformations.

Immigration Immigration is a good example of an issue on which the level of conflict among political elites, such as elected officials, is much higher than among the general public. In recent years, many immigration reform proposals have been debated in Congress but none have been enacted, as representatives and senators could not compromise on a proposal.[89] However, as Figure 5.11 shows, there is broad consensus among the American public for specific reforms. More than two-thirds of the sample favored guest worker programs that would allow illegal immigrants to become citizens after several years—and a comparable number favored fining businesses that hired illegal workers as well. The question, then, is why immigration reform has been stymied in Congress. The problem is not partisan divisions in the electorate. Other research has found that similar percentages of Republicans, Democrats, and independents support this kind of program, at least in the general

POLITICS IS CONFLICTUAL

High levels of conflict in Congress over a policy proposal, such as immigration reform, do not always reflect conflict among the American public. Members of Congress may disagree because of pressure from interest groups, because of their personal policy preferences, or because they believe that media coverage of the conflict will have some political benefit.

public.[90] These data suggest that the failure to reform immigration laws may have more to do with conflict within Congress or pressures from a small number of voters who have intense preferences.

Global Warming Although most Americans agree that global warming is happening, the public is split on what is causing it. And on this issue, unlike immigration reform, grouping respondents by their partisanship reveals sharp differences in opinion, as shown in Figure 5.12. If you are a Democrat, you are much more likely to believe that global warming is real and being caused by humans. If you are a Republican, you are more likely to believe that global warming isn't happening, or if it is, that it is a natural phenomenon that humans have no decisive role in creating. Given this split, it is no surprise that members of Congress and the president have been unable to agree on policies to combat global warming, since one party's supporters do not see it as a problem in the first place.

Social Issues Social issues are among the most divisive in American politics. Typically these issues involve the question of whether the government should restrict an individual's behavior in line with a particular moral code.

We looked at opinion data on abortion earlier in this chapter and saw that support for abortion rights, as measured in opinion surveys, varies substantially with small changes in question wording (see Table 5.3). Some Americans oppose abortions under any circumstances, while others view abortion as a personal choice that government should not control. But most people are in the middle, favoring access to abortion under some circumstances but not others. For these people, support for abortion laws depends on how the question is asked. This distribution of opinion has stayed roughly the same for over a generation.

POLITICS IS CONFLICTUAL

In some cases, such as global warming and many social issues, differences in Americans' opinions are strongly related to their partisanship, with most Democrats on one side of the issue and most Republicans on the other.

FIGURE 5.11 **OPINIONS ABOUT IMMIGRATION REFORM OPTIONS**

Immigration reform is a highly contentious issue in Congress. Do American voters agree on what should be done?

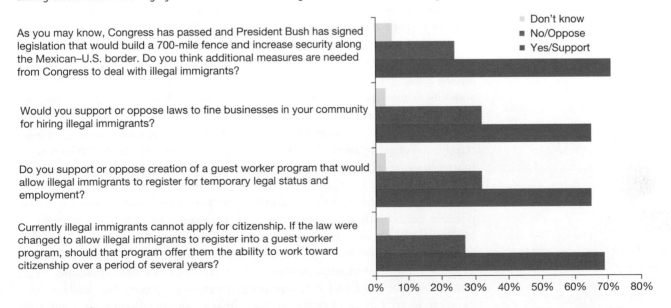

SOURCE: Quinnipiac University Poll, "Let Illegal Immigrants Become Citizens, U.S. Voters Tell Quinnipiac Poll," November 21, 2006, available at http://www.quinnipiac.edu/ x1284.xml?ReleaseID=988&What=700%20mile%20fence&strArea=;&strTime=120. The margin of sampling error is +/– 2.4 percentage points.

FIGURE 5.12   PARTISAN DIFFERENCES ON GLOBAL WARMING

Are opinions on global warming shaped by partisanship? Do Republican and Democratic voters tend to agree or disagree on the nature of global warming and what should be done about it?

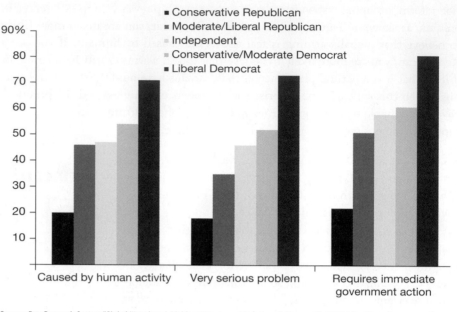

Source: Pew Research Center, "Global Warming: A Divide on Causes and Solutions," January 24, 2007, http://people-press.org/reports/display.php3?ReportID=303.

Table 5.3 suggests that it is easy to overstate the conflict in American society over abortion rights. While there are many pro-life and pro-choice protests, and abortion rights are a perennial campaign issue, a majority of Americans have two abortion-related views in common: they are uncomfortable about abortions but oppose outlawing the procedure. Whether these considerations could lead to a compromise proposal is an open question, but the debate over abortion rights in America does not consist of two large groups on opposite sides of the question. In fact, far more people are in the middle.

Another social issue, gay rights, shows a distribution of opinion that is similar to views on global warming. Survey data show that a majority of Americans favor allowing gay couples to form civil unions (partnerships that confer the same legal standing as marriage), but that less than one-third of Americans support allowing gay couples to marry.[91] Taking a closer look, Figure 5.13 shows that the conflict splits Americans in partisan terms, with a majority of Republicans favoring no legal recognition of gay relationships and a majority of Democrats favoring civil unions or marriage rights. Thus, while the data show high levels of conflict, they suggest that disagreements over gay rights are driven by partisan identification.

While these figures show how partisanship affects positions on issues, it is also possible, particularly over time, that issue positions could causes changes in an individual's party identification. For example, suppose a Republican decides that he favors gay marriage and supports an aggressive government effort to combat global warming, positions supported by more Democrats than Republicans. This inconsistency between his party identification and his preferences may lead the individual to identify as a Democrat, for the simple reason that Democratic candidates are more likely to share his position on these issues.

FIGURE 5.13   PARTISAN DIFFERENCES ON GAY RIGHTS

Americans narrowly favor some form of official recognition for same-sex partnerships. Are these attitudes influenced by partisanship?

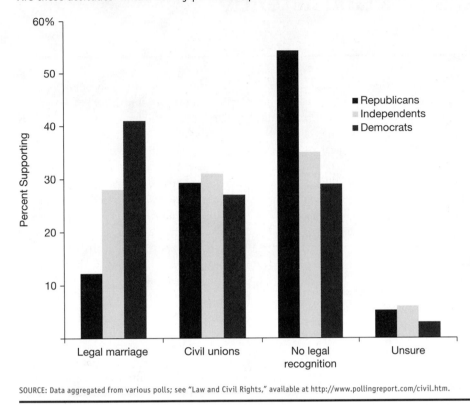

SOURCE: Data aggregated from various polls; see "Law and Civil Rights," available at http://www.pollingreport.com/civil.htm.

SECTION SUMMARY

1. Americans disagree about how the government should address many policy questions, from immigration to global warming.
2. However, in many areas, policy conflict reflects question wording or a disagreement on principles such as party affiliation. Thus, while conflict is a fact of American politics, it is easy to overstate its reach and its intensity.

Does Public Opinion Matter?

As we discussed at the beginning of this chapter, some observers of American politics have argued that most Americans have no real opinions about candidates, policies, or anything else. Others have claimed that these opinions exist but are ignored by government officials. The case of the Iraq war does not support either of these claims, as we showed in the chapter introduction. Having described what political scientists know about American public opinion, we can now analyze these claims.

To begin with, one of the most important pieces of evidence that public opinion remains highly relevant in American politics is the amount of time and effort politi-

How Many Americans Are Consistently Liberal or Conservative?

As Tables 5.5 and 5.6 show, Americans hold polarized opinions on several important political principles and policy questions, but there are also issues on which most people hold moderate opinions. On the whole, the data do not support claims of a polarized America divided into two opposing camps, regardless of the issue.

Additional evidence against polarization comes from looking at a series of opinion questions in order to determine the percentage of Americans who consistently answer on the same ideological side of these questions, either liberal or conservative. As we discussed in the beginning of the chapter, early studies of public opinion found little evidence of such consistency. Has

this property of American public opinion changed over the last thirty years?

A 2006 Pew Trust survey tested just this point by asking a series of questions about several politically divisive social issues: gay marriage, adoption of children by gay couples, abortion, stem cell research, and the morning-after pill. The researchers then calculated the number of times each respondent gave a socially conservative response to these questions, opposing gay marriage, adoption by gay couples, abortion, etc. If Americans hold consistently liberal or conservative views, most people should give either no conservative responses or all conservative responses. The first column in the graph shows that 22 percent of respondents expressed consistently liberal views on the five questions. Similarly, the right-hand column shows that 12 percent expressed consistent conservatism. In other words, only about a third of the sample held beliefs that aligned with only one of these ideological positions. The rest gave liberal responses on some issues and conservative responses on others. These findings provide another challenge to claims about a polarized America. Not only are there low levels of polarization on many policy questions, but most Americans give some liberal and some conservative responses to these questions. These data suggest that American public opinion is not very polarized—and that when someone identifies as a liberal or a conservative, she is expressing her average opinion or general tendency. ■

THE CONSISTENCY OF AMERICAN PUBLIC OPINION

Figure 5.5 showed that among Americans, self-described moderates outnumber both conservatives and liberals. Is this label consistent with citizen's positions on specific issues?

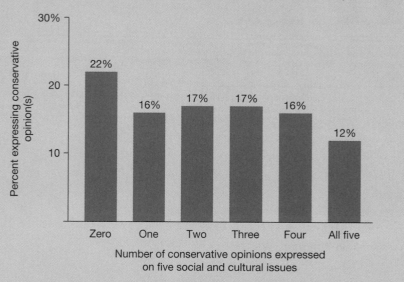

Number of conservative opinions expressed on five social and cultural issues

SOURCE: Pew Research Center, "Most Want Middle Ground on Abortion," August 3, 2006, available at http://people-press.org/reports/pdf/283.pdf.

cians, journalists, and political scientists spend trying to find out what Americans think. If people were just making up their opinions, there would be no point to carrying out elaborate, expensive public opinion surveys. The intense effort to find out what people think, as well as the importance given to these data by candidates, party leaders, and political strategists, provide the best evidence that these opinions matter.

Of course, it is easy to come up with examples in which public opinion appears to be ignored in the political process because policy has stayed the same despite a clear majority supporting change. And in many other cases, new policies have been enacted even though a majority preferred the status quo. But these examples do not mean that public opinion is irrelevant. Rather, they reflect the complexities of the policy-making process. As we have seen, it's not always possible to please a majority of citizens; politicians' willingness to do so depends on whether the majority is organized into interest groups, how much they care about the issue (and the intensity of the opposition), whether their demands are shared by elected officials, and many other factors. Moreover, the American system of checks and balances between the branches of government deliberately makes it hard to change most government policies.

Many of the arguments about the irrelevance of public opinion also hinge on misreading poll results. On many of the issues discussed here, an individual's support for a particular policy option hinges on how survey questions are worded. As you saw in the case of the Iraq conflict, support for withdrawing American troops depends on whether the current commitment is described as open-ended or temporary. Similarly, the percentage of people who say they favor abortion rights depends on whether the question describes the motivations for the procedure. Thus, depending on which poll results we use, the results of a particular policy can be made to look closely aligned with or completely contradictory to the opinions of a majority of Americans.

It is also important to remember that for most people, opinions are not predetermined, firm ideas. If you went out today and asked people what they want government to do, there is no guarantee that they would give the same answer the next day, week, or month. These shifts in opinion mean that it is often difficult to connect aggregate-level opinions (what Americans think as a group) with outcomes such as who wins an election or whether a proposal is enacted in Congress. In trying to connect outcomes to opinions, we are aiming at a moving target.

Even with all of these difficulties, it is clear that public opinion is the wellspring of politics in America, exerting conspicuous influence in widespread areas of government. The data on Americans' policy mood, for example, shows that significant policy mood changes were often followed by changes in government policy. Chapter 10, Congress, shows how legislators spend a great deal of time trying to determine what their constituents want and how constituents will respond to different actions. In Chapter 8, Elections, we will see how voters use retrospective evaluations to form opinions about who to vote for, and how candidates incorporate the public's views into campaign platforms that will attract support from the electorate. And Chapter 7, Political Parties, discusses how voters use candidates' party affiliations like brand names to determine how each party's candidates will behave if elected.

Recent events also speak to the influence of public opinion. In the case of the war in Iraq, as long as public support remained high, members of Congress voiced few criticisms of military strategy or reconstruction efforts. However, as public support waned, more and more House members and senators from both parties began to express reservations, disagree with President Bush's claims that conditions were getting better, and suggest that Congress needed to revise the war policy.[92] These comments no doubt reinforced the downward trend in public support for the war, and may have directly influenced the pro-Democratic shift in the 2006 election, in which Democrats gained majority control of the House and Senate (see Chapter 8). By 2008, voters' concerns over Iraq were overshadowed by worries about the economy, and the war receded significantly as an electoral issue.

The debate over global warming shows the same pattern. Public opinion on this issue has shifted dramatically in recent years, driving legislative efforts in 2007 and 2008 to limit carbon emissions. However, the lack of consensus on the causes of global warming and the partisan split in opinion meant that none of these efforts have succeeded.[93]

In fact, it is hard to find a major policy change that did not have majority support in the electorate at the time it was made. From relief and reconstruction efforts after Hurricane Katrina to the enactment of a prescription drug benefit for Medicare recipients to the minimum wage increase enacted by Democrats after they took control of the House of Representatives in 2007—all of these efforts reflected the demands of a majority of Americans, which is exactly what we should expect if public opinion is real and relevant to what happens in politics.

Failed efforts to change policies also demonstrate the importance of public opinion. The apparent consensus for health care reform falls apart once people are asked about specific proposals. Thus, it is no surprise that President Clinton's proposed reforms failed in 1994, and that no subsequent plan has attracted broad public support. Similarly, Bush's failed attempts to reform Social Security in 2005 show that it is virtually impossible to enact a major new piece of legislation if a strong majority of Americans oppose the proposal.

SECTION SUMMARY

1. On big issues that most Americans care about deeply, government policy generally reflects the opinions held by ordinary Americans.

2. Cases in which government policy appears to conflict with public opinion generally involve narrow splits in public opinion, a lack of consensus on what government should do, or a minority of the electorate that cares intensely about the issue.

Conclusion

Public opinion is real and it matters. Americans have ideas about what they want government to do and use these ideas to guide their political choices. American politicians are also extraordinarily sensitive to public opinion and reluctant to take actions that contradict the beliefs of large numbers of their constituents.

To put it another way, the role of public opinion in shaping policy on the Iraq war is not an exception but an example of how much public opinion matters in American politics. The average American is not an expert on military tactics or the history of the Middle East and knows relatively little about the progress of the war. But even this small amount of information is enough to inform beliefs about what America should do in Iraq. And the changes in the last few years in government policy, politicians' statements, and election outcomes all reflect changes in American public opinion on the war.

Likewise, very few Americans are experts about abortion rights, Social Security, or education policy. Their responses to questions about these issues may vary from day to day, but most Americans know enough to decide what they want government to do about these problems—and to act on these opinions. Politicians, in turn, take public opinion very seriously, as it provides the yardstick that measures citizens' judgments of their behavior in office.

CRITICAL THINKING

1. Given that many Americans cannot answer basic political questions (or answer them incorrectly), and many of the opinions they express vary from day to day without anything changing in the political world, how can we say that public opinion exists?
2. In light of the many problems with measuring public opinion, how should you read survey results?
3. How much conflict is there in American public opinion?

KEY TERMS

considerations (p. 147)
issue scale (p. 156)
ideological polarization (p. 164)
latent opinion (p. 147)
level of conceptualization (p. 144)
liberal–conservative ideology (p. 146)
mass survey (p. 156)
on-line processing (p. 147)
policy mood (p. 168)
political socialization (p. 150)
population (p. 156)
public opinion (p. 143)
random digit dialing (p. 158)
random sample (p. 156)
robo-poll (p. 159)
sample (p. 156)
sampling error (p. 156)

SUGGESTED READING

Alvarez, R. Michael, and John Brehm. *Hard Choices, Easy Answers.* Princeton, NJ: Princeton University Press, 2002.

Campbell, David. *Why We Vote: How Schools and Communities Shape Our Civic Life.* Princeton, NJ: Princeton University Press, 2006.

Carmines, Edward G., and James A. Stimson. *Issue Evolution: Race and the Transformation of American Politics.* Princeton, NJ: Princeton University Press, 1990.

Converse, Phillip E. "The Nature of Belief Systems in Mass Publics." In *Ideology and Discontent,* edited by David E. Apter, 206–61. Glencoe, IL: The Free Press of Glencoe, 1964.

Delli Carpini, Michael X., and Scott Keeter. *What Americans Know About Politics and Why It Matters.* New Haven, CT: Yale University Press, 1997.

Green, Donald P., Bradley Palmquist, and Eric Schickler. *Partisan Hearts and Minds.* New Haven, CT: Yale University Press, 2002.

Hibbing, John R., and Elizabeth Theiss-Morse. *Congress as Public Enemy: Public Attitudes Toward American Political Institutions.* New York: Cambridge University Press, 1995.

Jacobs, Lawrence R., and Robert Y. Shapiro. *Politicians Don't Pander: Political Manipulation and the Loss of Democratic Responsiveness.* Chicago: University of Chicago Press, 2000.

Lupia, Arthur, and Mathew D. McCubbins. *The Democratic Dilemma.* New York: Cambridge University Press, 1998.

Marcus, George E., John L. Sullivan, Elizabeth Theiss-Morse, and Sandra L. Wood. *With Malice Toward Some: How People Make Civil Liberties Judgments.* New York: Cambridge University Press, 1995.

Zaller, John. *The Nature and Origins of Mass Opinion.* New York: Cambridge University Press, 1992.

6

THE MEDIA

By the spring of 2001, Representative Gary Condit of California had served six terms in the House. As a member of the Intelligence Committee, he had high-level security clearance, and he was also a member of the Democratic Party's Steering and Policy Committee that formulates the party's agenda and tactics in the House. Aside from his hobby of riding a motorcycle on weekends back in his district and wearing cowboy boots on the House floor, Condit didn't stand out much from his colleagues; he seemed a smart, above-average representative and a good bet for a long career in office.

In April 2001, however, college student Chandra Levy vanished just before finishing an internship at the Federal Bureau of Prisons in Washington, DC. When it emerged that she and Condit had had an affair, press attention to her disappearance zeroed in on Condit. The story hit the front pages of many publications and became a cable and network television staple. Condit was hounded by reporters, both in Washington and during his trips back to California. Over the next two months, Condit acknowledged his relationship with Levy, but said he had nothing to do with her disappearance. The police interviewed him three times, but never named him as a suspect. Even so, a CNN/*USA Today*/Gallup poll found that 67 percent of respondents believed that Condit was somehow involved; over three-quarters believed he was dishonest and immoral.[1] Condit ran for reelection in 2002 and was defeated by a former aide. Press attention to Levy's disappearance dropped off after the terrorist attacks in September 2001. Her body was found a year later in a Washington, DC, park. The crime has not been solved.

Gary Condit's story illustrates the role of the news media as a provider of political information—the media watchdog monitors politicians, government actions, and policy debates and reports to citizens. However, the story also raises some important and disturbing issues. In retrospect, the Condit–Levy story was not of great national political consequence, and there was little reason to suspect Condit of foul play. But at the time, many newspapers, television programs, and political news Web sites treated the disappearance of Chandra Levy as one of the most important things happening in Washington—and all but named Gary Condit as the prime suspect. (Condit eventually won legal settlements for libel against some publishers and reporters.)

During spring 2006, intern Chandra Levy's disappearance made front-page news nationwide. Congressman Gary Condit became the prime suspect, even though no evidence suggested foul play by Condit. Some journalists had misgivings about the coverage, but for most, the story was too popular to ignore.

Condit's experience also illustrates the three themes of this book. One of the principle reasons that politics is everywhere is that so much air time and countless printed pages and Web sites are devoted to covering political issues and events. Thus, examining what the media report and how they report it is a crucial component of understanding what Americans know about the government. Politics not only provides the content of many news stories—its processes and outcomes also influence the news industry. Coverage is shaped by federal regulations that affect what can be printed or broadcast, as well as by the structure and ownership of media corporations, many of which need to make a profit to survive. These political influences on the media can, in turn, affect how Americans view officeholders, candidates, and events. Finally, media coverage often focuses on political conflicts and can also become a focus of contention itself, as elected officials and others involved in politics often complain of unfair treatment by the press.

Complaints about media coverage of American politics are common. Many observers blame the media for Americans' lack of knowledge about politics and public policy, low levels of civic engagement, and distrust of the federal government.[2] These observers want coverage that gives Americans a detailed appreciation of the complex policy questions facing elected officials and bureaucrats, and that holds elected officials accountable for their campaign promises and behavior in office—rather than a steady stream of scandals, failures, and poll results.[3]

Our discussion of the news media addresses these arguments. Who are the media and how do they cover politics? What determines which stories make the news and how they are reported? Is media coverage politically biased? Where do people get their political information? How are new, Internet-based information sources affecting both the media business and what Americans know about politics?

The News Media in America

This section describes the **mass media**, the many sources of political information available to the average American. It also describes the dramatic changes occurring in new forms of media, and how these changes affect not only the amount of political information available and how it is delivered, but also how people use this information.

HISTORY OF THE NEWS MEDIA IN AMERICA

The role of the media as an information source and the controversy over how they report about politics are nothing new. Since the Founding, politicians have understood that Americans learn about politics largely from the media. And they have complained about coverage and sought to influence both the media's selection of stories and the way they report on them.

In colonial America, newspapers like the Pennsylvania Gazette *reported on government policy, elections, and scandals.*

The Early Days Long before there was a United States, the news media were active in colonial America. One of the earliest newspapers, the *Pennsylvania Gazette,* was published by Ben Franklin beginning in 1729. For the most part, newspapers had relatively low circulations, due partly to their cost and partly to the fact that they were available only in major cities.[4] During the Revolutionary War, many newspapers offered a rationale for separation from Britain and chronicled the course of the conflict. Afterward, newspapers became the venue for debates over the proposed federal government.[5]

Despite the constitutional guarantee of freedom of the press, in 1798 Congress and President Adams enacted the Alien and Sedition Acts, which made it a crime to criticize the President or Congress.[6] While these press restrictions were either repealed a few years later or allowed to expire, they serve as a reminder that the American media have never been free of government regulation, both in terms of what is published and who can own a newspaper or other media source.

Penny Press, Yellow Journalism, and Muckrakers Beginning in the 1830s, a combination of new technologies, entrepreneurs, and political ambition transformed the news media. In 1833, the *New York Sun* began selling papers for a penny a copy, rather than the standard price of six cents—thus earning the label **penny press**. The price reduction, which was made possible by cheaper, faster printing presses, made the newspaper available to the mass public for the first time, and this increase in circulation made it possible, even with the lower price, to hire larger staffs of reporters.[7] The development of the telegraph also aided newspapers by allowing reporters on assignments throughout the country to quickly send stories back home for publication. The Associated Press, the first **wire service**, was formed in the 1840s by a group of newspapers in New York to share the benefits and costs of this new technology.[8]

Many other newspapers soon appeared. Many were unabashedly partisan, using their coverage of events to support a particular political party or position. For example, the *New York Tribune,* published by Horace Greeley, was strongly anti-slavery. By 1860, the *Tribune*'s circulation was larger than any other newspaper in the world, and its articles, "helped to add fuel to the fires of slavery and sectionalism that divided North and South."[9]

The period after the Civil War saw the beginning of **yellow journalism**, a new type of newspaper reporting that appealed to a wider audience by using bold headlines, illustrations, and sensational stories. The best example of yellow journalism was the *New York Journal*, published by William Randolph Hearst. During the months before the Spanish-American War, Hearst's reporter in Cuba cabled that there were no signs of war and asked whether he should return home. Hearst cabled back, "Please remain. You furnish the pictures and I'll furnish the war."[10] Of course, America did not fight the Spanish-American War just because Hearst's newspaper published daily articles calling for the conflict—but it appears that the paper had a significant impact on public opinion.

At the same time, other authors and reporters used newspapers and books to call for reforms to federal, state, and local governments. These **investigative journalists,** known as muckrakers, included Lincoln Steffens, who criticized corruption in municipal governments, and Upton Sinclair, who raised concerns about food safety and public health.[11] The year 1896 saw the purchase of a small New York newspaper by Arthur Ochs, who wanted to rebuild it around the goal of journalistic impartiality, accuracy, and complete coverage of events. He gave the *New York Times* a new motto: "All the News That's Fit to Print."[12]

New Technologies and Federal Regulation After World War I, new communications technology made it possible to broadcast news and entertainment programs over radio—and for many Americans to buy radios to hear these programs.[13] During the 1920s, hundreds of small, local stations were built, along with some larger stations that could broadcast across the country, and the beginnings of networks, groups of local radio (and later, TV) stations owned by one company that broadcast a common set of programs.

▲ *The* New York Journal's *advocacy of war with Spain did not cause the conflict—but its steady stream of pro-war coverage did shape public opinion.*

mass media Sources like newspapers, television networks, radio stations, and Web sites, that provide information to the average citizen.

penny press A term describing reduced-price newspapers sold for one cent in the 1830s, when more efficient printing presses made newspapers available to a larger segment of the population.

wire service An organization that gathers news and sells it to other media outlets. The invention of the telegraph in the early 1800s made this type of service possible.

yellow journalism A style of newspaper popular in the late 1800s, featuring sensationalized stories, bold headlines, and illustrations in order to increase readership.

investigative journalists Reporters who dig deeply into a particular topic of public concern, often targeting government failures and inefficiencies.

▲ With the development of national radio networks in the 1920s and 1930s, Americans throughout the nation could hear coverage of important events as they occurred.

The Communications Act of 1934 authorized the **Federal Communications Commission (FCC)** to regulate **broadcast media**, which at the time meant radio stations and has since come to include television stations, cable TV, and other communications technologies. FCC regulations reflected the assumption that the airways were public property, so no one had an inherent right to operate a radio or TV station. Rather, the owners of these stations were expected to serve the public interest, as defined by the FCC.

A central concern of the FCC was that one company or organization might buy enough stations to dominate the airwaves in a particular city or state, so that only one set of programs or one network's point of view would be available. Over the next two generations, the FCC developed regulations to limit the number of radio and TV stations a company could own in a community and the total nationwide audience that a company's TV stations could reach. As new technologies such as cable and satellite TV developed, these regulations were expanded to include them.[14]

The 1940s saw the rise of TV as Americans' primary news source. As we discuss later, television made it possible to report on stories using instantly accessible visual footage rather than printed words, a crucial distinction given that many citizens are not highly motivated to learn about political events and issues. One frequently cited argument about public opinion during the Vietnam War was that the decline in public support for the war was driven by the fact that, for the first time in American history, stories depicting the horror of the war first-hand were a staple on nightly news broadcasts.[15]

POLITICS IS EVERYWHERE

The FCC's equal time provision continues to affect programming decisions, from the content of news programs to whether a TV program can remain on the air if a cast member is running for political office.

In the late 1940s, the FCC also developed the **fairness doctrine** (no longer in place), which required TV and radio stations to offer a variety of political views in their programming.[16] This rule did not mean that stations sent two reporters, one Republican and one Democrat (or one liberal and one conservative), to cover each political event. Rather, stations offered editorials supporting different political positions as part of their news programs, as well as talk shows and interviews featuring a wide range of political figures.

The FCC also created the **equal time provision**, which states that if a radio or television station gives air time or space to a candidate outside its news coverage—such as during an entertainment show or a cooking program—they have to give equal time to other candidates running for the same office. For example, in 2003, when actor Arnold Schwarzenegger was running for governor of California, television stations stopped broadcasting his movies on grounds that if they did, the other 134 candidates running in the election would be entitled to an equal amount of television time.[17] Some observers argued that Republican Fred Thompson's entry

▼ As these stark images from Vietnam (left) and Iraq (right) illustrate, photos and videos of war have the potential to capture attention and shape public opinion.

into the 2008 presidential primaries meant that some reruns of *Law and Order* would have to be taken off the air, as Thompson had played a district attorney on the show for several seasons. However, since no one made a formal complaint to the FCC, the episodes featuring Thompson continued to be broadcast, although actor Sam Waterston took over Thompson's role in new episodes.[18] TV satirist Stephen Colbert's brief presidential candidacy in 2007 also raised the question of whether *The Colbert Report* would have to go off the air during the campaign, since news and interview shows are normally exempted from the equal time provision. The issue became moot when Colbert was not allowed to compete in the South Carolina primaries.

▲ *Under the FCC's equal time regulations, if comedian Stephen Colbert had campaigned for president while remaining host of* The Colbert Report, *other presidential candidates could have forced the Comedy Central cable channel to give them free air time.*

Deregulation The FCC's limits on ownership and content assumed that radio and TV stations were public trustees who had a responsibility to provide full, fair, and unbiased coverage of political events. This assumption changed over time, with the development of new communications technologies such as cable TV, satellite TV, and the Internet because with so many sources of information, if one broadcaster ignored a candidate or an issue, citizens could still find out what they wanted to know from another source. Pressure for deregulation also came from the owners of media companies, who wanted to buy more TV, radio, and cable stations, as well as book and magazine publishers, Internet service providers, and newspapers to become more efficient and increase profits.[19] After much debate, Congress enacted the Telecommunications Act of 1996, which gave the FCC the power to revise all of the ownership and content restrictions enacted over the last two generations. Over the last ten years, the FCC has abolished most ownership restrictions. (The equal time provision is still in place, but the fairness doctrine was eliminated in 1987.)[20]

These regulatory changes accelerated two trends in American news media. The first is **concentration**, which involves one company owning more than one media source in a town or community. For example, Clear Channel Communications owns multiple AM and FM radio stations in over thirty different cities. The second trend is **cross-ownership**, one company owning several different kinds of media outlets, often in the same community. The Tribune Company in Chicago owns the WGN radio station, the WGN TV station, and the *Chicago Tribune* daily newspaper. These trends in turn have given rise to **media conglomerates**, companies that control a wide range of news sources.[21] All four television networks (ABC, NBC, CBS, and Fox) are part of larger companies that each own many other broadcast and cable stations, movie production and distribution companies, radio stations, newspapers, and other media outlets. Nuts and Bolts 6.1 shows the diverse holdings of one such company, News Corporation.

One pro-deregulation FCC commissioner, Kathleen Abernathy, argued for deregulation saying, "Democracy and civic discourse were not dead in America when there were only three to four stations in most markets in the 1960s and 1970s, and they will surely not be dead in this century when there are, at a minimum, four to six independent broadcasters in most markets, plus hundreds of cable channels and unlimited Internet voices."[22] Other commissioners disagreed, arguing that concentration would limit citizens' choices and force programming to become increasingly homogenized. As one commissioner put it, "As big media companies get bigger, they're likely to broadcast even more homogenized programming that increasingly appeals to the lowest common denominator. If [television] is [like] the toaster with pictures, soon only Wonder Bread will pop out."[23] As of now, it is not clear which viewpoint is correct, although many organizations, including the FCC, are researching the implications of deregulation.[24]

The deregulation of the news media stands in sharp contrast to the FCC's ongoing and strong regulation of entertainment broadcasts. For example, the FCC fined CBS Broadcasting for Janet Jackson's "wardrobe malfunction," which momentarily

Federal Communications Commission (FCC) A government agency created in 1934 to regulate American radio stations, and later expanded to regulate television, wireless communications technologies, and other broadcast media.

broadcast media Communications technologies, such as television and radio, that transmit information over airwaves.

fairness doctrine An FCC regulation requiring broadcast media to present several points of view to ensure balanced coverage. It was created in the late 1940s and eliminated in 1987.

equal time provision An FCC regulation requiring broadcast media to provide equal airtime on any non-news programming to all candidates running for an office.

concentration The trend toward single-company ownership of several media sources in one area.

cross-ownership The trend toward single-company ownership of several kinds of media outlets.

media conglomerates Companies that control a large number of media sources across several types of media outlets.

Holdings of News Corporation

News Corporation is an example of a media conglomerate, a company that controls a variety of different media outlets throughout the world—it owns a cable television network, TV and radio stations, newspapers, movie production companies, magazines, and even sports teams. While this structure allows the company to operate more efficiently, as it can rebroadcast or reprint stories in different outlets, opponents are concerned that conglomerates might expand to control most or even all of the sources that are available to the average citizen, making it impossible to access alternate points of view.

FOX TELEVISION STATIONS
Fox Television Network:
35 U.S. stations

**SATELLITE AND
CABLE STATIONS**
DirecTV
Fox News Channel
17 other cable channels
worldwide

FILM COMPANIES
20th Century Fox
Fox Searchlight Pictures
Fox Television Studios
Blue Sky Studios

NEWSPAPERS
New York Post
Wall Street Journal
5 UK newspapers
20 Australian newspapers

BOOKS AND MAGAZINES
The Weekly Standard
TV Guide (partial)
3 other magazines
45 book publishers worldwide

OTHER HOLDINGS
Los Angeles Kings
(40 percent ownership)
Los Angeles Lakers (10 percent
ownership)
MySpace.com
15 other businesses

POLITICS IS EVERYWHERE

Deregulation allows companies to control multiple media sources within a single community. If people use relatively few sources of information to learn about politics, deregulation makes it more likely that they may be exposed to only a single provider's point of view.

POLITICS IS CONFLICTUAL

The FCC's deregulation decisions were approved by a 3–2 vote of the FCC Commissioners. The closeness of the vote reflects fundamental disagreements within the FCC and in Congress about the desirability of these reforms.

exposed her breast during broadcast of the 2004 Super Bowl halftime show. (A court later threw out the regulation that the fine was based on.)[25] A more extreme example of the FCC's regulatory actions concerns radio personality Howard Stern, whose talk radio program specialized in outrageous behavior, featuring "strippers, porn stars, and dwarves," among other things.[26] By the 1990s, the show was a nationwide hit, producing over $100 million per year in revenue and $50 million per year in profits for the owner, Infinity Broadcasting. Although the show was the subject of repeated FCC investigations and fines,[27] the large profits it generated made the fines just a tolerable cost of doing business.

The situation changed in 2004, when members of Congress and FCC commissioners threatened to review and possibly cancel the broadcast licenses of radio stations that played Stern's show, on grounds that broadcasting obscene material was not in the public interest.[28] In response, Stern moved his show onto Sirius Satellite Radio, receiving a large salary increase and placing the show beyond FCC regulations, as the FCC has no jurisdiction over satellite radio.[29] On the unregulated satellite radio airwaves, the show has become even more outrageous—but listeners have to buy a radio capable of receiving Sirius's signal and purchase a subscription. Stern's experience illustrates how pervasive politics is, in that defining obscenity is not a matter of abstract debate. The FCC's decisions about what qualifies as obscene determines what can be broadcast on free radio. Moreover, political processes also yielded the decision to keep satellite radio outside of the FCC's jurisdiction, meaning that while broadcasting on Sirius, Stern can say whatever he wants without fearing fines or other punishments.

MEDIA SOURCES

There are many sources of political information, from **mainstream media (MSM)** publications such as newspapers, TV and radio stations, books, and magazines, to countless Internet-based sources.

Newspapers National newspapers, such as the *New York Times, Washington Post, Los Angeles Times,* or *Wall Street Journal,* cover American politics using a large, world-wide staff. Foreign publications such as the United Kingdom's *Financial Times* also cover American politics. Smaller, regional and local papers are published in medium-to large-sized cities and smaller towns. They differ from national papers in their staffing (fewer or no reporters based in other cities or outside the country) and in their coverage (focusing on local news and using more articles reprinted from other sources, such as wire service reports).

Recent years have seen significant declines in newspaper readership as Americans shift to other information sources, most notably the Internet. The newspaper business has also seen many corporate changes. Most newspapers are now part of large conglomerates such as Gannett or News Corporation, and outside major cities such as New York and Washington it is rare to have more than one local daily newspaper. It is too early to say that newspapers are "dead," as some do, but the drop in newspapers' circulation and their decreasing advertising revenues are forcing many newspapers to cut foreign bureaus, some local reporters, and the amount of news in every edition.[30] Even so, newspapers remain a widely used information source; as of 2007, 51 million Americans bought a newspaper every day and 124 million regularly read one.[31]

▲ *Australian native Rupert Murdoch, chairman of News Corp, directs an international empire of media businesses, including the* Wall Street Journal, *Fox News,* National Geographic, *and many others.*

Magazines and Books Of the many magazines that cover politics, national weeklies such as *Time* and *Newsweek* often feature political events as front-page news. The British publication *The Economist* has a small but influential audience for its coverage of politics and business worldwide. Many other magazines occasionally cover political topics. Even *Reader's Digest, GQ,* or *Ladies' Home Journal* will sometimes run an article or two about political issues or a profile of a politician.

A small number of magazines offer extensive coverage of political events, including *National Journal, The New Republic, The Nation,* and *The National Review.* These publications typically have minuscule circulations. In fact, the list of the top 100 magazines in America (based on circulation) includes publications on just about every topic, from *Sports Illustrated* to *Vogue,* but none focused on politics and government.[32] In contrast, on the *New York Times* Hardcover Nonfiction Bestsellers list in July 2007, a wide range of political books ranked among the most popular, from the diary of former president Ronald Reagan to a biography of 2008 presidential hopeful Hillary Clinton and an analysis of global warming by former vice president (and past presidential candidate) Al Gore.

Wire Services Across the nation and worldwide, publications and freelance journalists sell their articles to wire services, which resell them to other newspapers and magazines for reprinting. Two examples are the *Associated Press* and *Reuters.* Many large newspapers such as the *New York Times* maintain similar operations to provide stories to smaller papers with more limited staff. Newspaper chains can also redistribute one paper's articles to other papers in the chain for reprinting.

Wire services and reprinting are enormously cost-effective for newspapers because a relatively small subscription or reprint fee allows them to offer readers a wide range of stories about political events across the United States and throughout the world. The value is particularly high given that the average newspaper simply could not

mainstream media (MSM) Media sources that predate the Internet, such as newspapers, magazines, television, and radio.

prime time Evening hours when television viewership is at its highest and networks often schedule news programs.

news cycle The time between the release of information and its publication, like the twenty-four hours between issues of a daily newspaper.

afford to station reporters in Washington or outside the country, or send someone there to cover a breaking story. The downside to using wire services or reprinting is that the same story is often printed by hundreds of papers throughout the nation. Even among thousands of daily newspapers, there may be relatively few different original sources of information about a particular political event.

Television The four national networks (ABC, CBS, Fox, and NBC) and many cable channels, such as CNN, offer nightly news as well as **prime-time** news programs. Local TV stations also cover some local political events in addition to running the national networks' programming. News coverage varies from the "talking head" format of a person behind a desk reading copy to the camera, to investigative reporting, where reporters and camera crews gather information in the field and assemble it for broadcast, or talk shows, where reporters interview political figures or other people of interest. Some programs combine these formats; one popular example is *The O'Reilly Factor*, a nightly show on the Fox News Network hosted by conservative commentator Bill O'Reilly. In a typical episode, O'Reilly reports news stories, offers political commentary, and interviews elected officials, party officials, journalists, and other prominent people in the news.

Radio The major radio networks such as ABC, CBS, and Clear Channel Communications offer brief news programs throughout the day, but most political content on the radio consists of talk radio programs such as *The Rush Limbaugh Show*, where a host discusses politics with listeners who phone in. The major nationwide talk radio shows generally offer a politically conservative point of view—and openly advertise this orientation.[33] While there are liberal talk radio programs, their audience is just a small fraction of the size of conservative programs' audience. Other political radio programs are broadcast by National Public Radio, an organization funded by the government and private donations. Overall, there are more than 13,000 radio stations in America. Just as with other media sources, only a fraction focus on delivering news or political coverage.

The Internet Political news sources on the Internet vary widely. Some are electronic versions of sources that originated in other kinds of media. You can read most of the *New York Times* for free on its Web site or listen to Rush Limbaugh's radio program on his site. Sometimes Internet sites for television news shows or print publications feature stories that are unavailable in other formats, which reflects a trend described throughout this chapter: as more and more people use the Internet, companies that own newspapers, magazines, TV stations, and radio networks are moving their content to the Web in an attempt to keep their audience and stay in business.

ARE ALL MEDIA THE SAME?

From how they look to how they cover the news, media sources are not the same. One difference is timeliness. Newspapers in particular are prisoners of the **news cycle** because they publish only once per day. Publishing a book can take months or even years from the time writing begins to the day it's available for sale. Radio and TV coverage is somewhat easier to produce and rearrange on short notice, but Internet sites are even faster. Just write some new content, upload pictures, and the information is out.

A second difference is breadth. Nightly news programs on the major networks have only thirty minutes to deliver their report (twenty-three minutes excluding commercials). As a result, even an important political event like the president's

▲ *Rush Limbaugh exemplifies the conservative dominance of AM talk radio in America.*

How the International Press Views American Politics

Interest in American politics extends beyond America's borders. Newspapers, TV stations, radio stations, magazines, and Internet sites in other nations offer extensive coverage of American elections and the federal government. This interest reflects the fact that America is the largest economic and military power in the world. As a result, American election outcomes and policy changes have important consequences for people living elsewhere, and these individuals look to the media for information about America just as Americans do.

Just like the American media, many foreign newspapers, TV stations, and magazines maintain Web sites that reproduce much of their content. Most of the time, stories about American politics in the foreign press are also translated into English. Examples of media outlets abroad that cover American politics include the government-sponsored *People's Daily* in China, the Itar-Tass news agency in Russia, the British Broadcasting Corporation (BBC), and Al Jazeera, an Arabic- and English-language news provider that has a large audience throughout the the Middle East. Many other sites, such as Watching America, offer links to a wide range of foreign media.[a]

These sources offer a unique window into American politics. In large part, their stories are about the same individuals and events that you would see in American media coverage, but with a slightly different perspective. Foreign media sources focus on elements of

▲ This cartoon from a Chinese newspaper criticizes U.S. politicians for attacking China's human rights policies while ignoring abuses by American troops in Iraq, such as the Abu Ghraib prison scandal.

American politics that are of interest to people living elsewhere. Thus, their stories emphasize the local (for them) consequences of American elections and government policies. Occasionally foreign press will cover stories that are simply ignored by the American media.

For example, if you consulted Watching America in March 2006, you would have seen a story from an Iranian newspaper maintaining that Iran would be receptive to negotiations with America over nuclear proliferation and the situation in Iraq, a story from a Taiwanese newspaper describing how some Taiwanese politicians expected the United States to provide advanced weaponry to

Taiwan for free in the event of a conflict with China, and a story from a Chinese newspaper arguing that America's emphasis on human rights in China was an attempt to forestall China's emergence as the world's dominant economic power.

Of course, there is no reason to think that foreign media are any less vulnerable than their American counterparts to filtering, framing, or sensationalizing the news. Even so, these sources provide a useful check on American coverage of politics, allowing readers to see whether important stories or aspects of stories are missing from domestic news coverage. ■

State of the Union address receives only a brief discussion. Many radio programs face similar constraints, although some, such as NPR's *All Things Considered* and many talk radio programs, run for several hours every day, allowing them to spend more time on in-depth coverage. Newspapers may have more flexibility in the depth of their coverage, although they aim to print a set number of pages per section and per issue, while Internet outlets are the least constrained. A third and closely related difference is the medium of communication. Newspapers convey information through printed words and pictures, while TV coverage is made up of spoken words and images. Radio programs cannot present images but can broadcast the spoken word. Internet sources can easily combine media including text, images, and voices.

A final difference is resources. Major newspapers and television networks have offices and reporters stationed throughout the world. Local TV and radio stations, most newspapers, and many Internet sites depend on stories first published elsewhere or they may hire freelance reporters from different regions as needed. Similarly, during a presidential campaign, reporters from the major newspapers and TV networks accompany the presidential candidates throughout the campaign, while smaller newspapers and local TV stations generally rely on stories, photos, and video generated by others.

These differences mean that media sources are not interchangeable—what you learn about politics depends on where you look. People who get their political information exclusively from the nightly local news learn less about politics than people who thoroughly read a major paper such as the *New York Times*.

SECTION SUMMARY

1. Throughout American history, some owners of media companies have used their control over what gets reported to support their preferred candidates, parties, and points of view.
2. The Federal Communication Commission has regulated broadcast media since the 1930s. Recent decisions have removed many constraints from media companies, accelerating the process of concentration, and facilitating cross-ownership and the growth of media conglomerates.
3. In the modern era, there are many different places to find political news, from daily newspapers to television, radio, magazines, and the Internet.
4. Media sources differ in terms of their timeliness, breadth, medium, and resources, which affects how each type of source covers politics.

What Difference Does the Internet Make?

The evolution of the Internet over the last couple of decades has made new kinds of political information available to the average citizen. Many sites offer the full text of government reports and analyses; anyone can download the president's annual budget request, new regulations published in The Federal Register, or evaluations of government programs released by the Government Accountability Office.[34] Twenty years ago, these documents were available only at major libraries.

The Internet also contains a wealth of analytic information. For example, the Brookings Institution, a Washington-based think tank, publishes a weekly report on Iraq including hundreds of charts that detail the attacks, casualties, oil production and other economic indicators, surveys of the population, and additional information.[35] Before the Internet, if such a compilation existed, it would be available only by subscription or circulated only among a small number of scholars and policy makers.

Another type of Internet site collects links to political information. The Center for Responsive Politics, for example, offers a searchable database of contributions to candidates and political organizations.[36] The *Pollster* site collects and analyzes public opinion surveys, including presidential election polls, and offers interpretations of the results as well as discussions of possible sources of bias.[37] Other Web sites offer somewhat less useful but entertaining political information. For example, when House Majority Leader Tom DeLay was indicted in 2005, a Web site, *The Smoking Gun*, published his police mug shot.[38]

Most American newspapers, television networks, radio stations, and cable stations offer free access to most or all of their daily news via Internet sites as well as providing some Web-only information. They also post blogs written by their reporters. For example, Chris Matthews, who anchors MSNBC's politics show *Hardball*, also writes the daily blog *Hardblogger*.[39] Similarly, one of the most influential conservative weekly magazines, *National Review*, has a Web version, *National Review Online*, where many of their reporters publish Web-exclusive stories between issues of the magazine.[40]

Other Internet-only news providers, such as ABC News's *The Note*, offer collections of links to daily political coverage throughout the nation or a preview of upcoming political events in Washington.[41] *SCOTUSblog* (Supreme Court of the United States blog) analyzes Supreme Court decisions, judicial nominations, and other legal questions.[42]

Search engines such as Yahoo! or Google allow you to search through thousands of newspapers, wire service stories, and other information sources. Other Internet news sites that concentrate on political coverage include *Politico* and *Slate*.[43] Some news sites are expressly partisan—*Salon* and *The Huffington Post* lean in the liberal direction, while *Power Line* and *Town Hall* offer a conservative point of view.[44] Finally, an enormous amount of professional and amateur video coverage of politics is available on YouTube. Various political organizations and candidates use MySpace, Facebook, and other social networking sites to recruit and organize supporters.

The Internet has lowered the barriers to publication. In 1961, journalist A. J. Liebling wrote that, "freedom of the press is guaranteed only to those who own one," meaning that it was all but impossible for average citizens to report on what they knew or present their analyses to the general public.[45] The Internet has created more opportunities for home-grown media, allowing a would-be political reporter to easily set up a Web site or blog, or post videos online. For example, a large number of civilians and military personnel in Iraq have chronicled their experiences on blogs.[46] These sites provide information that would have been completely unavailable to most people even a few years ago.

Similarly, YouTube has many videos of campaign events and even some campaign ads, many prepared by people with no official connections to the candidates. These videos have the potential to change elections: in the 2006 Virginia Senate race, a volunteer for challenger James Webb recorded incumbent George Allen using a Tunisian racial slur, "macaca," to refer to the volunteer, who was of Indian descent.[47] The episode, which was later picked up by the mainstream media, dogged Allen for the entire campaign. After initially seeming a shoo-in for reelection, Allen lost by more than 9,000 votes.

▲ During Virginia senator George Allen's 2006 reelection campaign, he was videotaped at a rally calling an opposition tracker "macaca." Millions saw the clip on YouTube, and many interpreted the term as a racial slur. Before the Internet, the incident would never have come to light, but it became one factor in Allen's defeat. Here, Allen concedes the race to Democratic challenger Jim Webb.

The Internet creates new opportunities for two-way interaction between citizens, reporters, and government officials. Many reporters host live chat sessions, allowing people to ask follow-up questions about published stories.[48] In 2005, when then-attorney general Alberto Gonzales wrote an **op-ed** article for the *Washington Post* that argued for reauthorization of the Patriot Act, he participated in a chat session with readers soon after it was published.[49]

The Internet also allows ordinary citizens to report on political events as they happen. For example, during the December 2005 Iraqi parliamentary elections, many Internet sites featured live reporting of the voting process, including videos.[50] Individuals located throughout Iraq reported on their impressions of voter turnout, which parties were receiving strong support, and whether there were any attacks on polling stations.

How much of a difference does all this information make? Some pundits argue that the Internet will transform American politics, leading to a better-informed, more politically active citizenry.[51] And it may—someday. While some studies show that Internet usage is associated with higher levels of political participation, others show no such association.[52] Moreover, there is no clear evidence that surfing the Web makes people more politically informed.[53]

Why hasn't the Internet created a better-informed citizenry? One answer is that not everyone uses the Internet. An April 2007 Pew Trust survey found that 30 percent of adults were not regular users of the Internet.[54] A second problem is that, to some extent, finding information on the Internet still requires doing your own research. Despite the availability of search engines, it is not always obvious where to look for political information. Suppose you wanted to learn more about the conflict in Iraq. A Google search in early 2008 on the terms "America," "Iraq," and "war" returned over 9 million Web pages, from reports on America's military strategy to pictures of Iraqi civilian casualties. Thus, the problem is not finding information but deciding which of the 9 million pages will help you to learn about the conflict.

Third, some of the vast quantity of information on the Internet is of questionable reliability. Though this problem also arises for major publications, these publications are so widely read that when mistakes show up in print, they are typically spotted and corrected. Most major publications also have extensive fact-checking operations, because their ability to attract an audience depends on upholding a reputation for accuracy. On the other hand, citizen-reporters who post information on lesser-known Web sites are unlikely to get the benefit of these correction mechanisms. For example, during the 2004 Presidential campaign, many Web sites posted a photo of Democratic candidate John Kerry together with actor Jane Fonda at a 1970s-era anti-Vietnam War rally. Because Fonda openly supported the North Vietnamese government during the war, the photo was potentially distasteful to the political moderates and conservatives whose support Kerry sought. However, the controversial photo was soon exposed as a fake. The original photographer produced the negative, which showed Kerry standing by himself—Fonda's image had been copied from a second picture and added using photo retouching software.[55]

The Kerry–Fonda photo is not an isolated example. The open-source online encyclopedia *Wikipedia* has been found to contain serious inaccuracies about political figures and events.[56] And in January 2007, the Web magazine *Insight* published a story claiming that the presidential campaign organization of Democrat Hillary Clinton would release information showing that rival Democratic candidate Barack Obama had attended a radical Islamic religious school, known as a madrassa, in

POLITICS IS EVERYWHERE

The Internet is full of sites offering information and analysis of American politics—and representing just about every point of view on virtually everything government does.

op-ed Short for "opinion editorial," this type of article is written by a journalist or guest writer who expresses his or her opinion on a given issue without necessarily attempting to be objective.

Indonesia when he was six years old.[57] Both the claim about Obama and the claim about the Clinton campaign were false. However, while the story was in play, it received much attention from major media outlets—and drew traffic to *Insight*'s Web site. At one level, these examples suggest the Internet is self-correcting, in that the errors were identified. However, in cases of false information, the instant accessibility of information on the Internet becomes a vice that allows untruths to spread very quickly. Moreover, such stories' corrective publicity might not be enough. Both the doctored Kerry–Fonda photo and the false story of Obama's early education still appeared on political blogs as of 2008.

A fourth explanation for the fact that the Internet hasn't caused dramatic change in the electorate is the **normalization hypothesis**, which suggests that as more people began to use the Internet, many news sources such as newspapers and TV networks began to publish their stories on the Internet as well as in print or on the air.[58] As a result, when people look to the Internet for information, they are likely to find many of the same stories available in other sources.

Finally, the Internet's minimal impact on what Americans know also reflects a lack of demand for information. There is no requirement that Americans attain some baseline level of knowledge about politics. Thus, despite the wealth of information on the Internet, there is no guarantee that people will sit down, search for what they want or need to know, distinguish true from false information, and assemble what they find into coherent conclusions.

normalization hypothesis The idea that media sources will increasingly make their news available online as more people begin using the Internet.

SECTION SUMMARY

1. The growth of the Internet has vastly increased the amount of political information available to the average American, from official reports to expert analyses.
2. The Internet has also lowered barriers to publication, making possible home-grown media sites where ordinary citizens post reports and videos of political events.
3. The growth of the Internet has not led to a better-informed American public. Some explanations include lack of Internet access for some Americans, the difficulty of finding information, the inconsistent reliability of information, and the lack of an incentive to seek out information in the first place.

How Reporters Work: Leaks, Sources, and Shield Laws

The reality of reporting on politics is that many people involved in the political process don't want the public to know everything they are doing—or only want their own version of events to see print. Politicians want media coverage that highlights their achievements in order to build public support and secure election (or reelection), bureaucrats want favorable attention for their programs, and interest groups want publicity to further their causes. The result is that coverage of American politics reflects complex trade-offs between reporters who want complete, accurate information and sources who want favorable coverage.

Reporters also face legal hurdles as they research stories. Notwithstanding freedom of the press guaranteed in the Bill of Rights, reporters are subject to legal limitations including the clear and present danger test and prior restraint. If the government can convince a judge that publication of a particular story would lead to immediate harm to a person or persons, a judge can halt publication; this action is called prior restraint. The clear and present danger test sets the bar extremely high for stopping publication of a story. The Supreme Court has held that such attempts carry "a presumption of unconstitutionality." Thus, as we discussed in Chapter 4, most attempts to prevent publication have been unsuccessful.

In late 2005, the *Washington Post* ran a story that described a network of secret prisons run by the Central Intelligence Agency (CIA) that were being used to hold suspected terrorists.[59] A month later, the *New York Times* published a story revealing that the National Security Agency (NSA), under orders from President Bush, had wiretapped thousands of international phone calls without court authorization.[60] Both stories relied on classified information, so how did the reporters learn about these secret programs? This information was **leaked** by people inside the government—their identities remain a mystery to this day.

Government officials have two tactics to deter leaks or influence the media's coverage of a story. First, there are laws prohibiting the disclosure of classified information. In the case of the NSA wiretaps, after the *New York Times* article was published, the Justice Department began an investigation to find and prosecute whomever had disclosed classified information about the program, intending to use the threat of prosecution to stop other officials from giving information to reporters.[61] In the mid-1980s, a government employee was convicted of giving classified pictures of a new Soviet aircraft carrier to a defense publication.[62] Ironically, the new carrier was identical to one already in service (and well-photographed). Even so, the employee was jailed until being pardoned by President Clinton in 2001.

Government officials also try to persuade reporters and editors to voluntarily refrain from publishing sensitive stories. In the case of the NSA wiretaps, the *New York Times* sat on the story for a full year, publishing only when it was rumored that another paper was ready to release its own version of the story.[63] And when the story of the secret CIA prisons broke, it did not name any of the countries in Eastern Europe where the prisons were allegedly located. The reporters had this information but agreed to keep it out of the story.

Why do reporters restrain their stories this way? Sometimes they agree that keeping secrets is in the national interest. Other times, reporters are rewarded for cooperating—they may get information about another government policy or future access to officials. Alternately, reporters may be coerced to back down from a story through threats, such as the possibility that if they go ahead with a story, they may lose access to people in government for future stories or even go to jail.

POLITICS IS CONFLICTUAL

Disagreements within government and in Congress are the driving force behind leaks of information to the press.

leak The release of either classified or politically embarrassing information by a government employee to a member of the press.

press conference Events at which politicians speak to journalists and, in most cases, answer their questions afterward.

on background or **off the record** Terms describing comments a politician makes to the press on the condition that they can be reported only if they are not attributed to that politician.

STAGING THE NEWS

People inside the federal government, from the president to the large numbers of bureaucrats, work to shape media coverage to suit their personal goals. Larry Speakes, the press secretary to President Reagan, had a sign in his office that said, "You don't tell us how to stage the news, and we won't tell you how to cover it."

Politicians try to influence coverage by providing select information to reporters. Sometimes they hold **press conferences** where they take questions from the media. Other times, they speak to single reporters or to a group **on background** or **off the record**, meaning that the reporter can use the information but cannot

Prior Restraint of Secret Information

The conflict between reporters and government officials is particularly sharp in the case of intelligence agencies. The Central Intelligence Agency (CIA), National Security Agency (NSA), and other government organizations need to keep their operations secret to operate effectively. For example, during the 1970s, one NSA operation involved using submarines to install recording equipment on Soviet underwater communications cables used to relay secret military data. Obviously, if the operation became public, the Soviets would stop using the cables until they could find and remove the recording equipment. (As it happened, the operation ended when a Soviet spy working for the CIA found out about it.) Intelligence agencies also need to keep the identities of their covert operatives secret. As Porter Goss, former director of the CIA argued, if someone living abroad is found to be an employee of the CIA, their ability to gather information will surely be compromised—in some places, their life might be in danger.[a]

Both of these arguments speak to the need for prior restraint, which gives the government the power to keep the details of secret operations and the names of covert operatives out of the newspapers and other media sources. But as we discussed in Chapter 4, attempts to invoke prior restraint are almost never successful. Why isn't keeping secrets an easy call?

The problem is accountability. If the media are restrained from publication, then there is a risk government officials will be able to do whatever they want; the public, and most elected officials, will not find out. Put another way, without media watchdogs, the small number of unelected bureaucrats who make decisions about secret operations will never have to answer for those decisions to the public or to elected representatives. Moreover, these same bureaucrats would decide which operations would be considered secret in the first place. In some cases, the ability to keep operations secret has allowed intelligence agencies to carry out programs that might have been prohibited had they been publicized from the start, such as the network of CIA prisons in Eastern Europe that was revealed in 2005.

In sum, decisions about prior restraint are difficult, precisely because they involve balancing off two important goals: allowing the government to carry out covert operations, and informing the public about government actions so that citizens can evaluate and respond to them. If you had to evaluate an intelligence agency's request for prior restraint, how would you decide whether to grant it? ◼

---

attribute it to the politician by name. Another strategy is to hold events aimed, at least in part, at securing favorable press coverage. In October 2007, officials at the Federal Emergency Management Agency (FEMA) held a press conference to detail its response to massive wildfires outside San Diego, California. The conference was attended only by television camera crews; FEMA allowed reporters to listen to the conference by phone, but they could not ask questions. So, who asked the questions? Other FEMA employees. Clearly, the event was designed to showcase the scope and effectiveness of FEMA's relief efforts, but the effort collapsed when the circumstances of the press conference came to light.

Of course, people who leak information to the media also have their own agendas. Consider the Watergate scandal. In 1972, 1973, and 1974, reporters for the *Washington Post* published a series of articles revealing that many senior members of the Nixon administration, including the president, had covered up a series of illegal programs run by the Committee to Reelect the President, including money laundering, provision

▲ The threat of prosecution is one way to deter government employees from leaking secret information to the press. U.S. intelligence analyst Samuel Morrison was convicted of espionage for giving this satellite image of a Soviet naval shipyard, and several other photos, to a reporter.

shield laws Legislation, which exists in some states but not at the federal level, that gives reporters the right to refuse to name the sources of their information.

of hush-money to potential witnesses, and break-ins to the Democratic Party headquarters. These stories were possible only because someone in the administration leaked information to the *Post*'s reporters—and the informant's identity remained unknown for more than thirty years. In 2005, he came forward as senior FBI official W. Mark Felt.[64] The authors of the stories, Bob Woodward and Carl Bernstein, were not sure why Felt was giving them information, although they suspected part of his motivation was resentment at not being promoted to a more senior position in the FBI. They believed his revelations only because they could confirm some of the details with other sources.

REVEALING SOURCES

Reporters covering important or controversial stories often promise their sources that they will remain anonymous in any coverage based on the information they provide. These assurances are an important factor in the decision to leak information, especially classified information. However, this assurance is not absolute.

POLITICAL PROCESS MATTERS

The lack of a federal shield law means that reporters who face judicial orders to reveal their sources must be willing to go to jail to keep those names confidential.

Reporters and their editors can, under certain circumstances, be compelled by a court to reveal the sources for their stories. While some states have **shield laws** that allow reporters to refuse to name their sources, there is no such law at the federal level—although there have been attempts to enact such a law in recent years. As a result, federal prosecutors can ask a judge to force reporters to name their sources, on grounds that the identity of the source is fundamental to their case. If the judge agrees, the reporter can be jailed for contempt for an indefinite period of time unless he or she provides the information.

In 2005, a high-profile federal case brought public attention to this process, and to the lack of a federal shield law. The complex case was rooted in a news story in which a veteran journalist revealed that Valerie Plame, supposedly a mid-level employee for a private firm, secretly worked as an undercover employee of the CIA. The leak of Plame's CIA employment to the press—and the decision to publish the information—became all the more significant because of Plame's husband, former ambassador Joseph Wilson. Before the invasion of Iraq, Wilson had been hired by the CIA to determine whether the country of Niger had supplied Iraq with uranium. Wilson found no evidence of such exports, which detracted from the Bush administration's claims that Iraq was working to produce nuclear weapons. Thus, Wilson's CIA-based connection to Plame was leaked in an attempt to discredit his findings with the implication of a conflict of interest.

Regardless of the complex political circumstances surrounding the case, leaking Plame's identity broke the law: it is illegal to reveal the name of clandestine CIA employees. The same source who originally leaked Plame's name for publication had also served as a source for another veteran journalist, *New York Times* reporter Judith Miller. Even though Miller did not publish information from this source, she was subpoenaed to reveal the name, and ultimately jailed for over three months for refusing to do so. At that point, and with encouragement from her source, she decided to tell the special prosecutor that her source was I. Lewis Libby, then-vice president Dick Cheney's chief of staff. Libby was later convicted of lying to the grand jury about his role in the Plame case, although President Bush later commuted his prison sentence.

▲ *The journalists who revealed Valerie Plame's status as a covert CIA employee received the information from White House officials. By leaking it to the press, the officials aimed to discredit a report Plame's husband wrote, which contradicted White House claims about Iraq purchasing nuclear bomb-making materials.*

1. Reporters and their sources often help each other, since reporters need information and sources want favorable press coverage.
2. The government can stop publication of a press story only under extreme circumstances. However, if leakers are found, they often can be fired or prosecuted.
3. People in government often try to stage events as a way of shaping press coverage.
4. Reporters often promise to keep their sources anonymous, although this protection is not absolute because there is no federal shield law.

How Do Americans Use the Media to Learn about Politics?

Americans now have many more ways to learn about politics than they did a generation or two ago. Imagine yourself in the 1940s. Suppose you want to learn about President Truman's State of the Union speech. You can't go to Washington to hear the speech in person. Where do you get your information? If you live in a big city, the speech will probably be covered in tomorrow's newspaper. If you live in a small town, your local paper may or may not have a story, and if they don't, you will need a subscription to either a big-city paper (arriving a week later) or a weekly or monthly news magazine, or a radio that can pick up a station broadcasting the speech.

Now consider the modern era in which major political events saturate the media, even if each event makes headlines only briefly. You can tune into one of the four television networks, numerous cable news channels, public TV stations, radio stations, or listen to live streaming of the speech on the Internet. Most TV stations will feature pundits' commentary on the speech and will interview prominent politicians and commentators about it. Jay Leno and David Letterman will make jokes about the speech in their opening monologues on late-night TV, and Jon Stewart and Stephen Colbert will skewer it on their shows. Miss the speech? Tomorrow it will be front-page news in most newspapers, and larger, national papers will publish the full text. Countless Internet sites will offer information and analyses. And you will be able to watch a video of the speech on YouTube and many other sites.

POLITICS IS EVERYWHERE

Major political events such as the State of the Union Speech are reported by a wide range of media sources, from newspapers to comedy shows.

The fact that there are many sources of political information in the modern era does not imply that the average American uses most of them. For the most part, Americans learn about politics just as they become aware of other things, a process explained by the **by-product theory of information transmission**.[65] This theory posits that for many Americans, political information is acquired accidentally. People read the sports pages of a newspaper and glance at front page stories along the way. They watch *The Daily Show* and learn about politics while laughing at Jon Stewart's monologue. They read a story on a political blog or Internet news site because the title catches their eye as they're looking for something else.

After encountering new information, the question of whether an individual either remembers that information later, or uses it to modify her thoughts about politicians or policies, depends on her level of interest. John Zaller's work on information processing shows that highly interested people are unlikely to change their minds when they learn something new, as they have already decided what they

by-product theory of information transmission The idea that many Americans acquire political information unintentionally rather than by seeking it out.

think. On the other hand, people who are uninterested in politics are less likely to encounter new political information in the first place. Thus, media coverage is most likely to affect the beliefs of people who take a moderate interest in politics.[66]

MEDIA USAGE TRENDS

Even though there are many news sources, none of them are used by everyone or even by most Americans (Table 6.1). As of 2006, about half of those surveyed watched local news and between a quarter and a third watched cable news, nightly network broadcasts, or got their news online. This table also highlights some important trends in media usage.[67] The percentage of people who read newspapers has declined by a third in the last fifteen years, and the percentage watching TV news has also declined, with the number watching nightly news broadcasts showing the largest drop, from 60 percent to only 28 percent. Finally, use of online sources has increased from 2 percent of those surveyed in 1995 to nearly a third of the sample in 2006. Table 6.2 focuses on these Internet news sources; note that of the top ten sites, seven are affiliated with traditional media providers, such as CNN or the *New York Times.* Very few people reported using blogs as a news source: only 4 percent used them regularly, and 80 percent didn't use them at all.[68]

News-gathering is only one of the things Americans do every day (Table 6.3), and while a majority of those surveyed accessed some news source every day, more people watched non-news television than used any of these sources—and remember, this survey asks about any kind of news, not just news about politics. Among young people, news-gathering ranks well below exercising, watching non-news TV, and surfing the Internet, and just above playing video games. Even these numbers might be inflated, as some people might be unwilling to admit that they did not read or watch the news. This table confirms the primacy of television news programs as a source of

---

| TABLE 6.1 | THE CHANGING NEWS LANDSCAPE |

In the last decade, the growth of the Internet has made a wide variety of new information sources available to the average American. Has this development changed the types of news sources that Americans regularly use?

	1993	1996	2000	2002	2004	2006
Regularly watch ...						
Local TV news	77%	65%	56%	57%	59%	54%
Cable TV news	—	—	—	33	38	34
Nightly network news	60	42	30	32	34	28
Network morning news	—	—	20	22	22	23
Listened/read yesterday ...						
Radio	47[a]	44	43	41	40	36
Newspaper	58[a]	50	47	41	42	40
Seek online news three or more days per week	—	2[b]	23	25	29	31

[a] From 1994
[b] From 1995
SOURCE: Pew Research Center, "Maturing Internet News Audience—Broader Than Deep," July 30, 2006, available at http://people-press.org/reports/pdf/282.pdf.

INTERNET NEWS SOURCES

Table 6.1 showed that Americans increasingly get their news from the Internet. Are they primarily consulting sources that originated on the Internet, aggregation sites that collect and collate information, or Internet versions of mainstream news sources?

WEB SITES USED MOST OFTEN	PERCENT USING	WEB SITES USED MOST OFTEN	PERCENT USING
MSNBC	31%	ABC	4%
Yahoo	23	Drudge Report	3
CNN	23	Cable provider homepage	3
Google	9	BBC	2
AOL	8	*Washington Post*	2
Fox News	8	CBS	1
New York Times	5	*Los Angeles Times*	1
USA Today	5	*Wall Street Journal*	1
ESPN and other sports sites	4	Other Web sites	39

Based on those who regularly get news online. Respondents could offer multiple Web sites.
SOURCE: Pew Research Center, "Maturing Internet News Audience—Broader Than Deep," July 30, 2006, available at http://people-press.org/reports/pdf/282.pdf.

NEWS FACES STIFF COMPETITION

Older Americans grew up without cable channels, the Internet, or even color TV. Are there generational differences in the use of different media sources? Are there generational differences in the propensity to gather information in the first place?

	AGE 18–29	30–49	50–64	65+
News yesterday. . .				
Watched TV news	49%	53%	63%	69%
Read a newspaper	24	36	47	58
Listened to radio news	26	43	39	27
Got news online	24	29	21	10
Other activities yesterday . . .				
Went online (home/work)	62	62	52	21
Watched non-news TV	61	60	69	66
Exercised/ran/sports	56	46	38	35
Watched movie at home	40	23	21	12
Read a book	41	34	39	39
Played a video game	28	15	14	11
Read a magazine	24	20	24	33

SOURCE: Pew Research Center, "Maturing Internet News Audience—Broader Than Deep," July 30, 2006, available at http://people-press.org/reports/pdf/282.pdf.

information for all age groups. It also reveals sharp generational differences in how Americans get their news. Young people are much more likely to use Internet sources and much less likely than older people to read a printed copy of a newspaper.

Figure 6.1 reinforces the by-product theory of information acquisition. Three-quarters of those surveyed reported that they found news accidentally while going online for some other purpose. In other words, the average American does not necessarily search the Web for political information. Rather, they may learn about the world, and about politics, in the course of doing other things.

DOES THE SOURCE MATTER?

As we have discussed, people acquire different kinds of information in different formats from each type of media source. A newspaper can report on an insurgent attack in Iraq in a fair amount of detail and may have a few pictures—whereas a TV news show can include footage of the attack and the aftermath, even in a less detailed story. Do people who rely on different kinds of media sources learn different things about politics? And do most people tend to accumulate broad, general political knowledge or information about specific topics?

In 2007, the Pew Trust asked people twenty-three questions about contemporary politics, defining "high-knowledge" individuals as those who answered fifteen or more questions correctly. They then divided people according to their principle source of political information, and calculated the percentage of high-knowledge people who used each news source. The results are shown in Table 6.4. For each source, the table also gives the percentage of people who answered four of the survey's specific political questions correctly: those who could identify Sunnis as a religious group in Iraq, "Scooter" Libby as the person convicted in the Valerie Plame

---

FIGURE 6.1 **FINDING NEWS ONLINE ACCIDENTALLY**

The by-product theory of information transmission states that Americans by and large gather information about politics in the course of doing other things. What do these data on Internet usage tell us about this theory?

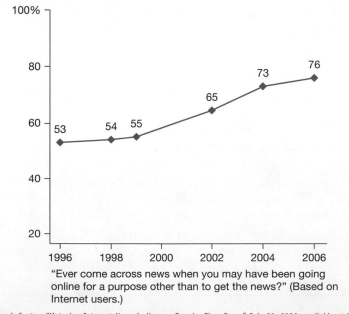

"Ever come across news when you may have been going online for a purpose other than to get the news?" (Based on Internet users.)

SOURCE: Pew Research Center, "Maturing Internet News Audience—Broader Than Deep," July 30, 2006, available at http://people-press.org/reports/pdf/282.pdf.

Are *The Daily Show*'s Viewers "Stoned Slackers"?

When Jon Stewart, host of *The Daily Show*, was a guest on Bill O'Reilly's talk show *The O'Reilly Factor* in September 2004, O'Reilly's complained about the influence that Stewart had over young voters. As he put it,

> You know what's really frightening? You actually have an influence on this presidential election. That is scary, but it's true. You've got stoned slackers watching your dopey show every night and they can vote.[a]

It is easy to dismiss O'Reilly's claims as sour grapes or something said in jest, but here we take the claim seriously. What kind of people watch *The Daily Show*?

It turns out viewers of *The Daily Show* score relatively well on a scale of political knowledge—much better than the population at large. At about the same time Stewart appeared on O'Reilly's show, the Annenberg Foundation released the results of a survey gauging the political knowledge of people who watched late-night TV programs. The poll asked respondents six questions about the 2004 presidential candidates, Democrat John Kerry and Republican George Bush. Here are the questions and answers:

▲ *Jon Stewart, host of* The Daily Show.

- Who favors allowing workers to invest some of their Social Security contributions in the stock market? (Bush)
- Who urged Congress to extend the federal law banning assault weapons? (Kerry)
- John Kerry says that he would eliminate the Bush tax cuts on those making how much money? (over $200,000 a year)
- Who is a former prosecutor? (Kerry)
- Who favors making the recent tax cuts permanent? (Bush)
- Who wants to make it easier for labor unions to organize? (Kerry)

Interestingly, the *Daily Show* viewers answered 60 percent of the questions right on average, versus 45 percent correct among the general population and 40 percent among respondents age eighteen to twenty-nine.[b]

This finding makes for a good news story, showing that a comedy show apparently provides real information about politics. However, it is important to keep two things in mind. First, *Daily Show* viewers also scored much higher than the general population on whether they followed politics closely (46 percent said they did, as opposed to 33 percent in the population at large) and on education (39 percent have college degrees to the general population's 24 percent). Second, a separate survey found that only 6 percent of *Daily Show* viewers rely on the program as their only source of political information.[c] In fact, the Annenberg survey found that people who watched *The Daily Show* were more likely than the rest of the population to watch cable news (51 percent versus 38 percent), to read a newspaper (53 percent versus 46 percent), and to go online for political information (30 percent versus 12 percent).

The conclusion: O'Reilly may or may not be right that people who watch *The Daily Show* are "stoned slackers," but his comments miss the fact that many of them are highly interested in politics and actively seek out political information. These efforts—not Stewart's entertaining take on American politics—probably drove the results of the Annenberg poll. ■

case, Vladimer Putin as the President of Russia, and who knew the approximate number of American combat deaths in Iraq. Regardless of the type of news source, the percentage of high-knowledge people rarely creeps above 50 percent, and the same is true for the percentage who could answer each of these four questions correctly. In other words, Americans are learning from news coverage, but very few learn enough to be considered current-events experts.

Table 6.4 also shows differences in the percentage of high-knowledge people who use the different media sources. *The Daily Show* and *The Colbert Report*, along with major online news sites, *The NewsHour* (a PBS nightly newscast), *The O'Reilly Factor*, National Public Radio, and *The Rush Limbaugh Show* were among those drawing the highest percentages of high-knowledge individuals. At the other extreme were groups who get their information from network evening news, blogs, the Fox News

TABLE 6.4 KNOWLEDGE LEVELS BY NEWS SOURCE

One of the most important questions about media usage is whether people who know a lot about politics get their information from different sources than people who don't know as much. Does this table show differences between high-information and low-information?

	HIGH-KNOWLEDGE GROUP	Percentage who could . . .			
		IDENTIFY SUNNIS	IDENTIFY LIBBY	IDENTIFY PUTIN	APPROXIMATE U.S. DEATHS IN IRAQ
Nationwide	35%	32%	29%	36%	55%
The audience of . . .					
The Daily Show/The Colbert Report	54%	50%	44%	52%	59%
Major newspaper Web sites	54	52	42	58	64
NewsHour with Jim Lehrer	53	46	45	54	67
The O'Reilly Factor	51	43	44	53	64
National Public Radio	51	49	43	51	66
Rush Limbaugh's radio show	50	40	42	52	70
Local daily newspaper	43	36	35	43	60
News from Google, Yahoo, etc.	41	44	33	44	60
CNN	41	38	36	41	60
Network evening news	38	31	33	37	61
Online news discussion blogs	37	35	32	36	57
Fox News Channel	35	32	29	38	58
Local TV news	35	30	30	35	57
Network morning shows	34	30	30	35	57

Entries show the percentage of regular viewers, readers or listeners of each outlet who fall in the high knowledge group (correctly answered at least 15 of 23 questions about politics and world affairs) and the percent who correctly answered some of the individual questions on the test.
SOURCE: Pew Research Center, "What Americans Know: 1989–2007," April 15, 2007, available at http://people-press.org/reports/pdf/319.pdf.

Network, local TV news and, at the bottom, network morning news. Of course, some of these differences may be due to other factors, such as variation in the education levels of those who prefer particular media sources, or some survey respondents' use of multiple sources.

SECTION SUMMARY

1. Americans use a variety of sources to learn about politics, with newspapers and televsion news programs ranking as the most popular.
2. There are clear generational differences in media usage patterns, with younger people relying more on the Internet and older people more likely to use newspapers.
3. The amount of political knowledge that people have is related to the particular media sources they use. Surprisingly, people who get political information from late-night comedy shows and from talk radio programs are often very well informed about politics.

Studying the Impact of Media Coverage on American Citizens

This section details what political scientists know about whether exposure to media coverage of politics changes what people think or do, the study of **media effects**. There is considerable evidence that media coverage influences its audience. However, much of the impact stems not from what is contained in stories about political events but from what is left out, how information is presented, or even whether a story is reported at all. Political scientists label these mechanisms as priming, filtering (also called agenda-setting), and framing.[69] In the remainder of this section, we will consider what political scientists know about each of these effects.

Among the first wave of scholars studying the media's impact on public opinion, there was little doubt of the media's power. Writing in the 1920s, Walter Lippman argued that by reading or listening to news coverage, Americans learned which issues they should care about, what government could do about these concerns, and the consequences of different policy choices.[70] This certainty was reversed beginning in the 1950s, when scholars began to test claims about media effects using survey data. The early studies yielded extremely negative results—as one scholar put it, media effects were governed by the "law of minimal consequences," meaning that they appeared to have little influence on what Americans knew about politics or their political behavior.[71] By the 1980s, however, these findings about the nonexistence of media effects were found to be incorrect: the result of bad surveys, inadequate statistics, and a narrow conception of what media effects would look like.[72]

Modern theories of media influence distinguish between several ways coverage can affect media consumers' beliefs and judgments. The most obvious mechanism is the use of the media as a forum for persuasion, in which an overt effort is made to talk people into changing their minds about a candidate or an issue. However, people are not always conscious of the ways media reports shape their beliefs. Theorists describe four media effects that work largely without consumers' awareness of their influence. The first effect is **filtering**, which results from journalists' and editors' decisions about which of many potential news stories to report. The second is **slant**, in which a story gives favorable coverage to one candidate or policy without providing "balanced" favorable coverage of the other side. The third effect, **priming**, happens when a story changes public opinion by publicizing a new argument or concern, such as when coverage of a candidate's background changes people's general impressions of a candidate. Finally, **framing** refers to the way the description or presentation of a story, including the details, explanations, and context offered in the report, can influence public opinion.

The existence of these media effects does not imply that reporters or editors try to mislead the public or sway public opinion to conform to their own ideas about a story. If you read an article about a particular issue and decide to change your position, this doesn't suggest that the story was inaccurate or biased. Your decision may well be justified by the facts of the situation. Similarly, when slanted campaign coverage praises one candidate and dismisses the other as unqualified, you might conclude that the author agrees with the first candidate's positions and wrote the story to help the candidate get elected. But what if the first candidate is actually more qualified? If so, then slanted coverage of the campaign might be objective.

The same is true for other media effects. Space limitations mean that some filtering is inevitable as reporters and editors decide which stories to cover. Similar kinds of decisions about what to report and how to present the information lead to

media effects The influence of media coverage on average citizens' opinions and actions.

filtering The influence on public opinion that results from journalists' and editors' decisions about which of many potential news stories to report.

slant The imbalance in a story that covers one candidate or policy favorably without providing similar coverage of the other side.

priming The influence on the public's general impressions caused by positive or negative coverage of a candidate or issue.

framing The influence on public opinion caused by the way a story is presented or covered, including the details, explanations, and context offered in the report.

▲ *The way a story is reported—which information is included in an article or which images area used—makes a big difference in what people learn from it. A story about the Palestinian–Israeli conflict, for example, might emphasize Israeli forces' destruction of Palestinians' homes (top), or suicide bombings by Palestinians in Israel (bottom).*

priming and framing effects. Even if everyone in the political media adhered to the highest standards of accuracy, these influences would still exist.

The modern conception of media effects is exemplified by James Druckman and Michael Parkin's 2005 study of a Senate race in Minnesota, which found that different newspapers covered the candidates differently, both in the amount of coverage they gave to each candidate and the percentage of positive versus negative stories they ran. They showed that a given paper's slant in coverage was correlated with endorsements, such that papers gave more coverage and more positive coverage to the candidates they endorsed. Voters who were regular readers of a paper that endorsed a particular candidate were more likely to hold a positive opinion of that candidate and more likely to vote for him.[73]

A study of priming by Jon Krosnick and Laura Brannon found that exposure to press coverage of the Persian Gulf War in 1990 and 1991 moved citizens to evaluate then-president George H. W. Bush based on his effectiveness in managing the war rather than other factors such as the state of the economy.[74] Such priming is more likely when citizens are politically knowledgeable about the issues being discussed and trust the authors of the related news stories.[75]

The concept of filtering is illustrated by Project Censored's annual list of Top Censored Stories. Their list for 2007 included warnings about the declining health of the world's oceans and increases in hunger and homelessness in the United States.[76] Their point is not that the government forces reporters to keep quiet; rather, the claim is that reporters and their editors are deciding against covering these stories, sometimes for political or self-serving reasons. Of course, everyone can come up with a list of stories that they believe deserve more attention than they are getting. However, because no media source can report on everything—they lack the space, the time, and the staff—some events or problems can easily fall through the cracks, receiving little or no attention despite their significance.

An example of framing was shown in a 2005 Pew Trust study of polls designed to assess public support for changes in Social Security. The study found that support varied depending whether the description emphasized the risks associated with private accounts or the possibility that they would bring higher returns.[77] The questions and responses are given in Table 6.5. The report also found that support depended on whether President Bush was identified as a supporter of the private account proposal. Mentioning Bush's sponsorship lowered support for the reform proposal—which reflected Bush's relatively low approval rating at the time.

Another study investigating the effects of framing had people watch one of two made-up television news stories.[78] Both stories described a proposed rally by the Ku Klux Klan in a nearby town. The first story emphasized the threat to public safety posed by the rally. The second story was identical except it omitted safety concerns, focusing instead on the free speech issues raised by the rally. The different frames for these stories are shown in Table 6.6a.

After watching one of the two stories, people answered a series of questions that measured their tolerance for the rally and for free speech, as well as how important they considered free speech and public order. The results for the two groups, shown in Table 6.6b, provided clear evidence of framing. People who saw the story that omitted safety concerns had a far greater tolerance for the rally than the people who saw the safety-focused story. The first group also placed a higher importance on free speech and a lower importance on public order. Additional research shows that frames work most effectively at shaping what people think when the frames are simple and easy to understand, and when there are no competing frames because a citizen is exposed to only one account of a particular political event.[79] In particular, news stories on television, which are short, simple, and present strong visual images, often have framing effects on their viewers.[80]

| TABLE 6.5 | FRAMING SOCIAL SECURITY REFORM |

One common criticism of political coverage is that the way reporters describe events or issues can influence their audience's beliefs. Does support for Social Security reforms vary with how the reforms are described? What factors appear to affect the way people respond to these questions?

Fox News/Opinion Dynamics (December 2004)	Should	Should not	Don't know
Do you think people should have the choice to invest privately up to 5 percent of their Social Security contributions, or not?	60%	27%	13%

Pew Research Center (December 2004)	Favor	Oppose	Don't know
Generally, do you favor or oppose this proposal (which would allow younger workers to invest a portion of their Social Security taxes in private retirement accounts, which might include stocks or mutual funds)?	54%	30%	16%

***Washington Post*/ABC News (December 2004)**	Support	Oppose	Don't know
Would you support or oppose a plan in which people who chose to could invest some of their Social Security contributions in the stock market?	53%	44%	3%

***Time*/SRBI (January 2005)**	Favor	Oppose	Don't know
President Bush favors changing the Social Security system to allow people to invest part of their Social Security payroll tax in stocks and bonds. Do you favor or oppose this proposed change to Social Security?	44%	47%	9%

NBC News/*Wall Street Journal* (January 2005)	Good idea	Bad idea	Don't know
In general, do you think that it is a good idea or a bad idea to change the Social Security system to allow workers to invest their Social Security contributions in the stock market?	40%	50%	10%

SOURCE: Pew Research Center, "Social Security Polling: Cross-Currents about Private Accounts," January 27, 2005, available at http://people-press.org/commentary/pdf/106.pdf.

IS MEDIA COVERAGE BIASED?

Surveys of the American electorate routinely find that many people believe that media coverage of politics is biased to some extent. Interestingly, Democrats generally think the media favors Republican candidates, while Republicans have the opposite belief.[81] In the main, a majority of Americans, regardless of their party affiliation, do not have great confidence in any of the mainstream media, as shown in Table 6.7.

It is easy to find examples of suspicious decisions by reporters and their editors. During the 2004 presidential campaign, the anchor of the CBS Evening News, Dan Rather, reported on documents that purportedly indicated President George W. Bush had neglected to show up for Air National Guard duty in the early 1970s. These documents were soon found to be forgeries, with help from several bloggers who discovered that the documents were written in a Microsoft Word font that did not exist in the 1970s. There were indications that Rather and others at CBS knew the documents were problematic but went ahead and reported the story without mentioning their doubts.[82] Critics charged that the story ran despite shaky evidence because Rather and CBS News favored Democrat John Kerry over Bush.

Similarly, the politically conservative Media Research Center argued in early 2006 that major news organizations were refusing to report good news about Iraq, instead offering "defeatist coverage" that exhibited a "pessimistic bias."[83] The Center's study found that 61 percent of the stories aired on the ABC, NBC, and CBS evening news programs during 2005 had a "negative or pessimistic bias," while only 24 percent were "balanced or neutral" and only 15 percent "positive or optimistic."[84] They concluded, "TV

POLITICS IS CONFLICTUAL

Republicans and Democrats disagree on the credibility of different media sources, although neither side has high confidence in any source.

TABLE 6.6a — FRAMING THE NEWS: TWO REPORTS ON A KU KLUX KLAN RALLY

These tables describe a framing experiment in which separate groups of people watched two different versions of a news story about a Ku Klux Klan rally, then answered questions about free speech and tolerance. How did variations in how the event was described affect people's responses to these questions?

	FREE SPEECH FRAME	PUBLIC ORDER FRAME
Theme	Members of the KKK and those protesting their appearance were determined to get out their message.	KKK rallies have the potential for disorder and physical violence between KKK supporters and those protesting their appearance.
Quotes	"No free speech for racists," on sign held by protester. "I came down here to hear what they have to say and I think I should be able to listen if I want to," spoken by a supporter of the KKK.	"Here you have a potential for some real sparks in the crowd," spoken by an observer. "The tension between Klan protesters and supporters came within seconds of violence," spoken by a reporter.
Images	Chanting of protesters. KKK leaders speaking before a microphone.	Police officers standing in front of Klan members protecting them from the protesters.
Interviews	Three of the four people interviewed were Klan supporters who wanted to hear the Klan's message.	All three people interviewed emphasized the violence and disruption of public order that they had witnessed.

TABLE 6.6b — MEASURING FRAMING EFFECTS

	FREE SPEECH FRAME	PUBLIC ORDER FRAME
Tolerance for rallies	3.96	3.31
Tolerance for speeches	4.17	3.54
Importance of free speech	5.49	5.25
Importance of public order	4.75	5.43

Higher numbers indicate greater tolerance
SOURCE: Thomas Nelson, Rosalee A. Clawson, and Zoe M. Oxley, "Media Framing of a Civil Liberties Conflict and Its Effect on Tolerance," *American Political Science Review* 91 (1997): 567-83.

journalists have spent much of their time following the terrorists' agenda of violence and mayhem, pushing the accomplishments of our soldiers off the public's radar screen."[85] These claims were echoed by the *Washington Times*, which began a series of editorials in 2005 highlighting "underreported news from Iraq," such as increases in primary school enrollment and increases in Iraq's gross domestic product (GDP). They found few mentions of these topics in other publications, leading them to conclude that most reporters were focusing on bad news from Iraq.[86]

Many journalists and commentators readily admit that they take an ideological or partisan perspective. Rush Limbaugh, the previously mentioned talk radio host, describes himself as a strong conservative. Many of the commentators on the Fox News Network make no secret of their conservative viewpoint. Similarly, the political news magazine *The Nation* describes itself as "a weekly journal of left/liberal opinion, covering national and international affairs as well as the arts."[87] These journalists' and organizations' points of view are well-known and easy to see. Some people might even find the bias useful. A liberal, for example, could use *The Nation*'s endorsements as a guide to which candidates they should support, and a conservative might listen to Rush Limbaugh to get the same information.

TABLE 6.7

PARTISANSHIP AND NEWS SOURCE CREDIBILITY

Do Americans consider all media sources equally reliable for learning about politics? Are there partisan differences in the sources people choose?

BELIEVE ALL OR MOST OF WHAT ORGANIZATION SAYS	REPUBLICANS	DEMOCRATS	GAP
NewsHour with Jim Lehrer	13%	32%	-19
National Public Radio	15	30	-15
Daily newspaper	12	26	-14
CBS News	15	26	-11
Local TV news	17	28	-11
CNN	22	32	-10
ABC News	18	27	-9
NBC News	19	26	-7
New York Times	16	23	-7
USA Today	15	22	-7
Time	20	23	-3
Wall Street Journal	29	26	-3
Fox News Channel	32	22	-10

Percentages are based on those who could rate each.
SOURCE: Pew Research Center, "The Media: More Voices, Less Credibility," January 25, 2005, available at http://people-press.org/commentary/pdf/105.pdf.

More generally, claims about media bias make strong assumptions about what fair coverage would look like, presuming, for example, that some of the news stories about Iraq should necessarily be optimistic or report positive developments along with negative ones. But what if critical coverage is justified? Suppose the Media Research Center's study is accurate, and some 61 percent of the stories they analyzed about Iraq were truly negative or pessimistic. Does that percentage mean the coverage was inaccurate? During 2005, hundreds of American troops and large numbers of civilians were killed in Iraq, and there were thousands of bombings, kidnappings, and other attacks by insurgent forces. Moreover, while some improvements were noted in school enrollments and the country's GDP, many other indicators, such as levels of oil exports, showed little change or even declined.[88] In other words, if the expectation is that the media should give an accurate picture of what's happening in Iraq, it is not clear that optimism was appropriate in 2005. In fact, after two stories, the *Washington Times* stopped publishing its "underreported news from Iraq" series.

Similarly, the evidence for priming, filtering, and framing does not support claims of either liberal or conservative media bias. Reporters move beyond "just the facts" because much of what happens in American politics requires interpretation. They must choose what to report because so many things happen every day, and decide how to report staged news, whether to reveal secrets, and which sources to rely on. Thus, filtering and framing of the news are virtually inevitable. There is no way to cover American politics, or any other topic, without choosing which stories to report and how to cover them. You may disagree with the decisions of a particular reporter or publication, but there is no such thing as completely objective

The Liberal Media?

One of the central criticisms of journalists in America is that a disproportionate number of them are liberals who, because of their own political leanings, tend to favor liberal politicians and liberal causes in their news coverage. As the late Michael Kelly, a well-known newspaper columnist once wrote in the *Washington Post*: "Does a largely liberal news media still exhibit a largely liberal bias? [This question] can be answered both as a matter of logic and as a matter of fact, and the answer is: sure."[a]

Are these claims of liberal media bias true? On the surface, the answer seems to be yes. The figure below gives the results of a 1997 survey conducted by the American Society of Newspaper Editors (ASNE), focusing on the party affiliations of newspaper reporters.[b] Reporters in this survey were much more likely to be Democrats rather than Republicans. Note that a majority said they were Democrats or liberals, or leaned in this direction, compared to only 15 percent who claimed a Republican or conservative affiliation.

A deeper look suggests a problem with this conclusion. The ASNE surveyed all journalists, not just those who cover politics. If you are interested in whether political reporting is biased in a liberal direction, it doesn't matter if restaurant reviewers are liberals, if the sports pages are dominated by Democrats, or even if the TV weather forecasters hate the Republican Party. The real question is whether an ideological bias exists among reporters who write about politics.

When you look at the ideological leanings of political reporters in particular, evidence for a liberal or pro-Democrat bias is weak. One survey sampled reporters based in Washington, DC, who cover national politics or the economy. The next figure shows their responses to a question about their ideological leanings. The figures reveal a complex ideological picture among political reporters. On social issues, there are more liberals than conservatives—but the pattern is reversed for economic issues. More importantly, on both sets of issues, the vast majority of reporters reported they were moderates.

These data suggest that the conventional wisdom about liberal reporters is only partly true. While reporters in general are predominately liberal or Democratic, those who cover politics and the economy look very different, with a much higher percentage of moderates, conservatives, and Republicans. These data do not prove that the media cover politics without bias, but they suggest that the people who write about politics have a range of political views. ■

ALL JOURNALISTS' SELF-REPORTED IDEOLOGIES

Allegations of a liberal bias in media coverage of politics center on the claim that reporters are predominantly liberals. Based on these data, what would you tell someone who made this claim?

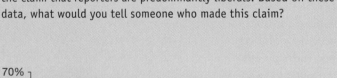

SELF-REPORTED IDEOLOGIES OF WASHINGTON REPORTERS WHO COVER POLITICS AND THE ECONOMY

This graph presents a more refined view of reporter ideology, focusing on Washington-based reporters who cover business, economics, or politics. Do these data support or refute claims of liberal media bias in political coverage?

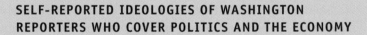
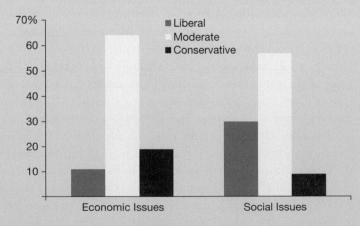

journalism; your preferred coverage would just involve a different frame, a different filter, and different kinds of priming.

Finally, it would be a mistake to argue that an overall media bias toward either liberal or conservative views must exist simply because so many Americans think it does. Analyses that compare media coverage to citizens' perceptions have found a **hostile media phenomenon**, in which people tend to view balanced coverage as biased against their preferred candidates. One study found that many Republicans believed that the newspapers and TV shows consistently gave favorable treatment to then-president Bill Clinton—even when a content analysis of these programs showed they were either balanced or only slightly favorable.[89] This hostile media phenomenon suggests that even though many Americans consider the media biased, the problem is not media coverage itself, so much as how this coverage is perceived.

SECTION SUMMARY

1. There is clear evidence of media effects; what citizens know or believe about politics often changes after they read or watch a political news story.
2. The mechanisms of media influence include priming, filtering, and framing. However, the evidence suggests that these phenomena are inherent to media coverage, rather than part of a conscious strategy to shape public opinion.
3. There is no evidence of a general media bias toward either liberal or conservative views.

hostile media phenomenon The idea that supporters of a candidate or issue tend to feel that media coverage is biased against their position, regardless of whether coverage is actually unfair.

attack journalism A type of increasingly popular media coverage focused on political scandals and controversies, which causes a negative public opinion of political figures.

horse race A description of the type of election coverage that focuses more on poll results and speculation about a likely winner than on substantive differences between the candidates.

soft news Media coverage that aims to entertain or shock, often through sensationalized reporting or by focusing on a candidate or politician's personality.

hard news Media coverage focused on facts and important issues surrounding a campaign.

Assessing Media Coverage of American Politics

In a democracy, the media's job is to provide citizens with information about politicians, government actions, and policy debates. In this section, we address complaints that media coverage of American politics falls far short of this goal. We will examine some of the reasons for journalists' and editors' choices, and the impact of those decisions on coverage and on what Americans know.

Scholars such as Larry Sabato and Thomas Patterson have documented the rise of **attack journalism**, where "bad news makes for good news," "the mere whiff of a controversy or scandal is grounds for a story," and "public officials are [portrayed as] an ineffective and untrustworthy lot."[90] Other researchers have argued that campaign coverage overemphasizes the **horse race** aspects of the campaign, such as which candidates are ahead and which are falling behind, rather than offering a complete description of each candidate's promises and analysis of how they are likely to behave in office.[91]

Media coverage of politics also emphasizes **soft news** (stories that are sensational or entertaining) over **hard news** (stories that focus on important issues and emphasize facts and figures).[92] At the same time, talk shows and those focused on entertainment have increased their political coverage mainly by reporting stories that emphasize scandals, personalities, and other topics that attract an audience rather than hard facts.[93] An oft-heard truism about local TV news is that "if it bleeds, it leads." An overemphasis on crime stories, coupled with a focus on the victims of crimes rather than on the causes and context of criminal events, leads people to overestimate the chances of being the victim of a violent crime.[94]

Moreover, citizens' perceptions of government may mirror press coverage. Many authors have suggested that citizens' low level of trust in government, as well as high levels of disapproval and dissatisfaction discussed in Chapter 5, may have more to do with how the media reports on American politics than with how government actually works.[95] The lack of hard information in much of the political coverage also fails to address the profound ignorance that many Americans have about the structure of the federal government, particular government policies, and how decisions are made.

Many journalists agree with these broad criticisms of their field. Figure 6.2 shows that a majority of journalists believe the media avoid complex stories and are too timid, and that coverage of events is becoming sloppier. Similarly, a 2000 survey of journalists found that 53 percent avoided stories that they thought were too complex for their target audience, and over 70 percent avoided stories that they believed were "important but dull."[96]

WHY MEDIA COVERAGE FALLS SHORT: MARKET FORCES

The deeper question about the American media's coverage of politics is *why* there is so much attack journalism, soft news, sensationalism, and scandal. If journalists are aware of the problem, why don't they take their role as political watchdogs for the public interest more seriously? One response is that journalists may feel the need to demonstrate their independence from politicians and government interests, and

---

FIGURE 6.2   **HOW JOURNALISTS VIEW THEIR PROFESSION**

Many observers complain about the quality of reporting on American politics. Do journalists share these concerns?

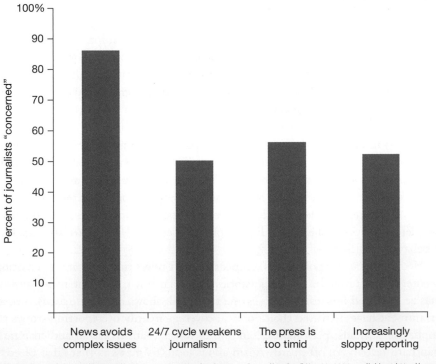

SOURCE: Pew Research Center, "Bottom-line Pressures Now Hurting Coverage, Journalists Say," May 23, 2004, available at http://people-press.org/reports/display.php3?ReportID=214.

perhaps counter or prevent claims of media bias. The result can be overly aggressive questioning of elected officials and cynical stories about the political process.[97]

The more significant explanation for the soft, sensationalistic nature of much political coverage is that reporters and their editors recognize that they are in a competitive business where the aim is to attract a paying audience. Describing the media as an information source for citizens makes sense in terms of how American politics works, but this description does not capture the sometimes-contradictory incentives facing journalists. Most American media outlets are for-profit enterprises. Because they need to produce coverage that attracts an audience, their strategy is often to create stories that consumers want to read and watch, and that are consistent with how members of their target audience think about politics.

For example, as we discussed in the context of public opinion (Chapter 5) and will return to in the next chapters, many Americans hold dismal evaluations of the Republican and Democratic parties, of Congress, and of the American political system in general. Given these perceptions, the prevalence of attack journalism is no surprise; journalists give the American people coverage of politics that fits their preconceptions. Americans are not changing what they think in response to attack stories and soft news. Rather, the way journalists cover politics reflects the tone of American public opinion.[98] Although journalists can and do shape public opinion—as the discussion of media effects showed—media coverage is also substantially shaped by the need to attract an audience. The shift in the tone and content of political coverage also reflects the expansion in the number of media sources and the competition among them for a finite audience. As longtime ABC reporter Sam Donaldson put it,

> We're trying desperately to hold onto an ever-shrinking audience, as far as the big commercial networks are concerned. . . . We're reaching out more and more for people who believe there are three-headed cows. . . . I'm part of the process of trying to find a larger audience of people who never really cared about news. . . . And to get them, we have to do things we didn't ever used to do before.[99]

The same factors can lead media sources to emphasize stories about Americans and America over coverage of important events in other countries. Coverage may also be shaped by a reporter's background—for example, someone who grew up in a middle-class neighborhood may have difficulty understanding or reporting accurately on the problems of the poor.[100]

Even if reporters tried to explain how government works, especially the need for compromise to get things done, it is unlikely that citizens would respond favorably. As researchers John Hibbing and Elizabeth Theiss-Morse discovered in their focus group studies, "Citizens . . . dislike being exposed to processes endemic to democratic government. People do not wish to see uncertainty, conflicting options, long debate, competing interests, confusion, bargaining, and compromised, imperfect solutions."[101] In other words, coverage that offered exclusively hard news, policy details, and sober analysis rather than at least some soft news, cynicism, scandals, and attack journalism, would probably not find much of an audience. Market forces also explain other aspects of the political media. The focus on campaigns as horse races, for example, reflects the kind of stories that the average voter finds interesting: who's ahead in the race, rather than the details of their campaign promises.[102] Similarly, the trend towards political coverage by soft news programs reflects the expectation that viewers want to see these stories covered by these programs to find out about the personalities rather than the facts.[103]

SECTION SUMMARY

1. Media coverage of American politics often falls short of the ideal of providing a full and complete understanding of the issues facing the government and what elected officials have done (or not done) to address these concerns.
2. Contemporary political coverage is marked by attack journalism and a focus on soft news and the horse race aspect of elections.
3. Market forces that fuel media outlets' desire to attract the largest possible audience are the principle explanation for this lapse.

Conclusion

The news media are the primary source of public information about American politics and policy. The considerable controversy about how well the media fulfill this role reflects both the importance of the task and the interest many people have in shaping political coverage. The news media landscape is currently undergoing a massive transition, as the Internet supports an ever-growing variety of new information sources, and fewer people rely on newspapers or television for news. Even so, these traditional sources remain the most popular for political information. Their coverage of politics is nowhere near perfect, but the media's imperfections are generally not the product of reporters and editors working to color coverage with biased views.

The story of Gary Condit neatly illustrates the causes and consequences of media coverage of American politics. In running story after story on Chandra Levy's disappearance and focusing on Condit as a suspect, media sources were responding to public demands for dramatic coverage. Americans might be better informed if they ignored political scandals and focused on the details of public policy, but sensational, lurid stories help attract and keep the audience that media companies need to stay in business.

Moreover, the Condit episode illustrates that the average American consults only a tiny fraction of the information provided by the media. Americans tend to learn about politics as a by-product of other activities, focusing on vivid, exciting stories regardless of their importance. While this process makes sense given the many demands people face every day, it can lead them to some peculiar conclusions, even about well-reported events—including continuing to suspect Gary Condit of involvement in Chandra Levy's disappearance even after the Washington, DC, police department concluded he had nothing to do with it. Even so, these shortcomings should not necessarily be read as an indictment of the news media or of the average American. Rather, they illustrate the simple fact that even though politics is everywhere, many Americans are not particularly interested in the political process and political outcomes.

CRITICAL THINKING

1. One argument against deregulating the media is that consolidation and the formation of media conglomerates will reduce the number of independent sources of information that are available to the average American. Based on the media sources that you and your friends use, do you agree or disagree with this argument? Why?
2. To what extent are journalists, editors, and the owners of media businesses to blame for the fact that the average American is often uninformed about and uninterested in politics?
3. What advice would you give to someone who wants to learn about American politics? What types of media sources should they seek, which ones should they avoid, and why?

KEY TERMS

attack journalism (p. 211)
broadcast media (p. 186)
by-product theory of information transmission (p. 199)
concentration (p. 187)
cross-ownership (p. 187)
equal time provision (p. 186)
fairness doctrine (p. 186)
Federal Communications Commission (FCC) (p. 186)
filtering (p. 205)
framing (p. 205)
hard news (p. 211)
horse race (p. 211)
hostile media phenomenon (p. 211)
investigative journalists (p. 185)
leak (p. 196)
mainstream media (MSM) (p. 189)
mass media (p. 184)
media conglomerates (p. 187)
media effects (p. 205)
news cycle (p. 190)
normalization hypothesis (p. 195)
off the record (p. 196)
on background (p. 196)
op-ed (p. 194)
penny press (p. 185)
press conference (p. 196)
prime time (p. 190)
priming (p. 205)
shield laws (p. 198)
slant (p. 205)
soft news (p. 211)
wire service (p. 185)
yellow journalism (p. 185)

SUGGESTED READING

Baum, Matthew A. *Soft News Goes to War: Public Opinion and American Foreign Policy in the New Media Age,* Princeton, NJ: Princeton University Press, 2003.

Braestrup, Peter. *How the American Press and Television Reported and Interpreted the Crisis of Tet 1968 in Vietnam.* New Haven, CT: Yale University Press, 1983.

Cappella, J. N., and K. H. Jamieson. *Spiral of Cynicism: The Press and the Public Good.* New York: Oxford University Press, 1997.

Iyengar, Shanto. *Is Anyone Responsible? How Television Frames Political Issues.* Chicago: University of Chicago Press, 1991.

Kuklinski, James H., and Lee Sigelman. "When Objectivity Is Not Objective." *The Journal of Politics* 54:3 (1992): 810–33.

Lippman, Walter. *Public Opinion.* 1922. Reprint, New York: Free Press, 1997.

Nelson, Thomas E., Rosalee A. Clawson, and Zoe M. Oxley. "Media Framing of a Civil Liberties Conflict and Its Effect on Tolerance," *American Political Science Review* 91 (1997): 567–83.

Norris, Pippa. *A Virtuous Circle? Political Communications in Post-Industrial Democracies.* New York: Cambridge University Press, 2000.

Patterson, Thomas. *Out of Order.* New York: Knopf, 1993.

Talese, Gay. *The Kingdom and the Power.* New York: Calder and Boyars, 1983.

POLITICAL PARTIES

A recent book on American political parties is titled *Why Parties?*—what role do political parties play in a democracy?[1] The answer may seem obvious. Parties and their candidates compete for control of the presidency, House and Senate, offering different visions of what government should do. Parties are everywhere in American politics—they help shape the way Americans think about candidates, policies, and vote decisions. In many cases, parties and their candidates define political conflicts. The way the parties are organized and the processes they follow influence their candidates during campaigns and in government. After the election, the winning party's candidates implement their vision, while the losers try to derail these efforts and develop an alternate vision that will attract support in the next election. In doing so, parties unify and mobilize disparate groups in society, simplify the choices facing voters, and bring efficiency and coherence to government policy making.

However, while political parties are a fundamental part of American politics, they often do not behave according to this job description. Consider Senator John Sununu, a Republican from New Hampshire (pictured at left with President George W. Bush). When he first ran for the Senate in 2002, one of Sununu's central campaign promises was to work with his Republican colleagues, including President Bush, to implement the Republican agenda. As President Bush put it during a joint campaign appearance, he wanted Sununu to be his "foot soldier in the Senate on the issues of Iraq and taxes, in particular, and to support [his] judicial appointees."[2] After his election to the Senate, Sununu was one of the most loyal members of the Republican conference, voting with his president and party over 90 percent of the time. Sununu also served as cochair of the 2004 Bush–Cheney reelection effort in New Hampshire. He voted for both of Bush's nominees to the Supreme Court, and supported the invasions of Iraq and Afghanistan.

By 2007, however, Senator Sununu's loyalty to his party and his president was much less evident. When Bush's attorney general, Alberto Gonzales, fired eight U.S. attorneys that year, Sununu was one of the first Republican Senators to demand Gonzalez's resignation.[3] Sununu cosponsored a resolution calling for an early withdrawal of American forces from Iraq.[4] And when Sununu was asked whether he wanted President Bush to campaign with him during his 2008 reelection bid, Sununu replied flatly, "I have no offers [of campaign help from the president]." One political commentator translated the comment this way: "'No, I would really prefer that he not come to raise money for me, but I am not going to insult the leader of the United States and my party."[5]

Sununu's experience is not unique. During the 2006 and 2008 elections, many Republican candidates opposed President Bush's policies on issues from the Iraq war to immigration. Rather than emphasizing their party label, many of these candidates did not mention it at all. Some Republican legislators refused to support proposals developed by their party's leaders in Congress. These actions were even more surprising given that many of these candidates had previously been just as loyal to President Bush and their party as Senator Sununu was.

The change in fortunes of the Republican Party illustrates that the question "why parties?" does not have an obvious answer—even though the influence of American political parties is everywhere. Most candidates for office run as major party nominees, and most Americans think of themselves as either Republicans or Democrats. Moreover, throughout American history, many of the major public policy conflicts have divided politicians and citizens according to party affiliation. However, while American political parties often have an obvious impact on elections and policy, the same organizations can look inept and irrelevant in many other situations. A good answer to "why parties?" must explain this variation. Why are American political parties sometimes powerful and in other cases powerless? The answer developed in this chapter rests on the notion that political process matters: understanding what parties do (and cannot do) requires an appreciation of how they are organized, as well as the rules and regulations that shape the behavior of party leaders, politicians, and citizens.

What Are Political Parties?

Political parties are organizations that run candidates for political office and coordinate the actions of officials elected under the party banner. There are many different kinds of parties. In many western European countries, political parties have millions of dues-paying members, and party leaders control what their elected officials do.

▲ American political parties have three separate, independent parts: the party in government, represented here by Democratic House Speaker Nancy Pelosi and her leadership team; the party organization, represented by Howard Dean, Chair of the Democratic National Committee; and the party in the electorate, exemplified by the crowd at a Barack Obama rally in May 2008.

In contrast, in many new democracies, candidates run as representatives of a party, but party leaders have no control over what candidates say during the campaign or how they act in office. America's major political parties, the Republicans and the Democrats, lie somewhere between these extremes. Many Americans have a deep, enduring connection to one of these parties, and these organizations' actions affect both election returns and policy outcomes.

However, rather than being unified organizations with party leaders at the top, candidates and party workers in the middle, and citizen-members at the bottom, American political parties are best described as a collection of **nodes**—groups and individuals who share a party label, but are under no obligation to work together.[6] For example, the Speaker of the House of Representatives is the leader of House members from her party, but she works independently from the party's national committee chair; neither one is in charge of the other. Similarly, while many Americans think of themselves as members of a political party, neither the Republicans or the Democrats have formal membership. Someone who identifies with the Republican Party does not have to work for or give money to the party, or vote for its candidates.

In light of this defining characteristic of American political parties, scholars describe these organizations as being comprised of three separate and largely independent pieces:[7] The **party organization** involves the structure of national, state, and local parties, including party leaders and workers. The **party in government** is made up of the politicians who were elected as candidates of the party. And the **party in the electorate** includes all the citizens who identify with the party. As you will see, organization matters: the fact that American political parties are split into three parts has important implications for what they do and for their impact on American politics.

nodes Groups of people who belong to, are candidates of, or work for a political party, but do not necessarily work together or hold similar policy preferences.

party organization A specific political party's leaders and workers at the national, state, and local levels.

party in government The group of officeholders who belong to a specific political party and were elected as candidates of that party.

party in the electorate The group of citizens who identify with a specific political party.

party system A period of time in which the names of the major political parties, their supporters, and the issues dividing them remain relatively stable.

POLITICS IS EVERYWHERE

Political parties in America are part of the debate in Washington (the party in government), organized throughout the country (the party organization), and shape the way ordinary citizens view politics (the party in the electorate).

History of American Political Parties

The Republican and Democratic parties have existed for a long time—the Republicans since 1854 and the Democrats since even earlier in the 1800s. The nickname for the Republican Party is the G.O.P. or "Grand Old Party," a play on G.A.R., the Grand Army of the Republic, which refers to the Union Army in the Civil War. The symbol for the Republicans is an elephant; for the Democrats, a donkey. This section shows that at certain points in history, both major American political parties have looked and acted very differently than they do today, and contemporary parties do not resemble their historical counterparts.

Political scientists use the term **party system** to describe periods in which the major parties' names, their groups of supporters, and the issues dividing them are all constant. As shown in Table 7.1, there have been six party systems in America.[8] For each party system, the table gives the names of the two major parties, says which party dominated (won the most presidential elections or controlled Congress), and describes the principle issues dividing the parties.

▼ *The symbols of the Republican and Democratic parties are an elephant and a donkey, respectively. They are often depicted feuding over government policy and refusing to compromise their differences.*

TABLE 7.1 AMERICAN PARTY SYSTEMS

PARTY SYSTEM	MAJOR PARTIES (Dominant party in boldface)	KEY ISSUES
First (1789–1828)	**Federalists,** Jeffersonian Democratic-Republicans	Location of the capital, financial issues (e.g., national bank)
Second (1829–1856)	**Democrats,** Whigs	Tariffs (farmers vs. merchants), slavery
Third (1857–1892)	Democrats, **Republicans**	Slavery (pre-Civil War), reconstruction (post-Civil War), industrialization
Fourth (1893–1932)	Democrats, **Republicans**	Industrialization, immigration
Fifth (1933–1968)	**Democrats,** Republicans	Size and scope of the federal government
Sixth (1969–present)	Democrats, Republicans (Neither party is dominant)	Size of the federal government, civil rights, individual liberties (e.g., abortion), foreign policy (e.g., Mid-East relations)

THE FIRST PARTY SYSTEM, 1789–1828

Political parties formed soon after the Founding of the United States. The first American parties, the Federalists and the Jeffersonian Democratic-Republicans, were primarily parties in government. As political scientist John Aldrich put it, members of Congress had ideas about what the new government should look like and what it should do, but they needed votes to translate these ideas into concrete policies.[9] The first parties were composed of like-minded legislators: Federalists wanted a strong central government and a national bank, and they favored assumption of state war debts by the national government; Jeffersonian Democratic-Republicans took the opposite positions based on their preference for concentrating power at the state level. These political parties were quite different from their modern counterparts. In particular, there were no national party organizations, few citizens thought of themselves as party members, and candidates for office did not campaign as representatives of a political party.

THE SECOND PARTY SYSTEM, 1829–1856

The second American party system began with the disintegration of the Federalist Party. Many Federalist legislators had opposed the War of 1812, and had supported a politically unpopular pay raise for members of Congress.[10] Ultimately, Federalist politicians were either defeated for reelection or switched their party affiliation, eliminating the Federalist Party as a political force in American politics.

The demise of the Federalists gave way to the Era of Good Feeling, a decade-long period when there was only one political party, the Jeffersonian Democratic-Republicans. Following the election of President Andrew Jackson in 1828, the organization that elected Jackson was transformed by him and by then-senator (later president) Martin Van Buren into the Democratic Party, the ancestor of the modern-day organization. At the same time, another new party, the Whigs, was formed and the Jeffersonian Democratic-Republican Party dissolved, with most of its politicians becoming Democrats.

The new Democratic Party embodied two important innovations. First, they cultivated electoral support as a way of strengthening the party's hold on power in Washington. The party built organizations at the state and local level to mobilize citizens to support the party's candidates. These efforts helped to bind citizens to the party, encouraging them to think of themselves as party members and creating the first American party in the electorate. The Democrats' second innovation was what Van Buren called the **party principle**, the idea that a party is not just a group of elected officials but an organization that exists apart from its candidates. Jackson and Van Buren also created the **spoils system**, whereby individuals who worked for the party were rewarded with benefits such as federal government jobs.

THE THIRD PARTY SYSTEM, 1857–1892

The issue of slavery split the second party system. Most Democratic politicians and party officials either supported slavery outright or wanted to avoid debating the issue.[11] The Whig Party was split between politicians who agreed with the Democrats and abolitionists who wanted to end slavery. Ultimately, antislavery Whigs left the party and formed a new organization, the Republican Party, which also attracted antislavery Democrats. As the remaining Whig candidates began to have difficulty winning office against both Republican and Democratic opponents, Whig officeholders left the party and joined one of these other more powerful parties, dividing the country into a largely Republican Northeast, a largely Democratic South, and politically split midwestern and border states.[12]

POLITICAL PROCESS MATTERS

☑ The decision to form the Republican Party around an antislavery platform put this issue on the political agenda and set the stage for the Civil War.

The demise of the Whigs and the rise of the Republican Party illustrates that parties exist only because elites, politicians, party leaders, and activists want them to. The Republican Party was created by people such as Abraham Lincoln who wanted to abolish slavery, and many other politicians subsequently joined the party because of ambition: they believed their chances of winning political office were higher as a Republican than as a Whig or a Democrat.

THE FOURTH PARTY SYSTEM, 1893–1932

While the Civil War settled the issue of slavery, it did not change the identity of the major American parties. In the post-war era, the Republicans and the Democrats remained the two prominent, national parties, and the same regional split persisted between these organizations. Slavery was no longer an issue, but the parties divided on related concerns such as the withdrawal of the Union Army from southern states. At about the same time, the rapid growth of American cities and increased immigration raised new debate over the size and scope of the federal government: should it help farmers and rural residents, inhabitants of rapidly expanding cities, or neither group? A related concern was whether the federal government should regulate America's fast-growing industrial base.

The political parties took opposing positions on this issue, leading to a new party system. Democrats, led by three-time presidential candidate William Jennings Bryan, attempted to build a coalition of rural and urban voters by proposing a larger, more active federal government and other policies that would help these groups. Although Bryan was never elected president, the issues he stood for divided the major parties and defined the debate in Washington for over a generation.

The move from the third to the fourth party system shows how American political parties reflect the basic divisions in society over what government should do. In

▲ Although Democrat William Jennings Bryan's three presidential campaigns failed (in 1896, 1900, and 1908), his passionate fight for policies to aid farmers and working-class city dwellers helped to create the fourth party system.

POLITICS IS CONFLICTUAL

Disagreement about public policy is the fundamental force that creates and sustains American political parties.

the third party system, the parties were divided over slavery and, after the Civil War, the pace of Reconstruction. Once these issues were settled, politicians and party leaders found new issues to campaign on—partly because they cared about these issues, and partly because taking these positions helped to attract votes and other forms of support to themselves and to their party.

THE FIFTH PARTY SYSTEM, 1933–1968

The fifth party system was born out of the Great Depression, a worldwide economic collapse. With millions unemployed, prices declining, and ever-growing soup lines of those unable to afford food becoming a common sight in major cities, the critical question was what the federal government should do to get things moving again.

Many Republican politicians, especially President Herbert Hoover, argued that conditions would improve given time, and that government intervention would be costly and do little good. Democratic challenger Franklin Roosevelt proposed new government programs that would help people in need and spur economic growth. Roosevelt won the 1932 presidential election, and voters also elected many new Democrats to Congress. Together, the president and Congress enacted the New Deal, a series of federal programs designed to stimulate the national economy, help needy people, and impose a variety of new regulations.

The debate over the New Deal produced a lasting change in American politics: it brought together the **New Deal Coalition** of African Americans, Catholics, Jewish people, union members, and white southerners who became strong supporters of Democratic candidates over the next generation.[13] This transformation established the basic division between the Republican and Democratic parties that would persist for the rest of the twentieth century, with Democrats generally favoring a large federal government that took an active role in managing the economy and regulating individual and corporate behavior, and Republicans believing that many of

New Deal Coalition The assemblage of groups who aligned with and supported the Democratic Party in support of New Deal policies during the fifth party system, including African Americans, Catholics, Jewish people, union members, and white southerners.

▲ A key issue in the 1932 election between Republican Herbert Hoover (left) and Democrat Franklin Roosevelt (right) was how the federal government should respond to the Great Depression. Roosevelt proposed expanding programs to feed the poor and put people back to work, while Hoover favored letting the economy recover on its own and relying on state, local, and private charities to assist the poor. Roosevelt won and enacted his New Deal policies, which gave rise to the fifth party system.

these programs should either be provided by state and local governments or kept entirely separate from government.

THE SIXTH PARTY SYSTEM, 1969–PRESENT

Changes in two areas drove the transition from the fifth to the sixth party system: political issues and technology. Beginning in the late 1940s, and more decisively during the 1960s, many Democratic candidates and party leaders, particularly outside the South, came out against the "separate but equal" system of racial discrimination in southern states, and in favor of programs designed to ensure equal opportunity for minority citizens throughout the nation.

At the same time, Democratic politicians, particularly President Lyndon Johnson, argued for expanding the federal government into health care funding (in the form of the Medicare and Medicaid programs), antipoverty programs, education, and public works. Johnson called his plan the Great Society. While some Republican politicians supported portions of the Great Society, particularly the civil rights reforms, there was considerable Republican opposition to expanding the role of government in society. This division, along with differences on new issues such as affirmative action, abortion rights, the war in Vietnam, and other foreign policy questions, produced a gradual but significant shift in the groups that identified with each party, with white southerners and some Catholics gradually moving to the Republican Party, and minorities, particularly African Americans, identifying more strongly as Democrats.

In the sixth party system, technological developments also brought changes in the party organizations. Both the Republican and Democratic parties became **parties in service**, involved in recruiting, training, and campaigning for their party's congressional and presidential candidates.[14] This change was driven in part by the increased use of television ads to mobilize supporters, but also by increased competition in Congress over control of policy. Just as in the first party system, the parties in government became more involved in elections as a way of electing like-minded colleagues who would vote with them to enact their preferred policies.

REALIGNMENTS

Each party system is separated from the next by a **realignment**, a change in the issues that divide the people who identify with each party (the party in the electorate). These shifts may cause similar changes in the policy preferences of officeholders (the party in government) and among activists and party workers (the party organization). A realignment begins with the emergence of a new question or issue debate that captures the attention of large numbers of ordinary citizens, activists, and politicians.[15] In order to spur a realignment, the issue has to be **crosscutting**, meaning that within each party coalition, people disagree on what government should do.

In the case of the second party system (1829–1856), recall that the new issue was slavery.[16] While most Democratic Party leaders and elected officials supported keeping slavery legal, the Whig Party was split between pro-slavery and abolitionist members. The result was the formation of a new political party, the Republicans, by antislavery Whigs and some Democrats. Within a few years, citizens and politicians moved to whichever party reflected their feelings about slavery, resulting in the realignment that yielded the third party system.

A realignment between the fifth party system (1933–1968) and the sixth (1969–present) produced the division between modern-day Republicans and Democrats.[17] The fifth party system was born during the Great Depression, when the

parties in service The role of the parties in recruiting, training, contributing to, and campaigning for congressional and presidential candidates. This aspect of party organization grew more prominent during the sixth party system.

realignment A change in the size or composition of the party coalitions or in the nature of the issues that divide the parties. Realignments typically occur within an election cycle or two, but they can also occur gradually over the course of a decade or longer.

crosscutting A term describing issues that raise disagreements within a party coalition or between political parties about what government should do.

parties were primarily divided by their positions on the appropriate size of the federal government and how much it should control the behavior of individuals and corporations, including issues such as the regulation of corporations, social welfare programs to help the poor and senior citizens, and public works. This conflict created the New Deal Coalition and gave the Democratic Party control of Congress and the presidency for most of the time between 1933 and 1969.

One of the new issues that drove the realignment between the fifth and sixth party systems was civil rights, and the question of whether the federal government should ensure that minority citizens were treated equally in all states, in terms of voting rights and access to public facilities.[18] Other new issues included the rights of people accused of crimes, the separation between church and state, freedom of speech, and abortion rights. Importantly, these volatile issues were crosscutting: within the Democratic and Republican parties, people disagreed about what government should do. Ultimately, the Democratic Party leaders and most of its politicians took a position generally favoring federal government intervention on these issues, while Republican Party officials and most Republican politicians generally favored a smaller, less active federal government.

These changes split the New Deal Coalition, with white southerners and evangelicals moving to the Republican Party, and African American voters becoming even stronger Democratic identifiers.[19] By the 1980s, the changes in the party coalitions and election outcomes were apparent, with control of Congress and the presidency divided between the two parties. Republicans gained House and Senate seats in southern states, and Democrats gained seats in the northeast, west, and southwest.[20]

SECTION SUMMARY

1. American parties have looked and operated very differently over time. In some party systems, there was little or no party in the electorate; in others, the party organization did relatively little to help their candidates get elected.
2. The variation in political parties across American history confirms that nothing about them is inevitable. Parties look and act as they do because many politicians, activists, and citizens support particular party features.
3. Realignments define the issues that separate American political parties, determine the balance of power between the parties, and lead to changes in government policy.
4. Realignments are rare because they occur only when a new crosscutting issue or set of issues captures the attention of large numbers of citizens and politicians.

Modern American Political Parties

In this section, we will examine the contemporary Democratic and Republican parties in terms of their party organization, party in government, and party in the electorate. In doing so, we will convey some basic information about the parties, show how each of their three distinct parts works, and consider some implications of this three-part structure.

THE PARTY ORGANIZATION

The principle policy-making body in each party organization is the **national committee**, which consists of representatives from state party organizations, usually one man and one woman per state. The state party organizations in turn are made up of some professional staff, plus thousands of party organizations at the county, city, and town levels.

Both parties also include a number of constituency groups (the Democrats' term) or teams (the Republicans' term), which are organizations within the party and work to attract the support of particular demographic groups considered likely to share the party's issue concerns—such as African Americans, Hispanics, people with strong religious beliefs, senior citizens, women, and many others—and assist in fund-raising.[21] In some cases, they also attempt to win over groups typically identified with the other party. For example, African Americans have long been strong supporters of Democratic candidates. Thus, the Democratic Party has a constituency group that informs African Americans about the party's candidates and works to convince these citizens to turn out and vote on Election Day. The Republican Party's corresponding constituency team works toward the opposite goal, trying to convince African Americans that Republican policies and candidates would better serve their interests.

Each party organization also includes a number of groups designed to gain support for or coordinate the efforts of particular individuals or politicians. These include the Democratic and the Republican Governors' Associations, the Young Democrats, the Young Republicans, and more specialized groups such as the Republican Lawyers' Organization or the Democratic Leadership Council (DLC), an organization of moderate Democratic politicians.[22] The parties use their college and youth organizations to help convince politically-minded students to work for the party and its candidates. President George W. Bush's chief political adviser, Karl Rove, got his start in politics as a leader of the Young Republicans.[23] Groups such as the Governors' Associations and the DLC hold meetings where elected officials discuss solutions to common problems and try to formulate joint strategies. People who work for a party organization carry out a wide range of tasks, from recruiting candidates and formulating political strategies to mobilizing citizens, fund-raising, filling out campaign finance reports, researching opposing candidates and parties, and even developing Web sites for the party and its candidates.

While some of the national-level leadership positions in the major parties are paid, full-time jobs, national party committee slots and most state and local party positions are held by unpaid volunteers. Compared to the national party organization, state and local party organizations are smaller, with proportionally more volunteers and fewer full-time staff. Local-level organizations, which are less common, are almost always staffed entirely by volunteers.

Many other groups, such as **political action committees (PACs)** or **527 organizations**, labor unions, and other interest groups are loosely affiliated with one of the major parties. For example, the organization MoveOn.org typically supports Democratic candidates. Similar organizations on the Republican side include the Club for Growth and the G.O.P. PAC (known as GOPAC), as well as many evangelical groups. While these groups often favor one party over the other, they are not part of the party organization and do not always agree with the party's positions or support its candidates. (Both PACs and 527 organizations are discussed in more detail in Chapter 9, Interest Groups.)

POLITICS IS EVERYWHERE

The large number of constituency groups or teams organized by the major political parties reflects the diversity of American society.

national committee An American political party's principal organization, comprised of party representatives from each state.

political action committees (PACs) Interest groups or divisions of interest groups that can raise money to contribute to campaigns or to spend on ads in support of candidates. The amount they can receive from each of their donors and their expenditures on federal electioneering are strictly limited.

527 organizations Tax-exempt groups formed primarily to influence elections through voter mobilization efforts and issue ads that do not directly endorse or oppose a candidate. Unlike political action committees, they are not subject to contribution limits and spending caps.

Brand Names, Inside Politics and Out

Thinking of party labels as brand names is a simple extension of how we think in everyday life. From morning to night, Americans see brand names everywhere they look. And their decisions about what to watch, buy, or consume are often driven by what these brand names call to mind.

If you need to be convinced, consider the results of a recent survey that asked college students to identify their favorite brands.[a] The ten most popular brands were:

1. Nike
2. Coca-Cola
3. American Eagle
4. Polo/Ralph Lauren
5. Sony
6. Gap
7. Adidas
8. Old Navy
9. Abercrombie & Fitch
10. Apple

▲ *Much like Nike or Apple, the Republican and Democratic party labels are often used as brand names that call to mind particular associations. Americans tend to associate each party's name with the policy preferences of its candidates.*

Think about the clothing manufacturers on the list: American Eagle, Polo, Gap, Adidas, Old Navy, and Abercrombie & Fitch. Each name calls to mind a different description of the clothing you'd find at that company's store. Where do these impressions come from? Perhaps you've shopped at these stores, or seen their ads, or seen other people wearing clothes bought there. Different people have their own associations with various brands and make different decisions about where to shop. But snap judgments, based on brand names, will probably help determine where you go the next time you shop.

Political parties' brand names work the same way. Knowing a candidate's party affiliation tells a voter what sorts of policies the candidate is likely to support and how he or she is likely to behave in office. Candidates are not selling a product, but they are trying to win votes and elections. And candidates use brand names in much same way as the corporations whose products you encounter in everyday life: like the cues brand names provide about products, a party label gives voters a simple, straightforward signal about what kinds of policies a particular candidate supports. ▪

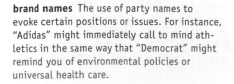

brand names The use of party names to evoke certain positions or issues. For instance, "Adidas" might immediately call to mind athletics in the same way that "Democrat" might remind you of environmental policies or universal health care.

Party Brand Names The Republican and Democratic Party organizations have well-established **brand names**. Because the parties stand for different things, both in terms of their preferred government policies, as well as their ideological leanings, the party names themselves become a short-hand way of providing information to voters about the parties' candidates.[24] Hearing the term "Democrat" or "Republican" calls to mind ideas about what kinds of positions the members of each party support, what kinds of candidates each party runs, and how these candidates will probably behave in office. Citizens can use these brand names as a voting cue to decide whom to vote for in an election. (See Chapter 8 for more information on voting cues.)

Figure 7.1 provides a general guide to the Democratic and Republican brand names. The figure reports voters' impressions of the two parties, measured on a liberal–conservative scale (1 = most liberal, 7 = most conservative). The figure shows voters' assessments beginning in 1970 and continuing into the present. The average American sees significant differences between the parties, placing the Democratic Party towards the liberal end of the ideological spectrum and the Republican Party towards the conservative end. The specific positions vary over the years, but the parties are always far apart in the average American's mind.

Additional information about party brand names comes from analyzing the beliefs held by the chairs of county-level party organizations, which are shown in Table 7.2. The table uses a 5-point scale to report the average response for

FIGURE 7.1 **REPUBLICAN AND DEMOCRATIC BRAND NAMES**

Over the last generation, Americans have consistently rated the Democratic Party as more liberal than the Republican Party. How might these perceptions shape candidates' decisions about which party to join and how to campaign?

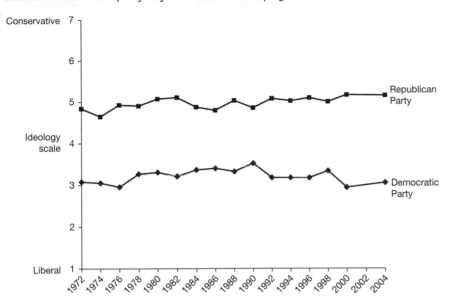

SOURCE: Calculated from the 1948–2004 American National Election Studies Cumulative Data File, available at http://www .electionstudies.org/studypages/cdf/cdf.htm.

TABLE 7.2 **ISSUE POSITIONS OF COUNTY PARTY CHAIRS**

This table shows the results a survey of county party chairs, in which the chairs were asked for their positions on a number of issues in terms of a 5-point scale: 1 = strongly agree, 2 = agree, 3 = no preference, 4 = disagree, 5 = strongly disagree. The results showed significant differences of opinion on many issues, including abortion rights, health insurance, and gun control. Are these differences consistent with how ordinary Americans see the parties?

	AVERAGE POSITION	
ISSUE	DEMOCRATS	REPUBLICANS
A woman's legal right to have an abortion	1.81	3.36
A constitutional amendment allowing organized prayer in the public schools	2.40	2.31
Government sponsored national health insurance	1.78	4.12
Increased government regulation to protect the environment	1.90	3.79
Affirmative action programs to increase minority representation in jobs and education	2.54	4.08
Increased government aid to the poor	2.21	3.71
The death penalty as punishment for certain serious crimes	2.85	1.90
Increased defense spending	2.22	1.83
Tax cuts to foster increased private investment in the economy	2.72	1.67
Increased public aid to education	1.71	3.13
Increased restrictions on purchasing fire arms	1.97	3.88

Source: Joel Paddock and Elizabeth Paddock, "Ideological Differences between Female and Male County Party Chairs," *The Social Science Journal* 41 (2004): 225–35.

political machine An unofficial patronage system within a political party that seeks to gain political power and government contracts, jobs, and other benefits for party leaders, workers, and supporters.

Democratic and Republican chairs about a number of issue positions—and shows sharp differences between the parties. In the case of firearms restrictions, for example, the average response for Democrats was 1.97 (supporting restrictions), while the average response for Republicans was 3.88 (opposing restrictions). Similar distinctions between the parties are found across the table. These data demonstrate that differences between the parties are not created for political advantage but reflect sincere differences of opinon about government policy between the people who make up the party organizations.

The Limits of the Party Organization The critical thing to understand about the Democratic and Republican party organizations is that they are not hierarchies. No one person or group in charge determines what either organization does. Since the Republican National Committee (RNC) and Democratic National Committee (DNC) are organized the same way, consider the example of Howard Dean, Chair of the DNC as of 2008. He has enormous influence over who works at the DNC. However, the party organization's issue positions are set not by Dean's employees but by DNC members from all fifty states. Since individual committee members are appointed by their state party organizations, they do not owe their jobs to Dean— and in fact, they can remove him from office if they like. If Dean and the Committee disagree, he can't force the committee members to do what he wants.

The national party organization is also unable to force state and local parties to share its positions on issues or comply with other requests. State and local parties make their own decisions about state- and local-level candidates and issue positions on their own. The national committee can cajole, it can threaten to withhold funds, and it can ask nicely. But if a state party organization, a group such as the Club for Growth, or even an individual candidate disagrees with the national committee, there's little the national committee can do to force compliance.

An example of friction between the national committees and their respective state party organizations occurred during spring and summer of 2007, as many state parties moved their states' presidential primaries and caucuses earlier in the primary season, such that one month into the five-month primary season, most states' delegates to the parties' presidential nominating conventions would already be committed to a candidate, based on the early-voting states' primary and caucus outcomes.[25] The Republican and Democratic national committees preferred a drawn-out process, in which many populous states with large numbers of delegates, such as New York and California, would not hold their primary or caucus until May or June. Both party organizations penalized states such as Florida and Michigan that held their primaries early without authorization by halving those states' convention delegations. But they were powerless to stop state party organizations from changing their primary dates in the first place.

Political Machines A **political machine** is a party organization built around the goal of gaining political power to enrich party leaders, party workers, and citizen supporters of the party.[26] Political machines give government services to citizens, government jobs to party workers, and government contracts to higher-level party officials and contributors. In return, the recipients of these benefits are expected to help by campaigning for machine candidates, contributing to the party, and voting for the machine's candidates.

Such patronage was at one time quite common in American politics; as discussed earlier, the Democratic Party was built on exactly this premise. One classic example of a political machine was Tammany Hall, an organization of Democratic Party politicians in New York City who were especially powerful during the late 1800s and early 1900s.[27] One of the most famous Tammany Hall politicians, George

The "Dime's Worth of Difference" between Republicans and Democrats

George Wallace, a Southern Governor and independent candidate for president in 1968, coined a classic phrase when he said of his rivals, Democrat Hubert Humphrey and Republican Richard Nixon, that there was "not a dime's worth of difference" between them—meaning that Wallace was the only candidate offering something different to the electorate.[a]

Given all the data in this chapter that shows disagreements between Republicans and Democrats, Wallace's claim may seem obsolete, something no one could conceivably argue in the modern era. Republicans and Democrats in Congress disagree on many issues, from raising the minimum wage to national defense policy. High levels of disagreement also exist among Republican and Democratic identifiers in the electorate. How could anyone say that the parties stand for the same things?

Oddly enough, people do. It is easy to find people and organizations who echo Wallace's claim. Ralph Nader, the Green Party presidential nominee in 2000 and an independent candidate in 2004 and 2008, argued that the major parties had "towering similarities," and that while some differences might exist, Nader believed that Democrats too often let the Republican view prevail.[b]

The Libertarian Party's Web site argues that Republican and Democratic politicians are united in their support for a large, expensive federal government, and that any differences in their positions are in the details.[c] The Green Party's site contrasts its positions on a series of issues with those of the Republicans and the Democrats, which the Green Party views as nearly identical.[d] And an article on the Constitution Party's Web site refers to the major parties as "Demopublicans" and "Republicrats."[e] The same article argued that George Wallace's "dime's worth of difference" had narrowed in recent years to a nickel or even a penny.

Are these individuals and organizations right about the similarities between Republicans and Democrats? And if they are, why do most Americans see real differences between the parties? Do minor parties have a keener sense of the American political system than the rest of us?

No; in the main, people who argue that the major parties in America are quite similar, if not the same, tend to hold relatively extreme positions on most issues. The Constitution Party, for example, advocates an end to government civil service regulations, a ban on compulsory school attendance laws, withdrawal of the United States from the United Nations and all international trade agreements, and abolishing foreign aid, the income tax, the Internal Revenue Service, and all federal welfare programs, and repealing all campaign finance legislation, the Endangered Species Act, and federal firearms regulations. They also propose that the United States take back the Panama Canal, and that senators be elected by state legislatures rather than a popular vote, as was the case before the ratification of the 17th Amendment.[f]

These positions are extreme, not in the sense of being silly or dangerous, but in the sense that relatively few Americans share the Constitution Party's agenda. As mentioned earlier, the Constitution Party's presidential candidate received very few votes in the 2008 election; it has elected precisely one candidate to political office, a state representative in Montana. And while there is no polling data on what Americans think of the party's proposals, it seems safe to say that few people would support taking back the Panama Canal or allowing state legislators to elect U.S. senators—although some children might favor the ban on compulsory school attendance. While the Greens, Libertarians, and Ralph Nader, do not agree with Constitution Party's positions, their agendas are similarly extreme.

Even so, it makes sense that someone who supported one of these organizations would believe that Republicans and Democrats agreed on most things. Given the large distance between the Constitution Party's positions and those espoused by its major party rivals, the distance between the two major parties may seem small indeed to Constitution Party members. (The same argument could be made about Wallace and his supporters a generation ago.) But for most Americans, whose preferences on most issues are relatively moderate and clustered around the Republican and Democratic brand names, the differences between the major parties are substantial. Put another way, the differences in platforms and brand names of the major American political parties are not as large as they could be—but from the perspective of the average American, there is much more than a dime's worth of difference. ∎

Washington Plunkitt, argued that political machines did not reduce the quality or increase the costs of local government, but just made sure that people who worked for the party would receive a disproportionate share of government money, a practice he labeled "honest graft."[28] Of course, there are numerous cases of political machines where the graft was not honest at all, where people who worked for the machine were given no-show jobs or contracts at inflated prices.

▲ *The Tammany Hall political machine, depicted here as a rotund version of one of its leaders, William "Boss" Tweed, controlled New York City politics for most of the nineteenth and early twentieth centuries. Their strategy was "honest graft," rewarding party workers, contributors, and voters for their efforts to keep the machine's candidates in office.*

While political machines were once common in cities and towns, American political parties at the national level have never operated as political machines—and very few machines have survived at the local level. Major party leaders do not control anywhere near the amount of resources they would need if they wanted to use a machine-like system to attract large numbers of workers to their organizations or to win support for candidates by providing services to citizens.

THE PARTY IN GOVERNMENT

The party in government consists of elected officials holding national, state, and local offices who took office as candidates of a particular party. Because the party in government is comprised of officeholders, it has a direct impact on government policy. Members of the party organization can recruit candidates, write platforms, and pay for campaign ads, but only those who win elections—the party in government—serve as members of Congress or as the executive officials, and actually propose, debate, vote on, and sign the legislation that determines what government does.

The party in government is largely independent of the party organization. Some elected officials or former elected officials serve as members of their party's national committee, or hold a position in a state or local organization, but most American politicians go through their entire political careers without holding a position in their party organization.

The Democratic and Republican parties in government in the U.S. House and Senate are organized around working groups—Democrats call theirs a **caucus**, and Republicans have a **conference**. The party caucus or conference serves as a forum for debate, compromise, and strategizing among a party's elected officials. For example, during 2007 and 2008, members of the House Democratic Caucus held numerous meetings to decide the party's position on the Iraq war, including whether the House should vote on a proposed funding resolution that included a timetable for withdrawal of American forces, and what should be proposed if President Bush vetoed such a resolution.[29] The Democrats' strategy for addressing these proposals reflected the consensus reached in the caucus. Each party's caucus or conference also meets to decide legislative committee assignments, leadership positions on committees, and leadership positions within the caucus or conference.[30] Caucus or conference leaders also serve as spokespeople for their respective parties, particularly when the president is from the other party. The party in government also contains elements of the party organization, such as groups that recruit and support candidates for political office. These are the Democratic Congressional Campaign Committee (DCCC), Democratic Senatorial Campaign Committee (DSCC), National Republican Senatorial Committee (NRSC), and the National Republican Congressional Committee (NRCC).

The modern Congress is **polarized**: in both the House and the Senate, Republicans and Democrats hold different views on government policy. Figure 7.2 compares legislators on the basis of their ideology, or their general feelings about government policy, as measured by a liberal–conservative scale, for two House sessions, the contemporary 108th House (served 2005–2007) and the 83rd House of almost sixty years ago (served 1953–1955). In the plots, a legislator's ideology is measured on the left–right scale using NOMINATE scores, which measure legislators' ideologies based on their legislative votes.[31]

POLITICS IS EVERYWHERE

The party in government, comprised of elected officials, serves as the public face of American political parties even though these individuals may operate largely independently from the party organizations they represent.

caucus (congressional) The organization of Democrats within the House and Senate that meets to discuss and debate the party's positions on various issues in order to reach a consensus and to assign leadership positions.

conference The organization of Republicans within the House and Senate who meet to discuss and debate the party's positions on various issues in order to reach a consensus and to assign leadership positions.

polarized A term describing the alignment of both parties' members with their own party's issues and priorities, with little crossover support for the other party's goals.

These graphs tell us two things. First, over the last sixty years, the magnitude of ideological differences between the parties in Congress has increased. In the 83rd House, there was some overlap between the positions of Democrats and Republicans, but it had disappeared by the 108th House.[32] These data confirm that disagreements between the parties reflect their very different ideas about what government should be doing.

Of course, the fact that Democrats and Republicans in Congress often disagree does not mean that compromise is impossible. For example, even as the parties clashed over funding the Iraq war in 2007 and 2008, they compromised on several trade agreements.[33] Democrats wanted the agreements to include guarantees about union organizing, a ban on child labor, and a commitment to enforce international environmental agreements; Republicans wanted the deals approved without these regulations. Ultimately, some of the provisions favored by Democrats were added, and the legislation was enacted by a large bipartisan majority.

There are also a few questions on which Democrats and Republicans find themselves in outright agreement. In spring 2007, during the controversy surrounding the firing of several U.S. attorneys by the Justice Department, senators repealed the provision of the U.S. Code that allowed U.S. attorneys to be appointed without a Senate vote (this provision had been included in 2006 as part of the reauthorization of the Patriot Act).[34] The vote on this measure was 94–2; that is, virtually all Senators, Republicans and Democrats alike, agreed on repeal.

The second fact that Figure 7.2 reveals is that both parties in government include a heterogeneous mixture of ideologies, not a homogenous or uniform consensus opinion. In the 83rd House plot, for example, Democrats vary from the relatively liberal left end of the scale to moderate (middle) and even somewhat conservative,

---

FIGURE 7.2 **IDEOLOGY OF THE PARTIES IN GOVERNMENT: HOUSE OF REPRESENTATIVES, 1952 AND 2004**

Over the last several decades, ideological differences between Democrats and Republicans in Congress have increased significantly. However, even in the 108th House, both parties still included a wide range of views. In light of these data, would you expect more or less partisan conflict in the modern Congress than there was fifty years ago? According to these data, would you expect House members in each party to agree on what policies to pursue?

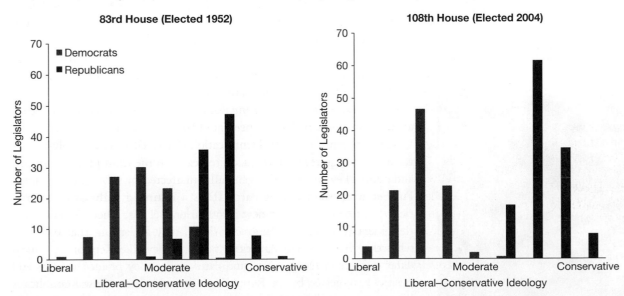

SOURCE: Calculated from Royce Carroll, Jeff Lewis, James Lo, Nolan McCarty, Keith Poole, and Howard Rosenthal, "DW-NOMINATE Scores with Bootstrapped Standard Errors," March 28, 2008, available at http://voteview.com/dwnl.htm.

party identification (party ID) A citizen's loyalty to a specific political party.

activists People who dedicate their time, effort, and money to supporting a political party or particular candidates.

running tally A frequently updated mental record that a person uses to incorporate new information, like the information that leads a citizen to identify with a particular political party.

POLITICS IS CONFLICTUAL

 Policy disagreements arise both within and between the Republican and Democratic parties in government.

toward the right side. Democrats in the 108th House were, on average, more liberal than their colleagues were in the 83rd, but a wide range of ideologies were still represented in the Democratic Caucus. The same is true for Republicans, who tend in the conservative direction in both the 108th and the 83rd House.

The heterogeneity of the party in government can create situations where a caucus or conference is divided on a policy question. In the last few years, congressional Democrats have been divided on issues such as funding for the war in Iraq. Republicans in Congress have also split on Iraq, as well as on immigration, federal spending, and Social Security reform. In some cases, such as the 2007 Democratic debate over war funding, members of a caucus or conference can find a compromise proposal they can all support.[35] However, compromise within a party caucus is not inevitable—even though legislators share a party label, they may not be able to find common ground. Consider the debate over immigration reform. Before the 2006 midterm elections, Republicans held majorities in the House and the Senate, so if they could agree on a proposal, they had enough votes to enact it. Furthermore, since President Bush was a Republican, he would likely sign the proposal into law. However, while some Republicans wanted to stiffen criminal penalties against illegal immigrants, others, including President Bush, favored allowing illegal immigrants to eventually gain citizenship.[36] Ultimately, Republicans in the Senate enacted a reform proposal with some Democratic support, but House Republicans were unable to come to an agreement.[37]

THE PARTY IN THE ELECTORATE

The party in the electorate consists of citizens who identify with a particular political party. Most Americans say they are either Democrats or Republicans, although the percentage has declined over the last two generations. **Party identification (party ID)** is a critical variable in understanding votes and other forms of political participation.

Americans can join a party if they like; both the Republicans and the Democrats have Web sites where people can sign up to receive e-mail alerts and to contribute to party causes. Joining a party does not give a citizen any direct influence over what the party does. Day-to-day decisions are made by party leaders and the candidates themselves. Party leaders and candidates often heed citizens' demands, but there is no requirement that they do so. However, real participation in party operations is open to citizens who become **activists** by working for a party organization or one of its candidates. Activists' contributions vary from stuffing envelopes to helping out with a phone bank, being a delegate to a party convention, attending campaign rallies, or campaigning door-to-door. Relatively few Americans are activists, perhaps 5 to 10 percent of the population.

Early theories of party identification described it as a deeply-felt attachment to a party that was acquired early in life from parents, friends, and political events, and was generally unaffected by subsequent events.[38] Further work showed that party ID is a **running tally** or an evaluation that takes account of new information.[39] Thus, when someone says they identify with the Republican Party, they are saying that based on what they have seen in American politics, they like Republican candidates more than Democratic candidates—that they prefer the ideas and positions suggested by the Republicans' brand name or how Republicans behave in office. New information tends to reinforce existing loyalties,

▼ Activist volunteers undertake most of the one-on-one efforts to mobilize support for a party and its candidates.

Citizen party identification is sensitive to events: during 2003 and 2004, the percentage of Republican identifiers increased given positive events in the Iraq war, and decreased given negative events. How would you expect party identification to be influenced by the state of the American economy?

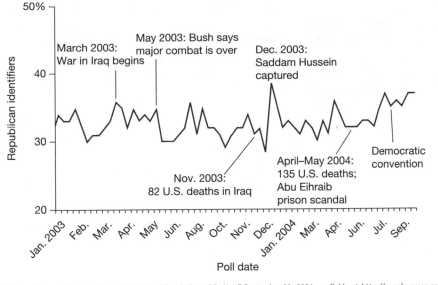

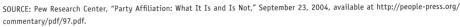

SOURCE: Pew Research Center, "Party Affiliation: What It Is and Is Not," September 23, 2004, available at http://people-press.org/commentary/pdf/97.pdf.

which is why Chapter 5, Public Opinion, described party identification as generally stable. However, citizens can revise their party identification when circumstances warrant.

Consider Figure 7.3, which shows the percentage of people who identified themselves as Republicans in Pew Trust surveys taken during 2003 and 2004. The figure also labels significant political events during that period, such as the 2004 Democratic Convention, the beginning of the Iraq war, and the capture of Iraqi former president, Saddam Hussein. The percentage of people surveyed who identified as Republicans varied from below 30 percent to nearly 40 percent. Good news in Iraq, such as the capture of Hussein, caused more people to identify with the Republican Party. Conversely, bad news about the war, such as the deaths of eighty-two American troops during a particularly violent month in Iraq, generated decreases. This pattern makes sense given that Republicans controlled Congress and the presidency during this time, and so were seen as responsible for the conduct of the war. Some citizens used events in Iraq to update their running tally on the Republican Party, which in turn caused some of them to switch their party affiliation.

Figure 7.4 gives data on party identification in America over the last sixty years. The first plot shows that the Democratic Party had a considerable advantage in terms of the number of citizens identifying with the party from the 1930s until the late 1980s. During the 1970s, nearly half of adults identified with the Democratic Party, and only about 20 percent identified with the Republicans. During the 1990s, the percentage of Democratic identifiers decreased significantly and the percentage of Republican identifiers increased slightly, to the point that in 2002 the

POLITICS IS EVERYWHERE

An individual's party identification influences vote decisions and other forms of political behavior.

In terms of party identification, the parties have moved from rough parity in the 1930s and 1940s, to a period of Democratic advantage that lasted from the 1950s to the 1980s. What events might have caused the late-1970s decline in Democratic identifiers?

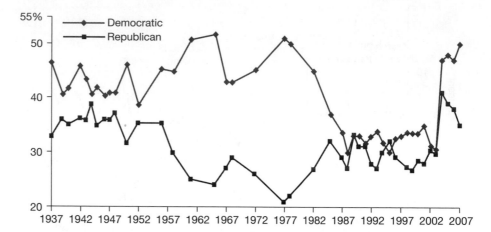

SOURCE: Pew Research Center, "The 2004 Political Landscape," November 3, 2003, available at http://people-press.org/reports/display .php3?PageID=750, and "Trends in Political Values and Core Attitudes, March 22, 2007, available at http:/:people-press.org/reports/ pdf/312.pdf.

parties had roughly the same percentage of identifiers.[40] However, in recent years, the Democrats have again opened up a significant advantage in terms of identifiers. The two lines in Figure 7.4 do not add up to 100 percent, and the difference represents the percentage of independent voters who do not identify with either party. The percentage of independents has increased significantly in the last fifty years, from about 20 percent in the 1950s to about 40 percent in recent years.

Some early analyses concluded that independents were unaffiliated with a party because they were in the process of shifting their identification from one party to the other.[41] Others saw independents as evidence of **dealignment**—a sign that more and more people saw the parties as irrelevant to their view of politics and their vote decisions.[42] The rise in the number of independents was also seen as an indication that Americans were becoming more politically savvy, learning more about candidates and not always blindly voting for the same party.[43]

More recent work has modified these findings. The percentage of independent voters has remained relatively constant over the last twenty years. The percentage of independents is also lower among regular voters. Moreover, many people who identify as independents actually have some weak attachment to one of the major political parties.[44] And while some independents are angry about or alienated from politics, most of them simply do not find the parties attractive enough to identify with either of them.[45] In any case, independents are not necessarily better informed about candidates, parties, or government policy than party identifiers. One of the few identifiable differences is that independents' vote decisions are more sensitive to things that happen during political campaigns.[46]

Looking more closely at vote decisions, Figure 7.5 shows how Democrats, Republicans, and independents voted in the 2008 presidential election. As you see, most Democrats voted for Barack Obama, the Democratic nominee, most Republicans

dealignment A decline in the percentage of citizens who identify with one of the major parties, usually over the course of a decade or longer.

voted for John McCain, the Republican nominee—and independent voters slightly favored Obama, but by a much smaller margin than Democrats did. Simply put, if you are trying to predict how someone will vote, the most important thing to know is their party identification.[47] Party ID shapes vote decisions even after we control for other factors. For example, economic issues dominated the 2008 election. Sixty percent of the people who were "very worried about economic conditions" voted for Barack Obama. However, among those who were concerned about the economy, the odds of voting for Obama increased if the voter was a Democrat.[48] Party ID also influences other kinds of political behavior. People whose identification is strong are more likely to work for the party or to make a contribution compared to people with weak party identification.[49]

Party Coalitions Data on party ID allows scholars to identify the **party coalitions,** or groups of citizens who identify with each party. Table 7.3 shows the contemporary Democratic and Republican party coalitions. As you see, some groups are disproportionately likely to identify as Democrats (African Americans), some are disproportionately likely to be Republicans (evangelicals), and in other groups there is no clear favorite party (people between the ages of thirty and fourty-nine).

The Republican and Democratic party coalitions differ systematically in terms of their policy preferences—what they want government to do—as shown in Table 7.4. The two columns give the percentages of Republican and Democratic identifiers who considered each item a priority. The right-hand column shows the differences between the Republican and Democratic Party coalitions, which disagree about the relative importance of issues like increasing the minimum wage, creating new jobs, providing health insurance to the uninsured, and defending the

---

FIGURE 7.5   **THE IMPACT OF PARTY IDENTIFICATION ON VOTE DECISIONS IN THE 2008 PRESIDENTIAL ELECTION**

Americans are much more likely to vote for candidates who share their party affiliation. What does this relationship tell us about the impact of campaign events (including speeches, debates, and gaffes) on vote decisions?

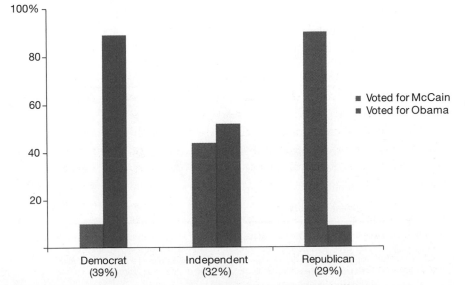

■ Voted for McCain
■ Voted for Obama

SOURCE: CNN Election Center, available at http://www.CNN.com/ELECTION/2008/results/polls/#val=USP00p1.

POLITICS IS CONFLICTUAL

❗ Although party identification is a strong predictor of policy preferences and vote decisions, the Republican and Democratic party coalitions are split on many policy questions—just like the parties in government.

United States against terrorism. On only a few issues, the percentages in both parties who consider the matter a priority are nearly the same, such as global trade. While the structure of the questions (asking about priorities rather than specific proposals) overstates the level of disagreement between Republicans and Democrats, these data demonstrate that party labels are meaningful: if you know someone is a Republican (or a Democrat), this information tells you something about what they probably want government to do, and how they will likely vote in the next election.

TABLE 7.3   **THE PARTY COALITIONS**

Many groups, such as African Americans and evangelicals, are much more likely to affiliate with one party rather than the other. What are the implications of these differences for the positions taken by each party's candidates?

		DEMOCRATIC	INDEPENDENT	REPUBLICAN
Gender	Male	30%	37%	33%
	Female	40	32	28
Age	18–29	34%	41%	21%
	30–49	33	35	32
	50–64	37	34	29
	65 and over	41	28	31
Race	White	31%	34%	35%
	African American	66	30	4
Region	Northeast	39%	36%	25%
	Midwest	35	35	30
	South	34	33	33
	West	34	34	32
Education	No college	39%	35%	26%
	Some college	33	35	32
	Completed college	30	33	37
	Postgraduate	36	34	28
Religion	Evangelical	27%	17%	56%
	Mainline Protestants	38	18	44
	African American Protestants	71	18	11
	Catholic	44	15	41
	Athiest/agnostic	54	27	19

SOURCE: Data on religion from the Bliss Institute, University of Akron, Fourth National Survey of Religion and Politics, March–May 2004, available at http://pewforum.org/publications/surveys/green-full.pdf. All other data from "Partisan Identification, by Groups," Gallup Poll, 2006, in Harold W. Stanley and Richard G. Niemi, *Vital Statistics on American Politics, 2007–2008,* (Washington, DC: CQ Press, 2007).

TABLE 7.4 ISSUE DIFFERENCES BETWEEN THE REPUBLICAN AND DEMOCRATIC PARTIES IN THE ELECTORATE

The Republican and Democratic Party coalitions hold different positions on many issues, from increasing the minimum wage to defending against terrorism—and on a few issues their differences are small, such as trade and cutting middle class taxes. Do these differences make sense in light of each party's "brand name"?

PERCENT CONSIDERING EACH AS A "TOP PRIORITY"	REPUBLICANS	DEMOCRATS	DIFFERENCE
Increasing minimum wage	28%	71%	−43%
Improving job situation	39	67	−28
Providing health insurance to uninsured	44	70	−26
Dealing with global warming	23	48	−25
Dealing with problems of poverty	48	67	−19
Dealing with energy problems	45	64	−19
Securing Medicare	53	70	−17
Reducing influence of lobbyists	28	44	−16
Reducing budget deficit	42	57	−15
Reducing crime	56	69	−13
Strengthening nation's economy	65	77	−12
Securing Social Security	62	72	−10
Improving educational system	65	74	−9
Reducing middle class taxes	49	54	−5
Dealing with global trade	33	35	−2
Dealing with moral breakdown	54	45	+9
Strengthening the military	56	42	+14
Reducing illegal immigration	63	48	+15
Defending U.S. against terrorism	93	74	+20

SOURCE: Pew Research Center, "Broad Support for Political Compromise in Washington," January 22, 2007, http://people-press.org/reports/pdf/302.pdf.

SECTION SUMMARY

1. The Republican and Democratic party organizations consist of thousands of groups at the national, state, and local levels, some of which are only informally connected to their party. Party organizations are not hierarchical, as neither party has one leader or group that all members have to obey.

2. The party in government is the public face of a political party, consisting of officials (members of Congress and the president) who were elected as party-affiliated candidates. Decisions made inside the party in government influence legislative strategies and policy outcomes.

3. The party in the electorate consists of voters who identify with a political party. Party identification has a strong influence on an individual's vote decisions and other aspects of political outlook and behavior. The Republican and Democratic party coalitions differ in terms of the groups that tend to identify with each party and what they want government to do.

The Role of Political Parties in American Politics

This section explains what political parties do in American politics, from contesting elections to building consensus across branches of government. It is important to remember, though, that these activities are not necessarily coordinated. Candidates and groups at different levels of a party organization may work together, refuse to cooperate, or even actively oppose each other's efforts.

CONTESTING ELECTIONS

In modern American politics, virtually everyone elected to a state or national political office is either a Republican or a Democrat. In the 110th Congress, elected in 2006, there were only two independent senators (Bernie Sanders of Vermont and Joe Lieberman of Connecticut) and no independent House members. In early 2008, all fifty states' governors were either Democrats or Republicans, and of more than 7,300 state legislators, only twenty-one were either independents or minor-party candidates.[50]

Recruiting and Nominating Candidates Actions taken inside party organizations shape citizens' choices on Election Day. Historically, recruiting candidates was left up to local party organizations. But in recent years, the process has become much more systematic, with national party leaders playing a central role in finding and recruiting candidates—and often promising those candidates help assembling a staff, organizing a campaign, and raising money.[51]

After the 2004 election, for example, members of the Democratic House and Senate Campaign Committees believed that the party could win seats in the 2006 midterms by running candidates with military experience who supported changing the U.S. policy on Iraq.[52] They began a two-year process of finding retired military men and women, persuading them to run, and training them in the art of campaigning (none had ever run for political office). In all, Democrats recruited sixty-one military veterans to run for two Senate and fifty-nine House seats, including Vietnam War veteran James Webb, who had served as President Ronald Reagan's secretary of the Navy, and retired admiral Joe Sestak.[53] The Democrats' strategy proved especially effective in the 2006 midterms, given the mounting public opposition to the war in Iraq.

For all of these efforts, parties do not control who runs in House or Senate races. In most states, candidates for these offices are selected in a **primary** election or a **caucus**, in which they compete for a particular party's spot on the ballot. (A few state parties use conventions to select candidates.) Nuts and Bolts 7.1 further explains these different ways that the parties select candidates.

POLITICAL PROCESS MATTERS

☑ As the example of the Democratic Party in 2006 demonstrates, strategic candidate-recruitment efforts can pay off in winning seats in the House and the Senate.

Types of Primaries and Caucuses

PRIMARY ELECTION	An election in which voters choose the major party nominees for political office, who subsequently compete in a general election.
Closed primary	A primary election system in which only registered party members can vote in their party's primary.
Nonpartisan primary	A primary election system in which candidates from both parties are listed on the same primary ballot. Following a nonpartisan primary, the two candidates who receive the most votes in the primary compete in the general election, even if they are from the same party.
Open ("crossover") primary	A primary election system in which any registered voter can participate in either party's primary, regardless of the voter's party affiliation.
CAUCUS ELECTION	A series of local meetings at which registered voters select a particular candidate's supporters as delegates who will vote for the candidate in a later, state-level convention. (In national elections, the state-convention delegates select delegates to the national convention.) Caucuses are used in some states to select delegates to the major parties' presidential nominating conventions. Some states' caucuses are open to members of any party, while others are closed.

Most party leaders remain neutral during primaries and then support whoever wins the party's spot on the ballot for the general election. An exception occurred in the 2006 Connecticut Democratic senatorial primary, where incumbent Joe Lieberman was upset by challenger Ned Lamont, in an election that hinged on Lieberman's strong support for the Iraq war.[54] While the state and national Democratic Party officially remained neutral, it was no secret that most party officials wanted Lieberman to win. After Lamont won the party's primary, Lieberman opted to run in the general election as an independent instead; most party leaders officially endorsed Lamont, but gave little support.

Running as a party's nominee is almost always the easiest way to get on the general election ballot. Many states give the Republican and Democratic nominees an automatic spot on the ballot; and even in states that don't automatically allocate ballot slots this way, the requirements for the major parties to get a candidate on the ballot are much less onerous than those for minor parties and independents. Nuts and Bolts 7.2 details these requirements, showing that in most states, the number of supporters' signatures required to earn a candidate a spot on the ballot are much lower for the major party candidates than for independent and minor party candidates. These advantages help explain why virtually all prominent candidates for Congress and the presidency run as Democrats or Republicans. They may not agree with all that the party stands for—but the party label gets them access to the general election ballot.

National parties also manage the nomination process for presidential candidates, which involves a series of primaries and caucuses held over a six-month period beginning in January of a presidential election year. The type of election (primary or caucus) and its date are determined by each state's legislature, although national

primary A ballot vote in which citizens select a party's nominee for the general election.

caucus (political) A local meeting in which party members select a party's nominee for the general election.

Should Parties Choose Their Candidates?

One of the facts of life for the leaders of the Democratic and Republican parties is that they cannot determine who runs as their party's candidate for Congress or for the presidency. They can encourage some candidates to run and attempt to discourage others by endorsing their favorites and funneling money, staff support, and other forms of assistance to the candidates they prefer. But in the end, candidates get on the ballot by winning a primary—or in the case of presidential candidates, a series of primaries and caucuses. The leaders of each party have to accept whoever emerges from the primary with the nomination.

As you have seen in this chapter, political parties don't always get the nominees that their leaders want, such as in the 2006 Connecticut Senate election when voters chose businessman Ned Lamont as the Democratic nominee over well-known incumbent Joe Lieberman. Other times, party leaders are unsuccessful in their efforts to recruit candidates for House and Senate seats. And party leaders cannot force candidates out of a race—in spring 2008, many Democratic Party leaders wanted Hillary Clinton to end her presidential candidacy as it became increasingly clear that Barack Obama would win the nomination. Clinton stayed in the race until the primaries ended, forcing Obama to campaign aggressively, spend additional campaign funds, and respond to attacks from the Clinton campaign.

Why not let party leaders pick their candidates? Many scholars have argued that giving party leaders more control over

▲ American political parties have little control over the nomination process. In Connecticut in 2006, most Democratic Party leaders preferred to nominate incumbent senator Joseph Lieberman, but they had to accept political newcomer Ned Lamont as their candidate when he defeated Lieberman in the Democratic primary election.

the process would increase the chances of getting experienced, talented candidates on the ballot.[a] After all, party leaders probably know more than the average primary voter about who would make a good candidate or elected official. Plus, party leaders have a strong incentive to find good candidates and convince them to run—their party's influence over government policy increases with the number of people they can elect to political office.

Why, then, do voters in America get to pick party nominees in primaries? Direct primaries were introduced in American politics during the late 1800s and early 1900s.[b] The goal was explicit: they wanted to take the

choice of nominees out of the hands of party leaders and give it to the electorate, with the assumption that voters should be able to influence the choice of candidates for the general election. Moreover, reformers believed that this goal outweighed the expertise held by party leaders.

Here is the trade-off. If party leaders select nominees, then they will likely choose electable candidates who share the policy goals held by party leaders. If voters choose nominees, they can pick whoever they want, using whatever criteria they like—but there is less guarantee that these candidates will be skilled general-election campaigners or effective in office. ■

nominating convention A meeting held by each party every four years at which states' delegates select the party's presidential and vice-presidential nominees and approve the party platform.

party committees can limit the allowable dates, using their control over seating delegates at the party conventions to motivate compliance. Voters in these primaries and caucuses don't directly select the parties' nominees for the presidential race. Instead, citizens' votes are used to determine how many of each candidate's supporters become delegates to the party's national **nominating convention**, where the delegates then vote to choose the party's presidential and vice-presidential nominees.

The national party organizations determine how many delegates each state will send to the convention based on factors such as state population, the number of votes the party's candidate received in each state in the last presidential election, and the number of House members and Senators from the party that each state elected.

Campaign Assistance Political scientist and party expert John Aldrich refers to America's contemporary political parties as parties in service, which reflects the idea that one of the parties' primary activities is helping candidates with their campaigns.[55] One of the most visible ways that the political parties support candidates is by contributing to and spending money on campaigns. Figure 7.6 shows the amount of money raised by the top groups within the Republican and Democratic

NUTS AND BOLTS

7.2

Getting on the Ballot: Requirements for Presidential Candidates

Many states are like California, where minor party and independent candidates must collect many more signatures to get on the ballot compared to major party nominees. Only a few states are like New Jersey, where the signature requirements for minor parties are relatively low—even lower than for the major parties. Only two states, Georgia and Connecticut, have the same signature requirements for all candidates.

Meeting these requirements is expensive. For example, when Ralph Nader ran as an independent candidate for president in 2004, his campaign attracted thousands of volunteers and spent millions of dollars.[a] Even so, Nader failed to get on the ballot in fifteen states, including California, Ohio, Pennsylvania, and Texas.[b]

EXAMPLE STATE	MAJOR PARTY SIGNATURES NEEDED	INDEPENDENT OR MINOR PARTY SIGNATURES NEEDED	STATES WITH SIMILAR LAWS
California	26,500	153,804 (1%)	Arizona, Arkansas, Florida, Illinois, Indiana, Maryland, Michigan, New York, North Carolina, Ohio, Oklahoma, Oregon, Pennsylvania, South Carolina, Texas, and West Virginia
Massachusetts	2,500	10,000	Minnesota, Idaho, Nevada, New Mexico, South Dakota, and Wisconsin
Alabama	500	5,000	Colorado, Delaware, Missouri, Hawaii, Kansas, Louisiana, North Dakota, Alaska, Maine, Nebraska, New Hampshire, and Tennessee
New Jersey	1,000	800	Iowa, Wyoming, Mississippi, Montana, New Jersey, Utah, Washington, Kentucky, Rhode Island, Vermont, and Virginia
Georgia	27,742 (1%)	27,742 (1%)	Connecticut

SOURCE: The Reform Institute, "Issue Overview: The Fight For Fair Access to the Ballot," July 30, 2007, available at http://www.reforminstitute.org/DetailPublications.aspx?pid=58&cid=2&tid=5&sid=7.

[a] Scott Shane, "The 2004 Election: The Independent; Nader Is Left with Fewer Votes, and Friends, after '04 Race," *New York Times*, November 4, 2004, p. 13.
[b] Mark Rodeffer, "The Nader Factor," CNN.com, Specials, November 1, 2004, available at http://www.cnn.com/ELECTION/2004/special/president/candidates/nader.ballot.html.

parties for the 2008 election (through October 27). The final figures show that parties raised more than $1.5 billion. The Democratic and Republican national committees (DNC and RNC) raised the most money, but the congressional campaign committees also raised significant sums. The RNC raised about $130 million more than the DNC because John McCain depended heavily on national party money, while Barack Obama raised more than $700 million on his own. (McCain accepted federal funding, which capped the amount that his campaign could spend directly.) Congressional Democratic committees, anticipating the vulnerability of Republican incumbents, substantially out-raised their Republican counterparts. State and local parties also raised nearly $400 million in the 2008 elections.[56]

The groups listed in Figure 7.6 clearly show the decentralized structure of American political parties. While the national committees raise the most cash by far, state parties and other groups raise an enormous amount by themselves—and decide independently how the money will be spent. During the 2004 presidential campaign, Democratic Party leaders wanted John Kerry to donate money left over from his primary campaign to congressional candidates from his party, to help the party win additional House and Senate seats.[57] And although Kerry surely wanted Democratic candidates to win their races, he refused; his surplus could be used for his own future campaigns, such as running for reelection to his Senate seat or making a second presidential run.

Such disagreements between candidates and party officials are not new. At the end of the 1996 presidential campaign, when incumbent Bill Clinton was a sure winner, Clinton's campaign managers decided against sending him to campaign with Democrats running for House and Senate seats.[58] They reasoned that although

FIGURE 7.6 **DEMOCRATIC AND REPUBLICAN FUND-RAISING IN THE 2007–2008 ELECTION CYCLE**

In the 2007–2008 election cycle, party committees raised about $1.5 billion in campaign funds. While most of this money was raised by the national committees, the state, local, and candidate committees also raised significant sums. To what extent might these funds allow the national committees to force candidates to run on the party platform?

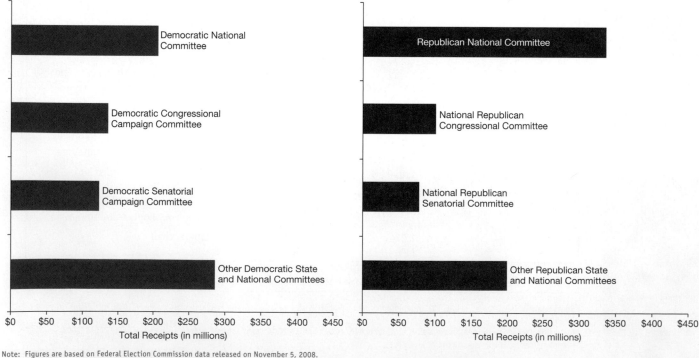

Note: Figures are based on Federal Election Commission data released on November 5, 2008.
SOURCE: Federal Election Commission data provided by the Center for Responsive Politics, available at http://www.opensecrets.org/parties/index.php.

the strategy would not reduce Clinton's chances of winning, spending time on congressional campaigning and tying Clinton to an unpopular Congress might reduce his popular vote total and his margin of victory in the electoral college. Many other presidential candidates, such as Ronald Reagan in 1984, have made similar calculations.[59]

Along with supplying campaign funds, party organizations give candidates other kinds of assistance, ranging from offering campaign advice (on which issues to emphasize, how to deal with the press, and the like) to conducting polls. Party organizations at all levels also undertake GOTV or get-out-the-vote activities, encouraging supporters to get to the polls. During the last few elections, the Republican Party has organized a "72-Hour Task Force" of volunteers to spend the days just before the election staffing phone banks and going door-to-door campaigning for candidates in close races.

A more general example of party assistance comes from the 2006 elections, when the Democratic Party formulated their "Fifty State Strategy," with the goal of recruiting strong candidates and helping to fund their campaigns in all fifty states (and 435 congressional districts) regardless of whether their Republican opponents seemed beatable.[60] As we discuss in more detail in Chapter 8, Elections, much of the Democrats' success in 2006 stemmed from congressional scandals, a weak economy, an unpopular war in Iraq, and low approval ratings for then-president Bush. However, the Democrats' efforts to recruit and fund candidates helped them capitalize on these events by giving voters a plausible alternative to Republican candidates.

▲ *During the final days of a campaign, the volunteers who staff candidate and party phone banks contact potential supporters to encourage them to go to the polls and vote on Election Day.*

Party Platforms The **party platform** is a set of promises about what candidates from the party will do if elected. The most widely-known party platform is the one approved at each party's presidential nominating convention, but the party organizations in the House and Senate also release platforms, as do other groups in the major parties. Party platforms generally reflect the brand name differences between the parties discussed earlier. For example, in the case of abortion rights, the 2008 Republican presidential platform advocates abstinence, adoption, and enactment of the Human Life Amendment, which would outlaw abortion under most circumstances. In contrast, the Democratic presidential platform in 2008 expressed support for a woman's right to choose, meaning abortion would be legal under a wider range of conditions.

In theory, party platforms describe differences between the major parties, capture each party's diagnosis of the problems facing the country, and give the party's plan for solving those problems. In this way, party platforms give citizens an easy way to make judgments about candidates. Rather than having to follow the individual campaigns by reading news stories and tracking political Web sites, they can simply read a short platform document to learn about what kinds of policies a candidate, or an entire slate of candidates, will support if elected.

However, candidates are not obligated to support their party's platform. For example, notwithstanding the consistently strong pro-choice position on abortion in the Democratic Party's presidential platforms over the last generation, some Democratic congressional candidates have promised to vote to restrict abortions if elected—a position much closer to the Republican platform.[61] For some of these candidates, this position reflected personal or religious beliefs; for others, it was driven by the desire to reflect the opinion of voters in their district or state.

Sometimes candidates will even repudiate a platform that was written for their campaign. In the 1996 presidential election, Republican candidate Bob Dole was asked to explain some differences between the issue stands he had taken during the primaries and his party's platform.[62] Dole replied that he had not read the platform. Of course, Dole knew what was in the Republican platform, but since he did not agree with some of its positions, he tried to ignore it as much as possible.

party platform A set of objectives outlining the party's issue positions and priorities—although candidates are not required to support their party's platform.

COOPERATION IN GOVERNMENT

conditional party government The theory that lawmakers from the same party will cooperate to develop policy proposals.

backbenchers Legislators who do not hold leadership positions within their party caucus or conference.

The theory of **conditional party government** describes parties as providing a forum for like-minded legislators to develop policy plans. However, there is no guarantee that legislators with a common party affiliation will be able to compromise their differences. While party leaders work to find agreements that are attractive to their **backbenchers**, there is no guarantee that they will be successful. And if they can't reach such an agreement, the party in government stays on the sidelines.

Developing Agendas Throughout the year, the parties in government meet to devise strategies for legislative action.[63] What proposals should they offer, and in what order should they be considered?[64] Should they try to make a deal with the president or with legislators from the other party? For example, after the Democrats gained majority control of the House in 2006, Democratic Caucus members met to develop an agenda for the first few days of the 110th Congress, which would convene in January 2007.[65] They agreed on seven proposals, including a measure to reduce student loan interest rates, encourage medical research on stem cells, and a resolution disapproving of President's Bush's policy in Iraq. The caucus also set a time limit: members wanted to debate and enact all of these measures in the first 100 hours of the new legislative session. Despite Republican protests, House Democrats enacted all of their proposals after forty-two hours.

In cases like these, it is easy to see how parties matter in legislative proceedings. The 100-hour plan was negotiated among members of the Democratic Caucus; Democratic leaders in the House used their control over when proposals would be considered, which amendments would be allowed, and how long debate would proceed to ensure speedy consideration and prevent Republicans from delaying votes or offering alternatives.

POLITICAL PROCESS MATTERS

Negotiations among members of the party in government often determine which proposals are brought up for debate in Congress and which are enacted into law.

Republican leaders in Congress did the same thing when they were in the majority. For example, during debate over Medicare Prescription Drug Benefit legislation in 2003, Republican congressional leaders, along with President Bush and his staff, worked to fashion a proposal that would attract widespread support from Republican legislators.[66] They changed details of the proposal, made deals on other legislation in return for support, and, in one case, threatened a retiring legislator that unless he voted yes, the party would not support the legislator's son in his bid to capture his father's House seat.[67] Ultimately, these efforts succeeded: the bill passed the House by a vote of 220 to 215—after Republican leaders held the vote open for over three hours while they worked to secure a few votes needed for passage.[68]

However, the party in government can act collectively this way only when its members can agree on what they want. Such agreement is not always forthcoming. In summer of 2006, the House Republicans, who were in the majority, split on immigration reform. Some members favored a proposal that created a path to citizenship for illegal immigrants, while others opposed amnesty and wanted to stiffen criminal penalties against them.[69] Ultimately, they never reached an agreement, and no reform measure came to a vote. The same thing would later happen under the Democratic majority in 2007. Similarly, during 2005, President Bush spent months giving speeches, holding town hall meetings, and meeting with legislators in an attempt to build support for his Social Security reforms, but the reforms were never brought to a vote. Why not? The principle reason was that with considerable opposition from Republican legislators, there were not enough supporters in the House or the Senate to enact the proposals.[70]

These defeats on immigration and Social Security are especially noteworthy because the Republicans held majorities in both houses of Congress. In other words, if Bush could have convinced Republican legislators to support his Social Security and immigration proposals, he would have carried the day, as the Republicans in the House and Senate had enough votes to enact the proposals without support from Democrats.

Much like President Bush's experience with Social Security reform, health care reform was one of President Bill Clinton's central goals during his first term in office. The Democrats held the majority in both the House and the Senate, but Clinton still had to abandon his reforms in the face of weak support from legislators in his own party.[71]

Coordination Political parties also can play an important role in coordinating the actions taken in different branches of government. Such coordination is extremely important for enacting new laws: unless supporters in Congress can amass a two-thirds majority to override a veto, they need the president's support. Similarly, the president needs congressional support to enact proposals that he or she favors. To these ends, the president routinely meets with congressional leaders from his party, and occasionally meets with the entire caucus or conference. The president also has staff in the Office of Legislative Liaison who meet with House and Senate members on a daily basis to present the president's proposals and hear what members of Congress from both parties want to enact.

During early 2007, President George W. Bush held many meetings with Republican members of Congress to lobby them to support his new Iraq policy, including an increase of American troops sent to the region and longer tours of duty for troops in Iraq. Bush even held a meeting with the entire House Republican Conference where he presented his policy and took questions from House Republicans. In the end, virtually all House Republicans sided with the president in opposing Democratic efforts to establish a timetable for withdrawal of American troops. However, Bush could not prevent Republican senator John Warner from proposing

▲ Presidents seeking legislative backing for their proposals must persuade their party's congressional leaders; they are unable to demand support. Even when the president's party holds a majority in both houses of Congress, he may have trouble getting policies approved, as did George Bush in the case of Social Security reforms, immigration policy changes, and other proposals.

a resolution opposing Bush's policy—and other Republican senators from announcing their support for Warner's proposal.[72]

Coordination can also occur between caucuses or conferences in the House and Senate. At the same time President Bush was meeting with Republican House members and senators, leaders from the House and Senate Democratic Caucuses were meeting to devise a strategy for opposing the president's new policy.[73] Their efforts to enact a withdrawal date for U.S. forces in Iraq were not successful. However, by presenting a unified front, the Democratic leadership forced congressional Republicans and President Bush to agree to time limits on war funding.

Such coordination efforts require real work and compromise since party leaders in the House and the Senate do not have authority over each other or over the elected members of their party. Nor can the president order a House member or senator to do anything, even if the legislator is from the president's own party. In 1993, for example, President Clinton needed one more vote in the Senate to enact a deficit reduction proposal.[74] One of the few undecided legislators was Democratic Senator Bob Kerrey of Nebraska. President Clinton met with Kerrey, held repeated telephone conversations with him, and offered various promises and enticements, all to secure his vote. Ultimately, Kerrey decided to vote for the proposal, but neither the president nor his party leaders could have forced him to support it.

Accountability One of the most important roles of political parties in a democracy is giving citizens identifiable groups to reward or punish for government actions, thereby providing a means for voters to focus their desire for accountability. By rewarding and punishing elected officials, often based on their party affiliation and other party members' behavior in office, voters use the party system to hold officials accountable for outcomes such as the state of the economy or America's relations with other nations.

During periods of **unified government**, when one party holds majorities in both the House and the Senate and controls the presidency, that party is the **party in power**; they have has enough votes to enact policies in Congress, and a good chance of having them signed into law by a president who shares their party. During times of **divided government**, when one party controls Congress but not the presidency or the House and Senate are controlled by different parties, the president's party is considered the party in power. Focusing on parties makes it easy for a citizen to issue rewards and punishments. Is the economy doing well? Then vote for the candidates from the party in power. But if the economy is doing poorly, or if a citizen feels that government is wasting tax money or enacting bad policies, he or she can vote for candidates from the party that is currently out of power. When citizens behave this way, they strengthen the incentive for elected officials from the party in power to work together to develop policies that address voters' concerns—on premise that if they do, then voters will reward them with another term in office.

American voters sometimes reward and punish elected officials in this way. In 1994, the Democratic Party lost fifty-four House seats, ten Senate seats, and control of both chambers of Congress, as voters punished them for a struggling economy, tax increases, congressional scandals, and President Clinton's performance in office. Likewise, in 2006, voters' disapproval of the Iraq war and President Bush's low approval ratings translated into Republican losses of thirty House seats and six Senate seats, giving control of the House and Senate to the Democrats.

Some political scientists have argued that legislators from the same party should be forced to work as a team—to run on the same campaign platform, work together in Washington to enact their platform, and be collectively held accountable in elections for whether their proposals worked or not. Political organizations that

unified government A situation in which one party holds a majority of seats in the House and Senate and the president is a member of that same party.

party in power Under unified government, the party that controls the House, Senate, and the presidency. Under divided government, the president's party.

divided government A situation in which the House, Senate, and presidency are not controlled by the same party, such as if Democrats hold the majority of House and Senate seats, and the president is a Republican.

function this way are called **responsible parties**,[75] and they have never existed in American politics, although they do exist in some European countries. If American parties worked this way, it is likely that more people would hold the party in power and its officeholders directly accountable for the state of the economy and other national-level outcomes.

In contrast to the responsible party model, the three-part structure of contemporary American parties complicates decisions about accountability. Suppose, for example, a legislator from the party in power opposed the policies enacted by her party. If so, it may not make sense for a voter to reward this legislator for good outcomes of those policies, or punish her for bad outcomes. Even though she is from the party in power, she did not cause the outcomes that the voter cares about. What should a voter do in this case?

Consider the 2006 election, when many Americans voted against Republican officeholders because of the poor situation in Iraq. While Republicans lost twenty-six seats to the Democrats, most Republican House members and Senators were returned to office. Why? Some were elected from states or districts where support for America's Iraq policy remained strong. But many others were reelected because they campaigned on a platform of changing America's policy, in effect saying, "Instead of punishing me for my party affiliation, reward me for working to change my party's position."

responsible parties A system in which each political party's candidates campaign on the party platform, work together in office to implement the platform, and are judged by voters based on whether they achieve the platform's objectives.

SECTION SUMMARY

1. During elections American political parties recruit and train candidates and provide ballot access, campaign cash, and a brand name.
2. In government, party groups set the legislative agenda, coordinate action across the branches of the federal government, and give voters a way to reward and punish officeholders for government performance.
3. The way party organizations operate is shaped by the way they are organized, and particularly by the distinction between the party in government and the party organization.

Minor Parties

So far, this chapter has focused on the major American political parties, the Republicans and the Democrats, and ignored other party organizations. The reason is that minor political parties in America are *so* minor that they are not significant players on the political stage. Many such parties exist, but few run candidates in more than a handful of races—and very few minor party candidates win political office. Very few Americans identify with minor parties. And most minor parties exist for only a short period of time.

Even so, you may think we're giving minor parties too little attention. Consider Ralph Nader, who ran as the Green Party nominee for president in 2000, winning almost 5 percent of the vote. In some states, the number of votes Nader received exceeded the margin separating Democrat Al Gore from Republican George Bush. In particular, in Florida, where Bush won by only a few hundred votes after a disputed recount, Nader received almost one hundred thousand votes—enough to swing the state, and the election, to Gore.

▲ *Minor party presidential candidates, such as Ralph Nader in 2000 and George Wallace in 1968, attract considerable press attention because of their distinctive, often extreme policy preferences—but they rarely affect election outcomes.*

However, the outcome of Nader's 2000 presidential campaign doesn't so much highlight the importance of minor parties as it illustrates the closeness of the 2000 presidential election. If Nader had not run, Gore might have received enough additional support to win. But given that Bush's margin of victory in Florida was so small, any number of seemingly minor events (a polling station closing early, or rain in some areas and sunshine in others) would have changed the outcome.

Minor parties did not play a decisive role in the 2008 presidential election, but in several swing states such as North Carolina and Missouri, they received more votes than the margin of difference between Obama and McCain. The most successful were the Independent Party (661,000 votes) and the Libertarian Party (491,000), while others like the Boston Tea Party and the U.S. Pacifist Party received far fewer votes (2,305 and 97, respectively). Minor parties won about 1.5 million votes in the 2008 presidential race, whereas the two major parties received 121 million votes.

Even if you look at lower offices, minor party candidates typically attract only meager support. The Libertarian Party claimed to have over 600 officeholders nationwide as of mid-2006. However, many of these officials hold unelected positions such as seats on county planning boards or relatively minor offices such as Justice of the Peace.[76]

Looking back in history, some minor party candidates for president have attracted a substantial percentage of citizens' votes. George Wallace ran as the candidate of the American Independent Party in 1968, receiving about 13 percent of the popular vote nationwide (over 9 million votes). Ross Perot, the Reform Party candidate for president in 1996, won 8.4 percent of the popular vote (about 8 million votes) in 1996. Perot also ran as an independent in 1992, winning 18.2 percent of the popular vote (over 19 million votes).

The differences between major and minor political parties in contemporary American politics grow even more substantial when considered in terms other than election outcomes. For most minor parties, the party in government does not exist, as few of their candidates win office. Many minor parties have virtually no organization beyond a small party headquarters and a Web site. Some minor parties, such as the Green Party, the Libertarian Party, and the Reform Party, have local chapters that meet on a regular basis. But these modest efforts pale in comparison to the nationwide network of offices, thousands of workers, and millions of dollars deployed by Republican and Democratic Party organizations.

Research by political scientists Steven Rosenstone, Roy Behr, and Edward Lazarus shows that people vote for minority party candidates because they find those candidates' positions more attractive than those of the major parties, and also because they believe that neither major party can govern effectively. That is, a vote for a minor party first requires a citizen to reject both the Democratic and Republican organizations.[77] In 2008, for example, presidential candidate Ralph Nader advocated an immediate withdrawal of American troops from Iraq, as well as deep cuts in defense spending.[78] To vote for Nader, a citizen would have to like Nader's issue stands and believe that neither of the major parties could effectively address these problems. However, precisely because minor parties appeal to the minority of Americans who want "something different" than what the major parties are offering, their platforms will not appeal to most Americans, whose goals and preferences are compatible with at least one major party platform.

The basic structure of the American political system also works against minor political parties. This principle is summed up by **Duverger's law**, which states that in a democracy that has **single-member districts** and **plurality voting** (as America does) there will be only two political parties that elect a significant number of candidates to political office. Given these electoral institutions (discussed further in Chapter 8), many people will consider a vote for a minor party candidate to be a wasted vote, as there is no chance that the candidate will attract enough votes to win office. As a result, well-qualified candidates are driven to affiliate with one of the major political parties, because they know that running as a minor party nominee will put them at a considerable disadvantage. These decisions reinforce citizens' expectations that minority party candidates have no chance of winning elections, and that a vote for them is a wasted vote.

Moreover, as shown earlier, minor party candidates also face significantly higher legal hurdles to get on the ballot. In 2007, when New York City mayor Michael Bloomberg considered running for president as an independent in the 2008 election, his staff estimated that he would need over 700,000 signatures to get on the ballot in all fifty states. And some states have additional hurdles: in Texas, for example, a candidate not affiliated with a major party needs signatures from registered voters who did not vote in either the last Democratic or Republican presidential primaries.[79]

Duverger's law The principle that in a democracy with single-member districts and plurality voting, like the United States, only two parties' candidates will have a realistic chance of winning political office.

single-member districts An electoral system in which every elected official represents a geographically defined area, such as a state or congressional district, and each area elects one representative.

plurality voting A voting system in which the candidate who receives the most votes within a geographic area wins the election, regardless of whether that candidates wins a majority (more than half) of the votes.

POLITICAL PROCESS MATTERS

 Current laws and the structure of America's electoral system defined in the Constitution both work against the development of minor political parties.

SECTION SUMMARY

1. While minor political parties offer citizens additional candidates and platforms to vote for, they only rarely elect candidates to national political office.
2. Minor parties face significant legal hurdles to getting their candidates on the ballot. Moreover, would-be candidates often find that their chances of winning are better if they run for a major-party nomination.

What Kind of Democracy Do American Political Parties Create?

Parties help political activists, party leaders, and citizens who identify with the party pursue their policy goals by focusing collective efforts on electing people to office who share their priorities. For politicians, parties provide ballot access, a brand name, campaign assistance, and a group of like-minded colleagues with whom they can coordinate, compromise, and strategize. For citizens, political parties provide information and a means of holding specific individuals accountable for what government does.

The question of whether political parties are good or bad for democracy depends on how the individual party members and officials carry out these tasks. Political parties can help democracy by filling the ballot with well-qualified candidates, helping them get elected, offering citizens clear, concise choices about government policies, informing citizens about platforms and candidates, motivating citizens to vote, and, after the election, helping elected officials enact the party platform, taking their rewards or punishments from voters in the next election, as the effects of these proposals become clear. The problem is that the people who make up American political parties are not primarily interested in democracy; they are interested in their own careers, policy goals, and winning political office. As a result, they are often led away from actions that would improve American democracy, in favor of pursuing their personal goals.

RECRUITING CANDIDATES

One of the most important things the Republican and Democratic parties can do for democracy is to recruit candidates for national political offices who can run effective campaigns and responsibly uphold their elected positions. After all, your choices as a voter are limited to the people on the ballot. If good candidates decide against running or are prevented from doing so, citizens will be dissatisfied no matter who wins the election.

The Republican and Democratic parties work to find good candidates and persuade them to run. However, the potential candidates have to decide for themselves whether their chances of winning justify the enormous investment of time and money needed to run a campaign. When a party is popular with the American public, such as Democrats in 2006 and 2008, party leaders can pick and choose among many well-qualified candidates, all of whom want to ride the party's popularity to a seat in the House or Senate. But when a party is unpopular, such as the Republicans in 2006 and 2008, the best potential candidates may decide to wait until the next election to run, leaving the already disadvantaged party with a relatively less competitive set of candidates.[80]

Moreover, even if party leaders can persuade a potential candidate to run, they cannot guarantee that person a position on the general election ballot; rather, voters choose the party's general election nominee for office in a primary election. Recall our previous discussion about Senator Joe Lieberman. In 2006, most state and national Democratic Party leaders wanted Lieberman, the incumbent Democratic senator, to be nominated for another term—but Democratic primary voters in Connecticut chose a different candidate, businessman Ned Lamont. Lieberman ultimately ran and won as an independent. However, if the Republican nominee had run a strong campaign, he might have won the seat, with Lieberman and Lamont splitting the Democratic vote.[81]

WORKING TOGETHER IN CAMPAIGNS

Parties can also work to simplify voters' choices by trying to get candidates to emphasize the same issues or take similar issue positions. That way, citizens know that when they vote for, say, a Democrat, they are getting someone whose policy positions differ in specific ways from those held by Republican candidates. The problem is that members of the party organization and the party in government do not always agree on what government should do. In recent years, issues such as national defense policy or immigration have split the Democratic and the Republican parties. Sometimes the differences within the parties reflect the candidates' genuine differences of opinion. Other times, candidates are trying to match the preferences of citizens in their state or district. Either way, the simple fact is that political parties in America generally speak with many voices, not one.

Why don't party leaders simply order their candidates to support the party platform or to work together in campaigns? As we have discussed, party leaders actually have very little power over candidates by way of rewards and punishments.[82] They can't kick a candidate off the ballot since candidates win the nomination in a primary election or at a convention. Even though parties have a lot of campaign money to dispense, their contributions typically make up only a fraction of what a candidate spends on their campaign. And incumbent candidates, who generally hold an advantage over their challengers when seeking reelection, are even less beholden to the party leaders. Even if party leaders could somehow prevent an incumbent from running for reelection, they would have to find another candidate to take the incumbent's place, which would mean losing the incumbent's popularity and reputation and reducing the party's chances of holding the seat.

WORKING TOGETHER IN OFFICE

Because candidates are not required to support their party's platform, there is no guarantee that that they will be able to work together with other members of the party in office. Sometimes, as with the Democrats' 100-hour plan in 2007, the members of a party can compromise to resolve their differences. However, there are also many examples in recent years of issues that split a party wide open, such as Democrats' divisions over Iraq war funding or the Republicans' disagreements about immigration reform and Social Security.

The fact that American political parties are heterogeneous means that elected members of the party may not agree on spending, policy—or anything else. In that sense, voters can't expect that putting one party in power is going to result in specific policy changes. Instead, policy outcomes depend on how (and whether) individual officeholders from the party can resolve their differences. Institutions such as the party caucuses or conferences provide a forum in which elected officials can meet and seek common ground, but there is no guarantee that they will find acceptable compromises.

ACCOUNTABILITY

The final task for a party is to serve as an accountability mechanism that gives citizens an identifiable group to reward when policies work well and to punish when

Party Organizations in Other Countries

Our description of American political parties highlights their lack of control over what their candidates say and do in elections and in government. Most American politicians—and nearly all officeholders—run as the candidate of a political party, but the major party organizations have little power to determine who gets their nominations.

The situation is very different in many other democracies. In most western European countries, the leaders of political parties can force candidates from their party to run on the party platform and, if elected, to vote according to the wishes of party leaders.[a] Where do they get this power? For one thing, the party organizations can determine which politicians are nominated to run for office. In some countries, party organizations routinely move candidates from one district to another, a practice known as parachuting. The national party organizations may also control most of the campaign resources. Finally, after the election, the leaders of the party that won the election often get to decide which of the elected politicians from their party will serve in the winning candidate's cabinet and wield policy-making power. This combination of incentives and threats makes most politicians in western Europe highly loyal to their party organization.

What are the consequences of these dif-

▲ In Germany, whose legislature is depicted here, candidates campaign as representatives of their party and must follow the dictates of their party leaders. Voters choose between party platforms rather than individual candidates, and they evaluate the winning party based on how successfully it has implemented its platform since the last election.

ferences? Legislatures in western Europe show high levels of party discipline—elected officials generally vote according to party leaders' instructions. Elections in these countries focus on party platforms rather than the promises made by individual candidates; instead of comparing candidates, citizens compare parties and their platforms when deciding how to vote.

Which system is better? It depends on what you think is important. The organization of western European parties helps them devise meaningful platforms and

coordinate the activities of their elected officials, and gives citizens a specific organization to hold accountable for government performance. However, precisely because candidates in these systems campaign as party members rather as individuals, they cannot tailor their appeals to the specific demands of voters in their district or state. As a result, western European voters in some areas may find that none of the candidates they see in an election are addressing the issues that matter to them. ■

policies fail. However, individual legislators also work to build a reputation and standing with the voters that is independent of their party label. They are happy to emphasize their party affiliation when it brings them support, but choose not to mention it when the party is associated with unpopular policies or outcomes. Republican legislators, for example, highlighted their party identification in the 2002 and 2004 elections, as the party was held in high regard by many voters.[83] However, by 2006, with voter evaluations of the party and President Bush at all-time lows, many Republican candidates deemphasized their connection to the party as much as possible.[84]

When politicians work to secure their own political future in this way, they make it harder for voters to use party labels to decide who should be rewarded and who should be punished for government performance. The result is that legislators are held accountable for their own performance in office, such as how they voted—but no one in Congress is accountable for large-scale outcomes such as the state of the economy or for foreign policy.

CITIZENS' BEHAVIOR

As you have seen, most Americans identify as either a Republican or a Democrat, and many citizens use party labels to cue their vote decisions. However, citizens are under no obligation to give money or time to the party they identify with or to any of the party's candidates. They don't have to vote for their party's candidates, or even to vote at all. All of these actions would strengthen party organizations, but citizens do not have to take them even if they strongly identify with a party.

Here again, citizens are free to choose how to participate in American politics, including the option of not participating at all. But many of the things citizens do—such as not contributing to campaigns or party organizations, voting for candidates from separate parties to hold different offices, or ignoring party affiliation in their retrospective evaluations—weaken party organizations and make it harder for them to operate as a team to enact policies and oversee the bureaucracy.

SECTION SUMMARY

1. The actions taken inside party organizations, parties in government, and parties in the electorate shape both election outcomes and policy outcomes in Washington.
2. American political parties are not organized as hierarchies; party leaders cannot control how their candidates campaign or what their elected officials do in office. The party also cannot force citizen members to support the party's candidates in elections.
3. As a result, many of the actions taken in party organizations, by elected party members in government, or by ordinary citizens who identify with the party, do not help American democracy work well.

Conclusion

American political parties help organize elections, unify disparate social groups, simplify the choices facing voters, and build compromises around party members' shared policy concerns. However, in all of these activities their success depends on whether individual party members—candidates, citizens, and party leaders—are willing to take the actions necessary to achieve these goals. Sometimes they are, but other times they decide that their own interests, or those of their constituents, are best served by ignoring or even working against party priorities. And when party members refuse to cooperate, political parties may be unable to do the things that help American democracy to work well.

The career of Senator John Sununu illustrates this phenomenon. When Sununu first ran for the Senate, he proclaimed his loyalty to the Republican Party and to

President Bush, a strategy that made sense given President Bush's high approval ratings at the time in Sununu's state of New Hampshire and the state's high percentage of Republican identifiers. Six years later, with President Bush's popularity much lower and declines in Republican identifiers, the best strategy for Sununu was to emphasize his independence from his president and party. Many other Republican candidates made the same decision, leaving the party hamstrung in its efforts to convince candidates to campaign on a common platform, or to enact policies in Congress.

CRITICAL THINKING

1. Suppose you are the leader of your party's caucus or conference in the House of Representatives. Why would you want to convince your party's elected officials to support the party's position on an issue? Why might you want to let them vote as they think best?
2. Is the spoils system a good idea or a bad idea? Why?
3. How would we know that a realignment is taking place in American politics?

KEY TERMS

activists (p. 232)
backbenchers (p. 244)
brand names (p. 226)
caucus (congressional) (p. 230)
caucus (political) (p. 239)
conditional party government (p. 244)
conference (p. 230)
crosscutting (p. 223)
dealignment (p. 234)
divided government (p. 246)
Duverger's law (p. 249)
527 organizations (p. 225)
national committee (p. 225)
New Deal Coalition (p. 222)
nodes (p. 219)
nominating convention (p. 240)
parties in service (p. 223)
party coalitions (p. 235)
party identification (party ID) (p. 232)
party in government (p. 219)
party in power (p. 246)
party in the electorate (p. 219)
party organization (p. 219)
party platform (p. 243)
party principle (p. 221)
party system (p. 219)
plurality voting (p. 249)
polarized (p. 230)

political action committees (PACs) (p. 225)
political machine (p. 228)
primary (p. 239)
realignment (p. 223)
responsible parties (p. 247)
running tally (p. 232)
single-member districts (p. 249)
spoils system (p. 221)
unified government (p. 246)

SUGGESTED READING

Aldrich, John. *Why Parties?* Chicago: University of Chicago Press, 1995.

Bartels, Larry M. "Partisanship and Voting Behavior, 1952–1996." *American Journal of Political Science* 44:1 (2000): 35–50.

Carmines, Edward G., and James A. Stimson. *Issue Evolution: Race and the Transformation of American Politics.* Princeton, NJ: Princeton University Press, 1989.

Cox, Gary. *Making Votes Count: Strategic Coordination in the World's Electoral Systems.* Cambridge, UK: Cambridge University Press, 1997.

Cox, Gary, and Mathew McCubbins. *Setting the Agenda: Party Government in the U.S. House of Representatives.* New York: Cambridge University Press, 2005.

Fiorina, Morris. *Retrospective Voting in American National Elections.* New Haven, CT: Yale University Press, 1981.

Green, Donald, Bradley Palmquist, and Eric Schickler. *Partisan Hearts and Minds.* New Haven, CT: Yale University Press, 2004.

Key, V. O. *Politics, Parties, and Pressure Groups.* New York: Crowell, 1956.

Polsby, Nelson. *Consequences of Party Reform.* New York: Oxford University Press, 1983.

Riordon, William L. *Plunkitt of Tammany Hall.* 1905. Reprint, New York: Dutton, 1963.

Rohde, David. *Parties and Leaders in the Post-Reform House.* Chicago: University of Chicago Press, 1991.

Schattschneider, E. E. *Party Government.* New York: McGraw-Hill, 1942.

Schlesinger, Joseph. *Political Parties and the Winning of Office.* Ann Arbor, MI: University of Michigan Press, 1994.

Stanley, Harold W., and Richard G. Niemi. "Partisanship, Party Coalitions, and Group Support, 1952–2004." *Presidential Studies Quarterly* 36:2 (2006): 172–88.

Sundquist, James L. *Dynamics of the Party System.* Rev. ed. Washington, DC: Brookings Institution, 1983.

Wattenberg, Martin P. *Where Have All the Voters Gone?* Cambridge, MA: Harvard University Press, 2002.

8

ELECTIONS

To appreciate why American elections are both fascinating and seemingly unexplainable, consider what happened to Republican senator John McCain during the 2008 presidential election. For a year or so after the 2006 midterm election, McCain was the obvious presidential front-runner: a good bet to win both his party's nomination and the general election. He had served as a naval aviator in the Vietnam War before being shot down and held as a prisoner of war for five and a half years. After the war, McCain had a distinguished career in the House and Senate, gaining national publicity for his efforts to hold down government spending. He ran for the Republican presidential nomination in 2000, calling his campaign bus the Straight Talk Express, and almost won—attracting considerable support from independents and Democrats. After 2000, McCain sought to build his support among conservative Republicans, working tirelessly for the party and its candidates during the 2002, 2004, and 2006 elections, including campaigning to reelect President George Bush, who defeated him for the 2000 Republican nomination.

Despite all of these political assets and plenty of prior planning, nothing went right for McCain in late 2007. His campaign organization was beset with discord, his fund-raising lagged behind that of other candidates, and his campaign events attracted few supporters. He soon lost front-runner status and began a slow, continual descent in the polls, firing much of his staff and even mothballing his campaign bus.

Then, at the Republican primary election in New Hampshire, a funny thing happened: McCain's campaign came back to life. Though he had lost the first contest, the Iowa caucuses, in early January, he won the New Hampshire primary and began a steady climb in national polls, followed by a string of wins in important primary states such as South Carolina and Florida. Other onetime favorites for the Republican nomination, former Massachusetts governor Mitt Romney and former New York City major Rudy Giuliani, dropped out of the race, and both endorsed McCain. By mid-February, McCain's nomination was assured.

McCain's success did not continue. Except for one brief period after the Republican National Convention, he consistently trailed Barack Obama in the polls. He was widely criticized for choosing Sarah Palin as his vice presidential nominee, and his attacks against Obama's inexperience, alleged ties to radicals, and plans to redistribute income, went nowhere. When the financial crisis hit in September, McCain was seen as having no solutions to offer. By Election Day, there was little question that he would lose.

▲ Early in the 2008 presidential primaries, most political observers had written off Republican candidate John McCain, shown here trying to refuel his stalled campaign bus, the Straight Talk Express. McCain's experience challenges theories of American elections: can we explain why a candidate thought to have no chance at all went on to win his party's nomination, then fail to win the presidency?

What happened to John McCain? How did the front-runner become a long-shot, and then revive to win the nomination, only to struggle in the general election? Was it his age, issue positions, campaign organization, or other factors? Answering these questions will help explain John McCain's fate as well as how American elections work.

As this example suggests, American national elections sometimes look bewilderingly complex and extremely conflictual. The conflict comes as no surprise: Americans disagree about what government should do, and these differences play out between candidates running for the House, Senate, and presidency. As prominent, public forums for Americans to debate policy preferences, elections provide further evidence that politics is everywhere. During election season, campaign coverage and ads for candidates become almost impossible to avoid. Even so, one of the most important tasks all campaigns face is getting citizens' attention and convincing them to listen to the candidate's appeals.

Elections also illustrate that political process matters. Candidates in American elections compete for a wide variety of offices. They are elected for different periods of time to represent districts, states, or the entire nation—places that vary tremendously in terms of what constituents want from government. A variety of rules determine who can run, who can vote, and how candidates can campaign. Even ballot layouts and how votes are cast and counted vary across states. Elections also differ in the amount of media coverage they receive, the level of involvement of political parties and other organizations, and the amount of attention citizens pay to the contests. All these aspects of the election process—who runs, how they campaign, and how voters respond—shape outcomes.

This chapter explains elections by focusing on the interactions between candidates and citizens. Candidates want to win political office, which requires that they convince citizens to vote for them. Citizens in turn decide how to respond to candidates' appeals. Understanding these interactions and the conditions surrounding them is the key to making sense of American elections.

By making the election process more comprehensible, we aim to demonstrate how and why elections matter. We will show that there are real differences between candidates running for national office, and that these distinctions have profound implications for public policy. And we will show that despite Americans' general detachment from politics, their votes reflect both their policy preferences and considerable insight into candidates' promises and performance.

American Elections: Basic Facts, Fundamental Questions

The first step in our analysis is to consider some basic information about recent American elections. Table 8.1 describes the outcomes of the last five presidential elections. Bolded candidates won their election; candidates followed by an asterisk were incumbent presidents running for reelection. In the 2008 election two candidates received more than 1 percent of the **popular vote**: Republican John McCain (46.1 percent), and Democrat Barack Obama (52.6 percent). However, McCain received 32 percent of the **electoral vote**, and Obama received 68 percent.

popular vote The votes cast by citizens in an election.

electoral vote Votes cast by members of the electoral college; after a presidential candidate wins the popular vote in a given state, that candidate's slate of electors will cast electoral votes for the candidate on behalf of that state.

In this election, 61 percent of people who were registered to vote actually voted, the highest turnout since 1968. In 2008, in addition to selecting a president, voters across the country chose between candidates for all 435 seats in the House and 35 of 50 Senate seats (as well as for 11 governorships and many state and local offices).

Table 8.1 raises a host of important questions: Where do candidates come from—how did McCain and Obama come to be the Republican and Democratic nominees? Why did Obama win—what issues did his campaign stress? How did people decide whether to vote and whom to support? Why was turnout so high? What is the difference between the popular vote and the electoral vote?

Table 8.2 reports the results of the last nine congressional elections, showing turnout; the **party ratios** for the newly-elected House and Senate, or how many Democrats and how many Republicans hold office in each chamber; the **seat shift**, or the change in the party ratio since the last Congress; and the percent of reelected incumbents in each chamber and party. To begin with, note that some (but not all) congressional elections are held in the same year as a presidential election. This regularity raises the question of whether the outcomes of the two elections are linked. Do voters take account of the president or the presidential candidates when deciding how to vote for congressional candidates?

The congressional election data suggest some of the same questions raised about presidential elections: Why do particular individuals become candidates for the House and Senate? How do they campaign—and how do voters decide? Why are congressional incumbents so successful at getting reelected? Does low congressional turnover imply that most voters are apathetic and alienated—or generally satisfied with the performance of their representatives?

The congressional election data also show a striking difference between two types of elections. Most congressional elections are **normal elections**, where seat shifts between the parties are small, and reelection rates for both parties are high.[1]

party ratio The proportions of seats in the House and Senate that are controlled by each major party.

seat shift A change in the number of seats held by Republicans and Democrats in the House or Senate.

normal election A typical congressional election in which the reelection rate is high, and the influences on House and Senate contests are largely local.

TABLE 8.1	PRESIDENTIAL ELECTION RESULTS, 1992–2008						
		REPUBLICAN		DEMOCRATIC		INDEPENDENT/MINOR PARTY	
YEAR	TURNOUT	POPULAR	ELECTORAL	POPULAR	ELECTORAL	POPULAR	ELECTORAL
1992	58.1%	George H. W. Bush*		**Bill Clinton**		Ross Perot (Reform)	
		37.4%	31% (168)	**43%**	**69% (370)**	18.9%	0
1996	51.7	Bob Dole		**Bill Clinton***		Ross Perot (Reform)	
		40.7%	30% (159)	**49.2%**	**70% (379)**	8.4%	0
2000	54.2	**George W. Bush**		Al Gore		Ralph Nader (Green)	
		47.9%	**51% (271)**	48.4%	49% (266)	2.4%	0
2004	60.3	**George W. Bush***		John Kerry		—	
		50.7%	**53% (286)**	48.3%	47% (251)		
2008	61.0	John McCain		**Barack Obama**		—	
		46.1%	32% (173)	**52.6%**	**68% (365)**		

*Denotes incumbent candidate. Election winner in boldface.

SOURCES: Calculated from statistics available from the Federal Election Commission at http://www.fec.gov, and the *Atlas of U.S. Presidential Elections* at http://www.uselectionatlas.org. Data for 2008 compiled from http://www.cnn.com/ELECTION and from Real Clear Politics, http://www.realclearpolitics.com.

TABLE 8.2 CONGRESSIONAL ELECTION RESULTS, 1992–2008

| | | HOUSE OF REPRESENTATIVES | | | | SENATE | | | |
YEAR	TURNOUT	PARTY RATIO	SEAT SHIFT	DEMOCRATS REELECTED	REPUBLICANS REELECTED	PARTY RATIO	SEAT SHIFT	DEMOCRATS REELECTED	REPUBLICANS REELECTED
1992	58.1%	258 D, 176 R	+ 9 R	86.7%	90.9%	57 D, 43 R	+1 D	82.4%	83.3%
1994	41.1	204 D, 230 R	+54 R	83.9	99.4	47 D, 53 R	+10 R	87.5	80.0
1996	51.7	207 D, 227 R	+3 D	98.3	91.4	45 D, 55 R	–	100	85.7
1998	38.1	211 D, 223 R	+4 D	99.5	97.2	45 D, 55 R	–	92.3	87.5
2000	54.2	212 D, 222 R	+1 D	98.0	97.5	50 D, 50 R	+5 D	93.3	64.3
2002	39.5	205 D, 229 R	+8 R	97.4	97.5	48 D, 51 R	+ 1 R	83.3	93.3
2004	60.3	201 D, 232 R	+3 R	97.4	99.0	44 D, 55 R	+4 R	92.9	100
2006	40.2	233 D, 202 R	+30 D	100	89.6	50 D, 49 R	+6 D	100	57.1
2008*	61.0	254 D, 173 R	+21 D	97.9	92.1	58 D, 41 R	+7 D	100	66.7

*Data for 2008 does not account for one Senate race unresolved as of December, 2008.

SOURCES: Calculated from Harold W. Stanley and Richard G. Niemi, *Vital Statistics on American Politics* (Washington, DC: CQ Press, 2007), Tables 1.1 and 1.10a, and from http://www.cnn.com/ELECTION.

Some congressional elections, such as 1994 and 2006, do not fit this description, however. In these cases, known as **nationalized elections**, turnover is much higher, and reelection rates are significantly lower for one party's incumbents. Results in these years also show a strong seat shift from one party to the other. In 2006, for example, Democrats won thirty-one House seats and six Senate seats, taking majority control of both chambers for the first time in twelve years. In 2008, Democrats gained twenty-one House seats and at least seven Senate seats, and 95 percent of House incumbents and nearly 90 percent of Senate incumbents who ran for another term were reelected (at publication one Senate race was unresolved). The Democrats' 2008 gains were not as large as some expected, but they nevertheless suggest that the contest was more nationalized than normal.

Whether a congressional election is normal or nationalized has important implications for what happens in government. Nationalized elections typically involve a change in party control of one or both houses of Congress or the presidency, and these changes can profoundly affect what government does. What determines whether an election will be normal or nationalized? Is it a change in how voters decide, or perhaps how candidates campaign? And what forces drive these changes?

The most important thing you can bring to this discussion is an open mind, since many seemingly obvious intuitions about American elections are open to multiple interpretations. Recall the discussion in Chapter 1 of the "Purple America" map of the 2008 presidential election results (Figure 1.2, p. 22). This map offers a different perspective on the outcome than a red state–blue state map like the one at the front of this book, which shows state-level results. Both maps are valuable, and we're better off not relying on just one.

▲ American candidates compete for different offices under a complex set of regulations. At the national level, their large campaign organizations often spend millions. Even so, elections are best understood in individual terms: one candidate trying to win one citizen's vote

WHAT DO ELECTIONS DO?

Our working assumption for explaining the behavior of candidates and voters in an election is that their actions are tied directly to what elections do: select representatives and give citizens the opportunity to reward and punish office-holders seeking reelection.

Selecting Representatives The most visible function of American national elections is the selection of officeholders: members of the House and Senate and the president and vice president. Candidates can be **incumbents** or **challengers**. America has a representative democracy, which means that by voting in elections, Americans have an indirect effect on government policy. Though citizens do not make policy choices themselves, they determine which individuals get to make these choices. In this way, elections are supposed to connect citizen preferences and government actions.

Accountability The election process also creates a way to hold incumbents accountable. When a citizen faces a choice between voting for either an incumbent or a challenger, he makes a **retrospective evaluation**. The citizen considers the incumbent's performance, and asks "has she done a good job on the issues I care about?"[2] Citizens who answer "yes" typically vote for the incumbent, while those who say "no" more likely vote for the challenger.

Retrospective evaluations are significant because they make incumbents reponsive to constituent demands.[3] If an elected official wants to be reelected and anticipates that some constituents will make retrospective evaluations, he will try to take actions that these constituents will like. If an incumbent ignores the possibility of voters' retrospective evaluations, voters can make these judgments and opt to remove people from office whose performance they disapprove of. Many Americans use retrospective evaluations to judge members of Congress and the president. One of the important differences between normal and nationalized elections is that in nationalized elections, voters' overall evaluations of Congress and the president are much more negative, leading more voters to vote against incumbents from the party in power.

nationalized election An atypical congressional election in which the reelection rate is relatively low for one party's House and Senate incumbents and national-level issues exert more influence than usual on House and Senate races.

incumbent A politician running for reelection to the office she currently holds.

challenger A politician running for an office that he does not hold at the time of the election. Challengers run against incumbents or in open-seat elections.

retrospective evaluation A citizen's judgment of an officeholder's job performance since the last election.

POLITICAL PROCESS MATTERS

☑ Voters elect members of Congress and the president, who in turn make policy choices ranging from budgetary decisions to approving new laws, and they also select judges and appoint the senior bureaucrats who head government departments. There is a lot at stake in an election.

SECTION SUMMARY

1. American national elections allow voters to select members of Congress, the president, and the vice president, and they create a mechanism for holding these elected officials accountable for their behavior in office.

2. The American political system is a representative democracy: Americans do not make policy choices themselves, but they vote for the individuals who get to make these choices.

How Do American Elections Work?

This section describes the rules and procedures that define American national elections. We begin with congressional elections, then examine presidential contests. The first step in any election is to define who can vote. The Constitution limits voting rights to American citizens who are at least eighteen years old. There are also

nomination The selection of a particular candidate to run for office in a general election as a representative of his or her political party.

open primary A primary election in which any registered voter can participate in the contest, regardless of party affiliation.

closed primary A primary election in which only registered members of a particular political party can vote.

general election The election in which voters cast ballots for House members, senators, and (every four years) a president and vice president.

numerous restrictions on voter eligibility that vary across states, as shown in Nuts and Bolts 8.1.

TWO STAGES OF ELECTIONS

House and Senate candidates face a two-step procedure. First, if the prospective candidate wants to run on behalf of a political party, she must first win the party's **nomination** in a primary election. If the would-be candidate wants to run as an independent, she needs to gather signatures on a petition to secure a spot on the ballot. Different states hold either **open primaries** or **closed primaries**, and the timing of these elections is set by state law.

The second step in the election process, the **general election**, is held throughout the nation on the first Tuesday in November, which is designated by federal law as Election Day. General elections are the contests that determine who wins elected positions in government. The offices at stake vary depending on the year. On-year elections are held every four years (2004, 2008 . . .). During an on-year election, Americans elect the entire House of Representatives, one-third of the Senate, and a president and vice president. During off-year elections (2006, 2010 . . .), there is no presidential contest, but the entire House and a third of the Senate are up for election.

For both primaries and general elections, the location of polling places varies across the nation. In some areas, people cast their votes in schools, fire stations, or

NUTS AND BOLTS

8.1

Voting Requirements across the States

REQUIREMENT	STATES WITH REQUIREMENT
Must be a U.S. citizen, at least eighteen years old on the day of the election, and residing in the state where you're registered	All states
Cannot have been convicted of a major crime and not pardoned	Alaska, Alabama, Arkansas, Connecticut, Delaware, Florida, Idaho, Iowa, Kentucky, Minnesota, Mississippi, Nebraska, Nevada, North Carolina, Rhode Island, Tennessee, Texas, Virginia, Washington, West Virginia, Wisconsin, and Wyoming
Cannot be in jail on Election Day	Alabama, California, Colorado, Georgia, Illinois, Indiana, Kansas, Louisiana, Maryland, Massachusetts, Michigan, Montana, New Jersey, New Mexico, New York, Ohio, Oklahoma, South Carolina, South Dakota, and Utah
Must have lived in the state where you are registered for at least a specified period before the election (usually thirty days)	Idaho, Indiana, Kentucky, Michigan, Mississippi, Montana, Nevada, New Jersey, New York, North Carolina, Pennsylvania, Rhode Island, Utah, and Wisconsin
Cannot have been ruled mentally incompetent by a court	**All states** *except* Alaska, Idaho, Illinois, Indiana, Maine, Michigan, New Hampshire, New Jersey, North Dakota, Oregon, Pennsylvania, Vermont, and Washington
Must swear an oath the state and/or U.S. Constitution	Alabama, Florida, and Vermont
Cannot bet on the election outcome	Wisconsin

SOURCE: Compiled from the Eagleton Institute of Politics, Rutgers University, available at http://www-rci.rutgers.edu/~eagleton/News-Research/NewVoters/VoterRegRequire.html.

other public buildings. Some communities use private homes as polling stations—as of 2006, one-third of the polling stations in Los Angeles County were in private homes.[4]

A new development in American elections is an increase in the practice of early voting, casting a general election vote prior to Election Day.[5] Early voting has always been an option for voters who could show that they could not vote on Election Day because of travel, illness, religious obligations, or similar reasons. These voters could cast an **absentee ballot**, typically by mailing it to a designated location. In recent years, many states have established no-excuse-required absentee ballots or simply allowed voters to vote early by mail or at polling stations. Oregon votes entirely by mail. While many Americans vote early (about 20 percent of registered voters in 2006 and over 30 percent in 2008), and studies show that early voters are more likely to have strong party identification (as well as high incomes and high commute times to work),[6] it is not clear whether early voting has changed election outcomes. If enough people voted early, it could have a significant impact on campaign tactics: for example, candidates would have to begin campaign advertising earlier to ensure that early voters saw these appeals.

CONSTITUENCIES: WHO CHOOSES REPRESENTATIVES?

Another critical feature of American elections is that officeholders are elected in single-member districts in which only the winner of the most votes takes office. (Although each state's senators both represent the whole state, they are elected separately; they are not the first- and second-place election winners.) Candidates for the Senate compete at the state level; House candidates compete in congressional districts. In most states, congressional district lines are drawn by state legislatures, while in a few states, nonpartisan commissions or committees of judges perform this function. In the main, district lines are revised after each national census, to make sure the boundary lines reflect shifts in population across and within states, although redistricting can take place at any time. (For details on redistricting, see Chapter 10.)

Changes in the size and shape of districts have important effects on who wins elections. By drawing lines one way or the other, the people in control of redistricting can determine whether a district is winnable by a Democrat or a Republican, which often makes the boundary-drawing process extremely contentious. For example, the Republican-controlled Texas legislature redistricted in 2003, with the goal of undoing a plan enacted by Democratic state legislators in 2001.[7] Many redistricting efforts (including Texas in 2001 and 2003) are designed to create districts that help one party's candidates win additional state legislative or congressional seats. Redistricting can also affect an incumbent House member's chances of winning by moving the district line to exclude former constituents and replace them with voters who do not know the incumbent.[8]

Because members of the House and Senate are elected from specific geographic areas, they often represent very different kinds of people, in terms of their age, race, income levels, and occupations, as well as their political leanings, including party affiliation and ideology. As a result, legislators elected from different areas of the country face very diverse demands from their constituents—leading them to pursue some very dissimilar kinds of policies.

For example, Democratic Senator Ted Kennedy, elected from Massachusetts, represents a fairly liberal state where gay marriage is legal, while Republican senator Orrin Hatch is from the conservative state of Utah. Suppose the Senate votes on a measure to ban gay marriage nationwide. Kennedy would know that most of his

absentee ballot A voting ballot submitted by mail before an election. Voters use absentee ballots if they will be unable to go to the polls on Election Day.

▲ Americans vote in all sorts of places—even private homes. Here, a voter leaves a polling station set up in an enclosed porch in Meridian, Oklahoma, for use in the 2008 presidential primaries.

Proportional Representation

While Congress and state legislatures are all elected using single-member districts, many other countries, particularly most Western European countries, use proportional representation.[a] Under this system, there are no districts or other geographic units that elect their own representatives. Instead, there is a single nationwide campaign in which each party runs a list of as many candidates as there are seats in the legislature. On Election Day, citizens vote for a party, not a candidate. Votes are then counted nationwide for each party, and the parties receive the number of seats in the legislature proportional to the percentage of the nation's votes it received.

As an example, suppose America had used proportional representation in the 1996 presidential election, and that people cast party votes in accordance with the votes they cast for presidential candidates. As shown in Table 8.1 (p. 259), in this election Republican Bob Dole received 40.7 percent of the popular vote, Democrat Bill Clinton received 49.2 percent, and Reform Party candidate Ross Perot received 8.4 percent. The 435 House seats would then be allocated proportionately to these results: the Republican Party would hold 177 seats (40.7 percent of 435), the Democrats would hold 214 seats, and the Reform Party would hold 39 seats.

This example illustrates the pros and cons of proportional representation. By counting votes nationwide rather than district-by-district, proportional representation enhances the political power of small interests that are organized into a political party. Under the system of single-member

▲ In countries such as Germany, where there is no president and many legislative seats are allocated by proportional representation, elections sometimes produce coalition governments in which multiple parties share control. Here, leaders of Germany's Social Democratic Party and Christian Social Union are shown on either side of German chancellor and Christian Democratic Union leader Angela Merkel after the signing of their 2005 power-sharing agreement.

districts and the electoral college, the Reform Party was a failure; its congressional candidates never won a House or Senate seat, and its presidential candidates never won any electoral votes. Under proportional representation, the Reform Party would be a force to be reasoned with. Its candidates would hold nearly 10 percent of House seats. More importantly, under proportional representation, in an election such as this one, the smaller party would hold the balance of power between the Republicans and the Democrats. Neither major party would hold enough seats to enact legislation on their own. Thus, in order to get anything done, they would be forced to find common ground with Reform legislators.

Some scholars have proposed proportional representation in America as a way to increase the political power of minority groups, or to give small ideological groups the opportunity to elect representatives to Congress.[b] However, because proportional representation enhances the power of small groups, countries that use this system tend to have many political parties, each of which elects some people to the legislature, with none of the parties even approaching holding a majority of seats. As a result, enacting new policies requires complex negotiations among many competing interests represented in the legislature. The implication is that enhancing representation for small groups through proportional representation comes at a price: the ability to get things done in the resulting legislature. ■

constituents would probably want him to vote against the proposal—and Hatch would know that most of his constituents would probably want him to vote for it. This example illustrates that in many cases, congressional conflicts over policy reflect differences in constituents' demands. Kennedy and Hatch may well hold different views on a gay marriage ban, but even if they agreed, their constituents' distinct demands would likely be enough to ensure that they voted differently.

The Constitution also shapes American elections. It imposes residency requirements on candidates for federal offices, as shown in Nuts and Bolts 8.2, and it sets the term of office (the number of years an officeholder serves before facing another election) for federal offices. The term of office for the House members is two years, and senators serve six-year terms. The president and vice president are elected to a four-year term.

DETERMINING WHO WINS

Most House and Senate contests involve **plurality voting**: the candidate who gets the most votes wins. However, some states use **majority voting**, meaning that a candidate needs a majority (more than 50 percent of the vote) to win. If no candidate has a majority, there is a **runoff election** between the top two finishers. Some candidates have lost runoff elections even though they received the most votes in the first contest. In a 2007 special election for Georgia's 10th District, Republican Paul Broun lagged more than 20 percentage points behind state senator Paul Whitehead after the first round of voting (in the first round, Whitehead received 43.5 percent of the vote in a ten-candidate race.)[9] Broun went on to defeat Whitehead by a few hundred votes in the runoff.

The two-step process of primary and general elections can have a similar effect on the election's outcome. Sometimes the winner of a primary is not a party's best candidate for the general election. You may recall from Chapter 7 that in the 2006 Connecticut Senate Democratic primary, politically inexperienced challenger Ned Lamont defeated incumbent Joe Lieberman.[10] Lieberman then went on to win the general election as an independent.

Americans vote using a wide range of machines and ballots,[11] and the choice of voting technology can affect election outcomes.[12] Some counties use paper keypunch ballots, on which voters use a stylus to punch out holes in a ballot card next to the names of their preferred candidates. Other counties use mechanical voting machines

plurality voting A voting system in which the candidate who receives the most votes within a geographic area wins the election regardless of whether he or she wins a majority (more than half) of the votes.

majority voting A voting system in which a candidate must win more than 50 percent of votes in order to win the election. If no candidate wins enough votes to take office, a runoff election is held between the top two vote-getters.

runoff election Under a majority voting system, a second election held only if no candidate wins a majority of the votes in the first general election. Only the top two vote-getters in the first election compete in the runoff.

NUTS AND BOLTS

8.2

Constitutional Requirements for Candidates

The Constitution sets age limits and residency requirements for candidates who run for federal government positions. Presidential candidates must be thirty-five years or older at the time they take office and born in the United States. (Thus, Arnold Schwarzenegger, U.S. citizen, actor, and governor of California, cannot be elected president: he was born in Austria.) A House candidate must be at least twenty-five when she takes office, and needs to have been a U.S. citizen for at least seven years. A senator must be at least thirty and needs to have been a citizen for nine years. House and Senate candidates are also required to reside in the state that they seek to represent. In addition, members of the electoral college cannot vote for a president and vice president who reside in the same state.

▲ Many different mechanisms are used to record votes in American elections, including paper keypunch ballots and computerized, electronic machines (above).

that require voters to pull a lever next to the name of their preferred candidates. Touch-screen voting machines are becoming increasingly popular, where votes are cast by pressing buttons on a terminal screen. A few localities still use paper ballots where voters mark their preferred candidate with an "X." The move to touch-screen voting is controversial because critics worry that the machines could be manipulated to change election outcomes.[13] Of course, earlier technologies aren't perfect either; vote totals in lever machines could also be manipulated, and paper ballots could be lost or altered. Moreover, the widespread use of touch screens in 2006 and 2008 occurred without major problems.[14] Many voting technology experts prefer optical scan voting in which voters indicate their preferences with a felt-tip pen on a paper ballot that is read by a scanner. The method is very accurate and inexpensive, and it leaves a paper trail.

Different voting methods also show different rates of **undervotes**, which happen when a voter either casts an unmarked ballot, votes in some races on the ballot but not others, or casts a ballot that cannot be counted for some reason. The various voting technologies are also associated with different rates of voter error, such as when a voter accidentally casts a ballot for someone other than his preferred candidate. (Of course, since votes are secret, it is impossible to be sure about these mistakes, but they have been observed in lab experiments involving hypothetical elections.) The confusion that surrounded the 2000 presidential election outcome in Palm Beach County, Florida showed what a difference ballot structure can make. Palm Beach County residents voted on punch cards in combination with something called butterfly ballots. This ballot listed the candidates on both sides of a center column. Voters indicate their preference on this kind of ballot by pressing down on the circle in the center column that corresponds to the name of their preferred candidate using a stylus. A punch card inserted underneath the ballot records the stylus marks, and votes are counted by counting holes in the punch cards.

This ballot structure appears to have caused some supporters of Al Gore in Palm Beach County to mistakenly vote for Pat Buchanan. As the picture shows,

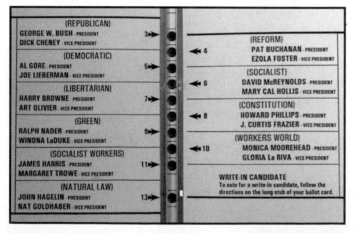

▲ The design of the infamous Palm Beach County, Florida, butterfly ballot, used in the 2000 presidential election, inadvertently led some people who intended to vote for Democrat Al Gore to select Reform Party candidate Patrick Buchanan.

Gore's name and Buchanan's were on facing pages at about the same level, so it would be easy for a voter to press down on the wrong circle, thereby voting for Buchanan when they intended to vote for Gore. Analyses suggested that the butterfly ballot cost Gore several thousand Palm Beach County votes—enough to change the results of the election in Florida, and thus the outcome of the 2000 Presidential election.[15] Keep in mind, though, that the butterfly ballot in Palm Beach County is only one example of the influence of a voting method on the election results. We don't know whether ballots used in other counties and states favored Gore or some other candidates. But it is clear that choices about how votes are structured can affect who wins elections.

Ballot counting adds additional complexities. Most states have laws that allow vote recounts if a race is sufficiently close (within 1 percent or less). In the 2006 Senate race in Virginia, incumbent George Allen could have asked for a recount, as he lost to challenger James Webb by just over 9,000 votes out of more than 2 million cast. Even when a recount occurs, it may be impossible to definitively determine who won a particular election, as the statutes that determine which ballots are valid are often vague and open to interpretation. The deeper lesson of these examples is that when an election is close, the question of which candidate wins may depend on how ballots are structured and votes counted. The problem is not that election officials are dishonest; rather, close elections inherently produce ambiguous outcomes.

undervote Casting a ballot that is either incomplete or cannot be counted.

There are often claims that officials manipulate election rules to guarantee wins by their favored candidates. In the 2004 election, some Democrats charged that Republican local officials had changed registration laws, the location of polling stations, ballot counting procedures, and other rules to help President Bush win Ohio.[16] It is difficult to definitively disprove these allegations, although investigations found no evidence of a conspiracy.[17] What is clear is that the election rules used affect the results. Particularly in close races, small changes in the rules governing elections can easily change outcomes. In the close 2008 Minnesota Senate race between Republican Norm Coleman and Democrat Al Franken, press reports suggested that some voters were turned away because of a shortage of voting supplies. If polling stations were required to stock extra supplies the election outcome might have been different.

▲ American presidential campaigns depend on thousands of paid and volunteer staff. Here, workers for Republican candidate John McCain contact potential supporters.

OTHER PLAYERS IN AMERICAN ELECTIONS

Elections involve many people and organizations. Political parties give candidates ballot access and electoral resources. The parties also organize the national conventions that nominate candidates for president and vice president. Interest groups, from the National Rifle Association to the Sierra Club endorse candidates, make contributions to campaigns, and run campaign ads that support their preferred candidates and criticize the ones they oppose, as we will see in more detail in Chapter 9.[18] Within campaigns, campaign consultants plan strategies, run public opinion polls, assemble ads and buy television time, and talk with members of the media on the candidate's behalf, to name just a few things required to run a successful campaign. For many consultants, electioneering is a full-time, year-round position. Many concentrate on electing candidates from one party, although some will work for whomever will pay them. Almost all campaigns also have paid and volunteer staff, ranging from the dozen or so people who work for a typical House candidate to the thousands needed to run a major-party candidate's presidential campaign.

Some campaign staff work full-time for an incumbent's campaign committee or are on the incumbent's congressional or presidential staff. With some exceptions for senior presidential staff, federal law prohibits government employees from engaging in campaign activities.[19] As a result, many congressional staffers take a leave of absence from their government jobs to work on their bosses' reelection campaign, and then return to working for the government after the election—assuming the incumbent is reelected.

PRESIDENTIAL ELECTIONS

Many of the rules governing elections, such as who can vote and how ballots are counted, are the same for both presidential and congressional elections. However, presidential contests have several unique rules regarding how nominees are determined and how votes are counted.

The Nomination: Primaries and Caucuses Presidential nominees from the Democratic and Republican parties are determined by a series of state-level **primaries** and **caucuses** over a five-month period beginning in January of an election year.[20] These elections select **delegates** to attend the nominating conventions that are held during the summer. At these conventions, the delegates cast the votes that determine their party's presidential and vice presidential nominees. The format of these elections, including their timing and the number of delegates selected per state, is determined on a state-by-state basis by the state and national party

primary A ballot vote in which citizens select a party's nominee for the general election.

caucus (political) Local meetings in which party members select a party's nominee for the general election.

delegates Individuals who attend their party's national convention and vote to select their party's nominee for the presidency. Delegates are elected in a series of primaries and caucuses that occur during winter and spring of an election year.

proportional allocation During the presidential primaries, the practice of determining the number of convention delegates allotted to each candidate based on the percentage of the popular vote cast for each candidate. All Democratic primaries and caucuses use this system, as do some states' Republican primaries and caucuses.

winner-take-all During the presidential primaries, the practice of assigning all of a given state's delegates to the candidate who receives the most popular votes. Some states' Republican primaries and caucuses use this system.

organizations.[21] In some states, each candidate preselects a list of delegates who will go to the convention if the candidate wins sufficient votes in the primary or caucus. In other states, candidates select delegates off a list developed by party leaders. In both cases, a candidate's principle goal is to win as many delegates as possible—and also to select delegates who will be reliable supporters at the convention. Surprisingly, neither party requires delegates to support the candidate who selected them, but there is an expectation that they will do so.

The details of translating primary and caucus votes into convention delegates vary from state to state, but some general rules apply. All Democratic primaries and caucuses use **proportional allocation** to divide each state's delegate seats between the candidates, which means that if a candidate receives 40 percent of the votes in a state's primary, 40 percent of the delegates on the candidate's slate are selected. Some Republican contests use proportional allocation, but some others are **winner-take-all**, so that the candidate who receives the most votes gets all of the state's convention delegates. These rules matter: in the race for the 2008 Republican nomination, John McCain's early victories in winner-take-all primaries helped him build a large lead in delegates that caused some other candidates to drop out. Overall, McCain won only 47 percent of the primary and caucus vote but claimed 72 percent of the delegates. In contrast, senators Hillary Clinton and Barack Obama each won about 48 percent of the vote, and they also divided the pledged delegates almost evenly (Obama had 52 percent to Clinton's 48 percent). If Republicans used proportional allocation, McCain would have faced tougher opposition through additional contests and might not have won the nomination.

The ordering of state primaries and caucuses is important because many candidacies do not survive beyond the early contests.[22] Most presidential candidates pour everything they have into the first few elections. Candidates who do well will attract contributions, campaign workers, endorsements, and additional media coverage, enabling them to move on to subsequent primaries or caucuses. But for candidates who do poorly in the first contests, contributions and coverage will dry up, and these candidates will usually drop out. The result is that the candidate who leads after the first several primaries and caucuses generally wins the nomination, as John McCain did to become the 2008 Republican nominee.[23] However, when the first few contests do not yield a clear favorite, as in the race for the 2008 Democratic nomination when Hillary Clinton and Barack Obama split the early primaries and caucuses, the race can continue until the last states have voted.

One candidate who downplayed the power of early momentum was 2008 Republican hopeful Rudy Giuliani, who devoted few resources to the early contests in Iowa, New Hampshire, and South Carolina, believing he would fare best by concentrating his efforts on the late-January Florida primary.[24] This strategy was partly driven by a calculation that most of the other candidates would devote their resources to the early contests, then most would perform poorly and drop out, allowing Giuliani to dominate the remaining contests. It also reflected the fact that as a moderate conservative, Giuliani was not expected to do well in the first few states' primaries and caucuses, as those states' Republican voters tend to be more conservative. Nonetheless, Giuliani's strategy backfired, as John McCain emerged from South Carolina as the clear frontrunner, then won the Florida primary by a significant margin. Giuliani dropped out of the race—and endorsed McCain—a few weeks later.

If a sitting president runs for reelection, as George Bush did in 2004, he typically faces little opposition for the party's general-election nomination—not because challengers defer to the president, but because most presidents are popular enough among their own party's faithful supporters that they can win the nomination without too much trouble. Only presidents with particularly low approval ratings have faced serious opposition in their nomination bids, as did Gerald Ford in 1976 and Jimmy Carter in 1980. Both won renomination but lost the general election.

Among the states, the presidential nomination process is always changing.[25] There has been a trend toward **regional primaries**, where all of the states in a geographic area elect delegates on the same day, as well as **frontloading**, where some states move their primaries earlier in the process. For many years, the states of Iowa and New Hampshire have held the first presidential nomination contests in late January, with the Iowa caucuses held a week before the New Hampshire primary. State party officials from other states often complained about the media attention given to these contests and the disproportionate influence of these states in winnowing the candidate pool. As a result, both parties' National Committees decided that in 2008 Nevada would hold its caucus just after the Iowa caucus, and South Carolina would hold its primary a week after New Hampshire.[26]

These changes encouraged many state legislatures to frontload their states' primaries and caucuses. As a result, twenty-one states held their presidential selections on "Super Tuesday," February 5, 2008, allotting a total of 2,084 delegates to the Democratic convention and 1,081 to the Republican convention on a single day. In Michigan and Florida, the state legislatures moved their primaries to mid- and late January, respectively, prompting Iowa and New Hampshire to hold their contests even earlier than usual in an effort to hold on to their privileged position. (These schedule changes by Michigan and Florida occurred despite both major parties' threats to punish both states for the early votes by refusing to seat their delegations at the nominating conventions, meaning that these states' votes would not count toward selecting the parties' general-election nominees. Ultimately, both parties seated the wayward states' delegations and gave them full voting rights—but only because each party's presumptive nominee had enough votes to win the nomination regardless of how these delegates voted.) As a result of these broad changes, a large fraction of both parties' convention delegates were selected by early February, about one month into the nomination process. On the Republican side in 2008, these changes helped John McCain to become the presumptive nominee by the middle of February. However, on the Democratic side, both Hillary Clinton and Barack Obama emerged from Super Tuesday with roughly equal delegate counts and continued to fight for the nomination until the end of the primary process in early June.

Another recent change that distinguishes the candidate selection processes of the two parties is that about one-fifth of delegates to the Democratic Convention are not supporters of a particular candidate, chosen to attend the convention through primary and caucus results. Rather, they are elected officials and party officials who are selected by their colleagues to serve as **superdelegates**. Most of them are automatically seated at the convention regardless of primary and caucus results, and they are free to support any candidate for the nomination. By forcing candidates to court support from superdelegates, the party aims to ensure that the nominee is someone these officials believe can win the general election, and whom they can work with if he or she is elected.[27] In the 2008 Democratic nomination contest, many superdelegates waited until the end of the primaries in early June to announce their support, leaving the race open until then.

The National Convention Presidential nominating conventions are held late in the summer of an election year. The main task is the selection of the party's presidential election nominee.[28] To get the nomination, a candidate needs the support of a majority of the delegates. If no candidate receives a majority after the first round of

regional primaries A practice whereby several states in the same area of the country hold presidential primaries or caucuses on the same day.

frontloading The practice of states moving their presidential primaries or caucuses to take place earlier in the nomination process, often in the hopes of exerting more influence over the outcome.

superdelegates Democratic members of Congress and party officials selected by their colleagues to be delegates at the party's presidential nominating convention. (Republicans do not have superdelegates.) Unlike delegates selected in primaries or caucuses, superdelegates are not committed to a particular candidate and can exercise their judgment when deciding how to vote at the convention.

voting at the convention, the voting continues until someone does. Some conventions have required many ballots to select a nominee (the record is 103 ballots at the 1924 Democratic Convention).[29] However, all recent conventions have needed only one ballot to select a nominee.

After the convention delegates nominate a presidential candidate, they select a vice presidential nominee. Typically the presidential nominee gets to choose whom to run with, and the convention delegates ratify this choice without much debate. Delegates also vote on the party platform that describes what the party stands for and what kinds of policies its candidates will supposedly seek to enact if they are elected.

The final purpose of a convention is to attract public attention to the party and its nominees. Public figures give speeches during the evening sessions when all of the major television networks have live convention coverage. In 2000, the nomination speech for Democrat Al Gore was given by the actor Tommy Lee Jones, Gore's undergraduate roommate. At some recent conventions, both parties have drawn press attention by recruiting speakers who support their political goals despite their association with the opposing party. Democratic senator Zell Miller spoke at the 2004 Republican Convention. The 2008 Republican Convention featured a speech by Connecticut senator Joe Lieberman, who had been Al Gore's running mate on the Democratic presidential ticket in 2000, while former Republican representative Jim Leech delivered a speech before the 2008 Democratic Convention.

Once presidential candidates are nominated, the general election campaign officially begins—though it often unofficially starts much earlier, as soon as the major parties' presumptive nominees are known. We will have more to say about presidential campaigns in a later section.

Counting Presidential Votes Despite the set-up in the voting booth where you choose between the candidates by name, citizens don't vote directly for presidential candidates. Rather, when you select your preferred candidate's name, you are choosing that person's slate of pledged supporters from your state to serve as electors, who will then vote to elect the president. The number of electors for each state equals the state's number of House members (which varies based on state population) plus the number of Senators (two per state). All together, the electors chosen by the citizens of each state constitute the **electoral college**, the body that formally selects the president. Small-population states, therefore, have few electoral votes—Delaware and Montana each have only three—while the highest-population state, California, has fifty-five. In most states, electoral votes are allocated on a winner-take-all basis: the candidate who receives the most votes from a given state's citizens gets all of that state's electoral votes. Two states, Maine and Nebraska, allocate most of their electoral votes at the congressional district level, which means that in those states, the candidate who wins the most votes in each congressional district wins that district's single electoral vote. Then, the remaining two electoral votes are given to the candidate who gets the most votes statewide.[30]

The winner-take-all method of allocating most states' electoral votes focuses candidates' attention on two kinds of states: high-population states with lots of electoral votes to be gained and **swing states** where the contest is relatively close. It's better for a candidate to spend a day campaigning in California, with its fifty-five electoral votes, than in Montana, where only three electoral votes are at stake. However, if one candidate is sure to win a particular state, both candidates will direct their efforts elsewhere. In 2004, when polls indicated that Democrat John Kerry was very likely to win California, both Kerry and Bush pulled most of their

POLITICAL PROCESS MATTERS

☑ The rules that govern elections or any other aspect of politics are never neutral; they always advantage some candidate or group.

electoral college The body that votes to select America's president and vice president based on the popular vote in each state. Each candidate nominates a slate of electors who are selected to attend the meeting of the college if their candidate wins the most votes in a state or district.

swing states In a presidential race, highly competitive states in which both major party candidates stand a good chance of winning the state's electoral votes.

staff and advertising out of California, and redeployed them to swing states like Ohio and Missouri.[31] As polls began to move against John McCain in October 2008, his campaign suspended advertising in Michigan and Wisconsin in favor of additional efforts in Ohio and Pennsylvania. Looking at the same polls, the Obama campaign redeployed advertising and volunteers to Ohio, Florida, Indiana, and even Arizona, McCain's home state. The result: Obama won all of these states except Arizona.

After citizens' votes are counted in each state, the chosen slates of electors meet in December in the state capitals. At their meetings, the electors almost always vote for the presidential candidate they have pledged to support. After the votes are certified by a special session of the Senate, the candidate who wins a majority of the nation's electoral votes (at least 270) is the new president. One peculiarity of the electoral college is that in some states, it is legal for an elector to vote for a candidate they are not pledged to or to abstain from voting.[32] Some electors have done so, although never in large enough numbers to alter the outcome of an election.[33] Such events are uncommon for the simple reason that electors are selected by the presidential candidates. A candidate is unlikely to pick someone to serve as an elector if there seems to be any chance that the person will switch candidates or opt not to vote.

If no candidate receives a majority of the electoral college votes, the members of the House of Representatives choose the winner using a procedure in which the House members from each state decide which candidate to support, then cast one collective vote per state, with the winner needing a majority of these state-level votes to win. This procedure has not been used since 1824, although it might be required if a third-party candidate won a significant number of electoral votes, or if a state's electors were unwilling to cast their votes.[34]

A presidential candidate can win the electoral college vote, and thus the election, despite receiving a minority of the votes cast by citizens—particularly if the vote is divided between more than two candidates. When a third-party candidate for president receives a substantial number of votes, the election winner can easily end up receiving more votes than any other candidate without winning a majority of the popular vote. Bill Clinton, for example, won a substantial electoral college majority in 1992, while receiving only 43 percent of the popular vote, due to the fact that Ross Perot, running as a third-party candidate, received almost 19 percent of the national popular vote but not enough support in any one state to win electoral votes.

In addition, because of the way popular votes translate into electoral votes, a candidate can receive a majority of the electoral vote even though another candidate won more popular votes. Thus, George Bush, the winner of the 2000 election, received about 540,000 fewer votes than his main rival, Al Gore. The other presidents who won the electoral college vote but lost the popular were John Quincy Adams in 1824, Rutherford B. Hayes in 1876, and Benjamin Harrison in 1888—and this almost occurred in 1960, when John F. Kennedy was elected, and in 1976, when Jimmy Carter won the presidency.

SECTION SUMMARY

1. American presidential elections are a two-step process: In primary elections and caucuses candidates secure the party's nomination, and in the general election officeholders are chosen.

2. Candidates for the House and Senate compete in single-member districts, with the winner decided using plurality (in some cases majority) voting. Presidential elections are decided by the electoral college vote.

3. Many groups and individuals are active in elections, such as party organizations, interest groups, and activists. Their activities include working for candidates, making campaign contributions, and campaigning on behalf of candidates they favor.
4. Election outcomes are shaped by who runs and how those people campaign—but also by the rules that govern electoral competition.

Electoral Campaigns

This section turns to the campaign process and what candidates do to convince people to go to the polls and vote for them on Election Day. Our emphasis is on things that candidates do regardless of the office they are running for, across the entire **election cycle,** the two-year period between general elections.

SETTING THE STAGE

On the day after an election, candidates, party officials, and interest groups all start thinking about the next election cycle: who won and who lost, which incumbents look like safe bets for reelection and which ones might be vulnerable, who might retire in the next couple of years or run for another office in the next election, and whether election returns reveal any new information about what kinds of campaigns or issues might increase turnout or support.

These calculations also reflect the costs of running for office. Challengers for House and Senate seats know that a campaign will take up a year or more of their time and deplete their financial resources, and presidential campaigns require even more money and effort. If a potential challenger for one of these offices already holds elected office, such as a state legislator running for the House or a House member running for the Senate, they may have to give up their current office in order to run for a new one.[35]

Party organizations and interest groups face similar constraints. They do not have the funds to offer significant support to candidates in all 435 congressional districts, thirty-three or thirty-four Senate races, and a presidential contest.[36] Which races draw their attention? The answer depends on many factors, such as how well incumbents did in the last election and how much money those who were reelected have on hand for the next election, whether party affiliation in the state or district favors Republicans or Democrats (and by how much), and whether the newly elected officeholders are likely to run for reelection.

Trends are also taken into account. After the 2004 race, the Cook Political Report ranked how the senators up for election in 2006 were likely to fare based on their constituents' level of support for President Bush in the 2004 presidential campaign.[37] In this calculation, the most vulnerable Democratic senator was Ben Nelson of Nebraska, a state that George Bush won by 33 percentage points. Nelson was considered vulnerable because he was a Democrat running for reelection in a strongly Republican state. The least vulnerable Democrat was Ted Kennedy of Massachusetts, as President Bush lost this state by 25 points. (In 2006, generally considered a bad year for Republicans, both Nelson and Kennedy were reelected.) The 2008 campaign included a few surprises. Senate Republican Susan Collins of Maine was thought to be in danger of losing her seat, but won convincingly, and Republican Senate leader Mitch McConnell of Kentucky, thought early on to have a safe seat, only narrowly won reelection. However, for the most part, early ratings in 2008 were

election cycle The two-year period between general elections.

strong predictors of outcomes. As predicted, no Democratic senators lost their seats, while Republican senators Elizabeth Dole and John Sununu were both defeated.

Party committees and candidates also consider the likelihood that incumbents might retire, creating an **open seat**. In the run-up to the 2008 election, many Republican House members and Senators announced their retirements. Open seats are of special interest to potential candidates and other political actors because incumbents generally hold an election advantage.[38] So, when a seat opens, candidates from the party that does not control that seat know that they may have a better chance to win because they will not have to run against an incumbent. Consequently, the incumbent's party leaders know that they have to recruit an especially strong candidate in order to hold the seat. Interest groups will watch all of these decisions with an eye towards deciding whom they should endorse or support with campaign donations and advertisements.

Presidential campaigns work the same way. Virtually all first-term presidents run for reelection. So, potential challengers in the opposing party study the results of the last election to see how many votes the president received, and how this support was distributed across the states, in order to figure out their own chances of winning a head-to-head contest against the president. Candidates in the president's party make the same calculations, although no sitting president in the twentieth century was denied renomination. Some Presidents (Harry Truman in 1952, Lyndon Johnson in 1968) retired because their chances of being renominated were not good, while others (Gerald Ford in 1976, Jimmy Carter in 1980) faced tough primary contests, as previously mentioned.[39]

Most candidates who run for Congress or the presidency do so because they want the prize: they want to hold political office.[40] This motivation can lead an individual to run even with a relatively small chance of winning. For example, many politically inexperienced, poorly funded challengers run against House and Senate incumbents who won by large margins in the previous election—and for these candidates, the decision to run is smarter than it first appears. These relatively unseasoned challengers have little chance of beating the stronger challengers seeking their party's nomination to compete in an open-seat contest. So it makes sense for them to enter an almost hopeless race against the incumbent: At least they win the party's nomination, and if the incumbent makes a serious mistake during the general election campaign, they may stand a chance of winning.[41]

Some candidates run for office in order to gain publicity for causes they support. During the 2004 and 2008 presidential campaigns, Representative Dennis Kucinich of Ohio ran for the Democratic presidential nomination. While Kucinich would have been happy to be the nominee, he knew that he had no realistic chance of winning the party's nomination. His goal was to focus the attention of other Democratic hopefuls on the war in Iraq, which he strongly opposed, and to pressure the eventual nominee to take a strong antiwar stance.[42] Similarly, Representative Ron Paul of Texas ran for the 2008 Republican nomination at least in part to draw attention to the conservative antiwar position and his libertarian ideology.

BEFORE THE CAMPAIGN

Most incumbent House members, senators, and presidents work throughout the election cycle to secure their reelection; political scientists label this activity the **permanent campaign**.[43] To stay in office, incumbents have to do two things: keep their constituents happy, and raise money for their campaign. As we will see in Chapter 10, congressional incumbents try to keep their constituents happy by taking actions that ensure voters can identify something good that the incumbent has done, which will boost those voters' retrospective evaluations at election time.[44]

open seat An elected position for which there is no incumbent.

permanent campaign The actions officeholders take throughout the election cycle to build support for their reelection.

▲ House member Dennis Kucinich (D-OH) ran for the Democratic presidential nomination in 2004 and 2008. Though his efforts never attracted many supporters, he succeeded in drawing media attention to his principal campaign issues, an end to the war in Iraq and enactment of government-funded health care for all Americans.

▲ Most officeholders are always campaigning—traveling around their states or districts, talking with constituents, and explaining their actions in office—all with the hope of winning and keeping support for the next election. Here, Senator Ted Kennedy (D-MA) makes a campaign stop at a diner.

Incumbent presidents make the same kinds of calculations. During Bill Clinton's first term, for example, many of his advisors argued that he had to sign welfare reform legislation, for which there was great public support, in order to gain support in the next election.[45] George W. Bush's advisors made a similar argument about the Medicare reform legislation in 2003.[46] Of course, many presidential actions are taken in response to events rather than initiated to gain voter support. Particularly in the case of wars and other conflicts, it is far-fetched to say that presidents initiate hostilities for political gain. Even so, presidents, just like other politicians, are keenly aware of the political consequences of their actions and the need to build a record they can run on in the next election.

Presidents can also use the federal bureaucracy to their own advantage and to help members of their party. During the 2006 congressional campaign, the Bush-appointed commissioner of the Internal Revenue Service ordered his staff to delay taxpayer audits, believing that people who received audit notices might take out their displeasure on Republican congressional candidates.[47] Some scholars have argued that presidents try to increase economic growth in the months prior to elections, with the aim of increasing support for themselves (if they are eligible to run for reelection) and for their party's candidates, a phenomenon called the **political business cycle**.[48] Given the size and complexity of the U.S. economy, and the fact the independent Federal Reserve System controls monetary policy, it is unlikely that these kinds of efforts could have much success. Even so, out of a desire to stay in office and help their party's candidates, it seems clear that presidents would want to be seen as having a positive impact on the economy.

Candidates for all offices, incumbents and challengers alike, also devote considerable time before the campaign to raising campaign funds. Fund-raising helps an incumbent president or member of Congress in two ways.[49] First, it ensures that if the incumbent faces a strong opponent, he will have enough money to run an aggressive campaign. Successful fund-raising also deters opposition. Potential challengers are less likely to run against an incumbent if they see that she is well-funded with a sizable campaign war chest. Political professionals refer to this early fund-raising and its meaning for a candidate's prospects as the **money primary**.[50]

The other thing candidates do before the campaign is to build their campaign organization. The process of recruiting staff, particularly at the presidential level, is labeled the **talent primary**.[51] Just like fund-raising, the talent primary is also read as a signal of a candidate's prospects: if experienced, well-respected people agree to work in a candidate's campaign, observers conclude that the candidate's prospects for being elected are probably good.

Clearly, it's hard to separate what candidates do at election time from what they do between elections—incumbents are *always* campaigning, which is part of the reason they are so likely to win reelection. In many cases, incumbent House members and senators also wind up running against poorly funded, inexperienced candidates. Stronger challengers see that the incumbent has been working hard to solidify a hold on the constituency, and they decide to wait until the incumbent retires, when they can run for an open seat. Thus, incumbents are not automatically favored for reelection, but they often win by large margins because of all the things they do while holding office in between elections.[52]

POLITICS IS EVERYWHERE

Many elected officials are perpetually running for reelection, in the sense that it is impossible to separate actions they take to change government policy from the actions taken to strengthen their prospects for reelection.

political business cycle Attempts by elected officials to manipulate the economy, increasing economic growth and reducing unemployment and inflation around election time, with the goal of improving evaluations of their performance in office.

money primary Fund-raising by candidates prior to the primaries or caucuses. The amounts that candidates manage to raise in this period are often considered indicative of their respective chances of winning.

talent primary Candidates' attempts to recruit well-respected consultants and campaign staff prior to the first primaries and caucuses. A candidate's ability to recruit a prestigious campaign team is often considered indicative of his or her electoral prospects.

Reelection Rates for Congressional Incumbents

As we have discussed throughout this chapter, in a typical congressional election, upwards of 90 percent of the sitting House members and Senators who run for reelection win. Even in a nationalized election, most incumbents from both political parties return to Washington for a new term. As one analysis of a House election in 2000 put it, "[the incumbent] has as much chance of losing Tuesday as he does of getting hit by a blimp."[a] Similarly, in an opinion piece written just before the 2006 midterms, two political scientists wrote that congressional incumbents "enjoy reelection rates that would have been the envy of the Supreme Soviet."[b]

Why are congressional reelection rates so high? Aside from their extreme claims, both articles make the same point: members of Congress have insulated themselves from electoral challenges through a few specific tactics that draw on their power as office-holders. They raise large sums of campaign cash well in advance of upcoming elections, use redistricting to give themselves a safe district populated by supporters, and enact pork-barrel legislation that provides government benefits and programs to their constituents.

The result of these actions, goes the argument, is that House incumbents can get reelected without breaking a sweat, especially since they typically find themselves facing weak, poorly funded challengers. If so, the high reelection rates for congressional incumbents are not a sign that voters are satisfied with Congress at all. Rather, they reflect the poor choices that voters are offered at election time. A lack of real opposition also means legislators need not fear retribution at the polls even if they ignore their constituents. As political scientists Samuel Issacharoff and Jonathan Nagler put it, "the clear losers are the voters. An insulated Congress is one that becomes increasingly inattentive to the preferences of the electorate."[c]

Political science research offers some important counters to these claims. First, if incumbents were so safe, they would not spend so much time in the permanent campaign, going home to their district or state nearly every weekend to meet with constituents, explain their behavior in Washington, and find out what they need to do to increase their chances of winning the next election.

Second, in nearly every congressional district, there are many state legislators, county executives, mayors, and other local elected officials who would love to serve in Congress. If they think an incumbent is unpopular or otherwise vulnerable, at least one of them would surely run against the incumbent in the next election.[d] Studies show that when such politically experienced candidates challenge a congressional incumbent, they are generally able to raise enough money to fund a credible campaign.[e]

Third, incumbents don't always win. In a nationalized election, incumbents from one party have significantly lower chances of reelection than their colleagues in the other party. And even in normal elections, a small number of incumbents lose a primary or a general election, and others retire because they know their chances of winning are problematic. Moreover, incumbent defeats don't happen at random: incumbents who lose have often cast votes that run counter to their constituents' demands or have become embroiled in a personal scandal.[f]

This evidence suggests that congressional incumbents are not necessarily safe from electoral defeat. Rather, their high reelection rates result from the actions they take every day, which are calculated to win favor with their constituents. As Congress scholar David Mayhew described it, "When we say, 'Congressman Smith is unbeatable,' we do not mean that there is nothing he could do that would lose him his seat. Rather we mean, 'Congressman Smith is unbeatable as long as he continues to do the things he is doing.'"[g] ∎

DURING THE CAMPAIGN

General election campaigns begin in early September. By this point, both parties have their presidential nominees and their congressional candidates. Interest groups, candidates, and party committees have raised most of the funds they will use or donate in the campaign. The race is on.

Having made numerous trips to the first primary and caucus states, trying to build their organization and attract mass support, presidential campaigns largely shift their focus once primaries and caucuses start to be held to focus on **wholesale politics**, in which candidates contact voters indirectly, such as through media coverage and campaign advertising. At this point, presidential campaign events generally involve large numbers of citizens, or, if they are smaller events or one-on-one encounters, they are designed to generate media coverage and thereby reach a larger

wholesale politics A mode of campaigning that involves indirect contact with citizens, such as running campaign ads.

audience. (Of course, people who work in a presidential campaign, particularly volunteers, pursue direct contacts with citizens throughout the campaign.) In contrast, some campaigns for the House and even a few Senate races primarily involve candidates or their staff contacting citizens directly, a mode of campaigning called **retail politics**. On the Sunday before the election in 2008, Connecticut representative Chris Shays spent time driving from church to church, hoping to meet people as they left services and persuade them to support his candidacy. While Shays also ran campaign ads, these one-on-one contacts were an integral part of his campaign.

Basic Campaign Strategies One of the most fundamental campaign strategies, particularly in congressional campaigns, is to build name recognition. Simply put, a citizen needs to know a candidate's name before thinking about voting for him. And since many citizens tend not to be well-informed about congressional candidates, efforts to increase a candidate's name recognition in these races can deliver a few extra percentage points of support—enough to turn a close defeat into a victory. (Practically all voters can identify the major party presidential candidates, so name recognition efforts are not as central to these elections.)

A second basic strategy is **mobilization**. Turnout is not automatic: just because a citizen supports a candidate does not mean that he or she will actually vote. Candidates have to worry just as much about making sure that their supporters vote as they do about winning support in the first place. Moreover, focusing on getting supporters to the polls is often a relatively efficient use of candidates' resources. Given that most people don't pay much attention to politics, it's much easier to get a supporter to go to the polls than it is to convert an opponent into a supporter.

Campaign professionals refer to these voter mobilization efforts as **GOTV** ("get out the vote") or the **ground game**.[53] Most campaigns for Congress or the presidency use extensive door-to-door canvassing to contact citizens, as well as **phone banks** and e-mail. In 2008, Barack Obama's campaign launched a massive get-out-the-vote operation, staffing offices around the country with thousands of workers who identified potential supporters and helped persuade them to vote for Obama on Election Day.[54] Both Republican and Democratic campaigns use sophisticated databases, combining voter registration, demographics, and even purchasing data to determine who their potential supporters are and how best to reach them.[55] Scholars have found clear evidence that these efforts boost a candidate's electoral support.[56]

Sometimes candidates also try to decrease support and turnout for their opponent. One tactic is **push polling**, in which a candidate or a group that supports a candidate conducts a voter "survey," typically by phone, that isn't actually designed to measure opinions so much as to influence them. Campaigns use these so-called polls to spread false or misleading information about another candidate by including this information in questions posed to large numbers of citizens.[57] Another strategy is to frighten people. In 2006, a staffer for a Republican House candidate in California sent letters to Latinos in their district, a group the campaign considered likely to support the opposing candidate, stating that it was illegal for immigrants to vote.[58] (If immigrants are U.S. citizens and registered, it is completely legal for them to vote.) The staffer was fired when the use of this tactic was publicized, and the candidate lost the election.

Promises and Platforms The next set of campaign decisions have to do with the candidate's **campaign platform**, which includes stances on issues and promises about how the candidate will act in office. Given that few voters are well-informed about public policy or inclined to learn, candidates do not win elections by trying to educate the electorate or making complex promises. The average voter is not motivated to listen to or think through the details of long arguments. What works in a campaign is to make promises and take positions that are simple and consistent with what the average voter believes, even if these beliefs are inconsistent with reality.

For example, many people believe that interest groups have too much power in Washington. But, as we will see in Chapter 9, interest groups' influence is far less powerful than most Americans believe. Even so, many candidates accuse their opponent of being beholden to interest groups—over 300 candidates ran ads along these lines in the 2006 election.[59] These claims may be far-fetched, but they work well politically because they play to citizens' perceptions. One such ad that ran against Senator James Talent of Missouri charged that Talent had received over $280,000 in contributions from oil companies—which sounds like a lot of money until you consider that Talent spent over $12 million on his reelection campaign. (He also lost.)

In writing their platform, candidates may be constrained by positions they have taken in the past or by their party affiliation. Chapter 7 showed that the parties have strong brand identities that lead many citizens to associate Democrats with liberal policies and Republicans with conservative ones. Candidates often find it difficult to make campaign promises that contradict these perceptions. In 2006, many Republican candidates tried to avoid talking about the war in Iraq, even though polls suggested that most voters were focused on this issue.[60] Why avoid the topic? Most Republican incumbents had previously supported the war, so voters might not see a newly adopted antiwar position as credible. Moreover, taking a strong stand against the war would place them at odds with Republican president George Bush. Democrats faced no such constraints: many had opposed the war from the start, or offered only reluctant, qualified support. For them, it was easy and politically popular to take a strong antiwar stand. The war was much less important for platforms in the 2008 contest. With American casualties decreasing, voters were more concerned about candidates' positions on the economy, energy, and health care.

Another influence on a candidate's positions is where he is running for office. In a state or district where there are many conservative or Republican voters, support for the Iraq war might be a winning electoral strategy (or, at a minimum, not a sure loser)—just as strong opposition to the war was essential for candidates running in states or districts where most voters are moderate to liberal or Democrats.

The two-step electoral process in American elections also influences candidate positions. To win office, candidates have to campaign twice, first in a primary and then in a general election. Voters in primary elections generally hold more extreme views than the average voter in a general election. As a result, in the typical congressional district, Republican candidates win primaries by taking conservative positions, while Democrats win their primaries by upholding liberal views. However, a position or promise that attracts votes in a primary election might not work so well in the general election, or vice versa. For example, in a 2006 Republican primary for the 8th District in Arizona, candidate Randy Graf won because of his strong anti-immigrant position.[61] Graf even opposed the immigration reform proposal developed by House Republicans because its penalties for illegal immigrants were not severe enough. While these positions helped Graf win the primary, they hurt his chances in the general election, since many voters strongly opposed his proposals. (Graf lost the general election.)

For all these reasons, different parties' candidates for the same office often make some similar campaign promises even though they disagree on other matters. During the 2008 North Carolina Senate race, candidates Elizabeth Dole and Kay Hagan held roughly the same positions on issues such as immigration, the Iraq war, and the government's bailout of financial firms. As a result, the race turned on other issues, such as Dole's low effectiveness ranking in a survey of Senate staff.

Real Campaign Platforms The excerpt from the campaign platforms of the 2008 presidential candidates shown in Table 8.3 illustrates the similarities and differences in the candidates' platforms in five issue areas that received considerable attention in the campaign: the economy, education, energy, immigration, and national security. As you see, in some areas McCain and Obama offered sharply different ideas of what government should do. In the case of the war in Iraq, for example, Obama pledged to withdraw American forces in sixteen months, while McCain opposed setting a firm timetable. And on the economic front, McCain favored making all of President Bush's temporary tax cuts permanent, while Obama proposed repealing them for households earning more than $250,000 per year.

However, even on controversial issues, there were some similarities between the candidates' platforms. In the case of immigration policy, for example, the candidates' positions were essentially identical, differing only in the details of their proposals. Both candidates supported merit pay for teachers, some amount of domestic offshore oil drilling, sending additional troops to Afghanistan, and many other policies.

Candidates from different parties agree on some things and disagree on many others. But no one watching the typical presidential or congressional contest would say the candidates were making the same promises about the future—or that they were taking diametrically opposed positions.

Issues matter in American elections. A candidate's issue positions help to mobilize supporters and attract volunteers, activists, interest-group endorsements, and contributions. Issue positions also define what's at stake in an election: what government will do differently depending on who gets elected. And as we will see in the next section, some citizens vote based on candidates' issue positions. Even so, there is considerable evidence that many voters do not know very much about

TABLE 8.3	PRESIDENTIAL CANDIDATES' ISSUE POSITIONS (SELECTED), 2008	
ISSUE	**JOHN McCAIN**	**BARACK OBAMA**
Economy	Make all Bush-era tax cuts permanent	Make Bush-era tax cuts permanent only for families earning under $250,000 per year
	Freeze most government spending	Increase regulation of financial firms
Education	Retain Bush-era No Child Left Behind program, but fund schools directly	Increase spending on teacher training and remedial and early-childhood education
	Institute merit-based pay for teachers	Institute merit-based pay for teachers
Energy	Allow a large increase in domestic offshore oil drilling	Allow a small increase in domestic offshore oil drilling
	Offer tax credits for buying eco-friendly cars; offer prizes for developing new battery technologies	Increase spending on alternative and renewable energy technologies
Immigration	Increase border security	Increase border security
	Allow illegal immigrates to gain citizenship after paying a fine and back taxes.	Allow illegal immigrants to gain citizenship after paying a fine and back taxes
National Security	Maintain open-ended commitment to keeping forces in Iraq	Set a timetable for withdrawing forces from Iraq
	Send additional troops to Afghanistan	Send additional troops to Afghanistan

SOURCE: Compiled from "Campaign Promises," *National Journal*, September 9, 2008, available at http://www.nationaljournal.com/campaigns/2008/wh08/promises.htm.

candidates' issue positions, particularly for House and Senate races. As a result, when a candidate wins a race, or a party wins seats across the country, it is risky to read the outcome as a sign that the winners had the most-popular set of issue positions.

For example, in the 1994 congressional races, many Republican House candidates ran on a common platform called the Contract with America. The Contract promised a House vote on a series of proposals, from banning any new congressional pay raises from taking effect until after the next election (keeping a given Congress from raising its own salary) to imposing all federal workplace regulations on congressional offices. Many observers attributed the 1994 Republican landslide to the popularity of the Contract.[62] However, subsequent surveys found that only a minority of the electorate knew what the Contract was. While there was a strong shift in support towards the Republicans in 1994, the Contract with America was not the deciding factor.

Confronting Other Candidates The final set of campaign strategies involves a candidate's opponent. Candidates seek to contrast their own records or positions with those of the opposing candidates, or make claims designed to lower citizens' opinions of their opponents. Sometimes these interactions occur during a formal debate. Most congressional campaigns involve one or more debates, before an audience of likely voters, a group of reporters, or the editorial board of a local newspaper. Typically candidates take questions from reporters, although in some cases candidates question each other, or answer questions from citizens in the audience.

Presidential campaigns involve multiple debates during the primary and caucus season. During the months before the first primaries and caucuses, each party's candidates gather for many single-party debates using a variety of formats. During the general election, the Republican and Democratic nominees meet for several debates. (The exact number and the format are negotiated by the campaigns and the Commission on Presidential Debates, a nonpartisan organization that hosts the debates.)[63] The 2008 presidential campaign featured three debates between the presidential nominees and one between the vice presidential nominees. Though the debates did not generate sharp shifts in voter support, they gave Barack Obama, who had spent less time than John McCain on the national stage, a chance to show his readiness for the presidency. By responding in a calm, detailed manner to the questions and McCain's criticisms, Obama partly assuaged fears that he was too inexperienced or naïve to be president.

As this example illustrates, the debates give candidates a chance to present themselves to the electorate. They offer extremely valuable free exposure, which is particularly important for candidates who do not have the money to run an extensive paid ad campaign. In 2008, the audience for each of the presidential and vice presidential debates was over 50 million people.[64] In a sense, the entire campaign functions like an extended debate, as candidates try to court support from citizens. Candidates work to put their own qualifications and records before the electorate, emphasizing facts, stances, and achievements that they believe citizens will evaluate favorably. And each candidate works to publicize aspects of her opponent's record that citizens seem likely to view unfavorably.

Given a relatively uninterested electorate, candidates must figure out how to present themselves to voters in a way that captures their attention and gains their support. Thus, in the 2004 presidential debates, George Bush's first remarks emphasized the September 11 attacks, arguing that the overthrow of the Taliban in Afghanistan and the invasion of Iraq had reduced the chances of another terrorist attack in America.[65] This argument was politically advantageous given that many Americans saw preventing a terrorist attack as a top priority—and at the time, gave Bush high marks for his performance on September 11. During the 2008 campaign, John McCain tried to dramatize his criticisms of Barack Obama's tax policies by describing how they might affect "Joe the Plumber" (whose real name is Samuel J. Wurzelbacher), who had been taped asking Obama about his tax plan at an Ohio campaign stop.

Candidates also attempt to win support by emphasizing their understanding of citizens' concerns and their willingness to address these problems, and campaigns provide an opportunity for questioners to test a candidate's knowledge of everyday life. For example, candidates often find themselves quizzed about the prices of everyday items, such as loaf of bread, a pound of coffee, or a gallon of milk, or how much citizens pay in property taxes or at the gas pump.[66] Questions like these are such a part of American political lore that candidates are routinely briefed about local prices before a debate.

Many campaign events are designed to reinforce the impression that candidates share voters' concerns and values. In the weeks before the 2008 Democratic primaries in Indiana and Pennsylvania, candidate Barack Obama visited a bowling alley in Pennsylvania where he bowled a game before a few startled patrons—and the entire group of reporters following his campaign.[67] A week later, rival Hillary Clinton visited a bar in Crown Point, Indiana, where she joined patrons in a round of beers and whiskey shots as reporters documented the event.[68] While these efforts don't always work as intended, there is no doubt what candidates are trying to do: convince would-be supporters that they are "just like them." Sometimes these attempts lead candidates into embarrassing situations: before the primaries, Republican presidential hopeful Mitt Romney claimed in town meetings that he had been a hunter "pretty much [his] whole life," but after press inquiries, had to admit that he had been hunting only twice.[69]

Candidates also try to raise doubts about opponents by citing politically damaging statements or unpopular past behavior. In the first 2004 presidential debate, John Kerry criticized the conduct of the war in Afghanistan and the failure to capture the architect of the September 11 attacks, Osama bin Laden, by charging that Bush had "outsourced the job to Afghan warlords."[70] Other politicians use push polls to achieve the same goals, or rely on endorsements or ads funded by interest groups. During the 2006 campaign, one liberal interest group even tried to influence the results of Google searches about Republican candidates. The group constructed Web sites and links so that citizens who searched for information about Jon Kyl, a senator running for reelection in Arizona, would find an article criticizing Kyl as their first search result.[71]

Candidates and interest groups also do **opposition research**, digging into an opponent's past for embarrassing incidents or personal indiscretions, either by the candidate or a member of the candidate's family or staff. Campaigns may then leak this information to the media or release it on their own. Candidates also use trackers, staff who attend their opponents' events with video cameras in the hopes of recording embarrassing behavior or statements. The resulting videos may then be posted on the Internet, given to the press, or used in a campaign ad. During the 2006 campaign, one tracker taped Montana senator Conrad Burns falling asleep during a congressional hearing.[72] Another tracker mentioned in Chapter 5 recorded Virginia senator George Allen referring

▲ During campaigns, candidates often seek to strengthen the perception that they share (or at least are sympathetic to) average Americans' beliefs and interests. Here, Democratic candidate Hillary Clinton enjoys a beverage with patrons in an Indiana bar during the 2008 presidential primaries.

to him as "macaca," a Tunisian term for monkey. (The tracker was of Indian descent; Allen's mother is Tunisian).[73] The video was posted on YouTube, and Allen's remarks remained a persistent story throughout the campaign. Allen later lost to challenger James Webb by just over 9,000 votes. While we can't be sure, a seemingly racist remark could easily have made the difference in such a close race.

The spread of trackers' candid and sometimes unflattering videos shows just one effect of how much easier the Internet makes distributing information about candidates. All of the Republican and Democratic presidential nominees in 2008 had Web sites as well as Facebook profiles and MySpace pages; many congressional candidates had them as well.[74] One blogger, citing the proliferation of Internet-distributed videos on candidates, labeled the 2006 election the "first YouTube election,"[75] and the YouTube influence persisted in 2008. Many campaign debates and videotapes of events were available on YouTube, and the cable news channel CNN ran Republican and Democratic presidential debates in which citizens submitted questions for the candidates in the form of YouTube videos.

However, much of the information about candidates that was available over the Internet during recent elections would likely have found other outlets in previous elections. For example, during the 1988 election, when the Internet was only a curiosity and Web browsers did not exist, voters learned through mainstream media sources that one of the Democratic presidential candidates, Joe Biden, had been accused of plagiarism while in law school—and that more recently Biden's speechwriter had lifted themes and text from a speech written by a party leader in Britain. If a candidate learns something that will help him win office or hurt an opponent's chances, he will find a way to get the information to the electorate. A more important use of the Internet in the 2008 campaign was Barack Obama's Web-based fund-raising operation. Obama raised over $600 million, much of it through the Internet. This surplus enabled him to force the McCain campaign to abandon efforts in some states to remain competitive in others.

Candidates who are well ahead in the polls with victory virtually assured often try to avoid mentioning their opponent at all, assuming that to mention the opponent would only provide free publicity. Conversely, as we discuss in the next section, candidates who are behind in the polls sometimes resort to **attack ads**, campaign ads that focus on criticisms of their opponents. These candidates hope that attack ads will gain voters' attention and give them a reason for rethinking their support for the front-runner.

The 2008 election featured attack ads on all levels. An ad against Republican representative Mary Bono featured a bobblehead version of Bono nodding as a Bush impersonator asked for her vote and thanked her for supporting him. In the presidential campaign, attack ads described Barack Obama as inexperienced, dishonorable, a socialist, and a friend of radicals. The general message was summed up in the ad calling Obama "a risk we can't take."

Do these strategies influence election outcomes? There are many stories of candidates who rode to victory on the back of some truly astounding claims. However, assertions about candidates' virtues or their opponents' vices shape outcomes only when they are consistent with voters' preexisting evaluations or beliefs. For Bono and Obama, it appears the attack ads had little effect, and both candidates won their elections.

CAMPAIGN ADVERTISING: GETTING THE WORD OUT

One of the realities of modern American electoral campaigns, particularly for the presidency, is that they are conducted largely through campaign advertising. As you saw earlier, candidates for office, party committees, and interest groups spend

attack ads Campaign advertising that criticizes a candidate's opponent—typically by making potentially damaging claims about the opponent's background or record—rather than focusing on positive reasons to vote for the candidate.

▲ *The so-called "Daisy" ad from the 1964 presidential campaign interspersed images of a child in a field of flowers and footage of a nuclear detonation. It was broadcast only once but caused much controversy—and helped to crystallize doubts about Republican candidate Barry Goldwater.*

over $1 billion during each election cycle on campaign-related activities. Most of that money is spent on campaign advertising, usually in the form of thirty-second television spots. Campaign advertising is critical because candidates cannot assume citizens will take the time to learn from other sources about the candidates, their qualifications, and their issue positions.

Campaign advertising has evolved considerably over the last generation.[76] During the early years of television, many campaign ads consisted of speeches by candidates or endorsements from supporters, and they usually ran several minutes in length, unlike today's ads which often run under one minute. In the 1964 presidential race, Lyndon Johnson's campaign ran a five-minute ad titled "Confessions of a Republican," featuring an actor talking about why he didn't want to vote for Republican Barry Goldwater.[77] The 1964 Johnson campaign also ran an ad that was a harbinger of political appeals yet to come: a one-minute ad, titled "Peace, Little Girl" and broadly nicknamed "Daisy," which featured a child counting the petals she is pulling from a daisy one by one, interspersed with a voice-over of a military countdown and images of the detonation of a nuclear bomb.[78] The implication was that electing Goldwater would increase the chances that nuclear weapons would be used in a future conflict. The ad ran only once, but it generated a great deal of controversy and remains one of the most iconic pieces of campaign advertising.

Much like the "Daisy" ad, modern campaign ads are typically short, with arresting images, and they often also use photo montages and bold text in attempts to engage a distracted citizenry. A classic example of an ad designed to capture viewers' attention ran during the 2006 campaign and featured actor Michael J. Fox.[79] The ad showed Fox, a longtime sufferer of Parkinson's disease, weaving back and forth in his chair and jerking uncontrollably because of the neurological symptoms of the disease. Fox's message: elect Missouri Democrat Claire McCaskill to the Senate because she supports stem cell research that might cure Parkinson's and other diseases. During the 2008 presidential primaries, Republican Mike Huckabee ran an ad that featured the actor Chuck Norris and Huckabee "endorsing" each other: Norris described Huckabee as a "lifelong hunter who will protect our 2nd Amendment rights"; Huckabee said that when Norris does a pushup, "he doesn't lift himself up, he pushes the earth down."[80]

As the main way that candidates reach the electorate, campaign ads abound in American elections.[81] A study of the 2002 midterm election found that the House and Senate races featured over half a million TV ads run by candidates, political parties, and interest groups. The number of ads in congressional races was similar in the 2000 elections, but there were an additional 250,000 ads pertaining to the presidential contest. About 60 percent of these ads were run by candidates' campaigns, with the rest from political parties, political action committees, or 527

▶ *During the 2006 Senate race, actor Michael J. Fox (left) appeared in a campaign ad for Missouri Democrat Claire McCaskill, highlighting her support for stem cell research. Early in the 2008 presidential primaries, actor Chuck Norris appeared with Republican candidate Mike Huckabee (far right) in an ad where they gave mutual endorsements. The Fox ad helped McCaskill to win election, while Huckabee was defeated.*

organizations (the next chapter looks closely at these latter two types of groups). These overall numbers translate into large numbers of ads in individual campaigns, particularly in close races. For example, during the 2002 campaign for a Senate seat in Missouri, incumbent Democrat Jean Carnahan ran over 7,000 campaign ads; Democratic Party committees ran over 7,000 ads, and interest groups ran an additional 1,000 pro-Carnahan ads.[82]

Virtually all kinds of political organizations run campaign ads. Table 8.4 shows the number of ads run by interest groups during the 2004 general election campaign for the presidency. Liberal groups ran the most ads in this particular election, although many ads came from all categories. (The proportion of ads from different sources varies; in the 2000 election, business groups ran over one-half of the total.) The total number of ads is concentrated among a few organizations: in 2004, the Media Fund ran over one-quarter of the total.

The content of campaign ads varies depending on who is running the ads. Table 8.5 shows data from the 2000 and 2004 presidential elections. As you see, campaigns, parties, and interest groups run a mix of positive ads extolling a candidate's record, background, or campaign promises, and negative ads citing an opponent's shortcomings or failures. An interesting feature of Table 8.5 is that of all the groups that run campaign ads, candidates themselves run the highest percentage of positive ads. On the other hand, note that in the 2000 election, the authors of the study could not find a single positive ad run by an advocacy group. Analyses of the 2008 campaign showed that there was little change. Advocacy ads in the primaries and the general election were overwhelmingly negative.

TABLE 8.4	CAMPAIGN ADVERTISING BY INTEREST GROUPS, 2004		
ORGANIZATION	**NUMBER OF ADS RUN**	**ORGANIZATION**	**NUMBER OF ADS RUN**
Liberal Groups, Total	**146,615**	**Labor Groups, Total**	**24,502**
Media Fund	74,915	AFL-CIO	10,962
MoveOn.org	43,143	National Education Association	5,238
New Democratic Network	10,609	United Auto Workers	2,664
Citizens for a Strong Senate	3,830	Service Employees International Union	2,213
League of Conservation Voters Municipal Employees	3,182 2,111	Association of Federal, State, County, and Municipal Employees	2,111
EMILY's List	2,399	Others	1,314
Others	3,143	**Business Groups, Total**	**11,114**
Conservative Groups, Total	**43,810**	Americans for Job Security	5,279
Progress for America	23,354	United Seniors Association	2,291
Swift Vets and POWs for Truth	8,690	National Association of Realtors	1,701
Club for Growth	8,151	American Medical Association	1,109
Americans United to Preserve Marriage	705	Others	734
National Rifle Association	1,083		
Others	1,827		

SOURCE: Robert Boatright, Michael Malbin, Mark Rozell, and Clyde Wilcox, "Interest Groups and Advocacy Organizations After BCRA," in *The Election After Reform*, ed. Michael Malbin (Washington, DC: Rowman and Littlefield, 2006), pp. 112–82.

One critical question about campaign advertising is whether ads work—whether they shape what people know, or influence their vote decisions or other forms of participation. Some observers have complained that campaign ads depress turnout and reinforce citizens' negative perceptions of government.[83] Many of these arguments focus on attack ads or negative campaigning. During the 2006 campaign, such ads accused candidates of breaches of judgment like using taxpayer dollars to pay for phone sex and dancing the night away at a college fraternity party.[84] (The latter charge was apparently true—the former was not.) Another candidate ran an ad linking his opponent to "Osama Bin Laden, gay marriage, 'lesbians and feminists,' activist judges, infanticide, flag-burning, racial quotas, space aliens, illegal immigrants, Jesse Jackson, and Al Sharpton."[85] Amazingly, a candidate running for Congress in another state took the ad, and without making substantial changes, ran it against his own opponent. Another attack ad during 2006 was aimed at an African American Senate candidate in Tennessee, Democrat Harold Ford. The ad, which was paid for by the Republican National Committee, featured a white woman in a low-cut shirt who claimed she had met Ford at a party at the Playboy Mansion.[86] The meeting never took place, but Ford and his campaign spent several days responding to the charge.

The question is, what do Americans learn from campaign ads? Do they simply believe what they are told, good and bad, or are they discerning about what they infer? Analyses suggest that Americans are reasonably thoughtful when assessing campaign ads. In 2008, an ad run by incumbent North Carolina senator Elizabeth Dole against her Democratic challenger, Kay Hagan, claimed that Hagan had taken "godless money" from the Godless Americans PAC. What, the ad asked, had she promised in return? The ad ended with a voice similar to Hagan's saying, "There is no God." In response, Hagan held a press conference with the minister of her church, who confirmed that she was a regular attendee and elder. Hagan also ran a counterattack ad accusing Dole of "bearing false witness against a fellow Christian." Exit polls suggested that Dole's initial ad backfired badly—if anything, voters considered it indicative of Dole's unworthiness to serve for another term in the Senate.

Surprisingly, the evidence suggests that campaign advertising has several beneficial effects. Scholars have found that people who are exposed to campaign ads tend to be more interested in the campaign and know more about the candidates.[87] Moreover, many campaign ads highlight real differences between the candidates and the parties.[88] Even so, average citizens are well aware that they cannot believe everything they see on television, so campaign advertising typically gets voters' attention without necessarily changing their minds.[89]

With regard to negative campaigning, early evidence suggested that attack ads depressed voter turnout, but later studies have shown that they do not have much of an effect.[90] Negative ads run by a candidate's campaign can also backfire, driving away supporters from the candidate who runs them. As a result, candidates often rely on party committees and interest groups to run negative ads, enabling them to run only positive ads (recall Table 8.5).

In the end, despite all of the money and effort poured into campaign advertising, these messages—like all other aspects of a campaign—must be designed to capture the attention of citizens whose interest in politics is relatively minimal, delivering a message that can be understood without too much interpretation. In this way, campaign advertising reflects an old political saying, that most things candidates do in campaigns are wasted efforts that have little impact on the election. The problem is that candidates don't know which of their actions will amount to wasted efforts and which will help them win, so they try them all.

Federal Election Commission The government agency that enforces and regulates campaign finance laws; made up of six presidential appointees, of whom no more than three can be members of the same party.

CAMPAIGN FINANCE

Campaign finance refers to money collected for and spent on campaigns and elections by candidates, political parties, and other organizations and individuals. The **Federal Election Commission** is in charge of administering election laws, including the complex set of regulations pertaining to how campaigns can spend money.

NUTS AND BOLTS

8.3

Contribution Limits in the 2008 Elections

The table below summarizes the Bipartisan Campaign Reform Act limitations on campaign contributions.[a] During the 2008 elections, individuals could contribute up to $2,300 to a candidate per election (donations to the primary and general elections count separately); $28,500 to a political party, $10,000 to a state party, $5,000 to a PAC, with an overall limit of about $100,000. Individuals can also make unlimited contributions to 527 organizations, which can use the money for voter mobilization efforts or issue advocacy as long as they do not directly support or oppose a particular candidate.

	INDIVIDUAL CANDIDATES	NATIONAL PARTY COMMITTEE	STATE PARTY	POLITICAL ACTION COMMITTEE	LIMIT ON TOTAL CONTRIBUTIONS
Individuals	$2,300	$28,500	$10,000	$5,000	$42,700 to candidates, $65,500 to organizations
Political action committees	$5,000	$15,000	$5,000	$5,000	—
Political party committees	$37,300 direct, $38,300 coordinated	—	—	—	—

SOURCE: Center for Responsive Politics, "Federal Campaign Finance Law: Contribution Limits," available at http://www.opensecrets.org/overview/limits.php.

[a] These details are taken from Michael Malbin, "Thinking about Reform," in *Life after Reform: When the Bipartisan Campaign Reform Act Meets Politics*, ed. Michael Malbin (Washington, DC: Rowman and Littlefield) and from the *More Soft Money Hard Law* site at http://www.moresoftmoney hardlaw.com, which is run by Robert Bauer, a Washington attorney and expert on campaign finance.

hard money Donations that are used to help elect or defeat a specific candidate.

soft money Contributions that can be used for voter mobilization or to promote a policy proposal or point of view as long as these efforts are not tied to supporting or opposing a particular candidate.

The most recent changes in campaign finance rules, which were passed as the Bipartisan Campaign Reform Act (BCRA), took effect after the 2002 elections, and have been modified by subsequent Supreme Court decisions.

The limits on campaign contributions in the BCRA—also known as the McCain–Feingold Act after its chief sponsors, John McCain (R-AZ) and Russell Feingold (D-WI)—vary depending on whether contributions are made by an individual or a group, and by the type of group (see Nuts and Bolts 8.3). Political action committees (PACs) are groups that aim to elect or defeat particular candidates or political parties. A company or organization can form a PAC and solicit contributions from employees or group members. As Nuts and Bolts 8.3 shows, the amount PACs can give to each candidate in an election is limited, but it's important to remember that these limits pertain to **hard money**, which means they restrict only the funds given directly to a candidate. PACs can also form 527 organizations, which can then accept unlimited amounts of **soft money,** which can be used to mobilize voters or advocate for a particular issue as long as these efforts are not tied to a specific candidate.

As discussed in Chapter 7, political party committees are entities within the Republican and Democratic parties. Both of the major parties have a national committee and a campaign committee in each house of Congress. Party committees are

NUTS AND BOLTS

8.4

Campaign Finance in Presidential Elections

During the presidential primary process, the federal government provides matching funds to candidates who raise $5,000 in each of at least twenty states in contributions of $250 or less. Once a candidate passes this fund-raising threshold, the government matches the first $250 of each subsequent contribution. In order to receive these funds, candidates must agree to an overall cap on the amount they will spend during the nomination process ($42.05 million in 2008), and to spending caps for each primary or caucus of 67 cents per voting-age person in the state.[a] If candidates forgo the federal matching funds, they can ignore these spending caps—a strategy followed by Democratic candidates Hillary Clinton and Barack Obama as well as all the major Republican candidates for the 2008 presidential nomination.

During the general election, presidential candidates can receive federal funding for their campaigns: $84.1 million in 2008, along with an extra $16.4 million for the nominating convention. Candidates do not have to accept this funding, although every major party nominee did so between 1976, when the law took effect and 2008, when Democrat Barack Obama became the first candidate to opt out. Funds are also given to minor political parties if their candidate received more than 5 percent of the vote in the previous election. Only one candidate has passed this threshold: John Anderson, who ran as an independent in 1980.

These federal funds are generated, in part, by money that taxpayers voluntarily allocate out of the taxes they pay to the federal government by checking off a particular box on their federal tax return form. In recent years, the amount of money an individual taxpayer can choose to put to this use is $3. (This donation does not reduce an individual's refund or increase their taxes.) In recent years, this voluntary check-off procedure has not allocated sufficient funds to pay for candidates' public funding, so the rest has been taken from general government revenues.[b]

[a] The spending caps are adjusted in each election for inflation.
[b] Campaign Finance Institute Task Force on Financing Presidential Nominations, "So the Voters May Choose: Reviving the Presidential Matching Fund System," April 2005, available at http://www.cfinst.org/president/pdf/VotersChoose.pdf.

Campaign Finance Regulations

Campaign finance regulations are complex and place real restrictions on what Americans can do to influence election outcomes. Suppose you are a wealthy person or the head of a corporation with deep pockets. Under current law, you and your corporation can only donate about $15,000 to a candidate's campaign; corporations have to form a political action committee to do so, and cannot pay for the contribution with business revenues. You can also form an organization called a 527 that can run campaign ads designed to help elect your preferred candidates, or donate to an existing 527. But if your goal is to help your favorite candidate directly, you face serious limits.

These limits on campaign spending arguably conflict with fundamental tenets of American democracy. The Bill of Rights states that Congress cannot abridge, "freedom of speech, or of the press; or the right of the people peaceably to assemble, and to petition the Government for a redress of grievances." One interpretation of the 1st Amendment is that people should be free to spend whatever they want on contesting elections—excluding bribes, threats, and other illegal actions, of course.

The principal argument for restricting campaign contributions is that money conveys political power. That is, if we let rich people spend as much as they wanted on electioneering, they could control election outcomes by giving their favored candidates enough money to win regardless of who ran against them. This argument implies that removing contribution restrictions would mean election outcomes driven purely by campaign spending rather than by voters' preferences.

▲ As this cartoon illustrates, many Americans believe there is too much money in politics and that a candidate can win only by raising more money than the opposition. The truth is more complicated: while a successful campaign requires substantial funds, particularly at the presidential level, many winning candidates have been significantly outspent.

As discussed elsewhere in this chapter, it is easy to overstate the value of money as a political asset. Even with unlimited funds, it is hard to get voters' attention—and harder still to change their minds. There are many examples of candidates who lost despite outspending their opponents. And there is no evidence in the corporate world that a company that spends enough on advertising can dominate its market and put its competitors out of business. People watch ads, but their purchasing decisions appear to be driven by other factors, such as their own budgets and preferences.

Even so, because money for ads is a necessary component of a political campaign, the possibility remains that a rich donor could change election outcomes by giving large sums to challengers in congressional elections. Many challengers never find out how voters would respond to their platforms because they lack the funds to prepare or air campaign ads. Though most poorly funded challengers would stand no chance of beating their incumbent opponents even with an unlimited advertising budget—some might.

Should unlimited contributions be allowed? In arriving at an opinion, consider these three questions:

1. Is the average underfunded candidate's problem simply a lack of money, or is their inability to attract campaign funds a symptom of a deeper problem, such as their lack of popularity with voters?

2. Should a candidate who faces a well-funded opponent be given public funds or some other advantage to counteract the opponent's spending?

3. If unlimited contributions are allowed, should candidates be made to disclose the identity of their contributors to ensure that voters can learn who is backing the candidates' ad campaigns? ■

limited in the amount of hard money they can give to a candidate's campaign, and in the amount they can spend on behalf of the candidate as a coordinated expenditure. However, a party committee can spend an unlimited amount in independent expenditures to elect a candidate or candidates. To be considered independent, expenditures must not be controlled, directed, or approved by any candidate's campaign. Independent expenditures can pay for campaign advertising, either to promote a party's candidate or to attack his opponent, but the candidate or candidates cannot be consulted on the specific messages.

Another type of group, called 527 organizations after the provision of the Internal Revenue Code that allows them, can raise unlimited soft money from individuals for voter mobilization and for issue advocacy, but these expenditures must not be coordinated with a candidate or party. Ads by 527s cannot advocate the election or defeat of a particular candidate or political party; any phrases in an ad that do so—and thereby change the ways the ad can be funded—are termed magic words.[91] Nuts and Bolts 8.4 describes the additional financial regulations for presidential elections,[92] and Chapter 9 looks more closely at PACs and 527s.

These complex campaign finance regulations reflect two simple truths. First, any limits on campaign activities involve balancing the right to free speech about candidates and issues with the idea that rich people or well-funded organizations should not be allowed to dominate what voters hear during the campaign. Striking this balance has created some arbitrary compromises: for example, BCRA originally prohibited unions and corporations from running ads within sixty days of an election, but did not apply the same restriction to 527s. This provision was stuck down by the Supreme Court. Second, an enormous amount of money is spent on American elections. Table 8.6 shows the amount raised by candidates, political parties, and others in 2004, 2006, and 2008. More than $2 billion was raised for the 2004 election, with 2006 not far behind and a big increase to over $5 billion in 2008. Moreover, campaign spending is concentrated among a relatively small number of organizations with sizable electioneering budgets. In each of the last several election cycles, the largest organizations have spent more than $50 million.

The principle concern about all this campaign cash is that the amount of money spent on a candidate's campaign might matter more than the candidate's qualifications or issue positions. That is, a candidate could get elected regardless of how good a job he would do, simply because he has more money than competing candidates to pay for campaign ads, polls, a large staff, and mobilization efforts. A second concern is that individuals and organizations that can afford to make large contributions (or to fund their own electioneering efforts) might be able to dictate election outcomes or, by funding campaigns, garner a disproportionate amount of influence over the subsequent behavior of elected officials.

Making Sense of Campaign Finance Campaign finance records are amazingly transparent. It is easy to find out which individuals or organizations gave money to a candidate, political party, or other organization.[93] Thus, if you are worried that a particular organization is using campaign contributions to influence elected officials, it is easy to find out which officeholders have received the group's donations. In fact, campaign finance records are so readily available that it is often easy to identify fraudulent organizations. During the 2008 primary campaign, a group called Californians for Obama solicited contributions for Democratic candidate Barack Obama via a Web site complete with descriptions of endorsements and fundraising events. However, none of these endorsements or events actually happened, and Obama never received funds from the organization.[94] After the scam became public, the organization's Web site was taken down, but no one was prosecuted,

TABLE 8.6   CANDIDATE, PARTY, AND INTEREST GROUP ELECTION FUND-RAISING, 2004–2008

Candidates and political parties raise and spend a great deal of money in their campaigns. How do these numbers help to explain the high reelection rates for members of Congress?

	2004	2006	2008
Presidential Candidates*			
Republican	(Bush) $367,228,801	—	(McCain) $360,000,000
Democrat	(Kerry) $328,479,245	—	(Obama) $639,000,000
Congressional Candidates			
House incumbents	$456,994,049	$198,137,808	$539,879,135
House challengers	$112,682,861	$27,680,023	$193,381,140
House open seat candidates	$127,084,712	$16,453,309	$150,938,532
Senate incumbents	$223,964,927	$190,492,258	$361,183,002
Senate challengers	$79,852,042	$44,307,619	$100,188,001
Senate open seat candidates	$239,197,856	$18,382,257	$59,328,470
Political Parties			
Republicans	$875,704,006	$598,127,532	$1,228,025,068
Democrats	$710,416,993	$493,311,599	$1,210,831,060
Interest Groups	$599,445,823	$294,934,997	$425,561,881
Totals	$4,121,051,315	$1,881,827,402	$5,268,316,289

*Presidential spending includes federal matching funds for the general election.

SOURCE: Data available as of November 6, 2008 compiled from the Center for Responsive Politics, http://www.opensecrets.org.

as the relatively small amount of money raised made it difficult to prove that the operation had broken the law.

When you look at campaign finance data, the first thing you will see is that a lot of money is spent trying to win elections. However, the raw data does not always tell the whole story. For example, the huge amounts make more sense when you consider what is at stake during each election cycle: control of the federal government, with a budget of about $3 trillion a year, and the power to start wars and regulate many aspects of citizens' lives. It's not surprising that so many organizations and individual donors invest in getting their preferred candidates elected. It is also important to keep in mind that the total amount spent on electioneering represents the sum of all the funding for the 435 House contests, thirty-three or thirty-four Senate races, and a presidential election. Moreover, one of the reasons why American campaigns are so expensive is the cost of television advertising. Nearly 80 percent of campaign expenditures are for television time. In major media markets, a thirty-second ad on a major television network can cost a candidate tens or even hundreds of thousands of dollars.[95] Given that even House campaigns may run hundreds of ads, and presidential campaigns run tens of thousands, it is easy to see why campaign costs pile up so quickly.

One way to put campaign expenses in context is to consider what major corporations pay in advertising expenses. In 2006, for example, Wal-Mart, the second-largest corporation in America, paid $1.6 billion for newspaper, magazine, and television ads.[96] Given this number, it's not surprising that American campaigns are so expensive. After all, Wal-Mart wants to contact average people and get their attention, just as candidates and other political organizations do. And corporations and candidates also use the same media, such as television ads, to deliver their messages to citizens.

More importantly, while money certainly matters in political campaigns, it cannot work miracles. Candidates for national political office need significant funding to have a realistic change of winning, but money does not ensure success. In 2004, thirty House and Senate candidates each spent more than $500,000 of their own money on their campaigns. Only one of these candidates was elected; half lost their primary races, and the rest either lost the general election or dropped out of the race.[97] In addition, many losing incumbents outspend their challengers. In the 2006 race, Pennsylvania senator Rick Santorum spent more than $23 million on his reelection campaign, versus the $17 million spent by his challenger, State Treasurer Robert Casey. Santorum lost by over 10 percentage points.

For political actors, such as parties, PACs, and 527s, it is also important to distinguish between the amount of money an organization collects and the amount it actually spends on electioneering. Consider EMILY's List, a political action committee that supports pro-choice, Democratic female candidates, which collected over $30 million during the 2004 election cycle.[98] Less than a third of this total was used for donations, advertising, phone banks, and other campaign activities. The rest was spent on the organization's payroll, office rent, and the direct mail operations that solicited the contributions.

Media coverage of campaign finance topics often takes an alarmist tone that is inconsistent with the actual content of the stories. One article reported on a 527 organization called Stop Her Now, whose main goal was to ensure the defeat of Senator Hillary Clinton in the 2008 presidential campaign—though she had not officially announced her candidacy at that time of the article.[99] In any case, the article reported that a single wealthy donor, Richard Collins, was the principle contributor to the 527, and had also donated money to a PAC founded by a potential Republican presidential candidate in 2008, former New York City mayor Rudolph Giuliani. However, if you read through to the end of the article, you'd find that Collins had donated only $80,000 to the 527 and $10,000 to the PAC. This is real money, but only a tiny fraction of the money needed to influence the outcome of an election.

There is also little evidence that campaign contributions alter legislators' behavior, or that contributors are rewarded with votes supporting their causes or favorable policies. Research suggests that most contributions are intended to help elect politicians whom contributors already like, with no expectation that these officials will do anything differently because they received a contribution.[100] Contributions may help contributors gain access, getting the contributor an appointment to present arguments to a politician or her staff. But people and organizations who contribute are already friendly with the politicians they support, and the politicians would likely hear their arguments in any case.

In sum, while money helps shape elections, claims about the power of large contributors and big spenders are typically overstated. Much of the campaign spending in American elections is not funded by large corporations or rich people but by average Americans making small donations. Moreover, no candidate or political organization has the ability to dominate the airwaves and crowd out other voices. In the end, citizens are exposed to campaign advertising from a variety of sources, and have to decide which arguments to take seriously—just like they do with all the other information they receive during the campaign.

SECTION SUMMARY

1. Strategizing for the next election begins the day after the last election, as would-be candidates, party leaders, and interest group staff begin to interpret the election results, and decide where to concentrate their efforts in the next contests.

2. Most incumbents work to secure their reelection throughout the entire election cycle. These efforts are known as the permanent campaign.

3. During the campaign, candidates try to build name recognition, mobilize supporters, and publicize their campaign platform. Other important tactics include emphasizing their knowledge of and sympathy to voters' concerns and going negative against their opponent.

4. Campaigns feature thousands of ads commissioned by candidates, parties, and interest groups. There is considerable evidence that campaign advertising shapes citizens' beliefs about candidates, as well as their propensity to participate in the political process.

5. Billions of dollars are spent on American elections. However, there is little evidence that money buys electoral success—or that the sum is excessive given the stakes and the cost of campaign advertising.

How Do Voters Decide?

All of the electoral activities we have considered so far are directed at citizens: making sure they are registered to vote, influencing their vote decisions, and getting them to the polls. In this section, we'll look more closely at how citizens respond. The first thing to understand is that the high level of attention, commitment, and energy exhibited by candidates and other campaign actors is not matched by ordinary citizens. We have seen throughout this chapter and others that politics is everywhere, and we have described elections as the primary mechanism that citizens have to control the federal government. Even so, the average American citizen is far from being an expert, enthusiastic participant in elections. Only a minority of citizens report high levels of interest in campaigns, many people know little about the candidates or the issues, and many people do not vote.[101]

THE DECISION TO VOTE

Politics is everywhere, but getting involved is your choice; voting and other forms of political participation are optional. Surprisingly, even a strong preference between two candidates may not drive a citizen to the polls because each citizen's vote is just one of many.[102] The only time a vote "counts," in the sense that it changes the outcome, is when the other votes are split evenly so that one vote breaks the tie. Although this scenario was used in the 2008 movie *Swing Vote*, in which Kevin Costner's character had to cast the deciding vote in a presidential election, it is highly unlikely in any real election. Thus, if a citizen's only motivation to vote is the possibility of single-handedly influencing the outcome, it is unlikely that she will experience any benefit of casting a ballot. Moreover, voting involves costs. Even if you don't attempt to learn about the candidates, you still have to get to the polls on Election Day. Thus, the **paradox of voting** is, why does anyone vote, given that voting is costly and the chances of affecting the outcome are small?

Among Americans, voter **turnout**—the percentage of registered voters who actually voted—in recent presidential elections has been between 65 and 70 percent, though the number shrinks below 50 percent if you include people who didn't vote because they opted not to register or were ineligible to register because of a felony conviction or other factors.[103] Turnout is significantly higher in presidential elections than in off-year elections and in primaries and caucuses. In the 2008 presidential primaries, for example, some states reported turnouts exceeding 30 percent, which were regarded as unusually high. For caucuses, which require individuals to spend several hours voting, turnout is generally only a few percentage points. (The turnout percentages reported in survey results are generally higher, as some people either misremember whether they voted or are unwilling to admit that they did not vote.)

Table 8.7 shows the considerable variation in turnout across different demographic groups. Turnout is higher for whites than nonwhites, and among older Americans compared to younger cohorts, and for college graduates relative to people with a high school education or less. Men and women, however, say they vote at roughly the same rate.

Table 8.8 shows how respondents explained their decisions about whether to go to the polls, and their reasons shed some light on these variations in turnout. People who vote regularly are more likely to see going to the polls as an obligation of citizenship, to feel guilty when they do not vote, and to believe that the election matters. These responses may help explain the paradox of voting. The first two reasons have to do with benefits an individual receives from the act of voting, rather than from the outcome of the election. The third reason suggests that if people believe that the election is important, this will be enough to drive them to the polls, even in the face of high odds that their votes will not change the outcome.

On the other hand, turnout is much lower among those who are angry with with the government, believe that government actions do not affect them, or think that voting will have no impact on government policy. Citizens who hold these beliefs are unlikely to care about the outcome of the election, and are unlikely to feel guilty for abstaining or see voting as an obligation.

These data demonstrate the importance of mobilization in elections. As we discussed earlier, many candidates for political office spend at least

TABLE 8.7	TURNOUT IN THE 2004 ELECTION		
	REGULAR VOTER	**VOTE SOMETIMES**	**RARE VOTER OR NONVOTER**
Total	35%	20%	45%
Men	36%	20%	44%
Women	34	21	45
White	37%	21%	42%
Black	31	23	45
Hispanic	24	16	60
18–29	22%	13%	65%
30–49	35	21	44
50–64	42	24	34
65+	41	22	37
College graduate	46%	22%	32%
Some college	38	20	43
High school or less	28	20	52

SOURCE: Pew Research Center, "Regular Voters, Intermittent Voters, and Those Who Don't," October 18, 2006, available at http://www.people-press.org/reports/pdf/292.pdf.

TABLE 8.8	HOW AMERICANS EXPLAIN THEIR DECISION TO VOTE		
	REGULAR VOTER	VOTE SOMETIMES	RARE VOTER OR NONVOTER
Percentage who agree . . .			
Duty as citizen to always vote	88%	80%	51%
This election matters more	83	74	67
Feel guilty when I don't vote	72	70	52
Angry with government	24	15	18
Issues in DC don't affect me	15	25	29
Voting doesn't change things	13	18	32
Difficult to get to polls	8	8	26
Lived in neighborhood less than one year	3	5	16

SOURCE: Pew Research Center, "Regular Voters, Intermittent Voters, and Those Who Don't," October 18, 2006, available at http://www.people-press.org/reports/pdf/292.pdf.

as much time trying to convince their supporters to vote as they do attempting to persuade others to become supporters in the first place. Because many Americans either do not vote or vote only sporadically, mobilization is a vital strategy for winning elections.

The reasons nonvoters abstain can also suggest what kinds of arguments might convince them to go to the polls. If a campaign can make nonvoters believe that the election matters and that it is their duty to vote, the chances that they will go to the polls on Election Day may increase. On the other hand, making people angry at Washington—perhaps with negative campaign ads—could lower turnout.

The turnout data provide another example of how the rules of the political process can shape outcomes. Among people who have moved within the last two years, turnout is extremely low, at least partly because moving often requires a citizen to re-register at his new address, and he must also locate his new polling place. Since passage of the Motor Voter Act in 1993, people have been able to register at the Department of Motor Vehicles at the same time that they renew their driver's license, which has increased turnout by a few percentage points.[104]

HOW DO PEOPLE VOTE?

The image of the average citizen as distracted and uninterested in the details of politics still holds, even among those who decide to vote. Some **issue voters** are highly interested in politics, collect all the information they can about the candidates, and vote based on this information.[105] However, most citizens do not invest the time and effort to become an issue voter because they are not interested enough in politics to want to spend their time that way, and they aren't so concerned with voting for the candidates that come closest to their preferences. Reliable information about candidates is also often difficult to find. While candidates, parties, and other organizations release a blizzard of endorsements, reports, and press releases throughout the campaign, much of this information may be difficult to interpret. It is a daunting task, even for the rare, highly motivated voter.

The combination of a lack of interest and a relatively complex task leads the majority of American voters to base their vote decision on easily interpretable pieces

issue voters People who are well-informed about their own policy preferences and knowledgeable about the candidates—and use all of this information when they decide how to vote.

▶ *In order to vote, citizens must be registered. Until recently, people who had either moved or turned eighteen just before an election often could not register in time to vote, but the 1993 Motor Voter Act lowered barriers to registration. The act required states to give citizens the opportunity to register to vote when applying for or renewing a driver's license.*

of information or **voting cues**.[106] Voters in American national elections use many kinds of cues including:

- *Incumbency*: Vote for the incumbent candidate.[107]
- *Partisanship*: Vote for the candidate whose party affiliation matches your own.[108]
- *Personal vote*: Vote for the incumbent if he or she has helped you get assistance from a government agency, or has helped your community benefit from desirable government projects.[109]
- *Personal characteristics*: Vote for the candidate whose personal characteristics (age, race, gender, ethnicity, or religious beliefs) match your own, or suggest you have common values, ideologies, or policy preferences.[110]
- *Retrospective evaluations*: Focus on a small set of votes the incumbent has cast while in office or other duties of the office that you care about, and vote for the incumbent if he or she has behaved the way you want in these circumstances.[111]
- *For (or against) the party in power*: Vote for a candidate based on a comparison of that candidate's party with an assessment of the party in power (the party that controls the presidency and has majorities in the House and Senate).[112]

Cues help voters shrink the complex question of whom they should support down to a more narrowly focused version that is easier to answer. They give people a low-cost way to cast what political scientist and campaign consultant Samuel Popkin called a **reasonable vote**—a vote that, more likely than not, is consistent with the voter's true preference between candidates.[113] Studies have found that citizens who use cues and are politically well-informed are more likely to cast a reasonable vote compared to those who also use cues but are otherwise relatively politically ignorant. In essence, information helps people to select the right cue.[114]

Consider the partisanship cue. As discussed earlier, Republican and Democratic candidates usually hold different positions on many important issues. As a result, a candidate's party affiliation tells a voter something about how the candidate is likely to behave if elected. The signal is not foolproof: a Republican voter who is pro-gay rights might use a partisan cue to vote for George Bush because he was the Republican nominee, even though more investigation would reveal that Bush's position on gay rights is the opposite of his own. Even so, because partisan cues are so easy to employ, they are a favorite voting strategy in American elections; as noted in Chapter 7, many voters use these cues when voting for president. Partisan cues also

voting cues Pieces of information about a candidate that are readily available, easy to interpret, and lead a citizen to decide to vote for a particular candidate.

reasonable vote A vote that is likely to be consistent with the voter's true preference about the candidates.

play a strong role in congressional elections, and the importance of this cue seems to have increased in recent elections.[115]

A candidate's personal characteristics also play a crucial role in vote decisions. As we saw in Chapter 5, information about race, ethnicity, gender, religion, or age provides a fairly solid basis for predictions about some of a person's ideological beliefs. Thus, when voters choose a candidate who "looks like them," they are not necessarily behaving irrationally. Rather, they may be using a cue that suggests they share the candidate's priorities. Exit polls in the 2008 election suggested that Americans with strong religious beliefs were more likely to vote for the McCain–Palin ticket, partly because of Sarah Palin's membership in a charismatic Christian church.

Cues can also involve retrospective evaluations. A citizen can vote for or against a House member or senator based on how that person voted on a specific issue—even a single vote—or on judgments about an incumbent's honesty or qualifications, willingness to do casework to help constituents, or success at attracting government spending to the constituents' area. While none of these factors tell the whole story about an incumbent's performance, each provides a rationale for deciding whether an incumbent deserves another term.[116] Similarly, a voter might use the state of the economy to decide whether the president deserves another term in office—or focus on America's success or failure in recent foreign affairs to judge presidential performance. In fact, economic conditions like the rates of growth, inflation, and unemployment are very good predictors of how many people will vote for a president running for reelection.[117]

Table 8.9, which is based on surveys of voters in 1990s congressional elections, gives examples of how these incumbent-based cues shape vote decisions. As you see, people were more likely to vote for a House or a Senate incumbent if they believed

---

TABLE 8.9 **VOTE DECISIONS IN CONGRESSIONAL ELECTIONS: CANDIDATE CUES**

Americans are much more likely to vote for candidates who keep in touch, respond to contacts, vote as they prefer, and are expected to do a good job on important problems. If you were a member of Congress who wanted to stay in office, what sorts of actions would you take in order to secure reelection?

QUESTION	RESPONSE	PERCENT VOTING FOR INCUMBENT	
		HOUSE	SENATE
How good a job does the incumbent do keeping in touch with people?	Very good	88%	87%
	Very poor	24	21
Level of satisfaction with incumbent's response to voter-initiated contact?	Very satisfied	90%	90%
	Not at all satisfied	13	26
Agreed or disagreed with incumbent's vote on particular bill?	Agreed	93%	—
	Disagreed	43	—
Which candidate would do a better job on the most important problem?	Incumbent	97%	—
	Challenger	11	—

Note: Latter questions were not asked in Senate survey.

SOURCE: Gary Jacobson, *The Politics of Congressional Elections*, 6th ed. (New York: Pearson Longman, 2004), Table 5.11.

Stereotyping

For the most part, American voters are cue-takers: rather than becoming well-informed about who the candidates are and what they are likely to do if elected, voters rely on cues, readily available, easily interpretable pieces of information that help them to decide which candidate is worth supporting. Voters use cues when they choose a particular candidate just because that person's party affiliation matches their own party identification, or when they vote for a candidate on the basis of gender or some other descriptive factor. It makes sense that voters use cues; it would be much more surprising if they did not—especially since most people regularly use many similar kinds of cues during ordinary interactions. Many political psychologists describe people as motivated tacticians, who "evaluate potential officeholders in much the same manner as they apprise the other people they encounter in their daily lives."[a]

How do motivated tacticians behave? During casual, everyday interactions, they rely on stereotypes, beliefs that link a person's visible characteristics or actions to a judgment about their beliefs, ideologies, or other attributes. Stereotypes can be based on almost anything—how someone dresses; what car a person drives; age, gender, or race; preference for a Mac or a PC; or whether the person is a vegetarian, vegan, or meat eater.

While stereotypes represent a simplification of the world, and may lead to inaccurate judgments, people are driven to use them because they need to form judgments about

▲ What sort of cues might John McCain have hoped voters would take from images of his service in Vietnam?

others quickly and with a minimum investment of effort. Walter Lippman, one of the first scholars to study public opinion, argued the point three generations ago:

> [M]odern life is hurried and multifarious, above all physical distance separates men who are often in vital contact with each other, such as employer and employee, officials and voter. There is neither time nor opportunity for intimate acquaintance. Instead we notice a

trait which marks a well-known type, and fill in the rest of the picture by means of the stereotypes we carry about in our heads. He is an agitator. That much we notice, or are told. Well, an agitator is this sort of person, and so *he* is this sort of person. He is an intellectual. He is a plutocrat. He is a foreigner. He is a "Southern European." He is from Back Bay. He is a Harvard Man. How different from the statement: he is a Yale Man. He is a regular fellow. He is a West Pointer. He is an old army sergeant. He is a Greenwich Villager: what don't we know about him, then, and about her?[b]

Some scholars argue that voters use a wider set of candidates' perceived personal characteristics as cues for their vote decisions. One version of this kind of judgment is solicited in some recent polls with the question, "Which candidate would you like to have a beer or a cup of coffee with?" In the 2004 presidential contest, citizens who answered this question favored George Bush over John Kerry, 56 percent to 44 percent.[c] While this question may appear to have little to do with what elections are supposed to be about—choosing people to determine what government does—it expresses a powerful truth about how average Americans view elections and vote decisions. Their decisions are made quickly, based on relatively little information, and they reflect general judgments about candidates rather than a detailed appreciation of what they are likely to do in office. ■

that the incumbent had done a good job keeping in touch with constituents, had responded well to requests for casework, and had voted (or would vote) in line with the respondent's preferences.

While cues are an important determinant of vote decisions, some Americans also look to the backgrounds and life experiences of the candidates. Table 8.10 offers some details on what these voters are looking for. Military service is an asset, particularly for Republicans, as is being a Christian. People from both parties like political experience and business experience. On the other side, Americans tend not to want a candidate who is an atheist, has never held an elected office, is over seventy, is a Muslim, or has several other features perceived by some as problematic.

These data are a reminder that even though the average American spends little effort to learn about the candidates in congressional or even presidential elections, information about the candidates still matters to voters. If people happen to learn about a candidate's life experiences or beliefs from media coverage or an opponent's ads, this information can have an enormous impact on their willingness to support the candidate.

TABLE 8.10 **PREFERRED CANDIDATE TRAITS**

When Americans evaluate candidates, they want military experience, Christian beliefs, and political experience. Many say they don't want atheists, Muslims, gays, or people who have had affairs or used drugs in the past. Do these preferences help to explain the success or failure of candidates in the 2008 presidential primaries?

More likely to support a candidate who . . .

	TOTAL	REPUBLICAN	DEMOCRAT	INDEPENDENT
Served in the military	48%	58%	38%	49%
Is Christian	39	61	32	31
Long-time DC politician	35	40	39	31
Former business executive	28	38	21	28
Attended prestigious university	22	24	28	15
Is in their 40s	18	14	24	15
Has been a minister	15	21	14	14
Is a woman	13	8	21	9
Is black	7	4	13	5
Never held elective office	7	5	5	9

Less likely to support a candidate who . . .

	TOTAL	REPUBLICAN	DEMOCRAT	INDEPENDENT
Does not believe in God	63%	86%	56%	57%
Never held elective office	56	64	59	50
Is in their 70s	48	42	60	43
Is Muslim	46	66	39	38
Is homosexual	46	64	37	42
Used drugs in the past	45	54	45	39
Had extramarital affair	39	62	25	36
Has been a minister	25	22	28	28
Smokes cigarettes	18	29	14	13
Long-time elected official	15	18	10	19
Is Hispanic	14	16	17	12
Former business executive	13	10	16	13
Is a woman	11	21	5	7

Note: Traits with 5 percent or fewer of the public saying "more likely to support" are not shown. Traits with 10 percent or fewer of the public saying "less likely to support" are not shown.

SOURCE: Pew Research Center, "Republicans Lag in Engagement and Enthusiasm for Candidates," February 23, 2007, available at http://people-press.org/reports/pdf/307.pdf.

NORMAL AND NATIONALIZED ELECTIONS

All of these strategies for making vote decisions are used to some extent in every election. However, in normal elections, when congressional reelection rates are high and the seat shift between the parties is small, voters generally use cues that focus on the candidates themselves, such as incumbency, partisanship, a personal connection to a candidate, the candidate's personal characteristics, or retrospective evaluations. This behavior is consistent with what Tip O'Neill, Speaker of the House from 1977 to 1987, was talking about when he said that "all politics is local," meaning that congressional elections are independent, local contests in which a candidates chances of winning depend on what voters think of the candidate in particular—not their evaluations of the president, Congress, or national issues. It also explains why electoral **coattails** are typically very weak in American elections, and why so many Americans cast **split tickets** rather than **straight tickets**. In the main, vote decisions in presidential and congressional elections are made independently of each other.

Nationalized elections occur when a large number of voters switch to using the anti-party in power cue, which leads them to vote against candidates from the president's party. Typically this kind of shift happens when many voters became highly concerned about a national issue such as the state of the economy or an international conflict. In the 1974 elections, voters focused on economic worries, and on the resignation of President Richard Nixon in connection with the Watergate scandal. In 1980, the crucial issue for many voters was the poor state of the economy. Economic concerns were salient again in 1994, along with disapproval of President Clinton and a recent tax increase. And in 2006, surveys showed that many voters rated the war in Iraq as the most important issue, and they generally disapproved of how the war was being conducted.[118]

National-level concerns such as these cause citizens to lower their evaluations of the president and of Congress, and to use different cues to guide their voting decisions.[119] Specifically, many voters look for someone to blame, focusing on members of Congress from the party in power. They then vote against these members, either as a protest vote, because they disapprove of their performance, or because they want to put different individuals in charge in the hopes that conditions will improve. Whether viewed in terms of voting against one party's incumbents or for the other party's challengers, these motivations lead to the same voting behavior; the difference is a matter of voters' attitudes and emphases. Recent nationalized elections have generally brought losses for the party in power, but this is not always the case. In 1964, for example, Democratic president Lyndon Johnson won reelection in a landslide over Republican Barry Goldwater, and congressional Democrats in both houses substantially increased their majorities.

As we have seen throughout this chapter, nationalized elections like the one in 2006 can produce sharp shifts in Washington, and exit polls showed that all politics was *not* local in 2006: the congressional shift toward the Democratic Party was born out of national-level issues. Many voters strongly opposed the war in Iraq, believed that Congress was bedeviled by ethical lapses and corruption, and disapproved of President Bush's performance in office.[120] As Table 8.11 shows, voters who had these concerns were much more likely to vote for Democratic candidates.

Nationalized elections are rare because most of the time, relatively few citizens are highly concerned about national issues or hold strong opinions of the president, Congress, or the overall state of the nation. Congressional incumbents also work hard to focus attention on the good things they have done for their constituents. And it is important to remember that even in nationalized elections, some voters still use the incumbent-centered cues described earlier. In a nationalized election,

coattails The idea that a popular president can generate additional support for candidates affiliated with his party. Coattails are weak or nonexistent in most American elections.

split ticket A ballot on which a voter selects candidates from more than one political party.

straight tickets A ballot on which a voter selects candidates from only one political party.

TABLE 8.11 ISSUES AND VOTING IN THE 2006 MIDTERM ELECTIONS

In the 2006 election, many Americans appear to have based their votes on the war in Iraq, congressional scandals, the state of the economy, and evaluations of President Bush. Do these findings suggest that Democratic candidates would be favored in the 2008 election? Was this expectation borne out?

ISSUE	OPINION	VOTE IN HOUSE RACE	
		DEMOCRAT	REPUBLICAN
War in Iraq	Approve	18%	81%
	Disapprove	80	18
How GOP leaders handled page scandal	Approve	26%	73%
	Disapprove	73	25
State of economy	Excellent or Good	28%	70%
	Not Good or Poor	77	21
President George W. Bush	Approve	14%	84%
	Disapprove	82	16

SOURCE: CNN.com, 2006 Exit Poll, November 7, 2006, available at http://www.cnn.com/ELECTION/2006/pages/results/states/US/H/00/epolls.0.html.

voters don't suddenly become better informed about politics than they are the rest of the time. Rather, some of them just switch to a different set of voting cues depending on the circumstances of the election.

SECTION SUMMARY

1. The decision to vote is driven by a citizen's sense of obligation; the closeness of the election and a citizen's preferences between the candidates have relatively little to do with the decision.
2. Very few people are issue voters who are well-informed about candidates, issues, and the election. The average voter uses a series of simple but powerful cues to make vote decisions.
3. During normal elections, voters tend to use cues that focus attention on individual candidates and their performance in office.
4. During nationalized elections, many voters focus on the party in power, leading them to vote against these candidates because of national-level issues such as a poor economy, a federal tax increase, or an international conflict.

Election 2008

The 2008 elections were a substantial win for Democrats at all levels. Democrat Barack Obama won the presidency with 365 electoral votes (270 needed to win) and over 52 percent of the popular vote. Democrats gained at least seven seats in the Senate

▲ *The forty-fourth American president-elect, Barack Obama, with vice president-elect, Joe Biden, waves to a crowd of celebrating supporters on November 4, 2008.*

and nineteen in the House (at publication several close 2008 races were unresolved). It is hard to find much good news in these results for the Republican Party or its officeholders.

Some characteristics of the 2008 contest distinguished it not only from recent elections, but from all previous American elections. For the first time, an African American was elected president. The election also included the first female candidate to have a significant chance of winning a major party's nomination for the presidency, Democrat Hillary Clinton, and only the second female vice presidential nominee, Alaska governor Sarah Palin. It was the first presidential race in half a century in which there was no incumbent president or vice president on the ballot. Obama was the first presidential candidate to decline federal funds for the general election campaign. For the first time since the 2000 election, the wars in Iraq and Afghanistan were not central issues. And, as the campaign unfolded, the American economy was faltering due to high energy prices, the failure of several large financial firms, the collapse of house prices, and banks' increasing unwillingness to lend money, even to well-established, secure firms.

As economic growth ground to a halt during the campaign, Americans began to evaluate candidates for the presidency and for Congress based on their proposals for handling this crisis. This focus favored Democratic candidates—as we discuss throughout the text, most Americans view Democrats as relatively more likely to favor government intervention in the economy and see Republicans as more inclined to oppose such efforts. Democrats also benefited from the fact that unpopular Republican president George Bush was in charge during the economic meltdown, which led some voters to attribute responsibility for the crisis to Republican officeholders and candidates. As a result, many Democratic candidates, including Obama, were able to turn the election into a referendum on the economic policies of the Bush administration by arguing that electing John McCain and other Republicans would bring "more of the same."

The wars in Afghanistan and Iraq did not loom large in the campaign: during the month prior to the election, fewer than 10 percent of the population cited the wars as the most important issue facing the country. This shift in public opinion reflected the decline in American casualties and insurgent attacks that began in 2007 and continued into 2008. The War on Terror and the need to prevent future attacks had faded from the headlines. Thus, as the election neared, they were no longer top considerations for the average voter—but the economy was.

Republican candidates, including McCain and Palin, worked to shift public attention away from the economy to issues that they believed would help their candidacy. McCain and Palin argued that Obama was inexperienced, that he associated with a known terrorist (a reference to William Ayers, a former member of the 1960s-era radical Weather Underground Organization, now a professor, who served with Obama on a foundation board and held a fund-raiser for Obama's first campaign), and that Obama would redistribute wealth away from middle- and upper-class people to fund new government programs for the poor. These arguments might have worked in the absence of an economic crisis, or if the Iraq war and terrorist attacks had remained central concerns. But the daily headlines about corporate bankruptcies, rising foreclosure rates, and a sagging stock market—coupled with Obama's steady performance during debates and his campaign's focus on the need for change—didn't allow McCain's and Palin's arguments to gain much traction. In addition, McCain's choice of Palin as his running mate became a liability after she committed several well-publicized gaffes that called into question her readiness for national office, while Barack Obama's choice of Delaware senator Joe Biden was generally considered a reasonable one.

The outcome of the 2008 contest was also shaped by the rules and procedures governing the process. One explanation for Republican losses in the House and Senate was that a disproportionate number of Republican officeholders retired rather than facing two more years in the minority, which gave Democrats opportunities to pick up open seats. Republicans also had to defend more Senate seats than their Democratic counterparts: in 2008, twenty-three Senate seats held by Republicans were up for reelection, versus only twelve for Democrats. Of course, given the propensity for voters to blame President Bush and the Republicans for the poor state of the American economy in 2008, Republicans faced an uphill fight from the start. Nevertheless, these structural factors certainly increased their troubles.

In the presidential nomination contests, Barack Obama benefited from the large number of Democratic caucuses. Because turnout for caucuses is extremely low, they benefit candidates like Obama who have a strong get-out-the-vote operation and many enthusiastic volunteers. In fact, were it not for Obama's performance in the caucuses, Senator Hillary Clinton would have won the Democratic nomination, as she tended to outperform Obama in states that held primary elections. On the Republican side, many state primaries allocated delegates using a winner-take-all rule. Mitt Romney, who dropped out of the contest after John McCain amassed an insurmountable delegate lead, noted that if the delegates had been awarded proportionally, he would have had more delegates than McCain.

In the general election, Obama's get-out-the-vote operation was far more elaborate than McCain's, which helped Obama win swing states such as Ohio, Indiana, and Pennsylvania. The Obama campaign did all the usual things, from knocking on doors to organizing shuttle vans to drive voters to the polls, but their operation was one of the largest and most effective ever seen in a presidential race. The Obama campaign was also notable for its extensive use of the Internet for communication and fund-raising, and the McCain campaign was unable to match these efforts.

There were real differences between Republican and Democratic candidates in 2008 on issues such as how to address economic problems, how to reform health care, and what to do in Iraq. Exit poll data showed that a clear majority of voters cited the economy as the most important issue, and that Obama was the favorite among people who wanted government action to address economic problems. McCain, in contrast, won more support from citizens who believed that less government involvement would help solve economic woes, as well as those who ranked national security as their primary concern.

Despite Obama's victory and the Democrats' gains in Congress, Obama probably will not be able to enact all the new policies he proposed in four years' time. For one thing, while the Democrats managed to significantly increase their majorities in both the House and the Senate, they still lack the sixty votes required to prevent filibusters and bring proposals to a vote in the Senate. There is also considerable disagreement among Democratic senators and House members about what the party's priorities should be. Fiscal constraints, including a large budget deficit, the costs of bailing out the banking system, and the wars in Iraq and Afghanistan, will limit new spending. Moreover, despite Americans' demands for action on the economy and in other areas, it is unclear whether there is broad public support for large, new government programs. These political and fiscal limits do not make action impossible—but they suggest that we should expect incremental rather than radical reforms.

POLITICAL PROCESS MATTERS

☑ Democratic and Republican candidates, from Obama and McCain on down, offered competing visions of what the federal government should do about many issues including the economy, the war in Iraq, health care reform, energy policy, and many others. It mattered who won the elections.

Elections Matter

It is easy to complain about American elections. Citizens are not experts about public policy. They often know little about the candidates running for office. Candidates sensationalize, attack, and dissemble, rather than giving details about who they are and what they would do if elected. Billions of dollars are spent electing members of Congress and the president. Even so, there are clear, systematic differences between Democratic and Republican candidates that translate into different government policies depending on who holds office. Moreover, the criteria that average Americans use to make vote decisions reflect these differences. People don't know everything about politics or about elections, but their votes are, by and large, reasonable.

Moreover, many examples of seemingly strange behavior pertaining to American elections make a lot more sense once you look at them closely. It makes sense that so few Americans are issue voters—and that many people decide to abstain. Both behaviors result from a lack of interest in politics and the almost nonexistant impact of each vote on the election outcome. For the same reasons, it makes sense that candidates trying to get the attention of distracted voters tend to emphasize sensationalism over sober discussion of policies. The outcome of the election, who wins and who loses, is the result of all these individual-level choices added together. In that sense, election outcomes reflect the preferences of the American people.

American elections are not perfect, but it is impossible to say that they are irrelevant. By determining who holds political office, elections determine what government does. The 2006 midterm election gave voters a clear choice: shift congressional power to the Democrats or leave it in the hands of Republicans, the party in power. The 2008 elections presented a choice between sustaining the shift toward the Democrats or returning the Republicans to power. You might prefer that voters were offered different choices, a detailed menu of policy options for Iraq and other questions. Even so, there is no ignoring the fact that voters faced an important choice, and that the results of the election had real policy consequences.

The weeks after the 2006 midterm elections illustrate this point. As a result of the switch in party control in Congress, Representative Nancy Pelosi of California became the first woman Speaker of the House and third in the line of succession to the presidency. Secretary of Defense Donald Rumsfeld, who had often been criticized for his direction of the war in Iraq, resigned the day after the election. The Secretary of the Treasury, Henry Paulson, offered new talks with congressional Democrats on Social Security reform. President Bush showed new interest in changing the nation's aims and strategy in Iraq, leading to the "troop surge" of 2007.

The same is true for the 2008 election, which strengthened the Democrats' hold on the House and Senate and transferred the presidency to Democrat Barack Obama. Because Obama won, U.S. troops will probably leave Iraq sooner than they would have under a McCain presidency. Financial firms will likely face new regulations. There may also be significant changes in energy and education policy, although these shifts hinge on Obama's ability to convince Republicans and Democrats in Congress to support his proposals. Finally, Obama's historical and cultural significance as the first African American president may help improve perceptions of America held by people in other countries. In Congress, Democrats gained seats in both the House and Senate, and while there is no guarantee that the caucuses will be able to find consensus on important issues, these increased majorities make it more likely that Democrats will get at least some of what they want. In sum, elections matter. The choices candidates offer, and how citizens assess those choices and make vote decisions, have important policy consequences.

SECTION SUMMARY

1. Elections matter because candidates from the Republican and Democratic parties stand for different things and behave differently in office.

2. Most citizens are not policy experts, but they cast reasonable votes.

3. Elections also create a way for citizens to hold elected officials accountable for their behavior in office.

4. Many of the seemingly irrational features of American elections are the product of sensible behavior by candidates, citizens, and other political actors.

Conclusion

Candidates in American national elections compete for different offices across the country using a variety of rules that determine who can run for office, who can vote, and how ballots are counted and winners determined. Election outcomes are shaped by who runs for office and how they campaign, who decides to vote and how they decide whom to support, but also by the rules that govern electoral competition.

What happened to John McCain in 2008? His strong stand in favor of the Iraq War was damaging in 2007, as public opinion turned sharply against American involvement—but probably helped his candidacy as support for the war began to increase again in late 2007 and early 2008. McCain also benefited from rules in crucial states that allowed independents and registered Democrats to cross party lines and vote in the Republican primary, and winner-take-all rules in some states that gave him a large majority of delegates despite winning less than 50 percent of the Republican primary vote.

Moreover, while McCain had some obvious drawbacks as a candidate—his age and lack of connection to the evangelical community that makes up a large portion of Republican primary voters—other candidates had even greater liabilities. Mitt Romney was handicapped among some voters by his Mormon religious beliefs and the perception that he had shifted positions on many issues to appeal to conservatives; Rudy Giuliani was seen as too politically moderate and had been through two complicated divorces. In the end, while McCain was not the perfect candidate for many Republicans, he was considered the best one in the race.

None of McCain's strengths helped him much in the general election. His steadfast support for the troop surge in Iraq was of little consequence given that the economy had displaced the war as most voters' top concern by the time of the election. Moreover, McCain's appeals to conservative Republicans during the primaries and the Republican Convention, symbolized by his selection of Alaska governor Sarah Palin for vice president, reduced his chances of winning support from independents and moderate Democrats—support that he needed to win the general election. Finally, McCain was also the victim of bad luck. The economic crisis that began in September 2008 brought about the swift collapse of the stock market and several major financial firms. These events gave voters two reasons to vote

Democratic: to punish Republicans for President Bush's economic policies, and to demand government intervention to mitigate the impact of the economic crisis. This second reason was bolstered by the economic measures that Obama and many other Democrats were proposing. McCain might well have lost even if the American economy had remained strong, but the economic meltdown destroyed any chance he had of winning the election.

CRITICAL THINKING

1. Can American elections be described as debates over government policy, given that the average voter knows so little about what government is doing or could do? Explain your answer.
2. Using cues to make vote decisions lowers the cost of voting, in terms of the time and effort involved in a voter's decision. Under what conditions will cues help a voter make the right choice in an election, defined as the same choice that would result from having complete information about the candidates? Under what conditions will cues lead a voter to make the wrong choice?
3. What kinds of candidates are helped by limits on campaign contributions by individuals and organizations such as PACs? What kinds of candidates do these restrictions hurt? Why do such limits affect these types of candidates differently?

KEY TERMS

absentee ballot (p. 263)
attack ads (p. 281)
campaign platform (p. 276)
caucus (political) (p. 267)
challenger (p. 261)
closed primary (p. 262)
coattails (p. 298)
delegates (p. 267)
election cycle (p. 272)
electoral college (p. 270)
electoral vote (p. 258)
Federal Election Commission (p. 285)
frontloading (p. 269)
general election (p. 262)
GOTV (p. 276)
ground game (p. 276)
hard money (p. 286)
incumbent (p. 261)
issue voters (p. 293)
majority voting (p. 265)
mobilization (p. 276)
money primary (p. 274)
nationalized election (p. 260)
nomination (p. 262)
normal election (p. 259)

open primary (p. 262)
open seat (p. 273)
opposition research (p. 280)
paradox of voting (p. 292)
party ratio (p. 259)
permanent campaign (p. 273)
phone banks (p. 276)
plurality voting (p. 265)
political business cycle (p. 274)
popular vote (p. 258)
primary (p. 267)
proportional allocation (p. 268)
push polling (p. 276)
reasonable vote (p. 294)
regional primaries (p. 269)
retail politics (p. 276)
retrospective evaluation (p. 261)
runoff election (p. 265)
seat shift (p. 259)
soft money (p. 286)
split ticket (p. 298)
straight ticket (p. 298)
superdelegates (p. 269)
swing states (p. 270)
talent primary (p. 274)
turnout (p. 292)
undervote (p. 266)
voting cues (p. 294)
wholesale politics (p. 275)
winner-take-all (p. 268)

SUGGESTED READING

Abramson, Paul, John Aldrich, and David Rohde. *Change and Continuity in the 2004 and 2006 Elections*. Washington, DC: CQ Press, 2007.

Bartels, Larry. *Presidential Primaries and the Dynamics of Public Choice*. Princeton, NJ: Princeton University Press, 1988.

Cramer, Richard Ben. *What It Takes: The Way to the White House*. New York: Vintage, 1993.

Donovan, Todd, and Shaun Bowler. *Reforming the Republic: Democratic Institutions for the New America*. New York: Pearson, 2007.

Fiorina, Morris P. *Retrospective Voting in American National Elections*. New Haven, CT: Yale University Press, 1981.

Jacobson, Gary. *The Politics of Congressional Elections,* 6th ed. New York: Pearson Longman, 2004.

Key, V. O. *The Responsible Electorate.* New York: Vintage, 1966.

Museum of the Moving Image, "The Living Room Candidate: Presidential Campaign Commercials, 1952–2004," online exhibit at http://livingroomcandidate.movingimage.us.

Niemi, Richard G., and Herbert F. Weisberg. *Controversies in Voting Behavior,* 4th ed. Washington, DC: CQ Press, 2001.

Popkin, Samuel. *The Reasoning Voter.* Chicago: University of Chicago Press, 1991.

9

INTEREST GROUPS

An unwritten law of Washington politics is that "all publicity is good publicity." It seems this rule does not apply, however, to being described on the cover of *Time* magazine as "the man who bought Washington." The man who earned that dubious distinction was Jack Abramoff, a longtime Washington lobbyist. Abramoff attracted a wide range of clients, from Indian tribes to African dictators to Microsoft and other corporations, all of whom hired Abramoff and his firm to argue for the policy and regulatory changes they favored before elected officials and bureaucrats.[1]

Though lobbying itself is legal, Abramoff's efforts to sway legislators on his clients' behalf went beyond the legal means of seeking influence, including offers of "golf junkets, meals at his restaurant, seats at sporting events, and, in some cases, old-fashioned cash."[2] The photograph shows Abramoff (left) on a golf outing in Scotland with his guests: conservative political activist Ralph Reed (on Abramoff's left, holding a club); former chief of staff of the General Services Administration, David Savafian; and Representative Bob Ney (R-OH, right), then-chair of the House Administration Committee. Abramoff was convicted in 2006 of conspiracy, fraud, and tax evasion; Ney, Savafian, and several congressional aides and high-level bureaucrats were also convicted of accepting Abramoff's bribes or making false statements about their relationship with him.[3] The Abramoff scandal is not the only recent example of lobbying misdeeds. In 2006, Representative Randy "Duke" Cunningham (R-CA) was convicted of taking $2.4 million in bribes from lobbyists in return for steering government contracts to their defense industry clients.[4]

These episodes come as no surprise to most Americans. A 2006 study found that three-quarters of respondents believed that interest groups and lobbyists had too much influence in Washington.[5] An even higher percentage, 82 percent, believed that lobbyists often bribe members of Congress. And while the survey found broad support for tighter lobbying regulations, a majority of respondents believed that such regulations would have little or no effect.

The large number and wide variety of interest groups in America exemplify the idea that politics is everywhere. Many Americans are dues-paying members of interest groups, such as the American Civil Liberties Union, the National Rifle Association, or the American Association of Retired Persons. And many of the clubs, groups, and organizations to which Americans belong have little-known yet extensive lobbying arms. These groups' work reflects the conflictual nature of politics, as

TIME

THE
MAN WHO
BOUGHT
WASHINGTON

Jack Abramoff took influence
peddling to new heights—and
depths. Now he's ready to tell all.
A TIME investigation of the lobbyist
who's turning Washington inside out

BY KAREN TUMULTY

▲ *When the scandals surrounding Jack Abramoff came to light, many Americans considered him a typical lobbyist who used gifts, bribes, and favors to get advantageous policy decisions from elected officials and bureaucrats. Abramoff's actions were illegal, but the question remains: are his tactics common in Washington, or was he a rare exception?*

interest groups Organizations of people who share common political interests and aim to influence public policy by electioneering and lobbying.

lobbying Efforts to influence public policy through contact with public officials on behalf of an interest group.

groups seek to persuade elected officials and bureaucrats to change to government policy—often by sidelining other competing demands to give the group what it wants.

The chapter will also focus on a surprising fact about interest groups: despite the proliferation of these organizations in America, some large groups of like-minded Americans have no identifiable interest group fighting for their policy concerns. Where, for example, are the groups that lobby for what college students want? This fact raises an important question: why do people's shared goals and interests lead them to form interest groups in some cases but not others?

To answer this question, we will draw on the book's third theme: political process matters. We will focus on how interest groups are organized, how they decide which issues to lobby, and the ways they influence government policy. Examining these factors will help us to assess how much influence these groups really have in Washington and where they get their power—as well as whether Jack Abramoff, Bob Ney, and Randy Cunningham are exceptional cases or examples of how business is usually done in Washington.

The Interest Group Universe

Interest groups are organizations that seek to influence government policy by helping to elect candidates who support their policy goals and by **lobbying** elected officials and bureaucrats. In its most basic form, lobbying involves persuasion—using reports, protests, informal meetings, or other techniques to convince an elected official or bureaucrat to help enact a law, craft a regulation, or do something else that a group wants. The members of an interest group can be individual citizens, local governments, businesses, foundations or nonprofit organizations, churches, or virtually any other entity. An interest group's employees or members may lobby on the group's behalf, or a group may hire a lobbyist or lobbying firm to do the work for them.

Interest groups and political parties share the goal of changing what government does, but there are three critical differences between these organizations. First, political parties focus on running candidates for office and coordinating the activities of elected officials. While interest groups also electioneer, they do not run candidates. Second, the major political parties hold certain legal advantages over even the largest interest groups when it comes to influencing policy, such as guaranteed positions on electoral ballots. Third, the elected members of political parties have a direct influence over government activity: they propose, debate, and vote on policies. Interest groups have, at best, an indirect influence: they must either persuade elected officials to support their point of view or help elect candidates who already share their goals.

Interest groups are a fundamental feature of democracy. The federal government has the power to set policies that affect the lives of all Americans, and Americans in turn have a wide variety of preferences as to how this power should be used. As James Madison wrote, "the urge to differ is universal."[7] Some Americans join interest groups with the goal of making their particular preferences a reality.

Sometimes interest groups are primarily political organizations. One such group is Public Citizen, which carries out research projects, lobbies legislators and bureaucrats, and tries to rally public opinion on a wide range of environmental, health, and energy issues. More commonly, though, lobbying is only one part of what an organization does. The National Rifle Association (NRA) is a group that

Interest Groups in Other Nations

Just as in America, people all over the world have ideas about what they would like government to do, and they organize to shape policies in line with their preferences, making interest groups a fundamental component of democracy.[a] Studies have even found that the longer a country has been a democracy, the more interest groups it has.[b] Interest groups in other countries are also structured similarly to those that operate in America. They are often either affiliated with or part of larger organizations, such as labor unions, ethnic associations, or religious groups. Citizens often belong to several interest groups—although, similar to Americans, they may not be aware of the groups' political activities.

Comparing countries reveals three important differences in how interest groups lobby. First, the targets of their lobbying vary. As discussed in Chapter 7, political parties are often much stronger in other countries than they are in America. Most European countries, such as Germany, France, Italy, and Great Britain have highly influential party organizations. When parties are strong, individual politicians have to follow the orders of party leaders or risk being either removed from office or prevented from running in the first place.[c] As a result, interest groups in these countries focus on lobbying party leaders rather than individual legislators, who ultimately have to do what party leaders demand.

Interest groups in other nations are also typically subject to stringent campaign finance restrictions.[d] In Great Britain, for ex-

▲ *Interest groups are active in almost every democracy. In Europe, these groups lobby both their national government and the European Union, whose legislators and bureaucrats determine policies that affect many local industries. Here, European farmers protest European Union plans to cut agricultural subsidies.*

ample, interest groups cannot contribute to the campaigns of individual candidates for Parliament. In many other European countries, interest groups can run campaign ads, but must cease doing so during the last days of the electoral campaign.

Differences in governmental institutions also change how interest groups lobby.[e] Consider parliamentary systems, in which the executive and legislative branches of government are linked. The party controlling the legislature selects not only the prime minister, who serves as the head of the government, but also the ministers who control specific organizations within the government. In the American system, the branches of government are often con-

trolled by different political parties, so interest groups face a choice. Should they lobby the executive branch to seek a regulation that suits their purposes, or should they lobby Congress for a budget request or new legislation? In a parliamentary system, this choice does not exist: interest groups can only lobby the party in power, which controls both branches of government.

A final difference in the way interest groups abroad lobby has to do with the influence of the European Union.[f] Interest groups in the member states who want a change in policy can lobby either their own government or the legislators and bureaucrats in the Union government, for policies that would apply to all member states. ■

promotes gun ownership rights whose members share interests in hunting, target shooting, and similar hobbies. The NRA is also an interest group that endorses candidates, contributes to campaigns, and lobbies elected officials. It also runs ads on television and other media to persuade the public to support the NRA position on guns. In other cases, interest group activity is almost hidden within an organization. Consider the Automobile Association of America (AAA). Most drivers know AAA as a provider of emergency roadside service and maps, but AAA is also an interest group that lobbies for increased funding for highways and less for mass transit.

▲ More than 4 million individuals belong to the National Rifle Association, one of the most powerful interest groups in America. At their national convention shown here, members debate the group's goals and select leaders.

As these descriptions suggest, interest groups and lobbying are ubiquitous in American politics. Many organizations have lobbying operations, or hire lobbyists to work on their behalf. You may think that you don't belong to a group that lobbies the federal government, but the odds are that you do.

POLITICS IS EVERYWHERE

The large number of interest groups in America, as well as their widespread membership, demonstrate the pervasiveness of political concerns.

In fact, one important view of American politics, pluralism, identifies interest groups as America's fundamental political actors.[8] Pluralists argue that most Americans participate in politics through their membership in interest groups like Public Citizen, the NRA, or even AAA. These groups lobby, electioneer, and negotiate among themselves to encourage legislators to pursue policies that benefit their members. Others describe America as an **interest group state**, meaning that these groups are involved whenever policy is made.[9]

THE BUSINESS OF LOBBYING

Interest group lobbying is heavily regulated.[10] Lobbying firms must file annual reports identifying their clients and specifying how much they were paid by each one. Similarly, interest groups and corporations must file reports listing staff members who spent more than 20 percent of their time lobbying Congress, and detailing expenditures to lobbying firms. Existing laws also require most executive or legislative branch employees who take lobbying jobs to refrain from lobbying people in their former office or agency for one year—though elected officials who become lobbyists must wait two years.

One thing is for sure: lobbying involves billions of dollars a year. Figure 9.1 shows annual lobbying expenditures for 2000 through 2007, compiled from the official reports that interest groups and lobbyists are required to file with the federal government. The data in Figure 9.2 show that a multitude of groups and organizations lobby the federal government—and the number has risen dramatically in the last generation.[11] The number of registered lobbyists doubled between 2000 and 2005, from about 15,000 to more than 30,000, and these numbers are dramatically higher than they were in the 1950s and 1960s.

interest group state A government in which most policy decisions are determined by the influence of interest groups.

MONEY SPENT ON LOBBYING, 2000–2007

These data show that in recent years, interest groups have spent several billion dollars lobbying the federal government—and their spending is steadily increasing. Does this amount seem surprisingly large or surprisingly small, given what lobbyists do?

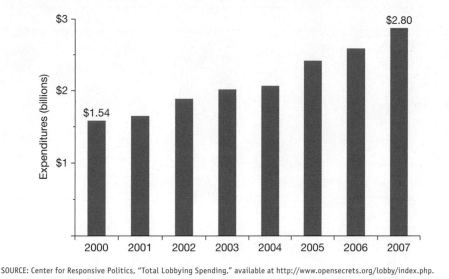

SOURCE: Center for Responsive Politics, "Total Lobbying Spending," available at http://www.opensecrets.org/lobby/index.php.

GROWTH IN FEDERAL SPENDING AND IN LOBBYING

These graphs show that as the federal government has grown, so has the number of lobbyists. One explanation is that lobbyists get the government to spend money that it otherwise would not. Is there an alternate explanation that is consistent with the data?

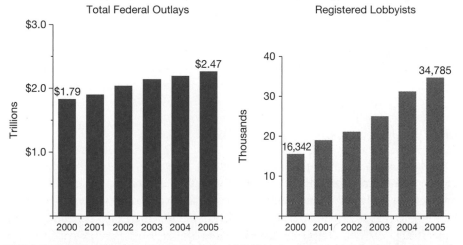

SOURCE: Jeffrey H. Birnbaum, "The Road to Riches Is Called K Street," *Washington Post*, June 22, 2005, p. A1; GPO Access, Budget of the United States Government, Historical Table 1.1 (FY 2009), available at http://www.gpoaccess.gov/usbudget/fy09/hist.html.

The number of interest groups has also shot up in recent years. In a 1999 study, two scholars found that the number of interest groups in the United States had risen from about 5,000 in 1959 to over 25,000 in 1995.[12] The current number is undoubtedly much higher: the 2006 *Encyclopedia of Associations* lists over 100,000 national and regional organized groups in America—though not all of these groups lobby the federal government.

Why are there so many interest groups and registered lobbyists, and why are their numbers increasing? The first graph in Figure 9.2 shows that this proliferation

Restrictions on Interest Group Lobbying

The case of Jack Abramoff and the congressmen and staff convicted of taking bribes from his organization suggest that some interest groups and lobbying firms are not playing by the rules. Rather than just making their case to officials, they are offering money and other inducements in return for policy change.

It seems that to solve this problem, interest groups and lobbying firms should be regulated to ensure that they cannot unfairly dominate the policy process, regardless of the public's opinion about their agendas, by buying support from members of Congress and bureaucrats. This proposal raises two questions. First, would new regulations prevent abuses of power? Second, are such abuses of power commonplace enough to justify a new regulation?

To place the argument for reform in context, consider the six-point lobbying reform proposal offered after the Abramoff scandal by a coalition of six groups: Public Citizen, Common Cause, Democracy 21, Public Campaign Legal Center, U.S. PIRG, and the League of Women Voters.[a]

1. Place low limits on interest groups' contributions to candidates.
2. Ban interest groups from providing subsidized travel to people in government.
3. Ban gifts from interest groups and their staff to members of Congress and congressional staff.
4. Establish an independent ethics review board to oversee interactions between lobbyists and both Congress and the bureaucracy, and increase penalties for ethics violations.
5. Ban former members of Congress, legislative staff, and bureaucrats from lobbying for two years after leaving office.
6. Require electronic filing of lobbying registration forms and congresspersons' financial disclosure forms.

Most of these proposals seem unobjectionable. For example, why should interest groups be allowed to give gifts to the officials they are lobbying? And in the age of the Internet, where all kinds of information is accessible to the average citizen, it makes sense that information about lobbying ac-

▲ This cartoon summarizes public assumptions about lobbying and its impact on members of Congress. In reality, Jack Abramoff's level of access and his criminal conduct are the exception rather than the rule among lobbyists.

tivities and gifts to legislators and bureaucrats should be readily available.

Even so, there are three fundamental problems with these restrictions. First, some of them violate freedoms that many Americans value. The campaign finance restrictions in point one would make it harder for people to organize to influence elections. For example, the amount that groups such as the NRA or the AARP contribute to political campaigns would be severely limited compared to the current rules. If you are not a member of these groups, the restriction probably sounds fine—but remember, the limits would apply to all groups, including those you belong to, which may make the trade-off unattractive. A second problem is that it is difficult to tell whether these regulations would work as intended. As discussed in this chapter, interest groups are already highly regulated in terms of who can lobby, how they can lobby, and what kinds of gifts and assistance they can offer to government officials. Giving legislators, staffers, or bureaucrats gifts in return for policy changes is already against the law, and if those laws aren't working, it is hard to see how new,

similar laws will solve the problem.

Finally, this chapter shows that these reforms are, to some extent, based on a misunderstanding of how interest groups operate. The case of Jack Abramoff is interesting precisely *because* it is a glaring exception. Most interest groups are small and have such limited resources that they couldn't offer gifts or threaten to withhold large campaign donations even if they wanted to. Moreover, interest groups tend to focus on offering advice and information to people in government who already support their goals. None of the reforms described here would change anything about those practices, except to add some additional reporting requirements and further limit their (already restricted) ability to hire people who used to work in government.

The case for reforming interest group regulations is therefore weaker than it first appears. If existing laws do not deter violations, will new laws do so? Are these reforms aimed at exceptional cases or at average groups? And are they effective enough to warrant limiting Americans' ability to organize in support of candidates or to petition for policy changes? ■

▲ Throughout the early and mid-2000s, the Boeing Corporation mounted an extensive lobbying campaign as part of its efforts to win a contract to build air refueling planes for the U.S. Air Force. This campaign involved meetings with elected officials and bureaucrats, as well as advertising in many national publications.

is related to the large size and widespread influence of the federal government. People get involved and lobby because they have a stake in what the government does. They want their company to get a government contract, or they want a new regulation to favor their business sector. They want the government to limit what citizens can do or relax restrictions on behavior. Simply put, the federal government does so many things and spends so much money that many individuals, organizations, and corporations have strong incentives for lobbying.

Changes in communication technology may also contribute to the increasing numbers of interest groups and lobbyists.[13] Television and the Internet make it easier for people to realize that they have common interests, while cell phones, e-mail, and other forms of electronic communication make it easier for large, geographically dispersed groups to organize and implement lobbying strategies. Even so, many like-minded groups in America remain **latent** or unorganized, without a group to represent them, suggesting that even when participation can be virtually effortless, many people still opt not to participate.

The expenditures shown in Figure 9.1 pay for many things. For example, beginning in 2003 lobbyists for the Boeing Corporation were working to secure a government contract with the U.S. military for Boeing to build tanker aircraft (planes that can refuel other planes in midair). A Boeing memo detailed the effort: along with meetings between Boeing employees and Department of Defense staff to negotiate the contact, Boeing's lobbyists and employees were meeting with members of Congress, congressional staff, senior members of President Bush's staff, and the leaders of labor unions whose members worked for Boeing.[14] Boeing also ran ads in Washington newspapers promoting their tanker proposal. Thus, in pursuing the contract, Boeing paid the salaries of its employees who planned and executed the lobbying effort, and paid for outside lobbyists and their meetings on Capitol Hill, as well as spending money on broader publicity efforts. As of late 2008, Boeing's efforts had not won them the contract, but the company was one of two finalists.

The disclosure data also reveal who the big spenders on lobbying are. As shown in Table 9.1, the list is dominated by corporations like General Electric, and groups

POLITICS IS CONFLICTUAL

Q The exponential growth in the numbers of interest groups and lobbyists reflects Americans' widespread differences of opinions about government policy.

latent A term describing a group of politically like-minded people that is not represented by any interest group.

of businesses such as the Chamber of Commerce. Two exceptions are the American Medical Association, which is a national organization of physicians, and the American Association of Retired Persons. Of General Electric's $11.4 million spent on lobbying in 2006, over $8 million was spent on GE employees, and the remaining $3 million paid for the services of a total of fourteen lobbying firms.[15]

Most interest groups or corporations spend much less on their lobbying efforts. The Sierra Club, for example, spent less than $100,000 on lobbying in 2006.[16] All of these funds helped pay the salaries of Sierra Club employees whose jobs include lobbying. Many other groups spend even less, barely scraping together enough cash to send someone to plead their case in Washington.

Other companies lobby through their membership in **trade associations** like the National Beer Wholesalers Association (NBWA), a nationwide group of local businesses that buy beer from brewers and resell it to stores and restaurants. The NBWA's principal lobbying goal is to ensure that laws remain in place requiring middlemen between beer producers and the stores, bars, and restaurants that sell

---

TABLE 9.1 **TOP TWENTY SPENDERS ON LOBBYING, 1996–2008**

This table shows the corporations and associations that spent the most on lobbying between January 1996 and March 2008. Why do you think each group spends so much on lobbying? What do these groups want from government?

LOBBYING CLIENT	EXPENDITURES
U.S. Chamber of Commerce	$380,014,680
American Medical Association	$184,147,500
General Electric	$167,230,000
American Hospital Association	$148,161,639
American Association of Retired Persons	$134,012,064
Pharmaceutical Research and Manufacturers of America	$130,643,400
Edison Electric Institute	$118,222,628
Northrop Grumman	$109,875,253
Business Roundtable	$109,070,000
National Association of Realtors	$104,190,380
Blue Cross/Blue Shield	$94,846,172
Freddie Mac	$92,624,048
Boeing Co.	$89,378,310
General Motors	$89,170,483
Lockheed Martin	$86,671,735
Exxon Mobil	$85,086,942
Verizon Communications	$84,145,610
Southern Co.	$83,480,694
SBC Communications	$79,851,656
Fannie Mae	$77,967,000

SOURCE: Center for Responsive Politics, "Top Spenders," available at http://www.opensecrets.org/lobby/top.php?indexType=s.

beer to consumers. If the rules change to allow beer producers to deal with the end-sellers directly, then the NBWA's members are out of a job.

While the amount of money spent on lobbying by interest groups may seem like a lot, it is small compared to how much is at stake.[17] The federal government now spends more than $3 trillion every year. In recent years, spending by interest groups and by the lobbying arms of organizations and corporations amounts to only $2 billion every year. That's a lot of money, but it's still less than 0.1 percent of total federal spending. This difference raises a critical question: if interest groups could control policy choices by spending money on lobbying, why aren't they spending more?

TYPES OF INTEREST GROUPS

Interest groups can be divided into three categories based on the type of concerns that drive their lobbying efforts: economic groups, citizen groups, and single-issue groups. Within each of these three broad categories there are several types of organizations with their own distinct policy goals.

The first type is the **economic groups**, such as corporations, trade associations, labor groups, and professional organizations. Economic interest groups aim to influence policy in ways that will help their members derive economic—that is, monetary—benefits. Trade associations, like the National Beer Wholesalers Association mentioned earlier, are one kind of economic group. In rare cases, a group that seems to be a trade association is actually a front for a single corporation's own lobbying efforts. The Coalition for Luggage Security, for example, lobbies for laws that would force airline passengers to pre-ship their luggage to their destination. The supposed goal is to prevent terrorists from getting explosives on commercial airliners by not allowing anyone to check bags in the first place. However, the Coalition's Web site shows that its president is also the head of a company that offers pre-shipping services. Moreover, the Coalition has no other members—no individuals, no corporations.[18] It is simply a lobbying arm of a corporation.

Labor organizations are another kind of economic group. The American Federation of Labor and Congress of Industrial Organizations (AFL-CIO) is a federation of fifty-five labor unions with over 10 million members. The AFL-CIO lobbies for several kinds of pro-union laws, including regulations that make it easy for workers to form labor unions, union shop laws that require workers at a company to join a union if one exists, and a wide range of other policies.[19] Professional organizations, a third type of economic group, also lobby for government policies that financially benefit their members. One such organization, the American Medical Association, is one of the top spenders on lobbying (see Table 9.1).

A second interest group category is **citizen groups** (also known as public interest groups). These groups are organized around a desire to change the federal government's spending, regulations, or new programs. One such group is the consumer advocacy organization Public Citizen, discussed earlier. Another is the Family Research Council, which describes itself as "promoting the Judeo-Christian worldview as the basis for a just, free, and stable society." This group lobbies for a wide range of policies, from legislation that defines marriage as between a man and a woman to the elimination of estate taxes.[20]

The third category of interest group is the **single-issue groups**. These groups focus their lobbying on a narrow range of topics, or even a single government program or piece of legislation. Examples include the National Right to Life Committee, which lobbies for restrictions on abortion rights, and NumbersUSA, which lobbies against guest worker programs for noncitizens.

▲ Many interest groups claim to speak for large numbers of Americans, but some lobby for changes that would benefit only a few people or a single corporation. The Coalition for Luggage Security, for example, has only one member: a company that specializes in shipping travelers' baggage, which would gain considerable business if the Coalition's lobbying efforts succeeded.

economic groups A type of interest group that seeks public policies that will provide monetary benefits to its members.

citizen groups A type of interest group that seeks changes in spending, regulations, or government programs concerning a wide range of policies (also known as public interest groups).

single-issue groups A type of interest group that has a narrowly focused goal, seeking change on a single topic, government program, or piece of legislation.

▲ *Dr. James Dobson heads Focus on the Family, a citizen group that lobbies for a wide range of policies, most stemming from the conservative, Christian orientation of the leaders and membership.*

Historically, economic interest groups outnumbered citizen groups and single-issue groups. However, while the number of all types of interest groups has increased in recent years, the increase in citizen groups has far outpaced the growth in economic groups.[21] This change might be due in part to the federal government's increased role in many aspects of citizens' everyday lives. The government has always regulated businesses to some degree, so businesses have always had a strong motivation to lobby. Since the 1960s, however, the government's increased role in regulating individual behavior may have given a similar boost to the number of citizen organizations.

ORGANIZATIONAL STRUCTURES

There are two main models of interest group structure. Most large, well-known organizations like the AARP and the NRA are **centralized groups.** These national organizations typically have headquarters in Washington, field offices in large state capitals, and members nationwide. The defining feature of a centralized group is that the organization's leadership is concentrated in its headquarters. These leaders have the power and the responsibility to determine the group's lobbying goals and tactics. The other structural model is a **confederation,** which is made up of largely independent, local organizations. For example, the National Independent Automobile Dealers Association (NADA) is made up of fifty separate, state-level organizations that provide most of the membership benefits to car dealers who join the organization, and raise much of the money that NADA contributes to candidates running for political office (several million dollars in recent elections).

Both of these organizational structures have advantages and disadvantages. A centralized organization controls all of the group's resources and can deploy them efficiently, but it can be challenging for these groups to find out what members want. In the late 1980s, for example, the AARP lobbied for a new federal insurance benefit for senior citizens, only to find that the overwhelming majority of its members opposed this program.[22]

Confederations have the advantage of maintaining independent chapters at the state and local levels, so it is easier for the national headquarters to learn what their members want—all they have to do is contact their local groups. But this strength of confederations is closely related to their main weakness. State and local chapters mostly function independently of the national headquarters, since they attract members and raise money largely on their own. The national headquarters depends on the local organizations for funds to pay its staff and make campaign contributions. Thus, the norm in most confederated organizations is that when local chapters send money to headquarters to be used for campaign contributions, they also specify which candidates they want to receive it.[23] As a result, confederated groups often are beset with conflict, as different local chapters have their own ideas about what to lobby for and which candidates to support.

STAFF

Interest group staff falls into two categories: experts on the group's focal policy areas, and people with useful government connections and knowledge of procedures. The first group includes scientists, engineers, and others with advanced degrees; the second is dominated by people who have worked inside government as elected

POLITICAL PROCESS MATTERS

☑ Organizational structures shape the ways interest groups lobby and help determine their policy goals.

centralized groups Interest groups that have a headquarters, usually in Washington, DC, as well as members and field offices throughout the country. In general, these groups' lobbying decisions are made at headquarters by the group leaders.

confederations Interest groups made up of several independent, local organizations that provide much of their funding and hold most of the power.

officials, bureaucrats, or legislative staff.[24] Sometimes these former members of the government are also policy experts, but their unique contribution is their knowledge of how government works and their relationships with officeholders and other former coworkers.

The practice of transitioning from government positions to working for interest groups or lobbying firms is known as the **revolving door**.[25] A 2005 study by Public Citizen found that from 1998 to 2005, over 40 percent of representatives leaving the House or the Senate joined a lobbying firm after their departure.[26] A separate study in June 2006 found that more than two-thirds of the Department of Homeland Security's original senior staff left their positions to work for corporations or lobbying firms.[27] The revolving door works in the other direction too: Andrew Card, who was President George W. Bush's chief of staff, had previously held positions at General Motors and at lobbying firms.[28]

The revolving door presents a dilemma. On one hand, people who have worked in industry or as lobbyists are likely to be familiar with a particular field and the relevant laws, making them well-qualified for the executive branch. Similarly, former officeholders, congressional staff, and bureaucrats are attractive to lobbying firms, as they have first-hand knowledge of how policies are made and have established relationships with people in government. On the other hand, the problem with the revolving door is that people in government may try to help particular firms and interest groups in return for a well-paid position after they leave government service. Or, when the influence works in the opposite direction, lobbyists-turned-lawmakers may favor the firms and organizations that once employed them.

In Washington during the 1970s and earlier, the offices of lobbying firms were concentrated along one street, K Street, although now they are scattered across the city. Still, the term **K Street** is used to refer collectively to Washington lobbyists.

MEMBERSHIP

Interest groups can also be distinguished on the basis of the size of their membership and the members' role in the group's activities. Some interest groups are **mass associations** with large numbers of dues-paying members. One example is the Sierra Club, which advertises itself as the "oldest, largest and most influential grassroots environmental organization."[29] The Sierra Club has over 750,000 members who each pay annual dues of about $30. Besides keeping its members informed about the making of environmental policy in Washington, the Sierra Club endorses judicial nominees and candidates for elected positions, and works with members of Congress to develop legislative proposals. The group's members elect the organization's board of directors.

Not all mass associations give members a say in selecting a group's leaders or determining its mission. To join the American Association of Retired Persons (AARP), which has over 35 million members, you don't have to be retired, but you have to be at least fifty years old and pay dues of $12.50 per year. Members get discounts on insurance, car rentals, and hotels, as well as driver safety courses and help doing their taxes. The AARP claims to lobby for policies its members favor, but members actually have no control over which legislative causes the group chooses. Moreover, the AARP does not poll members to determine its issue positions, nor do members pick the AARP leadership.

Peak associations have a different type of membership,[30] exemplified by the Business-Industry Political Action Committee (BIPAC). This association of several hundred businesses and trade associations aims to elect "pro-business individuals" to Congress.[31] Individuals cannot join peak associations—they may work for the association's member companies or organizations, but they cannot become dues-paying members on their own.

Finally, some interest groups have no members at all, which seems odd at first. Wouldn't group leaders want the money or the political power that comes from representing a lot of people? The answer is that getting people to join an organization, even one whose goals they agree with, is harder than you might expect, as we discuss later in the chapter. As a result, it often makes sense for interest groups to seek funding from foundations, corporations, or a few wealthy individuals rather than from broad-based membership.

RESOURCES

Interest groups use resources including people, money, and expertise to support their lobbing efforts. We will examine interest group strategies in a later section; for now, the important thing to understand is that a group's resources influence its set of available lobbying strategies. Some groups have sufficient funding and staff to pursue a wide range of strategies, while smaller groups with fewer resources have only a few lobbying options.

People One of the most important resources for most interest groups is members. Group members can write letters to elected officials, send e-mails, meet with elected officials, and even travel to Washington for demonstrations. A group's members may also offer its leaders expertise or advice. Even when the "members" of a group are corporations, as is the case with trade associations, CEOs and other corporate staff can help with the group's lobbying efforts.

Many mass organizations try to get their members involved in the lobbying process. MoveOn.org, for example, has a Web page that helps people send letters to the editors of various national and local newspapers. Many newspapers print selected letters from readers, so one way MoveOn hopes to bring public attention to its political priorities is by getting these Web-generated letters printed. Using their site, you provide your address, choose from a list of local and national papers to contact, and compose a message—using MoveOn's "talking points," which cover a wide range of issues—if you choose. The page automatically imports your message into correctly addressed e-mails to your selected newspapers.[32]

Similarly, the Web page of the Family Research Council alerts members to volunteer opportunities, announces where the organization's rallies will be held, and tells members how they can help local chapters by hosting dinners, stuffing envelopes, or similar activities.[33] And the National Paper Trade Association, which describes itself as "the Association for the paper, packaging, and supplies distribution channel," organized the CEOs of its member corporations to lobby senators about various pieces of legislation.[34]

Interest groups' ability to use people as a resource is limited by two major challenges. First, it requires members—and as you have seen, recruitment is sufficiently difficult and expensive that some interest groups opt not to have members. The second challenge is motivating members to participate, especially since those who don't participate will reap the same policy benefits as those who do if the group succeeds. As we discuss later, while there are instances where interest groups have changed government policy by persuading their members to write letters, e-mail, and visit elected officials, the more common situation is that interest groups ask for members' help but receive little response.[35]

▲ *Interest groups use a variety of tactics to draw attention to their concerns, including events designed to generate media coverage. Jon Davids, a Public Interest Research Group staffer, traveled nearly 20,000 miles across America with an eighteen-foot inflatable largemouth bass named Freddie to events that publicized the dangers of mercury pollution in lakes and streams.*

Money Virtually everything interest groups do, from meeting with elected officials to fighting for what they want in court, can be purchased as services by well-funded groups. Money can also be used to make campaign contributions, or to develop and run campaign ads, and of course, money is necessary to fund interest groups' everyday operations.

Well-funded interest groups have a considerable advantage in the lobbying process. If they need an expert, a lobbyist, or a lawyer, they can hire one. They can pay for campaign ads, and make campaign contributions, while groups with less cash are prevented from using these strategies. The importance of money for interest group operations can be seen in their funding appeals to members. If you look at the donations page from the Sierra Club's Web site, you'll see that supporters can give a membership as a gift, join as a life member, or give monthly. They can make commemorative or memorial gifts, set up a planned giving scheme, or donate stock. The group even offers gift-giving plans for non-U.S. residents, specific parameters for Canadian residents, and a Spanish-language version of their donations page.

Even so, money isn't everything, and there are many ways for groups to be effective without spending much. Groups can rely on members to lobby for them, hire staff willing to work for low pay because they share the group's goals, or cite already-published research rather than funding their own studies to bolster their case for policy change. Moreover, the fact that a group has lots of money is no guarantee that their lobbying efforts will succeed. The Luggage Security Coalition, for example, is unlikely to achieve its goal of preventing air travelers from checking baggage no matter how much money it has for lobbying.

Expertise Expertise takes many forms. Some interest group leaders know a lot about their members' preferences, or about what people in a community, congressional district, or state want.[36] Other groups can offer information to elected officials and bureaucrats, ranging from detailed reports on policy questions to concrete legislative proposals. This information is an asset group leaders can use to negotiate with elected officials or bureaucrats as part of a trade to get what the group wants.

Expertise can also involve knowledge of political factors, such as information about what kinds of policies party caucuses or individual legislators are willing to support, or information about the courts, such as the constitutionality of proposed laws and policies or the ideological leanings of different judges. Lobbying firms that employ ex-members of Congress and bureaucrats are a good source of this kind of information.

Consider the AARP, whose Web site offers a vast array of research and analyses, such as information about senior citizens' part-time employment, how people invest their 401(k) retirement accounts, and a comparison of long-term care policies in Europe and the United States.[37] The AARP's lobbyists then use this research when they argue for policy changes in their public testimony and in private meetings with members of Congress and congressional staff. For example, in September 2004 testimony before Congress, AARP staff presented the results of their research on trends in part-time work by senior citizens, the societal benefits of this trend, and what Congress could do to encourage it.[38]

Not all interest groups have such expertise. Some groups focus on mobilizing people outside government, expecting that elected officials will respond to this pressure by developing policy solutions. However, particularly for groups headquartered in Washington or state capitals, expertise often comes naturally. In the course of their jobs, interest group staff often become well-versed in the details of current policies and the policy options that pertain to their interests. They talk with members of Congress and bureaucrats on a daily basis, learning who their friends are—and what they need to do to change enemies into friends.

SECTION SUMMARY

1. The number of interest groups in America has increased dramatically over the last generation—largely due to the increasingly expansive role of government in American society.

2. Interest groups and other organizations interested in influencing policy spend billions of dollars on lobbying each year. However, most individual groups have relatively modest lobbying efforts.

3. Economic organizations, citizen associations, and single-issue groups differ in terms of their goals. Groups can be divided into membership organizations and peak associations.

4. The resources an interest group uses to lobby include money, people, and expertise.

Forming and Maintaining Interest Groups

An interest group's first task is to get organized: raise the money needed to hire staff, rent an office, set up a Web site, and begin to formulate policy goals and a lobbying strategy. Once organized, the group needs to continue to attract funds for ongoing operations. These tasks are not as easy as they might sound. Even if a group of people share the same goals, the challenge is to make them aware of these common interests and persuade them to donate time or money to a lobbying operation.

As discussed earlier, despite the fact that there are many interest groups in America, there are also plenty of latent, or unorganized, groups. This section seeks to explain this anomaly.

free riding The practice of relying on others to contribute to a collective effort, while failing to participate on one's own behalf and still benefiting from the group's successes.

THE LOGIC OF COLLECTIVE ACTION

Changes in government policy are public goods: if the government changes policy, such as increasing the size of college tuition grants, everyone who is eligible for the grants benefits from the increase. There's no way to exclude people based on whether they helped to initiate this change in some way, such as by joining an interest group that lobbied for it. Moreover, joining an interest group is voluntary. Group members can send letters asking students to join, they can call or send thousands of e-mails, but they cannot force anyone to join lobbying efforts or send in their dues.

> **POLITICAL PROCESS MATTERS**
>
> ✓ The logic of collective action influences whether interest groups form, what they lobby for, and what members receive from the group.

These circumstances make it hard to motivate people to contribute to collective efforts, since each would-be member can see that his contribution is but a minuscule portion of what the group needs to succeed. Regardless of how many other people join, an individual is better off **free riding**—refusing to join, and still enjoying the benefits of any successes the group might have. But if everyone acts on this calculation, no one will join the group and the organization will be unable to lobby for tuition grants or anything else.

The Prisoners' Dilemma The logic of collective action is an example of a broad class of situations called prisoners' dilemmas. The essence of a prisoners' dilemma situation is that all participants will be better off if they cooperate or coordinate their behavior, but each individual participant also has an incentive to defect or refuse to cooperate, in hopes of enjoying the benefits of the other participants' efforts without contributing themselves.

Prisoners' dilemmas get their name from the classic example used to describe these situations, in which two individuals are arrested on suspicion of having collaborated to commit a crime. Upon arriving at the police station, they are questioned in separate rooms. While the police are confident that the suspects are guilty, they lack concrete evidence, so they offer each of the suspects a deal: "Confess and implicate your partner," each suspect is told, "and you will be released outright. But if you remain silent and your partner talks, you will be convicted alone and receive a long jail sentence." If both suspects confess, they will be both convicted but receive moderate sentences, whereas when both suspects cooperate to defy the police and remain silent, they each receive a short sentence.

The police strategy creates the options depicted in Figure 9.3, in which the choices available to the first suspect are arranged in rows, while the second suspect's choices are arranged in columns. Each cell in Figure 9.3 shows the combinations of choices available to the suspects and the sentence that each one receives depending on whether both suspects, only one of them, or neither confess to the crime.

Figure 9.3 shows that each suspect receives a shorter sentence when he defects or implicates his partner, regardless of what the partner does. Consider the situation from Suspect 2's vantage point. If Suspect 1 attempts to cooperate (top row), then Suspect 2 could receive either a short sentence if he also cooperates (top, left), or no jail time if he defects and turns in his partner (top, right). However, if Suspect 1 defects instead (bottom row), then Suspect 2 could receive either a long sentence—

FIGURE 9.3   THE PRISONERS' DILEMMA

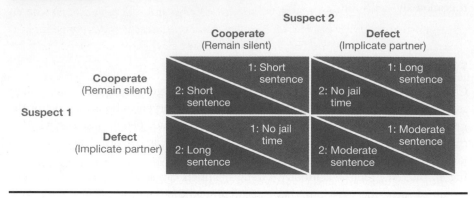

for attempting to cooperate with the partner who gave him up (bottom, left)—or a moderate sentence for joining his partner in confessing to the police (bottom, right). Given these payoffs, each individual suspect always fares better by defecting and taking the police deal, regardless of what the other suspect does. However, when *both* suspects defect, producing the bottom, right cell as the outcome, they will both receive moderate sentences—faring worse than if they had cooperated with each other to stay silent (top, left cell; short sentence).

The prisoners' dilemma will be familiar to anyone who watches police shows on TV. Programs like *Law and Order* frequently show situations in which two suspects thought to be in cahoots are interrogated separately, with the goal of getting one to implicate the other. The message to each suspect is always the same: we're going to be lenient with the first person to talk, and throw the book at the one who remains silent.

In politics, prisoners' dilemmas are common. Legislators may get involved in such situations when making deals involving vote trades, and nations face a variety of similar dilemmas involving security issues or environmental problems. In many cases, legislators can resolve such dilemmas easily, because both parties know that each specific negotiation is one of many in an ongoing relationship, and both can tell whether their partner is cooperating or defecting. This knowledge allows both negotiators to enforce cooperation by threatening to refuse to cooperate with a defector in the future. Thus, a senator might want to renege on her end of a vote trade with a colleague, but because she knows she will need to make many future deals with the colleague, she cooperates in order to preserve these future interactions.

Collective action problems involving interest groups are usually more difficult to resolve since there are typically more participants (the potential members of an interest group), and there is no way for each participant to know whether others are free riding or not. For example, suppose you favor government action against global warming, and you receive a letter from an organization that shares your goals, asking for a modest contribution to support its lobbying efforts. If you are like most people, you will feel a powerful incentive to free ride. After all, the results of the lobbying campaign will be the same regardless of whether you contribute. Furthermore, others who favor government action will not know whether you contributed and cannot punish a decision to free ride. Thus, interest groups need a different solution to the collective action problem.

POLITICS IS EVERYWHERE

The logic of collective action and the insights from the prisoners' dilemma apply to many kinds of group behavior inside politics and out, not just interest group organization.

Free Riding in Everyday Life

Environmental issues, such as global warming, air and water pollution, and unsustainable exploitation of renewable resources, are often described as collective action problems. One class of these problems involve renewable natural resources, such as a forest or fishery. The problem is that each participant can maximize profits by exploiting the resource as much as possible without worrying about whether this practice is sustainable. However, if everyone behaves this way, the common resource pool will be destroyed: all the fish will be caught; all the trees will be cut down.

Research into these common pool situations shows that participants are more likely to cooperate when they comprise a small, self-contained community in which they interact frequently over a long period. Under these conditions, people are likely to construct institutions that deter free riding. Why? Because the benefits of collective action are large enough in these cases that the participants urgently want to figure out a way to capture them. One kind of institution formed for this purpose allows people to monitor each other to determine whether everyone is cooperating. The group can then punish free riders, perhaps by denying them the benefits of collective action enjoyed by the rest of the community.

These kinds of problems are not limited

▲ Roommates' failure to help to keep shared living spaces clean is a classic case of free riding. This picture shows what happens when all roommates try to free ride.

to the kinds of resources and responsibilities overseen by the government. Anyone who has lived with a roommate or group knows that one perennial problem is the responsibility for common living spaces. Everyone typically agrees that these areas should be kept clean, but each resident sees an opportunity to free ride. Instead of cleaning up your mess, why not leave the task to someone else? But if everyone follows this incentive, it doesn't take long before the dishes start piling up in the sink, and the living room is littered with abandoned soda cans and months-old magazines.

How do people solve this collective action problem to maintain the common

resource of their dorm suite or apartment? Sometimes they don't. You probably have some neighbors who live in an incredible mess. Some of them undoubtedly prefer disorder over the costs of maintaining neatness, but others are struggling with a collective action problem. Though the roommates agree on the virtues of a clean apartment, each one attempts to reap the benefits of free riding.

To address this kind of collective action problem, you need one of the three mechanisms described in this chapter. One option is participation benefits: find people to live with who want a clean home enough that they are willing to clean regardless of whether you help. The second possibility is to set up a reward system to motivate you and your roommates to keep common spaces clean. A third strategy is coercion: sign a lease with a draconian landlord, whose willingness to return your security deposit depends on your willingness to keep the space clean throughout the term of the lease. A final option is to hire a cleaning service that everyone pays for. Without at least one of these mechanisms, you and your roommates may face a serious free rider problem. And the fact that common living spaces so often stay messy suggests that roommates are often unable implement one of these solutions. ■

groups often involve a small number of corporations or individuals, the costs of free riding are relatively high: one actor's efforts or contributions can significantly boost the likelihood of success, and one member's failure to contribute can likewise compromise the group's efforts. Thus, economic groups can often form on the strength of their shared policy or monetary goals, without coercion, selective incentives, or solidary benefits. In contrast, citizen groups, with many more potential members, typically need to use at least one of these three methods solve their collective action problems.

Finally, the logic also explains why some interest groups have no members at all. Sometimes interest groups, such as the Coalition for Luggage Security, are funded by a single wealthy company or individual. Other groups raise money from foundations or corporate donors.[50] Why not try to attract members? They can be surprisingly hard to find, and it takes even more time and money to convince them to participate.

SECTION SUMMARY

1. The logic of collective action shows that common interests or goals are not enough to motivate people to join or contribute to an interest group. Before groups can cooperate, they must solve the free rider problem.

2. Possible solutions to the free rider problem include solidary benefits, coercion, and selective incentives. Many successful groups use more than one of these solutions to motivate people to join the group and support its lobbying efforts.

3. The logic of collective action explains why some contingents remain latent or unorganized. It also explains why economic groups are more likely to form than citizen groups, and why some citizen groups have no members.

Interest Group Strategies

Having formed an interest group, the next task is to decide on the group's lobbying goals. You might think this question is decided before the group forms: how else could members be convinced to join, except with promises about fighting for a particular cause? But remember, sometimes people join interest groups because of selective incentives or coercion, without considering the group's lobbying efforts. Moreover, the average citizen does not know much about the details of American politics, including the lobbying activities of groups that he or she might join.

In some cases, group members play a role in lobbying decisions. Sierra Club members, for example, select the group's board of directors, who then set the group's agenda. In confederations, the group's local offices often vote to determine the group's policies. And in small trade associations, corporate representatives often meet to negotiate their goals. However, particularly in large citizen organizations, there is no mechanism for members to influence lobbying decisions. Who decides?

In most interest groups, the leaders of the group make these decisions. Members are essentially along for the ride, with no way to protest or disapprove of their group's lobbying decisions except by quitting the organization. Thus, there is not necessarily a connection between members' opinions and lobbying decisions. Leaders of a group can lobby on issues that their members are not interested in or take positions that a majority of their members oppose.

Once a group has organized and determined its goals, the next step is to decide how to lobby. Interest groups have a number of possible tactics, which fall into two categories: **inside strategies**, which are actions taken in Washington, and **outside strategies**, which involve actions taken outside Washington.[51]

INSIDE STRATEGIES

Direct Lobbying When interest group staff meet with officeholders or bureaucrats, they plead their case through **direct lobbying**, asking government officials to change policy in line with the group's goals.[52] Such contacts are very common. If you visit a congressional office, you are likely to see someone from an interest group waiting to meet with the legislator or someone from their staff. For example,

inside strategies Tactics used by interest groups within Washington, DC, to achieve their policy goals.

outside strategies Tactics used by interest groups outside Washington, DC, to achieve their policy goals.

direct lobbying Attempts by interest group staff to influence policy by speaking with elected officials or bureaucrats.

a search of disclosure data maintained by Congress found that over 47,000 groups and individuals lobbied members of Congress in 2007.[53]

Interest group representatives are not always middle-aged men in expensive suits. Some groups arrange visits from delegations of group members from a legislator's district to make the case that their issue matters to the legislator's constituents. Others use volunteers to represent the group. For example, the organization ProSpace, which encouraging space exploration through tax credits and regulatory reform, sponsors an annual event called March Storm in which citizens who share the group's agenda travel to Washington (in March) to meet with members of Congress and their staff.

Direct lobbying is generally aimed at elected officials and bureaucrats who are sympathetic to the group's goals.[54] In these efforts, interest groups and their representatives do not try to convert opponents into supporters; rather, they help like-minded legislators secure policy changes that they both want. Their help can take many forms, such as sharing information about the proposed changes, providing lists of legislators who might be persuadable, or even drafting legislative proposals or regulations.

The important thing to understand is that these efforts usually are not part of a trade, in which the groups expect certain legislative action in return for the group's help. Rather, the group's efforts function more like a subsidy, a way of helping a legislator to enact policies she prefers—and that the group prefers as well.[55] The legislator knows that a like-minded group has no reason to misrepresent their policy information. After all, the group and the legislator are on the same side and want to enact the same policies. In fact, the member and staff will be happy to meet with the group's representatives, as their information may be vital to the legislator's efforts to enact legislation, manage the bureaucracy, or keep the support of constituents back home in the district.[56] Interest groups also contact fence sitters—legislators who are not supporters or opponents—with the goal of converting them into supporters.

In contrast, interest groups spend little time on legislators and bureaucrats who oppose the group's goals. These opponents are unlikely to listen to an interest group's message; since they disagree with the group's position from the outset, they are also less likely to let an interest group's delegation visit them in the first place—and if they do meet, they may suspect that the group has stretched the truth to present the most favorable case for its preferred policies.

Who do these groups contact? Analysis of the annual disclosure forms that lobbyists are required to file shows that they contact people throughout the federal government, from elected officials to members of the president's staff as well as bureaucrats in the executive branch. They seek this wide range of contacts because different federal officials play distinct roles in the policy-making process, which means they have various types of influence to offer interest groups. Members of Congress shape legislation and budgets; presidential staff influence the formation of new policies and obtain presidential consent for new laws; and executive branch bureaucrats change the ways regulations are written and how policies are implemented.

Drafting Legislation and Regulations Another inside strategy involves writing draft versions of legislation or regulations. Interest groups sometimes draft legislative proposals and regulations, which they then deliver to legislators and bureaucrats as part of their lobbying efforts.[57] Surveys of interest groups found that over three-quarters of the groups surveyed reported drafting proposals for members of Congress.[58] A 2006 *USA Today* story on relatives of members of Congress who work as lobbyists found that twenty-two out of thirty had succeeded in getting specific changes that helped their clients added to legislative proposals.[59]

Interest groups don't give proposals to just anyone. As with direct lobbying, they seek out legislators who already support their cause and who have significant influence within Congress, either by being on a powerful committee or by having their colleagues' respect. A lobbying effort aimed at cutting interest rates on student loans would target supporters of this change who are also members of the congressional committee that has jurisdiction over student loan programs—preferably someone who chairs the committee or one of its subcommittees, or who holds some other leadership position.[60] Interest groups also lobby bureaucrats in order to shape the details of new regulations.[61] If the type of regulations involved can go into effect without congressional approval, then lobbying can give groups what they want directly. But even if new regulations require approval by Congress or White House staff, interest groups can increase their chances of success by getting involved in the initial drafting of new regulations.

Research Interest groups often prepare research reports on topics of interest to the group. For example, in March 2007, the Web site of Public Citizen featured a series of research reports on a diverse set of topics, such as alleged price and supply manipulations by oil companies, lobbyists' contributions to congressional candidates, and efforts to eliminate the estate tax (a tax on inherited wealth).[62] Such reports serve multiple purposes. They may sway public opinion or help persuade elected officials or bureaucrats. They also help interest group staff claim expertise on some aspect of public policy. Members of Congress are more likely to accept a group's legislative proposal if they believe that the group's staff have some research to back up their claims. Journalists are also more likely to respond to an interest group's requests for publicity if they believe that the group's staff has evidence supporting their claims.

Testimony Interest group staff often testify before congressional committees. In part, this activity is aimed at informing members of Congress about issues that matter to the group. For example, in fall 2006 the AARP's Web site showed that the group's staff had testified before Congress on topics such as bank lending to seniors, nursing home regulations, outsourcing of jobs, identity theft, the implementation of digital television, and enhancing mass transit for seniors.[63] Similarly, the NRA's Web site shows that its staff testified in favor of "right to carry" laws as well as in support of laws that would grant immunity to gun manufacturers for harm committed with weapons they had produced.[64]

Litigation Another inside strategy involves taking the government to court. In bringing their case, groups can argue that the government's actions are not consistent with the Constitution, or that the government has misinterpreted the provisions of existing law.[65] Groups can bring these actions using lawyers on their staff, by hiring a law firm to work for them, or by finding lawyers who are willing to work for free. Groups can also become involved in an existing case by filing *amicus curiae* or "friend of the court" briefs, documents that offer judges the group's rationale for how the case should be decided.

One famous example of interest group litigation was the legal battle waged by the National Association for Advancement of Colored People (NAACP) during the 1950s to desegregate public facilities in southern states.[66] Realizing that southern legislatures would not repeal their discriminatory laws, and that Congress was unlikely to order the states to do so, NAACP staff focused their efforts on legal action, challenging the constitutionality of the laws that allowed separate schools for whites and blacks. This strategy was successful: in 1954, the Supreme Court's *Brown v. Board of Education* decision held that segregated schools were unconstitutional, the first step in the process of overturning the "separate but equal" system.

▲ *The American Civil Liberties Union is an interest group that often uses litigation strategies in its efforts to change government policy. Here, an ACLU attorney describes the group's efforts to limit the Department of Homeland Security's use of "no fly lists" to screen airline passengers.*

Modern interest groups continue to use litigation strategies. The American Civil Liberties Union (ACLU) went to court in 2002 in an attempt to overturn parts of the Patriot Act, such as the provisions that made it easier for federal law enforcement authorities to gather information about American citizens without first obtaining a warrant from a judge.[67] The ACLU's logic was the same as the NAACP's a generation earlier. However, after Congress reauthorized the Patriot Act in 2006, the ACLU abandoned its litigation strategy, focusing instead on direct lobbying and grassroots efforts.

Working Together Interest groups can also work together in their lobbying efforts, formulating a common strategy and meeting, sometimes daily, to discuss progress and future plans. Generally these are short-term efforts focused on achieving a specific outcome, like when interest groups form coalitions to support or oppose confirmation of judicial and cabinet nominees.[68] Similarly, during enactment of the Medicare Prescription Drug Bill in 2003, a coalition of forty-nine interest groups, including the American Medical Association (AMA), the National Federation of Independent Businesses (NFIB), and the Christian Coalition, persuaded legislators to support the addition of medical savings accounts to the proposal.[69]

Why do groups work together? The most obvious reason is the power of large numbers; legislators are more likely to respond when many groups, with large, diverse memberships, are all asking for the same thing.[70] The groups involved may also have different kinds of resources to contribute to the effort. In the case of adding medical savings accounts to the Medicare Prescription Drug Bill, the AMA could offer expertise, while the NFIB and the Coalition could provide grassroots support.[71]

OUTSIDE STRATEGIES

Grassroots Lobbying Directly involving interest group members in lobbying efforts is called **grassroots lobbying**. Members may send letters, make telephone

grassroots lobbying A lobbying strategy that relies on participation by group members, such as a protest or a letter-writing campaign.

calls, participate in a protest, or express their demands in other ways. Many groups encourage grassroots lobbying. For example, the AARP's Web site has a page where members can find names and contact information for their representatives in Congress.[72] Other links allow members to e-mail or fax letters to their representatives that are pre-written by the AARP to express the group's positions on various proposals, such as pension protection legislation and proposals to curb identity theft. The AARP also organizes district meetings with elected officials and encourages their members to attend.

Mass protests are another form of grassroots lobbying. Some protests are aimed at stopping government action, such as when people lie down in front of a bulldozer to stop the building of new highway. A secondary goal is to gain media attention, with the idea of publicizing the group's goals and perhaps gaining new members or financial support. For example, a coalition of anti-abortion groups holds an annual protest called the March for Life in Washington on January 22, the anniversary of the Supreme Court's 1973 *Roe v. Wade* decision, which struck down a group of laws banning abortion. Each year's protest attracts considerable press attention, as thousands of people march and elected officials give speeches.[73]

Grassroots strategies are useful because elected officials are loath to act against a large group of citizens who care enough about an issue to express their position.[74] However, these member-based strategies work only for a small set of interest groups. To take advantage of them, groups first need a large number of members. Ten, twenty, or even a hundred letters are not necessarily going to spur a legislator to action. Legislators begin to pay attention to a letter-writing campaign only when they receive several thousand pieces of mail. (Remember, congressional districts contain roughly 700,000 citizens.)

In addition, for grassroots lobbying to be effective, the letters or other efforts have to come from a member's own constituents. For example, a representative who opposes increases in student aid is not going to worry about a letter-writing campaign if most of the letters come from people who don't live in her district. Moreover, grassroots lobbying works only if the leaders of an interest group can convince their members to participate. As noted earlier, participation is not inevitable, even if members really want their group's lobbying effort to succeed.

The effectiveness of grassroots lobbying also depends on perceptions of how much a group has done to motivate participation. Suppose a representative gets 10,000 e-mails demanding an increase in student aid. However, virtually all the

▲ Interest groups often hold mass protests, such as this 2007 anti-abortion rally in Olympia, Washington, to attract media attention and demonstrate the depth of public support for their goals.

messages contain the same appeal because they were generated and sent from a group's Web site. People in Washington refer to this sort of top-down organized grassroots lobbying as **astroturf lobbying**.[75] Given the similarity of the letters, the representative is likely to ignore the effort entirely, believing that it says more about the group's ability to make participation in its campaign accessible and easy than it does about the number of people in the district who strongly support an increase in student aid.

The evolution of the Internet has important implications for grassroots lobbying. As noted earlier, one argument is that technological developments such as blogs and e-mail make grassroots lobbying easier by lowering the costs of encouraging the members and would-be members of an interest group to get involved by writing a letter, sending an e-mail, making a phone call, or showing up for a protest. Certainly the Internet makes it easier to contact people and lowers the cost of getting involved in some kinds of lobbying efforts. However, if Internet-driven grassroots lobbying looks like astroturf lobbying, it will not achieve its goal of influencing the behavior of elected officials and bureaucrats.

Mobilizing Public Opinion A strategy related to grassroots lobbying involves trying to change what the public thinks about an issue. The goal is not to get citizens to do anything, but to influence public opinion in the hopes that elected officials will see this change and respond by enacting (or opposing) new laws or regulations in order to keep their constituents happy. Virtually all groups try to influence opinion. Most maintain a Web page that presents their message and write press releases to get media coverage of their demands, efforts, and successes. Any contact with citizens, whether to encourage them to join the group, contribute money, or engage in grassroots lobbying, also involves elements of persuasion—trying to transform citizens into supporters, and supporters into true believers.

A focused mobilization effort involves contacting large numbers of potential supporters through e-mail, phone calls, direct mail, television advertising, print media, and Web sites. In order to get legislators to respond, a group has to persuade large numbers of people to get involved; otherwise legislators will ignore the group's efforts. One example of mobilization occurs during congressional hearings on nominees to the Supreme Court or other federal judgeships. One study found that about one-third of the groups that lobbied for or against these nominees also deployed direct mail and leaflets, and ran phone banks to influence public opinion.[76] Similarly, a study of lobbying on health care policy found that interest groups and lobbyists from business, consumer groups, and others, routinely work to shape public opinion in order to build congressional support for their preferred outcomes.[77]

Electioneering Interest groups get involved in elections by contributing to candidates, mobilizing people (including their staff) to help in a campaign, endorsing candidates, funding campaign ads, or efforts to mobilize a candidate's or party's supporters. All of these efforts are aimed at trying to influence who gets elected, with the expectation that changing who gets elected will affect what government does.

Federal laws limit groups' electioneering efforts. Most interest groups are organized as **501(c) organizations**, a designation based on their Internal Revenue Service classification, which means that donations to the group are tax deductible. However, 501(c) organizations face sharp limits on the amount of political activities they can engage in (the formal limit is 20 percent of the group's activities or budget). Interest groups can get around these limits by forming a separate **political action committee (PAC)** or **527 organization** (another IRS designation). A PAC can solicit funds from group members or others to contribute to candidates or to spend on ads in support of candidates, while the 527 can spend money on voter mobilization and

astroturf lobbying Any lobbying method initiated by an interest group that is designed to look like the spontaneous, independent participation of many individuals.

501(c) organizations A tax code classification that applies to most interest groups; this designation makes donations to the group tax-deductible but limits the group's political activities.

political action committee (PAC) An interest group or division of and interest group that can raise money to contribute to campaigns or to spend on ads in support of candidates. The amount a PAC can receive from each of it donors and its expenditures on federal campaigning are strictly limited.

527 organization A tax-exempt group formed primarily to influence elections through voter mobilization efforts and issue ads that do not directly endorse or oppose a candidate. Unlike political action committees, they are not subject to contribution limits and spending caps.

issue advocacy, as long as their efforts do not support or oppose a particular candidate. Most interest groups have separate PACs and 527 organizations. Corporations can also form PACs and 527s, and can ask their employees to contribute.

In 2008, federally focused 527 organizations spent over $200 million on electioneering while PACs spent over $350 million.[78] Nuts and Bolts 9.1 reports campaign spending for the top ten 527 organizations. The top spending 527, the Service Employees International Union, spent over $25 million in 2008, and even the tenth listed organization, Alliance for a New America, spent over $4 million, which was more than the largest PAC. The box also shows that most of the large 527 organizations are strongly tied to one of the major parties. The leaders of these organizations are people with strong ties to either the Republican or the Democratic party, and the literature from these organizations leaves no doubt about their partisan leanings.

While some 527s spend a lot on electioneering, the average is lower than you might think. In the 2008 election, there were 292 active 527 organizations participating in the campaign that spent an average of only about $685,000 each. In other words, while some 527s run substantial ad campaigns across the entire nation, the average 527 only gets involved in a few races.

An example of a well-funded 527 organization is Swift Vets and POWs for Truth, which ran several well-publicized ads in the 2004 presidential race criticizing Democrat John Kerry's claims about his service on a Swift Boat during the Vietnam War.[79] It is hard to say how much these ads affected public perceptions of Kerry; a September 2004 survey found that only about one-quarter of the electorate was following the ads closely.[80] Even so, it is clear that Democratic groups spent much time and money responding to these ads, rather than making a positive case for their candidate.

PACs tend to spend less than 527s on electioneering. The data on the top ten PACs in 2008 is shown in Nuts and Bolts 9.2. Consider the largest PAC, the Na-

POLITICAL PROCESS MATTERS

☑ The rules governing interest group electioneering shape the organization of these groups, including their decisions to form 527 organizations and PACs.

NUTS AND BOLTS 9.1

Big Spenders in the 2008 Election: 527 Organizations

ORGANIZATION	GENERALLY SUPPORTS	TOTAL EXPENDITURES
Service Employees International Union	Democrats	$25,058,103
America Votes	Democrats	$19,672,551
American Solutions Winning the Future	Republicans	$17,470,711
The Fund for America	Democrats	$11,514,130
EMILY's List	Democrats	$10,349,746
GOPAC	Republicans	$8,100,840
College Republican National Committee	Republicans	$6,458,084
Citizens United	Republicans	$5,238,329
Gay and Lesbian Victory Fund	Democrats	$5,145,721
Alliance for a New America	Democrats	$4,890,620

SOURCE: Center for Responsive Politics, 527 Committees: "Top Fifty Federally Focused Organizations," available at http://www.opensecrets.org/527s/527cmtes.php. Based on data released by the FEC on October 27, 2008.

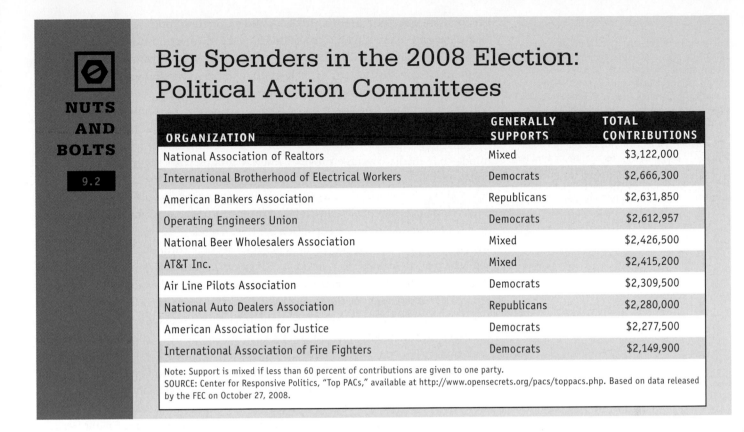

Big Spenders in the 2008 Election: Political Action Committees

ORGANIZATION	GENERALLY SUPPORTS	TOTAL CONTRIBUTIONS
National Association of Realtors	Mixed	$3,122,000
International Brotherhood of Electrical Workers	Democrats	$2,666,300
American Bankers Association	Republicans	$2,631,850
Operating Engineers Union	Democrats	$2,612,957
National Beer Wholesalers Association	Mixed	$2,426,500
AT&T Inc.	Mixed	$2,415,200
Air Line Pilots Association	Democrats	$2,309,500
National Auto Dealers Association	Republicans	$2,280,000
American Association for Justice	Democrats	$2,277,500
International Association of Fire Fighters	Democrats	$2,149,900

Note: Support is mixed if less than 60 percent of contributions are given to one party.
SOURCE: Center for Responsive Politics, "Top PACs," available at http://www.opensecrets.org/pacs/toppacs.php. Based on data released by the FEC on October 27, 2008.

tional Association of Realtors. They contributed just over $3 million to candidates in the 2008 election. By the time you get to the tenth largest PAC, run by the International Association of Fire Fighters, campaign contributions are only slightly over $2 million. Again, these organizations donating millions of dollars are the exception by a significant margin: in the 2008 election, the average PAC gave only $101,000 in contributions. Part of the reason for this lower spending is that PACs' direct contributions to candidates are capped at $5,000 per candidate, and their contributions to party committees are also strictly limited.

These data highlight a sharp difference in electioneering strategies between the very few large, well-funded interest groups and everyone else. A few 527s and PACs have the money to deploy massive advertising and mobilizing efforts for a candidate or issue they like or against those they don't. There are also some mass associations, such as labor unions or ideological groups, that can persuade large numbers of members to work for and vote for candidates the group supports or against candidates the group wants to defeat. But these strategies are not available to the vast majority of interest groups. They simply don't have the resources needed to make a real difference in an election. For the most part, they hope to use their contributions to give modest help to candidates who are sympathetic to the group's goals, and to generate access. That is, they donate to a campaign in the hopes that, once elected, the officeholder will remember the contribution when the group asks for a meeting. Some groups give money to both candidates in a race (as long as neither candidate actively opposes the group's position), figuring that regardless of who wins, they will be able to meet with the winner.[81] A few groups use an extreme version of this strategy, waiting until after the election to make their contribution to the winning candidate, a strategy known as **taking the late train.**

Media Contacts Media coverage helps a group publicize its concerns without spending any money—so most interest group leaders talk often with journalists about the group's goals and activities, suggesting news stories that pertain to the

taking the late train An interest group strategy for gaining access to future officeholders that involves donating money to the winning candidate after an election in hopes of securing a meeting with that person when she takes office.

initiative A direct vote by citizens on a policy change proposed by fellow citizens or organized groups outside government. Getting a question on the ballot typically requires collecting a set number of signatures from registered voters in support of the proposal. There is no mechanism for a national-level initiative.

referendum A direct vote by citizens on a policy change proposed by a legislature or another government body. While referenda are common in state and local elections, there is no mechanism for a national-level referendum.

group's issues and pursuing favorable coverage for the group. Such attention may lead people to join the group, contribute money, or demand that elected officials support the group's agenda. Favorable media coverage also helps a group's leaders assure members that they are actively working on member concerns.

Journalists listen when interest groups call if they believe that the group's story will catch their readers' attention or address their concerns. Smart interest group leaders make it easy for journalists to cover their cause, holding events that are designed to produce intriguing news stories. These stories may not change anyone's mind—but media coverage provides interest groups with free publicity for their policy agenda.

Bypassing Government: The Initiative Process A final outside strategy for interest groups bypasses government entirely: a group can work to get their proposed policy change voted on by the public in a general election through an **initiative** or a **referendum**. Referenda and initiatives allow citizens to vote on specific proposed changes in policy. The difference between these procedures lies in the source of the proposal. In a referendum, the legislature or another government body proposes the question that is put to a vote, whereas the initiative process allows citizens to put questions on the ballot, typically after gathering signatures of registered voters on a petition.

Initiatives can only occur in states and municipalities that have the appropriate procedures in place; there is no mechanism for a nationwide vote on an interest group's proposal. So, if a group wants to use this process to affect national change, it has to get its measure on the ballot in one state at a time. Moreover, only some states allow initiatives, while others permit this kind of vote only on a narrow range of issues. The champion state for initiatives is California, whose citizens often vote on dozens of initiatives in each general election, ranging from funding for stem cell research to limits on taxation and spending.[82]

POLITICAL PROCESS MATTERS

☑ The lack of an initiative or referendum process at the federal level means that groups have to either work through the process state by state or lobby elected officials and bureaucrats for policy changes. There is no straightforward way to bypass these individuals.

There are many examples of groups using the initiative process to change government policy. Most notably, advocates of term limits on state legislatures have used the initiative process to establish limits in twenty-one states, though some have since been overturned by legislative action or subsequent initiatives.[83]

One of the principle concerns about the initiative process is that it favors well-funded groups that can advertise heavily in support of their proposals and work to mobilize supporters to go to the polls on Election Day.[84] However, money often is not enough: even groups with substantial resources, have sometimes been unable to reform policy through the initiative process.[85]

CHOOSING STRATEGIES

Most groups give testimony, do research, contact elected officials and bureaucrats, talk with journalists, and develop legislative and regulatory proposals.[86] In fact, as Table 9.2 shows, most groups use more than one of these strategies. Some groups do not contact legislators and bureaucrats at all, and only a bare majority of interest groups engage in grassroots lobbying. Relatively few groups organize protests, endorse candidates, or provide campaign workers.

A particular group's decisions about which strategies to use depend partly on its resources and partly on what approach the group believes will be most effective in promoting its particular issues. Some strategies that work well for one group's agenda might not be appropriate for another group. The Humane Society is an organization that lobbies to protect against abuse and neglect of animals. It has

TABLE 9.2 INTEREST GROUP TACTICS

Most groups use both inside and outside strategies, and virtually all groups utilize a wide variety of inside strategies. Several outside strategies (advertising, endorsements, and protests) are used by relatively few groups. How might groups' resources drive these lobbying strategies?

TACTIC	PERCENTAGE USING
Inside Strategies	
Contacting journalists	72%
Direct lobbying	84
Drafting new legislation	78
Drafting new regulations	85
Litigation	60
Research reports	81
Testimony	95
Outside Strategies	
Electioneering	
Campaign workers or advertising	24%
Candidate endorsements	22
Campaign contributions	58
Grassroots lobbying	
Organizing protests	20
Soliciting letters or e-mails	68

SOURCE: After Table 8.1 in Frank Baumgartner and Beth Leech, *Basic Interests: The Importance of Groups in Politics and in Political Science* (Princeton, NJ: Princeton University Press, 1998), p. 152.

10 million members and a $120 million annual budget but only a small Washington office.[87] This is because the group focuses on grassroots lobbying and electioneering. In the 2006 election, the Humane Society helped enact an initiative in Arizona that limited the size of factory farms that raise pigs and other livestock, and defeated a Michigan initiative that would have legalized the hunting of mourning doves.

Other interest groups have money or expertise but few members. The Internet2 consortium is one such group comprised of universities, laboratories, and companies that are designing technical standards for a faster Internet. This organization has little money and few individual members, so strategies such as litigation and electioneering are impossible. What they have instead is expertise—knowledge of the demand for new kinds of Internet services, and the cost and feasibility of providing them—which representatives of Internet2 convey to members of Congress by giving testimony on these topics. In February 2006, the vice president of Internet2 testified against proposals to eliminate "net neutrality" (net neutrality prevents companies that control data transmission on the Internet from charging some users more than others).[88] The debate also involves major telecommunications companies such as Comcast and AT&T, who favor the elimination of net neutrality. These corporations deployed substantial funds for lobbying and electioneering as a way of achieving their policy goals.[89] The issue of net neutrality shows how differences in resources can shape groups' choices about lobbying strategies.

How Much Power Do Interest Groups Have?

In April 2005, Jeffrey Birnbaum, a highly regarded reporter for the *Washington Post*, criticized elected officials for focusing on what he saw as minor issues, such as appointing federal judges, while ignoring problems such as the rise in Americans' health care costs and major international issues such as poverty and AIDS. The problem, Birnbaum argued, is that elected officials let interest groups define their agenda:

> Like it or not, we increasingly live in a stage-managed democracy where highly orchestrated interests filter our priorities for us. These groups don't have absolute power, of course. In the nation's capital, home to 30,000 registered lobbyists, hundreds of elected politicians, thousands of journalists, and untold numbers of entrenched bureaucrats, no one's in charge. But long-established entities like the AARP, the Family Research Council, and the U.S. Chamber of Commerce mold our collective thinking and regularly dictate the language and tenor of our civil debates.[90]

Other critics echo Birnbaum's arguments. The Web site of the Alliance for Retired Americans includes detailed critiques of the Medicare Prescription Drug Benefit, arguing that key elements of the program, including the ban on importing cheaper prescription drugs from abroad, resulted from health care industry lobbying. As the Alliance sees it, drug companies got what they wanted; the rest of us did not. Interest groups are also thought to have enormous influence over the actions of unelected bureaucrats. The theory of bureaucratic capture posits that agencies are vulnerable to being "captured," or having their policy goals displaced by the aims of the individuals and corporations they are supposed to regulate. When this happens, bureaucrats become more interested in catering to interest groups rather than implementing policies that are good for the general population.[91] (See Chapter 12 for further discussion of bureaucratic capture.)

The scholarly evidence on interest group influence does not support these claims. Interest group scholars Frank Baumgartner and Beth Leech reviewed all the studies of interest group influence published in major political science journals, and concluded that the literature was a "maze of contradictions."[92] Half of the studies they analyzed found that interest group lobbying had some impact on policy, while the other half found the influence marginal or nonexistent.[93] It seems that some interest groups get what they want from government some of the time, but that success can prove elusive even for groups with many members and large budgets.

▲ While many observers credit lobbying by the pharmaceutical industry for policies such as the Medicare Prescription Drug Benefit (and its ban on importing medicines), favorable public opinion, the efforts of the AARP, and bureaucrats' independent judgments probably had greater influence on passing the Drug Benefit than the advertising, contributions, and direct contacts from industry representatives.

This conclusion makes sense in light of four truths about interest group influence. First, interest groups lobby their friends in government rather than their enemies, and tend to moderate their demands in the face of resistance. A high success rate for an interest group's efforts may reflect these kinds of calculations and compromises rather than supporting the case that they are extremely powerful. For example, the NRA leadership would probably favor a new federal law that made it legal to carry a concealed handgun throughout the nation, since the NRA has lobbied for these laws at the state level and sent their representatives to testify at congressional hearings.[94] Why doesn't the NRA demand federal legislation? There is no sign that Congress would enact this proposal. A proposal that would force states to honor concealed carry permits issued by other states has been introduced in Congress several times in the last decade but never brought up for debate or a vote.[95] Thus, the NRA's decision to forgo lobbying for a federal concealed carry law shows the limits of the organization's power.

Second, some complaints about the power of interest groups come from losers in the political process. As Senator Mitch McConnell (R-KY) once said, "My favorite definition of 'special interest' is a group [that's] against what I am trying to do."[96] Consider the Alliance for Retired Americans and its claims about the Medcare Prescription Drug Benefit mentioned above. The Alliance lobbied against the Medicare legislation just as the drug companies lobbied for it. However, the Alliance was on the losing side of the debate—many of the provisions they favored were not enacted, making them more prone to complain about the influence of "special interests."

Third, many interest groups claim responsibility for policies and election outcomes regardless of whether their lobbying made the difference. Consider former Senate minority leader Tom Daschle (D-SD), who was defeated in his 2004 reelection bid. Many interest groups funded ads criticizing Daschle or contributed to his opponent's campaign.[97] But did they defeat Daschle? They helped, but Daschle was also hurt by strong Republican Party support for his opponent, as well as by the popularity of President Bush, who carried Daschle's home state of South Dakota in the 2004 election.

POLITICS IS CONFLICTUAL

Any time a political outcome is reached, the losers in the policy process will likely bemoan the influence of groups that prevailed.

Finally, the sizable amounts that groups spend to lobby Congress can easily overshadow the more important issue of what they got for their money. Lobbying elected officials and bureaucrats can be expensive, regardless of whether the efforts bring about legislative or regulatory success. As the Challenging Conventional Wisdom box suggests, many lobbying efforts seem to have little effect on the legislative process. This is not to say that legislators ignore interest groups; one study found that lobbying efforts on a particular issue increased the amount of time that legislators spent thinking about or working on the related policy proposals.[98] However, such efforts do not prompt legislators to drop everything else and do what the group wants.

WHAT DETERMINES WHEN GROUPS SUCCEED?

Rather than asking why interest groups are so powerful, it makes more sense to ask when they are powerful.[99] Research points to two related factors that determine the success of lobbying efforts. The first is salience: how many Americans care about what a group is trying to do? The second is conflict: to what extent do other groups or the public oppose the policy change?

Salience Interest groups are more likely to succeed when their request has low salience, or attracts little public attention.[100] When the average voter does not know or care about a group's request, legislators and bureaucrats do not have to

salience The level of familiarity with an interest group's goals among general population.

Microsoft's Lobbying "Success"

The lobbying efforts by one of the world's most profitable corporations show that money doesn't always translate into influence.[a] In the late 1990s, the Department of Justice (DOJ) began antitrust proceedings against Microsoft, alleging that the corporation had used its position as a monopoly supplier of the Windows operating system to gain an unfair advantage over competitors making other kinds of software, such as Web browsers. Some DOJ lawyers argued that the only remedy for Microsoft's dominance was to break up the corporation into two or more separate companies.[b]

It seems likely that Microsoft would respond to the breakup threat by increasing its lobbying operations, asking members of Congress to pressure Justice Department officials to end the investigation or to propose less draconian remedies. Indeed, during the investigation and subsequent trial Microsoft went from spending $2.2 million on lobbying to over $12 million and increased contributions to candidates through its PAC from about $200,000 to nearly $1 million.

These contributions raise a puzzling question. Microsoft is one of the largest corporations in America, with yearly profits in the billions of dollars. Its CEO, Bill Gates, is the richest man in the world with a net worth of about $50 billion. Court proceedings threatened to tear the company apart. If there was ever a time for a corpo-

▲ Despite facing potentially costly federal antitrust proceedings in the late 1990s, Microsoft and its CEO, Bill Gates, spent only a modest amount on lobbying and campaign contributions.

ration to spend a lot of money on lobbying, this was it. But Microsoft spent only $12 million—a lot to the average citizen, but peanuts compared to what was at stake.

More to the point, what did Microsoft get for its money? Not much. The judicial proceedings ended in a settlement that kept Microsoft intact, fined the company, and required minor changes to its Window operating system. However, there is no evidence that Microsoft's lobbying made any difference, and some of the company's lobbyists did very little for their fees. Microsoft hired Ralph Reed, a well-known Republican activist and campaign consultant, to ask prominent supporters of then-presidential candidate George W. Bush to write the can-

didate on Microsoft's behalf. How many letters did Reed generate? Exactly one.[c]

Microsoft's fairly lackluster lobbying experience was not unusual. As discussed in this chapter, many studies of interest group lobbying find that efforts at changing officials' minds in Congress or the bureaucracy rarely succeed. In this regard, interest groups' situation has not changed much since the early 1960s, when an early study of lobbying found that most interest groups concentrated on providing information to legislators and bureaucrats who already agreed with their goals.[d] What about persuasion? According to these studies, most groups had modest funds, a small staff, and limited knowledge of the political situation in Washington. They might want to lobby aggressively to secure their preferred policy outcomes, but they were simply unable to do so. Microsoft's case suggests that many of this study's conclusions still apply.

If it was possible for a company to win policy concessions by lobbying, Microsoft could manage it. Yet even when the very existence of the corporation was in question, Microsoft had only a modest lobbying operation that seemed to make little or no difference in the suit's outcome. Legislators and bureaucrats are harder to persuade than many people think. As a result, lobbying is more focused on providing information to political allies and helping potential new allies get elected than it is about changing minds. ■

worry about the political consequences of giving the group what it wants. The only question is whether the officials themselves favor the request, or can be convinced that the group's desired change is worthwhile. In contrast, when salience is high, a legislator's response to lobbying will hinge on her judgment of constituent opinion: do voters favor what the group wants? As discussed in Chapter 8, the average legislator has a strong interest in reelection and is unlikely to act against her constituents' wishes. As a result, lobbying may count for nothing in the face of public opposition or be superfluous when the group's position already has public support.

Many of the policies that are the focus of lobbying efforts are not at all salient. Consider the National Turkey Federation, an association of turkey farmers and processors. The Foundation sponsors the annual ritual of presenting the president with a (live) Thanksgiving turkey, which is officially "pardoned" by the president and sent to a local petting zoo. In 2002, the Federation was successful in getting federal bureaucrats to change federally funded school lunch program regulations in a way that increased the allowable amount of turkey in various entrees. The policy change resulting from the Federation's lobbying efforts may not sound like a big deal; in fact, it attracted no publicity, which is precisely the point. When few people know of or care about a policy change, interest groups are able to dominate the policy-making process since their request concerns an issue that no one else cares about.

Low-salience issues are surprisingly common. The idea of interest group lobbying probably brings to mind titanic struggles on controversial issues, such as gun control, abortion rights, or judicial nominations, in which groups try to capture public attention as a way of pressuring people in government. In fact, most interest group lobbying is designed to attract little or no public attention—which is the very reason these efforts may stand a good chance of succeeding. This desire to keep their requests quiet may explain why many groups concentrate on inside strategies, avoiding actions that might bring their requests to the attention of the public. While outside strategies may win some public support, they may also generate public opposition, thereby short-circuiting the group's efforts.

Conflict There are two kinds of conflict over lobbying. One involves disagreements between groups: some prefer spending more on a given program, some less. The other involves differences between what a particular interest group wants and the opinions or preferences of the general public. Both kinds of conflict work against lobbying efforts.[101] In the case of the National Turkey Foundation, for example, virtually no one in the general public knew about their proposal, and no interest group lobbied against it. In essence, bureaucrats heard one group asking for something, and, hearing no opposition to the request, decided the policy change was worth making. The situation might have been very different if another group—perhaps the American Pork Producers, or the American Cattlemen—had lobbied against the Turkey Foundation. If so, satisfying one group would have required displeasing at least one other group. Faced with this no-win situation, bureaucrats or legislators would be less likely to give the group what it wanted.

You may wonder: if conflict is fundamental to politics, shouldn't there be at least one group opposing every lobbying effort? The answer is, not necessarily. Because some groups remain latent, there may be no organizations on one side of an issue. And even when opposition groups exist, they might decide against lobbying to concentrate their efforts on other matters. Finally, if only a small percentage of people oppose a group's lobbying effort, the opposition may have little power, even when they are represented by an interest group.

This discussion illustrates that being large or well-funded often does not help an interest group convince government officials to comply with its requests—which completely contradicts many Americans' views of interest groups. As mentioned earlier, many people worry that well-funded interest groups will use their financial resources to dominate the policy-making process, even if public opinion is against them, but these fears are largely unfounded.

Having more money or a large membership increases the number of lobbying strategies available to a group, but success also depends on what the group wants. If there is significant opposition from other groups or from the public, success is unlikely regardless of the group's resources. Think about one of the most powerful interest groups, the NRA, and its advocacy of concealed carry laws. Despite the

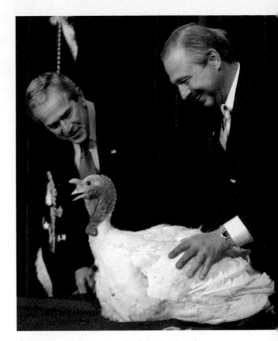

▲ If you have ever heard of the National Turkey Federation, it's probably because of their participation in the annual presidential "pardoning" of a turkey before Thanksgiving. The Federation's relative anonymity has been beneficial: its effort to increase the amount of turkey served in federally funded school lunches was aided by most Americans' lack of awareness of the proposal.

POLITICS IS CONFLICTUAL

Whether an interest group gets what it wants from government depends critically on whether other groups or the general public oppose the group's request.

NRA's millions of members and billion-dollar budget, it has little chance of getting a concealed carry law through Congress because of opposition by other groups and ordinary citizens.

Of course, it would be an overstatement to say that large, powerful interest groups *never* get what they want. Sometimes large groups lobby for uncontroversial policy changes and get them, or they may use the strategies described earlier to secure controversial policies. But when large, powerful groups ask for controversial changes, their resources are typically outmatched by the difficulty of the task. These groups can send staff to lobby, commission research reports, testify, bring lawsuits, and encourage grassroots activity—but these tactics are unlikely to prevail in the face of organized opposition or significant, albeit unorganized, opposition from the public.

Thus, interest groups matter, but they affect a different set of issues and policies than most people think. When legislators or bureaucrats make important, high-profile decisions, interest group lobbying is just one of many influences—and it is rarely the most important one. Lobbying is most effective on issues of interest to relatively few people.

This finding explains the surprising figures on interest group spending discussed earlier: even though groups spend a lot on lobbying each year, the amount is very small compared to total federal spending. Interest group lobbying succeeds without great expenditures on policy questions that are unfamiliar or unimportant to the public, and when only one group is lobbying or all the active groups want the same thing. From the interest groups' perspective, it is pointless to spend money lobbying on high-salience or high-conflict questions, since success is extremely unlikely.

Finally, many people claim that when interest groups get what they want, their efforts help only narrow segments of the population. Sometimes this is true, but all Americans are part of the political process, whether they know it or not, and whether they participate or not. The same points are true for interest groups. Many Americans belong to interest groups; others benefit from interest group lobbying, even though they knew nothing about a group's efforts or did nothing to help. Thus, while it is not clear that everyone wins when an interest group gets what it wants, interest group lobbying clearly benefits more of the population than is immediately apparent.

SECTION SUMMARY

1. Many observers claim that lobbying allows interest groups to get what they want from Congress regardless of what they ask for and whether the public supports the request.
2. Scholarly evidence suggests that these worries are unfounded: much of the time, lobbying by interest groups has little or no effect on policy.
3. The success of a group's lobbying efforts depends in part on the salience of their request and the amount of conflict it engenders.

Conclusion

The number of American interest groups and the amount those groups spend on lobbying have increased rapidly in recent years, bringing a larger variety of organizations and lobbying tactics. The image of slick lobbyists representing rich corporations or well-to-do individuals fits only a small fraction of American interest groups. Not everyone who lobbies in Washington looks like Jack Abramoff or acts as he did.

Contrary to the image of interest groups as powerful manipulators, one of the biggest challenges for these organizations is solving the free rider problem, which they must do in order to organize in the first place. Interest groups are more likely to get what they want when their demands attract little public attention and no opposition from other groups. When a group asks for a large or controversial policy change, it stands little chance of success, even if the group has many members, a large lobbying budget—or an unprincipled leader like Jack Abramoff directing its operation.

Finally, data on how groups lobby show that representatives Randy Cunningham and Bob Ney, who were both sent to prison for taking bribes from lobbyists, are by far the exception rather than the rule. By and large, interest groups shape policy by providing information to like-minded officials in Congress and the bureaucracy, focusing media attention, or mobilizing public outcry about an issue.

CRITICAL THINKING

1. The chapter describes the last few decades' massive increases in the number of interest groups and lobbyists and in the amount spent on lobbying. What factors could cause this increase to level off or even reverse?

2. A friend complains to you about the enormous power of organized interests in American politics, citing a group's recent victory in getting members of Congress to approve its policy proposal. Present three other possible explanations for this victory that do not have anything to do with the political power of the interest group.

3. As described in this chapter, college students are a latent group in American politics. Based on the logic of collective action, what would an interest group entrepreneur have to do to organize this group?

KEY TERMS

astroturf lobbying (p. 331)
centralized groups (p. 316)
citizen groups (p. 315)
coercion (p. 323)
confederations (p. 316)
direct lobbying (p. 326)
economic groups (p. 315)
501(c) organizations (p. 331)
527 organization (p. 331)
free riding (p. 321)
grassroots lobbying (p. 329)
initiative (p. 334)
inside strategies (p. 326)
interest group entrepreneurs (p. 324)
interest group state (p. 310)
interest groups (p. 308)
K street (p. 317)
latent (p. 313)
lobbying (p. 308)
mass association (p. 317)

outside strategies (p. 326)
peak association (p. 317)
political action committee (PAC) (p. 331)
purposive benefits (p. 323)
referendum (p. 334)
revolving door (p. 317)
salience (p. 337)
selective incentives (p. 323)
single-issue groups (p. 315)
solidary benefits (p. 323)
taking the late train (p. 333)
trade association (p. 314)

SUGGESTED READING

Ainsworth, Scott. *Analyzing Interest Groups: Group Influence on People and Policies.* New York: W. W. Norton, 2002.

Baumgartner, Frank, and Beth Leech. *Basic Interests: The Importance of Interest Groups in Politics and in Political Science.* Princeton, NJ: Princeton University Press, 1999.

Carpenter, Daniel. *The Forging of Bureaucratic Autonomy: Reputations, Networks, and Policy Innovation in Executive Agencies, 1862–1928.* Princeton, NJ: Princeton University Press, 2002.

Kollman, Kenneth. *Outside Lobbying: Public Opinion and Interest Group Strategies.* Princeton: Princeton University Press, 1998.

Lowi, Theodore. *The End of Liberalism: The Second Republic of the United States.* New York: W. W. Norton, 1979.

Olson, Mancur. *The Logic of Collective Action,* 2nd ed. Cambridge, MA: Harvard University Press, 1971.

Schattschneider, E. E. *The Semi-Sovereign People.* New York: Harper and Row, 1959.

Schlozman, Kay Lehman, and John Tierney. *Organized Interests and American Democracy.* New York: HarperCollins, 1986.

Verba, Sidney, Kay Lehman Schlozman, and Henry Brady. *Voice and Equality: Civic Participation in America.* Cambridge, MA: Harvard University Press, 1995.

Walker, Jack. *Mobilizing Interest Groups in America.* Ann Arbor, MI: University of Michigan Press, 1991.

10

CONGRESS

Recently, after one author's daughter's little league game, another parent wanted to talk politics. He asked, "What proportion of our members of Congress are crooks?" It is easy to see where the question came from given the scandals involving lobbyist Jack Abramoff and the resignations of several members of Congress, including former House majority leader Tom DeLay (R-TX), who left under an ethics cloud, and Representative Randy "Duke" Cunningham (R-CA), who was convicted of accepting $2.4 million in bribes and illegal gifts from a defense contractor, including a Rolls Royce, valuable rugs and antiques, and $700,000 in a fraudulent house deal.[1] The author tried to convince him that most politicians are hard-working, honest public servants. "Aw, c'mon," was the reply, "Most of those guys are on the take." Unfortunately, this view is all too common, even among the students in American politics classes, and such sentiments have been around for a long time. Mark Twain said, "It could probably be shown by facts and figures that there is no distinctly native criminal class except Congress." He also said, "Assume you are a fool. Now assume you are a member of Congress . . . but I repeat myself." Will Rogers, the popular American cowboy humorist of the early twentieth century said, "Congress is the best money can buy."[2]

But there is another side of Congress that is not as widely recognized by the public. John F. Kennedy's book *Profiles in Courage* examined the careers of eight U.S. senators who "exhibited the most admirable of human virtues." With "grace under pressure," these leaders endured "the risks to their careers, the unpopularity of their courses, the defamation of their characters, and sometimes, but sadly only sometimes, the vindication of their reputations and their principles."[3] Examples include Daniel Webster's powerful oration to try to stop the Civil War and Sam Houston's plea to keep Texas as part of the Union. These leaders made difficult choices that damaged their careers.

Such acts of heroism are not daily events in Congress, but they are more common than you might think. Recent examples include Senator Russ Feingold's (D-WI) actions to protect civil liberties after the terrorist attacks of September 11. Feingold was the only senator to vote against the Patriot Act, which enhanced law enforcement's surveillance powers. Four years later, his views received much broader support as forty Democratic and three Republican senators joined to block extension of the Patriot Act unless stronger protections were enacted for personal

▲ Members of Congress include the "criminal class" noted by Mark Twain—Representative Randy "Duke" Cunningham, shown with his wife, Nancy (left)—and the "profiles in courage" described by John F. Kennedy, such as Senator John McCain (R-AZ, center) and Senator Russ Feingold (D-WI, right), who co-sponsored legislation to reform campaign finance laws.

information such as library and medical records. Senator John McCain's (R-AZ) dogged determination in pushing through an anti-torture bill and Senator Arlen Specter's (R-PA) opposition to the National Security Agency's secret wire-tapping of American citizens' phone conversations—both over the strong objections of a president of their own party—certainly constitute acts of courage.[4]

Given the undeniable virtue, character, and even heroism of many members of Congress throughout history, why is the institution held in such low regard? Part of the reason is that Congress is not very well understood by the general public. Anyone who has watched congressional debates on CSPAN knows that legislative maneuvers can make your head spin, and the discussions can seem mind-numbing. We will show that the basic characteristics of Congress are straightforward, and the motivations that guide members' behavior and the way that Congress works are transparent. Why do members of Congress act the way they do? This chapter argues that members' behavior is driven by their desire to respond to constituent interests (and the closely related goal of reelection), and constrained by the institutional structures within which they operate (like the committee system, parties, and leadership). At the same time, members try to be responsible for the broader national interests, which can often be at odds with constituent interests and the desire to be reelected.

Resolving the tension between being responsible and responsive may not require acts of courage, but it requires members of Congress to make tough decisions, often involving political trade-offs and compromises. Should a House member vote for dairy price supports for her local farmers even if it means higher milk prices for families around the nation? Should a senator vote to subsidize the production of tobacco, the biggest cash crop in his state, despite the tremendous health costs it imposes on millions of Americans? Should a member vote to close a military base, as requested by the Pentagon, even if it means the loss of thousands of jobs back home? These are difficult questions (the tobacco example may seem like a no-brainer, but it is not easy for a legislator from a tobacco state).

Coming to terms with these questions often involves compromise and deal making. For example, when President Clinton needed votes to pass the North American Free Trade Agreement in 1993, he required support from Democrats who were inclined to vote against it because of pressure from constituents. To gain their support, he offered exemptions from portions of the treaty or promised support for a pet project in the future. More recently, when President George W. Bush needed to round up votes for the 2005 Central American Free Trade Agreement, he made

▲ Congress is often highly responsive to its constituents' needs, for example by providing funding for transportation projects such as new highways.

side deals with supporters of a transportation bill that he had previously threatened to veto. The trade agreement passed by a razor-thin margin in the House (217–215). Americans often view this type of wheeling and dealing as improper, but it is an essential part of the legislative process.

Conflicts between local and national interests—and the resulting political compromises—are built into the system. Failure to understand this point is one reason that Congress is held in such low regard. As John F. Kennedy observed nearly fifty years ago, "I am convinced that the decline [in support for Congress]—if there has been a decline—has been less in the Senate than in the public's appreciation of the art of politics, of the nature and necessity of compromise and balance, and of the nature of the Senate as a legislative chamber."[5]

The tension between responsiveness and responsibility illustrates the three themes of this book. Members of Congress regularly make decisions that affect our everyday lives. Indeed, they spend much of their time trying to respond to our desires, which means that many laws are relevant for our interests, such as government support for education, transportation, tax laws, and energy policy. The idea that political process matters is probably more evident in this chapter than any other. Controlling the legislative agenda, determining which amendments will be allowed on a given bill, or stacking an important committee with sympathetic partisans are all common aspects of the legislative process that affect political outcomes. Finally, the conflictual nature of politics is evident in the examples above that illustrate the tensions between responsiveness and responsibility. These trade-offs and compromises inherent to the lawmaking process often result in political conflict.

POLITICS IS CONFLICTUAL

The simultaneous need to represent local and national constituencies often creates conflict in Congress. For example, should members be more concerned about delivering benefits to their district or guarding against the higher taxes or deficits required to pay for those policies?

This chapter begins by examining the constitutional underpinnings of the representational tensions Congress must address. After exploring the issue of support for Congress in more detail, we will describe congressional elections and different ways of understanding representation, discuss Congress's central institutional features, and conclude by considering some potential reforms that might make Congress work better.

Congress's Place in Our Constitutional System

Congress was clearly the "first branch" in the early decades of our nation's history. The Constitution gave Congress the lead role in a vast array of enumerated powers, including regulating commerce, coining money, raising and supporting armies, creating the courts, establishing post offices and roads, declaring war, and levying taxes (see Article I, Section 8, of the Constitution in the Appendix). The president, in contrast, was given few explicit powers and played a much less prominent role in the early years of our history than he does today. Many of Congress's extensive powers come from its implicit powers that are rooted in the elastic clause of Article I, which gives Congress the power "to make all laws which shall be necessary and proper for carrying into execution the foregoing powers."

As noted in the Chapter 2, the compromises that gave rise to Congress's initial structure reflected an attempt to reconcile the competing interests of the day (large versus small states, northern versus southern interests, and proponents of strong

bicameralism The system of having two chambers within one legislative body, like the House and Senate in the U.S. Congress.

national power versus state power). These compromises included **bicameralism**, a two-chambered institution comprised of a popularly elected House and a Senate chosen by state legislatures, allowing slaves to count as three-fifths of a person for purposes of apportionment for the House, and setting longer terms for senators (six years, instead of two years for the House). But these compromises also laid the foundation for the split loyalties that members of Congress have between their local constituencies and the nation's interests. While the Founders hoped that Congress would pass legislation that emphasized the national good over local interests, they also recognized the importance of local constituencies. In *Federalist* 56, for example, Madison said that "it is a sound and important principle that the representative ought to be acquainted with the interests and circumstances of his constituents," and the two-year House term was intended to tie legislators to public sentiment.

At the same time, the *Federalist Papers* made it quite clear that the new government was by no means a direct democracy that would put all policy questions to the public. In *Federalist 57*, Madison pursued this line of thinking, asserting that "the aim of every political constitution is, or ought to be, first to obtain for rulers men who possess most wisdom to discern, and most virtue to pursue, the common good of society." This common good may often conflict with local concerns, as noted in the earlier examples. In these situations, members were expected to both "refine and enlarge the debate" to encompass the common good *and* represent their local constituents.

In general, the Founders viewed the Senate as the more likely institution to enlarge the debate and speak for the national interests; it was intended to check the more responsive and passionate House. Because senators were indirectly elected and served longer terms than House members, the Senate was more insulated from the people. A famous (though maybe fictional) story that points out the differences between the House and Senate involves an argument between George Washington and Thomas Jefferson. Jefferson did not think the Senate was necessary, while Washington supported having two chambers. During the argument, Jefferson poured some coffee he was drinking into his saucer. Washington asked him why he had done so. "To cool it," replied Jefferson. "Even so," said Washington, "we pour legislation into the senatorial saucer to cool it."

This idea of a more responsible Senate survived well into the twentieth century, even after ratification of the 17th Amendment in 1913, which began the direct, popular election of senators. Hubert H. Humphrey (D-MN), who served in the Senate from the 1949 to 1965 and 1970 to 1978 (serving as Johnson's vice president in between) summarized this view: "The first four years are for God and country and the last two years are for the folks back home."[6] Today the Senate is still somewhat more insulated than the House. Because of the six-year term, only one-third of the 100 Senate seats are contested in each election, while all 435 House members are elected every two years. However, differences between the House and Senate's representational roles have become muted as senators seem to campaign for reelection 365 days a year, every year, just like House members.[7] This "permanent campaign" means that senators are less insulated from electoral forces than they once were.

The relationship between the president and Congress has also evolved significantly since the Founding era. Congress's roots in geographic constituencies made it well-suited for the politics of the nineteenth century. In the first 125 years of U.S. history, several great presidents left their mark on national politics (George Washington, Andrew Jackson, and Abraham Lincoln, among others), but Congress dominated much of the day-to-day politics, which revolved around a relatively

POLITICAL PROCESS MATTERS

The six-year term for the Senate makes that body somewhat more insulated from the public than the House, where members are elected every two years.

limited range of issues such as the tariff (taxes on imported or exported goods), slavery, and internal improvements such as building roads and canals. Given the tendency to address these issues with patronage and the **pork barrel** (that is, jobs and policies targeted to benefit specific constituents), Congress was better suited for the task than the president was.

Starting around the turn of the twentieth century and accelerating with the New Deal of the 1930s that established modern social welfare and regulatory policies, the scope of national policy expanded and politics became more centered in Washington. With this nationalization of politics and the increasing importance of national security issues concerning World War II; the Cold War; wars in Korea, Vietnam, and Iraq; and the War on Terror, the president has assumed a more central policy-making role. However, the central tensions between representing local versus national interests remain a key factor in understanding the legislative process and the relationship between members of Congress and their constituents.

pork barrel Legislative appropriations that benefit specific constituents, created with the aim of helping local representatives win reelection.

SECTION SUMMARY

1. The Founders created Congress as the first branch of government, giving it extensive enumerated powers and vast implied powers through the elastic clause.
2. The debates at the Constitutional Convention over the nature of the legislative branch reflected the variety of regional and political interests of the day.
3. The resulting compromises, bicameralism and the representation of national and state interests, reflect that politics necessarily involves conflictual trade-offs about what government does. The Founders' process of creating Congress involved many trade-offs and compromises, and the resulting institution is at the core of American policy making.

Congress and the People

CONGRESS'S IMAGE PROBLEM

While Congress is not comprised of the kind of scoundrels described in the introduction to this chapter, public opinion polls show that most Americans would agree with Mark Twain and Will Rogers. Public approval of Congress bottomed out at 18 percent in March 1992, and stayed in the 20 to 30 percent range over the next few years. Approval inched up to around 50 percent by the end of the 1990s, and then, following the terrorist attacks of September 11, 2001, skyrocketed to 84 percent in one poll (though most polls were still in the 60 to 67 percent range). By May 2008, however, public approval had dropped back to around 19 percent, with one poll showing an all-time low of 16 percent approval.[8] The public's cynical view of Congress runs deep. Well over half of all Americans agree with statements such as "the government is pretty much run by a few big interests looking out for themselves." A NBC/*Wall Street Journal* poll found that 23 percent of respondents thought that "very few" members of Congress are "honest and trustworthy in their conduct," and another 18 percent thought that "fewer than half" of members were honest. An even more telling poll conducted by Fox News in June 2005, asked, "In general, which of the following do you think better describes most senators and representatives on Capitol Hill these days? (a) Statesmen doing service for their country; (b) Petty politicians fighting for personal gain." Only 17 percent answered "statesmen" while 63 percent said "petty politicians" (the rest said "mixed" or "unsure"). Only 18 percent of the public believed that "the best people are attracted to serve in public life." This is a dramatic change from twenty years ago when public approval of Congress was closer to 50 percent. Another poll found that members of Congress landed fifth from the bottom in a ranking of twenty-six professions in terms of perceived honesty and ethical standards. Only 14 percent of the public said that members of Congress had "very high" or "high" standards, which placed them just ahead of stockbrokers, insurance salesmen, advertisers, and car salesmen.[9]

Why does Congress have such an image problem? Some of the abuse heaped on Congress is self-inflicted. While political corruption for personal gain is rare in Congress (only three members have been indicted on bribery charges since 1980), there are periodic scandals such as the "check bouncing" incident involving members' accounts at the House bank and the misuse of House post office funds in the early 1990s, or public outrage over large pay increases for members of Congress.[10] More recently, then-House majority leader Tom DeLay (R-TX) was indicted on money laundering charges for his efforts on behalf of Republican state legislators in Texas. Many members of Congress, Democrats and Republicans alike, were implicated in the scandal surrounding lobbyist Jack Abramoff. Mark Foley (R-FL) brought even more shame on the House when his steamy e-mails to sixteen-year-old male House pages were revealed. Foley quickly resigned when his inappropriate behavior was exposed, but the scandal had important implications for the midterm elections. Simple inertia may also explain this continued cynicism. After years of a continual "blame game," in which the president and Congress point fingers at each other for failed policies, voters have gotten into the habit of believing that politicians are inept (see Challenging the Conventional Wisdom for an alternative view).

Media Influences Perhaps even more importantly, several studies show that the media are also in a cynical, negative mood about politics. While it is a time-worn tradition for politicians to blame the media for their poor standing in the polls, in this instance there is a solid basis for the complaints. One study showed that Congress's image problem may be due, at least in part, to its increasingly negative coverage on television network news. First, the amount of coverage of Congress has declined dramatically, from an average of 124 stories a month between 1972 and 1978 to forty-two stories a month from 1986 to 1992. Ironically, this drop coincides with the beginning of regular, live television coverage of House and Senate proceedings—which could have provided some juicy sound bites for the networks. Cable news shows may have made up for some of this decline in coverage, but the audience for cable news is much smaller than for networks news. More importantly, the study found that the coverage has become far more scandal-based and less concerned with policy developments. The authors of the study concluded, "Until the mid-1980s the networks broadcast about thirteen stories on policy matters for each report on ethical lapses. Since then the evening news has shown nearly one scandal story for every three issue stories."[11]

Research on coverage in the print media is more mixed. One study examined stories on Congress in various national newspapers and magazines during ten important political periods between 1946 and 1992 and concluded that coverage of Congress has always been somewhat superficial and negative, but this tendency has become much worse in recent decades. The study concluded that "press coverage of Congress focuses on scandal, partisan rivalry, and interbranch conflict rather than the more complex subjects such as policy, process, and institutional concerns."[12] From this perspective, the professional context of journalism, with its short news cycle and the need to produce a salable product, creates pressure for superficial coverage that perpetuates Congress's image problem. Burdett Loomis, a

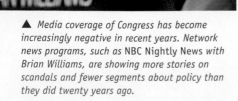

▲ Media coverage of Congress has become increasingly negative in recent years. Network news programs, such as NBC Nightly News with Brian Williams, are showing more stories on scandals and fewer segments about policy than they did twenty years ago.

Buying Votes in Congress

In a recent poll that revealed the common view of corruption in Congress, one question asked, "Do you think recent reports that lobbyists may have bribed members of Congress are isolated incidents, or do you think this kind of behavior is the way things work in Congress?"[a] Only 16 percent said "isolated incidents," while 77 percent said "the way things work." Even more revealing, 57 percent of those surveyed thought that "most" or "about half" of members of Congress "accept bribes or gifts that affect their votes," as opposed to only 36 percent who said "some" did this, and 5 percent who thought "hardly any." The figures showed a somewhat more positive view when people were asked about their own member of Congress, as opposed to members in general, but even then it wasn't a pretty picture. It probably doesn't help matters that members of Congress sometimes joke about the issue; former Senator John Breaux (D-LA) famously said, "My vote isn't for sale, but it can be rented." At least we hope he was joking!

As discussed in Chapter 9, despite this common perception research has not found much evidence that members of Congress even "rent" their votes. The problem is that people tend to contribute money to politicians they agree with, so it is almost impossible to disentangle a member's own views from the positions held by interest groups, lobbyists, and individual contributors. For example, the National Rifle Association supports gun ownership rights and is concerned about gun control laws, so it contributes money to politicians who share those views. When those members vote against gun control, it doesn't mean that the group's donations influenced the members' votes—they would very likely have voted that way anyway. Even the most sophisticated statistical analyses that take into account members' predispositions to vote for particular bills do not find that interest group contributions influence roll call voting.[b]

Despite this lack of evidence in support of the conventional wisdom, reformers raise another important point: even the *appearance* of a conflict of interest may raise questions of legitimacy that contribute to Congress's image problem. Bruce Ackerman of the Yale Law School suggests that campaign contributions should be funneled through a blind trust that would sever the link between contributors and members of Congress. Members of Congress would not know where the money came from, so they could not be influenced by their contributors. However, other experts have criticized the plan as unworkable, questioning whether people would still donate if they had to do so anonymously—and whether they could really remain anonymous.[c] A more workable, but politically controversial, way to limit the potential influence of donors would be to use public funds to finance congressional elections. ∎

congressional scholar, bets his students every year that they cannot find a post-1970 political cartoon that depicts Congress in an unambiguously positive light. In more than ten years, no student has been able to collect on the bet.[13] A more recent study examined more than 8,000 newspaper stories on members of Congress over a two-year period. It found that 70 percent of news stories were neutral, and of the 30 percent that had some spin, positive stories outnumbered negative stories five to one. However, letters to the editor and editorials or opinion pieces were evenly balanced between negative and positive viewpoints.[14] In the wake of the September 11 attacks, media coverage of Congress turned more positive and less critical for a brief period, but mounting opposition to the war in Iraq and the various congressional scandals outlined above have turned coverage more negative again.

The Responsibility–Responsiveness Dilemma Congress's image problem isn't simply a matter of negative media coverage or a cynical public. It is rooted in the basic representational conflicts that arise from Congress's dual roles discussed previously: responsibility for national policy making and responsiveness to local constituencies. This duality may make members of Congress appear to be simultaneously small-minded seekers of meaningless symbolic legislation and great leaders who debate

POLITICS IS EVERYWHERE

Broadcast news includes reports on Congress, but there are now fewer of these stories than a couple of decades ago, and they have a more negative focus, contributing to Congress's image problem.

important issues. Indeed, the range of issues that Congress must address is vast, from taxes and health care reform to overseeing the classification of black-eyed peas; from authorizing the war with Iraq and expanding free trade to declaring a "National Cholesterol Education Month." (The latter is an example of commemorative legislation, which now comprises about half of the laws Congress enacts.) Part of the national frustration with Congress, then, arises because we want our representatives to be responsible *and* responsive; we want them to be great national leaders *and* take care of our local and even, at times, personal concerns. But often it is impossible to satisfy both of these demands at the same time—difficult choices have to be made between being responsive or responsible. Rather than understanding these issues as inherent in the legislative process, we often accuse members of **gridlock** and partisan bickering when our conflicting demands are not met. For example, public opinion polls routinely show that the public wants lower taxes, more spending in many areas (such as education, the environment, and health care), and balanced budgets, but those three things cannot happen simultaneously. We often expect the impossible from Congress and then are frustrated when it doesn't happen.

Congress's Image and the Electoral Connection Another well-documented element of the complex relationship between the public and Congress is that citizens often think quite highly of their own representatives while disliking Congress as an institution. There is a persistent 30 to 40 percent gap between approval ratings for individual members and for the institution. As one of the leading congressional scholars of the twentieth century, Richard Fenno, put it, "If Congress is the 'broken branch,' why do we love our congressman so much?" This pattern is consistent with the trade-off between responsibility and responsiveness. Members of Congress tend to respond more to their constituents' demands than take on the responsibility of solving national problems. And when Congress becomes embroiled in debates about constituencies' conflicting demands, the institution may appear ineffectual. But as long as members of Congress keep the "folks back home" happy, their individual popularity will remain high.

A classic book by political scientist David Mayhew, *Congress: The Electoral Connection,* established these observations as the common wisdom.[15] Mayhew argues any member's individual goal is to make a career in politics, and thus in the short-run, to get reelected. This **electoral connection** is the essential factor for understanding congressional behavior and how the institution is structured. We will explore this connection in more detail later in this chapter.

For now, it is important to note that the electoral connection can help explain Congress's image problem in several ways. First, and most obviously, it feeds the cynical view that politicians are *only* interested in keeping their jobs rather than in true public service. Second, there is some evidence that voters are starting to question the value of pork-barrel spending, even when it is targeted to their district. For example, conservative Republicans who try to bring home the pork while criticizing the government for its huge budget deficits are likely to suffer electoral consequences.[16] Third, members' desire to please means that Congress has a difficult time refusing any group's demands, which may create incoherent and contradictory policies. Fourth, given that most members are experts at getting reelected (typically about 95 to 97 percent of House incumbents are reelected), they achieve a certain level of independence from the party leadership; that is, they do not depend on leaders for their reelection. This contributes to the fragmentation of Congress and creates difficulties for the leadership as they attempt to shepherd policies through the legislative maze. Finally, members are able to remain popular despite the negative public opinions of Congress as an institution because they have become adept at cultivating local contacts in forums such as town meetings, homecoming parades, and radio call-in shows.

REPRESENTATION AND THE CONSTITUENCY

Styles of Representation To understand congressional behavior, we must first examine the two basic components of the relationship between a constituency and its member of Congress: descriptive and substantive representation. The former is rooted in the politician's side of the relationship. Does the member of Congress "look like" the constituents, in demographic terms? Is the member African American, Latino, or white, male or female, Catholic, Protestant, or some other religion? Many people believe that such **descriptive representation** is a distinct value in itself. Having positive role models for various demographic groups helps create greater trust in the system, and there are benefits from being represented by someone who shares something as basic as skin color with constituents.

Descriptive representation is also related to the tension between responsiveness and responsibility. For example, African American members of Congress typically come from electorally safe districts where they enjoy high levels of support and trust from their constituents.[17] In general, constituents report higher levels of satisfaction with representatives who are of their same race. This means that descriptively represented constituents are more likely to assume that their interests are being represented than those who are not.[18] If you doubt that descriptive representation makes a difference, ask yourself whether it would be fair if all 435 House members and 100 Senators were white, male Protestants. While the demographics of Congress are considerably more diverse than this, the legislature does not come close to "looking like us" on a nationwide scale. Figure 10.1 shows that, although we still

---

FIGURE 10.1a WOMEN IN CONGRESS, 1937–2007

While Congress still does not have gender parity, there have been substantial gains in recent years. What difference does it make for policy to have more women in Congress?

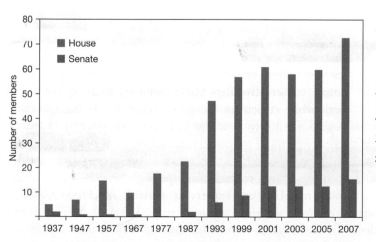

SOURCE: Data from U.S. Capitol, Office of the Clerk, Women in Congress, "Historical Data Overview," available at http://womenincongress.house.gov/data/index.html.

FIGURE 10.1b MINORITIES IN THE HOUSE, 1937–2007

Hispanics now comprise the largest ethnic minority in the United States, yet they still lag behind African Americans in terms of representation in the House. What do you think explains this difference? How might it affect policy?

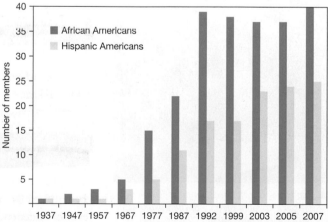

SOURCE: Compiled from Mildred L. Amer, "Black Members of the United States Congress: 1870–2005," Congressional Research Service Report RL30378, August 4, 2005, and recent election returns.

substantive representation When a member of Congress represents constituents' interests and policy concerns.

trustee A member of Congress who represents constituents' interests while also taking into account national, collective, and moral concerns that sometimes cause the member to vote against the preference of a majority of constituents.

delegate (congressional role) A member of Congress who loyally represents constituents' direct interests.

politico A member of Congress who acts as a delegate on issues that constituents care about (like civil rights) and as a trustee on more complex or less salient issues (like some foreign policy or regulatory matters).

have a long way to go, the nation is more descriptively represented now than at any point in history.

While descriptive representation is important, it only goes so far. As one political observer pointed out, we do not expect lunatics to be represented by crazy people.[19] More important than a member's race, gender, or religion, many argue, is the *substance* of what the member of Congress does. Merely because a representative shares some characteristics with you does not necessarily mean that he or she will represent your interests (though, as noted above, the two tend to be linked, especially for racial representation). **Substantive representation** moves beyond appearances to specify how the member serves constituents' interests. Two models go back at least until the eighteenth century: (1) the **trustee**, who represents the interests of constituents from a distance, weighing a variety of national, collective, local, and moral concerns, and (2) the **delegate**, who has a simple mandate to carry out the direct desires of the voters. Another way to think about these roles is that trustees are more concerned with being responsible while delegates are more interested in responsiveness.

One of the most famous examples of a representative acting as a trustee was Marjorie Margolies-Mezvinsky (D-PA) in a crucial 1993 vote on President Clinton's budget, which included some controversial tax increases and spending cuts to balance the budget. Hours before the vote, she told reporters that she would vote against the budget, but she had also promised President Clinton that she would support the bill if her vote was needed. As she walked down the aisle to cast the critical vote in the 218–216 cliffhanger (in which she fulfilled her promise to the president), Republican members chanted, "Goodbye Majorie," in an accurate forecast of her defeat in the next election.[20] Representative Margolies-Mezvinsky did what she thought was in the best long-term interests of her constituents and the nation, even though it ended her career.

A delegate, on the other hand, does not have to worry about incurring the wrath of angry voters because she simply does what the voters want—and examples are so numerous it is pointless to single out one member for attention: when it comes to tax cuts, agricultural subsidies, increases in Medicare payments, or new highway projects, hundreds of representatives act as delegates for their districts' interests.

Truth be told, the trustee/delegate distinction is mostly important as a theoretical point of departure for talking about the representation roles. Nearly all members act like trustees in some circumstances and like delegates in others. The third model of representation is the **politico**, who is more likely to act as a delegate on issues that are highly salient to the constituency, such as civil rights, but is more likely to be a trustee on less salient or very complex issues, such as some foreign policies. Therefore, the crucial component of representation is the nature of the constituency and how the member of Congress attempts to balance and represent constituents' conflicting needs and desires.

The Role of the Constituency Our characterization of the representative–constituency relationship raises a host of questions. How much do voters monitor their representatives' behavior? Can representation work if voters are not paying attention? The most demanding theory of representation, known as policy responsiveness, requires that voters express basic policy preferences, representatives respond to those desires, and then voters monitor and assess the politician's behavior. However, those conditions are rarely met because most constituents do not follow congressional politics.

Despite this lack of attention, representational links remain strong through indirect mechanisms. Members of Congress behave as if voters were paying attention,

▲ Representative Marjorie Margolies-Mezvinsky (D-PA) demonstrated the role of the trustee with her decisive vote on President Clinton's 1993 budget.

even when constituents are inattentive. Incumbents know that at election time, challengers may raise issues that become salient after the public thinks about them, so they try to deter challengers by anticipating what the constituents would want *if they were fully informed.*[21] For example, the public didn't know much about stem cell research until it became a big issue in the 2006 midterm elections. Savvy incumbents would have tried to preempt any vulnerability on that issue *before* a strong challenger raised the issue in a campaign by staking out a position consistent with what the voters would want once they knew more about the issue. Richard Fenno points out that some segments of the constituency are more attentive and more important for the member's reelection than others. These constituents will have a different representational relationship than those who occupy one of the more distant concentric circles in Fenno's characterization (Figure 10.2)[22]

Another way to examine the representative–constituency relationship is to look at differences across districts. A representative from South Dakota will have to address different concerns than one from New York City. How do districts vary? First, and most obviously, they differ in size: Senate "districts" (that is, states) vary in terms of area from Alaska to Delaware, and in terms of population from California to Wyoming. House districts all have about 700,000 people, but they vary tremendously in size (591,000 square miles for the at-large seat in Alaska to seven or eight square miles for several New York City districts). Districts also differ in terms of who lives there and what they want from government. Some districts are located in poor city neighborhoods, where voters often focus on economic development, crime control, antipoverty programs, and looser immigration regulations. Some are wealthy and urban, where citizens tend to demand foreign aid and support higher taxes to pay for domestic policy initiatives. Some are suburban, where funding for education and transportation are likely the critical issues. Some are conservative and rural, where agricultural policies typically dominate and support for tax cuts is strong. Districts vary from the religious to the secular, from domination by one industry to a diversified corporate base to no industry at all. Some consider government a force for good while others argue that government should get off the people's backs. And some districts are a mixture of all of these things.

Because districts have a variety of opinions, demands, and concerns, the legislators they elect differ from each other as well. Regardless of the office, most voters want to elect someone whose policy positions are as close to theirs as possible. As a result, legislators tend to reflect the central tendencies of their districts. At one level, electing a legislature that thinks like America sounds like a good thing. If legislators act and think like their districts, then the legislature will contain a good mixture of the demands and interests held across the country or state. The problem is that finding an acceptable compromise is not easy. We elect legislators to get things done, but they may be unable to agree on anything—not because they are stupid or unwilling to compromise, but because their disagreements are too fundamental to bridge. Again, consider abortion rights. The country is sharply divided on this issue, and the same divisions exist in the House and the Senate, and in most state legislatures. The fact that legislators have not arrived at a decision that puts this issue to rest is no surprise: just as citizens disagree, so do their elected representatives.

Despite the vast differences between congressional constituencies, voters want many of the same things: a healthy economy, a safe country (both in terms of national defense and local crime), good schools for their children, and effective health care. Figure 10.3 reports responses to a survey that asked citizens to rate the importance

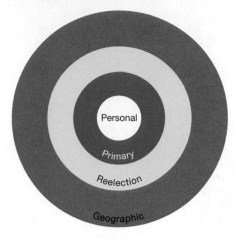

FIGURE 10.2 **FENNO'S CONCENTRIC CIRCLES**

Personal

Primary

Reelection

Geographic

SOURCE: Based on Richard F. Fenno, *Home Style: House Members in Their Districts* (Boston: Little, Brown, 1978).

POLITICAL PROCESS MATTERS

 Strong challengers can impose electoral accountability on incumbents by raising issues that might otherwise go unnoticed by the voters.

FIGURE 10.3 THE JOB OF A MEMBER OF CONGRESS

Congress is often criticized for passing pork-barrel policies that benefit specific districts. Yet this survey clearly shows that people want their "fair share" and are less concerned with whether their representative works on "national bills." Why do you think that is? Could it have to do with the wording of the questions?

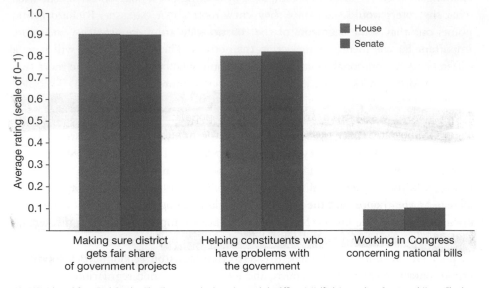

SOURCE: Adapted from Paul Gronke, *The Electorate, the Campaign, and the Office: A Unified Approach to Senate and House Elections* (Ann Arbor, MI: University of Michigan Press, 2001), Table 6.5.

of three aspects of a legislator's job: dealing with national issues, making sure that their district received its fair share of federal support, and helping individual constituents deal with government. The survey showed strong support for the theme of this chapter concerning tensions between local and national concerns. Citizens clearly want their elected officials to get them a fair share of the federal pie and do casework for the district, the classic indicators of responsiveness. But the respondents in this poll showed little interest in having the representatives "work in Congress concerning national bills." Thus, responsibilities for national interests may be more difficult for members of Congress to explain to their constituents.

REDISTRICTING

The final point to understand about the context of legislative constituencies concerns their physical boundaries. District boundaries determine who is eligible to vote in any given congressional race, and these boundaries are redrawn every ten years, after each national census. **Redistricting** is the task of state legislatures and its official purpose is to ensure that districts are roughly equal in population, which in turn ensures that every vote counts equally in determining the composition of the legislature. District populations vary over time as people move from state to state or from one part of a state to another. At the national level, states gain or lose legislative seats after each census through a process called **apportionment** as the fixed number of House seats (435) is divided among the states (that is, the states that are growing the fastest, like California, Florida, and Texas, gain seats, while those that are not growing as fast, such as New York and Michigan, lose seats). The one legislature in America that is not redistricted is the U.S. Senate, which by design elects two legislators per state, giving voters in small states more influence than those in large states.

redistricting Redrawing the geographic boundaries of legislative districts. This happens every ten years to ensure that districts remain roughly equal in population.

apportionment The process of assigning the 435 seats in the House to the states based on increases or decreases in state populations.

In theory, redistricting proceeds from a firm set of principles that define what districts should look like. One criterion has already been mentioned: districts should be roughly equal in population. Districts should also capture "communities of interest," meaning that they should group like-minded voters into the same district. There are also a variety of technical criteria such as compactness (districts should not have extremely bizarre shapes) and contiguity (one part of a district cannot be completely separated from the rest of the district). Mapmakers also try to respect traditional natural boundaries and avoid splitting municipalities, protect incumbents, preserve existing districts, and avoid diluting the voting power of racial minorities.

While these principles play an important role in redistricting, they are not the driving force in the redistricting process. Just as war is "diplomacy by other means," redistricting is electioneering by other means. Suppose a Democrat holds a state assembly seat from an urban district populated mainly by citizens with strong Democratic Party ties. After a census, the Republican-dominated state legislature develops a new plan that extends the representative's district into the suburbs, claiming that the change counteracts population declines within the city by adding suburban voters. However, these suburban voters will likely be Republicans, increasing the chance that the Democrat will face strong opposition in future elections, and maybe lose his seat. Such changes have an important impact on voters as well. Voters moved to a new district by a change in boundaries may be unable to vote for the incumbent they have supported for years, instead getting a representative who doesn't share their views.

In congressional redistricting, a reduction in the number of seats allocated to a state can lead to districting plans that put two incumbents in the same district, forcing them to run against each other. Needless to say, incumbents from one party use these opportunities to defeat incumbents from the other party. For example, when Pennsylvania lost two congressional seats after the 2000 census, the Pennsylvania state legislature, with Republican majorities in both Houses, created two districts in which Democratic incumbents faced each other in primary elections, thereby increasing the likelihood of a seat shift toward the Republicans. The most dramatic recent example of redistricting for partisan purposes was in Texas. Deviating from the standard practice of redrawing district lines only once every decade, Republicans decided to change the district boundaries that had only been in effect for one election. Democratic legislators were outraged by the partisan power grab and literally fled the state (they hid out in Oklahoma) to prevent the special session of the legislature from convening. Eventually Republicans were able to implement their plan and gain five House seats in the 2004 elections. The Supreme Court upheld the Texas plan, saying that even when partisan advantage is the only motivation for redistricting, this does not make the resulting plan unconstitutional (however, the Court left the door open for future challenges under the equal protection clause of the 14th Amendment).[23]

These attempts to use the redistricting process for political advantage are called **gerrymandering**, after Elbridge Gerry, a Massachusetts House member and governor, vice president under James Madison, and author of one of the original partisan redistricting plans (including a district with a thin, winding shape resembling a salamander). In addition to the partisan gerrymanders discussed above, there are several other types outlined in Nuts and Bolts 10.1.

Redistricting may yield boundaries that look highly unusual, even bizarre. Consider the 1992 redistricting in North Carolina, where the Justice Department told state legislators that they needed to create two districts with majority populations of minority voters (called minority-majority districts). Figure 10.4 shows the plan they enacted, in which the district boundaries look like a pattern of spider webs and ink

gerrymandering Attempting to use the process of redrawing district boundaries to benefit a political party, protect incumbents, or change the proportion of minority voters in a district.

Types of Gerrymanders

Partisan gerrymanders: Elected officials from one party draw district lines that benefit candidates from their party and hurt candidates from other parties. This usually occurs when one party has majorities in both houses of the state legislature and occupies the governorship, and can therefore enact redistricting legislation without votes from the minority party.

Incumbent gerrymanders: Lines are drawn to benefit the current group of incumbents. This usually occurs when control of state government is divided between parties, and support from both parties is required to enact a districting plan, or when plans must be approved by judges or bipartisan panels.

Racial gerrymanders: Redistricting is used to help or hurt the chances of minority legislative candidates. The Voting Rights Act (VRA) of 1965 mandated that districting plans for many parts of the South be approved by the U.S. Department of Justice or a Washington, DC, district court. Subsequent interpretation of the 1982 VRA amendments and Supreme Court decisions led to the creation of districts in which racial minorities are in the majority. The original aim of these majority-minority districts was to raise the percentage of African American and Latino elected officials. However, Republicans in some southern states have used this requirement to enact plans that elect minorities (who tend to be Democrats) in some districts, but favor Republicans in adjoining districts.

Candidate gerrymanders: District plans that favor certain individuals, particularly state legislators planning to run for the U.S. House. For example, a Republican state legislator would want to construct a congressional district with a high percentage of Republican voters and as many of his current constituents as possible.

blots. The most unusual is the 12th District, known as the "I-85 district," which began in Charlotte, proceeded up interstate I-85 to Greensboro, picked up some voters there, then followed the highway to Durham, where it gained additional voters. The strangest aspect of this plan was that in some areas the district was only as wide as I-85 itself, following the highway off an exit ramp, over a bridge, and down the entrance ramp on the other side. This unusual move prevented the I-85 district from bisecting the district through which it was traveling, which would have violated the state law requiring contiguous districts.

The North Carolina example shows how convoluted redistricting plans can become. Part of the complexity is due to the availability of census databases that allow line-drawers to divide voters as closely as they want, moving neighborhood by neighborhood, even house by house when developing their plans. Why bother with this level of detail? Redistricting influences who gets elected. Put another way, redistricting is not an academic exercise; it is active politicking in its most fundamental form. The North Carolina plan was ultimately declared unconstitutional by the Supreme Court—a ruling that only established that line-drawers could not get away with overtly outrageous plans. The current legal standard after a decade-long series of cases is that race cannot be the predominant factor in drawing congressional district lines, but it may be a factor. However, there is still plenty of room to create districts that have profound political consequences.

The obvious political implications of redistricting often lead to demands that district plans be prepared or approved by nonpartisan committees, or by panels of judges who are theoretically immune from political pressure. Some states have such requirements, but even districts drawn by unelected people have political consequences. For example, a plan that minimizes changes to district lines typically helps incumbents retain districts that they know they can win.

POLITICAL PROCESS MATTERS

 District boundaries may have an important impact on the type of House member who gets elected, in terms of party, race, and other factors.

FIGURE 10.4　NORTH CAROLINA REDISTRICTING, 1992

This set of House districts was the subject of the landmark Supreme Court ruling *Shaw v. Reno* (1993), in which the Court said that "appearances matter" when drawing district lines. Do you agree? Should other factors such as race, party, and competitiveness play a greater role than district shape?

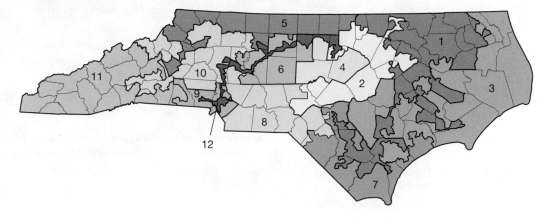

SOURCE: North Carolina General Assembly, 1992 Congressional Base Plan No. 10, available at http://www.ncga.state.nc.us/Redistricting/Archives/Defuncan10/92BP10_Map_Detail.pdf.

SECTION SUMMARY

1. Representing the interests of constituents always involves trade-offs, starting with the nature of the representation itself: is descriptive representation important? Should a member act more like a delegate, trustee, or politico?

2. Answering these questions depends on one's views of responsible versus responsive behavior from Congress. Should a member of Congress do what is right for the nation or for the district when those two constituencies want different things?

3. Parts of the constituency from different regions, races, classes, and ethnicities require another set of trade-offs, as do Fenno's concentric circles. These trade-offs are illustrated most dramatically in redistricting, but they are inherent in the concept of representation.

Elections and Member Behavior

The desire to be reelected influences House members' and senators' behavior both in the district and in Congress. Take, for example, the early career of Representative Tammy Baldwin (D-WI). In 1998 she became the first woman from Wisconsin and the first openly gay person ever elected to a freshman term in Congress.[24] In her first two elections, she won with the overwhelming support of liberal voters in Madison, but lost the surrounding rural areas and suburbs, narrowly winning district-wide with 52 percent and 51 percent of the vote. Baldwin recognized that she needed to shore up support outside Madison and spent considerable time over the next several years meeting with constituents in the rural and suburban parts of her district. She also spent a great deal of time on issues important to these voters, such as the dairy price support program and the problem of chronic wasting disease, which had infected Wisconsin deer. Having shored up her electoral base

▲ *Representative Tammy Baldwin (D-WI) meets with students at Edgewood High School in Madison, Wisconsin. This type of constituent meeting is an important way for incumbents to shore up their electoral support.*

incumbency safety The relative infrequency with which members of Congress are defeated in their attempts for reelection.

(and having benefited from favorable redistricting in 2002), she cruised to victories in her next two elections with 66 percent and 63 percent of the vote.

This story has been repeated hundreds of times across the country and members' success at pleasing constituents has produced large rewards. As Figure 10.5 shows, very few members are defeated in their reelection races. One way that political scientists have documented the growth of **incumbency safety** is to examine the electoral margins in House elections. If a member is elected with less than

---

FIGURE 10.5a **HOUSE INCUMBENCY REELECTION RATES, 1948–2006**

The rate of defeat for incumbent House members is very low, typically in the 5 to 10 percent range, while total turnover is quite a bit higher. Which data are more important for debates about the importance of term limits? Which data are more central to discussions of electoral accountability?

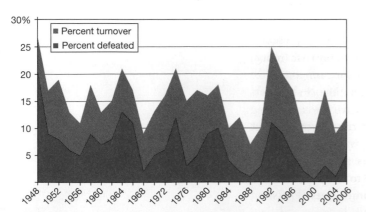

FIGURE 10.5b **SENATE INCUMBENCY REELECTION RATES, 1948–2006**

Incumbency reelection rates are noticeably more volatile in the Senate than in the House. What implications does this have for the Founders' belief that the Senate should be more insulated from popular control than the House? Does the Senate's six-year term help provide that insulation?

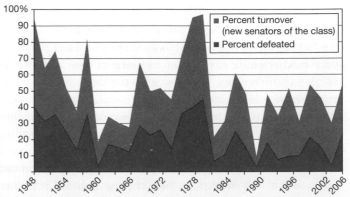

SOURCE: Compiled from Center for Responsive Politics, Reelection Rates over the Years, available at http://www.fecwatch.org/bigpicture/reelect.php?cycle=2006, and Norman J. Ornstein, Thomas E. Mann, and Michael J. Malbin, *Vital Statistics on Congress: 1999–2000* (Washington, DC: CQ Press, 2000), pp. 60–3.

55 percent of the vote, he or she is said to hold a marginal seat. Since the late 1960s, the number of marginal districts has been declining. Having fewer marginal districts does not necessarily translate into fewer incumbent defeats, but in the past two decades, incumbent reelection rates have been near record-high levels.[25] Even in 1992 and 1994, when there was a strong anti-incumbent mood in the nation, 93 percent of the incumbents who ran were reelected. In the 2004 general elections, only seven House incumbents were defeated—more than a 98 percent success rate—and four of them lost because of the partisan Texas redistricting. In 2006, the reelection rate was down a bit, but 94 percent of House incumbents (and all the Democratic incumbents) were reelected. Even in 2008, undoubtedly a historic election and one that many called "transformational," 95 percent of House incumbents were reelected. While the Democrats picked up some seats in the Senate, reelection remained the norm there as well. Why are incumbents so successful? Scholars have offered several reasons for this increase in incumbency safety.

In the District: Home Style One explanation for increasing incumbency safety is directly rooted in the diversity of congressional districts and states. Members typically respond to the diversity in their districts by developing an appropriate home style: a way of relating to the district.[26] More specifically, a home style shapes the way members allocate resources, the way incumbents present themselves to others, and the way they explain their policy positions.

Given the variation among districts, it makes sense that members' home styles vary as well. In some rural districts it is important for representatives to have local roots, and voters expect extensive contact with members. Candidates who relocate from other areas rarely succeed in such districts. Urban districts expect a different kind of style. They have a more mobile population so it is not crucial to be home-grown. Voters tend to expect less direct contact and place more emphasis on how members explain their policy positions. Incumbency safety may be explained in part by the skill with which members have cultivated their individual home styles in the last two decades. Members are spending more time at home and less time in Washington than was true a generation ago. This familiarity with the voters has certainly helped members remain in office, though a concrete measure of this variable is difficult to develop.

Nuts and Bolts 10.2 provides an example of how one member, Representative Tammy Baldwin, spends her time in Washington and in her district. In general, a legislator's workday in the Capitol is split between committee meetings, briefings, staff meetings, meetings with constituents, and various dinners and fundraisers with interest groups and other organizations, punctuated by dashes to the floor of the House or Senate to vote. Days in the district are spent meeting with constituents to explain what is happening in Washington and listen to voters' concerns.

Campaign Fund-Raising Raising money is also key to staying in office. Thomas "Tip" O'Neill, Speaker of the House in the 1970s and 1980s, used to say that "money is the mother's milk of politics." Incumbents need money to pay for campaign staff, travel, and advertising. It takes at least $750,000 to make a credible challenge to an incumbent in most districts, and in many areas with expensive media markets the minimum price tag is $1 million or more. Few challengers can raise that much money. The gap between incumbent and challenger spending has grown dramatically in the past decade, and incumbents now spend about six times as much, on average, as challengers. Incumbents have far greater potential to raise vast sums of money when it is needed, in part because political action committees (PACs) are typically unwilling to risk alienating an incumbent by donating to challengers. (See Chapter 9 for a complete discussion of PACs.)

Typical Work Days for Representative Tammy Baldwin (D-WI)

IN WASHINGTON, DC

(Votes scheduled throughout the day)

9:00–10:00 Briefing hosted by Sen. Clinton: Discussion of the "Federal Marriage Amendment" (Musgrave Amendment), hate crimes legislation, the Employment Non-Discrimination Act, federal benefits, and HIV-AIDS

10:00–12:00 Hearing, Judiciary Subcommittee on the Constitution: H.J.Res 56, the Federal Marriage Amendment

12:00–1:00 Lunch

1:00–1:15 Constituent meeting: Bankruptcy reform, deposit insurance reform, real estate brokerage legislation

1:15–2:15 Meeting with legislative staff

2:15–2:45 Prepare with staff for meeting on Federal Marriage Amendment

2:45–3:45 Meeting with other members on Federal Marriage Amendment

3:45–4:30 Meeting with Swiss Parliamentarians and Officials (New Glarus, WI, reflects the strong, continuing influence of early Swiss settlers and is home to The Swiss Center.)

4:30–7:00 Office time

7:30–10:00 Dinner hosted by Swiss ambassador with Swiss officials and other House members

IN THE DISTRICT

8:00–8:45 Travel to Jefferson, WI

9:00–9:45 Welcoming remarks, Jefferson County Grants Workshop: Presentations on securing federal grants

9:45–10:00 Military Service Medals Presentation to Ft. Atkinson World War II veteran at Jefferson County Courthouse

10:00–10:45 Travel to Madison, WI

11:00–12:00 Office time and lunch

12:00–1:00 Travel to Beloit, WI

1:00–2:00 Welcoming remarks, Rock County Grants Workshop: Presentations on securing federal grants

2:00–3:00 Travel to Madison, WI; consider remarks for evening speech

3:00–6:00 Office time: Research for speech on the Patriot Act

6:00–6:45 Dinner

6:45–7:00 Travel to University of Wisconsin campus

7:00–8:00 Speak to Political Science Honor Society on campus: Personal reflections on your life in politics, question and answer session.

Note: The authors would like to thank Representative Tammy Baldwin and her press secretary, Jerilyn Goodman, for sharing this information. Ms. Goodman emphasized that there really isn't a "typical day" for the member, but said that these two days were as good as any.

Money also functions as a deterrent to potential challengers. A sizeable reelection fund signals that an incumbent knows how to raise money (and can raise more), and will run a strong campaign. The aim is to convince would-be challengers that they have a slim chance of beating the incumbent—and to convince contributors and party organizations that there's no point in trying to find or support a challenger.

This last point is crucial in explaining incumbency safety because it is nearly impossible to beat an incumbent with a weak challenger. Political scientists Gary Jacobson and Samuel Kernell illustrate this point with a story about Representative Robert Leggett of California. Leggett was a principle target of the 1976 "Koreagate" investigation (a scandal involving several House members), but he was not considered vulnerable enough for any strong Republicans to challenge him. They note, "By the time it came out that he had fathered two children by an aide, had been supporting two households for years, and even forged his wife's name on a deed for the second house, the nominations had already been set. His Republican opponent was an obscure, retired state civil servant who thought that the outcome of the election 'was mostly up to God' and spent only $10,674 on the election."[27] Leggett managed to hang onto his seat for one more term. The moral of the story is that you cannot beat somebody with nobody. Only 10 to 15 percent of challengers in a typical election year have any previous elective experience; when such a high proportion of challengers are amateurs, it is not surprising so many incumbents win.

Constituency Service In addition to cultivating a home style and raising money, another thing incumbents do to get reelected is to "work their districts," taking every opportunity to meet with their constituents, listen to their concerns, and perform casework, helping constituents interact with government programs or agencies. Most legislators travel around their districts or states with several staffers whose job is to follow in the incumbent's wake, talk to people who have met the incumbent, and write down contact information and what the incumbent has promised to do. High levels of constituency service may help explain why some incumbents have become electorally secure.

Most House members work their districts to an extreme; they are said to be in the "Tuesday to Thursday Club," meaning they are only in Washington during the middle of the week, spending the rest of their time at home in their districts. These members go from diner to diner on Saturday mornings, having a chat over coffee, spending the day at public events and in their "Meet Your Representative" RV, then hitting the bowling alleys at night to meet a few more people. One member even told one of us that his wife has given up sending him out for groceries because he spends three hours talking with people while getting a loaf of bread.

What are incumbents trying to achieve by working their district? You might think they are trying to bamboozle the voters, talking just long enough and fast enough to win people's support. Actually, incumbents work their districts because in terms of constituent support, these sorts of activities are pure profit—no one is upset by an opportunity to meet and talk with the representative and benefit from some casework. In fact, many voters might give the incumbent some credit simply for being willing to listen, regardless of whether they agree with her positions.

Incumbents have a lot of built-in advantages over candidates who might run against them. By virtue of their position, they can help constituents who have problems with an agency or program. They attract media attention because of their actions in office; small local newspapers will even reprint members' press releases verbatim because they do not have the resources to do their own reporting. They can use the money and other resources associated with their position for casework and contact with voters (trips home to the district and the salaries of their staffers who do constituency service are taxpayer-funded). And they use their official position as a platform for raising campaign cash. A contributor who donates as a way to gain access to the policy-making process will be inclined to give to someone already in office. Finally, most incumbents represent states or districts whose partisan balance, the number of likely supporters of their party versus the number likely to prefer the other party, is skewed in their favor—if it wasn't, they probably wouldn't have won the seat in the first place.

Everything incumbents do between elections comes at a cost. One of the reasons Congress has come under such heavy fire recently is the perception that it has granted itself too many special privileges that are specifically aimed at securing reelection (such as funding for large staffs and the franking privilege of sending mail at no cost). Also, time spent actively campaigning takes time away from the responsibilities of enacting laws and overseeing their implementation. The fact that the average officeholder spends so much time away from formal responsibilities may strike you as a bad thing, and in some sense it is. But remember, incumbents work so hard at "meeting and greeting" because we, the voters, appreciate these activities enough to reward incumbents who do them. So constituents are also somewhat responsible for how incumbents allocate their time.

casework Assistance provided by members of Congress to their constituents in solving problems with the federal bureaucracy or addressing other specific concerns.

There is also another a more subtle consequence of the electoral connection. Because congressional politics tends to be local, voters are not usually strongly influenced by the president or the national parties. The president certainly can play a role in congressional elections, as George W. Bush's blitz of competitive House and Senate races demonstrated in 2002. Also, the national economy can have both direct and indirect influences on congressional races. However, the fact that most incumbents can insulate themselves from national forces makes it more difficult to hold the government accountable and may reduce the responsiveness of the political system. Many House candidates also distance themselves from the national party. In one of the more extreme examples from the 2002 midterms, Connie Morella, a Republican House member from a Democratic-leaning Maryland district, bashed her Democratic opponent for sounding too much like a Republican! (Morella was one of the few incumbents to lose in 2002.) However, as discussed in Chapter 8, in nationalized midterm elections, national issues can overwhelm the incumbents' attempts to insulate themselves. In 2006, many House Republicans tried to distance themselves from President Bush and the unpopular war in Iraq, but more than twenty were defeated. In 2008, Republicans faced more backlash against Bush, whose approval ratings had hit record lows. Republican members of Congress avoided being seen with him, while Democrats highlighted their opponents' earlier support for the president. Despite the Democrats' efforts to nationalize the election, only fourteen House Republicans were defeated in what could have been a much worse year for their party.

Overall, the localized nature of congressional elections promotes congressional stability in the face of presidential change. This has profound implications for governance because it increases the likelihood that the presidency and Congress will be controlled by different parties. This kind of divided government complicates accountability because the president and Congress have become adept at blaming each other when things go wrong.

In the Institution While the goal of reelection has a clear impact on members' behavior in the district, it also influences how they operate in the institution. Members of Congress are relatively independent, largely because the electorate, rather than the congressional leadership, holds the power to fire and hire members. The impact of the electoral connection also works in more subtle ways. Earlier in this chapter, we mentioned David Mayhew's argument about the importanct of the reelectoral goal for understanding members' behavior. While members certainly hold multiple goals, including making good policy, Mayhew argues that reelection must come first. That is, if members cannot maintain their seats, they cannot attain other goals in office.

Mayhew then asks the question, "Members of Congress may be electorally motivated, but are they in a position to do anything about it?"[28] After all, if they were unable to work toward reelection, this goal would not be a very useful basis for understanding their behavior. While individual members of Congress cannot do much to alter national economic or political forces, they can control their own activities in the House or Senate, and as we argued earlier, these factors often outweigh national or partisan considerations among constituents. The importance of the electoral incentive in explaining the behavior of members of Congress seems especially clear for marginal incumbents constantly trying to shore up their electoral base. But for those from safe districts (which is a large and growing number), why should they worry? Objectively, it looks as though about 90 percent of House members (and a large proportion of Senators) are absolutely safe, but incumbents realize that this security is not guaranteed. Even in elections with relatively low turnover, many incumbents are "running scared"; in every election, a few supposedly safe incumbents are unexpectedly defeated, and members tend to think that it could be them the next time around. Mayhew warns,

Congress and Constituency Service

Most members of Congress love doing constituency service because it is an easy way to make voters happy. If a member can help a constituent solve a problem, that person will be more likely to support the member in the future.[a] Therefore, most members devote a significant portion of their staff to constituency service, publish newsletters that tout their good deeds on behalf of constituents, and solicit citizens' requests for help through their newsletters and Web sites. Most House members have a link on their home page that says something like "How can I help?" with links to different categories like government agencies, grants, internships, service academies, visiting Washington, DC, and buying U.S. flags (you may purchase a five by eight foot cotton flag for $6.85, and if you want one that has flown over the U.S. Capitol, it only costs an additional $4.05). If you visit Washington, your member can get you passes to the House or Senate gallery and may even meet with you. An example of a more extensive offer of assistance comes from the Government Agencies link on Wisconsin representative Tammy Baldwin's Web site:

> *How I Can Help* I may be able to assist you if you have a problem involving federal agencies or programs, including the Social Security Administration, Medicare, the Internal Revenue Service,

▲ Members of Congress work hard to serve their constituents. In 2006, then-senator Barack Obama (D-IL) addressed the concerns of former employees and family members of two Naperville, Illinois, nuclear weapons plants during a town hall meeting. Obama later took up these issues with the Federal Advisory Board on Radiation and Worker Health.

Immigration and Naturalization, the Department of Veterans Affairs, federal Workers' Compensation or one of the military services.

What I Can Do for You My staff and I can help in communicating with federal agencies, and advocating on your behalf, if you have already gone through proper channels yourself and are facing difficulties. If you are not sure where to turn for help, we are here to help direct you to the right agency. Communicating with

federal agencies can be a frustrating process, and my office can act as a liaison between you and the agency. Also, if you have filed an application or petition and time has passed without a response, my office will be happy to check the status of your case. While I cannot force an agency to act in your favor, I can ask for full and fair consideration of a claim, for expeditious handling of a case or claim, and I can point out any failure to follow laws or regulations.[b] ■

"When we say 'Congressman Smith is unbeatable,' we do not mean that there is nothing he could do that would lose him his seat. Rather we mean, 'Congressman Smith is unbeatable as long as he continues to do the things that he is doing.'"[29] Members recognize that becoming inattentive to the district, being on the wrong side of a key string of votes, or failing to bring home the district's share of pork could cost them their seat. And a potential challenger is always waiting in the wings.

Mayhew outlines three ways that members promote their chances for reelection: advertising, credit claiming, and position taking. **Advertising** does not refer to the thirty-second spots on TV or radio during a campaign but to appeals or appearances

advertising Actions taken by a member of Congress that are unrelated to government issues but have the primary goal of making a positive impression on the public, like sending holiday cards to constituents and appearing in parades.

credit claiming The acceptance of credit by a member of Congress for legislation that specifically benefits his constituents.

position taking Any public statement in which a member of Congress makes her views on an issue known to her constituents.

without issue content that get the member's name before the public in a favorable way. Advertising includes the activities discussed above associated with "working the district," such as attending town meetings, appearing on a float in a homecoming parade, going to a local Rotary Club lunch, or sending letters of congratulation for high school graduations, birthdays, or anniversaries. Members of Congress also spend a fair amount of time meeting with constituents in Washington: school groups, tourists, and interest groups flock to their members' offices expecting to see their representative.

The second activity, **credit claiming**, involves the member of Congress taking credit for something of value to the voter—most commonly pork-barrel policies targeted to their specific constituents or district. The goodies must be specific and small-scale enough that the member of Congress may believably claim credit. In other words, it is far less credible to take credit for something like a national drop in violent crime or an increase in SAT scores than for the local veterans' hospital renovations or a highway improvement grant. The other main source of credit claiming is casework for individual constituents who request help with tasks like tracking down a lost Social Security check or expediting the processing of a passport. This activity, like advertising, has both district-based and Washington-based components, as the Politics Is Everywhere box explains.

Position taking refers to any public statement on something of interest to constituents or interest groups, roll call votes, speeches, editorials, or position papers. This may be the toughest aspect of a member's job because on many issues the member will alienate a certain segment of the population no matter what position she takes. Sometimes the congressional leadership will try to structure votes to help members duck some of the most controversial issues, but in many cases, members cannot avoid taking a definitive stance. In the pre-television era, members could present different positions to different audiences, but with a more vigilant press and video coverage of many events, this is no longer common. However, members still try to appeal to specific audiences within the district. For example, while speaking to the Veterans of Foreign Wars, a member might emphasize her support for a particular new weapons program, but in a meeting with college students, she might talk about her opposition to the war in Iraq.

SECTION SUMMARY

1. The goal of reelection is central to understanding congressional behavior.
2. By developing an effective home style, building up a campaign war chest to deter challengers, working the district, and serving constituents, most members of Congress establish relatively secure districts.
3. The electoral motivation also influences behavior within the Congress by encouraging advertising, credit claiming, and position taking.

The Structure of Congress

Much of the structure of the institution is set up to meet the electoral needs of its members. David Mayhew's key observation supporting this idea is that very little of what it takes to get reelected involves zero-sum processes, in which one person's gain is another's loss. If the institution were more zero-sum, then there would be more competition and rivalry. Instead, norms of universalism, reciprocity, and specialization, defined below, still dominate. There are several aspects of the structure of Congress that facilitate members' reelection including informal structures (norms) and formal structures (staff, the committee system, parties, and the leadership).

Despite the importance of the electoral connection, the goal of being reelected cannot explain everything about members' behavior and the congressional structure. This section will also examine some other explanations for the way Congress is set up: the policy motivations of members, the partisan basis for congressional institutions, and the informational advantages of the committee system.

INFORMAL STRUCTURES

Various norms provide an informal structure for the way that Congress works. Universalism is a norm stating that when benefits are being divided up, as many districts and states as possible should benefit. Thus, when it comes to handing out federal highway dollars or expenditures for the Pentagon's weapons programs, the benefits are broadly distributed across the entire country, which means that votes in support of these bills tend to be very lopsided. For example, the $286 billion 2005 transportation bill contained some federal spending in every part of the country and passed by a 91–4 vote in the Senate and a 412–8 margin in the House.[30]

Another norm, reciprocity, reinforces universalism with the idea that "if you scratch my back and I'll scratch yours." This norm (also called logrolling) leads members of Congress to support bills that they otherwise might not vote for in exchange for another member's vote on a bill that is very important to them. For example, a House member from a dairy state might vote for tobacco price supports even if there are no tobacco farmers in her state and in return, she would expect the member from the tobacco state to vote for the dairy price support bill. This norm can produce the wasteful pork-barrel spending noted above. For example, recall from Chapter 1 that the 2005 transportation bill had 6,371 earmarks worth $24 billion (of the bill's $286.5 billion total), so nearly everyone gained something by passing it. The You Decide box describes some of the fierce debates in Congress and among political commentators about the merit of this type of spending.[31]

The norm of specialization is also important, both for the efficient operation of Congress and for members' reelection. By specializing and becoming an expert on a given issue, members provide valuable information to the institution as a whole and also create a basis for credit claiming. This norm is stronger in the House where members often develop a few areas of expertise, whereas senators tend to be policy generalists. For example, Representative Henry Waxman (D-CA) has dedicated much of his decades-long House career to the issue of health care, while Senator John McCain (R-AZ) has had his hand in a wide variety of issues, including campaign finance and lobbying reform, tax policy, telecommunications and aviation issues, national defense, foreign policy, and immigration policy.

The seniority norm also serves individual and institutional purposes. This norm holds that the member with the longest service on a committee will chair the committee. While there have been numerous violations of the seniority norm in the past thirty years, whereby the most senior member is passed over for someone favored by the party leaders, the norm benefits the institution by providing for orderly succession in committee leadership.[32] The norm also benefits members by providing a tangible reason why voters should return them to Congress year after year. Many members of Congress make this point when campaigning, and the issue is more than just posturing. Committee chairs *are* better able to "bring home the bacon"

universalism The informal congressional norm of distributing the benefits of legislation in a way that serves the interests of as many states and districts as possible.

reciprocity The informal congressional norm whereby a member votes for a bill that he might not otherwise support because a colleague strongly favors it—in exchange for the colleague's vote for a bill that the member feels strongly about (also known as logrolling).

earmarks Federally funded local projects attached to bills passed through Congress.

specialization The expertise of a member of Congress on a specific issue or area of policy. Specialization is more common in the House than the Senate, where members tend to be policy generalists.

seniority The informal congressional norm of choosing the member who has served the longest on a particular committee to be the committee chair.

POLITICAL PROCESS MATTERS

The seniority norm means that the longer a member serves on a committee, the more likely he or she will become the chair or ranking minority member of that committee.

The Politics of Pork

The infamous "bridge to nowhere" in Ketchikan, Alaska, discussed in Chapter 1 is one of the most famous examples of wasteful pork-barrel spending, but it is unusual only in its scale rather than its kind. It is also unusual because the outcry over the bridge prompted Alaska to pull the plug on the project, whereas most pork-barrel spending survives. Pork typically takes the form of earmarked funding for a specific project that is not subjected to standard, neutral spending formulas or a competitive process. The number of earmarks has increased more than tenfold in recent years: four of the most heavily earmarked appropriations bills in 2000 contained 764 earmarks—and in 2005, that number was about 8,600.

One tactic legislators often use to win approval for pork is to insert it into emergency spending bills that are expected to pass, such as disaster relief for flood and hurricane victims, spending for national security after the September 11 attacks, or the bills funding the war in Iraq. For example, when the bill establishing the Department of Homeland Security passed the Senate by a narrow 52–47 vote on November 19, 2002, Senator Joseph Lieberman observed, "I fear some of my colleagues have seized upon the likely passage of this bill as an opportunity to load it up with unwise, inappropriate, and hastily considered provisions, many of which protect special interests."[a] The *Washington Post* cited three especially blatant examples of special interest legislation attached to the bill:

> The most contentious of the targeted provisions would limit legal liability for companies that produce vaccines, provide airport security and develop antiterrorism technologies. Another would relax a proposed ban on issuance of homeland security contracts to companies that establish foreign tax havens to avoid U.S. taxes. A third was described

▲ Surrounded by members of Congress, President Bush signs the Federal Funding Accountability and Transparency Act of 2006. The law is intended to "reduce incentives for wasteful spending"—that is, cut down on pork.

> by critics as stacking the deck for Texas A&M University, a favorite of some GOP leaders in both houses, as the choice for a new homeland security research center.[b]

Several moderate Republicans opposed these provisions so strongly that Minority Leader Trent Lott (R-MS) and Speaker Dennis Hastert (R-IL) had to make some last-minute deals to bring them back into the fold. They promised the moderates, Olympia Snowe and Susan Collins, Republicans from Maine, and Lincoln D. Chafee (R-RI), that these riders would be removed in the next legislative session. If these provisions had gone through the normal legislative process, they almost certainly would have failed.

Some broader definitions of pork include any benefit targeted to a particular political constituency (typically an important business in a member's district or a generous campaign contributor), even if the benefit is part of a stand-alone bill. Examples of this type of targeted federal largesse include the bill that provided federal support to the airlines after the September

11 attacks, which sailed through Congress without much debate, and the lucrative contracts to rebuild Iraq that were awarded to politically well-connected businesses.

Pork has plenty of critics. Citizens Against Government Waste, one of the most outspoken groups to tackle pork-barrel spending, compiles each year's federal pork-barrel projects into their annual *Pig Book* to draw attention to pork. Representative Dave Obey (D-WI) and Senator John McCain (R-AZ), among others, have been trying to get Congress to cut back on earmarks. The arguments against pork are especially urgent during a time of massive budget deficits. According to this view, the national interest in a balanced budget should take priority over localized projects.

However, some argue that pork is the "glue of legislating" since these small side-payments secure the passage of larger bills. If it takes a little pork for the home district or state in order to get important legislation through Congress, so be it. The motives of budget reform groups that call for greater fiscal discipline in Congress may also be questioned, since many of these groups oppose government spending in general—not just on pork. In some cases, policies they identify as pork have significant national implications: military readiness, road improvements to support economic infrastructure, or the development of new agricultural and food products. National interests can be served, in other words, by allowing local interests to take a dip into the pork barrel. Put another way, "pork is in the eye of the beholder," or one person's pork is another person's essential spending. Finally, defenders of pork point out that even according to the critics' own definition, pork spending constitutes less than 1 percent of the total federal budget. If you were a member of Congress, would you work hard to deliver pork to your district, or work to eliminate as much pork as you could from the budget? ■

than a junior member who is still learning where the bathrooms are. For example, Don Young, the former Transportation Committee chair in the House, was able to secure funding for the infamous "bridge to nowhere" in Alaska described in Chapter 1 (they were even going to name the connecting highway Don Young Way).

FORMAL STRUCTURES

Parties and Party Leaders Political parties are important for allocating power in Congress. Party leaders are always elected on straight party-line votes, and committee leadership, the division of seats on committees, and the allocation of committee resources are all determined by the majority party. Parties in Congress also become more important when the two chambers are controlled by opposing parties, as was the case between 1981 and 1987 when Republicans controlled the Senate and Democrats controlled the House, and in part of 2001 and 2002 when the opposite was true.

A leading theory of congressional organization points to the importance of parties in solving collective action problems in Congress. Without parties the legislative process would be much more fractured and decentralized because members would be autonomous agents in battle with each other. Parties provide a team framework that allows members to work together for broadly beneficial goals. Just think how difficult it would be for a member of Congress to get a bill passed if she had to build a coalition from scratch every time. Instead, parties provide a solid base from which coalition building may begin. As discussed in Chapter 7, political parties provide the collective good of brand name recognition for members.

The top party leader in the House—and the only House leader mentioned in the Constitution—is the **Speaker of the House,** who influences the legislative agenda, committee assignments, scheduling, and overall party strategy. The Speaker is aided by the **majority leader**, the majority whip, and the caucus chair (in addition to many other lower-level party positions). The majority leader is one of the national spokespersons for the party and also helps with the day-to-day operation of the legislative process. The majority whip oversees the extensive **whip system**, which has three important functions: information gathering, information dissemination, and coalition building. The whips meet regularly to discuss legislative strategy and scheduling. The whips then pass along this information to colleagues in their

Speaker of the House The elected leader of the House of Representatives.

majority leader The elected head of the party holding the majority of seats in the House or Senate.

whip system An organization of House leaders who work to disseminate information and promote party unity in voting on legislation.

▲ *Party leadership is central in the legislative process. As of 2008 the majority party leadership was (from left to right): House Majority Leader Steny Hoyer (D-MD), House Majority Whip James Clyburn (D-SC), House Speaker Nancy Pelosi (D-CA), Senate Majority Whip Richard Durbin (D-IL), and Senate Majority Leader Harry Reid (D-NV).*

The Legislature in the Political Process

The U.S. Congress is quite different from many other legislatures around the world in terms of how its members are elected, its relations to the executive, and its internal operations. Congressional representation is based on geographically determined single-member districts that hold plurality, winner-take-all elections, while (as discussed in Chapter 8) most other legislatures are elected using party lists and some version of proportional representation. In an election with party lists, each party makes a list of people who would serve in the legislature. Using proportional representation with party lists means that the number of people from each party's list who actually serve as legislators depends on how much support the party receives in the election. For example, if there are 100 seats in the legislature and a party wins 40 percent of the vote, in a strictly proportional system the party would take the first 40 people from their list and they would be the legislators from that party. Legislatures that are elected from national party lists are much more likely to concern themselves with national rather than parochial interests. There are no incentives to "bring home the pork" to your district if you are not elected from a district.

Examining the recent legislative elections in Iraq highlights the significance of these differences. Iraqi voters selected parties rather than candidates, and the country's 275 legislators were then taken from the party lists based on the proportion of votes each party received. This meant that

▲ The upper house of Parliament in The Hague, Netherlands.

even relatively small factions could elect a few people to the legislature as long as they could muster a small percentage of the national vote. This has the virtue of creating more proportional representation, but it also fractures political power more broadly. One hundred eleven parties competed and twelve won representation in the January 2005 elections. Party lists also allow more descriptive representation. Twenty-nine percent of Iraqi legislators are women because the law mandated that every third person on the party lists had to be a woman (only about 15 percent of members of the U.S. Congress are women).

There are too many other differences to describe them all in detail. Briefly, relations with the executive are much stronger in a parliamentary system than in a presidential system because the prime minister is elected from the legislature. Indeed, the lines between executive and legislative power are much more blurred in a parliamentary system. Parties tend to be highly unified in parliamentary systems and less so in presidential systems. Oversight powers, legislative capacity (ratifying treaties, amending constitutions, approving executive appointments, and impeachment power), the number of votes and how they are recorded, tenure and reelection rates, and the relative power of committees in the institution also vary tremendously.[a] ■

respective parties and indicate the party's position on a given bill. Whips also take a head-count of party members in the House on specific votes and communicate this to the party leaders.

If a vote looks close, whips try to persuade members to support the party's position (the term "whip" comes from the term "whipper-in" from English fox hunts, the person responsible for making sure that the hounds did not wander too far from the pack). Similarly, party whips try to ensure that members do not stray too far from the party position. The caucus chair (or the conference chair for the Republicans) runs the party meetings to elect floor leaders, make committee assignments, and set legislative agendas. The minority party in the House has a parallel structure: their leader is the **minority leader** and the second in command is the minority whip. The Democratic party made history in January 2007, when they elected Nancy Pelosi as the first woman Speaker of the House.

The Senate leadership does not have as much power as that of the House, mostly because individual senators have more power than House members because of the Senate's rule of unlimited debate. The majority leader and minority leader are the leaders of their respective parties, and those second in command are the assistant majority and minority leaders. The Senate also has a whip system, but it is not as developed as the House system. Republicans have a separate position for the conference chair, while the Democratic leader serves also as conference chair. The country's vice president is officially the president of the Senate, but he only appears in the chamber when needed to cast a tie-breaking vote. The Constitution also mentions the **president pro tempore** of the Senate, whose formal duties involve presiding over the Senate when the vice president is not there. This is typically the most senior member of the majority party, and the position does not have any real power (in fact, the actual president pro tempore rarely presides over the Senate and the task is typically given to a more junior senator).

Political parties in Congress also reflect the individualism of the institution. Compared to parliamentary systems, U.S. congressional parties are very weak (see Comparing Ourselves to Others). They do not impose a party line or penalize members who vote against the party. Indeed, they have virtually no ability to impose electoral restrictions (such as denying the party's nomination) on renegade members. Thus, from the perspective of a member seeking reelection, parties are more useful for what they are not—they do not force members to vote with the party— than what they are. While there are significant party differences on many issues, on about half of all **roll call votes**, majorities of both parties are on the same side!

Although still weaker than their overseas counterparts, parties in Congress have greatly strengthened since the 1960s (Figure 10.6). Partisanship—when party members stick together in opposition to the other party—reached its highest levels in the post–World War II era in the mid-1990s. About 70 percent of all roll call votes were **party votes**, in which a majority of one party opposed a majority of the other party. The proportion of party votes has since fallen but remains around 50 percent. **Party unity**, the percentage of party members voting together on party votes, soared during this period as well, especially in the House. The Democratic Party has become much more cohesive as southern Democrats have started to vote more like their northern counterparts, partly because of the increasing importance of African American voters in the South. Similarly there are fewer moderates within the Republican Party, as most regions of the country that used to elect them are now electing Democrats.[33]

Strong party leadership is referred to as conditional party government, which indicates that strong party government is possible, but conditional on the consent of party members.[34] Leaders' primary responsibility is to get their party's legislative agenda through Congress, but their negative powers are quite limited. The positive powers they have mostly take the form of agenda control and persuasion. Leaders' success largely depends on personal skills, communicative abilities, and trust. Some of the most successful leaders, such as Lyndon Johnson (D-TX), majority leader of the Senate from 1955 to 1961, and Sam Rayburn (D-TX), Speaker for over seventeen years, kept in touch with key members on a daily basis. Leaders also must have the ability to bargain and compromise. One observer noted, "To Senator Johnson,

minority leader The elected head of the party holding the minority of seats in the House or Senate.

president pro tempore A largely symbolic position usually held by the most senior member of the majority party in the Senate.

roll call vote A recorded vote on legislation; members may vote yes, no, abstain, or present.

party votes A vote in which the majority of one party opposes the position of the majority of the other party.

party unity The extent to which members of Congress in the same party vote together on party votes.

POLITICS IS CONFLICTUAL

 An important role of party leadership is to overcome the natural conflict in politics by forging compromises and building coalitions to pass legislation.

FIGURE 10.6a | PARTY VOTES IN CONGRESS, 1962–2006

These graphs make two important points. First, partisanship has increased in the last two decades, both in terms of the proportion of party votes and the level of party unity. Second, despite these increased levels of partisanship, only about half of all votes in the House and Senate divide the two parties. Given these potentially conflicting observations, how would you assess the argument that partisanship in Congress is far too intense?

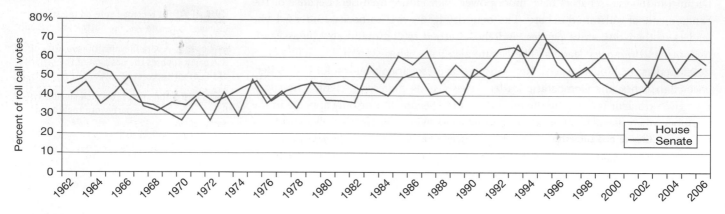

FIGURE 10.6b | PARTY UNITY IN CONGRESS, 1962–2006

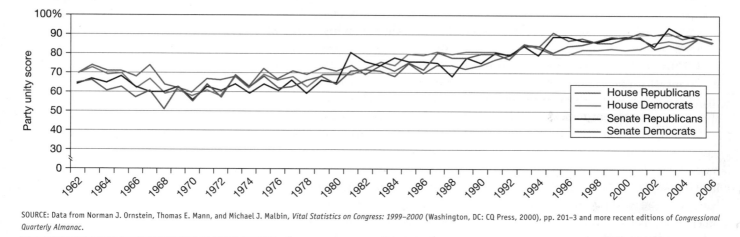

SOURCE: Data from Norman J. Ornstein, Thomas E. Mann, and Michael J. Malbin, *Vital Statistics on Congress: 1999–2000* (Washington, DC: CQ Press, 2000), pp. 201–3 and more recent editions of *Congressional Quarterly Almanac.*

public policy evidently was an inexhaustibly bargainable product."[35] Such leaders find solutions where none appear possible. Leaders also do favors for members (such as making campaign appearances, helping with fund-raising, contributing to campaigns, helping them get desired committee assignments, or guiding pet projects through the legislative process) to engender a feeling of personal obligation to the leadership when it needs a key vote.

The party's most powerful positive incentives are in the area of campaign finance. In recent years the congressional campaign committees of both parties and the national party organizations have been supplying candidates with money and resources in an attempt to gain more influence in the electoral process. Party leaders may also help arrange a campaign stop or a fundraiser for a candidate with party leaders or the president. For example, in November and December of 2005, President Bush attended fundraisers for two Senate candidates, one incumbent senator, and one incumbent House member.[36] Such events typically raise $500,000 to more than $1 million.

Despite these positive reinforcements, members' desire for reelection always comes before party concerns, and leadership will rarely try to force a member to vote against constituents' interests. For example, Democrats from rural areas, where most constituents support gun ownership and many are hunters, would not be expected to vote the party line favoring a gun-control bill. To be disciplined by the party, a member of Congress must do something much more extreme than not supporting them on roll call votes, for example supporting the opposing party's candidate for Speaker or passing strategic information to the opposition.

Two recent examples show that party leaders have limits in terms of how much they will tolerate. Former representative James Traficant of Ohio was a true maverick in the Democratic Party. He often took to the floor to give outrageous speeches, occasionally looking up to the ceiling, holding up his arms and blurting out, "Beam me up Scottie." In April 2002, Traficant was convicted and eventually jailed for bribery, racketeering, and tax evasion. When the House Ethics Committee was investigating him, his closing statement was,

> I want you to disregard all the opposing counsel has said. I think they are delusionary. I think they've had something funny for lunch in their meal. I think they should be handcuffed to a chain-link fence, flogged, and all of their hearsay evidence should be thrown the hell out. And if they lie again, I am going to go over and kick them in the crotch. Thank you very much.[37]

While he was still fighting the investigation, he voted for the Republican candidate for Speaker, Dennis Hastert. The Democratic Party leadership promptly stripped him of his committee assignments and let him know that he was no longer welcome in the party. Soon after that, Traficant became only the second representative since the Civil War (and only the fifth in U.S. history) to be expelled from the House.

Former senator Jim Jeffords (I-VT) also felt the pinch of party power. In 2001, when Jeffords left the Republican Party to become an independent, he became a hero to the Democratic Party, as his switch gave them control of the Senate. However, when Republicans retook control of the Senate in November 2002, they were in no mood to do any favors for Jeffords. Many in the party viewed him as a traitor and were not interested in extending the olive branch.

Despite these occasional strong-armed tactics, party leaders have moved toward a service-oriented leadership in the last decade, recognizing that their power is only as strong as the leeway granted by the rank-and-file membership. However, within this context, leaders can gain a fair amount of power, as demonstrated by Newt Gingrich's reign as Speaker between 1995 and 1999 and Tom DeLay's service as whip and majority leader between 1995 and 2005. Gingrich largely engineered the Republican takeover of the House in 1994, placed his loyalists in top leadership positions, and then tried to push through his Contract with America (a set of promises made to the American people about what Republicans would do if they became the majority party). DeLay, nicknamed "The Hammer," was a fundraising and election-strategy genius who tried to make Republicans the majority party for the next generation. As whip, he was a strong legislative tactician and head-counter who excelled at pushing through his party's agenda. He was forced to step down as majority leader late in 2005 when he was indicted for his fund-raising activities in Texas. The Democratic Party's success in the 2006 midterm elections was attributable in part to voters' reaction against this "culture of corruption."

The Committee System The committee system in the House and Senate is another crucial part of the legislative structure. There are four types of committees: standing, select, joint, and conference. **Standing committees**, which have ongoing membership and jurisdictions are where most of the work of Congress gets done. These committees draft legislation and oversee the implementation of the laws they pass. **Select committees** are typically created to address a specific topic for one or

▲ Party leaders, especially the president, can play an important role in campaigning for members of Congress. President Bush is shown here stumping for Senator Jim Talent (R-MO) at Missouri Southern State University just before the 2006 midterm elections.

standing committees Committees that are a permanent part of the House or Senate structure, holding more importance and authority than other committees.

select committees Committees in the House or Senate created to address a specific issue for one or two terms.

two terms, such as the Select House Committee on Homeland Security (which later became a standing committee). These committees do not have the same legislative authority as standing committees. **Joint committees** are comprised of members of the House and Senate, and rarely have legislative authority (the last joint committee to have such authority was the Joint Committee on Atomic Energy, disbanded in 1977). The Joint Committee on Taxation, for example, does not have authority to send legislation concerning tax policy to the floor of the House or Senate. Instead, it gathers information and provides estimates of the consequences of proposed tax legislation. Some joint committees take care of common administrative housekeeping tasks: the Joint Committee on the Library oversees the Library of Congress and the Joint Committee on Printing oversees the Government Printing Office. **Conference committees** are formed to resolve specific differences between the House and Senate versions of legislation that passes each chamber. These committees are mostly comprised of standing committee members from each chamber who worked on the bill. Nuts and Bolts 10.3 shows the policy areas covered by each type of committee.

The committee system creates a division of labor that helps reelection by supporting members' specialization and credit claiming. For example, a chair of the Agriculture Committee or of an important agricultural subcommittee may reasonably take credit

**NUTS
AND
BOLTS**

10.3

Congressional Committees

Equivalent or similar committees in both chambers are listed across from each other.

HOUSE COMMITTEES	SENATE COMMITTEES	JOINT COMMITTEES
Agriculture	Agriculture, Nutrition, and Forestry	Joint Economic Committee
Appropriations	Appropriations	Joint Committee on the Library
Armed Services	Armed Services	Joint Committee on Printing
Budget	Budget	Joint Committee on Taxation
Education and Labor	Health, Education, Labor, and Pensions	
Energy and Commerce	Commerce, Science, and Transportation	
Financial Services	Banking, Housing, and Urban Affairs	
Foreign Affairs	Foreign Relations	
Homeland Security and Governmental Affairs	Homeland Security and Governmental Affairs	
House Administration	Rules and Administration	
Select Committee on Intelligence	Select Committee on Intelligence	
Judiciary	Judiciary	
Natural Resources	Energy and Natural Resources	
Small Business	Small Business and Entrepreneurship	
Standards of Official Conduct	Select Committee on Ethics	
Transportation and Infrastructure	Environment and Public Works	
Veterans Affairs	Veterans Affairs	
Ways and Means	Finance	

The committees below are specific to one chamber.

Oversight and Government Reform	Special Committee on Aging
Rules	Select Committee on Indian Affairs
Science and Technology	
Select Committee on Energy Independence and Global Warming	

for passing an important bill for the farmers back home, such as the Cottonseed Payment Program that provides assistance to cottonseed farmers who lost crops due to hurricanes. The number of members who could make these credible claims expanded dramatically in the 1970s with the proliferation of subcommittees (there are ninety-seven in the House and sixty-eight in the Senate). One observer of Congress suggested, with some exaggeration, that if you ever forget a member's name, you can simply refer to him or her as "Mr. or Ms. Chairman," and you will be right about half the time. This view of congressional committees is based on the **distributive theory**, which is rooted in the norm of reciprocity and the incentive to provide benefits for the district. The theory holds that members will seek committee assignments to best serve their district's interests, the leadership will accommodate those requests, and the floor will respect the views of the committees in a big institution-level logroll (that is, committee members will support each other's legislation).

However, the committee system does not exist simply to further members' electoral goals. It is also a *corrective* to individualism because the structure of committees creates more expertise than if the policy process were more ad hoc.[38] This expertise, according to the **informational theory**, provides collective benefits to the rest of the members because it helps reduce uncertainty about policy outcomes. By deferring to expert committees, members are able to achieve beneficial outcomes while using their time more efficiently. This informational theory is also consistent with the argument made by Richard Fenno more than thirty years ago that members will serve on committees for reasons other than simply trying to achieve reelection (which is implied by the distributive theory). Fenno argued that members also were interested in achieving power within the institution and making good policy.[39] Others argue that goals will vary from bill to bill, and all members pursue reelection advantage, institutional power, and effective policy in different circumstances.[40] Thus, the committee system does not exist only to further members' electoral goals, but it often serves that purpose.

Committees also serve the policy needs of the majority party, especially the Rules Committee that structures the nature of debate in the House. The Rules Committee has become an arm of the majority party leadership, and in many instances it provides rules that support the party's policy agenda or protect its members from having to take controversial positions. For example, the Rules Committee could prevent an amendment on a health care bill that, if it came to a vote, would force members to take a position on abortion.

Congressional Staff The final component of the formal structure of Congress is Congressional staff. The size of personal and committee staff exploded in the 1970s and 1980s and has since leveled off. The total number of congressional staff is more than four times as large as it was forty years ago (Figure 10.7). Part of the motivation for this growth was to reduce the gap between the policy-making capability of Congress and the president, especially with regard to fiscal policy. The larger committee staffs gave members of Congress independent sources of information and expertise with which to challenge the president. The other primary motivation was electoral. By increasing the size of their personal staff, members were able to open multiple district offices and expand the opportunities for casework. When the Republicans took control of Congress in 1994, they vowed to cut the waste in the internal operation of the institution, in part by cutting committee staff. However, while they reduced committee staff by nearly a third, they made no cuts in personal staff.

The structure of Congress generally serves its members' needs. The norms of the institution and its formal structure facilitate members' electoral and policy goals. If any aspect of this structure were to hinder Congress's goals, it is within members' power to change that aspect of the institution.

distributive theory The idea that members of Congress will join committees that best serve the interests of their district and that committee members will support each other's legislation.

informational theory The idea that having committees in Congress made up of experts on specific policy areas helps to ensure well-informed policy decisions.

FIGURE 10.7   CONGRESSIONAL STAFF, 1935–2005

The size of congressional staff increased substantially in the late 1960s and early 1970s. What are some possible explanations for this increase? What impact might it have on Congress's policy-making capacity and ability to meet constituents' needs?

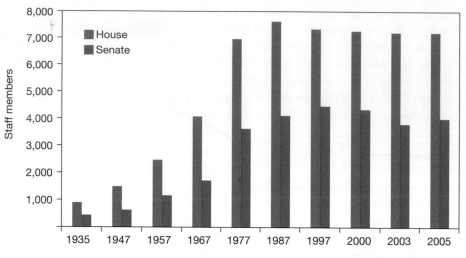

SOURCE: Data from Norman J. Ornstein, Thomas E. Mann, and Michael J. Malbin, *Vital Statistics on Congress: 2005–2006* (Washington, DC: CQ Press, 2008), available at http://library.cqpress.com/vsap/vsap07_figs5-2a.

SECTION SUMMARY

1. The structure of Congress is comprised of informal norms and formal institutions, both of which have an important impact on how legislation is produced.
2. Congress's informal norms include universalism, reciprocity, specialization, and seniority. The strength of these norms varies between the House and the Senate and changes over time.
3. Its formal structure includes political parties, leaders, committees, and staff.

How a Bill Becomes a Law

Every introductory textbook has the obligatory section, including the neat little diagram, on "how a bill becomes a law." This book is no exception; however, we will provide an important truth-in-advertising disclosure: many important laws do not follow this orderly path. In fact, Barbara Sinclair's book *Unorthodox Lawmaking* argues that "the legislative process for major legislation is now less likely to conform to the textbook model than to unorthodox lawmaking."[41] After presenting the standard view, we will describe the most important deviations from that path.

The details of the legislative process can be incredibly complex, but its basic aspects are fairly simple. The most important thing to understand about the process is that before a piece of legislation can become a law it must be passed *in identical form* by both the House and the Senate and signed by the president. If the president vetoes the bill, it can still be passed with a two-thirds vote in each chamber. The basic steps of the process are:

1. A member of Congress introduces the bill.
2. A subcommittee and committee craft the bill.

3. Floor action on the bill takes place in the first chamber (House or Senate).
4. Committee and floor action takes place in the second chamber.
5. The conference committee works out any differences between the House and Senate versions of the bill. (If the two chambers pass the same version, steps 5 and 6 are not necessary.)
6. Final approval of the conference committee version by the floor of each chamber.
7. The president either signs or vetoes the final version.
8. If the bill is vetoed, both chambers attempt to override the veto.

The first part of the process, unchanged from the earliest Congresses, is the introduction of the bill. Only members of Congress can introduce the bill, either by dropping it into the "hopper," a wooden box at the front of the chamber in the

FIGURE 10.8   **HOW A BILL BECOMES A LAW**

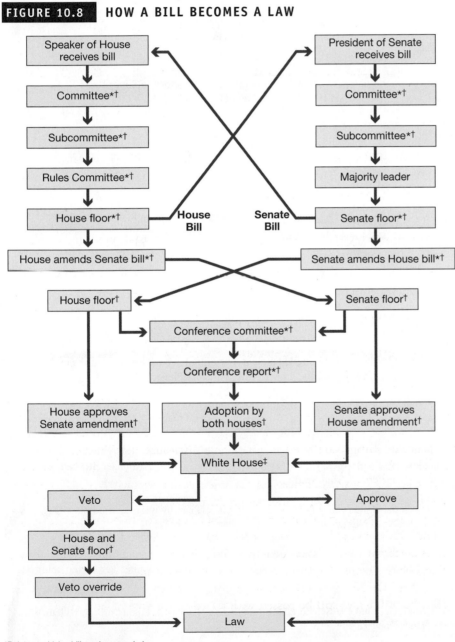

*Points at which a bill can be amended.
†Points at which a bill can die.
‡ If the president neither signs nor vetoes a bill within ten days while Congress is in session, it automatically becomes law.

POLITICS IS EVERYWHERE

Members of Congress routinely pass commemorative legislation that recognizes the achievements of their constituents, ranging from resolutions recognizing sports teams to naming post offices after local leaders.

House, or by presenting it to one of the clerks at the presiding officer's desk in the Senate. Even the president would need to have a House member or Senator introduce his bill. Each bill has one or more sponsors and often many cosponsors. Members may introduce bills on any topic they choose, but often the bills are related to a specific constituency interest. For example, Senate Resolution 441 was introduced by the four senators from New York and New Jersey to congratulate the New York Giants on winning Super Bowl XLII (Figure 10.9). Obviously, most legislation is more substantive, but members of Congress are always attentive to issues their constituents care about.

FIGURE 10.9 TAKING CARE OF THE FANS

110th CONGRESS
2d Session
S. RES. 441

Congratulating the New York Giants on their victory in Super Bowl XLII.
IN THE SENATE OF THE UNITED STATES

February 4, 2008

Mr. SCHUMER (for himself, Mrs. CLINTON, Mr. LAUTENBERG, and Mr. MENENDEZ) submitted the following resolution; which was considered and agreed to

RESOLUTION

Congratulating the New York Giants on their victory in Super Bowl XLII.

Whereas, on Sunday, February 3, 2008, the New York Giants defeated the New England Patriots by a score of 17-14 to win Super Bowl XLII;

Whereas the Giants, who were double-digit underdogs, overcame overwhelming odds to defeat the Patriots; [. . .]

Whereas Eli Manning, having led a game-winning drive for 83 yards at the end of the fourth quarter, was named the game's Most Valuable Player;

Whereas David Tyree's game-breaking catch will forever go down in Super Bowl history as one of the greatest plays ever;

Whereas the relentless onslaught of the Giants defensive line, highlighted by spectacular plays by Justin Tuck, Osi Umenyiora, and team Captain Michael Strahan, sacked Patriots quarterback Tom Brady five times;

Whereas the Giants capped off an amazing playoff run by winning all 4 playoff games on the road as underdogs; [. . .]

Whereas the Giants attract fans from New York, New Jersey, and Connecticut to their home games in East Rutherford, New Jersey, and to away games across the country; [. . .] Now, therefore, be it

Resolved, That the Senate congratulates the New York Giants on their victory in Super Bowl XLII.

SOURCE: Excerpted from S Res. 441, 110th Cong., 2nd sess. (February 4, 2008), available at http://thomas.loc.gov/cgi-bin/query/z?c110:S.RES.441.

The next step is to send the bill to the relevant committee. House and Senate rules specify committee jurisdictions (there are more than 200 categories) and the bill is matched with the committee that best fits its subject matter. In the House, major legislation may be sent to more than one committee in a practice known as multiple referral, but one of them is designated the primary committee, and the bill is reviewed by different committees sequentially, or in parts. The practice is less common in the Senate, in part because senators have more opportunities to amend legislation on the floor.

Once the bill goes to a committee, the chair refers it to the relevant subcommittee where much of the legislative work is done. The subcommittee holds hearings, calls witnesses, and gathers the information necessary to rewrite, amend, and edit the bill. The final language of the bill is determined in a collaborative process known as the **markup**. During this meeting, members debate aspects of the issue and offer amendments to change the language or content of the bill. After all amendments have been considered, a final vote is taken on whether to send the bill to the full committee. The full committee then considers whether to pass along the bill to the floor. They, too, have the option of amending the bill, passing it as-is, or tabling it (which kills the bill). Every bill sent to the floor by a committee is accompanied by a report and full documentation of all of the hearings. These documents constitute the bill's legislative history, which the courts, executive departments, and the public use to determine the purpose and meaning of the law.

When the bill makes it to the floor, it is placed on one of the various legislative calendars. Bills are removed from the calendar to be considered by the floor under a broad range of possible rules. (Some of the most important rules will be discussed below, when we outline some of the differences between the House and Senate, but most of the technical details are not central to the basic story.) When the bill reaches the floor, the majority party and minority party each designate a bill manager who is responsible for guiding the debate on the floor. In the House, debate proceeds according to tight time limits and rules governing the nature of amendments. Senate debate is much more open and unlimited in most circumstances (unless all the senators agree to a limit). If you have ever watched CSPAN, you know that often there are very few people on the floor during debates. Typically only the small number of people who are most interested in the bill (usually members of the committee that produced it) actively participate and offer amendments.

When debate is completed and all amendments have been considered, the presiding officer calls for a voice vote, with those in favor saying "aye," and those opposed "no." If it is unclear which side has won, any member may call for a "division vote," which requires members on each side to stand and be counted. At that point any member may call for a recorded vote (there is no way of recording members' positions on voice votes and division votes). If at least twenty-five members agree that a recorded vote is desired, an elaborate system of buzzers goes off in the office buildings and committee rooms, calling members to the floor for a the vote. Once they reach the floor, members vote by an electronic system in which they insert ATM-like cards into slots and each vote is recorded on a big board at the front of the House or Senate chamber.

If the bill passes the House and the Senate in different forms, the discrepancies have to be resolved. On many minor bills, one chamber may simply accept the other chamber's version to solve the problem. On other minor bills and some major bills, differences are resolved through process known as amendments between the chambers. In this case, one chamber modifies a bill passed by the other chamber and sends it back to them. These modifications can go back and forth several times before both houses agree on an identical bill. The most common way to resolve differences on major legislation is through a conference committee comprised of the key players in the House and the Senate. About three-fourths of major bills go

ON AGREEING TO THE RESOLUTION				
H CON RES 104				
	YEA	NAY	PRES	NV
REPUBLICAN	224		1	4
DEMOCRATIC	167	11	21	6
INDEPENDENT	1			
TOTALS	392	11	22	10
TIME REMAINING	0:00			

▲ *This CSPAN coverage of a House vote shows a relatively empty chamber. Few members are on the floor for most debates; they rush in to vote, then go back to other legislative work.*

markup One of the steps through which a bill becomes a law, in which the final wording of the bill is determined.

Types of Legislation

Bill: A legislative proposal that becomes law if it is passed by both the House and the Senate in identical form and approved by the president. Each is assigned a bill number, with "HR" indicating bills that originated in the House and "S" denoting bills that originated in the Senate. Private bills are concerned with a specific individual or organization and often address immigration or naturalization issues. Public bills affect the general public if enacted into law.

Simple resolution: Legislation used to express the sense of the House or Senate, designated by "H.Res." or "S.Res." Simple resolutions only affect the chamber passing the resolution, are not signed by the president, and cannot become public law. Resolutions are often used for symbolic legislation, such as congratulating sports teams (see Figure 10.9)

Concurrent resolution: Legislation used to express the sense of both chambers, to set the annual budget, or to fix adjournment dates. which are designated by "H.Con.Res" or "S.Con.Res." Concurrent resolutions are not signed by the president and therefore do not carry the weight of law.

Joint resolution: Legislation that has few practical differences from a bill unless it proposes a constitutional amendment. In that case, a two-thirds majority of those present and voting in both the House and the Senate, and ratification by three-fourths of the states, are required for the amendment to be adopted.

to a conference committee, but only 12 percent of all bills go this route.[42] Sometimes the conferees split the difference between the House and Senate versions, but other times the House and Senate approaches are so different that one must be chosen, an especially tricky prospect when different parties control the two chambers. Sometimes the conference cannot resolve differences and the bill dies. If the conference committee can agree on changes, each chamber must pass the final version, the conference report, by a majority vote and neither chamber is allowed to amend it.

The bill is then sent to the president. If he approves and signs the measure within ten days (not counting Sundays), it becomes law. If the president objects to the bill, he may **veto** it within ten days, sending it back to the chamber where it originated, along with a statement of objections. Unless both the House and the Senate vote to override the veto by a two-thirds majority, the bill dies. If the president does not act within ten days and Congress is in session, the bill becomes law without the president's approval. If Congress is not in session, the measure dies through what is known as a **pocket veto**. Each Congress is comprised of two one-year sessions, and there is some dispute whether pocket vetoes between sessions of Congress are legitimate, or whether they must happen at the end of the second session. Recent presidents have claimed that pocket vetoes between sessions are legitimate, but both Congress and the Washington, DC, Appeals Court disagreed. The Supreme Court has not offered a definitive ruling on this matter.[43]

One final point on how a bill becomes a law is important: any bill that appropriates money must pass through the two-step process of authorization and appropriation. In the authorization process, members debate the merits of the bill, determine its language, and limit the amount that can be spent on the bill. The appropriations process involves both the Budget Committees in the House and the Senate, which set the overall guidelines for the national budget, and the Appropriations Committees in the two chambers, which determine the actual amounts of money that will be spent.

DEVIATIONS FROM THE TEXTBOOK PROCESS

There are many ways in which legislation may not follow the typical path. First, in some congresses as many as 20 percent of *major* bills bypass the committee system. This may be done by a discharge petition, in which a majority of the members force

veto The president's rejection of a bill that has been passed by Congress. A veto can be overridden by a two-thirds vote in both the House and Senate.

pocket veto The automatic death of a bill passed by the House and Senate when the president fails to sign the bill in the last ten days of a legislative session.

a bill out of its assigned committee, or by a special rule in the House. Second, about one-third of major bills are adjusted post-committee in the legislation negotiated by supporters to increase the chances of passage. Sometimes the bill goes back to the committee after these changes, and sometimes it does not. Thus, while most of the legislative work is accomplished in committees, a significant amount of legislation bypasses committee review.

Third, summit meetings between the president and congressional leaders may bypass or jump-start the normal legislative process. For example, rather than going through the Budget Committees to set budgetary targets, the president may meet with top leaders from both parties and hammer out a compromise that is presented to Congress as a done deal. This technique is especially important on delicate budget negotiations, or when the president is threatening to use the veto. Often the congressional rank-and-file go along with the end product of the summit meeting, but occasionally they revolt and reject it.

Fourth, omnibus legislation—massive bills that run hundreds of pages long and cover many different subjects and programs—often requires creative approaches by the leadership to guide the bill through the legislative maze. Leadership task forces may be used in the place of committees, and alternatives to the conference committee may be devised to resolve differences between the two chambers. Also the massive legislation is often accompanied by riders—extraneous legislation attached to the "must pass" bill to get pet projects approved that would otherwise fail. This is a form of pork-barrel legislation and another mechanism used in the quest for reelection.

DIFFERENCES IN THE HOUSE AND SENATE LEGISLATIVE PROCESSES

There are three central differences in the legislative processes of the House and the Senate: (1) the continuity of the membership and the impact this has on the rules (2) how bills get to the floor, (3) and the structure of the floor process, including debate and amendments. First, as discussed earlier, the Senate is a continuing body, with two-thirds of its members returning to the next session without facing reelection (because of the six-year term), whereas all House members are up for reelection every two years. This has an important impact on the rules of the two chambers: there has been much greater stability in the rules of the Senate than the House. While the House adopts its rules anew at the start of each new session (sometimes with major changes and other times with only minor modifications), the Senate has not had a general reaffirmation of its rules since 1789. However, the Senate rules can be changed at the beginning of a session to meet the needs of the new members.

The other two differences between the House and Senate are even more important. The process by which a bill gets to the floor is much more complicated in the House than the Senate. In the House, when a bill is reported from a committee it goes to the bottom of the legislative calendar. However, the leadership can move a bill to the top of the agenda in several ways. One mechanism is to have the bill considered under suspension of the rules, which is mostly used for noncontroversial legislation. Debate is limited to forty minutes, no amendments are allowed, and bills must pass by a two-thirds vote. Another mechanism used for major legislation is for the Rules Committee to make a special rule that, if approved by a majority vote of the House, moves the bill to the top of the list for immediate consideration.

The procedure is much easier in the Senate. As in the House, certain bills have privileged status over others, such as conference reports and vetoed bills on which Congress will attempt an override. Because they are in the final stages of the process, they are promoted to the top of the list so they don't have to wait in line with newer bills. Other than privileging these bills, the Senate does not use special rules or

omnibus legislation Large bills that often cover several topics and may contain extraneous, or pork-barrel, projects.

suspension of the rules One way of moving a piece of legislation to the top of the agenda in the House: debate on the bill is limited to forty minutes, amendments are not allowed, and the bill must pass by a two-thirds vote.

▲ *The late senator Strom Thurmond (R-SC) still holds the record for the longest filibuster in Senate history.*

various calendars. If the majority leader wants action on a given bill, he will simply put it on the legislative agenda, either through a motion or unanimous consent.

The floor process is also much simpler and less structured in the Senate than in the House. In part, this is due to the relative size of the two chambers: the House with its 435 members needs to have more rules than the 100-person Senate. Ironically, however, the floor process is actually much easier to navigate in the House because of its structure. The House is a very majoritarian body (that is, a majority of House members can almost always have its way), while former Majority Leader Howard Baker compared leading the Senate to "herding cats." He said it was difficult "trying to make ninety-nine independent souls act in concert under rules that encourage polite anarchy and embolden people who find majority rule a dubious proposition at best."[44] Part of this difficulty is rooted in the fact that the Senate has unlimited debate and a very open amendment process. Unless restricted by a unanimous consent agreement, senators can speak as long as they want and offer any amendment to a bill, even if it isn't germane (that is, directly related to the underlying bill). Debate may be cut off only if a supermajority of sixty senators agrees in a process known as invoking **cloture.** Therefore, one senator can stop any bill by threatening to talk the bill to death if forty of his or her colleagues agree. This practice is known as a **filibuster.**

Before the 1960s, senators really did hold the floor for hours by reading from the phone book or reciting recipes. The late Strom Thurmond, the senator from South Carolina who was the longest serving and oldest senator until his retirement in January 2003 (at 100 years old and 48 years in the Senate), holds the record of twenty-four hours and eighteen minutes of continuous talking. Today it is rare for a filibuster to tie up Senate business, since a senator's threat to filibuster a bill is often enough to take the bill off the legislative agenda. If the bill is actually filibustered, it goes on a separate legislative track so it does not bring the rest of the business of the Senate to a halt. Alternatively, if supporters of the bill think they have enough votes, they can invoke cloture before a filibuster starts.

Because of the practice of unlimited debate in the Senate, much of its business is conducted under unanimous consent agreements by which senators agree to adhere to time limits on debate and amendments. However, because these are literally *unanimous* agreements, a single senator can obstruct the business of the chamber by issuing a hold on the bill. This practice is often a bargaining tool to extract concessions from the bill's supporters, but sometimes, especially late in a session when time gets tight, a hold can actually kill a bill by removing it from the active agenda.

In contrast the House is a more orderly, if complex, institution. The Rules Committee exerts great control over the legislative process, especially on major legislation, through special rules that govern the nature of debate on a bill. There are three general types of rules: **closed rules** do not allow any amendments to the bill, **open rules** allow any germane amendments, and **modified rules** allow some specific amendments but not others. Once a special rule is adopted and the Committee of the Whole convenes, general debate is tightly controlled by the floor managers. All amendments are considered under a five-minute rule, but this rule is routinely bent as members offer phantom "pro forma" amendments to, for example, "strike the last word" or "strike the requisite number of words." This means that the member is not really offering an amendment, but is simply going through the formal procedure of offering one in order to get an additional five minutes to talk about the amendment. So while the Senate is formally committed to unlimited debate, they often voluntarily place limits on themselves through unanimous consent, which makes them operate much more like the House. Similarly, while the House has very strict rules concerning debate and amendments, there are ways of bending those rules to make the House operate a bit more like the potentially free-wheeling Senate.

cloture A procedure through which the Senate can limit the amount of time spent debating a bill (cutting off a filibuster), if a supermajority of sixty senators agree.

filibuster A tactic used by senators to block a bill by continuing to hold the floor and speak—under the Senate rule of unlimited debate—until the bill's supporters back down.

closed rules Conditions placed on a legislative debate by the House Rules Committee prohibiting the addition of amendments to a bill.

open rules Conditions placed on a legislative debate by the House Rules Committee allowing the addition of relevant amendments to a bill.

modified rules Conditions placed on a legislative debate by the House Rules Committee allowing certain amendments to a bill while barring others.

SECTION SUMMARY

1. This overview of the structure and procedures of Congress only scratches the surface of the complex world of the legislative process. "How a bill becomes a law" is clearly more complicated than the basic diagram that captures the essence of the process.

2. There are many important differences between the House and Senate, and both chambers often use alternative policy-making processes. However, in both chambers (and in their differences) the rules governing political process shape outcomes. For example, the rules of the House mean that a majority can almost always have its way, whereas in the Senate, sixty votes are needed to pass legislation.

Oversight

Once a bill becomes a law Congress plays another crucial role by overseeing the implementation of the law to make sure the bureaucracy interprets it as Congress intended. Other motivations drive the oversight process as well, such as the desire to gain publicity that may help in the reelection quest, or to embarrass the president (if he is of the opposite party; for example, Democrats have promised to investigate fraud and cost-overruns in the Defense Department contracts to rebuild Iraq that went to corporations with close Republican Party ties). However, the basic motivation for oversight is to ensure that laws are implemented properly.

There are several mechanisms that Congress may use to accomplish this goal; these will be addressed in more detail in Chapter 12, The Bureaucracy, but will we will briefly describe them here. First, the bluntest instrument is the power of the purse. If members of Congress think an agency is not properly implementing their programs, they can simply cut off the funds. However, this approach to punishing agencies is rarely used because budget cuts often end up cutting good aspects of the agency along with the bad.

Second, Congress may hold hearings and investigations. By summoning administration officials and agency heads to a public hearing, Congress can use the media spotlight to focus attention on problems within the bureaucracy or on issues that have been overlooked. For example, Congress recently held extensive hearings on the enforcement of tax laws by the Internal Revenue Service (IRS). These hearings made front-page news for several days because everyone could relate to the issue. The hearings uncovered some real abuses, and the IRS vowed to clean up its act. Congress was also spurred to action by the Enron and WorldCom bankruptcies and a series of corporate scandals. Again, media attention was intense because many Americans were affected by the resulting decline in value of their stocks. This type of oversight is known as fire alarm oversight—that is, members wait until there is a crisis before they spring to action.[45] This is in contrast to police patrol oversight, which involves constant vigilance in overseeing the bureaucracy. Of the two, fire alarm oversight is far more common because Congress does not have the resources to constantly monitor the entire bureaucracy.

Third, Congress may use **legislative vetoes**, which resemble fire alarm oversight in being a reactive rather than proactive form of oversight. In writing laws, Congress often gives the bureaucracy broad discretion over how to implement policies, because it is impossible for Congress to foresee every scenario that might arise. However, Congress is reluctant to give full control to the implementing agencies.

▲ Corporate scandals have rocked Wall Street and Main Street in recent years, costing investors millions of dollars and thousands of workers their jobs. When major scandals happen, Congress wants to know why. The late Kenneth Lay, former Enron Corporation chairman, is sworn in before a Congressional hearing to testify about his role in the company's collapse.

Legislative vetoes resolve this dilemma by allowing Congress to overturn bureaucratic decisions. There are one-house or two-house versions of legislative vetoes and some even allow committees to exercise a veto. In 1983, the Supreme Court ruled that many forms of legislative vetoes are unconstitutional.[46] However, despite this ruling Congress continues to use this form of oversight.

Finally, the Senate exercises specific control over other executive functions through its constitutional responsibilities to provide "advice and consent" on presidential appointments and approval of treaties. The Senate will typically defer to the president on these matters, but it may assert its power, especially when constituent interests are involved. One current example would be the Senate's increasing skepticism about free trade agreements negotiated by the president's trade representatives.

The ultimate in congressional oversight is the process of removing the president, vice president, other civil officers, or federal judges through impeachment. The House and Senate share this power: the House issues articles of impeachment, which outline the charges against the official, and the Senate conducts the trial of the impeached officials. Two presidents have been impeached: Andrew Johnson in the controversy over Reconstruction after the Civil War, and Bill Clinton over the scandal involving White House intern Monica Lewinsky. However, neither president was convicted and removed by the Senate.

Reforming Congress

The pork-laden Homeland Security Bill and Transportation Bill are good examples of why many Americans are convinced that the entire political system is dysfunctional (see You Decide). This deep cynicism is rooted in the perception that government is not serving the public interest. Attempts to reform Congress address either Congress's external image or internal "quality of life" concerns. The former, which attempt to tackle the absence of institutional leadership and accountability, are difficult to address through congressional reforms. The only way to achieve complete accountability is through responsible party government (discussed in Chapter 7), though this is an elusive goal at best, even when the same party controls Congress and the presidency. However, in a decentralized, individualistic institution such as Congress, the only force for collective responsibility is the majority party. Specific reform proposals seeking to take advantage of this force include giving the Speaker more power over committee assignments (which Newt Gingrich briefly asserted in 1995), strengthening the role of the party caucus, and requiring the leadership to play a larger role in agenda setting. The latter could be accomplished through an annual "state of the Congress" address by congressional leaders, the creation of a specific agenda, and increased activism by the leadership in pushing the agenda. Unfortunately, providing the potential for stronger parties in Congress will not ensure that leaders use their new powers effectively. Some leaders may be reluctant to encroach on committees' turf. For example, Newt Gingrich, the strong Speaker during the mid-1990s, was much more willing to push committees to work with his agenda than was his successor to the speakership, Dennis Hastert.

Proposals aimed at improving the quality of life in Congress attempt to expand the time available to members for legislative work and reduce some of the external pressures. In a survey of members taken by the Joint Committee on the Organization of Congress in 1993, 58 percent said that "studying and reading about pending or future legislation or issues" was the first or second most important activity for which they would like to have more time. More than half also said they would like to spend more time "attending floor debate or watching it on TV." In contrast, only just over 1 percent listed "fundraising for your next campaign" and 5 percent mentioned "meeting personally with constituents when they are in Washington," as either of the top two activities they would like to spend more time doing. Specific proposals that address quality of life concerns include revoking some of the "sunshine reforms" of the 1970s, which opened up committee hearings to the general public. By closing more of these meeting, members would be more insulated from interest group pressure. Other proposals include having fewer recorded votes, reducing the number of committee and subcommittee assignments, public financing of congressional elections, giving serious consideration to the minority party's grievances, and creating an ombudsman (a person who investigates complaints) office to handle most constituency requests rather than having the members' staff do it.

Unfortunately, the two reform agendas are at odds with one another. Most steps that would improve the quality of life in Congress, such as insulating members from outside pressure, would not enhance its image; most people would see this as a way of shielding Congress from public accountability. Strengthening parties in Congress could come at the expense of more partisan in-fighting. The minority party typically prefers weaker party leadership, while the majority party is willing to tolerate strong leadership while maintaining a solid base in committee power. Efforts to truly strengthen party leadership are often met with howls of protest from the minority party and sometimes from junior members of the majority party, thus exacerbating quality of life concerns.

The one exception to this trade-off is campaign finance reform, which would both free up time for members (if public financing is adopted) and enhance Congress's image if the public accepts it as true reform. After a decade-long battle, Congress passed the Bipartisan Campaign Reform Act, also called the McCain–Feingold Act after two of its primary sponsors, banning so-called "soft money" and limiting issue ads (see Chapter 8 for a discussion of this legislation and campaign finance more generally). However, critics hold that this legislation was not comprehensive enough because the parties are already finding ways to circumvent it.

One other topic that continues to receive attention from congressional critics and reformers is term limits. Critics complain that incumbents are too entrenched and there is not enough turnover. They point to the fact that more than 95 percent of the House incumbents who ran for reelection between 1984 and 2008 were returned to office. This is much greater job security than most corporate presidents or blue-collar workers have. Most labor unions would readily accept a contract guaranteeing 95 percent of workers their jobs. As reaction to incumbency safety, a grassroots movement to limit terms started in 1990 and reached a fever pitch in 1992, as voters in ten states passed term limits for state legislators. Currently seventeen states limit terms for state legislators, but the movement appears to be losing steam. Twenty states had passed congressional term limits before the 5–4 Supreme Court decision in *U.S. Term Limits v. Thornton* (1995) ruled that terms limits on Congress could only be passed by constitutional amendment. Then in 1999, Mississippi voters rejected a state referendum that would have imposed term limits for their state legislature; in 2002 the Oregon state supreme struck down term limits that had been passed in 1992; and in 2002, Idaho became the first state to have its legislature repeal term limits.

There are two interesting ironies associated with the term limits movement. First, the Founders feared that the House would be an unstable body with excessive turnover and a lack of professionalism. Technically it *is* possible that 435 new members of Congress could be elected every two years, but obviously the opposite has happened. Second, as noted earlier, while the public is critical of Congress as an institution, most voters do not feel this way about their own individual representative. One bumper sticker opposing term limits succinctly captures this irony: "Stop me before I vote again." Thus, while many people claim to support term limits, they don't want to vote out their own members of Congress.

SECTION SUMMARY

1. Most efforts to reform Congress address either Congress's external image or internal "quality of life" concerns.

2. These two reform agenda tend to be at odds with one another: changes that would improve Congress's external image tend to worsen internal problems and vice versa.

3. Campaign finance reform may be the one type of reform that could address both concerns.

Conclusion

While the details of the legislative process and the institutions of Congress can be complicated, the basic explanations for member behavior are quite straightforward when viewed in terms of the trade-off between responsiveness and responsibility. Members of Congress want to be reelected, so they are generally quite responsive to constituents' interests. They spend considerable time on casework, meeting with people in the district, and delivering benefits for the district. At the same time, members are motivated to be responsible—to rise above local interests and attend to the nation's best interests. The conflict between these two impulses can create contradictory policies that contribute to Congress's image problem. For example, we subsidize tobacco farming at the same time that we spend billions of dollars to treat the health problems tobacco use creates. We have laws on water rights that encourage farmers to irrigate the desert at the same time we pay farmers to leave parts of their land unplanted in areas of the country that are well-suited for agriculture. These policies, and others, can be explained by the desire to serve local interests and by the norms of reciprocity and universalism.

Considering members' motivations is crucial to understanding how Congress functions, but their behavior is also constrained by the institutions in which they operate. The committee system is an important source of expertise and information, and it provides a platform from which members can take positions and claim credit. Parties in Congress provide coherence to the legislative agenda and help structure voting patterns on bills. Rules and norms constrain the nature of debate and the legislative process. While these institutions shape members' behavior, it is important to keep in mind that members can also change those rules and institutions. Therefore, Congress has the ability to evolve with changing national conditions and demands from voters, groups, and the president.

In this context, much of what Congress does can be understood in terms of the conflicts inherent in politics. How can members act responsibly without sacrificing responsiveness? Can Congress be structured in a way that allows members to be responsive (and therefore have a better chance of getting reelected) without losing the ability to make tough, unpopular decisions when needed, like cutting budget deficits? This chapter also sheds light on some of the ways that political process matters. With a better understanding of how Congress operates, you will be better able to assess the outputs of government. For example, this chapter provided a closer look at party leaders and pork-barrel spending: party leaders in Congress help members solve their collective action problems, rather than causing gridlock and policy failure, as is commonly assumed. Some pork may be wasteful, but in other cases it is important for the districts that receive the benefits and may serve broader collective interests as well. Congress does not always live up to the expectations of being the "first branch" of government, but it often does an admirable job balancing the conflicting pressures it faces.

CRITICAL THINKING

1. If you had to choose between having a responsive or responsible member of Congress, which would you choose and why? Would your answer depend on how other members of Congress were behaving?
2. If you were in charge of the Commission on Congressional Reform, what proposals would you make to change how Congress operates? Would your proposals have a chance of being implemented?
3. What types of activities do members undertake to work toward reelection? How do they structure the institutions of Congress to help themselves achieve this goal? Do these behaviors and institutions serve broader public interests as well as the narrower goal of reelection?

KEY TERMS

advertising (p. 363)
apportionment (p. 354)
bicameralism (p. 346)
casework (p. 361)
closed rules (p. 380)
cloture (p. 380)
conference committees (p. 372)
credit claiming (p. 364)
delegate (p. 352)
descriptive representation (p. 351)
distributive theory (p. 373)
earmarks (p. 365)
electoral connection (p. 350)
filibuster (p. 380)
gerrymandering (p. 355)
gridlock (p. 350)
incumbency safety (p. 358)
informational theory (p. 373)
joint committees (p. 372)
legislative veto (p. 381)
majority leader (p. 367)
markup (p. 377)
minority leader (p. 369)

modified rules (p. 380)
omnibus legislation (p. 379)
open rules (p. 380)
party unity (p. 369)
party votes (p. 369)
pocket veto (p. 378)
politico (p. 352)
pork barrel (p. 347)
position taking (p. 364)
president pro tempore (p. 369)
reciprocity (p. 365)
redistricting (p. 354)
roll call vote (p. 369)
select committees (p. 371)
seniority (p. 365)
Speaker of the House (p. 367)
specialization (p. 365)
standing committees (p. 371)
substantive representation (p. 352)
suspension of the rules (p. 379)
trustee (p. 352)
universalism (p. 365)
veto (p. 378)
whip system (p. 367)

SUGGESTED READING

Bianco, William T. *Trust: Representatives and Constituents.* Ann Arbor, MI: University of Michigan Press, 1994.

Canon, David T. *Race, Redistricting and Representation: The Unintended Consequences of Black Majority Districts.* Chicago: University of Chicago Press, 1999.

Fenno, Richard F. *Congressmen in Committees.* Boston: Little, Brown, 1973.

Hall, Richard L. *Participation in Congress.* New Haven, CT: Yale University Press, 1996.

Jacobson, Gary C. *The Politics of Congressional Elections,* 5th ed., New York: Addison-Wesley, 2001.

Mayhew, David R. *Congress: The Electoral Connection.* New Haven, CT: Yale University Press, 1974.

11

THE PRESIDENCY

During his presidency, George W. Bush was described as having "a conception of presidential power so spacious and peremptory as to imply a radical transformation of the traditional polity."[1] Though we have said throughout this book that politics matters, some critics of Bush have argued that if we accept his definition of presidential power, presidential elections will become the *only* ones that matter, because the president would have broad power to act on his own, regardless of public support, congressional consent, or judicial review.[2]

During his two terms, President Bush saw many of his preferred policies enacted, including large tax cuts, the No Child Left Behind education reforms, the Medicare Prescription Drug Benefit, a ban on some types of late-term abortion, and the appointment of two conservative Supreme Court judges, including Chief Justice John Roberts. In response to the September 11 attacks, Bush ordered American troops to invade and occupy Iraq and Afghanistan and restricted civil liberties, including increasing government surveillance of American citizens and limiting the legal rights of suspected terrorists. These accomplishments illustrate two of this book's themes. First, all of them drew criticism from opponents and became sources of political conflict. And second, taken together, they affected the lives of all Americans. Bush's record of prevailing in the face of political opposition raises serious questions about the limits—or lack thereof—on presidential power.

These questions are equally relevant for America's newest president, Barack Obama. Obama took office in the midst of the worst economic crisis since the Great Depression. He promised to restore economic growth, cut taxes for the middle class, and implement new financial industry regulations. He also promised to increase investment in green technologies, improve health care delivery, and withdraw American forces from Iraq. Can Obama enact these changes on his own? And if he can, is this power granted in the Constitution, or does it come from somewhere else?

The answer to these questions lies in the book's third theme: political process matters. In some situations, the powers allocated in the Constitution enable the president to change government policy unilaterally—unless two-thirds majorities of both houses of Congress are willing to override the change, or unless the Supreme Court rules the change unconstitutional. However, there are limits on this power. Congress and the Court can and do overturn presidential actions. Moreover, many policy changes require explicit congressional approval. This chapter shows that all

▲ *George Washington remains, for many Americans, the presidential ideal—a leader whose crucial domestic and foreign policy decisions shaped the growth of America's democracy.*

presidents face these opportunities and constraints, and their success in office depends on the particular challenges that arise, their personal policy goals, and their skill at using the power of the presidency.

America's Presidents

This section introduces America's presidents using the book's three themes. First, the impact of presidential actions are everywhere in American society.[3] However, presidents do not always achieve their political and policy-making goals. These presidential failures are just as significant as presidential successes because of what they reveal about the processes, rules, and procedures that grant power to the president and constrain its use. This section also shows that successful presidents must be skilled politicians who can find ways to mitigate the inevitable conflicts over government policy. The president needs citizens' support to get reelected, to help elect legislators from his party, and get his policy priorities through Congress. The president must also work closely with Congress, bargaining with legislators over budgets, laws, and regulations. As a result, a president's success in implementing his vision for America depends not only on his knowledge of government and public policy but also on his ability to win the support of the public and other politicians.

PRESIDENTS, POWER, AND POLITICS

As discussed in previous chapters, presidential power has expanded over time, probably beyond what many of the framers intended. Still, since the early years of the Republic, presidents' actions have had profound consequences for the nation. The first presidents, George Washington, John Adams, and Thomas Jefferson, helped forge compromises on issues such as choosing a permanent location for the nation's capital, setting up the federal courts, and deciding on a system for financing the government.[4] Presidents Andrew Jackson and Martin Van Buren were instrumental in forming the Democratic Party and its local party organizations.

Early presidents also made important foreign policy decisions, such as the Monroe Doctrine, issued by President James Monroe in 1823, which stated that America would remain neutral in wars involving European nations, and that these nations must cease attempts to colonize or occupy areas in North and South America.[5] Democrat James Polk oversaw the admission of Texas into the Union following the Mexican-American war, which ended with huge territorial concessions to the United States. Polk also negotiated the Oregon Treaty with Britain, which resulted in the acquisition of land that later became Oregon, Washington, Idaho and parts of Montana and Wyoming.[6]

Several presidents were also active in the many attempts to devise a lasting compromise on slavery prior to the Civil War, and to the prosecution of the war itself. President Millard Fillmore's support helped to enact the Compromise of 1850, which limited slavery in California. Democrat Franklin Pierce played a similar role when he supported the passage of the Kansas-Nebraska Act, which regulated slavery in these territories. Abraham Lincoln, who helped form the Republican Party in the 1850s, played a central role in setting policy as president during the Civil War. His orders raised the huge Union Army, and as commander in chief, he directed the

POLITICS IS EVERYWHERE

Since the Founding, presidential decisions about domestic and foreign policy have influenced the lives of ordinary Americans.

conduct of the bloody war that kept the southern states from seceding permanently. As part of his war strategy Lincoln issued the Emancipation Proclamation, which freed the slaves in the South and temporarily suspended the writ of habeas corpus, allowing the government to imprison people without filing charges against them.[7]

During the late 1800s and early 1900s, presidents were instrumental in the federal government's responses to the nation's rapid expansion and industrialization.[8] These changes in the country's size and its economy generated conflict over which services the federal government should provide to citizens, and how much the government should regulate individual and corporate behavior.[9] Republican president Theodore Roosevelt used the Sherman Antitrust Act to break up the Northern Securities Company, a nationwide railroad trust that was one of the largest companies of its day. He increased the power of the Interstate Commerce Commission to regulate businesses and expanded federal conservation programs. Democrat Woodrow Wilson further increased the government's role in managing the economy through his efforts to enact the Clayton Antitrust Act, the Federal Reserve Act, the first federal income tax, and legislation banning child labor.[10]

Wilson's foreign policy activities illustrate the limits of presidential power. While he campaigned in the 1916 election on a promise to keep America out of World War I, he ultimately changed his mind and ordered American troops to fight on the side of the Allies. After the war, Wilson offered a peace plan, the Fourteen Points, which proposed reshaping the borders of European countries in order to mitigate future conflicts; creating an international organization, the League of Nations, to prevent future conflicts; and taking other measures to encourage free trade and democracy.[11] However, America's allies rejected most of Wilson's proposals, and the Senate refused to allow American participation in the League of Nations, despite Wilson's intense lobbying efforts.

Presidential actions also defined the government's response to the Great Depression, a worldwide economic collapse in the late 1920s and 1930s marked by high unemployment, huge stock market declines, and bank failures. Republican president Herbert Hoover favored only modest government actions in response, arguing that more substantial efforts would be of little use.[12] After Hoover lost the 1932 election, the new president, Democrat Franklin Roosevelt, and his staff began fundamentally reshaping American government. Roosevelt's New Deal reforms created many federal agencies that helped individual Americans and imposed many new corporate regulations, from financial industry reforms to tougher regulation of the drug industry.[13] This federal government expansion continued under Roosevelt's successors. Even Republican Dwight Eisenhower, whose party had initially opposed many New Deal reforms, presided over the creation of new agencies and the building of the interstate highway system.[14]

Presidents were also instrumental in the civil rights reforms and expansion of the federal government in the 1960s. President John Kennedy established the Peace Corps, and began the process of bargaining with members of Congress over legislation that would guarantee voting rights and civil rights for African Americans. Democrat Lyndon Johnson, who assumed the presidency after Kennedy was assassinated in November 1963, campaigned for reelection on his proposals for the Great Society and a War on Poverty. Together with a Democratic Congress, Johnson created a wide range of domestic programs, such as the Department of Housing and Urban Development, Medicare, Medicaid, and federal funding for schools, and finished the job of enacting voting rights and civil rights legislation.

Both Johnson and his successor, Richard Nixon, directed America's involvement in the Vietnam War, with the goal of forcing the North Vietnamese to abandon

POLITICS IS CONFLICTUAL

In many cases, presidential proposals have met with substantial opposition in Congress. As a result, presidents have often been unsuccessful in changing domestic and foreign policy.

▲ During the Great Depression, people who lost their homes built camps of ramshackle structures on vacant land. These "Hoovervilles" were nicknamed for then-president Herbert Hoover, whom many people blamed for the economic calamity.

their plans to unify North and South Vietnam. Here again, presidential efforts did not meet with success: despite enormous deployments of American forces and more than 58,000 American casualties, Nixon eventually signed an agreement that allowed American troops to leave but did not end the conflict, which concluded only after a North Vietnamese victory in 1975.

The two presidents after Nixon, Republican Gerald Ford and Democrat Jimmy Carter, faced the worst economic conditions since the Great Depression, largely due to increased energy prices. Both presidents offered plans to reduce unemployment and inflation, restore economic growth, and enhance domestic energy sources. In both cases, however, their efforts were largely unsuccessful, which became a critical factor in their failed reelection bids.

In the last generation, the political and policy importance of presidential actions has only increased. The popularity of Republican Ronald Reagan's campaign platform of tax cuts, fewer regulations, smaller government, and a tougher stand against the Soviet Union helped Republicans gain majority control of the Senate in 1980 and attract many new voters to the party. While Democratic opposition in the House and a lack of public support limited Reagan's success in reducing the size of government, he and his staff worked to negotiate important arms control agreements with the Soviet Union, efforts that accelerated under Reagan's former vice president and successor to the presidency, George H. W. Bush. Bush led American and international participation in the Persian Gulf War during 1990 and 1991, in which an American-led coalition removed invading Iraqi forces from Kuwait with minimal American casualties.

Democrat Bill Clinton's presidency was marked by passage of the North American Free Trade Agreement, welfare reform, arms control agreements, successful peacekeeping efforts by U.S. troops in Haiti and the Balkans, one of the longest periods of economic growth in U.S. history, and the first balanced budgets since the 1960s. However, despite considerable efforts to drum up public support for health care reform, congressional and public opposition doomed Clinton's proposals. The same factors delayed peacekeeping efforts in Bosnia and Kosovo, and deterred American efforts to stop the murders of hundreds of thousands of people because of civil war in Rwanda. And, as noted in the introduction, whether you approve or disapprove of Republican George W. Bush's many far-reaching actions in office, there is no doubt of their magnitude. Barack Obama's campaign promises will, if implemented, have direct and lasting effects on the lives of ordinary Americans and on the world. However, a president's legacy is difficult to predict, and Obama's legacy will be determined as much by how he responds to unanticipated events as by his campaign promises.

POLITICAL PROCESS MATTERS

✓ The history of the American presidency shows that presidential elections matter. In areas ranging from America's relations with other countries to the size and activities of the federal government, presidents have left their mark on the nation.

SECTION SUMMARY

1. Presidents have done important things, such as expanding U.S. territory, fighting wars, and creating new domestic programs. It matters who gets elected president.
2. Many presidential accomplishments are made in the face of high levels of conflict between the president and Congress, the president and the courts, or between all three branches of government.
3. Presidents are politicians. They must court public support to get elected (and reelected), and bargain with legislators over laws, budgets, and regulations.

4. The president's ability to determine what government does is limited by constitutional restrictions on power and by the extent of his public and congressional support.

The President's Job Description

This section describes the presidency, focusing on both the president's **constitutional authority**, derived from the provisions of the Constitution that describe the president's governmental role, and on **statutory authority**, which comes from laws that give the president additional responsibilities. Throughout the section, our aim is to show how these provisions operate in modern-day American politics: what kinds of opportunities and constraints they create for the current president and future holders of the office.

HEAD OF THE EXECUTIVE BRANCH

The president's job description begins with the list of constitutional responsibilities of the office. The Constitution's **vesting clause,** "The executive Power shall be vested in a President of the United States of America," makes the president the **head of government**, granting authority over the executive branch, as well as **head of state**, or the symbolic and political representative of the country.

The Constitution also places the president in charge of the implementation of laws, saying, "he shall take Care that the Laws be faithfully executed." Sometimes the implementation of a law is nearly automatic, as was the case in the 2005 transportation bill that allocated over $280 billion to highway and mass transit construction nationwide—including, in its original form, funding for Ketchikan, Alaska's "bridge to nowhere" discussed in Chapter 1. In that case, all the president needed to do to implement the law was to ensure that bureaucrats in the Department of Transportation used proper, lawful procedures to choose contractors to complete these projects.

More commonly, the president's authority to implement the law requires using judgment to translate legislative goals into programs, budgets, and regulations. For example, the No Child Left Behind Act of 2001 mandated standardized tests for elementary and secondary students and cuts in government aid for schools with low test scores. This act allowed presidential appointees in the Department of Education to write the regulations that defined a "low score" and decide which tests would be used to assess student achievement.[15] Similarly, the Military Commissions Act of 2006 established the goal of using military tribunals to review evidence against terror suspects, but allowed President Bush and his appointees to determine these tribunals' procedures, such as whether defendants could see classified information that was part of the evidence against them, and whether evidence obtained through coercive interrogation could be used in the trials.[16]

Appointments The president appoints ambassadors, senior bureaucrats, and members of the federal judiciary, including Supreme Court justices.[17] As the head of the executive branch, the president controls about 8,000 positions, ranging from high-profile jobs such as the secretary of state, to mundane administrative and secretarial positions. About 1,200 of these appointments—generally high-level positions such as cabinet secretaries—require Senate confirmation. Though this sounds like a large

▲ The No Child Left Behind Act brought far-reaching changes in federal education policy and in the teaching in public elementary and secondary schools. For modern presidents, however, policy accomplishments are not enough. As this picture of George W. Bush at an event commemorating the reforms illustrates, presidents must also publicize their achievements to retain funding for their programs and boost their chances for reelection.

constitutional authority (presidential) Powers derived from the provisions of the Constitution that outline the president's role in government.

statutory authority (presidential) Powers derived from laws enacted by Congress that add to the powers given to the president in the Constitution.

vesting clause Article II, Section 1, of the Constitution, which states that "executive Power shall be vested in a President of the United States of America," making the president both the head of government and the head of state.

head of government One role of the president, through which he or she has authority over the executive branch.

head of state One role of the president, through which he or she represents the country symbolically and politically.

number of presidential appointees, remember that they are spread across the entire federal government.

In addition, presidents make a substantial number of nominations to the federal courts; Presidents Bill Clinton and George W. Bush each appointed more than 400 judges. Since federal judgeships are lifetime appointments, they allow the president to put people into positions of power who will remain after he leaves office. For example, President George W. Bush appointed two conservative justices to the Supreme Court, John Roberts and Samuel Alito, whose impact was immediately apparent in a series of Court decisions released in 2007 on issues such as abortion rights, gun control, and affirmative action.[18]

The need for Senate confirmation of the president's appointments to many high-level positions fundamentally limits this presidential power. Rather than demanding that the Senate vote on every nomination, presidents have typically withdrawn the most controversial names and found other candidates who are more satisfactory to the Senate. President Bush took this approach in 2005 when he allowed Bernard Kerik to withdraw his name from consideration for the position of secretary of homeland security following press reports that Kerik had, among other things, hired an illegal immigrant as a housekeeper.[19] In that same year, Bush also nominated then-White House counsel Harriet Miers to replace Sandra Day O'Connor on the Supreme Court, but Miers withdrew her name from consideration a few weeks later because her confirmation prospects were dim. Bush then nominated the eventual appointee, Samuel Alito, instead.

One way the president can temporarily dodge the need for Senate approval is to make a **recess appointment** during a period that Congress is not in session, to fill a position that normally requires Senate confirmation. These appointments, however, are temporary, lasting only for the rest of the legislative term. By making recess appointments, the president can fill vacant ambassadorships or designate heads of cabinet departments without waiting for a Senate vote. This provision was included in the Constitution because it was expected Congress would not be in session much of the year, but in the modern era, when Congress is in session almost continuously, recess appointments are sometimes used to by-pass the confirmation process for controversial nominees. On August 1, 2005, President Bush used this strategy to name John Bolton, a longtime critic of the United Nations, as a UN ambassador,[20] hoping that the Senate's opposition to Bolton would diminish over time so that he could be confirmed. Bolton was never confirmed, however, and left office in December 2006 when his recess appointment ended.

POLITICS IS CONFLICTUAL

Because presidential appointees to the judiciary and to positions in the executive branch wield real power over policy, disputes between presidents and members of Congress over the shape of government policy often lead to disagreements over presidential nominees to these positions.

Executive Orders Presidents also have the power to issue **executive orders**, proclamations that unilaterally change government policy without subsequent congressional consent.[21] One executive order issued by President Bush in 2001 mobilized members of the Army's Ready Reserve, some of whom served in Iraq or Afghanistan, while others were assigned elsewhere to replace soldiers sent to serve in these conflicts. Another 2004 order waived a provision of the Trade Act of 1974 that affected trade with the country of Belarus. A third created a Council on Bioethics to advise the president on various issues.

Political scientists Kenneth Mayer and Kevin Price estimated that over 1,000 executive orders issued between 1949 and 1999 were the subject of press coverage, congressional hearings, litigation, scholarly articles, or presidential public statements.[22]

recess appointment When a person is chosen by the president to fill a position, such as an ambassadorship or the head of a department, while the Senate is not in session, thereby by-passing Senate approval. Unless approved by a subsequent Senate vote, recess appointees serve only to the end of the congressional term.

executive orders Proclamations made by the president that change government policy without congressional approval.

How Executive Orders Affect Ordinary Americans

A president's executive orders typically attract little public attention and take effect without congressional consent, which raises important questions about how these orders affect government policy—and the lives of ordinary Americans. If their effects are significant, Americans might do well to keep a closer watch on a president's executive orders and perhaps even demand that their representatives in Congress work to repeal orders that are contrary to their wishes.

In fact, some executive orders have virtually no impact on citizens' lives. Consider some orders issued.[a] President Bush issued one such order in July 2007 in response to discoveries of dangerous contaminants in imported food and high levels of lead in some shipments of toys manufactured abroad. The order established a new interagency working group on import safety, but it gave no details about what this group would do. Another order issued at the same time changed the order of succession within the Department of Homeland Security—which subordinate would take over if the secretary was incapacitated. This order changed some of the department's procedures but had no real impact on the general public.

As these examples suggest, the changes implemented by executive orders are generally small—but the effects of even a "small" change can be important and far-reaching. An order issued in November

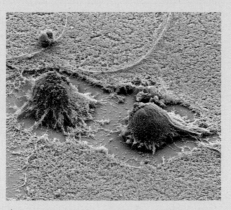

▲ President Bush's 2007 executive order allowing revision of restrictions on stem cell research may significantly impact the lives of ordinary Americans. This image shows two human embryonic stem cells.

2007, for example, was titled, "Executive Order: Establishing an Emergency Board to Investigate a Dispute between Metro-North Railroad and Its Maintenance of Way Employees Represented by the International Brotherhood of Teamsters." This order called for the formation of a board that would analyze and help solve a conflict between the Metro-North commuter railroad, which brings over 100,000 people each day to their jobs in New York City, and the railroad's labor union. Under current law, the union is prohibited from going on strike during the board's investigation of the conflict. Since a strike by these employees would cause considerable disruption for the thousands of people in New York, New Jersey, and Connecticut

who depend on the rail service, this order was anything but trivial.

Another executive order issued by President Bush in June 2007 was titled, "Expanding Approved Stem Cell Lines in Ethically Responsible Ways." The order gave the secretary of the Department of Health and Human Services the authority to revise restrictions limiting federal funding for research on stem cells. This cutting-edge research could lead to techniques for reversing damage to the heart, liver, and other organs, or even the possibility of creating replacement organs for transplant. However, since some stem cells are derived from human embryos (following in vitro fertilization and donated by patients undergoing fertility treatment), many people believe that such research is unethical. Whether you share these concerns, favor the research, or have a condition that might be treatable one day with stem cells, the president's order is clearly significant.

While some executive orders are truly unimportant for most citizens, some have a direct impact on the lives of millions of Americans. Others raise moral concerns that many Americans share or do things that many Americans favor, even if the changes have no discernable impact on their lives. To fully understand how government affects your life, you need to move beyond acts of legislation and regulatory decisions to consider executive orders as well. ■

Most, like the latter two examples noted above, dealt with relatively minor matters. However, some executive orders make significant policy changes. Bush's initial plan for holding terror suspects indefinitely without charges and his authorization of warrantless wiretapping of Americans' international phone calls were both implemented through executive orders.

Executive orders may appear to give the president authority to do whatever he wants, even in the face of strong opposition from Congress. However, a president's power to issue executive orders is limited. In all three examples listed above,

Congress had passed a law giving the president the authority to issue the executive order. If this had not been the case, and if members had instead objected to the policy changes, they could have passed a law overturning any of these executive orders or denied funding to implement them—although they would need support from two-thirds of both houses to override the expected presidential veto.

The president can, in theory, cite the Constitution as the sole source of his authority to issue an executive order, although this strategy is uncommon. If this happens, Congress can pass a law overturning the order, but the president could potentially refuse to abide by the new law, arguing that the constitutional grant of power can only be changed by amending the Constitution itself. Such a disagreement would likely end up before the Supreme Court, allowing the Court to decide whether the Constitution granted the president the authority he had claimed. If the Court disagreed with the president, their ruling would void the order.

Commander in Chief The Constitution makes the president the commander in chief of America's military forces, but gives Congress the power to declare war. These provisions are potentially contradictory, and the Constitution leaves open the broader question of who controls the military.[23] In practice, however, the president controls day-to-day military operations through the Department of Defense and has the power to order troops into action without explicit congressional approval. This happened most recently in 2002, when President George W. Bush deployed more than 100,000 troops, hundreds of aircraft, and dozens of warships in anticipation of action against Iraq. While Congress eventually passed a resolution authorizing combat operations against Iraq, this happened after the deployments had occurred.

Congress has the power to declare war, but this power by itself does not constrain the president. In fact, even though the United States has been involved in hundreds of military conflicts since the Founding, there have been only five declarations of war: the War of 1812, the Mexican-American War (1846), the Spanish-American War (1898), World War I (1917), and World War II (1941). However, especially in recent years, members of Congress have used other methods to constrain presidential war-making powers.

In particular, Congress enacted the War Powers Resolution in 1973; its provisions are described in Nuts and Bolts 11.1. However, a 2004 report by the Congressional Research Service found that between 1975 and 2003, despite dozens of U.S. military actions—ranging from embassy evacuations to large-scale operations, including the 1991 Persian Gulf War and the invasions of Iraq and Afghanistan—the War Powers

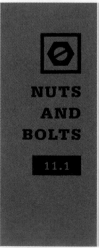

NUTS AND BOLTS

11.1

The War Powers Resolution of 1973

1. The President is required to report to Congress any introduction of U.S. forces into hostilities or imminent hostilities.

2. The use of force must be terminated within sixty days unless Congress approves of the deployment. The time limit can be extended to ninety days if the president certifies that additional time is needed to safely withdraw American forces.

3. The president is required whenever possible to consult with Congress before introducing American forces into hostilities or imminent hostilities.

4. Any congressional resolution authorizing the continued deployment of American forces will be considered under expedited procedures.

SOURCE: Richard F. Grimmett, "The War Powers Resolution: After Thirty Years," Congressional Research Service Report RL32267, March 11, 2004.

Resolution has been invoked only once.[24] Moreover, despite being in effect for over thirty years, the War Powers Resolution has never faced Supreme Court review. Some scholars have even argued that the resolution actually expands presidential power because it gives the president essentially unlimited control for the first ninety days of a military operation.[25]

Despite its limitations, the War Powers Resolution has forced presidents to gain congressional approval, in the form of congressional resolutions, for large-scale military actions such as the invasion of Iraq, as well as for lesser operations, such as the deployments of peacekeeping forces in Bosnia during the 1990s. Members of Congress can also curb a president's war-making powers through budget restrictions, legislative prohibitions, and, ultimately, through impeachment.[26]

POLITICAL PROCESS MATTERS

☑ While presidents and members of Congress often disagree about the constitutionality of the War Powers Resolution, its provisions have forced presidents to gain congressional approval before initiating military actions that generated significant opposition in Congress or among the American people.

Treaty Making and Foreign Policy Treaty-making power is shared between Congress and the president: presidents and their staff negotiate treaties, which are typically then sent to the Senate for approval, which requires the support of a two-thirds majority. In the case of treaties negotiated under **fast-track authority**, both the House and Senate vote on the treaty, with majority support in each chamber required for approval. However, the president has a **first-mover advantage** in the treaty-making process. Congress considers treaties only after negotiations have ended; there is no way for members of Congress to force the president to negotiate a treaty.

Presidents have two strategies for avoiding a congressional treaty vote. One is to announce that the United States will voluntarily abide by a treaty without ratifying it. President Clinton used this tactic to implement the 1997 Kyoto Protocol, an agreement that set limits on carbon emissions by industrialized nations.[27] It is also possible to structure a deal as an **executive agreement** between the executive branch and a foreign government, which does not require Senate approval. Relative to a ratified treaty, which remains in force after the president who negotiated it leaves office, both voluntary compliance and executive agreements have the disadvantage that a subsequent president can simply undo the action, as President George W. Bush did in the case of compliance with the Kyoto Protocol.

▲ While the Constitution mandates Senate approval for treaties before they take effect, the president has the authority to declare that the United States will voluntarily abide by a treaty without ratifying it. After the United Nations Framework Convention on Climate Change, President Clinton took this action, which does not require Senate consent, to implement the Kyoto Protocol.

fast-track authority An expedited system for passing treaties under which support from simple majority, rather than a two thirds majority, is needed in both the House and Senate, and no amendments are allowed.

first-mover advantage The president's power to initiate treaty negotiations. Congress cannot initiate treaties and can only consider them once they have been negotiated.

executive agreement An agreement between the executive branch and a foreign government, which acts as a treaty but does not require Senate approval.

▲ While many observers expected President Bill Clinton's administration to focus on domestic policy, he and his advisors spent much time dealing with international crises and commitments, such as the NATO peacekeeping mission in Kosovo.

The president also serves as the principle representative of the United States in foreign affairs other than treaty negotiations. These duties include communicating with foreign leaders and nongovernmental organizations to persuade them to do what the president believes will be in the United States' interest.

The amount of time the president devotes to foreign policy is subject to world events and therefore not entirely under his control. When President Bill Clinton took office in 1993, the expectation was that he would focus on domestic policy, partly because of his campaign promises to reform health care, increase employment opportunities, and cut the budget deficit, but also because the prominence of foreign policy issues seemed to decline with the end of the Cold War. Clinton certainly spent significant time on domestic issues, but he also ended up sending troops to Somalia, Haiti, Bosnia, and Kosovo; negotiating several arms control agreements; facilitating Russia's transition to democracy; and attempting to broker a peace agreement between Israel and the Palestinians.[28] Similarly, President George W. Bush campaigned on the priorities of tax cuts and education reform[29] and against nation-building abroad. Nonetheless, in response to the September 11 attacks, he initiated efforts to build stable democracies in Afghanistan and Iraq.[30]

Legislative Power The Constitution establishes lawmaking as a shared power between the president and Congress.[31] The president can recommend policies to Congress, most notably in the annual **State of the Union** address. The president and his staff also work with members of Congress to develop legislative proposals, and although the president cannot formally introduce legislation, it is typically easy to find a member of Congress willing to sponsor a presidential proposal.[32]

The president's legislative power also stems from the ability to veto legislation, as discussed in Chapter 10. Under the two-step legislative process set by the Constitution, once both Houses of Congress have passed a bill by simple majority, the president must decide within two weeks of congressional action whether to sign it or issue a veto. Signed bills become law, but vetoed bills return to the House and Senate for a vote to override the veto. If both chambers enact the bill again with at least two-thirds majorities, the bill becomes law; otherwise it is defeated. If Congress adjourns before the president has made his decision, the president can pocket veto the proposal simply by not responding to it. Pocket vetoes cannot be overridden, but congressional leaders can avoid them by keeping the Congress in session for two weeks after a bill is enacted, forcing the president to either sign the bill or veto it.

Presidential vetoes can have significant policy consequences. President Bill Clinton vetoed several bills that would have banned some types of late-term abortion. Supporters of these measures comprised a majority in both houses of Congress, but they could not amass the two-thirds majority required to override Clinton's veto.[33] After President Bush took office, however, the ban was approved by the House and Senate and signed into law.

Studies show that vetoes are most likely to occur under divided government, when a president from one party faces a House and Senate controlled by the other party.[34] Under these conditions, the veto allows the president to block proposals supported by legislators from the other party, producing gridlock when policy does not change.[35] Vetoes are much less likely under unified government, when one party's candidates control Congress and the presidency, because the chances are much higher that the president and legislators from his party will hold similar policy priorities.

Democratic president Bill Clinton faced divided government, working with a Republican-controlled Congress for all but the first two years of his eight years in

POLITICAL PROCESS MATTERS

The president's veto power allows him to block legislation unless its supporters in Congress can amass support from a two-thirds majority in both the House and the Senate.

State of the Union An annual speech in which the president addresses Congress to report on the condition of the country and recommend policies.

Who Leads Other Countries?

The American president serves as both head of state and head of government, an arrangement that gives the president an enormous opportunity to shape what government does. However, this also creates a huge workload for the president, even with the help of appointees to manage the federal government. How common is this arrangement among the world's democracies?

Scholars of comparative politics have identified three ways to structure a democracy. First, in a presidential system (or presidential republic), such as the United States, a single chief executive, who is elected separately from legislators, serves as both head of state and head of government.

Second, in a parliamentary system (or parliamentary monarchy), a member of the legislature—usually the leader of the majority party—serves as the head of government. Some of these countries do not have a head of state, and in those that do, the position is usually held by a king or queen

whose role is largely ceremonial. For example, Gordon Brown is Great Britain's prime minister, or head of government, and the country's head of state is Queen Elizabeth II. The queen delivers the annual message of the government to Parliament, which is the equivalent of the president's State of the Union address, but the speech is written by the prime minister and his staff; the queen simply reads the text.

The third type of democracy is a mixed republic (also called a semi-presidential system), which resembles a parliamentary system in that the head of government is chosen from the members of the legislature. Unlike a parliamentary system, however, a semi-presidential system also has a separately elected head of state or president. The powers of this chief executive vary widely between countries. In France the president focuses on foreign policy, while the prime minister handles domestic policy, but in some other countries, such as Germany and Israel, the president's job is largely ceremonial.

The table below reports the distribution of these three systems and several other forms of government across the world. The most common form of government worldwide is a mixed republic with a separate head of government and head of state. There are also a substantial number of parliamentary monarchies. However, most of the semi-presidential systems listed in the table actually work much like parliamentary systems. In these countries, the chief executive has relatively little power, just like the monarch in a parliamentary monarchy.

Moreover, while America is not alone in having a presidential system, most other countries that use this system are new, relatively small democracies in Central or South America or in Africa, such as Nicaragua, Argentina, Nigeria, or South Africa. Among democracies in the developed world, America's presidential system is highly unusual. ■

SYSTEMS OF GOVERNMENT WORLDWIDE

	PRESIDENTIAL REPUBLIC	PARLIAMENTARY MONARCHY	MIXED REPUBLIC	MONARCHY	MILITARY STATE	OTHER	TOTAL
Sub-Saharan Africa	17	1	27	1	1	2	49
Asia-Pacific	8	10	14	4	1	0	37
Central and Eastern Europe	0	0	26	0	0	1	27
Middle East	1	0	8	7	1	2	19
North America	2	1	0	0	0	0	3
Central and South America	16	9	7	0	0	0	32
Scandinavia	0	3	2	0	0	0	5
Western Europe	1	7	8	1	0	2	19
Total	45	31	92	13	3	7	191

SOURCE: Based on Pippa Norris, *Driving Democracy* (New York: Cambridge University Press, 2008), Table 5.1.

office. Republican President George W. Bush, in contrast, had divided government with Democratic control of the Senate during most of his first two years in office (Jim Jeffords, I-VT, left the Republican Party on May 24, 2001, giving control of the Senate to the Democrats), unified government for the middle four years, and divided government once again when the Democrats took control of the House and the Senate in the 2006 midterm elections. Clinton issued almost forty vetoes in his eight years in office, whereas Bush vetoed only eleven pieces of legislation in the same time. Bush's low number of vetoes was a consequence of the more unified government he enjoyed while in office.

While the veto is useful to block legislation or issue a threat that encourages legislators to negotiate before casting their votes, it cannot force members of Congress to enact a proposal they oppose.[36] The president and his staff bargain with legislators, trying to craft proposals that a majority will support and sometimes offering inducements to individual lawmakers, such as presidential support for other favored policies. House members and Senators from the president's party may feel obligated to help him, but it is very hard for a president to win over opponents in Congress, especially if helping the president will anger a legislator's constituents.

In one recent example, President Bush's chief domestic priority during 2005 was reforming Social Security. As mentioned in Chapter 5, Public Opinion, Bush made extensive efforts to win public and congressional support for raising the retirement age, stemming the growth in benefits, and partially privatizing the program. Despite his speeches, conferences, and town hall meetings, however, the ideas never took hold with the electorate, and members of Congress did not respond as Bush hoped: no reform proposal was seriously considered.[37] Bush was similarly unsuccessful in getting legislators to consider his immigration reform proposals in 2006 and in 2007, with pressure from constituents playing a major role in members' calculations.[38]

Other Duties and Powers The Constitution gives the president a number of additional powers, including the authority to pardon people convicted of federal crimes or commute their sentences. The only limit on this power is that a president cannot pardon anyone who has been impeached and convicted by Congress. (Thus, if a president is removed from office via impeachment, he can neither pardon himself nor be pardoned when his vice president assumes the presidency.)

While most presidential pardons attract little attention, some have been extremely controversial. Presidents have pardoned their own appointees for crimes committed while serving in their administrations, as well as campaign contributors and personal friends. In July 2007, President George W. Bush commuted a thirty-month jail term given to Lewis "Scooter" Libby, Vice President Dick Cheney's former aide. Libby had been convicted of lying to a grand jury about his role in leaking the name of Valerie Plame, a covert CIA agent, to several journalists. As mentioned in Chapter 6, this information was leaked to discredit a report written by Plame's husband that contradicted the administration's claims that Iraq was importing nuclear material for weapons development.[39]

The president's power to pardon raises the concern that pardons could become part of a tacit bargain between a president and his subordinates. That is, the possibility of a presidential pardon could allow executive branch employees to pursue the president's objectives with impunity, even if it meant breaking the law. Similarly, pardons granted to campaign contributors, such as President Bill Clinton's pardon of contributor Marc Rich, who had been convicted of tax evasion, could become a way to trade money for leniency. (There is, however, no evidence that Clinton made such a bargain.) Nonetheless, even when a pardon is controversial, there is no way to reverse a president's decision.

The Constitution also gives the president a number of largely ceremonial powers, such as the power to convene Congress or to adjourn it if legislators cannot agree on an adjournment date. This provision gave the president real power during the early days of the Republic, when Congress was in session for only a few months every year. Now that Congress is in session for most of the year, and party leaders set dates for the beginning and end of legislative sessions well in advance, this power is irrelevant. Similarly, the Constitution gives the president the responsibility for receiving ambassadors from other nations by officially recognizing that they speak on behalf of their countries' rulers. The president also signs commissions to formally appoint military officers.

Executive Privilege Finally, while it is not a formal power, all presidents have claimed to hold **executive privilege**, or the ability to shield themselves and their subordinates from revealing White House discussions, decisions, or documents (including e-mails) to members of the legislative or judicial branches of government.[40] The nature of executive privilege—exactly what it protects versus what Congress can force the president to release—is an unsettled question. Some constitutional scholars even argue that in legal terms, executive privilege doesn't exist.[41]

▲ In July 2007, President Bush commuted the prison sentence of former vice presidential chief of staff Lewis "Scooter" Libby, following Libby's conviction for lying to a grand jury about his role in the Valerie Plame affair.

A late-2006 incident focused public attention on questions about the limits of executive privilege after senior political appointees in the Justice Department decided to remove several U.S. attorneys from office.[42] U.S. attorneys are presidential appointees who investigate and prosecute crimes under federal law. While senior Bush administration officials and spokesmen initially claimed that the attorneys were removed because of poor performance, statements from the fired attorneys and lower-level Justice Department staff made it clear that the attorneys were dismissed because they were viewed as insufficiently loyal to President Bush. (The firings were not illegal, but they were embarrassing, as they suggested the Bush administration was more interested in political loyalty than job performance.) Several congressional committees subpoenaed Bush administration staff to testify about the matter, but President Bush refused to allow the testimony to take place, arguing that conversations about the removal of the attorneys fell under executive privilege, meaning he had the right to keep these conversations confidential.[43] Ultimately, some political appointees in the Justice Department, including Attorney General Alberto Gonzalez, testified before Congress, although others, such as Karl Rove, continued to refuse to testify. In this sense, the claim of executive privilege was upheld, but only because members of Congress did not enforce subpoenas to compel testimony.

Even though claims of executive privilege have been made since the ratification of the Constitution in 1789, it is still not clear exactly what falls under the privilege and what does not. In the 1974 case *United States v. Nixon*, a special prosecutor appointed by the Justice Department to investigate the Watergate scandal challenged President Nixon's claims of executive privilege to force him to hand over tapes of potentially incriminating Oval Office conversations involving Nixon and his senior aides. The Supreme Court ruled unanimously that executive privilege does exist, but that the privilege is not absolute. Their decision required Nixon to release the tapes, which proved his involvement with attempts to cover up the scandal—but the ruling did not clearly state the conditions under which a future president could withhold such information.[44]

executive privilege The right of the president to keep executive branch conversations and correspondence confidential from the legislative and judicial branches.

The Limits of Executive Privilege

Deciding which information a president can be compelled to release to the public or to other branches of government and what he can keep confidential requires confronting fundamentally political questions. There are no right answers, and the limits of executive privilege remain unclear.

On one hand, members of Congress need facts, predictions, and estimates from the executive branch in order to make good public policy. More importantly, members need to be able to weigh the pros and cons of a range of policy alternatives. Consider the controversy over the firing of eight U.S. attorneys in 2007 by senior staff in the Justice Department. It is clear that the attorneys were fired for reasons other than poor performance, although the precise motivations for the terminations are unclear. Nonetheless, critics of the firing decisions noted that one of the dismissed attorneys had received complaints from a Republican senator for not bringing charges in a voting fraud case against Democrats. Another was replaced with a former aide to Bush's one-time campaign strategist and deputy chief of staff, Karl Rove.[a]

The U.S. attorney case may seem like a situation in which executive privilege does not apply. Shouldn't the American people know the reasons for hiring and firing senior government employees? If the Justice Department staff did nothing wrong, why wouldn't the Bush administration let them explain the reasons for the firings to Congress?

First, testifying before Congress, or even releasing documents in response to a congressional request, is enormously time-

▲ Congressional concerns over the firing of eight U.S. attorneys, some of whom are shown here at a House hearing, led to demands for documents and testimony from White House officials about the reasons for the firings—and claims by White House officials that this information was shielded by executive privilege.

consuming and can be surprisingly expensive. Presidential appointees who have testified before Congress have faced legal bills of $100,000 or more. If members of Congress could require information and testimony of executive branch employees whenever they wanted, it would be hard for the executive bureaucracy to get anything done—and hard to convince anyone to work there.[b]

The second argument for invoking executive privilege in the case of the U.S. attorneys is that under current law, U.S. attorneys can be removed by the president at any time, even for purely political reasons. Thus, part of the motivation for these congressional requests for information was to force Bush administration officials to publicly reveal that politics played a role in their decisions. That goal has to do with

electoral politics—making Republicans look bad in the eyes of voters—as well as with members of Congress trying to acquire the information necessary to make sound decisions.

In sum, while being able to get information from a president can help members of Congress make better policy choices, there are situations where confidentiality helps the president and his staff make good choices as well. However, executive privilege can also be used to hide crimes or questionable political tactics, or to prevent members of Congress from embarrassing the president by publicizing his mistakes or private comments. Should presidents have an executive privilege? What limits should apply to congressional requests for information and testimony? You decide. ■

President Bill Clinton invoked executive privilege thirteen times on matters such as an investigation of Secretary of Agriculture Mike Espy, the firing of employees in the White House Travel Office, and the investigation of his own conduct with White House intern Monica Lewinsky.[45] In all of these cases, however, federal courts ordered the documents to be released.

Claims of executive privilege present a dilemma. On one hand, members of Congress need to know what is happening in the executive branch. In the case of President Nixon and the Watergate scandal, claims of executive privilege allowed the Watergate cover-up to continue for over a year and would have kept this information secret permanently if the Court had ruled in Nixon's favor.[46] At the same time, the president and his staff need to be able to communicate freely, discussing alternate strategies and hypothetical situations, without fearing that they will be forced to reveal conversations that could become politically embarrassing or costly. (Suppose the discussions included political strategies for the next election or a sarcastic remark about jailing their opponents.) Moreover, allowing aides to testify before Congress is enormously time-consuming and can be costly for the aides if they hire lawyers.

THE PRESIDENT AS POLITICIAN

As the head of the executive branch, the president has considerable influence over policy. However, much of what presidents do (or want to do) requires support from legislators, bureaucrats, and average citizens. As a result, the presidency is an inherently political office. The president has to take into account the political consequences of his decisions—both for his own reelection prospects and for the reelection of legislators from his party. He must also contend with the fact that achieving his policy goals often requires bargaining and compromising with others, both inside and outside of government.

Presidents try to deliver on their campaign promises not only because they believe in them, but also because fulfilling them is politically advantageous. President George W. Bush promised to cut taxes and enact education reforms, and he delivered on these promises.[47] To solidify conservative support in the months before the 2004 presidential election, Bush also proposed a constitutional amendment to define marriage to exclude gay and lesbian couples—although he did not work to build support for the proposal, which never came up for a vote.[48]

The president also typically keeps a close eye on **presidential approval**, a survey-based measurement of the percentage of the public who thinks he is doing a good job in office. Particularly during his first term, one of the president's primary concerns is to build a record that will get him reelected, and keeping approval levels as high as possible is a crucial part of this strategy. Figure 11.1, which shows the presidential approval ratings for the last six presidents who ran for reelection, reveals that first-term presidents with less than 50 percent approval are in real trouble. No recent president has been reelected with less than 50 percent approval.

All presidents have staff and consultants who regularly poll the public to discern its feelings about the president and find out what actions might increase approval. These findings influence but do not determine presidential actions. For example, poll results probably played no role in President Bush's decision to invade Iraq. While the invasion was initially popular, it is likely that Bush would have made the same decision even if he had faced much stronger public opposition. On the other hand, legislators' tepid support for Bush's proposed ban on gay marriage was driven, at least in part, by public opposition to the ban.[49]

While political considerations matter somewhat less to a second-term president (since running for reelection is not an option), politics still matters in the second term. Members of Congress are more likely to support policy initiatives proposed by a popular president, believing that this popularity reflects public support for

POLITICS IS EVERYWHERE

Though the president is the head of state and a symbol of the nation, politics remains an inescapable part of the office. Not only do presidential actions have policy consequences, but presidents must also cultivate public support in order to get reelected and to help elect candidates from their party.

presidential approval The percentage of Americans who feel that the president is doing a good job in office.

FIGURE 11.1   PRESIDENTIAL POPULARITY AND REELECTION

This figure shows the pre-election year average approval ratings for recent presidents who ran for reelection. It shows that a president's chances of winning reelection are related to their popularity. At what level of approval would you say that an incumbent president is likely to be reelected?

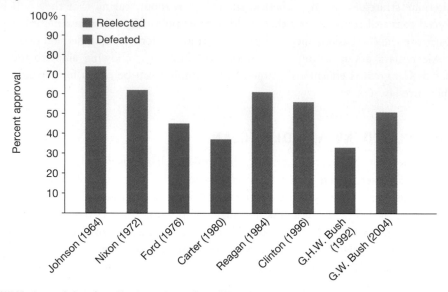

SOURCE: Approval data from The Roper Center for Public Opinion Research, University of Connecticut, "Data Access: Presidential Approval," available at http://webapps.ropercenter.uconn.edu/CFIDE/roper/presidential/webroot/presidential_rating.cfm.

the president's goals. Conversely, an unpopular president, such as President Bush in 2007 and 2008, will find it much harder to build support for new programs. For example, when Bush called on members of Congress to end the practice of earmarking federal funds for specific projects to benefit their own constituents, even members of Bush's party in the House and Senate ignored the proposal.[50]

The President as Party Leader The president is the unofficial head of his political party and generally picks the day-to-day leadership of the party, or at least has considerable influence over the selection. This process begins when a presidential candidate captures the party's nomination. For example, soon after Barack Obama became the presumptive Democratic Party nominee by amassing a majority of convention delegates, some of his senior aides and advisors took on leadership positions in the Democratic Party organization.[51]

The president's connection to the party reflects the fact that their interests are intertwined. The president needs support from his party members in Congress to enact legislation, and the party and its candidates need the president to compile a record of policy achievements that reflect well on the party, and to help raise the funds needed for the next election. Therefore, party leaders generally defer to a presidential candidate's (or a president's) staffing requests, and most presidents and presidential candidates take time to meet with national party leaders and the congressional leadership from their party to plan legislative strategies, make joint campaign appearances, and raise funds for the party's candidates. President Bush, for example, raised over $180 million for Republican House and Senate candidates in the 2002 midterm election.[52]

On the other hand, when presidential approval ratings drop to low levels, most members of Congress will see no political advantage to campaigning with the

Is the President Responsible for America's Economic Conditions?

During the 2008 presidential campaign, Republican candidate John McCain and Democratic candidate Barack Obama disagreed on many things, from how to reform America's health care system to the withdrawal of troops from Iraq. Nonetheless, one point of agreement between the candidates was their willingness to blame their predecessor, President George W. Bush, for the poor state of the American economy in 2008. During a speech in June 2008, Obama charged that "We did not arrive at the doorstep of our current economic crisis by some accident of history. . . . This was not an inevitable part of the business cycle that was beyond our power to avoid. It was the logical conclusion of a tired and misguided philosophy that has dominated Washington for far too long."[a] A month later, in a speech in Denver, Colorado, McCain differed with Obama on some of the specifics but agreed that President Bush deserved some of the blame for economic conditions, saying, "This Congress and this administration have failed to meet their responsibilities to manage the government. Government has grown by 60 percent in the last eight years. That is simply inexcusable."[b]

Many Americans hold similar views. In a February 2008 survey by the Pew Research Center, almost half of the respondents assigned President Bush a "great deal" of responsibility for economic conditions—many more than blamed Congress (31 percent), multinational corporations (31 percent), or Ben Bernanke, the Chairman of the Federal Reserve (6 percent).[c] These judgments fit a long-term pattern: as noted earlier, many incumbent presidents, such as Democrat Jimmy Carter (1980) and Republican George H. W. Bush (1992) have lost reelection bids because of poor economic conditions at the time they sought reelection.

For several reasons, it seems reasonable to hold the president accountable for the

▲ Americans often blame the president for economic hardships, such as the mortgage crisis of 2007 and 2008, in which housing prices dropped significantly and many homeowners abandoned their mortgages.

state of the economy. As discussed in this chapter, the president is head of the government's executive branch, with the power to propose legislation and budgets, negotiate treaties, control the implementation of new policies, and implement a variety of changes using executive orders.

However, if you consider the president's powers in light of the overall structure of the federal government, the president has much less control over the economy than one might think. As described in Chapter 10, Congress, the president cannot influence the economy by increasing government spending, cutting taxes, or establishing major new programs without congressional consent. And even if he could, these efforts might not have much effect given that the federal budget ($3.1 trillion in 2008) is only about one-fifth of the total American economy (more than $14 trillion in 2008). Moreover, the president has no direct control over the Federal Reserve, which can influence economic growth and inflation by changing inter-

est rates or the money supply. The Federal Reserve operates as an independent agency, which means that its decisions are not subject to review by the president or Congress. And finally, even if the president could single-handedly manipulate legislation, government spending, interest rates, and the money supply, his impact on the American economy would still be subject to conditions in the much larger world economy (approximately $65 trillion in 2008) as well as the price of crucial inputs such as oil.

Though American citizens and candidates for office often blame the sitting president for the state of the economy, this attribution is based on a misperception of the president's powers. The president can do many things that help shape economic conditions in America, particularly if members of Congress or the Federal Reserve are willing to cooperate in these efforts. But the president cannot guarantee Americans high rates of economic growth or low inflation and unemployment. ∎

go public A president's use of speeches and other public communications to appeal directly to citizens about issues the president would like the House and Senate to act on.

president or supporting his proposals, and they may become increasingly reluctant to comply with his requests. In the 2002 and 2004 elections, Republican legislators stressed their connection to President Bush and gladly accepted offers of joint campaign appearances. In 2006 and 2008, however, many Republican candidates tried to deemphasize their connection to the president and did not ask him to campaign with them.[53]

Going Public The president is in an excellent position to communicate with the American people because of his prominent role and the extensive media coverage devoted to anything he says to the nation. Broadcast and cable networks even give the president prime time slots for his State of the Union speech and other major addresses. The media attention that comes with the presidency provides the president with a unique strategy for shaping government policy: the ability to **go public**, or appeal directly to American citizens, in the hopes of getting the electorate to pressure members of the House and Senate to do what he wants.[54] By directly seeking the support of the electorate, the president can utilize what President Theodore Roosevelt called the bully pulpit—exploiting the fact that anything he says will receive a high level of public and media attention.[55]

The first American president to give a live nationwide address was Franklin Roosevelt, who used his 1936 State of the Union speech to argue against congressional attempts to undo his New Deal reforms.[56] Throughout his presidency, Roosevelt made thirty informal radio broadcasts, which he called fireside chats. While it is hard to say for sure, as political scientists do not have good polling data from the 1930s, it appears that Roosevelt's efforts helped to restore public confidence and built support for his New Deal proposals. Such public appeals are partly designed to persuade, but they also serve to bring an issue that the president considers important to the attention of citizens who already share his views, in the hope that they will urge their elected representatives to support the president's requests.

Of course, going public doesn't always bring success; the key to making it work is public opinion—whether people agree with what the president wants. In 1981 Ronald Reagan used televised speeches to build support for his tax cut proposals, which received a warm welcome from many Americans. In contrast, in 2006 and 2007, as public approval for the war in Iraq declined, President Bush gave several televised speeches in an attempt to regain support for the conflict, but these efforts had little effect.[57] Going public may also have political consequences for the president. It can alienate members of Congress, as it represents an attempt to go over legislators' heads to reach the American people directly, thereby getting Congress to agree with the president without the benefit of the usual bargaining and negotiations.[58]

POLITICS IS EVERYWHERE

The president is the only elected official who has regular opportunities to speak directly to the American people through televised speeches and consistent media coverage of actions in office. In some cases, such as Ronald Reagan's 1981 speeches on proposed tax cuts, these efforts can motivate congressional action by winning public support.

PRESIDENTIAL SUCCESSION

Under the Constitution, presidents are limited to two full terms in office. A vice president who becomes president in between elections can, if reelected, serve two more full terms even after taking over during the first half of their predecessor's term. Under the 25th Amendment, a vice president can also temporarily take over as president, a procedure used in 2007 when President George W. Bush had a medical procedure requiring anesthesia.[59]

If the president and the vice president were to both die or become incapacitated, the Speaker of the House of Representatives would become president. Next in line is the president pro tempore of the Senate, and then a list of cabinet secretaries in the order shown in Nuts and Bolts 11.2. Whenever the entire cabinet and Congress gather in one place, such as at the annual State of the Union address, at least one member of the cabinet is assigned to be somewhere else, so that in the event of a catastrophe, someone in the line of succession would survive to assume the presidency.

In the event that the vice president must be replaced due to resignation, impeachment, or incapacity, the 25th Amendment allows the president to nominate a new vice president, who must be confirmed by majority votes in the House and the Senate. This procedure was used twice in the 1970s, first to make Gerald Ford vice president under Richard Nixon (replacing Spiro Agnew), then, after Nixon's resignation, to make Nelson Rockefeller vice president under Ford.[60]

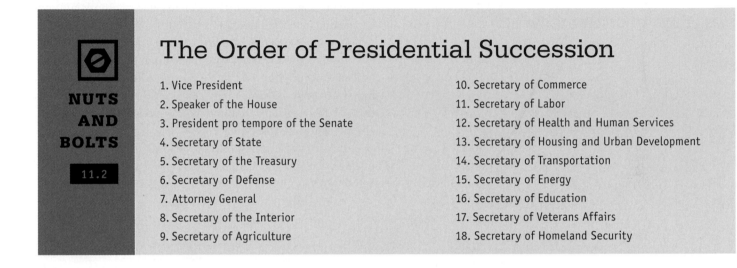

NUTS AND BOLTS

11.2

The Order of Presidential Succession

1. Vice President
2. Speaker of the House
3. President pro tempore of the Senate
4. Secretary of State
5. Secretary of the Treasury
6. Secretary of Defense
7. Attorney General
8. Secretary of the Interior
9. Secretary of Agriculture
10. Secretary of Commerce
11. Secretary of Labor
12. Secretary of Health and Human Services
13. Secretary of Housing and Urban Development
14. Secretary of Transportation
15. Secretary of Energy
16. Secretary of Education
17. Secretary of Veterans Affairs
18. Secretary of Homeland Security

SECTION SUMMARY

1. The president's duties include overseeing the implementation of legislation; appointing senior government officials and federal judges; issuing executive orders; serving as military commander in chief; directing America's foreign policy; proposing, signing, and vetoing legislation; and carrying out other duties.
2. The president is a politician who needs to cultivate citizens' support in order to get reelected, to pressure Congress to enact his proposals, and to help elect candidates from his party.
3. Even after 220 years of American history, the limits of presidential power in such areas as national security and executive privilege remain unclear.

The American Public and the President

As the last section described, presidents need to cultivate public support in order to get reelected and to enact their policy proposals. Thus, in order to understand what kinds of policy goals presidents set and how they seek to come across to the public, it is important to consider what Americans want from their presidents and which characteristics they associate with a successful president.

Table 11.1 shows the results of several surveys about the qualities Americans want in a president. Large majorities want the president to have good judgment and to be ethical and compassionate while smaller majorities want a president who says what he believes, holds consistent positions, and is forceful and decisive. A third or fewer want the president to be willing to compromise, to have political experience and savvy, to have Washington experience, or to be loyal to his party. Relatively few Americans consider military experience an important presidential asset.

The interesting part of this table lies in the comparison of items that received strong support (consistency, forcefulness, and decisiveness) with those that fewer people found appealing (compromise, political experience, political savvy, Washington experience, and party loyalty). We have seen that American politics is conflictual, which means that compromising and bargaining are fundamental parts of what successful politicians do. However, it seems that most Americans are not looking for a president who has the traits and experiences that facilitate negotiating and deal making. Moreover, presidents may face tough decisions between building a public reputation for firmness and making the compromises necessary to change or implement policies.

Consider, for example, the welfare reforms enacted by President Bill Clinton and Congress in 1996. The legislation was not Clinton's ideal; he opposed its five-year lifetime limit on benefits. However, Clinton supported other provisions in the bill

POLITICS IS CONFLICTUAL

The American public's conception of the ideal president does not include the skills and traits needed to handle the conflicts that are endemic to American politics.

TABLE 11.1 CITIZEN DEMANDS ON THE PRESIDENT

These data show that many Americans want the president to stick to his principles, say what he believes, and be forceful and decisive. Fewer consider political experience and willingness to compromise essential presidential qualities. How might the political necessity for bargaining and compromise affect a president's ability to satisfy citizens' expectations?

ESSENTIAL QUALITIES	1995	1999	2003
Sound judgment	76%	78%	76%
High ethical standards	67	63	67
Compassion	64	63	63
Saying what one believes	59	57	56
Consistent positions	51	50	52
Forcefulness and decisiveness	50	46	49
Willingness to compromise	34	33	38
Experience in public office	30	38	37
Political savvy	31	–	36
Experience in Washington	21	27	32
Party loyalty	25	33	30
Military experience	–	–	16

SOURCE: Pew Research Center, "Bush Reelect Margin Narrows to 45%–43%." news release, September 25, 2003, available at http://people-press.org/reports/pdf/194.pdf.

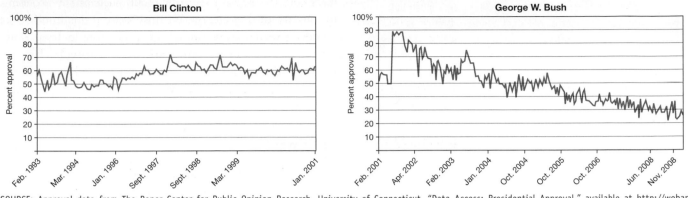

SOURCE: Approval data from The Roper Center for Public Opinion Research, University of Connecticut, "Data Access: Presidential Approval," available at http://webapps
.ropercenter.uconn.edu/CFIDE/roper/presidential/webroot/presidential_rating.cfm.

that increased funding for job-training and day-care programs designed to help welfare recipients transition to gainful employment. Taken together, the package was probably the best Clinton could hope for from a Republican-controlled Congress. Moreover, the proposal attracted a high level of public support. Signing the bill did not help Clinton's reputation as a man of unwavering principle, but it did implement real changes to welfare programs and increased his support among fiscally conservative voters in the 1996 election.

EXPLAINING PRESIDENTIAL APPROVAL

Questions about the public's approval of the president have been asked in mass surveys since Franklin Roosevelt was president. Figure 11.2 reports presidential approval data for the two most recent presidents, Bill Clinton and George W. Bush. The data for Clinton show a relatively rare pattern of steady improvement throughout his time in office. In contrast, George W. Bush's popularity steadily declined following the sharp spike upward after the September 11 attacks.

What explains this variation? Presidential approval generally spikes during national crises, such as the Iranian Hostage Crisis during Jimmy Carter's term, the Persian Gulf War during George H. W. Bush's term, or the September 11 attacks during George W. Bush's first term. Recall from our discussion of public opinion that this phenomenon has been called the "rally 'round the flag" effect,[61] comparing the electorate to troops gathering around a flag during a battle.

There are no such spikes in the chart for Bill Clinton, reflecting the fact that there were no national crises during his time in office. In such relatively calm times, presidential approval reflects the overall state of the nation including citizens' perceptions of economic conditions and national security. In Clinton's case, economic conditions steadily improved throughout his presidency, generating the increase in his approval ratings observed earlier. Even when Clinton was being impeached in 1998 and 1999, his popularity did not suffer.

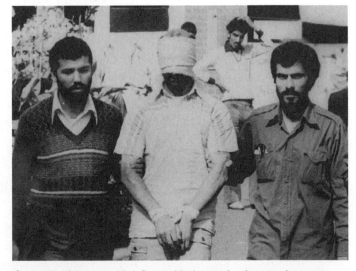

▲ Presidential approval is influenced by international events that concern Americans, such as the taking of American hostages by militant Iranian students in 1979. Then-president Jimmy Carter initially saw his approval ratings increase, but they declined steadily as the crisis continued into 1980.

POLITICS IS EVERYWHERE

Citizens' evaluations of the president are driven by their assessments of national conditions such as the state of the economy and national security.

This finding may suggest that even if Americans want an ethical president, they forgive misdeeds given good performance on the issues they care about, such as the economy. In contrast, during George W. Bush's two terms in office, he presided over an increasingly unpopular war in Iraq, along with a deteriorating economy, particularly during his last two years in office. Both of these factors contributed to the steady declines in Bush's approval ratings.

SECTION SUMMARY

1. Most Americans want the president to have good judgment and to be ethical and compassionate. Somewhat fewer Americans want a president who is politically experienced and willing to compromise.
2. Issues such as the economy and health care are perennially important in presidential elections. In recent elections, national security issues such as preventing terrorist attacks and managing the wars in Iraq and Afghanistan have also come to the fore.
3. Presidential approval ratings are driven by a president's performance on the major issues facing the country, such as the economy and national security.

The Executive Branch

As head of the executive branch, the president runs a huge, complex organization with hundreds of thousands of employees. This section describes the organizations and staff who help the president exercise his vast responsibilities, from managing disaster-response efforts to implementing policy changes.[62] Among these employees are appointees who hold senior positions in the government. These individuals serve as the president's eyes and ears in the bureaucracy, making sure that bureaucrats are following presidential directives.

Many other executive branch employees work within the Executive Office of the President (EOP), which has employed about 1,800 people in recent administrations. About one-third of these employees are concentrated in two offices, the Office of Management and Budget (OMB), which develops the president's budget proposals, monitors spending by government agencies, and the Office of the United States Trade Representative (USTR), which negotiates trade agreements with other nations.[63]

THE EXECUTIVE OFFICE OF THE PRESIDENT

Nuts and Bolts 11.3 lists the organizations that make up the **Executive Office of the President (EOP)** and one of its main components, the White House Office. Both include offices that have clear policy-related or political missions, such as the Office of Management and Budget mentioned above, or the Domestic Policy Council, whose staff are involved in all aspects of policy making, from developing proposals to monitoring their implementation.

Regardless of their official job title and policy responsibilities, one of the most important duties of EOP staff is helping the president and candidates from his

Executive Office of the President (EOP) The group of policy-related offices that serve as support staff to the president.

The Executive Office of the President

Council of Economic Advisors
Council on Environmental Quality
National Security Council
Office of Administration
Office of Management and Budget

Office of National Drug Control Policy
Office of Science and Technology Policy
Office of United States Trade Representative
President's Foreign Intelligence Advisory Board
White House Office

WHITE HOUSE OFFICE

Domestic Policy Council
Homeland Security Council
National Economic Council
Office of Faith-Based and Community Initiatives
Office of the First Lady

Office of National AIDS Policy
Privacy and Civil Liberties Oversight Board
USA Freedom Corps
White House Fellows Office
White House Military Office

party achieve their policy goals and get reelected. Consider the Office of National Drug Control Policy (ONDCP). Throughout 2006, representatives from the office traveled throughout the country to hold joint press conferences with Republican and Democratic members of Congress where they announced federal grants for drug abuse prevention programs. However, three months before that year's midterm elections, with Republicans in danger of losing majority control of the House and Senate, ONDCP officials began holding press conferences exclusively with Republican legislators.[64] An e-mail from the head of the office, John Walters, revealed that this strategy was an attempt to help vulnerable Republican candidates. In other words, while people in the ONDCP did not abandon their official duties, they also did everything they could to help Republicans in the 2006 election.

Even the small, lower level offices within the White House Office play political roles as they carry out their official responsibilities. One office that fulfils such a dual role is the Photo Office, whose official job is to "photographically document and maintain an archive of official events of the president, the first lady, the vice president, and his wife."[65] The office also photographs the president with political supporters, providing pictures that can be used to thank them for their contributions or other efforts.

The most influential EOP staff occupy the offices in the West Wing of the White House. The West Wing contains the president's office, known as the Oval Office, and space for the president's chief aide and personal secretary, as well as senior aides including the vice president, the president's press secretary, and the chief of staff who coordinates White House operations.

Most EOP staff members are presidential appointees who retain their positions only as long as the president who appointed them remains in office. These individuals are often drawn to government service out of loyalty to the president or because they share his policy goals. However, most leave their positions after a year or two to escape the pressures of the job, the long hours, and the relatively low government salaries.[66] Despite the fairly frequent turnover in many EOP positions, some EOP offices, such as the Office of Management and Budget (OMB), the Office of the United States Trade Representative, and the National Security Council, also have a significant number of permanent staff analysts and experts.[67]

When the president appoints people to EOP positions, his primary expectation of them is loyalty, rather than a concern for the general public or policy expertise.[68]

▲ The primary characteristic of senior presidential aides is loyalty to the president, as demonstrated by a long record of service in other political positions. These three Bush appointees (from left), Chief of Staff Josh Bolten, Deputy Chief of Staff Karl Rove, and White House Counselor Dan Bartlett, had all worked for Bush prior to their appointments in his administration—either when he was governor of Texas or during his first presidential campaign in 2000.

A look at the biographies of White House staffers shows that many had worked on the campaign of the president who appointed them, often from very early in the race for the party's general election nomination. The backgrounds of some of George W. Bush's prominent West Wing staffers underline this point. Karl Rove, who served as a deputy chief of staff, had been a political strategist and campaign manager for Bush since the beginning of his political career.[69] National Security Advisor Steve Hadley worked for Vice President Cheney when Cheney was secretary of defense, and he also worked as an advisor to Bush's 2000 presidential campaign.[70] Chief of Staff Joshua Bolten served as policy director for the same campaign before becoming Bush's director of OMB and later serving as White House chief of staff.[71]

The exceptions to the loyalty rule for appointees are individuals who received their jobs because of their expertise, their connections to the president's political party (as opposed to the president himself), or links to an important group outside the government. For example, President George W. Bush named Robert Gates to be secretary of defense in late 2006. Gates had no direct connection to President Bush, but he was an expert on defense policy who had held senior defense- and intelligence-related positions in previous administrations, and he had been a member of the Iraq Study Group, which produced a well-publicized report in late 2006 that led to significant changes in U.S. strategy in Iraq.

Why is loyalty so important? Put yourself in the position of a president whose packed day begins with an intelligence briefing and ends with a state dinner. All the while, crucial decisions about public policy are being made throughout the federal government. You have no time to make these decisions yourself or even to supervise those who make them, so you need staff who understand what you want the government to do and will dedicate themselves to implementing your vision.[72] The emphasis on loyalty in presidential appointments also has an obvious drawback: appointees may not know much about the jobs they are given, and may not be very effective at managing the agencies they are supposed to control. As discussed in Chapter 12, The Bureaucracy, many observers believe that delays in the provision of federal disaster relief after Hurricane Katrina stemmed in part from the fact that many of the senior positions in the Federal Emergency Management Agency were held by political appointees who knew little about such operations.[73]

POLITICS IS CONFLICTUAL

The emphasis on EOP employees' loyalty to the president reflects the size and complexity of the federal government, the difficulty of monitoring how policies are implemented, and the likelihood that the president may face opposition from legislators and bureaucrats.

THE VICE PRESIDENT

As set out in the Constitution, the vice president's job is to preside over Senate proceedings. This largely ceremonial job is usually delegated to the president pro tempore of the Senate, who in turn typically gives the duty to a more junior member. The vice president also has the power to cast tie-breaking votes in the Senate.[74] For example, in 2005, Vice President Cheney cast the deciding vote to pass a package of budget cuts to various government programs, including Medicare, Medicaid, and federally funded student loans.[75] As mentioned earlier, the vice president's other formal responsibility is to become president if the current president dies, becomes incapacitated, resigns, or is impeached. Of the forty-four people who have become president, nine were vice presidents who became president in midterm.

These rather limited official duties of the vice president pale in comparison to the influential role played by recent vice presidents. Vice President Dick Cheney, who served with President George W. Bush, exerted a significant influence over many policy decisions, including the rights of terror suspects, tax and spending policy, environmental decisions, and the writing of new government regulations.[76] Many critics claimed that Cheney had too much power, and some even described him as a co-president.[77]

Cheney's influence stemmed from his expertise. He served as President Gerald Ford's chief of staff, a long-time member of the Republican leadership in the House of Representatives, and as secretary of defense in President George H. W. Bush's administration. Moreover, Cheney and President George W. Bush held similar views on what government should do. In other words, Bush didn't blindly trust Cheney's judgment. Rather, he knew they usually agreed on what should be done.[78]

While Dick Cheney's level of influence was unique, other recent vice presidents have also had real power. For example, Vice President Al Gore was an important advisor to President Bill Clinton. He headed an interagency task force that aimed to reorganize and streamline the federal government, as well as the Gore–Chernomyrdin Commission, a joint U.S.–Russian group that worked to control Russia's surplus nuclear weapons material.

▲ George W. Bush's vice president, Dick Cheney, was one of the most influential vice presidents in American history.

The vice president's role as a senior advisor and trusted confidante is a recent development. Before this change, vice presidents were often chosen to provide political or regional balance to a presidential candidate's electoral appeal. Jack Garner, who was Franklin Roosevelt's first vice president, once said the office was "not worth a bucket of warm spit." Garner had been added to the ticket in an attempt to win southern votes in the 1932 election, but had been ignored by Roosevelt and his aides after the election and given little to do. Similarly, Dwight Eisenhower chose then-senator Richard Nixon as his vice president in order to appeal to conservative groups in the Republican Party, but excluded Nixon from many meetings once in office. However, the expansion of the federal government beginning in the 1960s appears to have led recent presidents to look beyond political or regional factors when choosing a vice president, to find a like-minded individual who can help them manage the bureaucracy and achieve their policy goals. Barack Obama's choice, longtime senator and chairman of the Senate Foreign Relations Committee, Joe Biden, reflected the same priorities, as Biden's foreign policy expertise was expected to offset Obama's relative inexperience in this area.

POLITICAL PROCESS MATTERS

☑ The vice presidency is not a trivial office. Not only have many vice presidents gone on to become president, but modern vice presidents serve as close presidential advisors with considerable influence over government policy.

THE PRESIDENT'S CABINET

The president's **cabinet** is composed of the heads of the fifteen executive departments in the federal government, along with other appointees given cabinet rank by the president. Nuts and Bolts 11.4 lists the cabinet positions. The cabinet members' principal job is to be the front-line implementers of the president's agenda in their executive departments. As we discuss in more detail in Chapter 12, they monitor the actions of the lower-level bureaucrats who retain their jobs regardless of who is president and who may not be sympathetic to the president's priorities.

Like other presidential appointees, cabinet members are chosen for a combination of loyalty to the president and expertise. Margaret Spellings, who served as

cabinet The group of fifteen executive department heads who implement the president's agenda in their respective positions.

Cabinet Positions

Secretary of Agriculture

Secretary of Commerce

Secretary of Defense

Secretary of Education

Secretary of Energy

Secretary of Health and Human Services

Secretary of Homeland Security

Secretary of Housing and Urban Development

Secretary of the Interior

Secretary of Labor

Secretary of State

Secretary of the Treasury

Secretary of Transportation

Secretary of Veterans Affairs

Vice President

White House Chief of Staff

Attorney General

Head of the Environmental Protection Agency

Head of the Office of Management and Budget

Head of the Office of National Drug Control Policy

United States Trade Representative

secretary of education in Bush's second term, had also worked for Bush when he was governor of Texas and was a domestic policy advisor to Bush during his first term. Condoleezza Rice, Bush's second-term secretary of state, was his main foreign policy advisor during the 2000 campaign and headed the National Security Council in Bush's first term.

SECTION SUMMARY

1. Political appointees in the Executive Office of the President, along with the vice president and appointees in executive departments and agencies, help the president manage the federal government and provide political assistance to the president and to candidates from his political party.
2. The primary mission of presidential appointees is to help the president achieve his or her policy goals. As such, loyalty to the President is generally valued over policy expertise.
3. Vice President Dick Cheney was the most powerful vice president in American history owing to his experience, expertise, and general agreement with President Bush.

Assessing Presidential Power

Throughout American history, presidents have realized major achievements. They have expanded the United States, fought wars, and enacted large government programs. Yet, as discussed earlier, the Constitution grants the president only rather limited powers. Assessing presidential power requires examining this contradiction.

Debates over the source and extent of presidential powers have a long history. In the 1790s, Alexander Hamilton and James Madison, writing anonymously as Helvidius and Pacificus, argued about whether George Washington needed congressional approval to declare the United States neutral in the war between Britain and France.[79] Even after more than two centuries, many of the limits to presidential powers—including which executive actions require congressional approval and which ones can be reversed by Congress—are not well-defined.

Recall the case of the president's war-making powers: the Constitution makes the president military commander in chief but gives Congress the power to declare war and to raise and support armies, without specifying which branch of government is in charge of the military. Thus, at least part of presidential authority must be derived or assumed from what the Constitution *does not say*—ways in which it fails to define or delineate presidential power.[80]

Presidency scholars Terry Moe and William Howell argue that constitutional ambiguities about presidential power have allowed presidents to take **unilateral action**, changing policy on their own without consulting Congress or anyone else. While Congress could, in theory, undo unilateral actions through legislation, court proceedings, or even impeachment, Moe and Howell argue that the costs of doing so, in terms of time, effort, and public perceptions, are often prohibitive. The result is that presidents can take unilateral action despite congressional opposition, knowing their actions stand little chance of being reversed.

The 2007 debate over funding the war in Iraq provides a good example of how constitutional ambiguities create opportunities for unilateral actions. During the debate, in which many Democrats in Congress wanted to cut off war funding to force the withdrawal of American forces from Iraq, supporters of the Bush administration responded with what they called the **unitary executive theory**. They argued that the Constitution's vesting clause allows the president to issue orders and policy directives that members of Congress cannot undo unless the Constitution explicitly gives them this power. In the case of funding the Iraq war, they maintained that the Constitution's description of the president as commander in chief of America's armed forces meant that even if Congress refused to appropriate funds for the war, the president could order American forces to stay in Iraq, and order the Department of the Treasury to spend any funds necessary to continue operations. Ultimately, members of Congress approved a funding resolution—but if they hadn't and the president had refused to withdraw American forces, the disagreement likely would have required resolution by the Supreme Court.

Many unilateral actions occurred throughout the Bush presidency. President Bush acted unilaterally when he restricted the legal rights of terror suspects, made strategic decisions about the wars in Iraq and Afghanistan, froze the financial assets of members of Al Qaeda and other terror organizations, reorganized America's intelligence agencies to create the Department of Homeland Security, and relaxed environmental regulations. Bush unilaterally withdrew the United States from the Anti-Ballistic Missile Treaty that limited U.S. and Soviet defensive missile installations, and he authorized wiretaps of Americans' international phone conversations without gaining warrants from the Foreign Intelligence Surveillance Court, a special federal court created to approve such requests.[81]

It is important to understand that Bush was not the first president to take (or threaten to take) broad, unilateral actions. Bill Clinton took unilateral action to expand health care benefits for federal employees, impose new penalties for companies that denied health coverage to the poor, mandated trigger locks be included with all firearms purchased for federal agencies, and, in the final days of his term, gave federal protection to millions of acres of land and issued several new environmental regulations.[82]

Moe and Howell cite many historical examples of unilateral presidential actions, such as the annexation of Texas, the freeing of slaves in the Emancipation Proclamation, the desegregation of the U.S. military, the initiation of affirmative action programs, and the creation of major agencies such as the Peace Corps.[83] Other studies found that the majority of federal administrative agencies had been created

unilateral action (presidential) Any policy decision made and acted upon by the president and his staff without the explicit approval or consent of Congress.

unitary executive theory The idea that the vesting clause of the Constitution gives the president the authority to issue orders and policy directives that cannot be undone by Congress.

signing statement A document issued by the president when signing a bill into law explaining his interpretation of the law, which often differs from the interpretation of Congress, in an attempt to influence how the law will be implemented.

by unilateral presidential actions and that over 90 percent of American agreements with other nations since the 1940s were concluded as executive agreements between the president and a foreign government, rather than as treaties requiring ratification by Congress.[84]

Presidents have also tried to control the interpretation and implementation of laws by issuing a **signing statement** when signing a bill into law. These documents, which explain the president's interpretation of the new law, are issued most often when the president disagrees with the interpretation of members of Congress who supported the legislation, but still wishes to approve the bill. Presidents issue signing statements so that if the courts have to resolve uncertainties about the bill's intent, judges can take into account not only the views expressed during congressional debates about the bill, but also the president's interpretation of it.[85] The president can also influence the implementation of a law through a signing statement, essentially telling the bureaucracy to follow his interpretation of the law rather than Congress's.

In some cases, presidents have found loopholes in laws designed to restrict their power. An analysis of several pieces of legislation designed to curb presidential power that were enacted in the 1970s (including the War Powers Resolution, the Ethics in Government Act, and measures dealing with budgets and intelligence agencies) found that subsequent presidents have actually used these laws to justify unilateral actions—the precise opposite of what was intended.[86] For example, current law requires the president to give congressional leaders "timely notification" of secret intelligence operations. During the Reagan administration, senior officials did not reveal the existence of ongoing operations for several months. When these operations were eventually discovered, these officials claimed they were within the letter of the law because it did not specify a time limit for notification.[87]

POLITICS IS CONFLICTUAL

Unilateral presidential actions are often driven by conflict. Presidents act unilaterally to avoid compromising with members of Congress.

Unilateral actions are especially likely in the last days of a presidency, especially if the next president is from the other party, as the outgoing president tries to influence as many important policies as possible before leaving office.[88] For example, in January 2001, President Bill Clinton finalized regulations that would lower the amount of arsenic allowed in drinking water by 2006. When President George W. Bush took office, he and his staff debated whether to rescind the regulations, believing they imposed too many economic costs, but decided against it. They did not want to publicly oppose a regulation that made water safer to drink. Bush's staff also looked into reversing Clinton's last-minute designation of millions of acres of land as federally protected national monuments, but found that the president only had the authority to create monuments, not to eliminate them.[89]

In theory, members of Congress can undo a president's unilateral action by enacting a law to overturn it, but this harder than it may sound.[90] Some members of Congress may approve of what the president has done or be indifferent to it. Moreover, enacting the resolution doesn't just require a simple majority in the House and Senate. Rather, as discussed earlier in this chapter, Congress needs to muster a two-thirds majority in both houses to override the assured presidential veto of the attempt to overturn his decree.

Members of Congress can also write laws in a way that limits the president's authority over their implementation.[91] The problem with this approach is that members of Congress delegate authority to the president or the executive branch bureaucracy for good reasons—either because it is difficult for legislators to predict how a policy should be implemented, or because they cannot agree among themselves on an implementation plan.[92] Members of Congress from the president's party

▲ *The president wields considerable power through the ability to take unilateral actions. Here, President Clinton signs an order establishing Utah's Grand Escalante National Monument on thousands of acres of federally owned land.*

▲ *Members of Congress as well as federal courts can undo unilateral presidential actions. A series of Supreme Court rulings forced the Bush administration to allow terror suspects like Salim Hamdan, an Al Qaeda member captured in Afghanistan, to challenge their imprisonment in federal courts. This courtroom sketch from Guantanamo U.S. Naval Base, Cuba, shows Hamdan (far left) and his legal team.*

may also want him to have the authority because they hold similar policy goals and would therefore benefit from the exercise of unilateral power.

Even if members of Congress tried to use these strategies to limit the president's authority, the president could still argue—along the lines of the unitary executive theory—that Congress could not overturn his actions because the Constitution did not explicitly gave the legislature this power. The only option for members of Congress would be to take the president to court, probably all the way to the Supreme Court, to demonstrate that the president overstepped his constitutional authority, which is not a very practical or expedient option. Aside from the fact that the Court might not side with Congress, these legal proceedings could take years.

Even so, opponents of some unilateral actions have used court decisions to limit presidential power. In 1952, when steel mill workers were going to go on strike, President Truman argued that federal control of the steel mills was necessary to sustain the United States' efforts in the Korean War. Ninety minutes before the steelworkers were to go on strike, President Truman went on national television to announce that the U.S. government would seize the nation's steel mills to keep them operating. However, the Supreme Court's ruling in *Youngstown Sheet and Tube v. Sawyer* reversed President Truman's actions.[93] More recently, in the 2006 case *Hamdan v. Rumsfeld* and the 2008 case *Boumediene v. Bush,* the Supreme Court reversed the Bush administration's actions that had denied terror suspects access to federal courts.[94]

Congress also has the power to remove the president or vice president from office through the **impeachment** process. However, impeaching a president is much more difficult than passing a law to undo a unilateral action. First, House members must impeach (indict) the president by majority vote, which accuses him of a crime or breach of his sworn duties. Then senators hold a trial, followed by a vote—in which a two-thirds majority is required to remove the president from office.

These procedures are rarely used; only two presidents have faced an impeachment vote: Andrew Johnson in 1866 and Bill Clinton in 1999. Johnson was involved in a political dispute over administration of the southern states after the Civil War; Clinton was alleged to have lied under oath in a sexual harassment lawsuit. Though

impeachment A negative or checking power of Congress over the other branches allowing them to remove the president, vice president, or other "officers of the United States" for abuses of power.

both of these presidents were impeached by the House, they were not convicted by the Senate, so they stayed in office. One reason impeachment is difficult is that members of Congress who are upset about certain presidential actions might nevertheless oppose removing the president from office. They might approve of his other initiatives, want to prevent the vice president from becoming president, or have concerns about the political backlash that impeachment could generate against them or their party.

In sum, ambiguities in the Constitution create opportunities for unilateral presidential action. These actions are subject to reversal through legislation, court decisions, and impeachment, but members of Congress face significant costs if they undertake any of these options. As long as the president is careful to limit exercise of unilateral power to actions that do not generate intense opposition in Congress, he can implement a wide range of policy goals without official congressional consent. Thus, presidential power has important consequences for government policy—but it is not unlimited.

SECTION SUMMARY

1. Ambiguities in the Constitution and in statutory authority allow the president to act unilaterally, that is, to change policies without congressional approval. All recent presidents have taken unilateral actions, especially on foreign policy and at the end of their terms.

2. Congress can try to undo unilateral presidential actions by passing legislation with a veto-proof, two-thirds majority. Even then, reversing the president's action may require a court challenge if the president claims he is using constitutional authority.

3. Congress also has the power to remove the president from office through the impeachment procedure. Impeachment is a cumbersome and politically risky strategy, however, and it has never been successfully used to remove a president.

Conclusion

A president's power over government policy is derived from constitutional authority, statutory authority, and ambiguities within these official grants of power that give the president a substantial ability to act unilaterally. Even so, presidential power is limited. The president shares many powers with Congress, including lawmaking, treaty-making, and war-making powers. Moreover, presidents are politicians who need public support, both to win reelection and to persuade members of Congress to approve their policy initiatives. The public evaluates the president based on how he handles issues that are a priority for many Americans, such as the economy, health care, and national security.

These factors suggest a very different explanation for the seemingly unusual, expansive power George W. Bush wielded as president. For one thing, Bush's policy successes are not unusual; many presidents have similar records of accomplishment. Moreover, while Bush enjoyed notable successes, he was also forced to concede defeat in a number of cases, in the face of insufficient congressional or public support, or reversal of his actions by the courts. Moreover, many of his successful unilateral actions concerned policy areas in which members of Congress and the public either favored his proposals or had no strong feelings about them. Thus, the president remains an important figure in American politics but is clearly not solely responsible for setting government policy.

CRITICAL THINKING

1. Why might bureaucrats who are not presidential appointees be more responsive to congressional mandates and demands than to the president's orders, even though the president heads the executive branch?

2. What can members of Congress do to stop a president from changing policy unilaterally? Which of these methods seems most effective, and why?

3. Why do you think Americans often hold the president more accountable than Congress for the state of the economy?

KEY TERMS

cabinet (p. 411)
constitutional authority (presidential) (p. 391)
executive agreement (p. 395)
Executive Office of the President (EOP) (p. 408)
executive orders (p. 392)
executive privilege (p. 399)
fast-track authority (p. 395)
first-mover advantage (p. 395)
go public (p. 404)
head of government (p. 391)
head of state (p. 391)
impeachment (p. 415)
presidential approval (p. 401)
recess appointment (p. 392)
signing statement (p. 414)
State of the Union (p. 396)
statutory authority (presidential) (p. 391)
unilateral action (presidential) (p. 413)
unitary executive theory (p. 413)
vesting clause (p. 391)

SUGGESTED READING

Canes-Wrone, Brandice. *Who Leads Whom? Presidents, Policy, and the Public.* Chicago: University of Chicago Press, 2006.

Draper, Robert. *Dead Certain: The Presidency of George W. Bush.* New York: Free Press, 2007.

Howell, William G. *Power without Persuasion: The Politics of Direct Presidential Action.* Princeton, NJ: Princeton University Press, 2003.

Klein, Joe. *The Natural: The Misunderstood Presidency of Bill Clinton.* New York: Random House, 2002.

Krehbiel, Keith. *Pivotal Politics: A Theory of U.S. Lawmaking.* Chicago: University of Chicago Press, 1998.

Lewis, David E. *Presidents and the Politics of Agency Design.* Palo Alto, CA: Stanford University Press, 2003.

Mayer, Kenneth. *With the Stroke of a Pen: Executive Orders and Presidential Power.* Princeton, NJ: Princeton University Press, 2001.

Moe, Terry M., and William G. Howell. "The Presidential Power of Unilateral Action," *Journal of Law, Economics, and Organization* 15 (1999): 132–46.

Neustadt, Richard E. *Presidential Power and the Modern Presidents: The Politics of Leadership from Roosevelt to Reagan.* New York: Free Press, 1990.

Rudalevige, Andrew. *Managing the President's Program: Presidential Leadership and Legislative Policy Formation.* Princeton, NJ: Princeton University Press, 2002.

Schlesinger, Arthur M., Jr. *The Crisis of the Old Order, 1919-1933.* Boston: Houghton Mifflin, 1957.

Skowronek, Stephen. *The Politics Presidents Make: Leadership From John Adams to Bill Clinton.* Cambridge, MA: Harvard University Press, 1997.

THE BUREAUCRACY

To many Americans, the bureaucracy signifies all the deficiencies of the federal government. Consider how the Federal Emergency Management Agency (FEMA) responded to Hurricane Katrina, the storm that hit New Orleans in August 2005. Despite widespread press coverage of massive damage and flooding, FEMA officials waited more than a day before starting relief operations. FEMA bought more than 150,000 trailers for use as temporary housing—many with identical locks. The organization also renovated a former Army base into a shelter for people who could not return to their homes at a cost of over $400,000 per evacuee, and provided over $10 million in disaster assistance to federal prisoners who had claimed, falsely, that their homes had been destroyed. To house thousands of relief workers, FEMA chartered three cruise ships, paying more than it would have cost to send the same number of people on a Caribbean cruise.[1]

It's easy to find other stories of bureaucratic inefficiency, fraud, and folly.

- Government agencies have lost over 1,000 laptop computers containing citizens' Social Security numbers and other personal information.[2]
- In 2007 investigations into the care of wounded American soldiers uncovered neglect, poor housing, inadequate medical and psychological treatment, and a "hopelessly complicated bureaucratic maze" of a medical system facing patients and their families.[3]
- An audit of government credit cards at the Department of Agriculture found over $5 million in employees' personal charges, including car payments, tattoos, and Ozzie Osborne concert tickets.[4]
- In 2007 new federal regulations took effect requiring Americans to show a passport as identification every time they entered the country. The resulting wave of passport applications from Americans traveling to Canada, Mexico, and the Caribbean swamped the State Department, to the point that new applications suddenly took months instead of weeks to process.[5]

On the other hand, there are also many cases of bureaucratic accomplishment, effectiveness, and even heroism. Consider some of the government employees awarded a Service to America Medal in recent years by the Partnership for Public Service, a nonprofit, nonpartisan organization.[6]

▲ *While many aspects of the federal government's response to Hurricane Katrina fit the stereotype of a bumbling, ineffectual bureaucracy, there were also many successes, such as the Coast Guard rescue operations after Katrina hit. Why do bureaucrats seem so competent in some cases but incompetent in others?*

- Doctors Douglas Lowy and John Schiller directed research at the National Institutes of Health that resulted in a new vaccine to prevent cervical cancer.
- The U.S. Geological Survey Hurricane Response Team led by Dr. Thomas Casadevall rescued hundreds of people in New Orleans after Hurricane Katrina.
- Internal Revenue Service employee Terrence Lutes developed the eFile system for filing tax returns over the Internet, cutting processing costs by 90 percent and allowing citizens to receive their tax refunds in as little as ten days.
- Mark S. Ward headed efforts by the Agency for International Development to aid victims of the Asian tsunami in 2004 and the earthquake that struck South Asia in 2005, rebuilding over fifty miles of roads and bridges, and providing shelter for over 550,000 people and food assistance to 1 million.

These examples—both the impressive and the confounding—illustrate the enormous range of the federal bureaucracy and its impact on life in America. The bureaucracy, it seems, is everywhere. Americans encounter the work of government employees every day: when they sort through mail delivered by the Postal Service, drive on highways funded by the Department of Transportation, or purchase food inspected by the Food and Drug Administration. The prices Americans pay to surf the Web, watch television, or use a cell phone are influenced by regulations issued by the Federal Communications Commission. When they go on vacation, their bags are inspected by the Transportation Security Administration, the aircraft and pilots are scrutinized by the Federal Aviation Administration, and the beaches may be maintained by the Army Corps of Engineers.

The paradox of the federal bureaucracy is that the same organization that does so many amazing things also does things that are inefficient, wasteful, and downright dumb. Do these shortcomings result from inevitable accidents—or are they the consequences of deliberate actions? In this chapter, we will show that many bureaucratic failures can be explained by the bureaucracy's procedures, including the complexity of the tasks it undertakes, and by the political conflicts that ensue when elected officials and interest groups attempt to control bureaucrats' actions. This chapter also shows that the public's disdain for bureaucrats is not uniform. Most Americans award higher ratings to government agencies and offices with which they have personal experience. Similarly, most bureaucrats believe deeply in their agency's mission and work hard to achieve its goals.

What Is the Federal Bureaucracy?

The American federal **bureaucracy** that makes up the government's executive branch is composed of millions of **civil servants**, who work for the government in permanent positions, and thousands of **political appointees** holding short-term, usually senior positions, who are appointed by and loyal to the president. Another name for the bureaucracy is the administrative state, which refers to the role bureaucrats play in administering government policies.[7]

WHAT DO BUREAUCRATS DO?

The task of the bureaucracy is to implement policies established by congressional acts or presidential decisions. Sometimes the tasks associated with putting these laws and resolutions into effect are very specific. For example, in the appropriations bill for fiscal year 2008, which set federal spending levels for October 1, 2007 to September 30, 2008, Congress mandated a 3.5 percent pay increase for military personnel and funds for new military equipment, including an aircraft carrier, a nuclear submarine, two destroyer warships, and twelve F-35 Joint Strike Fighter aircraft.[8] These provisions require no discretion on the part of the bureaucrats who implement them. Their tasks were limited to making the administrative changes necessary to raise military pay and following through with the purchase of the specified number of ships and planes.

More commonly, however, legislation determines only the general guidelines for meeting governmental goals, allowing bureaucrats to develop specific policies and programs. In these cases, bureaucrats' actions determine the essence of government action, deciding "who gets what, when, and how."[9] For example, the 1938 Federal Food, Drug, and Cosmetic Act gave the Food and Drug Administration (FDA; the agency that regulates the pharmaceutical industry, as well as food and cosmetics) the job of determining which drugs are safe and effective, but it allowed FDA bureaucrats to develop their own procedures for making these determinations.[10] Currently the FDA requires that drug manufacturers first test new drugs for safety, then conduct further trials to determine their effectiveness. An FDA advisory board of scientists and doctors reviews the results of these tests. Then FDA bureaucrats decide whether to allow the manufacturer to market the drug.

More generally, the job of the federal bureaucracy includes a wide range of activities, from regulating the behavior of individuals and corporations to buying everything from pencils to jet fighters for the government. These activities are inherently political and often conflictual—ordinary citizens, elected officials, and bureaucrats themselves often disagree about how these decisions should be resolved, and work to influence bureaucratic actions to suit their own goals.

Regulations A **regulation** is a government rule that affects the choices that individuals or corporations make, by either allowing or prohibiting behavior, setting out the conditions under which certain behaviors can occur, or assessing costs or granting benefits based on behavior. Regulations are developed in a

bureaucracy The system of civil servants and political appointees who implement congressional or presidential decisions; also known as the administrative state.

civil servants Employees of bureaucratic agencies within the government.

political appointees People selected by an elected leader, such as the president, to hold a government position.

regulation A rule that allows the government to exercise control over individuals and corporations by restricting certain behaviors.

POLITICAL PROCESS MATTERS

✓ Allowing bureaucrats to determine the details of new policies makes it possible for bureaucrats to have their own independent impact on what government does.

process known as the **notice and comment procedure**.[11] Before a new regulation developed by a government agency or organization can take effect, it must be published in the Federal Register, an official, daily publication that includes rules, proposed rules, and several other types of government documents. Individuals and companies that will be affected by the regulation can then respond to the agency that proposed it, either supporting the new regulation or opposing it, and offering different versions for consideration. Those potentially affected by the regulation can also appeal to members of Congress or to the president's staff for help getting the proposed rule revised. Based on the submitted comments, the proposing agency issues a revised regulation, which is also published in the Federal Register and put into effect.

The process of devising or modifying regulations is extremely political. Members of Congress and the president often have strong opinions about how new regulations should look—and even when they don't, they may still get involved in the process on behalf of a constituent or interest group who would be affected by the proposed regulation. Bureaucrats take account of these pressures from elected officials for two reasons. First, the bureaucrats' policy-making power may have been created by a statute that members of Congress could overturn if they disapprove of how bureaucrats use their power. Second, bureaucrats need congressional support to get larger budgets and more important tasks for their agency, and to prevent budget cuts. Thus, despite bureaucrats' hands-on power to implement—and thereby often shape—policies, their agencies' budgets, appointed leaders, and overall missions are subject to elected officials' oversight.

Many regulations are issued each year: the 2002 Federal Register contained over 75,000 pages of proposed regulations, new regulations, and changes to existing regulations. There were 4,167 final regulations, 135 of which were labeled "economically significant," meaning that they were estimated to have over $100 million in economic impact. Moreover, government bureaucrats issued over 36,000 final rules during the period between 1995 and 2002.[12] While virtually all government agencies issue regulations, most come from a few agencies, including the Federal Trade Commission, which regulates commerce; the Federal Communications Commission, which regulates the media companies that create content as well as the telecommunications companies that transmit information; and the Food and Drug Administration, which regulates drugs, medical products, food, and cosmetics.

Federal regulations affect every aspect of everyday life. Regulations influence the gas mileage of cars sold in the United States, the materials used to build roads, and the price of gasoline. Regulations determine the amounts that doctors charge senior citizens for medical procedures; the hours that medical residents can work; and the criteria used to determine who gets a heart, lung, or kidney transplant. Regulations set the eligibility criteria for student loans, limit how the military can recruit on college campuses, and describe what constitutes equal funding for men's and women's college sports teams. Regulations also shape contribution limits and spending decisions in political campaigns.

POLITICS IS EVERYWHERE

The power to regulate gives federal bureaucrats the ability to shape virtually every aspect of individual and corporate behavior in America.

Some regulations can have a life-or-death impact on individual Americans. In 2007 the Center for Medicare and Medicaid established criteria that hospitals performing organ transplant operations must meet in order for their transplant procedures to qualify for Medicare reimbursement. In plain terms, these regulations determine which hospitals senior citizens on Medicare can use if they need a transplant. In order to qualify for reimbursement, a hospital needs to perform a set number of transplants per year, meet minimum success rates for those operations, manage their patient waiting lists according to certain criteria, and provide particular services to transplant recipients and their families—including advising transplant recipients on their diets.[13]

Regulations are often controversial because they involve trade-offs between incompatible goals, as well as decisions made under uncertain circumstances. For example, the FDA drug approval process is designed to prevent harmful drugs from coming to market.[14] As a result, patients typically cannot get access to treatments that are still considered experimental because have not received FDA approval, even when a yet-unapproved treatment is a patient's only remaining option.[15] Advocates for patients have argued that people with dire prognoses should be allowed to use an experimental treatment as a potentially life-saving last resort.[16] However, current FDA regulations prevent them from doing so except under very unusual circumstances, arguing that unapproved treatments may do more harm than good, and that allowing wider access to these drugs may tempt manufacturers to market new drugs without adequate testing.

▲ *Federal regulations influence many aspects of everyday life that do not initially seem to be affected by government action. The increase in the number of women's intercollegiate athletic teams is partly due to regulations that required equal funding for men's and women's teams.*

Procurement Bureaucrats also handle government purchases, buying everything from pencils to aircraft carriers. The General Services Administration (GSA) manages over 8,300 buildings owned or leased by the government and a fleet of over 170,000 vehicles, and provides government agencies with most of their supplies.[17]

Procurement seems a straightforward task: agencies determine what they need, find out who can supply it, and choose the lowest-cost provider. However, procurement for the federal government can be surprisingly complicated. Consider the purchase of a new model of fighter plane or an attack submarine. Bureaucrats must devise criteria for choosing between designs with very different strengths and weaknesses. Procurement decisions are also shaped by congressional and executive mandates. For example, when the GSA searches for suppliers of a particular product, it often has to give a preference to small businesses or firms owned by minorities or veterans. These guidelines are the result of the political process, as elected officials try to shape government actions to suit their own policy goals.

POLITICAL PROCESS MATTERS

 Mandates established by elected officials, such as giving priority to small businesses or minority- or veteran-owned companies for government purchases, affect even basic procurement decisions by government bureaucrats.

Finally, high-profile procurement decisions are often made in times of crisis, with little opportunity for evaluation. For example, it is not unreasonable to criticize FEMA for overpaying for the cruise ships it used as hotels—but it is important to keep in mind that FEMA needed housing in severely flooded areas for large numbers of relief workers, and needed it right away. In the middle of the crisis, the cruise ships may well have been the best option, even at an inflated cost.

Providing Services **Street-level bureaucrats** provide services to help ordinary Americans.[18] For example, many job training programs are run by federal employees. The federal government provides disaster assistance, such as the benefits received by the residents of areas affected by Hurricane Katrina or the September 11 attacks. Federal employees manage tourist attractions from the National Zoo to the Statue of Liberty to Mount Rushmore. They inspect passenger baggage at airports, monitor aircraft maintenance, and direct aircraft in flight.

Research and Development Government scientists work in areas from medicine to astronomy to agriculture. Sometimes their work takes the form of basic research,

street-level bureaucrats Agency employees who directly provide services to the public, such as those who provide job training services.

state capacity The knowledge, personnel, and institutions that the government requires to effectively implement policies.

red tape Excessive or unnecessarily complex regulations imposed by the bureaucracy.

standard operating procedures Rules that lower-level bureaucrats must follow when implementing policies.

such as discoveries by scientists working for the National Institutes of Health of some of the mechanisms that govern cell reproduction and death. Government scientists also do applied research, from developing new cancer drugs to improving crop management techniques. Federal funds also support research in many universities and corporations that examines similar questions.

Managing and Directing Some bureaucrats spend their time supervising actions taken by people outside government. For example, the Department of Defense uses civilian contractors to provide support services in Iraq, from cooking and laundry to some maintenance work on planes, trucks, and ships. Many workers at government facilities and public works projects are employees for private corporations working on government contracts.

BUREAUCRATIC EXPERTISE AND ITS CONSEQUENCES

This description of what bureaucrats do highlights the fact that in the main, bureaucrats are experts. Even compared to most members of Congress or presidential appointees, the average bureaucrat is a specialist in a certain policy area, with a better grasp of his agency's mission and rationale. For example, people who hold scientific or management positions in the FDA usually know more about the benefits and risks of new drugs than people outside the agency. Their decision to deny unapproved drugs to seriously ill patients may look cruel, but it may also reflect a thoughtful balancing of two incompatible goals: preventing harmful drugs from reaching the market, and allowing people who have exhausted all other treatments access to risky, experimental products. A bureaucracy of experts is an important part of what political scientists call **state capacity**—the knowledge, personnel, and institutions needed to implement policies that change society.[19]

Despite bureaucrats' policy expertise, their decisions may often appear to take too much time, be based on arbitrary judgments of what is important, and have unintended consequences—to the point that actions designed to solve one problem may create new and even larger ones. Many critics of the modern bureaucracy cite the abundance of **red tape**, which refers to unnecessarily complex procedures, or **standard operating procedures**, which are the rules that lower-level bureaucrats must follow when implementing policies regardless of whether they are applicable to the situation at hand. FEMA's performance after Hurricane Katrina, as well as many of the other bureaucratic blunders mentioned in the introduction to this chapter, are classic examples of these phenomena.

There have been many attempts to make the bureaucracy operate more smoothly and effectively by mandating that bureaucrats make decisions using specific procedures or criteria. These efforts have added many acronyms to the language of Washington bureaucrats: PPBS, MBO, ZBB, PBB, and REGO.[20] While each of these efforts can claim some modest successes, none have fundamentally changed the way the government does business. The lesson seems to be that examples of poor performance by America's bureaucracy have little to do with the bureaucracy itself. Otherwise, one of these reform packages would have solved these problems, leaving a well-functioning bureaucracy.

These cases of bureaucratic ineptitude and the failure of reform efforts raise a critical and perplexing question: how can

▲ Despite their policy expertise, bureaucrats still sometimes make mistakes. When the Medicare program implemented the new Prescription Drug Benefit, information about the new coverage was available on an easy-to-read Web site, but the agency soon learned that many seniors who needed to access the information did not know how to use a Web browser.

an organization full of experts develop such dysfunctional ways of doing business? Bureaucrats are neither clueless nor malevolent. What, then, explains red tape and counterproductive standard operating procedures? The answer is the very strength of the American bureaucracy: its expertise.

Because bureaucrats know things that elected officials do not, and because bureaucrats have their own policy goals, it is hard for elected officials to evaluate what bureaucrats are doing. For example, FEMA's use of a cruise ship to house relief workers after Hurricane Katrina may have looked expensive, but the FEMA staffer who was on the scene and signed the contract may have found that all other options were either more expensive or simply impossible. Without knowing the specifics, it is impossible to judge the efficacy of the decision. Political scientists refer to the difficulty that elected officials and their staff face when they try to interpret or understand bureaucratic actions as the **problem of control**.[21]

The problem of control is a classic example of the **principal–agent game**, which describes a hypothetical interaction between two players: the principal, who needs something done, and the agent, whom the principal hires to complete the task.[22] In the federal government, the president and Congress are principals, and bureaucrats are agents. Each principal faces the challenge of motivating the agents to act in the principal's interests.[23] An agent may not want to work, or may prefer outcomes that the principal does not like. Moreover, because the agent is an expert at the task he has been given, he has private information inaccessible to the principal. The problem for the principal, then, is this: giving the agent explicit orders will prevent the agent from acting based on expertise. But if the principal gives the agent the freedom to make decisions based on expertise, the principal has no control over the agent's actions. For example, suppose Congress and the president direct the FDA to shorten its drug approval process. However, FDA officials might have mandated a lengthy process based on their expert assessment of the best way to screen out harmful drugs. By giving orders that supercede the FDA officials' screening process, the elected officials would be sacrificing the valuable bureaucratic expertise behind the policy and risking the hasty approval of unsafe drugs.

On the other hand, if Congress and the president allow FDA bureaucrats to devise their own procedures and regulations, there is a chance that the FDA could use this freedom to pursue goals that have nothing to do with drug safety. For example, critics of the FDA's procedures have complained that a drawn-out approval process favors large companies that already have drugs on the market over smaller companies trying to get approval for drugs that would compete with existing products.[24] These critics contend that the drug screening processes are the result of **regulatory capture**, a situation in which bureaucrats cater to a small number of people or corporations outside government, regardless of the impact these actions have on public welfare.

One case of a thoroughly "captured" bureaucrat involved the Boeing Corporation. In 2003, the Air Force negotiated a deal with Boeing to lease 100 aircraft as refueling planes. At the same time, Darleen Druyun, a senior Air Force official in charge of the negotiations, was offered a job at Boeing.[25] When the details of the unusually expensive fuel tanker lease became public—after Druyon had moved to her new job at Boeing—critics charged that Druyun had given Boeing a sweetheart deal in return for a well-paid position. Ultimately, Druyun pleaded guilty to slanting the contract in Boeing's favor and was jailed: it is illegal for government employees to negotiate for a job with a company while at the same bargaining with the company over the terms of a government contract. Ultimately, the Air Force

problem of control A difficulty faced by elected officials in ensuring that when bureaucrats implement policies, they follow these officials' intentions but still have enough discretion to use their expertise.

principal–agent game The interaction between a principal (like the president or Congress), who needs something done, and an agent (like a bureaucrat), who is responsible for carrying out the principal's orders.

regulatory capture A situation in which bureaucrats favor the interests of the groups or corporations they are supposed to regulate at the expense of the general public.

POLITICAL PROCESS MATTERS

 Because bureaucrats are experts compared to elected officials, and because they have the power to implement policies, elected officials face a problem of control: how to ensure that their goals and preferences are reflected in bureaucratic decisions.

awarded the contract to another firm but was forced to reopen the bidding process when Boeing protested.

You might think that the problem of control isn't too difficult to solve as long as bureaucrats act as impartial experts and leave their own policy goals (or future employment) out of their decisions. Many studies of bureaucracies, beginning with the work of the early political theorist Max Weber, argue for **neutral competence**, the idea that bureaucrats should provide information and expertise, and avoid taking sides on policy questions or being swayed by elected officials, people outside government, or their own policy goals.[26] However, bureaucrats' behavior doesn't always fit Weber's vision. Many enter the bureaucracy with their own ideas about what government should do and work to make decisions in line with those goals. Bureaucrats may also be tempted to favor interest groups or corporations in order to secure a better-paying job. However, even if bureaucrats wanted to remain completely dispassionate, they would face a government in which many other people with their own policy goals and interests attempted to influence their behavior. Members of Congress or the president sometimes try to use the bureaucracy to implement policies that reflect their personal preferences or reward their political supporters.[27]

SECTION SUMMARY

1. The bureaucracy or administrative state comprises the civil service employees, political appointees, and organizations that make up the executive branch of the federal government.
2. Bureaucrats develop regulations, procure goods and services for government agencies, provide services to citizens, carry out research and development, and manage government contractors.
3. Most bureaucrats are experts who know more about the policies administered by their agency than the average citizen or member of Congress.
4. Bureaucratic expertise creates a problem of political control. Thus, bureaucrats are not above or apart from politics but in the middle of the political process.

History of the American Bureaucracy

The evolution of America's federal bureaucracy was not steady or smooth. Rather, most of its important developments occurred during three fairly short periods: during the late 1890s and early 1900s, in the 1930s, and in the 1960s.[28] In all three eras, the driving force was a combination of new demands from citizens for enhanced government services and the desire of people in government, including elected officials, to either respond to these demands or to increase the size and scope of the federal government in line with their own policy goals.

neutral competence The idea, credited to theorist Max Weber, which suggests that bureaucrats should provide expertise without the influence of elected officials, interest groups, or their own political agendas.

THE BEGINNING OF AMERICA'S BUREAUCRACY

From the beginning of the United States until the election of Andrew Jackson in 1828, the staff of the entire federal bureaucracy numbered no more than in the low thousands. There were only three executive departments (State, Treasury, and War), along with a Postmaster General.[29] The early federal government also performed a narrow range of tasks. It collected taxes on imports and exports and delivered the mail. The national army consisted of a small Corps of Engineers and a few frontier patrols. The attorney general was a private attorney who had the federal government as one of his clients. Members of Congress outnumbered civil servants in Washington; the president had very little staff at all.[30]

The small size of the federal government during these years reflected Americans' deep suspicion towards government, especially unelected officials. In the Declaration of Independence, one of the charges against King George III was that he had "erected a multitude of new offices and sent hither swarms of officers to harass our people and eat out their substance."[31] Executive branch offices were formed only when absolutely necessary. Nonetheless, conflicts soon arose around control of the bureaucracy. The legislation that established the departments of State, Treasury, and War allowed the president to nominate the people in charge of these departments, but made these appointments subject to Senate approval. (The same is true today for the heads of all executive departments and many other presidential appointments.)

The election of Andrew Jackson in 1828 brought the first large-scale use of the spoils system, in which people who had worked in Jackson's campaign were rewarded with new positions in the federal government, usually working as local postmasters.[32] The spoils system was extremely useful to party organizations, as it gave them an extremely powerful incentive with which to convince people to work for the party.

The problem with the spoils system was to ensure that these government employees, who often lacked experience in their new fields, could actually carry out their jobs. The solution was to develop routines and procedures for these employees, so that they knew exactly what to do even if they had little or no experience or training.[33] These instructions became one of the earliest uses of standard operating procedures, and they ensured that the government could function even if large numbers of employees were hired only to reward them for political work rather than because of their qualifications.[34]

As America expanded in size, so did the federal government, which saw an almost eightfold increase in the size of the bureaucracy between 1816 and the beginning of the Civil War in 1861. This growth did not reflect a fundamental change in what the government did—in fact, much of the increase came in areas such as the Post Office, which needed to grow to serve a geographically larger nation—and, of course, to provide "spoils" for party workers in the form of government jobs.[35] Even by the end of the Civil War, the federal government still had very little involvement in the lives of ordinary Americans. Services such as education, public works, and welfare benefits were provided by state and local governments, if they were provided at all, with the federal government's role in daily life limited to mail delivery, collecting import and export taxes, and a few other areas.

▲ This cartoon of a monument to Andrew Jackson riding a pig decries his involvement in the spoils system, which allowed politicians to dole out government service jobs in return for political support.

BUILDING A NEW AMERICAN STATE: THE PROGRESSIVE ERA

Changes in the second half of the nineteenth century transformed America's bureaucracy, dramatically increasing its state capacity.[36] This transformation began after the Civil War, but the most significant changes took place during the Progressive Era, between 1890 and 1920. Many different laws and executive actions increased the government's regulatory power during this period, including the Sherman Antitrust Act of 1890, the Pure Food and Drug Act of 1906, the Meat Inspection Act, expansion of the Interstate Commerce Commission, and various conservation measures.[37] With these changes, the federal government was no longer simply a deliverer of mail and defender of borders; rather, it had an indirect impact on several aspects of everyday life. When Americans bought food or other products, went to work, or traveled on vacation, the choices available to them were shaped by the actions of federal bureaucrats in Washington and elsewhere.

These developments were matched by a fundamental change in the federal bureaucracy following the passage of the 1883 Pendleton Civil Service Act. This measure created the **federal civil service**, in which the merit system (qualifications, not political connections) would be the basis for hiring and promoting bureaucrats.[38] In other words, when a new president took office, he could not replace members of the civil service with his own campaign workers. Initially, only about 13,000 federal jobs were given civil service protections, but over the next two decades, many additional positions were incorporated into the civil service. In some cases, presidents gave civil service protections to people who had been hired under the spoils system, in order to prevent the next president from replacing these bureaucrats with their own loyalists.

Over time, these reforms created a bureaucracy in which people were hired for their expertise and allowed to build a career in government without having to fear being fired when a new president or Congress took office.[39] These changes also attracted government employees who were motivated primarily by their interest in shaping government policy. Studies of this transformation have found that one of the driving forces behind the changes was a shift in citizens' demands. People wanted a greater role for government, both in regulating the behavior of large corporations and delivering more services to citizens.[40]

When civil service reforms were adopted, their impact on party organizations was well-understood. As one New York City machine politician, George Washington Plunkitt, put it, "This civil service law is the biggest fraud of the age. It is the curse of the nation. . . . How are you going to interest our young men in their country if you have no offices to give them when they work for their party?"[41] What Plunkitt meant was that without the spoils system, organizations like his would be in serious danger of losing their hold on government, as they would be unable to use the promise of a government job to motivate people to help elect the machine's candidates. Members of Congress, some of whom were members of spoils-based organizations, enacted civil service legislation because of strong public pressure to reform the bureaucracy—and because the protections would apply to current federal workers, some of whom had received their position in return for partisan work.[42]

THE NEW DEAL, THE GREAT SOCIETY, AND THE REAGAN REVOLUTION

The New Deal The New Deal refers to the government programs implemented during Franklin Roosevelt's first term as president in the 1930s. At one level, these programs were a response to the Great Depression and the inability of local governments and private charities to respond to this economic crisis. Many advocates of the New Deal also favored an expanded role for government in American society, regardless of the immediate need for intervention.[43] Roosevelt's programs included reforms to the financial industry as well as efforts to help people directly and to stimulate employment, economic growth, and the formation of labor unions. The Social Security Act, which was the first federally funded pension program for all Americans, was also passed as part of the New Deal.[44]

These reforms represented a vast increase in the size, responsibilities, and capacity of the bureaucracy, as well as a large transfer of power to bureaucrats and

federal civil service A system created by the 1883 Pendleton Civil Service Act in which bureaucrats are hired on the basis of merit rather than political connections.

to the president.[45] While the Progressive Era reforms created an independent bureaucracy and increased its state capacity, the New Deal reforms increased the range of policy areas in which this capacity could be applied. Before the New Deal, the federal government influenced citizens' choices through activities such as regulating industries and workplace conditions. Afterwards, the federal government took on the role of delivering a wide range of benefits and services directly to individuals, from jobs to electricity.

The expansion of the federal government and the subsequent delegation of power to bureaucrats and to the president were controversial changes, both at the time they were enacted, and as they were implemented in subsequent years.[46] Many Republicans opposed New Deal reforms because they believed that the federal government could not deliver services efficiently, and that an expanded federal bureaucracy would create a modern spoils system. Many southerners worried that the federal government's increased involvement in everyday life would endanger the system of racial segregation in southern states.[47] Even so, Democratic supporters of the New Deal, aided by public support, carried the day.

POLITICS IS CONFLICTUAL

Expansion of the federal bureaucracy during the New Deal was not universally supported: policy concessions were used to gain votes from southern Democrats in Congress, such as assurances that their states and districts would be treated generously by the new federal programs.

The Great Society The Great Society was a further expansion in the size, capacity, and activities of the bureaucracy that occurred during the presidency of Lyndon Johnson (1963–69). During these years, President Johnson proposed and Congress enacted programs that funded bilingual education, loans and grants for college students, special education, preschools, construction of elementary and secondary schools, mass transit programs in many cities, health care for seniors and poor people, job training and urban renewal, enhanced voting rights and civil rights for minorities, environmental protection, and funding for the arts and cultural activities.[48] Members of Congress frequently attempted to control these new programs, with the goal of delivering valuable benefits to their own constituents. In the case of the Model Cities Program, which was designed to fund efforts to revitalize decaying urban areas, members of Congress demanded expansion of the program from a small set of experimental projects to a nationwide, 150-city effort. In return for this congressional support of the agencies associated with the program, members of Congress forced bureaucrats to fund lucrative projects in their districts.[49]

The Great Society programs had mixed success. Voting rights and civil rights reforms ended the "separate but equal" system of social order in southern states, and dramatically increased political participation by African Americans.[50] At the same time, many antipoverty programs were dismal failures. Poverty rates among most groups remained relatively constant, and other indicators, such as the rate of teen pregnancies, actually increased.[51] In retrospect, the people who designed and implemented these programs did not realize the complexities of the problems they were trying to address.[52] For example, many antipoverty programs were built on the assumption that most people receiving welfare needed job training programs in order to transition from welfare to permanent, paid employment. However, additional data that was available a decade later showed that most people receiving welfare do so for short periods of time, because of divorce or medical hardship— problems that the Great Society programs did not touch.[53] Despite these shortcomings, the expansion of the federal government during the New Deal and Great Society has remained in place over the last generation.

The Reagan Revolution The election of Ronald Reagan to the presidency in 1980, along with a Republican takeover of the Senate and significant Republican gains in the House of Representatives, created an opportunity for conservatives to roll back

▲ Reducing the number and complexity of government regulations was one of President Ronald Reagan's priorities in office, but his efforts were largely unsuccessful, and subsequent presidents have had similarly little success.

the size and scope of the federal government. However, after eight years of Reagan in office followed by four years of his vice president, George H. W. Bush, and Republican control of Congress during most of Democrat Bill Clinton's presidency as well as during most of the presidency of Republican George W. Bush, the growth of the federal government has not slowed. Few programs have been eliminated, and the federal budget has steadily increased.[54]

Moreover, even conservative presidents and members of Congress have enacted programs and regulations that increased the impact of government on society. For example, Republican President George W. Bush's administration added the No Child Left Behind education reforms, which imposed many new requirements on local schools; the new Medicare Prescription Drug Benefit, which was the biggest new health care program since the 1960s; the Sarbanes–Oxley Act, which increased financial reporting requirements for corporations; and a host of other regulations, from regulations on backyard play sets to inspections of baggage on commercial aircraft.[55]

SECTION SUMMARY

1. For several decades after the Founding, America's bureaucracy was small, with many employees hired because of their political activity.
2. The Progressive Era saw a vast increase in the state capacity of the federal government—the creation of a bureaucracy that was separate from Congress and the president, with the resources to implement policies to change society.
3. Other significant increases in the size of the bureaucracy and the scope of its activities occurred during the New Deal of the 1930s and the Great Society of the late 1960s.

The Modern Federal Bureaucracy

Figure 12.1 shows the structure of the executive branch of the federal government. As discussed in Chapter 11, the Executive Office of the President (EOP) contains organizations that support the president and implement presidential policy initiatives. Among its many offices, the EOP contains the **Office of Management and Budget (OMB)**, which prepares the president's annual budget proposal and monitors government spending as well as the development of new regulations. Below the EOP are the fifteen executive departments, from the Department of Agriculture to the Department of Veterans Affairs, which comprise the major divisions within the executive branch. The heads of these fifteen organizations make up the president's cabinet.

Each executive department contains many smaller organizations. Figure 12.2 shows the organizational chart for the Department of Agriculture. As you see, Agriculture includes offices that help farmers produce and sell their crops, as well as offices that ensure food safety, but it also houses the Forest Service, and offices that manage issues related to housing and utilities in rural areas. The Department of Agriculture also administers the food stamps program, even though the program has no direct connection to farming or food safety.

Below the executive departments, but not subordinate to them, are a set of agencies, commissions, and government corporations that are called **independent**

Office of Management and Budget (OMB) An office within the Executive Office of the President that is responsible for creating the president's annual budget proposal to Congress, reviewing proposed rules, and other budget-related tasks.

independent agencies Government offices or organizations that provide government services and are not part of an executive department.

FIGURE 12.1   THE EXECUTIVE BRANCH OF THE FEDERAL GOVERNMENT

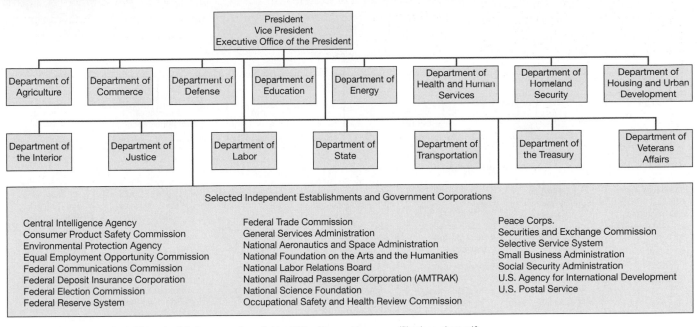

SOURCE: Based on GPO Access: Guide to the U.S. Government, available at http://bensguide.gpo.gov/files/gov_chart.pdf.

agencies or independent establishments to highlight that they are not part of an executive department. Most of these carry out specialized functions, such as the Federal Reserve, which manages the money supply, banking system, and interest rates. The figure only includes some noteworthy or well-known agencies; there are many more.

There are two important lessons to draw from these charts. First, the federal government serves an enormous range of functions. Second, the division of activities among executive departments and independent agencies does not have an obvious logic. Why, for example, does the Department of Agriculture administer rural utilities programs or food stamps? Similarly, it is not always clear why certain tasks are handled by an independent agency while others fall within the scope of an executive department.[56] Why is the Federal Reserve an independent agency rather than part of the Department of the Treasury?

Organizational decisions like these often reflect elected officials' attempts to shape agency behavior—and the extent to which political process matters. Part of the difference between independent agencies and the organizations contained within executive departments has to do with the president's ability to control these organizations' activities. Organizations that are housed within an executive department, such as the Internal Revenue Service, can be controlled by the president to some extent through his appointees.[57] In contrast, independent agencies have more freedom from oversight and control by the president and Congress. For example, the president nominates governors of the Federal Reserve, who, if they are confirmed by the Senate, serve for fourteen years. Outside the nomination and confirmation process, the president and Congress have very little control over the Federal Reserve's policies; the organization is self-financing, and its governors can be removed from office only after impeachment by Congress.

These details about the hiring and firing of bureaucrats and the location of agencies in the structure of the federal government matter because they determine

POLITICAL PROCESS MATTERS

 The president's ability to influence or control the actions of a government organization depends in part on whether the organization is an independent agency or part of an executive department.

FIGURE 12.2 **THE STRUCTURE OF THE DEPARTMENT OF AGRICULTURE**

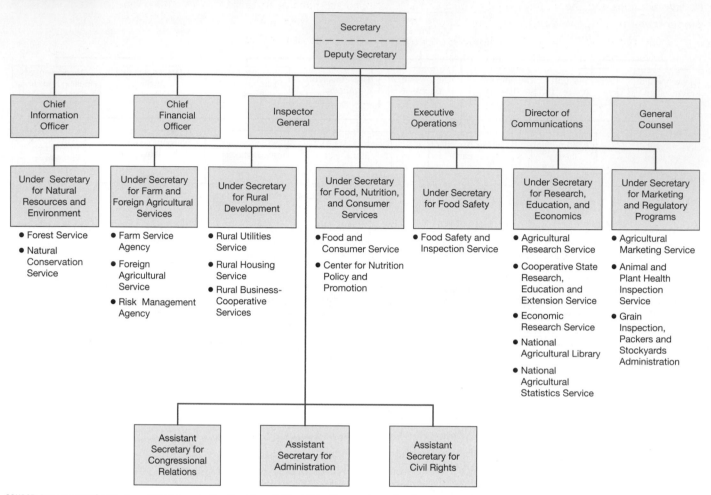

SOURCE: Department of Agriculture, "USDA Organization Chart," available at http://www.usda.gov/img/content/org_chart_enlarged.jpg.

the amount of political control that other parts of the government can exercise over an agency, as well as who gets to exercise this power. As political scientist Terry Moe puts it, "American public bureaucracy is not designed to be effective. The bureaucracy rises out of politics, and its design reflects the interests, strategies, and compromises of those who exercise political power."[58]

An extreme example of bureaucratic structure being driven by political concerns rather than efficiency or effectiveness comes from the use of intelligence agencies by the Bush administration in the months before the Iraq War. At the time, there was a spirited debate between members of the administration about the justification for war. Central Intelligence Agency reports expressed strong doubts about purported links between Al Qaeda and Iraq, and they believed that Iraq was nowhere near having an operational nuclear weapon.[59] Both of these conclusions weakened the case for war.

In response, senior leaders in the Bush administration, including Vice President Cheney, Defense Secretary Donald Rumsfeld, and Assistant Secretary of Defense Paul Wolfowitz, set up the Office of Special Plans (OSP) within the Department of Defense to develop an alternate view on Iraq's nuclear program, placing Douglas Feith, who favored war with Iraq, at its head.[60] The OSP used an information-gathering tactic known as stovepiping, relying on raw intelligence reports—including information from defectors—rather than summaries and interpretations of this information prepared by the CIA and other agencies. The resulting OSP reports made a strong case for invading Iraq, based on links between the country's leadership and terrorist organizations and the claim that the country had developed weapons of mass destruction—conclusions that later proved almost completely false. In retrospect, it is clear that the OSP was created and staffed to make the case for war that other agencies were unwilling to make based on the available evidence.

THE SIZE OF THE FEDERAL GOVERNMENT

The federal government employs millions of people. Table 12.1 reports the number of employees in each executive department and selected independent agencies.

TABLE 12.1   **EMPLOYMENT IN SELECTED FEDERAL ORGANIZATIONS**

Some federal agencies, such as the Department of Defense, have many employees, but many others are quite small. The Department of Education, for example, has only 4,000 employees. Does this variation in size make sense given the differences in the budgets and missions of these organizations?

ORGANIZATION	TOTAL EMPLOYEES
Cabinet Departments	
Defense	623,000
Veterans Affairs	239,000
Homeland Security	149,000
Treasury	109,000
Justice	105,000
Agriculture	92,000
Interior	66,000
Health and Human Services	60,000
Transportation	53,000
Commerce	39,000
Labor	16,000
Energy	15,000
State	14,000
Housing and Urban Development	10,000
Education	4,000
Independent agencies	
Social Security Administration	62,000
National Aeronautics and Space Administration	18,000
Environmental Protection Agency	18,000
Tennessee Valley Authority	12,000
General Services Administration	12,000
Federal Deposit Insurance Corporation	5,000

SOURCE: U.S. Bureau of Labor Statistics, Career Guide to Industries, "Federal Government, Excluding the Postal Service," Table 1, March 12, 2008, available at http://www.bls.gov/oco/cg/cgs041.htm.

FIGURE 12.3 THE SIZE OF THE FEDERAL BUDGET

The graph on the left shows that federal spending has increased sharply since the 1940s. However, the one on the right shows that as a percentage of gross domestic product, which measures the size of the American economy, the increase is much smaller, with essentially no change after 1980. What might these figures suggest about the increase in government spending?

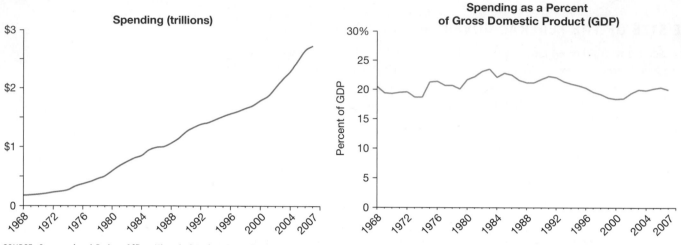

SOURCE: Congressional Budget Office, Historical Budget Data, "Revenues, Outlays, Deficits, Surpluses, and Debt Held by the Public," available at http://www.cbo.gov/budget/data/historical.shtml.

The Department of Defense is the largest cabinet department, with over 600,000 civilian personnel. The Department of Education is the smallest, with only 4,000. Many departments are quite small: five cabinet departments have fewer than 20,000 employees. Some independent agencies have even fewer. The General Services Administration, for example, has only 12,000 employees. And the numerous agencies not listed in the table have only 50,000 employees in total.

Figure 12.3 shows the size of the federal budget since 1968. As you see, the budget has steadily increased, to the point that annual spending in recent years is approximately $3 trillion per year. The best explanation for the size of the federal government is the size of America itself—a diverse population of over 300 million spread out over an area more than twice the size of the European Union—coupled with America's position as the most powerful nation in the world. However, some observers argue that the real explanation has to do with bureaucrats themselves. This view suggests that the government is so large because bureaucrats are **budget maximizers** who never pass up a chance to increase their own funding, regardless of whether the new spending is worthwhile.[61]

This argument misses some important points. First, the increase in total federal spending masks the fact that many agencies see their budgets shrink.[62] Particularly in recent administrations, one of the principle missions of presidential appointees, both in agencies and in the Executive Office of the President, has been to scrutinize budget requests with an eye to cutting spending as much as possible.[63] And every year, some government agencies are eliminated.[64]

Moreover, public opinion data provide an explanation for the overall growth in government: the American public's demand for services.[65] Despite complaints about the federal bureaucracy, polls find little evidence of demands for less government. When the Harris Poll asked people in 2007 to decide which two programs should have their spending cut as a way of reducing the budget deficit, a majority favored cutting relatively small programs: 51 percent picked the space program and 28 percent picked welfare programs, as shown in Table 12.2. Far fewer people favored

budget maximizers Bureaucrats who seek to increase funding for their agency whether or not that additional spending is worthwhile.

Who Are Bureaucrats?

Determining the size of the bureaucracy is not easy. While it is fairly straightforward to tally the number of civilian employees in the federal bureaucracy, the result understates the true size of the bureaucracy because it ignores other individuals who are paid by the government even though they are not government employees. Who are members of the bureaucracy?

The figure below reports data from a recent analysis of federal employment.[a] There are just under 2 million civilian employees who get a paycheck from the federal government. However, there are another 1.5 million members of the armed forces, plus about 900,000 Postal Service employees. An additional 5 million people who work for private companies are paid through government contracts with their employers. United Space Alliance, for one, is a private company that employs thousands of people to launch NASA space shuttles and to ready the shuttles for the next flight after each mission.

Finally, almost 3 million people work on programs funded by federal grants. On your college campus, for example, there are probably hundreds if not thousands of researchers paid from grants awarded by the National Science Foundation, the National Institutes for Health, or other agencies. Many local programs, such as job training, public works, and even after-school recreation for elementary students, are funded at least in part by federal grants.

Part of the reason for employing people to do government-funded work through contracts and grants rather than adding them to the federal payrolls may be to make the number of federal employees look artificially low. However, there is a second reason: since members of the civil service can be fired only for poor performance (and through cumbersome measures), hiring contractors allows staff size to be reduced according to a department's needs, such as when a particular project is finished or requirements change. Thus, while you may think that you don't know or regularly encounter any bureaucrats, think again: the federal bureaucracy is much larger than it may initially seem. ■

FEDERAL EMPLOYMENT

These data show that many people who work for the federal government are not actually federal employees. Instead, they may be employed by contractors, work on projects funded by federal grants, or work for the military or the Postal Service. Why doesn't the government simply hire more people rather than paying contractors and giving out grants?

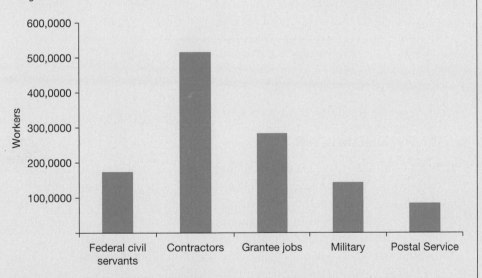

SOURCE: Data from Paul C. Light, "Fact Sheet on the True Size of Government," Brookings Institution, available at http://www.brookings.edu/gs/cps/light20030905.pdf.

cuts in the programs that account for the overwhelming majority of federal spending: defense, Medicare, and Social Security. In other words, while in the abstract Americans might want a smaller government that is less involved in everyday life, they do not support the large-scale budget cuts that would be necessary to achieve this goal. The public's desire for more government services is often encouraged by elected officials, who create new government programs (and expand existing ones in response to constituent demands), as a way of building support and improving their chances of reelection.

SECTION SUMMARY

1. The federal bureaucracy is organized into fifteen executive departments, each containing a number of agencies, and many independent agencies that operate outside executive departments' control.
2. Nearly 2 million people work for the federal government. Almost twice that number work for government contractors or are funded by federal grants.
3. Decisions about where an agency is located within the federal government structure have important implications for political control.
4. Public demand for government services provides the best explanation for the size of the federal government.

The Human Face of the Bureaucracy

The term "bureaucrat" applies to a wide range of people with different qualifications and job descriptions. Nuts and Bolts 12.1 shows data on the wide variety of types of jobs that federal workers do. There are a lot of managers (533,000 people) and administrative support staff (325,000), but there are also 55,000 scientists,

The Size of America's Government

Many Americans believe that taxes are too high, and that the federal government is wasteful and inefficient. These complaints raise the question of how U.S. government spending compares to spending by other countries. While the extent of the services provided by different governments varies considerably, generally speaking the United States provides a much narrower range of benefits to its citizens compared to other developed nations, such as the industrialized democracies of western Europe. Many other countries offer benefits such as government-funded health care, a free or low-cost college education, and more generous old-age pensions. Thus, if the United States spends more than these countries, this would suggest that the federal government really is wasteful and inefficient—spending more and delivering less.

The Organization for Economic Cooperation and Development (OECD) collects a large variety of economic statistics about its thirty-three member nations, which include the United States and most western European democracies. The figure reports government spending in some of these countries, measured as a percentage of gross domestic product (GDP), which includes the value of all the goods and services produced in an economy over a set time period—usually one year. (Note that much of recent U.S. spending on the wars in Iraq and Afghanistan is excluded from the figure.) We report government spending relative to the country's GDP rather than by itself because these countries differ greatly in terms of the overall size of their economies and populations. That is, a country that spends more than others in absolute terms might simply be richer or have a larger population than most. Considering spending as a percentage of GDP allows us to factor in the size of each country's population and economy to compare more accurately.

The data show that compared to other countries, the United States has one of the lowest levels of government spending. In fact, in some countries, such as Sweden, spending is almost double the level of spending in the United States. Of course, this doesn't imply that Swedish bureaucrats are doubly wasteful—rather, it reflects the fact that the Swedish government provides many services to its citizens, such as health care, child care, and unemployment compensation, that the U.S. government either does not provide or provides at lower levels. Still, the data do not suggest that the United States government spends more than other countries' governments.

No one likes to pay taxes. It is important to consider what Americans get from government for their contributions, or whether additional spending on new programs is warranted. It is also important to explore other ways of delivering services, such as substituting private companies for government operations. However, the fact that many Americans believe the government is too large does not mean it is inherently wasteful or harmful to the nation's economy. Also, as these data show, the U.S. government is actually small relative to other western democracies. ■

THE SIZE OF AMERICA'S GOVERNMENT COMPARED TO THOSE OF OTHER NATIONS

While the federal bureaucracy is very large and does many things, total federal spending as a percentage of the U.S. gross domestic product is one of the lowest for all industrialized countries. Based on these data, how would you respond to complaints about the magnitude of federal spending?

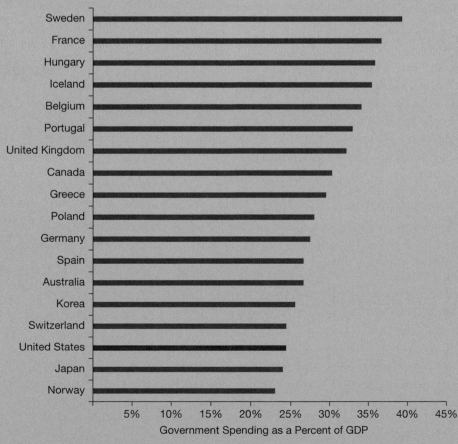

Government Spending as a Percent of GDP

SOURCE: Organization for Economic Cooperation and Development, "OECD in Figures," available at http://www.oecd.org/infigures.

Types of Federal Workers

OCCUPATION	EMPLOYEES	PERCENT OF FEDERAL WORK FORCE
Management, business, and financial jobs (e.g., purchasing agents, accountants, tax collectors)	650,000	33%
Professional and related jobs (e.g., scientists, engineers, computer specialists, lawyers, doctors, nurses)	642,000	33
Office and administrative support jobs (e.g., secretaries, record clerks)	279,000	14
Service jobs (e.g., jailers, police officers, detectives)	157,000	8
Installation, maintenance, and repair jobs (e.g., mechanics, electricians)	93,000	5
Transportation and moving jobs (e.g., air traffic controllers, transportation inspectors)	56,000	3
Farming, fishing, and forestry jobs (e.g., agricultural inspectors, farmworkers, loggers)	9,000	0.4

SOURCE: Based on the U.S. Bureau of Labor Statistics, Career Guide to Industries, "Federal Government, Excluding the Postal Service," Table 3, March 12, 2008, available at http://www.bls.gov/oco/cg/cgs041.htm#table3.

73,000 doctors and nurses, 68,000 computer specialists, and even 45,000 police officers and detectives.[66] The federal government includes so many different kinds of jobs because of the vast array of services it provides. This section describes who these people are and the terms of their government employment.

MOTIVATIONS

Figure 12.4 describes a 2003 survey that asked bureaucrats and people working for private firms whether their primary interest was job security or the desire to help the public.[67] The bars on the left show that a large majority of federal employees mentioned their salary and benefits as prime motivations. Even so, about one-third reported that their main incentive was an interest in public service or in what government does. The right side of Figure 12.4 shows that federal employees' motivations closely parallel those expressed by people working outside government. The percentages of government and private sector employees who gave each response are almost identical. Like everyone else, the average federal employee's work-related decisions are often driven by self-interest, including the desire to make money. However, just like people who work outside government, many federal employees have other motivations, including the desire to do a good job.[68]

CIVIL SERVICE REGULATIONS

One of the most important characteristics of most jobs in the federal bureaucracy is that they are subject to the civil service regulations mentioned earlier.[69] The current civil service system sets out a job description and pay ranges for virtually all federal jobs.[70] People with less than a college degree are generally eligible for clerical and low-level technical jobs. Like in the private sector, a college degree or an advanced degree and work experience qualify an individual for higher-level positions. Federal salaries are supposed to be comparable to what people earn in similar, private sector

FIGURE 12.4 MOTIVATIONS FOR EMPLOYMENT: COMPARING BUREAUCRATS AND PRIVATE SECTOR EMPLOYEES

This chart shows that the motivations of federal employees are much the same as private sector workers' reasons for pursuing particular jobs. Some join the bureaucracy for the pay and benefits, but a substantial proportion work for the government because of policy goals—they want to help people or make a difference in how government works. For an elected official worried that bureaucrats will ignore congressional directives in favor of their own preferences, are these results good news or bad news?

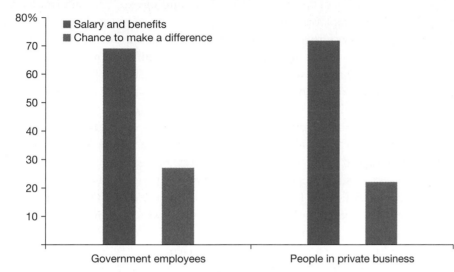

SOURCE: Data from Paul Light, "The Content of Their Character: The State of the Nonprofit Workforce," *The Nonprofit Quarterly* (Fall, 2002): 6–16.

positions, and salaries are increased somewhat for federal employees who work in areas with a high cost of living.

The civil service system also established a set of tests used to determine who is hired for low-level clerical and secretarial positions. These exams are given on set dates, and the people who receive the highest scores are hired as vacancies arise. A similar system is used for Postal Service employees and for federal air traffic controllers. Higher-level jobs are filled by comparing the qualifications and experience of candidates who meet the educational requirements for the position. Seniority, or the amount of time a person has worked for the government or at a particular type of position, is also used to determine which employees receive promotions.

Civil service regulations also provide job security. After three years of satisfactory performance, employees cannot be fired except "for cause," meaning the firing agency must cite a reason for the termination, such as poor performance. Civil service regulations set out a detailed, multistep procedure that has to be followed to fire someone, beginning with low performance evaluations, then moving to warning letters given to the employee, followed by a lengthy appeals process before a firing takes place. In simple terms, it is very hard to fire someone from the federal bureaucracy as long as they show up for work. One study calculated that fewer than 500 civil servants are fired in a given year.[71] A subpar performer may be given other duties, transferred to another office, or even given nothing to do in the hope that the person will leave voluntarily out of boredom.

Despite the difficulties associated with firing an individual underperforming bureaucrat, it is possible to reduce the size of the federal workforce through reductions in force (RIF), which are occasionally carried out when an entire office or program is terminated. Employees who have been laid off due to a RIF can apply for civil service positions in other parts of government. Another strategy for reducing the federal workforce is to simply not replace employees who decide to leave government service.

If you think civil service regulations look extraordinarily cumbersome, you're right.[72] The hiring criteria remove a manager's discretion to hire someone who would do an excellent job but lacks the education or work experience that the regulations specify as necessary for the position. The firing requirements make it extremely difficult to remove poor performers. The salary and promotion restrictions create problems with rewarding excellent performance or promoting the best employees rather than those with the most seniority.

Why do civil service requirements exist? Recall that the aim of these regulations was to separate politics from policy. The mechanism for achieving this goal was a set of rules and requirements that made it hard for elected officials to control the hiring and firing of government employees to further their own political goals. In effect, even though civil service regulations have the obvious drawbacks just described, they also provide this less apparent but very important benefit.

While loyalty to the president is a widely known and accepted criterion for hiring agency heads and other presidential appointees, professionals with permanent civil service positions are supposed to be hired on the basis of their qualifications, not their political beliefs. In fact, it is illegal to bring politics into these hiring decisions. However, there are well-documented cases in which administrations have made political beliefs a priority in hiring mid-level bureaucrats. For example, during the presidency of George W. Bush, Justice Department officials admitted to screening applicants based on their ideological leanings. Membership in a liberal organization such as Greenpeace listed on a candidate's resume reduced the likelihood of being hired, while membership in conservative organizations such as the Federalist Society boosted an applicant's chances.[73] While the Bush administration is the most severe known recent example of this practice, it is likely that other administrations have behaved similarly.

▲ Federal law prohibits the use of government money, facilities, or services for political activities. Here, former Republican representative Tom DeLay (left), whose Texas district included NASA's Johnson Space Center, attends an awards ceremony with NASA administrator Michael Griffin. Although Griffin flew to Houston on a government plane primarily to present awards to NASA employees, his trip was citied as an illegal use of funds because his speech praised DeLay, who was running for reelection.

LIMITS ON POLITICAL ACTIVITY

Federal employees are also limited in their political activities. The Hatch Act, enacted in 1939 and amended in 1940, prohibited federal employees from engaging in organized political activities.[74] Under the act, employees could vote and contribute to candidates, but could not work for candidates or for political parties. These restrictions were modified in the 1993 Federal Employees Political Activities Act, allowing federal employees to undertake a wider range of political activities, including fund-raising and serving as an officer of a political party.

Senior members of the president's White House staff are exempt from most of these restrictions, though they cannot use government resources for political activities. Thus, early in the 2006 election campaign, at a NASA awards ceremony, NASA administrator Michael Griffin referred to Congressman Tom DeLay, whose district contained NASA's Johnson Space Center, by saying, "The space program has had no better friend in its entire existence than Tom DeLay. He's still with us and we need to keep him there."[75] The problem was not what Griffin said; he was a political appointee and could endorse DeLay if he wanted to. Rather, the problem was that Griffin had flown to Texas for the NASA ceremony on a government aircraft, which, because of the endorsement, could be construed as using government resources for political purposes.

These regulations make life especially difficult for presidential appointees whose job duties often mix government service with politics, such as helping the president they work for get reelected. In order to comply with Hatch Act restrictions, these officials need to carry separate cell phones to make calls related to their political activities, and maintain separate e-mail accounts—usually provided by the party or campaign committee—for their political communications. Inevitably, some messages are sent using the wrong system. During the Bush administration, various political appointees used the Republican Party e-mail system to send messages relating to the controversial dismissal of several U.S. attorneys.[76]

It is not completely clear which activities are allowed or prohibited by these laws. For example, in spring 2007, congressional Democrats complained that Karl Rove, then-deputy White House chief of staff and a close political advisor to President George W. Bush, had given a series of briefings to senior political appointees on Republican losses in the 2006 midterm elections and plans for the 2008 campaign. Although these meetings had been approved as legal by the White House counsel, their political content is obvious. During one briefing, the head of the General Services Administration asked how her agency could help elect Republican candidates in 2008.[77] As a senior member of the White House staff, Rove is exempt from the Hatch Act's prohibitions, but the more junior White House staff involved in the briefings probably were not.

POLITICAL PROCESS MATTERS

The notice and comment procedure helps elected officials and other interested parties monitor bureaucratic actions.

POLITICAL APPOINTEES AND THE SENIOR EXECUTIVE SERVICE

Not every federal employee is a member of the civil service. The president appoints over 7,000 individuals to senior positions in the executive branch that are not subject to civil service regulations, such as the leaders of executive departments and independent agencies, as well as members of the Executive Office of the President. (In some cases, these nominees need to be confirmed by a majority vote in the Senate.) Some of these presidential appointees get their jobs as a reward for service during the campaign. They may have worked on the campaign staff, contributed substantial funds, or raised money from other donors. These individuals may not be given positions with real decision-making power. Some government agencies have the reputation of being "**turkey farms**," places where campaign stalwarts can be appointed without the risk that their lack of experience will lead to bad policy.[78]

The majority of a president's appointees are intended to act as the president's eyes, ears, and hands throughout the executive branch. They hold positions of power within government agencies, serving as secretaries of executive departments, agency heads, or senior deputies. Their jobs involve finding out what the president wants from their agency and ordering, persuading, or cajoling their subordinates to implement presidential directives.

In many agencies, people who serve in the top positions are members of the Senior Executive Service (SES), who are also exempt from civil service restrictions.[79] As of 2008, there were a few thousand SES members, most of whom were career government employees who held relatively high-level agency positions before moving to the SES. This change of employment status costs them their civil service protections but allows them to apply for senior leadership positions in the bureaucracy. Some political appointees are also given SES positions, although most do not have the experience or expertise held by career bureaucrats who typically move to the SES.

The president's ability to appoint bureaucrats in many different agencies helps him control the bureaucracy. By selecting people who are loyal or like-minded, a

▲ One of the problems for a new administration is finding appropriate government jobs for loyal campaign workers and contributors. Agencies that often employ these individuals despite their lack of qualifications are known as "turkey farms." These appointees generally serve without mishap, but the Bush administration's use of FEMA as a turkey farm was cited as one reason for the agency's inadequate response to Hurricane Katrina.

president can attempt to control the actions of lower-level bureaucrats and implement his policy agenda. The SES also gives civil servants an incentive to do their jobs well, as good performance in an agency position can help build a career that might allow them to transfer to the SES.

SECTION SUMMARY

1. Like employees in the private sector, bureaucrats are motivated by financial concerns, but many also take a strong interest in enacting good public policy.
2. Civil service regulations protect bureaucrats against being fired but also make it hard for supervisors to remove incompetent employees or reward top performers.
3. Federal employees face significant restrictions on their political activity.
4. The Senior Executive Service allows high-level bureaucrats to take leadership positions in government agencies, at the cost of removing their civil service protections.

How Americans See the Bureaucracy

Americans have mixed feelings about the bureaucracy. Figure 12.5 shows that a majority of survey respondents agreed that the federal government is typically inefficient and wasteful—although the percentage agreeing with this assessment in 2007 had declined significantly from its peak in 1994. A survey conducted in 1999 found similar results. Only 8 percent of respondents believed that the federal government has had a large number of policy successes, whereas a near-majority could not name a single government success.[80]

Why do Americans dislike bureaucrats? Many of these negative assessments result from low levels of trust in government, economic conditions, and media coverage that highlights examples of bureaucratic incompetence.[81] However, Americans tend to have more positive impressions of the government agencies with which they have personal experience.[82] A survey that targeted groups of people who had first-hand contact with a set of government agencies, such as professional tax preparers who often interact with bureaucrats from the Internal Revenue Service (IRS), found that a majority of the people who were familiar with an agency reported favorable impressions of its operations.

These studies have an important implication: if you want to know what Americans think about the bureaucracy, it depends on how you ask the question and whom you ask. Asked about government in general, most Americans will complain. However, if you ask about parts of the bureaucracy that people know something about, their impressions are much more likely to be favorable.

FIGURE 12.5 **HOW AMERICANS VIEW THE FEDERAL BUREAUCRACY**

Many Americans believe the bureaucracy is wasteful and inefficient. Note, however, that the magnitude of negative feelings varies over time. Consider the time frame represented on the graph. What happened during these years that might explain the changes in citizens' opinions about the government?

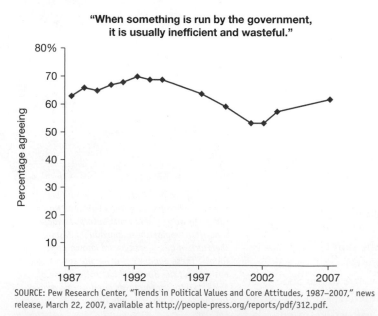

"When something is run by the government, it is usually inefficient and wasteful."

SOURCE: Pew Research Center, "Trends in Political Values and Core Attitudes, 1987–2007," news release, March 22, 2007, available at http://people-press.org/reports/pdf/312.pdf.

Bureaucratic Efficiency and the General Services Administration

The beginning of this chapter cited several examples of bureaucratic waste. Many researchers and political experts would see these instances as fitting into a broader pattern in which anything government does is sure to cost more than it should and deliver less of what people need. The public opinion data discussed earlier in this chapter show that many Americans agree. However, like most broad assertions about American politics, claims about bureaucratic waste need to be evaluated with data—and one agency in the federal bureaucracy is an ideal place to look: the General Services Administration.

The General Services Administration (GSA) provides management and purchasing services to the federal government. It manages and leases office space and other facilities for government agencies and procures everything from office supplies to liquid helium for resale to other government agencies. The GSA also has an airline ticketing service and a hotel reservation service for federal employees. GSA employees manage the federal government's real estate portfolio and its vehicle fleet, both of which are among the largest in the country. They even provided 520 SUVs to U.S. agencies working in Iraq after the invasion.

Because much of what the GSA does is similar to activities in private companies, is it possible to evaluate the GSA's operations by comparing what it pays for goods and services to the prices paid by private corporations? Specifically, do government agencies pay more by get-

▲ General Services Administration employees begin a renovation of the White House press briefing room.

ting their goods and services through the GSA than they would by using local realtors to find office space, buying cars through dealers, and getting their pencils, computers, and furniture at the local office supply store?

By law, the GSA must complete an annual performance review that measures its efforts against a variety of indicators, and its 2006 report completely contradicts conventional views about government waste and inefficiency.[a]

- The GSA pays 8.5 percent less rent for office space than private companies pay for comparable space.
- Service costs (heating, lighting, etc.) for GSA-managed buildings are 4.2 percent less than they are for compa-

rable, privately managed space. During 2006 the GSA reduced energy consumption in the buildings it managed by 4.4 percent.
- The vacancy rate in buildings operated by the GSA is only 1.5 percent, which is quite low compared to major corporations.
- The GSA buys cars at 39 percent below the invoice price, whereas most private citizens are doing well if they pay no *more* than the invoice price.

Contrary to the notion that the federal bureaucracy is necessarily wasteful, GSA bureaucrats appear to be working efficiently—at a low cost to taxpayers. ∎

Controlling the Bureaucracy

As the expert implementers of legislation and presidential directives, bureaucrats hold significant power to influence government policy. This situation creates the problem of political control illustrated by the principal–agent game: elected officials must figure out how to reap the benefits of bureaucratic expertise without simply giving bureaucrats free reign do whatever they want. One strategy is to take away discretion entirely and give bureaucrats simple, direct orders. One such case came to light in summer 2007 when outgoing surgeon general Richard Carmona revealed in a congressional hearing that he had been ordered to mention President Bush's name at least three times on every page of his speeches, and to refrain from criticizing administration policies in the controversial areas of stem cell research, abstinence-only sex education programs, and the "morning-after pill" method of birth control called Plan B.[83]

Similarly, after NASA scientist James Hansen gave a speech in 2006 calling for policies to combat global warming that did not reflect the Bush administration's preferences, he was told to submit all future papers, lectures, and interview requests to NASA political appointees for review.[84] In this case, NASA reversed the order after it received press attention, and Michael Griffin, then-head of NASA, released a statement supporting scientific openness.[85] Soon after this episode, however, NASA's official mission statement was modified to exclude studies of Earth, thereby choking off its studies of climate change entirely.[86]

Attempts like these to control the bureaucracy are fairly common. At the same hearing that featured Bush's outgoing surgeon general, David Satcher, who was surgeon general during the Clinton administration, testified that he had been ordered to not release a report on sexuality and public health in order to avoid embarrassing President Clinton, who was then being accused of having an extramarital affair with White House intern Monica Lewinsky.

The problem with eliminating bureaucrats' discretion is that this also limits the positive influence of their expertise. Particularly when new policies are being developed, taking away bureaucratic discretion is costly for legislators or presidential appointees, as it forces them to take the time to work out the policy details themselves—and may still produce less effective policies than those constructed by bureaucrats with specialized knowledge.[87] Moreover, preventing bureaucrats from using their judgment makes it impossible for them to craft policies that take into account new developments or unforeseen circumstances.[88]

For all of these reasons, elected officials must find ways to reduce or eliminate **bureaucratic drift**—that is, bureaucrats pursuing their own goals rather than their assignments from officeholders or appointees—while still reaping the benefits of bureaucratic expertise. This section describes two common strategies: changing the way agencies are organized and staffed, and using standardized procedures for monitoring agency actions. In both cases, the aim is to set up the agency so that bureaucrats can use their expertise, while making sure their actions are consistent with elected officials' wishes.[89]

AGENCY ORGANIZATION

Over the last twenty years, political scientists have shown how agencies can be organized to minimize bureaucratic drift.[90] Specifically, when an agency is set up or given new responsibilities, the officials who initiated the change don't simply tell the agency what to do. To make sure that they get the policies they want, they also

bureaucratic drift Bureaucrats' tendency to implement policies in a way that favors their own political objectives rather than following the original intentions of the legislation.

determine where the agency is located within the federal government structure and who runs it. These efforts may occur solely within Congress, involve both Congress and the president, or be arranged by presidential actions.[91]

For example, when legislation was written to form the Department of Homeland Security in 2002, the Bush administration pushed to have the Coast Guard transferred out of the Department of Transportation and into the new department. This move was designed to change the Coast Guard's priorities from search and rescue operations and routine patrol to a focus on port security, without increasing its budget. The shift worked: over the next few years, the amount of effort expended by Coast Guard personnel on port security increased from only a few percent of total effort to nearly 50 percent, with a corresponding decrease in other activities.[92]

Another strategy is to impose limits on who is allowed to run the agency. In the case of the Federal Communications Commission, for example, one of elected officials' principal concerns about the organization is that it will adopt regulations on political advertising that favor one political party over the other. To prevent this, the legislation that created the agency mandates that it will be run by five commissioners, all of whom are nominated by the president and confirmed by the Senate.[93] However, no more than three of the commissioners can be from the same political party. As a result, if a partisan majority on the commission tries to enact laws that favor one party, opponents only need to convince one supporter to switch positions in order to block the measure. The same rule is used to select commissioners for other agencies. The Federal Election Commission has six commissioners, three Democrats and three Republicans, to guard against one party gaining control of the agency and making biased decisions.[94] In many cases, commissioners are also prohibited from having a business relationship (as a consultant, stockholder, or otherwise) with any company that is subject to their agency's rulings.

▲ The transfer of the Coast Guard from the Department of Transportation to the Department of Homeland Security shifted the focus of Coast Guard operations from search and rescue to port security.

MONITORING

One of the most important ways elected officials prevent bureaucratic drift is to know what bureaucrats are doing or planning to do. Information gathering by members of Congress about bureaucratic actions is termed **oversight**. Congressional committees often hold hearings to question members of the bureaucracy, typically agency heads, secretaries of executive departments, or senior agency staff. Similarly, one of the primary responsibilities of presidential appointees is to monitor how bureaucrats are responding to presidential directives.

Advance Warning Members of Congress, the president, and his staff gain advance knowledge of bureaucratic actions through the notice and comment procedure described earlier in the chapter, which requires bureaucrats to disclose their proposed changes before they take effect.[95] This delay gives people who oppose a change the opportunity to register complaints with their congressional representatives, and it allows these legislators time either to pressure the agency to revise the regulation or even to enact another law undoing or modifying the agency action.

POLITICAL PROCESS MATTERS

 The notice and comment procedure helps elected officials and other interested parties monitor bureaucratic actions.

Investigations: Police Patrols and Fire Alarms Investigations involve Congress, legislative staff, or presidential appointees selecting some government program or office, and scrutinizing the organization, its expenditures, and its activities. The idea would be to investigate every agency as often as possible, with agencies that had large budgets or carried out important functions being investigated more frequently.

oversight Congressional efforts to make sure that laws are implemented correctly by the bureaucracy after they have been passed.

police patrol oversight A method of oversight in which members of Congress constantly monitor the bureaucracy to make sure that laws are implemented correctly.

fire alarm oversight A method of oversight in which members of Congress respond to complaints about the bureaucracy or problems of implementation only as they arise rather than exercising constant vigilance.

These investigations may involve fact-finding trips to local offices, interviews with senior personnel, audits of agency accounts, and even calls to the agency to see how they respond to citizens' requests. This method of investigation is called **police patrol oversight**.[96] Think of a police officer walking her beat, rattling doors to see if they are locked, checking out broken windows, and looking down alleys for suspicious behavior.

The disadvantage of police patrol oversight is that it is costly, both in terms of money and staff time. Moreover, these investigations often find that agencies are doing what they should. Because of these drawbacks, Congress and the president also look outside government for information on what bureaucrats are doing. Rather than undertaking a series of investigations, they wait until they receive a complaint about bureaucratic actions, then focus investigative efforts on those cases, a practice labeled **fire alarm oversight**.[97]

The so-called fire alarm can take many different forms. Representatives and their staff meet frequently with constituents who may let them know of a problem with the bureaucracy. Similarly, the president and his staff are often contacted by lobbyists, corporate executives, or even ordinary citizens with complaints about bureaucratic actions. Newspaper reporters and even Internet bloggers also provide information on what bureaucrats are doing. Some agencies have advisory committees that not only help make agency decisions but also serve to keep Congress and the president informed about them.[98]

The case of NASA climate change scientist James Hansen described earlier provides a clear example of fire alarm oversight. The order requiring that Hansen submit all his public statements and work for review became public when it was reported by the *New York Times* and other newspapers. The resulting firestorm of protest from members of Congress forced NASA head Michael Griffin to rescind the order.

These fire alarms provide exactly the sort of information that Congress and the president often lack about how bureaucrats are implementing laws and directives, including cases when bureaucrats are doing (or planning to do) something that contradicts their mandate. These communications tell Congress and the president where to focus their efforts to monitor the bureaucracy, drawing their attention to agencies or programs where problems have been reported, rather than trying to oversee the entire government at once.

CORRECTING VIOLATIONS

When members of Congress or the president find a case of bureaucratic drift, they can take steps to influence the bureaucrats' actions. Many tactics can be used to bring a wayward agency into line. Legislation or an executive order can send a clear directive to an agency or remove its discretion, tasks and programs can be moved to an agency more closely aligned with elected officials' goals, political appointees at an agency can be replaced, and agencies can be reorganized. In extreme situations, members of Congress can even fail to renew an agency's statutory authority, in effect putting the agency out of business. (This option was used to halt the work of the Federal Trade Commission for a short time in the early 1970s.)[99]

One of the most significant difficulties in dealing with bureaucratic drift is disagreement between members of Congress and the president about whether or not an agency is doing the right thing—regardless of whether the agency is following its original orders. Most of the tactics listed above require joint action by the president and congressional majorities. Without presidential support, members of Congress need a two-thirds majority to impose corrections. Without congressional support,

Is Political Control of the Bureaucracy Beneficial?

When working with bureaucrats, elected officials face the problem of political control: should they allow bureaucrats to exercise judgment when implementing policies or give them specific, narrow directives? Letting bureaucrats set policy allows them to base decisions on their expertise or private information, but it also gives them the freedom to ignore elected officials' policy goals and preferences in favor of their own.

Discretion also allows bureaucrats to say things that contradict the public statements of members of Congress or the President. Statements by NASA scientist James Hansen about the need to actively combat global warming, for example, contradicted then-president Bush's view that global warming deserved further study but nothing more. Such cases seem clear cut, suggesting that Americans should support bureaucrats, who often know more about the details of policy problems and solutions than members of Congress. Likewise, it seems obvious that government scientists such as Hansen should be allowed to conduct research without political intervention. Indeed, NASA's policy

▲ Attempts by NASA bureaucrats to suppress public comments about global warming by James Hansen, director of NASA's Goddard Institute for Space Studies, were abandoned after they attracted media coverage.

on scientific freedom notes the agency's commitment to "a culture of scientific and technical openness which values the free exchange of ideas, data and information, [and in which] scientific and technical information concerning agency programs and projects will be accurate and unfiltered."[a]

The problem with bureaucratic discretion is that it cuts both ways. Allowing bureaucrats to act as they think best means that they can disregard the stated goals of legislation or the preferences of elected officials and simply implement the policies they favor. Even bureaucrats' public statements can have policy consequences—they may influence public opinion and in turn shape government policy. When a scientist such as Hansen sounds the alarm, many people listen.

Another down side that comes with bureaucratic discretion is that bureaucrats are unelected and most are very difficult to fire because of their civil service protections. A misbehaving elected official can be removed from office via an election or impeachment; bureaucrats have more staying power. Moreover, if bureaucrats are given a great deal of leeway to use their judgment in policy making, it becomes very difficult to determine the criteria for judging whether their removal is warranted or not. How much discretion should elected officials allow bureaucrats to use? You decide. ■

---

the president can only threaten to cut an agency's proposed budget, change its home within the federal bureaucracy, or set up a new agency to do what the errant agency refuses to do. Such disagreements between the president and Congress can give an agency significant freedom, as long as it retains support of at least one branch of government. For example, a study of Federal Reserve policy making found that the Fed has been able to quash attempts to end its independence from political control by choosing monetary policies that are always considered acceptable by at least one branch of government, either Congress or the president.[100]

An agency may also be able to fend off elected officials' attempts to take political control if it has a reputation for expertise. For example, one reason that the attempts to pass legislation forcing the Food and Drug Administration to alter its drug approval process have met with

POLITICAL PROCESS MATTERS

Disagreements between the president and Congress create opportunities for bureaucratic drift.

little success is that FDA's process is thought to have worked mostly as intended, approving new drugs that are safe and effective and keeping ineffective or unsafe drugs off the market. At the same time, the FDA has also responded to pressure from Congress and the president to revise some rules on its own.[101]

Finally, agencies can sometimes fend off attempts to control their behavior by appealing to groups in society who benefit from agency actions.[102] For example, since the 1980s, the Occupational Safety and Health Administration (OSHA) has resisted attempts by Republican presidents and Republican members of Congress to eliminate the agency.[103] One element of their strategy has been to build strong ties to labor unions; as a result, OSHA is much more likely to receive complaints about workplace safety from companies with strong unions. The second prong of the strategy has involved building cooperative arrangements with large companies to prevent workplace accidents, an approach that not only protects workers but can save companies a lot of money over the long term. Moreover, when OSHA levies fines against companies that violate safety regulations, they are generally much less than would be allowed by law. As a result, when proposals to limit or eliminate OSHA are debated in Congress, members hear from unions as well as many large corporations in support of keeping the agency in place. Over time, this strategy has generated support for the agency from Democrats and Republicans in the House and Senate.

Many other agencies have followed similar strategies, even when the bureaucracy was much smaller. For example, during the early 1900s, bureaucrats in the Department of Agriculture and in the Forest Service won congressional approval to move the Forest Service out of the Department of the Interior and into their own department. Republicans in Congress opposed the move believing (correctly) that it would allow the Forest Service to impose user fees and limit grazing rights, which the Republican members opposed. The move happened because leaders in the Forest Service and the Department of Agriculture had cultivated the support of interest groups such as the Audubon Society, the Sierra Club, and organizations representing ranchers, all of whom lobbied Congress in favor of the change.[104]

SECTION SUMMARY

1. Elected officials can exercise political control over bureaucrats by giving them simple directives and little discretion. However, this strategy eliminates the benefits of allowing bureaucrats to act on their expertise.
2. To solve this problem, elected officials use agency organization, restrictions on agency leaders and staff, and oversight mechanisms such as police patrols and fire alarms.
3. In response, agencies work to build public and interest group support for their policies.
4. Agencies have more discretion when the president and members of Congress disagree on what the agency should be doing.

Explaining the Anomalies

This chapter began with two lists: one describing bureaucratic failures and embarrassments and another highlighting significant bureaucratic accomplishments. In light of the vast capabilities of the federal government, the accomplishments need little explaining, so this section focuses on explaining the failures. Put another way, how can a government that functions so well in some areas be a dismal failure in others?

The first reason for bureaucratic shortfalls is the complexity of the tasks that bureaucrats undertake. Even when members of Congress and the president agree on which problems deserve attention, bureaucrats are often given the much harder task of translating these officials' lofty problem-solving goals into concrete policies. Given the magnitude of this job, it is no surprise that even the best efforts of government agencies do not always succeed. Consider the Great Society's goal of eliminating poverty in America.[105] When these antipoverty programs were implemented in the 1960s, the causes of poverty were not well understood. Years later, it became clear that without a better understanding of the problem, it would be impossible to develop effective policies to help the poor.[106]

Second, the use of standard operating procedures is rooted partly in the complexity of bureaucrats' tasks—but also in the desire of agency heads and elected officials to control the actions of lower-level staff. Some of FEMA's failures after Katrina were the product of preset plans and procedures that did not anticipate a disaster of the magnitude faced in New Orleans. Similarly, while it sounds like a good idea to require passports at border crossings, the regulations failed to take into account how the State Department would cope with the crush of millions of new applications. And while the FDA's drug approval process succeeds for the most part at preventing harmful drugs from coming to market, the delays imposed by the process do prevent some patients from receiving life-saving treatments. However, in all of these cases, the decisions do not reflect incompetence or malice. Rules and procedures are needed in any organization to ensure that decisions are made fairly and that they reflect the goals of the organization. However, it is impossible to find procedures that will work this way in all cases, particularly for the kinds of policy decisions made by bureaucrats.

Dysfunctional bureaucratic behavior can also arise from the problem of political control. Requiring the surgeon general to mention the president's name three times on each page of his speeches sounds absurd, and perhaps it is—but it is also true that the president and his appointees are genuinely worried about being undercut by unelected bureaucrats who may disagree with their plans. Similarly, government reorganizations such as the formation of the Department of Homeland Security may be designed to bring about some bureaucratic "failures" as priorities shift and agencies' goals are redefined. That is, no one expects agencies like the Coast Guard to take on new responsibilities without shifting resources away from the jobs they are already doing. In a sense, the Guard has fallen short in its routine patrol mission since it became part of Homeland Security. But the reason for moving the Guard into the new department was to refocus its efforts on port security rather than its traditional missions. From the viewpoint of political control, the reorganization worked exactly as planned.

In sum, when government agencies do things that look bizarre or counterproductive, it would be wrong to immediately conclude that the organizations involved are inept or willfully shirking their responsibilities. Rather, they may be doing the best they can to achieve formidable goals, carrying out procedures that are often—but not always—productive, or responding to directives from elected officials.

Conclusion

Bureaucrats implement government policy—often in situations like Hurricane Katrina where the problems as well as potential solutions are vast and poorly understood, and in the face of sharp disagreements about what government should do. On the government's behalf, they spend money on everything from pencils to aircraft carriers. They formulate regulations that determine what can be created, produced, transported, bought, sold, consumed, and disposed of in America. Elected officials, from members of Congress to the president, want to control what bureaucrats do while also tapping into their expertise on policy matters.

These characteristics of the bureaucracy and the fundamentally political nature of bureaucrats' jobs explain many cases of bureaucratic ineptitude and red tape. Sometimes bureaucrats simply make mistakes, choosing the wrong policy because they—and, in some cases, everyone else—lack full information about the tasks they were given. Bureaucrats may drag their feet when they oppose their tasks on policy grounds. Policies may also reflect direct orders given by elected officials or political appointees. Attempts at political control also shape the structure of the bureaucracy, from influencing which agencies function independently and which are housed within executive departments to determining the qualifications for commissioners and agency heads and the rules they must follow when making decisions.

CRITICAL THINKING

1. Suppose you are a member of Congress who must decide whether to give bureaucrats in a particular agency direct orders that allow them little or no input, or to allow them to exercise their own discretion. What factors should you consider when making this decision?

2. What are the advantages and disadvantages of the fact that bureaucrats often have their own preferences about how to implement the policies they administer?

3. Why might bureaucrats pay more attention to orders and directives from members of Congress than those from the president or his political appointees?

KEY TERMS

budget maximizers (p. 434)
bureaucracy (p. 421)
bureaucratic drift (p. 444)
civil servants (p. 421)
federal civil service (p. 428)
fire alarm oversight (p. 446)
independent agencies (p. 430)
neutral competence (p. 426)
notice and comment procedure (p. 422)
Office of Management and Budget (OMB) (p. 430)
oversight (p. 445)
police patrol oversight (p. 446)

political appointees (p. 421)
principal–agent game (p. 425)
problem of control (p. 425)
red tape (p. 424)
regulation (p. 421)
regulatory capture (p. 425)
standard operating procedures (p. 424)
state capacity (p. 424)
street-level bureaucrats (p. 423)
turkey farms (p. 441)

SUGGESTED READING

Aaron, Henry J. *Politics and the Professors: The Great Society in Perspective.* Washington, DC: Brookings Institution Press, 1978.

Brehm, John, and Scott Gates. *Working, Shirking and Sabotage.* Ann Arbor, MI: University of Michigan Press, 1998.

Carpenter, Daniel P. *The Forging of Bureaucratic Autonomy: Reputations, Networks, and Policy Innovation in Executive Agencies, 1862–1928.* Princeton, NJ: Princeton University Press, 2001.

Epstein, David, and Sharyn O'Halloran. *Delegating Powers: A Transaction Cost Politics Approach to Policy Making Under Separate Powers.* New York: Cambridge University Press, 1999.

Huber, John D., and Charles R. Shipan. *Deliberate Discretion? The Institutional Foundations of Bureaucratic Autonomy.* New York: Cambridge University Press, 2002.

Lewis, David E. *Presidents and the Politics of Agency Design: Political Insulation in the United States Government.* Palo Alto, CA: Stanford University Press, 2003.

Light, Paul. *A Government Well-Executed: Public Service and Public Performance.* Washington, DC: Brookings Institution Press, 2003.

McCubbins, Mathew D., Roger G. Noll, and Barry R. Weingast. "Structure and Process as Solutions to the Politician's Principal–Agency Problem," *Virginia Law Review* 74 (1989): 431–82.

Miller, Gary. *Managerial Dilemmas: The Political Economy of Hierarchy.* New York: Cambridge University Press, 1987.

Moe, Terry M. "Political Control and the Power of the Agent," *Journal of Law, Economics, and Organization* 22 (2006): 1–21.

Nelson, Michael. "A Short, Ironic History of American National Bureaucracy," *Journal of Politics* 44 (1982): 747–78.

Skowronek, Stephen. *Building a New American State: The Expansion of National Administrative Capacities, 1877–1920.* New York: Cambridge University Press, 1982.

THE COURTS

Following the September 11 attacks and the invasion of Afghanistan, President Bush broadly interpreted his war powers to give him the right to declare terrorism suspects "unlawful enemy combatants" who could be held indefinitely without access to lawyers or to the courts. If the government brought charges against the suspects, they could be tried in military tribunals with different rules of procedure and fewer rights for the defendants. In a series of cases, the Supreme Court struck down those assertions of presidential power. The first case involved an American citizen, Yasser Esam Hamdi, who was arrested in Afghanistan for suspected terrorist activities. He was held for nearly two years without access to a lawyer and the Supreme Court ruled that he had been deprived of his due process rights and that he had the right to challenge his detention.[1] The second case expanded this decision by ruling that a British citizen, Shafiq Rasul, and other detainees at the Guantanamo facility were also allowed to challenge their detention in federal court.[2]

Two more recent cases were more far-reaching. The first case involved Salim Ahmed Hamdan, the former driver for Osama bin Laden; the central issues were whether military tribunals were legal and whether Congress had the power to remove pending cases from the jurisdiction of the courts. On both issues, the Court ruled against the administration, saying, "The executive is bound to comply with the rule of law that prevails in this jurisdiction." The Court ruled that military tribunals violate military law and the Geneva Conventions on the treatment of prisoners of war. Mr. Hamdan's lawyer said that Hamdan was "awe-struck that the court would rule for him and give a little man like him an equal chance. Where he's from, that is not true."[3]

Congress responded to the decision by passing the Military Commissions Act of 2006, which restored the military's ability to prosecute unlawful enemy combatants in military tribunals and stripped from federal courts their jurisdiction over appeals from prisoners being held at Guantanamo. However, two years later, the Supreme Court struck down parts of the law, restoring prisoners' right to challenge their indefinite detention, saying, "The practice of arbitrary imprisonments has been, in all ages, the favorite and most formidable instrument of tyranny."[4] In August 2008, a military commission found Hamdan guilty of providing material support for terrorism. He was acquitted of the more serious conspiracy charge and given a prison sentence of five and a half years, of which he was given credit for his sixty-one months in detention at Guantanamo.

▲ *The most widely recognized symbol of justice, a blindfolded woman holding a set of scales in one hand and a sword in the other, is represented at hundreds of courthouses around the world.*

While these cases are critical in determining the institutional boundaries and legal processes in the War on Terror, they also illustrate a broader point about the role of the Supreme Court: it is a policy-making institution and an equal partner in our system of separated powers. It may strike you as undemocratic that unelected judges tell the elected branches what to do, but this is a central part of our system of checks and balances. When the Supreme Court rules that military tribunals are unconstitutional, the president and Congress must scramble back to the drawing board and figure out what to do. The decision of which path to take in a given case is often very political, involving trade-offs and conflicts much like decision making in Congress.

That the Supreme Court is a policy-making and political institution may seem inappropriate. After all, the guiding principles of the "rule of law" in the American political system—embodied in the words carved above the entrance to the Supreme Court, "equal justice under the law," and the statue of Justice represented as a blindfolded woman holding a set of scales—seem to contradict the view of a political Court. The American people generally accept the legal principles that guide the Court and public approval of the Supreme Court is almost always higher than it is for the president or Congress. One leading scholar talked about the "mystic function" of the Supreme Court that underpins the moral approval and legitimacy of the Court.[5] Indeed, there is a certain aura that comes with the black robes, the formal architecture of the courtroom, and the secrecy of the judicial decision-making process (in Great Britain, some judges still wear powdered wigs to help maintain that aura).

This respect is also rooted in the perception, embodied in the blindfolded Justice statue, that the courts are "above politics." Judges (and a jury when relevant) are supposed to apply the law objectively in deciding who is right or wrong in civil cases and who is guilty or innocent in criminal cases. Higher courts handle appeals from lower courts to make sure that the law was applied correctly and that rulings are consistent with the national and state constitutions. While this all sounds simple enough, reality is a bit more complicated. Politics is an inherent part of the judiciary and a single set of objective standards is not always available for a given case. Judges have their own political views and opinions and these often shape their views of cases in part *because* there are usually multiple legal justifications for any case. For example, there is no simple or clear-cut way to determine objectively the relative legal merits of Justice Clarence Thomas's dissenting view that the *Hamdan* decision was "untenable" and "dangerous" or the majority's view that "Congress has not issued the executive a blank check" to pursue the War on Terror without oversight. To a large extent, this depends on the justices' views of the trade-offs between a broad view of presidential powers, legal due process, and our commitments under international treaties.

The role of the Court as a policy-making and political institution also illustrates the themes of this book. On one hand, the courts seem to resist our characterization that politics is everywhere. The aura, mystery, and prestige of the courts all seem to isolate them from the rest of the political process. However, most Americans will come into contact with the court system at some point in their lives, whether it is to contest a traffic ticket, fight a local zoning change, or serve on a jury (we will assume that none of you will be on the "wrong side" of the law). The relevance of the courts in national politics is similarly self-evident. Dramatic moments, such as the *Bush v. Gore* decision that decided the 2000 presidential election, are the most obvious examples of the relevance (and political nature!) of the courts. Less visible decisions that are handed down every day in the federal courts affect the lives of millions of Americans across a broad range of areas, including environmental policy, employment law, tax policy, civil rights, and civil liberties. In fact, some critics of the courts complain about an "imperial judiciary" that has become *too* powerful in the political system. This chapter will examine these issues about the proper place of the courts within our political system. How much power should unelected judges have? Are they a necessary check on the other branches of government or a source of unaccountable power that contradicts core principles of democracy? How do the courts interact with the other branches?

Courts may not be viewed as a policy-making institution, at least in the same way that Congress is, and therefore the theme "political process matters" may not seem to apply to the courts. However, the courts often *do* make policy and the manner in which they make decisions has an impact on outcomes. To see how political process matters for the courts it will be important to answer the following questions: What are the different roles of the courts? What is the structure of the judicial system? How do court decisions shape policy?

Finally, as detained terrorism suspects and military tribunal cases reveal, politics is conflictual. Congress, the president, and the Supreme Court may have very different ideas about specific powers that each branch should have in the War on Terror, and this produces conflict between the branches. Should the Court give the president broad powers during time of war, or should it uphold more general principles of due process? Should the Court focus on international treaties, such as the Geneva Conventions, or congressional statutes such as the Detainee Treatment Act in answering the previous question? Why does the Court choose one constitutional principle over another or decide to hear one case but not another? In a nutshell, what is the nature of judicial decision making? Before addressing these questions we will discuss how the Founders viewed the judicial system.

The Development of an Independent and Powerful Federal Judiciary

THE FOUNDERS' VIEWS OF THE COURTS: THE WEAKEST BRANCH?

The Federalists and Antifederalists did not see eye-to-eye on much, and the judiciary was no exception. Alexander Hamilton, writing in *Federalist 78*, said that the Supreme Court would be "beyond comparison the weakest of the three departments of power." On the other hand, the author of what came to be known as the *Antifederalist Papers* wrote, "The supreme court under this constitution would be exalted above all other power in the government and subjected to no control."[6] Hmmm, which is it, weakest or strongest? While the framers could not agree on their predictions of the relative power of the Court, there was surprisingly little debate at the Constitutional Convention about the judiciary, at least when compared to the more extended battles over Congress and the executive. Article III of the Constitution, which lays out the power of the Court, is much shorter than Article I or II. Article III created one Supreme Court and gave the courts independence by providing federal judges with lifetime terms (that is, they can serve during "good behavior") and stipulating that judges' salaries cannot be reduced during their terms in office.

The main disagreements at the Constitutional Convention about the judiciary had to do with how independent the courts should be vis-à-vis the other branches and how much power to give the courts. Some of the framers feared a tyrannical Congress and wanted to create a judicial and executive branch that could check this power. Some argued for making the executive and judicial branches much more

Judiciary Act of 1789 The law in which Congress laid out the organization of the federal judiciary. The law refined and clarified federal court jurisdiction and set the original number of justices at six. It also created the Office of the Attorney General and established the lower federal courts.

district courts Lower level trial courts of the federal judicial system that handle most U.S. federal cases.

closely related so they would be better able to balance Congress. A central debate on this topic was whether to give the judiciary some "revisionary power" over Congress, similar to the president's veto power. This idea of judicial review, which we will discuss more fully below, would have given the Supreme Court the power to strike down laws passed by Congress that violated the Constitution. The framers could not agree on the more general issue of judicial review, so the Constitution remained silent on the matter. As the power of judicial review has evolved, it has become a central part of the system of checks and balances discussed in Chapter 2.

Many details about the Supreme Court were left up to Congress, including its size, the time and place it would meet, and its internal organization. These details, and the system of lower federal courts, were outlined in the **Judiciary Act of 1789**. This law set the number of justices at six (one chief justice and five associates) who were to meet twice a year, in February and August. The number of justices gradually increased to ten by the end of the Civil War and was then restricted to seven (a target that would be reached through retirements) as part of the Reconstruction policies imposed on President Andrew Johnson. The number fell to eight and then was set at nine in 1869, where it has remained since.[7] The act also created a system of federal courts, which included thirteen **district courts** and three circuit courts. The district courts each had one judge, and the circuits were made up of two Supreme Court justices and one district judge. This odd arrangement for staffing the circuit courts remained in place for more than 100 years, over the objections of the justices who resented having to "ride circuit" in difficult traveling conditions.[8] Today, separate judges are appointed to fill the circuit courts. The other

---

NUTS AND BOLTS

13.1

Jurisdiction of the Federal Courts as Defined in Article III of the Constitution

JURISDICTION OF LOWER FEDERAL COURTS

- Cases involving the U.S. Constitution, federal laws, and treaties.
- Controversies between two or more states. (Congress passed a law giving the Supreme Court exclusive jurisdiction over these cases.)
- Controversies between citizens of different states.
- Controversies between a state and citizens of another state. (The 11th Amendment removed federal jurisdiction in these cases.)
- Controversies between a state or its citizens and any foreign states, citizens, or subjects.
- Cases affecting ambassadors, public ministers, and consuls.
- Cases of admiralty and maritime jurisdictions.

- Controversies between citizens of the same state claiming lands under grants of different states.

JURISDICTION OF THE SUPREME COURT

Original Jurisdiction

- Cases involving ambassadors, public ministers, and consuls.
- Cases to which a state is a party.

Appellate Jurisdiction

- Cases falling under the jurisdiction of the lower federal courts, "with such exceptions, and under such Regulations as the Congress shall make."

SOURCE: Lee Epstein and Thomas G. Walker, *Constitutional Law for a Changing America: Institutional Powers and Constraints*, 5th ed. (Washington, DC: CQ Press, 2004), 65.

most important part of the act refined and clarified the jurisdiction of the federal courts. One controversial provision along these lines was Section 25 of the act which expanded the Court's **appellate jurisdiction**, cases that are heard on appeal from lower courts, to include state supreme court cases involving conflicts between state law and federal law or treaties or the U.S. Constitution.

The Supreme Court had a rough start. Indeed, it seemed determined to prove Alexander Hamilton right that it was the weakest branch. Of the six original justices appointed by George Washington, one declined to serve and another accepted the appointment but never showed up for a formal session. The first sessions of the Court lasted only a few days because it did not have much business. In fact, the Court did not decide a single case in 1791 or 1792. When Justice Rutledge resigned in 1791 to take a state court position, two potential appointees turned down the job to keep their positions in their state legislatures! Such career decisions would be unimaginable today, as the Supreme Court is seen as the pinnacle of a legal career.[9]

JUDICIAL REVIEW AND *MARBURY V. MADISON*

The Court started to gain more power and stature when John Marshall was appointed chief justice by outgoing President John Adams in 1801. Marshall served in that position for thirty-four years and single-handedly transformed the Court into an equal partner in the system of checks and balances. The most important step toward that equal partnership was the decision *Marbury v. Madison* (1803) which gave the Supreme Court the power of judicial review. As we noted above, the framers were split on the wisdom of giving the Court the power to strike down laws passed by Congress. However, historians have established that a majority of the framers, including the most influential ones, favored **judicial review**. Why they chose to duck this important issue is a mystery. Given the silence of the Constitution, Marshall simply asserted that the Supreme Court had the power to determine when a law was unconstitutional.

The facts of *Marbury* and the legal reasoning through which the Court claimed the power of judicial review are fairly complicated, but they are worth explaining in some detail because this is one of the most important court cases in American history. The Federalists had just lost the election of 1800 to Thomas Jefferson and the Democratic-Republicans. In a last-minute power grab, the Federalist-controlled lame-duck Congress gave President Adams an opportunity to appoint forty-two new justices of the peace for the District of Columbia (the nation's capital moved to the District of Columbia in 1801) and Alexandria, Virginia. Adams made the appointments, and they were confirmed by the Senate, but time ran out before the new administration took over and the secretary of state John Marshall did not ensure that all of the legal documents concerning the appointments were delivered by midnight (the same Marshall who had just been confirmed as chief justice; as they say in mystery novels, "The plot thickens"). When President Jefferson assumed office, his secretary of state James Madison ordered that at least five of them not be delivered because of partisan differences with the outgoing administration (the historical record is mixed on the exact number of appointments affected). William Marbury was one of the people who did not receive his commission, so he appealed directly to the Supreme Court to have the Court issue an order giving him the position.

As leading figures in opposing parties, Chief Justice Marshall and President Jefferson did not really like each other. This put Marshall in an especially difficult position because he was very concerned that if he issued the order that Marbury

POLITICAL PROCESS MATTERS

 If Jefferson had followed the standard process and approved the commissions that the previous administration approved, one of the most important Supreme Court cases in American history would not have happened.

▲ *William Marbury was the plaintiff in* Marbury v. Madison *(1803), the case that established the principle of judicial review. Although Marbury never got the job he was seeking from his lawsuit, his case established the Supreme Court as an equal partner in the system of checks and balances.*

writs of mandamus Orders issued by a higher court to a lower court, government official, or government agency to perform acts required by law.

wanted (giving Marbury his job), Jefferson probably would ignore it (technically, former president Madison was the other party in the lawsuit, but by this point President Jefferson was calling the shots). Given the weakness of the Court, having such an order disregarded by the president could have been a final blow to its position in the national government. However, if the Court did not issue the order, it would be giving in to Jefferson, despite the merits of Marbury's case—he really had been cheated out of his job. It appeared that the Court would lose whether it issued the order or not.

To get out of the mess, Marshall established the idea of judicial review. While the idea was not original to Marshall (as noted above, the framers debated the issue and Hamilton endorsed it in some detail in *Federalist 78*), the Court had never asserted its authority to rule on the constitutionality of a federal law. Marshall's reasoning was quite clever: the Court's opinion said that Marbury was due his commission, but the Court did not have the power to give him his job because the part of the Judiciary Act of 1789 that gave it that power was unconstitutional! The core issue was Section 13 of the 1789 act which gave the Court the power to issue orders (**writs of mandamus**) to anyone holding federal office. This section of the act expanded the "original jurisdiction" of the Supreme Court, and that was where Congress overstepped its bounds, according to Marshall. The original jurisdiction of the Court is clearly specified in the Constitution, so any attempt by Congress to change that jurisdiction through legislation would be unconstitutional; the only way original jurisdiction could be changed was through a constitutional amendment.[10] Marshall writes, "The question, whether an act, repugnant to the constitution, can become the law of the land, is a question deeply interesting to the United States." He goes on to assert that the Court must answer that question: "It is emphatically the province and duty of the judicial department to say what the law is. . . . If two laws conflict with each other, the courts must decide on the operation of each. So if a law be in opposition to the Constitution . . . the courts must determine which of these conflicting rules governs the case. This is of the very essence of judicial duty."[11]

JUDICIAL REVIEW IN PRACTICE

While Chief Justice Marshall lost the battle—poor Mr. Marbury never did get his job and Jefferson was able to appoint the people he wanted to be justices of the peace—the Supreme Court clearly won the war. By asserting the power of the Court to review the constitutionality of laws passed by Congress, the Court became an equal partner in the institutional balance of power. While it would be more than fifty years until the Court would use judicial review again to strike down a law passed by Congress (in the unfortunate 1857 *Dred Scott* case concerning slavery that basically led to the Civil War), the reasoning of *Marbury* has never been challenged by subsequent presidents or congresses (but see Challenging Conventional Wisdom for an alternative view of *Marbury*).

Interpreting federal laws may be viewed as a logical responsibility for the Supreme Court, even if judicial review is not mentioned in the Constitution. But what about state laws? Should their constitutionality be a matter for state courts to decide, or should the Supreme Court have final say over state laws as well? As with its silence on the broader issue, the Constitution does not directly answer this question. However, the supremacy clause requires that the U.S. Constitution and national laws take precedence over state constitutions and state laws when they conflict. As noted above, the Judiciary Act of 1789 made it clear that the Supreme Court would rule on these matters.

The Irrepressible Myth of *Marbury*

Apparently nothing in the conventional wisdom is sacred: even the origins of judicial review in the landmark decision *Marbury v. Madison* are challenged by revisionist historians, legal scholars, and political scientists. One of the strongest challenges comes from Michael Stokes Paulsen, whose *Michigan Law Review* article is excerpted here:

Nearly all of American constitutional law today rests on a myth. The myth, presented as standard history both in junior high civics texts and in advanced law school courses on constitutional law, runs something like this: A long, long time ago—1803, if the storyteller is trying to be precise—in the famous case of *Marbury v. Madison,* the Supreme Court of the United States created the doctrine of "judicial review." Judicial review is the power of the Supreme Court to decide the meaning of the Constitution and to strike down laws that the Court finds unconstitutional. . . . Judicial review (the myth continues) thus serves as the ultimate check on the powers of the other branches of government, and is one of the unique, crowning features of our constitutional democracy. . . . Indeed, the Court's authority over constitutional interpretation by now must be regarded, rightly, as one of the pillars of our constitutional order, on par with the Constitution itself.

So the myth goes. But nearly every feature of the myth is wrong. For openers, *Marbury v. Madison* did not create the concept of judicial review, but (in this respect) applied well-established principles. . . . Moreover, and also contrary to the mythology that has come to surround *Marbury*, the power of judicial review was never understood by proponents and defenders of the Constitution as a power of judicial supremacy over the other branches, much less one of judicial exclusivity in constitutional interpretation. Nothing in the text of the Constitution supports a claim of judicial

supremacy. . . . Nothing in Chief Justice Marshall's opinion in *Marbury* makes such a claim of judicial supremacy either. The standard civics-book (and law school casebook) myth misrepresents and distorts what John Marshall and the Framers understood to be the power of judicial review: a coordinate, coequal power of courts to judge for themselves the conformity of acts of the other two branches with the fundamental law of the Constitution, and to refuse to give acts contradicting the Constitution any force or effect insofar as application of the judicial power is concerned. [. . .]

Alas, that is not the constitutional world we inhabit today. Instead, we live in a constitutional world in which the Supreme Court is sultan and a perversion of *Marbury v. Madison* is our governing constitutional myth. The myth is, by now, an ingrained one. The Supreme Court lives by the myth. The political branches by and large have accepted it. And it has been taught as Holy Writ to several generations of elementary school and law school students. Disentangling our political culture from the Myth of *Marbury* is not a mere day's work. On this, the occasion of *Marbury's* 200th anniversary, however, it is worth reflecting on the fact that The Myth is a betrayal of everything that *Marbury* stands for, and a betrayal of the written Constitution that *Marbury* identifies as the appropriate object of veneration.[a]

Pretty strong stuff! Once the hyperbole is stripped away (for example, it is unlikely that many elementary school students examine the intricacies of *Marbury*), Paulsen and the other revisionists make several important points.[b] Two of these are already incorporated into this book's account of judicial review and therefore are probably not as "revisionist" as the revisionists would like to think: (1) John Marshall did not invent judicial review. As we note, Hamilton developed the idea in *Federalist* 78 and it was discussed at the Constitutional Convention. (2) The Supreme Court

does not have a monopoly on constitutional interpretation, and Marshall himself did not make the claim of judicial supremacy (a point that is broadly accepted by constitutional scholars even if it is not well understood by the general public).

Three other points made by the revisionists are not as widely cited. (3) *Marbury* was not cited in subsequent Supreme Court cases as a precedent for judicial review until the late nineteenth century. Legal scholars in the early twentieth century were the first to promote the idea that *Marbury* was a landmark decision. (4) When the opinion was delivered in 1803, it was not controversial. Even the Jeffersonian Democrats, who were at odds with Marshall's Federalists, thought that it was a reasonable decision and not the institutional power-grab that is described in modern accounts. (5) Marshall made a very narrow case for judicial review, arguing that the Supreme Court could declare legislation that was contrary to the Court's interpretation of the Constitution null and void only if it concerned judicial powers. Revisionists argue that what appear to be broad claims of judicial power in *Marbury* (e.g., the Court has the power "to say what the law is") are taken out of the context of a much more narrow claim of power.

One reason the revisionist accounts have not received broader acceptance is that they often have a conservative, anti-court agenda. For example, in developing the argument that *Marbury* is significant for establishing the idea that the Constitution should be supreme and be interpreted by all three branches rather than having the courts at the center of this process, Paulsen goes on to say, "constitutional supremacy implies strict textualism as a controlling method of constitutional interpretation, not free wheeling judicial discretion."[c]

While these disputes cannot be resolved here, one key point of agreement between the revisionist and standard accounts of *Marbury* is that the decision established judicial independence by Marshall's assertion of the autonomy of the courts from the other branches. ∎

It didn't take long for the Court to assert its power in this area. In 1796 the Court heard a case concerning a British creditor who was trying to collect a debt from the state of Virginia. The state had passed a law canceling all debts owed by Virginians (or the state) to British subjects. However, the Treaty of Paris, which ended the Revolutionary War and achieved American independence, ensured the collection of such debts. This conflict was resolved when the Court struck down the state law and upheld Americans' commitments under the treaty.[12] While advocates of states' rights were not happy with this development, it was crucial for the national government that the Constitution be applied uniformly rather than be subject to different interpretations by every state. The precise contours of the relationship between the national government and the states were defined in large part by how active the Supreme Court was in asserting its power of judicial review and how willing it was to intervene in matters of state law. As outlined in Chapter 3, for much of the nineteenth century the Court embraced dual federalism, in which the national government and the states operated on two separate levels. Later, the Court became more willing to involve itself in state law as it moved toward a more active role for the national government in regulating interstate commerce and selectively incorporating the amendments that comprise the Bill of Rights under the 14th Amendment (discussed in Chapter 4).

All in all, the Court has struck down more than 160 acts of Congress and about 1,400 state acts. This sounds like a lot, but Congress passed more than 60,000 laws in its first 215 years, so only about one-quarter of 1 percent have been struck down by the Court. The number of state laws passed throughout history is more difficult to measure, but the percentage of state laws that have been struck down is also quite small. The Court has ruled on state laws in many important areas, including civil liberties, desegregation and civil rights, abortion, privacy, redistricting, labor laws, employment and discrimination, and business and environmental regulation.

POLITICS IS CONFLICTUAL

Q State and national laws often conflict with the Constitution. When this happens, the Supreme Court must interpret the laws and strike down those that it views as unconstitutional. This produces political conflict between the political branches and levels of government.

When the Supreme Court strikes down a congressional or state law, it is engaging in **constitutional interpretation**—that is, it determines that the law is unconstitutional. But the Supreme Court also engages in **statutory interpretation** on a regular basis: applying national and state laws to particular cases. Often the language of a statute may be unclear and the Court must interpret how the law should be applied. For example, should the protection of endangered species prevent economic development that may destroy the species' habitat? How does one determine if an employer is responsible for sexual harassment in the workplace? How should the voting rights of minorities be protected? In each of these cases, the Court must interpret the words of the relevant statutes and try to figure out what Congress really meant. Often, this involves the controversial practice of consulting legislative histories—floor debates, congressional hearings, and so on—to determine legislative intent. Justice Antonin Scalia argues that such searches are inherently subjective and that justices should confine themselves to interpreting the actual statutory text.

While judicial review is universally accepted by politicians and other political actors as a central part of the political system, critics of the practice are concerned about its antidemocratic nature. Why do we give nine unelected justices such awesome power over our elected representatives? Debates about the proper role for the Court will continue as long as it is involved in controversial decisions. We will take up this question later in the chapter when we address the concepts of judicial activism and judicial restraint.

The Use of Judicial Review

Scholars and philosophers have described and categorized judicial systems from the time the ancient Greek philosopher Plato examined the various rules of Greek city-states to come up with his ideal legal institutions. However, the practice of judicial review is a much more recent development. The early precursor to judicial review goes as far back as 1180 in the old German Reich, where judicial bodies dealt with disputes between individual rulers. However, the modern practice of judicial review, in which a high court strikes down a law of the national government, started with *Marbury v. Madison* in 1803.

The practice was slow to take hold in the rest of the democratic world. A recent study of judicial review explains why with this summary of British thinking on the subject: "Parliament had the 'right to make or unmake any law whatever; and further, that no person or body is recognized by the law of England as having a right to override or set aside the legislation of Parliament.'"[a] This thinking dominated Europe through the nineteenth and early twentieth centuries, as legislatures were seen as the truest expression of the will of the people. Norway had the first European court to estab-

▲ *Pakistani lawyers and party activists hold portraits of the deposed chief justice of the Supreme Court in May 2008. Then-president Pervez Musharraf sacked forty-one judges because of challenges to his controversial reelection, sparking a nationwide protest and demands for an independent judiciary. The controversy contributed to Musharraf's decision to resign in August 2008.*

lish judicial review in 1866 and several Scandinavian countries did not adopt the practice until a few years ago.[b] Today Great Britain remains one of the few democracies in which courts do not have judicial review of national legislation (though the House of Lords and the European Court of Justice can review the laws of Parliament).

Judicial review has spread dramatically during the "third wave" of democracy. Unlike our hybrid system of checks and balances and separation of powers, which has been largely shunned by established and emerging democracies in favor of the parliamentary form of government, judicial review has become an important American export. Of the seventy nations that became democratic between 1986 and 2000, twenty-nine have some form of judicial review by the courts (in eight of those nations, judicial review is shared with another special body), twenty-four have judicial review by a special body, and only seventeen have limitations on judicial review.[c] Of course, many of these nations have judicial review in name only, as the courts are largely compliant with the dominant regime. Nonetheless, the idea of a court that can check the power of the elected branches of government, especially to protect the political rights of the minority, has become an increasingly important component of democratic governance. ■

SECTION SUMMARY

1. The Founders had mixed views about the role of the Supreme Court. They knew they wanted an independent judicial institution but were not sure how much power it should have.

2. Judicial review made the Supreme Court an equal partner in the system of checks and balances and separation of powers. With the power to strike down the decisions of the other branches, the Court clearly plays a central role in deciding how the government exercises power.

3. Somewhat counter to the popular view of the Court, it is a very *political* institution. Rather than neutrally handing down decisions according to an objective standard, it regularly must resolve conflicts over alternative interpretations of the law. Politics truly is everywhere, even in the judicial system.

plaintiff The person or party who brings a case to court.

defendant The person or party against whom a case is brought.

verdict The final decision in a court case.

plea bargain An agreement between a plaintiff and defendant to settle a case before it goes to trial or the verdict is decided. In a civil case this usually involves an admission of guilt and an agreement on monetary damages; in a criminal case it often involves an admission of guilt in return for a reduced charge or sentence.

standard of proof The amount of evidence needed to determine the outcome of a case. The standard is higher in a criminal case than in a civil one.

burden of proof The responsibility of having to prove guilt; it rests with the plaintiff in criminal cases but could be with either party in a civil trial.

The American Legal and Judicial System

Two sets of considerations are necessary to understand the overall nature of our judicial system: the fundamentals of the legal system that apply to all courts in the United States and the structure of the court system within our system of federalism.

COURT FUNDAMENTALS

The general characteristics of the court system begin with the people who are in the court room. The **plaintiff** brings the case and the **defendant** is the person or party who is being sued or charged with a crime. If the case is appealed, the petitioner is the person bringing the appeal and the respondent is on the other side of the case. In a civil case, the plaintiff is suing to determine who is right or wrong and to gain something of value, such as monetary damages, the right to vote, or admission to a university. For example, imagine that your neighbor accidentally backs his car into the fence that divides your property, destroying a large section of it. The neighbor does not have adequate insurance to cover the damages and refuses to pay for the repairs out of his own pocket. You do not want to pay the $1,000 deductible on your insurance policy, so you (the plaintiff) sue your neighbor (the defendant) to see who is right and whether your neighbor has to pay for the repairs. In a criminal case, the plaintiff is the government and the prosecutor attempts to prove the guilt of the defendant (the person accused of the crime). Many, but not all, civil and criminal cases are heard before a jury that will decide the outcome in the case, which is called the **verdict**. Often cases get settled before they go to a trial (or even in the middle of the trial) in a process known as **plea bargaining**. In a civil case, this would mean that the plaintiff and defendant agree on a monetary settlement and admission of guilt (or not; in some cases the defendant may agree to pay a fine or damages but not have to admit guilt). In a criminal case, the defendant may agree to plead guilty in exchange for a shorter sentence or being charged with a lesser crime.

There are some important differences between civil and criminal cases, such as the **standard of proof** that is used to determine the outcome of the case. In civil cases the jury has to determine whether the "preponderance of evidence," that is, a majority of the evidence, proves that the plaintiff wins. In a criminal case, a much stiffer burden must be met—"beyond all reasonable doubt." Thus, when O. J. Simpson, the former star NFL running back, was accused of murdering his wife and her friend, he was not found guilty in criminal court but lost a civil case and had to pay significant monetary damages. Another difference is where the **burden of proof** lies. In criminal cases there is a presumption of "innocent until proven guilty." That is, the state must prove the guilt of the defendant. However, in civil cases the burden of proof may be on the plaintiff or the defendant depending on the underlying law that governs the case. To make matters even more complicated, in civil cases the plaintiff may have to prove certain points and the defendant other points. For example, in certain race-based voting rights cases, the plaintiff would have to prove that race was the predominant motivation for creating a black-majority congressional district. If that point is demonstrated, then the burden of proof shifts to the defendant to show that there was some "compelling state interest" to justify the use of race as a predominant factor.

▲ O. J. Simpson dons a pair of gloves as part of testimony in his double-murder trial in Los Angeles in June 1995. The jury was not convinced of his guilt "beyond all reasonable doubt" and thus acquitted Simpson in this criminal trial. However, a subsequent civil trial found that a "preponderance of evidence" was against him.

Our Litigious Society

Americans are very litigious—that is, we love to sue. One well-known case involved Stella Liebeck, a seventy-nine-year-old woman who successfully sued McDonald's for $160,000 in actual damages and $480,000 in punitive damages when she spilled a cup of coffee on her lap and received third-degree burns (the original jury award was for $2.9 million, but this was reduced by the court). But Stella is the model of a reasonable litigant compared to people who have sued fast-food chains for making them fat, or a man who sued musician John Fogerty for harming his hearing at a rock concert. Another farfetched suit was filed by the mother of a nineteen-year-old who was killed when he drove into a light pole at 90 miles per hour after drinking beer at a party; she sued Coors Brewing Company, claiming that it promotes underage drinking (the case was dropped).[a] Hot coffee burns you, Big Macs and super-sized fries make you fat, rock concerts are loud, and you shouldn't drive when drunk, especially at 90 miles per hour. Cases like these are headline-grabbers and the staples of late-night television, but they may trivialize an important part of our legal system that imposes accountability on businesses: the class action lawsuit.

Class action lawsuits are civil suits brought by a group of individuals on behalf of themselves and others in the general public who are in similar circumstances. The target of these suits may be corporations that produce hazardous or defective products, or illegal behavior by a company that harmed a particular group. For example, 1.6 million current and former female Wal-Mart employees have sued the retailing giant for sex discrimination, claiming that the store had a pattern of paying women less than men for the same work and promoting fewer women than men. Any woman who has worked at Wal-Mart would be part of the suit if she joined the "class." Suits are often filed on behalf of shareholders of companies that have lost

▲ Class action lawsuits can hold businesses accountable for fraud or selling dangerous products. The tobacco class action lawsuit filed by forty-six states' attorneys general led to the largest civil settlement in U.S. history.

value because of fraud committed by the corporate leaders. Enron, Tyco, WorldCom, Health South, and many other corporations have cost their shareholders billions of dollars through their illegal actions. Class action suits attempt to help shareholders recover some of those losses.

The most famous series of class action suits were filed by smokers against the tobacco industry. In an effort to limit potential liability, the industry reached a landmark settlement in 1998 with forty-six states in which they agreed to pay the states $206 billion over twenty-five years to compensate for the costs associated with smoking. A partial list of other products and industries with class action suits are the airline industry (for price fixing), asbestos, automobile manufacturers, computers and other high-tech devices (such as iPods, cell phones, etc.), Internet service providers, dietary supplements, racial and gender discrimination by many employers, wage disputes (such as failure to pay overtime wages), various environmental issues, the financial sector, the grocery industry, gun makers, the health care industry (especially drugs), the insurance industry, lead paint, oil companies, silicon

implants, tire makers, the tobacco industry, and toxic mold.

In each of these categories, class action suits range from frivolous to extremely important. Our favorite example of a frivolous suit came from a Web site that was trying to attract plaintiffs for the critical issue of "avocado-less guacamole dips." The Web site says, "Los Angeles consumer attorney Ray E. Gallo is investigating alleged fraud in the sale of so-called 'guacamole' that contains relatively little, if any, avocado. . . . If you or someone you know has purchased so-called guacamole dip made by Dean's, Marie's, Herr's, T. Marzetti's or Kraft, you may qualify for damages or remedies that may be awarded in a possible class action lawsuit. Please click on the link below to submit your complaint and we will have a lawyer review your complaint."[b] You have probably eaten some pretty bad guacamole, but are the pain and suffering caused by such "consumer fraud" severe enough to warrant going to court?

On the other hand, class action suits are a very important mechanism for providing accountability and justice in our economic system. Federal regulators do not have the ability to ensure the complete safety of food, drugs, and consumer products. Therefore, consumers rely on the legal system and class action lawsuits to provide businesses with the incentive to produce safe products. If businesses know they will be slapped with a multimillion- (or billion!) dollar lawsuit if they make fraudulent claims or produce a defective product, they will be more likely to operate in an above-board manner. The large settlements that plaintiffs sometimes win are not only to compensate them for actual damages but also to deter future misbehavior on the part of other businesses.

Class action suits have expanded the reach of the legal system to include virtually every American in one class or another, clearly illustrating that politics is everywhere. ■

There are several other characteristics of the judicial system that apply to all cases. First, ours is an **adversarial system** in which lawyers on both sides have an opportunity to present their case, challenge the testimony of the opposing side, and try to convince the court that their version of the events is true. The process of "discovery," in which both sides share the information that will be presented in court, ensures a fair process and few last-minute surprises (contrary to the "Perry Mason moments" that Hollywood loves so much, in which the star of the show comes up with some new evidence or a star witness just minutes before the closing arguments). Second, forty-nine of the fifty states and the federal courts operate under a system of **common law**, which means that legal decisions build from precedent established in previous cases and apply commonly throughout the jurisdiction of the court. The alternative, which is practiced only in Louisiana, is the civil law tradition that is based on a detailed codification of the law that is applied to each specific case.

The notion of **precedent** (or *stare decisis*—"let the decision stand"), deserves special attention. Precedent is a previously decided case or set of decisions that serves as a guide for future cases on the same topic. Lower courts are bound by Supreme Court decisions when there is a clear precedent that is relevant for a given case. In some cases, following precedent is not clear-cut because several precedents may seem relevant. The lower courts have a fair amount of discretion in sorting out which precedents are the most important. The Supreme Court tries to follow its own precedents, but in the past fifty years justices have been much more willing to deviate from earlier decisions when they think that the precedent is flawed. As shown in Table 13.1, there have been more than twice as many decisions overruled by the Court in the past 50 years than in the previous 164 years. Part of this can be explained by the relatively small number of precedents that *could* have been overturned in the first few decades of our history. Indeed, no precedents were overturned in the first three Courts and only a total of four in the first eighty-five years of the nation's history. But even accounting for this natural accumulation of more precedents to potentially overturn, recent courts have been much more willing to deviate from precedent than previous courts. As this record indicates, precedent is not a rule the Court must follow but a norm that constrains its behavior.

Finally, two more points must be considered before a case is filed. First, the person bringing the case must have **standing** to sue in a civil case, which means that there is a legitimate basis for bringing the case. This usually means that the individual must have suffered some direct and personal harm from the action that is being addressed in the court case. Standing is easy to establish for private parties— if your neighbor destroys your fence, you have been harmed. However, it gets more interesting when the government is a party. For example, when an environmental group challenged the Interior Department's interpretation of the Endangered Species Act, the Court ruled that it did not have standing because it did not demonstrate that the government's policy would cause "imminent" injury to the group.[13] Similarly the Court has ruled that thirty-one members of Congress did not have standing to challenge American bombing in Kosovo and taxpayers do not have standing to sue the government if they disagree with a specific policy.[14] Depending on your politics, you may not want your hard-earned cash going to buy school lunches for poor children or to fund the war in Iraq. However, your status as a taxpayer does not give you enough of a personal stake in these policies to challenge them in court. You would not have standing.

adversarial system A two-sided court structure in which lawyers on both sides of a case attempt to prove their argument over their opponents' version of the case.

common law Law based on the precedent of previous court rulings rather than on legislation. It is used in all federal courts and forty-nine of the fifty state courts.

precedent A legal norm established in court cases that is then applied to future cases dealing with the same legal questions.

standing Legitimate justification for bringing a civil case to court.

TABLE 13.1 **SUPREME COURT CASES OVERRULING PRECEDENT AND ACTS OF CONGRESS, 1789–2003**

The Supreme Court has overruled precedent in a far higher proportion of cases in the past 50 years than it did during the first 160 years of U.S. history. More acts of Congress have also been struck down in recent years—but even in some earlier periods, the Court has played an activist role. What do these data say about the role of Supreme Court within our constitutional system?

COURT (CHIEF JUSTICE)	YEARS	CASES OVERRULING PRECEDENT	PRECEDENTS OVERRULED	CASES OVERRULING ACTS OF CONGRESS	ACTS OVERRULED PER YEAR
Jay Court	1789–1795	0	0	0	0
Rutledge Court	1795	0	0	0	0
Ellsworth Court	1796–1800	0	0	0	0
Marshall Court	1801–1836	1	1	1	0.03
Taney Court	1836–1864	2	3	1	0.03
Chase Court	1864–1874	1	1	8	0.8
Waite Court	1874–1888	9	11	7	0.5
Fuller Court	1888–1910	3	4	13	0.52
White Court	1910–1921	4	4	10	1.1
Taft Court	1921–1930	5	6	13	1.44
Hughes Court	1930–1941	15	22	15	1.36
Stone Court	1941–1946	8	11	1	0.20
Vinson Court	1946–1953	6	11	2	0.28
Warren Court	1953–1969	37	53	23	1.44
Burger Court	1969–1986	46	62	31	1.82
Rehnquist Court	1986–2003	37	43	34	2

Note: This table only includes cases in which the reversal of precedent is clearly stated in the Court decision. A single case can overrule more than one precedent.

SOURCE: David G. Savage, *Guide to the Supreme Court*, 4th ed. (Washington, DC: CQ Press, 2004), p. 320.

The final general characteristic of the legal system is the **jurisdiction** of the court—when bringing a case before the court, you have to make sure you have chosen a court that actually has the power to hear your case. A simple example: if you want to contest a speeding ticket, you would not file your case in the state supreme court or the federal district court, but in your local traffic court. What if you believed you were the victim of discrimination in the workplace? Would you sue in state or federal court? You probably could do either, but the decision would be based on which set of laws would provide you more protection from discrimination. This obviously will vary by state, so the proper jurisdiction for a given case is often a judgment call based on specific legal questions (this practice of seeking the best court for your case is called "venue shopping").

STRUCTURE OF THE COURT AND FEDERALISM

The structure of the court system is just like the rest of the political system: it is divided within and across levels of government. Across the levels of government, the court system operates on two parallel tracks within the state and local courts and the national courts. Within each level of government, both tracks are comprised of courts of original jurisdiction, appeals courts, and courts of special jurisdiction (see Figure 13.1). There is much variation in the structure of state courts in terms of

jurisdiction The sphere of a court's legal authority to hear and decide cases.

FIGURE 13.1   THE STRUCTURE OF THE COURT SYSTEM

The system of federalism means that we have a two-track court system at the national and at the state and local levels. What advantages and disadvantages of this two-track system can you think of?

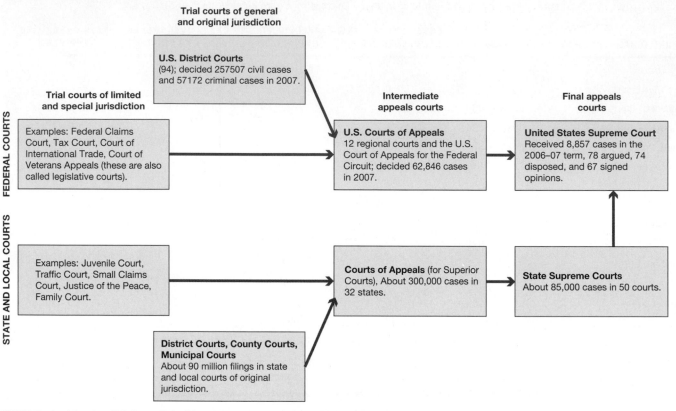

SOURCE: Caseload data from U.S. Courts, Federal Court Management Statistics, available at http://www.uscourts.gov/fcmstat/index.html; and U.S. Supreme Court, Chief Justice's Year-End Report on the Federal Judiciary, 2007, available at http://www.supremecourtus.gov/publicinfo/year-end/2007year-endreport.pdf.

their names and the number of levels of courts. However, they all follow the same general pattern of trial courts with limited and general original jurisdiction and appeals courts (either one or two levels, depending on the state).

The federal courts are also comprised of the general and limited jurisdiction courts, but there are some additional important differences between these types of courts at the federal level. The **constitutional courts**, which include the district courts, appeals courts, and Supreme Court, are established under Article III of the Constitution (and the legislative power granted to Congress under Article III to create new courts), while the limited jurisdiction courts are established under Article I, the legislative article of the Constitution. The Constitution gave Congress the power to "constitute tribunals inferior to the Supreme Court"; therefore, these courts are often called the **legislative courts**.

There are several important differences between the legislative and general courts. First, the legislative courts hear cases that are concerned with enforcing specific statutes within a given area, such as tax law or law concerning international trade. Second, these courts can have "quasi-judicial," administrative, or even legislative functions, whereas the general courts only have judicial roles. Third, while all federal judges are nominated by the president and confirmed by the Senate, judges on legislative courts serve fixed terms, whereas the other federal judges serve as long as they want during "good behavior."[15]

constitutional courts Those courts established under Article III of the Constitution (or under the legislative power granted to Congress in Article III to create new courts): the Supreme Court, district courts, and appeals courts.

legislative courts Limited jurisdiction courts created by Congress under Article I of the Constitution.

District Courts As we briefly outlined earlier, the lower federal courts were created by the Judiciary Act of 1789. The district courts are the workhorses of the federal system. District courts handle more than a quarter of a million filings a year, and their workload has steadily increased over the past half-century. There are eighty-nine districts in the fifty states, with at least one district court for each state. There are also district courts in Puerto Rico, the Virgin Islands, the District of Columbia, Guam, and the Northern Mariana Islands, to bring the total to ninety-four districts with 678 judges.[16] There are two limited jurisdiction district courts: the Court of International Trade, which addresses cases involving international trade and customs issues, and the United States Court of Federal Claims, which handles most claims for money damages against the United States, disputes over federal contracts, unlawful "takings" of private property by the federal government (a rapidly growing area of federal law), and other claims against the United States.

Appeals Courts The **appeals courts** (or "circuit courts," as they were called until 1980) are the intermediate courts of appeals, but in practice they are the final court for most federal cases that are appealed from the lower courts. The losing side in a federal case can appeal to the Supreme Court, but given that the highest court in the land hears so few cases, the appeals courts usually get the final word. Appeals courts did not always have this much power; in fact through much of the nineteenth century they were "judicial stepchildren."[17] They had very limited appellate jurisdiction and did not hear many significant cases. The only real effort to create an independent set of federal appellate courts in the first 100 years of our nation's history was the aborted effort by the outgoing Adams administration in 1800. As part of the Federalists' plan to stack the federal courts (recall the maneuver with the justice of peace positions which led to *Marbury v. Madison*), the Federalists created

---

FIGURE 13.2 **MAP OF THE FEDERAL APPEALS COURTS**

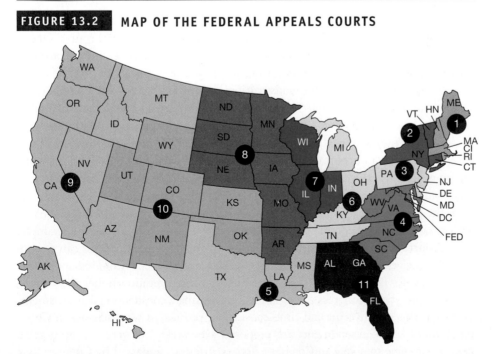

SOURCE: U.S. Courts, Circuit Map, available at http://www.uscourts.gov/courtlinks.

appeals courts The intermediate level of federal courts that hear appeals from district courts. More generally, an appeals court is any court with appellate jurisdiction.

eighteen appeals court judgeships that were filled at the last minute by President Adams and a sympathetic Senate. Rather than allow the Federalists to have that much power over the federal courts, the incoming Jefferson administration and the Democratic-Republican Congress simply abolished these courts the next year (possibly in violation of the Constitutional mandate of life tenure for federal judges, but that was a fight that Chief Justice John Marshall did not want to take on).

In 1869 the circuit courts finally were given some of their own judges rather than being staffed entirely by district court judges and Supreme Court justices, which meant the Supreme Court justices had to "ride circuit" only once every two years.[18] The Judiciary Act of 1891 created nine regional circuit courts and expanded their appellate jurisdiction to include most cases from the district courts. This process of expanding the power of the appeals courts was largely completed in the 1925 Judiciary Act.[19] Today the only appeals of district court cases that go directly to the Supreme Court and bypass the appeals court are cases that concern legislative reapportionment and redistricting, voting rights, and some issues related to the 1964 Civil Rights Act.[20] The number of appeals courts slowly expanded as the workload grew, to the current twelve regional courts (the eleven numbered districts shown in Figure 13.2, plus the appeals court for the District of Columbia) and the Court of Appeals for the Federal Circuit which handles specialized cases from all over the country. The smallest of the regional appeals courts is the First Circuit, which has nine judges, and the largest is the Ninth Circuit with twenty-eight judges.[21] In 2007, there were 179 appeals court judges and 96 "senior judges" (these numbers include the twelve judges and four senior judges of the appeals court for the federal circuit).[22] Senior judges are retired judges who hear certain cases to help out with the overall workload; they typically handle about 15 percent of the workload for the federal court system.

The Supreme Court The Supreme Court sits at the top of the federal courts. The rest of this chapter will outline many of the important aspects of the Court, including how cases get to the Court, nominations, decision making, and relations to the other branches. The immediate discussion concerns the Court's place within the judicial system and its relationship to the other courts. The Supreme Court is the "court of last resort" for cases coming from both the state and federal courts. One of the important functions of the Court is to resolve conflicts between lower courts, or between a state law and federal law, or between the states, to ensure that the application and interpretation of the Constitution is consistent across the United States. For example, before the Court took up the issue of affirmative action in higher education, there were several conflicting lower court decisions, which meant that affirmative action was legal in certain parts of the country and unconstitutional in other parts. A district court or appeals court ruling is applicable only for the specific region of that court, whereas Supreme Court rulings apply to the entire country.

While the Supreme Court is the most important interpreter of the Constitution, the president and Congress also interpret the Constitution on a regular basis. This means that the Supreme Court does not always have the final say. For example, if the Court strikes down a federal law for being overly vague, Congress can rewrite the law to clarify the offending passage. When this happens, Congress may have the final word. Even on matters of constitutional interpretation rather than statutory interpretation, Congress can fight back by passing a constitutional amendment. However, this is a difficult and time-consuming process; as we discussed in Chapter 2, hundreds of amendments are proposed every year, but very few even get a hearing or come to a vote in Congress, and even fewer are passed by Congress and submitted to the states for ratification. Nevertheless, that option is available as a way of overturning an unpopular Court decision. Perhaps the best example of this is the very first major case ever decided by the Supreme Court—*Chisholm v. Georgia* (1793). This case upheld the right of a citizen of one state to sue the citizens of another state in federal court. The states were shocked by this challenge to their sovereignty and a constitutional amendment to overturn the decision quickly made its way through Congress. By 1798 the 11th Amendment had been ratified and citizens of states could no longer sue each other in federal court.

HOW JUDGES ARE SELECTED

There are many different mechanisms for placing judges in courts. At the national level, which we will discuss in more detail below, the president makes the nominations with the advice and consent of the Senate, while there are many different methods used in the states.

State-Level Judges At the state level there are five different means for selecting judges for trial courts: appointment by the governor (two states), appointment by the state legislature (two states), partisan elections (nine states), nonpartisan elections (seventeen states), and the system called the Missouri Plan in which the governor makes appointments from a list that has been compiled by a nonpartisan screening committee (seventeen states; four more states use the Missouri Plan for some courts and another means for other courts).[23] With this last method, the appointed judge usually has to run in a retention election within several years of the appointment, making this system a hybrid of the political nomination and popular election routes to the court.

There is some controversy over the wisdom of electing judges. Elections certainly mean that courts will be more responsive to public opinion, but they may undermine the courts' role as the protector of unpopular minority rights. Also, even in states where judicial elections are officially nonpartisan, it is quite clear who the liberal and conservative candidates are, so judicial elections can be very partisan. Interest groups are often involved in the process, by making endorsements or running their own advertisements for or against the judicial candidates.

> ## POLITICAL PROCESS MATTERS
>
> ☑ The method of selecting judges has an impact on the courts' accountability. Thirty states have at least some elections for judges, allowing voters to remove judges with whom they are unhappy. All federal judges are appointed, have life tenure, and can be removed only by impeachment.

Federal Judges The Constitution does not specify requirements for serving on the federal courts, unlike the detailed stipulations for Congress and the president. Federal judges don't even have to have a law degree! (This is probably due to the limited number of law schools at the time of the founding; it was far more common for someone who wanted to be a lawyer to serve as an apprentice to learn the trade rather than going to a law school.) The president nominates federal judges with the "advice and consent" of the Senate.

The nomination battles for federal judges can be intense because the stakes are high. As the discussion of judicial review made clear, the Supreme Court plays a central role in the policy process, and because a justice has life tenure, a justice's impact can outlive the president and Senate who put him on the Court. While presidents can serve only eight years and the average tenure for a House member or Senator is around ten years, the justices serving in the last term of the Rehnquist Court (1986–2005) had an *average* of twenty years of experience. Chief Justice Rehnquist had the longest tenure at thirty-three and a half years; (the record is held by William O. Douglas at thirty-six and a half years). That group of justices had the second longest tenure together in history (from July 29, 1994, through September 29, 2005; the longest was just over twelve years, from 1812 to 1824 under John Marshall). When John Roberts replaced William Rehnquist as the new chief justice and Samuel Alito replaced Sandra Day O'Connor, the average tenure of the current Court fell, but it is still a safe bet that most justices will serve longer than the president or average member of Congress.

The Role of the President Given the Constitution's silence on the qualification of federal judges, presidents have broad discretion over whom to nominate. Presidents have always tried to influence the direction of the Court by picking people who share their views on important issues. Because the Senate often has different ideas about the proper direction for the Court, nomination disputes end up being a combination of debates over the merit and qualifications of a nominee and bare-fisted partisan battles about the ideological composition of the Court.

While presidents would *like* to influence the direction of the Court, it is not always possible to predict how judges will behave once they are on the Court. Earl Warren is probably the best example. He was appointed by Republican president Dwight Eisenhower and had been the Republican governor of California, yet he turned out to be one of the most liberal chief justices in the last century. Eisenhower called Warren's nomination the biggest mistake he ever made.[24] On the current Court, Justices Stevens and Souter were nominated by Republican presidents (Ford and Bush senior, respectively), but they regularly vote with the liberal bloc.

The president can make a good guess about how a justice is likely to vote based on the nominee's party affiliation and the nature of his or her legal writings and decisions (if he or she has prior judicial experience). Not surprisingly, 98 of 108 justices who have served on the Court have shared the president's party (just over 90 percent). Overall, more than 90 percent of the lower court judges appointed by presidents in the twentieth century have also belonged to the same party as the president. The lowest percentage of same-party appointments for any president in the twentieth century was 81 percent by Gerald Ford, who faced a strongly Democratic Senate when he became president after Richard Nixon resigned because of the Watergate scandal. Ford hoped that giving nearly a fifth of his judicial appointments to Democrats would help bring the country together.[25]

At the other extreme, the most partisan move to influence the Court was Franklin Delano Roosevelt's infamous plan to pack the Court. FDR was frustrated because the Court had struck down several pieces of important New Deal legislation, so to get a more sympathetic Court, he proposed nominating a new justice for every justice who was over seventy years old. Six justices were older than seventy, so this would have increased the size of the Court to fifteen. This effort to disguise the partisan power play as a humanitarian gesture (to help the old-timers with their work load) didn't fool anyone. The plan to pack the Court ran into opposition, but in what has been dubbed the "switch in time that saved nine," the Court started ruling in favor of the New Deal legislation, so the plan was dropped. In addition to the ideological considerations about whom to nominate, the president also considers the reputation of the potential nominee as a legal scholar and his personal relationship to the candidate, as well as the candidate's ethical standards, gender, and race (see Table 13.2 for data on the latter two points).

The other half of the equation to determine the composition of the federal courts is the Senate. The Senate has shifted from a very active role in providing its "advice and consent" on court appointments to a passive role and then back to an active role. One constant in the role of the Senate is that nominees are rarely rejected because of their qualifications, but rather for political reasons. Of twenty-eight nominees rejected by the Senate in the history of the United States (twelve by a roll call vote in the Senate and sixteen that were withdrawn or not acted upon), only two were turned down because they were seen as unqualified: George Williams in 1873 and G. Harold Carswell in 1970; serious questions were also raised about a third, cur-

TABLE 13.2 **THE DEMOGRAPHICS OF THE FEDERAL BENCH**

All presidents try to appoint qualified candidates to the federal courts; however, there is variation in the types of people they nominate. Identify some characteristics common to most judges and some that vary across presidents. Which traits vary by the president's party?

	W. BUSH**		CLINTON		BUSH		REAGAN		CARTER	
Experience										
Judicial	53%	(44)	52%	(159)	47%	(69)	46%	(134)	54%	(109)
Prosecutorial	51%	(42)	41%	(126)	39%	(58)	44%	(128)	38%	(77)
Neither	23%	(19)	29%	(88)	32%	(47)	29%	(83)	31%	(63)
Average age at nomination	50.3		49.5		48.2		48.6		49.6	
Law school education										
Public	53%	(44)	40%	(121)	53%	(78)	45%	(130)	52%	(105)
Private	40%	(33)	41%	(124)	33%	(49)	43%	(126)	31%	(63)
Ivy League	7%	(6)	20%	(60)	14%	(21)	12%	(34)	17%	(34)
Gender										
Male	80%	(66)	72%	(218)	80%	(119)	92%	(226)	86%	(173)
Female	21%	(17)	29%	(87)	20%	(29)	8%	(24)	14%	(29)
Ethnicity/race										
White	86%	(71)	75%	(229)	89%	(132)	92%	(268)	79%	(159)
African American	7%	(6)	17%	(53)	7%	(10)	2%	(6)	14%	(28)
Hispanic	7%	(6)	6%	(18)	4%	(6)	5%	(14)	7%	(14)
Asian	–	–	1.3%	(4)	–	–	0.7%	(2)	0.5%	(1)
Native American	–	–	0.3%	(1)	–	–	–	–	–	–
Percentage white male	69%	(57)	52%	(160)	73%	(108)	85%	(246)	68%	(137)
Political identification										
Democrat	7%	(6)	88%	(267)	6%	(9)	5%	(14)	91%	(184)
Republican	83%	(69)	6%	(19)	89%	(131)	92%	(266)	5%	(9)
Other	–	–	0.3%	(1)	–	–	–	–	–	–
None	10%	(8)	6%	(18)	5%	(8)	3%	(10)	5%	(9)
Net worth										
Under $200,000	5%	(4)	13%	(41)	10%	(15)	18%	(52)	36%*	(53)
$200–499,999	22%	(18)	22%	(66)	31%	(46)	38%	(109)	41%	(61)
$500–999,999	17%	(14)	27%	(82)	26%	(39)	22%	(63)	19%	(28)
$1+ million	57%	(47)	38%	(116)	32%	(48)	23%	(66)	4%	(6)
Total number of appointees	83		305		148		290		202	

*These figures are for appointees confirmed by the 96th Congress for all but six Carter district court appointees (for whom no data were available).
**Data through 2003.

SOURCE: Sheldon Goldman, Elliot Slotnick, Gerard Gryski, and Gary Zuk, "W. Bush Remaking the Judiciary: Like Father Like Son," *Judicature* 86:6 (2003): 304.

▲ Since the late 1960s the Senate has become more assertive in providing "advice and consent" on Supreme Court nominations. The confirmation hearings for Justice Clarence Thomas in 1991 were among the most contentious in recent decades. Thomas was confirmed by the second-narrowest margin in U.S. history for a Supreme Court justice (52–48).

rent justice Clarence Thomas, who had served for only eighteen months as a federal judge before being nominated to the Court. Thomas also was accused in a highly charged Senate Judiciary Committee hearing of sexual harassment by a former colleague. Thomas won confirmation by a 52–48 vote, the second narrowest successful margin in history. The other twenty-six nominees were rejected for political reasons. The most common reason is when a "lame duck" president makes a nomination and the Senate is controlled by the opposing party, the Senate often kills the nomination, hoping that its party will win the presidency and will nominate a justice more to its liking. John Tyler holds the record for having *five* nominations killed in the last fifteen months of his presidency (from January 1844 through March 1845) by a Senate controlled by the opposing party.

Throughout the nineteenth century the Senate was very willing to turn down Court nominations for political reasons. In fact, twenty-one nominees were not confirmed by the Senate from 1793 through 1894 (about a third of the total number of nominees). Then in the first half of the twentieth century the Senate allowed presidents to appoint whom they wanted. Between 1894 and 1968 only one nominee, Judge John Parker, nominated by Herbert Hoover in 1930, was defeated. The Senate did not even require nominees to testify throughout this period.

A rethinking of this passive role emerged in the late 1960s. President Nixon vowed to move the Court back from the "liberal excesses" of the Warren Court, but the Senate stiffened its spine and rejected two nominees in a row in 1969 (Clement Haynsworth) and 1970 (Harold Carswell). For Haynsworth there were some ethical problems having to do with his participation in cases in which he had a financial interest. As noted above, Carswell had a mediocre judicial record and civil rights groups raised questions about his commitment to enforcing antidiscrimination laws. Nixon must have thought that the Senate wouldn't reject him twice in a row! The most recent Senate rejection was of Judge Robert Bork, a brilliant, very conservative, and controversial figure. Liberal interest groups mobilized against him and the Senate rejected him by the widest margin of any nominee since 1846 (the vote was 42 to 58), giving the English language a new verb: to get "borked" means to have your character and record challenged in a very public way.

The contentious battles between the president and the Senate over nominees to the federal bench and the Supreme Court have recently expanded to include nominees to the district and appeals courts as well. For much of the nation's history the president did not play a very active role in the nomination process for district courts, instead deferring to the home-state senator of the president's party to suggest candidates—a norm called **senatorial courtesy**. If there was no senator of the president's party from the relevant state, the president would consult House members and other high-ranking party members from the state. The president typically has shown more interest in appeals court nominations. The Justice Department plays a key role in screening candidates, but the local senators of the president's party remain active as well.

For the last fifteen years, the process has become much more contentious. As Figure 13.3a shows, the confirmation rate for federal judges has gone from between about 80 and 100 percent to less than 50 percent in recent years. When Republicans took control of the Senate in 1995, they stopped more than sixty of President Clinton's nominees to the lower federal courts through a process of holds (when a single senator can stop a nomination) and committee action. The average length of delay from nomination to confirmation has increased from less than 50 days in the mid-1960s through the mid-1980s to more than 200 days in the most recent

POLITICS IS CONFLICTUAL

Recent confrontations between the president and the Senate raise central questions about the Senate's proper role in providing "advice and consent" in federal court nominations. Since there are no clear constitutional answers to this question, it will surely remain an area of political conflict.

senatorial courtesy A norm in the nomination of district court judges in which the president consults with his party's senators from the relevant state in choosing the nominee.

Advice and Consent: Principled Opposition or Obstructionism?

Battles over court nominations have become even more tense in the last few years as Senate Democrats stopped ten of President Bush's lower court nominees through the filibuster (recall that forty-one senators can stop action on any bill or nomination through a filibuster). After winning reelection in 2004, President Bush resubmitted seven nominees who had been rejected in the previous Senate (and thirteen more who were nominated in the previous term but did not come up for a vote). Heartened by the increase in the number of Republicans in the Senate from fifty-one to fifty-five, President Bush and Republican leaders in the Senate believed they could pick off enough moderate Democrats to get the sixty votes needed to stop a filibuster. However, the Democrats drew a line in the sand, indicating that they were not going to abandon the filibusters. In 2005, the Republican leadership in the Senate considered implementing the "nuclear option," which would have prevented filibusters on judicial nominations (this plan gets its name because Democrats threatened to basically shut down the Senate if they lost the filibuster). This crisis was defused when the "Gang of 14"—seven moderate Republicans and seven moderate Democrats—agreed to a compromise that preserved the Democrats' right to filibuster, but only in the most extreme cases.

Put yourself in the place of a Democratic senator on the Judiciary Committee. The nominee before you is William Myers III for the Ninth Circuit, which covers nine western states and large tracts of federal lands. Myers has no prior judicial experience and has served as the head attorney in the Interior Department since 2001. In his private practice in Boise, Idaho, he was primarily an advocate and lobbyist for the ranching and mining industries, including a stint as director of Federal Lands for the National Cattlemen's Beef Association from 1993 to 1997. Myers has strongly opposed many of the na-

▲ During President George W. Bush's second term, Republicans controlled the Senate for the first two years and Democrats for the second two. For the first two years, Democrats used the filibuster to throw a wrench into the gears and stop Bush's most conservative judicial nominees. After they controlled the majority, Democrats were in a stronger bargaining position with the president.

tion's environmental laws, comparing them to King George's "tyrannical" rule over the colonies, saying that they could lead to a "modern-day revolution" in western states. You come from a "red state" (that voted for President Bush), but many of your core supporters are strong environmentalists who opposed Myers's nomination. In general, you think that President Bush should be able to appoint whom he would like to the federal courts, but you are concerned that he has gone too far with this nomination. Myers doesn't seem very qualified and he could do some serious damage to the nation's environmental laws with his lifetime tenure on the court. How do you vote on the nomination?

Now put yourself in the place of a Republican senator. You strongly favor President Bush's right to nominate whom he wants to the federal courts. You favor the president's free-market, pro-business policies and believe that many of the nation's en-

vironmental laws are hurting the economy. Therefore, you think that Myers would be a great judge. However, the Democrats are dead-set opposed and are threatening to filibuster his nomination again. You have to decide whether to support the "nuclear option" to take away the Democrats' right to filibuster the nomination. There are at least fifty-six votes in favor of Myers, but not the sixty needed to cut off the filibuster. On the one hand, you don't think it is fair that Democrats are obstructing the vote. On the other hand, you were in the Senate back when the Republicans were in the minority, and you remember how important the filibuster was to protect the views of the minority party. You are worried that supporting the "nuclear option" would seriously damage the institution that you value and respect as the world's greatest deliberative body. What do you do? ■

Presidential nominations to the federal courts have had a tougher time in recent years, in terms of both the rejection rate and time it takes to get nominees confirmed by the Senate. What accounts for these changes?

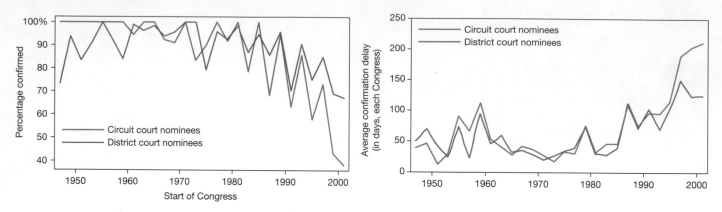

SOURCE: Forrest Maltzman, "Advice and Consent: Cooperation and Conflict in the Appointment of Federal Judges," in *The Legislative Branch*, ed. Paul J. Quirk and Sarah Binder (New York: Oxford University Press), pp. 410–11. Data compiled from Final Legislative and Executive Calendars, Senate Judiciary Committee, 80th–105th Congresses. Data for 106th and 107th Congresses compiled from the U.S. Senate Committee on the Judiciary, http://judiciary.senate.gov.

period (see Figure 13.3b). The situation has become even tenser in the last few years (see You Decide).

While there is no definitive answer to the battles over how active the Senate should be in giving its "advice and consent"—especially how much power a minority of forty-one senators should have—it is clear that the Founders intended the Senate to play an active role. The first draft of the Constitution gave the Senate the sole power to appoint Supreme Court justices. However, the final version of the Constitution made the appointment power a shared power with the goal of promoting responsibility through the president's role and "security" through the Senate's role. It was not expected that the Senate would compete with the president over whom to nominate, but it *was* assumed that it would exercise independent judgment as to the suitability of the president's nominees. Furthermore, the Founders did not expect the process to be free of politics, or that the Senate would be an essentially passive and subordinate player in a nominally joint enterprise. Even George Washington had two of his nominations turned down by the Senate for political reasons! Therefore, politics will continue to play an important role in deciding who serves on the federal bench.

SECTION SUMMARY

1. There are fundamental characteristics of the court system that distinguish the different types of cases: who can bring a case, which court has jurisdiction over the case, and what the burdens of proof are.

2. The federalist nature of the U.S. government defines another important characteristic of the court system: the parallel state and federal systems.

3. Within each system there is great variation in how judges are selected, but in all instances the contests over nominations reveal the political nature of the judicial branch of government.

Access to the Supreme Court

docket A calendar listing of cases that have been submitted to a court.

It is extremely difficult to have a case heard by the Supreme Court. Currently the Court hears fewer than 1 percent of the cases submitted (70 of about 8,000 to 9,000 cases). This section will explain how the Court decides which cases to hear. When a case is submitted to the Court, the clerk of the Court assigns it a number and places it on the **docket**. There used to be two dockets, one for poor people who could not afford the $300 filing fee (these cases are called *in forma pauperis* [IFP], which is Latin for "in the form of a pauper") and one for the regular cases, but since 1970 there has been a single docket. Now the only difference between regular cases and IFP cases is in how they are numbered and the number of copies of the brief that have to be filed with the Court.[26]

THE SUPREME COURT WORKLOAD

Statistics on the Supreme Court's workload initially suggest that the size of the docket has increased dramatically, from fewer than 5,000 cases a year in the 1970s to nearly 9,000 cases a year in recent sessions (see Figure 13.4). However, all of that increase has come from IFP cases, which have increased from about 2,200 cases a year in the 1970s and 1980s to more than 7,000 cases in the last session. The number of "paid" cases has actually dropped from about 2,500 cases a year in the 1980s to fewer than 1,800 in the past two terms.[27] Most of the IFP cases are frivolous and are dismissed after limited review. One law clerk described the IFP petitions as "sometimes handwritten, occasionally illegible, and often inscrutable."[28] The Court has become increasingly impatient with these frivolous petitions and has moved to prevent "frequent filers" from harassing the Court. One often-cited case involved Michael Sindram, who asked the Court to order the Maryland courts to remove a $35 traffic ticket from his record. Our favorite example concerned a wealthy drug dealer, Frederick W. Bauer, who was convicted on ten counts of dealing drugs (seven counts involved a total of 4,100 pounds of marijuana, two counts for nearly

---

FIGURE 13.4 THE COURT SEES MORE OPPORTUNITIES . . . BUT HEARS FEWER CASES

The Supreme Court's workload appears to be headed in two directions: the Court is receiving more cases but hearing fewer of them. What are the implications of having the Supreme Court hear fewer cases? Should something be done to try to get the Court to hear more cases?

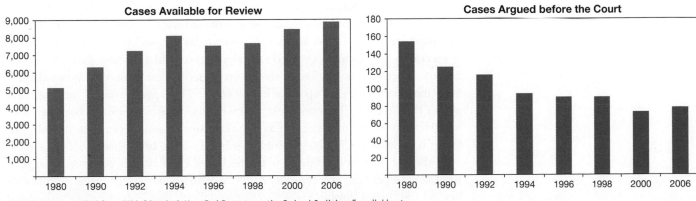

SOURCE: Data compiled from "Chief Justice's Year-End Reports on the Federal Judiciary," available at http://www.supremecourtus.gov/publicinfo/year-end/year-endreports.html.

250 pounds of cocaine, and one count for six gallons of hashish oil and a package of black gum hashish) and repeatedly petitioned the Court *in forma pauperis*. In his initial trial he applied for a court-appointed attorney (which is supplied for people who cannot afford their own legal counsel) but was turned down because a court hearing revealed that he had "unencumbered assets [that] totaled almost $500,000." The court found the petitioner's testimony that he was poor was "ambiguous, evasive and in many respects completely incredible."[29] Bauer petitioned the Court twelve times on various issues and finally the justices had had enough. They ruled that "Bauer has repeatedly abused this Court's certiorari and extraordinary writ processes" and directed "the Clerk not to accept any further petitions for certiorari or petitions for extraordinary writs from Bauer in noncriminal matters" unless he paid his docketing fees. They concluded that the order will "allow this Court to devote its limited resources to the claims of petitioners who have not abused our processes."[30]

While the increase in workload is not as significant as it appears, another change in how cases are handled by the Court is more important: the number of opinions issued by the Court has fallen by more than half in the past twenty years. The Court issued about 170 to 180 opinions a year through the 1980s, but this number has fallen to only 65 to 75 in recent years (see Figure 13.4).[31] The change is even more dramatic when one considers that the Court has reduced the number of "summary decisions" it issues (cases that do not receive a full hearing, but the Court rules on the merits of the case) from 150 a year in the 1970s to a handful today. The number of summary judgments declined when Congress gave the Court more control over its docket and virtually eliminated the number of cases that it was required to hear on appeal. However, there is no good explanation for why the Court issues half as many opinions as it used to, other than Chief Justices William Rehnquist and John Roberts think that the Court shouldn't issue so many opinions.[32]

RULES OF ACCESS

With the smaller number of cases that are being heard, it is even more important to understand the winnowing process. There are four paths that a case may take to get to the Supreme Court. First, Article III of the Constitution specifies that the Court has **original jurisdiction** in cases involving foreign ambassadors, foreign countries, or cases in which a state is a party. As a practical matter, the Court shares jurisdiction with the lower courts on these issues. In recent years, the Court invoked original jurisdiction only in cases involving disputes between two or more states over territorial or natural resource issues. For example, New Jersey and New York had a disagreement about which state should control about twenty-five acres of filled land that the federal government had added around Ellis Island. Another case involved a dispute between Kansas and Colorado over who should have access to water from the Arkansas River (recent disputes often concern water rights).[33] If original jurisdiction is granted and there are factual issues to be resolved, the Court will appoint a "special master" (usually a retired federal judge) to hold a hearing, gather evidence, and make a recommendation to the Court. This process is necessary because the Supreme Court is not set up to be a trial court. The "special master" arrangement allows the Court to function in its normal capacity as an appeals court by treating the master's recommendation as a lower court decision, even if technically the Court is a trial court in these original jurisdiction cases. In the history of our nation, only about 175 cases have made it to the Court through this path, an average of less than one per year, and typically these cases do not have any broader significance beyond the parties involved.[34]

The other three routes to the Court are all on appeal, either as a matter of right (usually called "on appeal"), through certification, or through the writ of certiorari.

Cases on appeal are those that Congress has determined to be so important that the Supreme Court must hear them. Before 1988 these cases comprised a larger share than today of the Court's docket and included cases in which a lower court declared a state or federal law unconstitutional or in which a state court upheld a state law that had been challenged as unconstitutional under the U.S. Constitution. As noted above, since 1988, Congress gave the Court much more discretion on these cases; the only ones that the Court is still compelled to take on appeal are some voting rights and redistricting cases. A **writ of certification** is when an appeals court asks the Court to clarify a federal law in a specific case. The Court can agree to hear the case, but given that appeals court judges are the only people who can make these requests, this path to the Court is very rare (in fact, in a search of Supreme Court cases in the past ten years, we could not find any that came to the Court through certification).

The third path is the most common: in fact, at least 95 percent of the cases in most sessions arrive through a **writ of certiorari** (from the Latin "to be informed"). In these cases, a litigant who lost in lower court can file a petition to the Supreme Court explaining why it should hear the case. If four justices agree, the case will get a full hearing (this is called, reasonably enough, the "Rule of Four"). While this may sound simple, the process of sifting through the 8,500 or so cases that the Court receives every year and deciding which 70 of them will be heard is daunting. Former justice William O. Douglas said that this winnowing process was "in many respects the most important and interesting of all our functions."[35]

▲ On rare occasions the Supreme Court serves as a court of original jurisdiction. One of those unusual times is when there is a dispute between two states, such as when the Court had to settle a disagreement between New York and New Jersey over Ellis Island.

THE COURT'S CRITERIA

How does the Court decide which cases to hear? Several factors come into play including the specific characteristics of the case and the broader politics surrounding it. While several criteria generally must be met before the Court will hear the case, justices still have leeway in defining the boundaries of these conditions.

Collusion, Mootness, and Ripeness First, there are the constitutional guidelines, which are sparse. The Constitution limits the Court to hearing actual "cases and controversies," which has been interpreted to mean that the Court cannot offer advisory opinions about hypothetical situations, but must be dealing with an actual case. The term "actual controversy" also includes several other concepts that limit whether a case will be heard: collusion, mootness, and ripeness. **Collusion** simply means that the litigants in the case cannot want the same outcome and cannot be testing the law without an actual dispute between the two parties.[36]

Mootness means that the controversy must still be relevant when the Court hears the case. For example, a student sued a law school for reverse discrimination, saying that he had not been admitted because of the university's affirmative action policy. A lower court agreed and ordered that the student be admitted. The appeals court reversed the decision, but the student was allowed to remain enrolled while the case was appealed to the Supreme Court. By the time the Court received the case, the student was in his last semester of law school and the university said that he would graduate no matter the outcome of the case. Therefore, the Court refused to hear the case because it was moot.[37] However, there have to be exceptions to this principle because some types of cases would always be moot by the time they got

cases on appeal Cases brought before the Supreme Court because Congress has determined that they require the Court's attention.

writ of certification An uncommon way in which a case is brought before the Supreme Court, whereby an appeals court asks the Court to clarify federal law in regards to a particular case.

writ of certiorari The most common way for a case to reach the Supreme Court, in which at least four of the nine justices agree to hear a case that has reached them via an appeal from the losing party in a lower court's ruling.

collusion Agreement between the litigants on the desired outcome of a case, causing a federal court to decline to hear the case. More generally, collusion can refer to any kind of conspiracy or complicity.

mootness The irrelevance of a case by the time it is received by a federal court, causing the court to decline to hear the case.

ripeness A criterion that federal courts use to decide whether a case is ready to be heard. A case's ripeness is based on whether its central issue or controversy has actually taken place.

cert pool A system initiated in the Supreme Court in the 1970s in which law clerks screen cases that come to the Supreme Court and recommend to the justices which cases should be heard.

to the Supreme Court. For example, exceptions have been made for abortion cases because a pregnancy lasts only nine months and the time that it takes to get a case from district court, to the appeals court, to the Supreme Court always takes longer than that.

Ripeness can be considered the opposite of mootness. With mootness the controversy is already over; with ripeness the controversy has not started yet. Just as you wouldn't want to eat a piece of fruit before it is ripe, the Court doesn't want to hear a case until it is ripe. Sometimes ripeness can affect standing. One example is the line item veto, which Congress gave to President Clinton at the start of his second term. Almost immediately some members of Congress challenged the constitutionality of the law because they believed that the president should not be able to veto part of a bill. A district court agreed with the members of Congress and ruled that the law was unconstitutional. The case was appealed to the Supreme Court, but it refused to hear the case: because the issue was not ripe, the members of Congress did not have standing. That is, President Clinton had not yet used the line item veto, so there was no controversy and the members had not been harmed. Two months later, Clinton used the veto, another case was filed, and the Court eventually struck down the law.[38] One other type of case will generally not be heard by the Court—those involving "political questions." We will return to this important topic later in the chapter.

Thousands of cases every year meet these basic criteria. One very simple guideline eliminates the largest number of cases: if a case does not involve a "substantial federal question" it will not be heard. This is clearly the vaguest criterion; it means that the Court does not have to hear a case if it does not think the case is important enough. This still leaves about 20 to 30 percent of the cases that are winnowed to the final list with the more specific guidance of Rule 10 in the Supreme Court rules (see Nuts and Bolts 13.2).

Internal Politics Not much is known about the actual discussions that determine which cases will be heard. The justices meet in conference with no staff or clerk. Leaks are rare, but a few insider accounts and the papers of retired justices have provided some insights into the process. First, since the late 1970s most justices have used a **cert pool** in which the law clerks take a first cut at the cases (the law clerks

POLITICAL PROCESS MATTERS

☑ The process of winnowing involves a great deal of discretion on the part of the justices, but a variety of basic requirements must be met before a case can be heard.

NUTS AND BOLTS

13.2

Rule 10 and Writs of Certiorari

A case is more likely to be heard by the Supreme Court when:

- there is conflict between appeals court opinions,
- there is conflict between a federal appeals court and a state supreme court on a substantial federal question,
- a lower court decision has "departed from the accepted and usual course of judicial proceedings,"
- a state court or appeals court has ruled on a substantial federal question that has not yet been addressed by the Court,
- a state supreme court or appeals court ruling conflicts with Supreme Court precedent.

Rule 10 also states that certiorari is unlikely to be granted when "the asserted error consists of erroneous factual findings or the misapplication of a properly stated rule of law."

SOURCE: U.S. Supreme Court, *Rules of the U.S. Supreme Court,* adopted January 27, 2003, effective May 1, 2003, available at http://www.supremecourtus.gov/ctrules/rulesofthecourt.pdf.

to the justices are the top graduates of the elite law schools in the nation who help justices with background research at several stages of the process). Clerks write joint memos about groups of cases, providing their recommendations about which cases should be heard. The ultimate decisions are made by the justices, but clerks have significant power to help shape the agenda. The only justice who does not use the cert pool is John Paul Stevens (his poor clerks have to sift through all of the cases!). Second, the chief justice has an important agenda-setting power: he decides the "discuss list" for a given day. Any justice can add a case to the list, but there is no systematic evidence on how often this happens. As noted above, only 20 to 30 percent of the cases are discussed in conference, which means that about three-quarters of the cases that are submitted to the Supreme Court are never even discussed by the Court. Of course, in most cases this is completely justified because of the high proportion of frivolous suits submitted to the Court.[39]

Many factors outside the legal requirements or internal processes of the Court influence access to the Court and which cases will be heard. Cases that have generated a lot of activity from interest groups or other governmental parties, such as the solicitor general, are more likely to be heard. The **solicitor general** is a presidential appointee who works in the Justice Department and supervises the litigation of the executive branch. In cases in which the federal government is a party, the solicitor general or someone from that office will represent the government in court. The Court accepts about 70 to 80 percent of cases in which the U.S. government is a party compared to fewer than 1 percent overall.[40]

Even with these influences, the Court has a great deal of discretion on which cases it hears. Well-established practices such as standing, ripeness, and mootness may be ignored (or at least modified) if the Court wants to hear a specific case. As legal scholar H. W. Perry points out, "What makes a case important enough to be certworthy is a case [the justices] consider important enough to be certworthy."[41] However, one final and very important point must be noted on this topic: while the justices may pick and choose their cases, they cannot set their own agenda. They can only select from the cases that come to them. If, for example, they thought that the Endangered Species Act was an unfair burden on the expansion of logging in old-growth forests, the justices could not make their opinions known on that issue until someone filed a lawsuit and there was an actual "case or controversy."

SECTION SUMMARY

1. Fewer than 1 percent of all appeals to the Supreme Court are actually heard by the Court.

2. Cases may reach the Supreme Court by original jurisdiction, on appeal, or a writ of certification, but by far the most common route to the Court is through a writ of certiorari.

3. Cases that are heard by the Court must be "cases and controversies" and must consider collusion, ripeness, and mootness.

4. Even after considering all of these factors, justices still have a great deal of discretion over which cases they will hear.

Hearing Cases before the Supreme Court

A surprisingly small proportion of the Court's time is actually spent hearing cases—only forty days in the 2007–08 term. The Court is in session from the first Monday in October through the end of June or early July. It hears cases on Mondays through Wednesdays in alternating two-week cycles in which it is in session from 10 A.M. to 3 P.M. with a one-hour break for lunch. In the other two weeks of the cycle, justices review briefs, write opinions, and sift through the next batch of petitions. On most Fridays when the Court is in session the justices meet in conference to discuss cases that have been argued and decide which cases they will hear. Opinions are released throughout the term, but the bulk of them come in May and June.[42]

The Court is in recess from July through September. Justices may take some vacation, but they mostly use the time for study, reading, writing, and preparing for the next term. During the summer the Court will also consider emergency petitions (such as stays of execution) and occasionally will hear important cases. For example, during the Watergate scandal of Richard Nixon's presidency, the Court was asked to decide whether the president had to hand over tapes of conversations that had been secretly recorded in the White House. In a unanimous ruling on July 24, 1974, the Court said that Nixon had to release the tapes. Two weeks later Nixon resigned.[43] More recently, on September 8, 2003 (a month before the fall session started), the Court heard a challenge to the Bipartisan Campaign Reform Act, more commonly known as the McCain–Feingold Act after its two principal sponsors. Congress urged the Court to give the law a speedy review given its importance for the upcoming 2004 elections. On December 10, 2003, the Court upheld most of the law's provisions.[44]

BRIEFS

During the regular sessions, the Court follows rigidly set routines. The justices prepare for a case by reading the **briefs** that are submitted by both parties. Because the Supreme Court hears only appeals, it does not call witnesses or gather new evidence. Instead, the parties present their arguments about why they either support the lower court decision or believe the case was improperly decided in tightly structured briefs of no more than fifty pages. Interest groups often submit ***amicus curiae*** ("friend of the court") briefs that convey their opinions to the Court; in fact, 85 percent of cases before the Supreme Court have at least one *amicus* brief. In a typical term in the 1990s there were about 400 *amici curiae* with an average of about 5 groups cosigning each brief for a total of about 1,800 organizational participants.[45] The federal government also files *amici curiae* on important issues such as school busing, school prayer, abortion, reapportionment of legislative districts, job discrimination against women, and affirmative action in higher education. It is difficult to determine the impact *amici curiae* have on the outcome of a case, but *amici curiae* that are filed early in the process increase the chances that the case will be heard. Interestingly, even *amici curiae* that are filed *against* a case increase the chances that the case will be heard.[46] Given the limited information that justices have about any given case, interest group involvement can be a strong signal about the importance of a case.

briefs Written documents prepared by both parties in a case, and sometimes by outside groups, presenting their arguments in court.

amicus curiae Latin for "friend of the court," referring to an interested group or person who shares relevant information about a case to help the Court reach a decision. Usually *amicus* participants register their opinions in briefs, but they also may participate in oral arguments if one of the parties in the case gives them some of their allotted time.

ORAL ARGUMENT

Once the briefs are filed and have been reviewed by the justices, cases are scheduled for **oral arguments**. Except in unusual circumstances, each case gets one hour, which is divided evenly between the two parties. In especially important cases, extra time may be granted. For example, the campaign finance case mentioned above had four hours of oral argument. Usually there is only one lawyer for each side who presents the case, but parties that have filed *amicus* briefs may participate if their arguments "would provide assistance to the Court not otherwise available." Given the tight time pressures, the Court is usually unwilling to extend the allotted time to allow "friends of the court" to testify (Court rules say that "such a motion will be granted in only the most extraordinary circumstances").[47] The relevant party can share part of its thirty minutes if it wants, but that doesn't happen often. Therefore, the participation of friends of the court is usually limited to written briefs rather than oral arguments.

The Court is strict about its time limits and uses a system of three lights to show the lawyers how much time is left. A green light goes on when the speaker's time begins, a white light provides a five-minute warning, and a red light means to stop. Most textbooks cite a few well-known examples of justices cutting people off in midsentence or walking out of the courtroom as the hapless lawyer drones on. One leading source on the Court implies that these anecdotes are generally revealing of Court procedure, saying, "Anecdotes probably tell as much about the proceeding of the Court during oral argument as does any careful study of the rules and procedures."[48] However, having a preference for "careful study" over anecdotes, we were curious about how common it was for justices to strictly impose the time limits. We examined forty-two cases from the 2004–05 term, using the online transcripts at the Court's Web site.[49] We found that most lawyers did not use all their allotted time, with 62 percent of the cases coming in under sixty minutes, 17 percent exactly an hour, and 21 percent over an hour. One-sixth of the lawyers still had at least five minutes left on the clock, which means they probably should have practiced their presentation a few more times in front of the mirror or the family dog. We found only two instances in which a justice cut someone off in midsentence after the person had gone over the one-hour limit. In one case an attorney asked, "May I finish this?" and then went on to speak another several sentences. Thus, while the Court

oral arguments Spoken presentations made in person by the lawyers of each party to a judge or appellate court outlining the legal reasons why their side should prevail.

▲ *Cameras are not allowed in the Supreme Court, so artists' sketches are the only images of oral arguments. This sketch shows George W. Bush's attorney general, Michael Mukasey (right), addressing the court.*

tries to stay within its time limits, it is not quite as draconian as some anecdotes may have us believe.

Some lawyers may not use all of their time because their train of thought is interrupted by aggressive questioning. Transcripts reveal that justices jump in with questions almost immediately and some attorneys never regain their footing. The frequency and pointedness of the questions vary by justice, with Justices Scalia, Breyer, and Ginsburg being the most aggressive on the current Court while Justice Thomas often goes months at a time without asking a single question. Cameras are not allowed in the courtroom, so most Americans have never seen the Court in action—though a small live audience is admitted every morning the Court is in session. However, if you are curious about oral arguments, audio recordings have been made of every case since 1995 and are available at http://www.oyez.org.

CONFERENCE

After oral arguments the justices meet in conference to discuss and then vote on the cases. As with the initial conferences, these meetings are conducted in secret. We know, based on notes in the personal papers of retired justices, that the conferences are orderly and structured but can become quite heated. The justices take turns discussing the cases and outlining the reasons for their positions. Justice Thurgood Marshall described the decision-making process in conference and the need for secrecy as

> a continuing conversation among nine distinct individuals on dozens of issues simultaneously. The exchanges are serious, sometimes scholarly, occasionally brash and personalized, but generally well-reasoned and most often cast in understated, genteel language. . . . The months-long internal debate on a case often focuses on how much law to change or make. Sometimes, cases come right down to the wire. . . . In other cases, a majority of justices start down one path, only to reverse direction. . . . This is the kind of internal debate that the justices have argued should remain confidential, taking the position that only their final opinions have legal authority. They have expressed concern that premature disclosure of their private debates and doubts may undermine the court's credibility and inhibit their exchange of ideas.[50]

OPINION WRITING

After justices indicate how they are likely to vote on a case, the most senior justice in the majority decides who will write the majority opinion. Usually this is the chief justice; for example, Warren Burger assigned 1,891 of the 2,201 opinions (about 86 percent) when he was chief justice in the 1970s and 1980s.[51] Many considerations come into play in deciding how a case will be assigned. First, the chief justice will try to ensure the smooth operation of the Court. Along these lines, in 1989, Chief Justice Rehnquist announced a change in how he assigned opinions. In his first three terms, he simply tried to give each justice the same number of cases, but he recognized that "this policy does not take into consideration the difficulty of the opinion assigned or the amount of work that the 'assignee' may currently have backed up in his chambers. . . . It only makes sense in the assignment of additional work to give some preference to those who are 'current' with respect to past work."[52] A second factor is the justices' individual areas of expertise. For example, Justice Blackmun had developed expertise in medical law when he was in private practice, including extensive work at the famous Mayo Clinic. This experience played a role in Chief Justice Burger's decision to assign Blackmun the majority opinion in the landmark abortion decision, *Roe v. Wade*. Likewise, Justice O'Connor developed expertise in racial redistricting cases and authored most of those decisions in the 1990s.

The final set of factors is more strategic and includes the Court's external relations, internal relations, and personal policy goals of the opinion assigner. The Court must be sensitive to how others might respond to its decisions because it must rely on the other branches to enforce its decisions. One famous example of this consideration in an opinion assignment came in a case from the 1940s that struck down a practice that had prevented African Americans from voting in Democratic primaries.[53] Originally, the opinion was assigned to Justice Felix Frankfurter, but Justice Robert Jackson wrote a memo suggesting that it might be unwise to have a liberal, politically independent Jew from the northeast write an opinion that was sure to be controversial in the South. Chief Justice Harlan Fiske Stone agreed and reassigned the opinion to Justice Stanley Reed, a Protestant and Democrat from Kentucky.[54] It may not seem that the Court is sensitive to public opinion, but these kinds of considerations happen fairly frequently in important cases. Internal considerations occasionally cause justices to vote strategically—different from the justice's sincere preference—in order to be in the majority so the justice can assign the opinion (often to himself or herself).

Justices may also assign opinions to help achieve their personal policy goals. The most obvious way to do this is for the chief justice to assign opinions to justices who are closest to his position. Obviously, this practice is constrained by the first point—ensuring the smooth operation of the Court. If the chief justice assigned all the opinions to the justices who are closest to him ideologically, then justices with other ideological leanings would get a chance to write opinions only in the 15 to 20 percent of cases in which the chief is in the minority. Clearly that wouldn't work. Charles Hughes, who was chief from 1930 to 1941, sometimes assigned opinions on liberal decisions to conservative justices and conservative opinions to liberal justices to downplay the importance of ideology on the Court.[55]

While these constraining factors prevent the assigning justice from using opinion assignments to further his policy goals in most cases, there is evidence of this type of behavior on the most important Court cases. One study found that on cases with a large number of *amicus* briefs (a good measure of importance), the justice who is closest to the chief is 61 percent more likely to get the assignment than the justice who is most distant from the chief.[56] This same study also found that the chief justice was more likely to assign the opinion to justices who were ideologically distant from the chief when it was necessary to hold together fragile coalitions. For example, a case decided by a 5–4 vote was more than twice as likely to go to a justice who was distant from the chief than a case that was decided by at least a 7–2 margin.[57] This shows that the chief justice is willing to set aside his own policy views when it is important to hold together a coalition. These same patterns tended to hold when associate justices made the assignments rather than the chief justice. The most significant difference was that associate justices were not quite as constrained by the desire to balance the workload.

After the opinions are assigned, the justices work on writing a draft. Law clerks typically help with this process. Some justices still insist on writing all of their opinions, while others allow a clerk to write the first draft. The drafts are circulated for comment and reactions to the other justices. Some bargaining may occur, in which a justice says he or she will withdraw support unless a provision is changed. Justices may join the majority opinion, they may write a separate concurring opinion, or they may dissent (see Nuts and Bolts 13.3 for details on the types of opinions).

Types of Supreme Court Decisions

Majority opinion: The core decision of the Court that must be agreed upon by at least five justices. The majority opinion presents the legal reasoning for the Court's decision.

Concurring opinion: Written by a justice who agrees with the outcome of the case but not with the legal reasoning. Concurring opinions may be joined by other justices. A justice may sign on to the majority opinion and write a separate concurring opinion.

Plurality opinion: Occurs when a majority cannot agree on the legal reasoning in a case. The plurality opinion is the one that has the most agreement (usually three or four justices). Because of the fractured nature of these opinions, they typically are not viewed as having as much clout as majority opinions.

Dissent: Submitted by a justice who disagrees with the outcome of the case. Other justices can sign on to a dissent or write their own, so there can be as many as four dissents. Justices can also sign on to part of a dissent but not the entire opinion.

Per curiam opinion: (Latin for "by the court") An unsigned opinion of the Court or a decision written by the entire Court. However, this is not the same as a unanimous decision that is signed by the entire Court. Per curiam opinions are usually very short opinions on noncontroversial issues, but not always. For example, *Bush v. Gore*, which decided the outcome of the 2000 presidential election, was a per curiam opinion. Per curiam decisions may also have dissents.

Two final points should be made about the process of writing and issuing opinions. First, until the 1940s there was a premium placed on unanimous decisions. This practice was started by John Marshall, who was chief justice from 1800 to 1835. Through the 1930s, about 80 to 90 percent of decisions were unanimous. This changed dramatically in the 1940s, when most cases had at least one dissent. In recent decades about two-thirds of cases have a dissent. Dissents serve an important purpose. Not only do they allow the minority view to be expressed, but they also often provide the basis for reversing a poorly reasoned case. When justices strongly oppose the majority opinion, they may take the unusual step of reading a portion of the dissent from the bench.

SECTION SUMMARY

1. There are several steps in the process of hearing a case before the Supreme Court. First, interested parties submit briefs to the Court outlining their arguments about how they think the case should be decided.
2. Next, the Court hears oral arguments, usually thirty minutes for each side.
3. After hearing the case, the justices meet in conference to discuss the case.
4. Finally, the opinions are assigned and written, outlining the reasons for the Court's decision. This part of the process involves a great deal of political maneuvering and bargaining among the justices.

Supreme Court Decision Making

There are many different influences on judicial decision making. The two main categories are legal and political. The legal factors include the precedent of earlier cases and norms that justices must follow the language of the Constitution. Political influences include the justices' preferences or ideologies, their stances on whether the Court should take a restrained or activist role with respect to the elected branches, and external factors such as public opinion and interest group involvement. Some scholars dispute these basic categories, arguing that all court behavior is political and that the use of legal factors is just a smoke screen for hiding personal preferences.

LEGAL FACTORS

Those who put forward the legal view usually present their position in normative terms; that is, justices *should* be led by precedent and the words of the Constitution. Advocates of this view recognize that justices often stray from these legal norms, but they criticize the interjection of personal preferences as a harmful politicization of the courts. Our view is that legal factors are often used as justification for political positions on the Court, but they also independently influence judicial decision making on a broad range of cases.

Precedent The most basic legal factor is *stare decisis* or precedent, which we discussed above. Precedent does not determine the outcome of any given case, because every case has a range of precedent that can be drawn upon to justify a justice's decision. The "easy" cases, in which settled law makes the outcome obvious, are less likely to be heard by the Court because of its desire to focus on the more controversial areas of unsettled law. However, there are areas of the law, such as free speech, the death penalty, and search and seizure, in which precedent is an important explanation in how justices decide a case.

The Language of the Constitution The various perspectives that emphasize the language of the Constitution all fall under the heading of **strict construction**. The most basic of these is the literalist view of the Constitution. Sometimes this view is also referred to as a textualist position because it sees the text of the document as determining the outcome of any given case. Literalists argue that justices need to look no farther than the actual words of the Constitution. Justice Hugo Black was one of the most famous advocates of this position. When the 1st Amendment says that "Congress shall make no law . . . abridging the freedom of speech," that literally means *no* law. Justice Black said, "My view is, without deviation, without exception, without any ifs, buts, or whereases, that freedom of speech means that government shall not do anything to people . . . either for the views they have or the views they express or the words they speak or write."[58] While that may be clear enough with regard to political speech, how about pornography, Internet speech, or symbolic speech, such as burning an American flag or wearing an armband to protest the Vietnam War? A literal interpretation of the Constitution does not necessarily help determine whether these forms of speech should be restricted. Indeed, Hugo Black was one of the two dissenters in a case that upheld students' right to wear armbands as a form of symbolic speech. Black believed that school officials should be allowed to decide whether a symbolic protest would be too disruptive in the classroom. So much for "without deviation, without exception"!

Critics of strict construction also point out that the Constitution is silent on many important points (such as a right to privacy) and could not have anticipated the changes in technology in the twentieth and twenty-first centuries that have many legal implications, such as eavesdropping devices, cloning, and the Internet. Also, while the language of the 1st Amendment is relatively clear, other equally important words of the Constitution such as "necessary and proper," "executive power,"

▲ Mary Beth Tinker and two other students in the Des Moines, Iowa, public schools were suspended for wearing armbands to protest the Vietnam War. The Supreme Court ruled that the 1st Amendment protected symbolic political speech, even in public schools. Mary Beth is shown here with her mother at the trial. (Photo by Dave Penney, Copyright 1965, The Des Moines Register and Tribune Company. Reprinted with permission.)

"equal protection," and "due process" are open-ended and vague. Some strict constructionists respond by arguing that if the words of the Constitution are not clear, the justices should be guided by what the Founders *intended*, a perspective called the **original intent** or originalist perspective. Clarence Thomas is the current justice who is most influenced by this view, especially on issues of federalism. Justice Antonin Scalia has a similar view, arguing that the text of the Constitution should be closely followed and if the text is ambiguous, justices should figure out what the words generally meant to people at the time they were written. This view leads Scalia to some unpopular positions, such as his view that the 6th Amendment provision that "in all criminal prosecutions the accused shall enjoy the right . . . to be confronted with the witnesses against him" applies even in the case of an accused child molester. The majority of the Court held that it was acceptable to have the child testify in front of the prosecutor and defense attorney, with the judge, jury, and the accused viewing from another room over closed-circuit television because of the potential trauma the child would experience by having to confront the defendant face-to-face.[59]

Critics of the strict constructionist view are often described as supporting a **living Constitution** perspective on the document. They argue that originalism or other versions of strict construction can "make a nation the prisoner of its past, and reject any constitutional development save constitutional amendment."[60] If the justices are bound to follow the literal words of the Constitution, *with the meaning they had when the document was written*, we certainly could be legally frozen in time. The option of amending the Constitution is a long and difficult process, so that is not always a viable way for the Constitution to reflect changing norms and values.

POLITICAL FACTORS

The living Constitution perspective points to the second set of influences on Supreme Court decision making: political factors. As we noted in the introduction to this chapter, many people are uncomfortable thinking about the Court in political terms and prefer to think of the image of "blind justice," in which constitutional principles are fairly applied. However, political influences are clearly evident in the Court—maybe less than in Congress or the presidency, but they are certainly present.

Political Ideology and Attitudes The most important political factor is the justice's ideology or attitudes about various issues (this is often called the **attitudinalist approach** to understanding Supreme Court decision making). Liberal judges are strong defenders of individual civil liberties, including defendants' rights, tend to be pro-choice on abortion, support regulatory policy to protect the environment and workers, support national intervention in the states, and favor race-conscious policies such as affirmative action. Conservative judges favor state regulation of private conduct (especially on moral issues), support prosecutors over defendants, tend to be pro-life on abortion, and support the free market and property rights over the environment and workers, states' rights over national intervention, and a color-blind policy on race. These are, of course, just general tendencies. However, they do provide a strong basis for explaining patterns of decisions, especially on some types of cases. For example, there were dramatic differences in the chief justices' rulings on civil liberties cases from 1953 to 2001: Earl Warren took the liberal position on 79 percent of the 771 cases he participated in, Warren Burger took the liberal position on 30 percent of 1,429 cases, and William Rehnquist took the liberal position on only 22 percent of his 2,127 cases.[61] If justices were

POLITICS IS EVERYWHERE

A variety of political factors enter into Supreme Court decision making despite the common view that justices are above politics and reach their decisions based on objective factors.

neutrally applying the law, there would not be such dramatic differences.

Proponents of the attitudinalist view also argue that justices who *claim* to be strict constructionists or originalists are really driven by ideology because they selectively use the text of the Constitution. For example, in the University of Michigan affirmative action case, Justice Thomas did not consider whether the authors of the 14th Amendment supported affirmative action (a brief review of the historical record would have shown that they did). Therefore, if Justice Thomas had been true to his originalist perspective, he would have supported affirmative action, but his ideology led him to oppose the policy.

▲ *Chapter 5 cited a survey in which most respondents were unable to name any Supreme Court justices. Just so you are not in danger of falling into that category, as of fall 2008 the justices are (front row, left to right) Anthony M. Kennedy, John Paul Stevens, John G. Roberts (chief justice), Antonin Scalia, and David Souter; (standing, left to right) Stephen Breyer, Clarence Thomas, Ruth Bader Ginsburg, and Samuel Alito Jr.*

The Strategic Model A strategic approach to understanding Supreme Court decision making focuses on justices' calculations about the preferences of the other justices, the president, and Congress, the choices that other justices are likely to make, and the institutional context within which they operate. After all, justices do not operate alone: at a minimum they need the votes of four of their colleagues if they want their position to prevail. Therefore, it makes sense to focus on the strategic interactions that take place to build coalitions. The median voter on the Court—the one in the middle when the justices are arrayed from the most liberal to the most conservative—has an especially influential role in the strategic model. For many years the median justice was Sandra Day O'Connor; when Samuel Alito replaced her, Anthony Kennedy became the new median. The four conservatives to his right (Thomas, Scalia, Roberts, and Alito) and the four liberals to his left (Breyer, Ginsberg, Souter, and Stevens) all would like to attract his vote. Research shows that at least one justice switches his or her vote at some stage in the process (from the initial conference to oral arguments to the final vote) on at least half of the cases, so strategic bargaining appears to be fairly common.[62] Our earlier discussion of opinion assignment and writing opinions to attract the support of a specific justice is more evidence in support of the strategic model.

Separation of Powers Another political influence on justices' decision making is their view of the place of the Court with respect to the democratically elected institutions (Congress and the president). Specifically, do they favor an activist or a restrained role for the Court? Advocates of **judicial restraint** argue that judges should defer to the elected branches and not strike down their laws or other actions. On the other hand, advocates of **judicial activism** argue that the Court must play an active role in interpreting the Constitution to protect minority rights even if it means overturning the actions of the elected branches. Yet another approach says that these normative arguments about how restraint or activism ought to work are fine and good, but they don't really matter because the Court usually follows public opinion and rarely plays a lead role in promoting policy change. One scholar found that three-fifths to two-thirds of Supreme Court decisions are consistent with public opinion when the public has a clear preference on an issue.[63] However, there are plenty of examples of when the Court has stood up for unpopular views, such as banning prayer in schools, allowing flag burning, and protecting criminal defendants' rights.

Often, assessments of the Court's role vary with the views of a specific line of cases. A political conservative may favor a series of "activist" decisions striking down

judicial restraint The idea that the Supreme Court should defer to the democratically elected executive and legislative branches of government rather than contradicting existing laws.

judicial activism The idea that the Supreme Court should assert its interpretation of the law even if it overrules the elected executive and legislative branches of government.

environmental laws or workplace regulations but oppose activist decisions that defend flag burning or defendants' rights. Political liberals may be the opposite—calling for judicial restraint on the first set of cases but activism when it comes to protecting civil liberties. Sometimes, the popular media mistakenly assert that liberal justices are more activist than conservative justices. In fact, that is not always the case. The current Court is quite conservative, but it is also activist.[64] The 1930s Court that struck down much of the New Deal legislation was also conservative and activist, but the Warren Court of the late 1950s and early 1960s was liberal and activist (see Table 13.1). Two conservatives, Justice Kennedy and Justice Thomas, have voted to overturn laws passed by Congress 93 percent and 81 percent of the time, respectively, whereas two of the most liberal justices, Breyer and Ginsburg, have taken the activist position in only 42 percent and 48 percent of the cases.[65]

A prominent legal journalist observed that the way the popular media describe activism and restraint typically boils down to ideology: if you like a decision, it is restrained; if you do not like a decision, it is activist. For example, *Bush v. Gore*, the decision that decided the outcome of the 2000 presidential election, shows that "most conservatives tie themselves in knots to defend judicial activism when they like the results and to denounce it when they do not. As the reaction to *Lawrence* [the recent gay sex case] and, earlier, *Roe* [the landmark abortion case] has shown, liberals have been no less selective in their outrage at judicial adventurousness."[66] There are instances in which restraint is more than ideology and preferences. Justice O'Connor, for example, took restrained positions on abortion and affirmative action, despite her personal views against these policies. However, it is important to define activism and restraint in terms of the Court's role in our system of separated powers: does it check the elected branches by overturning their decisions through judicial review? This is the only objective way to define activism and restraint.

Outside Influences: Interest Groups and Public Opinion Finally, there are external influences on the Court, such as public opinion and interest groups. We have already talked about the role of interest groups in filing *amicus* briefs. This is the only avenue of influence open to interest groups; other tactics such as lobbying or fundraising are either inappropriate or irrelevant (because justices are not elected). The role of public opinion is more complex. Obviously, justices do not consult public opinion polls the way elected officials do. However, there are several indirect ways that the Court expresses the public's preferences. The first was most colorfully expressed by Mr. Dooley, a fictional Irish American bartender who was created at the turn of the nineteenth century by a newspaper satirist named Finley Peter Dunne. Mr. Dooley offered keen insights on politics and general social criticism, including this gem on the relationship between the Supreme Court and the public, "no matter whether th' constitution follows th' flag or not . . . th' supreme coort always follows th' iliction returns."[67] That is, the public elects the president and the Senate, who nominate and confirm the justices. Therefore, sooner or later, the Court should reflect the views of the public. Subsequent work by political scientists has confirmed this to be largely the case,[68] especially in recent years when Supreme Court nominations have become more political and more important to the public.[69]

The second mechanism through which public opinion may influence the Court is more direct: when the public has a clear position on an issue that is before the Court, the Court tends to agree with the public. One study found that the "public mood" and Court opinions correlated very highly between 1956 and 1981, but their association was weaker through the rest of the 1980s.[70] Several high-profile examples support the idea that the Court is sensitive to public opinion: the Court's switch during the New Deal in the 1930s to support Roosevelt's policy agenda after standing in the way for four years, giving in to wartime opinion to support the internment of Japanese Americans during World War II, limiting an accused child molester's right to confront his accuser in a court room, declaring that the execution of mentally retarded defendants was "cruel and unusual punishment," and declaring that laws limiting sex between consenting gay adults were unconstitutional. In each of these cases the justices reflected the current public opinion of the nation rather than a strict reading of the Constitution or the Founders' intent. Sometimes the Court may shift its views to reflect *international* opinion.

The most recent example struck down the death penalty for minors in twelve states. Ruling by a 5–4 margin that the execution of sixteen- or seventeen-year-olds violated the 8th Amendment's prohibition against "cruel and unusual punishments," the majority opinion overturned a 1989 case and said the new decision was necessary to reflect the "evolving standards of decency" concerning the definition of "cruel and unusual punishments." Justice Kennedy, who voted on the other side of this issue sixteen years ago, wrote, "It is fair to say that the United States now stands alone in a world that has turned its face against the juvenile death penalty." Since 1990, he noted, only seven other countries have executed people for crimes they committed as juveniles, and all seven—Iran, Pakistan, Saudi Arabia, Yemen, Nigeria, China, and Congo—no longer execute minors. Justice Kennedy said that while the Court was not obligated to follow foreign developments, "it is proper that we acknowledge the overwhelming weight of international opinion" for its "respected and significant confirmation for our own conclusions." This explicit recognition of the role of public opinion firmly placed a majority of the Court on the side of the "living Constitution" perspective on this issue, while rejecting the strict constructionist view of the dissenters. Justice Ginsburg explicitly made this point in a concurring opinion in which she wrote, "Perhaps even more important than our specific holding today is our reaffirmation of the basic principle that informs the court's interpretation of the Eighth Amendment"—that the amendment's meaning has evolved rather than being fixed with an eighteenth-century understanding of the term.[71]

Another way that the Court may consider the public mood is to shift the timing of a decision. The best example here is the landmark school desegregation case, *Brown v. Board of Education*, that the Court sat on for more than two years—until after the 1952 presidential election—because it didn't think the public was ready for its bombshell ruling.[72] Others have argued that the Court rarely *changes* its views to reflect public opinion,[73] but at a minimum the evidence supports the notion that the Court is usually in step with the public.

SECTION SUMMARY

1. Supreme Court decision making is influenced by a variety of legal and political factors.
2. The power of precedent and the language of the Constitution explain many decisions, especially those involving areas of settled law.
3. Political factors such as justices' ideology, the strategic interactions among justices, and their views about judicial activism and restraint also come into play.
4. Outside considerations, such as involvement from interest groups and the views of the public, may also influence how justices decide a specific case.

▲ High school students in Maize, Kansas, join hands around a flagpole at the annual nationwide event calling Christian youth to pre-class schoolyard prayer at the start of the new school year. Enforcing the prohibition of school prayer and drawing the line between permissible and impermissible prayer have both been difficult for the Court.

The Role of the Court as a Policy Maker

We conclude with the topic addressed at the beginning of the chapter—the place of the Court within the political system. Is the Court the "weakest branch"? As Alexander Hamilton pointed out, the Court has "neither the power of the purse nor the sword." Therefore, it is not clear how it can enforce decisions. In some instances the Court can force its views on the other branches; in other cases it needs their support to enforce its decisions.

COMPLIANCE AND IMPLEMENTATION

To gain compliance with its decisions, the Court can rely only on its reputation and on the actions of Congress and the president to back them up. If the other branches don't support the Court, there isn't much it can do. The extreme example was the result of an ongoing feud between Chief Justice John Marshall and President Andrew Jackson in the 1830s. The case concerned a missionary, Samuel Worcester, who was arrested on Cherokee land in Georgia because he did not have the proper license to be there. Worcester claimed that the U.S. government, not the state of Georgia, should have control over the Cherokee Nation, and that therefore Georgia had no right to arrest him under its laws. Marshall agreed, writing, "The Cherokee Nation, then, is a distinct community, occupying its own territory, with boundaries accurately described, in which the laws of Georgia can have no force, and which the citizens of Georgia have no right to enter but with the assent of the Cherokees themselves or in conformity with treaties and with the acts of Congress."[74] After the decision, Jackson remarked, "John Marshall has made his decision. Now let him enforce it if he can." Georgia instead enforced its laws and ignored the Court—Worcester remained in jail for another year.

At the other extreme, some decisions of the Court are nearly self-enforcing because of their visibility and narrow application. If the decision primarily affects one party, the attention and focus on the case compels compliance. For example, Richard Nixon knew that he had to go along with the Court ruling forcing him to give up his secret tapes for the Watergate investigation or he would have been immediately impeached. But even cases that seem to have relatively narrow application, such as *Bush v. Gore*, which the Court tried to define narrowly, often are applied broadly by lower courts and future litigants. If the Court knows it is likely to face resistance, one thing it can do is attempt to get a unanimous vote, since even one dissent can provide a rationale for resisting a Court ruling.

The Court's lack of enforcement power is especially evident when a ruling applies broadly to millions of people who care deeply about the issue. One of the best examples is school prayer, which still exists in hundreds of public schools around the country despite having been ruled unconstitutional more than forty years ago. It is impossible to enforce the ban unless someone in the school complains and is willing to bring a lawsuit.

In most cases that involve a broad policy, the Court depends on the president for enforcement. After *Brown v. Board of Education*, the landmark school desegregation case, presidents Eisenhower and Kennedy had to send in the National Guard to desegregate public schools and universities. On the other hand, if presidents drag their feet, they can have a big impact on how the law is enforced. President Nixon attempted to lessen the impact of a school busing decision in 1971 that forced the integration of public schools by interpreting it very narrowly. Republican presidents who are opposed to abortion have limited the scope of *Roe v. Wade*, which legalized abortion in 1973, by denying federal support for abortions for people on Medicaid, banning abortions on military bases, and implementing a "gag rule," which prevented medical doctors from mentioning abortion as an option during pregnancy counseling. The Court must rely on its reputation and prestige to compel the president and Congress not to stray too far from its decisions.

RELATIONS WITH THE OTHER BRANCHES

The Court's relations with other branches may be strained as it has to rule on fundamental questions about institutional power. The Court has limited the power of the president in several high-profile cases, including Lincoln's suspension of the writ of habeas corpus during the Civil War, Truman's use of the National Guard to open steel mills that had been shut down by a labor dispute during the Korean War, Nixon's attempt to suppress information about the Vietnam War, and George W. Bush's suspension of civil liberties for "enemy combatants" during the War on Terror.[75] On the other hand, the Court has consistently upheld the president's broader war-making power, including Lincoln's blockade of southern ports when Congress was out of session in 1861 and unilateral military action in Vietnam, El Salvador, Grenada, Panama, the Persian Gulf, and Iraq.

The president and Congress often fight back when they think the Court is exerting too much influence, which can limit the Court's power as a policy-making institution. For the president this can escalate to open conflict, as in the battle between Jackson and Marshall over jurisdiction within the Cherokee Nation; the conflict between Jefferson and Marshall, which included the attempted impeachment of a Supreme Court justice for political reasons and the repeal of the 1801 Judiciary Act; and FDR's court-packing scheme, which was his response to the obstructionist New Deal Court. The president can also counter the Court's influence in a more restrained way by failing to enforce a decision as vigorously as he might otherwise, as we noted above. Congress can try to control the Court by blocking appointments it disagrees with (however, this often involves a disagreement with the president more than the Court), limiting the jurisdiction of the federal courts, or in the most extreme case, impeaching a judge. These latter two options are rarely used, but Congress often threatens to take these drastic steps. The most common way for Congress to respond to a Court decision that it disagrees with is simply to pass legislation that overturns the decision (if the case concerns the interpretation of a law). Sometimes these disputes can go on for a while, as with the recent flap over sentencing guidelines. Congress wanted the federal courts to get tougher on criminals, so it passed a law telling federal judges the range of sentences that they had to give for specific crimes. Chief Justice Rehnquist was upset when Congress passed the law without any input from the judiciary and said, "It seems that the traditional interchange between Congress and the judiciary broke down." The Court struck back when it invalidated the federal sentencing guidelines as an unfair imposition on the judiciary.[76]

In general, the Court is careful not to step on the toes of the other branches unless it is absolutely necessary. The Court often exercises self-imposed restraint and refuses to act on "political questions"—issues that are outside the judicial domain and should be decided by elected officials. One of the earliest applications was an 1804 dispute over whether a piece of land by the Mississippi River belonged to Spain or the United States. The Court observed, "A question like this, respecting the boundaries of nations, is, as has been truly said, more a political than a legal question, and in its discussion, the courts of every country must respect the pronounced will of the legislature."[77] A more recent application of the doctrine was a 1948 case in which the Court refused to review orders of the Civil Aeronautics Board granting or denying applications by citizen carriers to engage in overseas and foreign air transportation. The Court's reasons to avoid this issue show its deference to the elected branches on foreign policy:

> The very nature of executive decisions as to foreign policy is political, not judicial. Such decisions are wholly confided by our Constitution on the political departments of government, executive and legislative. They are delicate, complex, and involve large elements of prophecy. They are and should be undertaken only by those directly responsible to the people whose welfare they advance or imperil. They are decisions of a kind for which the Judiciary has neither aptitude, facilities, nor responsibility and which has long been held to belong in the domain of political power not subject to judicial instrument or inquiry.[78]

While this self-imposed limitation on judicial power is important, one must also recognize that the Court reserves the right to decide what a political question is. Therefore, one could argue that this is not much of a limit on judicial power after all. For example, for many decades the Court avoided the topic of legislative redistricting, saying that it did not want to enter that "political thicket." However, it changed its position in the 1960s in a series of cases that imposed the idea of "one-person, one-vote" on the redistricting process. The Court's ability to define the boundaries of political questions is an important source of its policy-making power.

This "big picture" question about the relationship of the Court to the other branches ultimately boils down to this: does the judiciary constrain the other branches, or does it defer to their wishes? Given the responsiveness of the elected branches to the will of the people, this question can alternatively be stated: does the Court operate in a countermajoritarian way as protector of minority interests, or does it defer to the popular will? The evidence on this is mixed.

Clearly the Court is activist on many issues, exercising judicial review, but on many other issues it defers to the elected institution. Sometimes an activist Court defends minority interests, on issues like criminal defendants' rights, school prayer, gay rights, and flag burning, but that is certainly not always the case. Is the Court acting undemocratically when it exercises its power of judicial review (or as critics would say, "legislates from the bench")? Or is it playing its vital role in our constitutional system as a check on the other branches?

The answers depend to some extent on one's political views. Conservatives would generally applaud the activism of the Rehnquist and Roberts Courts, while liberals would see it as an unwarranted check on the elected branches. Second, the role of the Court has varied throughout history: in some instances it defended unpopular views and strongly protected minority rights; in other cases it followed majority opinion and declined to play that important role. Clearly the Court has the *potential* to play an important policy-making role in our system of checks and balances; whether or not it actually plays that role depends on the political, personal, and legal factors outlined in this chapter.

SECTION SUMMARY

1. In some senses, the judiciary is the "weakest branch" in that it must rely on the other branches to enforce its decisions.

2. While the Court does not often check the other branches, deciding to not get involved in political questions, it may strike down actions by Congress or the president.
3. Defining the proper role of the Court within our system usually depends on one's political views concerning a specific case.

Conclusion

Politics is indeed everywhere, even in the courts, where you would least expect to see it. Despite the idealized image of Justice as a blindfolded woman holding a set of scales, politics affects everything the courts do, from the selection of judges to the decisions they make. Some characteristics of the federal courts, most importantly judges' lifetime tenure, insulate the system from politics more than the other branches. However, courts are influenced by judges' ideologies, interest groups, and the president and Senate, who try to shape their composition through the nomination process. The federal courts also demonstrate the other theme of the text. It shouldn't be surprising that political process matters in the courts. The rules of courtroom procedures, including discovery and how evidence is presented, can have an important impact on outcomes. Political process is also important for selecting judges and determining which cases get heard by the Supreme Court. Finally, the courts demonstrate that politics is conflictual. While plenty of unanimous Supreme Court decisions do not involve much conflict between the justices, many landmark cases deeply divide the Court on constitutional interpretation and how to balance those competing interpretations against other values and interests. These conflicts in the Court often reveal deeper fault lines in the broader political system.

Returning to the example that opened this chapter—the role of the courts in defining the government's role in the War on Terror—demonstrates the important role that the courts play in the political system. The federal courts may serve as a referee between the other branches, defining the boundaries of permissible conduct. In this case, they have limited the president's ability to unilaterally hold or try suspected terrorists without following established legal procedures. They also have forced Congress to clarify its laws to state more clearly what the executive branch can and cannot do in military tribunals. These cases illustrate another important role of the courts: standing up for the rights of individuals who would not be protected elsewhere in the political system. Protecting the rights of suspected terrorists may not strike some of you as an important role for the courts, but procedural fairness and the rule of law are the cornerstone of political freedom for all Americans.

CRITICAL THINKING

1. Should suspected terrorists receive the full protections of our legal system, or should the president have more leeway to identify "enemy combatants" and prosecute them under a different set of rules?
2. Should unelected judges have the ability to overturn laws passed by the elected branches? If so, should there be any mechanism for *political* accountability?
3. What is the proper role for the Senate in providing "advice and consent" on the selection of federal judges? Should the Senate play the role of an equal partner to the president, or simply approve most of the president's choices?

KEY TERMS

adversarial system (p. 464)
amicus curiae (p. 480)
appeals courts (p. 467)
appellate jurisdiction (p. 457)
attitudinalist approach (p. 486)
briefs (p. 480)
burden of proof (p. 462)
cases on appeal (p. 477)
cert pool (p. 478)
collusion (p. 477)
common law (p. 464)
constitutional courts (p. 466)
constitutional interpretation (p. 460)
defendant (p. 462)
district courts (p. 456)
docket (p. 475)
judicial activism (p. 487)
judicial restraint (p. 487)
judicial review (p. 457)
Judiciary Act of 1789 (p. 456)
jurisdiction (p. 465)
legislative courts (p. 466)
living Constitution (p. 486)
mootness (p. 477)
oral arguments (p. 481)
original intent (p. 486)
original jurisdiction (p. 476)

plaintiff (p. 462)
plea bargain (p. 462)
precedent (p. 464)
ripeness (p. 478)
senatorial courtesy (p. 472)
solicitor general (p. 479)
standard of proof (p. 462)
standing (p. 464)
statutory interpretation (p. 460)
strict construction (p. 485)
verdict (p. 462)
writ of certification (p. 477)
writ of certiorari (p. 477)
writs of mandamus (p. 458)

SUGGESTED READING

Baum, Lawrence. *Judges and Their Audiences: A Perspective on Judicial Behavior.* Princeton, NJ: Princeton University Press, 2006.

Cornell University Law School, Supreme Court Collection, available at http://supct/law.cornell.edu/supct.

Eisgruber, Christopher L. *Constitutional Self-Government.* Cambridge, MA: Harvard University Press, 2001.

Hansford, Thomas G., and James F. Spriggs II. *The Politics of Precedent on the U.S. Supreme Court.* Princeton, NJ: Princeton University Press, 2006.

Northwestern University, Oyez: Supreme Court Multimedia, available at http://www.oyez.org.

O'Brien, David M. *Storm Center: The Supreme Court in American Politics,* 6th ed. New York: W.W. Norton, 2002.

Rosen, Jeffrey. *The Most Democratic Branch: How the Courts Serve America.* New York: Oxford University Press, 2006.

Sunstein, Cass R., David Schkade, Lisa M. Ellman, and Andres Sawicki. *Are Judges Political? An Empirical Analysis of the Federal Judiciary.* Washington, DC: Brookings Institution, 2006.

Tushnet, Mark. *A Court Divided: The Rehnquist Court and the Future of Constitutional Law.* New York: W.W. Norton, 2006.

U.S. Supreme Court Web site, available at http://www.supremecourtus.gov.

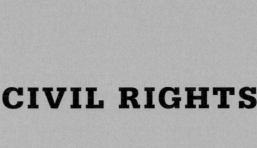

14

CIVIL RIGHTS

Y ou are driving home one night with a few of your friends after a party. It is late at night, but you have not had anything to drink and you are following all traffic laws. Your heart sinks as you see the red flashing lights of a squad car signaling you to pull over. As the police officer approaches your car, you wonder if you have been pulled over because you and your friends are African Americans driving in an all-white neighborhood. Have your civil rights been violated?

Change the scene to a car full of white teenagers with all the other facts the same. Can an officer pull you over just because he thinks that teenagers are more likely to be engaging in criminal activity than older people? Scenario two: you are a twenty-one-year-old Asian American woman applying for your first job out of college. After being turned down for the job at an engineering firm, you suspect that you didn't get the job because you are a woman and would not fit in with the "good ol' boy" atmosphere of the firm. Have your civil rights been violated?

Scenario three: you and your gay partner are told that "your kind" are not welcome in the apartment complex that you wanted to live in. Should you call a lawyer? Scenario four: you are a white male graduating from high school. You have just received a letter of rejection from the college that was first on your list. You are very disappointed but then you get angry when a friend tells you that one of your classmates got into the same school even though he had virtually the same grades as you and his SAT scores were a bit lower. Your friend says that it is probably because of the school's affirmative action policy—the classmate who was accepted is Latino. Are you a victim of "reverse discrimination?" Have your civil rights been violated? How about if you are a white contractor who lost a bid on a city contract to a minority-owned business because of a "set-aside" program put in place partly to reverse years of discrimination against minority-owned firms? Can you sue the city?

To answer these questions we must start with a definition of the term "civil rights." In general it means the right to be free from discrimination, but a more specific understanding of the term comes from the mission statement of the U.S. Commission on Civil Rights, a bipartisan, independent, federal commission that was established by the 1957 Civil Rights Act.[1] Its mission is to "appraise federal laws and policies," investigate complaints, and collect information with regard to citizens who are "being deprived of their right to vote," discriminated against, or being denied the "equal protection of the laws under the Constitution because of race, color, religion, sex, age, disability, or national origin." It investigates government actions, such as allegations of racial discrimination in the 2000 presidential election in Florida, and the actions of individuals in the workplace, commerce, housing, and education.

Given this definition and scope of coverage, all of the scenarios above would seem to be civil rights violations. However, some of them are, some are not, and two of them depend on additional considerations. Applying civil rights law can be very complex, but consistent with our argument that American politics makes sense, one of the central goals of this chapter is to highlight and summarize the central debates concerning civil rights policy today. A second goal of the chapter is to provide a better understanding of the origins of specific civil rights by examining the policy-making process. As is the case in all of the policy chapters of the text, we pull together much of what you learned in the first part of the text by explicitly discussing the role of Congress, the president, the courts, and other aspects of the policy-making process. Finally, this chapter will illuminate the three themes of the book. Civil rights policies are a good reminder that politics is everywhere: policies concerning discrimination in the workplace and in housing against women, minorities, gays, and the disabled affect millions of Americans every day. Debates over these policies are often very conflictual, illustrating the second theme of the book. And the role of the courts, the president, and Congress in creating and enforcing these policies shows that political process matters.

The Context of Civil Rights

Civil rights and civil liberties are often used interchangeably, but there are some important differences. Civil liberties refer to the freedoms guaranteed in the Bill of Rights, such as the freedom of speech, religious expression, and press, and the "due process" protection of the 14th Amendment, while **civil rights** protect all persons from discrimination and are rooted in laws and the equal protection clause of the 14th Amendment. Another difference is that civil liberties primarily limit what the government can do to you ("*Congress* shall make no law . . . abridging the freedom of speech"), whereas civil rights protect you from discrimination both by the government and by individuals. To oversimplify a bit, civil liberties are about freedom and civil rights are about equality.

It is somewhat surprising that neither civil liberties nor civil rights figured very prominently at the Constitutional Convention. Equality is not even mentioned in the Constitution or the Bill of Rights. The Bill of Rights is centrally concerned with freedom, but it was not added to the Constitution until the Antifederalists made it a condition for ratification, as discussed in Chapter 2. However, equality was very much on the Founders' minds, as is made clear in this ringing passage from the Declaration of Independence: "We hold these truths to be self evident, that all men are created equal, that they are endowed by the Creator with certain unalienable rights, that among these are life, liberty, and the pursuit of happiness." Despite the broad language, this was a limited conception of equality. Jefferson's reference to "men" was an intentional oversight of the other half of the population: women had virtually no political or economic rights in the late eighteenth century. Similarly, equality did not apply to the slaves or to Native Americans. Even propertyless white men did not have full political rights until several decades

POLITICS IS EVERYWHERE

Virtually everyone will be affected by civil rights laws at some point: race, ethnicity, gender, age, religion, and sexual orientation all receive varying degrees of protection under the Constitution, state law, and national law.

after the Constitution was ratified. Therefore, equality and civil rights in the United States have been a continually evolving work in progress.

AFRICAN AMERICANS

From the early nineteenth century, with the concerted efforts of the abolitionists, until the mid-twentieth century and the civil rights movement, the central focus of civil rights had been on the experiences of African Americans. Other groups received attention more gradually. Starting in the mid-nineteenth century, women began their fight for equal rights, and over the next century the civil rights movement expanded to include other racial and ethnic groups such as Native Americans, Latinos, and Asian Americans. Most recently, attention has turned to the elderly, the disabled, and gays and lesbians. The most divisive civil rights issue with the greatest long-term impact, however, has clearly been slavery and its legacy.

Slavery was part of the American economy and culture from nearly the beginning of our history. Dutch traders brought twenty slaves to Jamestown, Virginia, in 1619, a year before the Puritans came to Plymouth Rock. The number of slaves remained fairly small until the late seventeenth century, when three developments greatly increased the demand for slaves from Africa. First, the growth of the southern plantation system and the increased importance of tobacco as a cash crop created a need for labor. Second, the ready supply of indentured servants decreased rapidly.[2] Then, just as the demand for slaves started to wane Eli Whitney patented the cotton gin in 1794, which created an even greater demand for slaves. Between 1619 and 1808, when the importation of slaves was banned, about 600,000 to 650,000 slaves were imported from Africa to the United States.

It is impossible to overstate the importance of slaves to the southern economy. Slavery was everywhere in the South. The 1860 census shows that there were 2.3 million slaves in the Deep South, comprising 47 percent of the population of those states, and there were nearly 4 million slaves overall. While most slaves worked on plantations, they also worked in almost every part of the economy as shipyard workers, carpenters, bakers, stone masons, millers, spinners, weavers, and domestic servants. In the states that would secede from the Union, 30.8 percent of households owned slaves. Nearly a majority of households owned slaves in Mississippi and South Carolina. The economic benefits of slavery for the owners were clear. By 1860, the per capita income for whites in the South was $3,978; in the North it was $2,040. While the South had only 30 percent of the nation's free population, it had 60 percent of the wealthiest men.[3]

Abolitionists worked to rid the nation of slavery as its importance to the South grew, setting the nation on the collision course that would not be resolved until the Civil War. The Founders largely ducked the issue, as was discussed in Chapter 2, and subsequent legislatures and courts did not fare much better. The **Missouri Compromise** of 1820, which limited the expansion of slavery and kept the overall balance between slave states and free states, eased tensions for a while, but the issue would not go away. Slave owners became increasingly frustrated with the success of the Underground Railroad, which helped slaves escape to the North. The debate over admitting California as a free state or a slave state (or making it half free and half slave) threatened to split the nation once again. Southern states agreed to admit California as a free state, but only if Congress passed the Fugitive Slave Act, which required northern states to treat escaped slaves as property and return them to their owners. Soon after, Congress enacted the Compromise of 1850, which overturned the 1820 Compromise and allowed each new state to decide for itself whether to be a slave state or a free state. Northern states were not pleased with the possibility of

▲ Eli Whitney's cotton gin increased the demand for slaves on southern plantations by dramatically improving the efficiency of cotton production. His machine automated the process of separating the cottonseed from the raw cotton fibers.

Missouri Compromise An agreement between pro- and anti-slavery groups passed by Congress in 1820 in an attempt to ease tensions by limiting the expansion of slavery while also maintaining a balance between slave states and free states.

expansion of slavery in newly admitted states. All possibility of further compromise on the issue was killed by the misguided *Dred Scott v. Sandford* decision in 1857. The Supreme Court ruled that states could not be prevented from allowing slavery. It also held that slaves were property rather than citizens and had no legal rights. With Abraham Lincoln's victory in the 1860 presidential election, the southern states believed that slavery was in jeopardy, so they seceded from the Union and created the Confederacy.

The Civil War restored national unity and ended slavery, but the price was very high. More than 550,000 Americans died in the war and the casualty rate of 25 percent among combatants is nearly four times as high as that of any other war in which American soldiers participated.[4] Republicans moved quickly to ensure that the changes accomplished by the Civil War could not be easily undone by passing and adopting the Civil War Amendments: the 13th banned slavery, the 14th guaranteed that states could not deny the newly freed slaves the equal protection of the laws, and the 15th gave African American men the right to vote. These amendments were ratified in the five years following the war, though southern states resisted giving the newly freed slaves anything approaching the "equal protection of the laws" over the next 100 years.

In the Reconstruction Era (1866–77) blacks in the South gained considerable political power through institutions such as the Freedmen's Bureau and the Union League, with substantial help (some would argue manipulation and exploitation) from the Radical Republicans. When federal troops withdrew and the Republican Party abandoned the South, blacks were almost completely **disenfranchised** through the imposition of residency requirements, poll taxes, literacy tests, the **grandfather clause**, physical intimidation, other forms of disqualification. Later the practice known as the "white primary" allowed only whites to vote in Democratic primary elections; given that the Republican Party did not exist in most southern states, blacks were effectively disenfranchised. While most of these provisions claimed to be race neutral, their impact fell disproportionately on black voters. The most obvious of these was the grandfather clause, which was the way that illiterate whites were able to get around the literacy test.[5] Many states also had "understanding" or "good character" exceptions to the literacy tests, which gave election officials substantial discretion over who would be allowed to vote. The collective impact of these obstacles virtually eliminated black voting; for example, only 6 percent of blacks were registered to vote in Mississippi in 1890 and only 2 percent were registered in Alabama in 1906. After the last post-Reconstruction black congressman left the House in 1901, it was seventy-two years until another black represented a southern district in Washington, DC. In Mississippi, one county in 1947 had 13,000 blacks who were eligible to vote, but only six were actually registered. Despite the constitutional guarantees of the 14th and 15th Amendments, blacks had been effectively removed from the political system in the South, and they did not have much success in winning office at any level in the rest of the nation either.[6]

The social and economic position of blacks in the South followed a path similar to their political fortunes. In the years right after the Civil War, sympathetic Republicans passed the Civil Rights Acts of 1866 and 1875, which were supposed to outlaw segregation and provide equal opportunity for blacks. However, there were no enforcement provisions, and when Reconstruction ended in 1877, southern states swiftly moved to enact "black codes" or **Jim Crow laws** that led to the complete segregation of the races. The final blow came in 1883 when the Supreme Court ruled that the 1875 Civil Rights Act was unconstitutional because Congress did not have the power to forbid racial discrimination in private business. The Court argued that the 14th Amendment addresses the actions of state governments but not private citizens. This decision was interpreted by the South as a signal that the national government was unconcerned about protecting the rights of blacks. Jim Crow laws forbid interracial marriage and mandated the complete separation of the races in neighborhoods, hotels, apartments, hospitals, schools, restrooms, drinking fountains, restaurants, elevators, and cemeteries (even dead people were not allowed to mix across racial lines). In cases where it would have been too inconvenient to completely separate the races, as in public transportation, blacks had to sit in the back of the bus or in separate cars on the train and give up their seats to whites if asked. The Supreme Court validated these practices in *Plessy v. Ferguson* (1896) in establishing the **"separate but equal"** doctrine, officially permitting segregation as long as blacks had equal facilities.

In the first several decades after Reconstruction the rest of the nation mostly ignored the plight of blacks because at the turn of the century 90 percent of all African Americans lived in the South. But the northward migration of blacks to urban areas throughout the first half of the twentieth century dramatically transformed the demographic profile of the United States and changed racial politics. America's "race problem" was no longer a southern problem. While conditions for blacks were generally better outside the South, blacks still faced discrimination and lived largely segregated lives throughout the United States. In World Wars I and II black soldiers fought and died for their country in segregated units. Professional sports teams were segregated and black musicians and artists could not perform in many of the leading theaters across the nation, including in northern states. Blacks were largely relegated to the lowest-paying, menial jobs.

Progress was slow, but it began in the 1940s. The Supreme Court struck down the white primary in 1944, Jackie Robinson broke the color line in major league baseball in 1947, and the U.S. armed services were integrated in 1948 by Harry Truman's executive order. The most important civil rights development of the 1940s and 1950s was the landmark decision *Brown v. Board of Education* (1954), which rejected the "separate but equal" doctrine and then in *Brown II* (1955) ordered that public schools be desegregated "with all deliberate speed." This set the stage for the growing success of the civil rights movement that will be discussed later in this chapter.

▲ Jackie Robinson became the first player in the modern era to break the color barrier in major league baseball. Robinson played his first season on an all-white team in 1946 for the Brooklyn Dodgers minor-league affiliate, the Montreal Royals. He moved up to the Dodgers in 1947 and was named Rookie of the Year. He won many other honors and titles in his ten years with the Dodgers as one of the best players of his era.

LATINOS, ASIANS, AND NATIVE AMERICANS

While the legacy of slavery and the racial segregation in the South has been the dominant focus of civil rights policies in the United States, many other groups have also fought for equal rights over the past two centuries. One way to gauge the awareness of different racial and ethnic groups (if not their acceptance) is to track the changes in the U.S. Census categories. The census is taken every ten years, as required by the Constitution, to gather information about the size and characteristics of the U.S. population. In 1860 Native Americans became the second ethnic minority group to be acknowledged on the census (after African Americans); however, those living on reservations or in the Indian Territories were not counted in the U.S. population for purposes of congressional apportionment until 1890. Chinese were first listed as a separate group in 1860 only in California and then more generally in 1870, Japanese were added in 1890, and Asian and Pacific Islander categories were included in 1910 (including Hindu, Korean, and Filipino). While "Mexican" was designated as a race in the 1930 census and data had been collected previously

"separate but equal" The idea that racial segregation was acceptable as long as the separate facilities were of equal quality; supported by *Plessy v. Ferguson* and struck down by *Brown v. Board of Education*.

on mother tongue and Spanish surnames, the first attempt to identify Hispanics comprehensively was not until 1970.

The method for collecting information about race has also changed over the years. Before 1960, the census taker identified a person's race according to Census Bureau guidelines. In 1960 and 1970 a combination of direct interview and self-identification was used, and since 1980 people have identified their own race on census forms. In 2000, for the first time, people were allowed to check more than one racial category to reflect the growing reality of a multiracial United States. This evolution of census practices is significant because it shows that even though different racial groups have always been present in the United States, the way they are classified and counted varies significantly depending on the policies of a bureaucratic agency.

Each racial and ethnic group in the United States has a different history of interactions with the majority white population. In general, the history is not pretty: the majority population has done some awful things to minorities in addition to the civil rights abuses of African Americans outlined above, from the systematic eradication and removal of Native Americans from huge parts of the East and Midwest, to battles with and discrimination against Mexicans in the Southwest, to the poor treatment of Asian Americans on the West Coast and then their internment during World War II. This historical review is necessary to understand today's civil rights policies, which were not created in a vacuum but, at least in part, in response to historical events and current conditions.

The Native Americans were the first group to confront the European immigrants. While initial relations between the native population and the new arrivals were good in many places, the Europeans' appetite for more land and their insensitivity to Native American culture and traditions soon led to continual conflict. The Native Americans were systematically pushed from their land and placed on reservations. They had no political rights within the American system; indeed,

▲ Native Americans were continuously forced from their land from the beginning of European settlement until the early twentieth century. A religious leader known as Wovoka, who later went by the Anglo name Jack Wilson, prophesied peace between Native Americans and whites. His Ghost Dance, shown here being practiced by the Sioux in 1891, expressed his message of cross-cultural cooperation.

through much of the nineteenth century they were considered "savages" who should be eliminated. They did not gain the universal right to vote until 1924, just after women and well after black men. However, the U.S. government signed many treaties with them that treated the tribes as sovereign nations. (The Constitution does not consider Native American tribes to be foreign nations; as one Supreme Court case put it, they were "domestic dependent nations.")[7] Most of these treaties were routinely ignored by the U.S. government, and only in recent decades has the government started to uphold its obligations—though compliance has remained spotty. Native Americans have struggled to maintain their cultural history and autonomy in the face of widespread poverty and unemployment.

Latinos have had their own long fight for political and economic equality. The early history is rooted in the Mexican-American War (1846–48) and the conquest of much of current southwestern states by the United States. Since that time, Mexicans have resided in large numbers in that part of the country. While many Mexican Americans have roots that go back hundreds of years, a majority of Latinos have been in the United States for less than two generations. Consequently, Latinos have started to become a political force only recently, despite the fact that they now are the largest minority in the United States. Their relative lack of political clout when compared to African Americans can be explained by two factors. First, Latinos vote at a much lower rate than African Americans because of continued language barriers and the fact that about one-third of Latinos are not citizens (which is a requirement for voting). Second, unlike African Americans, Latinos are a relatively diverse group politically. Latinos include Mexican Americans, Cuban Americans, Puerto Ricans, Dominicans, and people from many other Latin American nations. Most Latino voters tend to be loyal to the Democratic Party, but Cuban Americans are strong Republicans. While this diversity means that Latino voters do not speak with one voice, it brings opportunity for increased political clout in the future. The diversity of partisan attachments among Latinos and their relatively low levels of political involvement mean that both parties are eager to attract them as new voters.

WOMEN AND CIVIL RIGHTS

When John Adams was at the Constitutional Convention in 1787, his wife Abigail advised him not to "put such unlimited power in the hands of the husbands. Remember, all men would be tyrants if they could. . . . If particular care and attention is not paid to the ladies, we are determined to foment a rebellion, and will not hold ourselves bound by any laws in which we have no voice or representation."[8] John Adams did not listen to his wife. The Constitution did not give women the right to vote, and they were not guaranteed that basic civil right until the 19th Amendment was ratified in 1920—though sixteen states, most of them western, allowed women to vote before then. Until the early twentieth century, women in most parts of the country could not hold office, serve on juries, bring lawsuits in their own name, own property, or serve as legal guardians for their children. A woman's identity was so closely tied to her husband that if she married a noncitizen, she automatically gave up her citizenship!

The rationale for these policies was called **protectionism**, which was similar to the offensive claims made by slave owners that the slaves were actually better off on the plantations than they would be as free people. For women the argument was that they were too frail to compete in the business world and that they needed to be protected by men. This rationale was used in many court cases to deny women equal rights. For example, in 1869 Myra Bradwell requested admission to the Illinois bar to practice law. She was the first woman to graduate from law school in Illinois, the

protectionism The idea under which some people have tried to rationalize discriminatory policies by claiming that some groups, like women or African Americans, should be denied certain rights for their own safety or well-being.

editor of Chicago Legal News, and held all the qualifications to be a lawyer in the state except for one—she was a woman. Her request was denied and she sued all the way to the Supreme Court, which ruled in 1873 that the prohibition against women lawyers did not violate the 14th Amendment's equal protection clause simply because the Constitution did not apply to women. Justice Joseph Bradley said:

> The civil law as well as nature itself has always recognized a wide difference in the respective spheres and destinies to man and woman. Man is, or should be, women's protector and defender. The natural and proper timidity and delicacy which belongs to the female sex evidently unfits it for many of the occupations of civil life. The constitution of the family organization which is founded in the divine ordinance, as well as the nature of things, indicates the domestic sphere as that which properly belongs to the domains and functions of womanhood.[9]

It would be interesting to see a judge try to make a similar argument today.

As recently as 1961, a court upheld a Florida law that automatically exempted women, but not men, from compulsory jury duty. The case involved a woman who killed her husband with a baseball bat after he admitted that he was having an affair and wanted to end the marriage. The woman argued that her conviction by an all-male jury violated her 14th Amendment guarantee of "equal protection of the laws" and that a jury with some women would have been more sympathetic to her "temporary insanity" defense. The court rejected this argument, ruling that the Florida law of granting women automatic exclusion from jury duty was reasonable because, "Despite the enlightened emancipation of women from the restrictions and protections of bygone years, and their entry into many parts of community life formerly considered to be reserved to men, woman still is regarded as the center of home and family life."[10] Apparently it was unthinkable to the all-male court that a man might have to stay home from work and take care of the kids while his wife served on a jury. Later in this chapter we will describe how the Supreme Court has moved away from this discriminatory position and rejected the protectionist way of thinking.

SECTION SUMMARY

1. Civil rights protect all persons from discrimination by the government and individuals. They are rooted in laws and the equal protection clause of the 14th Amendment.
2. The legacy of slavery and the racial segregation in the South has been the dominant focus of civil rights policies in the United States.
3. Starting in the mid-nineteenth century, women began their fight for equal rights, and over the next century the civil rights movement expanded to include other racial and ethnic groups such as Native Americans, Latinos, and Asian Americans.

A Color-Blind Society?

Why does all of this history matter for politics today? Indeed, one of the most common arguments against affirmative action or other policies aimed at making up for past discrimination is, "Why should I have to pay for the sins that were committed long before I was even born? Slavery ended a long time ago and besides, my relatives didn't even come to this country until long after slavery was abolished." There are two main responses. First, the effects of slavery and the Jim Crow laws are still quite evident. Legal racial segregation ended only forty-five years ago and its legacy, especially in the relative quality of education available to most whites and blacks, remains with us. Second, active discrimination is still evident in our society today. Given how important race is in the everyday lives of millions of Americans and how important it is for understanding American politics, a grasp of the history that got us to where we are today is an important starting point.

▲ Civil rights leader Martin Luther King Jr. waves to supporters from the steps of the Lincoln Memorial on August 28, 1963, in Washington, DC. The March on Washington drew an estimated 250,000 people who heard King deliver his famous "I Have a Dream" speech.

Martin Luther King Jr. presented the vision for a color-blind society in his "I Have a Dream" speech that he delivered before 250,000 people at the March on Washington on August 28, 1963. He said, "I have a dream that my four little children will one day live in a nation where they will not be judged by the color of their skin but by the content of their character." Most Americans share this dream of a color-blind society, but there are large differences of opinion about how close we are to that goal. Those who take the position that we must "move beyond race" argue that we already have achieved a level playing field on which people of different races have equal opportunities to succeed. Furthermore, they argue, efforts to make up for past discrimination or create additional opportunities for racial minorities through affirmative action only perpetuate racial discrimination by classifying people based on race. Others see race as central in everyday life and believe that discrimination is still an all-too-real part of life for racial minorities.

One simple test to see if you think we have reached the color-blind ideal described by King is to ask yourself what kinds of things you notice when you meet someone for the first time. Do you notice their hair color, height, body type, or whether they wear glasses or have a moustache? Do you notice their race? If you have met a person once or twice you may not remember hair color, whether he had a beard, or whether he had glasses. But you probably would remember someone's race as a defining feature. This is what people mean when they talk about a color-blind society—that race will be as unimportant for forming an opinion about someone as whether they wear glasses or have a beard. That is, people may or may not notice race, but this awareness of race will not affect their opinions or the way they behave. But people *do* still notice race, and mountains of research show that awareness of race does influence many people's opinions and behavior. People engage in racial stereotyping all the time, without necessarily being aware of it. Some intentionally discriminate against people based on their race.

We will give you two examples from personal experience in a liberal, northern midwestern city that prides itself on being tolerant and progressive. The first example represents unintentional stereotyping, while the second is clear racial discrimination. One Saturday morning one of the authors was at the checkout line at a local grocery store and the lady ahead of him was being given a hard time by the cashier. The woman had a large basket of groceries and the bill was well over $100. She wanted to pay for some of the groceries with food stamps and then the rest of them with a personal check. The cashier wanted to see a driver's license or two other forms of photo ID and the lady did not have them. The author wasn't close enough to see exactly what was going on, but she had some type of ID that was not adequate. After calling over the store manager and a lot of hemming and hawing, the cashier finally accepted her check. The author unloaded his similarly sized cart of groceries and paid by check, and the cashier never hesitated. In fact, he has never been asked for identification when paying by check in that store. The author would like to reach a different conclusion, but it seemed clear that the woman and he were treated so differently because she was black and using food stamps and he is white (see Politics Is Everywhere for the second example).

These kinds of stories, ranging from irritating and demeaning to a serious violation of the law, could be repeated by nearly every racial minority, woman, and gay person in the United States: the well-dressed businessman who cannot get a cab in a major city because he is black, the woman who is sexually harassed by her boss but is afraid to say anything because she doesn't want to lose her job, the teenage Latino who is followed around the music store by a clerk, the Arab American who must endure taunts about the head covering she wears, or the gay couple that has trouble finding an apartment. Discrimination is far too common in the United States and clearly indicates that we have not reached the color-blind (or gender and sexual orientation neutral) society desired by advocates of civil rights.

The election of Barack Obama as the first African American president may indicate the beginning of a new era in which race is a less significant factor in elections. Obama won 43 percent of the white vote, which is more than the percentages won by the last two Democratic presidential nominees, John Kerry in 2004 and Al Gore in 2000. Nine percent of voters said that race was an important factor in their vote, but of these, 53 percent voted for Obama. However, while race did not seem to have a big impact on the outcome of the election, this should not be seen as sufficient evidence that we have entered a period in which race doesn't matter.

The Racial Divide Today

In addition to the unequal treatment of racial minorities, women, and gays, a gulf remains between the objective condition of minorities and that of whites and the political views that they hold. While substantial progress has been made in bridging that divide, the political, social, and economic condition of racial minorities is not as good as it is for whites. The political divide is mostly evident in lower levels of voter turnout among racial minorities relative to whites (however, as noted above, the gap is largest between Latinos and whites). While different rates of voter turnout can mostly be accounted for by education and income—especially between blacks and whites—there are many examples of practices and institutions that are designed to depress minority turnout. The tactics include moving and reducing the number of polling places in minority-majority areas, changing from district-based to at-large elections, redistricting that dilutes minority voting power, withholding information about registration and voting procedures from blacks, and "causing or taking advantage of election day irregularities."[11] A personal example of such an "irregularity" was in the 1990 Senate election between an African American, Harvey Gantt, and Jesse Helms, one of the most conservative Republican senators, who exploited the racial divide in North Carolina for his political advantage throughout his career. Both authors of this text lived in North Carolina at the time and voted in a precinct that had a large African American population. Only half of the old, lever-style mechanical voting machines were working at the precinct—the others had been jammed with chewing gum. People had to wait several hours to vote and many simply became discouraged and left. Similar things happened throughout the

Racial and Gender Discrimination

A society that is free of discrimination is a goal shared by most Americans, yet we still have a long way to go. One example of discrimination that is still far too common in our society involved a graduate student in our department who is white and is married to an African American woman. They wanted to rent a bigger apartment, so they searched the want ads and made appointments to see the apartments. One landlord told them to meet him in front of the apartment at a specific time the next day. They waited where they were told, but the landlord didn't show up. After thinking about it, they remembered seeing a car that slowed down and almost stopped in front of the apartment but then sped away. They realized they had been victimized by a "drive-by landlord," that is, a landlord who checks out the race of the potential tenants from a distance; if they are not white, he or she will skip the appointment and tell them it is rented if they ask. Indeed, this is exactly what happened. They called the landlord and asked what had happened and were told the apartment was rented. To check their suspicions, they had some friends call and ask about the apartment and they were told it was available. Their friends (who were both white) made an appointment to meet the landlord, and this time the same car slowed down but pulled up and stopped. The landlord showed them around the apartment and was very friendly. The next day the graduate student slapped him with a racial discrimination lawsuit (he ended up winning a small settlement).

The plural of "anecdote" is not "data," but the national numbers clearly support

▲ Racial minorities are often subject to discrimination when they attempt to rent an apartment or get a job. Interracial couples are helping break down these racial barriers, but they, too, are subject to discrimination.

the claim that discrimination is still widespread in our society. In the 2007 fiscal year there were 82,792 charges filed at the Equal Employment Opportunity Commission, of which 36.9 percent were race-based complaints and 30 percent were gender based.[a] These formal complaints reflect only a relatively small proportion of actual discrimination in a given year. Many people do not know the law or have the resources to pursue a complaint if they believe they were discriminated against. Another recent study of 50,000 loans that were made in 2004 found that black and Hispanic home buyers pay higher interest rates than whites

who have similar credit ratings.[b] If you are a racial minority or woman, many of you probably have personal experiences of discrimination.

One other way to try to define the extent of discrimination is through experiments. Two economists examined how a person's race could influence their chances of getting a job interview. In their experiment they created résumés for job applicants who were well qualified and not as well qualified for a job. They then assigned names to their fictitious applicants that are common among blacks and whites (based on the ratio of black newborns and white newborns that are given specific names). For example, African American names included Kenya and Hakim and white names included Allison and Brad. Four résumés (high and low quality of each race) were then sent to actual job openings in Boston and Chicago for sales, administrative support, clerical, and customer service jobs. The study found that résumés with white names received 50 percent more calls for interviews than résumés with black names. In addition, 8.4 percent of the employers contacted at least one more white applicant than black applicant, while only 3.5 percent of employers contacted at least one more black applicant than white applicant. The value of a high quality résumé also varied between the two races. White résumés of high quality received 27 percent more calls than those of low quality, but for black résumés, the difference was only 8 percent in favor of the high quality ones.[c] This type of controlled experiment reveals that a person's race still matters for something as important as getting a job interview. ■

state and many were convinced that it was a systematic effort to hold down the vote for Harvey Gantt.[12]

More recent evidence for this claim comes from the 2000 presidential election in Florida, where the U.S. Commission on Civil Rights investigated dozens of complaints from minorities who were not allowed to vote. One target of the investigation was the "voter purge list" that the state had created to remove voters from the registration list who should not be allowed to vote. Most people on the list were supposed to be felons, who are not allowed to vote under Florida state law. The problem was that the list was created without cross-checking to make sure that the people on the list were felons. Thousands of people ended up on the list who had not committed any crime, but they had to clear their name before they were allowed to vote. Many people did not realize the problem until Election Day, and attempts to clear up the confusion usually failed. Given the racial composition of people who are convicted of crimes, minority voters were disproportionately affected by this policy. In addition, the commission described the use of police roadblocks close to voting places in predominantly minority neighborhoods as another practice that depressed minority voter turnout. Finally, the high incidence in minority areas of "spoiled ballots" that could not be counted could not be accounted for by differences in the income or education levels of voters.[13] Given that the outcome of the 2000 presidential election was decided by a few hundred votes in Florida, these efforts to depress minority turnout had an important impact on the election outcome (large majorities of African American voters supported Al Gore). Florida was not the only state in which such allegations were made. New Jersey, Missouri, Arkansas, and Louisiana also were accused of various tactics to depress minority turnout in recent elections.

The racial divide is also evident in social and economic terms. Nearly three times as many black families are below the poverty line as white families: 23.1 percent compared to 8.5 percent in 2007. The poverty rate of 19.5 percent for Hispanic families in 2007 was similar to that of black families.[14] Furthermore, while black median household income in 2006 was $32,373, only 62.9 percent of white family income, the gap in overall wealth is much more dramatic. The average white household has nearly six times the assets of the typical nonwhite family. In 2004 the median household net worth was $140,800 for whites and $24,900 for nonwhites. Figures for Hispanics are somewhat better, but the gaps are still large. Hispanic household income was 75.3 percent of white income, $38,747 compared to $51,429.[15] Poverty is not distributed equally throughout the United States, but rather is concentrated in areas where the minority population is the highest (see Figures 14.1a and 14.1b).

Other indicators show similar patterns. The rate of black, adult male unemployment has been about twice as high as that of white adult males for the past forty-five years (which is substantially higher than the nearly equal ratio of 1.26 in 1940). In January 2008, the unemployment rate among blacks was 9.2 percent compared to 4.4 percent for whites and 6.3 percent for Latinos.[16] The other most depressing statistic on the objective position of blacks is that only one-third of black children (34.6 percent) lived in two-parent households in 2004, compared to 73.8 percent of white children and 65.9 percent of Latino children. (In 1940, two-thirds of black children and 91 percent of white children lived with two parents.)[17] Blacks are more likely than whites to be victimized by crime, and some of the figures are stunning. A black male between the ages of eighteen and twenty-four is 10.5 times as likely to be murdered as a white male in that same age range.[18] On every measure of health—life expectancy, infectious diseases, infant mortality, cancer rates, heart disease, and strokes—the gaps between whites and blacks are large, and in many cases, they are growing. For example, in 2005, the life expectancy for blacks was five years shorter than for whites (73.2 years compared to 78.3), the infant mortality rate was more than double for blacks (13.69 deaths per 100,000 births compared

FIGURE 14.1a

PERCENTAGE OF PEOPLE IN POVERTY, 2006

Together, these maps show that the poverty rate in the United States is closely related to the minority population. How do you think these patterns might affect the politics of civil rights policies that are aimed at reducing discrimination in the workplace or housing?

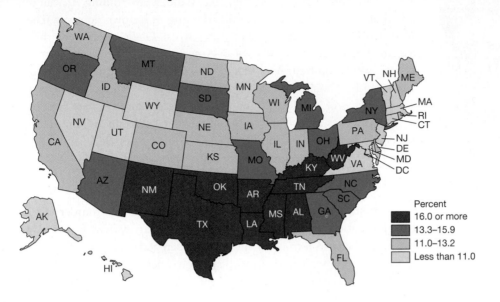

FIGURE 14.1b

PERCENTAGE OF THE POPULATION THAT IS WHITE, 2006

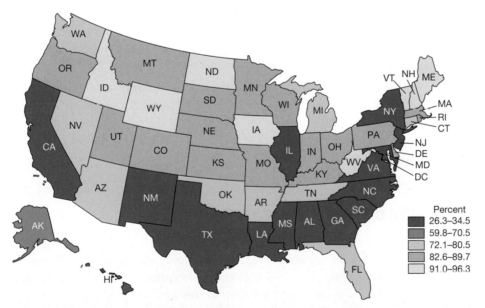

SOURCE: Poverty data from Bruce H. Webster Jr. and Alemayehu Bishaw, "Income, Earnings, and Poverty: Data from the 2006 American Community Survey," U.S. Census Bureau, August 2007, available at http://www.census.gov/prod/2007pubs/acs-08.pdf; race data from U.S. Census Bureau, State and County Quick Facts, available at http://quickfacts.census.gov/qfd/states/19000.html.

to 5.76 for whites), and in 2002 maternal mortality was more than quadruple (24.9 deaths per 100,000 births for blacks compared to 5.6 for whites). Similar gaps exist for incidence of cancer, diabetes, strokes, and heart attacks.[19]

The greatest disparity between racial minorities and whites may be in the criminal justice system. Racial profiling subjects many innocent blacks to intrusive searches. Recent studies have shown that blacks are not only more likely than whites to be convicted for the same crimes, but that blacks also serve longer sentences.[20]

▲ *James Byrd Jr. was murdered in Jasper, Texas, by three white supremacists who chained him to a pickup truck and dragged him down a road until he was decapitated. According to FBI statistics, there were about 4,000 race-related hate crimes in the United States in 2006.*

In many large American cities, tensions between police departments and minority communities periodically boil over. The largest race riots since 1990 were in Los Angeles in 1992 following the acquittal of four white police officers who had been videotaped brutally beating a black man, Rodney King. The riots left 54 people dead and more than 2,000 injured and caused more than $1 billion in damage. In 1999 New York police killed Amadou Diallo, a law-abiding African immigrant, in a hail of forty-one bullets as he was standing in his own doorway. The four officers were looking for a black suspect, and when Diallo reached for his wallet, they assumed it was a gun. The African American community was outraged when the officers were acquitted. A similar killing of an unarmed black man, nineteen-year-old Timothy Thomas, by police in Cincinnati in 2001 led to three days of rioting in which dozens of people were injured and more than 800 were arrested. The officer in this case was also acquitted. More recent cases include James Dennis, who was killed by Norfolk police in October 2007, and Sean Bell, who was shot dead in November 2006, in New York City hours before his wedding. Civil rights advocates point out that such incidents are far too common.

African Americans and other minorities are also subjected to hate crimes much more frequently than whites. One especially gruesome murder that received national attention in 1998 involved a black man, James Byrd Jr., who was chained to the back of a pickup truck by three white men and dragged to his death. Two of the murderers were sentenced to death and the other received life in prison. According the FBI's hate crime statistics, of the 7,722 hate crimes in 2006, 4,000 were race related. Of these, two-thirds were "anti-black," while only 22 percent were "anti-white," which means that rate of black hate crimes is more than five times what would be expected based on the percentage of African Americans in the United States, while the rate of white hate crimes is less than one-third as high as would be expected.[21]

This backdrop of racial inequality, discrimination, and violence provides continued motivation for civil rights activists to push their agenda in the three branches of government: legislative, executive, and judicial. In some instances, issues will be pursued in several arenas simultaneously; in others, redress will be sought in one arena after exhausting alternatives. The civil rights movement, which was crucial in the early policy successes, also continues to mobilize the grassroots. These various paths through the policy process will be explored in the next section.

SECTION SUMMARY

1. The dream of a color-blind society is shared by most Americans, but there is strong disagreement over how much progress we have made toward that goal.
2. While there are differences about *perceptions* of progress on racial differences, there are large gaps between whites and racial minorities on objective measures of political participation and social and economic well-being.

The Policy-Making Process and Civil Rights

It may not seem to make sense to talk about the policy-making process in terms of the distinct contributions of each of the three main branches of government. After all, our system of separated and shared powers almost ensures that each of the three branches has some say in making policy. However, each branch has played a central role at different points in history, depending on the political context. For example, in the 1940s and the 1950s the courts were seen as the most sympathetic branch for advancing the civil rights agenda because segregationist southern Democrats controlled key committees in Congress and none of the presidents of this era made civil rights a top priority (though some positive steps were taken, as we will discuss below). Then in the mid-1960s Congress took the lead role in civil rights policy by passing landmark legislation.

The policy-making process in the area of civil rights also provides insight into the importance of federalism. For African Americans' civil rights, the national government forced the southern states to desegregate the schools, allow blacks to vote, and generally dismantle the system of segregation, thus demonstrating the importance of nation-centered federalism. However, for gay rights—the most recent civil rights issue—the state and local governments have taken the lead role while the president and Congress have started to take steps to restrict gay rights, especially on the question of gay marriage. For women's rights, both the national and state governments have taken important actions at various times.

SOCIAL MOVEMENTS

While much of our discussion of civil rights focuses on the policy-making process, no discussion of this topic would be complete without noting the importance of social movements. From the early women's rights movement and abolitionists of the nineteenth century to the civil rights movement of the mid-twentieth century, activists pressured the political system to change its civil rights policies. Through collective action, social movements put issues on the policy agenda that otherwise would have been ignored by politicians. In some cases, as with the women's movement, politicians continued to ignore demands for many years. Women started to push for the right to vote at a convention in 1848 at Seneca Falls, New York. A constitutional amendment to give women the right to vote was regularly introduced in Congress between 1878 and 1913 but never was passed. After a parallel movement at the state level had some success, the conditions were finally right for passing the constitutional amendment in 1919 (it was ratified in 1920).

The civil rights movement of the 1950s and 1960s, aimed at ending segregation and gaining equal political and social rights for blacks, is the most famous example of a successful social movement (see Figure 14.2). The *Brown v. Board of Education* decision, which struck down the practice of segregation in public schools, gave the movement a boost, but nothing really changed in the daily lives of most blacks living in the South. White school boards and local governments resisted integration at all costs; change was not going to come easily. Black leaders became convinced that the courts could not be counted on to bring about change because of resistance to their decisions. The only way to change the laws was to get the public, both black and white, to demand change.

The spark that civil rights leaders had been waiting for came on December 1, 1955, in Montgomery, Alabama, when a woman named Rosa Parks refused to give up her seat on a bus to a white person, as she was required to do by law. Parks is often described as a seamstress who was tired after a long day's work and simply did not want to give up her seat. While that is true, there is a lot more to the story. Local civil rights leaders had been waiting for years for an opportunity to call a boycott of the local bus company because of its segregation policy. They needed a perfect test case—someone who would help draw attention to the cause.

Rosa Parks was just that person. She was a well-educated, law-abiding citizen who had been active in local civil rights organizations. In her book, *My Story*, Parks

FIGURE 14.2   CIVIL RIGHTS TIME LINE

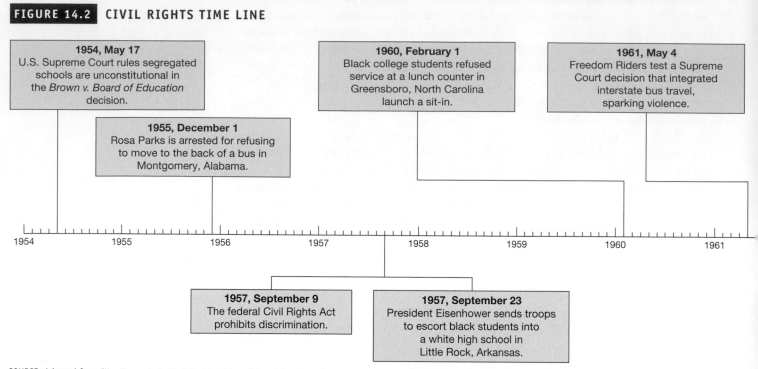

SOURCE: Adapted from "Key Moments in Civil Rights History," *Ann Arbor News*, January 11, 2004, available at http://www.mlive.com/news/aanews/index.ssf?/base/features-0/1073819921106320.xml.

says, "I was not tired physically, or no more tired than I usually was at the end of a working day. . . . No, the only tired I was, was tired of giving in."[22] When she was arrested for refusing to give up her seat, local civil rights leaders organized a boycott of the bus company that lasted more than a year. Whites in Montgomery tried everything to stop the boycott, including arresting and fining blacks who arranged a complex car pooling system to get to work: people waiting for a car to pick them up were arrested for loitering, and car pool drivers were arrested for not having the right kind of insurance or having too many people in their car. Martin Luther King Jr. was elected leader of the group, and he was subjected to harassment and violence—his house was firebombed and he was arrested several times. Finally a federal district court ruled that the segregation policy was unconstitutional, and the Supreme Court upheld that ruling.

Nonviolent Protest On February 1, 1960, four black students in Greensboro, North Carolina, went to a segregated lunch counter at a local Woolworth's and asked to be served. They sat there for an hour without being served and were forced to leave when the store closed. Twenty students returned the next day and the story was picked up by the national wire services. Within two weeks the sit-ins spread to eleven cities. In some cases the students were met with violence; in others they were simply arrested. However, the students continued to respond to the violence with passive resistance, and there was always another wave of protesters to replace those who were arrested. The Student Nonviolent Coordinating Committee (SNCC) was created to coordinate the protests. The Greensboro Woolworth's was integrated on July 26, 1961, but the protests continued in other cities. By August, 1961, the sit-ins had 70,000 participants and 3,000 arrests.[23] The sit-ins marked an important shift in the tactics of the civil rights movement away from the court-based approach and

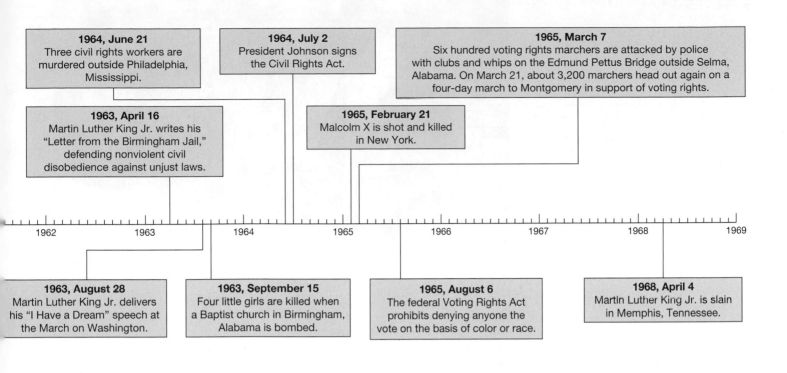

1964, June 21
Three civil rights workers are murdered outside Philadelphia, Mississippi.

1964, July 2
President Johnson signs the Civil Rights Act.

1965, March 7
Six hundred voting rights marchers are attacked by police with clubs and whips on the Edmund Pettus Bridge outside Selma, Alabama. On March 21, about 3,200 marchers head out again on a four-day march to Montgomery in support of voting rights.

1963, April 16
Martin Luther King Jr. writes his "Letter from the Birmingham Jail," defending nonviolent civil disobedience against unjust laws.

1965, February 21
Malcolm X is shot and killed in New York.

1962　1963　1964　1965　1966　1967　1968　1969

1963, August 28
Martin Luther King Jr. delivers his "I Have a Dream" speech at the March on Washington.

1963, September 15
Four little girls are killed when a Baptist church in Birmingham, Alabama is bombed.

1965, August 6
The federal Voting Rights Act prohibits denying anyone the vote on the basis of color or race.

1968, April 4
Martin Luther King Jr. is slain in Memphis, Tennessee.

toward the nonviolent civil disobedience that had been successful in Montgomery on a smaller scale.

Another important event during this period was the effort by the Freedom Riders to get President Kennedy to enforce two Supreme Court decisions that banned segregation in interstate travel, including bus terminals, waiting rooms, restaurants, and other public facilities related to interstate travel.[24] On May 4, 1961, a group of whites and blacks boarded two buses in Washington, DC, headed for New Orleans. The whites and blacks sat together and went into segregated areas of bus stations. The trip was uneventful until Rock Hill, South Carolina, where several of the Riders were beaten. Then in Anniston, Alabama, one bus had its tires slashed and was firebombed. The Riders were beaten as they fled the burning bus. The second group was confronted by an angry mob at the bus station in Birmingham and severely beaten with baseball bats and iron pipes. When it became clear that police protection would not be provided, the Riders abandoned the trip and regrouped in Nashville. After much internal debate, they decided to continue the rides. After more violence in Montgomery, President Kennedy intervened, and his brother, Robert Kennedy, the attorney general, worked out a deal in which the Riders would be provided police protection, federal troops would not intervene, and the Riders would have to face the local courts upon their arrest for "disturbing the peace." The Freedom Rides continued throughout the summer. More than 350 Riders were jailed and fined, and many others sustained permanent injuries from the beatings. The Freedom Rides successfully drew national attention to the continuing resistance in the South to desegregation rulings, forced the Kennedy administration to take a stand on this issue, and led to a stronger Interstate Commerce Commission ruling banning segregation in interstate travel.[25]

▲ *This attempt to integrate a lunch counter in Portsmouth, Virginia, in February 1960 was part of the sit-in movement that started in Greensboro, North Carolina. Through their nonviolent protests, civil rights activists pressured businesses to integrate.*

The Letter from the Birmingham Jail The next significant set of events was in Birmingham, Alabama, in 1963. Birmingham had more racial violence than any southern city, with eighteen unsolved bombings of black churches and homes in a six-year period (its nickname was "Bombingham" during this period). The city had closed its parks and golf courses rather than integrate them, and there was no progress on integrating the local schools. One of the leading supporters of integration had been castrated to intimidate other blacks who might advocate the policy. The city was run by the police chief "Bull" Connor, a strong segregationist who had allowed the attacks on the Freedom Riders. During a peaceful protest in early April 1963, Martin Luther King and many others were arrested. While in solitary confinement, King wrote his famous "Letter from the Birmingham Jail," an eloquent statement of the principles of nonviolent civil disobedience. The letter was a response to white religious leaders who told King in a newspaper ad that his actions were "unwise and untimely" and that "when rights are consistently denied, a cause should be pressed in the courts and in negotiations among local leaders, and not in the streets." King responded, "History is the long and tragic story of the fact that privileged groups seldom give up their privileges voluntarily." In arguing for direct action, he wrote, "I cannot sit idly by in Atlanta and not be concerned about what happens in Birmingham. Injustice anywhere is a threat to justice everywhere. We are caught in an inescapable network of mutuality tied in a single garment of destiny. Whatever affects one directly affects all indirectly."

In his letter King presented the justification for civil disobedience, writing that everyone had an obligation to follow just laws but an equal obligation to break unjust laws, which he defined in two ways. First, "A just law is a man-made code that squares with the moral law of the law of God. An unjust law is a code that is out of harmony with moral law." Second, an unjust law is "a code that a majority inflicts on a minority that is not binding on itself" or "a code that a majority inflicted upon a minority which that minority had no part in enacting or creating because they did not have the unhampered right to vote." This second component of defining an unjust law is very similar to the rationale that Thomas Jefferson laid out in the Declaration of Independence for resisting

POLITICS IS EVERYWHERE

The success of the civil rights movement was rooted in its ability to make the entire country aware of the plight of blacks in the South. By arguing that we are in "an inescapable network of mutuality," King was able to show that race was not just a southern concern.

British rule. The cry of "no taxation without representation" was heard from the colonists who dumped British tea in the Boston harbor because they viewed the tax on tea as unjust.

King also laid out the four steps of nonviolent campaigns: (1) collection of the facts to determine whether injustices are alive; (2) negotiation with white leaders to change the injustices; (3) self-purification, which involved training to make sure that the civil rights protesters would be able to put up with the abuse that they would receive; and (4) direct action to create the environment where change will be able to happen (such as the sit-ins and marches), but always in a nonviolent manner. By following these four steps, civil rights protesters ensured that their social movement would draw attention to their cause while turning public opinion against the violent tactics of their opponents.

King was released from jail shortly after writing his letter, but the situation escalated dramatically. The protest leaders decided to use children in the next round of demonstrations. After more than 1,000 children between the ages of six and eighteen were arrested and the jails were overflowing, the police turned powerful fire hoses and police dogs on the children to prevent them from continuing their march. Media coverage of the incident turned the tide of public opinion in favor of the civil rights marchers as the country expressed outrage over the violence in Birmingham. Similar protests occurred throughout the South, with more than 1,000 actions in over 100 different southern cities with more than 20,000 people arrested throughout the summer.

On June 11, 1963, President Kennedy gave a historic speech on civil rights, calling on Congress to take action. The next day Medgar Evers, a civil rights leader in Mississippi, was shot and killed in his driveway. A week later Kennedy sent his comprehensive civil rights bill to Congress that would guarantee equal social and political rights to blacks. On August 28, King delivered his "I Have a Dream" speech to a crowd of 250,000 people who had participated in the March on Washington (estimates of the crowd ranged from 200,000 to 500,000; it was clearly the largest political protest in the country's history up to that point). Two weeks later four African American girls were killed when a Birmingham church was bombed. President Kennedy was assassinated before his legislation could be passed, but the civil rights activists' courageous actions and concerted efforts over two decades played a key role in putting pressure on Congress to pass meaningful legislation. The details of this legislation will be discussed later in the chapter, in the section on the legislative arena.

With the passage of this landmark legislation, large-scale activity for civil rights for African Americans started to decline. However, mass protest became the preferred tool of many social movements. Vietnam War protesters marched on Washington by the hundreds of thousands in the late 1960s and early 1970s. The women's rights, gay rights, and environmental movements have staged many mass demonstrations in Washington and other major cities. Even groups outside the traditional civil rights movement, such as the Nation of Islam, have used the tactics of mass protest. The Million Man March in October 1995, was organized by Louis Farrakhan and attracted about 400,000 to Washington, DC. Traditional civil rights leaders had distanced themselves from Farrakhan in the past because of his racist and anti-Semitic views. However, the Million Man March helped establish Farrakhan as a political force that was difficult to ignore. Most recently,

▲ A seventeen-year-old civil rights demonstrator, defying an anti-parade ordinance, is attacked by a police dog in Birmingham, Alabama, on May 3, 1963. The next day, during a meeting at the White House, President Kennedy discussed this photo, which had appeared on the front page of the New York Times. Reaction against this police brutality helped spur Congress and the president to enact civil rights legislation.

large-scale demonstrations against international organizations, such as the International Monetary Fund and the World Trade Organization, and against the war in Iraq have swept the nation. The legacy of the civil rights movement was not only to help change unjust laws but also to provide a new tool for political action.

THE JUDICIAL ARENA

In the early years of the civil rights movement in the 1930s and 1940s, the Supreme Court provided most of the successes, especially in voting rights and desegregation. Later the attention of the Court would turn to discrimination cases in employment (in addition to cases in voting rights), and here its record was more mixed from the perspective of civil rights supporters. In two of the early voting rights cases the Court struck down the grandfather clause in 1915 and the white primary in 1944.[26] Both of these devices had prevented blacks from voting.

Challenging "Separate but Equal" in Education The National Association for the Advancement of Colored People (NAACP), which was formed in 1909 to fight for equal rights for blacks, started a concerted effort to nibble away at the "separate but equal" doctrine. Rather than tackle segregation head-on, the NAACP decided to challenge an aspect of segregation that would be familiar to the Supreme Court justices: the various ways in which states kept blacks out of all-white law schools. Another important part of the NAACP's strategy was to challenge admission practices in law schools outside the Deep South to demonstrate that segregation was not just a "southern problem" and to raise the chances for compliance with favorable Court decisions. A young attorney named Thurgood Marshall, who would later become the first African American Supreme Court justice, argued the NAACP's first successful case in 1936. This suit challenged the University of Maryland's practice of sending black students to an out-of-state law school rather than admitting them to the university's all-white law school. (The state gave black students a $200 scholarship, which was not adequate to cover the costs of tuition and travel and not available to all black students who wanted to attend law school.) The Maryland appeals court rejected this arrangement and ordered that black students be admitted to the University of Maryland law school.[27]

The Supreme Court's first ruling on these cases came two years later in a similar case from Missouri. Here, rather than providing a scholarship, the state paid the black students' tuition to attend an out-of-state school, while white students attended the in-state school tuition free. The state defended the practice under the separate but equal doctrine, pointing out that the law schools in the adjacent states were as good as the Missouri law school and had essentially the same curriculum. The state also distinguished their case from Maryland's by arguing that Missouri had a provision for creating a law school at Lincoln University, the state school for African Americans. The Court rejected both arguments in very strong terms, saying, "We think that these matters are beside the point." They expressed skepticism that the state would ever create a black law school that was equal in quality to the white school. The bottom line was that white students could go to law school in the state and similarly qualified black students could not, which violated the 14th Amendment's equal protection of the laws.[28]

In 1948 the Court ruled that a black student had to be admitted to the state law school in Oklahoma rather than being required to wait until a "separate but equal" black law school was constructed, or alternatively no white students could be admitted to law school until the equal school was available.[29] Another case from Oklahoma ruled that black students had to be fully integrated into a graduate program rather than being required to sit in a separate row in the classroom and at separate tables in the library and cafeteria.[30] While these cases were incremental steps toward eliminating segregation, the basic doctrine of "separate but equal" remained intact.

The next case chipped away at the principle itself. In 1950 Texas had a separate law school for black students, but it clearly was not equal to the law school for whites. When the lawsuit was brought, the law school for black students had only four part-time faculty, none of whom had offices at the school; no librarian in the law library; and a library with few of the promised books. The situation started to improve after the case was underway; the Court observed, "[The black law school] is apparently on the road to full accreditation. It has a faculty of five full-time professors; a student body of 23; a library of some 16,500 volumes serviced by a full-time staff; a practice court and legal aid association; and one alumnus who has become a member of the Texas Bar." However, and this is the crucial part of this case, the Court ruled that *this was not good enough*. There were more intangible aspects of the quality of law school that could not be measured by the number of books or faculty, such as the reputation of the school, the "position and influence of the alumni," and "traditions and prestige." This came very close to saying that "separate but equal" was a contradiction in terms, but the Court stopped just short of reaching that conclusion.[31]

After these victories there was a debate within the NAACP whether to continue the case-by-case approach against the separate but equal doctrine, striking down segregation where it clearly was unequal, or to directly challenge the principle itself. The latter approach was risky because it was not clear if the Court was ready to take this bold step and because defeat in the Court could set back the movement for many years. However, the signals increasingly indicated that the Supreme Court was ready to strike down the separate but equal doctrine. In addition to the law school cases, in 1948 the Court said that "restrictive covenants," clauses in real estate contracts that prevented the owner of a property from selling to an African American, could not be enforced by state or local courts because of the 14th Amendment's prohibition against a state denying blacks the "equal protection of the laws."

This application of the 14th Amendment was expanded in the landmark ruling *Brown v. Board of Education*. The case arrived on the Court's docket in 1951, was postponed for argument until after the 1952 elections, and then was reargued in December 1953. The ruling was postponed for so long (almost three years from when it first arrived) because the Court was keenly aware of the firestorm that would ensue. In its unanimous decision the Court ruled, "In the field of public education, the doctrine of separate but equal has no place. Separate educational facilities are inherently unequal, depriving the plaintiffs of the equal protection of the laws. Segregated facilities may generate in black children a feeling of inferiority that may affect their hearts and minds in a way unlikely ever to be undone."[32] The case was significant not only because it required all public schools in the United States to desegregate but also because it used the equal protection clause of the 14th Amendment in a way that had potentially far-reaching consequences.

However, the decision was limited in its scope by focusing on segregation in schools rather than segregation more generally and by focusing on the psychological damage done to the black school children because of segregation rather than on the broader claim that racial classification itself was not allowed by the Constitution. Chief Justice Earl Warren wanted a unanimous vote, and knew that two justices would not support a broader ruling that would overturn *Plessy* and rule segregation unconstitutional in all contexts. Even if segregation in other public places still was legal, the Court's *Brown* ruling provided an important boost to the civil rights movement.

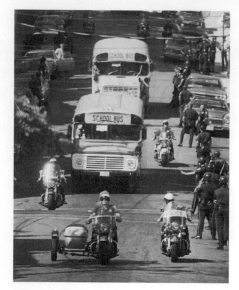

▲ *Some of the strongest reactions against court-ordered busing as a means of public school integration were outside the South. Black students being bused to a predominantly white and Irish part of South Boston required a heavy police escort in September 1974.*

The Push to Desegregate Schools In 1955, *Brown v. Board of Education II* addressed the implementation of desegregation and required the states to "desegregate with all deliberate speed."[33] The odd choice of words, "all deliberate speed," was taken as a signal by southerners that they could take their time with desegregation. The phrase does seem to be contradictory: being deliberate does not usually involve being speedy. Southern states engaged in a concerted effort of "massive resistance" to the desegregation order, as articulated by segregationist Virginia senator Harry F. Byrd, in some cases even closing public schools rather than integrating them—and then reopening the schools as "private," segregated schools for which the white students received government vouchers. However, the ruling did have some immediate impact: Maryland, Kentucky, Tennessee, Missouri, and the District of Columbia desegregated their schools within two years.

Eight years after *Brown I*, little had changed in the Deep South: fewer than 1 percent of black children attended school with white children.[34] The Supreme Court became frustrated with the lack of progress in desegregating the schools, saying that there was "too much deliberation and not enough speed."[35] Through the 1960s the courts had to battle against the continued resistance to integration. In 1971 the Court shifted its focus from **de jure** segregation—that is, segregation that was mandated by law—to **de facto** segregation—that is, segregation that existed because of segregated housing patterns—and approved school busing as a tool to integrate schools.[36] This approach was extremely controversial in many cities. The Court almost immediately limited the application of busing by ruling in a Detroit case that busing could not go beyond the boundaries of a city's school district; that is, students did not have to be bused from suburbs to cities unless it could be shown that the school district's lines were drawn in an intentionally discriminatory way.[37] This rule encouraged "white flight" from the cities to the suburbs in response to court-ordered busing. The Supreme Court retreated further from enforcing desegregation in 1991 when it said that a school district could be released from a court-ordered desegregation plan if the district had taken "all practicable steps" to desegregate. Furthermore, districts do not have to address segregation in public schools that is caused by segregated housing.[38] The Supreme Court ruled in 1995 that low minority achievement scores are not evidence of a district's failure to desegregate, and said that school districts cannot be forced by the courts to spend money to make magnet schools with special programs that could attract white students from the suburbs.[39]

POLITICAL PROCESS MATTERS

School districts may use a variety of tools to try to achieve racial integration, but ultimately those efforts must be consistent with the Supreme Court's interpretation of what is constitutionally permissible.

In what observers have called the most important decision on race in education since *Brown*, in 2007 the Court invalidated voluntary desegregation plans implemented by public school districts in Seattle and Louisville. Both districts set goals for racial diversity and denied assignment requests if they tipped the racial balance above or below certain thresholds. In a ringing endorsement of the color-blind approach, the majority opinion said, "The way to stop discrimination on the basis of race is to stop discriminating on the basis of race." In this case, the discrimination was against white students who wanted to be in schools with few minority students rather than black students who wanted to be in integrated schools. However, it was not immediately clear exactly how race could factor into school desegregation plans in the future, because only four justices signed on to the strict color-blind view. Justice Anthony Kennedy, who provided the fifth vote for some of the majority opinion, did not agree to substantial parts of it and articulated a position between the conservatives' position, that race may not be used to classify students, and the liberals' view, that it is necessary to achieve integrated schools.[40]

de jure Relating to actions or circumstances that occur "by law," such as the legally enforced segregation of schools in the American South before the 1960s.

de facto Relating to actions or circumstances that occur outside the law or "by fact," such as the segregation of schools that resulted from housing patterns and other factors rather than from laws.

Expanding Civil Rights The other significant Court rulings of this period in the area of civil rights struck down state laws that forbid interracial marriages (sixteen states had such laws), upheld all significant parts of the Civil Rights Act, and upheld and expanded the scope of the Voting Rights Act. The central cases ruled Congress had the power to eliminate segregation in public places, such as restaurants and hotels, under the commerce clause of the Constitution. The first case involved a 216-room hotel in Atlanta that was close to an interstate highway, advertised extensively on the highway, and had about 75 percent of its customers from out of state. The Court ruled that this establishment was clearly engaging in interstate commerce, so Congress had the right to regulate it.[41] The second case was a little more difficult. Unlike the Atlanta hotel, "almost all, if not all" of the patrons of Ollie's Barbeque in Birmingham, Alabama, were local. However, the Court pointed out that meat purchased for the restaurant came from out of state, and this comprised 46 percent of the total amount spent on supplies. Therefore, the practice of segregation would place significant burdens on "the interstate flow of food and upon the movement on products generally."[42] One aspect of this decision usually goes unnoticed: the white hotel owner claimed that his 13th Amendment rights were being violated by his being forced by Congress to serve black people. That is, he was claiming to have been forced into "involuntary servitude." The irony is pretty amazing—a white person who is discriminating against black people claiming that he was forced into slavery. The Court rejected that argument.

The next important area of cases came in employment law. In 1971 the Court ruled that employment tests, such as written exams or general aptitude tests, that are not related to job performance and that discriminate against blacks violate the 1964 Civil Rights Act.[43] The burden of proof was placed on the employer to show that the test is a "reasonable measure of job performance" and was not simply an excuse to exclude African Americans from certain jobs. Another important aspect of this **disparate impact standard** of discrimination is that the *intent* of the company or person who is discriminating does not matter, but whether the practice has an adverse *effect* on a racial group. This decision had a tremendous impact on integrating the workplace. In 1989, however, the Supreme Court reversed itself and placed the burden of proof on the employee to show that the discriminatory practice did not result from some business necessity.[44] This obviously made it much more difficult to prove workplace discrimination, and Congress subsequently overruled the Court on this issue, as we will discuss below (see Nuts and Bolts 14.1 for the legal definition of race-based workplace discrimination).

The Color-Blind Court and Judicial Activism The Roberts and Rehnquist Courts of the past two decades have been gradually imposing a "color-blind jurisprudence" over a broad range of issues. One area in which the color-blind approach had a big impact was in the racial redistricting that occurred in 1992 in which fifteen new U.S. House districts were specifically drawn to help elect African Americans and ten districts were drawn to provide an opportunity to elect Latino members. This dramatic change in the number of minorities in Congress (the increase was greater than 50 percent) was rooted in the 1982 amendments to the Voting Rights Act. Instead of mandating a fair *process*, this law and subsequent interpretation by the Supreme Court in the 1980s mandated that minorities be able to "elect representatives of their choice" when their numbers and configuration permitted. This shift meant that the legislative redistricting process now had to avoid discriminatory *results* rather than being concerned only with discriminatory *intent*. However, in a series of decisions starting with the 1993 landmark case *Shaw v. Reno*, the Supreme Court's adherence to a color-blind jurisprudence has thrown the constitutionality of black-

disparate impact standard The idea that discrimination exists if a practice has a negative effect on a specific group, whether or not this effect was intentional.

Race-Related Discrimination and Title VII as Defined by the Equal Employment Opportunity Commission

RACE-RELATED CHARACTERISTICS AND CONDITIONS

Discrimination based on physical characteristics associated with race, such as skin color, hair texture, or certain facial features violates Title VII, even though not all members of a race share the same characteristics. Title VII also prohibits discrimination based on any condition that predominantly affects one race unless the practice is job-related and necessary to do business. For example, since sickle cell anemia predominantly occurs in African Americans, a policy that excludes individuals with sickle cell anemia must be job-related and consistent with business necessity.

HARASSMENT

Harassment on the basis of race and/or color violates Title VII. Ethnic slurs, racial "jokes," derogatory comments, or other verbal or physical conduct based on an individual's race/color constitutes unlawful harassment if it creates an intimidating, hostile, or offensive working environment or interferes with the individual's work performance.

SEGREGATION AND CLASSIFICATION OF EMPLOYEES

Title VII is violated where employees who belong to a protected group are segregated by physically isolating them from other employees or from customer contact. Employers may not assign employees according to race or color, such as assigning primarily African Americans to predominantly African American establishments or geographic areas. It is illegal to exclude members of one group from particular positions or to categorize employees or jobs so that certain jobs are generally held by members of a certain protected group. Coding applications or resumes to designate an applicant's race constitutes evidence of discrimination where people of a certain race or color are excluded from employment or from certain positions.

PRE-EMPLOYMENT INQUIRIES

Requesting pre-employment information that discloses or tends to disclose an applicant's race strongly suggests that race will be used unlawfully as a basis for hiring. Therefore, if members of minority groups are excluded from employment, the request for such pre-employment information would likely constitute evidence of discrimination.

SOURCE: U.S. Equal Employment Opportunity Commission, "Race/Color Discrimination," available at http://www.eeoc.gov/types/race.html.

majority districts into doubt. The Court has ruled that black-majority districts are legal as long as they are "done right,"[45] but it has consistently held that if race is the predominant factor in drawing district lines, the districts are unconstitutional because they violate the equal protection clause of the 14th Amendment. This line of cases struck down black-majority districts in North Carolina, Georgia, Louisiana, Virginia, Texas, and Florida. The most recent case, in 2001, upheld the redrawn 12th District in North Carolina, which no longer was black majority, arguing that when race and partisanship are so intertwined—as they are when 90 percent of African Americans vote for the Democratic candidate—plaintiffs cannot simply assume that African Americans were placed together for racial reasons. This opens the door for a greater consideration of race than had been allowed in the previous cases. However, racial redistricting is an unsettled area of the law, and many other countries have used more aggressive policies such as quotas to ensure more equal representation for minorities and women (see Comparing Ourselves to Others).[46]

The racial redistricting cases illustrate a central concern in the institutional balance of power in the policy-making process that is also of great importance to

Representation of Women and Minorities

A central problem for representative democracy is to provide a voice for minority interests in a system that is dominated by the votes of the majority. The legitimacy and stability of any democracy depends, in part, on its ability to accomplish that difficult aim. The recent experiences in nation building in Iraq, Afghanistan, and Sudan provide dramatic evidence for this point: if minorities are excluded from the political process they often resort to violence and terrorism to gain a seat at the table. The American experiment in nation building in Philadelphia in 1787 faced similar, if less severe, divisions. The Founders' institutional solution of the separation of powers within and across levels of government provided multiple points of access for various interests and some assurance that no single interest would dominate government for extended periods. Majority tyranny was prevented by a pluralist politics in which "minorities rule," to use Robert Dahl's famous phrase. However, for at least forty years, scholars and politicians have recognized that our system did not provide adequate representation for certain groups in society, especially racial minorities and women (even if women are a numerical majority in most countries, they do not control the majority of political power).[a] Our pluralist system does not deal very well with specific racial, ethnic, or gender-based interests because our electoral system is based on single-member, winner-take-all (WTA) districts where the majority (or at least the plurality) clearly rule. While some U.S. communities are experimenting with different electoral mechanisms to enhance minority representation, many other countries have better formal representation of racial minorities and women than the United States.

Nations that have proportional representation are more likely to represent minority interests than those with WTA

▲ Many nations officially require proportional representation for party lists or reserved seats (a form of quotas) to ensure more equal representation of women in electoral office. Iraq, for example, requires that 25 percent of the members of parliament are women, a policy that Iraqi politician Nisreen Barwari strongly advocated.

systems. Usually there is a threshold that a party must meet (often 5 percent) before it is represented in a national legislature. Therefore, any racial or ethnic group with a strong common identity could conceivably gain representation in the national legislature with as little as 5 percent of the population. Some nations, such as Germany, Denmark, and Poland, even waive the threshold if the party is representing an ethnic minority. The strongest provision for the representation of racial, ethnic, and gender-based interests in legislatures is known as "reserved communal seats." For example, Jordan reserves 18 of its 80 seats for Christians, Circassians, and Bedouins, while Taiwan reserves 8 of its 225 seats for Aboriginals. Overall, at least seventeen countries use this mechanism to promote equal representation of racial and ethnic

minorities and twelve use it for gender equity.[b] This system of reserved seats, which is a form of quotas, was explicitly rejected in the 1982 Voting Rights Act amendments that provided minority voters in the United States an equal opportunity to elect candidates of their choice but said that the new law should not be seen as endorsing proportional representation or quotas.

Another mechanism that is commonly used to enhance representation for women but less so for racial and ethnic minorities is requiring that a certain percentage of candidates on the party list are women. In Iraq, for example, where women did not serve in public office under the previous regime, the new election laws require that parties reserve at least one-third of their slots for women as a way to meet the requirement of having at least 25 percent of the seats in parliament for women. As it turned out, one-third of the seats in the new parliament went to women. Twenty-three nations have party list requirements for women ranging from 50 percent to 5 percent. Ensuring representation of different racial and ethnic groups can also be an important mechanism for bringing peace to war-torn areas: Bosnia, Cyprus, Rwanda, Fiji, Sri Lanka, Zimbabwe, Kosovo, Macedonia, Afghanistan, and Iraq have all produced power-sharing settlements that require a certain number of seats for the various factions within their nations.

Finally, it is important to note that WTA systems can incorporate reserved seats into their system of district elections. India, Pakistan, and Samoa, among others, provide representation for minority interests through reserved seats even if they have single-member-district WTA elections. As the United States continues to struggle with issues of how to best represent its increasingly diverse electorate, it may learn some valuable lessons from other nations that have used a variety of techniques for many decades. ■

reasonable basis test The use of evidence to suggest that differences in the behavior of two groups can rationalize unequal treatment of these groups, such as charging sixteen- to twenty-one-year-olds higher prices for auto insurance than people over twenty-one because younger people have higher accident rates.

intermediate scrutiny standard The middle level of scrutiny the courts use when determining whether unequal treatment is justified by the effect of a law; this is the standard used for gender-based discrimination cases and for many cases based on sexual orientation.

strict scrutiny standard The highest level of scrutiny the courts use when determining whether unequal treatment is justified by the effect of a law. It is applied in all cases involving race. Laws rarely pass the strict scrutiny standard; a law that discriminates based on race must be shown to serve some "compelling state interest" in order to be upheld.

civil rights advocates: the Supreme Court is increasingly activist in civil rights. The Court is unwilling to defer to any other part of government if that branch disagrees with its view of discrimination and equal protection. Thus, as we discussed in Chapter 3, the Court was willing to overturn state laws in racial redistricting, congressional legislation with the Violence Against Women Act and the Americans with Disabilities Act (though the ruling only limited the scope of the law rather than striking it down entirely), U.S. executive branch contracting policies in cases that subjected racial "set-aside" programs to the "strict scrutiny" standard, the Florida State Supreme Court ruling on the 2000 presidential election, and California state law in a recent employment discrimination case.[47] This string of cases indicates that the Court's central tendency is not one of preferring state power to national power, as some have argued. Rather, it is a consistently activist assertion of judicial power over the elected institutions and a desire to have *its* interpretation of the law and of the Constitution rule rather than that of either of the other two branches. This trend illustrates that the Court's activism may be used either to further civil rights, as with the desegregation cases from the 1950s, or to limit civil rights.

Women's Rights The Supreme Court has also played a central role in determining women's civil rights. As mentioned earlier in this chapter, until relatively recently the Court did not apply the Constitution to women, despite the 14th Amendment's language that states may not deny any *person* the equal protection of the laws. Clearly women were not regarded as people when it came to political and economic rights in the nineteenth and early twentieth centuries. These protectionist notions were finally rejected in three cases between 1971 and 1976, when the Supreme Court made it much more difficult for states to treat men and women differently.

The first case involved an Idaho state law that said that a man was given priority over a woman when they were otherwise equally entitled to be the executor of a person's estate. This was justified on the "reasonable" grounds that it reduced the workload of the state courts by having an automatic rule that would limit challenges. However, the Court unanimously ruled that the law was arbitrary, did not meet the "reasonableness" test, and therefore violated the woman's equal protection rights under the 14th Amendment.[48] The second case involved a female Air Force officer who wanted to count her husband as a dependent for purposes of health and housing benefits. Under the current law a military man could automatically count his wife as a dependent, but a woman could claim her husband only if she brought in more than half the family income. The Court struck down this practice, saying protectionist laws "in practical effect, put women not on a pedestal, but in a cage."[49]

These two cases still relied on the **reasonable basis test** for the discrimination between men and women. It wasn't until 1976 that the Court established the new **intermediate scrutiny standard** in a case involving the drinking age. In the early 1970s some states had a lower drinking age for women than for men on the "reasonable basis" that eighteen- to twenty-year-old women are more mature than men of that age (states argued that women were less likely to be drunk drivers and less likely to abuse alcohol than men). The new intermediate scrutiny standard meant that this "reasonable basis" was not enough to justify the unequal treatment of men and women, so the law was struck down.[50]

Before this case only two standards were used to apply the 14th Amendment to different categories of people. Racial minorities received the strongest protection as the "suspect classification" where the **strict scrutiny test** is applied. Under this test there must be a "compelling state interest" to discriminate among people if race is involved. The suspect classification was first used in a case involving the internment of Japanese Americans during World War II. It is one of the few instances in which racial classification has survived strict scrutiny. In a controversial ruling, the Court said that the internment camps were justified on national security grounds.[51] The only other test before the new intermediate one said that it was acceptable to discriminate against a group of people as long as there was a "reasonable basis" for that state law (such as the efficiency argument made by the state of Idaho in the case involving control of an estate). Today, for example, states can pass a twenty-one-year-old drinking law on the grounds that traffic fatalities will be lower with a twenty-one-year-old drinking age rather than allowing eighteen-year-olds to drink.

The intermediate scrutiny test gives women stronger protections than the reasonable basis test, but it is not quite as strong as strict scrutiny. To use the legal jargon, the gender distinction would have to serve an "important government objective," but not a "compelling state interest," in order to withstand intermediate scrutiny. Some distinctions between men and women are still allowed. For example, in 1981 the Supreme Court said that gender differences influence combat roles and military needs and therefore justify male-only draft registration. This issue has not been relevant in recent years because of the all-volunteer armed services, but it would become relevant again if the draft were reinstated.[52]

In many instances, as with the Idaho case, the rights of women were strengthened by the new standard of equal protection. However, in other instances the rights of women and men were equalized by making things worse for women. For example, in the drinking age case, instead of dropping the drinking age for men to eighteen, states raised the age for women to twenty-one. Similarly, the Court struck down an Alabama divorce law in which husbands but not wives could be ordered to pay alimony.[53] Arguably women would have been better off in these two specific instances under the old discriminatory laws (because they could drink at eighteen instead of twenty-one and did not have to pay alimony in some states). However, the more aggressive application of the 14th Amendment for women was an important step in providing them the equal protection of the laws.

Two other areas where the Supreme Court helped advance women's rights were affirmative action and protection against sexual harassment. In 1987 the Court approved affirmative action in a case involving a woman who was promoted over a man despite the fact that he scored slightly higher than she did on a test. The Court ruled that this was acceptable to make up for past discrimination.[54] The Court made it easier to sue employers for sexual harassment in 1993, saying that a woman did not have to reach the point of a nervous breakdown before being able to claim that she was harassed; it was enough to demonstrate a pattern of "repeated and unwanted" behavior that created a "hostile workplace environment."[55] Later rulings stated that if a single act is flagrant the conduct did not have to be repeated to create a hostile environment. This was the standard used by Paula Jones to bring a lawsuit against President Clinton. She alleged that as governor of Arkansas, Clinton invited her to his hotel room and then exposed himself to her and asked her to perform oral sex (Jones was a state employee at the time, which is why she could argue that this incident was related to workplace harassment). The case was eventually settled out of court, but not before testimony in the case dredged up the Monica Lewinsky affair, which nearly brought down the Clinton presidency.

As with civil rights for minorities, the Court has also restricted the rights of women in some instances. In 1984 the Court ruled that Title IX of the Education Amendments of 1972, which prohibits sex discrimination in "any education pro-

▲ About 110,000 Japanese Americans were interned in "war relocation camps" during World War II. The Supreme Court upheld the practice, but that decision has been strongly criticized. Congress subsequently passed legislation apologizing for the internment and paid $1.6 billion in reparations to surviving internees and their heirs.

▲ Paula Jones sued President Clinton for sexual harassment when he was governor of Arkansas. Because Jones was a state employee, civil rights laws concerning a "hostile workplace environment" applied to her case. Testimony in this case revealed Clinton's affair with Monica Lewinsky, which nearly brought down his presidency.

gram or activity receiving Federal financial assistance," applied to private colleges and universities in which students received federal financial aid. However, in a blow to equal treatment for women, the Court said that only the specific program that received federal funds could not discriminate, rather than the institution as a whole. This ruling released many athletic programs from their obligation to provide equal opportunity for women athletes.[56] Congress overturned this ruling with the Civil Rights Restoration Act, which was passed in 1988 over a veto by Ronald Reagan. More recently, Lilly Ledbetter sued Goodyear Tire and Rubber Company for receiving lower pay than men for the same work over a twenty-year period, which she claimed was gender discrimination. However, the Court rejected her claim, saying that she did not meet the time limit required by the law, as the discrimination must have occurred within 180 days of the claim. Dissenters in the case pointed out pay discrimination usually occurs in small increments over long periods of time, so it would be impossible to recognize the discrimination within 180 days (in this instance, there was a 40 percent difference between Ledbetter's pay and that of her male colleagues after twenty years). Furthermore, workers do not have access to information about their fellow workers' pay, so it would be almost impossible to meet the standard set by the Court. The long-standing policy of the Equal Employment Opportunity Commission (EEOC) was that each new paycheck restarted the 180-day clock as a new act of discrimination, but the Court overturned that policy, making it almost impossible to sue for discriminatory pay based on gender or race under the Civil Rights Act.[57] As shown in Figure 14.3, significant pay disparities between men and women remain throughout much of the United States.

Other cases provide something for both sides of a dispute. A good example of this type of case was a sex discrimination suit brought under Title VII of the Civil

POLITICS IS EVERYWHERE

Some Supreme Court cases have a relatively narrow impact, but others potentially affect half of the wage earners in the country. The Ledbetter case, which makes it much more difficult for women to prove they were discriminated against, is a good example of one of those far-reaching cases.

FIGURE 14.3   **WOMEN'S EARNINGS AS A PERCENTAGE OF MEN'S EARNINGS, 2006**

There is a substantial difference between females' and males' earnings in the United States. What could account for this variation? How much do you think it has to do with levels of discrimination and how much with differences in the nature of the jobs that men and women hold?

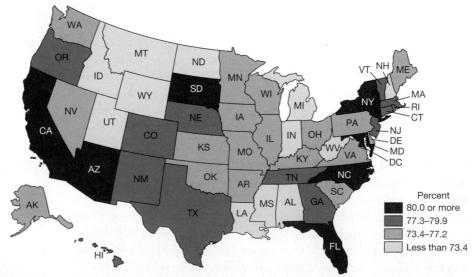

Percent
- 80.0 or more
- 77.3–79.9
- 73.4–77.2
- Less than 73.4

SOURCE: Bruce H. Webster Jr. and Alemayehu Bishaw, "Income, Earnings, and Poverty: Data from the 2006 American Community Survey," U.S. Census Bureau, August 2007, available at http://www.census.gov/prod/2007pubs/acs-08.pdf.

Rights Act.[58] Price Waterhouse, a large accounting firm, passed over a female employee for partnership in 1983. The company named forty-seven new partners that year, all men, and the person who brought the suit, Ann Hopkins, was the only woman among eighty-eight people up for promotion. Two lower courts agreed with her claim that she was discriminated against on the basis of sex. In job reviews she had been praised by her superiors for her "strong character, independence, and integrity," but others held these same qualities against her. One of her bosses said that she was "too macho" and another said that she would improve her chances of promotion if she would "walk more femininely, talk more femininely, dress more femininely, wear make-up, have her hair styled, and wear jewelry." She was fairly sure that her employer was not asking men to hit the gym and lose that pot-belly or buy a hair piece to cover their shiny domes, so she sued. The Supreme Court recognized that there had been discrimination but said there may have been other reasons that she was not promoted. So they sent the case back to the lower court, where Price Waterhouse would have to prove by the "preponderance of evidence" that they would not have promoted her to partner anyway, absent any sexual discrimination. This was an easier standard of proof than the previous standard of "clear and convincing evidence." So companies got a somewhat more favorable precedent out of the ruling, but even with this easier standard, the lower court awarded Hopkins $371,175 in back pay and partnership in the firm.

Gay Rights The Supreme Court has a similarly mixed record on gay rights. The early cases were not supportive of gay rights. One of the first cases concerned Georgia's law banning sodomy. The Supreme Court ruled in *Bowers v. Hardwick* that homosexual behavior was not protected by the Constitution and state laws banning it could be justified under the most lenient "reasonable basis" test.[59] In other recent cases the Supreme Court sidestepped the controversial issue of gay rights, choosing alternative constitutional grounds to reach its decision. For example, in 1995 the Court ruled that the South Boston Allied War Veterans Council did not have to let the Irish-American Gay, Lesbian, and Bisexual Group of Boston march in its St. Patrick's Day parade because of the veterans' 1st Amendment rights of free expression, thus ignoring the alternative "equal protection" claim made by the gay group.[60] A similar ruling held that the Boy Scouts of America did not have to admit an "avowed homosexual" as an assistant scoutmaster and ruled that New Jersey's public accommodations law did not require them to do so because of the Boy Scouts' 1st Amendment right of expressive association.[61]

In the first endorsement of civil rights for gays, the Supreme Court struck down an amendment to the Colorado state constitution that would have prevented gays from suing for discrimination in employment or housing. The Court said that gays' equal protection rights were violated by the state amendment because it "withdrew from homosexuals, but no others, specific legal protection from the injuries caused by discrimination."[62] The Court explicitly rejected the "reasonable basis" arguments made by the state and came close to putting gays in the "suspect classification" that has been restricted to racial and ethnic minorities.

An even more important ruling came seven years later in a case involving two Houston men. John Geddes Lawrence and Tyron Garner were prosecuted for same-sex sodomy after police entered Lawrence's apartment—upon receiving a false tip about an armed man in an apartment complex—and found the two having sex. Under Texas law, sodomy was illegal for gays but not for heterosexuals. In a landmark 6–3 ruling, the Supreme Court said that the liberty guaranteed by the 14th Amendment's due process clause allows homosexuals to have sexual relations. "Freedom presumes an autonomy of self that includes freedom of thought, belief, expression, and certain intimate conduct."[63] This reasoning is rooted in

substantive due process doctrine One interpretation of the due process clause of the 14th
Amendment; in this view the Supreme Court
has the power to overturn laws that infringe on
individual liberties.

the **substantive due process doctrine** that serves as the basis for the constitutional protections for birth control, abortion, and decisions about how to raise one's children. The decision explicitly overturned *Bowers v. Hardwick*, and the majority opinion had harsh words for that decision, saying it "was not correct when it was decided, and it is not correct today." Five members of the majority signed onto the broad "due process" reasoning of the decision, while Justice O'Connor wrote a concurring opinion in which she agreed that the Texas law was unconstitutional, but on narrower grounds. With the broader due process logic, a total of thirteen state laws that banned sodomy were struck down. Justice Scalia wrote a strong dissent and took the unusual step of reading part of his dissent from the bench when the decision was announced. He said the decision was "the product of a court that has largely signed on to the so-called homosexual agenda" and warned that the ruling "will have far-reaching implications beyond this case." He predicted that the ruling will serve as the basis for constitutional protections for gay marriage.

This summary of cases demonstrates that the courts can be a strong advocate of and impediment to civil rights. In general, however, the courts have a limited *independent* impact on policy. As Alexander Hamilton pointed out in *Federalist 78*, the Supreme Court has "neither the power of the purse nor the sword." That is, it must rely on the other branches of government to carry out its policy decisions, as the school desegregation cases so clearly demonstrate.

THE LEGISLATIVE ARENA

The bedrock of equal protection that exists today stems from landmark legislation passed by Congress in the 1960s, namely, the 1964 Civil Rights Act, the 1965 Voting Rights Act, and the 1968 Fair Housing Act. President Kennedy was slow to work actively for civil rights legislation for fear of alienating southern Democrats. The events in Birmingham prompted him to act, but he was assassinated before the legislation was passed. President Lyndon Johnson, a native Texan and former segregationist, helped push through the Civil Rights Act when he became president. The Civil Rights Act barred discrimination in employment based on race, sex, religion, or national origin, banned segregation in public places, and set up the Equal Employment Opportunity Commission as the enforcement agency for the legislation. One of the southern opponents of the legislation inserted the part about sex, thinking that it would defeat the bill (figuring, perhaps, that there would be a majority coalition of male chauvinists and segregationists), but it became law anyway.

The Voting Rights Act of 1965 (VRA) eliminated direct obstacles to minority voting in the South such as discriminatory literacy tests and other voter registration tests and also provided the means to enforce the law: federal marshals were charged with overseeing elections in the South, something that had not happened since Reconstruction. The VRA is often cited as one of the most significant pieces of civil rights legislation passed in our nation's history.[64] President Johnson compared the critical events at Selma, Alabama, in which voting rights marchers were brutally attacked by police with clubs and whips on the Edmund Pettus Bridge, and which helped provide impetus for passage of the VRA, to the American Revolution and the Civil War. He cited all three as moments when "history and fate meet at a single time in a single place to shape a turning point in man's unending search for freedom."[65] After its passage, President Johnson hailed the VRA as a "triumph for freedom as huge as any ever won on any battlefield."[66] The VRA precipitated an explosion in black political participation in the South. The most dramatic gains came in Mississippi, where black registration increased from 6.7 percent before the VRA to 59.8 percent in 1967. As one political scientist noted, "The act simply overwhelmed the major bulwarks of the disenfranchising system. In the seven states originally covered, black registration increased from 29.3 percent in March, 1965, to 56.6 percent in 1971–72; the gap between black and white registration rates narrowed from 44.1 percentage points to 11.2."[67] The last piece of landmark legislation, the Fair Housing Act of 1968, barred discrimination in the rental or sale of a house.

There have been many amendments to these laws since the 1960s. The most important changes were the 1975 amendments to the VRA that extended coverage of many of the provisions of the law to language minorities; the 1982 VRA amendments, which extended important provisions of the law for twenty-five years and made it easier to bring a lawsuit under the Act; the 1991 Civil Rights Act; and the 2006 extension of the VRA for another twenty-five years. The 1991 law overruled or altered parts of twelve Supreme Court decisions that had eroded the intent of Congress when it passed the civil rights legislation. It expanded earlier legislation and increased the costs to employers for intentional, illegal discrimination. Two of the central debates were over the standard that had to be met in discrimination cases and where the burden of proof should lie: on the employer or on the employee. After vetoing an earlier version of the bill, President George H. W. Bush ultimately agreed that the burden of proof should be on the employer. Thus, the central question was how to define the discriminatory standard. Democrats in Congress pushed for a relatively tough standard that discrimination be "essential to business practice" in order to be permitted. For example, if a university required all assistant professors to have a Ph.D., and it could be shown that more white applicants had Ph.D.s than minority applicants, the university would have the burden of proof to demonstrate that the Ph.D. was essential for doing the job. President Bush wanted a less stringent standard of "legitimate business objectives." Congress ended up adopting language that was somewhere in between: the employer must show that the practice is "job related for the position in question and consistent with business necessity."

The other most significant civil rights legislation of the 1990s was not passed into law. The Racial Justice Act would have permitted minority inmates on death row to use statistical data on discriminatory application of the death penalty to appeal their sentences. Government studies and academic research have conclusively demonstrated unequal application of the death penalty based on the race of the *victim*. A murderer is much more likely to be put on death row if he killed a white person than if he killed a black person (ranging from 4.3 times more likely in Georgia to 84 times more likely in Texas). However, in 1987 the Supreme Court ruled that a pattern of discrimination could not be the basis for a death sentence appeal; rather, actual discrimination in the specific case must be demonstrated.[68] The Congressional Black Caucus pushed for the Racial Justice Act as part of the $33.4 billion 1994 crime bill. It passed the House by a 217–212 margin and was defeated in the Senate 58 to 41. The provision was dropped in conference committee when President Clinton decided not to jeopardize the entire crime bill over the controversial act. Despite defeat on the specific provision, many political observers saw the 1994 crime bill as a victory for civil rights advocates, because for the first time the federal legislation included significant financial support for crime prevention measures ($6.1 billion), including some programs that were criticized by Republicans, such as "midnight basketball" aimed at keeping inner-city kids off the streets.

Women have also received extensive protection through legislation. As noted above, Title VII of the Civil Rights Act, which barred discrimination based on gender, was almost an accidental part of the bill (given that it was included by an opponent to the legislation). Indeed, the first executive director of the EEOC would

In November 2006 students from James Madison University rallied outside the Department of Education in Washington, DC, to protest the university's plan to cut ten of its men's athletic teams. The cuts were made to bring the school into compliance with the federal law requiring equity in men's and women's sports.

not enforce the gender part of the law because it was a "fluke." In 1966 the National Organization for Women (NOW) was formed to push for enforcement of the law. Its members convinced President Johnson to sign an executive order that eliminated sex discrimination in federal agencies and among federal contractors, but it was difficult to enforce. Finally in 1970 the EEOC started enforcing the law. Before long, one-third of civil rights cases involved sex discrimination, and those numbers have remained quite high in recent years (see Figure 14.4). In a breakthrough case in 1970, AT&T had to give its female workers $38 million in back pay because they had received lower wages than men for doing the same work.

Congress passed the next piece of important legislation for women in 1972: Title IX of the Higher Education Act. This law prohibits sex discrimination in institutions that receive federal funds and has had the greatest impact in women's sports. In the 1960s and 1970s the opportunities for women to play sports in college or high school were extremely limited. Very few scholarships were set aside for women at the college level, and budgets for women's sports were tiny when compared to the budgets for men. Though it took nearly thirty years to reach its goal of parity between men and women, most universities are now in compliance with Title IX. While the law has clearly been a great benefit for women athletes, it has its critics. Many men's sports, such as baseball, tennis, wrestling, and gymnastics, were cut at universities that had to bring the number of student athletes into rough parity (partly because the football program at most schools is so large). Critics argued that such cuts were not fair, especially given that the interest in women's sports was not as high. Defenders of the law argue that the gap in interest in women's and men's sports will not change until there is equal opportunity. There is some evidence to support that claim, as the interest is increasing in women's soccer and professional basketball with the WNBA, as well as continued interest in well-established women's professional sports such as golf and tennis.

FIGURE 14.4   **DISCRIMINATION CASES IN THE EQUAL EMPLOYMENT OPPORTUNITY COMMISSION, 2007**

Discrimination based on race and on sex are the two types that are most frequently reported, but there is a significant amount of discrimination based on age and disability as well. What types of discrimination do you think would be most likely to go unreported?

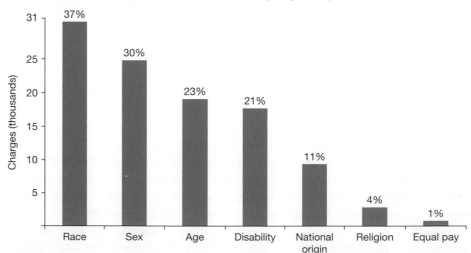

Note: Percentages do not sum to 100 because complaints may be filed in more than one category.

SOURCE: U.S. Equal Employment Opportunity Commission, Charge Statistics, available at http://www.eeoc.gov/stats/charges.html.

The other significant effort on behalf of women's rights during this period was the failed Equal Rights Amendment to the Constitution. The amendment passed in 1972 (it was first introduced in Congress in 1923!) and was sent to the states for ratification. The wording of the amendment was very simple: "Equality of rights under the law shall not be denied or abridged by the United States or any state on the account of sex." Many states passed it within months, but the process lost momentum, and the amendment fell three states short of the required thirty-eight states after the required seven years. The amendment received a three-year extension from Congress but still did not get the additional three states.

In 1994 Congress passed the Violence Against Women Act, which allowed women who were the victims of physical abuse and violence to sue in federal court. As mentioned above, this law was overturned by the Supreme Court, which ruled that Congress had exceeded its powers under the commerce clause.[69]

The other most important piece of civil rights legislation in recent years was the 1990 Americans with Disabilities Act, which provided strong federal protections for the 45 million disabled Americans. The law included tough language on workplace discrimination and access to public facilities. This law produced the curb-cuts in sidewalks, access for wheelchairs to public buses and trains, special seating in sports stadiums, and many other changes that have made the daily lives of the disabled a little easier and that provide them an equal opportunity to participate more fully in society. The scope of the law was narrowed by the Supreme Court when it ruled that it did not apply to state employees.[70]

Congress's track record in protecting gay rights is not quite as strong. In fact, most of the steps taken by Congress have been to restrict rather than expand gay rights. In 1996 Congress reacted to the possibility that some liberal states such as Hawaii would allow gay marriage by passing the Defense of Marriage Act. Its concern was rooted in the "full faith and credit clause" of the Constitution, which says that all states have to respect the laws of other states. So if gay marriages were allowed in one state, all other states would have to recognize that marriage as legal if the couple were to move to another state. President Clinton signed the bill even though he considered it unnecessary.

More recently Congress has proposed an amendment to the Constitution that would ban gay marriage. Acting on the fears expressed by Justice Scalia, members of Congress were concerned that the Supreme Court may strike down the Defense of Marriage Act. President George W. Bush endorsed the amendment, and Democrats have criticized it as a divisive gimmick to appeal to the conservative base of the Republican Party.

THE EXECUTIVE ARENA

The civil rights movement has also benefited greatly from presidential action, such as President Truman's integration of the armed services in 1948, and President Eisenhower's use of the National Guard to enforce a court order to integrate Central High School in Little Rock, Arkansas, in 1957. Executive orders by presidents Kennedy and Johnson in 1961 and 1965, respectively, established affirmative action; and in 1969 Richard Nixon expanded the "goals and numerical ranges" for hiring minorities. The most significant unilateral action taken by a president in the area of civil rights for gays was President Clinton's effort to follow through on his campaign promise to end the ban on gays in the military. Clinton was surprised by the strength of the opposition to his plan, so he ended up crafting a compromise policy of "don't ask, don't tell," which pleased no one. Under this policy the military would stop actively searching for gays in the military and recruits would not need to reveal their sexual orientation. However, if without an investigation the military somehow found out a person was gay, he or she still could be disciplined or discharged.

Clinton's experience with the policy on gays in the military and the low priority that recent presidential candidates have given to civil rights policy more generally means that it is less likely that significant and dramatic change will come from unilateral action by the president. Instead, attention to civil rights concerns in the executive branch has primarily been in two areas in the past fifteen years: racial diversity in presidential appointments and use of the bully pulpit to promote racial concerns and interests.

President Clinton excelled on both of these dimensions. In 1992, as a presidential candidate, Clinton promised a government that "looks like America." Clinton's cabinet, subcabinet, and judicial appointments achieved the greatest gender and racial balance of any in history. Fourteen percent of Clinton's first-year presidential appointments were African American (compared to 12 percent of the population in 1992), 6 percent were Hispanic (compared to 9.5 percent of the population), and the percentage of Asian American and Native American appointees was identical to their proportions in the population. Clinton truly delivered an administration that "looked like us." President Clinton also used the bully pulpit to advocate a civil rights agenda. For example, when affirmative action came under attack from the courts, he advocated an approach of "mend it, don't end it." More significant was Clinton's sustained effort to promote a "National Conversation on Race." Many critics dismissed the effort as empty symbolism, but Clinton's Race Initiative did help focus national attention on many of the problems faced by minorities.

While President George W. Bush did not achieve the same level of diversity in his appointments as Clinton, his administration was more diverse than that of other Republican presidents. Of his initial nineteen cabinet and cabinet-rank appointments, fifteen were men and four were women. There were two blacks (Secretary of State Colin Powell, who is Jamaican American, and Secretary of Education Rod Paige, who is African American), two Asian Americans (Secretary of Labor Elaine Chao and Secretary of Transportation Norman Mineta), one Cuban American (Secretary of Housing and Urban Development Mel Martinez), and one Arab American (Secretary of Energy Spencer Abraham). Since these initial appointments in 2001, two African Americans served in President Bush's second term: Condoleezza Rice served as secretary of state (she was the national security advisor in Bush's first term) and Alphonso Jackson as Housing and Urban Development secretary, as well as one Cuban American, Carlos Gutierrez, who served as commerce secretary, and one Mexican American, Alberto Gonzales, who served as attorney general for two and a half years. The rhetoric that surrounded these appointments, however, was not couched in terms of affirmative action, but rather merit. Critics argued that gender and race played a central role in these decisions, just as they did with Clinton, even if the rhetoric had a different tone. Despite the different approach, President Bush made serious overtures to minorities, especially Latinos, in his effort to expand the base of the Republican Party.

While it is too early to know the impact of the Obama presidency on the civil rights movement, the historical significance of his successful campaign is clear. At the 2008 Democratic National Convention, some African American delegates openly wept as Obama accepted the party's nomination. Many delegates had not expected that they would live to see an African American become a strong contender for the presidency. However, in some ways, Obama's victory may signal the beginning of a new "post-racial politics" that places less emphasis on race and devotes more attention to issues that concern all Americans, such as the economy, education, and heath care.

SECTION SUMMARY

1. The civil rights movement put pressure on the political system through non-violent protest and civil disobedience to enact far-reaching legislation to end segregation, prohibit discrimination, and guarantee equal voting rights.
2. The *Brown v. Board of Education* decision to end segregation in public schools was an important step toward ending legal segregation and discrimination in other parts of social life.
3. Starting in the 1980s the Supreme Court moved toward a "color-blind" jurisprudence that tried to minimize the impact of race in various social and political contexts. The Court has also played a central role in determining women's civil rights and gay rights.
4. The bedrock of equal protection for racial minorities that exists today stems from landmark legislation passed by Congress in the 1960s, namely, the 1964 Civil Rights Act, the 1965 Voting Rights Act, and the 1968 Fair Housing Act. Women have also received extensive protection through legislation, most importantly, Title VII of the Civil Rights Act and Title IX of the Higher Education Act.
5. Presidents have been very important in promoting civil rights, both through executive orders and through the "bully pulpit" of the presidency and symbolic politics.

Continuing and Future Civil Rights Issues

There is vigorous debate over the future direction of the civil rights movement as it moves into the new century. There are three main perspectives. The first group, whose views are articulated by such scholars as Stephan Thernstrom of Harvard University and Abigail Thernstrom of the Manhattan Institute, has suggested that our nation must "move beyond race." This group argues that on many social and economic indicators, the gap between blacks and whites has narrowed and that public opposition to race-based policies indicates that a new approach is needed. The Supreme Court has largely endorsed this view by implementing a "color-blind jurisprudence" over a broad range of issues. The second group is represented by traditional civil rights activists and groups such as the Congressional Black Caucus and the NAACP; it argues that the civil rights movement must continue to fight for the equality of opportunity by enforcing existing law and pushing for equality of outcomes by protecting and expanding racially targeted affirmative action programs and other policies that address racial inequality. These first two groups share the goal of racial equality and integration but differ on how much progress we have made in achieving those goals and how to make further progress. A final group does not support the goal of integration; instead, activists in this group such as Louis Farrakhan and the Nation of Islam argue for African American self-sufficiency and separation. They believe that African Americans can never gain equality within what they see as the repressive, white-dominated economic and political system.

A large majority of civil rights advocates endorse the second view. They argue that it would be a mistake to conclude that racial politics has become inconsequential at the turn of the new century in the United States or that the work of the civil rights movement is complete. They point to the resegregation of public schools, persistent gaps between whites and racial minorities in health and economic status, racial profiling, hate crimes, a backlash against immigrant groups, and continuing discrimination in employment and housing as ample evidence that our nation is not ready to "move beyond race." At the same time, this group rejects calls for racial separation as ultimately short-sighted and self-defeating.

The other two groups would respond by arguing that while the traditional civil rights agenda made important contributions to racial equality, further progress will require a different approach. Advocates of the color-blind approach argue that the only way toward progress on racial issues is to stop making distinctions between people based on race. Use government policies to make sure there is no overt discrimination and provide equal opportunity for all, and then let merit decide outcomes. The segregationists, who comprise a relatively small group, have basically given up on the civil rights agenda and believe that minorities can achieve success only on their own. Debates between advocates of these three views play out over a broad range of issues. Three of these issues are outlined in this last section of the chapter.

AFFIRMATIVE ACTION

The Civil Rights Act of 1964 ensured that, at least on paper, all Americans would enjoy equality of opportunity. But even after the act was passed, blacks continued to lag behind whites in socioeconomic status; that is, there was still a substantial gap between the equality of opportunity and the equality of outcomes (see Nuts and Bolts 14.2, President Johnson's speech on this topic). Beginning in 1965, President Johnson tried to address these inequalities with a policy of affirmative action. By executive order, Johnson required all federal agencies and government contractors to submit written proposals to hire certain numbers of blacks, women, Asian Americans, and Native Americans within various job categories. The policy was expanded and strengthened under President Nixon, and throughout the 1970s and 1980s, affirmative action programs grew in the private sector, higher education, and government contracting. Through such programs, employers and universities gave special opportunities to minorities and women, either to make up for past patterns of discrimination or to pursue the general goals of diversity.

Affirmative action takes many forms. The most passive type is extra effort to recruit women and minorities for employment or college admission by taking out ads in newspapers and magazines, visiting inner-city schools, or sending out targeted mailings. A more active form is to include race or gender as a "plus factor" in the admissions or hiring decision. That is, from a pool of qualified candidates, a minority applicant may be given an advantage over white applicants. (Women generally do not receive special consideration in admissions decisions, but gender may be a "plus factor" in some employment decisions; in fact, many selective schools have been quietly applying affirmative action for men because more highly qualified women apply than men.) The strongest form of affirmative action is the use of quotas—strict numerical targets to hire or admit a specific number of applicants from underrepresented groups.

Affirmative action has been a controversial policy, almost from its inception. Many whites view the policy as "preferential treatment" and "reverse discrimination." Polls indicate that minorities are much more supportive of the practice than whites. A majority of whites support more passive forms of affirmative action, such as "education programs to assist minorities in competing for college admissions," but draw the line at preferences, even when they are intended to make up for past discrimination.[71] This backlash against affirmative action has spilled over into

President Johnson's Commencement Address at Howard University

WASHINGTON, DC, JUNE 4, 1965

"To Fulfill These Rights"

[After outlining the legal protections for African Americans that had recently been provided by Congress, President Johnson presents his famous argument that true equality must be based on outcomes, not just opportunity.]

But freedom is not enough. You do not wipe away the scars of centuries by saying: Now you are free to go where you want, and do as you desire, and choose the leaders you please.

You do not take a person who, for years, has been hobbled by chains and liberate him, bring him up to the starting line of a race and then say, "you are free to compete with all the others," and still justly believe that you have been completely fair. Thus it is not enough just to open the gates of opportunity. All our citizens must have the ability to walk through those gates.

This is the next and the more profound stage of the battle for civil rights. We seek not just freedom but opportunity. We seek not just legal equity but human ability, not just equality as a right and a theory but equality as a fact and equality as a result.

For the task is to give 20 million Negroes the same chance as every other American to learn and grow, to work and share in society, to develop their abilities—physical, mental and spiritual, and to pursue their individual happiness.

To this end equal opportunity is essential, but not enough, not enough. Men and women of all races are born with the same range of abilities. But ability is not just the product of birth. Ability is stretched or stunted by the family that you live with, and the neighborhood you live in—by the school you go to and the poverty or the richness of your surroundings. It is the product of a hundred unseen forces playing upon the little infant, the child, and finally the man.

[President Johnson describes the persistent gulf between the socioeconomic status of blacks and whites, the causes of poverty, and some of the solutions to inequalities between whites and blacks.]

For what is justice? It is to fulfill the fair expectations of man. Thus, American justice is a very special thing. For, from the first, this has been a land of towering expectations. It was to be a nation where each man could be ruled by the common consent of all—enshrined in law, given life by institutions, guided by men themselves subject to its rule. And all—all of every station and origin—would be touched equally in obligation and in liberty. . . . This is American justice. We have pursued it faithfully to the edge of our imperfections, and we have failed to find it for the American Negro.

So, it is the glorious opportunity of this generation to end the one huge wrong of the American Nation and, in so doing, to find America for ourselves, with the same immense thrill of discovery which gripped those who first began to realize that here, at last, was a home for freedom.

All it will take is for all of us to understand what this country is and what this country must become. The Scripture promises: "I shall light a candle of understanding in thine heart, which shall not be put out." Together, and with millions more, we can light that candle of understanding in the heart of all America. And, once lit, it will never again go out.

SOURCE: *Public Papers of the Presidents of the United States: Lyndon B. Johnson, 1965,* vol. II, entry 301 (Washington, DC: Government Printing Office, 1966) pp. 635–40.

state politics in the past decade. California passed Proposition 209 in 1996, which banned the use of "race, sex, color, ethnicity or national origin as a criterion for either discriminating against, or granting preferential treatment to, any individual or group in the operation of the State's system of public employment, public education, or public contracting." Voters in Washington passed a similar resolution in 1999, Florida banned the use of race in college admission decisions in that year as well, and Michigan passed a broad ban on affirmative action in 2006. Several other state legislatures have considered taking up the issue, but the state and local decisions have been mixed. Voters in Houston, Texas, voted to continue affirmative action in their city in November 1997, perhaps illustrating the importance of the question wording on the resolution. In California the wording of Proposition 209 mentioned the hot-button term "preferential treatment," whereas the Houston resolution simply asked voters if they wanted to retain the city's affirmative action program.[72] Fifty-five percent of voters in California's and 58 percent in Michigan voted to get rid of "preferential treatment," while 55 percent of Houston's voters supported keeping the city's affirmative action program.

The Supreme Court has helped define the boundaries of this policy debate. The earliest cases concerning affirmative action in employment upheld preferential treatment and even rigid quotas when the policies were needed to make up for past discrimination. The cases involved a worker training program that set aside 50 percent of the positions for blacks (which meant that some less-qualified blacks were admitted into the program ahead of more-qualified whites), a labor union that was required to hire enough minorities to get its nonwhite membership to 29.23 percent, and the Alabama state police force, which was required to promote one black officer for every white even if there was a smaller pool of blacks who were eligible for promotion.[73] In each instance there had been a pattern of discrimination and exclusion that was the target of the affirmative action program.

The Supreme Court started moving in a "color-blind" direction in 1989 concerning "set-aside" programs in government contracting. In 1983 Richmond, Virginia, adopted a policy requiring contractors who had won city construction contracts to subcontract at least 30 percent of the work to minority-owned businesses. The city council noted that 50 percent of Richmond's population was black but only 0.67 percent of the city's prime construction contracts had gone to minority-owned businesses. A white-owned business, J. A. Croson, had bid for a city contract and lost to a minority-owned business. Croson sued, saying that his 14th Amendment equal protection rights had been violated. The Court agreed, ruling that set-asides were unconstitutional without specific evidence of patterns of discrimination against minorities and that any such programs had to be "narrowly tailored to meet a compelling state interest." "Generalized assertions" of past discrimination were not adequate to justify such rigid quotas.[74] This same reasoning was applied to federal contracting set-aside programs in 1995.[75]

The landmark decision for affirmative action in higher education is *University of California Regents v. Bakke* (1978).[76] Allan Bakke, a white student, sued when he was denied admission to medical school at the University of California, Davis, in successive years. Bakke showed that his test scores and GPA were significantly higher than those of some of the minority students who were admitted under the school's affirmative action program. Under that program, 16 of the 100 slots in the entering class were reserved for minority or disadvantaged students. The Supreme Court agreed with Bakke that rigid racial quotas were unconstitutional but allowed race to be used in admissions decisions as a "plus factor" to promote diversity in the student body. This standard was widely followed and largely unquestioned until 1996 when the Fifth Circuit Court of Appeals held that it was unconstitutional to consider race in law school admissions at the University of Texas. A circuit court in Washington reached the opposite conclusion in a different case.

Even more puzzling were two conflicting cases from the University of Michigan. A district court held that race-conscious undergraduate admissions were acceptable, but a decision a few months later in the same district court held that considering race in law school admissions was not constitutional. An appeals court reversed the law school decision, leaving the Supreme Court to sort out the mess. The Court's rulings were consistent with *Bakke*, saying that the law school's "holistic approach" that considered race as one of the factors in the admission decision

POLITICS IS CONFLICTUAL

 Affirmative action remains a controversial policy that reveals deep racial divisions concerning the merits of the policy.

Affirmative Action at the University of Michigan

If you were serving on the Supreme Court, how would you have decided the University of Michigan affirmative action cases? In the undergraduate case Jennifer Gratz had a high school GPA of 3.76 and an ACT score of 25 (eighty-third percentile), and Patrick Hamacher had a GPA of 3.37 and an ACT of 28 (eighty-ninth percentile), but they were denied admission to Michigan. The student in the law school case, Barbara Grutter, was a forty-three-year-old returning student who had an undergraduate GPA of 3.81 at Michigan State University and a 161 on the LSAT. All three students showed that they had higher scores than some of the minority students who were admitted under the university's affirmative action program. The legal question that the Court had to decide was whether the university's affirmative action program violated the equal protection clause of the 14th Amendment and civil rights laws barring discrimination on the basis of race, or if the program could be justified as serving a "compelling state interest" under the strict scrutiny standard.

The crucial point of contention in the debate over the use of race in college admissions decisions is "viewpoint diversity"; the claimed advantage of affirmative action is the diversity that it brings to classroom discussions. Advocates of affirmative action argue that viewpoint diversity is essential to learning and that having racial diversity in the student body is likely to produce more viewpoint diversity than having an all-white student body. Furthermore, proponents argue, the courts are not the proper place to decide these issues. Instead, as with the complex and highly charged topic of racial redistricting, the political branches of government are

▲ *University of Michigan students are shown hanging out on campus. Debates over the importance of racial diversity in the classroom have played a central role in court cases concerning affirmative action in higher education.*

where these decisions should be made. Advocates also make a very pragmatic argument that getting rid of affirmative action would almost certainly lead to a system that is *less* rooted in merit-based admissions than the current system, an odd position for political conservatives to hold. This is because states that get rid of race as a factor in admissions often adopt a "10 percent solution," which says that the top 10 percent of any graduating high school class can be admitted to the state university. This means that a student who may be in the top 20 percent of an excellent school might not be admitted even if she had better test scores and grades than a student who was in the top 10 percent of a high school that was not as good.

Opponents reply that supporters of affirmative action have not provided convincing evidence that racial diversity in colleges has any beneficial effects. They also argue that "viewpoint diversity" arguments assume that members of all racial minorities think alike, drawing a comparison to racial profiling in law enforcement. It is just as offensive, they say, that an admissions committee thinks that one black student has the same views as another black student as it is that a police officer may pull over a black teenage male just because he fits a certain criminal profile. Opponents also argue that affirmative action amounts to "reverse discrimination" and that any racial classification is harmful.

How would you decide these cases? To what extent should race be used as a "plus factor" to promote racial diversity and viewpoint diversity, if at all? How would you justify your decision? Is viewpoint diversity an important goal? Think of your own experiences from high school and college. Has racial diversity contributed to viewpoint diversity? ■

was acceptable but that the University of Michigan's more rigid approach to undergraduate admissions, which added 20 points to the 100 needed for admissions for minority students, was not acceptable.[77] While these two decisions affirmed *Bakke*, it was the first time that a majority of the Court clearly stated that "student body diversity is a compelling state interest that can justify the use of race in university admissions."[78]

MULTICULTURAL ISSUES

There are a host of issues involving the multicultural, multiracial nature of American society that will become more important as white people in the United States will no longer constitute a majority of the population by the middle of this century. Two of these issues are English as the official language and immigration.

The decision by many states to adopt laws establishing English as the official language has had practical consequences. For example, the Supreme Court upheld an Alabama state law that required that the state driver's license test be conducted only in English. A Mexican immigrant, Martha Sandoval, sued under Title VI of the 1964 Civil Rights Act, saying that the state law had a disparate impact on non–English-speaking residents. However, the Court held in *Alexander v. Sandoval*, 2001, that individuals may not sue federally funded state agencies over policies that have a discriminatory effect on minorities under Title VI. This decision could have far-reaching consequences for the use of the Civil Rights Act to fight patterns of discrimination. Two areas that could be affected are education policy (for example, civil rights advocates have challenged the use of standardized testing because of its disparate impact on minorities) and environmental policy (lawsuits brought under Title VI have alleged "environmental racism" in decisions to site hazardous waste dumps in predominantly minority areas).

The second increasingly prominent multicultural issue, immigration, was thrust back into center stage in the wake of the September 11 terrorist attacks. In light of these attacks, some people came to see immigration as a threat that must be curtailed. The government made it clear that it would not engage in racial profiling of Arab Americans, for example, subjecting them to stricter screening at airports, but many commentators argued that such profiling would be justified, and there was at least anecdotal evidence of an increase in discrimination against people of Middle Eastern descent.

In the past decade, immigration has been central in many political debates. Some of these debates are nominally about social welfare benefits, but deeper racial issues often are just below the surface (see Challenging Conventional Wisdom). For example, in 1994 voters in California adopted Proposition 187, which denied most public benefits to illegal immigrants but was viewed by critics as discriminatory to Mexican Americans. Debates over immigration have important political implications. Republicans were strongly in favor of Proposition 187, while Democrats opposed it. When the measure was struck down by the courts and Democrats won the 1998 gubernatorial race in California with the strong support of the newly galvanized and growing Hispanic population, Republicans softened their position on immigration. President George W. Bush was instrumental in trying to move the Republican Party in this direction. He actively cultivated the Hispanic vote, often presenting part of his speeches in Spanish, and won a record 44 percent of the Latino vote in 2004. Bush pushed for comprehensive immigration reform in 2006, making an alliance with Democratic Senator Ted Kennedy. However, anti-immigration Republicans in Congress rejected this effort and passed a strong measure aimed at enforcing existing immigration laws and building a barrier along the border with

Immigration

The long-standing conventional wisdom in the United States concerning immigration points to its central role in building our nation: we are a country of immigrants. America's ability to assimilate and integrate a broad range of people and cultures produced an image of a melting pot in which these diverse groups become something uniquely American. Others point to an image of a patchwork quilt in which different cultures are stitched together into the same American blanket while maintaining parts of their unique identity. Whatever the image, the Statue of Liberty in New York Harbor serves as the central symbol of this long-standing conventional wisdom and the noble words at the base of the statue are a warm welcome to generations of immigrants, "Give me your tired, your poor, your huddled masses yearning to breathe free, the wretched refuse of your teeming shore. Send these, the homeless, tempest tossed, to me: I lift my lamp beside the golden door."

Like most conventional wisdom, this has always had its dissenters. Immigrants have always been discriminated against as they try to make their new home, whether it was Italians, Germans, Irish, or Poles in the first wave of immigration in the nineteenth and early twentieth centuries or Asians, Mexicans, and other Latin Americans in the next wave. A recent expression of this nativist tradition in American politics has been evident in the debate over reforming immigration policy. Politicians such as James Sensenbrenner (R-WI), former chair of the House Judiciary Committee; media figures such as Lou Dobbs of CNN; and academics such as Harvard professor Samuel Huntington weighed in against President Bush's attempt to fashion a compromise between those who want to close the border with Mexico and deport all illegal immigrants and those who take a more forgiving line. Bush proposed to beef up border security while offering amnesty to illegal immigrants willing to pay fines and meet other conditions.

Sensenbrenner would have none of it, saying that we need to focus our efforts on keeping out illegal immigrants and making it a felony to assist anyone who is in the country illegally. That provision drew howls of protest from churches and charitable organizations that run homeless shelters and food banks, saying that many of their volunteers could be in violation of the law. The most sustained critique of the conventional wisdom on immigration comes from Huntington, who writes in *Who Are We: The Challenges to America's National Identity*,

> Americans like to boast of their past success in assimilating millions of immigrants into their society, culture, and politics. But . . . they have overlooked the unique characteristics and problems posed by contemporary Hispanic immigration. The extent and nature of this immigration differ fundamentally from those of previous immigration, and the assimilation successes of the past are unlikely to be duplicated with the contemporary flood of immigrants from Latin America.

He suggests that this development poses "a major potential threat to the cultural and possibly political integrity of the United States." Therefore, Huntington would argue that he isn't challenging the conventional wisdom on immigration as much as trying to uphold the traditional view of an assimilationist America that embraces new groups but expects them to adopt an American identity.

Huntington's critics point out that much of his evidence is pretty thin and that Mexican Americans and immigrants from other parts of Latin America appear to be assimilating at about the same rate as other immigrants. On some critical characteristics such as work ethic, family values, and religion, Mexican Americans already embrace many aspects of American culture. While only 5 percent of first-generation Mexican American immigrants speak English at home, by the third generation that figure is 60 percent.[a] There is some evidence that first-generation immigrants

depress wages for native low-income workers, but that effect is gone by the second generation (there are some difficult issues here, however, concerning the replacement of each generation with new immigrants, which continues to depress the wages of low-income workers). Overall, the evidence appears to support the conventional wisdom more than Huntington's view.

The American public is divided on this issue, in some cases sharing Huntington's pessimism and in other cases embracing a more optimistic view of immigration. A recent NBC News/*Wall Street Journal* poll asked, "Would you say that immigration helps the United States more than it hurts it, or immigration hurts the United States more than it helps it?" Forty-four percent thought it helped and 45 percent that it hurt. An AP poll found that 52 percent of Americans thought that immigrants had a "good influence on the way things are going in the United States," while 46 percent thought they had a bad influence. The same poll found that slightly more thought that immigrants helped improve their community (22 percent) than created problems (18 percent), but most (58 percent) thought they did not have much effect either way. The most negative view of immigrants tied them to crime: 19 percent said that immigrants were more likely than the native-born to be involved in crime, while 12 percent thought they were less likely, and 68 percent said no difference. The most positive view was that by huge margins (51 percent to 5 percent), Americans think that "immigrants work harder than people born here."[b] Given these mixed views, it is not surprising that a significant majority of Americans favored President Bush's compromise policy on this issue, which combined stronger border controls with an amnesty program. However, this compromise was rejected by conservatives in Congress who favored strengthening the border over providing a "path to citizenhip" for illegal immigrants. ∎

▲ *A United States Border Patrol vehicle cruises between the primary and secondary fence lines along the Mexican border in San Diego, California. Illegal immigration remains a controversial issue in national electoral and legislative politics. Attempts at major immigration policy reform broke down in 2006 and 2007.*

Mexico. Strong Latino turnout in 2006 is credited, at least in part, with a return of control of Congress to the Democrats. How to deal with immigration deeply divides the country and is likely to become even more controversial in the next decade.

Conclusion

We now can answer the questions about possible civil rights violations that introduced this chapter. The African American teenagers who were pulled over by the police may or may not have had their civil rights violated, depending on the laws in their state. In Massachusetts, for example, it is prohibited to consider the "race, gender, national or ethnic origin of members of the public in deciding to detain a person or stop a motor vehicle" except in "suspect specific incidents." That is, if the police officer was in pursuit of a specific African American suspect, it would have been legitimate to use racial profiling.[79] Pulling over the car full of white teenagers would have been acceptable as long as there was some "probable cause" to justify the stop. The Asian American woman who did not get the job could certainly talk to a lawyer about filing a "disparate impact" discrimination suit. Under the 1991 Civil Rights Act, the employer would have the burden of proof to show that she was not victimized by the "good ol' boy" network. The gay couple who could not get the apartment because of their sexual orientation may have a basis for a civil rights lawsuit based on the 14th Amendment; however, this would depend on where they live, given that there is no federal protection against discrimination against gays and lesbians. The recent Court decisions concerning affirmative action at the University of Michigan show that the white student who was not admitted to the university of his choice would just have to take his lumps, as long as the affirmative action program considered race as a general "plus factor" rather than assigning more or fewer points for it. Finally, the white contractor definitely could claim that he was a victim of reverse discrimination and sue the city. The burden of proof would be on the city to demonstrate a specific pattern of discrimination against minority-owned businesses to justify a "narrowly tailored" set-aside program.

While this review of civil rights policy has only highlighted some of the most important issues, it is clear that a broad and significant agenda remains. The civil rights movement will continue to use the multiple avenues of the legislative, executive, and judicial branches to secure equal rights for all Americans. Civil rights in the United States is an evolving work-in-progress.

CRITICAL THINKING

1. Have you ever faced discrimination based on your race, gender, or sexual orientation? If so, what did you learn in this chapter about whether your civil rights were violated?
2. Should government attempt to provide a level playing field by making sure that there is no discrimination, or should it go beyond providing equality of opportunity to also be concerned with the equality of outcomes?
3. Which policy-making institution has historically played the most important role in protecting the civil rights of Americans? Does that institution still play that role today?

KEY TERMS

civil rights (p. 498)
de facto (p. 518)
de jure (p. 518)
disenfranchised (p. 500)
disparate impact standard (p. 519)
grandfather clause (p. 500)
intermediate scrutiny standard (p. 522)
Jim Crow laws (p. 500)
Missouri Compromise (p. 499)
protectionism (p. 503)
reasonable basis test (p. 522)
"separate but equal" (p. 501)
strict scrutiny test (p. 522)
substantive due process doctrine (p. 526)

SUGGESTED READING

Canon, David T. *Race, Redistricting, and Representation: The Unintended Consequences of Black-Majority Districts*. Chicago: University of Chicago Press, 1999.

Dawson, Michael C. *Behind the Mule: Race and Class in African-American Politics*. Princeton, NJ: Princeton University Press, 1994.

Hochschild, Jennifer L. *Facing up to the American Dream: Race, Class, and the Soul of the Nation*. Princeton, NJ: Princeton University Press, 1995.

Katznelson, Ira. *When Affirmative Action Was White: An Untold History of Racial Inequality in Twentieth-Century America*. New York: W. W. Norton, 2005.

Kluger, Richard. *Simple Justice: The History of* Brown v. Board of Education *and Black America's Struggle for Equality*. New York: Vintage, 2004.

Kousser, J. Morgan. *Colorblind Injustice: Minority Voting Rights and the Undoing of the Second Reconstruction*. Chapel Hill, NC: University of North Carolina Press, 1999.

Lublin, David. *The Paradox of Representation: Racial Gerrymandering and Minority Interests in Congress*. Princeton, NJ: Princeton University Press, 1997.

Tate, Katherine. *Black Faces in the Mirror: African Americans and Their Representatives in Congress*. Princeton, NJ: Princeton University Press, 2003.

Thernstrom, Stephan, and Abigail Thernstrom. *America in Black and White One Nation, Indivisible: Race in Modern America*. New York: Simon and Schuster, 1997.

Appendix

The Declaration of Independence

In Congress, July 4, 1776

The unanimous Declaration of the thirteen united States of America,

When in the Course of human events, it becomes necessary for one people to dissolve the political bands which have connected them with another, and to assume among the powers of the earth, the separate and equal station to which the Laws of Nature and of Nature's God entitle them, a decent respect to the opinions of mankind requires that they should declare the causes which impel them to the separation.

We hold these truths to be self-evident, that all men are created equal, that they are endowed by their Creator with certain unalienable Rights, that among these are Life, Liberty and the pursuit of Happiness.—That to secure these rights, Governments are instituted among Men, deriving their just powers from the consent of the governed. —That whenever any Form of Government becomes destructive of these ends, it is the Right of the People to alter or to abolish it, and to institute new Government, laying its foundation on such principles and organizing its powers in such form, as to them shall seem most likely to effect their Safety and Happiness. Prudence, indeed, will dictate that Governments long established should not be changed for light and transient causes; and accordingly all experience hath shewn, that mankind are more disposed to suffer, while evils are sufferable, than to right themselves by abolishing the forms to which they are accustomed. But when a long train of abuses and usurpations, pursuing invariably the same Object evinces a design to reduce them under absolute Despotism, it is their right, it is their duty, to throw off such Government, and to provide new Guards for their future security.—Such has been the patient sufferance of these Colonies; and such is now the necessity which constrains them to alter their former Systems of Government. The history of the present King of Great Britain is a history of repeated injuries and usurpations, all having in direct object the establishment of an absolute Tyranny over these States. To prove this, let Facts be submitted to a candid world.

He has refused his Assent to Laws, the most wholesome and necessary for the public good.

He has forbidden his Governors to pass Laws of immediate and pressing importance, unless suspended in their operation till his Assent should be obtained; and when so suspended, he has utterly neglected to attend to them.

He has refused to pass other Laws for the accommodation of large districts of people, unless those people would relinquish the right of Representation in the Legislature, a right inestimable to them and formidable to tyrants only.

He has called together legislative bodies at places unusual, uncomfortable, and distant from the depository of their public Records, for the sole purpose of fatiguing them into compliance with his measures.

He has dissolved Representative Houses repeatedly, for opposing with manly firmness his invasions on the rights of the people.

He has refused for a long time, after such dissolutions, to cause others to be elected; whereby the Legislative powers, incapable of Annihilation, have returned to the People at large for their exercise; the State remaining in the mean time exposed to all the dangers of invasion from without, and convulsions within.

He has endeavoured to prevent the population of these States; for that purpose obstructing the Laws for Naturalization of Foreigners; refusing to pass others to encourage their migrations hither, and raising the conditions of new Appropriations of Lands.

He has obstructed the Administration of Justice, by refusing his Assent to Laws for establishing Judiciary powers.

He has made Judges dependent on his Will alone, for the tenure of their offices, and the amount and payment of their salaries.

He has erected a multitude of New Offices, and sent hither swarms of Officers to harrass our people, and eat out their substance.

He has kept among us, in times of peace, Standing Armies without the Consent of our legislatures.

He has affected to render the Military independent of and superior to the Civil power.

He has combined with others to subject us to a jurisdiction foreign to our constitution, and unacknowledged by our laws; giving his Assent to their Acts of pretended Legislation:

For Quartering large bodies of armed troops among us:

For protecting them, by a mock Trial, from punishment for any Murders which they should commit on the Inhabitants of these States:

For cutting off our Trade with all parts of the world:

For imposing Taxes on us without our Consent:

For depriving us in many cases, of the benefits of Trial by Jury:

For transporting us beyond Seas to be tried for pretended offences:

For abolishing the free System of English Laws in a neighboring Province, establishing therein an Arbitrary government, and enlarging its Boundaries so as to render it at once an example and fit instrument for introducing the same absolute rule into these Colonies:

For taking away our Charters, abolishing our most valuable Laws, and altering fundamentally the Forms of our Governments:

For suspending our own Legislatures, and declaring themselves invested with power to legislate for us in all cases whatsoever.

He has abdicated Government here, by declaring us out of his Protection and waging War against us.

He has plundered our seas, ravaged our Coasts, burnt our towns, and destroyed the lives of our people.

He is at this time transporting large Armies of foreign Mercenaries to compleat the works of death, desolation and tyranny, already begun with circumstances of Cruelty & perfidy scarcely paralleled in the most barbarous ages, and totally unworthy the Head of a civilized nation.

He has constrained our fellow Citizens taken Captive on the high Seas to bear Arms against their Country, to become the executioners of their friends and Brethren, or to fall themselves by their Hands.

He has excited domestic insurrections amongst us, and has endeavoured to bring on the inhabitants of our frontiers, the merciless Indian Savages, whose known rule of warfare, is an undistinguished destruction of all ages, sexes and conditions.

In every stage of these Oppressions We have Petitioned for Redress in the most humble terms: Our repeated Petitions have been answered only by repeated injury. A Prince whose character is thus marked by every act which may define a Tyrant, is unfit to be the ruler of a free people.

Nor have We been wanting in attentions to our Brittish brethren. We have warned them from time to time of attempts by their legislature to extend an unwarrantable jurisdiction over us. We have reminded them of the circumstances of our emigration and settlement here. We have appealed to their native justice and magnanimity, and we have conjured them by the ties of our common kindred to disavow these usurpations, which, would inevitably interrupt our connections and correspondence. They too have been deaf to the voice of justice and of consanguinity. We must, therefore, acquiesce in the necessity, which denounces our Separation, and hold them, as we hold the rest of mankind, Enemies in War, in Peace Friends.

We, Therefore, the Representatives of the United States of America, in General Congress, Assembled, appealing to the Supreme Judge of the world for the rectitude of our intentions, do, in the Name, and by Authority of the good People of these Colonies, solemnly publish and declare, That these United Colonies are, and of Right ought to be Free and Independent States; that they are Absolved from all Allegiance to the British Crown, and that all political connection between them and the State of Great Britain, is and ought to be totally dissolved; and that as Free and Independent States, they have full Power to levy War, conclude Peace, contract Alliances, establish Commerce, and to do all other Acts and Things which Independent States may of right do. And for the support of this Declaration, with a firm reliance on the protection of divine Providence, we mutually pledge to each other our Lives, our Fortunes and our sacred Honor.

The foregoing Declaration was, by order of Congress, engrossed, and signed by the following members:

John Hancock

NEW HAMPSHIRE
Josiah Bartlett
William Whipple
Matthew Thornton

MASSACHUSETTS BAY
Samuel Adams
John Adams
Robert Treat Paine
Elbridge Gerry

RHODE ISLAND
Stephen Hopkins
William Ellery

CONNECTICUT
Roger Sherman
Samuel Huntington
William Williams
Oliver Wolcott

NEW YORK
William Floyd
Philip Livingston
Francis Lewis
Lewis Morris

NEW JERSEY
Richard Stockton
John Witherspoon
Francis Hopkinson
John Hart
Abraham Clark

PENNSYLVANIA
Robert Morris
Benjamin Rush
Benjamin Franklin
John Morton
George Clymer
James Smith
George Taylor
James Wilson
George Ross

DELAWARE
Caesar Rodney
George Read
Thomas M'Kean

MARYLAND
Samuel Chase
William Paca
Thomas Stone
Charles Carroll,
   of Carrollton

VIRGINIA
George Wythe
Richard Henry Lee
Thomas Jefferson
Benjamin Harrison
Thomas Nelson, Jr.
Francis Lightfoot Lee
Carter Braxton

NORTH CAROLINA
William Hooper
Joseph Hewes
John Penn

SOUTH CAROLINA
Edward Rutledge
Thomas Heyward, Jr.
Thomas Lynch, Jr.
Arthur Middleton

GEORGIA
Button Gwinnett
Lyman Hall
George Walton

Resolved, That copies of the Declaration be sent to the several assemblies, conventions, and committees, or councils of safety, and to the several commanding officers of the continental troops; that it be proclaimed in each of the United States, at the head of the army.

The Articles of Confederation

Agreed to by Congress November 15, 1777;
ratified and in force March 1, 1781

To all whom these Presents shall come, we the undersigned Delegates of the States affixed to our Names, send greeting. Whereas the Delegates of the United States of America, in Congress assembled, did, on the fifteenth day of November, in the Year of Our Lord One thousand Seven Hundred and Seventy seven, and in the Second Year of the Independence of America, agree to certain articles of Confederation and perpetual Union between the States of Newhampshire, Massachusetts-bay, Rhodeisland and Providence Plantations, Connecticut, New-York, New-Jersey, Pennsylvania, Delaware, Maryland, Virginia, North-Carolina, South-Carolina and Georgia in the words following, viz. "Articles of Confederation and perpetual Union between the states of Newhampshire, Massachusettsbay, Rhodeisland and Providence Plantations, Connecticut, New-York, New-Jersey, Pennsylvania, Delaware, Maryland, Virginia, North-Carolina, South-Carolina and Georgia.

Art. I. The Stile of this confederacy shall be "The United States of America."

Art. II. Each state retains its sovereignty, freedom and independence, and every Power, Jurisdiction and right, which is not by this confederation expressly delegated to the United States, in Congress assembled.

Art. III. The said states hereby severally enter into a firm league of friendship with each other, for their common defence, the security of their Liberties, and their mutual and general welfare, binding themselves to assist each other, against all force offered to, or attacks made upon them, or any of them, on account of religion, sovereignty, trade, or any other pretence whatever.

Art. IV. The better to secure and perpetuate mutual friendship and intercourse among the people of the different states in this union, the free inhabitants of each of these states, paupers, vagabonds and fugitives from Justice excepted, shall be entitled to all privileges and immunities of free citizens in the several states; and the people of each state shall have free ingress and regress to and from any other state, and shall enjoy therein all the privileges of trade and commerce, subject to the same duties, impositions and restrictions as the inhabitants thereof respectively, provided that such restriction shall not extend so far as to prevent the removal of property imported into any state, to any other state, of which the Owner is an inhabitant; provided also that no imposition, duties or restriction shall be laid by any state, on the property of the united states, or either of them.

If any Person guilty of, or charged with treason, felony, or other high misdemeanor in any state, shall flee from Justice, and be found in any of the united states, he shall, upon demand of the Governor or executive power, of the state from which he fled, be delivered up and removed to the state having jurisdiction of his offence.

Full faith and credit shall be given in each of these states to the records, acts and judicial proceedings of the courts and magistrates of every other state.

Art. V. For the more convenient management of the general interests of the united states, delegates shall be annually appointed in such manner as the legislature of each state shall direct, to meet in Congress on the first Monday in November, in every year, with a power reserved to each state, to recall its delegates, or any of them, at any time within the year, and to send others in their stead, for the remainder of the Year.

No state shall be represented in Congress by less than two, nor by more than seven Members; and no person shall be capable of being a delegate for more than three years in any term of six years; nor shall any person, being a delegate, be capable of holding any office under the united states, for which he, or another for his benefit receives any salary, fees or emolument of any kind.`

Each state shall maintain its own delegates in a meeting of the states, and while they act as members of the committee of the states.

In determining questions in the united states, in Congress assembled, each state shall have one vote.

Freedom of speech and debate in Congress shall not be impeached or questioned in any Court, or place out of Congress, and the members of congress shall be protected in their persons from arrests and imprisonments, during the time of their going to and from, and attendance on congress, except for treason, felony, or breach of the peace.

Art. VI. No state without the Consent of the united states in congress assembled, shall send any embassy to, or receive any embassy from, or enter into any conference, agreement, or alliance or treaty with any King, prince or state; nor shall any person holding any office or profit or trust under the united states, or any of them, accept of any present, emolument, office or title of any kind whatever from any king, prince or foreign state; nor shall the united states in congress assembled, or any of them, grant any title of nobility.

No two or more states shall enter into any treaty, confederation or alliance whatever between them, without the consent of the united states in congress assembled, specifying accurately the purposes for which the same is to be entered into, and how long it shall continue.

No state shall lay any imposts or duties, which may interfere with any stipulations in treaties, entered into by the united states in congress assembled, with any king, prince or state, in pursuance of any treaties already proposed by congress, to the courts of France and Spain.

No vessels of war shall be kept up in time of peace by any state, except such number only, as shall be deemed necessary by the united states in congress assembled, for the defence of such state, or its trade; nor shall any body of forces be kept up by any state, in time of peace, except such number only, as in the judgment of the united states, in congress assembled, shall be deemed requisite to garrison the forts necessary for the defence of such state; but every state shall always keep up a well regulated and disciplined militia, sufficiently armed and accoutred, and shall provide and constantly have ready for use, in public stores, a due number of field pieces and tents, and a proper quantity of arms, ammunition and camp equipage.

No state shall engage in any war without the consent of the united states in congress assembled, unless such state be actually invaded by enemies, or shall have received certain advice of a resolution being formed by some nation of Indians to invade such state, and the danger is so imminent as not to admit of a delay, till the united states in congress asssembled can be consulted; nor shall any state grant commissions to any ships or vessels of war, nor letters of marque or reprisal, except it be after a declaration of war by the united states in congress assembled, and then only against the kingdom or state and the subjects thereof, against which war has been so declared, and under such regulations as shall be established by the united states in congress assembled, unless such state be infested by pirates; in which case vessels of war may be fitted out for that occasion, and kept so long as the danger shall continue, or until the united states in congress assembled shall determine otherwise.

Art. VII. When land-forces are raised by any state for the common defence, all officers of or under the rank of colonel, shall be appointed by the legislature of each state respectively, by whom such forces shall be raised, or in such manner as such state shall direct, and all vacancies shall be filled up by the state which first made the appointment.

Art. VIII. All charges of war, and all other expences that shall be incurred for the common defence or general welfare, and allowed by the united states in congress assembled, shall be defrayed out of a common treasury, which shall be supplied by the several states in proportion to the value of all land within each state, granted to or surveyed for any Person, as such land and the buildings and improvements thereon shall be estimated according to such mode as the united states in congress assembled, shall from time to time direct and appoint.

The taxes for paying that proportion shall be laid and levied by the authority and direction of the legislatures of the several states within the time agreed upon by the united states in congress assembled.

Art. IX. The united states in congress assembled, shall have the sole and exclusive right and power of determining on peace and war, except in the cases mentioned in the sixth article—of sending and receiving ambassadors—entering into treaties and alliances, provided that no treaty of commerce shall be made whereby the legislative power of the respective states shall be restrained from imposing such imposts and duties on foreigners, as their own people are subjected to, or from prohibiting the exportation of any species of goods or commodities whatsoever—of establishing rules for deciding in all cases, what captures on land or water shall be legal, and in what manner prizes taken by land or naval forces in the service of the united states shall be divided or appropriated—of granting letters of marque and reprisal in times of peace—appointing courts for the trial of piracies and felonies committed on the high seas and establishing courts for receiving and determining finally appeals in all cases of captures, provided that no member of congress shall be appointed a judge of any of the said courts.

The united states in congress assembled shall also be the last resort on appeal in all disputes and differences now subsisting or that hereafter may arise between two or more states concerning boundary, jurisdiction or any other cause whatever; which authority shall always be exercised in the manner following. Whenever the legislative or executive authority or lawful agent of any state in controversy with another shall present a petition to congress stating the matter in question and praying for a hearing, notice thereof shall be given by order of congress to the legislative or executive authority of the other state in controversy, and a day assigned for the appearance of the parties by their lawful agents, who shall then be directed to appoint by joint consent, commissioners or judges to constitute a court for hearing and determining the matter in question: but if they cannot agree, congress shall name three persons out of each of the united states, and from the list of such persons each party shall alternately strike out one, the petitioners beginning, until the number shall be reduced to thirteen; and from that number not less than seven, nor more than nine names as congress shall direct, shall in the presence of congress be drawn out by lot, and the persons whose names shall be so drawn or any five of them, shall be commissioners or judges, to hear and finally determine the controversy, so always as a major part of the judges who shall hear the cause shall agree in the determination: and if either party shall neglect to attend at the day appointed, without shewing reasons, which congress shall judge sufficient, or being present shall refuse to strike, the congress shall proceed to nominate three persons out of each state, and the secretary of congress shall strike in behalf of such party absent or refusing; and the judgment and sentence of the court to be appointed, in the manner before prescribed, shall be final and conclusive; and if any of the parties shall refuse to submit to the authority of such court, or to appear to defend their claim or cause, the court shall nevertheless proceed to pronounce sentence, or judgment, which shall in like manner be final and decisive, the judgment or sentence and other proceedings being in either case transmitted to congress, and lodged among the acts of congress for the security of the parties concerned: provided that every commissioner, before he sits in judgment, shall take an oath to be administered by one of the judges of the supreme or superior court of the state, where the cause shall be tried, "well and truly to hear and determine the matter in question, according to the best of his judgment, without favour, affection or hope of reward:" provided also, that no state shall be deprived of territory for the benefit of the united states.

All controversies concerning the private right of soil claimed under different grants of two or more states, whose jurisdictions as they may respect such lands, and the states which passed such grants are adjusted, the said grants or either of them being at the same time claimed to have originated antecedent to such settlement of jurisdiction, shall on the petition of either party to the congress of the united states, be finally determined as near as may be in the same manner as is before prescribed for deciding disputes respecting territorial jurisdiction between different states.

The united states in congress assembled shall also have the sole and exclusive right and power of regulating the alloy and value of coin struck by their own authority, or by that of the respective states—fixing the standard of weights and measures throughout the united states—regulating the trade and managing all affairs with the Indians, not members of any of the states, provided that the legislative right of any state within its own limits be not infringed or violated—establishing and regulating post-offices from one state to another, throughout all the united states, and exacting such postage on the papers passing thro' the same as may be requisite to defray the expences of the said office—appointing all officers of the land forces, in the service of the united states, excepting regimental officers—appointing all the officers of the naval forces, and commissioning all officers whatever in the service of the united states—making rules for the government and regulation of the said land and naval forces, and directing their operations.

The united states in congress assembled shall have authority to appoint a committee, to sit in the recess of congress, to be denominated "A Committee of the States," and to consist of one delegate from each state; and to appoint such other committees and civil officers as may be necessary for managing the general affairs of the united states under their direction—to appoint one of their number to preside, provided that no person be allowed to serve in the office of president more than one year in any term of three years; to ascertain the necessary sums of Money to be raised for the service of the united states, and to appropriate and apply the same for defraying the public expenses—to borrow money, or emit bills on the credit of the united states, transmitting every half year to the respective states an account of the sums of money so borrowed or emitted,—to build and equip a navy—to agree upon the number of land forces, and to make requisitions from each state for its quota, in proportion to the number of white inhabitants in such state; which requisition shall be binding, and thereupon the legislature of each state shall appoint the regimental officers, raise the men and cloath, arm and equip them in a soldier like manner, at the expense of the united states; and the officers and men so cloathed, armed and equipped shall march to the place appointed, and within the time agreed on by the united states in congress assembled: But if the united states in congress assembled shall, on consideration of circumstances judge proper that any state should not raise men, or should raise a smaller number than its quota, and that any other state should raise a greater number of men than the quota thereof, such extra number shall be raised, officered, cloathed, armed and equipped in the same manner as the quota of such state, unless the legislature of such state shall judge that such extra number cannot be safely spared out of the same, in which case they shall raise officer, cloath, arm and equip as many of such extra number as they judge can be safely spared. And the officers and men so cloathed, armed and equipped, shall march to the place appointed, and within the time agreed on by the united states in congress assembled.

The united states in congress assembled shall never engage in a war, nor grant letters of marque and reprisal in time of peace, nor enter into any treaties or alliances, nor coin money, nor regulate the value thereof, nor ascertain the sums and expenses necessary for the defence and welfare of the united states, or any of them, nor emit bills, nor borrow money on the credit of the united states, nor appropriate money, nor agree upon the number of vessels of war, to be built or purchased, or the number of land or sea forces to be raised, nor appoint a commander in chief of the army or navy, unless nine states assent to the same: nor shall a question on any other point, except for adjourning from day to day be determined, unless by the votes of a majority of the united states in congress assembled.

The congress of the united states shall have power to adjourn to any time within the year, and to any place within the united states, so that no period of adjournment be for a longer duration than the space of six Months, and shall publish the Journal of their proceedings monthly, except such parts thereof relating to treaties, alliances or military operations, as in their judgment require secrecy; and the yeas and nays of the delegates of each state on any question shall be entered on the Journal, when it is desired by any delegate; and the delegates of a state, or any of them, at his or their request shall be furnished with a transcript of the said Journal, except such parts as are above excepted, to lay before the legislatures of the several states.

Art. X. The committee of the states, or any nine of them, shall be authorised to execute, in the recess of congress, such of the powers of congress as the united states in congress assembled, by the consent of nine states, shall from time to time think expedient to vest them with; provided that no power be delegated to the said committee, for the exercise of which, by the articles of confederation, the voice of nine states in the congress of the united states assembled is requisite.

Art. XI. Canada acceding to this confederation, and joining in the measures of the united states, shall be admitted into, and entitled to all the advantages of this union: but no other colony shall be admitted into the same, unless such admission be agreed to by nine states.

Art. XII. All bills of credit emitted, monies borrowed and debts contracted by, or under the authority of congress, before the assembling of the united states, in pursuance of the present confederation, shall be deemed and considered as a charge against the united states, for payment and satisfaction whereof the said united states and the public faith are hereby solemnly pledged.

Art. XIII. Every state shall abide by the determinations of the united states in congress assembled, on all questions which by this confederation are submitted to them. And the Articles of this confederation shall be inviolably observed by every state, and the union shall be perpetual; nor shall any alteration at any time hereafter be made in any of them; unless such alteration be agreed to in a congress of the united states, and be afterwards confirmed by the legislatures of every state.

And Whereas it hath pleased the Great Governor of the World to incline the hearts of the legislatures we respectively represent in congress, to approve of, and to authorize us to ratify the said articles of confederation and perpetual union. Know Ye that we the undersigned delegates, by virtue of the power and authority to us given for that purpose, do by these presents, in the name and in behalf of our respective constituents, fully and entirely ratify and confirm each and every of the said articles of confederation and perpetual union, and all and singular the matters and things therein contained: And we do further solemnly plight and engage the faith of our respective constituents, that they shall abide by the determinations of the united states in congress assembled, on all questions, which by the said confederation are submitted to them. And that the articles thereof shall be inviolably observed by the states we respectively represent, and that the union shall be perpetual. In Witness whereof we have hereunto set our hands in Congress. Done at Philadelphia in the state of Pennsylvania the ninth day of July, in the Year of our Lord one Thousand seven Hundred and Seventy-eight, and in the third year of the independence of America.

The Constitution of the United States of America

[PREAMBLE]

We the People of the United States, in Order to form a more perfect Union, establish Justice, insure domestic Tranquility, provide for the common defence, promote the general Welfare, and secure the Blessings of Liberty to ourselves and our Posterity, do ordain and establish this Constitution for the United States of America.

Article I

SECTION 1

[LEGISLATIVE POWERS]

All legislative Powers herein granted shall be vested in a Congress of the United States, which shall consist of a Senate and House of Representatives.

SECTION 2

[HOUSE OF REPRESENTATIVES, HOW CONSTITUTED,
POWER OF IMPEACHMENT]

The House of Representatives shall be composed of Members chosen every second Year by the People of the several States, and the Electors in each State shall have the Qualifications requisite for Electors of the most numerous Branch of the State Legislature.

No Person shall be a Representative who shall not have attained to the Age of twenty five Years, and been seven Years a Citizen of the United States, and who shall not, when elected, be an Inhabitant of that State in which he shall be chosen.

Representatives and *direct Taxes*[1] shall be apportioned among the several States which may be included within this Union, according to their respective Numbers, *which shall be determined by adding to the whole Number of free Persons, including those bound to Service for a Term of Years, and excluding Indians not taxed, three fifths of all other Persons.*[2] The actual Enumeration shall be made within three Years after the first Meeting of the Congress of the United States, and within every subsequent Term of ten Years, in such Manner as they shall by Law direct. The Number of Representatives shall not exceed one for every thirty Thousand, but each State shall have at Least one Representative; *and until such enumeration shall be made, the State of New Hampshire shall be entitled to chuse three, Massachusetts eight, Rhode-Island and Providence Plantations one, Connecticut five, New-York six, New Jersey four, Pennsylvania eight, Delaware one, Maryland six, Virginia ten, North Carolina five, South Carolina five, and Georgia three.*[3]

When vacancies happen in the Representation from any State, the Executive Authority thereof shall issue Writs of Election to fill such Vacancies.

The House of Representatives shall chuse their Speaker and other Officers; and shall have the sole Power of Impeachment.

SECTION 3

[THE SENATE, HOW CONSTITUTED, IMPEACHMENT TRIALS]

The Senate of the United States shall be composed of two Senators from each State, *chosen by the Legislature thereof,*[4] for six Years; and each Senator shall have one Vote.

Immediately after they shall be assembled in Consequence of the first Election, they shall be divided as equally as may be into three Classes. The Seats of the Senators of the first Class shall be vacated at the Expiration of the second Year, of the second Class at the Expiration of the fourth Year, and of the third Class at the Expiration of the sixth Year, so that one third may be chosen every second Year; *and if Vacancies happen by Resignation, or otherwise, during the Recess of the Legislature of any State, the Executive thereof may make temporary Appointments until the next Meeting of the Legislature, which shall then fill such Vacancies.*[5]

No Person shall be a Senator who shall not have attained to the Age of thirty Years, and been nine Years a Citizen of the United States, and who shall not, when elected, be an Inhabitant of that State for which he shall be chosen.

The Vice President of the United States shall be President of the Senate, but shall have no Vote, unless they be equally divided.

The Senate shall chuse their other Officers, and also a President pro tempore, in the Absence of the Vice President, or when he shall exercise the Office of President of the United States.

The Senate shall have the sole Power to try all Impeachments. When sitting for that Purpose, they shall be on Oath or Affirmation. When the President of the United States is tried, the Chief Justice shall preside: And no Person shall be convicted without the Concurrence of two thirds of the Members present.

Judgment in Cases of Impeachment shall not extend further than to removal from Office, and disqualification to hold and enjoy any Office of honor, Trust or Profit under the United States: but the Party convicted shall nevertheless be liable and subject to Indictment, Trial, Judgment and Punishment, according to Law.

SECTION 4

[ELECTION OF SENATORS AND REPRESENTATIVES]

The Times, Places and Manner of holding Elections for Senators and Representatives, shall be prescribed in each State by the Legislature thereof; but the Congress may at any time by Law make or alter such Regulations, except as to the Places of chusing Senators.

The Congress shall assemble at least once in every Year, and such Meeting shall be on the first Monday in December, unless they shall by Law appoint a different Day.[6]

SECTION 5

[QUORUM, JOURNALS, MEETINGS, ADJOURNMENTS]

Each House shall be the Judge of the Elections, Returns and Qualifications of its own Members, and a Majority of each shall constitute a Quorum to do Business; but a smaller Number may adjourn from day to day, and may be authorized to compel the Attendance of absent Members, in such Manner, and under such Penalties as each House may provide.

---

[1]Modified by Sixteenth Amendment.
[2]Modified by Fourteenth Amendment.
[3]Temporary provision.
[4]Modified by Seventeenth Amendment.
[5]Modified by Seventeenth Amendment.
[6]Modified by Twentieth Amendment.

Each House may determine the Rules of its Proceedings, punish its Members for disorderly Behaviour, and, with the Concurrence of two thirds, expel a Member.

Each House shall keep a Journal of its Proceedings, and from time to time publish the same, excepting such Parts as may in their Judgment require Secrecy; and the Yeas and Nays of the Members of either House on any questions shall, at the Desire of one fifth of those Present, be entered on the Journal.

Neither House, during the Session of Congress, shall, without the Consent of the other, adjourn for more than three days, nor to any other Place than that in which the two Houses shall be sitting.

SECTION 6
[COMPENSATION, PRIVILEGES, DISABILITIES]

The Senators and Representatives shall receive a Compensation for their Services, to be ascertained by Law, and paid out of the Treasury of the United States. They shall in all Cases, except Treason, Felony and Breach of the Peace, be privileged from Arrest during their Attendance at the Session of their respective Houses, and in going to and returning from the same; and for any Speech or Debate in either House, they shall not be questioned in any other Place.

No Senator or Representative shall, during the Time for which he was elected, be appointed to any civil Office under the Authority of the United States, which shall have been created, or the Emoluments whereof shall have been encreased during such time; and no Person holding any Office under the United States, shall be a Member of either House during his Continuance in Office.

SECTION 7
[PROCEDURE IN PASSING BILLS AND RESOLUTIONS]

All Bills for raising Revenue shall originate in the House of Representatives; but the Senate may propose or concur with Amendments as on other Bills.

Every Bill which shall have passed the House of Representatives and the Senate, shall, before it become a Law, be presented to the President of the United States: If he approve he shall sign it, but if not he shall return it, with his Objections to that House in which it shall have originated, who shall enter the Objections at large on their Journal, and proceed to reconsider it. If after such Reconsideration two thirds of that House shall agree to pass the Bill, it shall be sent, together with the Objections, to the other House, by which it shall likewise be reconsidered, and if approved by two thirds of that House, it shall become a Law. But in all such Cases the Votes of both Houses shall be determined by yeas and Nays, and the Names of the Persons voting for and against the Bill shall be entered on the Journal of each House respectively. If any Bill shall not be returned by the President within ten Days (Sundays excepted) after it shall have been presented to him, the Same shall be a Law, in like Manner as if he had signed it, unless the Congress by their Adjournment prevent its Return, in which Case it shall not be a Law.

Every Order, Resolution, or Vote to which the Concurrence of the Senate and House of Representatives may be necessary (except on a question of Adjournment) shall be presented to the President of the United States; and before the Same shall take Effect, shall be approved by him, or being disapproved by him, shall be repassed by two thirds of the Senate and House of Representatives, according to the Rules and Limitations prescribed in the Case of a Bill.

SECTION 8
[POWERS OF CONGRESS]

The Congress shall have Power

To lay and collect Taxes, Duties, Imposts and Excises, to pay the Debts and provide for the common Defence and general Welfare of the United States; but all Duties, Imposts and Excises shall be uniform throughout the United States;

To borrow Money on the credit of the United States;

To regulate Commerce with foreign Nations, and among the several States, and with the Indian Tribes;

To establish an uniform Rule of Naturalization, and uniform Laws on the subject of Bankruptcies throughout the United States;

To coin Money, regulate the Value thereof, and of foreign Coin, and fix the Standard of Weights and Measures;

To provide for the Punishment of counterfeiting the Securities and current Coin of the United States;

To establish Post Offices and post Roads;

To promote the Progress of Science and useful Arts, by securing for limited Times to Authors and Inventors the exclusive Right to their respective Writings and Discoveries;

To constitute Tribunals inferior to the supreme Court;

To define and punish Piracies and Felonies committed on the high Seas, and Offences against the Law of Nations;

To declare War, grant Letters of Marque and Reprisal, and make Rules concerning Captures on Land and Water;

To raise and support Armies, but no Appropriation of Money to that Use shall be for a longer Term than two Years;

To provide and maintain a Navy;

To make Rules for the Government and Regulation of the land and naval Forces;

To provide for calling forth the Militia to execute the Laws of the Union, suppress Insurrections and repel Invasions;

To provide for organizing, arming, and disciplining, the Militia, and for governing such Part of them as may be employed in the Service of the United States, reserving to the States respectively, the Appointment of the Officers, and the Authority of training the Militia according to the discipline prescribed by Congress;

To exercise exclusive Legislation in all Cases whatsoever, over such District (not exceeding ten Miles square) as may, by Cession of particular States, and the Acceptance of Congress, become the Seat of the Government of the United States, and to exercise like Authority over all Places purchased by the Consent of the Legislature of the State in which the Same shall be, for the Erection of Forts, Magazines, Arsenals, dock-Yards, and other needful Buildings;—And

To make all Laws which shall be necessary and proper for carrying into Execution the foregoing Powers, and all other Powers vested by this Constitution in the Government of the United States, or in any Department or Officer thereof.

SECTION 9
[SOME RESTRICTIONS ON FEDERAL POWER]

The Migration or Importation of such Persons as any of the States now existing shall think proper to admit, shall not be prohibited by the Congress prior to the Year one thousand eight hundred and eight, but a Tax or duty may be imposed on such Importation, not exceeding ten dollars for each Person.[7]

The Privilege of the Writ of Habeas Corpus shall not be suspended, unless when in Cases of Rebellion or Invasion the public Safety may require it.

No Bill of Attainder or ex post facto Law shall be passed.

No Capitation, or other direct, Tax shall be laid, unless in Proportion to the Census or Enumeration herein before directed to be taken.[8]

No Tax or Duty shall be laid on Articles exported from any State.

---

[7]Temporary provision.
[8]Modified by Sixteenth Amendment.

No Preference shall be given by any Regulation of Commerce or Revenue to the Ports of one State over those of another; nor shall Vessels bound to, or from, one State, be obliged to enter, clear, or pay Duties in another.

No Money shall be drawn from the Treasury, but in Consequence of Appropriations made by Law; and a regular Statement and Account of the Receipts and Expenditures of all public Money shall be published from time to time.

No Title of Nobility shall be granted by the United States: And no Person holding any Office of Profit or Trust under them, shall, without the Consent of the Congress, accept of any present, Emolument, Office, or Title, of any kind whatever, from any King, Prince, or foreign State.

SECTION 10

[RESTRICTIONS UPON POWERS OF STATES]

No State shall enter into any Treaty, Alliance, or Confederation; grant Letters of Marque and Reprisal; coin Money; emit Bills of Credit; make any Thing but gold and silver Coin a Tender in Payment of Debts; pass any Bill of Attainder, ex post facto Law, or Law impairing the Obligation of Contracts, or grant any Title of Nobility.

No State shall, without the Consent of the Congress, lay any Imposts or Duties on Imports or Exports, except what may be absolutely necessary for executing its inspection Laws: and the net Produce of all Duties and Imposts, laid by any State on Imports or Exports, shall be for the Use of the Treasury of the United States; and all such Laws shall be subject to the Revision and Control of the Congress.

No State shall, without the Consent of Congress, lay any Duty of Tonnage, keep Troops, or Ships of War in time of Peace, enter into any Agreement or Compact with another State, or with a foreign Power, or engage in War, unless actually invaded, or in such imminent Danger as will not admit of delay.

Article II

SECTION 1

[EXECUTIVE POWER, ELECTION, QUALIFICATIONS OF THE PRESIDENT]

The executive Power shall be vested in a President of the United States of America. *He shall hold his Office during the Term of four Years, and, together with the Vice President, chosen for the same Term, be elected, as follows*[9]

Each State shall appoint, in such Manner as the Legislature thereof may direct, a Number of Electors, equal to the whole Number of Senators and Representatives to which the State may be entitled in the Congress: but no Senator or Representative, or Person holding an Office of Trust or Profit under the United States, shall be appointed an Elector.

The electors shall meet in their respective States, and vote by ballot for two Persons, of whom one at least shall not be an Inhabitant of the same State with themselves. And they shall make a List of all the Persons voted for, and of the Number of Votes for each; which List they shall sign and certify, and transmit sealed to the Seat of the Government of the United States, directed to the President of the Senate. The President of the Senate shall, in the Presence of the Senate and House of Representatives, open all the Certificates, and the Votes shall then be counted. The Person having the greatest Number of Votes shall be the President, if such Number be a Majority of the whole Number of Electors appointed; and if there be more than one who have such Majority, and have an equal Number of Votes, then the House of Representatives shall immediately chuse by Ballot one of them for President; and if no Person have a Majority, then from the five highest on the List the said House shall in like Manner chuse the President. But in chusing the President, the Votes shall be taken by States, the Representation from each State having one Vote; A quorum for this Purpose shall consist of a Member or Members from two thirds of the States, and a Majority of all the States shall be necessary to a Choice. In every Case, after the Choice of the President, the person having the greatest Number of Votes of the Electors shall be the Vice President. But if there should remain two or more who have equal Votes, the Senate shall chuse from them by Ballot the Vice President.[10]

The Congress may determine the Time of chusing the Electors, and the Day on which they shall give their Votes; which Day shall be the same throughout the United States.

No Person except a natural born Citizen, or a Citizen of the United States, at the time of the Adoption of this Constitution, shall be eligible to the Office of President; neither shall any Person be eligible to that Office who shall not have attained to the Age of thirty five Years, and been fourteen Years a Resident within the United States.

In Case of the Removal of the President from Office, or his Death, Resignation, or Inability to discharge the Powers and Duties of the said Office, the Same shall devolve on the Vice President, and the Congress may by Law provide for the Case of Removal, Death, Resignation or Inability, both of the President and Vice President, declaring what Officer shall then act as President, and such Officer shall act accordingly, until the Disability be removed, or a President shall be elected.

The President shall, at stated Times, receive for his Services, a Compensation, which shall neither be increased nor diminished during the Period for which he shall have been elected, and he shall not receive within that Period any other Emolument from the United States, or any of them.

Before he enter on the Execution of his Office, he shall take the following Oath or Affirmation:—"I do solemnly swear (or affirm) that I will faithfully execute the Office of President of the United States, and will to the best of my Ability, preserve, protect and defend the Constitution of the United States."

SECTION 2

[POWERS OF THE PRESIDENT]

The President shall be Commander in Chief of the Army and Navy of the United States, and of the Militia of the several States, when called into the actual Service of the United States; he may require the Opinion, in writing, of the principal Officer in each of the executive Departments, upon any Subject relating to the Duties of their respective Offices, and he shall have Power to grant Reprieves and Pardons for Offences against the United States, except in Cases of Impeachment.

He shall have Power, by and with the Advice and Consent of the Senate, to make Treaties, provided two thirds of the Senators present concur; and he shall nominate, and by and with the Advice and Consent of the Senate, shall appoint Ambassadors, other public Ministers and Consuls, Judges of the supreme Court, and all other Officers of the United States, whose Appointments are not herein otherwise provided for, and which shall be established by Law: but the Congress may by Law vest the Appointment of such inferior Officers, as they think proper, in the President alone, in the Courts of Law, or in the Heads of Departments.

The President shall have Power to fill up all Vacancies that may happen during the Recess of the Senate, by granting Commissions which shall expire at the End of their next Session.

SECTION 3

[POWERS AND DUTIES OF THE PRESIDENT]

He shall from time to time give to the Congress Information of the State of the Union, and recommend to their Consideration such Measures as he shall judge necessary and expedient; he may, on extraordinary Occasions, convene both Houses, or either of them, and in Case of Disagreement between them, with Respect to the Time of Adjournment, he may adjourn them to such Time as he shall think proper; he shall receive Ambassadors and other public Ministers; he shall take Care that the Laws be

---

[9]Number of terms limited to two by Twenty-second Amendment.
[10]Modified by the Twelfth and Twentieth Amendments.

faithfully executed, and shall Commission all the Officers of the United States.

SECTION 4
[IMPEACHMENT]

The President, Vice President and all civil Officers of the United States, shall be removed from Office on Impeachment for, and Conviction of, Treason, Bribery, or other high Crimes and Misdemeanors.

Article III

SECTION 1
[JUDICIAL POWER, TENURE OF OFFICE]

The judicial Power of the United States, shall be vested in one supreme Court, and in such inferior Courts as the Congress may from time to time ordain and establish. The Judges, both of the supreme and inferior Courts, shall hold their Offices during good Behaviour, and shall, at stated Times, receive for their Services, a Compensation, which shall not be diminished during their Continuance in Office.

SECTION 2
[JURISDICTION]

The judicial Power shall extend to all Cases, in Law and Equity, arising under this Constitution, the Laws of the United States, and Treaties made, or which shall be made, under their Authority;—to all Cases affecting Ambassadors, other public Ministers and Consuls;—to all Cases of admiralty and maritime Jurisdiction;—to Controversies to which the United States shall be a Party;—to Controversies between two or more States;—*between a State and Citizens of another State;*—between Citizens of different States,—between Citizens of the same State claiming Lands under Grants of different States, *and between a State,* or the Citizens thereof, *and foreign States, Citizens or Subjects.*[11]

In all Cases affecting Ambassadors, other public Ministers and Consuls, and those in which a State shall be Party, the supreme Court shall have original Jurisdiction. In all the other Cases before mentioned, the supreme Court shall have appellate Jurisdiction, both as to Law and Fact, with such Exceptions, and under such Regulations as the Congress shall make.

The Trial of all Crimes, except in Cases of Impeachment, shall be by Jury; and such Trial shall be held in the State where the said Crimes shall have been committed; but when not committed within any State, the Trial shall be at such Place or Places as the Congress may by Law have directed.

SECTION 3
[TREASON, PROOF, AND PUNISHMENT]

Treason against the United States, shall consist only in levying War against them, or in adhering to their Enemies, giving them Aid and Comfort. No Person shall be convicted of Treason unless on the Testimony of two Witnesses to the same overt Act, or on Confession in open Court.

The Congress shall have Power to declare the Punishment of Treason, but no Attainder of Treason shall work Corruption of Blood, or Forfeiture except during the Life of the Person attainted.

Article IV

SECTION 1
[FAITH AND CREDIT AMONG STATES]

Full Faith and Credit shall be given in each State to the public Acts, Records, and judicial Proceedings of every other State. And the Congress may by general Laws prescribe the Manner in which such Acts, Records and Proceedings shall be proved, and the Effect thereof.

SECTION 2
[PRIVILEGES AND IMMUNITIES, FUGITIVES]

The Citizens of each State shall be entitled to all Privileges and Immunities of Citizens in the several States.

A Person charged in any State with Treason, Felony or other Crime, who shall flee from Justice, and be found in another State, shall on Demand of the executive Authority of the State from which he fled, be delivered up, to be removed to the State having Jurisdiction of the Crime.

No person held to Service or Labour in one State, under the Laws thereof, escaping into another, shall, in Consequence of any Law or Regulation therein, be discharged from such Service or Labour, but shall be delivered up on Claim of the Party to whom such Service or Labour may be due.[12]

SECTION 3
[ADMISSION OF NEW STATES]

New States may be admitted by the Congress into this Union; but no new State shall be formed or erected within the Jurisdiction of any other State; nor any State be formed by the Junction of two or more States, or Parts of States, without the Consent of the Legislatures of the States concerned as well as of the Congress.

The Congress shall have Power to dispose of and make all needful Rules and Regulations respecting the Territory or other Property belonging to the United States; and nothing in this Constitution shall be so construed as to Prejudice any Claims of the United States, or of any particular State.

SECTION 4
[GUARANTEE OF REPUBLICAN GOVERNMENT]

The United States shall guarantee to every State in this Union a Republican Form of Government, and shall protect each of them against Invasion; and on Application of the Legislature, or of the Executive (when the Legislature cannot be convened), against domestic Violence.

Article V
[AMENDMENT OF THE CONSTITUTION]

The Congress, whenever two thirds of both Houses shall deem it necessary, shall propose Amendments to this Constitution, or, on the Application of the Legislatures of two thirds of the several States, shall call a Convention for proposing Amendments, which, in either Case, shall be valid to all Intents and Purposes, as Part of this Constitution, when ratified by the Legislatures of three fourths of the several States, or by Conventions in three fourths thereof, as the one or the other Mode of Ratification may be proposed by the Congress; *Provided that no Amendment which may be made prior to the Year One thousand eight hundred and eight shall in any Manner affect the first and fourth Clauses in the Ninth Section of the first Article;*[13] and that no State, without its Consent, shall be deprived of its equal Suffrage in the Senate.

Article VI
[DEBTS, SUPREMACY, OATH]

All Debts contracted and Engagements entered into, before the Adoption of this Constitution, shall be as valid against the United States under this Constitution, as under the Confederation.

---

[11]Modified by the Eleventh Amendment.
[12]Repealed by the Thirteenth Amendment.

This Constitution, and the Laws of the United States which shall be made in Pursuance thereof; and all Treaties made, or which shall be made, under the Authority of the United States, shall be the supreme Law of the Land; and the Judges in every State shall be bound thereby, any Thing in the Constitution or Laws of any State to the Contrary notwithstanding.

The Senators and Representatives before mentioned, and the Members of the several State Legislatures, and all executive and judicial Officers, both of the United States and of the several States, shall be bound by Oath or Affirmation, to support this Constitution; but no religious Test shall be required as a Qualification to any Office or public Trust under the United States.

Article VII
[RATIFICATION AND ESTABLISHMENT]

The Ratification of the Conventions of nine States, shall be sufficient for the Establishment of this Constitution between the States so ratifying the Same.[14]

Done in Convention by the Unanimous Consent of the States present the Seventeenth Day of September in the Year of our Lord one thousand seven hundred and Eighty seven and of the Independence of the United States of America the Twelfth. *In Witness* whereof We have hereunto subscribed our Names,

G:⁰ WASHINGTON—
Presidt. and deputy from Virginia

NEW HAMPSHIRE
John Langdon
Nicholas Gilman

MASSACHUSETTS
Nathaniel Gorham
Rufus King

CONNECTICUT
Wm. Saml. Johnson
Roger Sherman

NEW YORK
Alexander Hamilton

NEW JERSEY
Wil: Livingston
David Brearley
Wm. Paterson
Jona: Dayton

PENNSYLVANIA
B Franklin
Thomas Mifflin
Robt. Morris
Geo. Clymer
Thos. FitzSimons
Jared Ingersoll
James Wilson
Gouv Morris

DELAWARE
Geo: Read
Gunning Bedford jun
John Dickinson
Richard Bassett
Jaco: Broom

MARYLAND
James McHenry
Dan of St Thos. Jenifer
Danl. Carroll

VIRGINIA
John Blair—
James Madison Jr.

NORTH CAROLINA
Wm. Blount
Richd. Dobbs Spaight
Hu Williamson

SOUTH CAROLINA
J. Rutledge
Charles Cotesworth Pinckney
Charles Pinckney
Pierce Butler

GEORGIA
William Few
Abr Baldwin

Amendments to the Constitution

Proposed by Congress and Ratified by the Legislatures of the Several States, Pursuant to Article V of the Original Constitution.

Amendments I–X, known as the Bill of Rights, were proposed by Congress on September 25, 1789, and ratified on December 15, 1791.

Amendment I
[FREEDOM OF RELIGION, OF SPEECH, AND OF THE PRESS]

Congress shall make no law respecting an establishment of religion, or prohibiting the free exercise thereof; or abridging the freedom of speech, or of the press; or the right of the people peaceably to assemble, and to petition the Government for a redress of grievances.

Amendment II
[RIGHT TO KEEP AND BEAR ARMS]

A well regulated Militia, being necessary to the security of a free State, the right of the people to keep and bear Arms, shall not be infringed.

Amendment III
[QUARTERING OF SOLDIERS]

No Soldier shall, in time of peace be quartered in any house, without the consent of the Owner, nor in time of war, but in a manner to be prescribed by law.

Amendment IV
[SECURITY FROM UNWARRANTABLE SEARCH AND SEIZURE]

The right of the people to be secure in their persons, houses, papers, and effects, against unreasonable searches and seizures, shall not be violated, and no Warrants shall issue, but upon probable cause, supported by Oath or affirmation, and particularly describing the place to be searched, and the persons or things to be seized.

Amendment V
[RIGHTS OF ACCUSED PERSONS IN CRIMINAL PROCEEDINGS]

No person shall be held to answer for a capital, or otherwise infamous crime, unless on a presentment or indictment of a Grand Jury, except in cases arising in the land or naval forces, or in the Militia, when in actual service in time of War or in public danger; nor shall any person be subject for the same offence to be twice put in jeopardy of life or limb; nor shall be compelled in any criminal case to be a witness against himself, nor be deprived of life, liberty, or property, without due process of law; nor shall private property be taken for public use, without just compensation.

Amendment VI
[RIGHT TO SPEEDY TRIAL, WITNESSES, ETC.]

In all criminal prosecutions, the accused shall enjoy the right to a speedy and public trial, by an impartial jury of the State and district wherein the crime shall have been committed, which district shall have been previously ascertained by law, and to be informed of the nature and cause of the accusation; to be confronted with the witnesses against him; to have compulsory process for obtaining witnesses in his favor, and to have the Assistance of Counsel for his defence.

Amendment VII
[TRIAL BY JURY IN CIVIL CASES]

In suits at common law, where the value in controversy shall exceed twenty dollars, the right of trial by jury shall be preserved, and no fact tried by a jury, shall be otherwise reexamined in any Court of the United States, than according to the rules of the common law.

Amendment VIII
[BAILS, FINES, PUNISHMENTS]

Excessive bail shall not be required, nor excessive fines imposed, nor cruel and unusual punishments inflicted.

Amendment IX
[RESERVATION OF RIGHTS OF PEOPLE]

The enumeration in the Constitution, of certain rights, shall not be construed to deny or disparage others retained by the people.

Amendment X
[POWERS RESERVED TO STATES OR PEOPLE]

The powers not delegated to the United States by the Constitution, nor prohibited by it to the States, are reserved to the States respectively, or to the people.

Amendment XI
[*Proposed by Congress on March 4, 1794; declared ratified on January 8, 1798.*]
[RESTRICTION OF JUDICIAL POWER]

The Judicial power of the United States shall not be construed to extend to any suit in law or equity, commenced or prosecuted against one of the United States by Citizens of another State, or by Citizens or Subjects of any Foreign State.

Amendment XII
[*Proposed by Congress on December 9, 1803; declared ratified on September 25, 1804.*]
[ELECTION OF PRESIDENT AND VICE PRESIDENT]

The Electors shall meet in their respective states and vote by ballot for President and Vice-President, one of whom, at least, shall not be an inhabitant of the same state with themselves; they shall name in their ballots the person voted for as President, and in distinct ballots the person voted for as Vice-President, and they shall make distinct lists of all persons voted for as President, and of all persons voted for as Vice-President, and of the number of votes for each, which lists they shall sign and certify, and transmit sealed to the seat of the government of the United States, directed to the President of the Senate;—the President of the Senate shall, in presence of the Senate and House of Representatives, open all the certificates and the votes shall then be counted;—The person having the greatest number of votes for President, shall be the President, if such number be a majority of the whole number of Electors appointed; and if no person have such majority, then from the persons having the highest numbers not exceeding three on the list of those voted for as President, the House of Representatives shall choose immediately, by ballot, the President. But in choosing the President, the votes shall be taken by states, the representation from each state having one vote; a quorum for this purpose shall consist of a member or members from two-thirds of the states, and a majority of all the states shall be necessary to a choice. And if the House of Representatives shall not choose a President whenever the right of choice shall devolve upon them, before the fourth day of March next following, then the Vice-President shall act as President, as in the case of the death or other constitutional disability of the President.—The person having the greatest number of votes as Vice-President, shall be the Vice-President, if such number be a majority of the whole number of Electors appointed, and if no person have a majority, then from the two highest numbers on the list, the Senate shall choose the Vice-President; a quorum for the purpose shall consist of two-thirds of the whole number of Senators, and a majority of the whole number shall be necessary to a choice. But no person constitutionally ineligible to the office of President shall be eligible to that of Vice-President of the United States.

Amendment XIII

[*Proposed by Congress on January 31, 1865; declared ratified on December 18, 1865.*]

SECTION 1

[ABOLITION OF SLAVERY]

Neither slavery nor involuntary servitude, except as a punishment for crime whereof the party shall have been duly convicted, shall exist within the United States, or any place subject to their jurisdiction.

SECTION 2

[POWER TO ENFORCE THIS ARTICLE]

Congress shall have power to enforce this article by appropriate legislation.

Amendment XIV

[*Proposed by Congress on June 13, 1866; declared ratified on July 28, 1868.*]

SECTION 1

[CITIZENSHIP RIGHTS NOT TO BE ABRIDGED BY STATES]

All persons born or naturalized in the United States, and subject to the jurisdiction thereof, are citizens of the United States and of the State wherein they reside. No State shall make or enforce any law which shall abridge the privileges or immunities of citizens of the United States; nor shall any State deprive any person of life, liberty, or property, without due process of law; nor deny to any person within its jurisdiction the equal protection of the laws.

SECTION 2

[APPORTIONMENT OF REPRESENTATIVES IN CONGRESS]

Representatives shall be apportioned among the several States according to their respective numbers, counting the whole number of persons in each State, excluding Indians not taxed. But when the right to vote at any election for the choice of electors for President and Vice-President of the United States, Representatives in Congress, the Executive and Judicial officers of a State, or the members of the Legislature thereof, is denied to any of the male inhabitants of such State, being twenty-one years of age, and citizens of the United States, or in any way abridged, except for participation in rebellion, or other crime, the basis of representation therein shall be reduced in the proportion which the number of such male citizens shall bear to the whole number of male citizens twenty-one years of age in such State.

SECTION 3

[PERSONS DISQUALIFIED FROM HOLDING OFFICE]

No person shall be a Senator or Representative in Congress, or elector of President and Vice-President, or hold any office, civil or military, under the United States, or under any State, who, having previously taken an oath, as a member of Congress, or as an officer of the United States, or as a member of any State legislature, or as an executive or judicial officer of any State, to support the Constitution of the United States, shall have engaged in insurrection or rebellion against the same, or given aid or comfort to the enemies thereof. But Congress may by a vote of two-thirds of each House, remove such disability.

SECTION 4

[WHAT PUBLIC DEBTS ARE VALID]

The validity of the public debt of the United States, authorized by law, including debts incurred for payment of pensions and bounties for services in suppressing insurrection or rebellion, shall not be questioned. But neither the United States nor any State shall assume or pay any debt or obligation incurred in aid of insurrection or rebellion against the United States, or any claim for the loss or emancipation of any slave; but all such debts, obligations and claims shall be held illegal and void.

SECTION 5

[POWER TO ENFORCE THIS ARTICLE]

The Congress shall have power to enforce, by appropriate legislation, the provisions of this article.

Amendment XV

[*Proposed by Congress on February 26, 1869; declared ratified on March 30, 1870.*]

SECTION 1

[NEGRO SUFFRAGE]

The right of citizens of the United States to vote shall not be denied or abridged by the United States or by any State on account of race, color, or previous condition of servitude.

SECTION 2

[POWER TO ENFORCE THIS ARTICLE]

The Congress shall have power to enforce this article by appropriate legislation.

Amendment XVI

[*Proposed by Congress on July 2, 1909; declared ratified on February 25, 1913.*]
[AUTHORIZING INCOME TAXES]

The Congress shall have power to lay and collect taxes on incomes, from whatever source derived, without apportionment among the several States, and without regard to any census or enumeration.

Amendment XVII

[*Proposed by Congress on May 13, 1912; declared ratified on May 31, 1913.*]
[POPULAR ELECTION OF SENATORS]

The Senate of the United States shall be composed of two Senators from each State, elected by the people thereof, for six years; and each Senator shall have one vote. The electors in each State shall have the qualifications requisite for electors of the most numerous branch of the State legislatures.

When vacancies happen in the representation of any State in the Senate, the executive authority of such State shall issue writs of election to fill such vacancies: *Provided,* That the legislature of any State may empower the executive thereof to make temporary appointments until the people fill the vacancies by election as the legislature may direct.

This amendment shall not be so construed as to affect the election or term of any Senator chosen before it becomes valid as part of the Constitution.

Amendment XVIII

[*Proposed by Congress December 18, 1917; declared ratified on January 29, 1919.*]

SECTION 1
[NATIONAL LIQUOR PROHIBITION]

After one year from the ratification of this article the manufacture, sale, or transportation of intoxicating liquors within, the importation thereof into, or the exportation thereof from the United States and all territory subject to the jurisdiction thereof for beverage purposes is hereby prohibited.

SECTION 2
[POWER TO ENFORCE THIS ARTICLE]

The Congress and the several States shall have concurrent power to enforce this article by appropriate legislation.

SECTION 3
[RATIFICATION WITHIN SEVEN YEARS]

This article shall be inoperative unless it shall have been ratified as an amendment to the Constitution by the legislatures of the several States, as provided in the Constitution, within seven years from the date of the submission hereof to the States by the Congress.[1]

Amendment XIX

[*Proposed by Congress on June 4, 1919; declared ratified on August 26, 1920.*]
[WOMAN SUFFRAGE]

The right of citizens of the United States to vote shall not be denied or abridged by the United States or by any State on account of sex.

Congress shall have power to enforce this article by appropriate legislation.

Amendment XX

[*Proposed by Congress on March 2, 1932; declared ratified on February 6, 1933.*]

SECTION 1
[TERMS OF OFFICE]

The terms of the President and Vice President shall end at noon on the 20th day of January, and the terms of Senators and Representatives at noon on the 3d day of January, of the years in which such terms would have ended if this article had not been ratified; and the terms of their successors shall then begin.

SECTION 2
[TIME OF CONVENING CONGRESS]

The Congress shall assemble at least once in every year, and such meeting shall begin at noon on the 3d day of January, unless they shall by law appoint a different day.

SECTION 3
[DEATH OF PRESIDENT-ELECT]

If, at the time fixed for the beginning of the term of the President, the President elect shall have died, the Vice President elect shall become President. If a President shall not have been chosen before the time fixed for the beginning of his term, or if the President elect shall have failed to qualify, then the Vice President elect shall act as President until a President shall have qualified; and the Congress may by law provide for the case wherein neither a President elect nor a Vice President elect shall have qualified, declaring who shall then act as President, or the manner in which one who is to act shall be selected, and such person shall act accordingly until a President or Vice President shall have qualified.

SECTION 4
[ELECTION OF THE PRESIDENT]

The Congress may by law provide for the case of the death of any of the persons from whom the House of Representatives may choose a President whenever the right of choice shall have devolved upon them, and for the case of the death of any of the persons from whom the Senate may choose a Vice President whenever the right of choice shall have devolved upon them.

SECTION 5
[AMENDMENT TAKES EFFECT]

Sections 1 and 2 shall take effect on the 15th day of October following the ratification of this article.

SECTION 6
[RATIFICATION WITHIN SEVEN YEARS]

This article shall be inoperative unless it shall have been ratified as an amendment to the Constitution by the legislatures of three-fourths of the several States within seven years from the date of its submission.

Amendment XXI

[*Proposed by Congress on February 20, 1933; declared ratified on December 5, 1933.*]

SECTION 1
[NATIONAL LIQUOR PROHIBITION REPEALED]

The eighteenth article of amendment to the Constitution of the United States is hereby repealed.

SECTION 2
[TRANSPORTATION OF LIQUOR INTO "DRY" STATES]

The transportation or importation into any State, Territory, or Possession of the United States for delivery or use therein of intoxicating liquors, in violation of the laws thereof, is hereby prohibited.

SECTION 3
[RATIFICATION WITHIN SEVEN YEARS]

This article shall be inoperative unless it shall have been ratified as an amendment to the Constitution by conventions in the several States, as provided in the Constitution, within seven years from the date of the submission hereof to the States by the Congress.

---

[1]Repealed by the Twenty-first Amendment.

Amendment XXII

[*Proposed by Congress on March 21, 1947; declared ratified on February 27, 1951.*]

SECTION 1

[TENURE OF PRESIDENT LIMITED]

No person shall be elected to the office of President more than twice, and no person who has held the office of President or acted as President, for more than two years of a term to which some other person was elected President shall be elected to the office of the President more than once. But this Article shall not apply to any person holding the office of President when this Article was proposed by the Congress, and shall not prevent any person who may be holding the office of President, or acting as President, during the term within which this Article becomes operative from holding the office of President or acting as President during the remainder of such term.

SECTION 2

[RATIFICATION WITHIN SEVEN YEARS]

This article shall be inoperative unless it shall have been ratified as an amendment to the Constitution by the legislatures of three-fourths of the several States within seven years from the date of its submission to the States by the Congress.

Amendment XXIII

[*Proposed by Congress on June 16, 1960; declared ratified on March 29, 1961.*]

SECTION 1

[ELECTORAL COLLEGE VOTES FOR THE DISTRICT OF COLUMBIA]

The District constituting the seat of Government of the United States shall appoint in such manner as the Congress may direct:

A number of electors of President and Vice President equal to the whole number of Senators and Representatives in Congress to which the District would be entitled if it were a State, but in no event more than the least populous State; they shall be in addition to those appointed by the States, but they shall be considered, for the purposes of the election of President and Vice President, to be electors appointed by a State; and they shall meet in the District and perform such duties as provided by the twelfth article of amendment.

SECTION 2

[POWER TO ENFORCE THIS ARTICLE]

The Congress shall have power to enforce this article by appropriate legislation.

Amendment XXIV

[*Proposed by Congress on August 27, 1962; declared ratified on January 23, 1964.*]

SECTION 1

[ANTI-POLL TAX]

The right of citizens of the United States to vote in any primary or other election for President or Vice President, for electors for President or Vice President, or for Senator or Representative of Congress, shall not be denied or abridged by the United States or any State by reason of failure to pay any poll tax or other tax.

SECTION 2

[POWER TO ENFORCE THIS ARTICLE]

The Congress shall have power to enforce this article by appropriate legislation.

Amendment XXV

[*Proposed by Congress on July 6, 1965; declared ratified on February 10, 1967.*]

SECTION 1

[VICE PRESIDENT TO BECOME PRESIDENT]

In case of the removal of the President from office or his death or resignation, the Vice President shall become President.

SECTION 2

[CHOICE OF A NEW VICE PRESIDENT]

Whenever there is a vacancy in the office of the Vice President, the President shall nominate a Vice President who shall take the office upon confirmation by a majority vote of both houses of Congress.

SECTION 3

[PRESIDENT MAY DECLARE OWN DISABILITY]

Whenever the President transmits to the President pro tempore of the Senate and the Speaker of the House of Representatives his written declaration that he is unable to discharge the powers and duties of his office, and until he transmits to them a written declaration to the contrary, such powers and duties shall be discharged by the Vice President as Acting President.

SECTION 4

[ALTERNATE PROCEDURES TO DECLARE AND TO END PRESIDENTIAL DISABILITY]

Whenever the Vice President and a majority of either the principal officers of the executive departments, or of such other body as Congress may by law provide, transmit to the President pro tempore of the Senate and the Speaker of the House of Representatives their written declaration that the President is unable to discharge the powers and duties of his office, the Vice President shall immediately assume the powers and duties of the office as Acting President.

Thereafter, when the President transmits to the President pro tempore of the Senate and the Speaker of the House of Representatives his written declaration that no inability exists, he shall resume the powers and duties of his office unless the Vice President and a majority of either the principal officers of the executive department, or of such other body as Congress may by law provide, transmit within four days to the President pro tempore of the Senate and the Speaker of the House of Representatives their written declaration that the President is unable to discharge the powers and duties of his office. Thereupon Congress shall decide the issue, assembling within forty eight hours for that purpose if not in session. If the Congress, within twenty one days after receipt of the latter written declaration, or, if Congress is not in session, within twenty one days after Congress is required to assemble, determines by two-thirds vote of both Houses that the President is unable to discharge the powers and duties of his office, the Vice President shall continue to discharge the same as Acting President; otherwise, the President shall resume the powers and duties of his office.

Amendment XXVI

[*Proposed by Congress on March 23, 1971; declared ratified on July 1, 1971.*]

SECTION 1

[EIGHTEEN-YEAR-OLD VOTE]

The right of citizens of the United States, who are eighteen years of age or older, to vote shall not be denied or abridged by the United States or by any State on account of age.

SECTION 2

[POWER TO ENFORCE THIS ARTICLE]

The Congress shall have power to enforce this article by appropriate legislation.

Amendment XXVII

[*Proposed by Congress on September 25, 1789; declared ratified on May 8, 1992.*]

[CONGRESS CANNOT RAISE ITS OWN PAY]

No law varying the compensation for the services of the Senators and Representatives, shall take effect, until an election of representatives shall have intervened.

The Federalist Papers

No. 10: Madison

Among the numerous advantages promised by a well constructed Union, none deserves to be more accurately developed than its tendency to break and control the violence of faction. The friend of popular governments never finds himself so much alarmed for their character and fate, as when he contemplates their propensity to this dangerous vice. He will not fail therefore to set a due value on any plan which, without violating the principles to which he is attached, provides a proper cure for it. The instability, injustice, and confusion introduced into the public councils have, in truth, been the mortal diseases under which popular governments have everywhere perished, as they continue to be the favorite and fruitful topics from which the adversaries to liberty derive their most specious declamations. The valuable improvements made by the American constitutions on the popular models, both ancient and modern, cannot certainly be too much admired; but it would be an unwarrantable partiality to contend that they have as effectually obviated the danger on this side, as was wished and expected. Complaints are everywhere heard from our most considerate and virtuous citizens, equally the friends of public and private faith and of public and personal liberty, that our governments are too unstable, that the public good is disregarded in the conflicts of rival parties, and that measures are too often decided, not according to the rules of justice and the rights of the minor party, but by the superior force of an interested and overbearing majority. However anxiously we may wish that these complaints had no foundation, the evidence of known facts will not permit us to deny that they are in some degree true. It will be found, indeed, on a candid review of our situation, that some of the distresses under which we labor have been erroneously charged on the operation of our governments; but it will be found, at the same time, that other causes will not alone account for many of our heaviest misfortunes; and, particularly, for that prevailing and increasing distrust of public engagements and alarm for private rights which are echoed from one end of the continent to the other. These must be chiefly, if not wholly, effects of the unsteadiness and injustice with which a factious spirit has tainted our public administration.

By a faction I understand a number of citizens, whether amounting to a majority or minority of the whole, who are united and actuated by some common impulse of passion, or of interest, adverse to the rights of other citizens, or to the permanent and aggregate interests of the community.

There are two methods of curing the mischiefs of faction: the one, by removing its causes; the other, by controlling its effects.

There are again two methods of removing the causes of faction: the one, by destroying the liberty which is essential to its existence; the other, by giving to every citizen the same opinions, the same passions, and the same interests.

It could never be more truly said than of the first remedy, that it is worse than the disease. Liberty is to faction what air is to fire, an aliment without which it instantly expires. But it could not be a less folly to abolish liberty, which is essential to political life, because it nourishes faction, than it would be to wish the annihilation of air, which is essential to animal life, because it imparts to fire its destructive agency.

The second expedient is as impracticable, as the first would be unwise. As long as the reason of man continues fallible, and he is at liberty to exercise it, different opinions will be formed. As long as the connection subsists between his reason and his self-love, his opinions and his passions will have a reciprocal influence on each other; and the former will be objects to which the latter will attach themselves. The diversity in the faculties of men, from which the rights of property originate, is not less an insuperable obstacle to a uniformity of interests. The protection of these faculties is the first object of Government. From the protection of different and unequal faculties of acquiring property, the possession of different degrees and kinds of property immediately results; and from the influence of these on the sentiments and views of the respective proprietors, ensues a division of the society into different interests and parties.

The latent causes of faction are thus sown in the nature of man; and we see them everywhere brought into different degrees of activity, according to the different circumstances of civil society. A zeal for different opinions concerning religion, concerning Government, and many other points, as well of speculation as of practice; an attachment to different leaders ambitiously contending for pre-eminence and power; or to persons of other descriptions whose fortunes have been interesting to the human passions, have in turn divided mankind into parties, inflamed them with mutual animosity, and rendered them much more disposed to vex and oppress each other, than to co-operate for their common good. So strong is this propensity of mankind to fall into mutual animosities, that where no substantial occasion presents itself, the most frivolous and fanciful distinctions have been sufficient to kindle their unfriendly passions, and excite their most violent conflicts. But the most common and durable source of factions has been the various and unequal distribution of property. Those who hold and those who are without property have ever formed distinct interests in society. Those who are creditors, and those who are debtors, fall under a like discrimination. A landed interest, a manufacturing interest, a mercantile interest, a moneyed interest, with many lesser interests, grow up of necessity in civilized nations, and divide them into different classes, actuated by different sentiments and views. The regulation of these various and interfering interests forms the principal task of modern Legislation, and involves the spirit of party and faction in the necessary and ordinary operations of Government.

No man is allowed to be judge in his own cause, because his interest would certainly bias his judgment and, not improbably, corrupt his integrity. With equal, nay with greater reason, a body of men are unfit to be both judges and parties at the same time; yet what are many of the most important acts of legislation but so many judicial determinations, not indeed concerning the rights of single persons, but concerning the rights of large bodies of citizens; and what are the different classes of legislators but advocates and parties to the causes which they determine? Is a law proposed concerning private debts? It is a question to which the creditors are parties on one side and the debtors on the other. Justice ought to hold the balance between them. Yet the parties are, and must be, themselves the judges; and the most numerous party, or in other words, the most powerful faction must be expected to prevail. Shall domestic manufacturers be encouraged, and in what degree, by restrictions on foreign manufacturers? are questions which would be differently decided by the landed and the manufacturing classes, and probably by neither with a sole regard to justice and the public good. The apportionment of taxes on the various descriptions of property is an act which seems to require the most exact impartiality; yet there is, perhaps, no legislative act in which greater opportunity and temptation are given to a predominant party to trample on the rules of justice. Every shilling with which they overburden the inferior number is a shilling saved to their own pockets.

It is in vain to say that enlightened statesmen will be able to adjust these clashing interests and render them all subservient to the public good. Enlightened statesmen will not always be at the helm. Nor, in many cases, can such an adjustment be made at all without taking into view indirect and remote considerations, which will rarely prevail over the immediate interest which one party may find in disregarding the rights of another or the good of the whole.

The inference to which we are brought is that the *causes* of faction cannot be removed and that relief is only to be sought in the means of controlling its *effects*.

If a faction consists of less than a majority, relief is supplied by the republican principle, which enables the majority to defeat its sinister views by regular vote. It may clog the administration, it may convulse the society; but it will be unable to execute and mask its violence under the forms of the Constitution. When a majority is included in a faction, the form of popular government, on the other hand, enables it to sacrifice to its ruling passion or interest both the public good and the rights of other citizens. To secure the public good and private rights against the danger of such a faction, and at the same time to preserve the spirit and the form of popular government, is then the great object to which our enquiries are directed. Let me add that it is the great desideratum by which alone this form of government can be rescued from the opprobrium under which it has so long labored and be recommended to the esteem and adoption of mankind.

By what means is this object attainable? Evidently by one of two only. Either the existence of the same passion or interest in a majority at the same time must be prevented, or the majority, having such co-existent passion or interest, must be rendered, by their number and local situation, unable to concert and carry into effect schemes of oppression. If the impulse and the opportunity be suffered to coincide, we well know that neither moral nor religious motives can be relied on as an adequate control. They are not found to be such on the injustice and violence of individuals, and lose their efficacy in proportion to the number combined together, that is, in proportion as their efficacy becomes needful.

From this view of the subject it may be concluded that a pure Democracy, by which I mean a Society consisting of a small number of citizens, who assemble and administer the Government in person, can admit of no cure for the mischiefs of faction. A common passion or interest will, in almost every case, be felt by a majority of the whole; a communication and concert results from the form of Government itself; and there is nothing to check the inducements to sacrifice the weaker party or an obnoxious individual. Hence it is that such Democracies have ever been spectacles of turbulence and contention; have ever been found incompatible with personal security or the rights of property; and have in general been as short in their lives as they have been violent in their deaths. Theoretic politicians, who have patronized this species of Government, have erroneously supposed that by reducing mankind to a perfect equality in their political rights, they would at the same time be perfectly equalized and assimilated in their possessions, their opinions, and their passions.

A Republic, by which I mean a Government in which the scheme of representation takes place, opens a different prospect and promises the cure for which we are seeking. Let us examine the points in which it varies from pure Democracy, and we shall comprehend both the nature of the cure and the efficacy which it must derive from the Union.

The two great points of difference between a Democracy and a Republic are: first, the delegation of the Government, in the latter, to a small number of citizens elected by the rest; secondly, the greater number of citizens and greater sphere of country over which the latter may be extended.

The effect of the first difference is, on the one hand, to refine and enlarge the public views by passing them through the medium of a chosen body of citizens, whose wisdom may best discern the true interest of their country and whose patriotism and love of justice will be least likely to sacrifice it to temporary or partial considerations. Under such a regulation it may well happen that the public voice, pronounced by the representatives of the people, will be more consonant to the public good than if pronounced by the people themselves, convened for the purpose. On the other hand, the effect may be inverted. Men of factious tempers, of local prejudices, or of sinister designs, may, by intrigue, by corruption, or by other means, first obtain the suffrages, and then betray the interests of the people. The question resulting is, whether small or extensive Republics are most favorable to the election of proper guardians of the public weal; and it is clearly decided in favor of the latter by two obvious considerations.

In the first place it is to be remarked that however small the Republic may be, the Representatives must be raised to a certain number in order to guard against the cabals of a few; and that however large it may be they must be limited to a certain number in order to guard against the confusion of a multitude. Hence, the number of Representatives in the two cases not being in proportion to that of the Constituents, and being proportionally greatest in the small Republic, it follows that if the proportion of fit characters be not less in the large than in the small Republic, the former will present a greater option, and consequently a greater probability of a fit choice.

In the next place, as each Representative will be chosen by a greater number of citizens in the large than in the small Republic, it will be more difficult for unworthy candidates to practise with success the vicious arts by which elections are too often carried; and the suffrages of the people being more free, will be more likely to centre on men who possess the most attractive merit and the most diffusive and established characters.

It must be confessed that in this, as in most other cases, there is a mean, on both sides of which inconveniencies will be found to lie. By enlarging too much the number of electors, you render the representative too little acquainted with all their local circumstances and lesser interests; as by reducing it too much, you render him unduly attached to these, and too little fit to comprehend and pursue great and national objects. The Federal Constitution forms a happy combination in this respect; the great and aggregate interests being referred to the national, the local and particular to the State legislatures.

The other point of difference is the greater number of citizens and extent of territory which may be brought within the compass of Republican than of Democratic Government; and it is this circumstance principally which renders factious combinations less to be dreaded in the former than in the latter. The smaller the society, the fewer probably will be the distinct parties and interests composing it; the fewer the distinct parties and interests, the more frequently will a majority be found of the same party; and the smaller the number of individuals composing a majority, and the smaller the compass within which they are placed, the more easily will they concert and execute their plans of oppression. Extend the sphere and you take in a greater variety of parties and interests; you make it less probable that a majority of the whole will have a common motive to invade the rights of other citizens; or if such a common motive exists, it will be more difficult for all who feel it to discover their own strength and to act in unison with each other. Besides other impediments, it may be remarked, that where there is a consciousness of unjust or dishonorable purposes, communication is always checked by distrust in proportion to the number whose concurrence is necessary.

Hence, it clearly appears that the same advantage which a Republic has over a Democracy in controlling the effects of faction is enjoyed by a large over a small republic—is enjoyed by the Union over the States composing it. Does this advantage consist in the substitution of representatives whose enlightened views and virtuous sentiments render them superior to local prejudices and to schemes of injustice? It will not be denied that the representation of the Union will be most likely to possess these requisite endowments. Does it consist in the greater security afforded by a greater variety of parties, against the event of any one party being able to outnumber and oppress the rest? In an equal degree does the increased variety of parties comprised within the Union increase this security? Does it, in fine, consist in the greater obstacles opposed to the concert and accomplishment of the secret wishes of an unjust and interested majority? Here again the extent of the Union gives it the most palpable advantage.

The influence of factious leaders may kindle a flame within their particular States but will be unable to spread a general conflagration through the other States: a religious sect may degenerate into a political faction in a part of the Confederacy; but the variety of sects dispersed over the entire face of it must secure the national Councils against any danger from that source: a rage for paper money, for an abolition of debts, for an equal division of property, or for any other improper or wicked project, will be less apt to pervade the whole body of the Union than a particular member of it; in the same proportion as such a malady is more likely to taint a particular county or district than an entire State.

In the extent and proper structure of the Union, therefore, we behold a republican remedy for the diseases most incident to Republican Government. And according to the degree of pleasure and pride we feel in being republicans ought to be our zeal in cherishing the spirit and supporting the character of federalist.

PUBLIUS

No. 51: Madison

To what expedient, then, shall we finally resort, for maintaining in practice the necessary partition of power among the several departments as laid down in the constitution? The only answer that can be given is that as all these exterior provisions are found to be inadequate the defect must be supplied, by so contriving the interior structure of the government as that its several constituent parts may, by their mutual relations, be the means of keeping each other in their proper places. Without presuming to undertake a full development of this important idea I will hazard a few general observations which may perhaps place it in a clearer light, and enable us to form a more correct judgment of the principles and structure of the government planned by the convention.

In order to lay a due foundation for that separate and distinct exercise of the different powers of government, which to a certain extent is admitted on all hands to be essential to the preservation of liberty, it is evident that each department should have a will of its own; and consequently should be so constituted that the members of each should have as little agency as possible in the appointment of the members of the others. Were this principle rigorously adhered to, it would require that all the appointments for the supreme executive, legislative, and judiciary magistracies should be drawn from the same fountain of authority, the people, through channels having no communication whatever with one another. Perhaps such a plan of constructing the several departments would be less difficult in practice than it may in contemplation appear. Some difficulties, however, and some additional expense would attend the execution of it. Some deviations, therefore, from the principle must be admitted. In the constitution of the judiciary department in particular, it might be inexpedient to insist rigorously on the principle: first, because peculiar qualifications being essential in the members, the primary consideration ought to be to select that mode of choice which best secures these qualifications; second, because the permanent tenure by which the appointments are held in that department must soon destroy all sense of dependence on the authority conferring them.

It is equally evident that the members of each department should be as little dependent as possible on those of the others for the emoluments annexed to their offices. Were the executive magistrate, or the judges, not independent of the legislature in this particular, their independence in every other would be merely nominal.

But the great security against a gradual concentration of the several powers in the same department consists in giving to those who administer each department the necessary constitutional means and personal motives to resist encroachments of the others. The provision for defence must in this, as in all other cases, be made commensurate to the danger of attack. Ambition must be made to counteract ambition. The interest of the man must be connected with the constitutional rights of the place. It may be a reflection on human nature that such devices should be necessary to control the abuses of government. But what is government itself but the greatest of all reflections on human nature? If men were angels, no government would be necessary. If angels were to govern men, neither external nor internal controls on government would be necessary. In framing a government which is to be administered by men over men, the great difficulty lies in this: You must first enable the government to control the governed; and in the next place oblige it to control itself. A dependence on the people is, no doubt, the primary control on the government; but experience has taught mankind the necessity of auxiliary precautions.

This policy of supplying, by opposite and rival interests, the defect of better motives, might be traced through the whole system of human affairs, private as well as public. We see it particularly displayed in all the subordinate distributions of power, where the constant aim is to divide and arrange the several offices in such a manner as that each may be a check on the other; that the private interest of every individual may be a sentinel over the public rights. These inventions of prudence cannot be less requisite in the distribution of the supreme powers of the State.

But it is not possible to give to each department an equal power of self-defense. In republican government, the legislative authority necessarily predominates. The remedy for this inconveniency is to divide the legislature into different branches; and to render them, by different modes of election and different principles of action, as little connected with each other as the nature of their common functions and their common dependence on the society will admit. It may even be necessary to guard against dangerous encroachments by still further precautions. As the weight of the legislative authority requires that it should be thus divided, the weakness of the executive may require, on the other hand, that it should be fortified. An absolute negative on the legislature appears, at first view, to be the natural defense with which the executive magistrate should be armed. But perhaps it would be neither altogether safe nor alone sufficient. On ordinary occasions it might not be exerted with the requisite firmness, and on extraordinary occasions it might be perfidiously abused. May not this defect of an absolute negative be supplied by some qualified connection between this weaker branch of the stronger department, by which the latter may be led to support the constitutional rights of the former, without being too much detached from the rights of its own department?

If the principles on which these observations are founded be just, as I persuade myself they are, and they be applied as a criterion to the several State constitutions, and to the federal Constitution, it will be found that if the latter does not perfectly correspond with them, the former are infinitely less able to bear such a test.

There are, moreover, two considerations particularly applicable to the federal system of America, which place that system in a very interesting point of view.

First. In a single republic, all the power surrendered by the people is submitted to the administration of a single government; and usurpations are guarded against by a division of the government into distinct and separate departments. In the compound republic of America, the power surrendered by the people is first divided between two distinct governments, and then the portion allotted to each subdivided among distinct and separate departments. Hence a double security arises to the rights of the people. The different governments will control each other, at the same time that each will be controlled by itself.

Second. It is of great importance in a republic not only to guard the society against the oppression of its rulers, but to guard one part of the society against the injustice of the other part. Different interests necessarily exist in different classes of citizens. If a majority be united by a common interest, the rights of the minority will be insecure. There are but two methods of providing against this evil: The one by creating a will in the community independent of the majority—that is, of the society itself; the other, by comprehending in the society so many separate descriptions of citizens as will render an unjust combination of a majority of the whole very improbable, if not impracticable. The first method prevails in all governments possessing an hereditary or self-appointed authority. This, at best, is but a precarious security; because a power independent of the society may as well espouse the unjust views of the major as the rightful interests of the minor party, and may possibly be turned against both parties. The second method will be exemplified in the federal republic of the United States. Whilst all authority in it will be derived from and dependent on the society, the society itself will be broken into so many parts, interests and classes of citizens, that the rights of individuals, or of the minority, will be in little danger from interested combinations of the majority. In a free government the security for civil rights must be the same as that for religious rights. It consists in the one case in the multiplicity of interests, and in the other in the multiplicity of sects. The degree of security in both cases will depend on the number of interests and sects; and this may be presumed to depend on the extent of country and number of people comprehended under the same government. This view of the subject must particularly recommend a proper federal system to all the sincere and considerate friends of republican government: Since it shows that in exact proportion as the territory of the Union may be formed into more circumscribed Confederacies, or States, oppressive combinations of a majority will be facilitated; the best security, under the republican form, for the rights of every class of citizens, will be diminished; and consequently the stability and independence of some member of the government, the only other security, must be proportionally increased. Justice is the end of government. It is the end of civil society. It ever has been and ever will be pursued until it be obtained, or until liberty be lost in the pursuit. In a society under the forms of which the stronger faction can readily unite and oppress the weaker, anarchy may as truly be said to reign as in a state of nature, where the weaker individual is not secured against the violence of the stronger: And as, in the latter state, even the stronger individuals are prompted, by the uncertainty of their condition, to submit to a government which may protect the weak as well as themselves: So, in the former state, will the more powerful factions or parties be gradually induced, by a like motive, to wish for a government which will protect all parties, the weaker as well as the more powerful. It can be little doubted that if the State of Rhode Island was separated from the Confederacy and left to itself, the insecurity of rights under the popular form of government within such narrow limits would be displayed by such reiterated oppressions of factious majorities that some power altogether independent of the people would soon be called for by the voice of the very factions whose misrule had proved the necessity of it. In the extended republic of the United States, and among the great variety of interests, parties, and sects which it embraces, a coalition of a majority of the whole society could seldom take place on any other principles than those of justice and the general good; and there being thus less danger to a minor from the will of the major party, there must be less pretext, also, to provide for the security of the former, by introducing into the government a will not dependent on the latter, or, in other words, a will independent of the society itself. It is no less certain than it is important, notwithstanding the contrary opinions which have been entertained, that the larger the society, provided it lie within a practicable sphere, the more duly capable it will be of self-government. And happily for the *republican cause,* practicable sphere may be carried to a very great extent by a judicious modification and mixture of the *federal principle.*

PUBLIUS

Presidents and Vice Presidents

	PRESIDENT	VICE PRESIDENT
1	George Washington *(Federalist 1789)*	John Adams *(Federalist 1789)*
2	John Adams *(Federalist 1797)*	Thomas Jefferson *(Dem.-Rep. 1797)*
3	Thomas Jefferson *(Dem.-Rep. 1801)*	Aaron Burr *(Dem.-Rep. 1801)* George Clinton *(Dem.-Rep. 1805)*
4	James Madison *(Dem.-Rep. 1809)*	George Clinton *(Dem.-Rep. 1809)* Elbridge Gerry *(Dem.-Rep. 1813)*
5	James Monroe *(Dem.-Rep. 1817)*	Daniel D. Tompkins *(Dem.-Rep. 1817)*
6	John Quincy Adams *(Dem.-Rep. 1825)*	John C. Calhoun *(Dem.-Rep. 1825)*
7	Andrew Jackson *(Democratic 1829)*	John C. Calhoun *(Democratic 1829)* Martin Van Buren *(Democratic 1833)*
8	Martin Van Buren *(Democratic 1837)*	Richard M. Johnson *(Democratic 1837)*
9	William H. Harrison *(Whig 1841)*	John Tyler *(Whig 1841)*
10	John Tyler *(Whig and Democratic 1841)*	
11	James K. Polk *(Democratic 1845)*	George M. Dallas *(Democratic 1845)*
12	Zachary Taylor *(Whig 1849)*	Millard Fillmore *(Whig 1849)*
13	Millard Fillmore *(Whig 1850)*	
14	Franklin Pierce *(Democratic 1853)*	William R. D. King *(Democratic 1853)*

	PRESIDENT	VICE PRESIDENT
15	James Buchanan *(Democratic 1857)*	John C. Breckinridge *(Democratic 1857)*
16	Abraham Lincoln *(Republican 1861)*	Hannibal Hamlin *(Republican 1861)* Andrew Johnson *(Unionist 1865)*
17	Andrew Johnson *(Unionist 1865)*	
18	Ulysses S. Grant *(Republican 1869)*	Schuyler Colfax *(Republican 1869)* Henry Wilson *(Republican 1873)*
19	Rutherford B. Hayes *(Republican 1877)*	William A. Wheeler *(Republican 1877)*
20	James A. Garfield *(Republican 1881)*	Chester A. Arthur *(Republican 1881)*
21	Chester A. Arthur *(Republican 1881)*	
22	Grover Cleveland *(Democratic 1885)*	Thomas A. Hendricks *(Democratic 1885)*
23	Benjamin Harrison *(Republican 1889)*	Levi P. Morton *(Republican 1889)*
24	Grover Cleveland *(Democratic 1893)*	Adlai E. Stevenson *(Democratic 1893)*
25	William McKinley *(Republican 1897)*	Garret A. Hobart *(Republican 1897)* Theodore Roosevelt *(Republican 1901)*
26	Theodore Roosevelt *(Republican 1901)*	Charles W. Fairbanks *(Republican 1905)*
27	William H. Taft *(Republican 1909)*	James S. Sherman *(Republican 1909)*
28	Woodrow Wilson *(Democratic 1913)*	Thomas R. Marshall *(Democratic 1913)*

	PRESIDENT	VICE PRESIDENT		PRESIDENT	VICE PRESIDENT
29	Warren G. Harding *(Republican 1921)*	Calvin Coolidge *(Republican 1921)*	37	Richard M. Nixon *(Republican 1969)*	Spiro T. Agnew *(Republican 1969)*
					Gerald R. Ford *(Republican 1973)*
30	Calvin Coolidge *(Republican 1923)*	Charles G. Dawes *(Republican 1925)*	38	Gerald R. Ford *(Republican 1974)*	Nelson Rockefeller *(Republican 1974)*
31	Herbert Hoover *(Republican 1929)*	Charles Curtis *(Republican 1929)*	39	James E. Carter *(Democratic 1977)*	Walter Mondale *(Democratic 1977)*
32	Franklin D. Roosevelt *(Democratic 1933)*	John Nance Garner *(Democratic 1933)*	40	Ronald Reagan *(Republican 1981)*	George H. W. Bush *(Republican 1981)*
		Henry A. Wallace *(Democratic 1941)*	41	George H. W. Bush *(Republican 1989)*	J. Danforth Quayle *(Republican 1989)*
		Harry S. Truman *(Democratic 1945)*	42	William J. Clinton *(Democratic 1993)*	Albert Gore Jr. *(Democratic 1993)*
33	Harry S. Truman *(Democratic 1945)*	Alben W. Barkley *(Democratic 1949)*	43	George W. Bush *(Republican 2001)*	Richard Cheney *(Republican 2001)*
34	Dwight D. Eisenhower *(Republican 1953)*	Richard M. Nixon *(Republican 1953)*	44	Barack Obama *(Democratic 2009)*	Joseph R. Biden Jr. *(Democratic 2009)*
35	John F. Kennedy *(Democratic 1961)*	Lyndon B. Johnson *(Democratic 1961)*			
36	Lyndon B. Johnson *(Democratic 1963)*	Hubert H. Humphrey *(Democratic 1965)*			

Glossary

absentee ballot A voting ballot submitted by mail before an election. Voters use absentee ballots if they will be unable to go to the polls on Election Day.

activists People who dedicate their time, effort, and money to supporting a political party or particular candidates.

adversarial system A two-sided court structure in which lawyers on both sides of a case attempt to prove their argument over their opponent's version of the case.

advertising Actions taken by a member of Congress that are unrelated to government issues but have the primary goal of making a positive impression on the public, like sending holiday cards to constituents and appearing in parades.

amicus curiae Latin for "friend of the court," referring to an interested group or person who shares relevant information about a case to help the Court reach a decision. Usually *amicus* participants register their opinions in briefs, but they also may participate in oral arguments if one of the parties in the case gives them some of their allotted time.

Antifederalists Those at the Constitutional Convention who favored strong state governments over a strong national government.

appeals courts The intermediate level of federal courts that hear appeals from district courts. More generally, an appeals court is any court with appellate jurisdiction.

appellate jurisdiction The authority of a court to hear appeals from lower courts and change or uphold the decision.

apportionment The process of assigning the 435 seats in the House to the states based on increases or decreases in state populations.

Articles of Confederation Written in 1776, these were the first attempt at a new American government. It was later decided that the Articles restricted national government too much, and they were replaced by the Constitution.

astroturf lobbying Any lobbying method initiated by an interest group that is designed to look like the spontaneous, independent participation of many individuals.

attack ads Campaign advertising that criticizes a candidate's opponent—typically by making potentially damaging claims about the opponent's background or record—rather than focusing on positive reasons to vote for the candidate.

attack journalism A type of increasingly popular media coverage focused on political scandals and controversies, which causes a negative public opinion of political figures.

attitudinalist approach A way of understanding decisions of the Supreme Court based on the political ideologies of the justices.

backbenchers Legislators who do not hold leadership positions within their party caucus or conference.

bicameralism The system of having two chambers within one legislative body, like the House and Senate in the U.S. Congress.

Bill of Rights The first ten amendments to the Constitution; they protect individual rights and liberties.

block grants Federal aid provided to a state government to be spent within a certain policy area, which the state can decide how to spend within that area.

brand names The use of party names to evoke certain positions or issues. For instance, "Adidas" might immediately call to mind athletics in the same way that "Democrat" might remind you of environmental policies or universal health care.

briefs Written documents prepared by both parties in a case, and sometimes by outside groups, presenting their arguments in court.

broadcast media Communications technologies, such as television and radio, that transmit information over airwaves.

budget maximizers Bureaucrats who seek to increase funding for their agency whether or not that additional spending is worthwhile.

burden of proof The responsibility of having to prove guilt; it rests with the plaintiff in criminal cases but could be with either party in a civil trial.

bureaucracy The system of civil servants and political appointees who implement congressional or presidential decisions; also known as the administrative state.

bureaucratic drift Bureaucrats' tendency to implement policies in a way that favors their own political objectives rather than following the original intentions of the legislation.

by-product theory of information transmission The idea that many Americans acquire political information unintentionally rather than by seeking it out.

cabinet The group of fifteen executive department heads who implement the president's agenda in their respective positions.

campaign platform A candidate's description of his or her issue positions and the kinds of policies he or she will seek to enact in office.

cases on appeal Cases brought before the Supreme Court because Congress has determined that they require the Court's attention.

casework Assistance provided by members of Congress to their constituents in solving problems with the federal bureaucracy or addressing other specific concerns.

categorical grants Federal aid to state or local governments that is provided for a specific purpose, such as a mass transit program within the transportation budget or a school lunch program within the education budget.

caucus (congressional) The organization of Democrats within the House and Senate that meets to discuss and debate the party's positions on various issues in order to reach a consensus and to assign leadership positions.

caucus (political) A local meeting in which party members select a party's nominee for the general election.

centralized groups Interest groups that have a headquarters, usually in Washington, DC, as well as members and field offices throughout the country. In general, these groups' lobbying decisions are made at headquarters by the group leaders.

cert pool A system initiated in the Supreme Court in the 1970s in which law clerks screen cases that come to the Supreme Court and recommend to the justices which cases should be heard.

challenger A politician running for an office that he does not hold at the time of the election. Challengers run against incumbents or in open-seat elections.

checks and balances A system in which each branch of government has some power over the others.

citizen groups A type of interest group that seeks changes in spending, regulations, or government programs concerning a wide range of policies (also known as public interest groups).

caucus (congressional) The organization of Democrats within the House and Senate that meets to discuss and debate the party's positions on various issues in order to reach a consensus and to assign leadership positions.

caucus (political) A local meeting in which party members select a party's nominee for the general election.

centralized groups Interest groups that have a headquarters, usually in Washington, DC, as well as members and field offices throughout the country. In general, these groups' lobbying decisions are made at headquarters by the group leaders.

cert pool A system initiated in the Supreme Court in the 1970s in which law clerks screen cases that come to the Supreme Court and recommend to the justices which cases should be heard.

challenger A politician running for an office that he does not hold at the time of the election. Challengers run against incumbents or in open-seat elections.

checks and balances A system in which each branch of government has some power over the others.

citizen groups A type of interest group that seeks changes in spending, regulations, or government programs concerning a wide range of policies (also known as public interest groups).

civil liberties Basic political freedoms that protect citizens from governmental abuses of power.

civil rights Rights that guarantee individuals freedom from discrimination. These rights are generally grounded in the equal protection clause of the 14th Amendment and more specifically laid out in laws passed by Congress, such as the 1964 Civil Rights Act.

civil servants Employees of bureaucratic agencies within the government.

Civil War Amendments The 13th, 14th, and 15th Amendments to the Constitution, which abolished slavery and granted civil liberties and voting rights to freed slaves after the Civil War.

clash of civilizations The theory that terrorism is motivated by a hatred of Western culture and religion.

clear and present danger test Established in *Schenk v. United States*, this test allows the government to restrict certain types of speech deemed dangerous.

closed primary A primary election in which only registered members of a particular political party can vote.

closed rules Conditions placed on a legislative debate by the House Rules Committee prohibiting the addition of amendments to a bill.

cloture A procedure through which the Senate can limit the amount of time spent debating a bill (cutting off a filibuster), if a supermajority of sixty senators agree.

coattails The idea that a popular president can generate additional support for candidates affiliated with his party. Coattails are weak or nonexistent in most American elections.

coercion A method of eliminating nonparticipation or free riding by potential group members by requiring participation, as in many labor unions.

coercive federalism A form of federalism in which the federal government pressures the states to change their policies by using regulations, mandates, and conditions (often involving threats to withdraw federal funding).

Cold War The period of tension and arms competition between the United States and the Soviet Union that lasted from 1954 until 1991.

collective action problem A situation in which the members of a group would benefit by working together to produce some outcome, but each individual is better off refusing to cooperate and reaping benefits from those who do the work.

collusion Agreement between the litigants on the desired outcome of a case, causing a federal court to decline to hear the case. More generally, collusion can refer to any kind of conspiracy or complicity.

commerce clause Part of Article I, Section 8, of the Constitution that gives Congress "the power to regulate Commerce . . . among the several States." The Supreme Court's interpretation of this clause has varied, but today it serves as the basis for much of Congress's legislation.

commerce clause powers The powers of Congress to regulate the economy granted in Article I, Section 8, of the Constitution.

commercial speech Public expression with the aim of making a profit. It has received greater protection under the 1st Amendment in recent years but remains less protected than political speech.

common law Law based on the precedent of previous court rulings rather than on legislation. It is used in all federal courts and forty-nine of the fifty state courts.

competitive federalism A form of federalism in which states compete to attract businesses and jobs through the policies they adopt.

concentration The trend toward single-company ownership of several media sources in one area.

concurrent powers Responsibilities for particular policy areas, such as transportation, that are shared by federal, state, and local governments.

conditional party government The theory that lawmakers from the same party will cooperate to develop policy proposals.

confederal government A form of government in which states hold power over a limited national government.

confederations Interest groups made up of several independent, local organizations that provide much of their funding and hold most of the power.

conference The organization of Republicans within the House and Senate who meet to discuss and debate the party's positions on various issues in order to reach a consensus and to assign leadership positions.

conference committees Temporary committees created to negotiate differences between the House and Senate versions of a piece of legislation that has passed through both chambers.

consent of the governed The idea that government gains its legitimacy through regular elections in which the people living under that government participate to elect their leaders.

conservative One side of the ideological spectrum defined by support for lower taxes, a free market, and a more limited government; generally associated with Republicans.

considerations The many pieces of information a person uses to form an opinion.

constitutional authority (presidential) Powers derived from the provisions of the Constitution that outline the president's role in government.

constitutional courts Those courts established under Article III of the Constitution (or under the legislative power granted to Congress in Article III to create new courts): the Supreme Court, district courts, and appeals courts.

constitutional interpretation The process of determining whether a piece of legislation or governmental action is supported by the Constitution.

constitutional revolution A significant change in the Constitution that may be accomplished either through amendments (as in after the Civil War) or shifts in the Supreme Court's interpretation of the Constitution (as in the New Deal era).

containment An important feature of American Cold War policy in which the United States used diplomatic, economic, and military strategies in an effort to prevent the Soviet Union from expanding its influence.

cooperative federalism A form of federalism in which national and state governments work together to provide services efficiently. This form emerged in the late 1930s, representing a profound shift toward less concrete boundaries of responsibility in national–state relations.

Council of Economic Advisors (CEA) A group of economic advisers, created by the Employment Act of 1946, who provide objective data on

disenfranchised To have been denied the ability to exercise a right, such as the right to vote.

disparate impact standard The idea that discrimination exists if a practice has a negative effect on a specific group, whether or not this effect was intentional.

distributive theory The idea that members of Congress will join committees that best serve the interests of their district and that committee members will support each other's legislation.

district courts Lower level trial courts of the federal judicial system that handle most U.S. federal cases.

divided government A situation in which the House, Senate, and presidency are not controlled by the same party, such as if Democrats hold the majority of House and Senate seats, and the president is a Republican.

docket A calendar listing of cases that have been submitted to a court.

doctrine of interposition The idea that if the national government passes an unconstitutional law, the people of the states (through their state legislatures) can declare the law void. This idea provided the basis for southern secession and the Civil War.

double jeopardy Being tried twice for the same crime. This is prevented by the 5th Amendment.

dual federalism The form of federalism favored by Chief Justice Roger Taney in which national and state governments are seen as distinct entities providing separate services. This model limits the power of the national government.

due process clause Part of the 14th Amendment that forbids states from denying "life liberty or property" to any person without the due process of law. (A nearly identical clause in the 5th Amendment applies only to the national government.)

due process rights The idea that laws and legal proceedings must be fair. The Constitution guarantees that the government cannot take away a person's "life, liberty, or property, without due process of law." Other specific due process rights are found in the 4th, 5th, 6th, and 8th amendments, such as protection from self-incrimination and freedom from illegal searches.

Duverger's law The principle that in a democracy with single-member districts and plurality voting, like the United States, only two parties' candidates will have a realistic chance of winning political office.

earmarks Federally funded local projects attached to bills passed through Congress.

economic groups A type of interest group that seeks public policies that will provide monetary benefits to its members.

economic individualism The autonomy of individuals to manage their own financial decisions without government interference.

elastic clause Part of Article I, Section 8, of the Constitution that grants Congress the power to pass any law that is related to one of its expressed powers.

election cycle The two-year period between general elections.

electoral college The body that votes to select America's president and vice president based on the popular vote in each state. Each candidate nominates a slate of electors who are selected to attend the meeting of the college if their candidate wins the most votes in a state or district.

electoral connection The idea that congressional behavior is centrally motivated by members' desire for reelection.

electoral vote Votes cast by members of the electoral college; after a presidential candidate wins the popular vote in a given state, that candidate's slate of electors will cast electoral votes for the candidate on behalf of that state.

enumerated powers Powers explicitly granted to Congress, the president, or the Supreme Court in the first three articles of the Constitution. Examples include Congress's power to "raise and support armies" and the president's power as commander in chief.

equal time provision An FCC regulation requiring broadcast media to provide equal airtime on any non-news programming to all candidates running for an office.

establishment clause Part of the 1st Amendment that states, "Congress shall make no law respecting an establishment of religion," which has been interpreted to mean that Congress cannot sponsor or favor any religion.

exclusionary rule The principle that illegally or unconstitutionally acquired evidence cannot be used in a criminal trial.

executive agreement An agreement between the executive branch and a foreign government, which acts as a treaty but does not require Senate approval.

Executive Office of the President (EOP) The group of policy-related offices that serve as support staff to the president.

executive orders Proclamations made by the president that change government policy without congressional approval.

executive powers clause Part of Article II, Section 1, of the Constitution that states, "The executive Power shall be vested in a President of the United States of America." This broad statement has been used to justify many assertions of presidential power.

executive privilege The right of the president to keep executive branch conversations and correspondence confidential from the legislative and judicial branches.

factions Groups of like-minded people who try to influence the government. American government is set up to avoid domination by any one of these groups.

fairness doctrine An FCC regulation requiring broadcast media to present several points of view to ensure balanced coverage. It was created in the late 1940s and eliminated in 1987.

fast-track authority An expedited system for passing treaties under which support from simple majority, rather than a two thirds majority, is needed in both the House and Senate, and no amendments are allowed.

federal civil service A system created by the 1883 Pendleton Civil Service Act in which bureaucrats are hired on the basis of merit rather than political connections.

Federal Communications Commission (FCC) A government agency created in 1934 to regulate American radio stations, and later expanded to regulate television, wireless communications technologies, and other broadcast media.

Federal Election Commission The government agency that enforces and regulates campaign finance laws; made up of six presidential appointees, of whom no more than three can be members of the same party.

federal preemptions Impositions of national priorities on the states through national legislation that is based on the Constitution's supremacy clause.

federalism The division of power across the local, state, and national levels of government.

Federalist Papers A series of eighty-five articles written by Alexander Hamilton, James Madison, and John Jay that sought to sway public opinion toward the Federalists' position.

Federalists Those at the Constitutional Convention who favored a strong national government over strong state governments.

fighting words Forms of expression that "by their very utterance" can incite violence. These can be regulated by the government but are often difficult to define.

filibuster A tactic used by senators to block a bill by continuing to hold the floor and speak—under the Senate rule of unlimited debate—until the bill's supporters back down.

filtering The influence on public opinion that results from journalists' and editors' decisions about which of many potential news stories to report.

fire alarm oversight A method of oversight in which members of Congress respond to complaints about the bureaucracy or problems of implementation only as they arise rather than exercising constant vigilance.

first-mover advantage The president's power to initiate treaty negotiations. Congress cannot initiate treaties and can only consider them once they have been negotiated.

fiscal federalism A form of federalism in which federal funds are allocated to the lower levels of government though transfer payments or grants.

501(c) organization A tax code classification that applies to most interest groups; this designation makes donations to the group tax-deductible but limits the group's political activities.

527 organization A tax-exempt group formed primarily to influence elections through voter mobilization efforts and issue ads that do not directly endorse or oppose a candidate. Unlike political action committees, they are not subject to contribution limits and spending caps.

framing The influence on public opinion caused by the way a story is presented or covered, including the details, explanations, and context offered in the report.

free exercise clause Part of the 1st Amendment stating that Congress cannot prohibit or interfere with the practice of religion.

free market An economic system based on competition between businesses without government interference.

free rider problem The incentive to benefit from others' work without contributing that leads individuals in a collective action situation to refuse to work together.

free riding The practice of relying on others to contribute to a collective effort, while failing to participate on one's own behalf and still benefiting from the group's successes.

frontloading The practice of states moving their presidential primaries or caucuses to take place earlier in the nomination process, often in the hopes of exerting more influence over the outcome.

full faith and credit clause Part of Article IV of the Constitution requiring that each state's laws be honored by the other states. For example, a legal marriage in one state must be recognized across state lines.

gag order An aspect of prior restraint that allows the government to prohibit the media from publishing anything related to an ongoing trial.

general election The election in which voters cast ballots for House members, senators, and (every four years) a president and vice president.

general revenue sharing (GRS) A type of grant used in the 1970s and 1980s in which the federal government provided state governments with funds to be spent at each state's discretion. These grants provided states with more control over programs.

gerrymandering Attempting to use the process of redrawing district boundaries to benefit a political party, protect incumbents, or change the proportion of minority voters in a district.

go public A president's use of speeches and other public communications to appeal directly to citizens about issues the president would like the House and Senate to act on.

GOTV A campaign's efforts to "get out the vote" or make sure their supporters vote on Election Day (also known as the ground game).

government The system for implementing decisions made through the political process.

grandfather clause A type of law enacted in several southern states to allow those who were permitted to vote before the Civil War, and their descendants, to bypass literacy tests and other obstacles to voting, thereby exempting whites from these tests while continuing to disenfranchise African Americans and other people of color.

grassroots lobbying A lobbying strategy that relies on participation by group members, such as a protest or a letter-writing campaign.

Great Compromise A compromise between the large and small states, proposed by Connecticut, in which Congress would have two houses: a Senate with two legislators per state and a House of Representatives in which each state's representation would be based on population (also known as the Connecticut Compromise).

gridlock An inability to enact legislation because of partisan conflict within Congress or between Congress and the president.

ground game A campaign's efforts to "get out the vote" or make sure their supporters vote on Election Day (also known as GOTV).

hard money Donations that are used to help elect or defeat a specific candidate.

hard news Media coverage focused on facts and important issues surrounding a campaign.

hate speech Expression that is offensive or abusive, particularly in terms of race, gender, or sexual orientation. It is currently protected under the 1st Amendment.

head of government One role of the president, through which he or she has authority over the executive branch.

head of state One role of the president, through which he or she represents the country symbolically and politically.

horse race A description of the type of election coverage that focuses more on poll results and speculation about a likely winner than on substantive differences between the candidates.

hostile media phenomenon The idea that supporters of a candidate or issue tend to feel that media coverage is biased against their position, regardless of whether coverage is actually unfair.

ideological polarization The effect on public opinion when many citizens move away from moderate positions and toward either end of the political spectrum, identifying themselves as either liberals or conservatives.

ideology A cohesive set of ideas and beliefs used to organize and evaluate the political world.

impeachment A negative or checking power of Congress over the other branches allowing them to remove the president, vice president, or other "officers of the United States" (including federal judges) for abuses of power.

implied powers Powers supported by the Constitution that are not expressly stated in it.

incumbency safety The relative infrequency with which members of Congress are defeated in their attempts for reelection.

incumbent A politician running for reelection to the office she currently holds.

independent agencies Government offices or organizations that provide government services and are not part of an executive department.

informational theory The idea that having committees in Congress made up of experts on specific policy areas helps to ensure well-informed policy decisions.

initiative A direct vote by citizens on a policy change proposed by fellow citizens or organized groups outside government. Getting a question on the ballot typically requires collecting a set number of signatures from registered voters in support of the proposal. There is no mechanism for a national-level initiative.

inside strategies Tactics used by interest groups within Washington, DC, to achieve their policy goals.

interest group An organizations of people who share common political interests and aim to influence public policy by electioneering and lobbying.

interest group entrepreneurs The leaders of an interest group who define the group's mission and its goals and create a plan to achieve them.

interest group state A government in which most policy decisions are determined by the influence of interest groups.

grandfather clause A type of law enacted in several southern states to allow those who were permitted to vote before the Civil War, and their descendants, to bypass literacy tests and other obstacles to voting, thereby exempting whites from these tests while continuing to disenfranchise African Americans and other people of color.

grassroots lobbying A lobbying strategy that relies on participation by group members, such as a protest or a letter-writing campaign.

Great Compromise A compromise between the large and small states, proposed by Connecticut, in which Congress would have two houses: a Senate with two legislators per state and a House of Representatives in which each state's representation would be based on population (also known as the Connecticut Compromise).

Great Society The wide-ranging social agenda promoted by President Lyndon Johnson in the mid-1960s that aimed to improve Americans' quality of life through governmental social programs.

Greenspan Commission The informal name of the National Commission on Social Security Reform created by President Ronald Reagan in 1981 to address short-term and long-term problems facing the Social Security program.

gridlock An inability to enact legislation because of partisan conflict within Congress or between Congress and the president.

gross domestic product (GDP) The value of a country's economic output taken as a whole.

ground game A campaign's efforts to "get out the vote" or make sure their supporters vote on Election Day (also known as GOTV).

hard money Donations that are used to help elect or defeat a specific candidate.

hard news Media coverage focused on facts and important issues surrounding a campaign.

hate speech Expression that is offensive or abusive, particularly in terms of race, gender, or sexual orientation. It is currently protected under the 1st Amendment.

head of government One role of the president, through which he or she has authority over the executive branch.

head of state One role of the president, through which he or she represents the country symbolically and politically.

horse race A description of the type of election coverage that focuses more on poll results and speculation about a likely winner than on substantive differences between the candidates.

hostile media phenomenon The idea that supporters of a candidate or issue tend to feel that media coverage is biased against their position, regardless of whether coverage is actually unfair.

idealism The idea that a country's foreign policy decisions are based on factors beyond self-interest, including upholding important principles or values.

ideological polarization The effect on public opinion when many citizens move away from moderate positions and toward either end of the political spectrum, identifying themselves as either liberals or conservatives.

ideology A cohesive set of ideas and beliefs used to organize and evaluate the political world.

impeachment A negative or checking power of Congress over the other branches allowing them to remove the president, vice president, or other "officers of the United States" (including federal judges) for abuses of power.

implied powers Powers supported by the Constitution that are not expressly stated in it.

income support Government programs that provide support to low-income Americans, such as welfare, food stamps, unemployment compensation, and the Earned Income Tax Credit.

incumbency safety The relative infrequency with which members of Congress are defeated in their attempts for reelection.

incumbent A politician running for reelection to the office she currently holds.

independent agencies Government offices or organizations that provide government services and are not part of an executive department.

inflation The increase in the price of consumer goods over time.

informational theory The idea that having committees in Congress made up of experts on specific policy areas helps to ensure well-informed policy decisions.

initiative A direct vote by citizens on a policy change proposed by fellow citizens or organized groups outside government. Getting a question on the ballot typically requires collecting a set number of signatures from registered voters in support of the proposal. There is no mechanism for a national-level initiative.

inside strategies Tactics used by interest groups within Washington, DC, to achieve their policy goals.

interest group An organizations of people who share common political interests and aim to influence public policy by electioneering and lobbying.

interest group entrepreneurs The leaders of an interest group who define the group's mission and its goals and create a plan to achieve them.

interest group state A government in which most policy decisions are determined by the influence of interest groups.

intermediate scrutiny standard The middle level of scrutiny the courts use when determining whether unequal treatment is justified by the effect of a law; this is the standard used for gender-based discrimination cases and for many cases based on sexual orientation.

International Monetary Fund A nongovernmental organization established in 1944 to help stabilize the international monetary system, improve economic growth, and aid developing nations.

internationalism The idea that the United States should be involved in the affairs of other nations, out of both self-interest and moral obligation.

investigative journalists Reporters who dig deeply into a particular topic of public concern, often targeting government failures and inefficiencies.

isolationism The idea that the United States should refrain from involvement in international affairs.

issue scale A survey response format in which respondents select their answers from a range of positions between two extremes.

issue voters People who are well-informed about their own policy preferences and knowledgeable about the candidates—and use all of this information when they decide how to vote.

Jim Crow laws State and local laws that mandated racial segregation in all public facilities in the South, many border states, and some northern communities between 1876 and 1964.

joint committees Committees that contain members of both the House and Senate but have limited authority.

judicial activism The idea that the Supreme Court should assert its interpretation of the law even if it overrules the elected executive and legislative branches of government.

judicial restraint The idea that the Supreme Court should defer to the democratically elected executive and legislative branches of government rather than contradicting existing laws.

judicial review The Supreme Court's power to strike down a law or executive branch action that it finds unconstitutional.

Judiciary Act of 1789 The law in which Congress laid out the organization of the federal judiciary. The law refined and clarified federal court jurisdiction and set the original number of justices at six. It also created the Office of the Attorney General and established the lower federal courts.

jurisdiction The sphere of a court's legal authority to hear and decide cases.

national supremacy clause Part of Article VI, Section 2, of the Constitution stating that the Constitution is the "supreme Law of the Land," meaning national laws take precedent over state laws if the two conflict.

nationalized election An atypical congressional election in which the reelection rate is relatively low for one party's House and Senate incumbents and national-level issues exert more influence than usual on House and Senate races.

natural rights Also known as "unalienable rights," the Declaration of Independence defines them as "Life, Liberty, and the pursuit of Happiness." The Founders believed that upholding these rights should be the government's central purpose.

neutral competence The idea, credited to theorist Max Weber, which suggests that bureaucrats should provide expertise without the influence of elected officials, interest groups, or their own political agendas.

New Deal Coalition The assemblage of groups who aligned with and supported the Democratic Party in support of New Deal policies during the fifth party system, including African Americans, Catholics, Jewish people, union members, and white southerners.

New Jersey Plan In response to the Virginia Plan, smaller states at the Constitutional Conventions offered this plan in which each state would receive equal representation in the national legislature, regardless of size.

news cycle The time between the release of information and its publication, like the twenty-four hours between issues of a daily newspaper.

nodes Groups of people who belong to, are candidates of, or work for a political party, but do not necessarily work together or hold similar policy preferences.

nominating convention A meeting held by each party every four years at which states' delegates select the party's presidential and vice-presidential nominees and approve the party platform.

nomination The selection of a particular candidate to run for office in a general election as a representative of his or her political party.

normal election A typical congressional election in which the reelection rate is high, and the influences on House and Senate contests are largely local.

normalization hypothesis The idea that media sources will increasingly make their news available online as more people begin using the Internet.

notice and comment procedure A step in the rule-making process in which proposed rules are published in the *Federal Register* and made available for debate by the general public.

off the record A term describing comments a politician makes to the press on the condition that they can be reported only if they are not attributed to that politician (also known as "on background").

Office of Management and Budget (OMB) An office within the Executive Office of the President that is responsible for creating the president's annual budget proposal to Congress, reviewing proposed rules, and other budget-related tasks.

omnibus legislation Large bills that often cover several topics and may contain extraneous, or pork-barrel, projects.

on background A term describing comments a politician makes to the press on the condition that they can be reported only if they are not attributed to that politician (also known as "off the record").

on-line processing A way of forming a political opinion in which a person develops a preference regarding a candidate, party, or policy but does not remember the original reasons behind the preference.

op-ed Short for "opinion editorial," this type of article is written by a journalist or guest writer who expresses his or her opinion on a given issue without necessarily attempting to be objective.

open primary A primary election in which any registered voter can participate in the contest, regardless of party affiliation.

open rules Conditions placed on a legislative debate by the House Rules Committee allowing the addition of relevant amendments to a bill.

open seat An elected position for which there is no incumbent.

opposition research Attempts by a candidate's campaign or other groups of supporters to uncover embarrassing or politically damaging information about the candidate's opponent.

oral arguments Spoken presentations made in person by the lawyers of each party to a judge or appellate court outlining the legal reasons why their side should prevail.

original intent The theory that justices should surmise the intentions of the Founders when the language of the Constitution is unclear.

original jurisdiction The authority of a court to handle a case first, as in the Supreme Court's authority to initially hear disputes between two states.

outside strategies Tactics used by interest groups outside Washington, DC, to achieve their policy goals.

oversight Congressional efforts to make sure that laws are implemented correctly by the bureaucracy after they have been passed.

paradox of voting The question of why citizens vote even though their individual votes stand little chance of changing the election outcome.

parliamentary system A system of government in which legislative and executive power are closely joined. The legislature (parliament) selects the chief executive (prime minister) who forms the cabinet from members of the parliament.

parties in service The role of the parties in recruiting, training, contributing to, and campaigning for congressional and presidential candidates. This aspect of party organization grew more prominent during the sixth party system.

party coalitions The groups who identify with a political party, usually described in demographic terms, such as African American Democrats or evangelical Republicans.

party identification (party ID) A citizen's loyalty to a specific political party.

party in government The group of officeholders who belong to a specific political party and were elected as candidates of that party.

party in power Under unified government, the party that controls the House, Senate, and the presidency. Under divided government, the president's party.

party in the electorate The group of citizens who identify with a specific political party.

party organization A specific political party's leaders and workers at the national, state, and local levels.

party platform A set of objectives outlining the party's issue positions and priorities—although candidates are not required to support their party's platform.

party principle The idea that a political party exists as an organization distinct from its elected officials or party leaders.

party ratio The proportions of seats in the House and Senate that are controlled by each major party.

party system A period of time in which the names of the major political parties, their supporters, and the issues dividing them remain relatively stable.

party unity The extent to which members of Congress in the same party vote together on party votes.

party votes A vote in which the majority of one party opposes the position of the majority of the other party.

peak associations Interest groups whose members are businesses or other organizations rather than individuals.

penny press A term describing reduced-price newspapers sold for one cent in the 1830s, when more efficient printing presses made newspapers available to a larger segment of the population.

permanent campaign The actions officeholders take throughout the election cycle to build support for their reelection.

phone banks Groups of organized supporters who contact likely voters by phone to encourage support for their party or candidate.

picket fence federalism A more refined and realistic form of cooperative federalism in which policy makers within a particular policy area work together across the levels of government.

plaintiff The person or party who brings a case to court.

plea bargain An agreement between a plaintiff and defendant to settle a case before it goes to trial or the verdict is decided. In a civil case this usually involves an admission of guilt and an agreement on monetary damages; in a criminal case it often involves an admission of guilt in return for a reduced charge or sentence.

pluralism The idea that having a variety of parties and interests within a government will strengthen the system, ensuring that no group possesses total control.

plurality voting A voting system in which the candidate who receives the most votes within a geographic area wins the election, regardless of whether that candidates wins a majority (more than half) of the votes.

pocket veto The automatic death of a bill passed by the House and Senate when the president fails to sign the bill in the last ten days of a legislative session.

polarized A term describing the alignment of both parties' members with their own party's issues and priorities, with little crossover support for the other party's goals.

police patrol oversight A method of oversight in which members of Congress constantly monitor the bureaucracy to make sure that laws are implemented correctly.

policy mood The level of public support for expanding the government's role in society; whether the public wants government action on a specific issue.

political action committee (PAC) An interest group or division of and interest group that can raise money to contribute to campaigns or to spend on ads in support of candidates. The amount a PAC can receive from each of it donors and its expenditures on federal campaigning are strictly limited.

political appointees People selected by an elected leader, such as the president, to hold a government position.

political business cycle Attempts by elected officials to manipulate the economy, increasing economic growth and reducing unemployment and inflation around election time, with the goal of improving evaluations of their performance in office.

political machine An unofficial patronage system within a political party that seeks to gain political power and government contracts, jobs, and other benefits for party leaders, workers, and supporters.

political socialization The process by which an individual's political opinions are shaped by other people and the surrounding culture.

politico A member of Congress who acts as a delegate on issues that constituents care about (like civil rights) and as a trustee on more complex or less salient issues (like some foreign policy or regulatory matters).

politics The process that determines what government does.

popular vote The votes cast by citizens in an election.

population The group of people that a researcher or pollster wants to study, such as evangelicals, senior citizens, or Americans.

pork barrel Legislative appropriations that benefit specific constituents, created with the aim of helping local representatives win reelection.

position taking Any public statement in which a member of Congress makes her views on an issue known to her constituents.

positive externalities Benefits created by a public good that are shared by the primary consumer of the good and by society more generally.

power of the purse The constitutional power of Congress to raise and spend money. Congress can use this as a negative or checking power over the other branches by freezing or cutting their funding to punish executive agencies.

precedent A legal norm established in court cases that is then applied to future cases dealing with the same legal questions.

president pro tempore A largely symbolic position usually held by the most senior member of the majority party in the Senate.

presidential approval The percentage of Americans who feel that the president is doing a good job in office.

press conference Events at which politicians speak to journalists and, in most cases, answer their questions afterward.

primary A ballot vote in which citizens select a party's nominee for the general election.

prime time Evening hours when television viewership is at its highest and networks often schedule news programs.

priming The influence on the public's general impressions caused by positive or negative coverage of a candidate or issue.

principal–agent game The interaction between a principal (like the president or Congress), who needs something done, and an agent (like a bureaucrat), who is responsible for carrying out the principal's orders.

prior restraint A limit on freedom of the press that allows the government to prohibit the media from publishing certain materials.

privacy rights Liberties protected by several amendments in the Bill of Rights that shield certain personal aspects of citizens' lives from governmental interference, such as the 4th Amendment's protection against unreasonable searches and seizures.

privileges and immunities clause Part of Article IV of the Constitution requiring that states must treat non-state residents within their borders as they would treat their own residents. This was meant to promote commerce and travel between states.

problem of control A difficulty faced by elected officials in ensuring that when bureaucrats implement policies, they follow these officials' intentions but still have enough discretion to use their expertise.

proportional allocation During the presidential primaries, the practice of determining the number of convention delegates allotted to each candidate based on the percentage of the popular vote cast for each candidate. All Democratic primaries and caucuses use this system, as do some states' Republican primaries and caucuses.

protectionism The idea under which some people have tried to rationalize discriminatory policies by claiming that some groups, like women or African Americans, should be denied certain rights for their own safety or well-being.

public goods Services or actions (such as protecting the environment) that, once provided to one person, become available to everyone. Government is typically needed to provide public goods because they will be under-produced by the free market.

public opinion Citizens' views on politics and government actions.

purposive benefits Satisfaction derived from the experience of working toward a desired policy goal, even if the goal is not achieved.

push polling A type of survey in which the questions are presented in a biased way in an attempt to influence the respondent.

random digit dialing A method of random sampling used in telephone surveys, in which the interviewers call respondents by dialing random telephone numbers in order to include those with unlisted numbers.

random sample A subsection of a population chosen to participate in a survey through a selection process in which every member of the population has an equal chance of being chosen. This kind of sampling improves the accuracy of public opinion data.

realignment A change in the size or composition of the party coalitions or in the nature of the issues that divide the parties. Realignments typically occur within an election cycle or two, but they can also occur gradually over the course of a decade or longer.

reasonable basis test The use of evidence to suggest that differences in the behavior of two groups can rationalize unequal treatment of these groups, such as charging sixteen- to twenty-one-year-olds higher prices for auto insurance than people over twenty-one because younger people have higher accident rates.

reasonable vote A vote that is likely to be consistent with the voter's true preference about the candidates.

recess appointment When a person is chosen by the president to fill a position, such as an ambassadorship or the head of a department, while the Senate is not in session, thereby bypassing Senate approval. Unless approved by a subsequent Senate vote, recess appointees serve only to the end of the congressional term.

reciprocity The informal congressional norm whereby a member votes for a bill that he might not otherwise support because a colleague strongly favors it—in exchange for the colleague's vote for a bill that the member feels strongly about (also known as logrolling).

red tape Excessive or unnecessarily complex regulations imposed by the bureaucracy.

redistributive tax policies Policies, generally favored by Democratic politicians, in which taxation is used to attempt to create greater social equality, i.e. higher taxation of the rich to provide programs for the poor.

redistricting Redrawing the geographic boundaries of legislative districts. This happens every ten years to ensure that districts remain roughly equal in population.

referendum A direct vote by citizens on a policy change proposed by a legislature or another government body. While referenda are common in state and local elections, there is no mechanism for a national-level referendum.

regional primaries A practice whereby several states in the same area of the country hold presidential primaries or caucuses on the same day.

regulation A rule that allows the government to exercise control over individuals and corporations by restricting certain behaviors.

regulatory capture A situation in which bureaucrats favor the interests of the groups or corporations they are supposed to regulate at the expense of the general public.

remedial legislation National laws that address discriminatory state laws. Authority for such legislation comes from Section 5 of the 14th Amendment.

republican democracy A form of government in which the interests of the people are represented through elected leaders.

republicanism The belief that a form of government in which the interests of the people are represented through elected leaders is the best form of government.

responsible parties A system in which each political party's candidates campaign on the party platform, work together in office to implement the platform, and are judged by voters based on whether they achieve the platform's objectives.

retail politics A mode of campaigning in which a candidate or campaign staff contact citizens directly, as would happen at a rally, a talk before a small group, or a one-on-one meeting between a candidate and a citizen.

retrospective evaluation A citizen's judgment of an officeholder's job performance since the last election.

revolving door A term describing the movement of individuals from government positions to jobs with interest groups or lobbying firms, and vice versa.

ripeness A criterion that federal courts use to decide whether a case is ready to be heard. A case's ripeness is based on whether its central issue or controversy has actually taken place.

robo-poll A type of survey in which a computer program, rather than a live questioner, interviews respondents by telephone.

roll call vote A recorded vote on legislation; members may vote yes, no, abstain, or present.

running tally A frequently updated mental record that a person uses to incorporate new information, like the information that leads a citizen to identify with a particular political party.

runoff election Under a majority voting system, a second election held only if no candidate wins a majority of the votes in the first general election. Only the top two vote-getters in the first election compete in the runoff.

salience The level of familiarity with an interest group's goals among general population.

sample Within a population, the group of people surveyed in order to gauge the whole population's opinion. Researchers use samples because it would be impossible to interview the entire population.

sampling error A calculation that describes what percentage of the people surveyed may not accurately represent the population being studied. Increasing the number of respondents lowers the sampling error.

seat shift A change in the number of seats held by Republicans and Democrats in the House or Senate.

select committees Committees in the House or Senate created to address a specific issue for one or two terms.

selective incentives Benefits that can motivate participation in a group effort because they are available only to those who participate, such as member services offered by interest groups.

selective incorporation The process through which the civil liberties granted in the Bill of Rights were applied to the states on a case-by-case basis through the 14th Amendment.

senatorial courtesy A norm in the nomination of district court judges in which the president consults with his party's senators from the relevant state in choosing the nominee.

seniority The informal congressional norm of choosing the member who has served the longest on a particular committee to be the committee chair.

"separate but equal" The idea that racial segregation was acceptable as long as the separate facilities were of equal quality; supported by *Plessy v. Ferguson* and struck down by *Brown v. Board of Education*.

separation of powers The division of government power across the judicial, executive, and legislative branches.

shield laws Legislation, which exists in some states but not at the federal level, that gives reporters the right to refuse to name the sources of their information.

signing statement A document issued by the president when signing a bill into law explaining his interpretation of the law, which often differs from the interpretation of Congress, in an attempt to influence how the law will be implemented.

single-issue groups A type of interest group that has a narrowly focused goal, seeking change on a single topic, government program, or piece of legislation.

single-member districts An electoral system in which every elected official represents a geographically defined area, such as a state or congressional district, and each area elects one representative.

slander Spoken false statements that damage a person's reputation. Such statements can be regulated by the government but are often difficult to distinguish from permissible speech.

slant The imbalance in a story that covers one candidate or policy favorably without providing similar coverage of the other side.

soft money Contributions that can be used for voter mobilization or to promote a policy proposal or point of view as long as these efforts are not tied to supporting or opposing a particular candidate.

soft news Media coverage that aims to entertain or shock, often through sensationalized reporting or by focusing on a candidate or politician's personality.

solicitor general A presidential appointee in the Department of Justice who represents the federal government when it is a party to a case.

solidary benefits Satisfaction derived from the experience of working

proportional allocation During the presidential primaries, the practice of determining the number of convention delegates allotted to each candidate based on the percentage of the popular vote cast for each candidate. All Democratic primaries and caucuses use this system, as do some states' Republican primaries and caucuses.

protectionism The idea under which some people have tried to rationalize discriminatory policies by claiming that some groups, like women or African Americans, should be denied certain rights for their own safety or well-being.

public goods Services or actions (such as protecting the environment) that, once provided to one person, become available to everyone. Government is typically needed to provide public goods because they will be under-produced by the free market.

public opinion Citizens' views on politics and government actions.

purposive benefits Satisfaction derived from the experience of working toward a desired policy goal, even if the goal is not achieved.

push polling A type of survey in which the questions are presented in a biased way in an attempt to influence the respondent.

random digit dialing A method of random sampling used in telephone surveys, in which the interviewers call respondents by dialing random telephone numbers in order to include those with unlisted numbers.

random sample A subsection of a population chosen to participate in a survey through a selection process in which every member of the population has an equal chance of being chosen. This kind of sampling improves the accuracy of public opinion data.

realignment A change in the size or composition of the party coalitions or in the nature of the issues that divide the parties. Realignments typically occur within an election cycle or two, but they can also occur gradually over the course of a decade or longer.

realism The idea that a country's foreign policy decisions are motivated by self-interest and the goal of gaining more power.

reasonable basis test The use of evidence to suggest that differences in the behavior of two groups can rationalize unequal treatment of these groups, such as charging sixteen- to twenty-one-year-olds higher prices for auto insurance than people over twenty-one because younger people have higher accident rates.

reasonable vote A vote that is likely to be consistent with the voter's true preference about the candidates.

recess appointment When a person is chosen by the president to fill a position, such as an ambassadorship or the head of a department, while the Senate is not in session, thereby bypassing Senate approval. Unless approved by a subsequent Senate vote, recess appointees serve only to the end of the congressional term.

reciprocity The informal congressional norm whereby a member votes for a bill that he might not otherwise support because a colleague strongly favors it—in exchange for the colleague's vote for a bill that the member feels strongly about (also known as logrolling).

red tape Excessive or unnecessarily complex regulations imposed by the bureaucracy.

redistributive tax policies Policies, generally favored by Democratic politicians, in which taxation is used to attempt to create greater social equality, i.e. higher taxation of the rich to provide programs for the poor.

redistricting Redrawing the geographic boundaries of legislative districts. This happens every ten years to ensure that districts remain roughly equal in population.

referendum A direct vote by citizens on a policy change proposed by a legislature or another government body. While referenda are common in state and local elections, there is no mechanism for a national-level referendum.

regional primaries A practice whereby several states in the same area of the country hold presidential primaries or caucuses on the same day.

regressive A term describing taxes that take a larger share of poor people's income than wealthy people's income, such as sales taxes and payroll taxes.

regulation A rule that allows the government to exercise control over individuals and corporations by restricting certain behaviors.

regulatory capture A situation in which bureaucrats favor the interests of the groups or corporations they are supposed to regulate at the expense of the general public.

remedial legislation National laws that address discriminatory state laws. Authority for such legislation comes from Section 5 of the 14th Amendment.

republican democracy A form of government in which the interests of the people are represented through elected leaders.

republicanism The belief that a form of government in which the interests of the people are represented through elected leaders is the best form of government.

reserve requirement The minimum amount of money that a bank is required to have on hand to back up its assets.

responsible parties A system in which each political party's candidates campaign on the party platform, work together in office to implement the platform, and are judged by voters based on whether they achieve the platform's objectives.

retail politics A mode of campaigning in which a candidate or campaign staff contact citizens directly, as would happen at a rally, a talk before a small group, or a one-on-one meeting between a candidate and a citizen.

retrospective evaluation A citizen's judgment of an officeholder's job performance since the last election.

revolving door A term describing the movement of individuals from government positions to jobs with interest groups or lobbying firms, and vice versa.

ripeness A criterion that federal courts use to decide whether a case is ready to be heard. A case's ripeness is based on whether its central issue or controversy has actually taken place.

robo-poll A type of survey in which a computer program, rather than a live questioner, interviews respondents by telephone.

roll call vote A recorded vote on legislation; members may vote yes, no, abstain, or present.

running tally A frequently updated mental record that a person uses to incorporate new information, like the information that leads a citizen to identify with a particular political party.

runoff election Under a majority voting system, a second election held only if no candidate wins a majority of the votes in the first general election. Only the top two vote-getters in the first election compete in the runoff.

salience The level of familiarity with an interest group's goals among general population.

sample Within a population, the group of people surveyed in order to gauge the whole population's opinion. Researchers use samples because it would be impossible to interview the entire population.

sampling error A calculation that describes what percentage of the people surveyed may not accurately represent the population being studied. Increasing the number of respondents lowers the sampling error.

sanction A trade penalty that one nation places on another to encourage the penalized nation to change its actions or policies.

seat shift A change in the number of seats held by Republicans and Democrats in the House or Senate.

select committees Committees in the House or Senate created to address a specific issue for one or two terms.

selective incentives Benefits that can motivate participation in a group effort because they are available only to those who participate, such as member services offered by interest groups.

whip system An organization of House leaders who work to disseminate information and promote party unity in voting on legislation.

wholesale politics A mode of campaigning that involves indirect contact with citizens, such as running campaign ads.

winner-take-all During the presidential primaries, the practice of assigning all of a given state's delegates to the candidate who receives the most popular votes. Some states' Republican primaries and caucuses use this system.

wire service An organization that gathers news and sells it to other media outlets. The invention of the telegraph in the early 1800s made this type of service possible.

writ of certification An uncommon way in which a case is brought before the Supreme Court, whereby an appeals court asks the Court to clarify federal law in regards to a particular case.

writ of certiorari The most common way for a case to reach the Supreme Court, in which at least four of the nine justices agree to hear a case that has reached them via an appeal from the losing party in a lower court's ruling.

writs of mandamus Orders issued by a higher court to a lower court, government official, or government agency to perform acts required by law.

yellow journalism A style of newspaper popular in the late 1800s, featuring sensationalized stories, bold headlines, and illustrations in order to increase readership.

Endnotes

CHAPTER 1

1. Ronald D. Utt, "The Bridge to Nowhere: A National Embarrassment," (Washington, DC: The Heritage Foundation, October 20, 2005), available at http://www.heritage.org/Research/Budget/wm889.cfm (accessed 11/15/07).
2. Jonathan Weisman and Jim VandeHei, "Road Bill Reflects the Power of Pork," *Washington Post,* August 11, 2005, p. A1.
3. "Federal Spending on Collision Course," *Washington Post,* October 23, 2005, p. F2.
4. Carl Hulse, "Two 'Bridges to Nowhere' Tumble Down in Congress," *New York Times,* November 17, 2005, A18.
5. Governor Sarah Palin, "Gravina Access Project Redirected," press release, September 21, 2007, available at http://www.gov.state.ak.us/archive.php?id=623&type=1 (accessed 11/12/07).
6. Weisman and VandeHei, "Road Bill Reflects the Power of Pork."
7. See the Alaska Department of Transportation Web site at http://dot.alaska.gov/stwdplng/projectinfo/ser/Gravina/index1.shtml.
8. Governor Sarah Palin, "Gravina Access Project Redirected."
9. "Mr. Stevens's Tirade," *Washington Post,* October 23, 2005, p. B6.
10. For example, see the Federal Aviation Administration's report on funding the aviation infrastructure at http://www.gao.gov/new.items/d071104t.pdf; see the Government Accountability Office's report on the highway and bridge infrastructure at http://www.gao.gov/new.items/d02702t.pdf.
11. Thomas Hobbes, *Leviathan* (1651; repr., Indianapolis, IN: Bobbs, Merrill, 1958).
12. Alexander Hamilton, James Madison, and John Jay, *The Federalist Papers,* ed. Roy P. Fairfield 2nd ed., (1788; repr. Baltimore, MD: Johns Hopkins University Press, 1981), p. 160.
13. Hamilton, Madison, and Jay, *The Federalist Papers,* p. 18.
14. David Hume. *A Treatise of Human Nature,* T. H. Green and T. H. Grose, eds. (New York: Longmans, Green, and Co., 1898), p. 301.
15. Donald Green, Bradley Palmquist, and Eric Schickler, *Partisan Hearts and Minds* (New Haven, CT: Yale University Press, 2004); Christopher Achen, "Political Socialization and Rational Party Identification," *Political Behavior* 24:2 (2002): 151–70.
16. Robert S. Erikson, Michael B. Mackuen, and James A. Stimson, *The Macro Polity* (New York: Cambridge University Press, 2002).
17. Pew Research Center, "Two-in-Three Critical of Bush's Relief Efforts," September 8, 2005, available at http://people-press.org/reports/display.php3?ReportID=255 (accessed 1/13/08).
18. The origin of this quote is unknown; *Bartlett's Familiar Quotations* lists the author as "anonymous."
19. Here again, the author is unknown. Some people attribute the quote to the sociologist C. Wright Mills. Others give authorship to the feminist theorist Carol Hanisch. See http://research.umbc.edu/~korenman/wmst/pisp.html.
20. Sen. Jim Jeffords (VT) left the Republican party and became an Independent on May 24, 2001, giving control of the Senate to the Democrats until January 2003. Republicans controlled the House for Bush's first six years, and the Senate for the first five months of his presidency and then from January 2003, to January 2007.
21. Robert Barnes, "High Court Upholds Curb on Abortion," *Washington Post,* April 19, 2007, p. A1. The combined cases in this decision were *Gonzales v. Carhart et al.* and *Gonzales v. Planned Parenthood Federation of America.*
22. Associated Press, "Ozone Layer Should Keep Healing, UN Says," September 15, 2005, http://msnbc.msn.com/id/9369129.
23. Linda Feldmann, "How Lines of the Culture War Have Been Redrawn," *Christian Science Monitor,* November 15, 2004, available at http://www.csmonitor.com/2004/1115/p01s04=ussc.html (accessed 10/10/07).
24. Edward G. Carmines and James A. Stimson, *Issue Evolution: Race and the Transformation of American Politics* (Princeton, NJ: Princeton University Press, 1989).
25. Samuel Huntington, *Who Are We? The Challenges to America's National Identity* (New York: Simon and Schuster, 2004); Arthur M. Schlesinger Jr., *The Disuniting of America: Reflections on a Multicultural Society* (New York: Whittle Direct Books, 1991).
26. Charles Taylor, *Multiculturalism: Examining the Politics of Recognition,* ed. Amy Gutmann, with commentary by K. Anthony Appiah, Jürgen Habermas, Steven C. Rockefeller, Michael Walzer, and Susan Wolf. (Princeton, NJ: Princeton University Press, 1994); Will Kymlicka, *Multicultural Citizenship: A Liberal Theory of Minority Rights* (New York: Oxford University Press, 1995).
27. Morris P. Fiorina, with Samuel J. Abrams and Jeremy C. Pope, *Culture War: The Myth of a Polarized America,* 2nd ed. (New York: Pearson Longman, 2006), pp. 46–47.
28. Fiorina, *Culture War.*

CHAPTER 2

1. See the section of the Starr Report entitled "There Is Substantial and Credible Information that President Clinton Committed Acts that May Constitute Grounds for an Impeachment," available at http://icreport.loc.gov/icreport/7grounds.htm#L1 (accessed 11/10/07).
2. Deroy Murdock, "Ignorance and American Liberty," *National Review Online,* July 3, 2000 available at http://www.nationalreview.com (accessed 11/15/07).
3. Public Agenda "Knowing It by Heart: Americans Consider the Constitution and Its Meaning." Report for the National Constitution Center, September 17, 2002, pp. 15–16, available at http://www.constitutioncenter.org (accessed 1/21/08).
4. A classic text on the Founding period is Gordon S. Wood, *The Creation of the American Republic* (New York: W.W. Norton, 1969).
5. J. W. Peltason, *Corwin and Peltason's Understanding the Constitution,* 7th ed. (Hinsdale, IL: Dryden Press, 1976), p. 12.
6. The pamphlet sold 120,000 copies within a few months of publication, a figure that would leave the Harry Potter books in the dust in terms of the proportion of the literate public that purchased the book.
7. Thomas Hobbes, *Leviathan* (1651; repr. Indianapolis, IN: Bobbs, Merrill, 1958); John Locke, *Second Treatise of Government* (1690; repr. Indianapolis, IN: Bobbs, Merrill, 1952).
8. Charles A. Beard, *An Economic Interpretation of the Constitution of the United States* (New York: MacMillan, 1913).
9. David Brian Robertson, *The Constitution and America's Destiny* (New York: Cambridge University Press, 2005), p. 4.
10. Robert A. Dahl, *How Democratic Is the American Constitution?* (New Haven, CT: Yale University Press, 2001), p. 12.

11. Alexander Hamilton, John Jay, and James Madison, *The Federalist Papers* (1788; rept., edited by Roy P. Fairfield, 2nd ed. (Baltimore, MD: Johns Hopkins University Press, 1981), p. 22.
12. Quoted in Dahl, *How Democratic Is the American Constitution?*, p. 64.
13. Locke, *Second Treatise of Government*.
14. Quoted in Dahl, *How Democratic Is the American Constitution?*, p. 74.
15. Many delegates probably assumed that the electors would reflect the wishes of the voters in their states, but there is no clear indication of this in Madison's notes. (Hamilton makes this argument in *The Federalist Papers*.) Until the 1820s, many electors were directly chosen by state legislatures rather than by the people. In the first presidential election George Washington won the unanimous support of the electors, but in only five states were the electors chosen by the people.
16. Dahl, *How Democratic Is the American Constitution?*, p. 67.
17. The actual language of the section avoids the term "slavery." Instead it says, "The Migration or Importation of such Persons as any of the States now existing shall think proper to admit, shall not be prohibited by Congress prior to the Year one thousand eight hundred and eight." The ban on the importation of slaves was implemented on the earliest possible date, January 1, 1808.
18. The Avalon Project, Madison's notes to the convention, July 12, 1787; available at http://www.yale.edu/lawweb/avalon/debates/712.htm (accessed 11/15/07).
19. Roger A. Bruns, "A More Perfect Union: The Creation of the U.S. Constitution," National Archives, available at http://www.archives.gov/exhibits/charters/constitution_history.html (accessed 2/12/08).
20. Jefferson to John Adams, 1787, in *The Writings of Thomas Jefferson,* Memorial Edition, ed. Andrew A. Lipscomb and Albert Ellery Bergh, vol. 6, p. 370.
21. Louis Fisher, *Constitutional Conflicts between Congress and the President* (Lawrence, KS: University Press of Kansas, 1997), p. 244.
22. This ban prompted the White House to seek covert channels through which to support the Contras, which led to the ill-conceived secret arms deal with Iran (a nation that was under a complete U.S. trade embargo at the time) in which the money from the arms sales was funneled to the Contras.
23. Linda Greenhouse, "Chief Justice Attacks a Law as Infringing on Judges," *New York Times,* January 1, 2004.
24. William E. Gladstone, "Kin beyond Sea," *The North American Review,* September/October 1878, p. 185.
25. Dahl, *How Democratic is the American Constitution?*, p. 2.
26. Jefferson to James Madison, in *Thomas Jefferson on Democracy,* ed. Saul Padover (New York: Mentor Books, 1953), p. 153.
27. Cass R. Sunstein, "Making Amends," *The New Republic,* March 3, 1997, p. 42.
28. *Furman v. Georgia,* 408 U.S. 238 (1972).

Politics Is Everywhere

a. *Ohio v. Robinette*, 519 U.S. 33 (1996).

Comparing Ourselves to Others

a. "EU Voting Row Explained," BBC News, December 13, 2003, available at http://news.bbc.co.uk/1/hi/world/europe/3309773.stm; "From Jefferson's Brevity to Convolutions of Bureaucrats," *The Observer,* December 14, 2003, available at http://www.guardian.co.uk/eu/story/0,7369,1106851,00.html.

Challenging Conventional Wisdom

a. Albert P. Blaustein, "The U.S. Constitution: America's most Important Export," available at http://usinfo.state.gov/journals/itdhr/0304/ijde/blaustein.htm.

b. Graham K. Wilson, *Only in America? The Politics of the United States in Comparative Perspective* (Chatham, NJ: Chatham House Publishers, 1998), p. 7.

You Decide

a. Douglas Linder, "What in the Constitution Cannot be Amended?" *Arizona Law Review* 23 (1981): 717–33.
b. Kathleen M. Sullivan, "What's Wrong with Constitutional Amendments?" in *New Federalist Papers*, ed. Alan Brinkley, Nelson W. Polsby, and Kathleen M. Sullivan (New York: W.W. Norton, 1997), p. 63.
c. Jamin B. Raskin, "A Right to Vote," *The American Prospect*, August 27, 2001, pp. 10–12.

CHAPTER 3

1. Ronald Reagan, "Remarks on Signing a National Minimum Drinking Age Bill," July 17, 1984, The Public Papers of President Ronald W. Reagan, Ronald Reagan Presidential Library, available at http://www.reagan.utexas.edu/archives/speeches/1984/71784d.htm (accessed 2/29/08).
2. *South Dakota v. Dole,* 483 U.S. 203 (1987).
3. Marlene Markison and Jeffrey Lindley, Memo to NHTSA Regional Administrators and FHWA Division Administrators, October 22, 2007, National Highway Traffic Safety Administration, Washington, DC, available at http://www.nhtsa.dot.gov/nhtsa/whatsup/tea21/GrantMan/HTML/Joint%20Memo—Final—102207.pdf (accessed 2/29/08).
4. *Grutter v. Bollinger,* 539 U.S. 306 (2003). In this case, the Supreme Court upheld the affirmative action policy at the University of Michigan Law School.
5. See http://www.cisstat.com/eng/cis.htm for more information on the Commonwealth of Independent States.
6. Arthur S. Banks and Thomas Muller, eds., *Political Handbook of the World* (Binghamton, NY: CSA Publications, 1998), p. 1083
7. Pam Belluck, "Massachusetts Gay Marriage to Remain Legal," *New York Times,* June 14, 2007, available at http://www.nytimes.com/2007/06/15/us/15gay.html (accessed 10/18/07). The state supreme court decision that required the state legislature to recognize gay marriage was *Goodridge v. Dept. of Public Health,* 798 N.E.2d 941 (Mass. 2003).
8. *Nancy Wilson and Paule Schoenwether v. Richard Lake and John Ashcroft* (2005) No. 8:04-cv-1680-T-30TBM.
9. "The Supreme Court; Excerpts from Court's Welfare Ruling and Rehnquist's Dissent," *New York Times,* May 18, 1999, p. A20.
10. Stanley Elkins and Eric McKitrick, *The Age of Federalism* (New York: Oxford University Press, 1993).
11. John W. Wright, ed., *New York Times 2000 Almanac* (New York: Penguin Reference, 1999), p. 165.
12. *Mayor of City of New York v. Miln,* 36 U.S. (11 Pet.) 102 (1837).
13. *Cooley v. Board of Wardens of the Port of Philadelphia,* 53 U.S. 229 (1851).
14. *Slaughterhouse Cases,* 83 U.S. 36 (1873). See Ronald M Labbe and Jonathan Lurie, *The Slaughterhouse Cases: Regulation, Reconstruction, and the Fourteenth Amendment* (Lawrence, KS: University Press of Kansas, 2003).
15. *Civil Rights Cases,* 109 U.S. 3 (1883).
16. *United States v. E.C. Knight Co.,* 156 US 1 (1895).
17. *Hammer v. Dagenhart,* 247 U.S. 251 (1918).
18. *Lochner v. New York,* 198 U.S. 45 (1905).
19. *Schechter Poultry Corporation v. United States,* (1935).
20. Four key cases are *West Coast Hotel Company v. Parrish* (1937), *Wright v. Vinton Branch* (1937), *Virginia Railway Company v. System Federation*

(1937), and *National Labor Relations Board v. Jones & Laughlin Steel Corporation* (1937).

21. *Wickard v. Filburn,* 317 U.S. 111 (1942).

22. Martin Grodzins, *The American System* (New York: Rand McNally, 1966).

23. John Shannon, "Middle Class Votes Bring a New Balance to Federalism," February 1, 1997, policy paper 10 from the Urban Institute series "The Future of the Public Sector," available at http://www.urban.org/url.cfm? ID = 307051 (accessed 1/3/08).

24. Max Sawicky, "An Idea Whose Time Has Returned: Anti-recession Fiscal Assistance for State and Local Governments" (Washington, DC: Economic Policy Institute, briefing paper, October, 2001).

25. This number varies depending on which grants are counted. Tim Conlan finds 15 block grants in this period. See his *From New Federalism to Devolution* (Washington, DC: Brookings Institution, 1998).

26. *Brown v. Board of Education,* 347 U.S. 483 (1954); *Swann v. Charlotte-Mecklenburg Board of Education,* 402 U.S. 1 (1971).

27. *Baker v. Carr,* 369 U.S. 186 (1962); *Reynolds v. Sims,* 377 U.S. 533 (1964); and *Wesberry v. Sanders,* 376 U.S. 1 (1964). Martha Derthick, *Keeping the Compound Republic: Essays in American Federalism* (Washington, DC: Brookings Institution, 2001).

28. *Miranda v. Arizona,* 384 U.S. 436 (1966); *Mapp v. Ohio,* 367 U.S. 643 (1961).

29. John Kincaid, "Governing the American States," in *Developments in American Politics,* ed. Gillian Peele, Christopher J. Bailey, Bruce Cain, and Guy Peters (Chatham, NJ: Chatham House Publishers, 1995), pp. 208–16.

30. Paul Posner, "The Politics of Coercive Federalism in the Bush Era," *Publius* 37:3 (May, 2007): 390–412.

31. Barry Rabe, "Environmental Policy and the Bush Era: The Collision Between the Administrative Presidency and State Experimentation," *Publius* 37:3 (May, 2007): 413–31.

32. From a review of Michael S. Greve, *Real Federalism: Why It Matters, How It Could Happen* (Washington, DC: American Enterprise Institute Press, 1999), available at http://www.federalismproject.org/publications/ books (accessed 10/10/07).

33. Cass Sunstein, *Designing Democracy: What Constitutions Do* (New York: Oxford University Press, 2001), p. 107.

34. Linda Greenhouse, "The Nation: 5-to-4, Now and Forever; At the Court, Dissent Over States' Rights Is Now War," *New York Times,* June 9, 2002, section 4, p. 3.

35. Michael S. Greve, "Federalism on the Bench," *The Weekly Standard,* December 3, 2001, p. 34.

36. J. W. Peltason, *Corwin and Peltason's Understanding the Constitution,* 7th ed. (Hinsdale, IL: Dryden Press, 1976), p. 177.

37. *Garcia v. San Antonio Metropolitan Transit Authority,* 469 U.S. 528 (1985).

38. *Gregory v. Ashcroft,* 501 U.S. 452 (1991).

39. *New York v. United States* (1992) 112 S. Ct. at 2431-32. For a detailed discussion of these issues see "Constitution of the United States: Analysis and Interpretation" (Washington, DC: Government Printing Office, 2006), available at http://www.access.gpo.gov/congress/senate/constitution/con021.pdf.

40. *Printz v. United States,* 521 U.S. 898 (1997).

41. *Seminole Tribe v. Florida,* 517 U.S. 44 (1996).

42. *College Savings Bank v. Florida Prepaid Secondary Education Expense Board,* 527 U.S. 627 (1999) and *Florida Prepaid Post-Secondary Education Expense Board v. College Savings Bank,* 527 U.S. 666 (1999).

43. *Alden v. Maine,* 527 U.S. 706 (1999).

44. "A Narrow View of Federalism," *New York Times,* May 29, 2002, p. A20.

45. Jeffrey Segal and Harold Spaeth, "Supreme Court 5 Are on a Power Trip," *Newsday,* February 21, 2001, p. A31.

46. *City of Boerne v. Flores,* 521 U.S. 507 (1997), 520.

47. *Kimel et al. v. Florida Board of Regents,* 528 U.S. 62 (2000).

48. *Alabama v. Garrett,* 531 U.S. 356 (2001).

49. *Tennessee v. Lane,* 541 U.S. 509 (2004).

50. *Nevada Department of Human Resources v. Hibbs,* 538 U.S. 721 (2003).

51. *United States v. Lopez,* 514 U.S. 549 (1995).

52. *United States v. Morrison,* 529 U.S. 598 (2000).

53. *U.S. Term Limits, Inc. v. Thornton,* 514 U.S. 779 (1995).

54. *Romer v. Evans,* 517 U.S. 620 (1996).

55. *Atkins v. Virginia,* 536 U.S. 304 (2002).

56. Jonathan Turley, "Its Not the Cannabis, It's the Constitution," *Los Angeles Times,* August 5, 2002, Metro section, part 2, p. 11.

57. *Gonzales v. Raich,* 545 U.S. 1 (2005).

58. From a review of Greve, *Real Federalism.*

59. Martha Derthick, *Keeping the Compound Republic: Essays in American Federalism* (Washington, DC: Brookings Institution, 2001), pp. 9–32.

Comparing Ourselves to Others

a. Jonathan Rodden, "The Dilemma of Fiscal Federalism: Grants and Fiscal Performance Around the World," *American Journal of Political Science* 46:3 (July, 2002): 670–87.

b. Alfred Stepan, "Federalism and Democracy: Beyond the U.S. Model," *Journal of Democracy* 10:4 (1999): 19–34.

c. Spain has a unitary government, but it is often referred to as a "de facto federation" because it would be politically impossible for the central government to revoke the autonomy of Galicia, Catalonia, or the Basque Country.

Politics Is Everywhere

a. Frank M. Bryan, *Real Democracy: The New England Town Meeting and How It Works* (Chicago: University of Chicago Press, 2001).

Challenging Conventional Wisdom

a. Dale A. Krane, "The State of American Federalism, 2001–2002: Resilience in Response to Crisis," *Publius* 32:4 (Fall 2002): 1–27.

b. Kiki Caruson, Susan A. MacManus, Matthew Kohen, and Thomas A. Watson, "Homeland Security Preparedness: The Rebirth of Regionalism," *Publius* 35:1 (Winter, 2005): 143–71.

c. These data are from a September 2004 Gallup poll, available at http://www.pollingreport.com.

d. John Kincaid and Richard L. Cole, "Public Opinion on Issues of U.S. Federalism in 2005: End of the Post-2001 Pro-Federal Surge?" *Publius* 35:1 (Winter, 2005): 169–88. The only exception noted to the more positive image of state and local government is that the local property tax remains the most unpopular form of taxation.

CHAPTER 4

1. Darren W. Davis and Brian D. Silver, "Civil Liberties vs. Security: Public Opinion in the Context of the Terrorist Attacks on America," *American Journal of Political Science,* 48:1 (January, 2004): 33, 44.

2. Richard Morin and Claudia Deane, "Belief Erodes in the First Amendment," *Washington Post,* September 2, 2002.

3. Jane Mayer, "Outsourcing Torture: The Secret History of America's 'Extraordinary Rendition' Program," *The New Yorker,* February 14, 2005, available at http://www.newyorker.com/archive/2005/02/14/050214fa_fact6 (accessed 11/15/07).

4. Linda Greenhouse, "O'Connor Foresees Limits on Freedom," *New York Times,* September 29, 2001.

5. *Arar v. Ashcroft et. al,* 2006 WL 346439 (E.D.N.Y.). The case was also dismissed because Arar, a Canadian citizen, did not have standing to sue the U.S. government. Supporters of this decision (and the practice

more generally) say that it is an essential part of the War on Terror and that the enemy combatants who are arrested have no legal rights. Opponents say that the practice violates international law and our own standards of decency; furthermore, torture almost never produces useful information because people will say anything to get the torture to stop.

6. Mayer, "Outsourcing Torture."

7. President Bush expressed his opposition to the amendment by adding a signing statement to his official approval, in which he reserved the right to ignore the law on national security grounds. Charles Babington and Shailagh Murray, "Senate Supports Interrogation Limits 90–9; Vote on the Treatment of Detainees Is a Bipartisan Rebuff of the White House," *Washington Post,* October 6, 2005, p. A1. Eric Schmitt, "House Backs McCain on Detainees, Defying Bush," *New York Times,* December 15, 2005, p. A1. Charlie Savage, "Bush Could Bypass New Torture Ban: Waiver Right Is Reserved," *Boston Globe,* January 4, 2006.

8. Pew Research Center, "Trends in Political Values and Core Attitudes: 1987–2007," March 22, 2007, available at http://people-press.org/reports/display.php3?ReportID=312 (accessed 2/8/08).

9. *State v. Massey et al.,* Supreme Court of North Carolina, 51 S.E.2d 179 (1949). The case was appealed to the Supreme Court, but the Court declined to hear the case, which means that the state decision stands (*Bunn v. North Carolina,* 336 U.S. 942).

10. *Pennsylvania v. Miller,* Pennsylvania Court of Common Pleas, WL 31426193 (2002). However, supreme courts in Minnesota, Wisconsin, and several other states have decided that requiring the Amish to use orange SMV triangles violates their free exercise of religion.

11. *Wisconsin v. Yoder,* 403 U.S. 205 (1972).

12. Jeffrey Rosen, "Lemon Law," *The New Republic,* March 29, 1993, p. 17.

13. Max Farrand, ed., *The Records of the Federal Convention of 1787,* rev. ed. (New Haven, CT: Yale University Press), 1937, pp. 587–88, 617–618.

14. *The Papers of Thomas Jefferson,* J. Boyd, ed. (Princeton, NJ: Princeton University Press, 1958), 557–583, cited in *The Constitution of the United States of America: Analysis and Interpretation,* Lester S. Jayson, ed. (Washington, DC: U.S. Government Printing Office, 1973), p. 900.

15. Ralph Ketcham, *The Anti-Federalist Papers and the Constitutional Convention Debates* (New York, NY: Penguin Putnam, 2003), p. 237.

16. Ketcham, *The Anti-Federalist Papers and the Constitutional Convention Debates,* p. 247.

17. The two that were not ratified by the states were a complicated amendment on congressional apportionment and the pay raise amendment discussed later in this chapter.

18. Akhil Reed Amar, *The Bill of Rights* (New Haven, CT: Yale University Press, 1998), p. 292.

19. 1 *Annals of Congress* 755 (August 17, 1789), cited in Jayson, *The Constitution of the United States of America,* p. 898.

20. Henry J. Abraham and Barbara A. Perry, *Freedom and the Court: Civil Rights and Civil Liberties in the United States,* 8th ed. (Lawrence, KS: University Press of Kansas, 2003), p. 34.

21. *Barron v. Baltimore,* 32 U.S. 243 (1833), 250.

22. Amar, *The Bill of Rights,* p. 290.

23. There is an intense scholarly debate on the topic, but we believe the evidence indicates that the authors of the 14th Amendment intended for it to apply the Bill of Rights to the states. The strongest argument against this position is Raoul Berger's *The Fourteenth Amendment and the Bill of Rights* (1989) and a good book in support is Amar's *The Bill of Rights* (1998).

24. *The Slaughterhouse Cases,* 83 U.S. 36 (1873). The plaintiffs also made a 13th Amendment claim (that the monopoly forced them to work in "involuntary servitude") and a "due process" claim, but both of those were rejected by the Court as well. The Court focused on the "privileges and immunities" argument and the idea of dual citizenship.

25. Abraham and Perry, *Freedom and the Court,* p. 51.

26. *Chicago, Burlington, and Quincy Railroad v. Chicago,* 166 U.S. 226 (1897).

27. *Twining v. New Jersey,* 211 U.S. 78, 98 (1908).

28. *Gitlow v. New York,* 268 U.S. 652, 666 (1925).

29. The exceptions are the establishment clause of the 1st Amendment and the 6th Amendment right to a public trial. *Wolf v. Colorado* also came between the two periods of increased activity, but it only partially applied the 4th Amendment's prohibition against unreasonable searches and seizures. The Court said that states may not engage in such searches, but then allowed the state to use evidence gathered in an "unreasonable" search. It wasn't until *Mapp v. Ohio* in 1961 that the Court ruled that illegally obtained evidence could not be used in a trial, thus giving the incorporation of the 4th Amendment some teeth.

30. *Palko v. Connecticut,* 302 U.S. 319 (1937).

31. Abraham and Perry, *Freedom and the Court,* p. 65.

32. One of them, which said that Congress could not raise its pay until an election had been held, was ratified more than 200 years later in 1992 as the 27th Amendment! Usually time limits are set for the ratification of constitutional amendments, but the original Bill of Rights did not have a time limit. Only six of the original thirteen states ratified the pay raise amendment. By 1982 only eight states had ratified, but Gregory Watson, a student at the University of Texas, rediscovered the amendment when writing a term paper. He pushed the amendment through a letter-writing campaign, and his timing was perfect given the controversy over congressional pay raises in the 1980s and the generally low public opinion of Congress. See William T. Bianco, *Trust Representatives and Constituents* (Ann Arbor, MI: University of Michigan Press, 1994).

33. *Schenk v. United States,* 249 U.S. 47 (1919), 52.

34. Alan Dershowitz, *Shouting Fire: Civil Liberties in a Turbulent Age* (New York: Little, Brown, 2002).

35. *Debs v. United States* 249 U.S. 211 (1919); *Frohwerk v. United States,* 249 U.S. 204 (1919).

36. *Abrams v. United States,* 250 U.S. 616 (1919), 630–31.

37. *Dennis v. United States,* 341 U.S. 494 (1951).

38. *Brandenburg v. Ohio,* 395 U.S. 444 (1969).

39. *Smith v. Goguen,* 415 U.S. 566 (1974).

40. *Tinker v. Des Moines School District,* 393 U.S. 503 (1969).

41. *Spence v. Washington,* 418 U.S. 405 (1974).

42. *Spence v. Washington,* 409–410.

43. *Texas v. Johnson* 491 U.S. 397 (1989).

44. *United States v. Eichman,* 496 U.S. 310 (1990).

45. *United States v. O'Brien,* 391 U.S. 367, 376 (1968).

46. *Morse v. Frederick,* 127 S. Ct. 2618 (2007).

47. *Buckley v. Valeo* (1976), *McConnell v. Federal Election Commission* (2003).

48. *Board of Regents of the University of Wisconsin System et al., Petitioners v. Scott Harold Southworth et al.,* 529 U.S. 217 (2000).

49. Kermit L. Hall, "Free Speech on Public College Campuses: Overview," available at http://www.firstamendmentcenter.org/speech/pubcollege/overview.aspx (accessed 2/10/08).

50. Carolyn J. Palmer, Sophie W. Penney, Donald D. Gehring, and Jan A. Neiger, "Hate Speech and Hate Crimes: Campus Conduct Codes and Supreme Court Rulings," *National Association of Student Personnel Administrators Journal* 34:2 (1997), available at http://publications.naspa.org/naspajournal/vol34/iss2/art4 (accessed 12/18/07).

51. *City of St. Paul v. RAV,* 505 U.S. 377 (1992).

52. *Virginia v. Black,* 538 US 343 (2003).

53. *De Jonge v. State of Oregon*, 299 U.S. 353 (1937).

54. *Edwards v. South Carolina*, 372 U.S. 229 (1963).

55. The Supreme Court declined to review the case in *Smith v. Collin*, 439 U.S. 916 (1978), which meant that the lower court rulings stood (447 F.Supp. 676 (1978), 578 F.2d 1197 (1978)). See Donald A. Downs, *Nazis in Skokie: Freedom, Community and the First Amendment* (Notre Dame, IN: University of Notre Dame Press, 1985), for an excellent analysis of this important case.

56. *Forsyth County v. Nationalist Movement*, 505 U.S. 123 (1992).

57. *Frisby et al. v. Schultz et al.*, 487 U.S. 474 (1988).

58. *Near v. Minnesota*, 283 U.S. 697 (1931), 719–20.

59. *New York Times v. United States*, 403 U.S. 713 (1971).

60. *Nebraska Press Assn. v. Stuart*, 427 U.S. 539 (1976), 556–62. See Abraham and Perry, *Freedom and the Court*, pp. 209–10, for a discussion two cases that reversed and then reinstated the standard of allowing press coverage of trials except in exceptional cases.

61. Douglas Lee, "Gag Orders," available at http://www.firstamendment center.org/Press/topic.aspx?topic=gag_orders (accessed 2/10/08).

62. *Chaplinsky v. State of New Hampshire*, 315 U.S. 568 (1942).

63. *Chaplinsky v. State of New Hampshire*.

64. *New York Times v. Sullivan*, 376 U.S. 254 (1964), cited in Abraham and Perry, *Freedom and the Court*, p. 193.

65. *Hustler v. Falwell*, 485 U.S. 46 (1988).

66. *Hutchinson v. Proxmire*, 443 U.S. 111 (1979); *Wolston v. Reader's Digest Association*, 443 U.S. 157 (1979).

67. *Valentine v. Chrestensen*, 316 U.S. 52 (1942).

68. *Virginia State Board of Pharmacy v. Virginia Citizens Consumer Council, Inc.*, 425 U.S. 748 (1976); *City of Cincinnati v. Discovery Network, Inc. et al.*, 507 U.S. 410 (1993).

69. *Central Hudson Gas & Electric v. Public Service Commission*, 447 U.S. 557 (1980).

70. In 1996, Congress passed the Child Pornography Prevention Act. This law makes the possession, production, or distribution of child pornography a criminal offense punishable with up to fifteen years in jail and a fine. However, two parts of the law were struck down by the Court for being "overbroad and unconstitutional." *Ashcroft v. Free Speech Coalition*, 353 U.S. 234 (2002).

71. BBC News, "Curtains for Semi-nude Justice Statue," January 29, 2002, available at http://news.bbc.co.uk/2/hi/americas/1788845.stm (accessed 3/3/08).

72. *Jacobellis v. Ohio*, 378 U.S. 184, 197 (1964).

73. *Miller v. California*, 413 U.S. 15 (1973).

74. Kathleen Sullivan, "The First Amendment Wars," *The New Republic*, September 28, 1992, pp. 14, 35–40.

75. Walter Kendrick, *The Secret Museum: Pornography in Modern Culture* (Berkeley, CA: University of California Press, 1996), p. 219.

76. *Reno et al. v. American Civil Liberties Union et al.*, 521 U.S. 844 (1997).

77. *Ashcroft v. American Civil Liberties Union*, 535 U.S. 564 (2004).

78. James Hudson, "'A Wall of Separation,'" *Library of Congress Information Bulletin* 57:6 (June, 1998), available at http://www.loc.gov/loc/lcib/9806/danbury.html (accessed 3/3/08).

79. Abraham and Perry, *Freedom and the Court*, p. 300.

80. *Engle v. Vitale*, 370 U.S. 421 (1962).

81. *Wallace v. Jaffree*, 482 U.S. 38 (1985).

82. *Lee v. Weisman*, 505 U.S. 577 (1992), *Sante Fe Independent School District v. Doe*, 530 U.S. 290 (2000).

83. *Marsh v. Chambers*, 463 U.S. 783 (1983), *Jones v. Clear Creek Independent School*, 61 LW 3819 (1993).

84. *Lemon v. Kurtzman*, 403 U.S. 602 (1971).

85. *Lynch v. Donnelly*, 465 U.S. 668 (1984), 672–673.

86. Jeffrey Rosen, "Big Ten," *The New Republic*, March 14, 2004, p. 11.

87. *Van Orden v. Perry*, 03-1500 (2005), and *McCreary County et al. v. American Civil Liberties Union* of Kentucky, 03-1693 (2005).

88. *Zelman v. Simmons-Harris*, 536 U.S. 639 (2002).

89. *Zobrest v. Catalina School District*, 509 U.S. 1 (1993). A similar decision in 1997 allowed a public school teacher to teach in a special program in a parochial school, *Agostini v. Felton* 521 U.S. 203 (1997).

90. *Mitchell v. Helms*, 530 U.S. 793 (2000).

91. *Rosenberger v. University of Virginia*, 515 U.S. 819 (1995)

92. *Minersville School District v. Gobitis*, 310 U.S. 586 (1940).

93. *West Virginia Board of Education v. Barnette*, 319 U.S. 624 (1943), 642.

94. We will not cite all of the cases here. See Abraham and Perry, *Freedom and the Court*, Chap. 6, for a summary of cases on this topic, especially Tables 6.1 and 6.2.

95. *Employment Division, Department of Human Resources of Oregon v. Smith*, 494 U.S. 872 (1990), 878–80. This case is often erroneously reported as having banned the religious use of peyote. In fact, the Court said, "Although it is constitutionally permissible to exempt sacramental peyote use from the operation of drug laws, it is not constitutionally required."

96. *City of Boerne v. Flores*, 521 U.S. 527 (1997).

97. The court case was *Cutter v. Wilkinson*, No. 03-9877 (2005). See Linda Greenhouse, "Supreme Court Rules in Ohio Prison Case," *New York Times*, June 1, 2005, for a discussion of the broader debate.

98. *Gonzales v. O Centro Espirita Beneficiente Uniao Do Vegetal (UDV) et al.*, 546 U.S. 418 (2006).

99. *United States v. Miller*, 307 U.S. 174 (1939).

100. Robert J. Spitzer, *The Politics of Gun Control*, Chatham, NJ: Chatham House, 1995. Also see http://www.gunlawsuits.org/downloads/militiav.pdf for a complete list of the cases. The two cases recognizing the individual right to bear arms were *United States v. Timothy Joe Emerson*, 46 F. Supp. 2d 598, (1999) and the DC Circuit Court case that was appealed in the landmark ruling *Parker v. District of Columbia*, 478 F.3d 370 (DC Cir. 2007).

101. *District of Columbia v. Heller*, 554 U.S.____(2008).

102. Edward Walsh, "U.S. Argues for Wider Gun Rights; Supreme Court Filing Reverses Past Policy," *Washington Post*, May 8, 2002, p. A1. For a lengthy memo from the attorney general that explores the individual rights argument see http://www.usdoj.gov/olc/secondamendment2.htm#N_33_.

103. See Abraham and Perry, *Freedom and the Courts*, Chap. 4 for a discussion of these cases.

104. *Mapp v. Ohio*, 367 U.S. 643 (1961).

106. *United States v. Calandra*, 414 U.S. 338 (1974).

107. *Illinois v. Gates*, 462 U.S. 213 (1983).

108. *United States v. Leon*, 468 U.S. 897 (1984).

109. *Murray v. United States*, 487 U.S. 533 (1988).

109. *Vernonia School District v. Acton*, 515 U.S. 646 (1995), *Board of Education of Pottawatomie County v. Earls*, 536 U.S. 832 (2002).

110. Sharon L. Larson, Joe Eyerman, Misty S. Foster, and Joseph C. Gfroer, "Worker Substance Use and Workplace Policies and Programs," June, 2007, Substance Abuse and Mental Health Services Administration available at http://www.oas.samhsa.gov/work2k7/work.pdf (accessed 3/3/08).

111. *Chandler v. Miller*, 520 U.S. 305 (1997).

112. *Miranda v. Arizona*, 384 U.S. 436 (1966).

114. *New York v. Quarles*, 467 U.S. 649 (1984).

115. *Nix v. Williams*, 467 U.S. 431 (1984).

116. *Dickerson v. United States*, 530 U.S. 428 (2000).

116. *Benton v. Maryland*, 395 U.S. 784 (1969).

117. *Powell v. Alabama*, 287 U.S. 45 (1932).

118. *Gideon v. Wainwright*, 372 U.S. 335 (1963).

119. *Evitts v. Lucy,* 469 U.S. 387 (1985); *Wiggins v. Smith,* 539 U.S. 510 (2003). See Elizabeth Gable and Tyler Green, "*Wiggins v. Smith*: The Ineffective Assistance of Counsel Standard Applied Twenty Years After *Strickland,*" *Georgetown Journal of Legal Ethics* (Summer, 2004), for a discussion of many of these issues.

120. *Klopfer v. North Carolina,* 386 U.S. 213 (1967).

121. The law is 18 U.S.C. § 3161(c)(1) and the ruling is *Zedner v. United States,* 05-5992 (2006).

122. The case concerning African Americans is *Batson v. Kentucky,* 106 S. Ct. 1712 (1986); the case about Latinos is *Hernandez v. New York,* 500 U.S. 352 (1991); and the gender case is *J.E.B. v. Alabama ex rel. T.B.,* 511 U.S. 127 (1994).

123. *Furman v. Georgia,* 408 U.S. 238 (1972), *Gregg v. Georgia,* 428 U.S. 513 (1976).

124. See Abraham and Perry, Freedom and the Court, pp. 72–73, for a discussion of the earlier cases and Charles Lane, "5–4 Supreme Court Abolishes Juvenile Executions," *Washington Post,* March 2, 2005, p. A1, for a discussion of the 2002 and 2005 cases. The 2008 case was Kennedy v. Louisiana, 554 U.S.____(2008).

125. Lane, "5–4 Supreme Court Abolishes Juvenile Executions." Both sets of numbers on the increase in the number of states banning the death penalty include the twelve states that prohibit capital punishment in all instances.

126. *Baze and Bowling v. Rees,* 533 U.S. (2008).

127. Most of these statistics are reviewed in the Court case *McCleskey v. Kemp,* 481 U.S. 279 (1987). For a more complete discussion see David C. Baldus, George Woodworth, and Charles A. Pulaski, Jr., *Equal Justice and the Death Penalty: A Legal and Empirical Analysis* (Boston, MA: Northeastern University Press, 1990). The critical article in the *McClesky* decision was David C. Baldus, George Woodworth, and Charles A. Pulaski Jr., "Comparative Review of Death Sentences: An Empirical Study of the Georgia Experience," *Journal of Criminal Law & Criminology* 74:3 (1983): 661–753.

128. Republican Policy Committee, Senate Record Vote Analysis, Vote no. 106, 103rd Cong., 2nd sess., *Gift Ban and Racial Statistics in Death Penalty Cases,* S-5526 Temp. Record, May 11, 1994, available at http://www.mdcbowen.org/p2/rm/law/vote106.htm (accessed 3/4/08).

129. *Griswold v. Connecticut,* 381 U.S. 479 (1965), 482–86.

130. *Griswold v. Connecticut,* 512–13.

131. *Roe v. Wade,* 410 U.S. 113 (1973), 129.

132. *Planned Parenthood of Southeastern Pennsylvania v. Casey,* 505 U.S. 833 (1992).

133. Adam Liptak, "The New 5-to-4 Supreme Court," *New York Times,* April 27, 2007.

134. Department of Human Services, Office of Disease Prevention and Epidemiology, "Seventh Annual Report on Oregon's Death with Dignity Act," March 10, 2005, available at http://www.oregon.gov/DHS/ph/pas/docs/year7.pdf (accessed 2/10/08).

135. *Gonzales v. Oregon,* 546 U.S. 23 (2006).

You Decide

a. Linda Greenhouse, "Justices Decline to Rule on Limits for Drug-Sniffing Dogs," *New York Times,* April 5, 2005, p. A19.

Politics Is Everywhere

a. Leslie Cauley, "NSA Has Massive Database of Americans' Phone Calls," *USA Today,* May 11, 2006, p. 1.

b Lorraine Woellert and Dawn Kopecki, "The Snooping Goes Beyond Phone Calls," *Business Week,* May 29, 2006, p. 38; "Data Mining: Federal Efforts Cover a Wide Range of Uses," GAO Report 04-548, May 2004, available at http://www.gao.gov/new.items/dO4548.pdf.

Challenging Conventional Wisdom

a. *Lucas v. South Carolina Coastal Council,* 505 U.S. 1003 (1992).

b. The dissenters' argument was that when the plaintiff became the owner, the law was already in effect so the market value of the land would already be lower because the wetlands could not be developed. Therefore, having paid the lower price, the owner should not be able to claim that the land was devalued by the regulation (see the dissent in *Palazzolo v. Rhode Island,* 533 U.S. 606, 2001). This case gets a little more complicated because Palazzolo indirectly owned the land through shares he bought in a corporation in 1961 before the wetlands regulations had been passed. He became sole owner of the land after the regulation was enacted in the 1970s. Also, the Court ruled that he was not entitled, to compensation because a portion of the land still could be developed and was worth at least $200,000 so he had not been denied "all beneficial use of his property."

c. *Kelo v. City of New London,* 04-108 (2005).

d. Jeffrey Rosen, "The Unregulated Offensive," *New York Times Magazine,* April 17, 2005, pp. 42–9, 66, 128, 130.

Comparing Ourselves to Others

a. *Roper v. Simmons,* 30-633 (2005).

b. Charles Lane, "5–4 Supreme Court Abolishes Juvenile Executions," *Washington Post,* March 2, 2005, p. A1

c. *Roper v. Simmons.*

d. *Roper v. Simmons.*

e. Charles Lane, "Scalia Tells Congress to Mind Its Own Business," *Washington Post,* May 19, 2006, p. A19.

CHAPTER 5

1. Adam Nagourney and Megan Thee, "With Election Driven by Iraq, Voters Want New Approach," *New York Times,* November 2, 2006, p. A1.

2. For examples, see http://www.pollingreport.com, which collects poll results from many sources.

3. For examples of these claims, see Larry J. Sabato, *Feeding Frenzy: Attack Journalism and American Politics* (New York: Lanahan, 2000) and W. Lance Bennett and Robert M. Entman, *Mediated Politics: Communication in The Future of Democracy* (New York: Cambridge University Press, 2001).

4. For a review, see Arthur Lupia and Mathew D. McCubbins, *The Democratic Dilemma* (New York: Cambridge University Press, 1998).

5. Larry Bartels, "Partisanship and Voting Behavior, 1952–1996," *American Journal of Political Science* 44 (2000): 35–50.

6. Robert S. Erikson, Michael B. Mackuen, and James A. Stimson, *The Macro Polity* (New York: Cambridge University Press, 2002).

7. Angus Campbell, Phillip Converse, Warren Miller, and Donald Stokes, *The American Voter* (New York: Wiley, 1960); Phillip E. Converse, "The Nature of Belief Systems in Mass Publics," in *Ideology and Discontent,* ed. David E. Aptor (Glencoe, IL The Free Press of Glencoe, 1964), 209–61. For more modern versions of these arguments, see Eric R. A. N. Smith, *The Unchanging American Voter,* (Berkeley, CA: University of California Press, 1989); Phillip E. Converse, and Gregory Markus, "Plus ça Change . . .: The New CPS Election Study Panel," *American Political Science Review* 73:1 (March, 1979): 32–49.

8. Converse, "The Nature of Belief Systems in Mass Publics," p. 259.

9. Associated Press, "D'oh! More Know Simpsons than Constitution," *MSNBC,* March 1, 2006, available at http://www.msnbc.msn.com/id/11611015/ (accessed 2/20/08).

10. Ipsos News Center, "Most Americans Can't Name Any Supreme Court Justices, Says FindLaw.com Survey," press release, January 10, 2006,

available at http://www.ipsos-na.com/news/pressrelease.cfm?id=2933 (accessed 2/20/08).

11. Valerie Strauss, "Despite Lessons on King, Some Unaware of His Dream," *Washington Post,* January 15, 2007, p. B1.

12. Samuel Popkin, *The Reasoning Voter* (Chicago: University of Chicago Press, 1991).

13. John E. Sullivan, James E. Pierson, and Gregory E. Marcus, "Ideological Constraint in the Mass Public: A Methodological Critique and Some New Findings," *American Journal of Political Science* 23 (1978): 244–49.

14. Norman Nie, Sidney Verba, and John Petrocik, *The Changing American Voter* (Cambridge, MA: Harvard University Press, 1976).

15. Michael X. Delli Carpini and Scott Keeter, *What Americans Know About Politics and Why It Matters,* (New Haven, CT: Yale University Press, 1997).

16. For an example focusing on foreign policy opinions, see John Aldrich, John Sullivan, and Eugene Borgida, "Foreign Affairs and Issue Voting: Do Presidential Candidates Waltz Before a Blind Audience?," *American Political Science Review* 81: 123–41.

17. Donald Green, Bradley Palmquist, and Eric Schickler, "Macropartisanship: A Replication and Critique," *American Political Science Review* 93 (1998): 883–99; Robert S. Erikson, Michael B. Mackuen, and James A. Stimson, "What Moves Macropartisanship? A Response to Green, Palmquist, and Schickler," *American Political Science Review* 92 (1998): 901–12.

18. John Zaller, "Coming to Grips with V. O. Key's Concept of Latent Opinion" (unpublished paper, University of California, Los Angeles, 1998).

19. Milton Lodge, and Kathleen M. McGraw, "Introduction," in *Political Judgment,* ed. Milton Lodge and Kathleen M. McGraw (Ann Arbor, MI: University of Michigan Press, 1995).

20. Morris Fiorina, *Retrospective Voting in American National Elections* (Cambridge, MA: Harvard University Press, 1981).

21. John Zaller, *The Nature and Origins of Mass Opinion* (New York: Cambridge University Press, 1992).

22. R. Michael Alvarez, and John Brehm, *Hard Choices, Easy Answers* (Princeton, NJ: Princeton University Press, 2002).

23. John Zaller, and Stanley Feldman, "A Theory of the Survey Response: Revealing Preferences Versus Answering Questions," *American Journal of Political Science* 36 (1992): 579–616.

24. Janet M. Box-Steffensmeier and Susan DeBoef, "Macropartisanship and Macroideology in the Sophisticated Electorate," *Journal of Politics* 63:1 (2001): 232–48.

25. John Mueller, *War, Presidents, and Public Opinion* (Hoboken, NJ: Wiley, 1973).

26. Jack Citrin, Donald P. Green, Christopher Muste, and Cara Wong, "Public Opinion toward Immigration Reform: The Role of Economic Motivations," *American Journal of Political Science* 59:3 (1997): 858–82.

27. William G. Jacoby, "Issue Framing and Public Opinion on Government Spending," *American Journal of Political Science* 44:4 (2000): 750–67; L. M. Bartels, "Beyond the Running Tally: Partisan Bias in Political Perceptions," *Political Behavior* 24:2 (2002): 117–50.

28. Donald R. Kinder, "Exploring the Racial Divide: Blacks, Whites, and Opinion on National Policy," *American Journal of Political Science* 45:2 (2001): 439–49; Paul M. Sniderman and Thomas Piazza, *The Scar of Race* (Cambridge, MA: Harvard University Press, 1993).

29. Robert Huckfeldt, Jeffery Levine, William Morgan, and John Sprague, "Accessibility and the Political Utility of Partisan and Ideological Orientations," *American Journal of Political Science* 43:3 (July, 1999): 888–911.

30. George E. Marcus, John L. Sullivan, Elizabeth Theiss-Morse, and Sandra L. Wood, *With Malice Toward Some: How People Make Civil Liberties Judgments* (New York: Cambridge University Press, 1995).

31. Stanley Feldman and Marco R. Steenbergen, "The Humanitarian Foundation of Public Support for Social Welfare," *American Journal of Political Science* 45:3 (2001): 658–77

32. R. Michael Alvarez and John Brehm, "American Ambivalence towards Abortion Policy: Development of a Heteroskedastic Probit Model of Competing Values," *American Journal of Political Science* 39:4 (1995): 1055–82.

33. R. Michael Alvarez and John Brehm, "Are Americans Ambivalent towards Racial Policies?" *American Journal of Political Science* 41 (1997): 345–74.

34. Virginia Sapiro, "Not Your Parents' Political Socialization: Introduction for a New Generation," *Annual Review of Political Science* 7 (2004): 1–23.

35. Christopher Achen, "Parental Socialization and Rational Party Identification," *Political Behavior* 24 (2002): 151–70.

36. M. Kent Jennings and Richard G. Niemi, *Generations and Politics: A Panel Study of Young Adults and Their Parents* (Princeton, NJ: Princeton University Press, 1981).

37. Robert Putnam, *Bowling Alone: The Collapse and Revival of American Community* (New York: Simon and Schuster, 2000).

38. Richard G. Niemi and Mary Hepburn, "The Rebirth of Political Socialization," *Perspectives on Politics* 24 (1995): 7–16.

39. David Campbell, *Why We Vote: How Schools and Communities Shape Our Civic Life* (Princeton NJ: Princeton University Press, 2006).

40. Sidney Verba, Kay Schlozman, and Henry Brady, *Voice and Equality: Civic Volunteerism in American Politics* (Cambridge, MA: Harvard University Press, 1995).

41. Paul Allen Beck and M. Kent Jennings "Pathways to Participation," *American Political Science Review* 76 (1982): 94–108.

42. Fiorina, *Retrospective Voting in American National Elections.*

43. For an extended discussion, see Chapter 8.

44. Edward G. Carmines and James A. Stimson, *Issue Evolution: Race and the Transformation of American Politics* (Princeton, NJ: Princeton University Press, 1990).

45. Stephen Ambrose, *Citizen Soldiers* (New York: Touchstone Books, 1997) and Tom Brokaw *The Greatest Generation* (New York: Random House, 1998).

46. Suzanne Mettler and Eric Welch, "Civic Generation: Policy Feedback Effects of the BI Bill in Political Involvement Over the Life Course," *British Journal of Political Science* 34 (2004): 497–518.

47. Darren W. Davis and Brian D. Silver "Civil Liberties vs. Security: Public Opinion in the Context of the Terrorist Attacks on America," *American Journal of Political Science* 48:1 (2004): 28–46; Leonie Huddy, Nadia Khatib, and Theresa Capelos, "The Polls: Trends," *Public Opinion Quarterly* 66 (2002): 418–50.

48. See Pew Research Center, "Two-In-Three Critical of Bush's Relief Efforts," September 8, 2005, available at http://people-press.org/reports/display.php3?ReportID=255 (accessed 2/15/08) and "Katrina Relief Effort Raises Concern over Excessive Spending, Waste," October 9, 2005, available at http://people-press.org/reports/display.php3?ReportID=260 (accessed 2/13/08).

49. Robert S. Erikson, Michael B. Mackuen, and James A. Stimson, "Macropartisanship," *American Political Science Review* 83 (1989): 1125–42.

50. John Zaller, *The Nature and Origins of Mass Opinion* (New York: Cambridge University Press, 1992).

51. Richard Nadwau, et al., "Class, Party, and South-Nonsouth Differences," *American Politics Research* 32 (2004): 52–67.

52. James H. Kuklinski et al., "Racial Prejudice and Attitudes Toward Affirmative Action," *American Journal of Political Science* 41 (1997): 402–19.

53. Donald P. Green, Bradley Palmquist, and Eric Schickler, *Partisan Hearts and Minds* (New Haven, CT: Yale University Press, 2002).

54. Nicholas Lehmann, "The Controller: Karl Rove Is Working to Get George Bush Reelected, But He Has Bigger Plans," *The New Yorker,* May 12, 2003, pp. 68–83.

55. For elaboration on this point, see William T. Bianco, Richard G. Niemi, and Harold W. Stanley, "Partisanship and Group Support over Time: A Multivariate Analysis," *American Political Science Review* 80: (September, 1986): 969–76

56. Arthur Lupia and Mathew D. McCubbins, *The Democratic Dilemma* (New York: Cambridge University Press, 1998).

57. Lawrence R. Jacobs and Robert Y. Shapiro, *Politicians Don't Pander: Political Manipulation and the Loss of Democratic Responsiveness* (Chicago: University of Chicago Press, 2000).

58. Jacob Weisberg, "Bush's First Defeat," *Slate,* March 31, 2005, available at http://www.slate.com/id/2115141/ (accessed 2/21/08).

59. Pew Research Center, "Bush Failing in Social Security Push," March 2, 2005, available at http://people-press.org/reports/display.php3?ReportID=238 (accessed Feb 21, 2008).

60. David D. Kirkpatrick, "The Nation: Hanging In; He's Battered, But His Agenda Isn't Beaten," *New York Times,* March 5, 2006, section 4, p. 1.

61. Pollster.com, "IVR and Internet: How Reliable?" September 28, 2006, available at http://www.pollster.com/mystery_pollster/ivr_internet_how_reliable.php (accessed 2/21/08).

62. Alvarez and Brehm, "American Ambivalence Towards Abortion Policy."

63. For data on reported and actual turnout, see Chapter 8.

64. Gary Langer, "Two Years From Election, Looking at Early Polls," *ABC News,* January 18, 2007, available at http://abcnews.go.com/Politics/story?id=2802742&page=1 (accessed 2/21/08).

65. James H. Kuklinski et al., "Misinformation and the Currency of Democratic Citizenship," *The Journal of Politics* 62:3 (2000): 790–816.

66. Harris Interactive, "Iraq, 9/11, Al Qaeda, and Weapons of Mass Destruction: What the Public Believes Now, According to Latest Harris Poll," February 18, 2005, available at http://www.harrisinteractive.com/harris_poll/index.asp?PID=544 (accessed 2/27/08).

67. George H. Bishop, *The Illusion of Public Opinion: Fact and Artifact in Public Opinion Polls* (Washington, DC: Roman and Littlefield, 2004).

68. Delli Carpini and Keeter, *What Americans Know About Politics and Why It Matters.*

69. Harris Interactive, "Iraq, 9/11, Al Qaeda and Weapons of Mass Destruction."

70. Delli Carpini and Keeter, *What Americans Know About Politics and Why It Matters.*

71. Morris P. Fiorina, Samuel J. Abrams, and Jeremy C. Pope, *Culture War? The Myth of a Polarized America* (New York: Longman, 2002).

72. For data on how responses to these questions changed over time, see "Quick Tables for the GSS 1972–2004 Cumulative Datafile, available at http://sda.berkeley.edu:8080/quicktables/quickconfig.do?gss04 (accessed 2/13/08).

73. For a review of the literature on trust in government, see Karen Cook, Russell Hardin, and Margaret Levi, *Cooperation without Trust* (New York: Russell Sage Foundation, 2005) as well as Marc J. Hetherington, *Why Trust Matters: Declining Political Trust and the Demise of American Liberalism* (Princeton, NJ: Princeton University Press, 2004).

74. William T. Bianco, *Trust: Representatives and Constituents.* (Ann Arbor, MI: University of Michigan Press, 1994).

75. Sean M. Theriault, *The Power of the People: Congressional Competition, Public Attention, and Voter Retribution* (Columbus, OH: Ohio State University Press, 2005).

76. John R. Hibbing and Elizabeth Theiss-Morse, *Congress as Public Enemy: Public Attitudes Toward American Political Institutions* (New York: Cambridge University Press, 1995).

77. Thomas Rudolph and Jillian Evans, "Political Trust, Ideology, and Public Support for Government Spending," *American Journal of Political Science* 49 (2005): 660–71.

78. Patricia Moy and Michael Pfau, *With Malice Toward All? The Media and Public Confidence in Democratic Institutions* (Boulder, CO: Praeger, 2000).

79. Richard Fenno, *Home Style: U.S. House Members in Their Districts* (Boston: Little, Brown, 1978).

80. William T. Bianco, Daniel Lipinski, and Ryan W. Work, "What Happens When House Members 'Run With Congress'? The Electoral Consequences of Institutional Loyalty," *Legislative Studies Quarterly* 26 (2003): 413–27.

81. Robert S. Erikson, Michael B. Mackuen, and James A. Stimson, *The Macro Polity* (New York: Cambridge University Press, 2002).

82. James A. Stimson, *Public Opinion in America: Moods, Swings, and Cycles* (Boulder, CO: Westview Press, 1999).

83. Robert S. Erikson, Michael B. Mackuen, and James A. Stimson, "American Politics: The Model" (unpublished paper, Columbia University, 2000).

84. See, for example, Pew Research Center, "Iraq Looms Large in Nationalized Election," October 5, 2006, available at http://people-press.org/reports/display.php3?ReportID=290 as well as data at http://www.pollingreport.com.

85. Robin Toner and Jim Rutenberg, "Partisan Divide on Iraq Exceeds Split on Vietnam," *New York Times,* July 30, 2006, p. A1.

86. Pew Research Center, "Nation's Real Estate Slump Hits Wealthy Areas," October 11, 2007, available at http://people-press.org/reports/display.php3?ReportID=361 (accessed 5/5/08).

87. ABC News, Kaiser Family Foundation/*USA Today* Poll, "As Health Care Costs Take a Toll, Some Changes Win Broad Backing," October 6, 2006, available at http://abcnews.go.com/images/Politics/1021a1HealthCare.pdf (accessed 2/25/08).

88. Robert Kuttner, "The American Health Care System," *New England Journal of Medicine* 340 (1999): 163–168.

89. Hope Yen, "Frist Wants Immigration Vote This Week," ABC News, September 24, 2006, available at http://abcnews.go.com/Politics/wireStory?id=2484862 (accessed, 2/22/08).

90. Quinnipiac University Poll, "Let Illegal Immigrants Become Citizens, U.S. Voters Tell Quinnipiac Poll," November 21, 2006, available at http://www.quinnipiac.edu/x1284.xml?ReleaseID=988&What=700%20mile%20fence&strArea=;&strTime=120 (accessed 2/25/08).

91. Data aggregated from various polls; see Pollingreport.com, "Law and Civil Rights," available at http://www.pollingreport.com/civil.htm (accessed 2/25/08).

92. Thom Shanker and David S. Cloud, "The Reach of War: Bush's Plan for Iraq Runs Into Opposition in Congress," *New York Times,* January 12, 2007, p. A1.

93. Andrew Revkin, "A New Middle Stance Emerges in Debate over Climate," *New York Times,* January 1, 2007, p. 16.

CHAPTER 6

1. CNN.com, "Condits Cope With Life after Scandal," February 16, 2005, available at http://www.cnn.com/2005/US/02/11/condit.children (accessed 2/26/08).

2. Thomas E. Patterson, *Out of Order* (New York: Alfred A. Knopf, 1993); Robert D. Putnam, *Bowling Alone* (New York: Basic Books, 2000).

3. Thomas Patterson, "Bad News, Period," *Political Science and Politics* 29 (1996): 17–20.

4. Charles E. Clark, *The Public Prints: The Newspaper in Anglo-American Culture, 1665–1740* (New York: Oxford University Press, 1994).

5. William H. Riker, *The Strategy of Rhetoric: Campaigning for the American Constitution* (New Haven, CT: Yale University Press, 1996).

6. Geoffrey R. Stone, *Perilous Times: Free Speech in Wartime from the Sedition Act of 1798 to the War on Terrorism* (New York: W.W. Norton, 2004).

7. John D. Stevens, *Sensationalism and the New York Press* (New York: Columbia University Press, 1991).

8. Michael Schudson, *Discovering the News: A Social History of American Newspapers* (New York: Basic Books, 1978).

9. Robert C. Williams, *Horace Greeley: Champion of American Freedom* (New York: New York University Press, 2006).

10. W. Joseph Campbell, *Yellow Journalism: Puncturing the Myths, Defining the Legacies* (Boulder, CO: Praeger, 2003).

11. Lincoln Steffens, *The Shame of the Cities* (New York: McClure, Phillips & Co., 1904); Upton Sinclair, *The Jungle* (New York: Doubleday, Page, 1906).

12. Gay Talese, *The Kingdom and the Power* (New York: Calder and Boyars, 1983).

13. For a detailed history, see United States Early Radio History, available at http://www.earlyradiohistory.us.

14. This discussion draws on the summary Merging Media: How Relaxing FCC Ownership Rules Has Affected the Media Business, available at www.pbs.org/newshour/media/conglomeration/fcc2.html (accessed 2/26/08).

15. Peter Braestrup, *How The American Press and Television Reported and Interpreted the Crisis of Tet 1968 in Vietnam* (New Haven, CT: Yale University Press, 1983).

16. For an extended discussion of the fairness doctrine and related issues, see Fairness Doctrine: U.S. Broadcasting Policy, available at http://www.museum.tv/archives/etv/F/htmlF/fairnessdoct/fairnessdoct.htm.

17. For a discussion, see Michael Dorf, "Why Federal Law May Keep the Terminator off the Air until after California's Recall Election: A Primer," *FindLaw's Writ,* August 20, 2003, available at http://writ.news.findlaw.com/dorf/20030820.html.

18. Chris Cillizza and Shailagh Murray, "Contemplating a Run for Office Can Complicate Television Reruns," *Washington Post,* July 15, 2007, p. A2.

19. The Project for Excellence in Journalism, The State of the News Media, 2007: Ownership (2007), available at http://www.stateofthenewsmedia.org/2007/narrative_overview_ownership.asp?cat=5&media=1 (accessed 2/26/08).

20. The FCC Web site has a detailed discussion of the regulatory changes and the logic behind these revisions. See Strategic Goals: Media, available at http://www.fcc.gov/mediagoals.

21. The *Columbia Journalism Review* maintains a list of holdings for major media companies at Who Owns What, available at http://www.cjr.org/tools/owners.

22. Joanna Glasner, "Tech a Key in Media Rule Change," *Wired,* June 3, 2003, available at http://www.wired.com/techbiz/media/news/2003/06/59079 (accessed 2/26/08).

23. Glasner, "Tech a Key in Media Rule Change."

24. For details, see the FCC's Research Studies on Media Ownership, July 31, 2007, available at http://www.fcc.gov/ownership/studies.html.

25. Jacques Steinberg, "Howard Stern Prepares for Life Without Limits," *New York Times,* October 20, 2005; Stephen Labaton, "Decency Ruling Thwarts FCC on Vulgarities," *New York Times,* June 5, 2007.

26. Bryan Curtis, "The Shock Jock in Winter," *Slate,* March 2, 2004, available at http://www.slate.com/id/2096493 (accessed 2/26/08).

27. Adam Cohen, "Editorial Observer; Fighting for Free Speech Means Fighting for . . . Howard Stern," *New York Times,* May 3, 2004.

28. Cohen, "Editorial Observer; Fighting for Free Speech Means Fighting for . . . Howard Stern."

29. Jacques Steinberg, "Stern Likes His New Censor: Himself," *New York Times,* January 8, 2007.

30. See, for example, James J. Cramer, "Newspapers Still Stumble Online," RealMoney.com, May 2, 2005, available at http://www.thestreet.com/p/_rms/rmoney/jamesjcramer/10221101.html (accessed 2/26/08).

31. The Project for Excellence in Journalism, The State of the News Media, 2007: Ownership (2007), available at http://stateofthemedia.org/2007/narrative_newspapers_ownership.asp?cat=4&media=3 (accessed 2/26/08).

32. Magazine Publishers of America, "Average Circulation for Top 100 Magazines," available at http://www.magazine.org/Circulation/circulation_trends_and_magazine_handbook/1353.cfm (accessed 2/26/08).

33. Paul Starr, "Reclaiming the Air," *The American Prospect,* March 2004, pp. 57–61.

34. The President's current budget is available at http://www.whitehouse.gov/omb/budget, the Federal Register can be found at http://www.gpoaccess.gov/fr, and Government Accountability Office reports are available at http://www.gao.gov.

35. The Iraq Index is available at http://www.brookings.edu/iraqindex.

36. The Center for Responsive Politics, www.opensecrets.org.

37. *Pollster,* www.pollster.com.

38. Tom DeLay Mug Shot, *The Smoking Gun,* October 20, 2005, available at http://www.thesmokinggun.com/archive/1020051delay1.html.

39. *Hardblogger,* http://hardblogger.msnbc.msn.com.

40. *National Review Online,* www.nationalreview.com.

41. *The Note,* http://abcnews.go.com/Politics/TheNote.

42. *SCOTUSblog,* http://www.scotusblog.com/movabletype.

43. *Politico,* www.politico.com; *Slate,* www.slate.com.

44. *Salon,* www.salon.com; *The Huffington Post,* www.huffingtonpost.com; *Power Line,* http://www.powerlineblog.com; *Town Hall,* http://www.townhall.com.

45. A. J. Liebling, "Do You Belong in Journalism?" *The New Yorker,* May 14, 1960, p. 105

46. John Hockenberry, "The Blogs of War," *Wired,* August 2005, available at http://www.wired.com/wired/archive/13.08/milblogs.html (accessed 2/26/08).

47. The video, "Allen's Listening Tour," is available at http://youtube.com/watch?v=9G7gq7GQ71c (accessed 2/26/08).

48. The *Washington Post* has an archive of previous online discussions at "Post Politics Hour," available at http://www.washingtonpost.com/wp-dyn/content/linkset/2005/09/30/LI2005093000746.html.

49. A transcript of the online discussion with Gonzalez is available at http://www.washingtonpost.com/wpdyn/content/discussion/2005/12/13/DI2005121301425.html.

50. A good example is *Iraq the Model,* http://iraqthemodel.blogspot.com, as well as the many sites linked to its main page. As part of their coverage of the Iraq war, MSNBC maintains *Blogging Baghdad: The Untold Story,* http://baghdadblog.msnbc.com, where they presented numerous updates during Iraq's Election Day.

51. For a skeptical introduction to this argument, see the proceedings of "MeetUp, Craigslist, eBay: Has the Web Changed Politics?" a conference at the Harvard School of Law, December 9–11, 2004, available at http://cyber.law.harvard.edu/is2k4/home.

52. Bruce Bimber, "Information and Political Engagement in America: The Search for Effects of Information Technology at the Individual Level," *Political Research Quarterly* 54 (2001): 53–67; Caroline J. Tolbert and Ramona S. McNeal, "Unraveling the Effects of the Internet on Political Participation," *Political Research Quarterly* 56 (2003): 175–85.

53. Pew Research Center, "Public Knowledge of Current Affairs Little Changed by News and Information Revolutions," April 15, 2007, available at http://people-press.org/reports/display.php3?ReportID=319 (accessed 2/28/08).

54. Pew Research Center, "Percentage of American Adults Online," data from Pew Internet and American Life Project Surveys, March

2000–December 2006, available at http://www.pewinternet.org/trends/Internet_Adoption_4.26.07.pdf (accessed 2/28/08).

55. Ken Light, "The Real Fake," Digital Journalist, March 2004, available at http://www.digitaljournalist.org/issue0403/dis_light.html (accessed 2/28/08).

56. Katherine Q. Seelye, "Wikipedia Prankster Confesses," Seattle Times, December 11, 2005.

57. For details on the episode, see David Kirkpatrick, "Feeding Frenzy for a Big Story, Even if It's False," New York Times, January 29, 2007.

58. Michael Margolis and David Resnick, Politics as Usual (Los Angeles: Sage Publications, 2000).

59. Dana Priest, "CIA Holds Terror Suspects in Secret Prisons," Washington Post, November 2, 2005, p. A1. Various Bush administration staffers and Republicans in Congress demanded an investigation that would identify and prosecute the people who leaked information about the prison network.

60. James Risen and Eric Lichtblau, "Spying Program Snared U. S. Calls," New York Times, December 21, 2005, p. A1.

61. Scott Shane and David E. Sanger, "Criminal Inquiry Opened into Leak in Eavesdropping," New York Times, December 31, 2005, p. A1.

62. Federation of American Scientists, Secrecy and Government Bulletin, issue 64, January 1997, available at http://www.fas.org/sgp/bulletin/sec64.html (accessed 2/26/08).

63. David Folkenflik, "'Times' Held Story on U.S. Surveillance for a Year," All Things Considered, December 16, 2005, available at http://www.npr.org/templates/story/story.php?storyId=5058710 (accessed 2/26/08).

64. Bob Woodward, "How Mark Felt Became Deep Throat," Washington Post, June 2, 2005, p. A1.

65. Matthew A. Baum, Soft News Goes to War: Public Opinion and American Foreign Policy in the New Media Age (Princeton, NJ: Princeton University Press, 2003).

66. John Zaller, The Nature and Origins of Mass Opinion (New York: Cambridge University Press, 1992).

67. S. H. Chaffee, X. Zhao, and G. Leshner, "Political Knowledge and the Campaign Media of 1992," Communication Research 21 (1994): 305–24; Jeffrey J. Mondak, Nothing to Read: Newspapers and Elections in a Social Experiment (Ann Arbor, MI: University of Michigan Press, 1995).

68. Pew Research Center, "Maturing Internet News Audience—Broader Than Deep: Online Papers Modestly Boost Newspaper Readership," press release, July 30, 2006, available at http://people-press.org/reports/pdf/282.pdf (accessed 2/26/08).

69. For a discussion of these concepts, see Paul M. Sniderman and Sean M. Theriault, "The Structure of Political Argument and the Logic of Issue Framing," in Studies in Public Opinion, ed. William E. Saris and Paul M. Sniderman (Princeton, NJ: Princeton University Press, 2004); and Shanto Iyengar and Donald Kinder, News That Matters (Chicago: University of Chicago Press, 1987). See also Maxwell McCombs and Donald L. Shaw, "The Agenda-Setting Functions of Mass Media," Public Opinion Quarterly 36 (1972): 176–87; and Amos Tversky and Daniel Kahnemann, "The Framing of Decisions and the Psychology of Choice," Science 211 (1981): 453–58.

70. Walter Lippman, Public Opinion (1922; repr., New York: Free Press, 1997).

71. J. T. Klapper, The Effects of Mass Communication (New York: Free Press, 1960); see also Paul F. Lazarsfeld, Bernard Berelson, and Hazel Gaudet, The People's Choice (New York: Columbia University Press, 1944).

72. Stephen Ansolabehere, Roy Behr, and Shanto Iyengar, "The Evolution of Media Effects Research," in The Media Game: American Politics in the Television Age, ed. Stephen Ansolabehere, Roy Behr, and Shanto Iyengar (New York: MacMillan, 1993), 129–38. Steven E. Finkel, "Reexamining the 'Minimal Effects' Model in Recent Presidential Campaigns," The Journal of Politics 55 (1993): 1–21. Kathleen H. Jamieson, Everything You Think You Know about Politics . . . And Why You're Wrong

(New York: Basic Books, 2000). Shanto Iyengar and Adam Simon, "New Perspectives and Evidence on Political Communication and Campaign Effects," Annual Review of Psychology 51 (2000): 149–69.

73. James N. Druckman and Michael Parkin, "The Impact of Media Bias: How Editorial Slant Affects Voters," The Journal of Politics 67 (2005): 4, 1030–49; for similar results, see Kim Fridkin Kahn and Patrick J. Kenney, "The Slant of the News," American Political Science Review 96 (2002): 381–94.

74. Jon A. Krosnick and Laura Brannon, "The Impact of the Gulf War on the Ingredients of Presidential Evaluations: Multidimensional Effects of Political Involvement," American Political Science Review 87 (1993): 963–75.

75. Jon A. Krosnick and Joanne Miller, "News Media Impact on the Ingredients of Presidential Evaluations: Politically Knowledgeable Citizens Are Guided by a Trusted Source," American Journal of Political Science 44 (2000): 295–309.

76. Project Censored, Sonoma State University, "Top 25 Censored Stories of 2007," available at http://www.projectcensored.org/top-stories/category/y=2007 (accessed 2/26/08).

77. Pew Research Center, "Cross-Currents in Opinion about Private Accounts: Social Security Polling," January 27, 2005, available at http://people-press.org/commentary/display.php3?AnalysisID=106 (accessed 2/26/08).

78. Thomas E. Nelson, Rosalee A. Clawson, and Zoe M. Oxley, "Media Framing of a Civil Liberties Conflict and Its Effect on Tolerance," American Political Science Review 91 (1997): 567–83.

79. Dennis Chong and James N. Druckman, "A Theory of Framing and Opinion Formation in Competitive Elite Environments," Journal of Communication 57 (2007): 99–118.

80. Shanto Iyengar, Is Anyone Responsible? How Television Frames Political Issues (Chicago: University of Chicago Press, 1991).

81. Pew Research Center, "Cable and Internet Loom Large in a Fragmented Political Universe," January 11, 2004, available at http://people-press.org/reports/display.php3?ReportID=200 (accessed 2/26/08).

82. For details on these events, see CBS News, "CBS Ousts Four for Bush Guard Story," January 10, 2005, available at http://www.cbsnews.com/stories/2005/01/10/national/main665727.shtml (accessed 2/26/08).

83. Media Research Center, "Media Refusing to Report Positive News from Iraq," press release, January 16, 2006, available at http://www.mediaresearch.org/press/2006/press20060117.asp (accessed 2/29/08).

84. Richard Noyes, "TV's Bad News Brigade: ABC, CBS and NBC's Defeatist Coverage of the War in Iraq," Media Research Center Special Report, October 13, 2005, available at http://www.mrc.org/SpecialReports/2005/report101405_p1.asp (accessed 2/29/08).

85. Noyes, "TV's Bad News Brigade," p. 2.

86. See "Rumsfeld on Iraq," Washington Times, December 6, 2005, available at http://www.washingtontimes.com/op-ed/20051205-094913-3994r.htm (accessed 2/29/08); and "On Balance," Washington Times, December 7, 2005, available at http://www.washingtontimes.com/op-ed/20051206-091140-1752r.htm (accessed 2/29/08).

87. This description runs on the editorial masthead of every issue of The Nation.

88. For these and other data, see the Brookings Iraq Index, http://www.brookings.edu/iraqindex.

89. Paul Allen Beck, Russell J. Dalton, Steven Greene, and Robert Huckfeldt, "The Social Calculus of Voting: Interpersonal, Media, and Organizational Influences on Presidential Choices," American Political Science Review 96 (2002): 57–73.

90. Patterson, "Bad News, Period."

91. Iyengar, Is Anyone Responsible?

92. Thomas Patterson, "Doing Well and Doing Good: How Soft News and Critical Journalism Are Shrinking the News Audience and Weakening Democracy—And What News Outlets Can Do About It," (Cambridge, MA: Joan Shorenstein Center on the Press, Politics,

and Public Policy, Harvard University, 2000), available at http://www.ksg.harvard.edu/presspol/research_publications/reports/softnews.pdf (accessed 2/29/08).

93. Baum, *Soft News Goes to War.*

94. Frank D. Gilliam Jr. and Shanto Iyengar, "Prime Suspects: The Influence of Local Television News on the Viewing Public," *American Journal of Political Science* 44:3 (2000): 560–73.

95. Patterson, *Out of Order.*

96. Pew Research Center, "Self Censorship: How Often and Why: Journalists Avoiding the News," April 30, 2000, available at http://people-press.org/reports/display.php3?ReportID=39 (accessed 2/29/08).

97. T. E. Patterson, *The Vanishing Voter* (New York: Knopf, 2002); J. N. Cappella and K. H. Jamieson, *Spiral of Cynicism: The Press and the Public Good* (New York: Oxford University Press, 1997).

98. Pippa Norria, *A Virtuous Cycle* (New York: Cambridge University Press, 2003).

99. Baum, *Soft News Goes to War,* p. 57.

100. Brent Cunningham, "Across the Great Divide: Class," *Columbia Journalism Review* 3 (May/June 2004), available at http://cjrarchives.org/issues/2004/3/cunningham-class.asp (accessed 2/29/08).

101. John R. Hibbing and Elizabeth Theiss-Morse, *Congress as Public Enemy* (New York: Cambridge University Press, 1995); see also, John R. Hibbing and Elizabeth Theiss-Morse, "The Media's Role in Public Negativity toward Congress: Distinguishing Emotional Reactions and Cognitive Evaluations," *American Journal of Political Science* 42 (April 1998): 475–98.

102. Shanto Iyengar, Helmut Norpoth, and Kyu S. Hahn. "Consumer Demand for Election News: The Horserace Sells," *The Journal of Politics* 66:1 (2004): 157–75.

103. Baum, *Soft News Goes to War,* p. 57.

Comparing Ourselves to Others

a. For these sites, see the *People's Daily* at http://english.peopledaily.com.cn, Itar-Tass at http://www.itartass.com/eng, the BBC at http://www.bbc.co.uk, Al Jazeera at http://english.aljazeera.net, and Watching America at http://www.watchingamerica.com.

You Decide

a. Porter Goss, "Loose Lips Sink Spies," *New York Times*, February 10, 2006, p. 25.

Politics Is Everywhere

a. PR Newswire, "Bill O'Reilly Calls Viewers of *'The Daily Show with Jon Stewart'* A Bunch of 'Stoned Slackers' and 'Dopey Kids' During Interview with Jon Stewart on *'The O'Reilly Factor',*" September 30, 2004, available at http://www.prnewswire.com/cgi-bin/stories.pl?ACCT=109&STORY-/www/story/09-30-2004/0002262661&EDATE=Sept 30, 2004.

b. Annenberg Public Policy Center, "Daily Show Viewers Knowledgeable about Presidential Campaign, National Annenberg Election Survey Shows," press release, September 21, 2004, available at http://www.employeecomm.com/Media/MediaManager/2004_annenberg_election_survey.pdf.

c. Brian Wolly, "The Jon Stewart Fallacy," August 6, 2006, available at http://blogs.usatoday.com/gennext/2006/08/the_jon_stewart.html.

Challenging Conventional Wisdom

a. Michael Kelly, "Left Everlasting (Cont'd)," Washington Post, December 18, 2002, p. A35.

b. For details on the survey, see American Society of Newspaper Editors, Survey Report Page 19, July 7, 1997, available at http://www.asne.org/kiosk/reports/97reports/journalists90s/survey19.html and Fairness and Accuracy in Reporting, "Examining the 'Liberal Media' Claim,"

June 1, 1998, available at http://www.fair.org/reports/journalist-survey.html.

CHAPTER 7

1. John Aldrich, *Why Parties?* (Chicago: University of Chicago Press, 1995).

2. Jennifer Skalka, "Bush Tells Voters to Send Him an Ally; President says He needs Sununu with Him in Washington," *Concord Monitor,* October 6, 2002, p. A1.

3. Richard B. Schnitt and Richard Simon, "GOP Support for Gonzales Continues to Deteriorate," *Los Angeles Times,* April 21, 2007, p. A11.

4. Christopher Cooper, "Republican Strains Emerge Over Iraq," *Wall Street Journal,* June 16, 2005, p. A4. Jonathan Weisman, "GOP Divided Over Range and Severity of Spending Cuts," *Washington Post,* October 6, 2005, p. A7.

5. Quoted in Carrie Budoff, "Is Bush's Support Worse Than No Support?" *Politico,* July 16, 2007, available at http://www.politico.com/news/stories/0707/4960.html (accessed 3/24/08).

6. Joseph Schlesinger, *Political Parties and the Winning of Office* (Ann Arbor, MI: University of Michigan Press, 1994).

7. The three-part description first appeared in V. O. Key, *Politics, Parties, and Pressure Groups* (New York: Crowell, 1956). For a more recent description, see Paul Allen Beck and Marjorie Hershey, *Party Politics in America* (New York: Longman, 2004).

8. William Nesbit Chambers and Walter Dean Burnham, *The American Party Systems: Stages of Political Development* (Oxford, UK: Oxford University Press, 1966).

9. Aldrich, *Why Parties?*

10. Donald H. Hickey, "Federalist Party Unity and the War of 1812," *Journal of American Studies* 12 (April, 1978): 23–39; William T. Bianco, David B. Spence, and John D. Wilkerson, "The Electoral Connection in the Early Congress: The Case of the Compensation Act of 1816," *American Journal of Political Science* 40 (February, 1996): 145–71.

11. James MacPherson, *Battle Cry of Freedom: The Civil War Era* (New York: Oxford University Press, 1988).

12. Michael F. Holt, *The Rise and Fall of the Whig Party: Jacksonian Politics and the Onset of the Civil War* (New York: Oxford University Press, 1999).

13. Harold W. Stanley, William T. Bianco, and Richard G. Niemi, "Partisanship and Group Support over Time: A Multivariate Analysis," *American Political Science Review* 80 (1986): 969–76.

14. John Aldrich, *Why Parties?* re ed notes 15–20

15. James L. Sundquist, *Dynamics of the Party System,* rev. ed. (Washington, DC: Brookings Institution, 1983).

16. Aldrich, *Why Parties?*

17. John H. Aldrich and Richard G. Niemi, "The Sixth American Party System: Electoral Change, 1952–1992," in *Broken Contract: Changing Relationships between Americans and Their Governments* Steven Craig, ed. (Boulder, CO: Westview Press, 1993).

18. Edward G. Carmines and James A. Stimson, *Issue Evolution: Race and the Transformation of American Politics* (Princeton, NJ: Princeton University Press, 1989).

19. Harold W. Stanley and Richard G. Niemi, "Partisanship, Party Coalitions, and Group Support, 1952–2004," *Presidential Studies Quarterly* 36:2 (2006): 172–88.

20. Charles S. Bullock III, Donna R Hoffman, and Ronald Keith Gaddie "Regional Variations in the Realignment of American Politics, 1944–2004," *Social Science Quarterly* 87:3 (2006): 494–518.

21. The full list of Democratic constituency groups is available at http://www.democrats.org/communities.html. A list of Republican teams is available at http://www.gop.com/Teams/default.aspx.

22. Jon F. Hale, "The Making of the New Democrats," *Political Science Quarterly* 110:2 (1995): 207–32.

23. James C. Moore and Wayne Slater, *Bush's Brain: How Karl Rove Made George W. Bush Presidential* (New York: Wiley, 2003).

24. Gary Cox and Mathew McCubbins, *Legislative Leviathan* (Berkeley, CA: University of California Press, 1993); James M. Snyder and Michael M. Ting, "An Informational Rationale for Political Parties," *American Journal of Political Science* 46 (2002): 90–110.

25. Adam Nagourney and Cassi Feldman, "Early Primary Rush Upends '08 Campaign Plans," *New York Times,* March 12, 2007, p. A1; Linda Feldmann, "An Uproar Over '08 Primary Calendar," May 25, 2007, *Christian Science Monitor,* p. 2; Christopher Cooper, "Early Voting May Clip Iowa's Role," *Wall Street Journal,* May 22, 2007, p. A4.

26. Raymond Wolfinger, "Why Political Machines Have Not Withered Away and Other Revisionist Thoughts," *Journal of Politics* 34:2 (1972): 365–98.

27. For details on Tammany Hall, see William L. Riordon, *Plunkitt of Tammany Hall* (1905; repr., New York: Dutton, 1963) also available at http://www.marxists.org/reference/archive/plunkett-george/tammany-hall.

28. Riordan, *Plunkitt of Tammany Hall.*

29. Jonathan Weisman, "Democrats Split on Iraq Bill; Even Vote Counters Aren't Lined Up Behind Spending Measure," March 21, 2007, *Washington Post,* p. A13.

30. Jason Roberts and Steven Smith, "Procedural Contexts, Party Strategy, and Conditional Party Government," *American Journal of Political Science* 47:2 (2003): 205–317.

31. For details on NOMINATE scores, see Keith Poole and Howard Rosenthal, *Congress: A Political-Economic History of Roll Call Voting* (New York: Oxford University Press, 1997).

32. David Rohde, *Parties and Leaders in the Post-Reform House* (Chicago: University of Chicago Press, 1991).

33. Stephen Weisman, "Bush and Democrats in Accord on Trade Deals," *New York Times,* May 11, 2007.

34. Carl Hulse and Sheryl Gay Stolberg, "Changes Sought in Naming of Prosecutors," *New York Times,* March 20, 2007, p. A15.

35. Paul Kane, "Freshmen 42: A First Split on the Iraq War," *Washington Post,* May 17, 2007, available at http://blog.washingtonpost.com/capitolbriefing/2007/05/freshmen_42_a_first_split_on_t.html (accessed 3/27/08); Lois Romano, "Even with the Democratic Party's Right Wing, Bush's Iraq Plans Don't Fly," *Washington Post,* May 17, 2007, p. A15.

36. John Holusha, "Senate Continues Debate Over Immigration Reform," *New York Times,* April 4, 2006, p. A1.

37. Rachel Swarns, "Bill to Broaden Immigration Law Gains in Senate," *New York Times,* March 28, 2006, p. A1.

38. Donald Green, Bradley Palmquist, and Eric Schickler, *Partisan Hearts and Minds* (New Haven, CT: Yale University Press, 2004); Christopher Achen, "Political Socialization and Rational Party Identification," *Political Behavior* 24:2 (2002): 151–70.

39. Morris Fiorina, *Retrospective Voting in American National Elections* (New Haven, CT: Yale University Press, 1981).

40. Michael Meffert, Helmut Norpoth, and Anirudh V. S. Ruhil, "Realignment and Macropartisanship," *American Political Science Review* 95:4 (2001): 953–62.

41. Walter Dean Burnham, "The Reagan Heritage," in *The Election of 1988: Reports and Interpretations,* ed. Gerald M. Pomper, et al. (Chatham, NJ: Chatham House, 1989).

42. Martin P. Wattenberg, *The Decline of American Political Parties: 1952–1994* (Cambridge, MA: Harvard University Press, 1996).

43. David S. Broder, *The Party's Over: The Failure of Partisan Politics in America* (New York: Harper and Row, 1971).

44. Donald P. Green and Bradley Palmquist, "Of Artifacts and Partisan Instability," *American Journal of Political Science* 34:3 (August, 1990): 872–902.

45. Warren E. Miller and J. Merrill Shanks, *The New American Voter* (Cambridge, MA: Harvard University Press, 1996); Steven J. Rosenstone and John Mark Hansen, *Mobilization, Participation, and Democracy in America* (New York: Macmillan, 1993).

46. D. Sunshine Hillygus and Simon Jackman, "Voter Decision Making in Election 2000: Campaign Effects, Partisan Activation, and the Clinton Legacy," *American Journal of Political Science* 47 (2003): 583–96.

47. Larry M. Bartels, "Partisanship and Voting Behavior, 1952–1996," *American Journal of Political Science* 44:1 (2000): 35–50.

48. Data from CNN 2008 Election Center, available at http://www.cnn.com/ELECTION/2008/results/polls/#val=USP00p5 (accessed 11/5/08).

49. Martin P. Wattenberg, *Where Have All the Voters Gone?* (Cambridge, MA: Harvard University Press, 2002).

50. John F. Bibby, "Elections: Political Parties in the United States," in *United States Elections 2004,* ed. George Clack and Paul Malamud (Washington, DC: U.S. Department of State, Bureau of International Information Programs, September 2003), available at http://usinfo.state.gov/products/pubs/election04/parties.htm (accessed 3/27/08).

51. Jill Lawrence, "Party Recruiters Lead Charge for '06 Vote; Choice of Candidates to Run in Fall May Decide Who Controls the House," *USA Today,* May 25, 2006, p. A5.

52. James Dao and Adam Nagourney, "Soldier-Candidates: They Served, and Now They're Running," *New York Times,* February 19, 2006.

53. Jackie Calmes and Greg Hitt, "Can the Class of 2006 Save the Democrats?" *Wall Street Journal,* November 4, 2006, p. A1. For a full list of veteran Democratic candidates, see Fighting Dems for America, available at http://www.fighting-dems.com/node/25 (accessed 6/2/07).

54. Michael M. Grynbaum, "After Hard-Fought Senate Race, Lieberman Comes Out on Top," *Boston Globe,* November 8, 2006, p. A21.

55. Aldrich, *Why Parties?*

56. Data compiled from the Center for Responsive Politics, "Political Parties Overview: Election Cycle 2008," available at http://www.opensecrets.org/parties/index.php (accessed 11/5/08).

57. Rick Klein and Charlie Savage, "Some Democrats Decry Kerry's Unspent $16m," *Boston Globe,* November 19, 2004, available at http://www.boston.com/news/nation/articles/2004/11/19/some_democrats_decry_kerrys_unspent_16m (accessed 3/10/08).

58. Michael Duffy and Nancy Gibbs, "Our Journey Is Not Done: The Voters Hand Clinton a Historic Victory, but Send a Message: Work With the Republicans," *Time,* November 18, 1996.

59. Paul M. Weyrich, "Give President Bush Credit for Putting His Popularity to Work," *Enter Stage Right,* November 4, 2002, available at http://www.enterstageright.com/archive/articles/1102/1102politicalcapital.htm (accessed 3/27/08).

60. See Democratic Party, "A 50 State Strategy," available at http://www.democrats.org/a/party/a_50_state_strategy, (accessed 3/27/08).

61. Patricia Zapor, "Pro-life Democrats Describe Lonely Role, but See Improvements," *Catholic News Service,* July 28, 2004, available at http:// www.catholicnews.com/data/stories/cns/0404122.htm (accessed 3/27/08).

62. Jim Yardley, "Campaign Tests Bush's Balancing Skills," *New York Times,* April 16, 2000, p. 22.

63. Gary Cox and Mathew McCubbins, *Setting the Agenda: Party Government in the U.S. House of Representatives* (New York: Cambridge University Press, 2005).

64. Eric Schickler and Andrew Rich, "Controlling the Floor: Parties as Procedural Coalitions in the House," *American Journal of Political Science* 41:4 (1997): 1340–75.

65. For details on the 100-Hour Plan, see Carl Hulse, "After 42 Hours (or So), House Democrats Complete 100-Hour Push," *New York Times,* January 19, 2007.

66. Robin Toner, "Revamping Medicare: The Context; GOP Steals Thunder," *New York Times,* June 28, 2003.

67. Timothy Noah, "Who Tried to Bribe Defendant Smith?" *Slate,* December 1, 2003, available at http://www.slate.com/id/2091787 (accessed 3/27/08).

68. David S. Broder, "Time Was GOP's Ally on the Vote," *Washington Post,* November 23, 2003, p. A1.

69. John Holusha, "Senate Continues Debate Over Immigration Reform," *New York Times,* April 4, 2006, p. A1.

70. Jacob Weisberg, "Bush's First Defeat," *Slate,* March 21, 2005, available at http://www.slate.com/id/2115141 (accessed 3/27/08).

71. Theda Skocpol, *Boomerang: Health Care Reform and the Turn Against Government* (New York: W. W. Norton, 1997).

72. Jeff Zeleny and Carl Hulse, "The Struggle for Iraq; Key Republican Senator Offers Bipartisan Call to Reject Bush Plan for More Troops in Iraq," *New York Times,* January 23, 2007, p. 10.

73. Jeff Zeleny and Robin Toner, "Democrats Rally Behind a Pullout From Iraq in '08," *New York Times,* March 9, 2007, p. A1.

74. Bill Clinton, *My Life* (New York: Knopf, 2004), p. 536.

75. E. E. Schattschneider, *Party Government* (New York: McGraw Hill, 1942); Nelson Polsby, *Consequences of Party Reform* (New York: Oxford University Press, 1983).

76. See Libertarian National Committee, "Frequently Asked Questions about the Libertarian Party," available at http://www.lp.org/article_85.shtml (accessed 3/27/08).

77. Steven J. Rosenstone, Roy L. Behr, and Edward Lazarus, *Third Parties in America: Citizen Response to Major Party Failure* (Princeton, NJ: Princeton University Press, 1984).

78. Scott Shane, "The 2004 Election: The Independent; Nader Is Left with Fewer Votes, and Friends, After '04 Race," *New York Times,* November 6, 2004, p. A13.

79. Alan Nagourney and Jin Rutenberg, "For Two Years, Bloomberg Aides Prepared for Bid," *New York Times,* June 21, 2007.

80. Janet Hook and Peter Wallsten, "GOP Feels Sting of Candidates' Rejection," *Los Angeles Times,* October 10, 2005, p. A1.

81. Michael Powell, "Lieberman Holds Seat in Comeback," *Washington Post,* November 8, 2006, p. A35; Nicholas Confessore, "Lamont Boosts His Republican Opponent in Hope of Drawing Votes from Lieberman," *New York Times,* October 27, 2006, p. B5.

82. Gary Cox, *Making Votes Count: Strategic Coordination in the World's Electoral Systems* (Cambridge, UK: Cambridge University Press, 1997).

83. Thomas B. Edsall, "GOP Gains Advantage on Key Issues, Polls Say," *Washington Post,* January 27, 2002, p. A4.

84. John D. McKinnon, "Backing Away from Bush; Some Republican Candidates Avoid Ties with Unpopular President," *Wall Street Journal,* May 23, 2006, p. A4.

Politics Is Everywhere

a. Anderson Analytics, "GenX2Z Annual College Brand Survey, 2006," available at http://www.marketingsherpa.com/cs/anderson/genx2z.pdf.

Challenging Conventional Wisdom

a. Richard C. Pearson, "Former Alabama Governor George C. Wallace Dies," *Washington Post*, September 14, 1998, p. A1.

b. Nader made this claim throughout the campaign; for an example, see the transcript of his comments during a February 22, 2004 appearance on the television program *Meet the Press,* available at http://www.msnbc.msn.com/id/4304155.

c. Libertarian National Committee, "The Libertarian Party on Today's Issues," available at http://www.lp.org/issues/issues.shtml.

d. Green Party, "The Real Difference: Issue Comparison, " available at http://www.therealdifference.org/issues.html.

e. Gary Benoit, "Demopublicans vs. Republicrats," Constitution Party News Articles, November 3, 2006, available at http://www.constitutionparty.com/news.php?aid=357.

f. Constitution Party, "The Constitution Party National Platform," available at http://www.constitutionparty.com/party_platform.php#Preamble.

You Decide

a. Nelson Polsby, *Consequences of Party Reform* (New York: Oxford University Press, 1983).

b. Daniel A. Smith and Caroline J. Tolbert, *Educated by Initiative: The Effects of Direct Democracy on Citizens and Political Organizations in the American States* (Ann Arbor, MI: University of Michigan Press, 2004).

Comparing Ourselves to Others

a. Michael Gallagher, Michael Laver, and Peter Mair, *Representative Government in Western Europe* (New York: McGraw Hill, 2000).

CHAPTER 8

1. James Campbell, "The 2002 Midterm Election: A Typical or Atypical Midterm?" *Political Science and Politics* 36 (2003): 203–6.

2. Morris P. Fiorina, *Retrospective Voting in American National Elections* (New Haven, CT: Yale University Press, 1981); V. O. Key, *The Responsible Electorate* (New York: Vintage, 1966).

3. David Mayhew, *Congress: The Electoral Connection* (New Haven, CT: Yale University Press, 1973).

4. Melonyce McAfee, "Can I Vote Without Going Outside?" *Slate*, November 6, 2006, available at http://www.slate.com/id/2153111 (accessed 3/31/08).

5. For details on early voting, see the Early Voting Information Center site at http://earlyvoting.net/states.php.

6. Paul Gronke, "Early Voting Reforms and American Elections" (paper presented at the 2004 American Political Science Association Annual Meeting, Chicago, IL). For 2006 data, see Pew Research Center, "Public Cheers Democratic Victory," November 16, 2006, available at http://people-press.org/reports/display.php3?ReportID=296 (accessed 3/30/08).

7. For details on the Texas redistricting, see Sheryl Gay Stolberg, "The 2004 Campaign: The House; Bid for Control of Congress Plays Out in a Redrawn Texas," *New York Times,* October 18, 2004, p. 1. See also Carl Hulse, "The 2004 Campaign: The House; The Battle in Pennsylvania Isn't Just for President," *New York Times,* October 25, 2004, p. 18.

8. Bernard Grofman, "Criteria for Districting: A Social Science Perspective," *UCLA Law Review* 33 (1985): 77–96.

9. "Major Campaign Upset Brewing in Georgia's 10th District," *Politico,* July 18, 2007, available at http://www.politico.com/blogs/thecrypt/0707/Major_campaign_upset_brewing_in_Georgias_10th_District.html (accessed 3/31/08).

10. Anne Kornblut, "Status Quo in Senate Races: Menendez Retains His Senate Seat; Lieberman Finally Prevails Over Lamont," *New York Times,* November 8, 2006, p. 6.

11. For details, see the Caltech/MIT Voting Technology Project site at http://www.vote.caltech.edu.

12. Steven Ansolabehere and Charles Stewart, "Residual Votes Attributable to Technology," *Journal of Politics* 67 (2005): 365–80.

13. Randall Stross, "The Big Gamble on Electronic Voting," *New York Times,* September 24, 2006, p. 3.

14. An invaluable source for information on election technology, including reports on the use of touch screens in 2006, is the blog *Election Updates* written by California Institute of Technology professor Michael Alvarez and others at http://electionupdates.caltech.edu/blog.html.

15. Jonathan N. Wand, Kenneth W. Shotts, Jasjeet S. Sekhon, Walter R. Mebane, Michael C. Herron, and Henry E. Brady, "The Butterfly

Ballot Did It: The Aberrant Vote for Buchanan in Palm Beach County, Florida," *American Political Science Review* 95 (2001): 793–809.

16. Robert F. Kennedy Jr., "Was The 2004 Election Stolen?" *Rolling Stone,* June 1, 2006, available at http://www.rollingstone.com/news/story/10432334/was_the_2004_election_stolen (accessed 3/29/08).

17. Frhad Manjoo, "Was The 2004 Election Stolen? No," *Salon,* June 3, 2006, available at http://www.salon.com/news/feature/2006/06/03/kennedy (accessed 3/31/08).

18. Glen Justice, "The 2004 Election: Campaign Finance; Advocacy Groups Reflect on Their Role in the Election," *New York Times,* November 5, 2004, p. 23.

19. For details, see Committee on Standards of Official Conduct, "Rules and Standards of Conduct Relating to Campaign Activity," memorandum, March 2, 2000, available at http://www.house.gov/ethics/m_CampaignActivity2000.htm (accessed 3/29/08).

20. Minor party candidates are typically selected during party conventions.

21. Barbara Norrander, "Presidential Nomination Politics in the Post-Reform Era," *Political Research Quarterly* 49 (1996): 875–90.

22. Larry Bartels, *Presidential Primaries and the Dynamics of Public Choice* (Princeton, NJ: Princeton University Press, 1988).

23. William G. Mayer, "Forecasting Presidential Nominations or, My Model Worked Just Fine, Thank You," *Political Science and Politics* 36 (2003): 153–9.

24. Elisabeth Bumiller, "Edwards Is Out; Guiliani Quits and Backs McCain," *New York Times,* January 31, 2008.

25. Marty Cohen, David Karol, Hans Noel, and John Zaller, "Beating Reform: The Resurgence of Parties in Presidential Nominations, 1980 to 2000" (paper presented at the 2001 American Political Science Association Annual Meeting, San Francisco, CA).

26. Adam Nagourney, "Democrats Propose Moving Up Nevada in Presidential Caucuses," *New York Times,* July 23, 2006, p. 18.

27. Richard Herrera, "Are 'Superdelegates' Super?" *Political Behavior* 16 (1994): 79–93.

28. For a discussion of the 2004 conventions, see Kennedy School of Government, *Campaigning for President: The Managers Look at 2004* (New York: Rowman and Littlefield, 2005).

29. Robert K. Murray, *The 103rd Ballot: The Incredible Story of the Disastrous Democratic Convention in 1924* (New York: Harper and Row, 1976).

30. *FairVote,* "Maine and Nebraska," available at http://www.fairvote.org/e_college/me_ne.htm (accessed 3/31/08).

31. Adam Nagourney, "The 2004 Campaign: Strategy; Bush and Kerry Focus Campaigns in 11 Key States," *New York Times,* October 24, 2004, p. 1.

32. Robert Bennett, "The Problem of the Faithless Elector," *Northwestern University Law Review* 100 (2004): 121–30.

33. Timothy Noah, "Faithless Elector Watch: Ask Doctor Faithless," *Slate,* December 7, 2000, available at http://www.slate.com/id/1006644 (accessed 3/30/08).

34. James Q. Wilson, "Is The Electoral College Worth Saving?" *Slate,* November 3, 2000, available at http://www.slate.com/id/92663 (accessed 3/31/08).

35. Linda Fowler and Robert McClure, *Political Ambition: Who Decides to Run for Congress* (Ann Arbor, MI: University of Michigan Press, 1989).

36. Robin Kolodny, *Pursuing Majorities: Congressional Campaign Committees in American Politics* (Norman, OK: University of Oklahoma Press, 1999).

37. For these data, see Cook Political Report, "2006 Senate and Governor Race States: Bush Performance v. Kerry/Nader Performance," January 21, 2005, available at http://cookpolitical.com/races/report_pdfs/govsen.pdf (accessed 3/3/08).

38. Steven Ansolabehere and Allan Gerber, "Incumbency Advantage and the Persistence of Legislative Majorities," *Legislative Studies Quarterly* 22 (1997): 161–80.

39. For a discussion of Johnson's decision, see Robert A. Caro, *The Path to Power* (New York: Knopf, 1983).

40. Cherie Maestas, Sarah Fulton, Walter Stone, and L. Sandy Maisel, "When To Risk It: Institutions, Ambition and the Decision to Run for the U.S. House," *American Political Science Review* 100 (2006): 195–208.

41. Jeffrey A. Banks and D. Roderick Kiewiet, "Explaining Patterns of Candidate Competition in Congressional Elections," *American Journal of Political Science* 33 (1989): 997–1015.

42. Rick Lyman, "Down but Not Out, Kucinich Keeps on Fighting," *New York Times,* May 17, 2004, p. 18.

43. Thomas Mann and Norman Ornstein, *The Permanent Campaign and Its Future* (Washington, DC: American Enterprise Institute, 2000).

44. David Mayhew, *Congress: The Electoral Connection* (New Haven, CT: Yale University Press, 1973).

45. Joe Klein, *The Natural: The Misunderstood Presidency of Bill Clinton* (New York: Broadway, 2003).

46. Jacob Weisberg, "Drug Addled: Why Bush's Prescription Drug Plan Is Such a Fiasco," *Slate,* January 16, 2006, available at http://www.slate.com/id/2134456 (accessed 3/31/08).

47. David Johnston, "IRS Going Slow Before Election," *New York Times,* October 27, 2006, p. A1.

48. Henry Chappell and William Keech, "A New Model of Political Accountability for Economic Performance," *American Political Science Review* 79 (1985): 10–19.

49. Jonathan Krasno and Donald P. Green, "The Dynamics of Campaign Fundraising in House Elections," *Journal of Politics* 56 (1991): 459–74.

50. Michael J. Goff, *The Money Primary: The New Politics of the Early Presidential Nomination Process* (New York: Rowman and Littlefield, 2007).

51. Chris Cillizza, "Consulting Firms Face Conflict in 2008," *Roll Call,* June 20, 2005, p. 1.

52. Cherie Maestas, Walter Stone, and L. Sandy Maisel, "Quality Counts: Extending the Strategic Politician Model of Incumbent Deterrence," *American Journal of Political Science* 48 (2004): 479–90.

53. Matt Bai, "Turnout Wins Elections," *New York Times Magazine,* December 14, 2003, p. 100.

54. Bob Drogin and Robin Abcarian, "In Ohio, Obama's Ground Game Outguns McCain's," *Los Angeles Times,* November 3, 2008, p. A1.

55. Christopher Drew, "New Telemarketing Ploy Steers Voters on Republican Path," *New York Times,* November 6, 2006.

56. Donald Green and Alan Gerber, "The Effects of Canvassing, Phone Calls, and Direct Mail on Voter Turnout: A Field Experiment," *American Political Science Review* 94 (2000): 653–69; Lynn Vavreck, Constantine J. Spiliotes, and Linda L. Fowler, "The Effect of Retail Politics in the New Hampshire Primary," *American Journal of Political Science* 46 (2002): 595–610.

57. John Dickerson, "Weak Poll," *Slate,* October 30, 2006, available at http://www.slate.com/id/2152529 (accessed 3/31/08).

58. Sonya Geis, "California Campaign in Turmoil Over Letters," *Washington Post,* October 20, 2006, p. 4.

59. Jeffrey H. Birnbaum, "Candidates Taking Aim at Lobbyists," *Washington Post,* October 15, 2006, p. A1.

60. Adam Nagourney and Megan Thee, "With Election Driven by Iraq, Voters Want New Approach," *New York Times,* November 2, 2006, p. A1.

61. Jake Tapper and Avery Miller, "Border Politics on the Campaign Trail," *ABC News,* September 21, 2006, available at http://i.abcnews.com/WNT/story?id=2475262&page=1 (accessed 3/31/08).

62. For a detailed discussion of the debate over the Contract's effects in the 1994 election, see "Ignoring Evidence to the Contrary, *USA Today* Editorial Asserted 1994 'Contract with America' Was 'Effective . . . in Bringing Republicans to Power,'" October 20, 2006, available

at http://mediamatters.org/items/200610210001?show=1 (accessed 3/30/08).

63. For a history of presidential debates, see the Commission on Presidential Debates site at http://www.debates.org.

64. Compiled from Eric M. Appleman/Democracy in Action, "Debates: 2008 Presidential Campaign," available at http://www.gwu.edu/~action/2008/chrndebs08.html#1 (accessed 11/5/08).

65. See the transcript of the first debate: Commission on Presidential Debates, Debate Transcript, September 30, 2004, available at http://www.debates.org/pages/trans2004a.html (accessed 3/31/08).

66. For an example in the 2006 New Jersey Senate campaign, see Jonathan Tamari, "Senate Rivals Spar Over Iraq War," *Home News Tribune Online,* October 18, 2006, available at http://www.thnt.com/apps/pbcs.dll/article?AID=/20061018/NEWS/610180376/1001 (accessed 3/29/08).

67. Michael Powell, "Barack Bowl," *New York Times,* March 30, 2008, available at http://thecaucus.blogs.nytimes.com/2008/03/30/barack-bowl (accessed 4/15/08).

68. Maureen Dowd, "Eggheads and Cheese Balls," *New York Times,* April 16, 2008.

69. Michael Luo, "'Facts are Stubborn,' Romney Once Said, and He Should Know," *New York Times,* December 22, 2007.

70. Kerry made this charge in many speeches, most notably in the first presidential debate. See Commission on Presidential Debates, Debate Transcript, September 30, 2004: The First Bush-Kerry Presidential Debate, available at http://www.debates.org/pages/trans2004a_p.html (accessed 4/16/08).

71. Tom Zaller, "The 2006 Campaign: A New Campaign Tactic: Manipulating Google Data," *New York Times,* October 26, 2006, p. 20

72. "Smile, You're on . . . the Web: Gotcha," *USA Today Opinion,* October 11, 2006, available at http://blogs.usatoday.com/oped/2006/10/post_10.html (accessed 3/31/08).

73. Peter J. Boyer, "The Strangest Senate Race of the Year," *New Yorker,* September 30, 2006, pp. 23–45.

74. Helen A. S. Popkin and Ree Hines, "MySpace: A Place for Candidates," *MSNBC,* June 20, 2007, available at http://www.msnbc.msn.com/id/19337775 (accessed 3/31/08).

75. Jeff Matthews, *Jeff Matthews Is Not Making This Up,* "The First You-Tube Election, and Not the Last," November 9, 2006, available at http://jeffmatthewsisnotmakingthisup.blogspot.com/2006/11/first-youtube-election-and-not-last.html (accessed 3/31/08).

76. For a video library of presidential campaign ads, see Museum of the Moving Image, "The Living Room Candidate: Presidential Campaign Commercials 1952–2004," available at http://livingroomcandidate.movingimage.us/index.php (accessed 3/31/08).

77. Museum of the Moving Image, "The Living Room Candidate: 1964: Johnson vs. Goldwater," available at http://livingroomcandidate.movingimage.us/election/index.php?ad_id=1014 (accessed 3/31/08).

78. Museum of the Moving Image, "The Living Room Candidate: 1964: Johnson vs. Goldwater."

79. Katherine Shaver, "A Star Says He Finds Validation in Public Interest in Stem Cells," *Washington Post,* November 3, 2006, p. B4.

80. See "Hillary Clinton Sopranos Parody," available at http://www.youtube.com/watch?v=9BEPcJlz2wE (accessed 3/31/08) and "Mike Huckabee Ad: 'Chuck Norris Approved,'" available at http://www.youtube.com/watch?v=MDUQW8LUMs8 (accessed 3/31/08).

81. Kenneth Goldstein and Joel Rivlin, "Advertising in the 2000 and 2004 Elections: Findings from the 2000 Election," available at http://www.polisci.wisc.edu/tvadvertising/Analysis_Of_2000_Elections/cfi%20presentation.ppt, unpublished presentation, University of Wisconsin (accessed 3/31/08). For 2002 data, see Kenneth Goldstein and Joel Rivlin, *Political Advertising in the 2002 Elections,* unpublished manuscript, University of Wisconsin, available at http://www.polisci.wisc.edu/tvadvertising/Analysis%20of%20the%202000%20elections.htm (accessed 3/31/08).

82. Kenneth Goldstein and Joel Rivlin, *Political Advertising in the 2002 Elections,* unpublished manuscript, University of Wisconsin, available at http://www.polisci.wisc.edu/tvadvertising/Analysis%20of%20the%202000%20elections.htm (accessed 3/31/08).

83. For examples of this argument, see Thomas Patterson, *The Vanishing Voter* (New York: Knopf, 2002) and Jules Witcover, *No Way to Pick a President: How Money and Hired Guns Have Debased American Politics* (London, UK: Routledge, 2001).

84. Michael Grunwald, "The Year of Playing Dirtier," *Washington Post,* October 27, 2006, p. A1.

85. Jacob Weisberg, "Poisoned Politics," *Slate,* November 1, 2006, available at http://www.slate.com/id/2152671 (accessed 3/31/06).

86. Peter Whorisky, "Corker Grabs Narrow Victory Over Ford," *Washington Post,* December 8, 2006, p. A35.

87. Paul Freeman, Michael Franz, and Kenneth Goldstein, "Campaign Advertising and Democratic Citizenship," *American Journal of Political Science* 48 (2004): 723–41.

88. Constantine J. Spilotes and Lynn Vavreck, "Campaign Advertising: Partisan Convergence or Divergence," *Journal of Politics,* 64 (2002): 249–61.

89. Kathleen Hall Jameson, *Packaging the Presidency: A History and Criticism of Presidential Campaign Advertising* (New York: Oxford University Press, 1996).

90. Steven Ansolabehere and Shanto Iyengar, *Going Negative: How Political Advertisements Shrink and Polarize the Electorate* (New York: Free Press, 1997); Richard Lau, Lee Sigelman, Caroline Heldman, and Paul Babbitt, "The Effects of Negative Political Advertisements: A Meta-Analytic Analysis," *American Political Science Review* 93 (1999): 851–70.

91. Jonathan Krasno and Frank J. Sorauf, "For the Defense," *Political Science and Politics* 37 (2004): 777–80.

92. For the details on these rules, see Federal Election Commission, "Public Funding of Presidential Elections," February 2008, available at http://www.fec.gov/pages/brochures/pubfund.shtml (accessed 3/31/08).

93. Contribution and spending data are available from the Center for Responsive Politics at http://www.opensecrets.org.

94. Newser.com, "Fake Obama Group Keeps Donations," July 25, 2007, available at http://www.newser.com/story/4766.html (accessed 3/21/08).

95. Brian Stelter, "The Price of 30 Seconds," *New York Times,* October 1, 2007, available at http://tvdecoder.blogs.nytimes.com/2007/10/01/the-price-of-30-seconds, accessed (4/17/08).

96. Wal-Mart Stores, Inc., "Annual Report to Shareholders, 2006" March 29, 2006, available at http://www.sec.gov/Archives/edgar/data/104169/000119312506066792/dex13.htm (accessed 3/31/08).

97. Center for Responsive Politics, "The Big Picture, 2004 Cycle: Millionaire Candidates," available at http://www.opensecrets.org/bigpicture/millionaires.asp?cycle=2004 (accessed 3/31/08).

98. For the details on EMILY's List receipts and expenditures during the 2004 election cycle, see Center for Responsive Politics, "EMILY's List 2004 Pac Summary Data," available at http://www.opensecrets.org/pacs/lookup2.asp?strid=C00193433&cycle=2004 (accessed 3/31/08).

99. Raymond Hernandez, "Anti-Clinton Donor Reported as Donor to Giuliani," *New York Times,* November 29, 2006.

100. For a review of this literature, see Michael Malbin, *The Election After Reform: Money, Politics, and the Bipartisan Campaign Reform Act* (Washington, DC: Roman and Littlefield, 2006).

101. For a discussion, see Patterson, *The Vanishing Voter,* especially Chapter 1, "The Incredible Shrinking Electorate," pp. 3–22.

102. William H. Riker and Peter Ordeshook, "A Theory of the Calculus of Voting," *American Political Science Review* 62 (1968): 25–39.

103. Michael McDonald, The United States Elections Project, available at http://elections.gmu.edu (accessed 3/30/08).

104. Raymond Wolfinger and Jonathan Hoffman, "Registering and Voting with Motor Voter," *Political Science and Politics* 34 (2001): 85–92.

105. For a review of the literature on issue voters, see Jon K. Dalager, "Voters, Issues, and Elections: Are Candidates' Messages Getting Through?" *Journal of Politics* 58 (1996): 486–515.

106. Richard P. Lau and David P. Reslawsk, *How Voters Decide: Information Processing During Electoral Campaigns* (New York: Cambridge University Press, 2006).

107. Gary Cox and Jonathan Katz, "Why Did the Incumbency Advantage in U.S. House Elections Grow?" *American Journal of Political Science* 40 (1996): 478–96.

108. Charles Franklin, "Eschewing Obfuscation: Campaigns and the Perceptions of U.S. Senate Incumbents," *American Political Science Review* 85 (December, 1991): 1193–1214. Wendy M. Rahn, "The Role of Partisan Stereotypes in Information Processing about Political Candidates," *American Journal of Political Science* 37 (May, 1993): 472–96.

109. Bruce Cain, John Ferejohn, and Morris Fiorina, *The Personal Vote* (Cambridge, MA: Harvard University Press, 1985).

110. Jeffrey Koch, "Gender Stereotypes and Citizens' Impressions of House Candidates' Ideological Orientations," *American Journal of Political Science* 46 (2002): 453–62; Monica McDermott, "Candidate Occupations and Voter Information," *Journal of Politics* 67 (2005): 201–18; Carol Sigelman, Lee Sigelman, Barbara Walkosz, and Michael Nitz, "Black Candidates, White Voters: Understanding Racial Bias in Political Perceptions," *American Journal of Political Science* 39 (February, 1995): 243–65.

111. Fiorina, *Retrospective Voting in American National Elections;* Key, *The Responsible Electorate.*

112. Alfred J. Tuchfarber, Stephen E. Bennett, Andrew E. Smith, and Eric W. Rademacher, "The Republican Tidal Wave of 1994: Testing Hypotheses about Realignment, Restructuring, and Rebellion," *Political Science and Politics* 28 (1995): 689–93.

113. Samuel Popkin, *The Reasoning Voter* (Chicago: University of Chicago Press, 1991).

114. Richard R. Lau and David P. Redlawsk, "Advantages and Disadvantages of Cognitive Heuristics in Political Decision Making," *American Journal of Political Science* 45 (2001): 951–71.

115. Larry M. Bartels, "Partisanship and Voting Behavior, 1952–1996." *American Journal of Political Science* 44 (2000): 35–50.

116. Morris P. Fiorina, "Keystone Reconsidered," in *Congress Reconsidered,* 8th ed., ed. Lawrence Dodd and Bruce Oppenheimer (Washington, DC: CQ Press, 2004), pp. 159–177.

117. James Campbell and James Garrand, *Forecasting Presidential Elections* (Beverley Hills, CA: Sage Publications, 2000).

118. For 2006 exit poll data, see Pew Research Center, "Public Cheers Democratic Victory," November 16, 2006, available at http://people-press.org/reports/display.php3?ReportID=296 (accessed 3/31/08).

119. For data on presidential approval and evaluations of Congress in normal and nationalized elections, see Pew Research Center, "Democrats Hold Double-Digit Lead in Competitive Districts," October 6, 2006, available at http://people-press.org/reports/display.php3?ReportID=293 (accessed 3/31/08).

120. For 2006 exit poll data, see Pew Research Center, "Public Cheers Democratic Victory," November 16, 2006, available at http://people-press.org/reports/display.php3?ReportID=296 (accessed 3/31/08).

Comparing Ourselves to Others

a. For details on proportional representation in these countries, see Michael Gallagher, Michael Laver, and Peter Mair, *Representation of Government in Modern Europe* (London, UK: McGraw-Hill Europe, 2000).

b. Lani Guinier, "No Two Seats: The Elusive Quest for Political Equality," *Virginia Law Review* 77 (1991): 1414–28.

Challenging Conventional Wisdom

a. David Plotz, "The House Incumbent: He Can't Lose," *Slate*, November 3, 2000, available at http://www.slate.com/id/92692 (accessed 4/1/08).

b. Samuel Issacharoff and Jonathan Nagler, "Our Insulated Congress," *Pittsburgh Post-Gazette*, October 27, 2006, available at http://www.post-gazette.com/pg/06300/733341-109.stm (accessed 4/1/08).

c. Isscharoff and Nagler, "Our Insulated Congress."

d. Cherie Maestas, Sarah Fulton, Walter Stone, and L. Sandy Maisel, "When to Risk It: Institutions, Ambition and the Decision to Run for the U.S. House," *American Political Science Review* 100 (2006): 195–208.

e. Jonathan S. Krasno, Donald P. Green, and Jonathan A. Cowden, "The Dynamics of Campaign Fundraising in House Elections," *The Journal of Politics* 56 (1994): 459–74.

f. Brandice Canes-Wrone, David W. Brady, and John F. Cogan, "Out of Step, Out of Office: Electoral Accountability and House Members' Voting," *American Political Science Review* 96(2002): 127–40. Gary C. Jacobson and Michael A. Dimock, "Checking Out: The Effects of Bank Overdrafts on the 1992 House Elections," *American Journal of Political Science* 38 (1994): 601–24.

g. David Mayhew, *Congress: The Electoral Connection* (New Haven, CT: Yale University Press, 1973) p. 36.

Politics Is Everywhere

a. Wendy M. Rahn, "Candidate Evaluation in Complex Information Environments," in *Political Judgment*, ed. Milton Lodge and Kathleen M. McGraw (Ann Arbor, MI: University of Michigan Press, 1995) pp. 43–64. The term *motivated tactician* was coined by Susan Fiske; see Susan T. Fiske, "Social Cognition and Perception," *Annual Review of Psychology* 44 (1993): 155–94.

b. Walter Lippman, *Public Opinion* (New York: MacMillan, 1922), p. 89.

c. Morris P. Fiorina, Jon Krosnick, and Samuel J, Abrams, "The Economist/YouGov 2004 Presidential Election Internet Poll: Post-Conventions Report," 2004, available at http://www.economist.com/media/pdf/Post-Conventions.pdf (accessed 3/31/08).

CHAPTER 9

1. Massie Ritsch and Courtney Mabeus, "Casting off Abramoff," *Capital Eye,* April 6, 2006, Center for Responsive Politics, available at http://www.capitaleye.org/inside.asp?ID=210 (accessed 4/3/08).

2. Jacob Weisberg, "Three Cities, Three Scandals: What Jack Abramoff, Anthony Pellicano, and Jared Paul Stern have in Common," *Slate,* April 9, 2006, available at http://www.slate.com/id/2140238 (accessed 4/4/08).

3. Associated Press, "Others Caught Up in Abramoff Scandal," *New York Times,* March 23, 2007, available at http://www.nytimes.com/aponline/us/AP-Griles-Abramoff-Glance.htm (accessed 4/5/07). Associated Press, "Former Deputy Interior Secretary to Plead Guilty in Lobbyist Case," *New York Times,* March 23, 2007, available at http://www.nytimes.com/aponline/washington/AP-Griles-Abramoff.html (accessed 4/5/07).

4. Timothy Noah, "Duke Cunningham's Little Helpers," *Slate,* October 18, 2006, http://www.slate.com/id/2151748 (accessed 4/5/08).

5. Pew Research Center, "Public Disillusionment with Congress at Record Levels," April 20, 2006, available at http://people-press.org/reports/display.php3?ReportID=275 (accessed 4/6/08); Pew Research Center, "Americans Taking Abramoff, Alito and Domestic Spying in Stride," January 11, 2006, available at http://people-press.org/reports/display.php3?ReportID=267 (accessed 4/6/08).

6. Mancur Olson, *The Logic of Collective Action,* 2nd ed. (Cambridge, MA: Harvard University Press, 1971).

7. The quote is in *Federalist 10.* See John Jay, Alexander Hamilton, and James Madison, *The Federalist Papers* (1788; repr. New York: Modern Library, 2000).

8. Robert A. Dahl, *A Preface to Democratic Theory* (Chicago: University of Chicago Press, 1951); and David Truman, *The Governmental Process* (New York: Harper and Row, 1951).

9. Theodore Lowi, *The End of Liberalism: The Second Republic of the United States* (New York: W. W. Norton, 1979).

10. Lobbying regulations are often changed; the discussion here is just a general guide. Regular reports on past, current, and proposed lobbying regulations can be found on the Web site of the Congressional Research Service at http://www.opencrs.com.

11. Jeffrey Birnbaum, "The Road to Riches Is Called K Street," *Washington Post,* June 22, 2006, p. A1.

12. Frank Baumgartner and Beth Leech, *Basic Interests: The Importance of Interest Groups in Politics and In Political Science* (Princeton, NJ: Princeton University Press, 1999), p. 109.

13. Frances Cairncross, *The Death of Distance: How the Communication Revolution Is Changing Our Lives* (Cambridge, MA: Harvard Business School Press, 2001).

14. Leslie Wayne, "Documents Show Extent of Lobbying by Boeing," *New York Times,* September 3, 2003.

15. Center for Responsive Politics, Lobbying Spending Database, "General Electric Summary, 2006," available at http://www.opensecrets.org/lobbyists/clientsum.asp?txtname=General+Electric&year=2006 (accessed 4/7/08).

16. Center for Responsive Politics, Lobbying Spending Database, "Sierra Club Summary, 2006," available at http://www.opensecrets.org/lobbyists/clientsum.asp?txtname=Sierra+Club&year=2006 (accessed 4/7/08).

17. For more on this argument, see Tim Harford, "There's Not Enough Money in Politics," *Slate,* April 1, 2006, available at http://www.slate.com/id/2138874 (accessed 4/8/08); and Stephen Ansolabehere, John M. de Figueiredo, and James M. Snyder, "Why Is There So Little Money in American Politics?" *Journal of Economic Perspectives* 17 (2003): 105–30.

18. See Coalition for Luggage Security, "About the Coalition for Luggage Security," available at http://www.luggagesecuritycoalition.com/about.asp (accessed 4/9/08).

19. For details on the AFL-CIO's lobbying operations, see AFL-CIO, "Issues: Main Topics," available at http://www.aflcio.org/issues (accessed 4/8/08).

20. Family Research Council, "About Family Research Council," available at http://www.frc.org/get.cfm?c=ABOUT_FRC (accessed 4/8/08).

21. Baumgartner and Leech, *Basic Interests,* Chapter 6, pp. 100–19.

22. For a discussion of these events, see William Bianco, *Trust: Representatives and Constituents,* Chapter 6 (Ann Arbor, MI: University of Michigan Press, 1994) pp. 123–46.

23. John R. Wright, *Interest Groups and Congress: Lobbying, Contributions, and Influence* (New York: Longman, 1995).

24. Scott Ainsworth, *Analyzing Interest Groups: Group Influence on People and Policies* (New York: W. W. Norton, 2002).

25. Timothy Egan, "For Thirsty Farmers, Old Friends at Interior," *New York Times,* March 3, 2006, p. A1.

26. Public Citizen Congress Watch, "Congressional Revolving Doors: The Journey from Congress to K Street," July 2005, available at http://www.lobbyinginfo.org/documents/RevolveDoor.pdf (accessed 4/9/08).

27. Eric Lipton, "Former Antiterror Officials Find Industry Pays Better," *New York Times*, June 18, 2006, p. A1.

28. Revolving Door Working Group, "A Matter of Trust: How the Revolving Door Undermines Public Confidence in Government—And What to Do about It," October 2005, available at http://www.revolvingdoor.info/docs/matter-of-trust_final-full.pdf (accessed 4/7/08).

29. Sierra Club, http://www.sierraclub.org (accessed 5/22/08).

30. Robert H. Salisbury, John P. Heinz, Edward O. Laumann, and Robert L. Nelson, "Who Works with Whom? Interest Group Alliances and Opposition," *American Political Science Review* 81 (1987): 1217–34.

31. Business-Industry Political Action Committee, "About BIPAC," available at http://www.bipac.org/about/about.asp (accessed 4/8/08).

32. One example campaign is MoveOn.org Political Action Committee, "Letter to the Editor: Tell the Media: We Want to End the War. The President Wants Endless War," available at http://pol.moveon.org/lte/?lte_campaign_id=72 (accessed 4/8/08).

33. Focus on the Family, "Volunteers," available at http://www.focusonthefamily.com/volunteers (accessed 4/8/08).

34. National Paper Trade Association Alliance, "Senate Debate on EFCA to Begin," available at http://www.gonpta.com/report/articles/article.cfm?ArticleID=1491 (accessed 4/8/08).

35. Thomas Holyoke, "Choosing Battlegrounds: Interest Group Lobbying Across Multiple Venues," *Political Science Quarterly* 56 (2003): 325–36.

36. Scott Ainsworth, "Regulating Lobbyists and Interest Group Influence," *The Journal of Politics* 55 (1993): 41–55.

37. American Association of Retired Persons, "Policy and Research for Professionals in Aging," available at http://www.aarp.org/research/ppi (accessed 4/8/08).

38. "Breaking the Silver Ceiling," Testimony before the Senate Special Committee on Aging, September 20, 2004, available at http://www.aarp.org/research/press-center/testimony/a2004-09-22-aging.html (accessed 4/8/08).

39. Sidney Verba, Kay Lehman Schlozman, and Henry Brady. *Voice and Equality: Civic Participation in America* (Cambridge, MA: Harvard University Press, 1995).

40. John Clifford Green, Mark J. Rozell, and Clyde Wilcox, *Prayer in the Precincts: The Christian Right in the 1998 Elections* (Washington, DC: Georgetown University Press, 2000).

41. James Q. Wilson, *Political Organizations* (New York: Basic Books, 1974).

42. Casey Ichniowski and Jeffrey S. Zax, "Right to Work Laws, Free Riders, and Unionization in the Local Public Sector," *Journal of Labor Economics* 9 (1991): 255–69.

43. Sierra Club, "Join or Give," available at http://www.sierraclub.org/membership (accessed 4/8/08).

44. National Rifle Association, "Your NRA Membership," available at http://www.nra.org/benefits.aspx (accessed 4/8/08).

45. American Automobile Association, Foundation for Traffic Safety, available at http://www.aaafoundation.org/home (accessed 4/8/08).

46. Kenneth Kollman, *Outside Lobbying: Public Opinion and Interest Group Strategies* (Princeton, NJ: Princeton University Press, 1998).

47. Robert Salisbury, "An Exchange Theory of Interest Groups," *Midwest Journal of Political Science* 13 (1969): 1–32.

48. Jack Walker, *Mobilizing Interest Groups in America* (Ann Arbor, MI: University of Michigan Press, 1991).

49. Schattschneider, E. E. *The Semi-Sovereign People* (New York: Harper and Row, 1960).

50. Walker, *Mobilizing Interest Groups in America.*

51. Kollman, *Outside Lobbying.*

52. Walker, *Mobilizing Interest Groups in America.*

53. Derived from a search of the congressional lobbying disclosure database at http://idsearch.house.gov/idsearch.aspx (accessed 7/4/08).

54. John P. Heinz, Edward O. Laumann, and Robert Salisbury, *The Hollow Core: Private Interests in National Policymaking* (Cambridge, MA: Harvard University Press, 1993).

55. Richard L. Hall and Alan V. Deardorff, "Lobbying as Legislative Subsidy," *American Political Science Review* 100 (2006): 69–84.

56. Hall and Deardorff, "Lobbying as Legislative Subsidy."

57. Schlozman and Tierney, *Organized Interests and American Democracy.*

58. Baumgartner and Leech, *Basic Interests*, p. 152.

59. Matt Kelly and Peter Eisler, "Relatives Have 'Inside Track' on Lobbying for Tax Dollars," *USA Today*, October 17, 2006.

60. Christine A. DeGregorio, *Networks of Champions: Leadership, Access, and Advocacy in the U.S. House of Representatives* (Ann Arbor, MI: University of Michigan Press, 1992).

61. Daniel Carpenter, *The Forging of Bureaucratic Autonomy: Reputations, Networks, and Policy Innovation in Executive Agencies, 1862–1928* (Princeton, NJ: Princeton University Press, 2002).

62. For these and other Public Citizen reports, see http://www.citizen.org.

63. Derived from a search of the AARP site, http://www.aarp.org.

64. Derived from a search of the NRA Institute for Legislative Action site, http://www.nraila.org.

65. Kim Scheppele and Jack L. Walker, "The Litigation Strategies of Interest Groups," in *Mobilizing Interest Groups in America*, ed., Jack Walker (Ann Arbor, MI: University of Michigan Press, 1991).

66. Juan Williams and Julian Bond, *Eyes on the Prize: America's Civil Rights Years, 1954–1965* (New York: Penguin, 1988).

67. See American Civil Liberties Union, "USA PATRIOT Act," available at http://action.aclu.org/reformthepatriotact (accessed 4/8/08).

68. Lauren Cohen Bell, *Warring Factions: Interest Groups, Money, and the New Politics of Senate Confirmation* (Columbus, OH: Ohio State University Press, 2002).

69. Michael T. Meaney, "Brokering Health Policy: Coalitions, Parties, and Interest Group Influence," *Journal of Health Politics, Policy, and Law* 31 (2006): 887–923.

70. Kevin W. Hula, *Lobbying Together: Interest Group Coalitions in Legislative Politics.* (Washington, DC: Georgetown University Press, 1999).

71. Marie Hojnacki, "Interest Groups' Decisions to Join Alliances or Work Alone," *American Journal of Political Science* 41 (1997): 61–87

72. American Association of Retired Persons, "Elected Officials," available at http://capwiz.com/aarp/dbq/officials (accessed 4/8/08).

73. Michelle Boorstein, "Protesters See Mood Shift against 'Roe,'" *Washington Post*, January 24, 2006, p. A3.

74. Richard Fenno, *Home Style: U.S. House Members in Their Districts* (Boston: Little, Brown, 1978). See also Brandice Caines-Wrone, David W. Brady, and John F. Cogan, "Out of Step, Out of Office: Electoral Accountability and House Members' Voting," *American Political Science Review* 96 (2002) 127–40.

75. Kollman, *Outside Lobbying.*

76. Gregory Calderia, Marie Hojnacki, and John R. Wright, "The Lobbying Activities of Organized Interests in Federal Judicial Nominations," *The Journal of Politics* 62 (2000): 51–69.

77. Robert Pear, "Medicare Law Prompts a Rush for Lobbyists," *New York Times*, August 23, 2005.

78. For these and other campaign finance data, see the Federal Election Commission Web site at http://www.fec.gov, or the Center for Responsive Politics site at http://www.opensecrets.org.

79. The ads can be seen at the Swift Vets and POWs for Truth site, http://www.swiftvets.com.

80. Pew Research Center, "Kerry Support Rebounds, Race Again Even," September 16, 2004, available at http://people-press.org/reports/print.php3?PageID=879 (accessed 4/9/08).

81. John R. Wright, "PAC Contributions, Lobbying, and Representation," *Journal of Politics* 51:3 (August, 1989), 713–29.

82. John G. Matsusaka, "Direct Democracy and Fiscal Gridlock: Have Voter Initiatives Paralyzed the California Budget?" *State Politics and Policy* 5 (2005): 346–62.

83. Thad Kousser, *Term Limits and the Dismantling of State Legislative Professionalism* (New York: Cambridge University Press, 2004).

84. John G. Matsusaka, *For the Many or the Few: The Initiative, Public Policy, and American Democracy* (Chicago: University of Chicago Press, 2004).

85. Elizabeth R. Gerber, *The Populist Paradox: Interest Group Influence and the Promise of Direct Legislation* (Princeton, NJ: Princeton University Press, 1999).

86. Baumgartner and Leech, *Basic Interests,* Chapter 8, pp. 147-67.

87. Jeffrey Birnbaum, "The Humane Society Becomes a Political Animal," *Washington Post,* January 30, 2007, p. A15.

88. For this testimony, see "Testimony of Gary R. Bachula, Vice President, Internet2 before the Senate Committee on Commerce, Science and Transportation," Hearing on Net Neutrality, February 7, 2006, available at http://www.educause.edu/ir/library/pdf/EPO0611.pdf (accessed 4/9/08). For details on the net neutrality debate, see Tim Wu, "Network Neutrality FAQ," available at http://www.timwu.org/network_neutrality.html (accessed 4/9/08).

89. Tim Wu, "Does YouTube Really Have Legal Problems?" *Slate,* October 26, 2006, available at http://www.slate.com/id/2152264 (accessed 4/9/08); and Tim Wu, "Ma Bell Is Back: Should You Be Afraid?" *Slate,* January 4, 2007, http://www.slate.com/id/2156918 (accessed 4/9/08).

90. Jeffrey H. Birnbaum, "The Forces That Set the Agenda," *Washington Post,* April 24, 2005, p. B1.

91. For a review, see Carpenter, *The Forging of Bureaucratic Autonomy.*

92. Baumgartner and Leech, *Basic Interests*, Chapter 7, especially, Table 7.1 and Table 7.2, pp. 130 and 132.

93. Baumgartner and Leech, *Basic Interests*, p. 133.

94. National Rifle Association Institute for Legislative Action, "Fact Sheet: Right-to-Carry 2007," available at http://www.nraila.org/Issues/FactSheets/Read.aspx?ID=18 (accessed 4/9/08).

95. National Rifle Association Institute for Legislative Action, "Fact Sheet: Right-to-Carry: The Stearns/Boucher Right-to-Carry Reciprocity Bill," available at http://www.nraila.org/Issues/FactSheets/Read.aspx?id=189&issue=003 (accessed 4/9/08).

96. Quoted in William Saletan, "The Money Jungle," *Slate,* March 22, 2001, available at http://slate.msn.com/id/102994 (accessed 4/9/08).

97. Sheryl Gay Stolberg, "The 2004 Elections: Gracious but Defeated, Daschle Makes History," *New York Times*, September 8, 2004, p. 8.

98. Richard L. Hall and Frank W. Wayman, "Buying Time: Moneyed Interests and the Mobilization of Ideas in Congressional Committees," *American Political Science Review* 84 (1990): 797–820.

99. Baumgartner and Leech, *Basic Interests*, Chapter 7, pp. 120–46.

100. John M. Berry, *The Interest Group Society* (New York: Harper Collins, 1997); Raymond A. Bauer, Ithiel de Sola Pool, and Lewis Dexter, *American Business and Public Policy* (New York: Atherton Press, 1963).

101. David Austen-Smith and Jack Wright, "Counteractive Lobbying," *American Journal of Political Science* 38 (1994): 25–44; Baumgartner and Leech, "The Multiple Ambiguities of 'Counteractive Lobbying.'"

Comparing Ourselves to Others

a. Mancur Olson. *The Rise and Decline of Nations* (Cambridge, MA: Harvard University Press, 1984).

b. James E. Curtis, Douglas E. Baer, and Edward G. Grubb, "Nations of Joiners: Explaining Voluntary Association Membership in Democratic Societies," *American Sociological Review* 66 (2001): 783–805.

c. Michael Gallagher, Peter Mair, and Michael Laver, *Representative Government in Modern Europe* (New York: McGraw-Hill, 2005).

d. Fritz Plasser and Gunda Plasser, *Global Political Campaigning: A Worldwide Analysis of Campaign Professionals and Their Practices* (New York: Praeger, 2002).

e. Daniel Nelson, "Supplying Trade Reform: Political Institutions and Liberalization in Middle-Income Presidential Democracies," *American*

Journal of Political Science 47 (2003): 470–93; Nina Rudra, "Globalization and the Decline of the Welfare State in Less-Developed Countries," *International Organization* 56 (2002): 411–45.

f. Justin Greenwood, *Interest Representation in the European Parliament* (London, UK: Palgrave Macmillan, 2003).

You Decide

a. For the full text of this proposal, see League of Women Voters et al., "Ethics and Lobbying Reform: Six Benchmarks for Lobbying Reform," January 23, 2006, available at http://www.lwv.org.

Challenging Conventional Wisdom

a. Jacob Weisberg, "The Great Microsoft Lobbying Swindle," *Slate,* April 12, 2000, available at http://slate.msn.com/id/1005085 (accessed 4/12/08).

b. Amy Harmon, "U.S. vs. Microsoft: The Overview: Judge Backs Terms of U.S. Settlement in Microsoft Case," *New York Times,* November 2, 2002, p. A1.

c. Weisberg, "The Great Microsoft Lobbying Swindle."

d. Raymond A. Bauer, Ithiel de Sola Pool, and Lewis Dexter, *American Business and Public Policy* (New York: Atherton Press, 1963).

CHAPTER 10

1. Charles R. Babcock and Jonathan Weisman, "Congressman Admits Taking Bribes, Resigns: GOP's Cunningham Faces Jail Term," *Washington Post*, November 29, 2005, p. A1.

2. Quoted in Stephen Goode, "Congress: A Laughing Matter: History of Political Humor," *Insight on the News*, July 22, 1996, available at http://findarticles.com/p/articles/mi_m1571/is_n27_v12/ai_18486848. (accessed 5/3/08)

3. John F. Kennedy, *Profiles in Courage* (New York: Harper and Brothers, 1956), p. 1.

4. Joseph Martin Hernon, *Profiles in Character: Hubris and Heroism in the U.S. Senate, 1789–1990* (Armonk, NY: M. E. Sharpe, 1997) provides many other examples of responsible and even heroic actions in the Senate.

5. Kennedy, *Profiles in Courage*, p. 3.

6. Quoted in Alan I. Abramowitz and Jeffrey A Segal, *Senate Elections* (Ann Arbor, MI: University of Michigan Press, 1992), p. 231.

7. See Paul Gronke, *The Electorate, the Campaign, and the Office: A Unified Approach to Senate and House Elections* (Ann Arbor, MI: University of Michigan Press, 2000), for research showing the House and Senate elections share many similar characteristics. See Richard F. Fenno, *Senators on the Campaign Trail: The Politics of Representation* (Norman, OK: University of Oklahoma Press, 1996), for a good general discussion of Senate elections.

8. Five polls taken between April 28 and May 12, 2008, pegged Congress's approval rating between 16 and 22 percent, with a 19.2 percent average. PollingReport.com, "Congress: Job Rating in National Polls," available at http://www.pollingreport.com/CongJob.htm. (accessed 5/3/08)

9. All poll data except the poll comparing Congress to other occupations are from PollingReport.com (http://www.pollingreport.com). The occupations poll was cited in Karlyn Bowman and Everett Carll Ladd, "Public Opinion toward Congress: A Historical Look," in *Congress, the Press, and the Public*, ed. Thomas E. Mann and Norman J. Ornstein (Washington, DC: Brookings Institution Press, 1994), p. 50.

10. "Check bouncing" is in quotes because the checks did not actually bounce. The scandal involved penalty-free overdrafts permitted in members' accounts in the House bank (which allowed some members to abuse the privilege by using the overdrafts as short-term, interest-free loans). Many voters saw this as another unfair benefit to members of Congress, while others considered it a nonscandal because no taxpayers' money was at stake.

11. Robert S. Lichter and Daniel R. Amundson, "Less News Is Worse News: Television News Coverage of Congress, 1972–1992," in *Congress, the Press, and the Public*, ed. Thomas E. Mann and Norman J. Ornstein (Washington, DC: Brookings Institution Press, 1994), p. 136.

12. Mark J. Rozell, "Press Coverage of Congress, 1946–1992," in *Congress, the Press, and the Public,* ed. Thomas E. Mann and Norman J. Ornstein (Washington, DC: Brookings Institution Press, 1994), p. 110.

13. Burdett A. Loomis, *The Contemporary Congress* (Belmont, CA: Wadsworth, 2000), p. 47.

14. R. Douglas Arnold, *Congress, the Press, and Political Accountability* (Princeton, NJ: Princeton University Press, 2004), p. 80.

15. David R. Mayhew, *Congress: The Electoral Connection* (New Haven, CT: Yale University Press, 1974).

16. Patrick J. Sellers, "Fiscal Consistency and Federal District Spending in Congressional Elections," *American Journal of Political Science* 41:3 (July, 1997): 1024–41.

17. David T. Canon, *Race, Redistricting, and Representation: The Unintended Consequences of Black Majority Districts in the U.S. House* (Chicago: University of Chicago Press, 1999); Katherine Tate, *Black Faces in the Mirror: African Americans and Their Representatives in the U.S. Congress* (Princeton, NJ: Princeton University Press, 2003).

18. Claudine Gay, "Spirals of Trust? The Effect of Descriptive Representation on the Relationship between Citizens and Their Government," *American Journal of Political Science* 46:4 (October, 2002): 717–32; Tate, *Black Faces in the Mirror*, Chapter 7. However, Tate shows that African Americans who are represented by African Americans in Congress are not any more likely to vote, be involved in politics, or have higher overall approval rates of Congress than African Americans who are not descriptively represented.

19. A. Phillips Griffiths, quoted in Anne Phillips, *The Politics of Presence* (New York: Clarendon Press/Oxford University Press, 1995), p. 39. However, Senator Roman Hruska of Nebraska challenged Griffiths's argument, at least in the context of the Supreme Court. In defending President Nixon's appointee to the Supreme Court, G. Harrold Carswell, Hruska said, "Even if he were mediocre, there are a lot of mediocre judges and people and lawyers. They are entitled to a little representation, aren't they, and a little chance? We can't have all Brandeises and Frankfurters and Cardozos and stuff like that." Michael Barone, Grant Ujifusa, and Douglas Matthews, *The Almanac of American Politics* (New York: Dutton, 1975), p. 494. Note that "stuff like that" refers to three of the country's greatest justices.

20. Richard E. Cohen, *Changing Course in Washington: Clinton and the New Congress* (New York: Macmillian, 1994), pp. 210–11.

21. R. Douglas Arnold, *The Logic of Congressional Action* (New Haven, CT: Yale University Press, 1990), pp. 60–71.

22. Richard F. Fenno, *Home Style: House Members in Their Districts* (Boston: Little, Brown, 1978).

23. Dan Eggen, "Justice Staff Saw Texas Districting as Illegal: Voting Rights Finding on Map Pushed by DeLay Was Overruled," *Washington Post*, December 2, 2005, p. A1. The court case is *League of United Latin American Citizens v. Perry*, 547 U.S. (2006).

24. David T. Canon, "History in the Making: The 2nd District in Wisconsin," in *The Battle for Congress: Candidates, Consultants, and Voters,* ed. James A. Thurber (Washington, DC: Brookings Institution Press, 2001), pp. 199–238.

25. Gary C. Jacobson, *The Politics of Congressional Elections*, 5th ed. (New York: Longman, 2001), pp. 24–30.

26. Fenno, *Home Style.*

27. Gary C. Jacobson and Samuel Kernell, *Strategy and Choice in Congressional Elections* (New Haven, CT: Yale University Press, 1983).

28. Mayhew, *Congress*, p. 17.

29. Mayhew, *Congress*, p. 37.

30. Jonathan Weisman and Jim VandeHei, "Road Bill Reflects the Power of Pork; White House Drops Effort to Rein in Hill, *Washington Post,* August 11, 2005, p. A1.

31. Weisman and VandeHei, "Road Bill Reflects the Power of Pork."

32. An important qualification to the norm was imposed by Republicans in 1995 when they set a six-year term limit for committee and subcommittee chairs.

33. David W. Rohde, *Parties and Leaders in the Postreform House* (Chicago: University of Chicago Press, 1991).

34. David Rohde and John Aldrich, "The Transition to Republican Rule in the House: Implications for Theories of Congressional Politics," *Political Science Quarterly* 112:4 (Winter, 1997–1998): 541–67.

35. Nelson W. Polsby, *Congress and the Presidency,* 4th ed. (Englewood Cliffs, NJ: Prentice Hall, 1986), p. 111.

36. The beneficiaries of President Bush's fundraising assistance were Senate candidates Michael Steele of Maryland and Mark Kennedy of Minnesota, Senator Jon Kyl (R-AZ), and Representative Marilyn Musgrave (R-CO).

37. "James Traficant Hearing; Kick Them in the Crotch," available at http://www.youtube.com/watch?v=tQ5Os1400uc&feature=related. (accessed 5/7/08)

38. David E. Price, "Congressional Committees in the Policy Process," in *Congress Reconsidered,* 3rd ed., ed. Lawrence C. Dodd and Bruce I. Oppenheimer (Washington, DC: CQ Press, 1985), pp. 161–88.

39. Richard F. Fenno, *Congressmen in Committees* (Boston: Little, Brown, 1973).

40. Richard L. Hall, *Participation in Congress* (New Haven, CT: Yale University Press, 1996).

41. Barbara Sinclair, *Unorthodox Lawmaking* (Washington, DC: CQ Press, 2000), p. xiv.

42. Sinclair, *Unorthodox Lawmaking,* p. 59.

43. Louis Fisher, "The Pocket Veto: Its Current Status," Congressional Research Service Report RL30909, March 30, 2001. The appeals court case was *Barnes v. Kline* 759 F.2d 21 (D.C. Cir., 1985).

44. Howard H. Baker Jr., Leaders Lecture Series address to the Senate (Washington, DC, July 14, 1998) available at http://www.senate.gov/artandhistory/history/common/generic/ Leaders_Lecture_Series_Baker.htm. (accessed 5/7/08)

45. Mathew McCubbins and Thomas Schwartz, "Congressional Oversight Overlooked: Police Patrol versus Fire Alarm," *American Journal of Political Science* 28:1 (February, 1984): 165–77.

46. *Immigration and Naturalization Service v. Chadha,* 462 U.S. 919 (1983).

Challenging Conventional Wisdom

a. CBS News/*New York Times* poll, January 20–25, 2006, available at http://www.pollingreport.com/politics2.htm.

b. Grew Wawro, "A Panel Probit Analysis of Campaign Contributions and Roll-Call Votes," *American Journal of Political Science* 45:3 (July, 2001): 563–79; Janet M. Grenzke, "PACs and the Congressional Supermarket: The Currency Is Complex," *American Journal of Political Science* 33:1 (January, 1989): 1–24. However, one study found that money may buy more access on congressional committees, if not votes; see Richard L. Hall and Frank M. Wayman, "Buying Time: Moneyed Interests and the Mobilization of Bias in Congress," *American Political Science Review* 84 (1990): 797–820.

c. Kenneth R. Mayer, "Political Realities and Unintended Consequences: Why Campaign Finance Reform Is Too Important to Be Left to the Lawyers," *University of Richmond Law Review* 37:4 (May, 2003): 1069–110.

Politics Is Everywhere

a. Morris Fiorina, *Congress: Keystone of the Washington Establishment,* rev. ed. (New Haven: Yale University Press, 1989).

b. See Representative Tammy Baldwin's site, http://tammybaldwin.house.gov.

You Decide

a. Joseph Lieberman, "Lieberman Opposes Last Minute Republican Gifts to Special Interests," press statement, November 19, 2002, available at http://www.senate.gov/~govt-aff/111902press3.htm.

b. Helen Dewar, "Senate Passes Homeland Security Bill: Bush Calls Step 'Historic and Bold,'" *Washington Post,* November 20, 2002, p. A1.

Comparing Ourselves to Others

a. Information was drawn from John M. Carey, "Legislative Organization," in *Oxford Handbook of Political Institutions,* Sarah Binder, Rod Rhodes, and Bert Rockman, ed. (New York: Oxford University Press, 2005); Gerhard Lowenberg, Peverill Squire, and D. Roderick Kiewiet, ed., *Legislatures: Comparative Perspectives on Representative Assemblies* (Ann Arbor, MI: University of Michigan Press, 2002); and Gary W. Cox, "The Organization of Democratic Legislatures," in *Oxford Handbook of Political Economy,* Barry Weingast and Donald Wittman, ed. (New York: Oxford University Press, 2005).

CHAPTER 11

1. John Nichols, "The On-Line Beat: Arthur Schlesinger vs. the Imperial President," *The Nation,* March 1, 2007, available at http://www.thenation.com/blogs/thebeat?pid=170728 (accessed 4/29/08).

2. David G. Adler, "The Law: George Bush as Commander in Chief: Toward the Nether World of Constitutionalism," *Presidential Studies Quarterly* 36 (2006): 525–40.

3. Stephen Skowronek, *The Politics Presidents Make: Leadership From John Adams to Bill Clinton* (Cambridge, MA: Harvard University Press, 1997).

4. John Aldrich, *Why Parties?* (Chicago: University of Chicago Press, 1995).

5. Ernest R. May, *The Making of the Monroe Doctrine* (Cambridge, MA: Harvard University Press, 1975).

6. Arthur M. Schlesinger Jr., *The Age of Jackson* (Boston: Little, Brown, 1945).

7. David Greenberg, "Lincoln's Crackdown," *Slate,* November 30, 2001, available at http://www.slate.com/id/2059132 (accessed 4/29/08).

8. Steven Skowronek, *Building a New American State: The Expansion of National Administrative Capacities* (New York: Cambridge University Press, 1982).

9. Theda Skocpol, *Protecting Soldiers and Mothers: The Political Origins of Social Policy in the United States* (Cambridge, MA: Harvard University Press, 1995).

10. Kendrick Clements, *The Presidency of Woodrow Wilson* (Lawrence, KS: University Press of Kansas, 1992).

11. Thomas J. Knock, *To End All Wars: Woodrow Wilson and the Quest for a New World Order* (New York: Oxford University Press, 1992).

12. Arthur M. Schlesinger Jr., *The Crisis of the Old Order, 1919–1933* (Boston: Houghton Mifflin, 1957).

13. William E. Leuchtenburg, *FDR Years: On Roosevelt and His Legacy* (New York: Columbia University Press, 1995).

14. Chester Pach and Elmo Richardson, *The Presidency of Dwight D. Eisenhower* (Lawrence, KS: University Press of Kansas, 1991).

15. Alexander Russo, "Flunking Out," *Slate,* August 28, 2003, available at http://www.slate.com/id/2087654 (accessed 4/29/08).

16. Executive Order no. 13425, "Trial of Alien Unlawful Enemy Combatants by Military Commission," February 14, 2007, available at http://www.fas.org/irp/offdocs/eo/eo-13425.htm (accessed 4/29/08).

17. Thomas J. Weko, *The Politicizing Presidency: The White House Personnel Office, 1948–1994,* (Lawrence, KS: University Press of Kansas, 1995).

18. Walter Dellinger and Dahlia Lithwick, "A Supreme Court Conversation," *Slate,* June 22, 2007, available at http://www.slate.com/id/2168856/entry/2168959 (accessed 4/29/08).

19. Kevin Flynn and William K. Rashbaum, "An Aborted Nomination: The Nominee's Past; Beyond the Disclosure about Kerik's Nanny, More Questions Were Lurking," *New York Times,* December 13, 2004.

20. Helen Cooper, "Votes in Doubt, Bolton Resigns as Ambassador," *New York Times,* December 5, 2006.

21. Kenneth Mayer, *With the Stroke of a Pen: Executive Orders and Presidential Power* (Princeton, NJ: Princeton University Press, 2001).

22. Kenneth Mayer and Kevin Price, "Unilateral Presidential Powers: Significant Executive Orders, 1949–1999," *Presidential Studies Quarterly* 32 (2002): 367–85.

23. David G. Adler, "The Constitution and Presidential Warmaking: An Enduring Debate," *Political Science Quarterly* 103 (1988): 1–36.

24. Richard F. Grimmett, "The War Powers Resolution: After Thirty Years," Congressional Research Service Report RL32267, March 11, 2004.

25. Lewis Fisher and David G. Adler, "The War Powers Resolution: Time to Say Goodbye," *Political Science Quarterly,* 113:1 (1998): 1–20.

26. William G. Howell and Jon C. Pevehouse, *While Dangers Gather: Congressional Checks on Presidential War Powers* (Princeton, NJ: Princeton University Press, 2007).

27. John M. Broder, "The Climate Accord: The Overview; Clinton Adamant on Third World Role in Climate Accord," *New York Times,* December 12, 1997, pp. A1, A16.

28. Stephen M. Walt, "Two Cheers for Clinton's Foreign Policy," *Foreign Affairs* 79 (2000): 30–45.

29. Richard M. Stevenson, "The Nation; The High-Stakes Politics of Spending the Surplus," *New York Times,* January 7, 2001.

30. Ivo H. Daalder and James M. Lindsay, *America Unbound: The Bush Revolution in American Foreign Policy* (Washington, DC: Brookings Institution Press, 2003).

31. Mark A. Peterson, *Legislating Together: The White House and Capitol Hill from Eisenhower to Reagan* (Cambridge, MA: Harvard University Press, 1990).

32. Andrew Rudalevige, *Managing the President's Program: Presidential Leadership and Legislative Policy Formation* (Princeton, NJ: Princeton University Press, 2002).

33. "Campaign 2000: Today—Abortion; The Enduring Battle Over Choice," *New York Times,* October 11, 2000.

34. Charles Cameron and Nolan M. McCarty, "Models of Vetoes and Veto Bargaining," *Annual Review of Political Science* 7 (2004): 409–35.

35. Keith Krehbiel, *Pivotal Politics: A Theory of U.S. Lawmaking* (Chicago: University of Chicago Press, 1998).

36. Charles Jones, *The Presidency in a Separated System* (Washington, DC: Brookings Institution Press, 1994).

37. Jacob Weisberg, "Bush's First Defeat," *Slate,* March 21, 2005, available at http://www.slate.com/id/2115141 (accessed 4/29/08).

38. Mickey Kaus, "Has the GOP Found Its 2006 Issue?" *Slate,* March 20, 2006, available at http://www.slate.com/id/2138371 (accessed 4/29/08).

39. Michael Abramowitz, "Commuting Libby's Sentence 'Fair' Bush Says," *Washington Post,* July 13, 2007, p. A5.

40. Mark J. Rozell, "The Law: Executive Privilege: Definition and Standards of Application" *Presidential Studies Quarterly* 29:4 (1999): 918–30.

41. Raoul Berger, *Executive Privilege: A Constitutional Myth* (Cambridge, MA: Harvard University Press, 1974). For commentary, see Saikrisha Prakash, "A Comment on the Constitutionality of Executive Privilege," *Minnesota Law Review* 83:5 (May, 1999): 1143–89.

42. Bruce Fein, "Executive Nonsense," *Slate,* July 11, 2007, available at http://www.slate.com/id/2170247 (accessed 4/29/08).

43. Peter Baker and Dan Eggen, "New Privilege Claim by Bush Escalates Clash over Firings," *Washington Post,* July 10, 2007, p. A3.

44. See Oyez, United States v. Nixon, 418 U.S. 683 (1974), available at http://www.oyez.org/cases/1970-1979/1974/1974_73_1766 for a summary of the case.

45. Mark J. Rozell, "Something to Hide: Clinton's Misuse of Executive Privilege," *Political Science and Politics* 32 (1999): 550–53.

46. Mark J. Rozell, *Executive Privilege: The Dilemma of Secrecy and Democratic Accountability* (Baltimore, MD: Johns Hopkins University Press, 1994).

47. Edmund L. Andrews and Robin Toner, "Bush Promises in 2000: Some Fulfilled, Others Thwarted," *New York Times,* September 1, 2004.

48. Timothy Noah, "George W., Judicial Activist," *Slate,* February 24, 2004, available at http://www.slate.com/id/2096061 (accessed 4/29/08).

49. On both points, see Robert Draper, *Dead Certain: The Presidency of George W. Bush* (New York: Free Press, 2007).

50. David Kirkpatrick, "Question of Timing on Bush's Push on Earmarks," New York Times, January 29, 2008.

51. Ben Smith and David Paul Kuhn, "Obama Moves Quickly to Reshape DNC," Politico, June 13, 2008, available at http://www.politico.com/news/stories/0608/11045.html, accessed July 2, 2008.

52. Carrie Budoff, "Is Bush's Support Worse Than No Support?" *Politico,* July 16, 2007, available at http://www.politico.com/news/stories/0707/4960.html (accessed 4/29/08).

53. John D. McKinnon, "Backing Away From Bush; Some Republican Candidates Avoid Ties with Unpopular President," *Wall Street Journal,* May 23, 2006, p. A4; Budoff, "Is Bush's Support Worse Than No Support?"

54. George C. Edwards III, *The Public Presidency* (New York: St Martin's Press, 1983); George C. Edwards III, *On Deaf Ears* (New Haven, CT: Yale University Press, 2003).

55. Edmund Morris, *The Rise of Theodore Roosevelt* (New York: Collins, 1987).

56. Brandice Canes-Wrone, *Who Leads Whom: Presidents, Policy, and the Public* (Chicago: University of Chicago Press 2006).

57. For the text of the January 2007 speech, see "Bush: 'We Need to Change Our Strategy in Iraq,'" January 11, 2007, available at http://www.cnn.com/2007/POLITICS/01/10/bush.transcript/index.html (accessed 4/29/08).

58. Samuel Kernell, *Going Public: New Strategies of Presidential Leadership,* 2nd ed. (Washington, DC: Congressional Quarterly Press, 1993).

59. Associated Press, "Bush Regains Power after Colonoscopy," *New York Times,* July 21, 2007, available at http://www.nytimes.com/aponline/us/AP-Bush-Colonoscopy.html?hp (accessed 4/29/08).

60. Richard Cohen and Jules Witcover, *A Heartbeat Away: The Investigation and Resignation of Spiro T. Agnew* (New York: Viking, 1974).

61. John Mueller, *War, Presidents, and Public Opinion* (New York, John Wiley and Sons, 1973).

62. John Hart, *The Presidential Branch: From Washington to Clinton* (Chatham, NY: Chatham House Publishers, 1987).

63. John Hart, "President Clinton and the Politics of Symbolism: Cutting the White House Staff," *Political Science Quarterly* 110 (1995): 385–403.

64. Michael Fletcher, "White House Had Drug Officials Appear with GOP Candidates," *Washington Post,* July 18, 2007, p. A8.

65. See White House, "White House Offices," available at http://www.whitehouse.gov/government/off-descrp.html (accessed 4/29/08).

66. Kelly Chang, David Lewis, and Nolan McCarthy, "The Tenure of Political Appointees" (paper presented at the 2003 Midwest Political Science Association Annual Meeting, Chicago, IL, April 4).

67. David E. Lewis, "Staffing Alone: Unilateral Action and the Politicization of the Executive Office of the President, 1988–2004" *Presidential Studies Quarterly* 35 (2005): 496–514.

68. Charles E. Walcott and Karen M. Hult, "White House Staff Size: Explanations and Implications," *Presidential Studies Quarterly* 29 (1999), 638–56.

69. Mark Halperin and John F. Harris, *The Way to Win: Taking the White House in 2008* (New York: Random House, 2007).

70. White House, "National Security Council: Biography of Stephen Hadley, Assistant to the President for National Security Affairs," available at http://www.whitehouse.gov/nsc/hadleybio.html (accessed 4/29/08).

71. White House, "Joshua Bolten: White House Chief of Staff," available at http://www.whitehouse.gov/government/bolten-bio.html (accessed 4/29/08).

72. Karen M. Hult and Charles E. Walcott, *Empowering the White House: Governance Under Nixon, Ford, and Carter* (Lawrence, KS: University Press of Kansas, 2004).

73. David E. Lewis, "Political Appointments, Bureau Chiefs, and Federal Management Performance" (unpublished paper, Princeton University, 2003).

74. For a complete listing of votes, see Office of the Secretary of the Senate, "Occasions When Vice Presidents Have Voted to Break Tie Votes in the Senate," available at http://www.senate.gov/artandhistory/history/resources/pdf/VPTies.pdf (accessed 4/29/08).

75. Andrew Taylor, "Cheney Breaks Senate Tie on Spending Cuts," Associated Press, December 21, 2005.

76. For a series of articles detailing Cheney's role, see "Angler: The Cheney Vice Presidency," *Washington Post,* June 24–27, 2007, available at http://www.washingtonpost.com/cheney (accessed 4/29/08).

77. For example, see David Talbot, "Creepier Than Nixon," *Salon,* March 31, 2004, available at http://dir.salon.com/story/news/feature/2004/03/31/dean/index.html (accessed 4/29/08).

78. Barton Gellman and Jo Baker, "A Different Understanding with the President," *Washington Post,* June 24, 2007, p. A1.

79. Alexander Hamilton and James Madison, *The Pacificus-Helvidius Debates of 1793–1794: Toward the Completion of the American Founding,* ed. Martin J. Frisch, (1793; repr., Indianapolis, IN: The Liberty Fund, 2007).

80. Terry M. Moe and William G. Howell, "The Presidential Power of Unilateral Action," *Journal of Law, Economics, and Organization* 15 (1999): 132–46.

81. James Risen, and Eric Lichtblau, "Spying Program Snared U.S. Calls," *New York Times,* December 21, 2005, p. A1; David E. Sanger, "After ABM Treaty: New Freedom for U.S. in Different Kind of Arms Control," *New York Times,* December 15, 2001.

82. Howell, "Unilateral Powers: A Brief Overview."

83. These examples appear throughout Moe and Howell, "The Presidential Power of Unilateral Action"; see also William G. Howell, "Unilateral Powers: A Brief Overview," *Presidential Studies Quarterly* 35:3 (2005): 417–39.

84. David E. Lewis, *Presidents and the Politics of Agency Design* (Palo Alto, CA: Stanford University Press, 2003); William Howell and David Lewis, "Agencies by Presidential Design," *Journal of Politics* 64:4 (2002): 1095–114.

85. Louis Fisher, *Presidential War Power,* 2nd ed. (Lawrence, KS: University Press of Kansas, 2004); James M. Lindsay, "Deference and Defiance: The Shifting Rhythms of Executive–Legislative Relations in Foreign Policy," *Presidential Studies Quarterly* 33:3 (2003): 530–46; Lawrence Margolis, *Executive Agreements and Presidential Power in Foreign Policy* (New York: Praeger, 1985), 209–32.

86. Phillip Cooper, "George W. Bush, Edgar Allan Poe, and the Use and Abuse of Presidential Signing Statements," *Presidential Studies Quarterly* 35:3 (2005): 515–32.

87. Andrew Rudalevige, *The New Imperial Presidency: Renewing Presidential Power after Watergate* (Ann Arbor, MI: University of Michigan Press, 2005).

88. William G. Howell and Kenneth R. Mayer, "The Last One Hundred Days," *Presidential Studies Quarterly* 35:3 (2005): 533–53.

89. Juliet Eilperin, "GOP Won't Try to Halt Last Rules by Clinton," *Washington Post,* July 30, 2001, p. A1.

90. Christopher Deering and Forrest Maltzman, "The Politics of Executive Orders: Legislative Constraints on Presidential Power," *Political Research Quarterly* 52:4 (1999): 767–83.

91. David E. Lewis, *Presidents and the Politics of Agency Design: Political Insulation in the United States Government Bureaucracy, 1946–1997* (Palo Alto, CA: Stanford University Press, 2003).

92. David Epstein and Sharyn O'Halloran, *Delegating Powers* (Cambridge, UK: Cambridge University Press, 1999).

93. David G. Adler, "The Steel Seizure Case and Inherent Presidential Power," *Constitutional Commentary* 19 (2002): 155–208.

94. For a discussion of these and related cases, see Dahlia Lithwick and Walter Dellinger, "A Supreme Court Conversation," *Slate,* June 22, 2007, available at http://www.slate.com/id/2168856/entry/2168959 (accessed 7/4/08), and James Risen, "The Executive Power Awaiting the Next President," New York Times, June 22, 2008.

You Decide

a. For a summary of the charges and counter-charges, see Paul Gottsching and Dahlia Lithwick, "Who's Blaming Whom," *Slate,* March 27, 2007, available at http://www.slate.com/id/2162775.

b. Sam Coates, "Stress, Fees Mount for bush Aides Called to testify," *Washington Post,* September 18.2005; Adam Nagourney, "Working for clintons Can mean Big Legal Bills," *New York Times,* February 20,1998.

Challenging Conventional Wisdom

a. John M. Broder, "Obama, Adopting Economic Theme, Criticizes McCain," *New York Times,* June 10, 2008.

b. For excerpts of the speech, see Mark Halperin's The Page, "Excerpts of McCain's Speech in Denver, Colorado," *Time,* July 14, 2007, available at http://thepage.time.com/excerpts-of-mccains-speech-in-denver-colorado.

c. Pew Research Center, "Economic Discontent Deepens as Inflation Concerns Rise," February 14, 2008, available at http://people-press.org/report/395/economic-discontent-deepens-as-inflation-concerns-rise.

Politics Is Everywhere

a. A complete list of executive orders can be found on the White House site at http://www.whitehouse.gov/news/orders.

CHAPTER 12

1. These examples can be found in Spencer S. Hsu, "Order Shows FEMA Aid Shortcomings," *Washington Post,* December 3, 2006, p. A16; Eric Lipton, " 'Breathtaking' Waste and Fraud in Hurricane Aid," *New York Times,* June 27, 2006; Daniel Engber, "Who Unlocked My Trailer?" *Slate,* August 15, 2006, available at http://www.slate.com/id/2147790 (accessed 7/15/08); Shannon McCaffrey, Alison Young, and Seth Borenstein, "As New Orleans Flooded, Chertoff Discussed Avian Flu in Atlanta," Knight Ridder, September 15, 2005; Aaron C. Davis, "U.S. Paying a Premium to Cover Storm-Damaged Roofs," Knight Ridder, September 30, 2005; and Jonathan Weisman, "$236 Million Cruise Ship Deal Criticized," *Washington Post,* September 28, 2005, p. A1.

2. Douglass K. Daniel, "Commerce Dept. Lost 1,100 Laptops in Five Years," Associated Press, September 22, 2006, available at http://www.msnbc.msn.com/id/14946353 (accessed 7/15/08).

3. Michael Luo, "Soldiers Testify to Lawmakers Over Poor Care at Walter Reed," *New York Times,* March 6, 2007.

4. Brian M. Riedl, "Top 10 Examples of Government Waste," Heritage Foundation Backgrounder, available at http://www.heritage.org/Research/Budget/bg1840.cfm (accessed 7/15/08).

5. Jennifer Conlin, "A Heightened Summer Rush for Passports," *New York Times,* April 22, 2007.

6. For information on the Service to America Medals, see http://servicetoamericamedals.org/SAM/index.shtml.

7. Dwight Waldo, *The Administrative State: A Study of the Political Theory of American Public Administration* (1948; repr. Piscataway, NJ: Transaction Publishers, 2006).

8. Fred Kaplan, "House Democrats Back Down," *Slate,* May 10, 2007, available at http://www.slate.com/id/2165988 (accessed 7/15/08).

9. The original quote is from Robert Dahl, and was used in this context in David E. Lewis, *Presidents and the Politics of Agency Design: Political Insulation in the United States Government* (Palo Alto, CA: Stanford University Press, 2003).

10. For a history of the Food and Drug Administration, see John P. Swann, FDA History Office, "History of the FDA," available at http://www.fda.gov/oc/history/historyoffda/section2.html (accessed 7/15/08).

11. For details, see Cornelius Kerwin, *Rulemaking: How Government Agencies Write Law and Make Policy* (Washington, DC: CQ Press, 1999).

12. Clyde Wayne Crews Jr., "Ten Thousand Commandments: An Annual Snapshot of the Federal Regulatory State," 2003 ed. (Washington, DC: Cato Institute, 2003), available at http://www.cato.org/tech/pubs/10kc_2003.pdf (accessed 7/15/08).

13. The full text of the regulations and the rationale for them can be found at Centers for Medicare and Medicaid Services, "Transplants," available at http://www.cms.hhs.gov/certificationandcomplianc/20_transplant.asp (accessed 7/20/08).

14. Andrew Pollack, "New Sense of Caution at FDA," *New York Times,* September 29, 2006.

15. There are two exceptions. A patient can enroll in a clinical trial for a new drug during the approval process, but there is a good chance that the patient will get a placebo or a previously approved treatment rather than the drug being tested. The FDA does allow companies to provide some experimental drugs to patients who cannot participate in a trial, but only those drugs that have passed early screening trials.

16. Susan Okie, "Access Before Approval—A Right to Take Experimental Drugs?" *New England Journal of Medicine* 355 (2004): 437–40.

17. For details, see the U.S. General Services Administration site at http://www.gsa.gov.

18. Michael Lipsky, *Street Level Bureaucracy* (New York: Russell Sage Foundation, 1983).

19. Stephen Skowronek, *Building a New American State: The Expansion of National Administrative Capacities, 1877–1920* (New York: Cambridge University Press, 1982).

20. PPBS was Program Planning Budget System (Johnson administration), MBO was Management by Objectives (Nixon administration), ZBB was Zero-Based Budgeting (Carter administration), REGO was short for Reinventing Government (Clinton administration), and PBB (Performance Based Budgeting) was President George W. Bush's effort at bureaucratic reorganization. For details, see Cedilia Ferradino, "New Name, Old Challenges: Performance Budgeting's Continuing Struggle to Succeed in Washington." *Rockefeller College Review* 1:2 (2002): 6–23.

21. Terry Moe, "An Assessment of the Positive Theory of Congressional Dominance," *Legislative Studies Quarterly* 4 (1987): 475–98.

22. John Brehm and Scott Gates, *Working, Shirking and Sabotage* (Ann Arbor, MI: University of Michigan Press, 1998).

23. Gary Miller, *Managerial Dilemmas: The Political Economy of Hierarchy* (New York: Cambridge University Press, 1987).

24. Daniel P. Carpenter, "Protection without Capture: Approval by a Politically Responsive, Learning Regulator," *American Political Science Review* 98 (2004): 613–31.

25. R. Jeffrey Smith, "E-Mails Detail Air Force Push for Boeing Deal," *Washington Post,* June 7, 2005, p. A1.

26. Frances E. Rourke, "Responsiveness and Neutral Competence in American Bureaucracy," *Public Administration Review* 52 (1992): 539–46; Max Weber, *Essays on Sociology* (New York: Oxford University Press, 1958).

27. Terry M. Moe, "Power and Political Institutions," *Perspectives on Politics* 3 (2005): 215–33.

28. Karen Orren and Steven Skorownek, "Regimes and Regime Building in American Government: A Review of the Literature on the 1940s," *Political Science Quarterly* 113 (1998): 689–702.

29. Michael Nelson, "A Short, Ironic History of American National Bureaucracy," *Journal of Politics* 44 (1982): 747–78.

30. Nelson, "A Short, Ironic History of American National Bureaucracy."

31. Nelson, "A Short, Ironic History of American National Bureaucracy."

32. John Aldrich, *Why Parties?* (Chicago: University of Chicago Press, 1995).

33. Nelson, "A Short, Ironic History of American National Bureaucracy."

34. Matthew A. Crenson, *The Federal Machine: Beginnings of Bureaucracy in Jacksonian America* (Baltimore, MD: Johns Hopkins University Press, 1975).

35. James Q. Wilson, "The Rise of the Bureaucratic State," in *The American Commonwealth,* ed. Nathan Glazer and Irving Kristol (New York: Basic Books, 1976).

36. Stephen Skowronek, *Building a New American State.*

37. Robert Harrison, *Congress, Progressive Reform, and the New American State* (New York: Cambridge University Press, 2004).

38. The U.S. State Department has an excellent summary of the Pendleton Act at http://usinfo.state.gov/usa/infousa/facts/democrac/28.htm.

39. Lawrence C. Dodd and Richard L. Schott, *Congress and the Administrative State* (New York: John Wiley & Sons, 1979).

40. Richard F. Bensel, *The Political Economy of American Industrialization, 1877–1900* (New York: Cambridge University Press, 2000).

41. William Riordan, *Plunkitt of Tammany Hall: A Series of Very Plain Talks on Very Practical Politics* (1924; repr. New York: Signet Classics, 1995).

42. Sean Theriault, "Patronage, the Pendleton Act, and the Power of the People," *The Journal of Politics* 65 (2003): 50–68.

43. Ira Katznelson and Bruce Pietrykowski, "Rebuilding the American State: Evidence from the 1940s," *Studies in American Political Development* 5:2 (1991) 301–39.

44. David Plotke, *Building a Democratic Political Order: Reshaping American Liberalism in the 1930s and 1940s* (New York: Cambridge University Press, 1996).

45. Theda Skocpol and Kenneth Finegold, "State Capacity and Economic Intervention in the Early New Deal," *Political Science Quarterly* 97 (1999): 255–70.

46. Michael Brown, "State Capacity and Political Choice: Interpreting the Failure of the Third New Deal," *Studies in American Political Development* 9 (1995): 187–212.

47. Ira Katznelson, Kim Geiger, and Daniel Kryder, "Limiting Liberalism: The Southern Veto in Congress, 1933–1950," *Political Science Quarterly* 108 (1993): 283–306.

48. Joseph, Califano, "What Was Really Great about the Great Society," *Washington Monthly,* October 1999, available at http://www.washingtonmonthly.com/features/1999/9910.califano.html (accessed 7/16/08).

49. Douglas Arnold, *Congress and the Bureaucracy* (New Haven, CT: Yale University Press, 1978).

50. David T. Canon, *Race, Redistricting, and Representation: The Unintended Consequences of Black Majority Districts* (Chicago: University of Chicago Press, 1999).

51. Charles Murray, *Losing Ground: American Social Policy, 1950–1980* (New York: Basic Books, 1984).

52. Henry J. Aaron, *Politics and the Professors: The Great Society in Perspective* (Washington, DC: Brookings Institution Press, 1978).

53. Michael B. Katz, *In the Shadow of the Poorhouse: A Social History of Welfare in America* (New York: Basic Books, 1996).

54. Stephen Moore, "How the Budget Revolution Was Lost," Cato Policy Analysis no. 281, September 2, 1997, Cato Institute, available at https://www.cato.org/pubs/pas/pa-281.html (accessed 7/21/08).

55. Clyde Wayne Crews Jr., "Ten Thousand Commandments."

56. Andrew Rudalevige, "The Structure of Leadership: Presidents, Hierarchies, and Information Flow," *Presidential Studies Quarterly* 35 (2005): 333–60.

57. David E. Lewis, *Presidents and the Policy of Agency Design* (Palo Alto, CA: Stanford University Press, 2003).

58. Terry Moe, "An Assessment of the Positive Theory of Congressional Dominance," *Legislative Studies Quarterly* 4 (1987): 475–98.

59. Mark Hosenball, Michael Isikoff, and Evan Thomas, "Cheney's Long Path to War," *Newsweek,* November 17, 2003, pp. 34–40.

60. Eric Schmitt and Thom Shanker, "A CIA Rival: Pentagon Sets Up Intelligence Unit," *New York Times,* October 24, 2002, p. A1.

61. William A. Niskanen, *Bureaucracy and Public Economics* (Washington, DC: Edward Elgar Publishing, 1976); Robert Waples and Jac C. Heckelman, "Public Choice Economics: Where Is There Consensus?" *The American Economist* 49 (2005): 66–79.

62. Alan Schick and Felix LoStracco, *The Federal Budget: Politics, Process, Policy* (Washington, DC: Brookings Institution Press, 2000).

63. Joel D. Aberbach, "The Political Significance of the George W. Bush Administration,"*Social Policy and Administration* 39:2 (2005): 130–49.

64. David E. Lewis, "The Politics of Agency Termination: Confronting the Myth of Agency Immortality," *Journal of Politics* 64 (2002): 89–107.

65. Ronald A. Wirtz, "Put It on My . . . Er, His Tab: Opinion Polls Show a Big Gap Between the Public's Desire for Services and Its Willingness to Pay for These Services," *Fedgazette,* January 2004, available at http://www.minneapolisfed.org/pubs/fedgaz/04-01/tab.cfm (accessed 7/16/08).

66. John J. Brehm and Scott Gates, *Working, Shirking, and Sabotage.*

67. Paul Light, "Measuring the Health of the Public Service," in *Workways of Governance,* ed. Roger Davidson (Washington, DC: Brookings Institution Press, 2003).

68. John J. Brehm and Scott Gates, *Working, Shirking, and Sabotage.*

69. Paul Light, *A Government Well-Executed: Public Service and Public Performance* (Washington, DC: Brookings Institution Press, 2003).

70. This discussion of the details of the civil service system is based on Bureau of Labor Statistics, "Career Guide to Industries," March 12, 2008, available at http://www.bls.gov/oco/cg/cgs041.htm (accessed 7/16/08).

71. Chris Edwards and Tad DeHaven, "Federal Government Should Increase Firing Rate," *Tax and Budget Bulletin* 10, November 2002, Cato Institute, available at http://www.cato.org/pubs/tbb/tbb-0211-10.pdf (accessed 7/16/08).

72. Ronald N. Johnson and Gary D. Liebcap, *The Federal Civil Service System and the Problem of Bureaucracy* (Chicago: University of Chicago Press, 1993).

73. Eric Lichtblau, "Report Sees Illegal Hiring Practices at Justice Department," *New York Times,* June 25, 2008.

74. For the details of the Hatch Act, see Daniel Engber, "Can Karl Rove Plot Campaign Strategy on the Government's Dime?" *Slate,* April 21, 2006, available at http://www.slate.com/id/2140418 (accessed 7/16/08).

75. Samantha Levine, "NASA Denies Chief Made Formal DeLay Endorsement," *Houston Chronicle,* April 1, 2006.

76. Sheryl Gay Stolberg, "Advisers' E-Mail Accounts May Have Mixed Politics and Business, White House Says," *New York Times,* April 12, 2007.

77. Stephen Labaton and Edmund Andrews, "White House Calls Political Briefings Legal," *New York Times,* April 27, 2007.

78. Timothy Noah, "Low Morale at Homeland Security," *Slate,* September 14, 2005, available at http://www.slate.com/id/2126313 (accessed 7/17/08).

79. For details on the Senior Executive Service, see the Office of Personnel Management site at http://www.opm.gov/ses.

80. The survey was conducted by the Council for Excellence in Government. For the full survey results and interpretation, see Council for Excellence in Government, "Attitudes Toward Government" available at http://www.excelgov.org/index.php?keyword=a432949724f861 (accessed 7/20/08).

81. Susan Webb Yackee and David Lowery, "Understanding Public Support for the U.S. Federal Bureaucracy," *Public Administration Review* 7:4 (2005): 515–30.

82. C. T. Goodsell, *The Case for Bureaucracy* (Chatham, NJ: Chatham House Press, 1994).

83. Christopher Lee, "Ex-Surgeon General Says White House Hushed Him," *Washington Post,* July 11, 2007, p. A1.

84. Andrew C. Revkin, "Climate Expert Says NASA Tried to Silence Him," *New York Times,* January 29, 2006.

85. Andrew C. Revkin, "A Young Bush Appointee Resigns His Post at NASA," *New York Times,* February 8, 2006.

86. Andrew C. Revkin, "NASA's Goals Delete Mention of Home Planet," *New York Times,* July 22, 2006.

87. John D. Huber and Charles R. Shipan, *Deliberate Discretion? The Institutional Foundations of Bureaucratic Autonomy* (New York: Cambridge University Press, 2002).

88. David Epstein and Sharyn O'Halloran, *Delegating Powers: A Transaction Cost Politics Approach to Policy Making Under Separate Powers* (New York: Cambridge University Press, 1999).

89. Mathew D. McCubbins, Roger G. Noll, and Barry R. Weingast, "Structure and Process as Solutions to the Politician's Principal–Agency Problem," *Virginia Law Review* 74 (1989): 431–82.

90. Barry R. Weingast, "Caught in the Middle: The President, Congress, and the Political-Bureaucratic System," in *Institutions of American Democracy: The Executive Branch,* ed. Joel D. Aberbach and Mark A. Peterson (New York: Oxford University Press, 2006).

91. Keith Whittington and Daniel P. Carpenter, "Executive Power in American Institutional Development," *Perspectives on Politics* 1 (2003): 495–513.

92. Dara Cohen, Mariano-Florentino Cuéllar, and Barry R. Weingast, "Crisis Bureaucracy: Homeland Security and the Political Design of Legal Mandates," *Stanford Law Review* 59:3 (2006): 673–760.

93. Federal Communications Commission, "FCC Commissioners," April 1, 2008, available at http://www.fcc.gov/commissioners (accessed 7/17/08).

94. Federal Election Commission, "About the FEC: Commissioners," available at http://www.fec.gov/members/members.shtml (accessed 7/17/08); Federal Trade Commission, "Commissioners," available at http://www.ftc.gov/commissioners/index.shtml (accessed 7/17/08).

95. Roger Noll, Mathew McCubins, and Barry Weingast, "Administrative Procedures as Instruments of Political Control," *Journal of Law, Economics and Organization* 3 (1987): 243–77.

96. Mathew McCubbins and Thomas Schwartz, "Congressional Oversight Overlooked: Fire Alarms vs. Police Patrols," *American Journal of Political Science* 28 (1984): 165–79.

97. McCubbins and Schwartz, "Congressional Oversight Overlooked: Fire Alarms vs. Police Patrols."

98. Steven J. Balla and John R. Wright, "Interest Groups, Advisory Committees, and Congressional Control of the Bureaucracy," *American Journal of Political Science* 45 (2001): 799–812.

99. Moe, "An Assessment of the Positive Theory of Congressional Dominance."

100. Irwin Morris, *Congress, the President, and the Federal Reserve: The Politics of American Monetary Policy-Making* (Ann Arbor, MI: University of Michigan Press, 2000).

101. Daniel P. Carpenter, "The Gatekeeper: Organizational Reputation and Pharmaceutical Regulation at the FDA" (unpublished paper, Harvard University, 2006).

102. Terry M. Moe, "Political Control and the Power of the Agent" *Journal of Law, Economics, and Organization* 22 (2006): 1–29.

103. See David Weil, "OSHA: Beyond the Politics," *Frontline,* January 9, 2003, available at http://www.pbs.org/wgbh/pages/frontline/shows/workplace/osha/weil.html (accessed 7/17/08).

104. Daniel P. Carpenter, *The Forging of Bureaucratic Autonomy: Reputations, Networks, and Policy Innovation in Executive Agencies, 1862–1928* (Princeton, NJ: Princeton University Press, 2001).

105. Michael B. Katz, *In the Shadow of the Poorhouse.*

106. Henry J. Aaron, *Why Is Welfare So Hard to Reform?* (Washington, DC: Brookings Institution Press, 1973).

Politics Is Everywhere

a. Paul Light, 2005. "Fact Sheet on the New True Size of the Federal Government," http://www.brookings.edu/dybdocroot/gs/cps/light20030905.pdf.

Challenging Conventional Wisdom

a. These figures come from the General Services Administration, GSA Reports, available at http://www.gsa.gov/Portal/gsa/ep/contentView.do?contentId=9967&contentType=GSA_OVERVIEW.

You Decide

a. National Aeronautics and Space Administration, "NASA Public Affairs Policy FAQ," available at http://www.nasa.gov/pdf/145756main_comm_policy_faq.pdf.

CHAPTER 13

1. *Hamdi v. Rumsfeld,* 542 U.S. 507 (2004).

2. *Rasul v. Bush,* 542 U.S. 466 (2004).

3. Linda Greenhouse, "The Ruling on Tribunals: The Overview; Justices, 5–3, Broadly Reject Bush Plan to Try Detainees, *New York Times,* June 30, 2006, p. A18. *Hamdan v. Rumsfeld,* 126 S. Ct. 2749 (2006).

4. *Boumediene v. Bush,* 553 U.S. (2008).

5. Alexander M. Bickle, "Establishment and General Justification of Judicial Review," in *Classics in American Politics,* 2nd ed., ed. Pietro S. Nivola and David H. Rosenbloom (New York: St. Martin's Press, 1990), pp. 436–50; article originally published in 1962.

6. Ralph Ketcham, *The Anti-Federalist Papers and the Constitutional Convention Debates* (New York: Penguin Putnam, 2003), p. 304.

7. Lester S. Jayson, ed., *The Constitution of the United States of America: Analysis and Interpretation,* (Washington, DC: U.S. Government Printing Office, 1973), p. 585.

8. David G. Savage, *Guide to the U.S. Supreme Court,* 4th ed. (Washington, DC: CQ Press, 2004), p. 7.

9. Savage, *Guide to the U.S. Supreme Court,* 5–7.

10. Winfield H. Rose, "*Marbury v. Madison*: How John Marshall Changed History by Misquoting the Constitution," *Political Science and Politics* 36:2 (April, 2003): 209–14. Rose argues that in a key quotation in the case, Marshall intentionally left out a clause of the Constitution that suggests that Congress *did* have the power to expand the original jurisdiction of the Court. Other constitutional scholars reject this argument.

11. *Marbury v. Madison,* 1 CR. (5 U.S.) 137 (1803).

12. *Ware v. Hylton,* 3 U.S. 199 (1796).

13. *Lujan v. Defenders of Wildlife* (1992).

14. *Campbell v. Clinton,* 99-1843 (this was a District of Columbia appeals court decision; the Supreme Court refused to hear the appeal of the decision) and *Raines v. Byrd* (1997).

15. For a summary of other differences between these two types of federal courts see Henry J. Abraham, *The Judiciary: The Supreme Court in the Governmental Process,* 7th ed. (Boston: Allyn and Bacon, 1987), pp. 7–21.

16. U.S. Courts, Federal Court Management Statistics, 2007: District Courts, available at http://www.uscourts.gov/cgi-bin/cmsd2007.pl (accessed 3/18/08).

17. The "stepchildren" label and the rest of the information in this paragraph are drawn from J. Woodford Howard Jr., *Courts of Appeals in the Federal Judicial System* (Princeton, NJ: Princeton University Press, 1981), pp. 1–15.

18. Federal Judicial Center, "The Judiciary Act of 1869: An Act to Amend the Judicial System of the United States," available at http://www.fjc.gov/history/home.nsf/page/10a_bdy (accessed 7/18/08).

19. Federal Judicial Center, "The U.S. Courts of Appeals and the Federal Judiciary," available at http://www.fjc.gov/history/home.nsf/page/ca_bdy?OpenDocument (accessed 7/18/08).

20. Howard, *Courts of Appeals,* 5.

21. U.S. Courts, Federal Judiciary: Frequently Asked Questions, "Federal Judges," available at http://www.uscourts.gov/faq.html (accessed 3/18/08).

22. U.S. Courts, Federal Court Management Statistics, 2007: Courts of Appeals, available at http://www.uscourts.gov/cgi-bin/cmsa2007.pl (accessed 3/18/08).

23. "Judicial Selection in the States: Appellate and General Jurisdiction Courts," American Judicature Society, 2004, available at http://www.ajs.org/js/JudicialSelectionCharts_old.pdf (accessed 9/14/06).

24. Savage, *Guide to the U.S. Supreme Court,* 1003.

25. Sheldon Goldman, "Reagan's Second Term Judicial Appointments: The Battle at Midway," *Judicature* 70 (1986–87): 328, 331; 78.8 percent of Ford's district court nominees and 91.7 percent of his appeals court nominees were Republicans. See also Michael J. Gerhardt, *The Federal Appointment Process: A Constitutional and Historical Analysis* (Durham, NC: Duke University Press, 2000), especially Chapter 4.

26. The first regular case starts with the year and then cases are numbered sequentially (so 2009-1 is the first case for 2009), while the *in forma pauperis* cases start at 5001 (so the first case in 2009 would be 2009-5001).

27. The actual numbers for the 2002–2003 term were 1,869 paid cases and 6,386 indigent cases; the numbers for the 2003–2004 term were 1,722 and 6,092, respectively. Data gathered from the U.S. Supreme Court site at http://www.supremecourtus.gov (accessed 7/18/08).

28. Edward Lazarus, *Closed Chambers: The Rise and Fall of the Modern Supreme Court* (New York: Penguin, Putnam, 1998), p. 30.

29. Supreme Court of the United States *In Re Frederick W. Bauer,* On Petition for a Writ of Mandamus to the United States Court of Appeals for the Seventh Circuit, Brief for the United States in Opposition, No. 90-6351, March 4, 1991, available at http://www.usdoj.gov/osg/briefs/1990/sg900418.txt (accessed 7/18/08).

30. Supreme Court of the United States *In Re Frederick W. Bauer,* On Motion for Leave to Proceed in forma pauperis, No. 99-5440, Decided October 18, 1999, per curiam, available at http://supreme.lp.findlaw.com/supreme_court/decisions/99-5440.html (accessed 7/18/08).

31. John Roberts, U.S. Supreme Court, "2007 Year-End Report on the Federal Judiciary," January 1, 2008, available at http://www.supremecourtus.gov/publicinfo/year-end/2007year-endreport.pdf (accessed 3/17/08).

32. For a critical account of the Supreme Court's reduced case load, which dates back to the Rehnquist Court, see Philip Allen Lacovara, "The Incredible Shrinking Court," *The American Lawyer,* December 1, 2003, available at http://www.judicialaccountability.org/download/shrinkinusgcourt.htm (accessed 7/18/08).

33. *New Jersey v. New York,* No. 120 Orig., 118 S. Ct. 1726 (1998) and *Kansas v. Colorado,* No. 105 Orig., 125 S. Ct. 526 (2004).

34. Abraham, *The Judiciary,* p. 25, says that original jurisdiction has been invoked "about 150 times." A Lexis search revealed an additional twenty-seven original jurisdiction cases between 1987 and December 2004. See U.S. Department of Justice, Help/Glossary, available at http://www.usdoj.gov/osg/briefs/help.html for a basic discussion of the Supreme Court's original jurisdiction.

35. Savage, *Guide to the U.S. Supreme Court,* 848.

36. See Thomas G. Walker and Lee Epstein, *The Supreme Court of the United States: An Introduction* (New York: St. Martin's Press, 1993), pp. 80–85, for a more detailed discussion of these concepts and citations to the relevant court cases.

37. *DeFunis v. Odegaard,* 416 U.S. 312 (1974).

38. The appeals court case is *Byrd v. Raines,* 956 F. Supp. 25, and the case that was finally heard by the Court was *Clinton v. City of New York,* 524 U.S. 417 (1998).

39. Gregory A. Caldeira and John R. Wright, "The Discuss List: Agenda Building in the Supreme Court," *Law and Society Review* 24 (1990): 813.

40. Walker and Epstein, *Supreme Court,* 89.

41. H. W. Perry, "Agenda Setting and Case Selection," in *The American Courts: A Critical Assessment,* John B. Gates and Charles H. Johnson, eds. (Washington, DC: CQ Press, 1991), p. 237. Also see Perry's *Deciding to Decide: Agenda Setting in the United States Supreme Court* (Cambridge, MA: Harvard University Press, 1991).

42. U. S. Supreme Court, "The Court and Its Procedures," available at http://www.supremecourtus.gov/about/procedures.pdf (accessed 3/1708).

43. *United States v. Nixon,* 418 U.S. 683 (1974).

44. *McConnell v. Federal Election Commission,* 540 U.S. 93 (2003).

45. Lee Epstein, Jeffrey A. Segal, Harold J. Spaeth, and Thomas G. Walker, *The Supreme Court Compendium: Data, Decisions, and Developments,* 3rd ed. (Washington, DC: CQ Press, 2003), Table 7-25.

46. Gregory A. Caldeira and John R. Wright, "*Amicus Curiae* before the Supreme Court: Who Participates, When, and How Much?" *Journal of Politics* 52 (August, 1990): 803.

47. U.S. Supreme Court, Rules of the Supreme Court, adopted March 14, 2005, effective May 2, 2005, Rule 28.7, available at http://www.supremecourtus.gov/ctrules/rulesofthecourt.pdf (accessed 7/18/08).

48. Savage, *Guide to the U.S. Supreme Court,* 852.

49. U.S. Supreme Court, Argument Transcripts, available at http://www.supremecourtus.gov/oral_arguments/argument_transcripts.html (accessed 7/18/08).

50. Quoted in Savage, *Guide to the U.S. Supreme Court,* 854.

51. Forrest Maltzman, James F. Spriggs II, and Paul J. Wahlbeck, *Crafting Law on the Supreme Court: The Collegial Game* (New York: Cambridge University Press, 2000), 33.

52. William H. Rehnquist, "Memorandum to the Conference: Policy Regarding Assignments," November 24, 1989, papers of Justice Thurgood Marshall, Washington, DC: Library of Congress Manuscript Division, quoted in Maltzman, Spriggs, and Wahlbeck, *Crafting Law,* pp. 30–31.

53. *Smith v. Allwright,* 321 U.S. 649 (1944).

54. Walker and Epstein, *Supreme Court,* 110.

55. Savage, *Guide to the U.S. Supreme Court,* 854.

56. Maltzman, Spriggs, and Wahlbeck, *Crafting Law,* 51. This specific prediction was for a case that has fifteen *amicus* briefs.

57. Maltzman, Spriggs, and Wahlbeck, *Crafting Law,* 49–50.

58. Quoted in Lee Epstein and Thomas G. Walker, *Constitutional Law for a Changing America,* 5th ed. (Washington, DC: CQ Press, 2004) 29.

59. *Maryland v. Craig,* 497 U.S. 836 (1990).

60. Epstein and Walker, *Constitutional Law for a Changing America,* 31.

61. Epstein, Segal, Spaeth, and Walker, *Supreme Court Compendium,* Table 6-2.

62. Forrest Maltzman and Paul J. Wahlbeck, "Strategic Considerations and Vote Fluidity on the Burger Court," *American Journal of Political Science* 90 (1996): 581–92. Maltzman, Spriggs, and Wahlbeck, *Crafting Law.*

63. Thomas R. Marshall, *Public Opinion and the Supreme Court* (Boston: Unwin Hyman, 1989), 12; as cited in Epstein and Walker, *Constitutional Law for a Changing America,* 92.

64. Thomas M. Keck, *The Most Activist Supreme Court in History: The Road to Modern Judicial Conservatism* (Chicago: University of Chicago Press, 2004).

65. Marshall, *Public Opinion,* Table 6-8.

66. Jeffrey Rosen, "Has the Supreme Court Gone Too Far?" *Commentary* 116:3 (October, 2003).

67. Finley Peter Dunne, Paul Green, and Jacques Barzun, *Mr. Dooley in Peace and in War* (1898; repr., Champaign-Urbana, IL: University of Illinois Press, 2001).

68. Robert Dahl, "Decision-Making in a Democracy: The Supreme Court as a National Policy-Maker," *Journal of Public Law* 6 (1957): 279–95, is the classic work on this topic. More recent work challenged Dahl's methods but largely supports that idea that the Court follows the will of the majority.

69. Jeffrey A. Segal, Richard J. Timpone, and Robert M. Howard, "Buyer Beware? Presidential Success through Supreme Court Appointments," *Political Research Quarterly* 53:3 (September, 2000): 557–73; Gregory A. Caldeira and Charles E. Smith Jr., "Campaigning for the Supreme Court: The Dynamics of Public Opinion on the Thomas Nomination," *Political Research Quarterly* 58:3 (August, 1996): 655–81.

70. William Mishler and Reginald S. Sheehan, "The Supreme Court as a Countermajoritarian Institution? The Impact of Public Opinion on Supreme Court Decisions," *American Political Science Review* 87:1 (March, 1993): 87–101.

71. *Roper v. Simmons,* U.S. 03-633 (2005). See Linda Greenhouse, "Supreme Court, 5–4, Forbids Execution in Juvenile Crime," *New York Times,* March 2, 2005, p. A1, for a discussion of this case and Justice Scalia's dissent.

72. David O'Brien, *Storm Center: The Supreme Court in American Politics,* 4th ed. (New York: W. W. Norton, 1996).

73. Helmut Norpoth and Jeffrey A. Segal, "Popular Influence in Supreme Court Decisions," *American Political Science Review* 88 (1994): 711–16.

74. *Worcester v. Georgia,* 31 U.S. 515 (1832).

75. *Ex Parte Milligan,* 71 U.S. 2 (1866), *Youngstown Sheet and Tube v. Sawyer,* 343 U.S. 579 (1952), *New York Times v. U.S.* (1971).

76. Linda Greenhouse, "Chief Justice Attacks a Law as Infringing on Judges," *New York Times,* January 1, 2004, p. A1.

77. *Foster v. Neilson,* 27 U.S. 253 (1829).

78. *Chicago & Southern Airlines v. Waterman SS Corp,* 333 U.S. 103 (1948).

Challenging Conventional Wisdom

a. Michael Stokes Paulsen, "Judging Judicial Review: Marbury in the Modern Era: The Irrepressible Myth of *Marbury,*" *Michigan Law Review* 101 (August, 2003): 2706–43.

b. Robert Lowry Clinton, *Marbury v. Madison and Judicial Review* (Lawrence, KS: University Press of Kansas, 1989).

c. Paulsen, "Judging Judicial Review," 2710.

Comparing Ourselves to Others

a. Tom Ginsburg, *Judicial Review in New Democracies: Constitutional Courts in Asian Cases* (New York: Cambridge University Press, 2003), p. 1.

b. "Judicial Review of Parliamentary Legislation: Norway as a European Pioneer," Chief Justice Carsten Smith, The University of London Annual Coffin Memorial Lecture, April 3, 2000, http://www.hoyesterett.no/artikler/2694.asp.

c. Ginsburg, Table 1.1, 7–8. Also see Arne Mavcic, "Historical Steps in the Development of Systems of Constitutional Review and Particularities of Their Basic Models," for excellent tables on the legal systems of 150 countries, available at http://www.concourts/tab.

Politics Is Everywhere

a. The court cases come from a great Web site, Overlawyered (available at http://www.overlawyered.com), that gives examples of needless or frivolous law suits.

b. "Guacamole Dips Avocado-less Consumer Fraud," December 5, 2006, available at http://www.lawyersandsettlements.com/case/guacamole_dip_deceptive_advertising.

CHAPTER 14

1. There are eight commissioners on the Commission on Civil Rights, four appointed by the president and four by Congress. The commissioners serve six-year terms and do not require Senate confirmation, and no more than four members may be of the same political party.

2. Indentured servants were people who could not afford the price of a ticket for passage to the New World. In exchange for transportation, they gave up three to seven years of their freedom. The indentured servants worked in a variety of capacities. Some of them learned a valuable trade, but most of them worked in agriculture, performing tasks similar to those of the slaves who would later replace them.

3. Howard Dodson, "How Slavery Helped Build a World Economy," February 3, 2003, in *Jubilee: the Emergence of African-American Culture* (New York: Schomburg Center for Research in Black Culture, New York City Public Library).

4. Data from the Louisiana State University Civil War Center, available at http://www.cwc.lsu.edu/cwc/other /stats/warcost.htm (accessed 11/10/07).

5. V. O. Key Jr., Southern Politics in State and Nation (New York: Knopf, 1949), p. 538. For example, the Louisiana grandfather clause read, "No male person who was on January 1, 1867, or at any date prior thereto, entitled to vote under the Constitution of the United States, wherein he then resided, and no son or grandson of any such person not less than twenty-one years of age at the date of the adoption of this Constitution, . . . shall be denied the right to register and vote in this State by reason of his failure to possess the educational or property qualifications." Grandfather clauses as they applied to voting were ruled unconstitutional in 1915.

6. Chandler Davidson, "The Voting Rights Act: A Brief History," in *Controversies in Minority Voting: The Voting Rights Act in Perspective*, ed. Bernard Grofman and Chandler Davidson (Washington, DC: Brookings Institution, 1992), p. 21.

7. *Cherokee Nation v. Georgia* (1831).

8. Institute for Advanced Technology in the Humanities, University of Virginia, Abigail Adams to John Adams, March 31, 1776, available at http://www.iath.virginia.edu/seminar/unit1/text/adams.htm (accessed 7/30/08).

9. *Bradwell v. Illinois*, 83 U.S. 130 (1873).

10. *Hoyt v. Florida*, 368 U.S. 57 (1961).

11. Davidson, "The Voting Rights Act," p. 22. See U.S. Department of Justice, Civil Rights Division. "About Section 5 of the Voting Rights Act," available at http://www.usdoj.gov/crt/voting/sec_5/obj_activ.htm for a complete list of cases in which the Justice Department has denied "preclearance" of a change in an electoral practice under Section 5 of the Voting Rights Act.

12. Kenneth J. Cooper, "Helms Defeats Gantt: Poll Hours Disputed," *Washington Post*, November 6, 1990, p. A27.

13. United States Commission on Civil Rights, "Voting Irregularities in Florida During the 2000 Presidential Election," June 2001, available at http://www.usccr.gov/pubs/vote2000/report/main.htm (accessed 7/30/08).

14. U.S. Census Bureau, Annual Social and Economic Supplement, Current Population Survey, available at http://pubdb3.census.gov/macro/032007/pov/new01_100.htm (accessed 3/21/08).

15. Data on wealth are from the Federal Reserve, "2004 Survey of Consumer Finances," available at http://www.federalreserve.gov/pubs/oss/oss2/2004/scf2004home.html/1995/wlth95-1.html (accessed 3/21/08). Income data are from the U.S. Census Bureau, "Income, Earnings, and Poverty Data from the 2006 American Community Survey," August 2007, available at http://www.census.gov/prod/2007pubs/acs-08.pdf (accessed 3/21/08).

16. Labor Force Statistics data are from the U.S. Bureau of Labor Statistics, Current Population Survey, available at http://www.bls.gov/cps (accessed 3/21/08).

17. America's Families and Living Arrangements: 2006, U.S. Census Bureau, http://www.census.gov/population/www/socdemo/hh-fam/cps2006.html (accessed March 21, 2008).

18. Stephan Thernstrom and Abigail Thernstrom, *America in Black and White* (New York: Simon and Schuster, 1997), 265.

19. Life expectancy and infant mortality rates are from the Centers for Disease Control, available at http://www.cdc.gov/nchs/data/hestat/preliminarydeaths05_tables.pdf#A l; maternity mortality rates are from the National Center for Health Statistics, available at http://mchb.hrsa.gov/mchirc/chusa_04/pages/0409mm.htm (both accessed 3/21/08). Other health data are available from the Department of Health and Human Services, available at http://www.hhs.gov.

20. Hundreds of studies have examined these patterns, and, not surprisingly, there are divergent findings. However, most have found differences in sentencing based on race. A meta-analysis of eighty-five studies by Ojmarrh Mitchell and Doris L. MacKenzie funded by the U.S. Department of Justice found, "after taking into account defendant criminal history and current offense seriousness, African-Americans and Latinos were generally sentenced more harshly than whites." See Mitchell and MacKenzie, "The Relationship between Race, Ethnicity, and Sentencing Outcomes: A Meta-Analysis of Sentencing Research," December 2004, available at http://www.ncjrs.gov/pdffiles1/nij/grants/208129.pdf. For government studies of racial profiling see the Justice Department's "A Resource Guide on Racial Profiling Data Collection Systems," November 2000, available at http://www.ncjrs.gov/pdffiles1/bja/184768.pdf. For President Bush's statement on racial profiling, see Department of Justice, "Fact Sheet: Racial Profiling," June 17, 2003, available at http://www.usdoj.gov/opa/pr/2003/June/racial_profiling_fact_sheet.pdf. For a GAO study see "Racial Profiling: Limited Data on Motorist Stops," March 2000, available at http://www.gao.gov/new.items/gg00041.pdf. Government statistics on crime may be found on the Federal bureau of Investigation site at http://www.fbi.gov. (All documents accessed 3/21/08.)

21. Criminal Justice Information Services Division, Federal Bureau of Investigation, 2006 Hate Crime Statistics, available at http://www.fbi.gov/ucr/hc2006/table1.html (accessed 3/21/08).

22. Rosa Parks with James Haskins, *Rosa Parks: My Story* (New York: Dial Books, 1992), p. 116.

23. Clayborne Carson, David J. Garrow, Gerald Gill, Vincent Harding, and Darlene Clark Hine, eds., *The Eyes on the Prize Civil Rights Reader* (New York: Penguin Books, 1997).

24. *Boynton v. Virginia*, 363 U.S. 454 (1960).

25. David Halberstam, *The Children* (New York: Ballantine Books, 1999).

26. *Guinn v. United States*, 238 U.S. 347 (1915); *Smith v. Allwright*, 322 U.S. 718 (1944).

27. *Pearson v. Murray*, 169 Md. 478 (1936).

28. *Missouri ex rel. Gaines v. Canada*, 305 U.S. 377 (1938).
29. *Fisher v. Hurst*, 333 U.S. 147 (1948).
30. *McLaurin v. Oklahoma State Regents of Higher Education*, 339 U.S. 637 (1950).
31. *Sweatt v. Painter*, 339 U.S. 629 (1950).
32. *Brown v. Board of Education*, 347 U.S. 483 (1954).
33. *Brown v. Board of Education (II)* 349 U.S. 294 (1955).
34. Paul Brest and Sanford Levinson, *Process of Constitutional Decision Making: Cases and Material* (Boston: Little, Brown, 1982), pp. 471–80.
35. *Griffin et al. v. County School Board of Prince Edward County*, 377 U.S. 218 (1964).
36. *Swann v. Charlotte-Mecklenberg Board of Education*, 402 U.S. 1 (1971).
37. *Milliken v Bradley*, 418 U.S. 717 (1974).
38. *Board of Education of Oklahoma City v. Dowell*, 498 U.S. 237 (1991).
39. *Missouri v. Jenkins*, 515 U.S. 70 (1995).
40. *Parents Involved in Community Schools Inc. v. Seattle School District* 05-98 (2007); *Meredith v. Jefferson County (Ky.) Board of Education*, 551 U.S. (2007).
41. *Heart of Atlanta Motel, Inc. v. United States*, 379 U.S. 241 (1964).
42. *Katzenbach v. McClung*, 379 U.S. 294 (1964).
43. *Griggs v. Duke Power*, 401 U.S. 424 (1971).
44. *Wards Cove Packing Co. v. Atonio*, 490 U.S. 642 (1989).
45. *Easley v. Cromartie*, 532 U.S. 234 (2001), rehearing denied, 532 U.S. 1076 (2001).
46. *Easley v. Cromartie*, 532 U.S. 1076 (2001).
47. The set-aside case was *Adarand v. Pena* (1995), the Florida case was *Bush v. Gore* (2000), and the California discrimination case was *Circuit City Stores v. Adams* (2001).
48. *Reed v. Reed*, 404 U.S. 71 (1971).
49. *Frontiero v. Richardson*, 411 U.S. 677 (1973).
50. *Craig v. Boren*, 429 U.S. 190 (1976).
51. *Korematsu v. United States*, 323 U.S. 214 (1944).
52. *Rostker v. Goldberg*, 453 U.S. 57 (1981).
53. *Orr v. Orr*, 440 U.S. 268 (1979).
54. *Johnson v. Transportation Agency of Santa Clara*, 480 U.S. 616 (1987).
55. *Harris v. Forklift Systems*, 510 U.S. 17 (1993).
56. *Grove City College v. Bell*, 465 U.S. 555 (1984).
57. *Ledbetter v. Goodyear Tire & Rubber Co.*, 550 U.S. (2007).
58. *Price Waterhouse v. Hopkins*, 490 U.S. 228 (1989).
59. *Bowers v. Hardwick*, 478 U.S. 186 (1986), rehearing denied, 478 U.S. 1039 (1986).
60. *Hurley v. Irish-American Gay, Lesbian, and Bisexual Group of Boston*, 515 U.S. 557 (1995).
61. *Boy Scouts of America v. Dale*, 530 U.S. 640 (2000).
62. *Romer v. Evans*, 517 U.S. 620 (1996).
63. *Lawrence v. Texas*, 539 U.S. 558 (2003).
64. Drew S. Days III, "Section 5 Enforcement and the Justice Department," in *Controversies in Minority Voting: The Voting Rights Act in Perspective*, ed. Bernard Grofman and Chandler Davidson (Washington, DC: Brookings Institution Press, 1992), p. 52; Frank R. Parker, *Black Votes Count* (Chapel Hill, NC: University of North Carolina Press, 1990), p. 1.
65. Cited in *Congressional Record*, October 22, 1965, 28354.
66. Quoted in Voting Rights Act Extension: Report of the Subcommittee of the Constitution of the Committee on the Judiciary, U.S. Senate, 97th Congress, 2nd session, May 25, 1982, S. Rept. 97-417, 4.
67. Davidson, "The Voting Rights Act," p. 21.
68. *McClesky v. Kemp*, 481 U.S. 279 (1987).
69. *U.S. v. Morrison*, 529 U.S. 598 (2000).
70. *Board of Trustees of the University of Alabama v. Garrett*, 531 U.S. 356 (2001). However, in *State of Tennessee v. George Lane and Beverly Jones*, 541 U.S. 509 (2004) the Court ruled that the disabled must have access to courthouses.

71. *New York Times*/CBS poll, December 6–9, 1997. Fifty-nine percent of whites and 82 percent of blacks favored the education programs, while 57 percent of whites but only 23 percent of blacks opposed preferences in hiring and promotion "to make up for past discrimination."
72. The precise wording of the proposition was, "Shall the charter of the City of Houston be amended to end the use of affirmative action for women and minorities in the operation of City of Houston employment and contracting, including ending the current program and any similar programs in the future?"
73. The training program case was *United Steel Workers of America v. Weber*, 443 U.S. 193 (1979); the labor union case was *Sheet Metal Workers v. EEOC*, 478 U.S. 421 (1986); and the Alabama state police case was *U.S. v. Paradise*, 480 U.S. 149 (1987).
74. *Richmond v. J.A. Croson Co.*, 488 U.S. 469 (1989).
75. *Adarand Constructors, Inc. V. Pena*, 515 U.S. 200 (1995).
76. *Regents of Univ. of California v. Bakke*, 438 U.S. 265 (1978).
77. *Grutter v. Bollinger*, 123 S. Ct. 2325 (2003) was the law school case and *Gratz v. Bollinger*, 123 S. Ct. 2411 (2003) was the undergraduate admissions case.
78. In *Bakke*, Justice Lewis Powell was the only member of the Court who held this position, even if it became the basis for all affirmative action programs over the next twenty-five years. Four justices in the *Bakke* decision wanted to get rid of race as a factor in admissions, and another four thought that the "strict scrutiny" standard should not even be applied in this instance.
79. "An Act Providing for the Collection of Data Relative to Traffic Stops," Massachusetts state law, Chapter 228 of the Acts of 2000, available at http://www.mass.gov/legis/laws/seslaw00/sl000228.htm (accessed 7/22/08).

Politics Is Everywhere

a. U.S. Equal Employment Opportunity Commission, "Charge Statistics, FY 1997 through FY 2007," available at http://www.eeoc.gov/stats/charges.html.
b. Erik Eckholm, "Black and Hispanic Home Buyers Pay Higher Interest on Mortgages, Study Finds," *New York Times*, June 1, 2006, p. A20.
c. Kristie M. Engemann and Michael T. Owyang, "What's in a Name? Reconciling Conflicting Evidence on Ethnic Names," *The Regional Economic*, 2006, St. Louis Federal Reserve Bank, available at http://stlouisfed.org/publications/re/2006/a/pages/ethnic_names.html.

Comparing Ourselves to Others

a. A version of this paragraph appeared in David T. Canon, *Race, Redistricting, and Representation: The Unintended Consequences of Black Majority Districts* (Chicago: University of Chicago Press, 1999), p. 1. Robert Dahl's discussion of "minorities rule" appears in *Preface to Democracy Theory* (Chicago: University of Chicago Press, 1956), pp. 124–51.
b. Data on racial and ethnic minorities are from Andrew Reynolds, "Reserved Seats for National Legislatures: A Research Note," *Legislative Studies Quarterly* 30:2 (May, 2005): 301–10; data on gender are from Pippa Norris, "Increasing Women's Representation in Iraq: Which Strategies Would Work Best?" (unpublished paper, John F. Kennedy School of Government, Harvard University, February 16, 2004).

Challenging Conventional Wisdom

a. Daniel W. Drezner, "Hash of Civilizations," *The New Republic Online*, March 3, 2004, available at http://www.danieldrezner.com/policy/hash.htm.
b. All polling data are from PollingReport.com, available at http://www.pollingreport.com/immigration.htm.

Credits

FIGURES AND TABLES

Figure 1.2: Robert J. Vanderbei, Map: 2008 Presidential Election, Purple America. Reprinted by permission of Robert J. Vanderbei, Princeton University. Figure 5.1: From "Beyond Red vs. Blue: The 2005 Political Typology." Reprinted by permission of The Pew Research Center for the People & the Press. Table 5.1: From "American Attitudes Hold Steady in Face of Foreign Crises," Aug. 17, 2006, p. 4. Reprinted by permission of The Pew Research Center for the People & the Press. Unnumbered table, p. 158: Gallup, from "Topics A to Z." Reprinted by permission. Table 5.3: From "Abortion, the Court, and the Public," Oct. 3, 2005, p. 4. Reprinted by permission of The Pew Research Center for the People & the Press. Tables 5.5 and 5.6: From "Beyond Red vs. Blue: The 2005 Political Typology." Reprinted by permission of The Pew Research Center for the People & the Press. Table 5.7: From "Economic Discontent Deepens as Inflation Concerns Rise," Feb. 14, 2008, p. 2. Reprinted by permission of The Pew Research Center for the People & the Press. Table 5.8: From "Economic Discontent Deepens as Inflation Concerns Rise," Feb. 14, 2008, p. 1. Reprinted by permission of The Pew Research Center for the People & the Press. Figure 6.1: From "Maturing Internet News Audience—Broader Than Deep," July 30, 2006, p. 17. Reprinted by permission of The Pew Research Center for the People & the Press. Table 6.1: From "Maturing Internet News Audience—Broader Than Deep," July 30, 2006, p. 1. Reprinted by permission of The Pew Research Center for the People & the Press. Table 6.3: From "Maturing Internet News Audience—Broader Than Deep," July 30, 2006, p. 9. Reprinted by permission of The Pew Research Center for the People & the Press. Table 6.4: From "What Americans Know: 1989–2007," April 15, 2007, p. 2. Reprinted by permission of The Pew Research Center for the People & the Press. Table 6.5: From "Social Security Polling: Cross-Currents about Private Accounts," Jan. 27, 2005, p. 3. Reprinted by permission of The Pew Research Center for the People & the Press. Table 6.6: Thomas E. Nelson, Rosalee A. Clawson, and Zoe M. Oxley, 2 tables from "Media Framing of a Civil Liberties Conflict and Its Effect on Tolerance," *American Political Science Review* Vol. 91, No. 3 (Sept. 1997): 567–83. © 1997 American Political Science Association. Reprinted with the permission of Cambridge University Press. Table 6.7: From "Media: Trends 2005, More Voices, Less Credibility," Jan. 25, 2005, p. 51. Reprinted by permission of The Pew Research Center for the People & the Press. Figure 7.3: From "Party Affiliation: What It Is and What It Isn't," Sept. 23, 2004, p. 3. Reprinted by permission of The Pew Research Center for the People & the Press. Figure 7.4: From "2004 Political Landscape: Evenly Divided and Increasingly Polarized," Nov. 5, 2003, p. 19. Reprinted by permission of The Pew Research Center for the People & the Press. Table 8.8: From "Who Votes, Who Doesn't, and Why: Regular Voters, Intermittent Voters, and Those Who Don't," Oct. 16, 2006, p. 1. Reprinted by permission of The Pew Research Center for the People & the Press. Table 8.9: Table 5.11 from *The Politics of Congressional Elections, 6th Edition,* by Gary Jacobson. Copyright © 2004. Reprinted by permission of Pearson Education, Inc. Table 11.1: From "Once Again, Voters Say: It's the Economy; Bush Reelect Margin Narrows to 45%–43%," Sept. 25, 2003, p. 13. Reprinted by permission of The Pew Research Center for the People & the Press. Table 11.7: Pippa Norris, Table 5.1 from *Driving Democracy: Do Power Sharing Institutions Work?* © Pippa Norris 2008. Reprinted with the permission of Cambridge University Press. Figure 12.5: From "Trends in Political Values and Core Attitudes: 1987–2007," March 22, 2007, p. 45. Reprinted by permission of The Pew Research Center for the People & the Press.

PHOTOGRAPHS

p. 2: Chase Swift/Corbis; p. 5: (right) Kyle Niemi/U.S. Coast Guard/ZUMA/Corbis; (left) Photo courtesy Alaska Department of Transportation and Public Facilities; p. 7: (left) U.S. Army photo by staff Sgt. Russell Bassett; (right) AP Photo/Houston Chronicle, Brett Coomer; p. 8: Jupiter Images; p. 10: Bob Rowan/Progressive Image/Corbis; p. 12: AP Photo/Eric Risberg; p. 13: Justin Lane/epa/Corbis; p. 14: Jason Reed/Reuters/Corbis; p. 15: (top) Brooks Kraft/Corbis; (bottom) David McNew/Getty Images; p. 16: Brendan Smailowski/AFP/Getty Images; p. 18: AP Photo/Patti Longmire; p. 19: Bettmann/Corbis; p. 21: Sandy Felsenthal/Corbis; p. 24: © Wally McNamee/Corbis; p. 26: (top) AP Photo/Marta Lavandier; (bottom) AP Photo/Marty Lederhandler; p. 27: AP Photo/Seth Perlman; p. 34: Imagno/Getty Images; p. 35: North Wind Picture Archives; p. 43: (left) Leonard de Selva/Corbis; (right) North Wind Picture Archives; p. 45: Medford Historical Society Collection/Corbis; p. 46: Bettmann/Corbis; p. 47: Chris Hondros/Getty Images; p. 49: AP Photo/Evan Vucci; p. 53: AP/Alaa Al-Marjani; p. 59: National Archives/Time Life Pictures/Getty Images; p. 60: AP Photo/Gary Gardiner; p. 62: Philip Gould/Corbis; p. 64: (left) Michael Smith/Getty Images; (right) Alamy; p. 65: AP Photo/Mary Ann Chastain; p. 67: Bettmann/Corbis; p. 68: Bettmann/Corbis; p. 73: public domain; p. 75: Bettmann/Corbis; p. 81: AP Photo/Charles Rex Arbogast; p. 82: Terry Ashe/Time Life Pictures/Getty Images; p. 84: AP Photo/Chris O'Meara; p. 91: Kevin Moloney/Getty Images; p. 92: Joshua Adam Nuzzo/U.S. Navy via Getty Images; p. 93: Justin Sullivan/Getty Images; p. 97: AP Photo/David Zalubowski; p. 98: AP/Wide World Photos; p. 103: (left) AP Photo; (right) William Thomas Cain/Getty Images; p. 104: Newscom; p. 111: Bettmann/Corbis; p. 112: Hulton Archives/Getty/Newscom; p. 113: Al Crespo/Sipa Press/Newscom; p. 115: William Campbell/Sygma/Corbis; p. 117: AP Photo; p. 118: Zuma Photos/Newscom; p. 122: Jana Birchum/Getty Images; p. 126: Getty/Newscom; p. 127: Jim Morin/Miami Herald; p. 129: AP Photo/Pablo Martinez Monsivais; p. 131: Bettmann/Corbis; p. 132: Les Stone/Zuma/Corbis; p. 135: AP Photo/Missouri Department of Corrections; p. 137: Carlos Barria/Reuters/Corbis; p. 140: Justin Sullivan/Getty Images; p. 144: (left) Fox/Photofest; (right) Matthew Cavanaugh/epa/Corbis; p. 149: Ken Cedeno/Corbis; p. 151: (left) Tony Freeman/Photo Edit; (right) David Young-Wolff/Photo Edit; p. 152: (top) Margaret Bourke-White/Time Life Pictures/Getty Images; (bottom) CartoonArts International/NY Times Syndicate; p. 162: (left) AFP/Getty Images; (right) AP/Wide World Photos; p. 167: AP/Wide World Photos; p. 182: AP/Wide World Photos; p. 184: (top) Shawn Thew/Getty Images; (bottom) Rare Book & Manuscript Library, University of Pennsylvania; p. 185: The Granger Collection, New York; p. 186: (top) Taxi/Getty Images; (bottom left) Francoise De Mulder/Roger Viollet/Getty Images; (bottom right) Chris Hondros/Getty Images; p. 187: Alex Wong/Getty Images for Meet the Press; p. 189: Tom Stoddart/Getty Images; p. 190: Jim Sulley/epa/Corbis; 191: CartoonArts International; p. 193: AP/Wide World Photos; p. 197: Wikipedia Commons; p. 198: Stefan Zaklin/epa/Corbis; p. 203: AP Photo/Jason DeCrow; p. 206: (top) AP/Wide World Photos; (bottom) Ronen Zvulun/Reuters/Corbis; p. 216: AP Photo/Jim Cole; p. 218: (left) Chip Somodevilla/ Getty Images; (right)

Index

Page numbers in *italics* refer to illustrations. Page numbers in **boldface** refer to figures.

Catholicism, Catholics, 53
  party affiliation of, 222, 223
caucus (congressional), 230, 232, 251
caucus elections, 238–40, **239**, 267, 269, 279, 301
  voter turnout in, 292, 301
CBS Broadcasting, 187–88, 190, **201,** 207
CBS News, **159**
Census, U.S., **20,** 157, 502
  categories of, 501
  of 1860, 499
  of 1930, 501
Center for Medicare and Medicaid, 422–23
Center for Responsive Politics, 193
Central America, systems of government in, **397**
Central American Free Trade Agreement, 344–45
Central Europe, systems of government in, 397, **397**
Central Intelligence Agency (CIA), 100, 117, 128, 198, *198,*
    398
  Iraq reports of, 432, 433
  secret prisons of, 196, 197
centralized groups, 316
cert pool, 478–79
Chaffee, Lincoln, 366
challengers, 261
Chamber of Commerce, U.S., 314, **314,** 336
Chao, Elaine, 530
chat sessions, 194
checks and balances, 7, 34, 37, 39, 41, 45, 47–51, **48,** 69, 85, 92,
    94, 128, 179, 454–57
  other democracies' shunning of, 461
  Supreme Court in, 454, 456, 457, *458, 459*
Cheney, Dick, 53–54, 99, 117, 198, 217, 398, 410, 432
  expanded vice presidential role of, 411, *411*
Cherokee Nation, 490, 491
Chicago, Ill., *81*
Chicago Tribune, 187
child labor, 54, 75, 123, 389
child molesters, 489
Child Online Protection Act (1997), 120
children, 526
  in civil rights movement, 515
  racial divide and, 508–9
China, 34, 135, 191, 489
  human rights in, 191, *191*
  media in, 191, *191*
Chinese Americans, 501
Chisholm v. Georgia, 70, **74,** 469
chlorofluorocarbons (CFCs), 16
Christian Coalition, 323, 329
Christian Democratic Union (Germany), *264*
Christian Scientists, 123
Christian Social Union (Germany), *264*
Christmas, 121
Church of England, 53
Cincinnati, Ohio, police brutality in, 510
circuit courts, 456, 467, 468
  see also appeals courts

citizen groups, 81, 315, 316, *316,* 324, 325
Citizens Against Government Waste, 366
City of Boerne v. Flores, **90**
Civil Aeronautics Board, 492
civil disobedience, 511–15
civil liberties, 9, 99–139, 152
  ambiguity of, 101
  civil rights versus, **102,** 498
  communism and, 34
  conflict about, 100, 102–4, *103,* 124, 128
  as Constitutional Convention issue, 45, 46
  federalism and, 73, 74, 74, 96, 104–6
  international, 135
  origins of, 103–9
  public awareness of, 144, *144*
  public opinion on, 99, 100–101, **101,** 103, 110, 152, **166,** 169,
    170
  restriction of, 34, 99–101, 343, 387, 491
  Supreme Court rulings on, 486–87, 491
  see also Bill of Rights, U.S.; *specific amendments and liberties*
civil rights, *19,* 55, 74, 75, 82, 90, 94, 96, 106–7, 115, 133, 152,
    223, 224, 497–539
  affirmative action and, 532–36
  of African Americans, 498–502, 505–22, *505,* 526–27,
    529–36
  of Asian Americans, 499, 501, 502, 530, 532
  civil liberties versus, **102,** 498
  color-blind society and, 504–6
  context of, 498–504
  continuing and future issues in, 531–38
  of the disabled, 499, 522, **528,** 529
  of the elderly, 499, **528**
  executive arena and, 389, 501, 529–30
  of gays, 499, 511, 515, 525–26, 529
  Great Society and, 429
  judicial arena and, 516–26
  of Latinos, 499, 501–2, 503, 506, 507, 519, 530
  legislative arena and, 526–29
  multicultural issues in, 536–38
  of Native Americans, 498, 499, 501–3, *502,* 530, 532
  policy-making process and, 510–31
  racial divide today in, 506–10, *507,* **509**
  social movements for, 511–16, **512–13,** *514, 515*
  of women, 498, 499, 503–4, 511, 515, 521–25, *521,* 527–29,
    532
Civil Rights Act (1866), 500
Civil Rights Act (1875), 74, *75,* 500
Civil Rights Act (1957), 497
Civil Rights Act (1964), 83, 89, 468, 515, 519, 524, 526, 532
  Title VII of, 520, 524–25, 527–28
  Title VI of, 536
Civil Rights Act (1991), 527
civil rights movement, 501, 505, *505,* 510–16, *514, 515,* 526
  future of, 531–32
  nonviolent protest in, 512–15
  timeline for, **512–13**
Civil Rights Restoration Act (1988), 524

frontloading, in primaries, 269
Fugitive Slave Act (1850), 499

G

gag orders, 116, 117
Gallo, Ray E., 463
Gallup polls, 158, 183
gambling, 18, 87, **90**
Gannett, 189
Gantt, Harvey, 506–7
Garner, Jack, 411
Garner, Tyron, 525
gas prices, **173**
    effect of government policy on, 13, *13*
Gates, Bill, 338, *338*
Gates, Robert, 410
gays, gay rights, 22, 91, 114, 146, 160, **166**, 176, **177**, 178, 499,
    511, 515, 525–26, 529
    marriage and, 12, *12,* 18, 19, 21, **57**, 59, 70, 92, 176, 178, 263–
        65, 284, 401, 511, 526, 529
    military and, 529–30
    sex and, 488, 489, 525–26
gender:
    hate speech and, 114
    juries and, 134
    laws concerning, 89, **90**
    political influence of, 19, 20, 142, 153, **154**
    relationship of voting patterns to, 19, **236**
    as source of political conflict, 20
gender discrimination, 463, 507, 527
    in education, 523–24
    EEOC and, 527–28, **528**
general election, 262, 277, 279
    federal funding in, **286**
General Electric, 313, 314, **314**
General Motors, **314,** 317
General Services Administration (GSA), 423, 441
    bureaucratic efficiency and, 443, *443*
    number of employees in, **433,** 434
General Social Survey, 154, 164, 165
Geneva Conventions, 453, 455
Geological Survey Hurricane Response Team, U.S., 420
George III, King of England, 38, 427, 473
Georgia, 130, 136, 265, 490, 519, 520
    death penalty in, 527
    signature requirements for presidential candidates in, 241
German Empire, 112
Germany, 40, 53, 67, 68, *252, 264,* 309, 521
    government spending in, **437**
    judicial review in, 461
    mixed government in, 397
Gerry, Elbridge, 104, 105, 355
gerrymandering, 355, **356**
get-out-the-vote activities, 243, 276, 301
Gettysburg, Pa., *45*

Ghost Dance, *502*
Gibbons v. Ogden, 72
G.I. Bill, 152, *152*
Gideon v. Wainwright, **108,** 133
Gingrich, Newt, 371, 382
Ginsburg, Ruth Bader, 482, 487, *487,* 488, 489
Gitlow v. New York, **108,** 109
Giuliani, Rudolph, 257, 268, 290, 303
Gladstone, W. E., 52
global warming, 175, **176,** 180, 444, 447, *447*
Gobitis, Lillian and William, 123
going public, 404
Goldwater, Barry, 282, *282,* 298
Gonzales, Alberto, 99, 194, 217, 399, 530
Gonzales v. Oregon, 93
Goodyear Tire and Rubber Company, 524
Google, 193, 194, **201, 204,** 280
Google News, 11, *11*
G.O.P. PAC, 225
Gore, Al, 189, 270, 506
    expanded vice presidential role of, 411
    in 2000 election, 25–26, 28, 247–48, **259,** 266, *266,* 271, 508
Gore-Chernomyrdin Commission, 411
Goss, Porter, 197
government, federal:
    Articles of Confederation period of, 30–33
    branches of, 7, 28, 47–51, **48**
    criticism of, 72, 99, 109, 110, 111–12, *111,* 113
    deception by, 116, 128
    Democratic vs. Republican views on size and role of, **220,** 221,
        222–23, *222,* 224, 300
    Federalist and Antifederalist views of, 35, 36, 220, **220**
    forms of, **9,** 67–68, *67*
    health care debate and, 223, **227**
    influence on everyday life of, 10–11, 12–13, *12,* 63–65, *64,*
        66–67, 76, 81, *81,* 316
    interest groups and influence on, 277, 307, 308, 318, 336–37,
        336, 338, 339–41
    limited, 21, 30, 46, 78, 92, 104, 143, 168
    Madison's views on, 7, 8, 34
    media and, 10, 11, *11*
    order as goal of, 6–7
    poverty programs and, 222, *222,* 223, **227**
    power of, 7, 29, 30–31, 34, 35–36, 37–39, 41–42, 45, 46, 47–
        52, 54–55, 58, 63–97, 99–100, 105–6, 107, 112
    public goods provided by, 8, 9
    public opinion on, 83–85, 141–43, 146, 149, 152, *152,* 165–68,
        166, 167, 168, 173, 212
    purpose of, 6–9
    relationships between levels of, 76–77, *77,* 84, 93–94
    religion and, 103, 120–24, 224
    size of, 12, **13,** 78, 82, 168, 427, 430, 433–35, **433–36,** 437
    spending by, *see* spending, federal
    state aid by, 78–80, 82, 124
    waste in, 3, 4–5, 6
    welfare as goal of, 8–9
    workforce of, 12, **13,** 130

H

O

P

spending:
    attempts to regulate, **57**
    concurrent powers of, **66**
    Congressional authority over, 47, 63, 64, *64,* **66,** 82, 124
    on defense, **227,** 249
    federal, 3–6, 12–13, **13,** 78–79, 80, **80,** 82, *92,* 94, 100, 160,
        161, 168, **173,** 232, **311,** 315, 340, 403, 434–35, **434, 436,**
        437, **437**
    ideological views on, 18, 21, 78
    on lobbying efforts, 310, **311,** 313–15, **314,** 337, 338, *338,* 340
    public opinion on, 84, 143, 147, 160, **161,** 434–35, **436**
    state and local, 78–79, 80, **80,** 82, 96
    U.S. compared with other nations for, 437, **437**
Spirit of Justice, 119
split tickets, casting of, 298
spoils system, 221, 427, *427,* 428
sports, *129,* 130
Sports Illustrated, 189
spying:
    domestic, 100, 104, 116, 117, 127, *127,* 128, 139, 170
    foreign, 128
Sri Lanka, 521
standard of proof, 462
standard operating procedures, 424
standing, 464
standing committees, 371
Starr, Kenneth, 26
state capacity, 424, 428
State Department, U.S., 427, 431
    number of employees in, **433**
    passport applications to, 419, 449
state laws, judicial review of, 458, 460
State of the Union address, 396, 404, 405
    media coverage of, 192, 199
states:
    economic differences among, 95, **95**
    lawsuits between, 459
    political differences among, 18, 21–22, **22,** 125
states' rights, 72, 73, 74, 78, 79, 83–85, 86–91, 92, 93, 105–6,
        107, 109, 111, 115, 125, 138, 460
Statue of Liberty, 537
statutory interpretation, 460
Stearns, Junius Brutus, *46*
Steffens, Lincoln, 185
stem cell research, 18, 21, 178, 282, *282,* 353, 444
    executive order on, 393, *393*
stereotyping, of political candidates, 296
Stern, Howard, 188
Stevens, John Paul, 132, 470, 479, 487, *487*
Stevens, Ted, 4, 5
Stewart, Jon, 199, 203, *203*
Stewart, Potter, 119
Stone, Harlan Fiske, 483
Stop Her Now, 290
straight tickets, casting of, 298
street-level bureaucrats, 423
strict construction, 485–86, 487, 489

strict scrutiny standard, 522, 535
strikes, 393
student activity fees, 114, 122–23
student loans, federally funded, 410
Student Nonviolent Coordinating Committee (SNCC), 512
substantive due process doctrine, 526
substantive representation, 352
Sudan, 135, 521
Sullivan, Kathleen, 59, 119
Sunstein, Cass, 85
Sununu, John, 217–18, 253–54, 273
Super Bowl (2004), 187–88
superdelegates, 269
Supreme Court, U.S., *49,* 193, 217, 328, 330, 331, 453–60, **466,**
        468–70, 474–94
    access to, 475–79, **475, 478**
    allocation of power to, 7, **32,** 48, 51, 70
    amicus curiae and, 480, 488
    appellate jurisdiction of, **456,** 457, 468
    appointments to, 14, *15, 49,* 51, 72, 86, 92
    attitudinalist approach and, 486–87
    briefs for, 480
    campaign finance reforms and, 286, 288
    case criteria of, 477–79
    chief justices of, *49,* 73, 105, 457
    civil liberties and, 101–4, 105–9, 110–24, 125–38
    civil rights issues and, 500, 501, 504, 512, 513, 516–20, 522–
        27, 529, 531, 534, 536
    color-blind jurisprudence of, 519–20, 522, 531, 534
    constitutional amendments to overturn decisions of, 56, 59, 70,
        113
    constitutional interpretation by, 27, 28, 42, 54–55, 58, 60, *60,*
        61, 70, 71, 72, 73, *73,* 74, 87, 88–91, **90,** *91,* 92, 93, 101–4,
        104, 105–9, 110–20, 121–24, 125–38, 387, 394, 413, 460,
        468, 485–86, 487, 489
    decision making of, 484–89, **484,** *485*
    docket of, 475, 477
    executive privilege ruling of, 399
    FDR's court-packing plan for, 470, 491
    federalism and, 63, 65, 70, 71, 72, 73–75, *73,* 74, 75–76, *75,*
        82, *82,* 86–91, **90,** 92, 93, 96, 105–6, 107, 109, 124, 125,
        129, 137, 460
    G. W. Bush's appointments to, 387, 392
    hearing cases before, 480–84, *481*
    interpretation of laws by, 7, 14, *15,* 16, *19,* 26, 48, **48,** 51, 63,
        65, 72, 76, 86, 88, 92, 93, 120, 460
    judicial activism of, 487–88, 519–20, 522
    judicial restraint of, 487–88
    judicial review by, 48, 51, 456–61, *458,* 488, 492
    justices' conference in, 482
    legislative vetos and, 382
    opinion writing in, 482–84
    oral argument in, 481–82, *481*
    original intent and, 486, 487
    original jurisdiction of, **456,** *458,* 476, 477
    pocket vetos and, 378
    policy implications of composition of, 14, *15,* 51, 72, 86, 92

W

Physical/Political Map of the United States

0   150   300 mi
0   150   300 km

Pacific Ocean

Calgary
Saskatoon
S. Saskatchewan R.
Bow R.
Qu'Appelle R.
Regina

Vancouver
Str. of Juan de Fuca
Cape Flattery
Victoria
Seattle
Tacoma
Olympia
Cape Disappointment
WASHINGTON
Spokane
Coeur d'Alene
Columbia R.
Snake R.
Walla Walla
Bitterroot Range
Missoula
Helena
MONTANA
Milk R.
Missouri R.
Little Missouri R.
Williston
NORTH

Portland
Salem
Eugene
Willamette R.
OREGON
CASCADE RANGE
COLUMBIA PLATEAU
Yellowstone R.
Billings
Bighorn R.
SOUTH

Cape Blanco
COAST RANGES
IDAHO
Boise
Idaho Falls
Snake R.
Pocatello
Jackson
WYOMING
Belle Fourche R.
Black Hills
GREAT
Cheyenne R.
Niobrara R.
NEB

Cape Mendocino
Sacramento R.
Reno
GREAT
Great Salt Lake Desert
Great Salt Lake
Salt Lake City
Casper
N. Platte R.
PLAINS

Point Reyes
San Francisco
Oakland
Sacramento
Carson City
Lake Tahoe
NEVADA
BASIN
SIERRA NEVADA
San Joaquin R.
UTAH
Green R.
Laramie
Cheyenne
Steamboat Springs
S. Platte R.

San Jose
Monterey Bay
Salinas
Monterey
Fresno
CALIFORNIA
Death Valley
MOJAVE
Las Vegas
DESERT
Lake Mead
Glenwood Springs
Colorado R.
Moab
Denver
COLORADO
Colorado Springs
Pueblo
MOUNTAINS

Point Conception
Santa Barbara
Channel Islands
Bakersfield
Lancaster
Oxnard
Pasadena
Los Angeles
Long Beach
ROCKY
Lake Powell
COLORADO PLATEAU
Little Colorado R.
Flagstaff
Santa Fe
Rio Grande
Albuquerque
NEW MEXICO
Canadian R.
Amarillo
High

Oceanside
Escondido
San Diego
Tijuana
Salton Sea
ARIZONA
SONORAN
Phoenix
Gila R.
DESERT
Tucson
Pecos R.
Llano Estacado
Lubbock

BAJA CALIFORNIA
Ciudad Juárez
El Paso
Odessa
Colora

Vizcaíno Bay
SIERRA MADRE OCCIDENTAL
Hermosillo
TE
Edw Plat

Mulege
Gulf of California
MEXICO
SIERRA MADRE ORIENTAL
Rio Grande
Nuevo Laredo
Monte

HAWAII

0   100 mi
0   100 km

Kauai
Niihau
Kauai Channel
Oahu
Kaulakahi Channel
Honolulu
Kaiwi Channel
Molokai
Lanai
Maui
Kahoolawe
Alenuihaha Channel
Pacific Ocean
Mauna Kea
Hilo
Mauna Loa
Hawaii

ALASKA

0   400 mi
0   400 km

Beaufort Sea
Chukchi Sea
North Slope
BROOKS RANGE
Kotzebue Sound
Seward Peninsula
Yukon R.
Fairbanks
CANADA
St. Lawrence Island
Norton Sound
ALASKA
ALASKA RANGE
St. Elias Mountains
Nunivak Island
Kuskokwim Mountains
Anchorage
Juneau
Kuskokwim Bay
Iliamna Lake
Kenai Peninsula
Bering Sea
Bristol Bay
Alaska Peninsula
Gulf of Alaska
Alexander Archipelago
Aleutian Islands
Kodiak Island
Queen Charlotte Islands